W9-BZC-637

Fodor's

NEW
ENGLAND

30th Edition

Fodor's Travel Publications   New York, Toronto, London, Sydney, Auckland
www.fodors.com

FODOR'S NEW ENGLAND

Writers: Bethany Cassin Beckerlegge, Seth Brown, Pippa Jack, Josh Rogol, Eliot Sloan, Mary Ruoff, Laura V. Scheel, Janine Weisman

Editor: Salwa Jabado
Editorial Contributors: Bethany Cassin Beckerlegge, Penny Phenix

Production Editor: Carolyn Roth
Maps & Illustrations: Mark Stroud and David Lindroth, *cartographers;* Rebecca Baer, *map editor;* William Wu, *information graphics*
Design: Fabrizio La Rocca, *creative director;* Tina Malaney, Chie Ushio, Jessica Ramirez, *designers;* Melanie Marin, *associate director of photography;* Jennifer Romains, *photo research*
Cover Photos: Front cover: (Farmhouse, Vermont) SIME/eStock Photo. Back cover (from left to right): Ron and Patty Thomas/iStockphoto; Chee-Onn Leong/Shutterstock; Denis Jr. Tangney/iStockphoto. Spine: Babar760lDreamstime.com.
Production Manager: Angela L. McLean

30th Edition

ISBN 978–0–307–92926–6

ISSN 0192-3412

SPECIAL SALES

This book is available at special discounts for bulk purchases for sales promotions or premiums. Special editions, including personalized covers, excerpts of existing books, and corporate imprints, can be created in large quantities for special needs. For more information, write to Special Markets/Premium Sales, 1745 Broadway, MD 3-1, New York, NY 10019, or e-mail specialmarkets@randomhouse.com.

AN IMPORTANT TIP & AN INVITATION

Although all prices, opening times, and other details in this book are based on information supplied to us at press time, changes occur all the time in the travel world, and Fodor's cannot accept responsibility for facts that become outdated or for inadvertent errors or omissions. So **always confirm information when it matters,** especially if you're making a detour to visit a specific place. Your experiences—positive and negative—matter to us. If we have missed or misstated something, **please write to us.** Share your opinion instantly through our online feedback center at fodors.com/contact-us.

PRINTED IN CHINA

10 9 8 7 6 5 4 3 2 1

CONTENTS

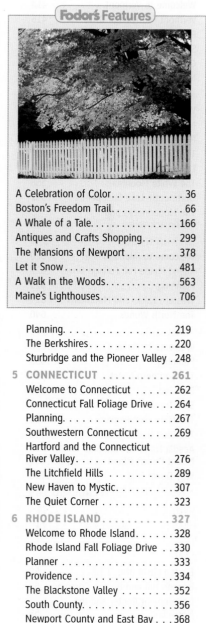

Fodor's Features

ABOUT
THIS GUIDE

Fodor's Ratings

Everything in this guide is worth doing—
we don't cover what isn't—but exceptional sights, hotels, and restaurants are
recognized with additional accolades.
Fodor's Choice ★ indicates our top recom-
mendations; ★ highlights places we deem
highly recommended. Care to nominate a
new place? Visit Fodors.com/contact-us.

Trip Costs

We list prices wherever possible to help
you budget well. Hotel and restaurant
price categories from $ to $$$$ are noted
alongside each recommendation. For
hotels, we include the lowest cost of a
standard double room in high season.
For restaurants, we cite the average price
of a main course at dinner or, if dinner
isn't served, at lunch. For attractions,
we always list adult admission fees; dis-
counts are usually available for children,
students, and senior citizens.

Hotels

Our local writers vet every hotel to recom-
mend the best overnights in each price cat-
egory, from budget to expensive. Unless
otherwise specified, you can expect pri-
vate bath, phone, and TV in your room.
For expanded hotel reviews, facilities, and
deals visit Fodors.com.

Restaurants

Unless we state otherwise, restaurants are
open for lunch and dinner daily. We men-
tion dress code only when there's a specific
requirement and reservations only when
they're essential or not accepted. To make
restaurant reservations, visit Fodors.com.

Credit Cards

The hotels and restaurants in this guide
typically accept credit cards. If not, we'll
say so.

Ratings
- ★ Fodor's Choice
- ★ Highly recommended
- ☺ Family-friendly

Listings
- ⊠ Address
- ⊠ Branch address
- ☎ Telephone
- 🖷 Fax
- ⊕ Website
- ✉ E-mail
- 🎫 Admission fee
- ☉ Open/closed times
- Ⓜ Subway
- ⌖ Directions or Map coordinates

Hotels & Restaurants
- 🛏 Hotel
- ⇆ Number of rooms
- ⦿ Meal plans
- ✕ Restaurant
- ✍ Reservations
- 👔 Dress code
- ⊟ No credit cards
- Ⓢ Price

Other
- ⇨ See also
- ☞ Take note
- ⛳ Golf facilities

1

Experience
New England

WHAT'S WHERE

The following numbers refer to chapters.

2 Boston. Massachusetts's capital city is also New England's hub. Boston's many universities make it a cosmopolitan town, but there are also blue-collar roots in the distinct neighborhoods. This is the cradle of American democracy, a place where soaring skyscrapers cast shadows on Colonial graveyards.

3 Cape Cod, Nantucket, and Martha's Vineyard. Great beaches, delicious seafood, and artisan-filled shopping districts fill scenic Cape Cod, chic Martha's Vineyard, and cozy Nantucket.

4 The Berkshires and Western Massachusetts. The mountainous Berkshires live up to the storybook image of rural New England; there's also a thriving arts community. Farther east, the Pioneer Valley is home to a string of historic settlements.

5 Connecticut. The densely populated southwest region contrasts with the sparsely populated northeastern Quiet Corner, known for antiquing. Small shoreline villages line the southeastern coast and are near a pair of casinos. The Connecticut River Valley and Litchfield Hills have grand old inns, rolling farmlands, and state parks.

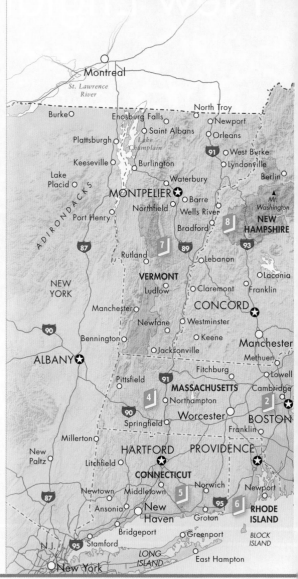

6 **Rhode Island.** The smallest of the six New England states is home to great sailing and glitzy mansions in Newport. South County has sparsely populated beaches and rolling farmland; scenic Block Island is just a short ferry ride away.

7 **Vermont.** Vermont has farms, freshly starched New England towns, quiet back roads, and bustling ski resorts.

8 **New Hampshire.** Portsmouth is the star of the independent state's 18-mile coastline. The Lakes Region is a popular summertime escape; the White Mountains' dramatic vistas attract photographers and adventurous hikers farther north.

9 **Inland Maine.** The largest New England state's rugged interior, including the Western Lakes and vast North Woods regions, attracts skiers, hikers, campers, anglers, and other outdoors enthusiasts.

10 **The Maine Coast.** Classic townscapes, rocky shorelines punctuated by sandy beaches, and picturesque downtowns draw vacationers to Maine like a magnet. Acadia National Park is where majestic mountains meet the coast; Bar Harbor is the park's gateway town.

NEW ENGLAND PLANNER

Average Temperatures

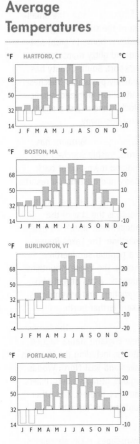

When to Go

All six New England states are year-round destinations. Winter is popular with skiers, summer draws families and beach lovers, and fall delights those who love the bursts of autumnal color. Spring can also be a great time, with sugar shacks transforming maple sap into all sorts of tasty things. ■TIP➜ **You'll probably want to avoid rural areas during mud season (April) and black-fly season (mid-May to mid-June).**

Memorial Day signals migration to the beaches and the mountains, and summer begins in earnest on July 4. Those who want to drive to Cape Cod in July or August, beware: on Friday and Sunday weekenders clog the overburdened U.S. 6. The same applies to the Maine Coast and its feeder roads, Interstate 95 and U.S. 1.

In the fall, a rainbow of reds, oranges, yellows, purples, and other vibrant hues emerges. The first scarlet and gold colors appear in mid-September in northern areas; "peak" color occurs at different times from year to year. Generally, it's best to visit the northern reaches in late September and early October and move south as October progresses.

CLIMATE

In winter, coastal New England is cold and damp; inland temperatures may be lower, but generally drier conditions make them easier to bear. Snowfall is heaviest in the interior mountains and can range up to several hundred inches per year in northern Maine, New Hampshire, and Vermont. Spring is often windy and rainy; in some years winter appears to segue almost immediately into summer. Coastal areas can be quite humid in summer, while inland, particularly at higher elevations, there's a prevalence of cool summer nights. Autumn temperatures can be mild even into October.

Getting Here and Around

⇨ *For more information, see Travel Smart New England.*

Air Travel: The main gateway to New England is Boston's Logan International Airport (BOS). Other New England airports include Bradley International Airport (BDL, 12 miles north of Hartford), T.F. Green Airport (PVD, just outside Providence), Manchester Boston Regional Airport (MHT, in New Hampshire about an hour from Boston), Portland International Jetport (PWM, in Maine), and Burlington International Airport (BTV, in Vermont).

Car Travel: New England is best explored by car. Areas in the interior are largely without heavy traffic and congestion, and parking is consistently easy to find. Coastal New England is considerably more congested, and parking can be hard to find or expensive in Boston, Providence, and many smaller resort towns along the coast. Still, a car is typically the best way to get around even on the coast (though once you arrive, you may want to explore on foot, on a bike, or by local transit and cabs). In New England's interior, public transportation options are more limited and a car is almost necessary.

Train Travel: Amtrak offers frequent daily service to several New England destinations, including Boston; Portland, Maine; coastal New Hampshire; several points in Vermont; and Pittsfield, Springfield, Worcester, and Framingham, Massachusetts. The Massachusetts Bay Transportation Authority (MBTA) connects Boston with outlying areas.

TRAVEL TIMES FROM BOSTON:	BY AIR	BY CAR	BY BUS	BY TRAIN
Acadia National Park (ME)	1 hour	5 hours	not applicable	not applicable
Burlington, VT	no direct flight	3½ hours	4½–5 hours	8¾ hours
Hartford, CT	no direct flight	1¾ hours	2–2¾ hours	4½–5¼ hours
New York, NY	¾–1 hour	4 hours	4½–7 hours	3½–4¼ hours
Portland, ME	no direct flight	2 hours	2¼ hours	2½ hours
Providence, RI	no direct flight	1 hour	1 hour	½–¾ hour
Provincetown, MA	½ hour	2¼ hours	3–3½ hours	not applicable

Visitor Information

Each New England state provides a helpful free information kit, including a guidebook, map, and listings of attractions and events. All include listings and advertisements for lodging and dining establishments. Each state also has an official website with material on sights and lodgings; most of these sites have a calendar of events and other special features.

Contacts Greater Boston Convention & Visitors Bureau ☎ 888/733–2678 ⊕ www.bostonusa.com.

Connecticut Commission on Culture & Tourism ☎ 888/288–4748 ⊕ www.ctvisit.com.

Maine Office of Tourism ☎ 888/624–6345 ⊕ www.visitmaine.com.

Massachusetts Office of Travel and Tourism ☎ 800/227–6277, 617/973–8500 ⊕ www.massvacation.com.

New Hampshire Division of Travel and Tourism Development ☎ 800/386–4664, 603/271–2665 ⊕ www.visitnh.gov.

Rhode Island Tourism Division ☎ 800/556–2484 ⊕ www.visitrhodeisland.com.

Vermont Department of Tourism and Marketing ☎ 802/828–3237, 800/837–6668 brochures ⊕ www.vermontvacation.com.

NEW ENGLAND TODAY

The People

The idea of the self-reliant, thrifty, and often stoic New England Yankee has taken on almost mythic proportions in American folklore, but in some parts of New England—especially in rural Maine, New Hampshire, and Vermont—there still is some truth to this image, which shouldn't come as a surprise. You need to be independent if you farm an isolated field, live in the middle of a vast forest, or work a fishing boat miles off the coast. Like any part of the country, there are stark differences between urban New Englanders and those you encounter outside the cities. Both, though, are usually fiercely proud of the region, its rugged beauty, and its contributions to the nation. New Englanders also tend to be well educated.

In terms of ethnicity, Vermont, Maine, and New Hampshire are three of the nation's four whitest states. African American and Asian populations are increasing, especially in Massachusetts and Connecticut. In northern Maine, there is a heavy French influence from nearby Québec.

The Politics

Though they're often portrayed as a bunch of loony liberals, the political views of New Englanders are actually more complex. The region's representation in both the U. S. Senate and the House of Representatives is heavily Democratic. Voters in New Hampshire, which hosts the nation's first primary each presidential election season, tend to lean conservative, but with a distinctly libertarian slant, as do residents in many rural portions of New England.

During the civil rights era in the 1960s, racial tension in Boston was high, with people clashing in the streets over public school segregation. In 2006, however, Massachusetts residents elected Deval Patrick, the second black governor ever to be elected in the United States. In 2004, Massachusetts became the first state to allow same-sex marriage, and four of the six states that permit gay marriage are in New England (Massachusetts, Vermont, New Hampshire, and Connecticut).

The Economy

Long gone are the days since New England's shoe and textile industries sailed overseas, when many a mill town suffered blows to employment and self-image. In recent years, the unemployment rate has fallen below the national average (though Rhode Island has one of the highest in the country at 11%). In Maine, the lobster-fishing industry (about 70% of the state's seafood industry) is hoping to rebound after a number of tough years. Between 2005 and 2009 lobster prices dropped nearly two dollars per pound, however prices have recovered somewhat since 2010 and in 2011 Maine fishermen hauled in lobster at a record-setting pace.

Exports are a major part of the modern New England economy, consisting heavily of computer and other electronics, chemicals, and specialized machinery. The Boston area is home to a thriving biotech industry. The service industries are also strong, especially in the insurance and financial sectors, which have a long history in Hartford. Some towns are known for a particular export: Groton, Connecticut, and Bath, Maine, both have naval shipyards supplying the military with high-technology ships and submarines; Springfield, Massachusetts, is a gun-manufacturing center; and Barre, Vermont, quarries granite. Assorted foods produced include maple syrup, blueberries, cranberries, lobster, and other seafood.

Sports

Fans from parts of all five states follow Massachusetts's sports teams as if they were their own. The state's capital is home to three of the region's four major sports teams—Boston Red Sox baseball, Boston Bruins hockey, and Boston Celtics basketball. The New England Patriots (football) play in the small suburb of Foxborough, about 30 miles southwest of Downtown Boston.

New England is currently enjoying a period of unprecedented sports success, as the region's teams have racked up seven titles since 2002. The most recent squad to claim a championship (the franchise's first since 1972) is the Boston Bruins, after besting the Vancouver Canucks in the 2011 Stanley Cup Finals.

Red Sox fans, often referred to as Red Sox Nation, are some of the most fanatical in the country. The 2004 World Series marked the pinnacle of bliss for many New Englanders after witnessing their beloved BoSox win, ending an 86-year drought. The Sox would do it again just three years later, in 2007.

The Patriots charged into the 21st century, winning three out of four Super Bowls, from 2002 to 2005, but the Pats' last two trips to the big game ended in heartbreak after upsets in both 2008 and 2012 to the New York Giants.

Not to be left out, the Celtics advanced their status as one of basketball's marquee franchises, capturing an NBA record 17th title in 2008 (the rival Los Angeles Lakers have since equaled the Celtics' title bounty, besting Boston in the 2010 Finals).

The Language

As people move around, the local accents have begun to blend, creating more of a general New England accent. (In fact, in some urban areas, you may not hear any accent.) Linguistic differences, however, are still evident in some places, especially close to the coast.

Boston's distinct accent is similar in tone to that of New York City's Bronx and is noted by the dropping of the R in certain places, as in the pronunciation of the famous sports arena "the Gahden." Bostonians also lengthen their vowels, so chowder sounds like "chowdah." Town names in Massachusetts are often spoken very differently than they are spelled; Gloucester, for example, becomes "Glawstuh." Bostonians also rush their speech, so "Hi, how are you?" is "hihawaya?" and "Did you eat?" sounds like "Jeet?"

Connecticut, Maine, and Rhode Island also have a Boston-like accent with nuanced differences. Rhode Islanders drop their R's at the end of words and use an "aw" sound for the O or A in words like "coffee" or "talk" but an "ah" sound for the short O's in words like "Providence" and "mom." In Connecticut and New Hampshire the accent is not nearly as strong, but it comes out in certain words, like how locals pronounce Concord ("Cahn-cuhd").

Meanwhile, true Mainers drop or soften their R's—making their favorite dish "lobstah"; they also often accentuate the vowel, so a one-word syllable can be pronounced like two, meaning "here" may become "hee-yuh."

QUINTESSENTIAL NEW ENGLAND

Fall Foliage

It's impossible to discuss New England without mentioning that time of year when the region's deciduous (leaf-shedding) trees—maples, oaks, birches, and beeches—explode in reds, yellows, oranges, and other rich hues. Autumn is the most colorful season in New England, but it can be finicky, defined as much by the weather as it is by the species of trees; a single rainstorm can strip trees of their grandeur. What happens in one area of the region doesn't necessarily happen in another, and if you have the time you can follow the colors from one area to the next. You'll be competing with thousands of other like-minded leaf peepers, so be sure to book lodging early. Your preparedness will pay off the first time you drive down a winding country road aflame in the bright sun of a New England autumn day.

The Coast

The coast of New England is both workplace and playground. From the 17th century, boatbuilders sprung up in one town after another to support the shipping and fishing trades. Today, the boatyards are far fewer than in historical times, but shipping and especially fishing remain important to the economy on the coast and beyond. It's not all work and no play—some of the classic wooden sailboats now serve cruise goers, and some fishermen have traded in their lobster boats for whale-watching vessels. The coast's lighthouses are another New England staple; more than 60 of these beacons of light line Maine's jagged coast like sentinels along the shore. In Massachusetts, Cape Cod is a beachcombers' paradise, and the relatively chilly waters of the North Atlantic don't scare away swimmers come summertime.

New Englanders are a varied group joined by a shared past and a singular pride in their roots. It's therefore no surprise that New England spans a spectrum of activities and locales, yet offers visitors and residents alike distinct experiences that still can perfectly define the region.

Food, Glorious Food

Maine lobster. Vermont Grade A maple syrup. Portuguese sausage from Cape Cod. Blueberries from Maine. Fine food prepared under the influence of every region of Italy in Boston's North End (there's plenty of Italian to go around Atwells Avenue in Providence's Federal Hill, too). This is just a sampling to whet your appetite. New England dining is truly a feast for the gastronomist, and it runs the gamut from the simply prepared to the most artistic of presentations: from blueberry pie just as Grandma used to make to molecular gastronomy in some Boston restaurants. Local ingredients and sustainable methods are common in foodie-focused cities and also Vermont. Chefs who grew up here sometimes leave to learn their trade, only to return and enrich the dining scene, but the region is attracting newcomers as well.

Artisans

New England's independent artisans have built a thriving cottage industry. Some of the finest potters spin their wheels on the coast, and one-off, often whimsical jewelry is wrought in silver, pewter, and other metals. Modern furniture makers take classic simple New England designs, including those of the Shakers and Quakers, and refine them for buyers the world over who are willing to pay thousands for craftsmanship that has withstood the test of time. The varied landscapes of Vermont and New Hampshire, with their respective Green and White Mountains; Massachusetts, with its Berkshire Mountains, Pioneer Valley, and historic coast; Connecticut, with its southern shore; and Rhode Island, with its oceanfront cliffs, have patiently sat for thousands of painters, whose canvases are sold in small shops and local museums.

NEW ENGLAND TOP ATTRACTIONS

Acadia National Park

(A) Hosting more than 2 million visitors annually, this wonder of the Maine Coast was the first national park established east of the Mississippi River. It is regularly one of the most visited in the United States. In the warmer months, take a drive around Mount Desert Island's 20-mile Park Loop Road to acquaint yourself with the area and indulge in spectacular views of the mountains and the sea. Head to the top of Cadillac Mountain for amazing 360-degree views (especially popular at sunrise) or bike the scenic 45-mile carriage-road system, inspecting each of the 17 stone bridges along the way. Go on a park ranger–led boat trip in search of local wildlife such as porpoises, seals, and seabirds or cruise to the fjordlike bay of Somes Sound, where steep rocky cliffs jut out of the sea. Adorable Bar Harbor is the park's gateway town.

Appalachian Trail

(B) The 2,180-mile Appalachian Trail, running from Springer Mountain, Georgia, to Katahdin, Maine, cuts through five of New England's six states: Connecticut, Massachusetts, New Hampshire, Vermont, and Maine. Though the trail is best known as a weeks-long endurance test for expert hikers, many short stretches can be walked in a few hours. "AT" terrain in Maine and New Hampshire can be quite challenging; the trail is a bit more manageable in southern New England. If you're a complete novice, you can also drive to many of the trailheads—if only to say you've set foot on the most famous walk in the country.

Baxter State Park

(C) Over the span of 32 years, from 1930 to 1962, former Maine governor Percival Baxter began buying and donating parcels of land, with the goal of creating a natural park in the wilds of northern Maine.

The result is Baxter State Park: more than 200,000 acres containing numerous lakes and streams, plus Mt. Katahdin, Maine's tallest peak and the northern terminus of the Appalachian Trail. Offering frequent sightings of moose, white-tailed deer, and black bear, and attracting only 60,000 visitors a year, Baxter State Park provides a wilderness experience not found elsewhere in New England.

Boston

(D) New England's largest and most cosmopolitan city is the region's hub for modern commerce, education, and culture, and the early history of the United States is never far from view. Orient yourself with a 360-degree view from the Prudential Skywalk Observation Deck before you hit the ground exploring. The 50-acre Boston Common is the oldest city park in the nation; across the street is the Public Garden, where a ride on a Swan Boat has been a popular pastime and a harbinger of spring since 1877. Two lanterns hung from the Old North Church kicked off the Revolutionary War and made Paul Revere a legend; the Freedom Trail is a 2.5-mile route that winds past 16 of the city's most historic landmarks. Be sure to include a visit to the Museum of Fine Arts, containing more than 450,000 works of art from almost every corner of the world, including Egyptian mummies and Asian scrolls.

Cape Cod National Seashore

(E) Comprising 40 miles of sandy beaches and nearly 44,000 acres of a landscape that has been the muse of countless painters and photographers, the Cape Cod National Seashore features the best of what New England has to offer. Since its designation in 1961 by President John F. Kennedy, it has become the perfect place for explorers and strollers looking for an untouched stretch of coastline. An exhaustive amount of programs—from guided bird walks to surf rescue demonstrations

to snorkeling in Wellfleet's kettle ponds—take place year-round; most are free.

Green Mountains

(F) Vermont takes its nickname (the Green Mountain State) and its actual name (*verts monts* is "green mountains" in French) from this 250-mile-long mountain range that forms the spine of the state. Part of the Appalachian Mountains, the Green Mountains are a wild paradise filled with rugged hiking trails (most notably the Long Trail and the Appalachian Trail), unspoiled forests, quaint towns, and some of the East Coast's best ski resorts. About 400,000 acres are protected in Green Mountain National Forest.

Lake Winnipesaukee

(G) As fun to fish as it is to pronounce, the largest (and longest) lake in New Hampshire is home to three species of trout, small- and largemouth bass, bluegill, and more. The 72-square-mile lake and its more than 250 islands also contain beaches, arcades, water parks, and countless other fun family diversions. In summer, Winnipesaukee buzzes with activity as travelers flock to resort towns like Wolfeboro, Weirs Beach, and Meredith.

Maine Coast

(H) Counting all its nooks, crannies, and crags, Maine's coast would stretch for thousands of miles if you could pull it straight. The Southern Coast is the most visited section, stretching north from Kittery to just outside Portland, but don't let that stop you from heading farther "Down East" (Maine-speak for "up the coast"). Despite the cold North Atlantic waters, beachgoers enjoy miles of sandy—or, more frequently, rocky—beaches, with sweeping views of lighthouses, forested islands, and the wide-open sea.

Mt. Washington

(I) New England's highest mountain, this New Hampshire peak has been scaled by many a car (as the bumper stickers will

attest). You can also take a cog railway to the top or, if you're an intrepid hiker, navigate a maze of trails. The weather station here recorded a wind gust of 231 mph in April 1934—the highest wind speed ever recorded at a surface station until it was surpassed in 1996 by a 253 mph gust on Australia's Barrow Island. Bundle up if you make the trek—the average temperature at the summit is below freezing.

Mystic

(J) Home to two great museums—Mystic Seaport (known for its collection of historic ships and re-creation of a 19th-century seaside village) and the Mystic Aquarium and Institute for Exploration—this Connecticut seaside town is one of the state's biggest draws. When you finish touring the town's two impressive institutions, peruse the boutiques and galleries downtown.

Newport

(K) Rhode Island's treasure trove has preserved Colonial buildings and Gilded Age mansions like no other city in the country. Here you'll find more than 200 pre-Revolutionary structures and scores of jaw-dropping, ridiculously over-the-top castles from the late 19th century. Newport is also a picturesque seaside town and one of the world's great sailing capitals.

Portland Head Light

(L) One of the most-photographed lighthouses in the nation, the historic white stone Portland Head Light was commissioned by George Washington and completed in 1791 for the whopping sum of $2,250. It welcomes nearly 1 million visitors each year and features an informative museum in the Victorian-style innkeeper's cottage. The lighthouse is in Fort Williams Park, about 2 miles from the town center of Cape Elizabeth, at the southwest entrance of Portland harbor.

TOP EXPERIENCES

Peep a Leaf

Tourist season in most of New England is concentrated in the late spring and summer, but a resurgence happens in September and October, especially in the northern states, when leaf peepers from all corners descend by the car- and busload to see the leaves turn red, yellow, orange, and all shades in between. Foliage season can be fragile and unpredictable—temperature, winds, latitude, and rain all influence when the leaves turn and how long they remain on the trees—but that makes the season even more precious. Apple picking at a local orchard or searching for the perfect pumpkin for a jack-o'-lantern among the falling leaves are quintessential New England experiences.

Comb a Beach

Whether sandy or rocky, New England beaches can be filled with flotsam and jetsam. Anything from crab traps unmoored by heavy waves to colored sea glass worn smooth by the water to lost watches, jewelry, and the like can appear at your feet. Also common are shells of sea urchins, clams, and other bivalves. During certain times of the year sand dollars of all sizes and colors are plentiful—you may even find one still whole.

Take Yourself Out to a Ballgame

Fenway Park has been the home of the Boston Red Sox since it opened in 1912 and is the oldest ballpark in the major leagues. Though the cheapest seats and farthest from the field, the bleachers are quite popular with the faithful, who gather to drink beer in plastic cups and watch as batters attempt to clear the 37-foot-tall left-field wall known as the Green Monster. Seat 21 of Section 42, Row 37 in the right-field bleachers is painted red in honor of the longest measurable home run

ever hit at Fenway, Ted Williams's legendary 502-foot blast on June 9, 1946. To get an up-close and inexpensive look at some of the game's next rising stars, visit the Red Sox triple-A farm team, the Paw Sox, located in Pawtucket, Rhode Island. During the summer, the Cape Cod Baseball League features some of the nation's best young collegiate talent.

Hit the Slopes

Though the mountain snow in New England is not as legendary as the powder out west (and, in fact, can be downright unpleasant when packed snow becomes crusty ice), skiing is quite popular here. Vermont has several ski areas, with Killington being the largest resort in the Northeast: its 200 trails span seven mountains. New Hampshire's White Mountains and Massachusetts's Berkshires also cater to snow-sport lovers, while Sunday River and Sugarloaf in Maine are perennial favorites with advanced intermediate and expert skiers. Beginners (and lift-ticket bargain hunters) can choose from a number of small but fun hills throughout northern New England.

Eat a Maine Lobster

Maine lobsters are world-renowned, and lobstermen and fish markets all along the coast will pack a live lobster in seaweed for overnight shipment to almost anywhere nationwide. These delectable crustaceans are available throughout New England, but without a doubt the best place to eat them is near the waters of origin. Lobster meat is sweet, especially the claws, and most agree that simple preparation is the best way to go: steamed and eaten with drawn butter or pulled into chunks and placed in a hot dog bun—the famous New England lobster roll. There are two types of lobster rolls to try: a cold

lobster salad with a leaf of lettuce and the barest amount of mayonnaise, and the Connecticut lobster roll, served warm with drawn butter and no mayo. Don't forget to save room for New England's other culinary treasure: *chowdah*. No two clam chowders taste the same, but they're all delicious.

Rise and Shine at a B&B

New England's distinctive architecture, much of it originating in the 18th and 19th centuries, has resulted in beautiful buildings of all shapes and sizes, many of which have been restored as bed-and-breakfasts. These inns typify the cozy, down-home, and historic feel of New England, and are an ideal lodging choice. This is especially true when the weather is cold, and the warm ambience of many of these inns more than justifies the slightly higher prices you'll pay here versus a hotel or motel.

Watch a Whale

The deep, cold waters of the North Atlantic serve as feeding grounds and migration routes for a variety of whales, including the fin, humpback, the occasional blue, and endangered white whales. Cape Cod and Maine's Southern Coast and Mid-Coast regions are the best places to hop aboard a whale-watching boat, but tours also depart from Boston Harbor. Some boat captains go so far as to guarantee at least a single sighting. The tours head to the whale feeding grounds about 20 miles offshore, where the majestic animals are numerous. The whale-watching season varies by tour skipper, but generally runs from April through October.

Fair Thee Well

New Englanders love their fairs and festivals. Maine-iacs celebrate the moose, clam, lobster, and blueberry, and a fair highlights organic farmers and their products. Maple sugar and maple syrup are feted in Vermont, while "live free or die" New Hampshire honors American independence. Newport, Rhode Island, hosts two highly regarded music festivals, one folk and one jazz. Many rural communities throughout New England hold agricultural fairs in late August and September.

Find the Perfect Souvenir

Artists and craftspeople abound in New England, meaning that finding the perfect souvenir of your vacation will be an enjoyable hunt. Whether you choose a watercolor of a picturesque fishing village, a functional and beautiful piece of handmade pottery, or a handcrafted piece of jewelry, you'll be supporting the local economy while taking a little piece of the region home with you.

Get Up Close and Personal with Nature

New England might be known for its flashy foliage in the fall and spectacular slopes in the winter, but the outdoors in the spring and summer delights all the senses as well. You can breathe in the ocean air as you drive along the Maine Coast or amble on Newport's 3½-mile Cliff Walk. Alternatively, enjoy the fragrance of the mountains and forests in the Berkshires, Vermont's Green Mountains, and New Hampshire's White Mountains while hiking along the Appalachian Trail. You may observe such animals as moose and bear. Close to the ocean there are numerous chances to see birds, seals, dolphins, and whales.

Savor Sweet Stuff

Summer vacations in New England go hand in hand with sweet treats; it's difficult to visit without sampling homemade

fudge at an old-fashioned candy store, buying an ice cream for your sweetie, or bringing home some saltwater taffy to share with the folks back at the ranch. Be sure to try a Maine specialty—the whoopie pie. Made from two chocolate circles of cake with vanilla cream filling in between, it's a delectable Maine tradition. If you are visiting Maine when the tiny but succulent wild blueberry is in season, take every opportunity to savor this flavorful fruit, whether in pie, muffin, or pancake form, and you'll understand its legendary culinary status. In Vermont, go on a factory tour at Ben & Jerry's, and have a delicious cone afterward. The Green Mountain state's favorite sons by no means have the market cornered on ice cream goodness; you'll find excellent frozen treats in every corner of the region (Cape Cod is an especially blessed area). In Boston, head to the Italian North End for a legendary cannoli. You can even have dessert for breakfast when you top your pancakes with Vermont's maple syrup.

Check Out Lighthouses

Maine's long and jagged coastline is home to more than 60 lighthouses, perched high on rocky ledges or on the tips of wayward islands. Though modern technology in navigation has made many of the lights obsolete, lighthouse enthusiasts and preservation groups restore and maintain many of them and often make them accessible to the public. Some of the state's more famous lights include Portland Head Light, commissioned by President George Washington in 1790 and immortalized in one of Edward Hopper's paintings; Two Lights, a few miles down the coast in Cape Elizabeth; and West Quoddy Head, on the easternmost tip of land in the United States. Some lighthouses are

privately owned and others accessible only by boat, but plenty are within easy reach and open to the public, some with museums and tours. At the Maine Lighthouse Museum in Rockland, visitors can view a collection of Fresnel lenses and Coast Guard artifacts.

Sail the Coast

The coastline of northern New England is a sailor's paradise, complete with hidden coves, windswept islands, and picture-perfect harbors where you can pick up a mooring for the night. With nearly 3,500 miles of undulating, rocky shoreline, you could spend a lifetime of summers sailing the waters off the Maine Coast and never see it all. If you're not one of the lucky few with a sailboat to call your own, there are many companies that offer sailboat charters, whether for day trips or weeklong excursions. It might sound like an expensive getaway, but as meals and drinks are usually included, an overnight sailing charter might not cost any more than a seaside hotel room, plus you have the advantage of an experienced captain to provide history and insight along the voyage.

Get the First Sight of First Light

At 1,530 feet, Cadillac Mountain, in Maine's Acadia National Park, is the highest mountain on the New England coast—so what better place to view the sunrise? Drive the winding and narrow 3.5-mile road to the summit before dawn (not accessible when the Loop Road is closed in the winter), and you could be the first person in the United States to see the summer sun's rays. (Note that this depends on the time of year; sometimes the first sunrise is at West Quoddy Head Lighthouse in Lubec, Maine).

NEW ENGLAND WITH KIDS

Children's Museum, Boston. Make bubbles, climb through a maze, and while away some hours in "Adventure Zone" at this fun museum just for tykes in Downtown Boston. A special play area for those under three lets them run around in a safe environment. Festivals happen throughout the year. (⇨ *Chapter 2.*)

Hampton Beach, New Hampshire. This seaside diversion draws families to its almost Coney Island–like fun. Along the boardwalk, kids enjoy arcade games, parasailing, live music, and an annual children's festival. They can even learn how saltwater taffy is made. (⇨ *Chapter 8.*)

Magic Wings Butterfly Conservatory & Gardens, Deerfield, Massachusetts. Almost 4,000 free-flying native and tropical butterflies are the star attraction here, contained within an 8,000-square-foot glassed enclosure that keeps the temperature upward of 80 degrees year-round. Relax around the Japanese koi pond on one of numerous benches and watch the kids chase the colorful creatures as they flit about. Or walk outside to the Iron Butterfly Outdoor Gardens, where flowers attract even more butterflies. (⇨ *Chapter 4.*)

Mystic Aquarium and Institute for Exploration, Mystic, Connecticut. This aquarium and research institute is one of only four North American facilities to feature endangered Steller sea lions, and New England's only beluga whale calls the aquarium home. Kids can touch a cownose ray, and you'll also see African penguins, harbor seals, graceful sea horses, Pacific octopuses, and sand tiger sharks. Nearby Mystic Seaport is another great attraction for kids and families. (⇨ *Chapter 5.*)

Montshire Museum of Science, Norwich, Vermont. This interactive museum uses more than 60 hands-on exhibits to explore nature and technology. The building sits amid 110 acres of woodlands and nature trails. Live animals are on-site as well. (⇨ *Chapter 7.*)

Massachusetts Audubon Wellfleet Bay Wildlife Sanctuary, South Wellfleet, Massachusetts. With its numerous programs and its beautiful salt-marsh surroundings, this is a favorite migration stop for Cape vacationers year-round. Five miles of nature trails weave throughout the sanctuary's 1,100 acres of marsh, beach, and woods. If you're careful and quiet, you might be able to get close to seals basking in the sun or birds such as the Great Blue Heron. Naturalists are on hand for guided walks and lectures. (⇨ *Chapter 3.*)

Plimoth Plantation, Plymouth, Massachusetts. Want to know what life was like in Colonial America? A visit to this living-history museum is like stepping into a time machine and zooming back to the year 1627. Curators are dressed in period costume and act like early-17th-century Pilgrims. (⇨ *Chapter 2.*)

Shelburne Farms, Shelburne, Vermont. This working dairy farm is also an educational and cultural resource center. Visitors can watch artisans make the farm's famous cheddar cheese from the milk of more than 100 purebred and registered Brown Swiss cows. A children's farmyard and walking trails round out the experience. (⇨ *Chapter 7.*)

Southworth Planetarium, Portland, Maine. This University of Southern Maine facility offers classes such as night-sky mythology and introductory astronomy. The 30-foot dome houses a star theater complete with lasers, digital sounds, and a star projector that displays more than 5,000 heavenly bodies. (⇨ *Chapter 10.*)

FLAVORS OF NEW ENGLAND

The locavore movement has finally hit New England. New farms, greenmarkets, and gourmet food shops are sprouting up every day and chefs are exploring more seasonably-based, farm-to-table options.

FOOD FESTIVALS

Wilton Blueberry Festival, Wilton, Maine. You can pick your own wild blueberries and sample baked goods from pancakes to pies at the annual Wilton Blueberry Festival (⊕ *www.wiltonbbf.com*), which takes place in early August.

Keene Pumpkin Festival, Keene, New Hampshire. Locals attempt to set the world record for most lit pumpkins at this yearly gathering (⊕ *pumpkinfestival2011.org*), which takes place in mid-to-late October. Enjoy hayrides and contests from pie-eating to pumpkin-seed-spitting.

Maine Lobster Festival, Rockland, Maine. Stuff your face with lobster tails and claws during this lobstravaganza (⊕ *www. mainelobsterfestival.com*) in early August. With almost 20,000 pounds of delicious crustacean at your finger tips, leaving hungry is unthinkable.

Vermont Cheesemakers Festival, Shelburne, Vermont. Artisanal cheeses and local beer and wine highlight this daylong festival (⊕ *www.vtcheesefest.com*) in late July. Sample more than 100 cheese varieties from 40 local cheesemakers in the Coach Barn of Shelburne Farms.

Chowderfest, Boston, Massachusetts. Thousands gather at City Hall Plaza for the annual Chowderfest (⊕ *www. bostonharborfest.com*) in early July. The chowder cook-off is part of Harborfest, Boston's yearly festivities centered around Independence Day.

SPECIALTIES BY STATE

Massachusetts

Concord grapes started growing in the namesake Massachusetts village way back in 1849. **Cranberries** are cultivated on marshy bogs, mostly in Massachusetts. Known as "Little Italy," Boston's **North End** contains almost 90 Italian restaurants; you'll find everything from hole-in-the-wall pizza joints to elegant eateries serving regional cuisine from every corner of the boot. No trip here is complete without a post-dinner **cannoli** from Mike's Pastry.

For more than 100 years fisherman and whalers of Portuguese and Azorean decent have called the seaside village of Provincetown home. Some say Provincetown Portuguese Bakery's decadent *malassadas* (fried dough dusted with sugar) are worth the trip alone.

Connecticut

The iconic **New Haven–style pizza,** a decidedly thin-crust pie cooked in a brick oven, can be found at several pizzerias in the Yale-infused town. The original creator, Frank Pepe Pizzeria Napoletana, has been around since 1925, while two blocks away is Sally's Apizza, established in 1938. If you prefer a newcomer, try BAR, a nightclub-cum-microbrewery popular with the college crowd. At any of the above, ask for fresh *mootz* (mozzarella in East Coast speak). **Connecticut-style lobster rolls,** warm lobster meat served on a bun doused with drawn butter, are another statewide specialty.

Over the past decade the state has also become known for its **vineyards.** Chardonnay, Riesling, Cabernet Sauvignon, and many other grape varietals are grown to produce local wines throughout New England, but Connecticut's wine production

stands out. The **Connecticut Wine Trail** is a collection of 24 vineyards, separated into the Western Trail in the Litchfield Hills and the Eastern Trail located near the southeastern shore. Hopkins Vineyard (Western Trail) overlooking Lake Waramaug and Jonathan Edwards Winery (Eastern Trail) are two of the most admired stops along the trail.

Rhode Island

Rhode Islanders are partial to **Jonnycakes,** a cornmeal flatbread that was once a staple of early American gastronomy. They also like to sip **cabinets**—milkshakes, often made with coffee and celery salt (also known as frappes in other parts of New England).

The Ocean State may be a small one, but its capital's food reputation is big, thanks to its status as the home of **Johnson & Wales,** an upper-echelon culinary academy. Some of its graduates have opened restaurants in Providence, drawing discriminating diners from near and far. Savor **Italian** food along Providence's Atwells Avenue in the **Federal Hill** neighborhood or nosh with the posh at upscale river-view establishments in downtown Providence.

Vermont

Vermonters are big on **maple syrup** straight up and in candies, but dairy products take top billing in this state. Milk and cream from the region's dairy farms are used in cheeses, like the famous **Vermont cheddars;** and in **ice cream,** like famed Ben & Jerry's. Willow Hill Farm in Milton, Vermont, is famous for their sheep's milk cheeses. Try their savory Vaquero Blue, a blue cheese made from both sheep and cow's milk. For a family-friendly stop, check out Shelburne Farms' children's farmyard. On the shores of Lake Champlain, Shelburne Farms uses only purebred Brown Swiss cows to make their famous farmhouse cheddar. In addition to the Vermont Cheesemakers Festival, Shelburne attracts visitors year round to taste mouthwatering cheeses and explore walking trails.

New Hampshire

Northern New Hampshire's cuisine carries a heavy French-Canadian influence. One of the most enticing francophone creations is *poutine* (french fries covered with cheese curds and gravy). The local **corn chowder** substitutes clams for corn and bacon, putting a twist on a Northeastern classic. **Smuttynose Brewing Company,** a craft brewery in Portsmouth, offers tours and tastings.

Maine

Lobster classics include **boiled lobster**—a staple at "in the rough" picnic-bench-and-paper-plate spots along the Maine Coast—and **lobster rolls,** a lobster meat–and-mayo or melted-butter preparation served in a toasted hot dog bun.

Blueberries, strawberries, raspberries, and blackberries grow wild (and on farms) all over the Northeast in summertime. Blueberry pancakes with maple syrup, blueberry muffins, and blueberry pies are very popular especially in coastal Maine. Mainers also love **whoopie pies,** cake-like cookies sandwiched together with frosting.

Portland's waterfront Commercial Street is bookended by two typical Maine diners, **Gilbert's Chowderhouse** and **Becky's Diner.** The former has one of the state's finest lobster rolls and homemade clam cakes; the latter opens for breakfast at 4 am to feed the fishermen before they head out to sea. Order a slice of fresh pie or buy one whole to take with you.

OUTDOOR
ADVENTURES

BEACHCOMBING
AND SWIMMING

Long, wide beaches edge the New England coast from southern Maine to southern Connecticut, with dozens dotting the shores of Cape Cod, Martha's Vineyard, and Nantucket. Many of the beaches have lifeguards on duty in season; some have picnic facilities, restrooms, changing facilities, and concession stands. Depending on the locale, you may need a parking sticker to use the lot.

When to Go

The waters are at their warmest in August, though they're cold even at the height of summer along much of Maine. Inland, small lake beaches abound, most notably in New Hampshire and Vermont. The best time to beach-comb is after the tide has gone out, when the retreating water has left behind its treasures. Early spring is an especially good time to see sand dollars washed up on beaches.

What to Look For

The best part of beachcombing is that you never quite know what you'll find at your feet. Sea glass—nothing more than man-made glass worn smooth from its seaward journeys—is common and most prized in rare shades of blue. You'll also find shells in abundance: blue mussels, tiny periwinkles, razor, or "jackknife" clams, ridged scallops, and oysters, with their rough outside shell and lovely mother-of-pearl interiors.

Best Beaches

Block Island, Rhode Island. Twelve miles off Rhode Island's coast, this 11-square-mile island has 12 miles of shoreline, 365 freshwater ponds, and plenty of hiking trails. Due to its rolling green hills,

some liken the island to Ireland. Take the hour-long ferry from Port Judith.

Cape Cod National Seashore, Massachusetts. With more than 150 beaches—roughly 40 miles worth—Cape Cod has enough to keep any beachcomber happy and sandy year-round. They range from the tourist-packed sand in Dennis to the almost untouched stretches of coast protected by the Cape Cod National Seashore. Favorite activities include swimming, bicycling, and even off-road ("over sand") travel (permit required).

Gloucester Beaches, Massachusetts. Along the North Shore, Gloucester is the oldest seaport in the nation. Its trio of beaches—Good Harbor Beach, Long Beach, and Wingaersheek Beach—cools those coming north of Boston for some sun and sand.

Hampton Beach State Park, New Hampshire. The Granite State's ocean shore is short, but this state park along historic Route 1 takes full advantage of the space it has. In addition to swimming and fishing, there are campsites with full hookups for RVs and an amphitheater with a band shell for fair-weather concerts.

Old Orchard Beach, Maine. Think Coney Island on a smaller scale. There's a white-sand beach to be sure (lapped by cold North Atlantic waters), but many come to ride the Pirate Ship at Palace Playland, drop quarters at the arcade, and browse the multitude of trinket-and-T-shirt shops.

Reid State Park, Maine. The water is cold much of the year, but this beach just east of Sheepscot Bay on Georgetown Island is a beautiful and quiet place to look for sand dollars or climb the rocks at low tide, exploring tidal pools. Great views can be had from the park's rocky Griffith Head.

BICYCLING

Biking on a road through New England's countryside is an idyllic way to spend a day. Many ski resorts allow mountain bikes in summer.

Bike Tours

There are a multitude of tour operators and magnificent trails throughout New England and many bike shops rent and repair bicycles. Urban Adventours in Downtown Boston provides both tours and rentals complete with helmet, lock, and Boston bike map. Bike New England offers cycling routes and maps throughout the Northeast.

Safety

On the road, watch for trucks and stay as close as possible to the side of the road, in single file. On the trail, ride within your limits and keep your eyes peeled for hikers and horses (both of which have the right of way), as well as dogs. Always wear a helmet and carry plenty of water.

Best Rides

Acadia National Park, Maine. At the heart of this popular park is the 45-mile network of historic carriage roads covered in crushed rock that bicyclists share only with equestrians and hikers. Hybrid or mountain bikes are the way to go here, leave your road bike at home. Fit and experienced riders can ascend the road to the top of Cadillac Mountain, but take caution: heavy traffic in the high season can make this a dangerous proposition.

All Along the Coast. U.S. 1, Maine. The major road that travels along the Maine Coast is only a narrow two-lane highway for most of its route, but it is still one of the country's most historic highways. As a result, it's very popular in spring, summer, and fall with serious long-distance bike riders.

Boston, Massachusetts. Commuters, students, and hard-core cyclists alike buzz along the streets and bike paths of New England's largest city. For a scenic ride, the 17-mile-long Dr. Paul Dudley White Bike Path can't be beat. It hugs the Charles River, with great views of practicing crew teams, the spires of Harvard University, and the Boston skyline. Or, for a bit of history with your ride, hop on the Minuteman Bikeway, which runs from the Alewife T stop (on the Red Line, in North Cambridge) to Lexington. From here, you can cycle to Concord, following the path the minutemen traveled on the first day of the American Revolution.

Cape Cod, Massachusetts. Cape Cod has miles of bike trails, some paralleling the national seashore, most on level terrain. On either side of the Cape Cod Canal is an easy 7-mile straight trail with views of the canal traffic. Extending 28 miles from South Dennis to Wellfleet, the Cape Cod Rail Trail is a converted rail bed that is now a paved, mostly flat bike path passing through a handful of the Cape's scenic towns, offering plenty of opportunity to take side trips.

Killington Resort, Vermont. Following the lead of many ski resorts in the western United States, Killington allows fat-tire riders on many of its ski trails after the snow has melted. Stunt riders can enjoy the jumps and bumps of the mountain bike park.

Portland, Maine. The paved **Eastern Prom Trail** extends from the edge of the Old Port to East End Beach, then to Back Bay for a 6-mile loop, before returning.

BOATING

Along many of New England's larger lakes, sailboats, rowboats, canoes, kayaks, and outboards are available for rent at local marinas. Sailboats are available for rent at a number of seacoast locations, but you may be required to prove your seaworthiness. Lessons are frequently available.

What to Wear

It can get cold on the water, especially while sailing so dress in layers and bring along a windbreaker and fleece even if it's warm on land. Don't wear cotton or jeans: once they get wet, they stay wet and will leave you chilled. Sunscreen, sunglasses (with Croakies so they don't fall overboard), and a hat are also musts, as are drinking water and high-energy snacks, especially for canoe and kayak expeditions.

Best Boating

Allagash Wilderness Waterway, Maine. This scenic and remote waterway—92 miles of lakes, ponds, rivers, and streams—is part of the 740-mile Northern Forest Canoe Trail, which floats through New York, Vermont, Québec, and New Hampshire as well as Maine.

Lake Champlain, Vermont. Called by some the sixth Great Lake, 435-square-mile Lake Champlain is bordered by Vermont's Green Mountains to the east and the Adirondacks of New York to the west. Burlington, Vermont, is the largest lakeside city and a good bet for renting a boat—be it canoe, kayak, rowboat, skiff, or motorboat. Attractions include numerous islands and deep-blue water that's often brushed by pleasant New England breezes.

Lakes Region, New Hampshire. Lake Winnipesaukee is the largest lake in New Hampshire, but there are many puddles large and small worth dipping a paddle into. Squam Lake is a tranquil lake made famous by *On Golden Pond*, Lake Wentworth has a state park with a boat launch, bathhouse, and picnic tables.

Mystic, Connecticut. The world's largest maritime museum, Mystic Seaport, is also a good place to get out on the water. A wide variety of sailing programs are available here—including lessons on a 61-foot schooner—as is instruction on powerboating. If you're eager to test your skills against other sailors, there's also a weekly race series.

Newport and Block Island, Rhode Island. Narragansett Bay, Newport Harbor, and Block Island Sound are among the premier sailing areas in the world. (Newport hosted the America's Cup, yachting's most prestigious race, from 1930 to 1983. San Francisco is scheduled to host in 2013.) Numerous outfitters provide public and private sailing tours, sailing lessons, and boat rentals.

Rockland, Maine. For a guided trip on the water, consider a windjammer excursion out of Rockland, Camden or Rockport. From day sails to multiday cruises, trips cost between $50 and $1,000, and include meals. Check Maine Windjammer Association (⊕ *www.sailmainecoast. com*) or Windjammer Cruises (⊕ *www. mainewindjammercruises.com*) for more information.

GOLF

Golf caught on early in New England. In fact, Newport Country Club hosted the first-ever U.S. Open Championship in 1895 and The Country Club in Brookline, Massachusetts, has since hosted the major tournament three times. It is one of the five founding members of the U.S. Golf Association and recognized as one of the first 100 golf clubs in America.

The region has an ample supply of public and semiprivate courses, many of which are part of distinctive resorts or even ski areas. One dilemma facing golfers is keeping their eye on the ball instead of the scenery. The views are marvelous at Balsams Wilderness grand resort in Dixville Notch, New Hampshire, and the nearby course at the splendid old Mount Washington Hotel in Bretton Woods. During prime season, make sure you reserve ahead for tee times, particularly near urban areas and at resorts.

Best Tees

The Gleneagles Golf Course at the Equinox, Vermont. One of the stateliest lodging resorts in all of New England, the Equinox opened in 1769 and has hosted the likes of Teddy Roosevelt and Mary Todd Lincoln. The golf course is par-71 and 6,423 yards, and is especially alluring in the fall when the trees that line the fairways explode in color. After golf, go to the 13,000-square-foot spa for some pampering. The resort is ringed by mountain splendor.

Newton Commonwealth Golf Course, Massachusetts. Minutes from Downtown Boston, this municipal golf course is open to the public seven days a week. Even with 18 holes it isn't a long course, but it can't be beat for a quick break from sightseeing in Beantown.

Pinehills Golf Club, Massachusetts. Located in Plymouth, less than an hour from Boston, Pinehills features a pair of five-star golf courses—one designed by Jack Nicklaus and the other by Rees Jones. Shaped by two of the world's premier golf course architects and adorned with top-notch facilities, this public course is widely recognized as one of the best in New England.

Samoset Resort on the Ocean, Maine. Few things match playing 18 holes on a championship course that's bordered by the North Atlantic. In Rockport, Maine, along Penobscot Bay, Samoset Resort's course is open from May through October. Book a room at the luxurious hotel here to make it a complete golf vacation.

HIKING

Probably the most famous trails in the region are the 270-mile Long Trail, which runs north–south through the center of Vermont, and the Maine-to-Georgia Appalachian Trail, which runs through New England on both private and public land. The Appalachian Mountain Club (AMC) maintains a system of staffed huts in New Hampshire's Presidential Range, with bunk space and meals available by reservation. State parks throughout the region afford good hiking.

Safety

There are few real hazards to hiking, but a little preparedness goes a long way. Know your limits, and make sure the terrain you are about to embark on doesn't exceed your abilities. Check the trail map carefully and pay attention to elevation changes, which make a huge difference in the difficulty of a hike (a steep 1-mile-long trail is much tougher to negotiate than a flat 2- or even 3-mile trail). Bring layers of clothing to accommodate changing weather and always carry enough drinking water. Before you go, be sure to tell someone where you're going and how long you expect to be gone.

Best Hikes

Appalachian Trail, Massachusetts, Connecticut, Vermont, New Hampshire, Maine. This path from Georgia to Maine is as great for a short day hike as it is for a challenging six-month endurance test. The AT is marked by rectangular white blazes which are kept up and relatively easy to follow. ⇨ *For a guide to the best day hikes and more information on hiking the AT, see "A Walk in the Woods: Hiking the Appalachian Trail" feature in Chapter 8.*

Mt. Washington, New Hampshire. The cog railroad and the auto road to the summit are popular routes up New England's highest mountain, but for those with stamina and legs of steel it's one heck of a hike. There are a handful of trails to the top, the most popular beginning at Pinkham Notch Visitor Center. Be sure to dress in layers and have some warm clothing for the frequent winds toward the peak.

The Long Trail, Vermont. Following the main ridge of the Green Mountains from one end of Vermont to the other, this is the nation's oldest long-distance trail. In fact, some say it was the inspiration for the Appalachian Trail. Hardy hikers make a go of its 270-mile length, but day hikers can drop in and out at many places along the way.

HISTORY YOU CAN SEE

History lies thick on the ground in New England—from Pilgrims to pirates, witches to whalers, the American Revolution to the Industrial Revolution.

Pilgrim's Progress

The story of the Pilgrims comes alive when you visit New England. From Provincetown (where the *Mayflower* actually first landed) to Plymouth and throughout Cape Cod, these early New England settlers left an indelible mark on the region. Their contemporaries, the Puritans, founded the city of Boston. Both groups, seeking religious freedom, planted the seeds for the founding of the United States.

What to See:

In Plymouth (south of Boston) you can visit **Plimoth Plantation**, *Mayflower II*, the **National Monument to the Forefathers**, and, of course, **Plymouth Rock** itself (⇨ *Side Trips from Boston in Chapter 2*). On Cape Cod, visit **First Encounter Beach** in Eastham and the **Pilgrim Monument** in Provincetown (⇨ *Cape Cod in Chapter 3*).

Talkin' 'Bout a Revolution

New England is the cradle of democracy. Home to many of the patriots who launched the American Revolution and the war's first battles, here you can see real evidence of the events you read about in history class. From battlefields to the Boston Tea Party ship, New England (and especially Massachusetts) is filled with touchstones of our national story.

What to See:

In Boston, walk the **Freedom Trail** (⇨ *Boston in Chapter 2*) or just be on the look-out for markers and plaques as you walk around Downtown—you can literally trip over history wherever you step. Outside the city, **Lexington** and **Concord** (⇨ *The North Shore and South of Boston in Chapter 2*) are easy visits for a quick primer on the start of the American Revolution.

Sea to Shining Sea

New England has a proud (and long) maritime history. From the *Mayflower* to boatbuilders in Maine who still produce wooden ships, you'll feel New England's seafaring traditions anywhere on the coast here. Many museums tell the story of the region's contributions to shipbuilding, nautical exploration, and whaling. And although the latter is no longer a pillar of the local economy, today you can go visit Earth's largest mammals on whale-watching expeditions that leave from many points along the New England coast.

What to See:

Arguably the nation's most famous ship, the USS *Constitution*, is docked in Charlestown, Massachusetts, just outside of Boston (⇨ *Exploring Boston in Chapter 2*). The **Maine Maritime Museum** in Bath, Maine, is the last remaining intact shipyard in the United States to have built large wooden sailing vessels (⇨ *Portland and Environs in Chapter 10*). But the granddaddy of New England maritime experiences is undoubtedly **Mystic Seaport**, where almost 500 vessels are preserved (⇨ *New Haven to Mystic in Chapter 5*).

Frozen in Time

New England preserves its past like no other region of the United States. In addition to countless museums, historic sites, refurbished homes, and historical markers, the area has several wonderfully preserved villages, each trying to capture a specific moment in time.

What to See:

A mile-long stretch of Main Street in Deerfield, Massachusetts, contains a remarkably well-preserved portion of an 18th-century village. **Historic Deerfield** (⇨ *The Pioneer Valley in Chapter 4*) contains 13 homes built between 1730 and 1850, all maintained as interpretive museums. Together, they house more than 25,000 artifacts harking back to a quintessential New England town.

One of the country's finest re-creations of a Colonial-era village, **Old Sturbridge Village** (⇨ *The Pioneer Valley in Chapter 4*) emulates an early-19th-century New England town, with more than 40 historic buildings moved here from other communities. Staff interpreters, clad in period costumes, do the sort of activities that villagers did back in the day: farmers plow, blacksmiths pound, and bakers bake. Though you might think it a static, if re-enactive, slice of quintessential New England life, the village represents a period of transition brought about by the growing significance of commerce and manufacturing, improvements in agriculture and transportation, and various social changes.

Near Lake Champlain, the **Shelburne Museum** (⇨ *Northern Vermont in Chapter 7*) spans 39 exhibition halls—many of which are restored 18th- and 19th-century buildings relocated here from locales throughout New England and New York. The sheer size and breadth of the museum's collections are dizzying. On display are more than 150,000 artifacts and works of art, as well as period structures that include a one-room schoolhouse, a lighthouse, a covered bridge, and even the 220-foot steamboat *Ticonderoga,* which once sailed Lake Champlain and is the last side-wheel steamboat of its

kind. Landscaping recalls a classic New England village and features more than 400 lilac trees and various gardens.

Writing the Story of America

The list of New England writers who have shaped American culture is long indeed. Massachusetts alone has produced great poets in every generation: Anne Bradstreet, Phillis Wheatley, Emily Dickinson, Henry Wadsworth Longfellow, William Cullen Bryant, e.e. cummings, Robert Lowell, Elizabeth Bishop, Sylvia Plath, and Anne Sexton. Bay State writers include Louisa May Alcott, author of the enduring classic *Little Women*; Nathaniel Hawthorne, who re-created the Salem of his Puritan ancestors in *The Scarlet Letter*; Herman Melville, who wrote *Moby-Dick* in a house at the foot of Mt. Greylock; Eugene O'Neill, whose early plays were produced at a makeshift theater in Provincetown on Cape Cod; Lowell native Jack Kerouac, author of *On the Road*; and John Cheever, chronicler of suburban angst. Mark Twain, arguably the most famous American author of all, lived in Connecticut for much of his writing career (in Hartford and later Redding).

What to See:

Many homes of famous New England writers are preserved. An especially rich stop is **Concord, Massachusetts,** where you can see the homes of Alcott, Ralph Waldo Emerson, Henry David Thoreau, and Hawthorne (as well as Thoreau's Walden Pond). You can visit their graves (as well as those of other authors) in the Author's Ridge section of the town's **Sleepy Hollow Cemetery** (⇨ *Side Trips from Boston in Chapter 2*). Another favorite stop is the **Mark Twain House** in Hartford, Connecticut (⇨ *Hartford and the Connecticut River Valley in Chapter 5*).

GREAT
ITINERARIES

NEW ENGLAND HIGHLIGHTS

In a nation where distances can often be daunting, New England packs its top attractions into a remarkably compact area. Understanding Yankeedom might take a lifetime—but it's possible to get a good appreciation for the six-state region in a 2½-week drive. The following itinerary assumes you're beginning your trip in Hartford, Connecticut (which is about three hours northeast of New York City). Of course, a trip to just a few of these locations would be rewarding and give you a good sampling of what the region has to offer.

Day 1: Hartford
The **Mark Twain House** resembles a Mississippi steamboat beached in a Victorian neighborhood (adjacent to it is the **Harriet Beecher Stowe House** museum). Downtown, you can visit Connecticut's ornate **State Capitol** and the **Wadsworth Atheneum**, which houses fine impressionist and Hudson River School paintings. For the sports buff, the **Naismith Memorial Basketball Hall of Fame** is only a quick detour up I-91 to Springfield, where Dr. James Naismith invented basketball in 1891. (⇨ *Hartford and the Connecticut River Valley in Chapter 5 and the Berkshires and Western Massachusetts in Chapter 4.*)

Day 2 and 3: Lower Connecticut River Valley and Block Island Sound
Here centuries-old towns such as **Essex**, **Chester**, and **Mystic** coexist with a well-preserved natural environment. In Rhode Island, sandy beaches dot the coast in **Watch Hill**, **Charlestown**, and **Narragansett**. (⇨ *Hartford and the Connecticut River Valley in Chapter 5 and South County in Chapter 6.*)

Day 4: Newport
Despite its Colonial downtown and seaside parks, to most people Newport means mansions—the most opulent, cost-be-damned enclave of private homes ever built in the United States. Turn-of-the-20th-century "cottages" such as the **Breakers** and **Marble House** are beyond duplication today. (⇨ *Newport County in Chapter 6.*)

Day 5: Providence
Rhode Island's capital holds treasures like **Benefit Street**, with its Federal-era homes, and the **Museum of Art at the Rhode Island School of Design**. Be sure to savor a knockout Italian meal on **Federal Hill** and visit **Waterplace Park and Riverwalk**. In the summer, catch a Paw Sox baseball game at McCoy Stadium in the neighboring town of Pawtucket. (⇨ *Providence in Chapter 6.*)

Day 6 and 7: Cape Cod
Meander along Massachusetts's beach-lined arm-shaped peninsula and explore **Cape Cod National Seashore**. Fun **Provincetown**, at the Cape's tip, is Bohemian, gay, and touristy, a Portuguese fishing village built on a Colonial foundation. In season, you can also whale-watch here. (⇨ *Cape Cod in Chapter 3.*)

Day 8: Plymouth
"America's hometown" is where 102 weary settlers landed in 1620. You can climb aboard the replica *Mayflower II*, then spend time at **Plimoth Plantation**, staffed by costumed "Pilgrims." (⇨ *The North Shore and South of Boston in Chapter 2.*)

Day 9–11: Boston
In Boston, famous buildings such as **Faneuil Hall** are not merely civic landmarks but national icons. From the **Boston Common**, the 2.5-mile **Freedom Trail** links treasures of American liberty such as the USS *Constitution* ("Old Ironsides") and the **Old North Church** (of "one if by land, two if by sea" fame). Be sure to walk the gas-lighted streets of **Beacon Hill**, too. On your second day, explore the massive **Museum**

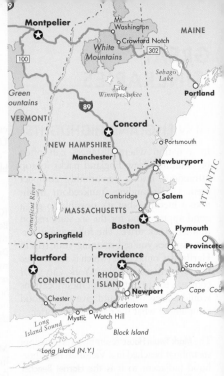

of Fine Arts and the grand boulevards and shops of **Back Bay**. On your third day, visit colorful **Cambridge, Harvard University,** and its museums. (⇨ *Boston, Chapter 2.*)

Day 12: Salem and Newburyport

In Salem, many sites, including the **Peabody Essex Museum,** recall the dark days of the 1690s witch hysteria and the fortunes amassed in the China trade. Newburyport's Colonial and Federal-style homes testify to Yankee enterprise on the seas. (⇨ *The North Shore in Chapter 2.*)

Day 13: Manchester and Concord

Manchester, New Hampshire's largest city, holds the **Amoskeag Mills,** a reminder of New England's industrial past. Smaller Concord is the state capital. Near the **State House** is the fine **Museum of New Hampshire History,** housing one of the locally built stagecoaches that carried Concord's name throughout the West. (⇨ *The Monadnocks and Merrimack Valley in Chapter 8.*)

Day 14 and 15: Green Mountains and Montpelier

From Concord, head northwest on I–89 and shortly after entering Vermont, hop on Route 100 North toward Montpelier. Route 100 runs along the eastern edge of the Green Mountains' rounded peaks and begins near **Green Mountain National Forest** in Vermont's southwest corner. The state's vest-pocket capital, Montpelier, has the gold-dome **Vermont State House,** the quirky **Vermont Museum,** and is also a relatively short ride (130 miles) from the French Canadian city of Montreal. (⇨ *Central Vermont and Northern Vermont in Chapter 7.*)

Day 16 and 17: White Mountains

U.S. 302 threads through New Hampshire's White Mountains, passing beneath brooding **Mt. Washington** and through **Crawford Notch,** before extending all the way to the coastal city of Portland,

Maine. In Bretton Woods, the **Mt. Washington Cog Railway** still chugs to the summit, and the **Mount Washington Hotel** recalls the glory days of White Mountain resorts. (⇨ *The White Mountains in Chapter 8.*)

Day 18: Portland

Maine's maritime capital shows off its restored waterfront at the **Old Port.** Nearby, two lighthouses on Cape Elizabeth, **Two Lights** and **Portland Head,** still stand vigil. (⇨ *Portland in Chapter 10.*)

THE SEACOAST

Every New England state except Vermont borders on saltwater. For history buffs, vivid links to the days when the sea was the region's lifeblood abound; for watersports enthusiasts, the sea guarantees fun.

Day 1–3: Southeastern Connecticut and Newport

Begin in **New London,** Connecticut home of the **U.S. Coast Guard Academy,** and board the USCGS *Eagle* (when in port) or tour the on-site museum that details more than 200 years of Coast Guard maritime history. In Mystic, the days of wooden ships and whaling adventures live on at **Mystic Seaport.** In Rhode Island, savor the Victorian resort of **Watch Hill** and the Block Island Sound beaches. See the extravagant summer mansions in **Newport.** (⇨ *New Haven to Mystic in Chapter 5, South County and Newport County in Chapter 6.*)

Day 4–7: Massachusetts's South Shore and Cape Cod

New Bedford was once a major whaling center; exhibits at the **New Bedford Whaling Museum** capture this vanished world. In **Plymouth,** visit the *Mayflower II* and **Plimoth Plantation,** the re-created Pilgrim village. **Cape Cod** can be nearly all things to all visitors, with quiet Colonial villages and lively resorts, gentle bayside wavelets, and crashing surf. (⇨ *South of Boston in Chapter 2 and Chapter 3.*)

Day 8–10: Boston and the North Shore

To savor Boston's centuries-old ties to the sea, take a half-day stroll by **Faneuil Hall** and **Quincy Market** or a boat tour of the harbor (you can even head out on a whale-watching tour from here). In **Salem,** the **Peabody Essex Museum** and the **Salem Maritime National Historic Site** chronicle the country's early shipping fortunes. Spend a day exploring more of the North Shore, including the old fishing port of **Gloucester** and **Rockport,** one possible place to buy that seascape painted in oils. **Newburyport,** with its Federal-style ship-owners' homes, is home to the Parker River National Wildlife Refuge, beloved by birders and beach walkers. (⇨ *Chapter 2.*)

Day 11–12: New Hampshire and Southern Maine

New Hampshire fronts the Atlantic for a scant 18 miles, but its coastal landmarks range from honky-tonk **Hampton Beach** to

quiet **Odiorne Point State Park** in Rye and pretty **Portsmouth,** where the cream of pre-Revolutionary society built Georgian- and Federal-style mansions—visit a few at the **Strawbery Banke Museum** and elsewhere. Between here and Portland, Maine's largest city, lie ocean-side resorts such as **Kennebunkport.** Near Portland is **Cape Elizabeth,** with its **Portland Head** and **Two Lights** lighthouses. (⇨ *Chapter 8 and Chapter 10.*)

Day 13–15: Down East

Beyond Portland ranges the ragged, island-strewn coast of Down East Maine. Some highlights are the retail outlets of **Freeport,** home of **L.L. Bean; Brunswick,** with the museums of Bowdoin College; and **Bath,** with the **Maine Maritime Museum.** Perhaps you'll think about cruising on one of the majestic schooners that sail out of **Rockland.** In **Camden** and **Castine,** exquisite inns occupy homes built from inland Maine's gold, timber. On your second day, visit the spectacular rocky coast of **Acadia National Park,** near the resort town of **Bar Harbor.** (⇨ *Chapter 10.*)

A CELEBRATION

Picture this: one scarlet maple offset by the stark white spire of a country church, a whole hillside of brilliant foliage foregrounded by a vintage barn or perhaps a covered bridge that straddles a cobalt river. Such iconic scenes have launched a thousand postcards and turned New England into the ultimate fall destination for leaf peepers.

OF COLOR

By Susan MacCallum-Whitcomb

Mother Nature, of course, puts on an annual autumn performance elsewhere, but this one is a showstopper. Like the landscape, the mix of deciduous (leaf-shedding) trees is remarkably varied here and creates a broader than usual palette. New England's abundant evergreens lend contrast, making the display even more vivid. Every September and October, leaf peepers arrive to cruise along country lanes, join outdoor adventures, or simply stroll on town greens.

Did you know the brilliant shades actually lurk in the leaves all year long? Leaves contain three pigments. The green chlorophyll, so dominant in summer that it obscures the red anthocyanins and orangey-yellow carotenoids, decreases in fall and reveals a crayon box of color.

Above, Vermont's Green Mountains are multicolored in the fall (and often white in winter).

PREDICTING THE PEAK

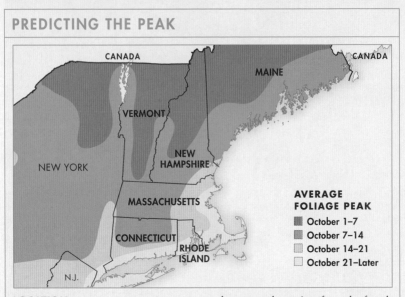

AVERAGE
FOLIAGE PEAK
- ■ October 1–7
- ■ October 7–14
- ☐ October 14–21
- ☐ October 21–Later

LOCATION

Pinning down precisely when colors will appear remains an inexact science, although location plays a major role. Typically, the transformation begins in the highest and northernmost parts of New England in mid-September, then moves steadily into lower altitudes and southern sectors throughout October.

For trip planning, think in terms of regions rather than states. In Maine (a huge state that runs north–south) leaf color can peak anytime from the fourth week of September to the third week of October, depending on the locale.

WEATHER

Early September weather is another deciding factor. From the foliage aficionado's perspective, the ideal scenario is calm, temperate days capped by nights that are cool but still above freezing. If the weather is too warm, it delays the onset of the season. If it's too dry or windy, the leaves shrivel up or blow off.

COLOR CHECK RESOURCES

Curious about current conditions? In season, each state maintains a dedicated Web site reporting on foliage conditions. Weather Channel has peak viewing maps and Foliage Network uses a network of spotters to chart changes.

- ■ **Connecticut:** ☎ 800/282–6863 ⊕ www.ct.gov/dep
- ■ **Foliage Network:** ⊕ www.foliagenetwork.com
- ■ **Maine:** ☎ 888/624–6345 ⊕ www.maine.gov/doc/foliage
- ■ **Massachusetts:** ☎ 617/973–8500 ⊕ www.massvacation.com
- ■ **New Hampshire:** ☎ 800/258–3608 ⊕ www.visitnh.gov
- ■ **Rhode Island:** ☎ 800/556–2484 ⊕ www.visitri.com
- ■ **Vermont:** ☎ 800/837–6668 ⊕ www.foliage-vermont.com
- ■ **Weather Channel:** ⊕ www.weather.com

TOP TREES FOR COLOR

A AMERICAN BEECH. This tree's smooth, steel-gray trunk is crowned with gold, copper, and bronze-tinted leaves in autumn, giving it a metallic sheen. Though the elliptical leaves sometimes hang on all winter, its "fruit" goes fast because beechnuts are a popular snack for birds, squirrels, and even bears.

B NORTHERN RED OAK. The upside of oaks is that they retain their fall shading until late in the season—the downside is that, for most species, that color is a boring brown. Happily, the northern red isn't like other members of the oak family. Its elongated, flame-shaped leaves turn fiery crimson and incandescent orange.

C QUAKING ASPEN. Eyes and ears both prove useful when identifying this aspen. Look for small, ovate leaves that usually become almost flaxen. Or listen for the leaves' quake: a sound, audible in even a gentle breeze, which the U.S. Forest Service likens to that made by "thousands of fluttering butterfly wings."

D SUGAR MAPLE. The leaf of the largest North American maple species is so lovely that Canada put it on its national flag. Each generally has five multi-pointed lobes—plus enough anthocyanin to produce a deep red color. The tree itself produces plentiful sap and is the cornerstone of New England's syrup industry.

E WHITE ASH. This tall tree typically grows to between 65 to 100 feet. Baseball enthusiasts admire the wood (which is used to craft bats); while foliage fans admire the compound leaves, each consisting of five to nine slightly serrated, tapering leaflets. They range in hue from burgundy and purple to amber.

F WHITE BIRCH. A papery, light, bright bark makes this slender hardwood easily recognizable. Centuries ago, Native Americans used birch wood to make everything from canoes to medicinal teas. Today's photographers know the bark also makes great pictures since it provides a sharp contrast to the tree's vibrant yellow leaves.

FANTASTIC FALL ITINERARY

The Berkshires

Fall is the perfect time to visit New England—country roads wind through dense forests exploding into reds, oranges, yellows, and purples. For inspiration, here is an itinerary for the truly ambitious that links the most stunning foliage areas; choose a section to explore more closely. Like autumn itself, this route works its way south from northern Vermont into Connecticut, with one or two days in each area.

VERMONT

NORTHWEST VERMONT

In Burlington, the elms will be turning colors on the University of Vermont campus. You can ride the ferry across Lake Champlain for great views of Vermont's Green Mountains and New York's Adirondacks. After visiting the resort town of Stowe, detour off Route 100 beneath the cliffs of Smugglers' Notch. The north country's palette unfolds in Newport, where the blue waters of Lake Memphremagog reflect the foliage. (⇨ *Northern Vermont in Chapter 7.*)

NORTHEAST KINGDOM

After a side trip along Lake Willoughby, explore St. Johnsbury, where the Fairbanks Museum and St. Johnsbury Athenaeum reveal Victorian tastes in art and natural-history collecting. In Peacham, stock up for a picnic at the Peacham Store. (⇨ *Northern Vermont in Chapter 7.*)

NEW HAMPSHIRE

WHITE MOUNTAINS AND LAKES REGION

In New Hampshire, Interstate 93 narrows as it winds through craggy Franconia Notch. Get off the interstate for the sinuous Kancamagus Highway portion of Route 112 that passes through the mountains to Conway. In Center Harbor, in the Lakes Region, you can ride the *MS Mount Washington* for views of the Lake Winnipesaukee shoreline, or ascend to Moultonborough's Castle in the Clouds for a falcon's-eye look at the colors. (⇨ *The White Mountains and Lakes Region in Chapter 8.*)

MT. MONADNOCK

In Concord, stop at the Museum of New Hampshire History and the State House. Several trails climb Mt. Monadnock, near Jaffrey Center, and colorful vistas extend as far as Boston. (⇨ *The Monadnocks and Merrimack Valley in Chapter 8.*)

⇨ For local drives perfect for an afternoon, also see our Fall Foliage Drive Spotlights in Chapters 4 (Western Massachusetts), 5 (Connecticut), 6 (Rhode Island), 7 (Vermont), 8 (New Hampshire), and 9 (Inland Maine).

THE MOOSE IS LOOSE!

Take "Moose Crossing" signs seriously because things won't end well if you hit an animal that stands six feet tall and weighs 1,200 pounds. Some 40,000 reside in northern New England. To search out these ungainly creatures in the wild, consider an orgaznized moose safari in northern New Hampshire or Maine.

MASSACHUSETTS

THE MOHAWK TRAIL

In Shelburne Falls, Massachusetts, the Bridge of Flowers displays the last of autumn's blossoms. Follow the Mohawk Trail section of Route 2 as it ascends into the Berkshire Hills—and stop to take in the view at the hairpin turn just east of North Adams (or drive up Mt. Greylock, the tallest peak in New England, for more stunning vistas). In Williamstown, the Sterling and Francine Clark Art Institute houses a collection of impressionist works. (⇨ *The Pioneer Valley and the Berkshires in Chapter 4.*)

THE BERKSHIRES

The scenery around Lenox, Stockbridge, and Great Barrington has long attracted the talented and the wealthy. Near U.S. 7, you can visit the homes of novelist Edith Wharton (the Mount, in Lenox), sculptor Daniel Chester French (Chesterwood, in Stockbridge), and diplomat Joseph Choate (Naumkeag, in Stockbridge). (⇨ *The Berkshires in Chapter 4.*)

CONNECTICUT

THE LITCHFIELD HILLS

This area of Connecticut combines the feel of upcountry New England with exclusive urban polish. The wooded shores of Lake Waramaug are home to country inns and wineries in pretty towns. Litchfield has a perfect village green—an idealized New England town center. (⇨ *The Litchfield Hills in Chapter 5.*)

FOLIAGE PHOTO HINT

Don't just snap the big panoramic views. Look for single, brilliantly colored trees with interesting elements nearby, like a weathered gray stone wall or a freshly painted white church. These images are often more evocative than big blobs of color or panoramic shots.

LEAF PEEPER PLANNER

Hot-air balloons and ski-lift rides give a different perspective on fall's color.

Enjoying fall doesn't necessarily require a multistate road trip. If you are short on time (or energy), a simple autumnal stroll might be just the ticket: many state parks even offer free short ranger-led rambles.

HIKE AND BIKE ON A TOUR

You can sign on for foliage-focused hiking holidays with **Country Walkers** (☎ *800/464–9255* ⊕ *www.countrywalkers.com*) and **Boundless Journeys** (☎ *800/941–8010* ⊕ *www.boundlessjourneys.com*); or cycling ones with **Bike Vermont** (☎ *800/257–2226* ⊕ *www.bikevt.com*) and **VBT Bicycling Vacations** (☎ *800/245–3868,* ⊕ *www.vbt.com*). Individual state tourism boards list similar operators elsewhere.

SOAR ABOVE THE CROWDS

New Hampshire's Cannon Mountain (☎ *603/823–8800* ⊕ *www.cannonmt.com*) is only one of several New England ski resorts that provides gondola or aerial tram rides during foliage season. Area hot-air balloon operators, like **Balloons of Vermont, LLC** (☎ *802/369–0213* ⊕ *www.balloonsofvermont.com*), help you take it in from the top.

ROOM AT THE INN?

Accommodations fill quickly in autumn. Vermont's top lodgings sell out months in advance for the first two weeks in October. So book early and expect a two-night minimum stay requirement. If you can't find a quaint inn, try basing yourself at a B&B or off-season ski resort. Also, be prepared for some sticker shock; if you can travel midweek, you'll often save quite a bit.

RIDE THE RAILS OR THE CURRENT

Board the **Essex Steam Train** for a ride through the Connecticut countryside (☎ *800/377–3987* ⊕ *www.essexsteamtrain.com*) or float through northern Rhode Island on the **Blackstone Valley Explorer** riverboat (☎ *401/724–2200* ⊕ *www.rivertourblackstone.com*).

Boston and Environs

WORD OF MOUTH

"We loved The Freedom Trail as it gave us an opportunity to explore the history of Boston and to have a good look at parts of this gorgeous city."

—cathies

WELCOME TO BOSTON AND ENVIRONS

TOP REASONS TO GO

★ **Freedom's Ring:** Walk through America's early history on the 2½-mile Freedom Trail that snakes through town.

★ **Ivy-Draped Campus:** Hang in Harvard Square like a collegiate or hit the university's museums: the Sackler (ancient art), the Botanical Museum, the Peabody (archeology), and the Natural History Museum.

★ **Posh Purchases:** Strap on some stilettos and join the quest for fashionable finds on Newbury Street, Boston's answer to Manhattan's 5th Avenue.

★ **Sacred Ground:** Root for (or boo) the Red Sox at baseball's most hallowed shrine, Fenway Park.

★ **Painted Glory:** Check out the beautiful Isabella Stewart Gardner Museum or stop by the Museum of Fine Arts, and view works by French masters Edouard Manet, Camille Passarro, and Pierre-Auguste Renoir, and American painters Mary Cassatt, John Singer Sargent, and Edward Hopper.

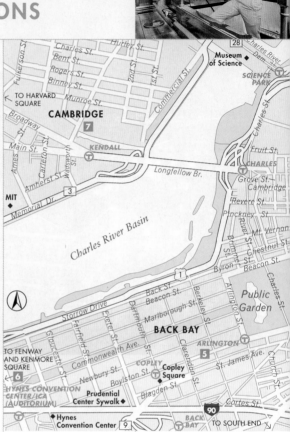

1 Beacon Hill, Boston Common, and the Old West End. The Brahmins' old stomping ground has many landmarks (Boston Common and the State House among them). The Old West End has the Museum of Science and TD Garden.

2 Government Center and the North End. The sterile Government Center area is home to lovely Faneuil Hall and the trio of restored buildings that share its name. The small North End is full of history and a strong Italian influence.

3 Charlestown. Charlestown's Freedom Trail sights can't be missed—literally. The Bunker Hill Monument is a towering tribute to a pivotal 1775 battle; the USS Constitution, a towering tangle of masts and rigging, highlights the neighborhood's naval heritage.

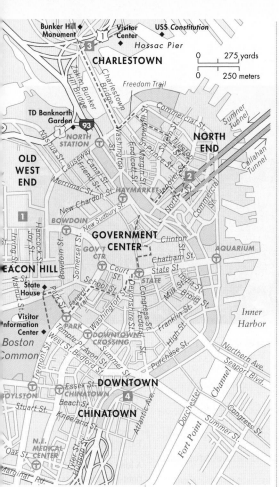

2

GETTING ORIENTED

With such a complex identity, it's no surprise that Boston, despite its relatively small size, offers visitors a diverse set of experiences. History buffs—and just about everyone else—will spend a day or more following the thick red line of the Freedom Trail and tracing Revolutionary history through town. Shopaholics can join the quest for fashionable finds on Newbury Street, while sports fiends gravitate toward Fenway Park for a tour (or if very lucky, a game) of the beloved Boston Red Sox's home. The Museum of Fine Art's expansive catalog of French impressionists and American painters, the Isabella Stewart Gardner Museum's palazzo of painting masters, and the Institute of Contemporary Art's modern works satisfy any artistic taste.

4 Downtown. This maze-like section of central Boston encompasses the Financial District and Downtown Crossing (a retail zone); as well as Chinatown, the revived Theater District, plus portions of the Freedom Trail and HarborWalk.

5 The Back Bay. Back Bay's chichi shops, upscale restaurants, and deluxe lodgings sit alongside attractions like the Public Garden and Public Library.

6 The Fenway. Sox fans, art lovers, and college students all frequent the Fens. Fenway Park, the Museum of Fine Arts, and the Isabella Stewart Gardner Museum are here.

7 Cambridge. A separate city across the Charles River, Cambridge has long been a haven for intellectuals and iconoclasts. Along with Harvard and MIT, you'll find bookstores, cafés, and funky boutiques.

FENWAY PARK
BOSTON AND ENVIRONS

For baseball fans Fenway Park is Mecca: a trip there is a religious pilgrimage to the home of former baseball greats such as Ted Willams and Carl Yastrzemski. The Boston Red Sox have played here since 1912, making Fenway the oldest Major League ballpark. The scoreboard is still operated by hand, and fans still clamor for cramped, uncomfortable seats.

For much of the ballpark's history Babe Ruth's specter loomed large. After winning five titles by 1918 (including the first World Series in 1903), the team endured an 86-year title drought after trading away the Sultan of Swat. The team vexed generations of fans with colossal late-season collapses, post-season bungles, and losses to the hated New York Yankees. The Sox snapped the spell in 2004, defeating the Yanks in the American League Championship Series after being down 3–0 and sweeping the St. Louis Cardinals in the World Series. The Red Sox won it all again in 2007, completely exorcising "The Curse."

(above) Take yourself out to a ballgame at legendary Fenway Park. (lower right) Iconic sox mark the park walls. (upper right) Flags adorn the epicenter of Red Sox Nation.

FUN FACT

A lone red seat in the right-field bleachers marks where Ted Williams' 502-foot shot—the longest measurable home run hit inside Fenway Park—landed on June 9, 1946.

TICKET TIPS

Can't get tickets? At Gate E two hours before the game, a handful of tickets are sold. There's a one-ticket limit, so everyone must be in line.

THE NATION
The Red Sox have the most rabid fan base in baseball. They follow the team with an intensity usually seen in religious cults. The Pats and Celtics may be champion-caliber teams, too, but this is first and foremost a Red Sox town.

THE MONSTER
Fenway's most dominant feature is the 37-foot-high "Green Monster," the wall that looms over left field. It's just over 300 feet from home plate and in the field of play, so deep fly balls that would have been outs in other parks sometimes become home runs. The Monster also stops line drives that would have been over the walls of other stadiums.

THE MUSIC
Fans sing "Take Me Out to the Ballgame" during the 7th inning stretch in every ballpark...but at Fenway, they also sing Neil Diamond's "Sweet Caroline" in the middle of the 8th. If the Sox win, the Standell's "Dirty Water" blasts over the loudspeakers at the game's end.

THE CURSE
In 1920 the Red Sox traded pitcher Babe Ruth to the Yankees, where he became a home-run-hitting baseball legend. Some fans—most famously *Boston Globe* columnist Dan Shaughnessy, who wrote a book called *The Curse of the Bambino*—blamed this move for the team's 86-year title drought, but others will claim that "The Curse" was just a media-driven storyline used to explain the team's past woes. Still, fans who watched a ground ball roll between Bill Buckner's legs in the 1986 World Series or saw Aaron Boone's winning home run in the 2003 American League Division Series swear the curse was real.

THE SPORTS GUY
For an in-depth view of the psyche of a die-hard Red Sox fan, pick up a copy of Bill Simmons's book *Now I Can Die in Peace*. Simmons, a native New Englander, writes for ESPN.com and is the editor-in-chief of Grantland.com.

VISIT THE NATION
Can't get tickets but still want to experience the excitement of a Red Sox game? Then head down to the park and hang out on Yawkey Way, which borders the stadium. On game days it's closed to cars and filled with vendors, creating a street-fair atmosphere. Duck into a nearby sports bar (there are many) and enjoy the game with other fans who couldn't secure seats. A favorite is the Cask'n Flagon, at Brookline Avenue and Lansdowne Street, across the street from Fenway. The closet you can get to Fenway without buying a ticket is the **Bleacher Bar** (✉ *82A Lansdowne St.*), which actually has a huge window in the center field wall overlooking the field. If you want to see a game from this unique vantage point, get here early—it starts filling up a few hours before game time.

Updated
by Bethany
Cassin
Beckerlegge

There's history and culture around every bend in Boston—skyscrapers nestle next to historic hotels, while modern marketplaces line the antique cobblestone streets. But to Bostonians, living in a city that blends yesterday and today is just another day in their beloved Beantown.

It's difficult to fit Boston into a stereotype because of the city's many layers. The deepest is the historical one, the place where musket-bearing revolutionaries vowed to hang together or hang separately. The next tier, a dense spread of Brahmin fortune and fortitude, might be labeled the Hub. It was this elite caste of Boston society, descended from wealthy English Protestants who first settled the state. They funded and patronized the city's universities and cultural institutions, gaining Boston the label "the Athens of America" and felt only pride in the slogan "Banned in Boston." Over that layer lies Beantown, home to the Red Sox faithful and the raucous Bruins fans who crowded the old Boston "*Gah*-den"; this is the city whose ethnic loyalties account for its many distinct neighborhoods. Crowning these layers are the students who converge on the area's universities and colleges every fall.

PLANNING

WHEN TO GO

Summer brings reliable sunshine, sailboats to Boston Harbor, concerts to the Esplanade, and café tables to assorted sidewalks. If you're dreaming of a classic shore vacation, summer is prime.

Weather-wise, late spring and fall are the optimal times to visit Boston. Aside from mild temperatures, the former offers blooming gardens throughout the city and the latter sees the surrounding countryside ablaze with brilliantly colored foliage. At both times expect crowds.

Autumn attracts hordes of leaf-peepers, and more than 250,000 students flood into the area each September; then pull out in May and June. Hotels and restaurants fill up quickly on move-in, move-out, and graduation weekends.

Winters are cold and windy.

PLANNING YOUR TIME

If you have a couple of days, hit Boston's highlights—Beacon Hill, the Freedom Trail and the Public Garden—the first day, and then check out the Museum of Fine Arts or the Isabella Stewart Gardner Museum the morning of the second day. Reserve day two's afternoon for an excursion to Harvard or shopping on Newbury Street.

GETTING HERE AND AROUND

AIR TRAVEL

Boston's major airport, Logan International (BOS), is across the harbor from Downtown, about 2 miles outside the city center, and can be reached by taxi, water taxi, or bus/subway via MBTA's Silver or Blue line). Logan has four passenger terminals, identified by letters A, B, C, and E. A free airport shuttle runs between the terminals and airport hotels. Some airlines use different terminals for international and domestic flights; most international flights arrive at Terminal E. A visitor center in Terminal C offers tourist information. T. F. Green Airport, in Providence, Rhode Island, and the Manchester Boston Regional Airport in Manchester, New Hampshire, are both about an hour from Boston.

Airport Information Logan International Airport (Boston) ✉ *I–90 east to Ted Williams Tunnel* ☎ *800/235–6426* ⊕ *www.massport.com/logan/* Ⓜ *Airport.* **Manchester Boston Regional Airport** ✉ *Off I–293/Rte. 101, Exit 2, Manchester, NH* ☎ *603/624–6556* ⊕ *www.flymanchester.com.* **T. F. Green Airport** ✉ *Off I–95, Exit 13, Providence, RI* ☎ *888/268–7222, 401/691–2471* ⊕ *www.pvdairport.com.*

CAR TRAVEL

In a place where roads often evolved from cow paths, driving is no simple task. A surfeit of one-way streets and inconsistent signage add to the confusion. Street parking is hard to come by, as much of it is resident-permit-only. Your own car is helpful if you're taking side trips, but for exploring the city it will only be a burden. Also, Bostonians give terrible directions since few of them actually drive.

PUBLIC TRANSIT

The "T," as the Massachusetts Bay Transportation Authority's subway system is nicknamed, is the cornerstone of an efficient, far-reaching public transit network that also includes aboveground trains, buses, and ferries. Its five color-coded lines will put you within a block of almost anywhere you want to go. Subways operate from about 5:30 am to 12:30 pm, as do buses, which crisscross the city and reach into suburbia.

A standard adult subway fare is $1.70 with a CharlieCard or $2 with a ticket or cash. For buses it's $1.25 with a CharlieCard or $1.50 with a ticket or cash (more if you are using an Inner or Outer Express bus). Commuter rail and ferry fares vary by route; yet all options charge seniors and students reduced prices, and kids under 12 ride free with a paying adult. Contact the MBTA (☎ *617/222–3200 or 800/392–6100* ⊕ *www.mbta.com*) for schedules, routes, and rates.

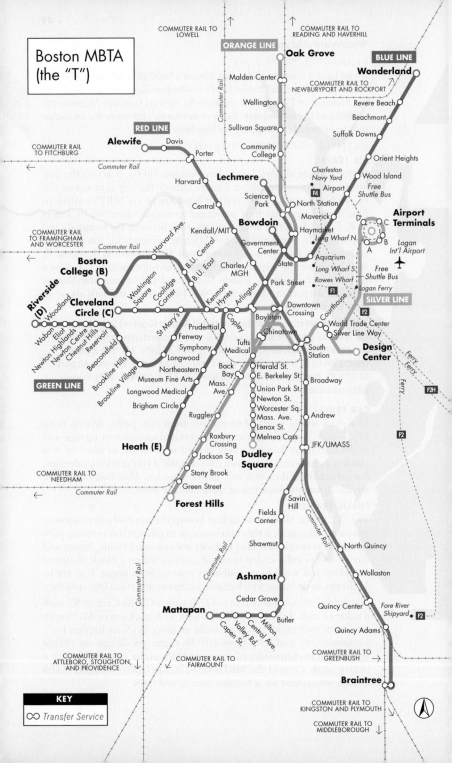

Boston MBTA (the "T")

ORANGE LINE

BLUE LINE

RED LINE

GREEN LINE

SILVER LINE

COMMUTER RAIL TO LOWELL

COMMUTER RAIL TO READING AND HAVERHILL

Oak Grove

Malden Center

Wellington

Sullivan Square

Community College

Wonderland

COMMUTER RAIL TO NEWBURYPORT AND ROCKPORT

Revere Beach

Beachmont

Suffolk Downs

Orient Heights

Wood Island

Airport

Free Shuttle Bus

Maverick

Alewife

Davis

Porter

Harvard

Central

Kendall/MIT

Charles/MGH

COMMUTER RAIL TO FITCHBURG

Commuter Rail

Lechmere

Science Park

North Station

Charleston Navy Yard

F4

Bowdoin

Government Center

Haymarket

Long Wharf N.

State

Aquarium

Long Wharf S.

Rowes Wharf

Airport Terminals

D

C

B

A

Logan Int'l Airport

Free Shuttle Bus

Logan Ferry

F1

Boston College (B)

COMMUTER RAIL TO FRAMINGHAM AND WORCESTER

Commuter Rail

Washington Square

Coolidge Corner

Harvard Ave.

B.U. Central

B.U. East

Kenmore

Hynes

Arlington

Park Street

Boylston

Downtown Crossing

Chinatown

Courthouse

World Trade Center

Silver Line Way

Design Center

F2

Riverside (D)

Cleveland Circle (C)

Woodland

Waban

Eliot

Newton Highlands

Newton Centre

Chestnut Hill

Reservoir

Beaconsfield

Brookline Hills

Brookline Village

St Mary's

Fenway

Prudential

Symphony

Longwood

Museum Fine Arts

Longwood Medical

Brigham Circle

Copley

Back Bay

Mass. Ave.

Tufts Medical

Herald St.

E. Berkeley St.

Union Park St.

Newton St.

Worcester Sq.

Mass. Ave.

Lenox St.

Melnea Cass

South Station

Broadway

Andrew

JFK/UMASS

Ferry

F2H

Heath (E)

Ruggles

Roxbury Crossing

Jackson Sq

Stony Brook

Green Street

Dudley Square

COMMUTER RAIL TO NEEDHAM

Commuter Rail

Forest Hills

Savin Hill

Fields Corner

Shawmut

North Quincy

Wollaston

Quincy Center

Fore River Shipyard

F2

Ashmont

Cedar Grove

Milton

Butler

Quincy Adams

Mattapan

Valley Rd.

Central Ave.

Capen St.

COMMUTER RAIL TO ATTLEBORO, STOUGHTON, AND PROVIDENCE

COMMUTER RAIL TO FAIRMOUNT

COMMUTER RAIL TO GREENBUSH

Braintree

COMMUTER RAIL TO KINGSTON AND PLYMOUTH

COMMUTER RAIL TO MIDDLEBOROUGH

KEY

∞ *Transfer Service*

TAXI TRAVEL

Cabs are available 24/7. Rides within the city cost $2.60 for the first 1/7 mile and 40¢ for each 1/7 mile thereafter (tolls, where applicable, are extra).

VISITOR INFORMATION

Contact the city and state tourism offices for details about seasonal events, discount passes, trip planning, and attraction information. The National Park Service has a Boston office for Boston's historic sites that provides maps and directions. The Welcome Center and Boston Common Visitor Information Center offer general information. The Cambridge Tourism Office's information booth is in Harvard Square, near the main entrance to the Harvard T stop.

Contacts Boston Common Visitor Information Center ⊠ *148 Tremont St., where Freedom Trail begins, Downtown* ☎ *888/733–2678* ⊕ *www. thefreedomtrail.org/visitor/boston-common.html.* **Boston National Historical Park Visitor Center** ⊠ *15 State St., Downtown* ☎ *617/242–5642* ⊕ *www. nps.gov/bost.* **Cambridge Tourism Office** ⊠ *4 Brattle St., Harvard Sq., Cambridge* ☎ *800/862–5678, 617/441–2884* ⊕ *www.cambridge-usa.org.* **Greater Boston Convention and Visitors Bureau** ⊠ *2 Copley Pl., Suite 105, Back Bay* ☎ *888/733–2678, 617/536–4100* ⊕ *www.bostonusa.com.* **Massachusetts Office of Travel and Tourism** ⊠ *State Transportation Bldg., 10 Park Plaza, Suite 4510, Back Bay* ☎ *800/227–6277, 617/973–8500* ⊕ *www.massvacation.com.*

ONLINE RESOURCES

Boston.com, home of the *Boston Globe* online, has news and feature articles, ample travel information, and links to towns throughout Massachusetts. The site for Boston's arts and entertainment weekly, the *Boston Phoenix* (⊕ *www.bostonphoenix.com*) has nightlife, movie, restaurant, and arts listings. The Bostonian Society (⊕ *bostonhistory.org*) answers some frequently asked questions about Beantown history on their website. The iBoston (⊕ *www.iboston.org*) page has wonderful photographs of architecturally and historically important buildings. *The Improper Bostonian* (⊕ *www.improper.com*) and *WickedLocal* (⊕ *www.wickedlocal.com*) provide a more relaxed (and irreverent) take on Boston news and information.

EXPLORING BOSTON

BEACON HILL AND BOSTON COMMON

Past and present home of the old-money elite, contender for the "Most Beautiful" award among the city's neighborhoods, and hallowed address for many literary lights, Beacon Hill is Boston at its most Bostonian. The redbrick elegance of its narrow streets sends you back to the 19th century just as surely as if you had stumbled into a time machine. But Beacon Hill residents would never make the social faux pas of being out of date. The neighborhood is home to hip boutiques and trendy restaurants. Beacon Hill is bounded by Cambridge Street on the north, Beacon Street on the south, the Charles River Esplanade on the west, and Bowdoin Street on the east.

Fodor's Choice
★
☯
Boston Common. Nothing is more central to Boston than the Common, the oldest public park in the United States and undoubtedly the largest and most famous of the town commons around which New England settlements were traditionally arranged. Dating from 1634, Boston Common started as 50 acres where the freemen of Boston could graze their cattle. (Cows were banned in 1830.) Latin names are affixed to many of the Common's trees; it was once expected that proper Boston schoolchildren be able to translate them.

On Tremont Street near Boylston stands the 1888 **Boston Massacre Memorial**; the sculpted hand of one of the victims has a distinct shine from years of sightseers' caresses. The Common's highest ground, near the park's Parkman Bandstand, was once called Flagstaff Hill. It's now surmounted by the **Soldiers and Sailors Monument,** honoring Civil War troops. The Common's only body of water is the **Frog Pond,** a tame and frog-free concrete depression used as a children's wading pool during steamy summer days and for ice-skating in winter. It marks the original site of a natural pond that inspired Edgar Allan Poe to call Bostonians "Frogpondians." In 1848 a gushing fountain of piped-in water was created to inaugurate Boston's municipal water system.

On the Beacon Street side of the Common sits the splendidly restored **Robert Gould Shaw 54th Regiment Memorial,** executed in deep-relief bronze by Augustus Saint-Gaudens in 1897. It commemorates the 54th Massachusetts Regiment, the first Civil War unit made up of free blacks, led by the young Brahmin Robert Gould Shaw. He and half of his troops died in an assault on South Carolina's Fort Wagner; their story inspired the 1989 movie *Glory.* The monument—first intended to depict only Shaw until his abolitionist family demanded it honor his regiment as well—figures in works by the poets John Berryman and Robert Lowell, both of whom lived on the north slope of Beacon Hill in the 1940s. This magnificent memorial makes a fitting first stop on the Black Heritage Trail. ⊠ *Bounded by Beacon, Charles, Tremont, and Park Sts., Beacon Hill* Ⓜ *Park St.*

Central Burying Ground. The Central Burying Ground may seem an odd feature for a public park, but remember that in 1756, when the land was set aside, this was a lonely corner of the Common. It's the final resting place of Tories and Patriots alike, as well as many British casualties of the Battle of Bunker Hill. The most famous person buried here is Gilbert Stuart, the portraitist best known for his likenesses of George and Martha Washington; he died a poor man in 1828. The Burying Ground is open daily 9–5. ⊠ *Boylston St. near Tremont, Beacon Hill* Ⓜ *Park St.*

Fodor's Choice
★
Granary Burying Ground. "It is a fine thing to die in Boston," A. C. Lyons, an essayist and old Boston wit, once remarked, alluding to the city's cemeteries, among the most picturesque and historic in America. If you found a resting place here at the Old Granary, as it's called, chances are your headstone would have been elaborately ornamented with skeletons and winged skulls. Your neighbors would have been impressive, too: among them are Samuel Adams, John Hancock, Paul Revere, and Benjamin Franklin's parents. Note the winged hourglasses carved into

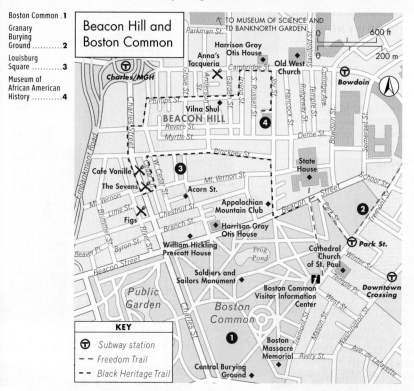

the stone gateway of the burial ground; they are a 19th-century addition, made more than 150 years after this small plot began receiving the earthly remains of colonial Bostonians. ⊠ *Entrance on Tremont St., Beacon Hill* ☉ *Daily 9–5* Ⓜ *Park St.*

★ **Louisburg Square.** One of Beacon Hill's most charming corners, Louisburg Square (proper Bostonians always pronounce the "s") was an 1840s model for a town-house development that was never built on the Hill because of space restrictions. Today, the grassy square, enclosed by a wrought-iron fence, belongs collectively to the owners of the houses facing it. The statue at the north end of the green is of Columbus, the one at the south end of Aristides the Just; both were donated in 1850 by a Greek merchant who lived on the square. The houses, most of which are now divided into apartments and condominiums, have seen their share of famous tenants, including author and critic William Dean Howells at Nos. 4 and 16, and the Alcotts at No. 10 (Louisa May not only lived but died here, on the day of her father's funeral). In 1852 the singer Jenny Lind was married in the parlor of No. 20. Louisburg Square is also the current home of Massachusetts Senator John Kerry.

There's a legend that Louisburg Square was the location of the Rev. William Blaxton's spring, although there's no water there today. Blaxton, or Blackstone, was one of the first Bostonians, having come to

DID YOU KNOW?

For a taste of Boston's watery side, take a walk on the 47-mile HarborWalk between major attractions (like the New England Aquarium), picturesque piers, working wharves, and even urban beaches.

the Shawmut Peninsula in the mid-1620s. When the Puritans, who had settled in Charlestown, found their water supply inadequate, Blaxton invited them to move across the river, where he assured them they would find an "excellent spring." Just a few years later, he sold them all but 6 acres of the peninsula he had bought from the Native Americans and decamped to Rhode Island, seeking greater seclusion; a plaque at 50 Beacon Street commemorates him. ⊠ *Between Mt. Vernon and Pickney Sts., Beacon Hill* Ⓜ *Park St.*

DID YOU KNOW?

Beacon Hill's north slope played a key part in African American history. A community of free blacks lived here in the 1800s; many worshipped at the African Meeting House, established in 1805 and still standing. It came to be known as the "Black Faneuil Hall" for the fervent antislavery activism that started within its walls.

FodorsChoice ★ ☾ **Museum of African American History.** Ever since runaway slave Crispus Attucks became one of the famous victims of the Boston Massacre of 1770, the African American community of Boston has played an important part in the city's history. Throughout the 19th century, abolition was the cause célèbre for Boston's intellectual elite, and during that time, blacks came to thrive in neighborhoods throughout the city. The Museum of African American History was established in 1964 to promote this history. The umbrella organization includes a trio of historic sites: the Abiel Smith School, the first public school in the nation built specifically for black children; the African Meeting House, where in 1832 the New England Anti-Slavery Society was formed under the leadership of William Lloyd Garrison; and the African Meeting House on the island of Nantucket, off the coast of Cape Cod. Park Service personnel continue to lead tours of the **Black Heritage Trail**, starting from the Shaw Memorial. The museum is the site of activities, including lectures, children's storytelling, and concerts focusing on black composers. ⊠ *46 Joy St., Beacon Hill* ☎ *617/725–0022* ⊕ *www.afroammuseum.org* ⊠ *$5* ☾ *Mon.–Sat. 10–4* Ⓜ *Park St.*

THE OLD WEST END

A few decades ago, this district—separated from Beacon Hill by Cambridge Street—resembled a typical medieval city: thoroughfares that twisted and turned, maddening one-way lanes, and streets that were a veritable hive of people. Today, little remains of the *old* Old West End except for a few brick tenements and a handful of monuments, including the first house built for Harrison Gray Otis. The biggest surviving structures with any real history are two public institutions, Massachusetts General Hospital and the former Suffolk County Jail, which dates from 1849. The onetime prison is now part of the luxurious, and wryly named, Liberty Hotel. Here you'll also find TD Banknorth Garden, the home away from home for loyal Bruins and Celtics fans. In addition, the innovative Museum of Science is one of the neighborhood's more modern attractions. The newest addition to the skyline here is the Leonard P. Zakim Bunker Hill Bridge, which spans the Charles River just across from the TD Banknorth Garden.

Fodor's Choice
★
Ⓒ

Museum of Science. With 15-foot lightning bolts in the Theater of Electricity and a 20-foot-long *Tyrannosaurus rex* model, this is just the place to ignite any child's scientific curiosity. Occupying a compound of buildings north of Massachusetts General Hospital, the museum sits astride the Charles River Dam. More than 550 exhibits cover astronomy, astrophysics, anthropology, medical progress, computers, the organic and inorganic earth sciences, and much more. The emphasis is on hands-on education.

The Charles Hayden Planetarium, with its sophisticated multimedia system based on a Zeiss planetarium projector, produces exciting programs on astronomical discoveries. The museum also includes the Mugar Omni Theater, a five-story dome screen. ⊠ *Science Park at Charles River Dam, Old West End* ☏ *617/723–2500* ⊕ *www.mos.org* 🖭 *$22* ⊙ *July 5–Labor Day, Sat.–Thurs. 9–7, Fri. 9–9; after Labor Day–July 4, Sat.–Thurs. 9–5, Fri. 9–9* Ⓜ *Science Park.*

Ⓒ **TD Garden.** Diehards still moan about the loss of the old Boston Garden, a much more intimate venue than this mammoth facility, which opened in 1995. A decade after it opened as the FleetCenter, the home of the Celtics (basketball) and Bruins (hockey) is once again known as the good old "Gah-den," and its air-conditioning, comfier seats, improved food selection, 1,200-vehicle parking garage, and nearly double number of bathrooms, has won grudging acceptance. The Garden occasionally offers public-skating sessions in the winter; call ahead for hours and prices. ⊠ *100 Legends Way, Old West End* ☏ *617/624–1050* ⊕ *www.tdbanknorthgarden.com* Ⓜ *North Station.*

Sports Museum of New England. The fifth and sixth levels of the TD Garden house the Sports Museum of New England, where displays of memorabilia and photographs showcase local sports history and legends. Take a tour of the locker and interview rooms (off-season only), test your sports knowledge with interactive games, or see how you stand up to life-size statues of heroes Carl Yastrzemski and Larry Bird. The museum is open daily 10–4, with admission allowed only on the hour. Last entrance is at 3 pm on most days, 2 pm on game days; admission is $10. ⊠ *Use west premium-seating entrance* ☏ *617/624–1234* ⊕ *www.sportsmuseum.org* 🖭 *$10*

GOVERNMENT CENTER

This is a section of town Bostonians love to hate. Not only does Government Center house what they can't fight—City Hall—but it also contains some of the bleakest architecture since the advent of poured concrete. But though the stark, treeless plain surrounding City Hall has been roundly jeered, the expanse is enlivened by feisty political rallies, free summer concerts, and the occasional festival.

★ **Faneuil Hall.** The single building facing Congress Street is the real Faneuil Hall, though locals often give that name to all five buildings in this shopping complex. Bostonians pronounce it *Fan*-yoo'uhl or *Fan*-yuhl. Like

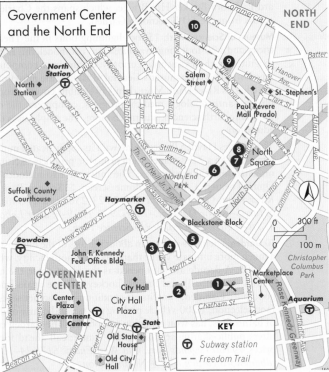

Government Center and the North End

other Boston landmarks, Faneuil Hall has evolved over many years. It was erected in 1742, the gift of wealthy merchant Peter Faneuil, who wanted the hall to serve as both a place for town meetings and a public market. It burned in 1761 and was immediately reconstructed according to the original plan of its designer, the Scottish portrait painter John Smibert (who lies in the Granary Burying Ground). In 1763 the political leader James Otis helped inaugurate the era that culminated in American independence when he dedicated the rebuilt hall to the cause of liberty.

In 1772 Samuel Adams stood here and first suggested that Massachusetts and the other colonies organize a Committee of Correspondence to maintain semiclandestine lines of communication in the face of hardening British repression. In later years the hall again lived up to Otis's dedication when the abolitionists Wendell Phillips and Charles Sumner pleaded for support from its podium. The tradition continues to this day: in presidential-election years the hall is the site of debates between contenders in the Massachusetts primary.

Faneuil Hall was substantially enlarged and remodeled in 1805 according to a Greek Revival design of the noted architect Charles Bulfinch; this is the building you see today. Its purposes remain the same: the balconied Great Hall is available to citizens' groups on presentation of a request signed by a required number of responsible parties; it also plays host to regular concerts.

Inside Faneuil Hall are dozens of paintings of famous Americans, including the mural *Webster's Reply to Hayne*, Gilbert Stuart's portrait of Washington at Dorchester Heights. Park rangers give informational talks about the history and importance of Faneuil Hall on the hour and half hour. The rangers are a good resource, as interpretive plaques are few. Brochures about Faneuil Hall's history, distributed by the National Park Service, make lighthearted references to the ongoing commercialism nearby by reprinting a 1958 ditty by Francis Hatch: "Here orators in ages past / Have mounted their attacks / Undaunted by proximity / Of sausage on the racks." Faneuil Hall has always sat in the middle of Boston's main marketplace: when such men as Andrew Jackson and Daniel Webster debated the future of the Republic here, the fragrances of bacon and snuff—sold by merchants in **Quincy Market** across the road—greeted their noses. Today the aroma of coffee wafts through the hall from a snack bar. The shops at ground level sell New England bric-a-brac. ⊠ *Faneuil Hall Sq., Government Center* ☎ *617/523–1300* ⊕ *www.cityofboston.gov/freedomtrail/faneuilhall.asp* 🎟 *Free* ☉ *Great Hall daily 9–5; informational talks every ½ hr. Shops Mon.–Sat. 10 am–9 pm, Sun. 11–6 pm* Ⓜ *Government Center, Aquarium, State.*

The Haymarket. Loud, self-promoting vendors pack this exuberant maze of a marketplace at Marshall and Blackstone streets on Friday and Saturday from 7 am until midafternoon (all vendors will likely be gone by 5). Pushcart vendors hawk fruits and vegetables against a backdrop of fish, meat, and cheese shops. The accumulation of debris left every evening has been celebrated in a whimsical 1976 public-arts project—Mags Harries's *Asaroton*, a Greek word meaning "unswept floors"—consisting of bronze fruit peels and other detritus smashed into pavement. Another Harries piece, a bronze depiction of a gathering of stray gloves, tumbles down between the escalators in the Porter Square T station in Cambridge. At Creek Square, near the Haymarket, is the **Boston Stone.** Set into the brick wall of the gift shop of the same name, this was a marker long used as milepost zero in measuring distances from Boston. ⊠ *Marshall and Blackstone Sts., Government Center* ☉ *Fri. and Sat. 7 am–midafternoon* Ⓜ *Government Center.*

Holocaust Memorial. At night its six 50-foot-high glass-and-steel towers glow like ghosts. During the day the monument seems at odds with the 18th-century streetscape of Blackstone Square behind it. Shoehorned into the north end of Union Park, the Holocaust Memorial is the work of Stanley Saitowitz, whose design was selected through an international competition; the finished memorial was dedicated in 1995. Recollections by Holocaust survivors are set into the glass-and-granite walls; the upper levels of the towers are etched with 6 million numbers in random sequence, symbolizing the Jewish victims of the Nazi horror. Manufactured steam from grates in the granite base makes for a particularly haunting scene after dark. ⊠ *Union St. near Hanover St., Government Center.*

Quincy Market. Not everyone likes Quincy Market, also known as Faneuil Hall Marketplace; some people prefer grit to polish, and disdain the shiny cafés and boutiques. But there's no denying that this pioneer effort at urban recycling set the tone for many similar projects throughout the country, and that it has brought tremendous vitality to a once-tired corner of Boston. Quincy Market continues to attract huge crowds of tourists and locals throughout the year. In the early '70s, demolition was a distinct possibility for the decrepit buildings. Fortunately, with the participation of the Boston Redevelopment Authority, architect Benjamin Thompson planned a renovation of Quincy Market, and the Rouse Corporation of Baltimore undertook its restoration, which was completed in 1976. Try to look beyond the shop windows to the grand design of the market buildings themselves; they represent a vision of the market as urban centerpiece, an idea whose time has certainly come again.

> ## THE STORY BEHIND THE GRASSHOPPER
>
> Why is the gold-plated weather vane atop Faneuil Hall's cupola in the shape of a grasshopper? One apocryphal story has it that Sir Thomas Gresham—founder of London's Royal Exchange—was discovered in a field in 1519 as a babe by children chasing grasshoppers. He later placed a gilded metal version of the insect over the Exchange to commemorate his salvation. Years later Peter Faneuil admired the critter (a symbol of good luck) and had a model of it mounted over Faneuil Hall. The 8-pound, 52-inch-long grasshopper is the only unmodified part of the original structure.

The market consists of three block-long annexes: **Quincy Market, North Market,** and **South Market,** each 535 feet long and across a plaza from Faneuil Hall. The structures were designed in 1826 by Alexander Parris as part of a public-works project instituted by Boston's second mayor, Josiah Quincy, to alleviate the cramped conditions of Faneuil Hall and clean up the refuse that collected in Town Dock, the pond behind it. The central structure, made of granite, with a Doric colonnade at either end and topped by a classical dome and rotunda, has kept its traditional market-stall layout, but the stalls now purvey international and specialty foods: sushi, frozen yogurt, bagels, calzones, sausage-on-a-stick, Chinese noodles, barbecue, and baklava, plus all the boutique chocolate-chip cookies your heart desires. This is perhaps Boston's best locale for grazing. ⊠ *Bordered by Clinton, Commercial, and Chatham Sts., Government Center* ☎ *617/523–1300* ⊕ *www.faneuilhallmarketplace.com* ☉ *Mon.–Sat. 10–9, Sun. 11–6. Restaurants and bars generally open daily 11 am–2 am; food stalls open earlier* Ⓜ *Government Center, Aquarium, State.*

Union Oyster House. Billed as the oldest restaurant in continuous service in the United States, the Union Oyster House first opened its doors as the Atwood & Bacon Oyster House in 1826. Charles Forster of Maine was the first American to use the curious invention of the toothpick on these premises. And John F. Kennedy was also among its patrons; his favorite booth has been dedicated to his memory. The charming facade is constructed of Flemish bond brick and adorned with Victorian-style signage. With its scallop, clam, and lobster dishes—as well as the de rigueur oyster—the menu hasn't changed much since the restaurant's early days (though the prices have). ✉ *41 Union St., Government Center* ☎ *617/227–2750* ⊕ *www.unionoysterhouse.com* ☾ *Sun.–Thurs. 11–9:30, Fri. and Sat. 11–10; bar open until midnight* Ⓜ *Haymarket.*

2

THE NORTH END

The warren of small streets on the northeast side of Government Center is the North End, Boston's Little Italy. In the 17th century the North End *was* Boston, as much of the rest of the peninsula was still under water or had yet to be cleared. Here the town grew rich for a century and a half before the birth of American independence. The quarter's dwindling ethnic character lingers along Salem or Hanover Street where you can still hear people speaking with Abruzzese accents.

Copp's Hill Burying Ground. An ancient and melancholy air hovers like a fine mist over this Colonial-era burial ground. The North End graveyard incorporates four cemeteries established between 1660 and 1819. Near the Charter Street gate is the tomb of the Mather family, the dynasty of church divines (Cotton and Increase were the most famous sons) who held sway in Boston during the heyday of the old theocracy. Also buried here is Robert Newman, who crept into the steeple of the Old North Church to hang the lanterns warning of the British attack the night of Paul Revere's ride. Look for the tombstone of Captain Daniel Malcolm; it's pockmarked with musket-ball fire from British soldiers, who used the stones for target practice. Across the street at 44 Hull is the **narrowest house in Boston**—it's a mere 10 feet across. ✉ *Intersection of Hull and Snowhill Sts., North End* ☾ *Daily 9–5* Ⓜ *North Station.*

Hanover Street. This is the North End's main thoroughfare, along with the smaller and narrower Salem Street. It was named for the ruling dynasty of 18th- and 19th-century England; the label was retained after the Revolution, despite a flurry of patriotic renaming (King Street became State Street, for example). Hanover's business center is thick with restaurants, pastry shops, and Italian cafés; on weekends, Italian immigrants who have moved to the suburbs return to share an espresso with old friends and maybe catch a soccer game broadcast via satellite. Hanover is one of Boston's oldest public roads, once the site of the residences of the Rev. Cotton Mather and the Colonial-era patriot Dr. Joseph Warren, as well as a small dry-goods store run by Eben D. Jordan—who went on to launch the Jordan Marsh department stores.

Fodor'sChoice ★ **Old North Church.** Standing at one end of the **Paul Revere Mall** is a church famous not only for being the oldest one in Boston (built in 1723) but for housing the two lanterns that glimmered from its steeple on the night of April 18, 1775. This is Christ, or Old North, Church, where Paul Revere and the young sexton Robert Newman managed that night to signal the departure by water of the British regulars to Lexington and Concord.

Although William Price designed the structure after studying Christopher Wren's London churches, Old North—which still has an active

Episcopal congregation (including descendants of the Reveres)—is an impressive building in its own right. Inside, note the gallery and the graceful arrangement of pews; the bust of George Washington, pronounced by the Marquis de Lafayette to be the truest likeness of the general he ever saw; the brass chandeliers, made in Amsterdam in 1700 and installed here in 1724; and the clock, the oldest still running in an American public building. The pews—No. 54 belonged to the Revere family—are the highest in the United States because of the little charcoal-burning foot warmers. Try to visit when changes are rung on the bells, after the 11 am Sunday service; they bear the inscription, "We are the first ring of bells cast for the British Empire in North America." On the Sunday closest to April 18, descendants of the patriots reenact the raising of the lanterns in the church belfry during a special evening service.

Behind the church is the **Washington Memorial Garden,** where volunteers cultivate a plot devoted to plants and flowers favored in the 18th century. The garden is studded with several unusual commemorative plaques, including one for the Rev. George Burrough, who was hanged in the Salem witch trials in 1692; Robert Newman was his great-grandson. In another niche hangs the "Third Lantern," dedicated in 1976 to mark the country's bicentennial celebration. ⊠ *193 Salem St., North End* ☎ *617/523–6676* ⊕ *www.oldnorth.com* ⊙ *Jan. and Feb., Tues.–Sun. 10–4; Mar.–May, daily 9–5; June–Oct., daily 9–6; Nov. and Dec., daily 10–5. Sun. services at 9 and 11 am* Ⓜ *Haymarket, North Station.*

🔆 **Paul Revere House.** Originally on the site was the parsonage of the Second Church of Boston, home to the Rev. Increase Mather, the Second Church's minister. Mather's house burned in the great fire of 1676, and the house that Revere was to occupy was built on its location about four years later, nearly a hundred years before Revere's 1775 midnight ride through Middlesex County. Revere owned it from 1770 until 1800, although he lived there for only 10 years and rented it out for the next two decades. Pre-1900 photographs show it as a shabby warren of storefronts and apartments. The clapboard sheathing is a replacement, but 90% of the framework is original; note the Elizabethan-style overhang and leaded windowpanes. A few Revere furnishings are on display here, and just gazing at his silverwork—much more of which is displayed at the Museum of Fine Arts—brings the man alive.

■ TIP➔ Special events are scheduled throughout the year, many designed with children in mind.

The immediate neighborhood also has Revere associations. The little park in North Square is named after Rachel Revere, his second wife, and the adjacent brick **Pierce-Hichborn House** once belonged to relatives of Revere. The garden connecting the Revere house and the Pierce-Hichborn House is planted with flowers and medicinal herbs favored in Revere's day. ⊠ *19 North Sq., North End* ☎ *617/523–2338* ⊕ *www. paulreverehouse.org* ▭ *$3.50, $5.50 with Pierce-Hichborn House* ⊙ *Jan.–Mar., Tues.–Sun. 9:30–4:15; Nov. and Dec. and 1st 2 wks of Apr., daily 9:30–4:15; mid-Apr.–Oct., daily 9:30–5:15* Ⓜ *Haymarket, Aquarium, Government Center.*

Pierce-Hichborn House. One of the city's oldest brick buildings, this structure, just to the left of the Paul Revere House, was once owned by Nathaniel Hichborn, a boatbuilder and Revere's cousin on his mother's side. Built about 1711 for a window maker named Moses Pierce, the Pierce-Hichborn House is an excellent example of early Georgian architecture. The home's symmetrical style was a radical change from the wood-frame Tudor buildings, such as the Revere House, then common. Its four rooms are furnished with modest 18th-century furniture, providing a peek into typical middle-class life. ✉ *29 North Sq., North End* ☎ *617/523–2338* 🎟 *$2, $5.50 with Paul Revere House* ☉ *Guided tours only; call to schedule* Ⓜ *Haymarket, Aquarium, Government Center.*

> **A STICKY SUBJECT**
>
> Boston has had its share of grim historic events, from massacres to stranglers, but on the sheer weirdness scale, nothing beats the Great Molasses Flood. In 1919 a steel container of molasses exploded on the Boston Harbor waterfront, killing 21 people and 20 horses. More than 2.3 million gallons of goo oozed onto unsuspecting citizenry. Some say you can still smell molasses on the waterfront during steamy weather.

CHARLESTOWN

Boston started here. Charlestown was a thriving settlement a year before colonials headed across the Charles River at William Blaxton's invitation to found the city proper. Today the district's attractions include two of the most visible—and vertical—monuments in Boston: the Bunker Hill Monument, which commemorates the grisly battle that became a symbol of patriotic resistance against the British, and the USS *Constitution,* whose masts continue to tower over the waterfront where she was built more than 200 years ago.

Fodor's Choice ★ **Bunker Hill Monument.** Three misunderstandings surround this famous monument. First, the Battle of Bunker Hill was actually fought on Breed's Hill, which is where the monument sits today. (The real Bunker Hill is about ½ mile to the north of the monument; it's slightly taller than Breed's Hill.) Bunker was the original planned locale for the battle, and for that reason its name stuck. Second, although the battle is generally considered a colonial success, the Americans lost. It was a Pyrrhic victory for the British redcoats, who sacrificed nearly half of their 2,200 men; American casualties numbered 400–600. And third: the famous war cry "Don't fire until you see the whites of their eyes" may never have been uttered by American Colonel William Prescott or General Israel Putnam, but if either one did shout it, he was quoting an old Prussian command made necessary by the notorious inaccuracy of the musket. No matter. The Americans did employ a deadly delayed-action strategy on June 17, 1775, and conclusively proved themselves worthy fighters, capable of defeating the forces of the British Empire.

Among the dead were the brilliant young American doctor and political activist Joseph Warren, recently commissioned as a major general but fighting as a private, and the British Major John Pitcairn, who two months before had led the redcoats into Lexington. Pitcairn is believed to be buried in the crypt of Old North Church.

In 1823 the committee formed to construct a monument on the site of the battle chose the form of an Egyptian obelisk. Architect Solomon Willard designed a 221-foot-tall granite obelisk, a tremendous feat of engineering for its day. The Marquis de Lafayette laid the cornerstone of the monument in 1825, but because of a nagging lack of funds, it wasn't dedicated until 1843. Daniel Webster's stirring words at the ceremony commemorating the laying of its cornerstone have gone down in history: "Let it rise! Let it rise, till it meets the sun in his coming. Let the earliest light of the morning gild it, and parting day linger and play upon its summit."

The monument's zenith is reached by a flight of 294 steps. There's no elevator, but the views from the observatory are worth the effort of the arduous climb. A statue of Colonel Prescott stands guard at the base. In the Bunker Hill Museum across the street, artifacts and exhibits tell the story of the battle, while a detailed diorama shows the action in miniature. ⊠ *Monument Square, Charlestown* ☎ *617/242–5641* ⊕ *www.nps. gov/bost/historyculture/bhm.htm.* 🎫 *Free* ⊙ *Museum daily 9–5, monument daily 9–4:30* Ⓜ *Community College.*

Fodor's Choice
★
Ⓒ
USS *Constitution*. Better known as "Old Ironsides," the USS *Constitution* rides proudly at anchor in her berth at the Charlestown Navy Yard. The oldest commissioned ship in the U.S. fleet is a battlewagon of the old school, of the days of "wooden ships and iron men"—when she and her crew of 200 succeeded at the perilous task of asserting the sovereignty of an improbable new nation. Every July 4th and on certain other occasions she's towed out for a turnabout in Boston Harbor, the very place her keel was laid in 1797.

The venerable craft has narrowly escaped the scrap heap several times in her long history. She was launched on October 21, 1797, as part of the nation's fledgling navy. Her hull was made of live oak, the toughest wood grown in North America; her bottom was sheathed in copper, provided by Paul Revere at a nominal cost. Her principal service was during Thomas Jefferson's campaign against the Barbary pirates, off the coast of North Africa, and in the War of 1812. In 42 engagements her record was 42–0.

The nickname "Old Ironsides" was acquired during the War of 1812, when shots from the British warship *Guerrière* appeared to bounce off her hull. Talk of scrapping the ship began as early as 1830, but she was saved by a public campaign sparked by Oliver Wendell Holmes's poem "Old Ironsides." She underwent a major restoration in the early 1990s, and only about 8%–10% of her original wood remains in place, including the keel, the heart of the ship. Today she continues, the oldest commissioned warship afloat in the world, to be a part of the U.S. Navy.

The men and women who look after the *Constitution*, regular navy personnel, maintain a 24-hour watch. Sailors show visitors around the ship, guiding them to her top, or spar, deck, and the gun deck below. Another treat when visiting the ship is the spectacular view of Boston across Boston Harbor. ■TIP→ Instead of taking the T, you can get closer to the ship by taking MBTA Bus 92 to Charlestown City Square or Bus 93 to Chelsea Street from Haymarket. Or you can take the Boston Harbor Cruise water shuttle from Long Wharf to Pier 4. ⊠ *Charlestown Navy Yard, 55 Constitution Rd., Charlestown* ☎ *617/242–7511* ⊕ *www.history. navy.mil/ussconstitution* 🎫 *Free* ⊙ *Apr. 1–Sept., Tues.–Sun. 10–6; Oct., Tues.–Sun. 10–4; Nov.–Mar., Thurs.–Sun. 10–4; last tour at 3:30* Ⓜ *North Station.*

DOWNTOWN

Boston's commercial and financial districts—the area commonly called Downtown—are in a maze of streets that seem to have been laid out with little logic; they are village lanes now lined with modern 40-story office towers. Just as the Great Fire of 1872 swept the old Financial District clear, the Downtown construction in more-recent times has obliterated many of the buildings where 19th-century Boston business-men sat in front of their rolltop desks. Yet historic sites remain tucked among the skyscrapers; a number of them have been linked together to make up a fascinating section of the Freedom Trail.

The area is bordered by State Street on the north and by South Station and Chinatown on the south. Tremont Street and the Common form the west boundary, and the harbor wharves the eastern edge. Locals navigate the tangle of thoroughfares in between, but few of them man-age to give intelligible directions, so carry a map.

☼ **Boston Tea Party Ships & Museum.** After a lengthy renovation, the museum is, as of this writing, scheduled to reopen in the summer of 2012 (though the opening date has been pushed out numerous times). The *Beaver II,* a reproduction of one of the ships forcibly boarded and unloaded the night Boston Harbor became a teapot, is supposed to return to the Fort Point Channel at the Congress Street Bridge and be joined by two tall ships, the *Dartmouth* and the *Eleanor.* Visitors are promised a chance to explore the ships and museum exhibits, meet reenactors, or drink a cup of tea in a new Tea Room. ⊠ *Fort Point Channel at Congress St. Bridge, Downtown* ⊕ *www.bostonteapartyship.com* ⊙ *Check website for updated information* Ⓜ *South Station.*

Fodor'sChoice ★ ☼ **Children's Museum.** Most children have so much fun here that they don't realize they're actually learning something. Creative hands-on exhibits demonstrate scientific laws, cultural diversity, and problem solving. After completing a massive 23,000-square-foot expansion in 2007, the museum has updated a lot of its old exhibitions and added new ones. Some of the most popular stops are also the simplest, like the bubble-making machinery and the two-story climbing maze. At the Japanese House you're invited to take off your shoes and step inside a two-story silk merchant's home from Kyoto. The "Boston Black" exhibit stimu-lates dialogue about ethnicity and community, and children can play at a Cape Verdean restaurant and the African Queen Beauty Salon. In the toddler PlaySpace, children under three can run free in a safe environment. There's also a full schedule of special exhibits, festivals, and performances. ⊠ *308 Congress St., Downtown* ☎ *617/426–6500*

Continued on page 73

BOSTON'S FREEDOM TRAIL

by Mike Nalepa

The Freedom Trail is more than a collection of historic sites related to the American Revolution or a suggested itinerary connecting Boston's unique neighborhoods. It's a chance to walk in the footsteps of our forefathers—literally, by following a crimson path on public sidewalks—and pay tribute to the figures all school kids know, like Paul Revere, John Hancock, and Ben Franklin. In history-proud Boston, past and present intersect before your eyes not as a re-creation but as living history accessible to all.

Boston played a key role in the dramatic events leading up to the American Revolution. Many of the founding fathers called the city home, and many of the initial meetings and actions that sparked the fight against the British took place here. In one day, you can visit Faneuil Hall—the "Cradle of Liberty"—where outraged colonial radicals met to oppose British authority; the site of the incendiary Boston Massacre; and the Old North Church, where lanterns hung to signal Paul Revere on his thrilling midnight ride. Colonists may have originally landed in Jamestown and Plymouth, but if you really want to see where America began, come to Boston.

Boston Common, Founder's Statue

⊕ www.nps.gov/bost
⊕ www.thefreedomtrail.org

☎ 617/242-5642

📧 Admission to the Freedom Trail itself is free. Several museum sites charge for admission. However, most attractions are free monuments, parks, and landmarks.

The 1729 Old South Meeting House, where many protesters gathered during the American Revolution.

PLANNING YOUR TRAIL TRIP

THE ROUTE

The 2½-mi Freedom Trail begins at Boston Common, winds through Downtown, Government Center, and the North End, and ends in Charlestown at the USS *Constitution*. The entire Freedom Trail is marked by a red line on the sidewalk; it's made of paint or brick at various points on the Trail. ⇨ *For more information on Freedom Trail sites, see listings in Neighborhood chapters.*

GETTING HERE AND BACK

The route starts near the Park Street T stop. When you've completed the Freedom Trail, head for the nearby Charlestown water shuttle, which goes directly to the downtown area. For schedules and maps, visit ⊕ *www.mbta.com.*

TIMING

If you're stopping at a few (or all) of the 16 sites, it takes a full day to complete the route comfortably. ■TIP➔ If you have children in tow, you may want to split the trail into two or more days.

VISITOR CENTERS

There are Freedom Trail information centers in Boston Common (Tremont Street), at 15 State Street (near the Old State House), and at the Charlestown Navy Yard Visitor Center (in Building 5).

TOURS

The National Park Service's free 90-minute Freedom Trail walking tours begin at the Boston National Historical Park Visitor Center at 15 State Street and cover sites from the Old South Meeting House to the Old North Church. Check online for times; it's a good idea to show up at least 30 minutes early, as the popular tours are limited to 30 people.

Half-hour tours of the USS *Constitution* are offered Tuesday through Sunday. Note that visitors to the ship must go through security screening.

FUEL UP

The trail winds through the heart of Downtown Boston, so finding a quick bite or a nice sit-down meal isn't difficult. Quincy Market, near Faneuil Hall, is packed with cafés and eateries. Another good lunch choice is one of the North End's wonderful Italian restaurants.

WHAT'S NEARBY

For a short break from revolutionary history, be sure to check out the major attractions nearby, including the Boston Public Garden, New England Aquarium, and Union Oyster House.

Above: In front of the Old State House a cobblestone circle marks the site of the Boston Massacre.

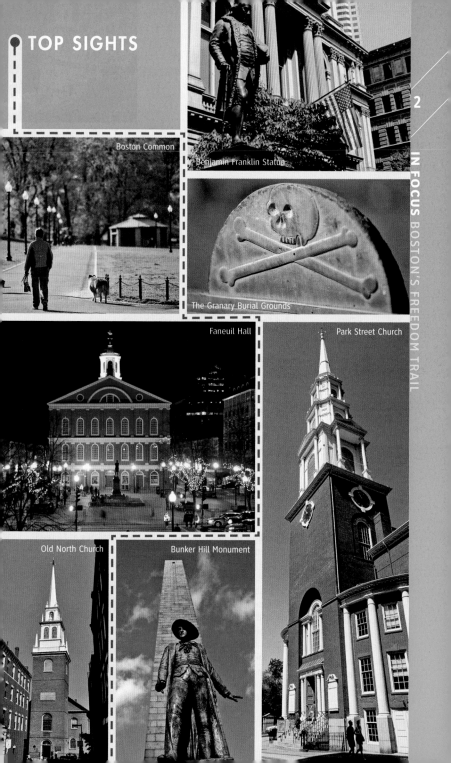

TOP SIGHTS

Boston Common

Benjamin Franklin Statue

The Granary Burial Grounds

Faneuil Hall

Park Street Church

Old North Church

Bunker Hill Monument

BOSTON COMMON TO FANEUIL HALL

Old State House

Cambridge St.

0   100 yards
0   100 meters

Hancock St.
Joy St.

BEACON HILL

Walnut St.

Mt. Vernon St.

Beacon St.

Bowdoin St.

Somerset St.

State House

Park St.

Boston Common

Park Street Church

T PARK ST.

Start: near the Park Street T stop.

Boston National Historic Park Visitor Center

GOVERNMENT CENTER

Court St.

School St.

King's Chapel and Burying Ground

Granary Burying Ground

Ben Franklin Statue

Old Corner Bookstore

Old South Meeting House

Washington St.

Clinton St.

Faneuil Hall

Boston Massacre Site

Old State House

State St.

Chatham St.

Boston National Historic Park Visitor Center

Kilby St.

Congress St.

Devonshire St.

Federal St.

Arch St.

Milk St.

Broad

Franklin

KEY

- - - Freedom Trail

Many of the Freedom Trail sites between Boston Common and the North End are close together. Walking this 1-mile segment of the trail makes for a pleasant morning.

THE ROUTE

Begin at ★ **Boston Common**, then head for the **State House**, Boston's finest example of Federal architecture. Several blocks away is the **Park Street Church**, whose 217-foot steeple is considered to be the most beautiful in New England. The church was actually founded in 1809, and it played a key role in the movement to abolish slavery.

Reposing in the church's shadows is the ★ **Granary Burying Ground**, final resting place of Samuel Adams, John Hancock, and Paul Revere. A short stroll to Downtown brings you to **King's Chapel**, founded in 1686 by King James II for the Church of England.

Follow the trail past the **Benjamin Franklin statue** to the **Old Corner Bookstore** site, where Hawthorne, Emerson, and Longfellow were published. Nearby is the **Old South Meeting House**, where arguments in 1773 led to the Boston Tea Party. Overlooking the site of the Boston Massacre is the city's oldest public building, the **Old State House**, a Georgian beauty.

In 1770 the Boston Massacre occurred directly in front of here—look for the commemorative stone circle.

Cross the plaza to ★ **Faneuil Hall** and explore where Samuel Adams railed against "taxation without representation." ■ TIP➜ A good mid-trail break is the shops and eateries of Faneuil Hall Marketplace, which includes Quincy Market.

Old Corner Book Store Site

★ = **Fodor's**Choice   ★ = Highly Recommended   ☾ = Family Friendly

NORTH END
TO CHARLESTOWN

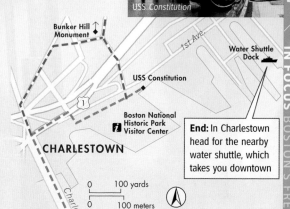

USS *Constitution*

Freedom Trail sites be-
tween Faneuil Hall and
Charlestown are more
spread out along
1½ miles. The sites here,
though more difficult to
reach, are certainly worth
the walk.

THE ROUTE

When you depart Faneuil Hall,
follow the red stripe to the
North End, Boston's Little Italy.

The ☾ **Paul Revere House**
takes you back 200 years—
here are the hero's own
saddlebags, a toddy warmer,
and a pine cradle made from
a molasses cask. It's also
air-conditioned in the summer, so try to stop here in
mid-afternoon to escape the
heat. Next to the Paul Revere
House is one of the city's
oldest brick buildings, the
Pierce-Hichborn House.

Next, peek inside a place
guaranteed to trigger a wave
of patriotism: the ★ **Old
North Church** of "One if by
land, two if by sea" fame.
Then head toward **Copp's**

Paul Revere House

**Hill Burying
Ground**, where
you can view
graves from the late
17th century through
the early 19th century.
Afterward, cross the
bridge over the Charles and
check out that revered icon,
the ☾ USS *Constitution*,
"Old Ironsides." It's open until
6 PM (4 PM November through
March), and you'll need about
an hour for a visit, so plan
accordingly.

The perfect ending to the
trail? A walk to the top of the
☾ **Bunker Hill Monument**
for the incomparable vistas.
The hill was the site of one of
the first battles of the Revolutionary War. Though the
colonial rebels actually lost,
they inflicted large casualties
on the better-trained British,
proving themselves against
the empire.

Bunker Hill ↑
Monument ◆

USS Constitution

Boston National
ℹ Historic Park
Visitor Center

CHARLESTOWN

Water Shuttle
Dock ⛴

End: In Charlestown
head for the nearby
water shuttle, which
takes you downtown

1st Ave.

Charlestown Bridge

| 0 | 100 yards |
| 0 | 100 meters |

**NORTH
END**

Commercial St.

Copp's Hill
◆ Burying Ground

Hull St.

Charter St.

Snow Hill St.

Salem St.

Tileston St.

Old North
◆ Church

Prince St.

Endicott St.

Margin St.

Pierce-
Hichborn
House

Paul Revere
◆ House

Hanover St.

North St.

Richmond St.

**GOVERNMENT
CENTER**

Clinton
St.

◆ Faneuil Hall

State St.

DID YOU KNOW?

If the Freedom Trail leaves you eager to see more Revolutionary War sites, drive about 30 minutes to Lexington and Concord, where the "shot heard 'round the world" launched the first battles in 1775.

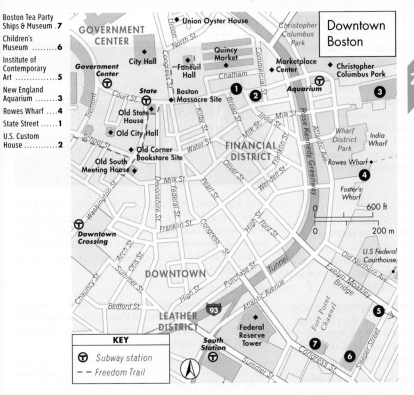

Downtown Boston

KEY

Ⓣ Subway station

-- Freedom Trail

🌐 *www.bostonkids.org* ✉ *$12, Fri. 5–9 $1* 🕑 *Sat.–Thurs. 10–5, Fri.
10–9* Ⓜ *South Station.*

Fodor's Choice **Institute of Contemporary Art.** Housed in a breathtaking cantilevered edi-
★ fice that juts out over the Boston waterfront, the ICA moved to this
site in 2006 as part of a massive reinvention that's seeing the museum
grow into one of Boston's most exciting attractions. Since its foundation
in 1936, the institute has cultivated its cutting-edge status: it's played
host to works by Edvard Munch, Egon Schiele, and Oskar Kokoschka.
Early in their careers, Andy Warhol, Robert Rauschenberg, and Roy
Lichtenstein each mounted pivotal exhibitions here. Now the ICA is
building a major permanent collection for the first time in its history,
while continuing to showcase innovative paintings, videos, installations, and multimedia shows. The performing arts get their due in the
museum's new theater, and the newly refurbished Water Café features
cuisine from local seasonal ingredients. ✉ *100 Northern Ave., South
Boston* ☎ *617/478-3100* 🌐 *www.icaboston.org* ✉ *$15, free Thurs. 5–9,
free for families last Sat. of every month* 🕑 *Tues. and Wed. 10–5, Thurs.
and Fri. 10–9, weekends 10–5. Tours on select weekends at 2 and select
Thurs. at 6* Ⓜ *Courthouse.*

Rowes Wharf. Take a Beacon Hill redbrick town house, blow it up to
the nth power, and you get this 15-story Skidmore, Owings & Merrill

NEW ENGLAND AQUARIUM

⊠ *Central Wharf between Central and Milk Sts., 1 Central Wharf, Downtown* ☎ *617/973–5200* ⊕ *www. neaq.org* 🎟 *$22.95, IMAX $9.95* ⊙ *July–early Sept., Sun.–Thurs. 9–6, Fri. and Sat. 9–7; early Sept.–June, weekdays 9–5, weekends 9–6* Ⓜ *Aquarium, State.*

This aquarium challenges you to really imagine life under and around the sea. Seals bark outside the West Wing, its glass-and-steel exterior constructed to mimic fish scales. Inside the main facility you can see penguins, sea otters, sharks, and other exotic sea creatures—more than 2,000 species in all.

TIPS

■ If you are planning to see an IMAX show as well as check out the aquarium, buy a combo ticket; you'll save $3.95 for the adult ticket.

■ Also, buy the combo ticket if you'd like to do the whale watch and the Aquarium, you'll save $7.95 over purchasing them separately.

■ Save yourself the torture of waiting in long weekend lines, and purchase your tickets ahead of time online at www.neaq.org. You can skip ahead of the crowd and pick up your tickets at the Will Call window, or print them out at home.

■ Want to make your day at the aquarium really special for the kids? Call ahead for a reservation to play with the seals! For $45, kids 9 and up can go behind the scenes and help feed and entertain the seals. Call Central Reservations at 617/973–5206 for more information.

HIGHLIGHTS

In the semienclosed outdoor space of the New Balance Foundation Marine Mammal Center, visitors enjoy the antics of northern fur seals while gazing at a stunning view of Boston Harbor.

One of the aquarium's exhibits, Amazing Jellies, features thousands of jellyfish, many of which were grown in the museum's labs.

Get up close and personal with sharks and rays at the Trust Family Foundation Shark and Ray Touch Tank, the largest of its kind on the East Coast.

Some of the aquarium's 2,000 sea creatures make their home in the four-story, 200,000-gallon ocean-reef tank, one of the largest of its kind in the world. Ramps winding around the tank lead to the top level and allow you to view the inhabitants from many vantage points. Don't miss the five-times-a-day feedings; each lasts nearly an hour and takes divers 24 feet into the tank.

From outside the glassed-off Aquarium Medical Center you can watch veterinarians treat sick animals—here's where you can see an eel in a "hospital bed." At the Edge of the Sea exhibit, children can gingerly pick up starfish and other creatures, while the Curious George Discovery Corner is a fun spot for younger kids. Whale-watch cruises leave from the aquarium's dock from April to October, and cost $39.95. Across the plaza is the aquarium's Education Center; it, too, has changing exhibits. The 6½-story-high IMAX theater takes you on virtual journeys from the bottom of the sea to the depths of outer space with its 3-D films.

extravaganza from 1987, one of the more welcome additions to the Boston Harbor skyline. From under the complex's gateway six-story arch, you can get great views of Boston Harbor and the yachts docked at the marina. Water shuttles pull up here from Logan Airport—the most intriguing way to enter the city. A windswept stroll along the HarborWalk waterfront promenade at dusk makes for an unforgettable sunset on clear days. ⊠ *Atlantic Ave. south of India Wharf, Downtown* Ⓜ *Aquarium.*

State Street. During the 19th century, State Street was headquarters for banks, brokerages, and insurance firms; although these businesses have spread throughout the Downtown District, "State Street" still connotes much the same thing as "Wall Street" does in New York. The early commercial hegemony of State Street was symbolized by Long Wharf, built in 1710 and extending some 1,700 feet into the harbor. If today's Long Wharf doesn't appear to be that long, it's not because it has been shortened but because the land has crept out toward its end. State Street once met the water at the base of the Custom House; landfill operations were pursued relentlessly through the years, and the old coastline is now as much a memory as such Colonial State Street landmarks as Governor Winthrop's 1630 house and the Revolutionary-era Bunch of Grapes Tavern, where Bostonians met to drink and wax indignant at their treatment by King George. ⊠ *Downtown* Ⓜ *State.*

U.S. Custom House. This 1847 structure resembles a Greek Revival temple that appears to have sprouted a tower. It's just that. This is the work of architects Ammi Young and Isaiah Rogers—at least, the bottom part is. The tower was added in 1915, at which time the Custom House became Boston's tallest building. It remains one of the most visible and best loved structures in the city's skyline. To appreciate the grafting job, go inside and look at the domed rotunda. The outer surface of that dome was once the roof of the building, but now the dome is embedded in the base of the tower.

The federal government moved out of the Custom House in 1987 and sold it to the city of Boston, which, in turn, sold it to the Marriott Corporation, which has converted the building into hotel space and luxury time-share units, a move that disturbed some historical purists. You can now sip a cocktail in the hotel's Counting Room Lounge, or visit the 26th-floor observation deck. The magnificent Rotunda Room sports maritime prints and antique artifacts, courtesy of the Peabody Essex Museum in Salem. ⊠ *3 McKinley Sq., Downtown* ☎ *617/310–6300* Ⓜ *State, Aquarium.*

THE BACK BAY

In the folklore of American neighborhoods, the Back Bay stands as a symbol of propriety and high social standing. Before the 1850s it really was a bay, a tidal flat that formed the south bank of a distended Charles River. The filling in of land along the isthmus that joined Boston to the mainland (the Neck) began in 1850, and resulted in the creation of the South End. To the north a narrow causeway called the Mill Dam (later Beacon Street) was built in 1814 to separate the Back Bay from the

Charles. By the late 1800s Bostonians had filled in the shallows to as far as the marshland known as the Fenway, and the original 783-acre peninsula had been expanded by about 450 acres. Thus the waters of Back Bay became the neighborhood of Back Bay.

Heavily influenced by the then-recent rebuilding of Paris according to the plans of Baron Georges-Eugène Haussmann, the Back Bay planners created thoroughfares that resemble Parisian boulevards. Almost immediately, fashionable families began to decamp from Beacon Hill and South End and establish themselves in the Back Bay's brick and brownstone row houses. By 1900 the streets between the Public Garden and Massachusetts Avenue had become the smartest, most desirable neighborhood in all of Boston.

Today the area retains its posh spirit, but mansions are no longer the main draw. Locals and tourists flock to the commercial streets of Boylston and Newbury to shop at boutiques, galleries, and the usual mall stores. Many of the bars and restaurants have patio seating and bay windows. The Boston Public Library, Symphony Hall, and numerous churches ensure that high culture is not lost amid the frenzy of consumerism.

TOP ATTRACTIONS

Fodor's Choice
★
☾

Boston Public Garden. Although the Boston Public Garden is often lumped together with Boston Common, the two are separate entities with different histories and purposes and a distinct boundary between them at Charles Street. The Common has been public land since Boston was founded in 1630, whereas the Public Garden belongs to a newer Boston, occupying what had been salt marshes on the edge of the Common. By 1837 the tract was covered with an abundance of ornamental plantings donated by a group of private citizens. The area was defined in 1856 by the building of Arlington Street, and in 1860 the architect George Meacham was commissioned to plan the park.

The central feature of the Public Garden is its irregularly shaped pond, intended to appear, from any vantage point along its banks, much larger than its nearly 4 acres. Near the Swan Boat dock is what has been described as the world's smallest suspension bridge, designed in 1867 to cross the pond at its narrowest point.

The Public Garden is America's oldest botanical garden, and has the finest formal plantings in central Boston. The beds along the main walkways are replanted for spring and summer. The tulips during the first two weeks of May are especially colorful, and there's a sampling of native and European tree species.

The dominant work among the park's statuary is Thomas Ball's equestrian **George Washington** (1869), which faces the head of Commonwealth Avenue at the Arlington Street gate. This is Washington in a triumphant pose as liberator, surveying a scene that, from where he stood with his cannons at Dorchester Heights, would have included an immense stretch of blue water. Several dozen yards to the north of Washington (to the right if you're facing Commonwealth Avenue) is the granite-and-red-marble **Ether Monument,** donated in 1866 by Thomas Lee to commemorate the advent of anesthesia 20 years earlier at nearby Massachusetts General Hospital. Other Public Garden monuments include statues of the Unitarian preacher and transcendentalist William Ellery Channing, at the corner opposite his Arlington Street Church; Edward Everett Hale, the author (*The Man Without a Country*) and philanthropist, at the Charles Street Gate; and the abolitionist senator Charles Sumner and the Civil War hero Colonel Thomas Cass, along Boylston Street.

The park contains a special delight for the young at heart; follow the children quack-quacking along the pathway between the pond and the park entrance at Charles and Beacon streets to the *Make Way for Ducklings* bronzes sculpted by Nancy Schön, a tribute to the 1941 classic children's story by Robert McCloskey. ⊠ *Bounded by Arlington, Boylston, Charles, and Beacon Sts., Back Bay* Ⓜ *Arlington.*

Swan Boats. The pond has been famous since 1877 for its foot-pedal-powered (by a captain) Swan Boats, which make leisurely cruises during warm months. The pond is favored by ducks and swans, and for the modest price of a few boat rides you can amuse children here for an hour or more. ☎ *617/522–1966* ⊕ *www.swanboats.com* 🖃 *Swan Boats $2.75* ☉ *Swan Boats mid-Apr.–June 20, daily 10–4; June 21–Labor Day, daily 10–5; day after Labor Day–mid-Sept., weekdays noon–4, weekends 10–4.*

★ **Boston Public Library.** This venerable institution is a handsome temple to literature and a valuable research library. The Renaissance Revival building was opened in 1895; a 1972 addition emulates the mass and proportion of the original, though not its extraordinary detail; this skylighted annex houses the library's circulating collections.

You don't need a library card to enjoy the magnificent art. The murals at the head of the staircase, depicting the nine muses, are the work of the French artist Puvis de Chavannes; those in the book-request processing room to the right are Edwin Abbey's interpretations of the Holy Grail legend. Upstairs, in the public areas leading to the fine-arts, music, and rare-books collections, is John Singer Sargent's mural series on the *Triumph of Religion*, shining with renewed color after its cleaning and restoration in 2003. The corridor leading from the annex opens onto the Renaissance-style **courtyard**—an exact copy of the one in Rome's Palazzo della Cancelleria—around which the original library is built. A covered arcade furnished with chairs rings a fountain; you can bring books or lunch into the courtyard, which is open all the hours the library is open, and escape the bustle of the city. Beyond the courtyard is the main entrance hall of the 1895 building, with its immense stone lions by Louis St. Gaudens, vaulted ceiling, and marble staircase. The corridor at the top of the stairs leads to **Bates Hall**, one of Boston's most sumptuous interior spaces. This is the main reference reading room, 218 feet long with a barrel-arch ceiling 50 feet high. ⊠ *700 Boylston St., at Copley Sq., Back Bay* ☎ *617/536–5400* ⊕ *www.bpl.org* ☉ *Mon.–Thurs. 9–9, Fri. and Sat. 9–5, Sun. 1–5. Free guided art and architecture tours Mon. at 2:30, Tues. and Thurs. at 6, Fri. and Sat. at 11, Sun. at 2 (Nov.–May only)* Ⓜ *Copley.*

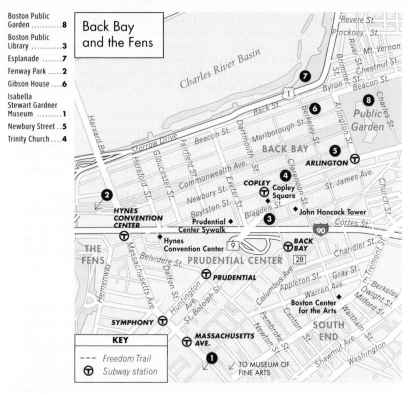

**Back Bay
and the Fens**

KEY

- - - *Freedom Trail*

🇹 *Subway station*

**QUICK
BITES**

Courtyard. You can take a lunch break at the Courtyard or the MapRoom Café, adjoining restaurants in the Boston Public Library. Breakfast and lunch are served in the 1895 map room, and the main restaurant, which overlooks the courtyard, is open for lunch and afternoon tea. The Courtyard is open weekdays 11:30–4, and the MapRoom Café is open Monday–Saturday 9–5. ⊠ *700 Boylston St., at Copley Sq., Back Bay* ☎ *617/859–2251* ⊕ *www.thecateredaffair.com/bpl/index.html.*

★ **Trinity Church.** In his 1877 masterpiece, architect Henry Hobson Richardson brought his Romanesque Revival style to maturity; all the aesthetic elements for which he was famous come together magnificently—bold polychromatic masonry, careful arrangement of masses, sumptuously carved interior woodwork—in this crowning centerpiece of Copley Square. A full appreciation of its architecture requires an understanding of the logistical problems of building it here. The Back Bay is a reclaimed wetland with a high water table. Bedrock, or at least stable glacial till, lies far beneath wet clay. Like all older Back Bay buildings, Trinity Church sits on submerged wooden pilings. But its central tower weighs 9,500 tons, and most of the 4,500 pilings beneath the building are under that tremendous central mass. The pilings are checked regularly for sinkage by means of a hatch in the basement.

Richardson engaged some of the best artists of his day—John LaFarge, William Morris, and Edward Burne-Jones among them—to execute the paintings and stained glass that make this a monument to everything that was right about the pre-Raphaelite spirit and the nascent aesthetic of Morris's Arts and Crafts movement. LaFarge's intricate paintings and ornamented ceilings received a much-needed overhaul during the extensive renovations that wrapped up in 2005. Along the north side of the church, note the Augustus Saint-Gaudens statue of Phillips Brooks—the most charismatic rector in New England, who almost single-handedly got Trinity built and furnished. Shining light of Harvard's religious community and lyricist of "O Little Town of Bethlehem," Brooks is shown here with Christ touching his shoulder in approval. For a nice respite, try to catch one of the Friday organ concerts beginning at 12:15. ■TIP→ The 11:15 Sunday service is followed by a free guided tour. ⊠ *206 Clarendon St., Back Bay* ☎ *617/536–0944* ⊕ *www.trinityboston.org* ✉ *Church free, guided and self-guided tours $6* ⊘ *Mon., Fri., and Sat. 9–5, Tues.–Thurs. 9–6, Sun. 1–6; services Sun. at 7:45, 9, and 11:15 am and 6 pm. Tours take place several times daily; call to confirm times* Ⓜ *Copley.*

WORTH NOTING

Esplanade. Near the corner of Beacon and Arlington streets, the Arthur Fiedler Footbridge crosses Storrow Drive to the Esplanade and the **Hatch Memorial Shell.** The free concerts here in summer include the Boston Pops' immensely popular televised July 4th performance. For shows like this, Bostonians haul lawn chairs and blankets to the lawn in front of the shell; bring a take-out lunch from a nearby restaurant, find an empty spot—no mean feat, so come early—and you'll feel right at home. An impressive stone bust of the late maestro Arthur Fiedler watches over the walkers, joggers, picnickers, and sunbathers who fill the Esplanade's paths on pleasant days. Here, too, is the turn-of-the-20th-century **Union Boat Club Boathouse,** headquarters for the country's oldest private rowing club.

Gibson House. Through the foresight of an eccentric bon vivant, this house provides an authentic glimpse into daily life in Boston's Victorian era. One of the first Back Bay residences (1859), the Gibson House is relatively modest in comparison with some of the grand mansions built during the decades that followed; yet its furnishings, from its circa-1790 Willard clock to the raised and gilded wallpaper to the multipiece faux-bamboo bedroom set, seem sumptuous to modern eyes. Unlike other Back Bay houses, the Gibson family home has been preserved with all its Victorian fixtures and furniture intact. The house serves as the meeting place for the New England chapter of the Victorian Society in America; it was also used as an interior for the 1984 Merchant-Ivory film *The Bostonians.* ■TIP→ Though the sign out front instructs visitors not to ring the bell until the stroke of the hour, you will have better luck catching the beginning of the tour if you arrive a few minutes early and ring forcefully. ⊠ *137 Beacon St., Back Bay* ☎ *617/267–6338* ⊕ *www. thegibsonhouse.org* ✉ *$9* ⊘ *Tours Wed.–Sun. at 1, 2, and 3 and by appointment* Ⓜ *Arlington.*

Shoppers take a break at a Newbury Street café.

Newbury Street. Eight-block-long Newbury Street has been compared to New York's 5th Avenue, and certainly this is the city's poshest shopping area, with branches of Chanel, Brooks Brothers, Armani, Burberry, and other top names in fashion. But here the pricey boutiques are more intimate than grand, and people live above the trendy restaurants and hair salons, giving the place a neighborhood feel. Toward the Massachusetts Avenue end, cafés proliferate and the stores get funkier, ending with Newbury Comics, Urban Outfitters, and Best Buy. ⊠ *Back Bay* Ⓜ *Hynes, Copley.*

THE FENWAY

The marshland known as the Back Bay Fens gave this section of Boston its name, but two quirky institutions give it its character: Fenway Park, home of Boston's beloved Red Sox, and the Isabella Stewart Gardner Museum, the legacy of a high-living Brahmin who attended a concert at Symphony Hall in 1912 wearing a headband that read, "Oh, You Red Sox." Not far from the Gardner is another major cultural magnet: the Museum of Fine Arts. Kenmore Square, a favorite haunt for Boston University students, adds a bit of funky flavor to the mix.

Fodor'sChoice **Fenway Park.** For 86 years, the Boston Red Sox suffered a World Series
★ dry spell, a streak of bad luck that fans attributed to the "Curse of the Bambino," which, stories have it, struck the team in 1920 when they sold Babe Ruth (the "Bambino") to the New York Yankees. All that changed in 2004, when a maverick squad broke the curse in a thrilling seven-game series against the team's nemesis in the series semifinals. This win against the Yankees was followed by a four-game sweep of

St. Louis in the finals. Boston, and its citizens' ingrained sense of pessimism, hasn't been the same since. The repeat World Series win in 2007 cemented Bostonians' sense that the universe had finally begun working correctly and made Red Sox caps the residents' semiofficial uniform. ⇨ *See the Fenway Park spotlight in the Sports and the Outdoors chapter for more information.* ⊠ *4 Yawkey Way, between Van Ness and Lansdowne Sts., The Fenway* ☎ *877/733–7699 box office, 617/226–6666 tours* ⊕ *www. redsox.com* ⊠ *Tours $12* ⊙ *During baseball season, tours daily 9–4 on the hr; off-season tours daily 10–2 on the hr. On game days, last tour is 3 hrs before game time* Ⓜ *Kenmore.*

> ### FRUGAL FUN
>
> Take a cue from locals and sign up for one of the Boston Park Rangers' programs. Top picks include a visit to the city stables to meet the Mounties and their horses, regularly scheduled readings of Robert McCloskey's *Make Way for Ducklings* in Boston's Public Garden, and city scavenger hunts geared for families. Contact **Boston Parks and Recreation** (☎ *617/635–7487* ⊕ *www.cityofboston.gov/parks/ parkrangers*).

FodorśChoice
★

Isabella Stewart Gardner Museum. A spirited young society woman, Isabella Stewart had come in 1860 from New York—where ladies were more commonly seen and heard than in Boston—to marry John Lowell Gardner, one of Boston's leading citizens. "Mrs. Jack" promptly set about becoming the most un-Bostonian of the Proper Bostonians. She decided to build the Venetian palazzo to hold her collected arts in an isolated corner of Boston's newest neighborhood. Her will stipulated that the building remain exactly as she left it—paintings, furniture, and the smallest object in a hall cabinet—and that is as it has remained. Today, it's probably America's most idiosyncratic treasure house.

Gardner's palazzo contains a trove of amazing paintings—including such masterpieces as Titian's *Europa,* Giotto's *Presentation of Christ in the Temple,* Piero della Francesca's *Hercules,* and John Singer Sargent's *El Jaleo.* Spanish leather panels, Renaissance hooded fireplaces, and Gothic tapestries accent salons; eight balconies adorn the majestic Venetian courtyard. There's a Raphael Room, Spanish Cloister, Gothic Room, Chinese Loggia, and a magnificent Tapestry Room for concerts, where Gardner entertained Henry James and Edith Wharton. An adjacent gallery houses the works of participants in museum's artist-in-residence program.

There are some conspicuously bare spots on the walls. On March 18, 1990, the Gardner was the target of a sensational art heist. Thieves disguised as police officers stole 12 works, including Vermeer's *The Concert.* To date, none of the art has been recovered, despite a $5 million reward. Because Mrs. Gardner's will prohibited substituting other works for any stolen art, empty expanses of wall identify spots where the paintings once hung.

A new addition to the museum is slated to open in 2012. The Renzo Piano–designed building will house a music hall, exhibit space, classrooms, and conservation labs, where the Gardner's works can be

MUSEUM OF FINE ARTS

✉ *465 Huntington Ave., The Fenway* ☎ *617/267–9300*
⊕ *www.mfa.org* 🖃 *$22*
🕐 *Sat.–Tues. 10–4:45, Wed.–Fri. 10–9:45. 1-hr tours daily; call for scheduled times*
Ⓜ *Museum.*

TIPS

■ From October to April, take a much-needed break from the art viewing and enjoy tea that is served from 2:30 to 4 in the second-floor Upper Rotunda.

■ The year-round cocktail party "MFA Fridays," from 5:30 to 9:30—held weekly in summer and monthly at other times—has become quite the social event. Stop by to admire the art in a festive atmosphere.

■ Be aware that the museum will require you to check any bag larger than 11"x15", even if it's your purse. So save that oversize bag for another day and bring along only the essentials.

■ With such extensive collections, you could easily spend a whole afternoon perusing the galleries, but if you only have an hour, head to the second floor and take in the Monets.

Count on staying a while if you have any hope of seeing what's here. Eclecticism and thoroughness, often an incompatible pair, have coexisted agreeably at the MFA since its earliest days. From Renaissance and baroque masters to impressionist marvels to African masks to sublime samples of Native American pottery and contemporary crafts, the collections are happily shorn of both cultural snobbery and shortsighted trendiness.

HIGHLIGHTS

The MFA's collection of approximately 450,000 objects was built from a core of paintings and sculpture from the Boston Athenaeum, historical portraits from the city of Boston, and donations by area universities. The MFA has more than 60 works by John Singleton Copley; major paintings by Winslow Homer, John Singer Sargent, Fitz Hugh Lane, and Edward Hopper; and a wealth of American works ranging from native New England folk art and Colonial portraiture to New York abstract expressionism of the 1950s and 1960s. Also of particular note are the John Singer Sargent paintings adorning the Rotunda. They were specially commissioned for the museum in 1921, and make for a dazzling first impression on visitors coming through the Huntington Street entrance.

The museum also owns one of the world's most extensive collections of Asian art under one roof. Its Japanese art collection is the finest outside Japan, and Chinese porcelains of the Tang Dynasty are especially well represented. The Egyptian rooms display statuary, furniture, and exquisite gold jewelry; a special funerary-arts gallery exhibits coffins, mummies, and burial treasures.

French impressionists abound; many of the 38 Monets (the largest collection of his work outside France) vibrate with color. There are canvases by Renoir, Pissarro, Manet, and the American painters Mary Cassatt and Childe Hassam.

repaired and preserved. ✉ *280 The Fenway, The Fenway* ☎ *617/566–1401, 617/566–1088 café* ⊕ *www.gardnermuseum.org* 🎟 *$12* 🕐 *Museum Tues.–Sun. 11–5, open some holidays; café Tues.–Fri. 11:30–4, weekends 11–4.* Ⓜ *Museum.*

EXPLORING CAMBRIDGE

Updated by Bethany Cassin Beckerlegge

Across the Charles River is the überliberal academic enclave of Cambridge. The city is punctuated at one end by the funky tech-noids of MIT and at the other by the grand academic fortress that is Harvard University. Civic life connects the two camps into an urban stew of 100,000 residents who represent nearly every nationality in the world, work at every kind of job from tenured professor to taxi driver, and are passionate about living on this side of the river.

The Charles River is the Cantabrigians' backyard, and there's virtually no place in Cambridge more than a 10-minute walk from its banks. Strolling, running, or biking here is one of the great pleasures of Cambridge, and views include graceful bridges, the distant Boston skyline, crew teams rowing through the calm water, and the elegant spires of Harvard soaring into the sky.

No visit to Cambridge is complete without an afternoon in Harvard Square. It's home to every variation of the human condition; Nobel laureates, homeless buskers, trust-fund babies, and working-class Joes mill around the same piece of real estate. Walk down Brattle Street past Henry Wadsworth Longfellow's house. Farther along Massachusetts Avenue is Central Square, an ethnic melting pot of people and restaurants. Ten minutes more brings you to MIT, with its eclectic architecture from postwar pedestrian to Frank Gehry's futuristic fantasyland. In addition to providing a stellar view, the Massachusetts Avenue Bridge, spanning the Charles from Cambridge to Boston, is also notorious in MIT lore for its Smoot measurements.

Harvard Art Museums. The artistic treasures of the ancient Greeks, Egyptians, and Romans are a major draw here. Make a beeline for the Ancient and Asian art galleries, the permanent installations on the fourth floor, which include Chinese bronzes, Buddhist sculptures, Greek friezes, and Roman marbles. Currently, the Sackler is the only one of the university's art museums open to the public. The Busch-Reisinger and Fogg museums closed in 2008. At present, visitors to the Sackler will enjoy a sampling of works culled from both. In 2013 the combined collections of all three museums will be represented under one roof under the umbrella name Harvard Art Museum. Works include Picasso, Klee, Toulouse-Lautrec, and Manet. ✉ *485 Broadway, Cambridge* ☎ *617/495–9400* ⊕ *www.harvardartmuseums.org* 🎟 *$9* 🕐 *Tues.–Sat. 10–5* Ⓜ *Harvard.*

Fodor's Choice
★
☾

Harvard Museum of Natural History. Many museums promise something for every member of the family; the vast Harvard Museum complex actually delivers. Swiss naturalist Louis Agassiz, who founded the zoology museum, envisioned a museum that would bring under one roof the

study of all kinds of life: plants, animals, and humankind. The result is three distinct museums, all accessible for one admission fee.

The **Museum of Comparative Zoology** traces the evolution of animals and humans. You literally can't miss the 42-foot-long skeleton of the underwater *Kronosaurus*. Dinosaur fossils and a zoo of stuffed exotic animals can occupy young minds for hours. The museum is old-fashioned. You can almost feel the brush of the whiskers of the ardent explorers and the naturalists who combed the world for these treasures. It's also the right size for kids—not jazzy and busy, a good place to ask and answer quiet questions. ■ TIP➔ **Check the website for children's events and special engagements, which occur throughout the year.**

Oversize garnets and crystals sparkle at the **Mineralogical and Geological Museum,** founded in 1784. The museum also contains an extensive collection of meteorites.

Perhaps the most famous exhibits of the museum complex are the glass flowers in the **Harvard University Herbaria (Botanical Museum),** created as teaching tools that would never wither and die. This unique collection holds 3,000 models of 847 plant species. Each one is a masterpiece, meticulously created in glass by a father and son in Dresden, Germany, who worked continuously from 1887 to 1936. Even more amazing than the colorful flower petals are the delicate roots of some plants; numerous signs assure the viewer that everything is, indeed, of glass. ✉ *26 Oxford St., Cambridge* ☎ *617/495–3045* ⊕ *www.hmnh. harvard.edu* ✉ *$9; free for Massachusetts residents Sun. 9–noon year-round and Wed. 3–5 Sept.–May* ☉ *Daily 9–5* Ⓜ *Harvard.*

Fodor's Choice
★
ⓒ

Harvard Square. Tides of students, tourists, political-cause proponents, and bizarre street creatures are all part of the nonstop pedestrian flow at this most celebrated of Cambridge crossroads.

Harvard Square is where Massachusetts Avenue, coming from Boston, turns and widens into a triangle broad enough to accommodate a brick peninsula (above the T station). The restored 1928 kiosk in the center of the square once served as the entrance to the MBTA station (it's now Out of Town News, a fantastic newsstand). Harvard Yard, with its lecture halls, residential houses, libraries, and museums, is one long border of the square; the other three are composed of clusters of banks and a wide variety of restaurants and shops.

On an average afternoon you'll hear earnest conversations in dozens of foreign languages; see every kind of youthful uniform from Goth to impeccable prep; wander by street musicians playing Andean flutes, singing opera, and doing excellent Stevie Wonder or Edith Piaf imitations; and watch a tense outdoor game of pickup chess between a street-tough kid and an older gent wearing a beard and a beret while you slurp a cappuccino or an ice-cream cone (the two major food groups here). An afternoon in the square is people-watching raised to a high art; the parade of quirkiness never quits.

As entertaining as the locals are, the historic buildings are worth noting. Even if you're only a visitor (as opposed to a prospective student), it's still a thrill to walk though the big brick-and-wrought-iron gates to

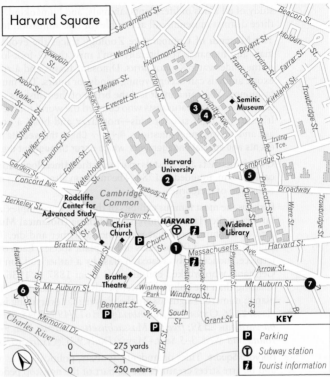

Harvard Yard, past the residence halls and statues, on up to Widener Library.

Across Garden Street, through an ornamental arch, is **Cambridge Common,** decreed a public pasture in 1631. It's said that under a large tree that once stood in this meadow George Washington took command of the Continental Army on July 3, 1775. A stone memorial now marks the site of the "Washington Elm." Also on the Common is the Irish Famine Memorial by Derry artist Maurice Herron, unveiled in 1997 to coincide with the 150th anniversary of "Black '47," the deadliest year of the potato famine. It depicts a desperate Irish mother sending her child off to America. At the center of the Common a large memorial commemorates the Union soldiers and sailors who lost their lives in the Civil War. On the far side of the Common (⊠ *Waterhouse St. between Garden St. and Massachusetts Ave.)* is a fantastic park. ⊕ *www.harvardsquare. com* Ⓜ *Harvard.*

QUICK BITES

Broadway Marketplace. The Broadway Marketplace is just around the corner from Harvard Yard. Besides the excellent fresh produce, there's a selection of sandwiches and prepared meals; choose one to be heated up and then grab a seat for a quick, delicious (if pricey) bite. ⊠ *468 Broadway, Cambridge* ☎ *617/547–2334* ⊕ *www.broadwaymarketplace.com.*

★ **Harvard University.** The tree-studded, shady, and redbrick expanse of Harvard Yard—the very center of Harvard University—has weathered the footsteps of Harvard students for more than 300 years. In 1636 the Great and General Court of the Massachusetts Bay Colony voted funds to establish the colony's first college, and a year later chose Cambridge as the site. Named in 1639 for John Harvard, a young Charlestown clergyman who died in 1638 and left the college his entire library and half his estate, Harvard remained the only college in the New World until 1693, by which time it was firmly established as a respected center of learning. Local wags refer to Harvard as WGU—World's Greatest University—and it's certainly the oldest and most famous American university. It boasts numerous schools or "faculties," including the Faculty of Arts and Sciences, the Medical School, the Law School, the Business School, and the John F. Kennedy School of Government.

Although the college dates from the 17th century, the oldest buildings in Harvard Yard are from the 18th century (though you'll sometimes see archaeologists digging here for evidence of older structures). Together the buildings chronicle American architecture from the Colonial era to the present. **Holden Chapel,** completed in 1744, is a Georgian gem. The graceful **University Hall** was designed in 1815 by Charles Bulfinch. An 1884 statue of John Harvard by Daniel Chester French stands outside; ironically for a school with the motto of *Veritas* ("Truth"), the model for the statue was a member of the class of 1882, as there is no known contemporary likeness of Harvard himself. **Sever Hall,** completed in 1880 and designed by Henry Hobson Richardson, represents the Romanesque revival that was followed by the neoclassical (note the pillared facade of Widener Library) and the neo-Georgian, represented by the sumptuous brick houses along the Charles River, many of which are now undergraduate residences. **Memorial Church,** a graceful steepled edifice of modified Colonial Revival design, was dedicated in 1932. Just north of the Yard is **Memorial Hall,** completed in 1878 as a memorial to Harvard men who died in the Union cause; it's High Victorian both inside and out. It also contains the 1,166-seat Sanders Theatre, which serves as the university's largest lecture hall, site of year-round concerts by students and professionals, and the venue for the festive Christmas Revels.

Many of Harvard's cultural and scholarly facilities are important sights in themselves, including the **Harvard Museum of Natural History,** the **Peabody Museum of Archaeology & Ethnology,** and the **Widener Library.** Be aware that most campus buildings, other than museums and concert halls, are off-limits to the general public. ✉ *Bounded by Massachusetts Ave. and Mt. Auburn, Holyoke, and Dunster Sts., Cambridge* ☎ *617/495–1000* ⊕ *www.harvard.edu* Ⓜ *Harvard.*

Harvard University Events & Information Center. Harvard University Events & Information Center, run by students, includes a small library, a video-viewing area, computer terminals, and an exhibit space. It also distributes maps of the university area and has free student-led tours of Harvard Yard. The tour doesn't include visits to museums, and it doesn't take you into campus buildings, but it provides a fine orientation. The information center is open year-round (except during

spring recess and other semester breaks), Monday through Saturday 9 to 5. Tours are offered September through May, weekdays at 10 and 2 and Saturday at 2 (except during university breaks). From the end of June through August, guides offer three tours Monday through Saturday at 10, 12 and 2. Groups of 20 or more can schedule their tours ahead. ⊠ *Holyoke Center, 1350 Massachusetts Ave., Cambridge* ☎ *617/495–1573* ⊕ *www.harvard.edu*

★ **Longfellow House-Washington's Headquarters.** If there's one historic house to visit in Cambridge, this is it. Henry Wadsworth Longfellow, the poet whose stirring tales of the Village Blacksmith, Evangeline, Hiawatha, and Paul Revere's midnight ride thrilled 19th-century America, once lived in this elegant mansion. One of several original Tory Row homes on Brattle Street, the house was built in 1759 by John Vassall Jr. and George Washington lived here during the Siege of Boston from July 1775 to April 1776. Longfellow first boarded here in 1837 and later received the house as a gift from his father-in-law on his marriage to Frances Appleton, who burned to death here in an accident in 1861. For 45 years Longfellow wrote his famous verses here and filled the house with the exuberant spirit of his own work and that of his literary circle, which included Ralph Waldo Emerson, Nathaniel Hawthorne, and Charles Sumner, an abolitionist senator. Longfellow died in 1882, but his presence in the house lives on—from the Longfellow family furniture to the wallpaper to the books on the shelves (many the poet's own). The home is preserved and run by the National Park Service. ■TIP→ Longfellow Park, across the street, is the place to stand to take photos of the house. The park was created to preserve the view immortalized in the poet's "To the River Charles." ⊠ *105 Brattle St., Cambridge* ☎ *617/876–4491* ⊕ *www.nps.gov/long* 🖼 *Free* ☉ *Check website for seasonal tour schedules* Ⓜ *Harvard.*

Massachusetts Institute of Technology. Celebrated for both its brains and its cerebral sense of humor, this once-tidy engineering school at right angles to the Charles River is growing like a sprawling adolescent, consuming old industrial buildings and city blocks with every passing year. Once dissed as "the factory," particularly by its Ivy League neighbor, MIT mints graduates that are the sharp blades on the edge of the information revolution. It's perennially in the top five of *U.S. News and World Report*'s college rankings.

Founded in 1861, MIT moved to Cambridge from Copley Square in the Back Bay in 1916. It has long since fulfilled the predictions of its founder, the geologist William Barton Rogers, that it would surpass "the universities of the land in the accuracy and the extent of its teachings in all branches of positive science." Its emphasis shifted in the

1930s from practical engineering and mechanics to the outer limits of scientific fields.

Architecture is important at MIT. Although the original buildings were obviously designed by and for scientists, many represent pioneering designs of their times. MIT maintains an information center in the Rogers Building, and offers free tours of the campus weekdays at 11 and 3. Check the schedule, as the tours are often suspended during school holidays. General hours for the information center are weekdays 9–5. ⊠ *77 Massachusetts Ave., Cambridge* ☎ *617/253–4795* ⊕ *www.mit. edu* Ⓜ *Kendall/MIT.*

Peabody Museum of Archaeology & Ethnology. With one of the world's outstanding anthropological collections, the Peabody focuses on Native American and Central and South American cultures; there are also interesting displays on Africa. The Hall of the North American Indian is particularly outstanding, with art, textiles, and models of traditional dwellings from across the continent. The Mesoamerican room juxtaposes ancient relief carvings and weavings with contemporary works from the Maya and other peoples. ⊠ *11 Divinity Ave., Cambridge* ☎ *617/496–1027* ⊕ *www.peabody.harvard.edu* 🏷 *$9, includes admission to Harvard Museum of Natural History, accessible through the museum; free for Massachusetts residents only Sun. 9–noon year-round and Wed. 3–5 Sept.–May* ☉ *Daily 9–5* Ⓜ *Harvard.*

SPORTS AND THE OUTDOORS

Updated by Bethany Cassin Beckerlegge

Everything you've heard about the zeal of Boston fans is true; you cheer, and you pray, and you root some more. "Red Sox Nation" witnessed a miracle in 2004, with the reverse of the curse and the team's first World Series victory since 1918.

Then in 2007 they proved it wasn't just a fluke with another Series win. In 2008 the Celtics ended their 18-year NBA championship drought with a victory over longtime rivals the LA Lakers. And three-time champions the New England Patriots are still a force to be reckoned with.

Bostonians' fervor for sports is equally evident in their leisure-time activities. Harsh winters keep locals wrapped up for months, only to emerge at the earliest sign of oncoming spring. Once the mercury tops freezing and the snows begin to melt, Boston's extensive parks, paths, woods, and waterways teem with sun worshippers and athletes.

NATURAL PARKS AND BEACHES

Arnold Arboretum. The sumptuously landscaped Arnold Arboretum is open all year to joggers and in-line skaters. Volunteer docents give free walking tours in spring, summer, and fall. ⊠ *125 Arborway, Jamaica Plain* ☎ *617/524–1718* ⊕ *www.arboretum.harvard.edu* Ⓜ *Forest Hills.*

Fodor'sChoice
★
ᘓ

Boston Harbor Islands National Park Area. Comprising 34 islands and peninsulas, the Boston Harbor Islands National Park Area is somewhat of a hidden gem for nature lovers and history buffs, with miles of lightly traveled trails and shoreline and several little-visited historic sites to explore. The focal point of the national park is 39-acre Georges Island, where you'll find the partially restored pre–Civil War Fort Warren that once held Confederate prisoners. Other islands worth visiting include Peddocks Island, which holds the remains of Fort Andrews, and Lovells Island, a popular destination for campers. Lovells, Peddocks, Grape, and Bumpkin islands allow camping with a permit from late June through Labor Day. There are swimming areas at the four camping-friendly islands as well, but only Lovells has lifeguards. Pets and alcohol are not allowed on the Harbor Islands. ☎ 617/223–8666 ⊕ www.bostonislands.com.

National Park Service. The National Park Service is a good source for information about camping, transportation, and the like. ☎ 617/223–8666 ⊕ www.bostonislands.com.

Charles River Reservation. Runners, bikers, and in-line skaters crowd the Charles River Reservation at the Esplanade along Storrow Drive, the Memorial Drive Embankment in Cambridge, or any of the smaller and less-busy parks farther upriver. Here you can cheer a crew race, rent a canoe or a kayak, or simply sit on the grass, sharing the shore with packs of hard-jogging university athletes, in-line skaters, moms with strollers, dreamily entwined couples, and intense academics, often talking to themselves as they sort out their intellectual—or perhaps personal—dilemmas. ☎ 617/626–1250 ⊕ www.mass.gov/dcr/parks/CharlesRiver.

Fodor's Choice
★
☼
Emerald Necklace. The six large public parks known as Boston's Emerald Necklace stretch 5 miles from the Back Bay Fens through Franklin Park, in Dorchester; the natural treasure also includes Arnold Arboretum, Jamaica Pond, Olmstead Park, and the Riverway. Frederick Law Olmsted's design heightened the beauty of the Emerald Necklace, which remains a well-groomed urban masterpiece. Locals take pride in and happily make use of its open spaces and its pathways and bridges connecting rivers and ponds.

Emerald Necklace Conservancy. The Emerald Necklace Conservancy maintains a regular calendar of nature walks and other events in the parks. ⊠ 125 The Fenway ☎ 617/522–2700 ⊕ www.emeraldnecklace.org.

Boston Parks & Recreation Department. Rangers with the Boston Parks & Recreation Department lead tours highlighting the area's historic sites and surprising ecological diversity. ⊠ 1010 Massachusetts Ave. ☎ 617/635–4505 ⊕ www.cityofboston.gov/parks/parkrangers.

Harbor Express. To reach the Harbor Islands, take the Harbor Express from Long Wharf (Downtown) or the Hingham Shipyard to Georges Island or Spectacle Island. High-speed catamarans run daily from May through mid-October and cost $14. Other islands can be reached by the free interisland water shuttles that depart from Georges Island. ☎ 617/770–0400 ⊕ www.harborexpress.com.

PARTICIPANT SPORTS

BICYCLING

★ It's common to see suited-up doctors, lawyers, and businessmen commuting on two wheels through Downtown; unfortunately, bike lanes are few and far between. Boston's dedicated bike paths are well used, as much by joggers and in-line skaters as by bicyclists.

Back Bay Bicycles. Back Bay Bicycles has road bikes for $65 per day and full-suspension mountain bikes for $100 per day (weekly rates are also available). Staff members also lead group mountain-bike rides on nearby trails. ⊠ *362 Commonwealth Ave., Back Bay* ☏ *617/247–2336* ⊕ *www.backbaybicycles.com.*

Community Bicycle Supply. Community Bicycle Supply rents cycles from April through October. ⊠ *496 Tremont St., at E. Berkeley St., South End* ☏ *617/542–8623* ⊕ *www.communitybicycle.com.*

Department of Conservation & Recreation (*DCR*). For other path locations, consult the Department of Conservation & Recreation website. ⊕ *www.mass.gov/dcr.*

Dr. Paul Dudley White Bike Path. The Dr. Paul Dudley White Bike Path, about 17 miles long, follows both banks of the Charles River as it winds from Watertown Square to the Museum of Science.

Massachusetts Bicycle Coalition (*MassBike*). The Massachusetts Bicycle Coalition, an advocacy group working to improve conditions for area cyclists, has information on organized rides and sells good bike maps of Boston and the state. Thanks to MassBike's lobbying efforts, the MBTA now allows bicycles on subway and commuter-rail trains during nonpeak hours. ⊠ *171 Milk St., Suite 33, Downtown* ☏ *617/542–2453* ⊕ *www.massbike.org.*

BOATING

Except when frozen over, the waterways coursing through the city serve as a playground for boaters of all stripes. All types of pleasure craft, with the exception of inflatables, are allowed from the Charles River and Inner Harbor to North Washington Street on the waters of Boston Harbor, Dorchester inner and outer bays, and the Neponset River from the Granite Avenue Bridge to Dorchester Bay.

Boat Drop Sites. There are several boat drop sites along the Charles.

Clarendon Street ⊠ *Back Bay.*

Hatch Shell ⊠ *Embankment Rd., Back Bay.*

Pinckney Street Landing ⊠ *Back Bay.*

Brooks Street ⊠ *Nonantum Rd., Brighton.*

Richard T. Artesani Playground ⊠ *Off Soldiers Field Rd., Brighton.*

Charles River Dam, Museum of Science ⊠ *Cambridge.*

Watertown Square ⊠ *Charles River Rd., Watertown.*

Christopher Columbus Waterfront Park. Sailboats can be rented from one of the many boathouses or docks along the Charles. Downtown, public landings and float docks are available at the Christopher Colum-

Many of the local University teams row on the Charles River.

bus Waterfront Park with a permit from the Boston harbormaster. ✉ *Commercial St., Boston Harbor, North End* ☎ *617/635–4505.*

Charles River Watershed Association. The Charles River Watershed Association publishes detailed boating information on its website. ☎ *781/788–0007* ⊕ *www.charlesriver.org.*

SPECTATOR SPORTS

⇨ *See the Fenway Park spotlight.*

BASKETBALL

★ **Boston Celtics.** The Boston Celtics, one of the most storied franchises in the National Basketball Association, have won the NBA championship 17 times since 1957, more than any other team in the league. The last title came in 2008, after a solid defeat of longtime rivals the LA Lakers ended an 18-year championship dry spell. Basketball season runs from late October to April, and playoffs last until mid-June. ✉ *TD Garden, Old West End* ☎ *866/423–5849, 617/931–2222 Ticketmaster* ⊕ *www.celtics.com.*

FOOTBALL

New England Patriots. Boston has been building a football dynasty over the past decade, starting with the New England Patriots come-from-behind victory against the favored St. Louis Rams in the 2002 Super Bowl. Coach Bill Belichick and heartthrob quarterback Tom Brady then brought the team two more championship rings in 2004 and 2005, and have made Patriots fans as zealous as their baseball counterparts. Exhibition football games begin in August, and the season runs through the playoffs in January. The state-of-the-art Gillette Stadium is in Fox-borough, 30 miles southwest of Boston. ⊠ *Gillette Stadium, Rte. 1, off I–95 Exit 9, Foxborough* ☎ *800/745–3000 Ticketmaster* ⊕ *www. patriots.com.*

HOCKEY

Beanpot Hockey Tournament. Boston College, Boston University, Harvard, and Northeastern teams face off every February in the Beanpot Hockey Tournament at the TD Garden. The colleges in this fiercely contested tournament traditionally yield some of the finest squads in the country. ⊕ *www.beanpothockey.com.*

Boston Bruins. The Boston Bruins are on the ice from September until April, frequently on Thursday and Saturday evenings. Playoffs last through early June. ⊠ *TD Garden, 100 Legends Way, Old West End* ☎ *617/624–2327* ⊕ *www.bostonbruins.com.*

RUNNING

Fodor's Choice ★

Boston Marathon. Every Patriots' Day (the third Monday in April), fans gather along the Hopkinton–to–Boston route of the Boston Marathon to cheer on more than 25,000 runners from all over the world. The race ends near Copley Square in the Back Bay.

Boston Athletic Association. For information, call the Boston Athletic Association. ☎ *617/236–1652* ⊕ *www.bostonmarathon.org.*

SHOPPING

Updated by Bethany Cassin Beckerlegge

Boston's shops are generally open Monday through Saturday from 10 or 11 until 6 or 7 and Sunday noon to 5. Many stay open until 8 pm one night a week, usually Thursday. Malls are open Monday through Saturday from 9 or 10 until 8 or 9 and Sunday noon to 6.

MAJOR SHOPPING DISTRICTS

Boston's shops and department stores are concentrated in the area bounded by Quincy Market, the Back Bay, and Downtown. There are plenty of bargains in the Downtown Crossing area. The South End's gentrification creates its own kind of consumerist milieus, from house-wares shops to avant-garde art galleries. In Cambridge you can find lots of shopping around Harvard and Central squares, with independent boutiques migrating west along Massachusetts Avenue (or Mass Ave., as almost everyone else calls it) toward Porter Square and beyond.

BOSTON

Charles Street. Pretty Charles Street is crammed beginning to end with top-notch antiques stores such as Judith Dowling Asian Art, Eugene Galleries, and Devonia, as well as a handful of independently owned fashion boutiques whose prices reflect their high Beacon Hill rents. River Street, parallel to Charles Street, is also an excellent source for antiques. Both are easy walks from the Charles Street T stop on the Red Line. ⊠ *Beacon Hill.*

Copley Place. Two bold intruders dominate Copley Square—the **John Hancock Tower** off the southeast corner and the even more assertive

Copley Place skyscraper on the southwest. An upscale, glass-and-brass urban mall built between 1980 and 1984, Copley Place includes two major hotels: the high-rise Westin and the Marriott Copley Place. Dozens of shops, restaurants, and offices are attractively grouped on several levels, surrounding bright, open indoor spaces. ⊠ *100 Huntington Ave., Back Bay* Ⓢ *Shopping galleries Mon.–Sat. 10–8, Sun. noon–6* Ⓜ *Copley.*

Downtown Crossing. Downtown Crossing is a pedestrian mall with a Macy's, H&M, and TJ Maxx. Millennium Place, a 1.8-million-square-foot complex with a Ritz-Carlton Hotel, condos, a massive sports club, a 19-screen Loews Cineplex, and the brand-new W Hotel turned this once seedy hangout into a happening spot. ⊠ *Washington St. from Amory St. to about Milk St., Downtown* Ⓜ *Downtown Crossing, Park St.*

Faneuil Hall Marketplace. Faneuil Hall Marketplace is a huge complex that's also hugely popular, even though most of its independent shops have given way to Banana Republic, Urban Outfitters, and other chains. The place has plenty of history, one of the area's great à la carte casual dining experiences (Quincy Market), and carnival-like trappings: push-carts sell everything from silver jewelry to Peruvian sweaters, and buskers perform crowd-pleasing feats such as break dancing. ⊠ *Bounded by Congress St., Atlantic Ave., the Waterfront, and Government Center, Downtown* ☎ *617/523–1300* ⊕ *www.faneuilhallmarketplace.com* Ⓜ *Government Center.*

★ **Newbury Street.** Newbury Street is Boston's version of New York's 5th Avenue. The entire street is a shoppers' paradise, from high-end names such as Brooks Brothers to tiny specialty shops such as the Fish and Bone. Upscale clothing stores, up-to-the-minute art galleries, and dazzling jewelers line the street near the Public Garden. As you head toward Mass Ave., Newbury gets funkier and the cacophony builds, with skateboarders zipping through traffic and garbage-pail drummers burning licks outside the hip boutiques. The big-name stores run from Arlington Street to the Prudential Center. ⊠ *Back Bay* Ⓜ *Arlington, Copley, Hynes.*

South End. South End merchants are benefiting from the ongoing gentrification that has brought high real-estate prices and trendy restaurants to the area. Explore the chic home-furnishings and gift shops that line Tremont Street, starting at Berkeley Street. The MBTA's Silver Line bus runs through the South End. ⊠ *South End* Ⓜ *Back Bay/South End.*

CAMBRIDGE

Central Square. Central Square has an eclectic mix of furniture stores, used-record shops, ethnic restaurants, and small, hip performance venues. ⊠ *East of Harvard Sq., Cambridge* Ⓜ *Central.*

Harvard Square. Harvard Square takes up just a few blocks but holds more than 150 stores selling clothes, books, records, furnishings, and specialty items. (⇨ *Harvard Square spotlight for more information.*) ⊠ *Cambridge* Ⓜ *Harvard.*

Galleria. The Galleria has various boutiques and a few decent, independently owned restaurants. ⊠ *57 JFK St., Cambridge* Ⓜ *Harvard.*

Brattle Street. A handful of chains and independent boutiques are clustered on Brattle Street. ⊠ *Behind Harvard Sq., Cambridge* Ⓜ *Harvard.*

Porter Square. Porter Square has distinctive clothing stores, as well as crafts shops, coffee shops, natural-food stores, restaurants, and bars with live music. ⊠ *West on Mass Ave. from Harvard Sq., Cambridge* Ⓜ *Porter.*

SHOPPING BY NEIGHBORHOOD

BEACON HILL

ANTIQUES

Boston Antique Company. This flea market–style collection of dealers has been in business for 32 years and is still going strong. Occupying the lower level of the building, the company contains everything from vintage photos and paintings to porcelain, silver, bronzes, and furniture. ⊠ *119 Charles St., Beacon Hill* ☎ *617/227–9810* ⊙ *Mon.–Sat. 10–6, Sun. noon–5* Ⓜ *Charles/MGH.*

Judith Dowling Asian Art. Judith Dowling's sophistication results from spareness and restraint. High-end Asian artifacts range from Japanese pottery to scrolls, Buddha figures, painted screens, cabinets, and other furnishings. ⊠ *133 Charles St., Beacon Hill* ☎ *617/523–5211* ⊕ *www. judithdowling.com* ⊙ *Thurs.–Sat. 11–5, and by appointment.*

GIFTS

The Flat of the Hill. There's nothing flat about this fun collection of seasonal items, toiletries, toys, pillows, and whatever else catches the fancy of the shop's young owner. Her passion for pets is evident—pick up a Fetch & Glow ball and your dog will never again have to wait until daytime to play in the park. ⊠ *60 Charles St., Beacon Hill* ☎ *617/619– 9977* Ⓜ *Charles/MGH.*

BACK BAY

BOOKS

Trident Booksellers & Café. Browse through an eclectic collection of books, tapes, and magazines, then settle in with a snack. It's open until midnight daily, making it a favorite with students. ⊠ *338 Newbury St., Back Bay* ☎ *617/267–8688* ⊕ *tridentbookscafe.com* ⊙ *Daily 8 am– midnight* Ⓜ *Hynes.*

CLOTHING AND SHOES

★ **Alan Bilzerian.** Satisfying the Euro crowd, this store sells luxe men's and women's clothing by such fashion darlings as Yohji Yamamoto and Ann Demeulemeester. ⊠ *34 Newbury St., Back Bay* ☎ *617/536–1001* ⊕ *www.alanbilzerian.com* ⊙ *Mon.–Sat. 10–6. Closed Sun.* Ⓜ *Arlington.*

Anne Fontaine. You can never have too many white shirts—especially if they're designed by this Parisienne. The simple, sophisticated designs are mostly executed in cotton and priced around $160. ⊠ *318 Boylston St., Back Bay* ☎ *617/423–0366* Ⓜ *Arlington, Boylston.*

Betsy Jenney. Ms. Jenney herself is likely to wait on you in this small, personal store, where the well-made, comfortable lines are for women who cannot walk into a fitted size-4 suit—in other words, most of the female population. The designers found here, such as Nicole Miller, are fashionable yet forgiving. ✉ *114 Newbury St., Back Bay* ☎ *617/536–2610* ⊕ *www.betsyjenney.com* Ⓜ *Copley.*

Daniela Corte. Local designer Corte cuts women's clothes that flatter from her sunny Back Bay studio. Look for gorgeous suiting, flirty halter dresses, and sophisticated formal frocks that can be bought off the rack or custom tailored. ✉ *211 Newbury St., Back Bay* ☎ *617/262–2100* Ⓜ *Copley.*

Grettaluxe. Drop by Copley's sassy little boutique and pick up the latest "it" pieces—from velour hoodies by Juicy Couture to the must-have Stella McCartney design du moment. There are also jewelry, handbags, and other accessories. ✉ *Westin Hotel, 10 Huntington Ave., Back Bay* ☎ *617/536–1959* Ⓜ *Copley.*

DEPARTMENT STORES

★ **Barneys New York.** The hoopla (not to mention the party) generated by this store's arrival was surprising in a city where everything new is viewed with trepidation. But clearly Boston's denizens have embraced the lofty, two-story space because it's filled with cutting-edge lines like Comme des Garçons and Nina Ricci, as well as a few bargains in the second-level Co-op section. ✉ *100 Huntington Ave., Back Bay* ☎ *617/385–3300* ⊕ *www.barneys.com* Ⓜ *Copley.*

Lord & Taylor. This is a reliable (if somewhat overstuffed with merchandise) stop for classic clothing by such designers as Anne Klein and Ralph Lauren, along with accessories, cosmetics, and jewelry. ✉ *760 Boylston St., Back Bay* ☎ *617/262–6000* ⊕ *www.lordandtaylor.com* Ⓜ *Prudential Center.*

Neiman Marcus. The flashy Texas-based retailer known to many as "Needless Markup" has three levels of swank designers and a jaw-dropping shoe section, as well as cosmetics and housewares. ✉ *5 Copley Pl., Back Bay* ☎ *617/536–3660* ⊕ *www.neimanmarcus.com* Ⓜ *Back Bay/South End.*

Saks Fifth Avenue. The clothing and accessories at Saks run from the traditional to the flamboyant. It's a little pricey, but an excellent place to find high-quality merchandise, including shoes and cosmetics. ✉ *The Shops at Prudential Center, 800 Boylston St., Back Bay* ☎ *617/262–8500* ⊕ *www.saksfifthavenue.com* Ⓜ *Prudential Center.*

GIFTS

★ **Fresh.** You won't know whether to wash with these soaps or nibble on them. The shea butter–rich bars come in such scents as clove-hazelnut and orange-cranberry. They cost $6 to $7 each, but they carry the scent to the end. ✉ *121 Newbury St., Back Bay* ☎ *617/421–1212* ⊕ *www. fresh.com* ⊗ *Mon.–Sat. 10–7, Sun. noon–6* Ⓜ *Copley.*

DOWNTOWN

BOOKS

Brattle Bookshop. The late George Gloss built this into Boston's best used- and rare-book shop. Today his son Kenneth fields queries from passionate book lovers. If the book you want is out of print, Brattle has it or can probably find it. ✉ *9 West St., Downtown* ☎ *617/542–0210, 800/447–9595* ⊕ *www.brattlebookshop.com* Ⓜ *Downtown Crossing.*

CLOTHING AND SHOES

Fodor's Choice ★ **Louis Boston.** Impeccably tailored designs, subtly updated classics, and the latest Italian styles highlight a wide selection of imported clothing and accessories. Visiting celebrities might be trolling the racks along with you as jazz spills out into the street from the adjoining Sam's Restaurant. ⊠ *60 Northern Ave., South Boston* ☎ *617/262–6100* ⊕ *www. louisboston.com* ☉ *Mon.–Wed. 11–6, Thurs.–Sat. 11–7, Sun. 11:30–5* Ⓜ *South Station.*

DEPARTMENT STORES

Macy's. Three floors offer men's and women's clothing and shoes, housewares, and cosmetics. Although top designers and a fur salon are part of the mix, Macy's doesn't feel exclusive; instead, it's a popular source for family basics. ⊠ *450 Washington St., Downtown* ☎ *617/357–3000* ⊕ *www.macys.com* Ⓜ *Downtown Crossing.*

CAMBRIDGE

ANTIQUES

Cambridge Antique Market. Off the beaten track this may be, but it has a selection bordering on overwhelming: five floors of goods ranging from 19th-century furniture to vintage clothing, much of it reasonably priced. There are two parking lots next to the building. ⊠ *201 Monsignor O'Brien Hwy., Cambridge* ☎ *617/868–9655* Ⓜ *Lechmere.*

BOOKS

Fodor's Choice ★ **Harvard Book Store.** The intellectual community is well served here, with a slew of new titles upstairs and used and remaindered books downstairs. The collection's diversity has made the store a favored destination for academics. ⊠ *1256 Massachusetts Ave., Cambridge* ☎ *617/661–1515* ⊕ *www.harvard.com* Ⓜ *Harvard.*

GIFTS

Buckaroo's Mercantile. It's Howdy Doody time at Buckaroo's—a great destination for the kitsch inclined. Find pink poodle skirts, lunch-box clocks, Barbie lamps, *Front Page Detective* posters, and everything Elvis. ⊠ *5 Brookline St., Cambridge* ☎ *617/492–4792* Ⓜ *Central.*

NIGHTLIFE AND THE ARTS

NIGHTLIFE

Updated by Bethany Cassin Beckerlegge

BEACON HILL

BARS

Cheers. Formerly known as the Bull & Finch Pub, Cheers was dismantled in England, shipped to Boston, and reassembled here. Though it was the inspiration for the TV series of the same name, it doesn't look anything like the bar in the show. Addressing that complaint, however, an additional branch in Faneuil Hall is an exact reproduction of the TV set. ⊠ *Hampshire House, 84 Beacon St., Beacon Hill* ☎ *617/227–9605* ⊕ *www.cheersboston.com* Ⓜ *Park St., Charles/MGH.*

The Sevens. There's nothing stuffy or pretentious at this laid-back alternative to the tony atmosphere of Beacon Hill (think dark, simple, with darts), just good pints and old-fashioned mixed drinks, plus darts and the televised game of the night. ✉ *77 Charles St., Beacon Hill* ☎ *617/523–9074* Ⓜ *Charles/MGH.*

GOVERNMENT CENTER

BARS

★ **Bell in Hand Tavern.** The country's oldest continuously operating pub is named after the occupation of its original owner, a town crier. It's on the perimeter of Faneuil Hall and has live music every night of the week. If you're brave, you can join the Tuesday-night karaoke. ✉ *45–55 Union St., Faneuil Hall, Government Center* ☎ *617/227–2098* ⊕ *www. bellinhand.com* Ⓜ *Haymarket.*

Black Rose. The Black Rose is decorated with family crests, pictures of Ireland, and portraits of the likes of Samuel Beckett, Lady Gregory, and James Joyce—just like a Dublin pub. Its Faneuil Hall location draws as many tourists as locals, but nightly shows by traditional Irish and contemporary performers make it worth braving the crowds. ✉ *160 State St., Faneuil Hall, Government Center* ☎ *617/742–2286* ⊕ *www. irishconnection.com/blackrose.html* Ⓜ *Aquarium, State.*

THE NORTH END

COMEDY CLUBS

★ **ImprovAsylum.** ImprovAsylum features comedians who weave audience suggestions into seven weekly shows blending topical sketches with improv in shows such as "Lost in Boston" and "New Kids on the Blog." Tickets start at around $20; students can pay $10 apiece with a two-for-one deal. Sunday shows are free—just be sure to get there plenty early to get a seat. ✉ *216 Hanover St., North End* ☎ *617/263–6887* ⊕ *www. improvasylum.com* Ⓜ *Haymarket, North Station.*

CHARLESTOWN

BARS

Warren Tavern. Massachusetts' oldest watering hole is more than 200 years old, and was once frequented by Paul Revere (even George Washington drank here). Today it caters mostly to tourists and Charlestown professionals. It's an easy stop for a pint en route to the Bunker Hill Monument or historic Navy Yard. Ask for the house-made potato chips with your ale of choice. ✉ *2 Pleasant St., Charlestown* ☎ *617/241–8142* ⊕ *www.warrentavern.com* Ⓜ *Community College.*

DOWNTOWN

COMEDY CLUBS

Comedy Connection. Comedy Connection, now residing at the Wilbur Theatre, has a mix of local and nationally known acts such as Tracy Morgan, Aziz Ansari, and Wayne Brady. ✉ *246 Tremont St., in Wilbur Theatre, Downtown* ☎ *617/931–2000* ⊕ *www.thewilburtheatre.com* Ⓜ *Boylston.*

DANCE CLUBS

Gypsy Bar. Gypsy Bar calls to mind the decadence of a dark European castle, with its rich red velvet and crystal chandeliers. Rows of video screens broadcast the Fashion Network, adding a sexier, more modern touch. Thirtysomething revelers and European students snack on lime-and-ginger-marinated tiger shrimp and sip "See You in Church"

The Harvard Coop has peddled books to university students since 1882.

martinis (vodka with fresh marmalade) while the trendy dance floor throbs to Top 40 and house music. ✉ *116 Boylston St., Theater District, Downtown* ☎ *617/482–7799* ⊕ *www.gypsybarboston.com* Ⓜ *Boylston.*

BACK BAY

BARS

Cactus Club. One of the few places in Boston that make a decent margarita, the Cactus Club has a popular outdoor patio for kicking back, sipping frozen drinks, and watching the stylish Back Bay crowds pass by. ✉ *939 Boylston St., Back Bay* ☎ *617/236–0200* ⊕ *www.bestmargaritas. com* Ⓜ *Hynes.*

THE SOUTH END

BARS

Franklin Café. This neighborhood institution is known for great martinis, microbrews on tap, and upscale pub food. There's no placard bearing its name; just look for the martini sign (or the crowd waiting for a dinner table) to know you're there. ✉ *278 Shawmut Ave., South End* ☎ *617/350–0010* ⊕ *www.franklincafe.com* Ⓜ *Back Bay/South End.*

THE FENWAY

BARS

Boston Beer Works. This is a "naked brewery," with all the works exposed—the tanks, pipes, and gleaming stainless-steel and copper kettles used in producing beer. Seasonal brews, in addition to 16 microbrews on tap, draw students, young adults, and tourists alike to the original location (its sibling by the TD Garden is popular, too). The atmosphere is too crowded and noisy for intimate chats, and good luck trying to get in when there's a home game. ✉ *61 Brookline Ave., The*

Fenway ☎ *617/536–2337* ⊕ *www. beerworks.net* Ⓜ *Kenmore.*

ALLSTON
ROCK CLUBS

Fodor'sChoice ★ **Paradise Rock Club.** This small place is known for hosting big-name talent like U2, Coldplay, and local stars such as the Dresden Dolls. Two tiers of booths provide good sight lines anywhere in the club, as well as some intimate and out-of-the-way corners, and four bars quench the crowd's thirst. The 18-plus crowd varies with the shows. The newer Paradise Lounge, next door, is a more intimate space to experience local, often acoustic songsters, as well as literary readings and other artistic events. It serves dinner. ✉ *967–969 Commonwealth Ave., Allston* ✛ *Near Boston University* ☎ *617/562–8800* ⊕ *www.thedise.com* Ⓜ *Pleasant St.*

> ## THE REAL CHEERS
>
> TV's *Cheers* may have ended in 1993, but that doesn't stop die-hard fans from paying their respects at the "real" Cheers bar on Beacon Street (or its second location in Faneuil Hall). Although the inspiration for the TV show doesn't quite look like its fictional double, the same atmosphere of good spirits persists. You can find your own kind of notoriety here by devouring the double-decker "Giant Norm burger" and adding your name to the Hall of Fame.

CAMBRIDGE
BLUES AND R&B CLUBS

★ **Cantab Lounge/Third Rail.** The Cantab Lounge/Third Rail hums every night with live Motown, rhythm and blues, folk, or bluegrass. The Third Rail bar, downstairs, holds poetry slams, open-mike readings and bohemia nights. It's friendly and informal, with a diverse under-forty crowd. ✉ *738 Massachusetts Ave., Cambridge* ☎ *617/354–2685* ⊕ *www.cantab-lounge.com* ⊟ *No credit cards* Ⓜ *Central.*

JAZZ CLUBS

Regattabar. Regattabar is host to some of the top names in jazz, including Sonny Rollins and Herbie Hancock. Tickets for shows are $15–$35. Even when there's no entertainment, the large, low-ceiling club is a pleasant (if expensive) place for a drink. ✉ *Charles Hotel, 1 Bennett St., Cambridge* ☎ *617/661–5000, 617/395–7757* ⊕ *www.regattabarjazz. com* Ⓜ *Harvard.*

★ **Ryles Jazz Club.** Soft lights, mirrors, and greenery set the mood for first-rate jazz. The first-floor stage is one of the best places for new music and musicians. Upstairs is a dance hall staging regular tango, salsa, and merengue nights, often with lessons before the dancing starts. Ryles also holds occasional open-mike poetry slams and a Sunday jazz brunch (call for reservations). It's open nightly, with a cover charge. ✉ *212 Hampshire St., Cambridge* ☎ *617/876–9330* ⊕ *www.ryles.com* Ⓜ *Bus 69, 83, or 91.*

ROCK CLUBS

★ **Middle East Restaurant & Nightclub.** The Middle East Restaurant & Nightclub manages to be both a Middle Eastern restaurant and one of the area's most eclectic rock clubs, with three rooms showcasing live local and national acts. Local phenoms the Mighty Mighty Bosstones got their start here. Music-world celebs often drop in when they're in town. There's also belly dancing, folk, jazz, and even the occasional country-tinged rock band. ✉ *472–480 Massachusetts Ave., Cambridge* ☎ *617/497–0576, 617/864–3278* ⊕ *www.mideastclub.com* Ⓜ *Central.*

THE ARTS

BEACON HILL

CONCERTS

★ **Hatch Memorial Shell.** On the bank of the Charles River, this wonderful acoustic shell is where the Boston Pops perform its famous free summer concerts (including the traditional July 4 show, broadcast live nationwide on TV). Local radio stations also put on music shows and festivals here from April through October. ✉ *Off Storrow Dr. at embankment, Beacon Hill* ☎ *617/626–4970* ⊕ *www.mass.gov/dcr/hatch_events.htm* Ⓜ *Charles/MGH, Arlington.*

DOWNTOWN AND SOUTH BOSTON

CONCERTS

Bank of America Pavilion. Bank of America Pavilion gathers up to 5,000 people on the city's waterfront for summertime concerts. National pop, folk, and country acts play the tentlike pavilion from about mid-June to mid-September. ✉ *290 Northern Ave., South Boston* ☎ *617/728–1600* Ⓜ *South Station.*

Boston Opera House. The Boston Opera House hosts plays, musicals, and traveling Broadway shows and also has booked diverse performers such as David Copperfield, B.B. King, and Pat Metheny. The occasional children's production may schedule a run here as well. ✉ *539 Washington St., Downtown* ☎ *617/259–3400* ⊕ *www.bostonoperahouseonline.com* Ⓜ *Boylston, Chinatown, Downtown Crossing, Park St.*

BACK BAY

CONCERTS

Berklee Performance Center. Associated with Berklee College of Music, Berklee Performance Center is best known for its jazz programs, but it's also host to folk performers such as Joan Baez and pop and rock stars such as Andrew Bird, Aimee Mann, and Henry Rollins. ✉ *136 Massachusetts Ave., Back Bay* ☎ *617/747–2261 box office* ⊕ *www. berkleebpc.com* Ⓜ *Hynes.*

★ **New England Conservatory's Jordan Hall.** New England Conservatory's Jordan Hall, one of the world's acoustic treasures, is ideal for chamber music yet large enough to accommodate a full orchestra. The Boston Philharmonic and the Boston Baroque ensemble often perform at the relatively intimate 1,000-seat hall. ✉ *30 Gainsborough St., Back Bay* ☎ *617/585–1260 box office* ⊕ *necmusic.edu/calendar_event* Ⓜ *Symphony.*

Symphony Hall. Acoustics rather than aesthetics make this hall, the home of the Boston Symphony Orchestra and the Boston Pops, special for performers and concertgoers. Although acoustical science was a brand-new field of research when Professor Wallace Sabine planned the interior, not one of the 2,500 seats is a bad one—the secret is the box-within-a-box

The first club in the United States to host U2, Paradise Rock Club has offered big names in an intimate venue since 1977.

design. ✉ *301 Massachusetts Ave., Back Bay* ☎ *888/266–1200 box office, 617/638–9390 tours* ⊙ *Free walk-up tours Oct.–May, Wed. at 4 and some Sat. at 2* Ⓜ *Symphony.*

OPERA

Boston Lyric Opera. Boston Lyric Opera stages four full productions each season at Citi Performing Arts Center, which usually include one 20th-century work. Recent highlights have included Musto's *The Inspector* and Verdi's *Macbeth.* ☎ *617/542–4912, 617/542–6772 audience services office* ⊕ *www.blo.org* Ⓜ *Boylston.*

THEATER

Huntington Theatre Company. Boston's largest resident theater company consistently performs a high-quality mix of 20th-century plays, new works, and classics under the leadership of artistic director Peter DuBois, and commissions artists to produce original dramas. The Huntington performs at two locations: at the Boston University Theatre and at the Calderwood Theatre Pavilion in the South End. ✉ *Boston University Theatre, 264 Huntington Ave., Back Bay* ☎ *617/266–0800 box office* ⊕ *www.huntingtontheatre.org* Ⓜ *Symphony* ✉ *Calderwood Theatre Pavilion, Boston Center for the Arts, 527 Tremont St., South End* ☎ *617/426–5000* ⊕ *www.bcaonline.org* Ⓜ *Back Bay/South End, Copley.*

THE SOUTH END

BALLET

★ **Boston Ballet.** The city's premier dance company performs at the Boston Opera House. In addition to a world-class repertory of classical and high-spirited modern works, it presents an elaborate signature

Nutcracker during the holidays. ⊠ *19 Clarendon St., South End* ☎ *617/695–6950* ⊕ *www.bostonballet.org* Ⓜ *Back Bay.*

THEATER

Boston Center for the Arts. Of Boston's multiple arts organizations, this city-sponsored arts-and-culture complex is the one that is closest to "the people." Here you can see the work of budding playwrights, view exhibits on Haitian folk art, or walk through an installation commemorating World AIDS Day. The BCA houses four theaters, a community music center, the Mills Art Gallery, and studio space for some 40 Boston-based contemporary artists. ⊠ *539 Tremont St., South End* ☎ *617/426–5000* ⊕ *www.bcaonline.org* 🎫 *Free* ⊙ *Weekdays 9–5; Mills Gallery Wed. and Sun. noon–5, Thurs.–Sat. noon–9* Ⓜ *Back Bay/South End.*

CAMBRIDGE

BALLET

José Mateo's Ballet Theatre. José Mateo's Ballet Theatre is a troupe building an exciting, contemporary repertory under Cuban-born José Mateo, the resident artistic director-choreographer. The troupe's performances include an original *Nutcracker* and take place October through April at the **Sanctuary Theatre,** a beautifully converted former church at Massachusetts Avenue and Harvard Street in Harvard Square. ⊠ *400 Harvard St., Cambridge* ☎ *617/354–7467* ⊕ *www.ballettheatre.org* Ⓜ *Harvard.*

FILM

Brattle Theatre. Brattle Theatre shows classic movies, new foreign and independent films, theme series, and directors' cuts. Tickets sell out every year for its acclaimed Bogart festival, scheduled around Harvard's exam period; the Bugs Bunny Film Festival in February; and *Trailer Treats,* an annual fund-raiser featuring an hour or two of classic and modern movie previews in July. At Christmastime, it has screenings of holiday movies such as *It's a Wonderful Life.* ⊠ *40 Brattle St., Harvard Sq., Cambridge* ☎ *617/876–6837* ⊕ *www.brattlefilm.org* Ⓜ *Harvard.*

Harvard Film Archive. Harvard Film Archive screens works from its vast collection of classics and foreign films that are not usually shown at commercial cinemas. Actors and directors frequently appear to introduce newer work. The theater was created for student and faculty use, but the general public may attend regular screenings for $9 per person. ⊠ *Carpenter Center for the Visual Arts, 24 Quincy St., Cambridge* ☎ *617/495–4700* ⊕ *hcl.harvard.edu/hfa* Ⓜ *Harvard.*

THEATER

★ **American Repertory Theater.** American Repertory Theater stages experimental, classic, and contemporary plays, often with unusual lighting, stage design, or multimedia effects. With new director Diane Paulus bringing in immersive theater performances, like *The Donkey Show* and *Sleep No More* (where audience and actors interact), the A.R.T. is selling out shows at its multiple venues. Its home at the Loeb Drama Center has two theaters; the smaller also holds productions by the Harvard-Radcliffe Drama Club. A modern theater space down the street, called Oberone, has a more flexible stage design for electrifying contemporary productions. ⊠ *64 Brattle St., Harvard Sq., Cambridge* ☎ *617/547–8300* ⊕ *www.amrep.org* Ⓜ *Harvard.*

2

WHERE TO EAT

Updated by John Blodgett

In a city synonymous with tradition, Boston chefs have spent recent years rewriting culinary history. The stuffy, wood-paneled formality is gone; the endless renditions of chowdah, lobster, and cod have retired. A crop of young chefs has ascended, opening small, upscale neighborhood spots that use New England ingredients to delicious effect.

Traditional eats can still be found (Durgin-Park remains as the best place to get baked beans), but many diners now gravitate toward innovative food in understated environs. Whether you're looking for casual French, down-home Southern cooking, some of the best sushi in the country, or Vietnamese *banh mi* sandwiches, Boston restaurants are ready to deliver. The fish and shellfish brought in from nearby shores continue to inform the regional cuisine: expect to see several seafood options on local menus, but don't expect them to be boiled or dumped into the lobster stew that JFK loved. Instead, you might be offered swordfish with salsa verde, cornmeal-crusted scallops, or lobster cassoulet with black truffles.

In many ways, though, Boston remains solidly skeptical of trends. If you close your eyes in the North End, Boston's Little Italy, you can easily imagine you're in Rome circa 1955. And over in the university culture of Cambridge, places like East Coast Grill and Oleana espoused the locovore and slow-food movements before they became buzzwords. *Prices in the reviews are the average cost of a main course at dinner or, if dinner is not served, at lunch.*

Use the coordinate (✥ B2) at the end of each listing to locate a site on the Where to Eat and Stay in Boston map.

BACK BAY AND SOUTH END

$$ SEAFOOD Fodor's Choice ★ 🍴 **B&G Oysters.** B&G Oysters' Chef Barbara Lynch (of No. 9 Park, the Butcher Shop, and Sportello fame) has made yet another fabulous mark on Boston with a style-conscious seafood restaurant that updates New England's traditional bounty with flair. Designed to imitate the inside of an oyster shell, the iridescent bar glows with silvery, candlelighted tiles and a sophisticated crowd. They're in for the lobster roll, no doubt—an expensive proposition at $27, but worth every cent for its decadent chunks of meat in a perfectly textured dressing. If you're sans reservation, be prepared to wait: the line for a seat can be epic. [$] *Average main: $20* ✉ *550 Tremont St., South End* ☎ *617/423–0550* 🌐 *www.bandgoysters.com* ✍ *Reservations essential* [M] *Back Bay/South End* ✥ *E6.*

$ AMERICAN 🍴 **The Butcher Shop.** Chef Barbara Lynch has remade the classic meat market as a polished wine bar–cum–hangout, and it's just the kind of high-quality, low-pretense spot every neighborhood could use. Stop in for a glass of wine, chat with any of the friendly but cosmopolitan clientele, and grab a casual, quick snack of homemade prosciutto and salami, daily pasta and sandwich specials, or a plate of artisanal cheeses. Reservations are accepted for parties of six or more. [$] *Average main: $12* ✉ *552 Tremont St., South End* ☎ *617/423–4800* 🌐 *www.thebutchershopboston.com* [M] *Back Bay/South End End* ✥ *E6.*

Candlepin Bowling

CLOSE UP

Back in 1880 Justin White adjusted the size of his pins at his Worcester, Massachussetts, bowling hall, giving birth to candlepin bowling, a highly popular pint-sized version of ten-pin bowling. Now played almost exclusively in northern New England and in the Canadian Maritime Provinces, candlepin bowling is a game of power and accuracy.

Paradoxically, candlepin bowling is both much easier and far more difficult than regular bowling. The balls are significantly smaller, weighing less than 3 pounds. There are no finger holes, and players of all ages and abilities can whip the ball down the alley. But because both the ball and the pins are lighter, it is far more difficult to bowl strikes and spares. Players are allowed three throws per frame, and bowlers may hit fallen pins (called wood) to knock down other pins. There has never been a perfect "300" score. The top score is 245. Good players score around 100 to 110, and novice players should be content with a score of 90.

A handful of alleys are in and around Boston, and many of them maintain their own quirky charm and history.

Needham Bowlaway. One of the area's oldest bowling alleys, this tiny place has eight cramped lanes in a tucked-away facility down a flight of stairs. Fans say Bowlaway is like bowling in your own basement. ⊠ 16 Chestnut St., Needham ☎ 781/444–9614 ⊕ www.needhambowl.com.

Boston Bowl. Open 24 hours a day, Boston Bowl attracts a more adult crowd. It has pool tables, a game room, and both 10-pin and candlestick bowling. ⊠ 820 Morrissey Blvd., Dorchester ☎ 617/825–3800 ⊕ www.bostonbowl.com.

Sacco's Bowl Haven. Sacco's Bowl Haven is proud that its '50s decor "makes bowling the way it was, the way it is." Run by the fourth generation of the Sacco family, the alley was recently renovated to include a Flatbread pizza restaurant. ⊠ 45 Day St., Somerville ☎ 617/776–0552.

$$$$
FRENCH
Fodor's Choice
★

✕ **Clio.** Years ago, when Ken Oringer opened his snazzy leopard skin–lined hot spot in the tasteful boutique Eliot Hotel, the hordes were fighting over reservations. Things have quieted down since then, but the food hasn't. Luxury offerings including foie gras, Maine lobster, and Kobe sirloin share menu space with fail-safe crispy chicken and Scottish salmon. A magnet for romantics and foodies alike, the place continues to serve some of the city's most decadent and well-crafted meals. New: A 2012 face-lift promises to double the size of the bar and make things less formal and more relaxed. $ *Average main: $39* ⊠ *Eliot Hotel, 370 Commonwealth Ave., Back Bay* ☎ 617/536–7200 ⊕ *www.cliorestaurant.com* ⌖ *Reservations essential* ⊙ *No lunch* Ⓜ *Hynes End* ✛ *B5.*

$$
AMERICAN
Fodor's Choice
★

✕ **Eastern Standard Kitchen and Drinks.** A vivid red awning beckons patrons of this spacious brasserie-style restaurant. The bar area and red banquettes are filled most nights with Boston's power players (members of the Red Sox management are known to stop in), thirtysomethings, and students from the nearby universities all noshing on raw-bar specialties

BEST BETS FOR BOSTON DINING

and comfort dishes such as lamb-sausage rigatoni, rib eye, and burgers. It's a Sunday brunch hot spot, especially on game days (the Big Green Monster is a very short walk away). The cocktail list is one of the best in town, filled with old classics and new concoctions, and in addition to a boutique wine list there is a reserve list for rare beers. A covered, heated patio offers alfresco dining year-round. $ *Average main: $22* ✉ *528 Commonwealth Ave., Kenmore Sq., Back Bay* ☎ *617/532–9100* ⊕ *www.easternstandardboston.com* Ⓜ *Kenmore* ✥ *A5.*

$ ✕**Flour Bakery + Café.** When the neighbors need coffee, a sandwich, or
AMERICAN a muffin—or just a place to sit and chat—they come here. A communal
☺ table in the middle acts as a gathering spot, around which diners enjoy classic sandwiches and a few specialties, like the grilled chicken with Brie and arugula, or the BLT with applewood-smoked bacon. Take-out dinner specials range from pecan-encrusted chicken to garlic-herb meat loaf with goat-cheese mashed potatoes. Flour has proved so popular that owner Joanne Chang opened a second location in the up-and-coming Fort Point Channel neighborhood. $ *Average main: $7* ✉ *1595 Washington St., South End* ☎ *617/267–4300* ⊕ *www.flourbakery.com* ⚏ *Reservations not accepted* Ⓜ *Massachusetts Ave.* ✥ *E6.*

$ ✕**Franklin Café.** This place has jumped to the head of the class by keep-
AMERICAN ing things simple yet effective. (The litmus test: local chefs gather here

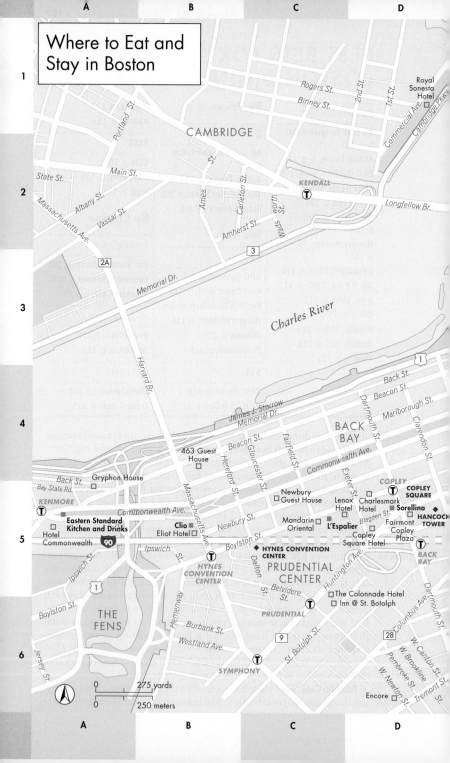

Where to Eat and Stay in Boston

A   **B**   **C**   **D**

1

CAMBRIDGE

Rogers St.
Binney St.
Royal Sonesta Hotel
Commercial Ave.
Cambridge Pkwy.
2nd St.
1st St.

Portland St.

State St.
Main St.
Albany St.
KENDALL
Longfellow Br.
Vassar St.
Ames St.
Carleton St.
Amherst St.
wadsworth St.
2A
3
Memorial Dr.

2

Massachusetts Ave.

3

Harvard Br.

Charles River

1

Back St.
Beacon St.
Dartmouth St.
Marlborough St.
Clarendon St.

BACK BAY

4

James J. Storrow Memorial Dr.

463 Guest House
Beacon St.
Gloucester St.
Hereford St.
Fairfield St.
Commonwealth Ave.
Exeter St.

Back St.
Gryphon House
Bay State Rd.
KENMORE
Commonwealth Ave.
Newbury Guest House
COPLEY
COPLEY SQUARE
Lenox Hotel
Charlesmark Hotel
Sorellina
HANCOCK TOWER

5

Hotel Commonwealth
Eastern Standard Kitchen and Drinks
90
Clio
Eliot Hotel
Massachusetts Ave.
Newbury St.
Mandarin Oriental
Boylston St.
L'Espalier
Blagden St.
Fairmont Copley Plaza
Copley Square Hotel
BACK BAY
Ipswich St.
HYNES CONVENTION CENTER
HYNES CONVENTION CENTER
Dalton St.
PRUDENTIAL CENTER
Huntington Ave.

6

Ipswich St.
1
Boylston St.
THE FENS
Hemenway St.
Burbank St.
Westland Ave.
Belvidere St.
PRUDENTIAL
The Colonnade Hotel
Inn @ St. Botolph
Columbus Ave.
28
W. Canton St.
W. Brookline St.
Pembroke St.
W. Newton St.
Tremont St.
Jersey St.
SYMPHONY
9
St. Botolph St.
Encore
Dartmouth St.

0   275 yards
0   250 meters

A   **B**   **C**   **D**

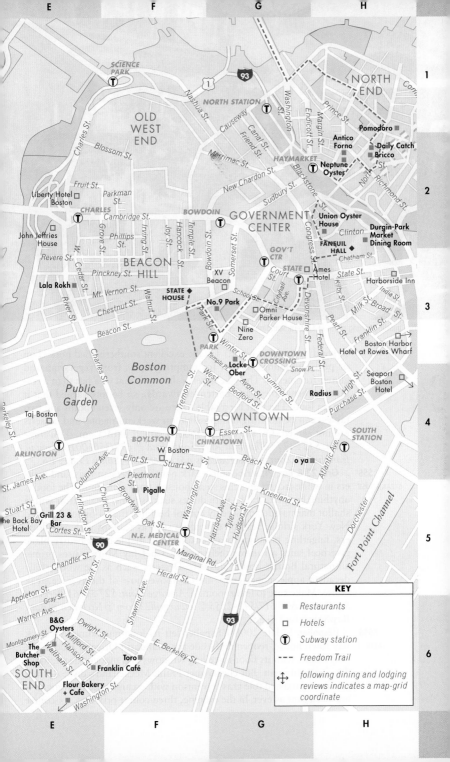

The bustling dining room at Eastern Standard Kitchen and Drinks.

to wind down after work.) Try the excellent southern-fried pork chop or pork dumplings, or opt for tempting items from vegetarian and gluten-free menus. The vibe is generally more that of a bar than a restaurant (hence the many bartender awards), so be forewarned that it can get loud. The wait for a table (there are only seven booths and two tables) can be downright impossible on weekend nights, and desserts are not served. On the upside, food is served until 1 am. [$] *Average main: $12* ✉ *278 Shawmut Ave., South End* ☎ *617/350–0010* 🌐 *www.franklincafe.com* ✍ *Reservations not accepted* [M] *South End* ✥ *E6.*

$$$ STEAKHOUSE

🍴 **Grill 23 & Bar.** Pinstripe suits, dark paneling, Persian rugs, and waiters in white jackets give this steak house a posh demeanor. The food is anything but predictable, with dishes such as prime steak tartar with a shallot marmalade and weekly cuts of beef like the 14-ounce dry-aged New York sirloin. Seafood specialties such as scallops with cauliflowers, fingerling potatoes, pearl onions, and maple-curry beurre blanc give beef sales a run for their money. Chef Jay Murray uses prime, all-natural Brandt beef exclusively. Desserts, such as the wonderfully decadent apple-quince crisp, are far above those of the average steak house. Make sure to leave room. [$] *Average main: $27* ✉ *161 Berkeley St., Back Bay* ☎ *617/542–2255* 🌐 *www.grill23.com* 🕓 *No lunch* [M] *Back Bay/South End* ✥ *E5.*

$$$$ FRENCH Fodor's Choice ★

🍴 **L'Espalier.** In late 2008 L'Espalier left its longtime home in a Back Bay town house, reopening beside the Mandarin Oriental Hotel. The new locale, with its floor-to-ceiling windows and modern decor, looks decidedly different. But chef-owner Frank McClelland's dishes—from caviar and roasted foie gras to venison with escargots de Bourgogne—are as elegant as ever. In the evening, three-course prix-fixe, six-course

2

seasonal degustation, and ten-course chef's journey menus tempt discriminating diners. A budget-minded power lunch as well as à la carte options are available weekday afternoons. Finger sandwiches and sublime sweets are served for weekend tea. $ *Average main: $85* ✉ *774 Boylston St., Back Bay* ☎ *617/262–3023* ⊕ *www.lespalier.com* ⚄ *Reservations essential* Ⓜ *Copley* ✛ *C5.*

$$ ✕ **Sonsie.** Café society blossoms along Newbury Street, particularly at
AMERICAN   Sonsie, where a well-heeled crowd sips coffee up front or angles for places at the bar. Lunch and dinner dishes, such as charcoal duck breast and leg with brown rice and five-spice turnips, are basic bistro fare with an American twist. The restaurant is a terrific place for weekend brunch, when the light pours through the long windows, and is at its most vibrant in warm weather, when the open doors make for colorful people-watching. A downstairs wine room meanwhile offers more intimacy. The late-night menu (nightly until 12:30 am) is perfect for those after-hours cravings. $ *Average main: $22* ✉ *327 Newbury St., Back Bay* ☎ *617/351–2500* ⊕ *www.sonsieboston.com* Ⓜ *Hynes.*

$$$ ✕ **Sorellina.** Everything about this upscale Italian spot is oversized, from
ITALIAN   its space near Copley Square to its portions. The sexy, all-white dining room is filled with well-heeled locals (some live in the gorgeous apartment building above it) who come for the modern twist on basic Italian dishes. Crudo, various versions of carpaccio, and the signature tuna tartare dot the list of starters, while veal saltimbocca with Maitake mushrooms and truffled whipped potato takes the spotlight. Just save room for dessert: it's always a highlight here. $ *Average main: $35* ✉ *1 Huntington Ave., Back Bay* ☎ *617/412–4600* ⊕ *www.sorellinaboston. com* ☽ *No lunch* Ⓜ *Copley, Back Bay* ✛ *D5.*

$ ✕ **Toro.** The buzz from chefs Ken Oringer and Jamie Bissonnette's tapas
SPANISH   joint still hasn't quieted down—for good reason. Small plates such as
Fodor's Choice   grilled corn with alioli and cotija cheese are hefty enough to make
★   a meal out of many, or share the regular or vegetarian paella with a group. An all-Spanish wine list complements the plates. Crowds have been known to wait it out for more than an hour. $ *Average main: $12* ✉ *1704 Washington St., South End* ☎ *617/536–4300* ⊕ *www. toro-restaurant.com* ⚄ *Reservations not accepted* Ⓜ *Massachusetts Ave.* ✛ *F6.*

BEACON HILL

$ ✕ **Lala Rokh.** Persian miniatures and medieval maps cover the walls
MIDDLE EASTERN   of this beautifully detailed fantasy of food and art. The focus is on the Azerbaijanian corner of what is now northwest Iran, including exotically flavored specialties and dishes such as familiar (and superb) eggplant puree, pilaf, kebabs, *fesanjoon* (the classic pomegranate-walnut sauce), and lamb stews. The staff obviously enjoys explaining the menu, and the wine list is well selected for foods that often defy wine matches. $ *Average main: $17* ✉ *97 Mt. Vernon St., Beacon Hill* ☎ *617/720–5511* ⊕ *www.lalarokh.com* ☽ *No lunch weekends* Ⓜ *Charles/MGH* ✛ *E3.*

A smoked salmon amuse bouche served at L'Espalier.

$$$$ EUROPEAN Fodor's Choice ★ 🍴 **No. 9 Park.** The stellar cuisine at Chef Barbara Lynch's first restaurant continues to draw plenty of well-deserved attention from its place in the shadow of the State House's golden dome. Settle into the plush but unpretentious dining room and indulge in pumpkin risotto with rare lamb or the memorably rich prune-stuffed gnocchi drizzled with bits of foie gras, the latter of which is always offered even if you don't see it on the menu. The wine list bobs and weaves into new territory, but is always well chosen, and the savvy bartenders are of the classic ilk, so you'll find plenty of classics and very few cloying, dessertlike sips here. [$] *Average main: $39* ✉ *9 Park St., Beacon Hill* ☎ *617/742–9991* 🌐 *www.no9park.com* [M] *Park St.* ✥ *G3.*

DOWNTOWN

$$$$ EUROPEAN 🍴 **Locke-Ober.** Chef Paul Licaris is relatviely new, but the kitchen here continues to turn out classics with flair. Traditionalists needn't worry; many favorites remain on the menu, including the restaurant's signature JFK lobster stew, broiled Dover sole, and Lobster Savannah. There is valet parking after 6 pm. [$] *Average main: $38* ✉ *3 Winter Pl., Downtown* ☎ *617/542–1340* 🌐 *www.lockeober.com* ✍ *Reservations essential* ⏲ *Closed Sun. No lunch* [M] *Downtown Crossing* ✥ *G3.*

$$$$ JAPANESE Fodor's Choice ★ 🍴 **o ya.** Despite its side-street location and hidden door, o ya isn't exactly a secret: dining critics from the *New York Times*, *Bon Appetit*, and *Food & Wine* have all named this tiny, improvisational sushi spot among the best in the country. Chef Tim Cushman's nigiri menu features squid-ink bubbles, homemade potato chips—even foie gras. Other dishes offer a nod to New England, such as the braised pork with Boston baked beans

CLOSE UP

Refueling

If you're on the go, you might want to try a local chain restaurant where you can stop for a quick bite or get some takeout. The places listed below are fairly priced, committed to quality, and use decent, fresh ingredients.

B.Good. This chainlet's avocado- and salsa-topped veggie burgers, baked sweet-potato fries, and sesame-ginger chicken salad are redefining fast food in Boston.

Bertucci's. Thin-crust pizzas fly fast from the brick ovens here, along with pastas and a decent tiramisu.

BoLoCo. For quick, cheap, healthful, and high-quality wraps and burritos, this is easily the city's most

dependable (and also locally based) chain. BoLoCo's menu also includes smoothies and breakfast options, and its hours are some of the longest in this notoriously early-to-bed city.

Finagle A Bagel. Find fresh, doughy bagels in flavors from jalapeño cheddar to triple chocolate, plus sandwiches and salads. Service is swift and efficient.

UBurger. Better-than-average burgers with toppings that lean toward the gourmet (sautéed mushrooms, blue cheese) and a great chocolate frappe (Boston-ese for milkshake) make this spot the East Coast's answer to California's much-loved In-n-Out.

and grilled lobster with a light shiso tempura. Cushman's wife Nancy oversees an extensive sake list that includes sparkling and aged varieties. $ *Average main: $36* ⊠ *9 East St., Leather District* ☎ *617/654–9900* ⊕ *www.oyarestaurantboston.com* ⊗ *Closed Sun. and Mon. No lunch* Ⓜ *South Station* ✦ *G4.*

$$$　✕ **Pigalle.** A quaint, 20-table spot, Pigalle is a romantic destination
FRENCH　to hit before taking in a show in the neighboring Theater District.
Fodor's Choice　Chef Marc Orfaly spices up basic French fare by throwing in the occa-
★　sional Asian-inspired special. He plays around with global flavors, so don't be alarmed to find spicy tempura tuna roll or grilled squid with paella stuffing on the menu next to the steak frites and cassoulet. For a delicious, cozy meal, this spot consistently has some of the best service in town. In late 2011, the bar and its menu were both extended, offering more casual fare such as burgers. $ *Average main: $32* ⊠ *75 Charles St. S, Theater District, Downtown* ☎ *617/423–4944* ⊕ *www. pigalleboston.com* ⚏ *Reservations essential* ⊗ *Closed Mon. No lunch* Ⓜ *Boylston* ✦ *F5.*

$$$　✕ **Radius.** Acclaimed chef Michael Schlow's notable contemporary
FRENCH　French cooking lures scores of designer- and suit-clad diners to the
Fodor's Choice　Financial District. The decor and menu are minimalist at first glance,
★　but closer inspection reveals equal shares of luxury, complexity, and whimsy. Peruse the menu in the dining room for choices such as ginger-poached duck, a selection of seviches, buttery Scottish salmon, or huckleberry-and-goat-cheese cheesecake for dessert. At the bar they serve a phenomenal (and award-winning) burger. Either way, it's a meal made for special occasions and business dinners alike. $ *Average main: $30* ⊠ *8 High St., Downtown* ☎ *617/426–1234* ⊕ *www.*

radiusrestaurant.com ⚖ *Reservations essential* ⊘ *Closed Sun. No lunch Sat.* Ⓜ *South Station* ✛ *H4.*

GOVERNMENT CENTER/FANEUIL HALL

$$
AMERICAN

✕ **Durgin-Park Market Dining Room.** You should be hungry enough to cope with enormous portions, yet not so hungry you can't tolerate a long wait (or sharing a table with others). Durgin-Park was serving its same hearty New England fare (Indian pudding, baked beans, corned beef and cabbage, and a prime rib that hangs over the edge of the plate) back when Faneuil Hall was a working market instead of a tourist attraction. The service is as brusque as it was when fishmongers and boat captains dined here, but that's just part of its charm. Ⓢ *Average main: $18* ✉ *340 Faneuil Hall Market Pl., North Market Bldg.* ☎ *617/227-2038* ⊕ *www. arkrestaurants.com/durgin_park.html* Ⓜ *Government Center* ✛ *H2.*

$$$
SEAFOOD

✕ **Union Oyster House.** Established in 1826, this is Boston's oldest continuing restaurant, and almost every tourist considers it a must-see. If you like, you can have what Daniel Webster had—oysters on the half shell at the ground-floor raw bar, which is the oldest part of the restaurant and still the best. The rooms at the top of the narrow staircase are dark and have low ceilings—very Ye Olde New England—and plenty of nonrestaurant history. The small tables and chairs (as well as the endless lines and kitschy nostalgia) are as much a part of the charm as the simple and decent (albeit pricey) food. On weekends, especially in summer, make reservations a few days ahead or risk enduring waits of historic proportions. There is valet parking after 5:30 pm Monday through Saturday. One cautionary note: Locals hardly ever eat here. Ⓢ *Average main: $25* ✉ *41 Union St., Government Center* ☎ *617/227-2750* ⊕ *www.unionoysterhouse.com* Ⓜ *Haymarket* ✛ *H2.*

NORTH END

$
ITALIAN
Fodor's Choice
★

✕ **Antico Forno.** Many of the menu choices here come from the eponymous wood-burning brick oven, which turns out surprisingly delicate pizzas simply topped with tomato and fresh buffalo mozzarella. But though its pizzas receive top billing, Antico excels at a variety of Italian country dishes. Don't overlook the hearty baked dishes and handmade pastas; the specialty, gnocchi, is rich and creamy but light. The joint is cramped and noisy, but also homey and comfortable—which means that your meal will resemble a raucous dinner with an adopted Italian family. Ⓢ *Average main: $17* ✉ *93 Salem St., North End* ☎ *617/723-6733* ⊕ *www.anticofornoboston.com* Ⓜ *Haymarket* ✛ *H2.*

$$$$
ITALIAN

✕ **Bricco.** A sophisticated but unpretentious enclave of nouveau Italian, Bricco has carved out quite a following. And no wonder: the handmade pastas alone are argument for a reservation. Simple but well-balanced main courses such as roast chicken marinated in seven spices and a brimming *brodetto* (fish stew) with half a lobster and a pile of seafood may linger in your memory. You're likely to want to linger in the warm room, too, gazing through the floor-to-ceiling windows while sipping a glass of Sangiovese from the Italian and American wine list. Ⓢ *Average* *main: $37* ✉ *241 Hanover St., North End* ☎ *617/248–6800* ⊕ *www. bricco.com* ⌕ *Reservations essential* ⊗ *No lunch* Ⓜ *Haymarket* ✛ *H2.*

$ ✕ **Daily Catch.** You've just got to love this place—for the noise, the
SEAFOOD intimacy, the complete absence of pretense, and, above all, the food. Shoulder-crowdingly small and always brightly lighted, the storefront restaurant, a local staple for more than 30 years, specializes in calamari dishes, black-squid-ink pastas, and linguine with clam sauce. There's something about a big skillet of linguine and calamari that would seem less perfect if served on fine white china. 💲*Average main: $15* ✉ *323 Hanover St., North End* ☎ *617/523–8567* ⊕ *www.dailycatch.com* ⌕ *Reservations not accepted* ▭ *No credit cards* Ⓜ *Haymarket* ✛ *H2.*

$$ ✕ **Neptune Oyster.** This tiny oyster bar, the first of its kind in the neigh-
SEAFOOD borhood, has only 20 chairs, but the long marble bar has extra seating for about 20 more patrons, and mirrors hang over the bar with hand-written menus. From there, watch the oyster shuckers as they deftly undo handfuls of bivalves. The *plateau di frutti di mare* is a gleaming tower of oysters and other raw-bar items piled over ice that you can order from the slip of paper they pass out listing each day's crusta-cean options. Dishes change seasonally, but a couple of favorites to count on year round include the signature North End Cioppino (fish stew) and the lobster roll that, hot or cold, overflows with meat. Ser-vice is prompt even when it gets busy (as it is most of the time). Go early to avoid a long wait. 💲*Average main: $20* ✉ *63 Salem St., North End* ☎ *617/742–3474* ⊕ *www.neptuneoyster.com* ⌕ *Reservations not accepted* Ⓜ *Haymarket* ✛ *H2.*

$$ ✕ **Pomodoro.** This teeny trattoria—just eight tables—is worth the wait,
ITALIAN with excellent country Italian favorites such as rigatoni with white beans and arugula, a veal scaloppini with sweet onion balsamic glaze, and a light-but-filling zuppa di pesce. The best choice could well be the classic linguini, accompanied by a bottle of Vernaccia. Pomodoro doesn't serve dessert, but it's easy to find great espresso and pastries in the cafés on Hanover Street. 💲*Average main: $24* ✉ *319 Hanover St., North End* ☎ *617/367–4348* ⌕ *Reservations essential* ▭ *No credit cards* ⊗ *No lunch weekdays* Ⓜ *Haymarket* ✛ *H1.*

CAMBRIDGE

Use the coordinate (✛ B2) at the end of each listing to locate a site on the Where to Eat and Stay in Cambridge map.

$ ✕ **All Star Sandwich Bar.** This place has a strict definition of what makes
AMERICAN a sandwich: no wraps. It has put together a list of classics, like crispy,
Fodor's Choice overstuffed Reubens and beef on weck, which are served quickly from
★ an open kitchen. Its famous Atomic Meatloaf Meltdown has been high-lighted on a number of foodie and other television networks. Burgers have joined the hot dog as the only nonsandwich options on the board. With bright colors and the personality of a beloved sandwich joint, the place has about a dozen tables that fill up at lunchtime. At dinner, choose from a small selection of beer and wine. 💲*Average main: $6* ✉ *1245 Cambridge St.* ☎ *617/868–3065* ⊕ *www.allstarsandwichbar. com* ⌕ *Reservations not accepted* Ⓜ *Central/Inman* ✛ *A4.*

$$$
ECLECTIC
Fodor'sChoice
★

✕**Chez Henri.** French with a Latin twist—odd bedfellows, but it works for this restaurant. The dinner menu gets serious, with pan-seared sea scallops glazed in a grapefruit barbecue sauce and sinfully sweet desserts like ginger-spiced shortcake. At the cozy bar you can sample conch fritters, grilled homemade chorizo, and a pressed Cuban sandwich. The place fills quickly with Cantabrigian locals—an interesting mix of students, professors, and sundry intelligentsia. The closest T stop (Harvard Square) is about a mile away. $ *Average main: $28* ⊠ *1 Shepard St.* ☎ *617/354–8980* ⊕ *www.chezhenri.com* ⊘ *No lunch* Ⓜ *Harvard* ✛ *A1.*

$$
AMERICAN

✕**East Coast Grill and Raw Bar.** Owner-chef-author Chris Schlesinger built his national reputation on grilled foods and red-hot condiments. The Texas-style beef brisket and North Carolina shredded pork are still here, but this restaurant has made an extraordinary play to establish itself in the front ranks of fish restaurants. Spices and condiments are more restrained, and Schlesinger has compiled a wine list bold and flavorful enough to match the highly spiced food. The dining space is completely informal. A killer brunch (complete with cornbread-crusted French toast and a do-it-yourself Bloody Mary bar) is served on Sunday. Patrons can park in the lot across the street for $5. $ *Average main: $24* ⊠ *1271 Cambridge St.* ☎ *617/491–6568* ⊕ *www.eastcoastgrill.net* ⊘ *No lunch* Ⓜ *Central* ✛ *A4.*

$$
AMERICAN
Ⓒ

✕**Full Moon.** Here's a happy reminder that dinner with children doesn't have to mean hamburgers. Choices include child pleasers like homemade mac and cheese as well as grown-up entrées that include roasted salmon fillet with tomato-raisin salsa. Youngsters can spread out with plenty of designated play space and juice-filled sippy cups, while parents weigh the substantial menu and a well-paired wine list. Folks visiting sans child may want to ask for one of the grown-ups' tables in the quiet, screened-off area near the front, but they also might want to consider another restaurant altogether: diners have compared the place to a day-care center or romper room. $ *Average main: $18* ⊠ *344 Huron Ave.* ☎ *617/354–6699* ⊕ *www.fullmoonrestaurant.com* ⚱ *Reservations not accepted* Ⓜ *Harvard* ✛ *B1.*

$$
SOUTHERN
Fodor'sChoice
★

✕**Hungry Mother.** You'll forget you're well above the Mason-Dixon line when you enter this Kendall Square gem, where Virginia-born chef Barry Maiden whips up Southern-inspired comfort food with a hint of French sophistication—and New England ingredients. From fried green tomatoes to cornbread with sorghum butter, from Berkshire pork loin to apple bread pudding, this cozy two-story bistro serves up decidedly soul-warming fare. (And if you need an extra shot of warmth, the expert bartenders create excellent house-mixed drinks, such as the Stirred, a rye-cynar-zirebenz-claret syrup-grapefruit bitters concoction.) $ *Average main: $20* ⊠ *233 Cardinal Medeiros Ave., Kendall Square* ☎ *617/499–0090* ⊘ *Closed Mon. No lunch* Ⓜ *Kendall/MIT* ✛ *B6.*

$$
MEDITERRANEAN
Fodor'sChoice
★

✕**Oleana.** Chef-owner Ana Sortun is one of the city's culinary treasures—and so is Oleana. Here flavors from all over the Eastern Mediterranean sing loud and clear, in the hot, crispy fried mussels starter and in the smoky eggplant puree beside tamarind-glazed beef. Lamb gets jacked up with Turkish spices, while the rabbit is accented by Moroccan-spiced almonds. In warm weather the back patio is a hidden

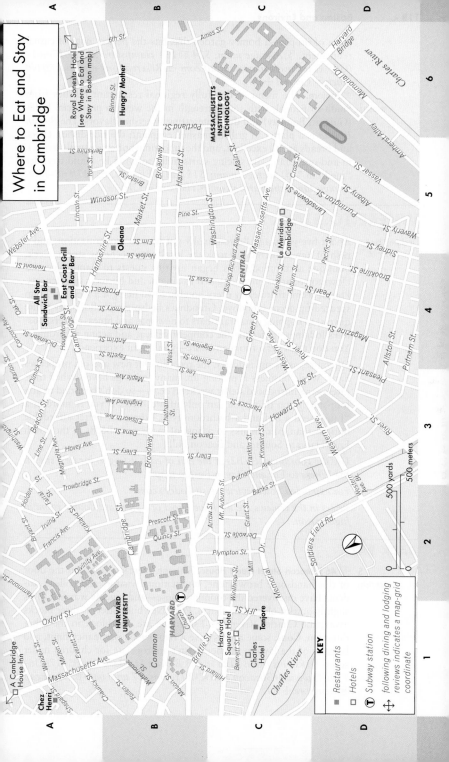

Where to Eat and Stay in Cambridge

Royal Sonesta Hotel
(see Where to Eat and
Stay in Boston map)

■ Hungry Mother

MASSACHUSETTS
INSTITUTE OF
TECHNOLOGY

Oleana ■

All Star
Sandwich Bar ■

East Coast Grill
and Raw Bar ■

□ Le Meridien
Cambridge

Ⓣ CENTRAL

□ A Cambridge
House Inn

Chez
Henri ■

HARVARD
UNIVERSITY

Ⓣ HARVARD

Harvard
Square Hotel □

□ Bennett St.

Charles
Hotel □

Tanjore ■

Common

Charles River

KEY

■ Restaurants

□ Hotels

Ⓣ Subway station

↕ following dining and lodging
reviews indicates a map-grid
coordinate

0   500 yards

0   500 meters

piece of utopia—a homey garden that hits the perfect note of casual refinement. [$] *Average main: $24* ✉ *134 Hampshire St.* ☎ *617/661–0505* 🌐 *www.oleanarestaurant.com* ✍ *Reservations essential* 🕒 *No lunch* [M] *Central* ✥ *B5.*

$ INDIAN ✕ **Tanjore.** The menu at this fully regional restaurant reaches from Sindh to Bengal, with some strength in the western provincial foods (Gujarat, Bombay) and their interesting sweet-hot flavors. The *Baigan Bhurta* is a platter of grilled, mashed eggplant; the rice dishes, chais, and breads are all excellent, and the lunchtime buffet is usually a quick in-and-out affair. The spicing starts mild, so don't be afraid to order "medium." [$] *Average main: $15* ✉ *18 Eliot St.* ☎ *617/868–1900* 🌐 *www.tanjoreharvardsq.com* [M] *Harvard* ✥ *C1.*

WHERE TO STAY

Updated by John Blodgett

About five years ago Boston finally got wise to modernization, and a rush of new construction took the local hotel scene by storm. Sleek, boutique accommodations began inviting guests to Cambridge and Downtown, areas once relegated to alumni and business traveler sets. Plus, it seems that nearly every hotel in town just got a face-lift. From spruced-up decor (goodbye, Grandma's bedspread; hello, puffy white duvets) to hopping restaurant-bars to new spas and fitness centers, Boston's lodgings are feeling the competitive heat and acting accordingly. You don't just get a room anymore—you get an experience.

Of course, as in any industry, the recession hit new and old properties hard. While business is picking up, many lodgings have slashed their rates—and introduced stellar weekend deals—so don't be afraid to aim four-star if you think you can only afford three. If you're more of a "I just need a bed and a bathroom type," there are better affordable options than ever, thanks to a host of made-over B&Bs in the South End, Harvard Square, and Beacon Hill.

Use the coordinate (✥ B2) at the end of each listing to locate a site on the Where to Eat and Stay in Boston map.

For expanded hotel reviews, visit Fodors.com.

Prices in the reviews are the lowest cost of a standard double room in high season.

BACK BAY

$ B&B/INN 🏨 **463 Beacon Street Guest House.** Though there's no sign on the door of this handsome brownstone, international visitors and college students have discovered the rooming house—and quickly warmed to its slightly quirky, old-auntie charm. **Pros:** Newbury Street is three blocks away; the Charles River and Esplanade are one block in the other direction. **Cons:** some rooms have a two-person occupancy limit, and because of the layout, the house isn't appropriate for children under seven. [$] *Rooms from: $125* ✉ *463 Beacon St., Back Bay* ☎ *617/536–1302* 🌐 *www.463beacon.com* 🛏 *20 rooms, 17 with bath* 🍴 *No meals* [M] *Kenmore* ✥ *B4.*

	NEIGHBORHOOD VIBE	PROS	CONS
Beacon Hill and Boston Common	Old brick and stone buildings host luxe boutique hotels and B&Bs on the hill or along busy, preppy Charles Street; some skyscraper lodging right on Boston Common.	Safe, quaint area with lamp-lit streets; chain-free upscale shopping and dining; outdoor fun abounds in the park; good T access.	Street parking is extremely hard to come by; not budget friendly; very close to noisy hospital; hills can be very steep.
Downtown	The city's financial center hums with activity and busy hotels during the week; new boutique lodging is moving in to compete with the big-box chains.	Excellent area for business travelers; frequent low weekend rates; good T and bus access; walking distance to Theater District and some museums.	All but dead at night; expensive garage parking during the day; Downtown Crossing is mobbed at lunchtime and on weekends; poorly marked streets.
The Back Bay	High-priced hotels in the city's poshest neighborhood, home to excellent shops, restaurants, bars, spas, and salons. Commonwealth Avenue is lined with historic mansions.	Easy, central location; safe, beautiful area to walk around at night; ample T access; excellent people-watching.	Rooms, shopping, and eating can be ridiculously expensive; Newbury Street is overcrowded with tourists on weekends.
The South End	Small, funky lodgings in a very hip and happening (and gay-friendly) area packed with awesome independent restaurants and shops.	The city's best dining scene; easy T and bus access; myriad parks; walking distance from the Back Bay and Downtown; safe along the main avenues at night.	Some bordering blocks turn seedy after dusk; difficult street parking (and few garages); only a handful of hotel options.
The Fenway and Kenmore Square	A sampling of large and small hotels and inns, plus two hostels; the area is a mix of students, young professionals, and die-hard Sox fans.	Close to Fenway Park (home of the Red Sox); up-and-coming dining scene; less expensive than most 'hoods; very accessible by T.	Impossible street parking on game days (and pricey garages); expect big crowds for concert and sporting events; some bars are loud and tacky.
Boston Outskirts	Mostly midsize chain hotels in student neighborhoods full of coffee shops, convenience stores, and rowdy college bars.	Serviceable airport lodging near Logan; cheap rates on rooms in Brighton, Allston, and parts of Brookline; easier driving than Downtown.	No overnight street parking in Brookline; far from Boston center and museums, shopping, and the river; some areas get dicey at night; T rides into the city proper can take an hour.
Cambridge	A mix of grand and small hotels pepper the hip, multi-university neighborhood; expect loads of young freethinkers and efficient (if laid-back) service.	Hallowed academia; verdant squares; good low- and high-cost eating and lodging; excellent neighborhood restaurants; very few chain anythings.	Spotty T access; less of a city feel; a few areas can be very quiet and slightly dodgy at night; lots of one-way streets make driving difficult.

BEST BETS FOR BOSTON LODGING

Fodor's Choice ★

Boston Harbor Hotel at Rowes Wharf, $$$$, p. 122

Charles Hotel, $$$, p. 125

Charlesmark Hotel, $$, p. 120

Eliot Hotel, $$$$, p. 121

Gryphon House, $$$, p. 124

Hotel Commonwealth, $$, p. 124

Inn@St. Botolph, $$$, p. 121

Liberty Hotel Boston, $$$$, p. 122

Nine Zero, $$$, p. 122

By Price

$

463 Beacon Street Guest House, p. 118

John Jeffries House, p. 121

$$

Charlesmark Hotel, p. 120

Encore, p. 124

Hotel Commonwealth, p. 124

$$$

Charles Hotel, p. 125

Colonnade Hotel, p. 120

Fairmont Copley Plaza, p. 121

Gryphon House, p. 124

Inn@St. Botolph, p. 121

Nine Zero, p. 122

Seaport Boston Hotel, p. 124

$$$$

Boston Harbor Hotel at Rowes Wharf, p. 122

Copley Square Hotel, p. 120

Eliot Hotel, p. 121

Le Meridien Cambridge, p. 125

Liberty Hotel Boston, p. 122

Mandarin Oriental Boston, p. 121

XV Beacon, p. 122

By Experience

BEST LOCATION

Charles Hotel, p. 125

Nine Zero, p. 122

$$ **Charlesmark Hotel.** Hipsters and romantics who'd rather spend their
HOTEL cash on a great meal than a hotel bill have put this late 19th-century
Fodor's Choice former residential row house on the map. **Pros:** fantastic price for
★ the location; free Wi-Fi. **Cons:** some might feel crowded by compact
rooms and hallways. $ *Rooms from: $239 ⊠ 655 Boylston St., Back
Bay* ☎ 617/247–1212 ⊕ *www.thecharlesmarkhotel.com* ⟿ *40 rooms*
⊚ Breakfast Ⓜ *Copley* ⊹ *D5.*

$$$ **Colonnade Hotel.** The Colonnade's $25-million makeover—a spruced-
HOTEL up facade, new windows, updated room decor—was a hit. **Pros:** roof-
☾ deck pool; across from Prudential Center shopping; good Red Sox
packages. **Cons:** Huntington Avenue can get clogged with rush-hour
traffic; on summer days the pool is packed by 11 am. $ *Rooms from:
$399* ⊠ *120 Huntington Ave., Back Bay* ☎ 617/424–7000, 800/962–
3030 ⊕ *www.colonnadehotel.com* ⟿ *276 rooms, 9 suites* ⊚ *No meals*
Ⓜ *Prudential Center* ⊹ *C6.*

$$$$ **Copley Square Hotel.** Thanks to an $18-million renovation, the Copley
HOTEL Square Hotel has hurtled into the present with high-tech registration
pods, cushy mattresses, and in-room iPod docks. **Pros:** free Wi-Fi; free
nightly wine tastings; cool bar and club scene. **Cons:** small rooms; those
facing Huntington Avenue can be noisy; not ideal for older couples seeking peace and quiet. $ *Rooms from: $499* ⊠ *47 Huntington Ave., Back*

Bay 🕾 *617/536–9000* ⊕ *www.copleysquarehotel.com* ⤴ *143 rooms* ⦿*No meals* Ⓜ *Copley* ✛ *D5.*

$$$$
HOTEL
Fodor's Choice
★

🏨 **Eliot Hotel.** Have you ever imagined that you live on posh Commonwealth Avenue, modeled after Paris's epic Champs Élysées? **Pros:** super location; top-notch restaurants; pet-friendly; beautiful rooms. **Cons:** very expensive; some complain of elevator noise. 💲*Rooms from: $485* ✉ *370 Commonwealth Ave., Back Bay* 🕾 *617/267–1607, 800/443–5468* ⊕ *www.eliothotel.com* ⤴ *16 rooms, 79 suites* ⦿*No meals* Ⓜ *Hynes* ✛ *B5.*

$$$
HOTEL
☾

🏨 **Fairmont Copley Plaza.** Past guests, including one Judy Garland, felt at home in the decadent, unabashedly romantic hotel, which underwent a $20-million renovation in early 2012. **Pros:** very elegant. **Cons:** tiny bathrooms with scratchy towels; charge for Internet access (no charge on Fairmont Gold level). 💲*Rooms from: $369* ✉ *138 St. James Ave., Back Bay* 🕾 *617/267–5300, 866/540–4417* ⊕ *www.fairmont. com/copleyplaza* ⤴ *366 rooms, 17 suites* ⦿*No meals* Ⓜ *Copley, Back Bay/South End* ✛ *D5.*

$$$
B&B/INN
Fodor's Choice
★
☾

🏨 **Inn@St. Botolph.** Like its sister property, XV Beacon, the 16-room inn packs plenty of style. **Pros:** affordable style; great location; posh yet homey; free satellite TV and Wi-Fi; "preferred" pricing at and free transit to top area restaurants. **Cons:** DIY parking; for those who need hand-holding, there's no front desk. 💲*Rooms from: $349* ✉ *99 St. Botolph St., Back Bay* 🕾 *617/236–8099* ⊕ *www.innatstbotolph.com* ⤴ *16 rooms* ⦿*Breakfast* Ⓜ *Prudential* ✛ *C6.*

$$$$
HOTEL
☾

🏨 **Mandarin Oriental Boston.** Since opening in 2008, the 148-room hotel has helped redefine luxury in town (pay attention, Ritz and Four Seasons), and offers services many guests are calling "out of this world." **Pros:** amazing service; very quiet; good-size rooms; too many amenities to list. **Cons:** small fitness center; exorbitantly expensive; average views. 💲*Rooms from: $600* ✉ *776 Boylston St., Back Bay* 🕾 *617/535–8888* ⊕ *www.mandarinoriental.com/boston* ⤴ *136 rooms, 12 suites* ⦿*No meals* Ⓜ *Prudential, Copley* ✛ *C4.*

$$$
HOTEL
☾

🏨 **Taj Boston Hotel.** Old-school elegance reigns at the Taj, formerly the landmark Ritz-Carlton Boston. **Pros:** white-glove service; great views; proximity to shopping, dining, and the park. **Cons:** occasionally snobby staff; frequently barren restaurant. 💲*Rooms from: $399* ✉ *15 Arlington St., Back Bay* 🕾 *617/536–5700* ⊕ *www.tajhotels.com* ⤴ *273 rooms, 45 suites* ⦿*No meals* Ⓜ *Arlington* ✛ *E4.*

BEACON HILL

$
B&B/INN

🏨 **John Jeffries House.** Right next to the Charles/MGH stop, the John Jeffries isn't only easily accessible, it's affordable—a veritable home run in this city. **Pros:** great Beacon Hill location; free Wi-Fi; good value. **Cons:** the busy (and noisy) hospital across the street; no spa or gym facilities. 💲*Rooms from: $149* ✉ *14 David G. Mugar Way, Beacon Hill* 🕾 *617/367–1866* ⊕ *www.johnjeffrieshouse.com* ⤴ *23 rooms, 23 suites* ⦿*Breakfast* Ⓜ *Charles/MGH* ✛ *E2.*

$$$$ HOTEL Fodor's Choice ★ **Liberty Hotel Boston.** When it opened in late 2007, the buzz around the Liberty was deafening. **Pros:** Scampo's mouthwatering house-made mozzarella bar; bustling nightlife; proximity to the river and Beacon Hill. **Cons:** loud in-house nightlife; long waits at bars and restaurants. [$] *Rooms from: $699* ✉ *215 Charles St., Beacon Hill* ☎ *617/224–4000* 🌐 *www.libertyhotel.com* 🛏 *288 rooms, 10 suites* 🍴 *No meals* [M] *Charles/MGH* ⊕ *E2.*

$$$$ **XV Beacon.** The 1903 Beaux-Arts exterior of one of the city's first small luxury hotels is a study in understated class and elegance. **Pros:** in-room massages; chef Jamie Mammano's steak house, Mooo; for a fee, pets get their own pampering and sitting programs. **Cons:** some rooms are very small; mattresses are just average; can be expensive on weekends during peak months (May, June, September, October). [$] *Rooms from: $575* ✉ *15 Beacon St., Beacon Hill* ☎ *617/670–1500, 877/982–3226* 🌐 *www.xvbeacon.com* 🛏 *63 rooms* 🍴 *No meals* [M] *Government Center, Park St.* ⊕ *G3.*

DOWNTOWN

$$$ HOTEL **Ames Hotel.** One of the newest players on the Boston scene, the Ames opened to quiet fanfare in November 2009. **Pros:** very cool design; cushy beds; limo service. **Cons:** far from South End and Back Bay shopping. [$] *Rooms from: $350* ✉ *1 Court St., Downtown* ☎ *617/979–8100, 800/697–1791* 🌐 *www.ameshotel.com* 🛏 *114 rooms* 🍴 *No meals* [M] *State St.* ⊕ *H3.*

$$$$ HOTEL Fodor's Choice ★ **Boston Harbor Hotel at Rowes Wharf.** Boston has plenty of iconic landmarks—the "salt and pepper" bridge, Fenway Park, the Public Garden ducklings. But none are as synonymous with über-hospitality as the Boston Harbor Hotel's 80-foot-tall outdoor archway and rotunda. **Pros:** high-quality Meritage and Sea Grille restaurants; easy walk to Faneuil Hall; water shuttle to Logan Airport. **Cons:** pricey; the spa gets booked up early; less convenient to the Back Bay and South End. [$] *Rooms from: $495* ✉ *70 Rowes Wharf, Downtown/Waterfront* ☎ *617/439–7000, 800/752–7077* 🌐 *www.bhh.com* 🛏 *204 rooms, 26 suites* 🍴 *No meals* [M] *Aquarium, South Station* ⊕ *H3.*

$$$ Fodor's Choice ★ **Nine Zero.** Nine Zero knows that hotel rooms can get a little lonely. **Pros:** pet-friendly; kid-friendly; lobby wine-tasting every evening (from 5 to 6); Etro bath products. **Cons:** smallish rooms; high parking fees. [$] *Rooms from: $349* ✉ *90 Tremont St., Downtown* ☎ *617/772–5800, 866/906–9090* 🌐 *www.ninezero.com* 🛏 *185 rooms, 5 suites* 🍴 *No meals* [M] *Park St., Government Center* ⊕ *G3.*

$$$ HOTEL 👶 **Omni Parker House.** In 2008 America's oldest continuously operating hotel got a $30-million makeover, so you can still steep yourself in Boston history . . . while watching a flat-screen TV. **Pros:** historic property; near Downtown Crossing on the Freedom Trail. **Cons:** small rooms, some quite dark; thin-walled rooms can be noisy. [$] *Rooms from: $339* ✉ *60 School St., Downtown* ☎ *617/227–8600, 800/843–6664* 🌐 *www.omniparkerhouse.com* 🛏 *551 rooms, 21 suites* 🍴 *No meals* [M] *Government Center, Park St.* ⊕ *G3.*

Charlesmark Hotel

Eliot Hotel

Boston Harbor Hotel at Rowes Wharf

Liberty Hotel Boston

Charles Hotel

Hotel Commonwealth

$$$ HOTEL 👶 🏨 **Seaport Boston Hotel.** Chances are, if you've ever been to Boston on business, you've already stayed at the Seaport. **Pros:** the Wave Health & Fitness Club; a no-tipping policy; close to water taxi; free Wi-Fi. **Cons:** far from city center; limited nearby dining options; pricey room service. [$] *Rooms from: $369* ✉ *World Trade Center, 1 Seaport La., Downtown/Seaport District* ☎ *617/385–4000, 800/440–3318* 🌐 *www.seaportboston.com* 🛏 *428 rooms* 🍴 *No meals* [M] *World Trade Center* ✥ *H4.*

$$$$ HOTEL 🏨 **W Boston.** This 235-room glass tower is fronted by a metal-and-glass "awning" that is outfitted with soft, color-changing neon lights that cast a cheeky glow on passersby. **Pros:** Bliss spa on-site; signature W feather-top beds; fashion scene. **Cons:** fee for Wi-Fi in rooms; area theater and bar crowds can be loud; expensive parking. [$] *Rooms from: $400* ✉ *100 Stuart St., Downtown/Theater District* ☎ *617/261–8700* 🌐 *www.whotels.com/boston* 🛏 *235 rooms* 🍴 *No meals* [M] *Boylston, Tufts Medical Center* ✥ *F4.*

SOUTH END

$$ B&B/INN 🏨 **Encore.** Innkeepers Reinhold Mahler and David Miller know a thing or two about ambience. **Pros:** trendy South End location; free Wi-Fi; Bang & Olufson sound systems; David and Reinhold are gracious hosts. **Cons:** small breakfast nook; two-night minimums on weekends; no elevator. [$] *Rooms from: $250* ✉ *116 W. Newton St., South End* ☎ *617/247–3425* 🌐 *www.encorebandb.com* 🛏 *3 rooms* 🍴 *Breakfast* [M] *Back Bay, Mass. Ave* ✥ *D6.*

KENMORE SQUARE

$$$ B&B/INN Fodor's Choice ★ 🏨 **Gryphon House.** The suites in this four-story 19th-century brownstone are thematically decorated: one evokes rustic Italy; another is inspired by neo-Gothic art. **Pros:** awesome value; free Wi-Fi; elegant suites are lush and spacious; gas fireplaces in all rooms; helpful, friendly staff. **Cons:** may be too fussy for some; there's no elevator or handicapped access. [$] *Rooms from: $300* ✉ *9 Bay State Rd., Kenmore Sq.* ☎ *617/375–9003, 877/375–9003* 🌐 *www.innboston.com* 🛏 *8 suites* 🍴 *Breakfast* [M] *Kenmore* ✥ *A5.*

$$ HOTEL Fodor's Choice ★ 👶 🏨 **Hotel Commonwealth.** Rumor has it that Bono and the Boss have walked the hallways of the Hotel Commonwealth. **Pros:** down bedding; perfect locale for Red Sox fans; happening bar scene at Eastern Standard. **Cons:** area is mobbed during Sox games; small gym. [$] *Rooms from: $299* ✉ *500 Commonwealth Ave., Kenmore Square* ☎ *617/933–5000, 866/784–4000* 🌐 *www.hotelcommonwealth.com* 🛏 *149 rooms, 5 suites* 🍴 *No meals* [M] *Kenmore* ✥ *A5.*

CAMBRIDGE

Use the coordinate (✛ B2) at the end of each listing to locate a site on the Where to Eat and Stay in Cambridge map.

$$$
HOTEL
Fodor's Choice
★
☾
Charles Hotel. It used to be that the Charles was *the* place to stay in Cambridge. **Pros:** free Wi-Fi; free domestic calls; kid-friendly; on-site jazz club and hip Noir bar; outdoor skating rink in winter. **Cons:** luxury comes at a price; less convenient for Downtown Boston trips. $ *Rooms from: $399* ⊠ *1 Bennett St.* ☎ *617/864–1200, 800/882–1818* ⊕ *www.charleshotel.com* ⤳ *249 rooms, 45 suites* Ⓜ *Harvard* ✛ *C1.*

$$$$
HOTEL
Le Meridien Cambridge. When the Meridien chain took over the cult favorite geek-chic Hotel at MIT, some fans worried the Cambridge spot would lose its charm. **Pros:** free Wi-Fi; tech-savvy rooms and surroundings; 24-hour fitness center; great off-season rates. **Cons:** a 10-minute walk to the T; pricey high-season rates; good area dining hard to come by. $ *Rooms from: $503* ⊠ *20 Sidney St.* ☎ *617/577–0200, 800/543-4300* ⊕ *www.lemeridien.com/cambridge* ⤳ *196 rooms, 14 suites* ⓄⅠ *No meals* Ⓜ *Central, Kendall/MIT* ✛ *C5.*

$$$
HOTEL
Royal Sonesta Hotel. Right next to the Charles River, the Sonesta has one of the best city skyline and sunset views in Boston. **Pros:** free Wi-Fi; nice pool; certified green hotel. **Cons:** a bit sterile; close to the Museum of Science but a far walk from the Back Bay and South End. $ *Rooms from: $379* ⊠ *40 Edwin Land Blvd., off Memorial Dr.* ☎ *617/806–4200, 800/766–3782* ⊕ *www.sonesta.com/boston* ⤳ *379 rooms, 21 suites* ⓄⅠ *No meals* Ⓜ *Lechmere* ✛ *A6.*

SIDE TRIPS FROM BOSTON

LEXINGTON

16 miles northwest of Boston.

Discontent with the British, American colonials burst into action in Lexington in April 1775. On April 18, patriot leader Paul Revere alerted the town that British soldiers were approaching. The next day, as the British advance troops arrived in Lexington on their march toward Concord, the minutemen were waiting to confront the redcoats in what became the first skirmish of the Revolutionary War.

These first military encounters of the American Revolution are very much a part of present-day Lexington, a modern suburban town that sprawls out from the historic sites near its center. Although the downtown area is generally lively, with ice-cream and coffee shops, boutiques, and a great little movie theater, the town becomes especially animated each Patriots' Day (April 19 but celebrated on the third Monday in April), when costume-clad groups re-create the minutemen's battle maneuvers and Paul Revere rides again.

To learn more about the city and the 1775 clash, stop by the **Lexington Visitor Center.**

GETTING HERE AND AROUND

Massachusetts Bay Transportation Authority (MBTA) operates bus service in the greater Boston area and serves Lexington.

ESSENTIALS

Bus Contacts MBTA ☎ *800/392–6100, 617/222–3200, 617/222–5146 TTY* ⊕ *www.mbta.com.*

Visitor Information Lexington Visitors Center ⊠ *1875 Massachusetts Ave.* ☎ *781/862–1450* ⊕ *www.lexingtonchamber.org* ⊙ *Apr.–Nov, daily 9–5; Dec.–Mar, daily 10–4.*

Tours Liberty Ride. Liberty Ride offers guided trolley tours (April through October) that visit many of the historic sites in Lexington and Concord. Tickets are good for 24 hours and allow on-off privileges. Dial extension 702. ☎ *781/862–0500* ⊕ *www.libertyride.us* ⊠ *$25.*

EXPLORING

Battle Green. It was on this 2-acre triangle of land, on April 19, 1775, that the first confrontation between British soldiers, who were marching from Boston toward Concord, and the Colonial militia known as the minutemen took place. The minutemen—so called because they were able to prepare themselves at a moment's notice—were led by Captain John Parker, whose role in the American Revolution is commemorated in Henry Hudson Kitson's renowned 1900 *Minuteman* statue. Facing downtown Lexington at the tip of Battle Green, the statue's in a traffic island, and therefore makes for a difficult photo op.

Buckman Tavern. While waiting for the arrival of the British on the morning of April 19, 1775, the Minutemen gathered at this 1690 tavern. A half-hour tour takes in the tavern's seven rooms, which have been restored to the way they looked in the 1770s. Among the items on display is an old front door with a hole made by a British musket ball. ⊠ *1 Bedford St.* ☎ *781/862–1703* ⊕ *www.lexingtonhistory.org* ⊠ *$7; $12 combination ticket includes Hancock-Clarke House and Munroe Tavern* ⊙ *Apr.–Oct., daily 10–4.*

Hancock-Clarke House. On April 18, 1775, Paul Revere came here to warn patriots John Hancock and Sam Adams (who were staying at the house while attending the Provincial Congress in nearby Concord) of the advance of British troops. Hancock and Adams, on whose heads the British king had put a price, fled to avoid capture. The house, a parsonage built in 1698, is a 10-minute walk from Lexington Common. Inside are the pistols of the British major John Pitcairn, as well as period furnishings and portraits. ⊠ *36 Hancock St.* ☎ *781/862–1703* ⊕ *www.lexingtonhistory.org* ⊠ *$7; $12 combination ticket includes Buckman Tavern and Munroe Tavern* ⊙ *Apr.–May, weekends 10–4; June–Oct., daily 10–4.*

★ **Minute Man National Historical Park.** West of Lexington's center stretches
Ⓒ this 1,000-acre, three-parcel park that also extends into nearby Lincoln and Concord *(⇨ Concord, Exploring)*. Begin your park visit at Lexington's **Minute Man Visitor Center** to see its free multimedia presentation, "The Road to Revolution," a captivating introduction to the events of April 1775. Then, continuing along Highway 2A toward Concord,

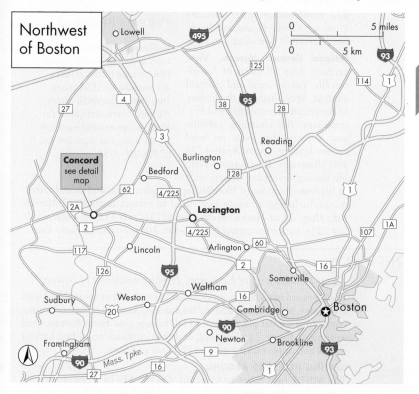

you pass the point where Revere's midnight ride ended with his capture by the British; it's marked with a boulder and plaque, as well as an enclosure where rangers sometimes give educational presentations. You can also visit the 1732 **Hartwell Tavern** (open mid-April through late May, weekends 9:30–5:30, and late May through late October, daily 9:30–5:30), a restored drover's (driver's) tavern staffed by park employees in period costume; they frequently demonstrate musket firing or open-hearth cooking, and children are likely to enjoy the reproduction Colonial toys. ⊠ *250 North Great Rd.(Hwy. 2A), ¼ mile west of Hwy. 128* ☎ *978/369–6993* ⊕ *www.nps.gov/mima* ☉ *North Bridge Visitor Center, mid-Mar.–Oct., daily 9–5; Nov., daily 9–4; Dec.–Mar., daily 11–3. Minute Man Visitor Center, mid-Mar.–Oct., daily 9–5; Nov., daily 9–4.*

Munroe Tavern. As April 19, 1775, dragged on, British forces met fierce resistance in Concord. Dazed and demoralized after the battle at Concord's Old North Bridge, the British backtracked and regrouped at this 1695 tavern 1 mile east of Lexington Common, while the Munroe family hid in nearby woods. The troops then retreated through what is now the town of Arlington. After a bloody battle there, they returned to Boston. Tours of the tavern last about 30 minutes. ⊠ *1332 Massachusetts Ave.* ☎ *781/862–1703* ⊕ *www.lexingtonhistory.org* ☒ *$7;*

$12 combination ticket includes Hancock-Clarke House and Buckman Tavern ⊙ June–Oct., noon–4.

National Heritage Museum. View artifacts from all facets of American life, put in social and political context. Specializing in the history of American Freemasonry and Fraternalism, the changing exhibits and lectures also focus on local events leading up to April 1775 and illustrates Revolutionary-era life through everyday objects such as blacksmithing tools, bloodletting paraphernalia, and dental instruments, including a "tooth key" used to extract teeth. ⊠ *33 Marrett Rd., Hwy. 2A at Massachusetts Ave.* ☎ *781/861–6559* ⊕ *www.monh. org* ✉ *Donations accepted ⊙ Wed.–Sat. 10–4:30. Closed Sun.–Tues.*

> **TOUR BY PHONE**
>
> Half-hour cell-phone audio tours of various parts of Minute Man National Historical Park are available for $5.99 apiece. They start at the visitor center, Hartwell Tavern, and Concord's North Bridge entrance—just look for the audio tour signs and call ☎ *703/286–2755.*

CONCORD

About 10 miles west of Lexington, 21 miles northwest of Boston.

The Concord of today is a modern suburb with a busy center filled with arty shops, places to eat, and old bookstores. Autumn lovers, take note: Concord is a great place to start a fall foliage tour. From Boston, head west along Route 2 to Concord, and then continue on to find harvest stands and apple picking around Harvard and Stow.

GETTING HERE AND AROUND

The MBTA runs buses to Concord. On the MBTA Commuter Rail, Concord is a 40-minute ride on the Fitchburg Line, which departs from Boston's North Station.

ESSENTIALS

Bus and Train Contact MBTA ☎ *617/222–3200, 800/392–6100* ⊕ *www.mbta. com.*

Visitor Information Concord Visitor Center ⊠ *58 Main St.* ☎ *978/369–3120* ⊕ *www.concordchamberofcommerce.org* ⊙ *Apr.–Oct., daily 10–4.*

EXPLORING

Concord Museum. The original contents of Emerson's private study, as well as the world's largest collection of Thoreau artifacts, reside in this 1930 Colonial Revival building just east of the town center. The museum provides a good overview of the town's history, from its original Native American settlement to the present. Highlights include Native American artifacts, furnishings from Thoreau's Walden Pond cabin (there's a replica of the cabin itself on the museum's lawn), and one of the two lanterns hung at Boston's Old North Church to signal that the British were coming by sea. If you've brought the children, ask for a free family activity pack. ⊠ *200 Lexington Rd., entrance on Cambridge Tpke.* ☎ *978/369–9763* ⊕ *www.concordmuseum.org* ✉ *$10 ⊙ Jan.–Mar., Mon.–Sat. 11–4, Sun. 1–4; Apr.–Dec, Mon.–Sat. 9–5, Sun. noon–5; June–Aug., daily 9–5.*

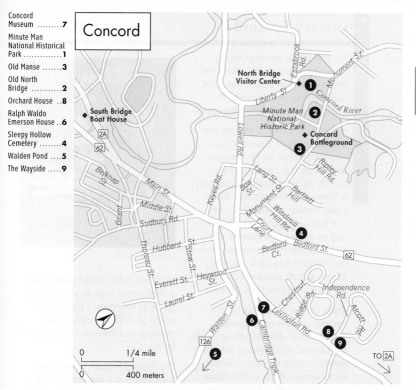

Concord

★ **Minute Man National Historical Park.** Along Highway 2A is a three-parcel
park with 1,000 acres. The park contains many of the sites important to
Concord's role in the Revolution, including Old North Bridge, as well as
two visitor centers, one each in Concord and Lexington (⇨ *Lexington,
What to See).* Although the initial Revolutionary War sorties were in
Lexington, word of the American losses spread rapidly to surrounding
towns: when the British marched into Concord, more than 400 minutemen were waiting. A marker set in the stone wall along Liberty Street,
behind the North Bridge Visitor Center, announces, "On this field the
minutemen and militia formed before marching down to the fight at
the bridge." ⊠ *Bounded by Monument St., Liberty St., and Lowell Rd.*
⊕ *www.nps.gov/mima* ⊗ *Grounds daily dawn–dusk.*

North Bridge Visitor Center. The park's North Bridge Visitor Center
is open from April through October, daily 9–5, and November, daily
9–4 (call for winter hours). ⊠ *174 Liberty St.* ☎ *978/369–6993.*

Old Manse. The Reverend William Emerson, grandfather of Ralph
Waldo Emerson, watched rebels and redcoats battle from behind his
home, which was within sight of the Old North Bridge. The house, built
in 1770, was occupied continuously by the Emerson family for almost
two centuries, except for a 3½-year period during which Nathaniel
Hawthorne rented it. Furnishings date from the late 18th century. Tours

Literary Concord

The first wholly American literary movement was born in Concord, the tiny town west of Boston that, quite coincidentally, also witnessed the beginning of the American Revolution.

Under the influence of essayist and poet Ralph Waldo Emerson, a group eventually known as the Transcendental Club (but called the Hedges Club at the time) assembled regularly in Emerson's Concord home. Henry David Thoreau, a fellow townsman and famous proponent of self-reliance, was an integral club member, along with such others as pioneering feminist Margaret Fuller and poet Ellery Channing, both drawn to Concord simply because of Emerson's presence.

Louisa May Alcott

These are the names that have become indelible bylines in high school anthologies and college syllabi, but Concord also produced beloved authors outside the Transcendentalist movement. These writers include Louisa May Alcott of *Little Women* fame and children's book author Harriet Lothrop, pseudonymously known as Margaret Sydney. Even Nathaniel Hawthorne, whose various temporary homes around Massachusetts constitute a literary trail all their own, resided in Concord during the early and later portions of his career.

The cumulative inkwells of these authors have bestowed upon Concord a literary legacy unique in the United States, both for its influence on literature in general and for the quantity of related sights packed within such a small radius. From Alcott's Orchard House to Hawthorne's Old Manse, nearly all of their houses remain standing, well-preserved and open for tours.

The Thoreau Institute, within walking distance of a reconstruction of Thoreau's famous cabin in the woods at Walden Pond, is a repository of his papers and original editions. Emerson's study sits in the Concord Museum, across the street from his house. Even their final resting places are here, on Authors Ridge in Sleepy Hollow Cemetery, a few short blocks from the town common. **Concord Bike Tours** (☎ 978/697-1897 ⊕ *www. concordbiketours.com*) will guide you through the sites on two wheels, usually April through November (weather permitting).

run throughout the day and last 45 minutes, with a new tour starting within 15 minutes of when the first person signs up. ⊠ *269 Monument St.* ☎ *978/369-3909* ⊕ *www.thetrustees.org/places-to-visit/greater-boston/old-manse.html* ⊠ *$8* ⊙ *Mid-Apr.–Oct., Mon.–Sat. 10–5, Sun. noon–5; Nov.–Mar. Tours Thurs. and Fri. 2, 3, and 4 pm and weekends noon–4:30 (weather permitting).*

2

Old North Bridge. A half mile from Concord center, at this bridge, the Concord minutemen turned the tables on the British on the morning of April 19, 1775. The Americans didn't fire first, but when two of their own fell dead from a redcoat volley, Major John Buttrick of Concord roared, "Fire, fellow soldiers, for God's sake, fire." The minutemen released volley after volley, and the redcoats fled. Daniel Chester French's famous statue *The Minuteman* (1875) honors the country's first freedom fighters. Inscribed at the foot of the statue are words Ralph Waldo Emerson wrote in 1837 describing the confrontation: "By the rude bridge that arched the flood / Their flag to April's breeze unfurled / Here once the embattled farmers stood / And fired the shot heard round the world." The lovely wooded surroundings give a sense of what the landscape was like in more rural times.

Orchard House. The dark brown exterior of Louisa May Alcott's family home sharply contrasts with the light, wit, and energy so much in evidence inside. Named for the apple orchard that once surrounded it, Orchard House was the Alcott family home from 1857 to 1877. Here Louisa wrote *Little Women*, based on her life with her three sisters; and her father, Bronson, founded his school of philosophy—the building remains behind the house. Because Orchard House had just one owner after the Alcotts left, and because it became a museum in 1911, many of the original furnishings remain, including the semicircular shelf-desk where Louisa wrote *Little Women*. ⊠ *399 Lexington Rd.* ☎ *978/369–4118* ⊕ *www.louisamayalcott.org* ⊠ *$9* ⊙ *Apr.–Oct., Mon.–Sat. 10–4:30, Sun. 1–4:30; Nov. and Dec. and Jan. 3–Mar., weekdays 11–3, Sat. 10–4:30, Sun. 1–4:30. Half-hour tours begin every 30 mins Apr.–Oct.; call for off-season schedule.*

Ralph Waldo Emerson House. The 19th-century essayist and poet Ralph Waldo Emerson lived briefly in the Old Manse in 1834–35, then moved to this home, where he lived until his death in 1882. Here he wrote the *Essays*. Except for artifacts from Emerson's study, now at the nearby Concord Museum, the Emerson House furnishings have been preserved as the writer left them, down to his hat resting on the newel post. You must join one of the half-hour-long tours to see the interior. ⊠ *28 Cambridge Tpke., at Lexington Rd.* ☎ *978/369–2236* ⊕ *www.rwe.org/emersonhouse* ⊠ *$8* ⊙ *Mid-Apr.–mid-Oct., Thurs.–Sat. 10–4:30, Sun. 1–4:30; call for tour schedule.*

Sleepy Hollow Cemetery. In the Author's Ridge section of this cemetery are the graves of American literary greats Louisa May Alcott, Ralph Waldo Emerson, Henry David Thoreau, and Nathaniel Hawthorne. Each Memorial Day, Alcott's grave is decorated in commemoration of her death. ⊠ *Bedford St. (Hwy. 62)* ☎ *978/318–3233* ⊙ *Daily dawn–dusk.*

Fodor's Choice ★ **Walden Pond.** For lovers of early American literature, a trip to Concord isn't complete without a pilgrimage to Henry David Thoreau's most famous residence. Here, in 1845, at age 28, Thoreau moved into a one-room cabin—built for $28.12—on the shore of this 100-foot-deep kettle hole formed by the retreat of an ancient glacier. Living alone for the next two years, Thoreau discovered the benefits of solitude and the beauties of nature. The essays in *Walden*, published in 1854, are a

Retrace Henry David Thoreau's steps at Walden Pond.

mixture of philosophy, nature writing, and proto-ecology. The site of the first cabin is staked out in stone. A full-size, authentically furnished replica of the cabin stands about ½ mile from the original site, near the Walden Pond State Reservation parking lot. Even when it's closed, you can peek through its windows. Now, as in Thoreau's time, the pond is a delightful summertime spot for swimming, fishing, and rowing, and there's hiking in the nearby woods. To get to Walden Pond State Reservation from the center of Concord—a trip of only 1½ miles—take Concord's Main Street a block west from Monument Square, turn left onto Walden Street, and head for the intersection of Highways 2 and 126. Cross over Highway 2 onto Highway 126, heading south for ½ mile. ⊠ *915 Walden St.(Hwy. 126)* ☎ *978/369–3254* ⊕ *www.mass.gov/dcr/parks/walden* ⌑ *Free, parking $5* ☉ *Daily 8 am–sunset, weather permitting.*

The Wayside. Nathaniel Hawthorne lived at the Old Manse in 1842–45, working on stories and sketches; he then moved to Salem (where he wrote *The Scarlet Letter*) and later to Lenox (*The House of the Seven Gables*). In 1852 he returned to Concord, bought this rambling structure called The Wayside, and lived here until his death in 1864. The subsequent owner, Margaret Sidney, wrote the children's book *Five Little Peppers and How They Grew* (1881). Before Hawthorne moved in, the Alcotts lived here, from 1845 to 1848. An exhibit center, in the former barn, provides information about the Wayside authors and links them to major events in American history. Hawthorne's tower-study, with his stand-up writing desk, is substantially as he left it. ⊠ *455 Lexington Rd.*

☎ 978/318–7863 🌐 *www.nps.gov/archive/mima/wayside* 🎟 *$5* 🕒 *Open by guided tour only, May–Oct.; call for reservations.*

SPORTS AND THE OUTDOORS

BOATING **South Bridge Boat House.** You can reach the North Bridge section of the Minute Man National Historical Park by water if you rent a canoe or kayak at the South Bridge Boat House and paddle along the Sudbury and Concord rivers. You can even paddle all the way to Sudbury or up to Billerica. ✉ *496 Main St.* ☎ *978/369–9438* 🌐 *www.canoeconcord.com* 🎟 *Canoes $14/hr weekdays, $17/hr weekends; kayaks $16/hr single, $18/hr double* 🕒 *Apr.–Nov. weekdays 10–1 hr before dusk, weekends and holidays 9–1 hr before dusk.*

WHERE TO EAT

$ AMERICAN ★ 🍴 **Main Streets Market & Cafe.** Cyclists, families, and sightseers pack into this brick building, which was used to store munitions during the Revolutionary War. Wood floors and blackboard menus add a touch of nostalgia, but the extensive menu includes many modern hits. Breakfast offerings include a quiche and breakfast sandwich of the day. At lunch, the grilled panini are excellent; they also serve flatbread pizza and pub fare. At night heartier offerings dominate the menu, including baked lobster mac and cheese, scallop and shrimp risotto, and a Yankee pot roast dinner. There's a full bar, live music five nights a week, and in summer the small alley outside leads to a counter that serves ice cream. [$] *Average main: $3* ✉ *42 Main St.* ☎ *978/369–9948* 🌐 *www.mainstreetsmarketandcafe.com.*

$ AMERICAN 🍴 **Walden Grille.** Chowders, salads, and sandwiches are typical fare at this old brick firehouse-turned-dining room. Start with the Philly spring rolls or crispy fried oysters. Sandwiches include burgers and BLTs, plus more creative options like the chicken curry roll-up or croque monsieur. Entrées run the gamut from braised short ribs to rock shrimp risotto. [$] *Average main: $17* ✉ *24 Walden St.* ☎ *978/371–2233* 🌐 *www.waldengrille.com.*

THE NORTH SHORE

The slice of Massachusetts's Atlantic Coast known as the North Shore extends past Boston to the Cape Ann region just shy of the New Hampshire border. In addition to miles of woods and beaches, the North Shore's highlights include Marblehead, a classic New England sea town; Salem, which thrives on a history of witches, writers, and maritime trades; Gloucester, the oldest seaport in America; Rockport, rich with crafts shops and artists' studios; and Newburyport, with its redbrick center and clapboard mansions, and a handful of typical New England towns in between. Bustling during the short summer season and breathtaking during the autumn foliage, the North Shore is calmer (and colder) between November and June. Many restaurants, inns, and attractions operate on reduced hours during the off-season.

MARBLEHEAD

17 miles north of Boston.

Marblehead, with its narrow and winding streets, beautifully preserved clapboard homes, sea captains' mansions, and harbor, looks much as it must have when it was founded in 1629 by fishermen from Cornwall and the Channel Islands. One of New England's premier sailing capitals, Marblehead attracts boats from along the Eastern Seaboard each July during Race Week—first held in 1889. Parking in town can be difficult; lots at the end of Front Street or on State Street by the Landing restaurant are the best options.

ESSENTIALS

Visitor Information Marblehead Chamber of Commerce Information Booth ✉ *62 Pleasant St.* ☎ *781/631–2868* 🌐 *www.visitmarblehead.com.*

EXPLORING

Abbott Hall. The town's Victorian-era municipal building, built in 1876, displays Archibald Willard's painting *The Spirit of '76.* Many visitors, familiar since childhood with this image of the three Revolutionary veterans with fife, drum, and flag, are surprised to find the original in an otherwise unassuming town hall. Also on-site is a small naval museum exploring Marblehead's maritime past. ✉ *188 Washington St.* ☎ *781/631–0000* 🎟 *Free* 🕒 *Call for hrs.*

Fort Sewall. Marblehead's magnificent views of the harbor, the Misery Islands, and the Atlantic are best enjoyed from this fort built in 1644 atop the rocky cliffs of the harbor. Used as a defense against the French in 1742 as well as during the War of 1812, Fort Sewall is today open to the public as community parkland. Barracks and underground quarters can still be seen, and Revolutionary War reenactments by members of the modern-day Glover's Marblehead Regiment are staged at the fort annually. ✉ *End of Front St.* 🌐 *www.essexheritage.org/sites/fort_sewall.shtml* 🎟 *Free* 🕒 *Daily sunrise–sunset.*

WHERE TO EAT AND STAY

For expanded hotel reviews, visit Fodors.com.

$ SEAFOOD 🍴 **The Landing.** Decorated in nautical blues and whites, this pleasant restaurant sits right on Marblehead harbor, with a deck that's nearly in the water. The restaurant offers classic New England fare like clam chowder and broiled scrod, and serves brunch on Sunday. The pub area has a lighter menu and local feel. [$] *Average main: $12* ✉ *81 Front St.* ☎ *781/639–1266* 🌐 *www.thelandingrestaurant.com.*

$ Fodor's Choice ★ 🏨 **Harbor Light Inn.** Housed in a pair of adjoining 18th-century mansions in the heart of Old Town Marblehead, this elegant inn features many rooms with canopy beds, brick fireplaces, and Jacuzzis. **Pros:** nice location amid period homes; on-site tavern with pub menu. **Cons:** limited parking; many one-way and narrow streets make this town somewhat confusing to get around in by car and the inn tricky to find. [$] *Rooms from: $175* ✉ *58 Washington St.* ☎ *781/631–2186* 🌐 *www.harborlightinn.com* 🛏 *20 rooms, 3 apartments.*

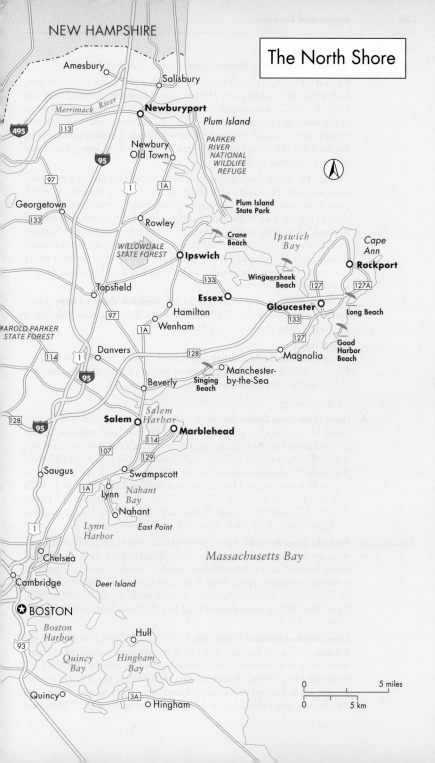

The North Shore

NEW HAMPSHIRE

Amesbury

Salisbury

Merrimack River

Newburyport

113

495

Plum Island

Newbury
Old Town

PARKER
RIVER
NATIONAL
WILDLIFE
REFUGE

97

Plum Island
State Park

1

1A

Georgetown

133

Rowley

Crane
Beach

*Ipswich
Bay*

Cape
Ann

WILLOWDALE
STATE FOREST

Ipswich

Rockport

133

127

127A

Topsfield

Wingaersheek
Beach

Essex

Gloucester

Long Beach

97

Hamilton

133

HAROLD PARKER
STATE FOREST

1A

Wenham

127

114

Danvers

128

Magnolia

Good
Harbor
Beach

1

95

Beverly

Singing
Beach

Manchester-
by-the-Sea

128

Salem

*Salem
Harbor*

95

Marblehead

114

107

129

Swampscott

Saugus

1A

*Nahant
Bay*

Lynn

Nahant

*Lynn
Harbor*

East Point

Massachusetts Bay

1

Chelsea

Deer Island

Cambridge

93

⭐ BOSTON

*Boston
Harbor*

Hull

*Quincy
Bay*

*Hingham
Bay*

Quincy

3A

Hingham

0   5 miles

0   5 km

SALEM

16 miles northeast of Boston, 4 miles west of Marblehead.

Known for years as the "Witch City," Salem is redefining itself. But first, a bit on its bewitched past. The witchcraft hysteria emerged from the trials of 1692, when several Salem-area girls fell ill and accused some of the townspeople of casting spells on them. More than 150 men and women were charged with practicing witchcraft, a crime punishable by death. After the trials later that year, 19 people were hanged and one man was crushed to death.

Though the witch trials might have built Salem's infamy, it'd be a mistake to ignore the town's rich maritime and creative traditions, which played integral roles in the country's evolution. Frigates out of Salem opened the Far East trade routes and generated the wealth that created America's first millionaires. Among its native talents are writer Nathaniel Hawthorne, the intellectual Peabody Sisters, navigator Nathaniel Bowditch, and architect Samuel McIntire. This creative spirit is today celebrated in Salem's museums, waterfront shops and restaurants, galleries, and wide common.

To learn more on the area, stop by the **Regional Visitor's Center**. Innovatively designed in the Old Salem Armory, the center has exhibits, a 27-minute film, maps, and a gift shop.

ESSENTIALS

Visitor Information Destination Salem ⊠ *54 Turner St.* ☎ *978/744–3663, 877/725–3662* ⊕ *www.salem.org.* **Regional Visitor's Center** ⊠ *2 New Liberty St.* ☎ *978/740–1650* ⊕ *www.nps.gov/ner/sama* ⊘ *Daily 9–5.*

EXPLORING

★ **House of the Seven Gables.** Immortalized in Nathaniel Hawthorne's classic novel, this site itself is a literary treasure. Built in 1668 and also known as the Turner-Ingersoll Mansion, the house includes a secret staircase, a garret containing an antique scale model of the house, and some of the finest Georgian interiors in the country. Also on the property is the small house where Hawthorne was born in 1804; built in 1750, it was moved from its original location a few blocks away. ⊠ *115 Derby St.* ☎ *978/744–0991* ⊕ *www.7gables.org* 🖭 *$12.50* ⊘ *Nov., Dec., and mid-Jan.–June, daily 10–5; July–Oct., daily 10–7.*

Fodor'sChoice **Peabody Essex Museum.** Salem's world-class museum celebrates maritime art, history, and the spoils of the Asian export trade. Its 30 galleries, housed in a contemplative blend of modern design, represent a diverse range of styles, from American decorative and seamen's art to idea studios and photography. ⊠ *East India Sq.* ☎ *978/745–9500, 866/745–1876* ⊕ *www.pem.org* 🖭 *$15* ⊘ *Tues.–Sun. 10–5; holiday Mondays 10–5.*

Salem Maritime National Historic Site. Near Derby Wharf, this 9¼-acre site focuses on Salem's heritage as a major seaport with a thriving overseas trade. It includes an orientation center with an 18-minute film; the 1762 home of Elias Derby, America's first millionaire; the 1819 Customs House, made famous in Nathaniel Hawthorne's *The Scarlet Letter*; and a replica of the *Friendship*, a 171-foot, three-masted 1797 merchant vessel. There's also an active lighthouse dating from 1871, as well as the nation's last surviving 18th-century wharves. The West India Goods Store, across the street, is still a working 19th-century store, with glass jars of spices, teas, and coffees. New to the site is the 1770 Pedrick Store House, moved from nearby Marblehead and reassembled right on Derby Wharf; the two-story structure once played a vital role in the lucrative merchant seaside trade. ✉ *193 Derby St.* ☎ *978/740–1650* 🌐 *www.nps.gov/sama* 🎟 *Site free, tours $5* 🕓 *Hrs vary; check website or call ahead.*

Salem Witch Museum. An informative, if somewhat hokey, introduction to the 1692 witchcraft hysteria, this museum has a short walk-through exhibit, "Witches: Evolving Perceptions," that describes witch hunts through the years. ✉ *Washington Sq. N* ☎ *978/744–1692* 🌐 *www.salemwitchmuseum.com* 🎟 *$9* 🕓 *Sept.–June, daily 10–5; July and Aug., daily 10–7.*

Salem Witch Trials Memorial. Dedicated by Nobel Laureate Elie Wiesel in 1992, this melancholy space—an antidote to the relentless marketing of the merry-witches motif—honors those who died because they refused to confess that they were witches. A stone wall is studded with 20 stone benches, each inscribed with a victim's name, and sits next to Salem's oldest burying ground. ✉ *Off Liberty St. near Charter St.* 🌐 *www.salemweb.com/memorial/memorial.shtml.*

ARTS AND ENTERTAINMENT

THEATER **Cry Innocent: The People versus Bridget Bishop.** This show, the longest continuously running play north of Boston, transports audience members to Bridget Bishop's trial of 1692. After hearing historical testimonies, the audience cross-examines the witnesses and must then decide the verdict. Actors respond in character revealing much about the Puritan frame of mind. Each show is different and allows audience members to play their "part" in history. ✉ *Old Town Hall, 32 Derby Sq.* ☎ *978/867–4767* 🌐 *www.gordon.edu/historyalive* 🎟 *$10* 🕓 *July–Oct., showtimes vary.*

WHERE TO EAT AND STAY

For expanded hotel reviews, visit Fodors.com.

$$$ STEAKHOUSE Fodor's Choice ★ 🍴 **43 Church.** Formerly the Lyceum, the new name of this long-established restaurant came with a changing of the guard: the second generation of the Harrington family has taken the helm of this well-established and much-loved dining spot. Always a hit for classy fare, the restaurant takes advantage of its historic building, where Alexander Graham Bell made the first long-distance phone call. Steaks are the house specialty here, but local seafood is given fine treatment as well. There's a nice brunch served on weekends. [$] *Average main: $32* ✉ *43 Church St.* ☎ *978/745–7665* 🌐 *www.43church.com.*

$ HOTEL 🏨 **The Hawthorne Hotel.** Elegantly restored, this full-service landmark hotel celebrates the town's most famous writer. **Pros:** lovely, historic lobby; parking available behind hotel; easy walking access to all the town's features. **Cons:** many rooms are small. [$] *Rooms from: $114* ✉ *18 Washington Sq. W* ☎ *978/744–4080, 800/729–7829* 🌐 *www.hawthornehotel.com* 🛏 *93 rooms.*

The First Witch Trial

It was in Danvers, not Salem, that the first witch trial was held, originating with the family of Samuel Parris, a minister who moved to the area in 1680 from Barbados, bringing with him two slaves, including one named Tituba. In 1691 Samuel's daughter, Betty, and niece, Abigail, began having "fits." Tituba, who had told Betty and Abigail stories of magic and witchcraft from her homeland, baked a "witch cake" to identify the witches who were harming the girls. The girls in turn accused Tituba of witchcraft. After

three days of "questioning," which included beatings from Samuel and a promise from him to free her if she cooperated, Tituba confessed to meeting the devil (in the form of a black hog or dog). She also claimed there were other witches in the village, confirming the girls' accusations against Sarah Good and Sarah Osborne, but she refused to name any others. Tituba's trial prompted the frenzy that led to the deaths of 20 accused "witches."

GLOUCESTER

37 miles northeast of Boston, 8 miles northeast of Manchester-by-the-Sea.

On Gloucester's fine seaside promenade is a famous statue of a man steering a ship's wheel, his eyes searching the horizon. The statue, which honors those "who go down to the sea in ships" was commissioned by the town citizens in celebration of Gloucester's 300th anniversary in 1923. The oldest seaport in the nation (with some of the North Shore's best beaches) is still a major fishing port. Sebastian Junger's 1997 book *A Perfect Storm* was an account of the fate of the *Andrea Gail*, a Gloucester fishing boat caught in "the storm of the century" in October 1991.

ESSENTIALS

Visitor Information Cape Ann Chamber of Commerce ✉ *33 Commercial St.* ☎ *978/283–1601* ⊕ *www.capeannchamber.com/.*

EXPLORING

The Cape Ann Historical Association. Downtown in the Captain Elias Davis 1804 house, this is Gloucester's surprising museum and gallery. It reflects the town's commitment to artists, and has the world's largest collection by maritime luminist Fitz Henry (Hugh) Lane. There's also an excellent exhibit on Gloucester's maritime history. ✉ *27 Pleasant St.* ☎ *978/283–0455* ⊕ *www.capeannmuseum.org* ✉ *$8* ⊙ *Tues.–Sat. 10–5, Sun. 1–4.*

Hammond Castle Museum. Inventor John Hays Hammond Jr. built this structure in 1926 to resemble a "medieval" stone castle. Hammond is credited with more than 500 patents, including inventions associated with the organ that bears his name. The museum contains medieval-style furnishings and paintings, and the Great Hall houses an impressive 8,200-pipe organ. From the castle you can see Norman's Woe Rock, made famous by Longfellow in his poem "The Wreck of the Hesperus." ✉ *80 Hesperus Ave., south side of Gloucester off Rte. 127*

☎ *978/283–2080, 978/283–7673* 🌐 *www.hammondcastle.org* 🎟 *$9* 🕒 *May–early June, weekends and mid-June–Oct., daily. Call for hrs.*

Rocky Neck. The town's creative side thrives in this neighborhood, the first-settled artists' colony in the United States. Its alumni include Winslow Homer, Maurice Prendergast, Jane Peter, and Cecilia Beaux. ✉ *53 Rocky Neck Ave.* ☎ *978/282–0917* 🌐 *www.rockyneckartcolony.org* 🕒 *Galleries 10–10, May 15–Oct. 15. Call or check website for winter hrs.*

SPORTS AND THE OUTDOORS

BEACHES Gloucester has some of the best beaches on the North Shore. From Memorial Day through mid-September, parking costs $20 on weekdays and $25 on weekends, when the lots often fill by 10 am.

Good Harbor Beach. Good Harbor Beach is a huge, sandy, dune-backed beach, with showers and snack bar, and a rocky islet just offshore. ✉ *Easily signposted from Rte. 127A* 🎟 *Parking $20 per car; $25 on weekends and holidays.*

Long Beach. For excellent sunbathing, visit Long Beach. ✉ *Off Rte. 127A on Gloucester-Rockport town line.*

Wingaersheek Beach. Wingaersheek Beach is a well-protected cove of white sand and dunes, with the white Annisquam lighthouse in the bay. ✉ *Exit 13 off Rte. 128* 🎟 *Limited parking, $20/car; $25 on weekends and holidays.*

BOATING **Thomas E. Lannon.** Consider a sail along the harbor and coast aboard the 65-foot schooner Thomas E. Lannon, crafted in Essex in 1996 and modeled after the great boats built a century before. From mid-May through mid-October, there are several two-hour sails, including trips that let you enjoy the sunset or participate in a lobster bake. Tickets are $40. ✉ *63 Rear Rogers St., Seven Seas Wharf* ☎ *978/281–6634* 🌐 *www.schooner.org.*

WHERE TO EAT AND STAY

For expanded hotel reviews, visit Fodors.com.

$$ AMERICAN 🍴 **Franklin Cape Ann.** This contemporary nightspot offers bistro-style chicken, roast cod, and steak frites, perfect for the late-night crowd (it's open until midnight). Live jazz is on tap most Tuesday evenings. Look for the signature martini glass over the door. [$] *Average main: $20* ✉ *118 Main St.* ☎ *978/283–7888* 🕒 *No lunch.*

$ ECLECTIC 🍴 **Passports.** With an eclectic lunch and dinner menu—hence the name—Passports is a bright and airy café with French, Spanish, and Thai dishes, as well as lobster sandwiches. Early risers can opt for breakfast, which is served only on Sunday mornings. The fried calamari and house haddock are favorites here, and there's always local art hanging on the walls for patrons to buy. Occasionally there are wine tastings. [$] *Average main: $15* ✉ *110 Main St.* ☎ *978/281–3680.*

$ RESORT 🏨 **Cape Ann's Marina Resort & Spa.** This year-round hotel less than a mile from Gloucester comes alive in summer. **Pros:** guests get a free river cruise during summer. **Cons:** "resort" is a misnomer—the hotel is surrounded by parking lots; expect motel quality. [$] *Rooms from:*

Kids enjoy the white sands of Wingaersheek Beach in Gloucester.

$175 ⊠ 75 Essex Ave. ☎ *978/283–2116, 800/626–7660* ⊕ *www. capeannmarina.com* ⊅ *31 rooms.*

$ 🏨 **Cape Ann Motor Inn.** On the sands of Long Beach, this three-story, shingled motel has no-frills rooms except for the balconies and ocean views. **Pros:** exceptional view from every room; kids under five stay free. **Cons:** thin walls; motel quality; summer season can be loud and crowded. 💲 *Rooms from: $175* ⊠ *33 Rockport Rd.* ☎ *978/281–2900, 800/464–8439* ⊕ *www.capeannmotorinn.com* ⊅ *30 rooms, 1 suite* ⦿ *Breakfast.*

ROCKPORT

41 miles northeast of Boston, 4 miles northeast of Gloucester on Rte. 127.

Rockport, at the very tip of Cape Ann, derives its name from local granite formations. Many Boston-area structures are made of stone cut from its long-gone quarries. Today the town is a tourist center with a well-marked, centralized downtown that is easy to navigate on foot. Walk past shops and colorful clapboard houses to the end of Bearskin Neck for an impressive view of the Atlantic Ocean and the old, weather-beaten lobster shack known as "Motif No. 1" because of its popularity as a subject for amateur painters and photographers.

ESSENTIALS

Visitor Information Rockport Chamber of Commerce ⊠ *33 Commercial St., Gloucester* ☎ *978/546–6575* ⊕ *www.rockportusa.com.*

2

WHERE TO EAT AND STAY

For expanded hotel reviews, visit Fodors.com.

$$ SEAFOOD 🍴 **Brackett's Ocean View.** A big bay window in this quiet, homey restaurant provides an excellent view across Sandy Bay. The menu includes chowders, fish cakes, and other seafood dishes. [$] *Average main: $18* ✉ *25 Main St.* ☎ *978/546–2797* 🌐 *www.bracketts.com* ⏲ *Closed Mon. and Tues. and Nov.–mid-Apr.*

$ ★ 🏨 **Addison Choate Inn.** Just a minute's walk from both the center of Rockport and the train station, this 1851 inn sits in a prime location. **Pros:** proximity to the ocean, shopping, and train station. **Cons:** only one bedroom on the first floor. [$] *Rooms from: $159* ✉ *49 Broadway* ☎ *978/546–7543, 800/245–7543* 🌐 *www.addisonchoateinn.com* 🛏 *5 rooms* ⏲ *Closed Nov.–Mar.* 🍽 *Breakfast.*

$ Fodor's Choice ★ 🏨 **Sally Webster Inn.** This inn was named for a member of Hannah Jumper's "Hatchet Gang," teetotalers who smashed up the town's liquor stores in 1856 and turned Rockport into the dry town it remained until as recently as 2007. **Pros:** homey atmosphere in an excellent location with attentive staff. **Cons:** some rooms accessed via stairs. [$] *Rooms from: $120* ✉ *34 Mt. Pleasant St.* ☎ *978/546–9251* 🌐 *www.sallywebster.com* 🛏 *7 rooms* 🍽 *Breakfast.*

ESSEX

35 miles northeast of Boston, 12 miles west of Rockport.

The small seafaring town of Essex, once an important shipbuilding center, is surrounded by salt marshes and is filled with antiques stores and seafood restaurants.

GETTING HERE AND AROUND

Head west out of Cape Ann on Rte. 128, turning north on Rte. 133.

ESSENTIALS

Visitor Information Escape to Essex 🌐 www.visitessexma.com.

EXPLORING

👶 **Essex Shipbuilding Museum.** At what is still an active shipyard, this museum traces the evolution of the American schooner, which was first created in Essex. The museum sometimes offers shipbuilding demonstrations. One-hour tours take in the museum's many buildings and boats, especially the *Evelina M. Goulart*—one of only seven remaining Essex-built schooners. ✉ *66 Main St.(Rte. 133)* ☎ *978/768–7541* 🌐 *www.essexshipbuildingmuseum.org* 🎟 *$7* ⏲ *Mid-Oct.–mid-May, weekends 10–5; mid-May–mid-Oct., Wed.–Sun. 10–5.*

WHERE TO EAT

$ SEAFOOD Fodor's Choice ★ 🍴 **Woodman's of Essex.** According to local legend, this is where Lawrence "Chubby" Woodman invented the first fried clam back in 1916. Today this sprawling wooden shack with indoor booths and outdoor picnic tables is *the* place for seafood in the rough. Besides fried clams, you can tuck into clam chowder, lobster rolls, or the popular "downriver" lobster combo. [$] *Average main: $16* ✉ *121 Main St.(Rte. 133)* ☎ *978/768–2559, 800/649–1773* 🌐 *www.woodmans.com.*

IPSWICH

30 miles north of Boston, 6 miles northwest of Essex.

Quiet little Ipswich, settled in 1633 and famous for its clams, is said to have more 17th-century houses standing and occupied than any other place in America; more than 40 were built before 1725. Information and a booklet with a suggested walking tour are available at the **Ipswich Visitor Information Center**.

ESSENTIALS

Visitor Information Ipswich Visitor Information Center ⊠ *36 S. Main St. (Rte. 1A)* ☎ *978/356–8540* ⊕ *www.ipswichma.com* ⊙ *Closed Nov.–Apr..*

EXPLORING

Castle Hill on the Crane Estate. This 59-room Stuart-style mansion, built in 1927 for Richard Crane—of the Crane plumbing company—and his family, is part of the Crane Estate, a stretch of more than 2,100 acres along the Essex and Ipswich rivers, encompassing Castle Hill, Crane Beach, and the Crane Wildlife Refuge. Although the original furnishings were sold at auction, the mansion has been elaborately refurnished in period style; photographs in most of the rooms show their original appearance. The Great House is open for one-hour tours and also hosts concerts and other events. Inquire about seasonal programs like fly-fishing or kayaking. If you're looking for an opulent and exquisite overnight stay, book a room at the on-site Inn at Castle Hill. ⊠ *Argilla Rd.* ☎ *978/356–4351* ⊕ *www.thetrustees.org* ▱ *Fees vary; call or check website* ⊙ *Memorial Day–Columbus Day weekend, Wed.–Sat., call for hrs.*

SPORTS AND THE OUTDOORS

BEACHES
★
Crane Beach. Crane Beach, one of New England's most beautiful beaches, is a sandy, 4-mile-long stretch backed by dunes and a nature trail. Public parking is available, but on a nice summer weekend it's usually full before lunch. There are lifeguards, a snack bar, and changing rooms. Check ahead before visiting mid-July to early August, when greenhead flies terrorize sunbathers. ■ TIP➔ **The Ipswich Essex Explorer bus runs between the Ipswich train station and Crane Beach weekends and holidays from June to September; the $5 pass includes round-trip bus fare and beach admission. Contact the Ipswich Visitor Information Center for information.** ⊠ *Argilla Rd.* ☎ *978/356–4354* ⊕ *www.thetrustees.org* ▱ *$2 on foot or by bike; additional charges apply if you arrive by car. Check website for details. Parking $15 weekdays, $25 weekends mid-May–early Sept.; $7 early Sept.–mid-May* ⊙ *Daily 8–sunset.*

HIKING
Ipswich River Wildlife Sanctuary. The Massachusetts Audubon Society's Ipswich River Wildlife Sanctuary has trails through marshland hills, where there are remains of early Colonial settlements as well as abundant wildlife. Make sure to grab some birdseed and get a trail map from the office. Enjoy bridges, man-made rock structures, and other surprises on the Rockery Trail. ⊠ *87 Perkins Row, southwest of Ipswich, 1 mile off Rte. 97, Topsfield* ☎ *978/887–9264* ⊕ *www.massaudubon.org* ▱ *$4* ⊙ *Office May–Oct., Tues.–Sun. 9–5; Nov.–Apr., Tues.–Sun. 9–4. Trails Tues.–Sun. dawn–dusk. Also open Mon. holidays.*

WHERE TO EAT

$ SEAFOOD Fodor's Choice ★ 🍴 **Clam Box.** Shaped like a giant fried clam box, this small roadside stand is the best place to sample Ipswich's famous bivalves. Since 1938 locals and tourists have been lining up for clams, oysters, scallops, and onion rings. [$] *Average main: $14* ✉ *246 High St.(Rte. 1A)* ☎ *978/356–9707* 🌐 *www.ipswichma.com/clambox* ✍ *Reservations not accepted* 🕒 *Closed late Nov.–Feb.*

$ SEAFOOD 🍴 **Stone Soup Café.** This cheery café provides consistently good food. Excellent breakfasts include omelets, French toast, and assorted pancakes; lunch features chowders, pot roast, or delicious Cuban sandwiches. Its clam chowder took home the town's annual prize six years in a row. Dinner can include lobster bisque, porcini ravioli, or whatever contemporary fare the chef is inspired to cook from the day's farm-stand finds. [$] *Average main: $8* ✉ *141 High St., off Rte. 1A* ☎ *978/356–4222* 💳 *No credit cards* 🕒 *Closed Tues. Call for off-season hrs.*

NEWBURYPORT

38 miles north of Boston, 12 miles north of Ipswich on Rte. 1A.

Newburyport's High Street is lined with some of the finest examples of Federal-period (roughly, 1790–1810) mansions in New England. The city was once a leading port and shipbuilding center; the houses were built for prosperous sea captains. Although Newburyport's maritime significance ended with the decline of the clipper ships, the town was revived in the 1970s. Today the town has shops, restaurants, galleries, and a waterfront park and boardwalk. Newburyport is walker-friendly, with well-marked restrooms and free parking all day down by the water.

A stroll through the **Waterfront Park and Promenade** offers a view of the harbor as well as the fishing and pleasure boats that moor here.

A causeway leads from Newburyport to a narrow piece of land known as Plum Island, which harbors a summer colony at one end.

EXPLORING

Custom House Maritime Museum. Built in 1835 in Greek Revival style, this museum contains exhibits on maritime history, ship models, tools, and paintings. ✉ *25 Water St.* ☎ *978/462–8681* 🌐 *www.customhousemaritimemuseum.org* 🎫 *$7* 🕒 *Mid-May–mid-Dec., Tues.–Sat. 10–4, Sun. noon–4.*

SPORTS AND THE OUTDOORS

Parker River National Wildlife Refuge. On Plum Island, this 4,662-acre refuge of salt marsh, freshwater marsh, beaches, and dunes is one of the few natural barrier beach–dune–salt marsh complexes left on the Northeast coast. Here you can bird-watch, fish, swim, and pick plums and cranberries. The refuge is a popular place in summer, especially on weekends; cars begin to line up at the gate before 7 am. There's no restriction on the number of people using the beach, but only a limited number of cars are let in; no pets are allowed in the refuge. ✉ *6 Plum Island Tpke.* ☎ *978/465–5753* 🌐 *www.fws.gov/northeast/parkerriver* 🎫 *$5 per car, bicycles and walk-ins $2* 🕒 *Daily dawn–dusk. Beach usually closed during nesting season in spring and early summer.*

BEACH Fodor's Choice ★ **Salisbury Beach State Reservation.** Relax at the long sandy beach, launch a boat, or just enjoy the water. From Newburyport center, follow Bridge Road north, take a right on Beach Road, and follow it until you reach State Reservation Road. The park is popular with campers; reservations in summer are made many months ahead to ensure a spot. ✉ *Rte. 1A, 5 miles northeast of Newburyport, Salisbury* ☎ *978/462–4481* 🌐 *www.mass.gov/dcr/parks/northeast/salb.htm* 🎟 *Beach free, parking $9.*

SHOPPING

Todd Farm Flea Market. A New England tradition since 1971, the Todd Farm Flea Market features up to 240 vendors from all over New England and New York. It's open every Sunday from mid-April through late November, though its busiest months are May, September, and October. Merchandise varies from antique furniture, clocks, jewelry, recordings, and tools to fishing rods, golf accessories, honey products, cedar fencing, vintage toys, and seasonal plants and flowers. Antiques hunters often arrive before the sun comes up for the best deals. ✉ *285 Main St., Rte. 1A, Rowley* ☎ *978/948–3300* 🌐 *www.toddfarm.com* 🕒 *Apr.–Nov., Sun. 5 am–3 pm.*

WHERE TO EAT AND STAY

For expanded hotel reviews, visit Fodors.com.

$$ SEAFOOD 🍴 **Glenn's Restaurant & Cool Bar.** A block from the waterfront parking lot, Glenn's offers creative combinations from around the world, with the occasional New England twist. The ever-changing menu might include sesame-crusted yellowfin tuna or house-smoked baby-back ribs. There's live jazz or blues on Sunday. [$] *Average main: $23* ✉ *44 Merrimac St.* ☎ *978/465–3811* 🌐 *www.glennsrestaurant.com* 🕒 *Closed Mon. No lunch.*

$ ★ 🏨 **Clark Currier Inn.** Once the home of the 19th-century sea captain Thomas March Clark, this 1803 Federal mansion has been beautifully restored. **Pros:** easy to find; close to shopping and the oceanfront; good for couples looking for a peaceful and quiet experience. **Cons:** children under 10 not allowed; rooms can get hot in summer. [$] *Rooms from: $145* ✉ *45 Green St.* ☎ *978/465–8363* 🌐 *www.clarkcurrierinn.com* 🛏 *7 rooms, 1 suite* 🍽 *Breakfast.*

SOUTH OF BOSTON

People from all over the world travel south of Boston to visit Plymouth for a glimpse into the country's earliest beginnings. The two main stops are the Plimoth Plantation, which re-creates the everyday life of the Pilgrims; and the *Mayflower II*, which gives you an idea of how frightening the journey across the Atlantic must have been. As you may guess, November in Plymouth brings special events focused on Thanksgiving. Farther south, New Bedford recalls the world of whaling.

EN ROUTE

While driving from Boston to Plymouth, stop at **Quincy**, to visit the Adams National Historic Park.

Adams National Historic Park. The Adams National Historic Park contains the birthplaces, homes, and graves of Presidents John Adams and his son John Quincy Adams. You can stop by for a guided visit or see it as part of a trolley tour of the property and family church. ⊠ *Carriage house, 135 Adams St., visitor center and bookstore, 1250 Hancock St., Quincy* ☎ *617/770–1175* ⊕ *www.nps.gov/adam* ☎ *$5* ⊙ *Tours 9–5 daily; last tour at 3:15, mid-Apr.–mid-Nov.*

PLYMOUTH

40 miles south of Boston.

On December 26, 1620, 102 weary men, women, and children disembarked from the *Mayflower* to found the first permanent European settlement north of Virginia. Today Plymouth is characterized by narrow streets, clapboard mansions, shops, antiques stores, and a scenic waterfront. To mark Thanksgiving, the town holds a parade, historic-house tours, and other activities. Historic statues dot the town, including depictions of William Bradford, Pilgrim leader and governor of Plymouth Colony for more than 30 years, on Water Street; a Pilgrim maiden in Brewster Gardens; and Massasoit, the Wampanoag chief who helped the Pilgrims survive, on Carver Street.

ESSENTIALS

Visitor Information Plymouth Visitor Information Center ⊠ *170 Water St., at Hwy. 44* ☎ *508/747–7533, 800/872–1620* ⊕ *www.visit-plymouth.com.*

EXPLORING

★ **Mayflower II.** This seaworthy replica of the 1620 *Mayflower* was built in England through research and a bit of guesswork, then sailed across the Atlantic in 1957. As you explore the interior and exterior of the ship, sailors in modern dress answer your questions about both the reproduction and the original ship, while costumed guides provide a 17th-century perspective. Plymouth Rock is nearby. ⊠ *State Pier* ☎ *508/746–1622* ⊕ *www.plimoth.org/features/mayflower-2* ☎ *$10, $28 with admission to Plimoth Plantation* ⊙ *Late Mar.–Nov., daily 9–5.*

Fodor's Choice **Plimoth Plantation.** Over the entrance to this popular attraction is the cau-
★ tion: You are now entering 1627. Believe it. Against the backdrop of the
☺ Atlantic Ocean, and 3 miles south of downtown Plymouth, this Pilgrim village has been carefully re-created, from the thatch roofs, cramped quarters, and open fireplaces to the long-horned livestock. Throw away your preconception of white collars and funny hats; through ongoing research, the Plimoth staff has developed a portrait of the Pilgrims that's more complex than the dour folk in school textbooks. Listen to the accents of the "residents," who never break out of character. You might see them plucking ducks, cooking rabbit stew, or tending gardens. Feel free to engage them in conversation about their life, but expect only curious looks if you ask about anything that happened after 1627. "Thanksgiving: Memory, Myth & Meaning," an exhibit in the visitor center, offers a fresh perspective on the 1621 harvest celebration that is now known as "the first Thanksgiving." Note that there's not a lot of shade here in summer. ⊠ *137 Warren Ave.(Hwy. 3A)* ☎ *508/746–1622* ⊕ *www.plimoth.org* ☎ *$24, $28 with Mayflower II* ⊙ *Late Mar.–Nov., daily 9–5.*

2

★ **Plymouth Rock.** This landmark rock, just a few dozen yards from the *Mayflower II*, is popularly believed to have been the Pilgrims' stepping-stone when they left the ship. Given the stone's unimpressive appearance—it's little more than a boulder—and dubious authenticity (as explained on a nearby plaque), the grand canopy overhead seems a trifle ostentatious.

Sparrow House. Built in 1640, this is Plymouth's oldest structure. It is among several historic houses in town that are open for visits. You can peek into a pair of rooms furnished in the spartan style of the Pilgrims' era. The contemporary crafts gallery also on the premises seems somewhat incongruous, but the works on view are of high quality. ✉ *42 Summer St.* ☎ *508/747–1240* ⊕ *www.sparrowhouse.com* ☛ *House $2, gallery free* ⊙ *Open daily 10–5.*

WHERE TO EAT AND STAY

For expanded hotel reviews, visit Fodors.com.

$ ✕ **Blue-eyed Crab Grille & Raw Bar.** Grab a seat on the outside deck over-
SEAFOOD looking the water at this friendly, somewhat funky (plastic fish dangling from the ceiling), fresh-fish shack. If the local Island Creek raw oysters are on the menu, go for them! Otherwise start with thick crab bisque full of hunks of floating crabmeat or the steamed mussels. Dinner entrées include seafood stew with chorizo and sweet potatoes and the classic fish-and-chips. Locals come for the brunch specials, too, like grilled shrimp and poached eggs over red-pepper grits, the lobster omelet, and banana-ginger pancakes. $ *Average main: $17* ✉ *170 Water St.* ☎ *508/747–6776* ⊕ *www.blueeyedcrab.com.*

$ ▦ **Best Western Cold Spring.** Walk to the waterfront and downtown Plymouth from this clean, family-friendly, two-story motel. **Pros:** half mile from Plymouth Rock and *Mayflower II;* some of the best wallet-pleasing rates in the area; friendly owners. **Cons:** basic rooms without much character. $ *Rooms from: $140* ✉ *188 Court St.* ☎ *508/746–2222, 800/678–8667* ⊕ *www.bestwesternmassachusetts.com* ⟿ *56 rooms.*

$ ▦ **John Carver Inn & Spa.** This three-story Colonial-style redbrick building is steps from Plymouth's main attractions. **Pros:** waterfront setting. **Cons:** pool is noisy and often overcrowded; some rooms need updating. $ *Rooms from: $99* ✉ *25 Summer St.* ☎ *508/746–7100, 800/274–1620* ⊕ *www.johncarverinn.com* ⟿ *74 rooms, 6 suites.*

NEW BEDFORD

45 miles southwest of Plymouth, 50 miles south of Boston.

In 1652 colonists from Plymouth settled in the area that now includes the city of New Bedford. The city has a long maritime tradition, beginning as a shipbuilding center and small whaling port in the late 1700s. By the mid-1800s it had developed into a center of North American whaling. Today New Bedford has the largest fishing fleet on the East Coast. Although much of the town is industrial, the restored historic district near the water is a delight. It was here that Herman Melville set his masterpiece, *Moby-Dick*, a novel about whaling.

ESSENTIALS

Visitor Information New Bedford Office of Tourism ✉ *Waterfront Visitor Center, Pier 3* ☎ *800/508–5353* 🌐 *www.newbedford-ma.gov/Tourism/DestinationNB/visitorcenter.html.*

EXPLORING

👋 **New Bedford Whaling Museum.** Established in 1903, this is the world's largest museum of its kind. A highlight is the skeleton of a 66-foot blue whale, one of only three on view anywhere. An interactive exhibit lets you listen to the underwater sounds of whales, dolphins, and other sea life—plus the sounds of a thunderstorm and a whale-watching boat—as a whale might hear them. You can also peruse the collection of scrimshaw, visit exhibits on regional history, and climb aboard an 89-foot, half-scale model of the 1826 whaling ship *Lagoda*—the world's largest ship model. A small chapel across the street from the museum is the one described in *Moby-Dick*. ✉ *18 Johnny Cake Hill* ☎ *508/997–0046* 🌐 *www.whalingmuseum.org* 🎟 *$10* 🕒 *Jan.–May, Mon.–Sat. 9–4, Sun. noon–4; June–Dec., daily 9–5.*

New Bedford Whaling National Historical Park. The city's whaling tradition is commemorated at this park that takes up 13 blocks of the waterfront historic district. The park visitor center, housed in an 1853 Greek Revival building that was once a bank, provides maps and information about whaling-related sites. Free walking tours of the park leave from the visitor center at 10:30, 12:30, and 2:30 in July and August. ✉ *33 William St.* ☎ *508/996–4095* 🌐 *www.nps.gov/nebe* 🎟 *Free* 🕒 *Daily 9–5.*

WHERE TO EAT

$ PORTUGUESE 🍴 **Antonio's.** Expect the wait to be long and the dining room to be loud, but it's worth the hassle to sample the traditional fare of New Bedford's large Portuguese population at this friendly, unadorned restaurant. Dishes include hearty portions of pork and shellfish stew, *bacalau* (salt cod), and grilled sardines, often on plates piled high with crispy fried potatoes and rice. [$] *Average main: $15* ✉ *267 Coggeshall St., near intersection of I–195 and Hwy. 18* ☎ *508/990–3636* 🌐 *www.antoniosnewbedford.com* 💳 *No credit cards.*

$ SEAFOOD 🍴 **Davy's Locker.** A huge seafood menu is the main draw at this spot overlooking Buzzards Bay. Choose from more than a dozen shrimp preparations, or a choice of healthful entrées—dishes prepared with olive oil, vegetables, garlic, and herbs. For landlubbers, chicken, steak, ribs, and the like are also available. [$] *Average main: $14* ✉ *1480 E. Rodney French Blvd.* ☎ *508/992–7359* 🌐 *www.davyslockerrestaurant.com.*

Cape Cod, Martha's Vineyard, and Nantucket

WORD OF MOUTH

"Route 6A is known as 'Old Kings Highway,' and traveling along this incredibly scenic two-lane road is like a trip back to Colonial days. Lots of old sea captains' homes (especially in Brewster), antiques shops, taverns and inns, art galleries, museums, and peeks of Cape Cod Bay here and there along the way."

— caper64

WELCOME TO CAPE COD, MARTHA'S VINEYARD, AND NANTUCKET

TOP REASONS TO GO

★ **Beaches:** Cape Cod's picturesque beaches are the ultimate reason to go. The high sand dunes, gorgeous sunsets, and never-ending sea will get you every time.

★ **Visiting Lighthouses:** Lighthouses rise along Cape Cod's coast like architectural exclamation marks. Highlights include Eastham's beautiful Nauset Light and Chatham and Nobska Lights for their spectacular views.

★ **Biking the Trails:** The Cape Cod Rail Trail from South Dennis to south Wellfleet is the definitive bike route, with 25 miles of relatively flat terrain. Martha's Vineyard and Nantucket have dedicated bike paths.

★ **Setting Sail:** Area tour operators offer everything from sunset schooner cruises to charter fishing expeditions. Mid-April through October, whale-watching adventures are popular.

★ **Browsing the Galleries:** The Cape was a prominent art colony in the 19th century and today it has a number of galleries.

1 Cape Cod. Typically divided into regions—the Upper, Mid, Lower, and Outer—Cape Cod is a place of many moods. The Upper Cape (closest to the bridges) has Cape Cod's oldest towns, plus fine beaches and fascinating little museums. The Mid Cape has sophisticated Colonial-era hamlets but also motels and miniature golf courses. In the midst of it all sits Hyannis, the Cape's unofficial capital. The Lower Cape has casual clam shacks, lovely lighthouses, funky art galleries, and stellar natural attractions. The narrow "forearm" of the Outer Cape is famous for sand dunes, crashing surf, and scrubby pines. Frenetic and fun-loving Provincetown is a leading gay getaway.

2 Martha's Vineyard. The Vineyard lies 5 miles off the Cape's southwest tip. The Down-Island towns are the most popular and most populated, but much of what makes this island special is found in its rural Up-Island reaches where dirt roads lead past crystalline ponds, cranberry bogs, and conservation lands.

3 **Nantucket.** Nantucket, or "Far Away Island" in the Wampanoag tongue, is some 25 miles south of Hyannis. Ferries dock in pretty Nantucket Town, where tourism services are concentrated. The rest of the island is mostly residential (trophy houses abound), and nearly all roads terminate in tiny beach communities.

GETTING ORIENTED

3

Henry David Thoreau, who famously traveled the sparsely populated mid-19th-century Cape Cod, likened the peninsula to "a bare and bended arm." Indeed—looking at a map the outline is obvious, and many people hold their own arm aloft and point to various places from shoulder to fist when asked for directions. There are three main roads that travel, more or less, the entire Cape: U.S. Highway 6, Route 28, and Route 6A, a designated historic road also called the Old King's Highway. Most visitors stick to these main byways, though the back roads can save time and aggravation in summer. The Cape is surrounded by water, though it's not a true island. Several bodies of water define the peninsula's land and seascapes: Just off the mainland to the southeast are the gentler, warmer waters of Buzzards Bay, Vineyard Sound, and Nantucket Sound. Cape Cod Bay extends north to the tip of Provincetown, where it meets the Atlantic Ocean.

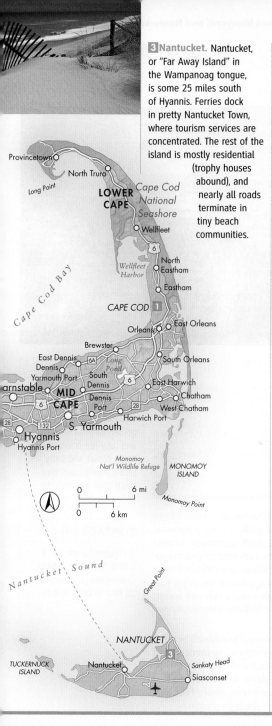

CAPE COD NATIONAL SEASHORE

John F. Kennedy certainly knew a good thing when he saw it. During his presidency, Kennedy marked off a magnificent 40-mile swath of the Massachusetts coast, protecting it for future generations. Today the Cape Cod National Seashore remains the Cape's signature site.

Encompassing more than 44,000 acres of coastline from Chatham to Provincetown, the park is truly a national treasure. Without protection, such expansive beauty would surely have been lost to rampant overdevelopment long ago. Within its borders are extraordinary ocean beaches, dramatic dunes, ancient swamps, salt marshes, and wetlands; pitch-pine and scrub-oak forest; much wildlife; and a number of historic structures open for touring.

There's no question that the National Seashore's beaches are the main attractions for sunbathers, swimmers, and surfers. It's not at all uncommon for the parking lots to fill up by 11 am on hot, sunny days. Arrive early to find your spot on the sand, or venture out on some of the less-traveled trails to find solitude in the high season.

BEST TIME TO GO

Swimming is best in summer; the park becomes sublime in the fall with golden salt-marsh grasses and ruby-red cranberry bogs. Winter and early spring nearly guarantee you'll have the place to yourself.

CONTACT INFO

✉ *Doane Rd. off U.S. 6 02642* ☎ *508/255–3421* ⊕ *www.nps.gov/caco* 🎟 *Free* ⏱ *Daily 9–4:30*

BEST WAYS TO EXPLORE

TAKE A WALK

Walking the marked trails, beaches, and wooded fire roads is an excellent way to truly experience the diverse natural splendor within the park. There are 11 self-guided trails that begin at various points, leading through shaded swamps, alongside marshes, and through meadows, forest, and dunes. Most of the terrain is flat and sometimes sandy.

RIDE A BIKE

Three well-maintained bicycle trails run through parts of the park. In Eastham, the short Nauset Trail heads from the Salt Pond Visitor Center through the woods and out to Coast Guard Beach. Truro's Head, off the Meadow Trail, edges a large salt meadow that's an ideal place for birding. The most physically demanding—and most dramatic—of the park's bike trails is the Province Lands Trail, more than 7 miles of steep hills and hairpin curves through forest and sand dunes. Mountain bikers can make their own trails on the miles of fire roads.

SEE THE SIGHTS

Several historic homes and sites are open for touring; there are also a few notable overlooks easily accessible by car. Climb the steep steps of lighthouses in Eastham and Truro or see rescue reenacts at the Old Harbor Life-Saving Station in Provincetown. Scenic overlooks include Eastham's exquisite Fort Hill area; Wellfleet's Marconi Station Site, where the first transatlantic wireless message was sent in 1903; Truro's Pilgrim Heights; and Provincetown's scenic 2-mile Race Point Road.

TOUR WITH A RANGER

From mid-April through Thanksgiving there is a full schedule of mostly free ranger-guided activities. Combining history, folklore, science, and nature, rangers take visitors right to the source, whether for a full-moon hike in the dunes, a campfire on the beach, a paddling trip, or a photography workshop.

SHIFTING SANDS

Forged by massive moving glaciers more than 20,000 years ago, Cape Cod's landscape is still in perpetual motion, continually shaped by the powerful forces of sand, wind, and water. The Cape's land is slowly giving way to rising ocean levels and erosion, losing an average of nearly 4 feet of outer beach per year. Many a home or structure has succumbed to the unrelenting ocean over the years; some—like Truro's Highland Light and Eastham's Nauset Light—have been moved to safety. Eventually Cape Cod will likely be lost to the sea, though not for thousands of years.

You'll see many signs on beaches and trails asking walkers to keep off the dunes. Take heed, for much of the fragile landscape of the outer Cape is held together by its dune formations and the vegetation that grows within them.

CAPE COD, MARTHA'S VINEYARD, AND NANTUCKET BEST BEACHES

Blessed by a great variety of surrounding waters, Cape Cod, Martha's Vineyard, and Nantucket boast some of the world's best beaches. They face the wild, bracing surf of the Atlantic Ocean on one side, while the warmer and gentler waters of Cape Cod Bay or the Nantucket Sound sweep the opposite shores.

Cape Cod alone has more than 150 beaches—enough to keep the most inveterate beachcomber busy all year long. One can still capture that sense of adventure that enchanted Thoreau so long ago while walking the isolated stretches of towering dune-backed beaches from Eastham to Provincetown. Families love the easy access and more placid beaches of the bay and sound, which tend to be more crowded. If saltwater isn't your thing, the Cape has dozens of freshwater kettle holes inland that were carved in the far-distant past by receding glaciers. Aside from warm, salt-free water, some—like Scargo Lake in Dennis—are also blessed with sandy beaches.

HISTORY LESSON

In this centuries-old area even a fun-in-the-sun day can double as a history lesson. In the Lower Cape, Eastham's popular **First Encounter Beach** has a bronze plaque that marks the spot where Myles Standish and his *Mayflower* buddies first encountered Native Americans in 1620.

UPPER CAPE

For Families: Parents love **Old Silver**—a long crescent of soft white sand in North Falmouth—for its comparatively calm, warm water, and kids like poking around the shallow tidal pools full of sea life.

MID CAPE

For Wanderers: Stretching some 6 miles across a peninsula that ends at Sandy Neck Light, **Sandy Neck Beach** in West Barnstable offers a spectacular combination of sand, sea, and dunes perfect for strolling and watching the plentiful birdlife.

For Active Types: Encompassing 1.5 miles of soft white sand on Nantucket Sound, busy West Dennis Beach has plenty of space to try windsurfing, play a game of beach volleyball, or just sit back and enjoy the people-watching.

LOWER CAPE

For Traditionalists: Locals contend that Eastham's **Nauset Light Beach and Coast Guard Beach**, both set within the **Cape Cod National Seashore**, are the quintessential beaches. Combining serious surf, sweeping expanses of sand, magnificent dunes, and mesmerizing views, these spots deliver on the wow factor.

For Bird-Watchers: On the barrier beaches of the **Monomoy National Wildlife Refuge,** accessible by boat tours from Chatham, you're bound to see more sandpipers and plovers than people. Summer

through early fall, shorebirds and waterfowl flock here to nest, rest, and feast in tidal flats.

OUTER CAPE

For Surfers: Wave-blasted **White Crest Beach** in Wellfleet is one of the preeminent places on the peninsula to Hang 10.

For Views: After the winding drive amid the dunes and scrub in the National Seashore, **Race Point Beach** in Provincetown literally is the end of the road. Cape Cod Bay and the Atlantic meet here in a powerful tumbling of waves; views are vast and include extraordinary sunsets as well whale sightings.

For Night Owls: After-hours it's tough to beat **Cahoon Hollow Beach** in Wellfleet. The water here is chilly but the music at the Beachcomber bar and restaurant is hot.

MARTHA'S VINEYARD

For Photographers: Perhaps no beach in this camera-ready region is more photogenic than that below the **Aquinnah Cliffs**. The multicolored clay cliffs face west allowing for gorgeous shots at sunset.

NANTUCKET

For Sand Castle Connoisseurs: Jetties Beach has the finest sand castle building material. Hordes gather to prove it during Sandcastle & Sculpture Day, held annually in mid-August.

Updated by Laura V. Scheel

Even if you haven't visited Cape Cod and Islands, you can likely—and accurately—imagine "sand dunes and salty air, quaint little villages here and there." As the 1950s Patti Page song promises, "you're sure to fall in love with old Cape Cod."

Cape Codders are fiercely protective of the environment. Despite some occasionally rampant development, planners have been careful to preserve nature and encourage responsible, eco-conscious building. Nearly 30% of the Cape's 412 square miles is protected from development, and another 35% has not yet been developed (on Nantucket and Martha's Vineyard, the percentages of protected land are far higher). Opportunities for sports and recreation abound, as the region is rife with biking and hiking trails, serene beaches, and waterways for boating and fishing. One somewhat controversial potential development has been a large-scale "wind farm" in Nantucket Sound, comprising some 130 turbines, each about 260 feet tall and several miles offshore.

The area is also rich in history. Many don't realize that the Pilgrims landed here first: in November 1620, the lost and travel-weary sailors dropped anchor in what is now Provincetown Harbor and spent five weeks here, scouring the area for food and possible settlement. Were it not for the aid of the resident Native Americans, the strangers would have barely survived. Even so, they set sail again for fairer lands, ending up across Cape Cod Bay in Plymouth.

Virtually every period style of residential American architecture is well represented on Cape Cod, including—of course—that seminal form named for the region, the Cape-style house. These low, one-and-a-half-story domiciles with clapboard or shingle (more traditionally the latter in these parts) siding and gable roofs have been a fixture throughout Cape Cod since the late 17th century. You'll also find grand Georgian and Federal mansions from the Colonial era, as well as handsome Greek Revival, Italianate, and Second Empire houses that date to Victorian times. Many of the most prominent residences were built for ship captains and sea merchants. In recent decades, the region has seen an influx of angular, glassy, contemporary homes, many with soaring windows and skylights and massive wraparound porches that take advantage of their enviable sea views.

PLANNING

WHEN TO GO

The Cape and Islands teem with activity during high season: roughly late June to Labor Day. If you're dreaming of a classic shore vacation, this is prime time.

However, with the dream come daunting crowds and high costs. Fall has begun to rival summer in popularity, at least on weekends through late October, when the weather is temperate and the scenery remarkable. Many restaurants, shops, and hotels remain open in winter, too, making the area desirable even during the coldest months. The region enjoys fairly moderate weather most of the year, with highs typically in the upper 70s and 80s in summer, and in the upper 30s and lower 40s in winter. Snow and rain are not uncommon during the cooler months, and it can be windy any time.

HYANNIS AVG. TEMPS.

JAN.	FEB.	MAR.	APR.	MAY	JUNE
40°F/4°C	41°F/5°C	42°F/6°C	53°F/12°C	62°F/17°C	71F 22C

JULY	AUG.	SEPT.	OCT.	NOV.	DEC.
78°F/26°C	76°F/24°C	70°F/21°C	59°F/15°C	49°F/9°C	40F 4C

PLANNING YOUR TIME

The region can be enjoyed for a few days or a few weeks, depending on the nature of your trip. As the towns are all quite distinct on Cape Cod, it's best to cater your trip based on your interests: an outdoors enthusiast would want to head to the National Seashore region; those who prefer shopping and amusements would do better in the Mid-Cape area. As one Fodors.com forum member noted, the Cape is generally "not something to see . . . instead, people go to spend a few days or weeks, relax, go to the beach . . . that sort of thing." A full-day trip to Nantucket to wander the historic downtown is manageable; several days is best to appreciate Martha's Vineyard's diversity.

GETTING HERE AND AROUND

⇨ See specific towns for more information.

AIR TRAVEL

The major air gateways are Boston's Logan International Airport and Providence's T. F. Green International Airport. Smaller municipal airports are in Barnstable, Martha's Vineyard, Nantucket, and Provincetown.

CAR TRAVEL

Cape Cod is easily reached from Boston via Route 3 and from Providence via I–195. Once you cross Cape Cod Canal, you can follow U.S. 6. Without any traffic, it takes about an hour to 90 minutes to reach the canal from either Boston or Providence. Allow an extra 30 to 60 minutes' travel time in peak periods.

Parking, in general, can be a challenge in summer, especially in congested downtowns and at popular beaches. If you can walk, bike, carpool, or cab it somewhere, do so. But unless you are planning to focus your attention on a single community, you'll probably need a car. Taking a vehicle onto the island ferries is expensive and requires reservations (another option is renting upon arrival).

FERRY TRAVEL
Martha's Vineyard and Nantucket are easily reached by passenger ferries (traditional and high-speed boats) from several Cape towns. Trip times vary from as little as 45 minutes to about two hours and range in price from about $8 one-way up to $35. In season, ferries connect Boston and Plymouth with Provincetown.

RESTAURANTS
Cape Cod kitchens have long been closely associated with seafood—the waters off the Cape and Islands yield a bounty of lobsters, clams, oysters, scallops, and myriad fish that make their way onto local menus. In addition to the region's strong Portuguese influence, globally inspired and contemporary fare commonly flavor restaurant offerings. Also gaining in popularity is the use of locally—and often organically—raised produce, meat, and dairy.

Note that ordering an expensive lobster dinner may push your meal into a higher price category than this guide's price range shows for the restaurant.

You can indulge in fresh local seafood and clambakes at seat-yourself shanties for a lower price than at their fine-dining counterparts. Often, the tackier the style (plastic fish on the walls), the better the seafood. These laid-back local haunts usually operate a fish market on the premises and are in every town on the Cape. *Prices in the reviews are the average cost of a main course at dinner or, if dinner is not served, at lunch.*

HOTELS
Dozens of heritage buildings now welcome overnight guests, so you can bed down in a former sea captain's home or a converted church. Scores of rental homes and condominiums are available for long-term stays. Several large resorts encompass numerous amenities—swimming, golf, restaurants, children's programs—all on one property, but often lack the intimate charm and serenity of the smaller establishments. Large chain hotels exist in very small numbers in the region; the vast majority of lodging properties are locally owned. You'll want to make reservations for inns well in advance during peak summer periods. Smoking is prohibited in all Massachusetts hotels. For more information on the state-park camping areas on Cape Cod, contact the Massachusetts Department of Conservation and Recreation (☎ 617/626–1250 ⊕ *www. mass.gov/dcr/forparks.htm*). *Prices in the reviews are the lowest cost of a standard double room in high season.*

CAPE COD

Continually shaped by ocean currents, this windswept land of sandy beaches and dunes has compelling natural beauty. Everyone comes for the seaside, yet the crimson cranberry bogs, forests of birch and beech, freshwater ponds, and marshlands that grace the interior are just as splendid. Local history is fascinating; whale-watching provides an exhilarating experience of the natural world; cycling trails lace the landscape; shops purvey everything from antiques to pure kitsch; and you can dine on simple fresh seafood, creative contemporary cuisine, or most anything in between.

Separated from the Massachusetts mainland by the 17.5-mile Cape Cod Canal—at 480 feet, the world's widest sea-level canal—and linked to it by two heavily trafficked bridges, the Cape is likened in shape to an outstretched arm bent at the elbow, its Provincetown fist turned back toward the mainland.

Each of the Cape's 15 towns is broken up into villages, which is where things can get complicated. The town of Barnstable, for example, consists of Barnstable, West Barnstable, Cotuit, Marston Mills, Osterville, Centerville, and Hyannis. The terms Upper Cape and Lower Cape can also be confusing. Upper Cape—think upper arm, as in the shape of the Cape—refers to the towns of Bourne, Sandwich, Falmouth, and Mashpee. Mid Cape includes Barnstable, Hyannis, Yarmouth, and Dennis. Brewster, Harwich, Chatham, Orleans, and Eastham make up the Lower Cape. The Outer Cape consists of Wellfleet, Truro, and Provincetown. ⇨ *The towns have been arranged geographically, starting with the Upper Cape and ending with the Outer Cape.*

ESSENTIALS

Visitor Information Cape Cod Chamber of Commerce ⊠ *Shoot Flying Hill Rd., Exit 6 off U.S. 6 and U.S. 132, Hyannis* ☎ *508/362–3225* ⊕ *www.capecodchamber.org.*

SANDWICH

3 miles east of Sagamore Bridge, 11 miles west of Barnstable.

★ The oldest town on Cape Cod, Sandwich was established in 1637 by some of the Plymouth Pilgrims and incorporated on March 6, 1638. Today, it is a well-preserved, quintessential New England village with a white-columned town hall and streets lined with 18th- and 19th-century houses.

ESSENTIALS

Visitor Information Sandwich Chamber of Commerce ⊠ *502 Rte. 130, Sandwich Center* ☎ *508/833–9755* ⊕ *www.sandwichchamber.com.*

EXPLORING

Fodor's Choice ★ ℭ **Heritage Museums and Gardens.** These 100 beautifully landscaped acres overlooking the upper end of Shawme Pond are one of the region's top draws. Paths crisscross the grounds, which include gardens planted with hostas, heather, herbs, and fruit trees. Rhododendrons are in full glory from mid-May through mid-June, and daylilies reach their peak

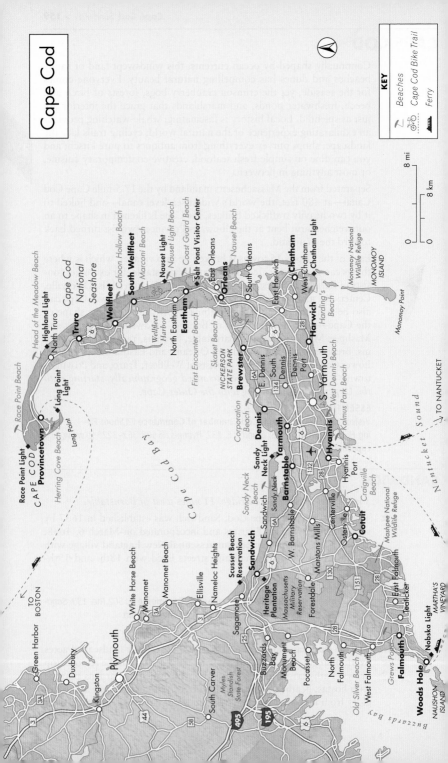

Cape Cod

KEY

⚓ Beaches
🚲 Cape Cod Bike Trail
⛴ Ferry

0   8 mi
0   8 km

from mid-July through early August. In 1967, pharmaceuticals magnate Josiah K. Lilly III purchased the estate and turned it into a nonprofit museum. A highlight is the Shaker Round Barn, which showcases classic and historic cars—including a 1919 Pierce-Arrow, a 1915 Milburn Light Electric, a 1911 Stanley Steamer, and a 1930 yellow-and-green Duesenberg built for movie star Gary Cooper. The history museum houses a semipermanent exhibit called "A Bird in the Hand," as well as seasonal exhibitions. The art museum has an extraordinary collection of New England folk art, including paintings, weather vanes, Nantucket baskets, and scrimshaw. Both adults and children can enjoy riding on a Coney Island–style carousel dating from the early 20th century. Other features include Hidden Hollow, an outdoor activity center for families with children.

A shuttle bus—equipped with a wheelchair lift and space to stow baby strollers—transports visitors on certain days. In summer, concerts are held in the gardens, often on Wednesday or Saturday evening or Sunday afternoon. The center of the complex is about ¾ mile on foot from the in-town end of Shawme Pond. ⊠ *67 Grove St., Sandwich Center* ☎ *508/888–3300* ⊕ *www.heritagemuseumsandgardens.org* 🖃 *$15* ☽ *Apr.–Nov., daily 10–5.*

Sandwich Boardwalk. For a view of the bay, you can walk to Town Neck Beach on the Sandwich Boardwalk, built over a salt marsh, creek, and low dunes. After Hurricane Bob destroyed the previous boardwalk in 1991, locals donated planks to rebuild it. Some are inscribed with a donor's name; others have jokes ("get off our board") and words of wisdom ("simplify/Thoreau"). The long sweep of Cape Cod Bay stretches out around the beach at the end of the walk, where a platform provides fine views, especially at sunset. You can look out toward Sandy Neck, Wellfleet, and Provincetown or toward the white cliffs beyond Sagamore. Near this mostly rocky beach are dunes covered with rugosa roses, which have a delicious fragrance; this is a good place for birding. The creeks running through the salt marsh make for great canoeing. From the town center it's about a mile to the boardwalk; cross Route 6A on Jarves Street, and at its end turn left, then right, and continue to the boardwalk parking lot. ⊠ *End of Jarves St., Sandwich Center.*

Sandwich Glass Museum. With its more than 10,000 square feet of exhibits, the Sandwich Glass Museum has information about the history of the shimmering glass that was manufactured here more than a century ago. There is a diorama showing how the factory looked in its heyday, an "ingredient room" showcasing a wide spectrum of glass colors along with the minerals added to the sand to obtain them, and an outstanding collection of blown and pressed glass in many shapes and hues. Large lamps, vases, and pitchers are impressive, as are the hundreds of candlesticks and small saucers on display. There are daily glass-blowing demonstrations on the hour between 10 and 3. The extensive, ornate gift shop sells some handsome reproductions, including some made by local and national artisans. The museum also hosts historic walking tours on Wednesday June through August. ⊠ *129 Main St., Sandwich Center* ☎ *508/888–0251* ⊕ *www.sandwichglassmuseum.org* 🖃 *$6* ☽ *Apr.–Dec., daily 9:30–5; Feb. and Mar., Wed.–Sun. 9:30–4.*

SHOPPING

Fodor's Choice ★ **Titcomb's Bookshop.** You'll find used, rare, and new books, including a large collection of Cape and nautical titles and Americana, as well as an extensive selection of children's books here. ✉ *432 Rte. 6A, East Sandwich* ☎ *508/888–2331* 🌐 *www.titcombsbookshop.com.*

NIGHTLIFE

British Beer Company. There is a traditional British "public house" atmosphere here and a great menu that includes fish, ribs, and pizza. Sunday evenings feature karaoke; a variety of bands play Thursday through Saturday nights. The British Beer Company also has two other Cape locations in Falmouth and Hyannis. ✉ *46 Rte. 6A* ☎ *508/833–9590* 🌐 *www.britishbeer.com.*

WHERE TO EAT AND STAY

For expanded hotel reviews, visit Fodors.com.

$$$ B&B/INN Fodor's Choice ★ 🏨 **Belfry Inne & Bistro.** This one-of-a-kind inn comprises a 1901 former church, an ornate wood-frame 1882 Victorian, and an 1827 Federal-style house clustered on a main campus. Room themes in each building nod to their respective histories: The Painted Lady's charmingly appointed rooms, for example, are named after former inhabitants; the luxurious rooms in the Abbey, named for the six days of the creation, have whirlpool tubs and gas fireplaces, and are set along a corridor overlooking the restaurant below. **Pros:** great in-town location; bright, beautiful, and spacious rooms. **Cons:** some steep stairs. [$] *Rooms from: $299* ✉ *8 Jarves St.* ☎ *508/888–8550, 800/844–4542* 🌐 *www.belfryinn.com* 🛏 *20 rooms* ⏲ *Closed Jan.* 🍴 *Breakfast.*

$$ B&B/INN ★ 🏨 **1750 Inn at Sandwich Center.** Across from the Sandwich Glass Museum, this 18th-century house with fine Colonial and Victorian furnishings is listed on the National Register of Historic Places. **Pros:** easy access to town center; intimate and friendly atmosphere. **Cons:** some steep; narrow stairs. [$] *Rooms from: $189* ✉ *118 Tupper Rd.* ☎ *508/888–6958, 800/249–6949* 🌐 *www.innatsandwich.com* 🛏 *5 rooms* ⏲ *Closed Jan.–Mar.* 🍴 *Breakfast.*

FALMOUTH

15 miles south of Bourne Bridge, 20 miles South of Sandwich.

Falmouth, the Cape's second-largest town, was settled in 1660. Much of Falmouth today is suburban, with a mix of old and new developments and a large year-round population. Many residents commute to other towns on the Cape, to southeastern Massachusetts, and even to Boston. The town has a quaint village center, with a typically old New England village green and a shop-lined Main Street. South of town center, Falmouth faces Nantucket Sound and has several often-crowded beaches popular with families. To the east, the Falmouth Heights neighborhood mixes inns, B&Bs, and private homes, nestled close together on residential streets leading to the sea. Bustling Grand Avenue, the main drag in Falmouth Heights, hugs the shore and the beach.

DID YOU KNOW?

Frappe is Massachusetts speak for milk shake. Try a frappe or get the scoop on the best ice cream flavors from your server at a local take-out window.

The village of Woods Hole, part of Falmouth, is home to several major scientific institutions, and is a departure point for ferries to Martha's Vineyard.

GETTING HERE AND AROUND

Heading from the Bourne Bridge toward Falmouth, County Road and Route 28A are prettier alternatives to Route 28, and Sippewisset Road meanders near Buzzards Bay between West Falmouth and Woods Hole.

If you're coming from Falmouth to Woods Hole, either ride your bicycle down the straight and flat Shining Sea Trail or take the Cape Cod Regional Transit Authority's WHOOSH trolley. In summer, the basically one-street village overflows with thousands of visiting scientists, students, and tourists heading to the islands. Parking, limited to a relatively small number of metered spots on the street, can be nearly impossible.

ESSENTIALS

Transportation Contacts Cape Cod Regional Transit Authority ☎ *800/352–7155* ⊕ *www.capecodtransit.org.*

Visitor Information Falmouth Chamber of Commerce & Visitor Center ✉ *20 Academy La.* ☎ *508/548–8500, 800/526–8532* ⊕ *www.falmouthchamber.com.*

EXPLORING

Marine Biological Laboratory–Woods Hole Oceanographic Institution Library. This is one of the best collections of biological, ecological, and oceanographic literature in the world. The library has access to more than 200 computer databases and subscribes to more than 5,000 scientific journals in 40 languages, with complete collections of most. The Rare Books Room contains photographs, monographs, and prints, as well as journal collections that date from 1665.

Unless you are a scientific researcher, the only way you can get in to see the library is by taking the hour-long tours offered weekdays at 1 and 2 from late June to late August. The tours, led by retired scientists, include an introductory slide show as well as stops at the library and the marine resources center. Reservations are required. ✉ *7 Marine Biological Laboratory St., off Water St., Woods Hole* ☎ *508/289–7423 for library, 508/289–7623 for tours* ⊕ *www.mbl.edu.*

Nobska Light. This imposing lighthouse has spectacular views from its base of the nearby Elizabeth Islands and of Martha's Vineyard, across Vineyard Sound. The 42-foot cast-iron tower, lined with brick, was built in 1876 with a stationary light. It shines red to indicate dangerous waters or white for safe passage. Since the light was automated in 1985, the adjacent keeper's quarters have been the headquarters of the Coast Guard group commander—a fitting passing of the torch from one safeguarder of ships to another. The interior is open to the public only sporadically. ✉ *Church St., Woods Hole* ⊕ *www.lighthouse.cc/nobska.*

☾ **Waquoit Bay National Estuarine Research Reserve.** This state park is one of 27 research reserves in the country. It encompasses 3,000 acres of estuary, woodlands, salt marshes, and barrier beach, making it a good site for walking, kayaking, fishing, and birding. The visitor center includes displays about the area. An interactive exhibit, outside on the lawn, lets kids trace the path of a raindrop through its journey from cloud to land to river. In July and August there are nature programs for families, including an outdoor lecture series on Tuesday evenings.

South Cape Beach is part of the reserve; you can lie out on the sand or join one of the interpretive walks. **Flat Pond Trail** runs through several different habitats, including fresh- and saltwater marshes. You can reach **Washburn Island** on your own by boat, or by joining a Saturday-morning tour. It offers 330 acres of pine barrens and trails, swimming, and 10 wilderness campsites (an advance reservation and permit are required). ⊠ *149 Rte. 28, 3 miles west of Mashpee rotary, Waquoit* ☎ *508/457–0495* ⊕ *www.waquoitbayreserve.org* ⊙ *Visitor center open weekdays, 10–4; Sat. 10–4.*

Fodor'sChoice ★ ☺ **Woods Hole Science Aquarium.** This impressive facility displays 16 large tanks and many more smaller ones filled with regional fish and shellfish. The rooms are small, but they are crammed with stuff to see. Magnifying glasses and a dissecting scope help you examine marine life. Several hands-on pools hold banded lobsters, crabs, snails, starfish, and other creatures. The stars of the show are two harbor seals, on view in the outdoor pool near the entrance; watch their feedings weekdays at 11 and 4. ⊠ *166 Water St., Woods Hole* ☎ *508/495–2001* ⊕ *aquarium. nefsc.noaa.gov* ✉ *Free* ⊙ *Tues.–Sat. 11–4.*

SPORTS AND THE OUTDOORS

BEACHES

★ **Old Silver Beach.** This long, beautiful crescent of soft white sand is bordered by the Sea Crest Beach Resort at one end. It's especially good for small children because a sandbar keeps it shallow at the southern end and creates tidal pools full of crabs and minnows. The beach has lifeguards, restrooms, showers, and a snack bar. There's a $20 fee for parking in summer. ⊠ *Off Quaker Rd., North Falmouth.*

BIKING

Fodor'sChoice ★ **Shining Sea Bikeway.** The wonderful Shining Sea Bikeway is an 11-mile paved bike path through four of Falmouth's villages, running from Woods Hole to North Falmouth. It follows the shore of Buzzards Bay, providing water views, and dips into oak and pine woods; a detour onto Church Street takes you to Nobska Light. A brochure is available at the trailheads. If you're going to Martha's Vineyard with your bike, you can park your car in one of Falmouth's Steamship Authority lots and ride the Shining Sea Bikeway to the ferry. The free shuttle buses between the Falmouth lots and the Woods Hole ferry docks also have bike carriers. ⊠ *Along Buzzard's Bay from Woods Hole to North Falmouth.*

FISHING

Eastman's Sport & Tackle. Freshwater ponds are good for perch, pickerel, trout, and more; you can obtain the required license (along with rental gear) at tackle shops, such as Eastman's Sport & Tackle. They're also a good resource if you are looking for local guide services. ⊠ *783 Rte. 28, Falmouth Center* ☎ *508/548–6900* ⊕ *www.eastmanstackle.com.*

Continued on page 172

A WHALE OF A TALE

by Steve Larese

WHALING IN NEW ENGLAND TIMELINE

mid-1600s	America enters whaling industry
1690	Nantucket enters whaling industry
1820	*Essex* ship sunk by sperm whale
1840s	American whaling peaked
1851	*Moby-Dick* published
1927	The last U.S. whaler sails from New Bedford
1970s	Cape Cod whale-watching trips begin
1986	Ban on whaling by the International Whaling Commission
1992	Stellwagen Bank National Marine Sanctuary established

Cameras have replaced harpoons in the waters north of Cape Cod. While you can learn about New England's whaling history and perhaps see whales in the distance from shore, a whale-watching excursion is the best way to connect with these magnificent creatures—who may be just as curious about you as you are about them.

Once relentlessly hunted around the world by New Englanders, whales today are celebrated as intelligent, friendly, and curious creatures. Whales are still important to the region's economy and culture, but now in the form of ecotourism. Easily accessible from several ports in Massachusetts, the 842-square-mi Stellwagen Bank National Marine Sanctuary attracts finback, humpback, minke, and right whales who feed and frolic here twice a year during their migration. The same conditions that made the Stellwagen Bank area of the mouth of Massachusetts Bay a good hunting ground make it a good viewing area. Temperature, currents, and nutrients combine to produce plankton, krill, and fish to feed marine mammals.

(opposite) Whaling museum custodian and a sperm whale jaw in the 1930s. (top) Hunted to near extinction, humpbacks today number about 60,000, and are found in oceans worldwide.

ON LAND: MARINE AND MARITIME MUSEUMS

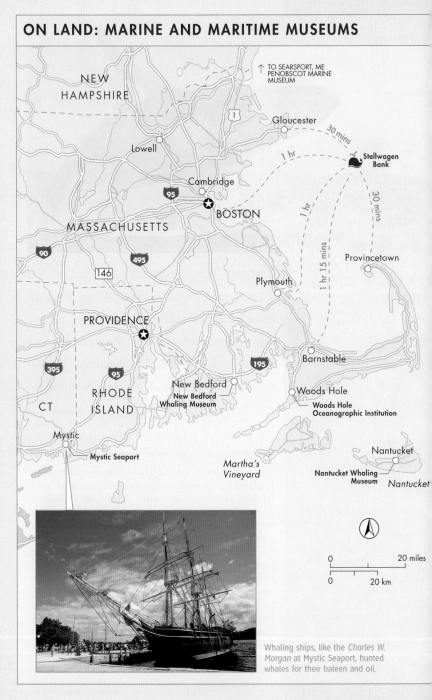

NEW HAMPSHIRE

↑ TO SEARSPORT, ME
PENOBSCOT MARINE
MUSEUM

Gloucester

1

30 mins

Stellwagen
Bank

1 hr

Lowell

Cambridge

95

BOSTON

MASSACHUSETTS

1 hr

30 mins

90

495

Provincetown

146

Plymouth

1 hr 15 mins

PROVIDENCE

Barnstable

395

195

RHODE
ISLAND

New Bedford
New Bedford
Whaling Museum

Woods Hole
Woods Hole
Oceanographic Institution

CT

95

Mystic
Mystic Seaport

Nantucket

Martha's
Vineyard

Nantucket Whaling
Museum   Nantucket

0 _____ 20 miles

0 _____ 20 km

Whaling ships, like the *Charles W.
Morgan* at Mystic Seaport, hunted
whales for their baleen and oil.

Even landlubbers can learn about whales and whaling at these top New England institutions.

Nantucket Whaling Museum. This former whale-processing center and candle factory was converted into a museum in 1929. See art made by sailors, including masterful scrimshaw—intricate nautical scenes carved into whale bone or teeth and filled in with ink ⊠ *Nantucket, Massachusetts* ☎ *508/228–1894* ⊕ *www.nha.org.*

★ **New Bedford Whaling Museum.** More than 200,000 artifacts are collected here, from ships' logbooks to harpoons. A must-see is the 89-foot, half-scale model of the 1826 whaling ship *Lagoda* ⊠ *New Bedford, Massachusetts* ☎ *508/997–0046* ⊕ *www.whalingmuseum.org.*

New Bedford Whaling National Historical Park. The visitor center for this 13-block waterfront park provides maps and information about whaling-related sites, including a sea captain's mansion and restored whaling schooner. ⊠ *New Bedford, Massachusetts,* ☎ *508/996–4095* ⊕ *www.nps.gov/nebe.*

★ **Mystic Seaport.** Actors portray life in a 19th-century seafaring village at this 37-acre living-history museum. Don't miss the 1841 *Charles W. Morgan,* the world's only surviving wooden whaling ship ⊠ *Mystic, Connecticut* ☎ *860/572–5302* ⊕ *www.mysticseaport.org.*

Penobscot Marine Museum. Maine's seafaring history and mostly shore-whaling industry is detailed inside seven historic buildings ⊠ *Searsport, Maine* ☎ *207/548–2529* ⊕ *www.penobscotbayhistory.org.*

Nantucket Whaling Museum

New Bedford Whaling Museum

THE GREAT WHITE WHALE

Herman Melville based his 1851 classic *Moby-Dick: or, The Whale* on the true story of the *Essex,* which was sunk in 1821 by huge whale; an albino sperm whale called Mocha Dick; and his time aboard the whaling ship *Acushnet.*

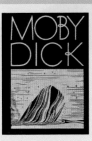

Mystic Seaport

★ = Fodor's Choice

AT SEA: WHALE-WATCHING TOURS

COMMON NORTH ATLANTIC SPECIES

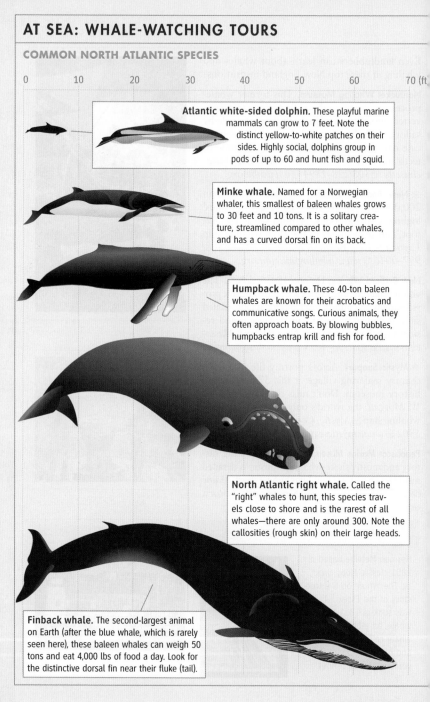

0   10   20   30   40   50   60   70 (ft)

Atlantic white-sided dolphin. These playful marine mammals can grow to 7 feet. Note the distinct yellow-to-white patches on their sides. Highly social, dolphins group in pods of up to 60 and hunt fish and squid.

Minke whale. Named for a Norwegian whaler, this smallest of baleen whales grows to 30 feet and 10 tons. It is a solitary creature, streamlined compared to other whales, and has a curved dorsal fin on its back.

Humpback whale. These 40-ton baleen whales are known for their acrobatics and communicative songs. Curious animals, they often approach boats. By blowing bubbles, humpbacks entrap krill and fish for food.

North Atlantic right whale. Called the "right" whales to hunt, this species travels close to shore and is the rarest of all whales—there are only around 300. Note the callosities (rough skin) on their large heads.

Finback whale. The second-largest animal on Earth (after the blue whale, which is rarely seen here), these baleen whales can weigh 50 tons and eat 4,000 lbs of food a day. Look for the distinctive dorsal fin near their fluke (tail).

SEAWORTHY TRIP TIPS

When to Go: Tours operate April through October; May through September are the most active months in the Stellwagen Bank area.

Ports of Departure: Boats leave from Barnstable and Provincetown on Cape Cod, and Plymouth, Boston, and Gloucester, cutting across Cape Cod Bay to the Stellwagen area. Book tours at least a day ahead in the height of the summer season. Hyannis Whale Watcher in Barnstable, the Dolphin Fleet, Portuguese Princess and Captain John's Whale Watch in Plymouth, and the New England Aquarium, and Boston Harbor Cruises in Boston are just a few of your options. *See Thar She Blows box in this chapter for more information.*

Cost: Around $40. Check company Web sites for coupons.

What to Expect: All companies abide by guidelines so as not to harass whales. Tours last 3 to 4 hours and almost always encounter whales; if not, vouchers are often given for another tour. Passengers are encouraged to watch the horizon for water spouts, which indicate a surfaced whale clearing its blowhole to breathe air. Upon spotting an animal, the boat slows and approaches the whale to a safe distance; often, whales will approach an idling boat and even swim underneath it.

What to Bring: Plastic bags protect binoculars and cameras from damp spray. Most boats have a concession stand, but pack bottled water and snacks. ■ TIP➔ Kids (and adults) will appreciate games or other items to pass the time in between whale sightings.

What to Wear: Wear rubber-soled footwear for slick decks. A waterproof outer layer and layers of clothing will help in

Hyannis Whale Watcher Cruises, Cape Cod Bay

varied conditions, as will sunscreen, sunglasses, and a hat that can be secured. Most boats have cabins where you can warm up and get out of the wind.

Comforting Advice: Small seat cushions like those used at sporting events may be appreciated. Consider taking motion-sickness medication before setting out. Ginger candy and acupressure wristbands can also help. If you feel queasy, get some fresh air and focus your eyes on a stable feature on the shore or horizon.

Photo Hints: Use a fast shutter speed, or sport mode, to avoid blurry photographs. Most whales will be a distance from the boat; have a telephoto lens ready. To avoid shutter delay on your point-and-shoot camera, lock the focus at infinity so you don't miss that breaching whale shot.

DID YOU KNOW?

Most boats have a naturalist aboard to discuss the whales and their environment. Many companies contribute to population studies by reporting the individual whales they spot. Whale tails, called flukes, are distinct and used like fingerprints for identification.

SHOPPING

★ **Bean & Cod.** This specialty food shop sells cheeses, breads, and picnic fixings, along with pastas, coffees and teas, and unusual condiments. The store also packs and ships gift baskets. ⊠ *140 Main St. (Rte. 28), Falmouth Center* ☎ *508/548–8840.*

NIGHTLIFE AND THE ARTS

Nimrod Inn. Nimrod Inn presents jazz and contemporary music at least six nights a week year-round. The Nimrod is also a great spot for late-night dining. ⊠ *100 Dillingham Ave., Falmouth Center* ☎ *508/540–4132* ⊕ *www.thenimrod.com.*

WHERE TO EAT AND STAY

For expanded hotel reviews, visit Fodors.com.

$$ ✕ **The Clam Shack.** Fried clams top the menu at this basic seafood joint
SEAFOOD right on Falmouth Harbor. The clams are crisp and fresh; the meaty lobster roll and the fish-and-chips platter are good choices, too. Place your order at the counter and then take your tray to the picnic tables on the roof deck for the best views. More tables are on the dock in back, or you can squeeze into the tiny dining room. Just don't plan on a late night here—the Shack closes most evenings around 8. $ *Average main: $14* ⊠ *227 Clinton Ave., Falmouth Harbor* ☎ *508/540–7758* ⊟ *No credit cards* ☉ *Closed early Sept.–mid May.*

$$ ✕ **La Cucina Sul Mare.** Northern Italian and Mediterranean cooking is the
ITALIAN specialty at this classy, popular place. The staff is friendly and the setting
Fodor'sChoice is both intimate and festive, if a bit crowded. Calamari, warm green
★ salad with goat cheese and cranberries, a classic lemon chicken sautéed with shallots and capers, and a variety of specials—including plenty of local fresh fish—adorn the menu. The *zuppa de pesce,* a medley of seafood sautéed in olive oil and garlic and finished in a white-wine, herb-and-tomato broth, is a specialty. Make sure to come hungry—the portions here are huge—and expect a long wait during prime hours in season. ■ TIP→ **Use the call-ahead wait list to get a jump on the line.** $ *Average main: $22* ⊠ *237 Main St., Falmouth Center* ☎ *508/548–5600* ⊕ *www.lacucinasulmare.com* ⚖ *Reservations not accepted.*

$$$ 🗖 **The Captain's Manor Inn.** With its deep, landscaped yard and wrought-
B&B/INN iron fence, this elegant inn with a wraparound porch resembles a private
★ estate. **Pros:** walk to town center; elegant setting. **Cons:** long stairway to second-floor rooms. $ *Rooms from: $275* ⊠ *27 W. Main St., Falmouth Center* ☎ *508/388–7336* ⊕ *www.captainsmanorinn.com* ⤳ *8 rooms* ⍾I *Breakfast.*

$$$ 🗖 **Coonamessett Inn.** At this delightful old-Cape-style inn, five buildings
B&B/INN of one- and two-bedroom suites ring a landscaped lawn that leads to a scenic wooded pond. **Pros:** lush grounds; high marks in romantic-dining setting. **Cons:** weddings are a constant here. $ *Rooms from: $240* ⊠ *311 Gifford St., at Jones Rd.* ☎ *508/548–2300* ⊕ *www.capecodrestaurants. org/coonamessett* ⤳ *28 suites, 1 cottage* ⍾I *Breakfast.*

HYANNIS

23 miles east of the Bourne Bridge, 21 miles northeast of Falmouth.

Perhaps best known for its association with the Kennedy clan, the Hyannis area was also a vacation site for President Ulysses S. Grant in 1874 and later for President Grover Cleveland. A bustling year-round hub of activity, Hyannis has the Cape's largest concentration of businesses, shops, malls, hotels and motels, restaurants, and entertainment venues.

GETTING HERE AND AROUND

There's plenty of public parking around town, on both sides of Main Street as well as in several public parking lots. The island ferry companies have designated parking lots (daily fee is about $15 in summer season) with free shuttles to the docks. Hyannis is the Cape's transit hub and is served by a number of bus routes.

ESSENTIALS

Transportation Contacts Hyannis Transportation Center ⊠ *215 Iyanough Rd.* ☎ *508/775–8504* ⊕ *www.capecodtransit.org.*

Visitor Information Hyannis Chamber of Commerce ⊠ *397 Main St.* ☎ *508/775–2201* ⊕ *www.hyannis.com.*

EXPLORING

John F. Kennedy Hyannis Museum. In Main Street's Old Town Hall, this museum explores JFK's Cape years (1934–63) through enlarged and annotated photographs culled from the archives of the JFK Library near Boston, as well as a seven-minute video narrated by Walter Cronkite. Also on-site is the **Cape Cod Baseball League Hall of Fame and Museum,** housed in several rooms in the basement of the JFK museum (which is appropriately referred to as "The Dugout"). Plaques of Hall of Famers, autographed items from former players who went on to play professional ball, and other Cape League memorabilia are on view; several films about the league and baseball itself are played continuously. ⊠ *397 Main St.* ☎ *508/790–3077* ⊕ *www.jfkhyannismuseum.org* ⊡ *$5; $8 for joint admission with baseball museum* ⊙ *Late Feb.–Mar., Thurs.–Sat. 10–4, Sun. noon–4; mid-Apr.–Memorial Day, Mon.–Sat. 10–4, Sun. noon–4; Memorial Day–Oct., Mon.–Sat. 9–5, Sun. noon–5; Nov., Fri.–Sat. 10–4, Sun. noon–4. Closed Dec. and Jan.*

SPORTS AND THE OUTDOORS

BEACH

Kalmus Park Beach. Kalmus Park Beach, at the south end of Ocean Street in Hyannis, is a fine, wide sandy beach with an area set aside for windsurfers and a sheltered area that's good for kids. It has a snack bar, restrooms, showers, and lifeguards. From late June through Labor Day, daily parking is $15 during the week and $20 on weekends.

NIGHTLIFE AND THE ARTS

Cape Cod Melody Tent. In 1950 actress Gertrude Lawrence and her husband, producer-manager Richard Aldrich, opened the Cape Cod Melody Tent to showcase Broadway musicals and concerts. Today it's the Cape's top venue for pop concerts and comedy shows. Performers who have played here, in the round, include the Indigo Girls; Lyle Lovett; Tony Bennett; Diana Krall; and Crosby, Stills & Nash. The Tent also holds an 11 am Wednesday children's theater series in July and August. ⊠ *21 W. Main St.* ☎ *508/775–5630* ⊕ *www.melodytent.com.*

WHERE TO EAT

$$$

BRAZILIAN

Fodor'sChoice

★

✕**Brazilian Grill.** The Cape has a large Brazilian population, and you can find many of these residents, plus plenty of satisfied visitors, at this all-you-can-eat *churrascaria* (Brazilian barbecue). Be prepared for some serious feasting: this experience is not for light eaters or vegetarians. Waiters circulate through the dining room offering more than a dozen grilled meats—beef, pork, chicken, sausage, even quail—on long sword-like skewers. You can help yourself to a buffet of salads and side dishes, including *farofa* (a couscous-like dish made of manioc, also known as cassava or yuca), plantains, rice, and beans. The atmosphere is often loud and jovial. For dessert, the homemade flan is the best anywhere. Dine on the redbrick patio in warm weather. $ *Average main: $28* ⊠ *680 Main St.* ☎ *508/771–0109* ⊕ *www.braziliangrill-capecod.com* ⊗ *No lunch on weekends.*

$$$

ECLECTIC

Fodor'sChoice

★

✕**Naked Oyster.** In a favored location on Main Street, this restaurant is known, not surprisingly, for its oysters, and with its own oyster farm in nearby Barnstable, the kitchen—and diners—benefit from near-daily deliveries of the succulent bivalves; more than 1,000 oysters are eaten here on an average summer weekend. You'll always find close to two dozen raw and "dressed" oyster dishes (such as barbecue oysters on the half shell with blue cheese, caramelized onions, and bacon) plus a nice range of non-oyster entrees, salads and appetizers. The oyster stew is also out of this world. Exposed brick walls inside and a few street-side tables outside add to the pleasurable dining experience. $ *Average main: $28* ⊠ *410 Main St.* ☎ *508/778–6500* ⊕ *www.nakedoyster.com.*

$$$

EUROPEAN

★

✕**The Paddock.** The Paddock is synonymous with tried-and-true for-mal dining on the Cape, with sumptuous upholstery in the main din-ing room and old-style wicker on the breezy summer porch creating authentic Victorian style, complementing a menu that is traditional yet subtly innovative—fresh ingredients are combined in novel ways: Cha-tham scrod comes with lemon thyme bread crumbs and a rich lobster sauce. The steak au poivre, with several varieties of crushed pepper-corns, is masterful; the fire-roasted salmon is stuffed with lobster, goat cheese, and finished with a beurre blanc. $ *Average main: $26* ⊠ *20 Scudder Ave.* ☎ *508/775–7677* ⊕ *www.paddockcapecod.com* ⊗ *Closed mid-Nov.–Mar.*

WHERE TO STAY

For expanded hotel reviews, visit Fodors.com.

$$$

HOTEL

★

⌨ **Anchor-In.** Most rooms at this small-scale motel on the north end of Hyannis Harbor have harbor views and small balconies overlooking the water. **Pros:** easy walk to downtown; great harbor views. **Cons:** no elevator—second-floor rooms accessed via stairs. $ *Rooms from: $299* ⊠ *1 South St.* ☎ *508/775–0357* ⊕ *www.anchorin.com* ⇥ *42 rooms* ⦿| *Breakfast.*

CLOSE UP

Clam Shacks

Cape Codders have been clamming for generations, and their iconic mollusks are a celebrated part of the culture here. Classic clam shacks are known for their bountiful baskets of crispy fried clams, which, according to Cape Codders, should always be ordered "whole"—that is, with the bellies. Fried clams are never the only item on the menu. Typical fare also includes clam chowder, lobster rolls, fried fish, scallops, shrimp, coleslaw, fries, potato salad, and other non-seafood items. The quintessential experience usually involves ordering at one window, picking up at another, and eating at a picnic table—hopefully one with a beach or harbor view! A few of our favorites on Cape Cod include The Clam Shack in Falmouth, Mac's Seafood in Wellfleet, and Arnold's Lobster & Clam Bar in Eastham. The Bite in Menemsha on Martha's Vineyard is also worth a try.

$
RENTAL

Breakwaters. These privately owned, weathered gray-shingle cottages, which rent by the week in summer or nightly in spring and fall, are in a relaxed setting on a quiet dead-end lane and most have water views. **Pros:** excellent waterfront location; ideal for families. **Cons:** hard to reserve unless you're staying for a week; no credit cards. $ *Rooms from: $110* ⊠ *432 Sea St.* ☎ *508/775–6831* ⊕ *www. thebreakwaters.com* ⇆ *19 cottages* ▭ *No credit cards* ۞ *Closed mid-Oct.–Apr.* ۞ *No meals.*

BARNSTABLE

4 miles north of Hyannis.

With nearly 50,000 year-round residents, Barnstable is the largest town on the Cape. It's also the second oldest (founded in 1639). You can get a feeling for its age in Barnstable Village, on and near Main Street (Route 6A), a lovely area of large old homes.

SPORTS AND THE OUTDOORS

BEACHES

Sandy Neck Beach. Sandy Neck Beach stretches some 6 miles across a peninsula that ends at **Sandy Neck Light.** The beach is one of the Cape's most beautiful—dunes, sand, and bay spread endlessly east, west, and north. The marsh used to be harvested for salt hay; now it's a haven for birds, which are out and about in the greatest numbers in morning and evening. The lighthouse, standing a few feet from the eroding shoreline at the tip of the neck, has been out of commission since 1952. It was built in 1857 to replace an 1827 light, and it used to run on acetylene gas. The main beach at Sandy Neck has lifeguards, a snack bar, restrooms, and showers. As you travel east along Route 6A from Sandwich, Sandy Neck Road is just *before* the Barnstable line, although the beach itself is in West Barnstable. ⊠ *Sandy Neck Rd., West Barnstable* ۞ *Daily 8 am–9 pm, but staffed only until 5 pm.*

WHERE TO STAY

For expanded hotel reviews, visit Fodors.com.

$$ B&B/INN ★ **Beechwood Inn.** This lovely yellow-and-pale-green 1853 Queen Anne house has gingerbread trim and is wrapped by a wide porch with wicker furniture and a glider swing, but inside, it's all Victorian splendor: mahogany and red velvet in the parlor, with lighter style antiques in the guest rooms. **Pros:** afternoon tea; seven beaches within a 5-mile radius. **Cons:** narrow, curved stairs. [$] *Rooms from: $209* ✉ *2839 Rte. 6A* ☎ *508/362–6618, 800/609–6618* 🌐 *www.beechwoodinn.com* 🛏 *6 rooms* 🍴 *Breakfast.*

$$$ B&B/INN Fodor's Choice ★ **Honeysuckle Hill.** Innkeepers Nancy and Rick provide plenty of little touches in this 1810 Queen Anne-style cottage and the airy, country-style guest rooms have lots of white wicker, checked curtains, and pastel-painted floors. **Pros:** gracious and generous innkeepers; lush gardens on the grounds; tasteful, large rooms; very short drive to Sandy Neck Beach. **Cons:** most rooms are accessed via steep stairs. [$] *Rooms from: $225* ✉ *591 Rte. 6A, West Barnstable* ☎ *508/362–8418, 866/444–5522* 🌐 *www.honeysucklehill.com* 🛏 *4 rooms, 1 suite* 🍴 *Breakfast.*

YARMOUTH

Yarmouth Port is 3 miles east of Barnstable Village; West Yarmouth is 2 miles east of Hyannis.

Once known as Mattacheese, or "the planting lands," Yarmouth was settled in 1639 by farmers from the Plymouth Bay Colony. By then the Cape had begun a thriving maritime industry, and men turned to the sea to make their fortunes. Many impressive sea captains' houses—some now B&Bs and museums—still line enchanting Route 6A and nearby side streets, and Yarmouth Port has some real old-time stores in town. West Yarmouth has a very different atmosphere, stretched on busy commercial Route 28 south of Yarmouth Port.

ESSENTIALS

Visitor Information Yarmouth Chamber of Commerce ✉ *425 Rte. 28, West Yarmouth* ☎ *508/778–1008, 800/732–1008* 🌐 *www.yarmouthcapecod.com.*

EXPLORING

★ 👶 **Bass Hole Boardwalk.** One of Yarmouth Port's most beautiful areas is Bass Hole, which stretches from Homer's Dock Road to the salt marsh. Bass Hole Boardwalk extends over a marshy creek; amid the salt marshes, vegetated wetlands, and upland woods. Gray's Beach is a little crescent of sand with still water good for kids—but don't go beyond the roped-in swimming area, the only section where the current isn't strong. At the end of the boardwalk, benches provide a place to relax and look out over abundant marsh life and, across the creek, the beautiful, sandy shores of Dennis's Chapin Beach. At low tide you can walk out on the flats for almost a mile. ✉ *Center St., near Gray's Beach parking lot.*

★ 👶 **Edward Gorey House Museum.** Explore the eccentric illustrations and off-beat humor of the late acclaimed artist. The regularly changing exhibitions, arranged in the downstairs rooms of Gorey's former home, include drawings of his oddball characters and reveal the mysterious psyche of

the sometimes dark but always playful illustrator. ✉ *8 Strawberry La.* ☎ *508/362–3909* 🌐 *www.edwardgoreyhouse.org* 🎫 *$5* 🕒 *Mid-Apr.–June, Thurs.–Sat. 11–4, Sun. noon–4; July–early Oct., Wed.–Sat. 11–4, Sun. noon–4; mid-Oct.–late Dec., Fri. and Sat. 11–4, Sun. noon–4.*

QUICK BITES

Jerry's Seafood and Dairy Freeze. Jerry's Seafood and Dairy Freeze, open year-round, serves fried clams and onion rings, along with thick frappes (milk shakes), frozen yogurt, and soft-serve ice cream at good prices. ✉ ***654 Rte. 28, West Yarmouth*** ☎ ***508/775–9752.***

SHOPPING

Peach Tree Designs. Peach Tree Designs carries home furnishings and decorative accessories; some are from local craftspeople, all are beautifully made. ✉ *173 Rte. 6A* ☎ *508/362–8317* 🌐 *www.peachtreedesigns.com.*

Oliver's. Oliver's has live music in a variety of genres in its Planck's Tavern on weekends year-round. ✉ *6 Bray Farm Rd., off Rte. 6A* ☎ *508/362–6062.*

WHERE TO EAT AND STAY

For expanded hotel reviews, visit Fodors.com.

$$$ JAPANESE Fodor's Choice ★

🍴 **Inaho.** Yuji Watanabe, chef-owner of the Cape's best Japanese restaurant, makes early-morning journeys to Boston's fish markets to shop for the freshest local catch. His selection of sushi and sashimi is vast and artful, and vegetable and seafood tempura come out of the kitchen fluffy and light. If you're a teriyaki lover, you can't do any better than the chicken's beautiful blend of sweet and sour. One remarkable element of the restaurant is its artful lighting: small pinpoint lights on the food accentuate the presentation in a dramatic way. Can't decide what to order? For a price ($$$$), the chef designs a varied and generous tasting menu. The serene and simple Japanese garden out back has a traditional koi pond. [$] *Average main: $26* ✉ *157 Main St. (Rte. 6A)* ☎ *508/362–5522* 🌐 *www.inahocapecod.com* 🕒 *Closed Sun. No lunch.*

$ BRITISH

🍴 **The Optimist Café.** From the outside, this bold Gothic Victorian looks like something out of a Brothers Grimm tale, with its steeply pitched roof, turrets, elaborate gingerbread trim, and deep rose-and-green paint job—inside, vibrant yellow walls help convey the café's mission to "turn a frown upside down," and chances are you'll be delighted with the great selection for breakfast (served all day) and lunch, featuring traditional English fare like the Ploughman's Lunch. Other British Isles favorites include several curries, smoked fish options, scones, and crumpets. Royalty or no, you're bound to be most pleased with the afternoon tea. Try *The Majesty*, a fine offering of scones with whipped cream, a variety of finger sandwiches and desserts, a pot of tea, and a bubbling flute of champagne. [$] *Average main: $12* ✉ *134 Rte. 6A* ☎ *508/362–1024* 🌐 *www.optimistcafe.com* 🕒 *No dinner.*

$$$ HOTEL ★

🏨 **Bayside Resort.** A bit more upscale than most of the properties along Route 28, the Bayside overlooks pristine salt marshes and, beyond them, Lewis Bay, and although it's not right on the water, there is a small beach and a large outdoor pool with a café (there's also an indoor pool). **Pros:** ideal for families with children; close to attractions of busy Route 28. **Cons:** no beach swimming; not for those seeking intimate surroundings. $ *Rooms from: $269* ✉ *225 Rte. 28, West Yarmouth* ☎ *508/775–5669, 800/243–1114* ⊕ *www.baysideresort.com* ⤶ *128 rooms* ⦿ *Breakfast.*

$$$

B&B/INN

Fodor'sChoice

★

⛉ **Liberty Hill Inn.** Smartly but traditionally furnished common areas— including the high-ceiling parlor, the formal dining room, and the wrap-around porch—are a major draw to this dignified 1825 Greek Revival house. **Pros:** tasteful surroundings; beautiful grounds. **Cons:** some steep stairs; some bathrooms have only small shower stalls; not a waterfront location. $ *Rooms from: $255* ✉ *77 Rte. 6A* ☎ *508/362–3976* ⊕ *www. libertyhillinn.com* ⤶ *8 rooms, 1 suite* ⦿ *Breakfast.*

DENNIS

Dennis Village is 4 miles east of Yarmouth Port; West Dennis is 1 mile east of South Yarmouth.

The backstreets of Dennis Village still retain the Colonial charm of its seafaring days. The town, which was incorporated in 1793, was named for the Reverend Josiah Dennis. There were 379 sea captains living here when fishing, salt making, and shipbuilding were the main industries, and the elegant houses they constructed—now museums and B&Bs—still line the streets.

ESSENTIALS

Visitor Information Dennis Chamber of Commerce ✉ *238 Swan River Rd., West Dennis* ☎ *508/398–3568, 800/243–9920* ⊕ *www.dennischamber.com.*

EXPLORING

Cape Cod Museum of Art. This museum on the grounds of the Cape Playhouse has a permanent collection of more than 850 works by Cape-associated artists. Important pieces include a portrait of a fisherman's wife by Charles Hawthorne, the father of the Provincetown art colony; a 1924 portrait of a Portuguese fisherman's daughter by William Paxton, one of the first artists to summer in Provincetown; a collection of wood-block prints by Varujan Boghosian, a member of Provincetown's Long Point Gallery cooperative; an oil sketch by Karl Knaths, who painted in Provincetown from 1919 until his death in 1971; and works by abstract expressionist Hans Hoffman and many of his students. ✉ *60 Hope La., Dennis Village* ☎ *508/385–4477* ⊕ *www.ccmoa.org* ⛉ *$8* ⊙ *Late May–mid-Oct., Mon.–Sat. 10–5, Sun. noon–5; mid-Oct.–Dec. and May, Tues.–Sat. 10–5, Sun. noon–5; Jan.–Mar., Thurs.–Sat. 10–5, Sun. noon–5; Apr., Wed.–Sat. 10–5, Sun. noon–5. Late opening, till 8 pm, every Thurs. year-round.*

SPORTS AND THE OUTDOORS

BEACHES Parking at all Dennis beaches is $20 a day in season ($25 on weekends) for nonresidents.

Corporation Beach. Corporation Beach has lifeguards, showers, restrooms, and a food stand. Once a packet landing owned by a corporation of the townsfolk, the beautiful crescent of white sand backed by low dunes now serves a decidedly noncorporate purpose as a public beach. ✉ *Corporation Rd., Dennis Village.*

NIGHTLIFE AND THE ARTS

THEATER

Fodor's Choice
★
☺

Cape Playhouse. For Broadway-style dramas, comedies, and musicals, as well as kids' plays, you can attend a production (June through September) at the Cape Playhouse, the oldest professional summer theater in the country. In 1927 Raymond Moore, who had been working with a theatrical troupe in Provincetown, bought an 1838 former Unitarian meetinghouse and converted it into a theater. The original pews still serve as seats. The opening performance was *The Guardsman*, starring Basil Rathbone. Other stars who performed here in the early days—some in their professional stage debuts—include Bette Davis (who first worked here as an usher), Gregory Peck, Lana Turner, Ginger Rogers, Humphrey Bogart, Tallulah Bankhead, and Henry Fonda, who appeared with his then-unknown 20-year-old daughter, Jane. Behind-the-scene tours are also given in season; call for a schedule. The playhouse offers children's theater on Friday morning during July and August. Also on the 26-acre property, now known as the Cape Playhouse Center for the Arts, are a restaurant, the **Cape Cod Museum of Art**, and the **Cape Cinema**. ✉ *820 Rte. 6A, Dennis Village* ☎ *508/385–3911, 877/385–3911* ⊕ *www.capeplayhouse.com* ☉ *Call for tour schedule.*

NIGHTLIFE

Harvest Gallery Wine Bar. Harvest Gallery Wine Bar is right at home near the Cape Cod Museum of Art, Cape Cod Cinema, and the Cape Playhouse. There's an extensive wine list; a good variety of hors d'oeuvres, salads, and desserts; eclectic artwork; and live music. ✉ *776 Main St., Dennis Village* ☎ *508/385–2444* ⊕ *www.harvestgallerywinebar.com* ☉ *Closed mid-Jan.–early Apr.*

WHERE TO EAT AND STAY

For expanded hotel reviews, visit Fodors.com.

$
SEAFOOD
Fodor's Choice
★

✕ **Cap'n Frosty's.** A great stop after the beach, this is where locals go to get their fried seafood. This modest joint has a regular menu that includes ice cream, a small specials board, and a counter where you order and take a number written on a french-fries box. The staff is young and hardworking, pumping out fresh fried clams and fish-and-chips on paper plates. All frying is done in 100% canola oil, and rice pilaf is offered as a substitute for fries. There's seating inside as well as outside on a shady brick patio. $ *Average main: $14* ✉ *219 Rte. 6A, Dennis Village* ☎ *508/385–8548* ⊕ *www.captainfrosty.com* ⌂ *Reservations not accepted* ☉ *Closed early Sept.–Mar.*

$$$
AMERICAN
Fodor's Choice
★

✕ **Red Pheasant.** This is one of the Cape's best cozy country restaurants, with a consistently good kitchen where creative American food, much of it locally sourced and organic, is prepared with elaborate sauces and herb combinations—sautéed day-boat scallops are served with butternut squash risotto, pumpkin seeds, and a ginger syrup, and an exquisitely roasted rack of lamb Persillade is another menu favorite; in fall, look for the specialty game dishes, including venison and quail. Try to reserve a table in the more intimate Garden Room. The expansive wine list is excellent. "Don't miss the opportunity to try this place," says Fodors.com reader ciaotebaldi. $ *Average main: $26* ✉ *905 Rte.*

6A, Dennis Village ☎ *508/385–2133* 🌐 *www.redpheasantinn.com* ✍ *Reservations essential* ⏲ *No lunch.*

$$ B&B/INN Fodor's Choice ★ 🏨 **Isaiah Hall B&B Inn.** Lilacs and pink roses trail along the white-picket fence outside this 1857 Greek Revival farmhouse on a quiet residential road near the bay, where innkeepers Jerry and Judy Neal set the scene for a romantic getaway. **Pros:** beautiful grounds; near beaches and attractions. **Cons:** some very steep steps; some rooms are on the small side. [$] *Rooms from: $189* ✉ *152 Whig St., Box 1007, Dennis Village* ☎ *508/385–9928* 🌐 *www.isaiahhallinn.com* 🛏 *10 rooms, 2 suites* 🍴 *Breakfast.*

3

BREWSTER

7 miles northeast of Dennis, 20 miles east of Sandwich.

Brewster's location on Cape Cod Bay makes it a perfect place to learn about the region's ecology. The Cape Cod Museum of Natural History is here, and the area is rich in conservation lands, state parks, forests, freshwater ponds, and brackish marshes. When the tide is low in Cape Cod Bay, you can stroll the beaches and explore tidal pools up to 2 miles from the shore on the Brewster flats.

ESSENTIALS

Visitor Information Brewster Chamber of Commerce ✉ *Town Hall, 2198 Rte. 6A* ☎ *508/896–3500* 🌐 *www.brewstercapecod.org.*

EXPLORING

Brewster Store. Built in 1852 as a church, this local landmark is a typical New England general store with such essentials as the daily papers, groceries, penny candy, gifts, and benches out front for conversation. Out back, the Brewster Scoop serves ice cream mid-June to early September. Upstairs, memorabilia from antique toys to World War II bond posters is displayed. Downstairs there's a working antique nickelodeon; locals warm themselves by the old coal stove in the colder months. ✉ *1935 Rte. 6A* ☎ *508/896–3744* 🌐 *www.brewsterstore.com.*

Fodor's Choice ★ 🐤 **Cape Cod Museum of Natural History.** A short drive west from the heart of Brewster, this spacious museum and its pristine grounds include a shop, a natural-history library, and exhibits such as a working beehive and a pond- and sea-life room with live specimens. Walking trails wind through 80 acres of forest, marshland, and ponds, all rich in birds and other wildlife. The exhibit hall upstairs has a wall display of aerial photographs documenting the process by which the famous Chatham sandbar was split in two. In summer there are guided field walks, nature programs, and art classes for preschoolers through ninth graders. ✉ *869 Rte. 6A, West Brewster* ☎ *508/896–3867* 🌐 *www.ccmnh.org* 🎟 *$10* ⏲ *June–Sept., daily 9:30–4; Feb. and Mar., Thurs.–Sun. 11–3; Oct.–Dec., Apr. and May, Wed.–Sun. 11–3. Closed Jan. Trails open year-round.*

🐤 **Nickerson State Park.** These 1,961 acres were once part of a vast estate belonging to Roland C. Nickerson, son of Samuel Nickerson, a Chatham native who founded the First National Bank of Chicago. Roland and his wife, Addie, lavishly entertained such visitors as President

Learn about the Cape's marshlands, forests, and ponds at the Cape Cod Museum of Natural History in Brewster.

Grover Cleveland at their private beach and hunting lodge in English country-house style, with coachmen dressed in tails and top hats and a bugler announcing carriages entering the front gates. The grand stone mansion built in 1908 is now part of the Ocean Edge resort. In 1934 Addie donated the land for the state park in memory of Roland and their son, who died during the 1918 flu epidemic.

The park consists of acres of oak, pitch pine, hemlock, and spruce forest speckled with seven freshwater kettle ponds formed by glaciers. Some ponds are stocked with trout for fishing. You can swim canoe, sail, and kayak in the ponds, and bicycle along 8 miles of paved trails that have access to the Cape Cod Rail Trail. Bird-watchers seek out the thrushes, wrens, warblers, woodpeckers, finches, larks, cormorants, great blue herons, hawks, owls, ospreys, and other species. Red foxes and white-tailed deer are occasionally spotted in the woods. Both tent and RV camping are popular here, and nature programs are offered in season. ⊠ *3488 Rte. 6A, East Brewster* 🕾 *508/896–3491* ⊕ *www.mass.gov/dcr* 🎫 *Free* ☉ *Daily dawn–dusk.*

SPORTS AND THE OUTDOORS
WATER SPORTS
Jack's Boat Rentals. Jack's Boat Rentals rents canoes, kayaks, Seacycles, Sunfish, pedal boats, and sailboards at two locations in Nickerson State Park. Sign up for sailing lessons offered at Cliff Pond. ⊠ *Flax Pond, Cliff Pond, Nickerson State Park, Rte. 6A, East Brewster* 🕾 *508/896–8556* ⊕ *www.jacksboatrental.com.*

SHOPPING

★ **Brewster Book Store.** Brewster Book Store prides itself on being a special Cape bookstore. It's filled to the rafters with all manner of books by local and international authors and has an extensive fiction selection and kids section. A full schedule of author signings and children's story times continues year-round. ✉ *2648 Rte. 6A, East Brewster* ☎ *508/896–6543, 800/823–6543* 🌐 *www.brewsterbookstore.com.*

Satucket Farm Stand. Open from Memorial Day through Labor Day, the Satucket Farm Stand is a real old-fashioned farm stand and bakery. There is plenty of local produce as well as some homemade baked goods and other treats. ✉ *76 Harwich Rd. (Rte. 124)* ☎ *508/896–5540* 🌐 *www.satucketfarm.com.*

BIKE THE RAIL TRAIL

The Cape's premier bike path, the **Cape Cod Rail Trail** (🌐 *www.mass.gov/dcr*), follows the paved right-of-way of the old Penn Central Railroad. About 25 miles long, the easy-to-moderate trail passes salt marshes, cranberry bogs, and ponds.

The trail starts at the parking lot off Route 134 south of U.S. 6, near Theophilus Smith Road in South Dennis, and it ends at the post office in South Wellfleet. Access points in Brewster are Long Pond Road, Underpass Road, and Nickerson State Park. There's also a spur off the trail that goes to Chatham.

THE ARTS

Cape Cod Repertory Theatre Co. Several impressive productions, from original works to classics, are staged in this indoor Arts and Crafts–style theater way back in the woods, in a season that runs from May to November. Mesmerizing entertainment for children, in the form of lively outdoor (and often interactive) theater, is provided here, too, and hour-long puppet shows and age-appropriate productions are given Monday through Wednesday mornings at 10 from late June through August. The theater is just west of Nickerson State Park. ✉ *3299 Rte. 6A, East Brewster* ☎ *508/896–1888* 🌐 *www.caperep.org.*

WHERE TO EAT AND STAY

For expanded hotel reviews, visit Fodors.com.

$$$ ECLECTIC ★ 🍴 **Bramble Inn.** Inside an inviting 1860s white house in Brewster's historic village center, this romantic property presents well-crafted, globally inspired contemporary fare in four dining rooms with floral wallpaper or wood-paneled walls, hung with gilt-framed mirrors and watercolor and oil paintings (much of the artwork is for sale). During the warmer months, dine on a patio amid fragrant flower beds. The menu changes often but always includes the assorted seafood curry—the house favorite—which combines lobster, shrimp, scallops, and cod in a light curry sauce with grilled banana, toasted coconut, sliced almonds, and house chutney. If you'd rather graze, opt for the Bramble Bites—choose from risottos, skillet roasted mussels, salmon Niçoise, and the like—served in the bar as well as the garden patios. [$] *Average main: $31* ✉ *2019 Rte. 6A, East Brewster* ☎ *508/896–7644* 🌐 *www.brambleinn.com* 🕒 *Closed Mon. and Tues. No lunch. Closed Jan.–early Apr.*

$$$$ ✕ **Chillingsworth.** One of the crown jewels of Cape restaurants, Chilling-
FRENCH sworth combines formal presentation with an excellent French menu
Fodor'sChoice and a diverse wine cellar to create a memorable dining experience.
★ Super-rich risotto, roast lobster, and grilled Angus sirloin are favorites. Dinner in the main dining rooms is prix-fixe and includes seven
courses—appetizer, soup, salad, sorbet, entrée, "amusements," and
dessert, plus coffee or tea. Less-expensive à la carte options for lunch,
dinner, and Sunday brunch are served in the more casual, patio-style Bistro. There are also a few guest rooms here for overnighting. $ *Average
main: $70* ⊠ *2449 Rte. 6A, East Brewster* ☎ *508/896–3640* ⊕ *www.
chillingsworth.com* ⊗ *Closed Thanksgiving–mid-May.*

$$ ▦ **Old Sea Pines Inn.** With its white-column portico and wraparound
B&B/INN veranda overlooking a broad lawn, Old Sea Pines, which housed a
Fodor'sChoice "charm and personality" school in the early 1900s, resembles a vintage
★ summer estate. **Pros:** not far from town; beautiful grounds; reasonable
rates. **Cons:** some rooms have shared baths; steep stairway to upper
floors. $ *Rooms from: $165* ⊠ *2553 Rte. 6A* ☎ *508/896–6114* ⊕ *www.
oldseapinesinn.com* ⇆ *24 rooms, 19 with bath; 5 suites* ⊗ *Closed Dec.–
mid-Apr.* ▮◯▮ *Breakfast.*

HARWICH

6 miles south of Brewster, 5 miles east of Dennis.

The Cape's famous cranberry industry took off in Harwich in 1844,
when Alvin Cahoon was its principal grower. Today you'll still find
working cranberry bogs throughout Harwich. Three naturally sheltered
harbors on Nantucket Sound make the town, like its English name-
sake, popular with boaters. You'll find dozens of elegant sailboats and
elaborate yachts in Harwich's harbors, plus plenty of charter fishing
boats. Each year in August the town pays celebratory homage to its
large boating population with a grand regatta, Sails Around the Cape.

ESSENTIALS

Visitor Information Harwich Chamber of Commerce ⊠ *1 Schoolhouse Rd. and
Rte. 28, Harwich Port* ☎ *508/432–1600, 800/442–7942* ⊕ *www.harwichcc.com.*

WHERE TO STAY

For expanded hotel reviews, visit Fodors.com.

$$$ ▦ **Winstead Inn and Beach Resort.** Comprising two distinct properties, the
B&B/INN Winstead Inn and Beach Resort offer a two-for-one Cape Cod experi-
★ ence: Harking back to an earlier era, the airy, attractive Beach Resort
sits on a private beach overlooking Nantucket Sound, and you can
gaze at the sweep of coast and surrounding grasslands while enjoying
a generous Continental breakfast from rockers and umbrella tables on
the deck and wraparound porches; at the other end of the spectrum, the
Winstead Inn sits along a quiet street on the edge of downtown. **Pros:**
most rooms have water views; spacious, elegant rooms. **Cons:** numerous
stairs; not for those on a budget. $ *Rooms from: $305* ⊠ *114 Parallel
St.* ☎ *508/432–4444, 800/870–4405* ⊕ *www.winsteadinn.com* ⇆ *18
rooms, 4 suites* ⊗ *Closed Nov.–Easter* ▮◯▮ *Breakfast* $ *Rooms from:
$305* ⊠ *4 Braddock La., Harwich Port* ⇆ *14 rooms* ▮◯▮ *No meals.*

CHATHAM

5 miles east of Harwich.

At the bent elbow of the Cape, with water nearly surrounding it, Chatham has all the charm of a quietly posh seaside resort, with plenty of shops but none of the crass commercialism that plagues some other towns on the Cape. The town has gray-shingle houses with tidy awnings and cheerful flower gardens, an attractive Main Street with crafts and antiques stores alongside dapper cafés, and a five-and-dime. Although it can get crowded in high season—and even on weekends during shoulder seasons—Chatham remains a true New England village.

ESSENTIALS

Visitor Information Chatham Chamber of Commerce ⊠ *2377 Main St. and 533 Main St.* ☎ *508/945–5199, 800/715–5567* ⊕ *www.chathaminfo.com.*

EXPLORING

★ **Atwood House Museum.** Built by sea captain Joseph C. Atwood in 1752, this museum has a gambrel roof, variable-width floor planks, fireplaces, an old kitchen with a wide hearth and a beehive oven, and some antique dolls and toys. The New Gallery displays portraits of local sea captains. The Joseph C. Lincoln Room has the manuscripts, first editions, and mementos of the Chatham writer, and antique tools are displayed in a room in the basement. The 1974 Durand Wing has collections of seashells from around the world and threaded Sandwich glass, as well as Parian-ware figures, unglazed porcelain vases, figurines, and busts. In a remodeled freight shed are the stunning and provocative murals (1932–45) by Alice Stallknecht Wight portraying religious scenes in Chatham settings. On the grounds are an herb garden, the old turret and lens from the Chatham Light, and a simple camp house rescued from eroding North Beach. ⊠ *347 Stage Harbor Rd., West Chatham* ☎ *508/945–2493* ⊕ *www.chathamhistoricalsociety.org* ⊡ *$6* ⊙ *Mid-May–Oct., Tues.–Sat. 1–4; July and Aug., Tues.–Sat. 10–4.*

★ **Chatham Light.** The view from this lighthouse—of the harbor, the sandbars, and the ocean beyond—justifies the crowds. The lighthouse is especially dramatic on a foggy night, as the beacon's light pierces the mist. Coin-operated telescopes allow a close look at the famous "Chatham Break," the result of a fierce 1987 nor'easter that blasted a channel through a barrier beach just off the coast. The U.S. Coast Guard auxiliary, which supervises the lighthouse, offers free tours April through October on most Wednesdays. The lighthouse is also open on three special occasions during the year: Seafest, an annual tribute to the maritime industry held in mid-October; mid-May's Cape Cod Maritime Week; and June's Cape Heritage Week; otherwise, this working lighthouse is off-limits. There is free but limited parking in front of the lighthouse facing the beach: the 30-minute time limit is closely monitored. ⊠ *Main St., near Bridge St., West Chatham.*

Fodor'sChoice
★ **Monomoy National Wildlife Refuge.** This 2,500-acre preserve includes the Monomoy Islands, a fragile 9-mile-long barrier-beach area south of Chatham. Monomoy's North and South islands were created when a storm divided the former Monomoy Island in 1978. A haven for

bird-watchers, the refuge is an important stop along the North Atlantic Flyway for migratory waterfowl and shorebirds—peak migration times are May and late July. It also provides nesting and resting grounds for 285 species, including gulls—great black-backed, herring, and laughing—and several tern species. White-tailed deer wander the islands, and harbor and gray seals frequent the shores in winter. The only structure on the islands is the **South Monomoy Lighthouse,** built in 1849.

Monomoy is a quiet, peaceful place of sand and beach grass, tidal flats, dunes, marshes, freshwater ponds, thickets of bayberry and beach plum, and a few pines. Because the refuge harbors several endangered species, activities are limited. Certain areas are fenced off to protect nesting areas of terns and the threatened piping plover. Get trail maps and information at the small visitor center. ⊠ *Wikis Way, Morris Island* ☎ *508/945–0594* ⊕ *www.fws.gov/northeast/monomoy.*

SPORTS AND THE OUTDOORS

Harding's Beach. Harding's Beach, west of Chatham center and on the calmer and warmer waters of Nantucket Sound, is open to the public and charges daily parking fees to nonresidents in season (late June to early September). Lifeguards are stationed here in summer. This beach can get crowded, so plan to arrive early or late. Nonresident parking fees at Chatham beaches are $15 daily, $60 weekly, and $125 seasonally. ⊠ *Harding's Beach Rd., off Barn Hill Rd., West Chatham.*

SHOPPING

★ **Chatham Jam and Jelly Shop.** Chatham Jam and Jelly Shop sells delicious concoctions like rose-petal jelly, apple-lavender chutney, and wild beach plum jelly, as well as all the old standbys. All preserves are made on-site in small batches, and about 75 of the 120-plus varieties are available for sampling (which is encouraged). ⊠ *10 Vineyard Ave., at Rte. 28, West Chatham* ☎ *508/945–3052* ⊕ *www.chathamjamandjellyshop.com.*

Yankee Ingenuity. Yankee Ingenuity stocks a varied selection of unique jewelry and lamps and a wide assortment of unusual, beautiful trinkets at reasonable (especially for Chatham) prices. The name doesn't mean the items are all from New England, however. ⊠ *525 Main St.* ☎ *508/945–1288* ⊕ *www.yankee-ingenuity.com.*

NIGHTLIFE AND THE ARTS

Chatham Squire. With four bars—including a raw bar—this is a rollicking year-round local hangout, drawing a young crowd to the bar side and a mixed crowd of locals to the restaurant. There's live entertainment on weekends. ⊠ *487 Main St.* ☎ *508/945–0945* ⊕ *www.thesquire.com.*

WHERE TO EAT AND STAY
For expanded hotel reviews, visit Fodors.com.

$$$ ╳ **Impudent Oyster.** A cozy, festive tavern with an unfailingly cheerful
SEAFOOD staff and superb but reasonably priced seafood, this always-packed res-
★ taurant sits inside a dapper house just off Main Street. It's a great place for a romantic meal or dinner with the kids, and the menu offers light burgers and sandwiches as well as more-substantial fare. The mussels with white-wine sauce is a local favorite. The dining room is split-level,

with a bar in back. There's not a ton of seating, so reserve on weekends. $ *Average main: $29* ✉ *15 Chatham Bars Ave.* ☎ *508/945–3545.*

$$$ B&B/INN ★ 🏨 **Queen Anne Inn.** Some of the large guest rooms at the Queen Anne have hand-painted murals, working fireplaces, balconies, and hot tubs, and lingering and lounging are encouraged. **Pros:** spacious rooms; historic setting; heated outdoor pool. **Cons:** long walk to the town center; some steep stairs. $ *Rooms from: $260* ✉ *70 Queen Anne Rd.* ☎ *508/945–0394, 800/545–4667* 🌐 *www.queenanneinn.com* 🛏 *33 rooms* 🕓 *Closed Jan.–Mar.* 🍴 *Breakfast.*

ORLEANS

8 miles north of Chatham, 35 miles east of Sagamore Bridge.

Orleans has a long heritage in fishing and seafaring, and many beautifully preserved homes remain from the Colonial era in the small village of East Orleans, home of the town's Historical Society and Museum. In other areas of town, such as down by Rock Harbor, more modestly grand homes stand near the water's edge.

GETTING HERE AND AROUND

A bus connecting Hyannis and Orleans serves the Lower Cape region. Year-round transport on the Flex service goes from Harwich to Provincetown, serving the towns of Brewster, Orleans, Eastham, Wellfleet, and Truro along the way.

ESSENTIALS

Visitor Information Orleans Chamber of Commerce ✉ *Eldredge Pkwy., off Rte. 6A* ☎ *508/255–1386, 800/856–1386* 🌐 *www.capecod-orleans.com.*

EXPLORING

Rock Harbor. A walk along Rock Harbor Road leads to the bay-side Rock Harbor, site of a War of 1812 skirmish in which the Orleans militia kept a British warship from docking. In the 19th century Orleans had an active saltworks, and a flourishing packet service between Rock Harbor and Boston developed. Today the former packet landing is the base of charter fishing and party boats in season, as well as of a small commercial fishing fleet. Sunsets over the harbor are spectacular. Parking is free here; it's a great place to watch the boats go by and do some limited swimming and sunbathing.

NEED A BREAK? **Cottage St. Bakery. Delicious artisanal breads, pastries, cakes, and sweets are made here, as well as healthful breakfast and lunch fare, from soups to homemade granola and hefty sandwiches.** ✉ *5 Cottage St.* ☎ *508/255–2821.*

SPORTS AND THE OUTDOORS

BEACHES

Nauset Beach. This town-managed beach—not to be confused with Nauset Light Beach on the National Seashore—is a 10-mile sweep of sandy ocean beach with low dunes and large waves good for bodysurfing or board surfing. The beach has lifeguards, restrooms, showers, and a food concession. Despite its size, the massive parking lot often fills up when the sun is strong; arrive quite early or in the late afternoon if you want to claim a spot. The beach is open to off-road vehicles with a special permit. Daily parking fees are $15. ✉ *Beach Rd., Nauset Heights* ☎ *508/240–3780.*

Skaket Beach. Skaket Beach on Cape Cod Bay is a sandy stretch with calm, warm water good for children. There are restrooms, lifeguards, and a snack bar. Daily parking fees are the same as at Nauset Beach. The parking lot fills up fast on hot August days; try to arrive before 11 or after 2. The many tide pools make this a favorite spot for families. Sunsets here draw a good crowd. ✉ *Skaket Beach Rd.* ☎ *508/240–3775.*

There is a daily parking fee of $15 from mid-June to Labor Day for both beaches.

BOATING AND FISHING

Arey's Pond Boat Yard. There's a sailing school here, with individual and group lessons. They also rent sailboats. ✉ *43 Arey's La., off Rte. 28, South Orleans* ☎ *508/255–0994* 🌐 *www.areyspondboatyard.com.*

Many of Orleans's freshwater ponds offer good fishing for perch, pickerel, trout, and more.

Goose Hummock Shop. The required fishing license, along with rental gear, is available at the Goose Hummock Shop, which also rents kayaks and gives kayaking lessons and tours. ✉ *15 Rte. 6A* ☎ *508/255–0455* 🌐 *www.goose.com.*

WHERE TO EAT AND STAY

For expanded hotel reviews, visit Fodors.com.

$$$ MEDITERRANEAN Fodor's Choice ★

🍴 **Abba.** Abba serves inspired Pan-Mediterranean cuisine in an elegant and intimate setting. Chef and co-owner Erez Pinhas skillfully combines Middle Eastern, Asian, and southern European flavors in such dishes as herb-crusted rack of venison with shiitake risotto and asparagus in port sauce, and grilled tuna with vegetable nori roll tempura in a balsamic miso-and-mustard sauce. Cushy pillows on the banquettes and soft candlelight flickering from Moroccan glass votives add a touch of opulence. A Fodors.com member gives Abba a perfect score, saying, "Everything is prepared with care and creativity." Reservations are suggested. [$] *Average main: $32* ✉ *89 Old Colony Way* ☎ *508/255–8144* 🌐 *www.abbarestaurant.com* ⏲ *No lunch.*

$$$ B&B/INN Fodor's Choice ★

🏨 **A Little Inn on Pleasant Bay.** This gorgeously decorated inn occupies a 1798 building on a bluff beside a cranberry bog and many of the rooms look clear out to the bay (others face the lush gardens)—there's even a small private beach with its own dock. **Pros:** great water views; abundant buffet breakfast; spacious, modern baths. **Cons:** not an in-town location. [$] *Rooms from: $280* ✉ *654 S. Orleans Rd., South Orleans* ☎ *508/255–0780, 888/332–3351* 🌐 *www.alittleinnonpleasantbay.com* 🛏 *9 rooms* ⏲ *Closed Oct.–Apr.* 🍽 *Breakfast.*

EASTHAM

3 miles north of Orleans, 6 miles south of Wellfleet.

Often overlooked on the speedy drive up toward Provincetown on U.S. 6, Eastham is a town full of hidden treasures. Unlike other towns on the Cape, it has no official town center or Main Street; the highway bisects it, and the town touches both Cape Cod Bay and the Atlantic. Amid the gas stations, convenience stores, restaurants, and large motel complexes, Eastham's wealth of natural beauty takes a little exploring to find.

ESSENTIALS

Visitor Information Eastham Chamber of Commerce ✉ *1700 Rte. 6, at Governor Prence Rd.* ☎ *508/240–7211* 🌐 *www.easthamchamber.com.*

EXPLORING

Fodor's Choice ★ **Cape Cod National Seashore.** ⇨ *See the highlighted listing, "Cape Cod National Seashore".*

SPORTS AND THE OUTDOORS

Fodor's Choice ★ **Nauset Light Beach.** Adjacent to Coast Guard Beach, this beautiful beach continues the National Seashore landscape of long, sandy beach backed by tall dunes, grass, and heathland. It has showers and lifeguards in summer, but as with other National Seashore beaches, there's no food concession. Nauset charges $15 daily per car, but you can buy an annual pass for $45 (valid for all six National Seashore beaches, Eastham to Provincetown). Parking here fills up very quickly in summer; plan to arrive early or you may have to go elsewhere. ✉ *Off Ocean View Dr.* 🌐 *www.nps.gov/caco.*

WHERE TO EAT AND STAY

For expanded hotel reviews, visit Fodors.com.

$$ SEAFOOD 🍴 **Arnold's Lobster & Clam Bar.** You can't miss this hot spot on the side of Route 6: look for the riot of colorful flowers lining the road and the patient folks waiting in long lines in the parking lot. That crowd is testament to the freshness and flavors that come out of this busy kitchen for lunch, dinner, and takeout, putting forth everything from grilled burgers to 3-pound lobsters. Unusual for a clam shack like this is the full bar, offering beer, wine, mixed drinks, and the house specialty, margaritas. There's ice cream and an artfully designed miniature-golf course to keep the kids happy. [$] *Average main: $16* ✉ *3580 State Hwy. (U.S. 6), Eastham* ☎ *508/255–2575* 🌐 *www.arnoldsrestaurant.com* ⏲ *Closed Nov.–Apr.*

$$ ITALIAN 🍴 **Fairway Restaurant and Pizzeria.** The friendly family-run Fairway specializes in Italian comfort food and pizzas—try the eggplant Parmesan, fettucine and meatballs, or a well-stuffed calzone—and is also very popular for breakfast. Attached to the Hole in One Donut Shop (a favorite among locals for early-morning coffee and exceptional donuts and muffins), the Fairway puts a jar of crayons on every paper-covered table and sells its own brand of root beer. The pizzas are hearty and filling, rather than the thin-crust variety. [$] *Average main: $15* ✉ *4295 U.S. Rte. 6, North Eastham* ☎ *508/255–3893* 🌐 *www.fairwaycapecod.com* ⏲ *No lunch.*

$$$ B&B/INN ★ 🏨 **Penny House Inn & Spa.** Tucked behind a wave of privet hedge, this rambling gray-shingle inn's spacious rooms are furnished with antiques, collectibles, and wicker, but the luxurious accommodations are cozy rather than stuffy. **Pros:** private and secluded, ideal for a romantic getaway; full range of spa services. **Cons:** off busy U.S. 6; no water views or beachfront. [$] *Rooms from: $235* ✉ *4885 County Rd.(U.S.*

6) ☎ *508/255–6632, 800/554–1751* 🌐 *www.pennyhouseinn.com* 🛏 *10 rooms, 3 suites* 🍴 *Breakfast.*

$$ B&B/INN Fodor'sChoice ★ 📷 **Whalewalk Inn & Spa.** This 1830 whaling master's home, on three landscaped acres, has wide-board pine floors, fireplaces, and 19th-century country antiques to provide historical appeal. **Pros:** beautiful grounds; elegantly appointed rooms; decadent spa treatments. **Cons:** no water views or beachfront. [$] *Rooms from: $220* ✉ *220 Bridge Rd.* ☎ *508/255–0617, 800/440–1281* 🌐 *www.whalewalkinn.com* 🛏 *11 rooms, 6 suites* 🕐 *Closed Dec.–Mar.* 🍴 *Breakfast.*

WELLFLEET AND SOUTH WELLFLEET

6 miles north of Eastham, 13 miles southeast of Provincetown.

Still famous for its world-renowned and succulent namesake oysters, Wellfleet is today a tranquil community; many artists and writers call it home. Less than 2 miles wide, it's one of the most attractively developed Cape resort towns, with a number of fine restaurants, historic houses, art galleries, and a good old Main Street in the village proper.

ESSENTIALS

Visitor Information Wellfleet ✉ *Rte. 6, near the post office, South Wellfleet* ☎ *508/349–2510* 🌐 *www.wellfleetchamber.com.*

EXPLORING

★ **Marconi Station.** On the Atlantic side of the Cape is the site of the first transatlantic wireless station erected on the U.S. mainland. It was from here that Italian radio and wireless-telegraphy pioneer Guglielmo Marconi sent the first American wireless message to Europe—"most cordial greetings and good wishes" from President Theodore Roosevelt to King Edward VII of England—on January 18, 1903. An outdoor shelter contains a model of the original station, of which only fragments remain as a result of cliff erosion. Underneath a roofed structure at Marconi Station is a mock-up of the spark-gap transmitter Marconi used. There's a lookout deck that offers a vantage point of both the Atlantic and Cape Cod Bay. Off the parking lot, a 1½-mile trail and boardwalk lead through the **Atlantic White Cedar Swamp,** one of the most beautiful trails on the seashore; free maps and guides are available at the trailhead. **Marconi Beach,** south of the Marconi Station on Marconi Beach Road, is one of the National Seashore's lovely ocean beaches. ✉ *Marconi Site Rd., South Wellfleet* ☎ *508/349–3785* 🌐 *www.nps.gov/caco* 🎟 *Free* 🕐 *Daily dawn–dusk.*

Fodor'sChoice ★ 👶 **Massachusetts Audubon Wellfleet Bay Wildlife Sanctuary.** This reserve, encompassing nearly 1,000-acres, is home to more than 250 species of birds. The jewel of the Massachusetts Audubon Society, the sanctuary is a superb place for walking, birding, and watching the sun set over the salt marsh and bay. The **Esther Underwood Johnson Nature Center** contains two 700-gallon aquariums that offer an up-close look at marine life common to the Cape's tidal flats and marshlands. From the center you can hike five short nature trails, including a fascinating Boardwalk Trail that leads over a salt marsh to a small beach—or you can wander through the Butterfly Garden. The Audubon Society is host

DID YOU KNOW?

With 40 miles of beach along the National Seashore, lifeguards are on duty only at certain sections. Coast Guard Beach is one area that also has practical facilities, making it popular with families.

to naturalist-led wildlife tours around the Cape, including trips to the Monomoy Islands, year-round. The sanctuary also has camps for children in July and August and weeklong field schools for adults. ⊠ *291 U.S. 6, South Wellfleet* ☎ *508/349–2615* ⊕ *www.massaudubon.org/ wellfleetbay* ⊠ *$5* ☉ *Trails daily 8 am–dusk; nature center late May– mid-Oct., daily 8:30–5; mid-Oct.–late May, Tues.–Sun. 8:30–5.*

SPORTS AND THE OUTDOORS

BEACHES

Cahoon Hollow Beach. Lifeguards, restrooms, and a restaurant and music club on the sand are the main attractions at Cahoon Hollow Beach, which tends to draw younger and slightly rowdier crowds; it's a big Sunday-afternoon party place. There are daily parking fees of $15 for nonresidents in season only (beginning around the 3rd week of June until Labor Day); parking is free for those with beach stickers. Space is limited, though the Beachcomber restaurant has paid parking. ⊠ *Ocean View Dr., Greater Wellfleet.*

White Crest Beach. White Crest Beach is a prime surfer hangout where the dudes often spend more time waiting for waves than actually riding them. Lifeguards are on duty daily 9 am to 5 pm from July through Labor Day weekend. If you're up to the challenge, join one of the spontaneous volleyball games that frequently pop up. There are daily parking fees of $15 for nonresidents in season only; parking is free for those with beach stickers. ⊠ *Ocean View Dr., Greater Wellfleet.*

BOATING

Jack's Boat Rental. Canoes, kayaks, Sunfish, pedal boats, surfboards, boogie boards, and sailboards are available at two locations in Wellfleet; one right on Gull Pond. Jack's also offeres sailing lessons and guided kayak tours. ⊠ *Gull Pond, U.S. 6 and Cahoon Hollow Rd., Greater Wellfleet* ☎ *508/349–9808, 508/349–7553* ⊕ *www.jacksboatrental.com.*

NIGHTLIFE AND THE ARTS

Wellfleet Drive-In Theater. The drive-in movie is alive and well on Cape Cod at the Wellfleet Drive-In Theater, which is right by the Eastham town line. Regulars spend the night in style: chairs, blankets, and picnic baskets. Films start at dusk nightly from May to September, and there's also a standard indoor cinema with four screens, a miniature-golf course, and a bar and grill. A summer evening here is a classic Cape experience for many families. It's also the home of the beloved Wellfleet Flea Market, held weekends from late spring to mid-October. ⊠ *51 U.S. 6, South Wellfleet* ☎ *508/349–7176* ⊕ *www.wellfleetcinemas.com.*

WHERE TO EAT

$$ ✕ **Finely JP's.** Chef John Pontius consistently turns out wonderful,
AMERICAN   affordable food full of the best Mediterranean and local influences and ingredients at his beloved restaurant along U.S. 6. Housed in a handsome Arts and Crafts–inspired structure, this spot has long been a local favorite. Appetizers are especially good, among them oysters baked in a white wine-cream sauce and jerk-spiced duck salad with a raspberry vinaigrette. The Wellfleet paella and the roast duck with cranberry-orange sauce draw rave reviews. Early birds can take advantage of the very reasonable three-course prix-fixe menu for $22. Off-season

Artists and birders flock to the Wellfleet Bay Wildlife Sanctuary, protected by the Massachusetts Audubon Society.

hours vary, so call ahead. $ *Average main: $22* ✉ *554 U.S. Rte. 6, South Wellfleet* ☎ *508/349–7500* ⊕ *www.finelyjps.com* ⌂ *Reservations not accepted* ⊘ *Closed some nights during off-season. No lunch. No brunch June–Sept.*

$$
SEAFOOD
✕ **Mac's Seafood.** Right at Wellfleet Harbor, this ambitious little spot has some of the freshest seafood around. There's not a whole lot of seating here—just some outside picnic tables on the sand—but when you've got a succulent mouthful of raw oyster or fried scallop, who cares? You can always sit along the pier and soak up the great water views while you chow down. This place serves a vast variety of seafood, plus sushi, Mexican fare (grilled-scallop burritos), *linguica* sausage sandwiches, raw-bar items, and ice cream. There's also a selection of smoked fish, pâtés, lobster, and fish you can take home to grill yourself. Mac's also has **Mac's Shack** (*91 Commercial St.* ☎ *508/349–6333* ⊘ *Closed Mon. and mid-Oct.–mid-May*), a funky sit-down restaurant in a rambling mid-19th-century barn overlooking Duck Creek, with a lobster boat on the roof. $ *Average main: $18* ✉ *Wellfleet Town Pier, 265 Commercial St., Wellfleet Harbor* ☎ *508/349–9611* ⊕ *www.macsseafood. com* ⊘ *Closed mid-Sept.–late May.*

EN ROUTE Edward Hopper summered in **Truro** from 1930 to 1967, finding the Cape light ideal for his austere brand of realism. One of the largest towns on the Cape in terms of land area—almost 43 square miles—it's also the smallest in population, with about 1,400 year-round residents. Truro is also the Cape's narrowest town, and from a high perch you can see the Atlantic Ocean on one side and Cape Cod Bay on the other. Its **Highland Light,** also called Cape Cod Light, is the Cape's oldest lighthouse and truly a breathtaking sight. Tours ($4) of the lighthouse are given daily from mid-May to October.

PROVINCETOWN

9 miles northwest of Wellfleet, 62 miles from Sagamore Bridge.

★ Many people know that the Pilgrims stopped here at the curved tip of Cape Cod before proceeding to Plymouth. Historical records suggest that an earlier visitor was Thorvald, brother of Viking Leif Erikson, who came ashore here in AD 1004 to repair the keel of his boat and consequently named the area Kjalarness, or Cape of the Keel. Bartholomew Gosnold came to Provincetown in 1602 and named the area Cape Cod after the abundant codfish he found in the local waters.

Incorporated as a town in 1727, Provincetown was for many decades a bustling seaport, with fishing and whaling as its major industries. In the late 19th century, groups of Portuguese fishermen and whalers began to settle here, lending their expertise and culture to an already cosmopolitan town. Fishing is still an important source of income for many Provincetown locals, but now the town ranks among the world's leading whale-watching—rather than whale-hunting—outposts.

Artists began coming here in the late 1890s to take advantage of the unusual Cape Cod light—in fact, Provincetown is the nation's oldest continuous art colony. By 1916, with five art schools flourishing here, painters' easels were nearly as common as shells on the beach. This bohemian community, along with the availability of inexpensive summer lodgings, attracted young rebels and writers as well, including John Reed (*Ten Days That Shook the World*) and Mary Heaton Vorse (*Footnote to Folly*), who in 1915 began the Cape's first significant theater group, the Provincetown Players. The young, then unknown Eugene O'Neill joined them in 1916, when his *Bound East for Cardiff* premiered in a tiny wharf-side East End fish house.

America's original gay resort, Provincetown today is as appealing to artists as it is to gay and lesbian—as well as straight—tourists. The awareness brought by the AIDS crisis and, more recently, Massachusetts's legalization of same-sex marriage has turned the town into the most visibly gay vacation community in America.

GETTING HERE AND AROUND

AIR TRAVEL   Year-round flight service by Cape Air connects Provincetown with Boston's Logan Airport.

CAR TRAVEL   The busiest travel time is early morning—especially on rainy days—when it seems that everyone on Cape Cod is determined to make it to Provincetown. Traffic is heaviest around Wellfleet and it can be slow going. Driving the 3 miles of Provincetown's main downtown thoroughfare, Commercial Street, in season could take forever. Parking is not one of Provincetown's better amenities, so bike and foot are the best ways to explore the downtown area.

FERRY TRAVEL   Bay State Cruise Company offers standard and high-speed ferry services between Commonwealth Pier in Boston and MacMillan Wharf in Provincetown. High-speed service runs a few times daily from mid-May through September ($83 round-trip); the ride takes 90 minutes. Standard service runs Saturdays only from early July through early September ($46 round-trip); the ride takes three hours. Boston Harbor Cruises runs a fast ferry from Long Wharf in Boston mid-May to mid-October for $83 round-trip. From the State Pier in Plymouth, the Plymouth to Provincetown Express Ferry operates a 90-minute ferry daily from mid-June to mid-September ($42 round-trip).

SHUTTLE **The Shuttle,** run by the Cape Cod Regional Transit Authority, provides
TRAVEL a seasonal (mid-June–mid-September) route from Truro, heading into town, with trips to Herring Cove Beach, Race Point Beach, and the Provincetown Airport. Bikes are accommodated.

ESSENTIALS

Transportation Contacts Bay State Cruise Company ☎ *617/748–1428, 877/783–3779* ⊕ *www.baystatecruisecompany.com.* **Boston Harbor Cruises** ☎ *617/227–4321, 877/733–9425* ⊕ *www.bostonharborcruises.com.* **Cape Air** ☎ *866/227–3247, 508/771–6944* ⊕ *www.flycapeair.com.* **Cape Cod Regional Transit Authority** ☎ *800/352–7155* ⊕ *www.capecodtransit.org.* **Provincetown Express Ferry** ☎ *508/747–2400, 800/225–4000* ⊕ *www.provincetownferry.com.*

Visitor Information Provincetown Chamber of Commerce ✉ *Information booth, 307 Commercial St., Box 1017, Downtown Center* ☎ *508/487–3424* ⊕ *www.ptownchamber.com.* **Provincetown Business Guild (gay and lesbian)** ✉ *3 Freeman St., Box 421–94, Downtown Center* ☎ *508/487–2313, 800/637–8696* ⊕ *www.ptown.org.*

EXPLORING

★ **Commercial Street.** Take a casual stroll by the many architectural styles (Greek Revival, Victorian, Second Empire, and Gothic, to name a few) used in the design of the impressive houses for wealthy sea captains and merchants. The Provincetown Historical Society puts out a series of walking-tour pamphlets, available for about $1 each at many shops in town. The center of town is where the crowds and most of the touristy shops are; people-watching here is supreme. The East End is mostly residential, with an increasing number of nationally renowned galleries; the similarly quiet West End has a number of small inns with neat lawns and elaborate gardens.

QUICK
BITES

Spiritus. The local bars close at 1 am, at which point the pizza joint/coffee stand Spiritus becomes the town's epicenter. It's the ultimate place to see and be seen, slice in hand and witty banter at the ready. In the morning, the same counter serves restorative coffee and croissants as well as delectable ice cream from Emack & Bolios, Häagen-Dazs, and Giffords of Maine. ✉ *190 Commercial St., Downtown Center* ☎ *508/487–2808* ⊕ *www.spirituspizza. com* ▭ *No credit cards* ☉ *Closed Nov.–Apr.*

★ **Pilgrim Monument.** The first thing you'll see in Provincetown is this grandiose edifice, which seems somewhat out of proportion to the rest of the low-rise town. The monument commemorates the Pilgrims' first landing in the New World and their signing of the Mayflower Compact (the first Colonial-American rules of self-governance) before they set off from Provincetown Harbor to explore the mainland. Climb the 116 steps and 60 short ramps of the 252-foot-high tower for a panoramic view—dunes on one side, harbor on the other, and the entire bay side of Cape Cod beyond. At the tower's base is a museum of Lower Cape and Provincetown history, with exhibits on whaling, shipwrecks, and scrimshaw. ✉ *1 High Pole Hill Rd., Downtown Center* ☎ *508/487–1310* 🌐 *www.pilgrim-monument.org* 🎫 *$7* ⏲ *Apr.–late May, mid–Sept.–early Dec., daily 9–5; late May–mid-Sept., daily 9–7; closed Dec.–Mar.*

SPORTS AND THE OUTDOORS

Fodor's Choice ★ **Art's Dune Tours.** Art's Dune Tours has been taking eager passengers into the dunes of Province Lands since 1946. Bumpy but controlled rides (about one hour) transport you through sometimes surreal sandy vistas peppered with beach grass and along a shoreline patrolled by seagulls and sandpipers. On Sunday there is a special Race Point Lighthouse Tour; or head out at sunset for a stunning ride, available with or without a clambake feast. ✉ *4 Standish St., Downtown Center* ☎ *508/487–1950, 800/894–1951* 🌐 *www.artsdunetours.com* 🎫 *Regular tours start at $27.*

Fodor's Choice ★ **Race Point Beach.** Race Point Beach, one of the Cape Cod National Seashore beaches in Provincetown, has a wide swath of sand stretching far off into the distance around the point and Coast Guard station. Because of its position facing north, the beach gets sun all day long. ✉ *Race Point Rd., east of U.S. 6* ☎ *508/487–1256* 🌐 *www.nps.gov/caco/index.htm* 🎫 *Parking: $15 per day late June–early Sept. and weekends late May–late June and early Sept.–end Sept.; $3 for bike/foot entry.*

WHALE-WATCHING

Dolphin Fleet. Tours are accompanied by scientists from the Center for Coastal Studies in Provincetown, who provide commentary while collecting data on the whales they've been monitoring for years. They know many of them by name and will tell you about their habits and histories. ■ **TIP→ Check the website and local print resources for discount coupons; also ask for AAA or AARP discounts.** ✉ *Ticket office: Chamber of Commerce building at MacMillan Wharf, Downtown Center* ☎ *508/240–3636, 800/826–9300* 🌐 *www.whalewatch.com* 🎫 *$42* ⏲ *Tours mid-Apr.–Oct.*

NIGHTLIFE

Atlantic House. Atlantic House is the grandfather of the gay nightlife scene. ✉ *4 Masonic Pl., Downtown Center* ☎ *508/487–3821* 🌐 *www.ahouse.com.*

WHERE TO EAT

$$$ AMERICAN Fodor's Choice ★ 🍴 **Devon's.** This unassuming tiny white cottage—with a dining room that seats just 42 lucky patrons—serves up some of the best food in town, judging by the continual crowds that wait for seats. Specialties from the oft-changing menu include brown butter and herb-roasted Atlantic halibut or grilled Provincetown day-boat scallops. Save some room for knockout desserts like blackberry mousse over ginger-lemon polenta cake with wild-berry coulis. Devon's is also a good spot for breakfast. [$] *Average main: $27* ✉ *401½ Commercial St., Downtown Center* ☎ *508/487–4773* 🌐 *www.devons.org* ✍ *Reservations essential* ⏲ *Closed Wed. and Nov.–mid-May. No lunch.*

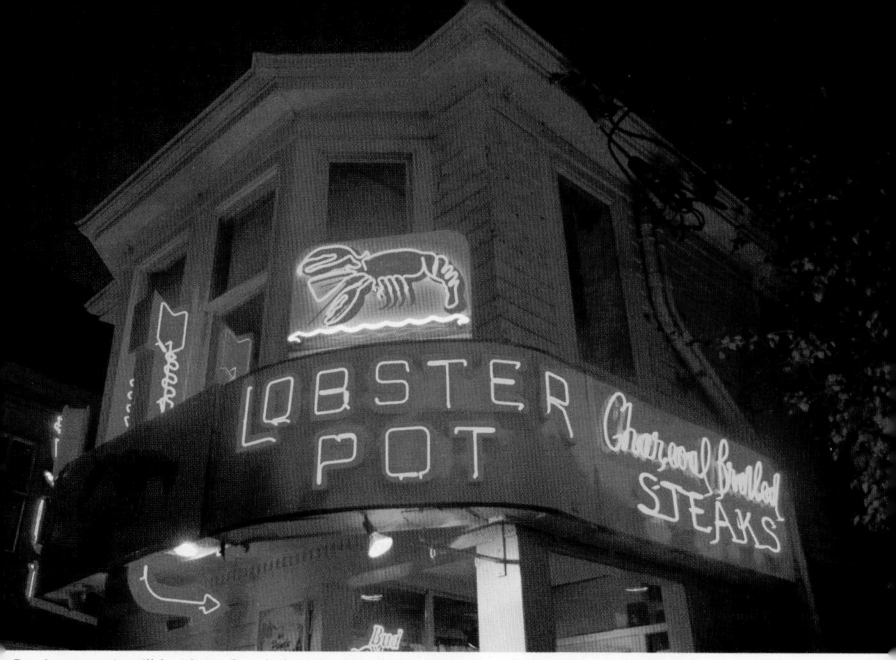

Provincetown is still bustling after dark, especially the late-night food scene and gay nightlife.

$$$ SEAFOOD 🍴 **Lobster Pot.** Provincetown's Lobster Pot is fit to do battle with all the lobster shanties anywhere (and everywhere) else on the Cape—it's often jammed with tourists, but the crowds reflect the generally high quality. The hardworking kitchen turns out classic New England cooking: lobsters, generous and filling seafood platters, and some of the best chowder around. Eat like a local and try the barbeque pepper shrimp. [$] *Average main: $27* ✉ *321 Commercial St., Downtown Center* ☎ *508/487–0842* 🌐 *www.ptownlobsterpot.com* ✍ *Reservations not accepted* ⏲ *Closed Jan.*

$$$ AMERICAN Fodor's Choice ★ 🍴 **The Mews.** This perennial favorite with magnificent harbor views focuses on seafood and grilled meats with a cross-cultural flair—popular entrées include roasted vegetable and polenta lasagna with a tomato-olive sauce and Shaking Beef, a Vietnamese-inspired dish of beef tenderloin sautéed with scallions and red onions and a lime-black pepper sauce; there's also a lighter bistro menu for smaller appetites. The view of the bay from the bar is nearly perfect, and the gentle lighting makes this a romantic spot to have a drink. The restaurant claims its vodka bar is New England's largest, with more than 275 varieties. Sunday brunch is served from Mother's Day to Columbus Day; fall and winter Monday nights get lively with the very popular open-mike coffeehouse. [$] *Average main: $26* ✉ *429 Commercial St., East End* ☎ *508/487–1500* 🌐 *www.mews.com* ⏲ *No lunch. Brunch Sun. only.*

WHERE TO STAY

For expanded hotel reviews, visit Fodors.com.

$$$

B&B/INN

Fodor's Choice

★

Brass Key. One of the Cape's most luxurious small resorts, this meticulously kept year-round getaway comprises a beautifully restored main house—originally a sea captain's home built in 1828—and several other carefully groomed buildings and cottages. **Pros:** ultraposh rooms; beautiful and secluded grounds; pool on-site. **Cons:** among the highest rates in town; rooms close to Bradford Street can get a bit of noise; significant minimum-stay requirements in summer. $ *Rooms from: $319* ⊠ *67 Bradford St., Downtown Center* ☎ *508/487–9005, 800/842–9858* ⊕ *www.brasskey.com* ⊅ *43 rooms* ¶ *Breakfast.*

$$

B&B/INN

Snug Cottage. Noted for its extensive flower gardens and enviable perch atop one of the larger bluffs in town, this convivial Arts and Crafts-style inn dates to 1825 and is decked in smashing English country antiques and fabrics. **Pros:** steps from East End dining and shopping; stunning grounds and gardens; most units are extremely spacious. **Cons:** rooms close to Bradford Street can get some noise; a bit of a walk to West End businesses; top suites aren't cheap. $ *Rooms from: $225* ⊠ *178 Bradford St., east of Downtown Center* ☎ *508/487–1616, 800/432–2334* ⊕ *www.snugcottage.com* ⊅ *3 rooms, 5 suites* ¶ *Breakfast.*

MARTHA'S VINEYARD

Far less developed than Cape Cod—thanks to a few local conservation organizations—yet more cosmopolitan than neighboring Nantucket, Martha's Vineyard is an island with a double life. From Memorial Day through Labor Day the quieter (some might say real) Vineyard quickens into a vibrant, star-studded place.

The busy main port, Vineyard Haven, welcomes day-trippers fresh off ferries and private yachts to browse in its array of shops. Oak Bluffs, where pizza and ice cream emporiums reign supreme, has the air of a Victorian boardwalk. Edgartown is flooded with seekers of chic who wander tiny streets that hold boutiques, stately whaling captains' homes, and charming inns.

Summer regulars have included a host of celebrities over the years, among them Carly Simon, Ted Danson, Spike Lee, and Diane Sawyer. If you're planning to stay overnight on a summer weekend, be sure to make reservations well in advance; spring is not too early. Things stay busy on September and October weekends, a favorite time for weddings, but begin to slow down soon after. In many ways the Vineyard's off-season persona is even more appealing than its summer self, with more time to linger over pastoral and ocean vistas, free from the throngs of cars, bicycles, and mopeds.

Except for Oak Bluffs and Edgartown, the Vineyard is "dry," but many restaurants allow you to bring your own beer or wine. The town of Vineyard Haven has recently allowed beer and wine—but no liquor—to be sold in restaurants only.

ESSENTIALS
Visitor Information **Martha's Vineyard Chamber of Commerce** ⊠ *34 Beach Rd., Vineyard Haven* ☎ *508/693–0085, 800/505–4815* ⊕ *www.mvy.com.*

VINEYARD HAVEN (TISBURY)

7 miles southeast of Woods Hole, 3½ miles west of Oak Bluffs, 8 miles northwest of Edgartown.

Most people call this town Vineyard Haven because of the name of the port where ferries arrive, but its official name is Tisbury. Not as high-toned as Edgartown or as honky-tonk as Oak Bluffs, Vineyard Haven blends the past and the present with a touch of the bohemian. Visitors step off the ferry right into the bustle of the harbor, a block from the shops and restaurants of Main Street.

GETTING HERE AND AROUND

It can be handy to have a car to see all of Martha's Vineyard and travel freely. Instead of bringing one over on the ferry in summer it's some-times easier and more economical to rent a car once you're on the island for the days you plan on exploring. The Martha's Vineyard Transit Authority (VTA) provides regular service to all six towns on the island. The buses can accommodate a limited number of bicycles and the island has an excellent network of well-maintained bike trails. The VTA also has free in-town shuttle-bus routes in Edgartown and Vineyard Haven.

AIR TRAVEL   Cape Air has regular, year-round flight service to the island from Hyan-nis, Boston, and Providence's T. F. Green Airport. From New York's LaGuardia Airport, Philadelphia, and Washington, D.C., U.S. Airways Express provides seasonal service.

FERRY TRAVEL   The Steamship Authority runs the only car ferries to Martha's Vineyard, which make the 45-minute trip from Woods Hole on Cape Cod to Vine-yard Haven year-round and to Oak Bluffs from late May through mid-October ($8 for passenger fare; $3 for bicycles; $42.50–$68 for a car). In summer and on autumn weekends, you must have a reservation if you want to bring your car; passenger reservations are never necessary.

The Island Queen makes the 35-minute trip from Falmouth Harbor to Oak Bluffs from late May through early October. Credit cards are not accepted for payment ($20 round-trip). The Vineyard Fast Ferry offers high-speed passenger service to Martha's Vineyard from North Kingstown, Rhode Island—a half hour south of Providence and a half-hour northwest of Newport. The ride takes 90 minutes, making this a great option for those flying in to T. F. Green Airport, just south of Providence. Service is from late May through early October and costs $49 one-way or $74 round-trip.

Hy-Line offers both high-speed and conventional ferry service to Mar-tha's Vineyard from Hyannis. The regular ferries offer a 95-minute run ($22.50) from Hyannis to Oak Bluffs early May to late October. The 55-minute high-speed ferry ($36) runs from late May through late November. Call to reserve a parking space in high season.

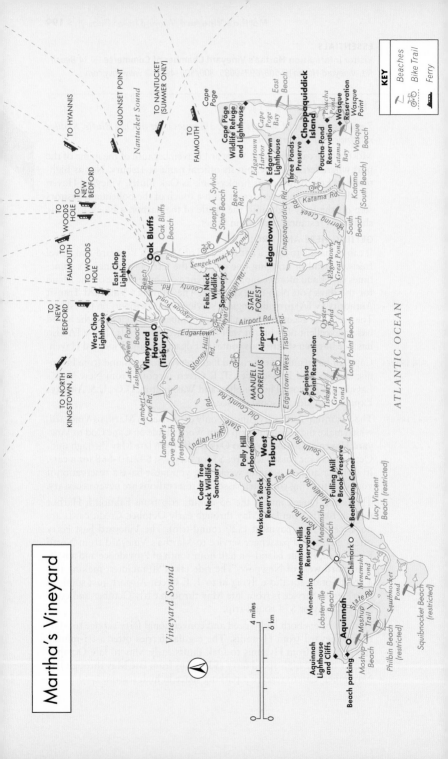

Martha's Vineyard

KEY

- Beaches
- Bike Trail
- Ferry

TO HYANNIS
TO QUONSET POINT
TO NANTUCKET (SUMMER ONLY)
TO FALMOUTH
TO WOODS HOLE
TO NEW BEDFORD
TO FALMOUTH
TO WOODS HOLE
TO NEW BEDFORD
TO NORTH KINGSTOWN, RI

Nantucket Sound

Cape Poge

Cape Poge Wildlife Refuge and Lighthouse

Cape Poge Bay

East Beach

Chappaquiddick Island

Poucha Pond Reservation

Poucha Pond

Wasque Reservation

Wasque Point

Katama Bay

Wasque Beach

Three Ponds Preserve

Edgartown Harbor

Edgartown Lighthouse

Edgartown

Chappaquiddick Rd.

Katama Rd.

Katama (South Beach)

Herring Creek

South Katama Rd.

Edgartown Great Pond

South Beach

Oak Bluffs
Oak Bluffs Beach

Beach Rd.

Joseph A. Sylvia State Beach

Sengekontacket Pond

Felix Neck Wildlife Sanctuary

County Rd.

Vineyard Haven Rd.

Beach Rd.

STATE FOREST

Airport Rd.

AIRPORT

MANUEL F. CORRELLUS

Edgartown-West Tisbury Rd.

Vineyard Sound

East Chop Lighthouse

West Chop Lighthouse

Vineyard Haven (Tisbury)

Lake Tashmoo

Owen Park Beach

Tashmoo Beach

Lambert's Cove Rd.

Lambert's Cove Beach (restricted)

Cedar Tree Neck Wildlife Sanctuary

Stoney Hill Rd.

Edgartown-Vineyard Haven Rd.

Indian Hill Rd.

State Rd.

Old County Rd.

Polly Hill Arboretum

Waskosim's Rock Reservation

West Tisbury

Sepiessa Point Reservation

Oyster Pond

Tisbury Great Pond

Long Point Beach

ATLANTIC OCEAN

Tea La.

North Rd.

Middle Rd.

Fulling Mill Brook Preserve

Beetlebung Corner

Lucy Vincent Beach (restricted)

Menemsha Hills Reservation

Menemsha

Lobsterville Beach

Menemsha Beach

Chilmark

Menemsha Pond

Squibnocket Pond

Squibnocket Beach (restricted)

State Rd.

Aquinnah

Moshup Trail

Moshup Beach

Aquinnah Lighthouse and Cliffs

Beach parking

Philbin Beach (restricted)

4 miles
6 km

Seastreak makes the hour-long trip by high-speed catamaran ($35) from New Bedford to Oak Bluffs and Vineyard Haven from May to the end of October several times daily.

ESSENTIALS

Transportation Contacts Martha's Vineyard Transit Authority (*VTA*). ☎ *508/693–9940* 🌐 *www.vineyardtransit.com.*

3

SPORTS AND THE OUTDOORS

BEACHES

Lake Tashmoo Town Beach. Swimmers have access to the warm, relatively shallow, brackish Lake Tashmoo from this beach—or cooler, gentler Vineyard Sound. ✉ *End of Herring Creek Rd..*

Owen Park Beach. This small, sandy harbor beach, is just steps away from the ferry terminal in Vineyard Haven, making it a great spot to catch some last rays before heading home. ✉ *Off Main St.*

Tisbury Town Beach. This public beach is next to the Vineyard Haven Yacht Club. ✉ *End of Owen Little Way, off Main St.*

SHOPPING

Fodor's Choice ★ **Rainy Day.** As the name suggests, Rainy Day carries gifts and amusements that are perfect for one of the island's gloomy rainy days, when you just need a warm, dry diversion. You'll find toys, crafts, cards, soaps, home accessories, gifts, and more. ✉ *66 Main St.* ☎ *508/693–1830* 🌐 *www.rainydaymv.com.*

WHERE TO EAT AND STAY

For expanded hotel reviews, visit Fodors.com.

$$$ AMERICAN 🍴 **Black Dog Tavern.** This island landmark—more popular with tourists than locals—lies just steps from the ferry terminal in Vineyard Haven. In July and August, the wait for breakfast (with an expansive omelet assortment) can be as much as an hour. Why? Partly because the character inside—roaring fireplace, dark-wood walls, maritime memorabilia, and a grand view of the water—makes everyone feel so at home. The menu is heavy on local fish, chowders, and chops. [$] *Average main: $25* ✉ *25 Water St., Vineyard Haven Harbor* ☎ *508/693–9223* 🌐 *www.theblackdog.com* ✍ *Reservations not accepted* 🕒 *October–May, no dinner Sun.–Wed.*

$$$$ B&B/INN ★ 🏨 **Crocker House Inn.** This 1890 farmhouse-style inn is tucked into a quiet lane off Main Street, minutes from the ferries and Owen Park Beach, and provides rooms that are decorated casually with understated flair. **Pros:** great owners; short walk from town; easygoing vibe. **Cons:** you pay a premium for this location; books up quickly in summer. [$] *Rooms from: $395* ✉ *12 Crocker Ave.* ☎ *508/693–1151, 800/772–0206* 🌐 *www.crockerhouseinn.com* 🛏 *8 rooms* 🍽 *Breakfast.*

$$$ B&B/INN 🏨 **Hanover House.** On a half-acre of landscaped lawn beside a busy road—but within walking distance of the ferry—this three-property, children-friendly inn consists of a classic, home-style B&B, a country inn, and a carriage house. **Pros:** good value; 10-minute walk to shops and dining. **Cons:** on busy road; no water or beach views from most units. [$] *Rooms from: $230* ✉ *28 Edgartown Rd.* ☎ *508/693–1066,*

800/696–8633 ⊕ *www.hanoverhouseinn.com* ⤸ *13 rooms, 2 suites* ↿◯⇂ *Breakfast.*

OAK BLUFFS

3½ miles east of Vineyard Haven.

Circuit Avenue is the bustling center of the Oak Bluffs action, with most of the town's shops, bars, and restaurants. Colorful gingerbread-trimmed guesthouses and food and souvenir joints enliven Oak Bluffs Harbor, once the setting for several grand hotels (the 1879 Wesley Hotel on Lake Avenue is the last remaining one). This small town is more high-spirited than haute, more fun than refined.

EXPLORING

East Chop Lighthouse. This lighthouse was built out of cast iron in 1876 to replace an 1828 tower (used as part of a semaphore system of visual signaling between the island and Boston) that burned down. The 40-foot structure stands high atop a 79-foot bluff with spectacular views of Nantucket Sound. ⊠ *E. Chop Dr.* ☎ *508/627–4441* ⊕ *www.mvmuseum.org* ⊠ *$5* ☉ *Late-June–mid-Sept., Sun. 1½ hrs before sunset–½ hr after sunset.*

Flying Horses Carousel. A National Historic Landmark, this is the nation's oldest continuously operating merry-go-round. Handcrafted in 1876 (the horses have real horsehair and glass eyes), the ride gives children a taste of entertainment from a TV-free era. ⊠ *Oak Bluffs Ave.* ☎ *508/693–9481* ⊠ *Rides $2* ☉ *Late May–early Sept., daily 10–10; Easter–late May, weekends 10–5; early Sept.–mid-Oct., weekdays 11–4:30, weekends 10–5.*

SPORTS AND THE OUTDOORS

BEACHES

Joseph A. Sylvia State Beach. This 6-mile-long sandy beach has a view of Cape Cod across Nantucket Sound, and food vendors and calm, warm waters make it a popular spot for families. Get there early or late in high summer: the parking spots fill up quickly. ⊠ *off Beach Rd., between Oak Bluffs and Edgartown.*

FISHING

Dick's Bait & Tackle. You can rent gear, buy accessories and bait, and check out a current copy of the fishing regulations here. ⊠ *108 New York Ave.* ☎ *508/693–7669.*

GOLF

Farm Neck Golf Club. A semiprivate club on marsh-rimmed Sengekontacket Pond, Farm Neck Golf Club has a driving range and 18 holes in a championship layout. ⊠ *1 Farm Neck Way, off County Rd.* ☎ *508/693–3057* ⊕ *www.farmneck.net.*

NIGHTLIFE

Offshore Ale. The island's only family brewpub, Offshore Ale, hosts live Latin, folk, and blues year-round and serves its own beer and ales and a terrific pub menu. Cozy up to the fireplace with a pint on cool nights. ⊠ *Kennebec Ave.* ☎ *508/693–2626* ⊕ *www.offshoreale.com.*

WHERE TO EAT AND STAY

For expanded hotel reviews, visit Fodors.com.

$$
MEXICAN
★
× **Sharky's Cantina.** Sharky's serves tasty—somewhat creative—Mexican and Southwestern fare and great drinks, and you may wait awhile to get a table, but once you're in, savor spicy tortilla soup, lobster quesadillas, chicken mole, and gaucho-style skirt steak. There's an extensive margarita list (they're strong here), and for dessert try apple-pie empanadas drizzled with caramel sauce. Limited items from the menu are served until around midnight during the summer season. They have a second location in Edgartown. ⓢ *Average main: $16* ⊠ *31 Circuit Ave.* ☎ *508/693–7501* ⊕ *www.sharkyscantina.com* ⌦ *Reservations not accepted.*

$$$$
AMERICAN
Fodor's Choice
★
× **Sweet Life Café.** Housed in a charming Victorian house, this island favorite's warm tones, low lighting, and handsome antique furniture will make you feel as if you've entered someone's home, but the cooking is more sophisticated than home-style—dishes are prepared in inventive ways (and change often with the seasons): sautéed halibut is served with sweet-pea risotto, pine nuts, and a marjoram beurre blanc, while the white gazpacho is filled with steamed clams, toasted almonds, sliced red grapes, and paprika oil. The desserts are superb; try the warm chocolate fondant with toasted-almond ice cream. There's outdoor dining by candlelight in a shrub-enclosed garden. ⓢ *Average main: $37* ⊠ *63 Upper Circuit Ave., at far end of town* ☎ *508/696–0200* ⊕ *www.sweetlifemv. com* ⌦ *Reservations essential* ⊗ *Closed Jan.–Mar. No lunch.*

$$$
B&B/INN
Pequot Hotel. The furniture in this casual cedar-shingle inn on a tree-lined street is quirky but comfortable—the old wing has the most atmosphere. **Pros:** steps from shops and dining; reasonable rates; charmingly offbeat. **Cons:** some rooms are small. ⓢ *Rooms from: $225* ⊠ *19 Pequot Ave.* ☎ *508/693–5087, 800/947–8704* ⊕ *www.pequothotel.com* ⌥ *31 rooms, 1 apartment* ⊗ *Closed mid-Oct.–Apr.* ⦿ *Breakfast.*

EDGARTOWN

6 miles southeast of Oak Bluffs.

Once a well-to-do whaling center, Edgartown remains the Vineyard's toniest town and has preserved parts of its elegant past. Sea captains' houses from the 18th and 19th centuries, with well-manicured gardens and lawns, line the streets.

EXPLORING

★
☺
Felix Neck Wildlife Sanctuary. The 350-acre Massachusetts Audubon Society preserve, 3 miles outside Edgartown toward Oak Bluffs and Vineyard Haven, has 4 miles of hiking trails traversing marshland, fields, woods, seashore, and waterfowl and reptile ponds. Naturalist-led events include sunset hikes, stargazing, snake or bird walks, and canoeing. ⊠ *100 Felix Neck Rd., off Edgartown–Vineyard Haven Rd.* ☎ *508/627–4850* ⊕ *www.massaudubon.org* ⊡ *$4* ⊗ *June–Aug., Mon.– Sat. 9–4, Sun. 10–3; Sept.–May, weekdays 9–4, Sat. 10–3, Sun. noon–3. Trails daily sunrise–dusk.*

OFF THE BEATEN PATH

A sparsely populated area with many nature preserves, where you can fish, **Chappaquiddick Island,** 1 mile southeast of Edgartown, makes for a pleasant day trip or bike ride on a sunny day. The "island" is actually connected to the Vineyard by a long sand spit that begins in South Beach in Katama. It's a spectacular 2¾-mile walk, or you can take the ferry, which departs about every five minutes. On the island's Mytoi preserve, a boardwalk runs through part of the grounds, where you're apt to see box turtles and hear the sounds of songbirds. Elsewhere you can fish, sunbathe, or even dip into the surf—use caution, as the currents are strong.

SHOPPING

Edgartown Books. David Le Breton, the owner of Edgartown Books, is a true bibliophile. He carries a large selection of current and island-related titles and will be happy to make a summer reading recommendation. ✉ *44 Main St.* ☎ *508/627–8463* 🌐 *www.edgartownbooks.net* 🕒 *Closed Jan.*

Old Sculpin Gallery. The Martha's Vineyard Art Association have their headquarters at this gallery, which exhibits the works of local juried artists on a weekly-changing schedule; on summer Sunday evenings it hosts opening receptions beginning at 5 pm. ✉ *58 Dock St.* ☎ *508/627–4881* 🌐 *www.oldsculpingallery.org* 🕒 *Open June–mid-Oct., daily 9–9.*

QUICK BITES

Morning Glory Farm. This farm store is full of incredible goodies, most made or grown on the premises, including fresh farm greens in the salads and vegetables in the soups, and homemade pies, breads, quiches, cookies, and cakes. A picnic table and grass to sit on while you eat make this an ideal place for a simple country lunch. ✉ *W. Tisbury Rd.* ☎ *508/627–9003* 🌐 *www.morninggloryfarm.com* 🕒 *Closed late Dec.–early May.*

WHERE TO EAT AND STAY

For expanded hotel reviews, visit Fodors.com.

$$$$ FRENCH

🍴 **Alchemy Bistro and Bar.** According to the menu, the dictionary meaning of *alchemy* is "a magic power having as its asserted aim the discovery of a panacea and the preparation of the elixir of longevity"—lofty goals for a French-style bistro. This high-class version has elegant gray wainscoting, classic paper-covered white tablecloths, old wooden floors, and an opening cut into the ceiling to reveal the second-floor tables. The only things missing are the patina of age and experience—and French working folks' prices—but you can expect quality and imagination. One example is the skillet-roasted pork tenderloin with crispy shallots. The alcohol list, long and complete, includes cognacs, grappas, and beers. On balmy evenings, the half-dozen outdoor tables on the candlelit brick patio are highly coveted. [$] *Average main: $35* ✉ *71 Main St.* ☎ *508/627–9999* 🕒 *No lunch.*

$$$$ B&B/INN ★

🏨 **Charlotte Inn.** From the moment you walk up to the dark-wood Scottish barrister's desk to check in at this regal 1864 inn, you'll be surrounded by the trappings and customs of a bygone era—beautiful antique furnishings, objets d'art, and paintings fill the property. **Pros:** over-the-top lavish; quiet yet convenient location; beautifully landscaped. **Cons:** can feel overly formal; intimidating if you don't adore museum-quality antiques. $\boxed{\text{\$}}$ *Rooms from: $550* $\boxtimes$ *27 S. Summer St.* ☎ *508/627–4751, 800/735–2478* ⊕ *www.charlotteinn.net* ⤴ *23 rooms, 2 suites.*

WEST TISBURY

8 miles west of Edgartown, 6½ miles south of Vineyard Haven.

West Tisbury retains its rural appeal and maintains its agricultural tradition at several active horse and produce farms. The town center looks very much like a small New England village, complete with a white-steepled church.

EXPLORING

Sepiessa Point Reservation. A paradise for bird-watchers, Sepiessa Point Reservation consists of 164 acres on splendid Tisbury Great Pond, with expansive pond and ocean views, walking trails around coves and saltwater marshes, bird-watching, horse trails, swimming, and a boat launch. $\boxtimes$ *New La., which becomes Tiah's Cove Rd.* ☎ *508/627–7141* 🎫 *Free* ⊙ *Daily sunrise–sunset.*

SHOPPING

Alley's General Store. Step back in time with a visit to Alley's General Store, a local landmark since 1858. Alley's sells a truly general variety of goods: everything from hammers to housewares and dill pickles to sweet muffins as well as great things you find only in a country store. There's even a post office inside. $\boxtimes$ *299 State Rd.* ☎ *508/693–0088.*

AQUINNAH

6½ miles west of Menemsha, 10 miles southwest of West Tisbury, 17 miles southwest of Vineyard Haven.

Aquinnah, called Gay Head until the town voted to change its name in 1997, is an official Native American township. The Wampanoag tribe is the guardian of the 420 acres that constitute the Aquinnah Native American Reservation. Aquinnah (pronounced a-*kwih*-nah) is Wampanoag for "land under the hill." You can get a good view of Menemsha and Nashaquitsa ponds, the woods, and the ocean beyond from Quitsa Pond Lookout on State Road. The town is best known for the red-hued Aquinnah Cliffs.

EXPLORING

Fodor's Choice
★

Aquinnah Cliffs. A National Historic Landmark, the spectacular Aquinnah Cliffs are part of the Wampanoag Reservation land. These dramatically striated walls of red clay are the island's major attraction, as evidenced by the tour bus–filled parking lot. Native American crafts and food shops line the short approach to the overlook, from which you can see the Elizabeth Islands to the northeast across Vineyard Sound and Noman's Land Island—a wildlife preserve—3 miles off the Vineyard's southern coast. $\boxtimes$ *State Rd.*

Aquinnah Lighthouse. This brick lighthouse (also called Gay Head Lighthouse) is stationed precariously atop the rapidly eroding cliffs. Bad weather may affect its opening hours. $\boxtimes$ *Lighthouse Rd.*

☎ *508/627–4441* ⊕ *www.mvmuseum.org* 📧 *$5* ⊙ *Mid-June–early Sept., daily 10–5, plus sunset hours: late June–July, Fri. and Sat. 7–9, Aug., Fri. and Sat. 6–8; late May–mid-June & mid-Sept., weekends 10–5.*

NANTUCKET

At the height of its prosperity in the early 19th century, the little island of Nantucket was the foremost whaling port in the world. Its harbor bustled with whaling ships and merchant vessels; chandleries, cooperages, and other shops crowded the wharves. Burly ship hands loaded barrels of whale oil onto wagons, which they wheeled along cobblestone streets to refineries and candle factories. Sea breezes carried the smoke and smells of booming industry through town as its inhabitants eagerly took care of business. Shipowners and sea captains built elegant mansions, which today remain remarkably unchanged, thanks to a very strict building code initiated in the 1950s. The entire town of Nantucket is now an official National Historic District encompassing more than 800 pre-1850 structures within 1 square mile.

Day-trippers usually take in the architecture and historical sites, dine at one of the many delightful restaurants, and browse in the pricey boutiques, most of which stay open from mid-April through December. Signature items include Nantucket lightship baskets, originally crafted by sailors whiling away a long watch; artisans who continue the tradition now command prices of $700 and up, and the antiques are exponentially more expensive.

NANTUCKET TOWN

30 miles southeast of Hyannis, 107 miles southeast of Boston.

Nantucket Town has one of the country's finest historical districts, with beautiful 18th- and 19th-century architecture and a museum of whaling history.

GETTING HERE AND AROUND

Arriving by ferry puts you in the center of town. There is little need for a car here to explore; ample public transportation and smoothly paved bike paths can take you to the further reaches with ease. The Nantucket Regional Transit Authority (NRTA) runs shuttle buses from in town to most areas of the island. Service is generally available from late May to mid-October.

AIR TRAVEL   Year-round flight service to Nantucket from Boston and Hyannis is provided by Cape Air, Island Airlines, and Nantucket Airlines. U.S. Airways Express offers seasonal service to the island from Washington, D.C., Philadelphia, and New York's LaGuardia; from Newark Airport in New Jersey, Continental Express provides a seasonal route to the island.

FERRY TRAVEL   Hy-Line's high-end, high-speed Grey Lady ferries run between Hyannis and Nantucket year-round in an hour ($39). Hy-Line's slower ferry makes the roughly two-hour trip from Hyannis between early May and

Sacred to the Wampanoag Tribe, the red-hued Aquinnah Cliffs are a popular attraction on Martha's Vineyard.

late October. The MV *Great Point* offers a first-class section ($28) with a private lounge and a bar or a standard fare ($22.50).

The Steamship Authority runs car-and-passenger ferries from Hyannis year-round, a 2¼-hour trip ($17.50 for passenger fare; $140–$200 for a car). There's also high-speed passenger ferry service, which takes only an hour, from late March through late December ($35).

In season, the passenger-only (some bikes allowed) ferry from Harwich Port to Nantucket is a less hectic alternative to the Hyannis crowd. The Freedom Cruise Line runs express high-speed 75-minute ferries between late May and early October ($39).

ESSENTIALS

Transportation Contacts Nantucket Regional Transit Authority ⊠ *3 E. Chestnut St.* ☎ *508/228–7025* ⊕ *www.nrtawave.com.*

Visitor Information Nantucket Chamber of Commerce ⊠ *Zero Main St., Nantucket* ☎ *508/228–1700* ⊕ *www.nantucketchamber.org.* **Nantucket Visitor Services and Information Bureau** ⊠ *25 Federal St., Nantucket* ☎ *508/228–0925* ⊕ *www.nantucket-ma.gov.*

EXPLORING

Nantucket Historical Association (NHA). The Nantucket Historical Association (NHA) maintains an assortment of venerable properties in town. A $20 pass gets you into all of the association's sites, including the glorious Whaling Museum. A $6 pass excludes the Whaling Museum but includes Hadwen House and Oldest House. ☎ *508/228–1894* ⊕ *www. nha.org.*

Each beach on Nantucket has a unique approach—sometimes getting there is half the fun.

African Meeting House. When the island abolished slavery in 1773, Nantucket became a destination for free blacks and escaping slaves. The African Meeting House was built in the 1820s as a schoolhouse, and it functioned as such until 1846, when the island's schools were integrated. A complete restoration has returned the site to its authentic 19th-century appearance. ⊠ *29 York St.* ☏ *508/228–9833* ⊕ *www. afroammuseum.org* 🎫 *$5* ⊙ *June–Oct., weekdays 11–3, Sat. 11–1, Sun. 1–3.*

Brant Point Light. The promontory where this 26-foot-tall, white-painted beauty stands offers views of the harbor and town. The point was once the site of the second-oldest lighthouse in the country (1746); the present, much-photographed light was built in 1901. ⊠ *End of Easton St., across footbridge.*

★ **First Congregational Church.** The tower of this church provides the best view of Nantucket—for those willing to climb its 94 steps. Rising 120 feet, the tower is capped by a weather vane depicting a whale catch. Peek in at the church's 1852 trompe l'oeil ceiling. ⊠ *62 Centre St.* ☏ *508/228–0950* ⊕ *www.nantucketfcc.org* 🎫 *Tower tour $5* ⊙ *Mid-June–mid-Oct., Mon.–Sat. 10–4; services Sun. 10 am.*

Fodor'sChoice
★
☾
Whaling Museum. With exhibits that include a fully rigged whaleboat and a skeleton of a 46-foot sperm whale, this museum—a complex that includes a restored 1846 spermaceti candle factory—is a must-see attraction that offers a crash course in the island's colorful history. Items on display include harpoons and other whale-hunting implements; portraits of whaling captains and their wives (a few of whom went whaling as well); the South Seas curiosities they brought home; a large collection

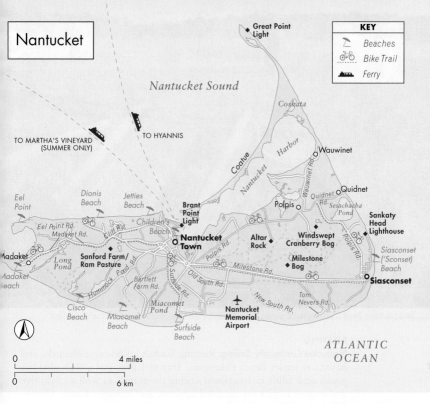

Nantucket

KEY
- Beaches
- Bike Trail
- Ferry

Nantucket Sound

Great Point Light

Coskata

TO MARTHA'S VINEYARD (SUMMER ONLY)

TO HYANNIS

Wauwinet

Coatue

Nantucket

Harbor

Eel Point

Dionis Beach

Jetties Beach

Brant Point Light

Polpis

Quidnet

Quidnet Rd.

Sesachacha Pond

Sankaty Head Lighthouse

Eel Point Rd.

Madaket Rd.

Cliff Rd.

Children's Beach

Nantucket Town

Altar Rock

Windswept Cranberry Bog

Polpis Rd.

Madaket

Long Pond

Sanford Farm/ Ram Pasture

Polpis Rd.

Milestone Bog

Siasconset ('Sconset) Beach

Madaket Beach

Bartlett Farm Rd.

Hummock Pond Rd.

Surfside Rd.

Old South Rd.

Milestone Rd.

New South Rd.

Siasconset

Cisco Beach

Miacomet Pond

Miacomet Beach

Surfside Beach

Nantucket Memorial Airport

Tom Nevers Rd.

ATLANTIC OCEAN

0   4 miles

0   6 km

of sailors' crafts, a full-size tryworks once used to process whale oil; and the original 16-foot-high 1850 lens from Sankaty Head Lighthouse. The Children's Discovery Room provides interactive-learning opportunities. Be sure to climb—or take the elevator—up to the observation deck for a view of the harbor. ⊠ *13–15 Broad St.* ☎ *508/228–1894* ⊕ *www.nha. org* ⊠ *$17, $20 combination pass includes Hadwen House and Oldest House* ⊙ *Early Feb.–late Apr., weekends 11–4; May–mid-Oct., daily 10–5; mid-Oct.–mid-Dec., Thurs.–Mon. 11–4. Closed Jan.*

SPORTS AND THE OUTDOORS

BEACHES

★ **Jetties Beach.** A short bike- or shuttle-bus ride from town, Jetties Beach is a popular family beach because of its calm surf, lifeguards, bathhouse, restrooms, and snack bar. It's a good place to try out water toys: kayaks, sailboards, and Day Sailers are rented in summer. On shore it's a lively scene, with playground and volleyball nets on the beach and adjacent public tennis courts. There is a boardwalk to the beach (special wheelchairs are available). You'll have a good view of passing ferries—and an even better one if you clamber out on the jetty itself (careful, it's slippery). ⊠ *Bathing Beach Rd., 1½ miles NW of Straight Wharf.*

When farmers flood cranberry fields during harvest season, the ripe crimson fruit floats to the surface.

BOATING

Nantucket Community Sailing. Renting Sunfish sailboats, sailboards, and kayaks at Jetties Beach (Memorial Day to Labor Day), NCS also has youth and adult instructional sailing programs, as well as adaptive water-sport clinics for disabled athletes. Its Outrigger Canoe Club—a Polynesian tradition—heads out several evenings a week (depending on interest) in season. ⊠ *4 Winter St.* ☎ *508/228–6600* ⊕ *www.nantucketcommunitysailing.org.*

SHOPPING

ARTWORK

Artists' Association of Nantucket. This is the best place to get an overview of the art scene on the island, with a schedule of exhibitions (including opening receptions); many members have galleries of their own. ⊠ *19 Washington St.* ☎ *508/228–0294* ⊕ *www.nantucketarts.org.*

★ **Nantucket Looms.** Luscious woven-on-the-premises textiles and chunky Susan Lister Locke jewelry are the focus of Nantucket Looms, among other adornments for self and home. ⊠ *51 Main St.* ☎ *508/228–1908* ⊕ *www.nantucketlooms.com.*

NIGHTLIFE AND THE ARTS

Chicken Box (*The Box*). Live music—including some big-name bands—plays six nights a week in season, and weekends throughout the year. ⊠ *14 Dave St.* ☎ *508/228–9717* ⊕ *www.thechickenbox.com.*

Muse. This is a year-round venue hosting live bands, including the occasional big-name act. The crowd—the barnlike space can accommodate nearly 400—can get pretty wild. ⊠ *44 Surfside Rd.* ☎ *508/228–6873.*

WHERE TO EAT AND STAY

For expanded hotel reviews, visit Fodors.com.

$ AMERICAN 👍 🍴 **Fog Island Café.** Cherished year-round for its exceptional breakfasts (e.g., pesto scrambled eggs), Fog Island is just as fine a spot for lunch. The storefront space is cheerily decked out in a fresh country style (echoed in the friendly service), and chef-owners Mark and Anne Dawson—both Culinary Institute of America grads—seem determined to provide the best possible value to visitors and local residents alike. [$] *Average main: $12* ✉ *7 S. Water St.* ☎ *508/228–1818* 🌐 *www.fogisland.com* 🕒 *No dinner; no lunch Sun.*

$$$ MODERN AMERICAN Fodor's Choice ★ 🍴 **Straight Wharf.** This loftlike restaurant with a harborside deck has enjoyed legendary status since the mid-'70s, when chef Marion Morash used to get a helping hand from culinary buddy Julia Child; the young couple now in command—Gabriel Frasca and Amanda Lydon—were fast-rising stars on the Boston restaurant scene, but their approach here is the antithesis of flashy and, if anything, they have lent this venerable institution a more-barefoot air, appropriate to the place and season: hurricane lamps lend a soft glow to well-spaced tables lined with butcher paper, and dish towels serve as napkins. Intense champions of local crops and catches, the chefs concoct stellar dishes like oysters with Meyer lemon granita, and line-caught halibut with garlic-chive spaetzle. Their style could be synopsized as simplicity that sings. For a lower-priced preview, explore the menu at the adjoining bar. [$] *Average main: $32* ✉ *6 Harbor Sq.* ☎ *508/228–4499* 🌐 *www.straightwharfrestaurant.com* ✍ *Reservations essential* 🕒 *Closed mid-Oct.–mid-May. No lunch.*

$$$$ B&B/INN ★ 🏨 **Nantucket Whaler.** Let's not mince words: the suites carved out of this 1850 Greek Revival house are gorgeous—neither Calliope Ligelis nor Randi Ott, the New Yorkers who rescued the place in 1999, had any design experience, but they approached the project as if preparing to welcome friends; each suite has a private entrance and a kitchen and the spacious bedrooms are lavished with flowers, well-chosen antiques, and plush robes. **Pros:** pretty rooms; well appointed; romantic. **Cons:** no common room; the usual in-town noise. [$] *Rooms from: $495* ✉ *8 N. Water St.* ☎ *508/228–6597, 888/808–6597* 🌐 *www.nantucketwhaler.com* 🛏 *4 rooms, 6 suites* 🕒 *Closed Dec.–Mar.* 🍽 *No meals.*

$$$$ B&B/INN Fodor's Choice ★ 🏨 **Union Street Inn.** Ken Withrow worked in the hotel business, Deborah Withrow in high-end retail display, and guests get the best of both worlds in this 1770 house, a stone's throw from the bustle of Main Street. **Pros:** pampering by pros; pervasive good taste. **Cons:** bustle of town; some small rooms. [$] *Rooms from: $499* ✉ *7 Union St.* ☎ *508/228–9222* 🌐 *www.unioninn.com* 🛏 *11 rooms, 1 suite* 🕒 *Closed Nov.–late Apr., except for Christmas stroll* 🍽 *Breakfast.*

SIASCONSET

7 miles east of Nantucket Town.

★ First a fishing outpost and then an artist's colony (Broadway actors favored it in the late 19th century), Siasconset—or 'Sconset, in the local vernacular—is a charming cluster of rose-covered cottages linked by driveways of crushed clamshells; at the edges of town, the former fishing shacks give way to magnificent sea-view mansions. The small town center consists of a market, post office, café, lunchroom, and a combination liquor store–lending library.

EXPLORING

Altar Rock. A dirt track leads to the island's highest point, Altar Rock, at an elevation of 101 feet, and the view is spectacular. The hill overlooks approximately 4,000 acres of coastal heathland (a rare habitat) laced with paths leading in every direction. ✉ *Altar Rock Road, 3 miles W of Milestone Rd. Rotary on Polpis Rd.*

SPORTS AND THE OUTDOORS

BIKING

'Sconset Bike Path. This 6.5-mile bike path starts at the rotary east of Nantucket Town and parallels Milestone Road, ending in 'Sconset. It is mostly level, with some gentle hills. Slightly longer (and dippier) the 9-mile Polpis Road Path, veering off to the northeast, is far more scenic and leads to the turnoff to Wauwinet.

WHERE TO EAT AND STAY

For expanded hotel reviews, visit Fodors.com.

$$$$ MODERN AMERICAN ★ 🍴 **Topper's.** The Wauwinet, a lavishly restored 19th-century inn on Nantucket's northeastern shore, is where islanders and visitors alike go to experience utmost luxury, and that includes the food; chef Kyle Zachary likes to source locally as much as possible—try the succulent local lightship diver scallops—though he will go farther afield with options like the buffalo short ribs or the Hudson Valley foie gras. In the creamy-white dining room, awash with lush linens and glorious flowers, you can choose from a three-course prix fixe or à la carte menu, and more casual fare is on offer out on the deck. Inside or out, you won't be disappointed with the spectacular views. Many visitors take advantage of the *Wauwinet Lady* (a complimentary launch docked at the White Elephant, a sister property) to frame the journey with a scenic harbor tour; jitney service is also offered. [$] *Average main: $35* ✉ *120 Wauwinet Rd., Wauwinet* ☎ *508/228–8768* 🌐 *www.toppersrestaurant.com* ✍ *Reservations essential* ⏲ *Closed Nov.–Apr. Brunch Sun. only.*

$$$$ RESORT Fodor's Choice ★ 🏨 **The Wauwinet.** This resplendently updated 1850 resort straddles a "haulover" poised between ocean and bay—which means beaches on both sides—and you can head out by complimentary van or launch to partake of utmost pampering (the staff-to-guest ratio exceeds one-on-one). **Pros:** solicitous staff; dual beaches; peaceful setting. **Cons:** distance from town; overly chichi. [$] *Rooms from: $750* ✉ *120 Wauwinet Rd., Wauwinet* ☎ *508/228–0145* 🌐 *www.wauwinet.com* 🛏 *32 rooms, 5 cottages* ⏲ *Closed Nov.–Apr.* 🍽 *Breakfast.*

The Berkshires and Western Massachusetts

WORD OF MOUTH

"The Clark, in Williamstown, usually has something good in a lovely setting, and the Williams College Museum should not be ignored."

—Ackislander

WELCOME TO THE BERKSHIRES AND WESTERN MASSACHUSETTS

TOP REASONS TO GO

★ **The Countryside:** Rolling hills, dense stands of forest, open pastures, even a few mountains.

★ **Early American History:** Visit preserved villages, homes, and inns where memories of Colonial history and personalities are kept alive.

★ **Summer Festivals:** Watch renowned dance companies perform against the Berkshire mountains backdrop at Jacob's Pillow or have the Boston Symphony Orchestra accompany your lawn picnic at Tanglewood in Lenox.

★ **Under-the-Radar Museums:** Western Massachusetts has an eclectic collection of institutions, from the Eric Carle Museum of Picture Book Art to the Basketball Hall of Fame.

★ **College Towns:** The Pioneer Valley is home to some lovely academic centers: Amherst (University of Massachusetts, Amherst College, and Hampshire College), Northampton (Smith College), and South Hadley (Mount Holyoke College).

1 The Berkshires. The "hills" you'll see here are actually a continuation of the same range that contains Vermont's Green Mountains. And though it's only a few hours from Boston or New York City, a trip to the Berkshires is a complete escape from all things urban. This is a place of ski resorts and winding forest drives, leaf peeping and gallery browsing. There are extreme sports and extreme spas. If you're looking for a place to recharge your batteries and your soul, you'll be hard-pressed to find a better option in the Northeast.

2 Sturbridge and the Pioneer Valley. Often overshadowed by Boston to the east and the Berkshires to the west, the Pioneer Valley is filled with historic settlements and college towns, natural treasures, and unique museums. Old Sturbridge Village, a re-created early-19th-century village with restored historic buildings, reenactments, and activities, is the premier attraction here. The main city, Springfield, is home to the Naismith Memorial Basketball Hall of Fame, but most of the area is quite rural—this is where the idyllic New England countryside you've imagined comes to life.

Williamstown · North Adams · Mt. Greylock (highest point Mass. 3,491) · Adams · Hancock · Onota Lake · Dalton · Pittsfield · Lenox · Lee · Housatonic · Great Barrington · NEW YORK · THE BERKSHIRES · CONNECTICUT · 0 6 mi · 0 6 km

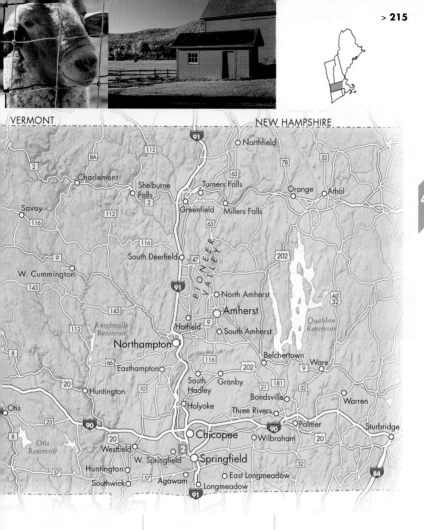

GETTING ORIENTED

Interstate 90 (the Massachusetts Turnpike) leads west from Boston to the Berkshires. The main north–south road within the Berkshires is U.S. 7. Highway 2 runs from the northern Berkshires to Greenfield at the head of the Pioneer Valley and continues across Massachusetts into Boston. The scenic section of Highway 2 known as the Mohawk Trail runs from Williamstown to Orange. Interstate 91 runs north–south in the Pioneer Valley in Western Massachusetts.

MASSACHUSETTS FALL FOLIAGE DRIVE

When fall foliage season arrives, the Berkshires are the place to appreciate the autumnal grandeur. Winding roads lined with dramatic trees ablaze—notably maples, birches, and beeches—pass alongside meadows, pasture, farmland, mountains, rivers, and lakes.

Although this complete scenic loop is only about 35 miles, you could easily spend the day making your way leisurely along the circuit. Begin in North Adams, a city transformed by art, and spend some time at the Massachusetts Museum of Contemporary Art (MASS MoCA). Just west of downtown off Route 2, the Notch Road leads into the **Mt. Greylock State Reservation**, ambling upward to the summit. At 3,491 feet, it's the state's highest point and affords expansive views of the countryside. Hike any of the many trails throughout the park, picnic at the peak, or stay for a meal at the rustic **Bascom Lodge**. Continue your descent on the Notch Road to Rockwell Road to exit the park and join Route 7 South.

BEST TIME TO GO

Peak season for leaf viewing in the Berkshires generally happens in mid-October. Trees growing near waterways—and they are plentiful in the area—tend to have more vibrant colors that peak a bit sooner than those elsewhere. The state regularly updates fall foliage information by phone and online (☎ *800/632–8038* ⊕ *www.massvacation. com*).

Follow Route 7 South into the small town center of Lanesborough, where you'll turn left onto Summer Street. Horse farms
and wide-open pastures make up the landscape, with distant
mountain peaks hovering grandly in the background. If you
want to pick your own apples, take a 1½-mile detour off Summer Street and stop at **Lakeview Orchard**.

Summer Street continues to tiny Berkshire Village, where
you'll pick up Route 8 heading back toward North Adams.
Running parallel to Route 8 from Lanesborough to Adams,
is the paved **Ashuwillticook Rail Trail** for biking and walking. Right in the midst of two mountain ranges, the trail
abuts wetlands, mixed woodland (including beech, birch, and
maple trees), the Hoosac River, and the Cheshire Reservoir. In
Cheshire, **Whitney's Farm Market** is busy on fall weekends
with pony rides, pumpkin picking, a corn maze, and hayrides;
plus they sell baked goods like the pumpkin whoopie pie.

Continuing on Route 8, you'll start to leave farm country as
you make your way back to North Adams. Once a part of its
much larger neighbor, the town of Adams still has active mills
and the **Susan B. Anthony Birthplace Museum** opened
in 2010. The 1817 Federal home of her birth has been fully
restored.

NEED A BREAK?

Bascom Lodge. Built in
the 1930s, this mountain-
top lodge retains its rustic
charm with no-frills but
comfortable lodging and
a restaurant in a stunning
setting. ⊠ *Summit, Mt.
Greylock State Reservation,
Adams* ☎ *413/743–1591*
⊕ *www.bascomlodge.net*
⊘ *Closed Nov.–May.*
Lakeview Orchard. At
Lakeview Orchard pick
your own bushel of apples
(among other fruits) and
sample freshly pressed
hot cider. Try some
cider donuts if you get
the chance. ⊠ *94 Old
Cheshire Rd., Lanesboro*
☎ *413/448–6009* ⊕ *www.
lakevieworchard.com*
⊘ *Open Tues.–Sun., early
July through Halloween.*
**The Susan B. Anthony
Birthplace Museum.**
The Susan B. Anthony
Birthplace Museum cel-
ebrates the extraordinary
life and legacy of Susan
B. Anthony and her fam-
ily. ⊠ *67 East Rd., Adams*
☎ *413/743–7121* ⊕ *www.
susanbanthonybirthplace.
com* ⊠ *$5* ⊘ *Late May–
mid-Oct., Thurs.–Mon.
10–4; mid-Oct.–late May,
Thurs.–Sat. 10–4.*

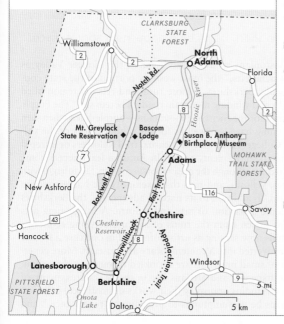

Updated by
Seth Brown

Rolling terrain defines the landscape of Western Massachusetts. The Pioneer Valley, which runs north to south through the heart of the Bay State, is home to the famed "Five College Consortium," a group of elite institutions including Amherst, Hampshire, Mount Holyoke, UMASS Amherst, and Smith. As a result there are some very college-focused areas, and while it may lack the collegiate density (or bustling metropolis feel) of Boston, areas like Northampton embody the vibrancy that comes from a large population of college students, with various cultural venues and culinary possibilities. In short, it can be a happening sort of place.

While most Bostonians would surely refer to the Pioneer Valley as "Western Massachusetts," the most westerly portion of the state consists of the bucolic Berkshires, a more rural and relaxed region filled with rolling hills and winding mountain roads. Therein sits "The Purple Valley," so named for the encircling mountains—purple-hued when seen through an evening haze—as well as for the school colors of the valley's Williams College. Hikers, be they casual trail followers or intrepid mountain climbers, have plenty to see. In Autumn leaf peepers come from all over to drive through the area renowned for its fall foliage, with vibrant oranges, yellows, and reds that exemplify the harvest season in New England. In addition to its natural advantages, the Berkshires have also become a bastion of arts and culture. A burgeoning arts community has arisen from the ruins of a manufacturing economy, with former mills now serving as artist lofts, and in one case a former electric plant converted into a contemporary art museum. More generally, a number of small museums are sprinkled throughout the region, and myriad craftspeople and artisans live in the Berkshires, many of whom have open studios or display their works in small local galleries. It would perhaps be presumptuous to proclaim a "renaissance," and yet it cannot be denied that the large concentration of arts and culture in the Berkshires has transformed it to a certain degree. The past few decades have seen not only an influx of artists, but of other revitalizing culture, ranging from boutique shopping to international cuisine, transforming a once depressed post-industrial area into a hot spot for festivals celebrating everything from ice sculptures to the spoken word.

PLANNING

WHEN TO GO

The dazzling foliage and cool temperatures make fall the best time to visit Western Massachusetts, but the Berkshires and the Pioneer Valley are increasingly a year-round destination. Visit in spring, and witness the burst of color that signals winter's end. Summer is a time of festivals, adventure sports, and outdoor concerts.

Many towns save their best for winter—inns open their doors to carolers and shops serve eggnog. The off-season is the perfect time to try cross-country skiing or spend a night by the fire, tucked under a quilt, catching up on books by Nathaniel Hawthorne or Henry David Thoreau.

GETTING HERE AND AROUND

AIR TRAVEL

Bradley International Airport in Windsor Locks, Connecticut, 18 miles south of Springfield on Interstate 91, serves the Pioneer Valley and the Berkshires.

Most travelers arrive at Boston's Logan International Airport, the state's major airline hub. From Boston, you can reach most parts of the Pioneer Valley in less than two hours by car, and the Berkshires are about three hours' drive from Bean Town.

Other airport alternatives include Manchester Boston Regional Airport in New Hampshire, 50 miles northwest of Boston, and T. F. Green International Airport in Providence, Rhode Island, 59 miles south of Boston.

CAR TRAVEL

Public transportation can be a bit spotty in this region, with buses that don't run on Sundays or during the evenings, so you'll almost certainly need a car. But you'll want one anyway so you can take leisurely drives down routes 2, 7, and 8 to see the fall foliage. Be warned that mountain roads are very winding and not for the fainthearted; if you care less about mountaintop views than you do about settled innards, skip the hairpin turn on Route 2 and approach North Adams from the South instead of the east.

TRAIN TRAVEL

The Northeast Corridor and high-speed Acela services of Amtrak link Boston with the principal cities between it and Washington, D.C. Amtrak's Lake Shore Limited, which stops at Springfield and Pittsfield in the Berkshires, carries passengers from Chicago to Boston. For destinations north and west of Boston, trains depart from Boston's North Station.

Train Information Amtrak. No ticket booth, must purchase in advance. Unstaffed station. ⊠ *1355 East St., Pittsfield* ☎ *800/872–7245* ⊕ *www.amtrak.com.*

RESTAURANTS

At country inns in the Southern Berkshires and the Pioneer Valley you can find traditional New England dinners strongly reminiscent of old England: double-cut pork chops, rack of lamb, game, Boston baked beans, Indian pudding, and the dubiously glorified "New England boiled dinner" (meat and vegetables slow-boiled). For those who come to the Berkshires to taste historical tradition, there is plenty of it on the menu.

If you prefer more creative contemporary fare, however, you will not be disappointed. There are various modern cafés and trendy watering holes with inventive menus ranging from fusion cuisine to pizza with inspired toppings.

Perhaps most enticingly, an influx of multiculturalism to the Berkshires has resulted in a number of excellent international food options, especially in the Northern/Central region. In addition to the standard Chinese, Indian, and Thai, visitors can sample Peruvian, Spanish, Columbian, Malaysian, and much more. *Prices in the reviews are the average cost of a main course at dinner or, if dinner is not served, at lunch.*

HOTELS

The signature type of accommodations outside Boston is the country inn; in the Berkshires, where magnificent mansions have been converted into lodgings, the inns reach a very grand scale indeed. Less extravagant and less expensive are bed-and-breakfast establishments, many of them in private homes. Make reservations for inns well in advance during peak periods (summer through winter in the Berkshires). Smoking is banned in all Massachusetts hotels.

Campers can pitch their tents amid acres of pine forest dotted with rivers and lakes or in the shadows of the rolling Berkshire Hills. The camping season in Massachusetts generally runs from Memorial Day to Columbus Day. For more about camping, contact the Massachusetts Department of Conservation and Recreation (☎ *617/626–1250* ⊕ *www.mass.gov/dcr/forparks.htm*). *Prices in the reviews are the lowest cost of a standard double room in high season.*

VISITOR INFORMATION

Massachusetts Office of Travel & Tourism ⊠ *10 Park Plaza, Suite 4510, Boston* ☎ *617/973–8500, 617/973–8500 brochures* ⊕ *www.massvacation.com.*

THE BERKSHIRES

Occupying the far western end of the state, the Berkshires are only about 2½ hours by car from Boston and New York City, yet the region lives up to the storybook image of rural New England, with wooded hills, narrow winding roads, and compact historic villages. Summer brings cultural events, including the renowned Tanglewood classical music festival in Lenox. The foliage blazes in fall, skiing is popular in winter, and spring is the time for maple sugaring. The scenic Mohawk Trail runs east to west across the northern section of the Berkshires.

ESSENTIALS

Bus Information Berkshire Regional Transit Authority ☎ 413/499–2782, 800/292–2782 ⊕ www.berkshirerta.com.

Visitor Information Berkshires Visitors Bureau ✉ 3 Hoosac St., Adams ☎ 413/743–4500, 800/237–5747 ⊕ www.berkshires.org.

NORTH ADAMS

130 miles northwest of Boston; 73 miles northwest of Springfield; 20 miles south of Bennington, Vermont.

If you're looking for a Berkshires getaway that combines culture with outdoor fun (and a cool place to stay), put North Adams on your short list. Established as the military outpost Fort Massachusetts in the mid-18th century, North Adams started out as a part of East Hoosac and then became part of Adams before incorporating as its own city in the late 19th century. By then its economy had become dependent upon its textile industry. After North Adams became a strong producer of electrical and radio parts, its fortunes waned following World War II.

In the recent past, however, the city has staged an impressive comeback as a center of contemporary art. In addition to the Massachusetts Museum of Contemporary Arts (Mass MoCA), North Adams has mills and factory buildings that have been converted to artists' studios and residences. (The town's Downstreet Art boasts 33 galleries in a four-block area.) The Porches Inn, a row of eye-catching multihued Victorians, has added an additional helping of hip to downtown. In addition, the 11-mile Ashuwillticook Rail Trail is easily accessible in nearby Adams, as is Mount Greylock State Reservation, if you explore it by foot via one of the local trailheads.

GETTING HERE AND AROUND

The best way to get to North Adams is either from the South via Pittsfield, or from the east via Williamstown. Either way, once you're in town you can see it all on foot if the weather is good, with almost everything within a few blocks of the town's Main Street—Natural Bridge Park is the exception, but it's still a reasonable walk.

EXPLORING

Fodor'sChoice **Massachusetts Museum of Contemporary Arts.** It's not just the dimensions—13 acres, 27 buildings, more than 250,000 square feet—that are impressive here. The nation's largest center for contemporary visual and performing arts is also one of the finest in the world, drawing equally huge attendances for its exciting gallery exhibits, art shows, concerts, dance, and film presentations. The enormous space in the main gallery allows for massive exhibits that simply wouldn't fit anywhere else, such as one showcasing six actual cars suspended overhead in various states of explosion, or Robert Rauschenberg's monumental *The ¼ Mile or 2 Furlong Piece*. The building, formerly housing the Sprague Electrical Co., is in itself a worthwhile exhibit, and also includes studios, cafés, shops, and the inspiring Kidspace gallery and studio. ✉ *87 Marshall St.* ☎ *413/664–4111* ⊕ *www.massmoca.org* ⊒ *$15* ☽ *July and Aug., daily 10–6; Sept.–June, Wed.–Mon. 11–5.*

★ **North Adams Museum of History & Science.** North Adams's best kept secret, this museum has three floors with more than 25 permanent exhibits including a kid-friendly model of the solar system, train set, and full-sized model of the Fort Massachusetts Barracks Room. The building was once part of a railroad yard, and a store sells local historical society publications. ⊠ *Bldg 5A, Western Gateway Heritage State Park* ☎ 413/664–4700 ⊕ *www.northadamshistory.org* 🖅 *Free* ☉ *Nov.–Apr., Sat. 10–4, Sun. 1–4; May–Oct., Thurs.–Sat. 10–4, Sun. 1–4.*

★ **Western Gateway Heritage State Park.** This park occupies the old Boston & Maine Railroad yard, where the visitor center houses exhibits that trace the impact of train travel on the region. A 30-minute documentary provides a look at the intense labor that went into the construction of the nearby Hoosac Tunnel, and a pedestrian bridge a block from the park offers a good view of tracks going into the tunnel. ⊠ *115 State St.* ☎ 413/663–6312 ⊕ *www.mass.gov/dcr/parks/western/wghp.htm* 🖅 *Free* ☉ *Visitor center daily 10–5.*

QUICK BITES

Jack's Hot Dog Stand. A North Adams institution since 1917, Jack's Hot Dog Stand is where locals go for a few hot wieners and hamburgers, with optional cheese and chili. This hole-in-the-wall also serves sweet sausage, onion rings, and fries. It's cash only, closes at 7 pm, and during lunch hour you'll be lucky to find a free stool at the counter. ⊠ *12 Eagle St.* ☎ 413/664–9006 ⊕ *www.jackshotdogstand.com* ☉ *Closed Sun.*

SPORTS AND THE OUTDOORS

PARK

★ **Natural Bridge State Park.** The city's 48-acre Natural Bridge State Park was named for the 30-foot span that crosses Hudson Brook, and offers numerous appealing views of rocky chasms. The marble arch at the park's center rises in what was a marble quarry from the early 1880s to the mid-1900s. There are picnic sites, hiking trails, and well-maintained restrooms. In winter the park is popular for cross-country skiing. ⊠ *McCauley Rd., Hwy. 8* ☎ 413/663–6392 ⊕ *www.mass.gov/dcr/parks/western/nbdg.htm.*

KAYAKING

Berkshire Outfitters. If you're itching to explore the Cheshire (Hoosac) lakes by kayak, Ashuwillticook Rail Trail by bike, or Mt. Greylock's summit on snowshoes, visit Berkshire Outfitters. Just 300 yards from the Rail Trail, this shop rents bicycles, kayaks, canoes, Nordic skis, and snowshoes, and has a very knowledgeable staff—as well as DCR trail maps. ⊠ *169 Grove St., Hwy. 8, Adams* ☎ 413/743–5900 ⊕ *www.berkshireoutfitters.com.*

THE ARTS

Down Street Art. Down Street Art is a public art project with 33 member art galleries in downtown North Adams. (The city has more contemporary art spaces than any town in the Berkshires.) Catch an Open Studios weekend to see the converted artist lofts at the Eclipse Mills as well. ⊠ *51 Main St., MCLA's Berkshire Cultural Resource Center* ☎ 413/663–5253 ⊕ *www.downstreetart.org.*

WHERE TO EAT

$ ✕ **Baer's Den Bakery and Deli.** Surprisingly homey and inviting for a deli,
DELI   the Baer's Den has a wood floor, tin ceiling, piano, pellet stove, and
★   curated art shows on the walls. Amiable owners chat with the customers
over the counter while serving up freshly made sandwiches on breads
mostly baked on-site. You can smell the rye bread while you sink your
teeth into the hearty corned beef Reuben. Among the rotating soups du
jour is a thick and rich fish chowder with a subtle sweetness. Get there
early if you want to try the famed Sam Adams Chili before the day's
supply runs out, and get there early for lunch: they close at 2 pm on
weekdays and 11 am on Saturday. $ *Average main: $6* ⊠ *3 East Hoosac
Street, Adams* ☎ *413/776–7310* ⊕ *www.baersbakery.com* ⌿ *Reservations not accepted* ▭ *No credit cards* ☾ *Closed Sun.*

$$ ✕ **Espana.** Chef Galo Lopez offers an ever-changing array of appeal-
TAPAS   ing tapas with a side order of good service and a tasteful atmosphere.
Fodor'sChoice   You may try a roast vegetable soup, crab cake, or cheese plate, but
★   the real must-have dish is the Caracoles, a plate of tender snails and
caramelized onion in a rich tomato-based sauce. If you prefer an
entrée, the paella comes with a half-hour wait, but it's worth it. Don't
miss the Tarta de Santiago for dessert. $ *Average main: $19* ⊠ *896
State Road* ☎ *413/346–4099* ⌿ *Reservations not accepted* ☾ *Closed
Mon.–Tues. No lunch.*

$$ ✕ **Gramercy Bistro.** Within the Mass MoCA complex, the mood and
FRENCH FUSION   style of this upscale casual eatery makes it easy to forget you are inside
★   a former factory building, and the eclectic menu, ranging from sautéed
sweetbreads to paella, has helped draw a loyal following. Chef-owner
Alexander Smith relies on organic meats and locally grown produce
when possible, adding serious zip with sauces made from wasabi and
fire-roasted poblano peppers. Come by on weekends for the memorable brunch. $ *Average main: $22* ⊠ *87 Marshall St.* ☎ *413/663–5300*
⊕ *www.gramercybistro.com* ☾ *No lunch. Brunch weekends only.*

$ ✕ **The Sushi House.** Right on the main drag, this Pan-Asian restaurant
ASIAN   offers some of the best dishes in Chinese, Thai, Korean, and Japanese
cooking. Start with seaweed salad, then consider a classic noodle dish
like pad thai (sweet stir-fried rice noodles) or *pad see ew* (wide, flat
noodles with meat and Chinese broccoli). The best food comes in a
hot clay pot, whether you order the Massaman curry (a peanut and
potato curry), the spicy *bibim bap* (a bowl of rice and veggies topped
with meat, a fried egg, and hot chili sauce), or the incredible melange
of rich flavors that is the Seafood Hotpot. Ironically, the only thing that
isn't uniformly excellent is the sushi, but it's still generally good and you
can watch two big-screen TVs from the sushi bar. $ *Average main: $14*
⊠ *45 Main Street* ☎ *413/664-9388.*

WHERE TO STAY

For expanded hotel reviews, visit Fodors.com.

$$$ ⊟ **Porches Inn.** These once-dilapidated mill-workers' houses dating
B&B/INN   from the 1890s were refurbished and connected with one long porch
Fodor'sChoice   to become one of New England's quirkiest hotels; they now strike a
★   perfect balance between high-tech and historic—rooms have a mix of
retro 1940s and '50s lamps and bungalow-style furnishings, along with

stunning bathrooms with slate floors, hot tubs, and mirrors fashioned out of old window frames. **Pros:** outdoor heated pool and hot tub (hot tub is open all year); large guest rooms; walk to town. **Cons:** small breakfast room. [$] *Rooms from: $229* ✉ *231 River St.* ☎ *413/664–0400* 🌐 *www.porches.com* 🛏 *47 rooms, 12 suites* 🍴 *Breakfast.*

$$ B&B/INN ★ **Topia Inn.** Park your shoes and your toiletries at the door—this Adams property, which opened in 2007 just off the Ashuwillticook Rail Trail, is the greenest inn in the Berkshires: innkeepers Nana Simopoulous and Caryn Heilman transformed a derelict downtown Colonial into an LEED-rated marvel, with a solar electric system, soybean oil heating, and natural clay walls; beds and linens are organic cotton; nontoxic toiletries are provided; and rooms are decorated by the innkeepers' artsy pals, with themes such as Morocco, Ancient Greece, Native American, and Retro 1960s. **Pros:** organic toiletries in guest rooms; organic breakfast; steam showers and spa tubs. **Cons:** next door to a bar; may be too eco-focused for some. [$] *Rooms from: $210* ✉ *10 Pleasant St., Adams* ☎ *413/743–9600* 🌐 *www.topiainn.com* 🛏 *10 rooms* 🍴 *Breakfast.*

WILLIAMSTOWN

5 miles west of North Adams.

When Colonel Ephraim Williams left money to found a free school in what was then known as West Hoosac, he stipulated that the town's name be changed to Williamstown. Williams College opened in 1793, and even today life in this placid town revolves around it. Graceful campus buildings like the Gothic cathedral, built in 1904, line Main Street. Along Spring Street are a handful of upscale shops and lively eateries.

GETTING HERE AND AROUND

Williamstown includes a lot of farms and rolling hills, but essentially Williamstown proper sits around Route 2, which bisects Williams College. On the college campus you can walk to Spring Street and Water Street, while anything else you want to see is probably just a short drive and brief turn off Route 2 (or a hop onto the BRTA bus).

EXPLORING

Fodor's Choice ★ **Clark Art Institute.** One of the nation's notable small art museums, the Clark Art Institute has a large Renoir collection (on tour from 2011 to 2014) as well as canvases by Monet and Camille Pissarro. *The Little Dancer,* an important sculpture by Degas, is another exceptional work on view. Other items include English silver, European and American photography from the 1840s through the 1910s, and 17th- and 18th-century Flemish and Dutch masterworks. ✉ *225 South St.* ☎ *413/458–2303* 🌐 *www.clarkart.edu* 🎟 *June–mid-Oct. $15, mid-Oct.–May free* 🕒 *Sept.–June, Tues.–Sun. 10–5; July and Aug., daily 10–5.*

Fodor's Choice ★ 👶 **Williams College Museum of Art.** The collections at this fine museum focus on American and 20th-century art. One of the country's best college art museums, the WCMA's 14,000 objects also span a range of eras and cultures. The original octagonal structure facing Main Street was built as a library in 1846, and the rainbow wall painting above the stairs is a Sol LeWitt, painted in situ in 2001. ✉ *15 Lawrence Hall Dr., Rte.*

Winslow Homer's *West Point, Prout's Neck* is just one of the notable paintings at Williamstown's Clark Art Institute.

2 ☏ 413/597–2376 ⊕ *wcma.williams.edu* ✉ *Free* ☉ *Tues.–Sat. 10–5, Sun. 1–5.*

SPORTS AND THE OUTDOORS

Mt. Greylock State Reservation. The centerpiece of this 10,327-acre reservation, to the south of Williamstown, is Mt. Greylock, at 3,491 feet the highest point in Massachusetts. The reservation has facilities for cycling, fishing, horseback riding, camping, and snowmobiling. Many treks—including a portion of the Appalachian Trail—start from the parking lot at the summit, an 8-mile drive from the mountain's base. The Bascom Lodge (⊕ *www.bascomlodge.net*) and Veterans War Memorial are at the peak. ✉ *30 Rockwell Rd., Lanesboro* ☏ *413/499–4262, 413/499–4263* ⊕ *www.mass.gov/dcr/parks/mtgreylock.*

SHOPPING

The Library Antiques. On downtown Williamstown's main drag, this antiques shop has an array of prints, folk art, jewelry, antiquarian books, and distinctive gifts. ✉ *70 Spring St.* ☏ *413/458–3436* ⊕ *www. libraryantiques.com.*

Toonerville Trolley CDs & Records. Some people consider this tiny place to be the best music store in the world. Toonerville carries hard-to-find jazz, rock, and classical recordings, curated by a friendly and knowledgeable owner. ✉ *131 Water St.* ☏ *413/458–5229* ⊕ *toonervilletrolleycds.com.*

☻ **Where'd You Get That?** Jam-packed with every imaginable toy and game, as well as some novelty items you'd never have imagined at all, Where'd

The Berkshires

Pownal

Green Mountain
National Forest

Readsboro

Stamford

7

VERMONT

Williamstown

Clarksburg

8

North Adams

Florida

Hoosac Tunnel

2

8A

2

Charlemont

*Mt Greylock
(highest point
Mass. 3,491)*

Adams

Cherryplain

7

New Ashford

116

Savoy

43

NEW YORK

8A

Plainfield

43

22

Cheshire

8

8A

9

116

0   5 mi

0   5 km

Hancock

Lanesboro

Onota Lake

Windsor

West Cummington

9

20

New Lebanon

9

9

Dalton

8

Pittsfield

143

22

20

Hinsdale

Worthington Corners

143

Chesterfield

Hancock Shaker Village

7

8

112

T H E   B E R K S H I R E S

90

41

Lenox

8

South Worthington

West Stockbridge

Becket

Knightville Reservoir

41

Lee

90

Chester

Knightville

22

South Lee

183

7

Stockbridge

20

Housatonic

Monument Mountain Reservation

Santarella Museum and Gardens

Tyringham

Huntington

Great Barrington

71

Monterey

23

8

Otis

90

23

23

Blandford

South Egremont

7

New Marlborough

Otis Reservoir

Cobble Mountain Res.

41

Sheffield

Standisfield

New Boston

Bartholomew's Cobble

183

8

57

Granville

Colebrook River Lake

Barkhamsted Reservoir

Canaan

CONNECTICUT

You Get That? also benefits from the enthusiasm of owners Ken and Michele Gietz. ✉ *100 Spring St.* ☎ *413/458–2206* 🌐 *www.wygt.com.*

THE ARTS

Fodor's Choice ★ **Williamstown Theatre Festival.** At the '62 Center for Theatre and Dance of Williams College, the Williamstown Theatre Festival is summer's hottest ticket. From June through August, the long-running festival presents well-known theatrical works with famous performers on the Main Stage and contemporary works on the Nikos Stage. ✉ *1000 Main St.* ☎ *413/597–3400, 413/597–3399* 🌐 *www.wtfestival.org.*

WHERE TO EAT

$$ AMERICAN Fodor's Choice ★ 🍴 **'6 House Pub.** Set in an old cow barn at the 1896 House Inn, this rustic, dark wood-paneled pub has buckets of character and an interesting array of upholstered furniture at the tables, so you can sit in an old wingback chair if you like. Chef Matt Schilling's extensive menu runs the gamut from traditional pub food (burgers and mozzarella sticks) to upscale vegetarian such as grilled plum salad with Granny Smith apples, Gorgonzola, glazed walnuts over mixed greens, or wild mushroom and cheese ravioli alfredo. If you love lobster you will appreciate the Lobster Martini appetizer, or the all-meat lobster roll. Daily specials include prime rib and pasta combos, but there's plenty to try on the standard menu. [$] *Average main: $17* ✉ *910 Cold Spring Rd., Rte. 7* ☎ *413/458–1896, 888/999–1896* 🌐 *www.6housepub.com* 🕓 *No lunch weekdays Oct.–May.*

$$ ECLECTIC ★ 🍴 **Mezze Bistro & Bar.** After their riverfront location burned, and after then leaving their second Water St. location, Mezze has now taken over the former Le Jardin restaurant, a beautiful hilltop location with charming grounds. It can get crowded especially in summer, when everyone wants to rub elbows with stars from the Williamstown Theatre Festival. The menu, heavily focused on local and seasonal ingredients, is always in flux, but is bound to contain some fancy options such as roast veal with duck-fat potatoes, or calf's liver with bacon lardons. [$] *Average main: $24* ✉ *777 Cold Spring Road, Routes 7 and 2* ☎ *413/458–0123* 🌐 *www.mezzerestaurant.com* ✍ *Reservations essential* 🕓 *No lunch.*

$ VIETNAMESE 🍴 **Saigon Vietnamese.** Formerly located in the middle of a bowling alley, Saigon's new location on Spring Street is more convenient, even if the atmosphere—upbeat music and flashing lights—feels like a bizarre club; still, the food is pleasing, from the first shrimp chips as they tingle on your tongue to the last sip of *pho* (noodle soup). The menu has many traditional Vietnamese favorites, such as *banh xeo* (rice pancake with pork and bean sprouts) and rice vermicelli with pork, that are all competently done. Keep a look out for specials like the marinated quail, covered in a dark, sweet, finger-lick-worthy sauce. [$] *Average main: $12* ✉ *66 Spring Street* ☎ *413/458–3588.*

WHERE TO STAY

For expanded hotel reviews, visit Fodors.com.

$$ B&B/INN ★ 🏨 **Guest House at Field Farm.** Built in 1948, this guesthouse contains a fine collection of art on loan from Williams College and the Whitney Museum. **Pros:** great views of the Berkshires; luxury (Frette) robes and towels plus high-thread-count linens. **Cons:** no TV in rooms.

[$] *Rooms from: $175* ✉ *554 Sloan Rd.* ☎ *413/458–3135* 🌐 *www.guesthouseatfieldfarm.org* 🛏 *5 rooms* 🕒 *Closed Jan.–Mar.* 🍴 *Breakfast.*

$$$ HOTEL ★ 🏨 **Orchards Hotel.** Although it's near Highway 2 and surrounded by parking lots, this thoroughly proper hostelry compensates with a courtyard filled with fruit trees and a pond stocked with koi; English antiques furnish most of the spacious accommodations—the inner rooms, which look onto the courtyard, are best for summer stays, while some of the outer rooms (with less distinguished views) have fireplaces to add appeal for winter visits. **Pros:** good beds; flat-screen TVs; good alternative to B&Bs and chain hotels. **Cons:** no coffeemakers in rooms; some guests complain of service lapses; minor signs of wear and tear. [$] *Rooms from: $250* ✉ *222 Adams Rd.* ☎ *413/458–9611, 800/225–1517* 🌐 *www.orchardshotel.com* 🛏 *49 rooms* 🍴 *No meals.*

$ B&B/INN ★ 🏨 **River Bend Farm.** Listed on the National Register of Historic Places, this 1770 Georgian Colonial is not on a river, nor is it a farm, but this rustic inn is a great place to discover simpler times, before TV. **Pros:** good breakfast; friendly innkeepers. **Cons:** set on a busy road with train sounds at night; guests share two bathrooms. [$] *Rooms from: $120* ✉ *643 Simonds Rd.* ☎ *413/458–3121* 🌐 *www.riverbendfarmbb.com* 🛏 *4 rooms without bath* 💳 *No credit cards* 🕒 *Closed Nov.–Mar.* 🍴 *Breakfast.*

HANCOCK

15 miles south of Williamstown.

Tiny Hancock, the village closest to the Jiminy Peak ski resort, comes into its own in winter. It's also a great base for outdoors enthusiasts year-round, with biking, hiking, and other options in summer.

GETTING HERE AND AROUND

Situated between Williamstown and Lanesborough, Hancock is an oft-overlooked destination for the outdoors person. You can take Route 43 from Williamstown, Route 7 from Pittsfield, or the BRTA bus from Lanesborough, with plenty of mountain views and trees along the way. The only place to walk around is the Shaker Village.

EXPLORING

👶 **Ioka Valley Farm.** Established in the 1930s, this 600-acre farm is one of the best-known pick-your-own farms in the Berkshires. You can pick berries all summer, then apples and pumpkins in fall. In winter you can cut your own Christmas tree. Other activities include hayrides, pedal tractors for kids, and a petting zoo with pigs, sheep, goats, and calves. ✉ *Hwy. 43* ☎ *413/738–5915* 🌐 *iokavalleyfarm.com* 🕒 *Seasonal, call ahead.*

SPORTS AND THE OUTDOORS

SKI AREA **Jiminy Peak.** This is the only full-service ski and snowboard resort in the Berkshires and the largest in southern New England, with a vertical of 1,150 feet, 44 trails, and nine lifts. It's mostly a cruising mountain—trails are groomed daily, and only on some are small moguls left to build up along the side of the slope. The steepest black-diamond runs are on the upper head walls; longer, outer runs make for good intermediate terrain. There's skiing nightly, and snowmaking covers

93% of the skiable terrain. Jiminy also has three terrain parks and a mountain coaster (weekends and holidays only), a two-person cart shoots down the mountain at speeds of up to 25 mph. ⊠ *37 Corey Rd.* ☎ *413/738–5500, 888/454–6469* ⊕ *www.jiminypeak.com.*

WHERE TO STAY

For expanded hotel reviews, visit Fodors.com.

$$$
RESORT
🏨 **Country Inn at Jiminy Peak.** Massive stone fireplaces in its lobby and lounge lend this hotel a ski-lodge atmosphere, and the condo-style suites—privately owned but put into a rental pool—accommodate up to four people and have couches and kitchenettes separated from living areas by bars with high stools; the roomiest units are on the second and third floors, and the suites at the rear of the building overlook the slopes. **Pros:** John Harvard's Restaurant is on-site; bathrooms are nice; rooms have eat-in kitchenettes. **Cons:** hallways are a bit dark; outdoor pool is small. ⑤ *Rooms from: $279* ⊠ *37 Corey Rd.* ☎ *413/738–5500, 800/882–8859* ⊕ *www.jiminypeak.com* 🛏 *105 suites* ⦿*No meals.*

PITTSFIELD

21 miles south of Williamstown, 11 miles southeast of Hancock.

Pittsfield is a workaday city without the quaint, rural demeanor of the comparatively small Colonial towns that surround it. There's a positive buzz in Pittsfield these days, though. Symbols of resurgence include the gorgeous Colonial Theatre, which was restored in 2007 and hosts 250 nights of performances per year, and a spate of new shops and eateries along North Street. City-sponsored art walks and a major renovation of the venerable Berkshire Museum are more evidence of Pittsfield's comeback.

GETTING HERE AND AROUND

Whether a train or bus drops you at the Intermodal Transportation Station, you'll be just a block from Pittsfield's expansive North Street, along which you can walk to find theatres, museums, interesting stores, and all sorts of restaurants. Bus routes go to the mall and Allendale, elsewhere you'll need to drive.

EXPLORING

★
🅒 **Berkshire Museum.** Opened in 1903, this "universal" museum has a little bit of everything: fine art including paintings from the Hudson River School; Alexander Calder's mobiles and toys; natural history, including animals and minerals; and local history. The latter is exemplified by the Hall of Innovation, which showcases Berkshire innovators whose creations range from special effects for *Star Wars* to the paper used for U.S. currency. The 10-foot-high *stegosaurus* outside the museum advertises the dinosaur gallery where families can sift through the dig pit for bones, but don't miss the ancient gallery featuring an Egyptian mummy, or the aquarium with a touch tank in the basement. Add to this rotating exhibits, such as Audubon's Birds, and the in-house cinema, and the Berkshire Museum has something for everyone. ⊠ *39 South St.* ☎ *413/443–7171* ⊕ *www.berkshiremuseum.org* 🎟 *$13* ⊙ *Mon.–Sat. 10–5, Sun. 11–5.*

HOLISTIC HIDEAWAYS

Kripalu

The Berkshires have become known for holistic retreats that send you home with the ultimate souvenir: a new-and-improved you, with a refreshed spirit, revitalized body, and healthier habits. Here are two places you might like to try.

Canyon Ranch. The Berkshires' outpost of Canyon Ranch in Lenox couldn't be more elegantly old-fashioned; the famous spa is set in Bellefontaine Mansion, a 1897 replica of Le Petit Trianon in Versailles. Looks can be deceiving, though. This holistic spa is home to a state-of-the-art, 100,000-square-foot fitness center, with the latest classes and the best equipment—perfect for gym junkies. Choose from among more than 40 fitness classes per day, plus lifestyle management workshops and private consultations with wellness experts in the field of medicine, nutrition, behavior, and physiology, while trying new fitness techniques, eating great food (even chocolate

sauce, craftily made from white grape juice and cocoa), and enjoying the Berkshires countryside on hikes and paddling excursions. ✉ *165 Kemble St., Rte. 7a, 9 miles south of Pittsfield, Lenox* ☎ *800/742–9000, 413/637–4400* ⊕ *www.canyonranch. com.*

Kripalu Center. You'll see many people sitting peacefully on the grounds as you search for a parking place at this health and yoga retreat in Stockbridge. Kripalu means grace, and there is even a hatha yoga method named after the institution. ✉ *57 Interlaken Rd., Rt. 183, 13 miles south of Pittsfield, Stockbridge* ☎ *866/200–5203, 800/741-7353* ⊕ *www.kripalu.org.*

The Option Institute. Here, it's all about learning to make emotional choices that enhance your life experience. Founded in 1983 by author Barry Neil Kaufman (*Happiness Is a Choice*) and Samahria Lyte Kaufman, the Option Institute is based on the premise that emotions like misery, fear, anger, and distress are optional, not inevitable. Personal growth workshops are designed to help participants develop tools that will improve the quality of their relationships, leading to a happier life. "Energizing" and "empowering" are words used by happy fans to describe their experience. Participants stay in rustic guesthouses and eat veggie meals served family-style. ✉ *2080 South Undermountain Rd., Sheffield* ☎ *800/714-2779* ⊕ *www. option.org.*

Many of New England's back roads are lined with historic split-rail fences or stone walls.

Fodor's Choice
★ **Hancock Shaker Village.** The third Shaker community in America, Hancock was founded in the 1790s. At its peak in the 1840s, the village had almost 300 inhabitants, who made their living farming, selling seeds and herbs, making medicines, and producing crafts. The religious community officially closed in 1960, but visitors today can still see craft demonstrations of blacksmithing, woodworking, and more. Many examples of Shaker ingenuity are visible at Hancock today: the **Round Stone Barn** and the **Laundry and Machine Shop** are two of the most interesting buildings. Also on-site are a farm (with a wonderful barn), some period gardens, a museum shop with reproduction Shaker furniture, a picnic area, and a café. Visit in April and catch the Baby Animals on Shaker Farm. ⊠ *Rtes. 20 & 41, 6 miles west of Pittsfield* ☎ *413/443–0188, 800/817–1137* ⊕ *www.hancockshakervillage.org* ✉ *$17* ⊗ *Apr.–Oct., daily 10–4.*

SPORTS AND THE OUTDOORS

Bousquet Ski Area. Prices and hours may change annually, but most winters here you can ski from 9 am to 9 pm every day except Sunday, starting at $20 midweek. With a 750-foot vertical drop, Bousquet technically has 23 trails if you count merging slopes separately. Some good beginner and intermediate runs, with a few steeper pitches. There are three double chairlifts, two carpet lifts, and a small snowboard park. Ski instruction is given twice daily on weekdays and thrice on weekends and holidays for children ages 5 and up.

If it's summer instead of ski season, Bousquet offers waterslides, disc golf, a large activity pool, a minigolf course, 32-foot climbing wall, go-karts, a bounce castle, an adventure park, and a zip line. ⊠ *101 Dan Fox*

Dr., off U.S. 7 near Pittsfield Airport ☎ 413/442–8316, 413/442–2436 snow conditions ⊕ www.bousquets.com

THE ARTS

South Mountain Concerts. For the serious music lover, this is one of the country's most distinguished centers for chamber music events. On the wooded slope of South Mountain, the 500-seat auditorium presents concerts every Sunday in September at 3. ⊠ *South Street, U.S. 7 and 20, 2 miles south of Pittsfield center* ☎ *413/442–2106* ⊕ *www. southmountainconcerts.org.*

WHERE TO EAT

$ ✕ **Aroma Bar and Grill.** In the middle of a nondescript shopping plaza, INDIAN the tasteful interior is almost surprising. After passing the bar and fish tank at the front, you are seated in the back half of the restaurant, where you can order from an extensive menu of Indian classics, ranging from *Kashmiri rogan josh* (cubes of lamb cooked with butter, onions and spices) to *mango chicken jalfrezie* (sautéed with mango and mixed vegetables). The real prize here is the weekend lunch buffet, which in addition to various main dishes boasts an endless supply of delectable appetizers like *vegetable pakoras* (deep-fried in chickpea batter) and *aloo samosas* (turnovers with seasoned potatoes and peas). $ *Average main: $14* ⊠ *Allendale Shopping Center, 5 Cheshire Road, Unit 32* ☎ *413/499–6500* ⊕ *www.aromabarandgrill.com* ☾ *Closed Mon.*

$$ ✕ **Elizabeth's.** You'd never guess this little white house just off Route 9 ITALIAN was a restaurant, let alone one serving some of the best Italian food ★ in the state. But Elizabeth's, in spite of feeling like dinner at a friend's house, offers a playful menu of simple entrees made from high-quality ingredients. From the four-cheese lasagna with caramelized onion, to the classic *pasta puttanesca* (olives, garlic, capers, hot pepper), all entrées are rich and served with bread and an impressive salad featuring a mixture of seasonal greens, vegetables, fruits, and cheeses. If everyone orders an entrée, you won't need an appetizer, but get the *bagna cauda* (a hot dipping bath of anchovy, garlic, and olive oil) anyway and take some salad home. Cash only. $ *Average main: $21* ⊠ *1264 East St.* ☎ *413/448–8244* ⚏ *Reservations essential* ▭ *No credit cards* ☾ *Closed Sun.–Tues. No lunch.*

$ ✕ **La Fogata Restaurante (Cocina Latina).** A few shelves of South American SOUTH foods, on your right as you walk in, comprise a small in-restaurant AMERICAN grocery started by owner and chef Miguel Gomez, because no place in ★ the area stocked the ingredients for true Colombian cooking. You may want to buy a jar of mole paste to take home, but it can wait until after you've dined at one of the small tables in this casual atmosphere with an open kitchen just behind the counter. It's hard to go wrong, whether you order a "typical platter" (grilled steak, fried egg, rice, beans, plantain, avocado, corn patty, and pork rind) or split a *picada La Fogata* (a tray brimming with five kinds of meats) with a friend. Vegetarian options are somewhat uninspiring, but if you eat meat, or even seafood, you will eat very well. $ *Average main: $13* ⊠ *770 Tyler Street* ☎ *413/443–6969.*

LENOX

10 miles south of Pittsfield, 130 miles west of Boston.

The famed Tanglewood music festival has been a fixture in upscale Lenox for decades, and it's a part of the reason the town remains fiercely popular in summer. Booking a room here or in any of the nearby communities can set you back dearly when music or theatrical events are in town. Many of the town's most impressive homes are downtown; others you can only see by setting off on the curving, tortuous back roads that traverse the region. In the center of the village, a few blocks of shabby-chic Colonial buildings contain shops and eateries.

GETTING HERE AND AROUND

Just off I–90 after passing through Lee, Lenox is a small town a bit south of Pittsfield. Be warned that while the Berkshires are usually blessedly free of traffic, Lenox and environs during the summer Tanglewood season is a notable exception.

ESSENTIALS

Visitor Information Lenox Chamber of Commerce ⊠ *Lenox Library, 18 Main St.* ☎ *413/637–3646* ⊕ *www.lenox.org.*

EXPLORING

Berkshires Scenic Railway Museum. In a restored 1903 railroad station in central Lenox, this museum displays antique rail equipment, vintage exhibits, and a large working model railway. It was previously the starting point for the diesel-hauled **Berkshire Scenic Railway,** a 1½-hour narrated round-trip train ride between Lenox and Stockbridge, but the train rides are on indefinite hiatus without permission from track owners, the Housatonic Railroad Company. ⊠ *10 Willow Creek Rd.* ☎ *413/637–2210* ⊕ *www.berkshirescenicrailroad.org* ⊿ *Free; charge for train rides should they recommence* ⊘ *Late May–Oct., weekends 9–4.*

Frelinghuysen Morris House & Studio. This modernist property on a 46-acre site exhibits the works of American abstract artists Suzy Frelinghuysen and George L. K. Morris as well as contemporaries including Pablo Picasso, Georges Braque, and Juan Gris. In addition to the paintings, frescoes, and sculptures, a 57-minute documentary on Frelinghuysen and Morris plays on a continuous loop in the classroom. ⊠ *92 Hawthorne St.* ☎ *413/637–0166* ⊕ *www.frelinghuysen.org* ⊿ *$12* ⊘ *Late June–early Sept., Thurs.–Sun. 10–3; early Sept.–mid-Oct., Thurs.–Sat. 10–3.*

Fodor's Choice ★ **The Mount.** This mansion built in 1902 with myriad classical influences was the summer home of novelist Edith Wharton. The 42-room house and 3 acres of formal gardens were designed by Wharton, who is considered by many to have set the standard for 20th-century interior decoration. In designing the Mount, she followed the principles set forth in her book *The Decoration of Houses* (1897), creating a calm and well-ordered home. Nearly $15 million has been spent to date on an extensive, ongoing restoration project. Take one of the guided tours (daily June through August; otherwise on weekends) for $2, or schedule a private "ghost tour" after hours. ⊠ *2 Plunkett St.* ☎ *413/551–5111,*

888/637–1902 ⊕ *www.edithwharton.org* ⌦ *$16* ⊘ *Grounds: dawn to dusk daily. House: May–Oct., daily 10–5; Nov.–Dec., weekends 10–5.*

Ventfort Hall Mansion and Gilded Age Museum. Built in 1893, Ventfort Hall was the summer "cottage" of Sarah Morgan, the sister of financier J. P. Morgan, and appeared in the film *The Cider House Rules*. Lively, information-packed tours offer a peek into the lifestyles of Lenox's super-rich "cottage class," and although the property is under restoration, many rooms are open, showing original stained glass and woodwork. The museum has rotating exhibits that explore the role of Lenox and the Berkshires as the era's definitive mountain retreat. Occasional evening plays and concerts are presented. ⊠ *104 Walker St.* ☎ *413/637–3206* ⊕ *www.gildedage.org* ⌦ *$15 single floor, $25 both floors* ⊘ *Weekdays 10–5, weekends 10–3.*

SPORTS AND THE OUTDOORS
HIKING
Kennedy Park. Town-owned Kennedy Park offers hiking and cross-country skiing on old carriage roads, plus nearly 15 miles of trails within a hardwood forest known as "Woolsey Woods." ⊠ *Main St. or West Dugway St.*

Pleasant Valley Wildlife Sanctuary. Part of the Massachusetts Audubon Society's system, the sanctuary abounds with beaver ponds, meadows, hardwood forests, and woodlands. A whiteboard at the entrance lists recent wildlife sightings, so you know what to watch for on your walk, and the various forest trails include loops that range in difficulty from a half-hour stroll around a pond, to a three-hour hike up a mountain. Hiking trails are open for cross-country skiing and snowshoeing in winter. ⊠ *472 W. Mountain Rd.* ☎ *413/637–0320* ⊕ *www.massaudubon. org* ⌦ *$4* ⊘ *Nature Center Tues.–Fri. 9–4, Sat.–Mon. 10–4. Trails daily dawn to dusk.*

HORSEBACK RIDING
Berkshire Horseback Adventures. Travel along the shaded trails of Kennedy Park and Lenox Mountain and enjoy breathtaking views of Berkshire County when you book an hour, half-day, or overnight ride. ⊠ *293 Main St.* ☎ *413/637–9090* ⊕ *www.berkshirehorseback.net.*

SHOPPING
Hoadley Gallery. One of the foremost crafts centers in New England, Hoadley Gallery, shows and sells American arts and crafts with a strong focus on pottery, jewelry, and textiles. ⊠ *21 Church St.* ☎ *413/637–2814* ⊕ *www.hoadleygallery.com.*

R. W. Wise. High-quality jewelry is designed on site and the store also sells estate and antique pieces. ⊠ *81 Church St.* ☎ *413/637–1589* ⊕ *www.rwwise.com* ⊘ *Closed Sun. and Mon., except July and Aug.*

THE ARTS
Fodor'sChoice ★ **Tanglewood.** Tanglewood, the 200-acre summer home of the Boston Symphony Orchestra (BSO), attracts thousands every year to concerts by world-famous performers from mid-June to Labor Day. The 5,000-seat main shed hosts larger concerts; the Seiji Ozawa Hall (named for the former BSO conductor) seats around 1,200 and is used for recitals,

Lawn tickets are a great way to experience the Boston Symphony Orchestra at Tanglewood—don't forget your blanket and picnic.

chamber music, and more intimate performances by summer-program students and soloists. One of the most rewarding ways to experience Tanglewood is to purchase lawn tickets, arrive early with blankets or lawn chairs, and have a picnic. Except for the occasional celebrity concert, lawn tickets remain below $20, and concerts can be clearly heard from just about any spot. Inside the shed, tickets vary in price, with most of the good seats costing between $38 and $100. ■TIP→ If you don't demand a seamless performance, consider an open rehearsal, offering much of the same music at a fraction of the price. ⊠ *297 West St., off Hwy. 183* ☎ *617/266–1492, 888/266–1492* ⊕ *www.tanglewood.org.*

Shakespeare & Company. The works of William Shakespeare and various others are performed in three theaters, in a schedule that's now expanded to include fall/winter in addition to the summer season. The Rose Footprint Theatre, however, is only open in summer, being a lawn-seating tent set up to resemble the dimensions of Shakespeare's first London theater, the Rose Playhouse. ⊠ *70 Kemble St.* ☎ *413/637–1199, 413/637–3353 tickets* ⊕ *www.shakespeare.org.*

WHERE TO EAT

$

PERUVIAN

★

✗ **Alpamayo.** Don't let this hole-in-the-wall fool you; what it lacks in pretension it more than makes up for in taste. Just order a plate of the much-lauded skewered beef hearts, and you'll quickly forget the atmosphere. Seviche is the specialty of the house, so if you aren't ordering it for your main course, consider a taste as an appetizer. Other options range from typical steaks and seafood to the delectable mishmash that is *lomo saltado* (angus beef, onions, tomatoes, french fries, sautéed together)—a microcosm of the restaurant; not much to look at, but a satisfyingly rich flavor. The carmel custard is a generous serving that two can share, unless one has a sweet tooth. $ *Average main: $13* ✉ *60 Main Street, Lee* ☎ *413/243-6000* ⊕ *www.alpamayorestaurant. com* ⊘ *Closed Mon.*

$$
FRENCH

✕ **Bistro Zinc.** Crisp walls, warm tile floors, and tall windows are bright and inviting in this stylishly modern French bistro, which feels like a country house in Provence. The kitchen turns out expertly prepared and refreshingly simple classics like steak *frites* (with fries), grilled pork loin, and coq au vin. The long, zinc-topped wood bar, always full and determinedly sophisticated, is the best Lenox can offer for nightlife. $ *Average main: $24* ✉ *56 Church St.* ☎ *413/637–8800* ⊕ *www. bistrozinc.com.*

$$$
ITALIAN

✕ **Café Lucia.** *Bistecca alla fiorentina* (porterhouse steak grilled with olive oil, garlic, and rosemary) and linguini *con melanzane* (with mozzarella-stuffed breaded eggplant) are among the dishes that change seasonally at this northern Italian restaurant with a nice porch. Weekend reservations are essential, especially during the Tanglewood music festival. $ *Average main: $28* ✉ *80 Church St.* ☎ *413/637–2640* ⊕ *www. cafelucialenox.com* ⌦ *Reservations essential* ⊘ *Closed Mon.; also closed Sun. Nov.–June. No lunch.*

$
BAKERY
Fodor's Choice
★

✕ **Chocolate Springs Cafe.** Escape into chocolate bliss here, where even the aroma is intoxicating. This award-winning chocolatier offers wedges of decadent cakes, store-made ice cream and sorbets, and a dazzling array of chocolates all made on-site from the top 10% of cocoa beans. Whether you like your chocolate dark and pure, sugar-free, or even filled with curry, you can't go wrong. You can eat at one of a handful of leather couches or wooden chairs and tables, but don't expect so much as a salad or a wrap—it's all chocolate, all the time. $ *Average main: $6* ✉ *Aspinwell Shops, 55 Pittsfield/Lenox Rd.* ☎ *413/637–9820* ⊕ *www.chocolatesprings.com.*

$$
CAFÉ

✕ **Church Street Café.** More laid-back than its nearby competitors, Church Street Café offers a minimalist rustic aesthetic, with hardwood floors, recycled metal chairs, and black-and-white photos on the walls. In contrast to the extensive wine list, the menu is a small but intriguing array of globally inspired dishes. From the baked onion-and-Manchego-cheese tart to the cioppino fish stew and the braised bison short ribs, the dishes served are an international culinary treat that changes seasonally. In warm weather you can dine on a shaded outdoor deck. $ *Average main: $24* ✉ *65 Church St.* ☎ *413/637–2745* ⊕ *churchstreetlenox.com* ⊘ *Closed Sun. and Mon.*

WHERE TO STAY

For expanded hotel reviews, visit Fodors.com.

$$
B&B/INN

🛏 **Brook Farm Inn.** Tucked away in a beautiful wooded glen a short distance from Tanglewood, this 1880s inn is hosted by attentive innkeepers who are history and music aficionados and often have classical music playing in the fireplace-lighted library; on request, there are occasional poetry readings, or stories from the innkeeper. $ *Rooms from: $179* ✉ *15 Hawthorne St.* ☎ *413/637–3013, 800/285–7638* ⊕ *brookfarm. com* ⌦ *15 rooms* ❚⊙❚ *Breakfast.*

$$$ B&B/INN Fodor'sChoice ★ 🏨 **Devonfield Inn.** This grand, yellow-and-cream Federal house sits atop a birch-shaded hillside, dotted with a few quaint outbuildings and 32 acres of rolling meadows.**Pros:** charming innkeepers; good breakfasts; nice pool and lawn, flat-screen TVs. **Cons:** not for families with young kids. [$] *Rooms from: $275* ✉ *85 Stockbridge Rd., Lee* ☎ *413/243–3298, 800/664–0880* 🌐 *www.devonfield.com* 🛏 *6 rooms, 3 suites, 1 cottage* 🍴 *Breakfast.*

$$ B&B/INN Fodor'sChoice ★ 🏨 **Gateways Inn.** The 1912 summer cottage of Harley Procter (as in Procter & Gamble) has had numerous owners during its tenure as a country inn, but after a quarter-million dollars in renovations from new innkeepers Michele and Eiran Gazit who took over in 2012, it looks better than ever. **Pros:** great location in the heart of Lenox; late-night food available in the piano bar. **Cons:** lots of stairs; wedding ceremonies sometimes take over the lobby. [$] *Rooms from: $200* ✉ *51 Walker St.* ☎ *413/637–2532* 🌐 *www.gatewaysinn.com* 🛏 *11 rooms, 1 suite* 🍴 *Breakfast.*

$ HOTEL ★ 🏨 **Yankee Inn.** Custom-crafted Amish canopy beds, gas fireplaces, and high-end fabrics decorate the top rooms at this immaculately kept, two-story motor inn, one of several modern hotels and motels along U.S. 7—the more economical units contain attractive, if nondescript, country-style furnishings; if you can, avoid the wings of the motel and stay in the main building for a nicer, less motel-y experience. **Pros:** convenient location to attractions; good value. **Cons:** closer to Pittsfield than Lenox; very small bar/lounge; dreary pool area. [$] *Rooms from: $119* ✉ *461 Pittsfield-Lenox Rd., off U.S. 7 and 20* ☎ *413/499–3700, 800/835–2364* 🌐 *www.yankeeinn.com* 🛏 *96 rooms* 🍴 *Breakfast.*

OTIS

20 miles southeast of Lenox.

A more rustic alternative to Stockbridge and Lenox, Otis, with a ski area and 20 lakes and ponds, supplies plenty of what made the Berkshires desirable in the first place—the great outdoors. Dining and lodgings options are slim; you can stay in Lee or Great Barrington or head southwest to Old Marlborough and stay at the Old Inn on the Green, where you can sample chef Peter Platt's swoon-worthy cuisine. Nearby Becket hosts the outstanding Jacob's Pillow Dance Festival in summer.

GETTING HERE AND AROUND

I–90 to Lee is the fastest way here for many coming from afar; locally Otis lies at the intersection of Routes 8 and 23. With no public transport, Otis is a place you'll be driving to or through.

EXPLORING

Deer Run Maples. This is one of several sugarhouses where you can spend the morning tasting freshly tapped maple syrup that's been drizzled onto a dish of snow. Sugaring season varies with the weather; it can be anytime between late February and early April. Call before coming to confirm opening hours. ✉ *135 Ed Jones Rd.* ☎ *413/269–7588* 🎟 *Free* 🕒 *Late Feb.–early Apr., hrs vary.*

SPORTS AND THE OUTDOORS

SKI AREA

Otis Ridge. The least expensive ski area in New England, Otis Ridge has long been a haven for beginners and families, but experts will find slopes here, too. The remote location is quite stunning, the buildings historic. Eleven downhill trails are serviced by four lifts, with 100% snowmaking coverage and night skiing Wednesday through Sunday. ⊠ *159 Monterey Rd., Hwy. 23* ☏ *413/269–4444* ⊕ *www.otisridge.com.*

THE ARTS

Fodor'sChoice ★ **Jacob's Pillow Dance Festival.** For nine weeks each summer, the tiny town of Becket, 8 miles north of Otis, becomes a hub of the dance world during the Jacob's Pillow Dance Festival, which showcases world-renowned performers of ballet, modern, and international dance. Before the main events, works in progress and even some of the final productions are staged outdoors, often free of charge. ⊠ *358 George Carter Rd., at U.S. 20, Becket* ☏ *413/243–9919, 413/243–0745 tickets* ⊕ *www. jacobspillow.org.*

STOCKBRIDGE

20 miles northwest of Otis, 7 miles south of Lenox.

Stockbridge is the quintessence of small-town New England charm, untainted by large-scale development. It is also the blueprint for small-town America as represented on the covers of the *Saturday Evening Post* by painter Norman Rockwell (the official state artist of Massachusetts). From 1953 until his death in 1978, Rockwell lived in Stockbridge and painted the simple charm of its buildings and residents. James Taylor sang about the town in his hit "Sweet Baby James," as did balladeer Arlo Guthrie in his famous Thanksgiving anthem "Alice's Restaurant," in which he tells what ensued when he tossed some garbage out the back of his Volkswagen bus down a Stockbridge hillside.

Indeed, Stockbridge is the stuff of legend. Travelers have been checking into the Red Lion Inn on Main Street since the 18th century, and Stockbridge is only slightly altered in appearance since that time. In 18th- and 19th-century buildings surrounding the inn are a handful of engaging shops and eateries. The rest of Stockbridge is best appreciated via a country drive or bike ride over its hilly, narrow lanes.

GETTING HERE AND AROUND

Stockbridge is easily accessible from West Stockbridge or Lee, both of which are exits off the Mass Pike. Once here, you can easily walk around the village and drive around the larger area.

ESSENTIALS

Visitor Information Stockbridge Chamber of Commerce ⊠ *50 Main St.* ☏ *413/298–5200, 413/298–5200* ⊕ *www.stockbridgechamber.org.*

EXPLORING

Berkshire Botanical Gardens. This 15-acre garden contains perennial, rose, daylily, and herb gardens of exotic and native plantings—some 2,500 varieties in all—plus greenhouses, ponds, and nature trails. Catch a free (with admission) tour on Friday or Saturday morning.

CLOSE UP

Norman Rockwell: Illustrating America

I was showing the America I knew and observed to others who might not have noticed. My fundamental purpose is to interpret the typical American. I am a storyteller.

—Norman Rockwell

If you've ever seen old copies of the *Saturday Evening Post*, no doubt you're familiar with American artist Norman Rockwell. He created 321 covers for the well-regarded magazine, and the *Post* always sold more copies when one of Rockwell's drawings was on the front page. The accomplished artist also illustrated Boy Scouts of America calendars, Christmas cards, children's books, and even a few stamps for the U.S. Postal Service—in 1994, a stamp bearing his image came out in his honor. His illustrations tended to fit the theme of Americana, family, or patriotism.

Born in New York City in 1894, the talented designer had a knack for art early on but strengthened his talent with instruction at the National Academy of Design and the Art Students League. He was only 22 when he sold his first cover to the *Post*. He was married three times and had three sons by his second wife. He died in 1978 in Stockbridge, Massachusetts, where he had lived since 1953.

Norman Rockwell 1920 magazine cover.

Famous works include his *Triple Self-Portrait* and the *Four Freedoms* illustrations done during World War II. They represent freedom of speech, freedom to worship, freedom from want, and freedom from fear. In a poetic twist, in 1977, President Gerald R. Ford bestowed on Rockwell the Presidential Medal of Freedom, the highest civilian honor a U.S. citizen can be given. Ford praised Rockwell for his "vivid and affectionate portraits of our country."

—Debbie Harmsen

✉ *5 West Stockbridge Rd., Rtes.183 & 102* ☎ *413/298–3926* ⊕ *www.berkshirebotanical.org* 🎟 *$12* ☉ *May–Oct., daily 10–5.*

Fodor's Choice ★ **Chesterwood.** For 33 years, this was the summer home of the sculptor Daniel Chester French (1850–1931), who created *The Minuteman* in Concord and the Lincoln Memorial's famous seated statue of the president in Washington, D.C. Tours are given of the house, which is maintained in the style of the 1920s, and of the studio, where you can view the casts and models French used to create the Lincoln Memorial. The beautifully landscaped 122-acre grounds also make for an enchanting stroll, bedecked with a contemporary sculpture show during the summer. If you are in the area on Memorial Day, come for the annual

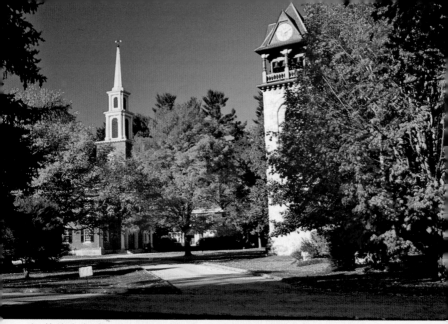

Stockbridge's churches are just some of the charming buildings on Main Street.

classic car show. ⊠ *4 Williamsville Rd., off Hwy. 183* ☎ *413/298–3579* ⊕ *www.chesterwood.org* ✉ *$16* ☉ *May–Oct., daily 11–4, grounds daily 10–5.*

★ **Naumkeag.** This Berkshire cottage once owned by Joseph Choate, a successful New York lawyer and an ambassador to Great Britain during President William McKinley's administration provides a glimpse into the gracious living of the gilded era of the Berkshires. The 26-room gabled mansion, designed by Stanford White in 1886, sits atop Prospect Hill. Its many original furnishings and art span three centuries; the collection of Chinese porcelain is also noteworthy. The meticulously kept 8 acres of formal gardens designed by Fletcher Steele are worth the visit. ⊠ *5 Prospect Hill Rd.* ☎ *413/298–3239* ⊕ *www.thetrustees.org* ✉ *$12* ☉ *Memorial Day–Columbus Day, daily 10–5.*

Norman Rockwell Museum. This charming museum traces the career of one of America's most beloved illustrators, beginning with his first *Saturday Evening Post* cover in 1916. The crown jewel of the 570 Rockwell illustrations is the famed "Four Freedoms" gallery, although various works—including self-portraits—are equally charming. The museum also mounts exhibits by other artists. Rockwell's studio was moved to the museum grounds and is complete in every detail. Stroll the 36-acre site, picnic on the grounds, or relax at the outdoor café (open from Memorial Day to Columbus Day). A child's version of the audio tour ($5 adults/$4 children) with a scavenger-hunt theme, as well as the kid's creativity center with art materials, make this museum more fun for kids. The museum shop makes it more fun for adults. ⊠ *9 Rte. 183,*

2 miles from Stockbridge ☎ *413/298–4100* ⊕ *www.nrm.org* ✉ *$16* ⊘ *May–Oct., daily 10–5; Nov.–Apr., weekdays 10–4, weekends 10–5.*

SHOPPING

Schantz Galleries. After nearly three decades working with Holsten Galleries, Jim Schantz bought the gallery, and though it's small and tucked away behind a bank, it features some of the finest glasswork in the world. With items from 55 contemporary glass artists—including Dale Chihuly (who did the Bellagio's ceiling in Vegas) and Lino Tagliapietra—the museum-quality glasswork is truly stunning. ⊠ *3 Elm St.* ☎ *413/298–3044* ⊕ *www.schantzgalleries.com.*

Williams & Sons Country Store. This traditional country store has penny candy, maple goods, candles, jams, and an authentic country feel. ⊠ *38 Main St.* ☎ *413/298–3016.*

THE ARTS

Berkshire Theatre Festival. Since 1929, this festival has presented plays nightly in summer. The four plays performed each summer on the Main Stage tend to be better-known vehicles with established actors. The Unicorn, a smaller theater, mounts experimental and new works. Festival shows are also now presented at the Colonial Theatre in Pittsfield. ⊠ *6 Main St.* ☎ *413/298–5576, 413/298–5576 box office* ⊕ *www.berkshiretheatregroup.org.*

WHERE TO EAT AND STAY

For expanded hotel reviews, visit Fodors.com.

$$$
ECLECTIC
✕ **Once Upon a Table.** A cute little name for a cute little upscale casual restaurant in the pedestrian alley off Stockbridge's Main Street. Cute and little also applies to the menu and the dishes themselves, a small but appealing selection of Continental and contemporary American cuisine that includes seasonal dishes and daily specials. After a sourdough rosemary roll, you can try "escargot potpie" (a puff pastry over a few snails in garlic butter), or entrées like seared crab cakes with capers, rack of lamb with garlic mashed potatoes, or a half duck in raspberry sauce. Ⓢ *Average main: $25* ⊠ *36 Main St.* ☎ *413/298–3870* ⊕ *www.onceuponatablebistro.com* ⟜ *Reservations essential* ⊘ *No breakfast weekdays.*

$$$
FRENCH
Fodor's Choice
★
✕ **Rouge.** In West Stockbridge, 5 miles northwest of Stockbridge, this little house with gray-green shingles, an illuminated small red sign, and simple and comfortable interior is reminiscent of a restaurant in the French countryside. Owner-chef William Merelle is indeed from Provence, where he met his American wife (and co-owner), Maggie, formerly a wine merchant. Try the steak au poivre with arugula, *pommes frites* (french fries), and cognac sauce or the braised free-range duck. Ⓢ *Average main: $28* ⊠ *3 Center St., West Stockbridge* ☎ *413/232–4111* ⊕ *www.rougerestaurant.com* ⟜ *Reservations essential* ⊘ *Closed Mon. and Tues. No lunch.*

$$$
B&B/INN
Fodor's Choice
★
▦ **The Inn at Stockbridge.** Antiques and feather comforters are among the accents in the rooms of this 1906 Georgian Revival inn run by the attentive Alice and Len Schiller, who serve breakfast in their elegant dining room, and provide wine and cheese every evening; each of the rooms in the adjacent "cottage" building has a decorative theme. **Pros:** beautiful

Massachusetts Farms

Living like a locavore is easy in the Berkshires and Western Massachusetts. The area's many farms, farm stands, and farmers' markets make everything from produce, dairy, and meat to maple syrup, flowers, and Christmas trees. There's spinach, asparagus, maple syrup, and flowers in the spring, an endless array of fruits and veggies at every farm stand in summer, and apples, cranberries, pumpkins, and squash seem to mimic the palette of the fall foliage.

FARM STANDS
A great place to find farm stands is south of Routes 7 and 8. More than 30 run along or just off these routes.

Whitney's Farm. Whitney's Farm sells fresh produce, plants and flowers, herbs, and dairy products. There is also a deli and bakery in the main building. ✉ 1775 S. State Rd., Rte 8, Cheshire ☎ 413/442–4749 ⊕ www. whitneysfarm.com ⏱ Mon.–Sat. 8–7, Sun. 9–6.

Sidehill Farm. Sidehill Farm, a little farther east (closer to Route 2 and Interstate 91), has yogurt (year-round) and raw milk (April through November) from grass-fed cows. Vegetables are generally available year-round, although veggie production went on hiatus in 2012. ✉ 137 Beldingville Rd., Ashfield ☎ 413/625–0011 ⊕ www.sidehillfarm.net.

YOU-PICK FARMS
Farms where you pick your own produce are very popular in Massachusetts. It's often berry farms and fruit orchards, but there are also many pick-your-own pumpkin patches, cornfields, and other vegetable farms.

FOR MORE INFORMATION
Berkshire Grown. To learn more about Berkshire farms, food producers, farm-to-table restaurants, workshops, and other events, check out Berkshire Grown. ✉ 314 Main St., Great Barrington ☎ 413/528–0041 ⊕ www. berkshiregrown.org.

Northeast Organic Farming Association. This organization offers a comprehensive resource for organic produce in Masssachusetts, including an interactive map. ✉ 411 Sheldon Rd., Barre ☎ 978/355–2853 ⊕ www. nofamass.org.

—Jen Laskey

grounds; good breakfast. **Cons:** noise from MA turnpike (most noticeable in suites); not within walking distance to town. [$] *Rooms from: $299* ✉ 30 East St., Rte. 7 N ☎ 413/298–3337, 888/466–7865 ⊕ *www. stockbridgeinn.com* 🛏 *10 rooms, 8 suites* 🍴 *Breakfast.*

$$
B&B/INN
Fodor's Choice
★

🏠 **The Red Lion Inn.** An inn since 1773, the Red Lion has hosted presidents, vice presidents, senators, and other celebrities, and consists of a large main building and nine annexes, each of which is different—one is a converted fire station—so if you like historic buildings filled with antiques, request a room in the main building (many of these units are small, but this is the authentic inn); if you want more space and more modern furnishings, request a room in one of the annex buildings. **Pros:** inviting lobby with fireplace; array of rocking chairs on porch; quaintly romantic. **Cons:** overpriced dining; puny fitness center; no cell reception.

The Red Lion Inn is a classic New England lodging experience: romantic, intimate, and historic.

$ Rooms from: $155 ✉ 30 Main St. ☎ 413/298–5545, 413/298–1690 🌐 www.redlioninn.com 🛏 125 rooms, 25 suites 🍽 Breakfast.

GREAT BARRINGTON

7 miles southwest of Stockbridge; 13 miles north of Canaan, Connecticut.

The largest town in South County became, in 1781, the first place in the United States to free a slave under due process of law and was also the birthplace, in 1868, of W. E. B. DuBois, the civil rights leader, author, and educator. The many ex–New Yorkers who live in Great Barrington expect great food and service, and the restaurants here deliver complex, delicious fare. The town is also a favorite of antiques hunters, as are the nearby villages of South Egremont and Sheffield.

GETTING HERE AND AROUND

The nearest international airports are Bradley International Airport in Windsor Locks, Connecticut, and Albany International Airport in Albany, New York, but you are better off driving in on Route 7 from either Stockbridge or Canaan, Connecticut. Great Barrington is also on the BRTA bus line from Stockbridge. There's plenty of parking in town, most of which is walkable as well.

ESSENTIALS

Visitor Information Southern Berkshire Chamber of Commerce ✉ *362 Main St.* ☎ *413/528–1510, 800/269–4825* 🌐 *southernberkshirechamber.com.*

SPORTS AND THE OUTDOORS
BICYCLING

The region's terrain is tremendously varied, and it tends to be hilly, but the Berkshires are relatively uncongested and extremely popular for biking, affording cycling enthusiasts of all abilities miles of great riding. The Ashuwillticook (pronounced *Ash*-oo-will-ti-cook) Rail Trail runs from the Pittsfield–Cheshire town line north up through Adams. Partly paved, it traces the old rail line and passes through rugged woodland and alongside Cheshire Lake. This is also a great venue for strolling, jogging, in-line skating, and cross-country skiing. The Berkshires Visitors Bureau distributes a free Berkshire Bike Touring Route, which is a series of relatively short excursions along area roads.

Ashuwillticook Rail Trail. Passing through the Hoosac River Valley, walkers and cyclists enjoy the paved 11-mile Ashuwillticook Rail Trail. ☎ 413/442–8928 ⊕ www.mass.gov/dcr/parks/western/asrt.htm.

HIKING

Bartholomew's Cobble. This natural rock garden beside the Housatonic River (the Native American name means "river beyond the mountains") is filled with trees, ferns, wildflowers, and 5 miles of hiking trails. The 277-acre site has a visitor center and museum. ⊠ 105 Weatogue Road (U.S. 7A), Ashley Falls, Sheffield ☎ 413/229–8600 ☜ $5 ⊙ Daily dawn–dusk.

A 90-mile swath of the Appalachian Trail cuts through the Berkshires. You'll also find hundreds of miles of trails elsewhere throughout the area's forests and parks.

Appalachian Trail. On Highway 23, about 4 miles east of where U.S. 7 and Highway 23 intersect, is a sign for the Appalachian Trail and a parking lot. Enter the trail for a moderately strenuous 45-minute hike. At the top of the trail is Ice Gulch, a gorge so deep and cold that there is often ice in it even in summer. Follow the Ice Gulch ridge to the shelter and a large flat rock from which you can see a wide panorama of the valley. ⊠ Lake Buel Road, Highway 23 ⊕ www.appalachiantrail.org.

Monument Mountain. For great views with minimal effort, hike Monument Mountain, famous as a spot for literary inspiration. Nathaniel Hawthorne and Herman Melville trekked it on August 5, 1850, and sought shelter in a cave when a thunderstorm hit. In the cave, they discussed ideas that would become part of a novel called Moby-Dick. While poet William Cullen Bryant stayed in the area, he penned a lyrical poem, "Monument Mountain," about a lovesick Mohican maiden who jumped to her death from the cliffs. Feel like hiking? An easy 2.5-mile loop is reachable via a parking lot. ⊠ Rte. 7, near Rte. 102, 4 miles north of Great Barrington ☎ 413/298–3239 ⊕ www.thetrustees.org.

SKI AREAS

Catamount Ski Area. With a 1,000-foot vertical drop, 99% snowmaking capacity, and even grades, Catamount Ski Area is ideal for family skiing. It has the most varied terrain in the Berkshires. There are 33 trails, served by six lifts, plus a snowboard area called Catamount Terrain Park, and a 400-foot half-pipe. The Sidewinder, an intermediate cruising trail, is more than 1 mile from top to bottom. There's also lighted nighttime boarding and skiing. ⊠ *3290 State Hwy. 23, South Egremont* ☎ *413/528–1262, 413/528–1262 snow conditions* ⊕ *www. catamountski.com.*

Ski Butternut. There are good base facilities here, in addition to pleasant skiing, 100% snowmaking capabilities, and the longest quad lift in the Berkshires. For snowboarders there are top-to-bottom terrain parks and a beginner park, and eight lanes are available for snow tubing. For downhill skiing, only a steep chute or two interrupt the mellow terrain on 22 trails. Eleven lifts, including 4 carpet lifts, keep skier traffic spread out. Ski and snowboard lessons are available. In summer Butternut usually hosts a crafts show. ⊠ *380 State Rd., Route 23* ☎ *413/528–2000, 413/528–4433 ski school, 800/438–7669 snow conditions* ⊕ *www. skibutternut.com.*

SHOPPING
ANTIQUES
The Great Barrington area, including the small towns of Sheffield and South Egremont, has the Berkshires' greatest concentration of antiques stores. Some shops are open sporadically, and many are closed on Tuesday.

Elise Abrams Antiques. Elise Abrams Antiques sells fine antique china, glassware, and furniture. ⊠ *11 Stockbridge Rd., U.S. 7* ☎ *413/528–3201* ⊕ *www.eliseabrams.com.*

Great Barrington Antiques Center. At the Great Barrington Antiques Center 50 dealers crowd onto one floor, selling Oriental rugs, furniture, and smaller decorative pieces. ⊠ *964 S. Main St., U.S. 7* ☎ *413/644–8848* ⊕ *www.greatbarringtonantiquescenter.com.*

FOOD AND COOKWARE
Bizalion. Bizalion, a French specialty foods shop and café, has imported cheeses, 10 different olive oils, cured meats, and brick-oven-baked baguettes and pastries. ⊠ *684 Main St.* ☎ *413/644–9988* ⊕ *www. bizalions.com.*

Boardman Farm. Boardman Farm offers fresh vegetables and is open all day, every day, on an honor system from mid-July through Thanksgiving. ⊠ *64 Hewins St., Sheffield* ☎ *413/229–8554.*

Howden Farm. Howden Farm has raspberries for picking from mid-August through mid-October and pumpkin picking from late September through October. They also run a bed-and-breakfast. ⊠ *303 Rannapo Rd., Sheffield* ☎ *413/229–8481* ⊕ *www.howdenfarm.com* ☉ *Mid-Aug.–mid-Oct., daily 11–5; mid-Oct–end Oct., weekends 11–5.*

Taft Farms. Taft Farms has raspberries from early July through mid-October, and pick-your-own pumpkins from September through October. ⊠ *119 Park St. N, Great Barrington* ☎ *413/528–1515* ⊕ *www. taftfarms.com* ☉ *Early July–Oct., daily 9–6.*

THE ARTS
Mahaiwe Performing Arts Center. Catch a classic movie or a performance by, perhaps, Judy Collins or the Daedalus Quartet at the Mahaiwe Performing Arts Center. This stunning 1905 theater offers a year-round schedule of live music, dance, and film, with performances that range

from famed country musicians and stand-up comedians to opera and modern dance. ✉ *14 Castle St.* ☎ *413/528–0100* 🌐 *www.mahaiwe.org.*

WHERE TO EAT

$ PIZZA 🍴 **Baba Louie's Sourdough Pizza Co.** Pizza good enough to merit the lines that oft stretch out the door? Quite possibly. Enjoy the trattoria rustica interior, and try to ignore the din of the crowd. Baba Louie's offers interesting crusts, with a choice of a mild sourdough or an organic wheat and spelt-berry. But the real interest here is the inspired topping combinations, like roasted sweet potatoes and parsnips, shaved fennel, caramelized onions, and fresh mozzarella with a hint of balsamic vinegar (on the Isabella Pizzarella), or ricotta, red onions, shrimp, pineapple, prosciutto, green chili, and a dusting of coconut (on the Hannah Jo). Weird, but good. [$] *Average main: $12* ✉ *286 Main St.* ☎ *413/528–8100* 🌐 *www.babalouiessourdoughpizzacompany.com* ✍ *Reservations not accepted.*

$$ CAFÉ ★ 🍴 **Castle Steet Café.** Chef-owner Michael Ballon wins raves for his simple-but-elegant cuisine and masterful hand with fresh local produce. Local artwork, hardwood floors, and sleek furnishings create an understated interior—a perfect backdrop for oysters on the half shell, linguini Provençal, or duck with black currant sauce. There's an extensive wine list, and the breadbasket has warm specialty bread from Berkshire Mountain Bakery. The frequent evening jazz may seem ear-splittingly loud if you aren't a fan. [$] *Average main: $23* ✉ *10 Castle St.* ☎ *413/528–5244* 🌐 *www.castlestreetcafe.com* ⏲ *Closed Tues.*

STURBRIDGE AND THE PIONEER VALLEY

A string of historic settlements lines the majestic Connecticut River, the wide and winding waterway that runs through Western Massachusetts. The bustling city of Springfield, known for its family-friendly attractions and museums, along with a cluster of college towns and quaint, rural villages is part of the Pioneer Valley, which formed the western frontier of New England from the early 1600s until the late 1900s.

Educational pioneers came to this region and created a wealth of major colleges including Mount Holyoke (the first college in the country for women), Amherst, Smith, Hampshire, and the University of Massachusetts. Northampton and Amherst serve as the valley's cultural hubs today; both have become increasingly desirable places to live, drawing former city dwellers who relish the ample natural scenery, sophisticated cultural venues, and lively dining and shopping.

SPRINGFIELD

90 miles west of Boston; 30 miles north of Hartford, Connecticut.

Springfield, easily accessed from Interstates 90 and 91, is the busy hub of the Pioneer Valley. Known as the birthplace of basketball (the game was devised by Canadian gym instructor James Naismith in 1891 as a last-ditch attempt to keep a group of unruly teenagers occupied in winter), the city has a cluster of fine museums and family attractions.

The Pioneer Valley

VERMONT

Northfield

Shelburne Falls

Turners Falls

Greenfield

Millers Falls

Orange

Athol

Deerfield

Montague

Locks Village

New Salem

South Deerfield

Sunderland

Shutesbury

Wheately

North Hatfield

North Amherst

University of Massachusetts

Amherst

Amherst College

Hatfield

South Amherst

Quabbin Reservoir

Northampton

Smith College

Hampshire College

Easthampton

South Hadley

Granby

Belchertown

Ware

Mount Holyoke College

Southampton

Westover Air Force Base

Bondsville

Warren

Holyoke

THE PIONEER VALLEY

Three Rivers

Palmer

Westfield

W. Springfield

Chicopee

Wilbraham

Old Sturbridge Village

Springfield

Southwick

Agawam

Longmeadow

East Longmeadow

Congamond Lakes

Sherwood Manor

CONNECTICUT

5 mi

5 km

GETTING HERE AND AROUND

Springfield is roughly the center of Massachusetts, which means it's easily accessible by bus, train, or Interstates 90 and 91. Parts of Springfield are walkable, but you're better off with a car, or using the PVTA local bus routes.

ESSENTIALS

Visitor Information Greater Springfield Convention & Visitors Bureau ✉ *1441 Main St.* ☎ *413/787–1548, 800/723–1548* ⊕ *www.valleyvisitor.com.* **Sturbridge Area Tourist Association** ✉ *380 Main St., Sturbridge* ☎ *800/628–8379, 508/347–2761* ⊕ *www.sturbridgetownships.com.*

EXPLORING

Fodor'sChoice ★ ☾ **Naismith Memorial Basketball Hall of Fame.** Along the banks of the Connecticut River, this 80,000-square-foot facility is dedicated to Canadian phys-ed instructor, Dr. James Naismith, who invented the game here in 1891 during his five years at Springfield's YMCA Training Center. It includes a soaring domed arena where you can practice jumpers, walls of inspirational quotes, dozens of interactive exhibits, and video footage and interviews with former players. The Honors Rings pay tribute to the hall's nearly 300 enshrinees. It's easy to find—just look for the 15-story spire with an illuminated basketball on top. ✉ *1000 W. Columbus Ave.* ☎ *413/781–6500, 877/446–6752* ⊕ *www.hoophall. com* ✇ *$19* ☾ *Sun.–Fri. 10–4, Sat. 10–5.*

☾ **Six Flags New England.** Containing more than 160 rides and shows, this mega attraction is the region's largest theme park and water park. Rides include the Bizarro Superman Ride, which is more than 20 stories tall and has a top speed of 77 mph. ✉ *1623 Main St., Route 159, 4 miles southwest of Springfield, Agawam* ☎ *413/786–9300* ⊕ *www. sixflags.com/newengland* ✇ *$50* ☾ *Hrs vary. Check website or call for information.*

★ ☾ **Zoo in Forest Park and Education Center.** At this leafy, 735-acre retreat hiking paths wind through the trees, paddleboats navigate Porter Lake, and hungry ducks float on a small pond. The zoo, where Theodore Geisel—better known as Dr. Seuss—found inspiration for his children's books, is home to nearly 200 animals, from black bears and bobcats to emus, lemurs, and wallabies. It's manageable in size, and spotting animals in the exhibits is fairly easy, which makes this an especially good stop for families with small children. Another plus: you can purchase small bags of food from the gift shop and feed many of the animals. Leave time to explore the park after you finish the zoo. ✉ *302 Sumner Ave.* ☎ *413/733–2251* ⊕ *www.forestparkzoo.org* ✇ *$7* ☾ *Daily 10–6.*

QUICK BITES

La Fiorentina Pastry Shop. Springfield's South End is the home of a lively Little Italy with some excellent restaurants, as well as La Fiorentina Pastry Shop, which has been doling out heavenly pastries, butter cookies, and coffees since the 1940s. ✉ *883 Main St.* ☎ *413/732–3151* ⊕ *www. lafiorentinapastry.com* ☾ *Mon.–Sat. 8–6, Sun. 8–2.*

★ ☾ **Springfield Museums.** One of the most ambitious cultural venues in New England, this complex includes five impressive facilities, all for one ticket:

The **Connecticut Valley Historical Museum,** the most modest of the group, presents changing exhibits drawn from its collections of furniture, silver, industrial objects, autos, and firearms; its main draw is the in-depth genealogical library, where folks from all over the world come to research their family trees. The must-see **George Walter Vincent Smith Art Museum** houses a fascinating private art collection that includes 19th-century American paintings by Frederic Church and Albert Bierstadt. A Japanese antiquities room is filled with armor, textiles, and porcelain, as well as carved jade and rock-crystal snuff bottles. The **Museum of Fine Arts** has paintings by Paul Gauguin, Claude Monet, Pierre-Auguste Renoir, Edgar Degas, Winslow Homer, and J. Alden Weir, as well as 18th-century American paintings and contemporary works by Georgia O'Keeffe, Frank Stella, and George Bellows. Rotating exhibits are open throughout the year. The **Springfield Science Museum** has an Exploration Center of touchable displays, the oldest operating planetarium in the United States, an extensive collection of stuffed and mounted animals, dinosaur exhibits, and the African Hall, through which you can take an interactive tour of that continent's flora and fauna. The **Museum of Springfield History** opened in 2009 and tells the story of the town's manufacturing heritage. (Springfield was home to the former Indian Motorcycle Company, and the museum has a rich collection of Indian bikes and memorabilia.) Also on the grounds is the free **Dr. Seuss National Memorial Sculpture Garden,** an installation of five bronze statues depicting scenes from Theodore Geisel's famously whimsical children's books. Born in Springfield in 1904, Geisel was inspired by the animals at Forest Park Zoo, where his father served as director. The statues include a 4-foot Lorax, a giant "Horton Court" featuring the elephant and Things 1 and 2, Giesel at his desk, and a 10-foot-high book inscribed with the entire text of *Oh the Places You'll Go!* ⊠ *220 State St., at Chestnut St.* ☎ *413/263–6800* ⊕ *www.springfieldmuseums. org* ✉ *$12.50* ⊙ *Museums Tue.–Sat. 10–5, Sun 11–5. Springfield History Library Archives, Tues.–Fri. 11–4. Outdoor Dr. Seuss Sculpture Garden, daily 9–5.*

OFF THE BEATEN PATH

Old Sturbridge Village. Old Sturbridge Village, modeled on an early-19th-century New England town, is a re-creation of a 1790–1840s era village with more than 40 historic buildings that were moved here from other towns. Some of the homes are filled with canopy beds and elaborate furnishings; in the simpler, single-story cottages, interpreters wearing period costumes demonstrate home-based crafts like spinning, weaving, and shoe making. There are several industrial buildings, including a working sawmill. Take an informative stagecoach ride, or boat ride along the Quinebaug River where you can learn about river life in 19th-century New England and catch a glimpse of ducks, geese, turtles, and other local wildlife. Nearby is the tiny town of Brimfield, home to one of the country's largest antiques fairs, held several times a year. ⊠ *1 Old Sturbridge Village Rd.* ☎ *508/347–3362, 800/733–1830* ⊕ *www.osv. org* ✉ *$24* ⊙ *Apr.–late Oct., daily 9:30–5; late Oct.–Mar., Wed.–Sun. 9:30–4 Dec. select evenings only. Open all Mon. holidays.*

Costumed historians are part of the 19th-century Old Sturbridge Village.

WHERE TO EAT

$ — CAJUN — ✕ **Big Mamou.** If you're cravin' Creole, you can't miss this casual joint, with seriously good, uncomplicated Louisiana cuisine. Owner/chef Wayne Booker stands behind the kitchen counter, and his hometown recipes, like Louisiana Lenny's sausage and chicken ya-ya (chicken breast wrapped around andouille sausage with Creole spices), shrimp-and-sausage jambalaya, barbecue pulled pork, and Bayou meatloaf. Added bonus: You can bring your own bottle. $ *Average main: $13* ✉ *63 Liberty St.* ☎ *413/732–1011* ⊕ *www.chefwaynes-bigmamou.com* ⚑ *Reservations not accepted* ⊙ *Closed Sun.*

$ — VIETNAMESE — ★ — ✕ **Pho Saigon.** This ethnic eatery, which is small, tastefully understated, and a little out of the way, serves up some of the best authentic Vietnamese cuisine in the city at wallet-pleasing prices. Enjoy full-of-flavor, made-from-scratch soups, the shrimp cakes with shredded yam, and the vermicelli dishes. There are lots of rice dishes and vegetarian options, as well as house specialties like the delectable fried soft-shell crab or the Vietnamese "happy pancake," a rice batter crepe stuffed with shrimp and chicken. Just be warned that you'll have to drive through Springfield's infamously bad intersection, "The X." $ *Average main: $10* ✉ *400 Dickinson St.* ☎ *413/781–4488* ⊙ *Closed Wed.*

WHERE TO STAY

For expanded hotel reviews, visit Fodors.com.

$ — B&B/INN — ★ — ⌂ **Naomi's Inn.** This elegantly restored house in a residential neighborhood has three individually decorated suites, all with lush comfort and artistic flair: the Louis XIV suite has two large rooms, 19th-century armoires, a down-filled sofa, and custom-tiled bath; the French Market suite has a custom-made iron king-sized bed, tiled bath, and an adjoining room with two twin beds, making it perfect for families. **Pros:** elegantly designed; deluxe linens and baths; warm and knowledgeable hosts; massage and/or babysitting available on request. **Cons:** near the hospital, so you may hear sirens. $ *Rooms from: $140* ⊠ *20 Springfield St.* ☎ *413/433–6019, 888/762–6647* ⊕ *www.naomisinn.net* ➳ *6 suites* ⦿ *Breakfast.*

$

B&B/INN

Fodor's Choice

★

☖ **The Publick House.** Step back in time at this rambling 1771 inn, where rooms are Colonial in design, with wide plank floors, period antiques and reproductions, and canopy beds; public areas, including several dining rooms and a tavern, have original woodwork and fireplaces, and the whole property, with 60 surrounding acres, sits on the picturesque Town Green. **Pros:** Colonial ambience and architecture; historical significance; log fires and candlelight throughout. **Cons:** rattling pipes; thin walls; small bathrooms. $ *Rooms from: $109* ⊠ *277 Main St., Route 131, Sturbridge* ☎ *508/347–3313, 800/782–5425* ⊕ *www. publickhouse.com* ➳ *14 rooms, 3 suites in main inn* ⦿ *No meals.*

SOUTH HADLEY

12 miles north of Springfield.

Nestled in the heart of Pioneer Valley, this small, quiet college town, with a cluster of Main Street cafés and stores, is surrounded by rolling hills and farmlands. It's best known for the Mount Holyoke College Art Museum, one of the finest in the region.

GETTING HERE AND AROUND

With Bradley International Airport and the Springfield Amtrak station to the south, South Hadley is reasonably convenient. You can walk around Mount Holyoke campus, but you'll need to drive to get most anywhere else.

EXPLORING

Mount Holyoke College. Founded in 1837, Mount Holyoke was the first women's college in the United States. Among its alumnae are poet Emily Dickinson and playwright Wendy Wasserstein. The handsome wooded campus, encompassing two lakes and lovely walking or riding trails, was landscaped by Frederick Law Olmsted. ⊠ *50 College St.* ☎ *413/538–2000* ⊕ *www.mtholyoke.edu.*

Mount Holyoke College Art Museum. Next to the college greenhouse, this museum contains some 11,000 works, including Asian, European, and American paintings and sculpture, as well as rotating exhibits. ⊠ *Lower Lake Rd. and Church Street* ☎ *431/538–2245* ⊕ *www.mtholyoke.edu* ☑ *Free* ⦿ *Tues.–Fri. 11–5, weekends 1–5.*

SHOPPING

The Odyssey Bookshop. In addition to stocking 50,000 new and used titles, the Odyssey Bookshop has readings and book signings by locally and nationally known authors. ⊠ *9 College St.* ☎ *413/534–7307* ⊕ *www.odysseybks.com.*

4

WHERE TO EAT

$$ ✕ **Food 101 Bar & Bistro.** There's nothing basic about this popular, oh-so-
ECLECTIC calm, candle-lighted eatery across from the Mount Holyoke campus.
Fodor'sChoice Dishes are complicated but mostly successful, like the lobster risotto;
★ the upscale *pommes frites* (french fries) with spicy ketchup and wasabi
mayonnaise; and the pan-seared sea scallops with cauliflower risotto,
crab and mâche salad, and warm curry oil. This spot is a magnet for
foodies, yuppies, and college students on their parents' tab. $ *Average
main: $24* ⊠ *19 College St.* ☎ *413/535–3101* ⊕ *www.food101bistro.
com* ⊙ *Closed Mon. No lunch weekends.*

NORTHAMPTON

10 miles northeast of South Hadley.

The cultural center of Western Massachusetts is without a doubt the
city of Northampton (nicknamed "Noho"), whose vibrant downtown
is packed with interesting eateries, lively clubs, and offbeat boutiques.
The city attracts artsy types, academics, activists, lesbians and gays, and
just about anyone else seeking the culture and sophistication of a big
metropolis but the friendliness and easy pace of a small town.

GETTING HERE AND AROUND

Northampton is served by buses from nearby Springfield's train station,
although most people will probably arrive by car on I–91. Downtown
is crossed by routes 5, 9, and 10, and walking to most downtown loca-
tions is not only possible, but an excellent way to spend an afternoon.
Local PVTA buses are also available.

ESSENTIALS

Visitor Information Greater Northampton Chamber of Commerce ⊠ *99
Pleasant St.* ☎ *413/584–1900, 800/238–6869* ⊕ *www.explorenorthampton.com.*

EXPLORING

Forbes Library. The Calvin Coolidge Presidential Library and Museum,
within the Forbes Library, contains a collection of President Cal-
vin Coolidge's papers and memorabilia. Northampton was the 30th
president's Massachusetts home. He practiced law here and served as
mayor from 1910 to 1911. ⊠ *20 West St.* ☎ *413/587–1011* ⊕ *www.
forbeslibrary.org* ⊙ *Coolidge Library and Museum: Mon. and Wed.
3–9, Tues. and Thurs. 1–5.*

> QUICK
> BITES

Herrell's Ice Cream. On the lower level of Thorne's Marketplace, Herrell's
Ice Cream is famous for its chocolate pudding, vanilla malt, and cinnamon
nutmeg flavors, as well as delicious homemade hot fudge. ⊠ *8 Old South
St.* ☎ *413/586–9700* ⊕ *www.herrells.com.*

Smith College. The nation's largest liberal arts college for women opened
its doors in 1875 (thanks to heiress Sophia Smith). Renowned for its
School of Social Work, Smith has a long list of distinguished alum-
nae, among them activist Gloria Steinem, chef Julia Child, and writer
Margaret Mitchell. One of the most serene campuses in New England,
Smith is also a leading center of political and cultural activity. Two sites
on Smith's campus, the Lyman Plant House and the Botanic Garden

of Smith College, should be visited. The flourishing **Botanic Garden of Smith College** covers the entirety of Smith's 150-acre campus. ⊠ *College Lane* ⊕ *www.smith.edu.*

Lyman Plant House. On the Smith College campus, the Lyman Plant House is home to more than 2,500 species of plants. ⊠ *College Lane* ☎ *413/585–2740* ⊕ *www.smith.edu/garden* ☉ *Daily 8:30–4*

Smith College Museum of Art. A floor of skylighted galleries, an enclosed courtyard for performances and receptions, and a high-tech art-history library make up this museum, where highlights of the permanent collection include European masterworks by Paul Cézanne, Degas, Auguste Rodin, and Georges Seurat, and works by woman artists like Mary Cassatt and Alice Neel. ⊠ *Brown Fine Arts Center, 22 Elm St. at Bedford Terrace* ☎ *413/585–2760* ⊕ *www.smith.edu/artmuseum* 🖃 *$5* ☉ *Tues.–Sat. 10–4, Sun. noon–4*

William Cullen Bryant Homestead. About 20 miles northwest of Northampton, in the scenic hills west of the Pioneer Valley, is the country estate of the 19th-century poet and author William Cullen Bryant. Come on a summer Saturday to tour the Dutch Colonial mansion filled with furnishings and collectibles from Bryant's life, work, and travels. Outside, the 195-acre grounds overlooking the Westfield River Valley are a great venue for bird-watching, cross-country skiing, snowshoeing, fishing, hiking, and picnics. ⊠ *207 Bryant Rd., Rte. 112, Cummington* ☎ *413/634–2244* 🖃 *Grounds free; house tour $5* ☉ *Grounds daily sunrise–sunset. House guided tours July and Aug., Sat. 1pm and 3pm.*

SPORTS AND THE OUTDOORS

Norwottuck Rail Trail. Part of the Connecticut River Greenway State Park, this is a paved 10-mile path that links Northampton with Belchertown by way of Amherst. Great for biking, rollerblading, jogging, and cross-country skiing, it runs along the old Boston & Maine Railroad route. Free trail maps are available. ⊠ *Hwy. 9 at Damon Rd., near Coolidge Bridge. Also accessible in Hadley at Hwy. 9 at River Dr. (Hwy. 47 N)* ☎ *413/586–8706.*

NIGHTLIFE AND THE ARTS

Diva's Nightclub. This spacious club serves the region's sizable lesbian and gay community with great music that draws people to the cavernous dance floor. ⊠ *492 Pleasant St.* ☎ *413/586–8161* ⊕ *www.divasofnoho. com* ☉ *Closed Sun. and Mon.*

Fitzwilly's. A reliable choice for a night out, Fitzwilly's draws a friendly mix of locals and tourists for drinks and tasty pub fare. Try the sliders. ⊠ *23 Main St.* ☎ *413/584–8666* ⊕ *www.fitzwillys.com.*

Hugo's. The dimly lighted and somewhat dive-y Hugo's has cheap beer, affordable pool, a rocking jukebox, and all the local color you'll ever want to see. ⊠ *315 Pleasant St.* ☎ *413/387-6023.*

WHERE TO EAT

$$
ITALIAN
✕ **Mulino's Restaurant.** In sleek quarters (which also contain the upstairs Bishop's Lounge), this modern trattoria carefully prepares Sicilian-inspired, home-style Italian food. You'll rarely taste a better carbonara sauce this side of the Atlantic, but don't overlook the wild mushroom

and Gorgonzola tossed with penne or the melt-in-your-mouth veal saltimbocca. Portions are huge, and the wine list is extensive. Parents like to take their college kids here for a special night out. $ *Average main: $17* ⊠ *41 Strong Ave.* ☎ *413/586–8900* ⊕ *mulinosrestaurant. com* ⊗ *No lunch.*

$$ ✕ **Northampton Brewery.** In a rambling building in Brewster Court, this
AMERICAN   noisy and often-packed pub and microbrewery has extensive outdoor seating on a deck. The kitchen serves an array of sandwiches and tasty comfort food, including Cajun catfish bites, chicken-and-shrimp jamba-laya, and the blackened blue burger (with blue cheese and caramelized onions). $ *Average main: $16* ⊠ *13 Old South St.* ☎ *413/584–9903* ⊕ *www.northamptonbrewery.com* ⌔ *Reservations not accepted.*

$ ✕ **Spoleto.** A Noho mainstay since the 1980s, Spoleto, in the heart of
ITALIAN   downtown, offers a something-for-everyone menu: basic beef, chicken,
Fodor's Choice   seafood, and pasta dishes served with a dash of creative flair and fla-
★   vor. The beef carpaccio and angel-hair crab cakes are first-rate. You'll find typical lasagna and chicken Parmesan dishes alongside the more adventurous *rollatini* (chicken with cheese, mushrooms, and asparagus). The Gorgonzola bread is a nice side dish. $ *Average main: $14* ⊠ *50 Main St.* ☎ *413/586–6313* ⊕ *www.spoletorestaurants.com* ⊗ *No lunch.*

AMHERST

8 miles northeast of Northampton.

★   One of the most visited spots in all of New England, Amherst is known for its scores of world-renowned authors, poets, and artists. The above-average intelligence quotient of its population is no accident, as Amherst is home to a trio of colleges—Amherst, Hampshire, and the University of Massachusetts. The high concentration of college-age humanity bolsters Amherst's downtown area, which includes a wide range of art galleries, music stores, and clothing boutiques.

GETTING HERE AND AROUND

Amherst is a stop on the Amtrak line, and the closest airline is Bradley International in Connecticut. Once you're in town, the PVTA buses are probably your best bet.

ESSENTIALS

Visitor Information Amherst Area Chamber of Commerce ⊠ *28 Amity St.* ☎ *413/253–0700* ⊕ *www.amherstarea.com.*

EXPLORING

Emily Dickinson Museum. The famed Amherst poet lived here her entire life (1830–86) in this brick Federal-style home. Admission is by guided tour only, and the highlight is getting to stand in the sunlit bedroom where the poet wrote many of her works. The museum is outfitted with period accoutrements, including original wall hangings and lace curtains. To say that the tour guides are knowledgeable in Dickinson's story would be a massive understatement. ⊠ *280 Main St.* ☎ *413/542–8161* ⊕ *www. emilydickinsonmuseum.org* ⌔ *$10* ⊗ *Mar.–May and Sept.–mid-Dec., Wed.–Sun. 11–4; June–Aug., Wed.–Sun. 10–5.*

The Evergreens. Next door is The Evergreens, an imposing Italianate Victorian mansion in which Emily's brother Austin and his family resided for more than 50 years. Unlike the Dickinson homestead, which has few of the family's original possessions, the Evergreens is packed with Austin's family's heirlooms. ⊠ *214 Main St.* ☎ *413/253–5272.*

QUICK BITES

The Black Sheep. Newspapers and books are strewn about the tables at this funky downtown café specializing in coffees and creative sandwiches, salads, and soups. It's a great place to pick up on the college vibe; free Wi-Fi, too. ⊠ *79 Main St.* ☎ *413/253–3442* ⊕ *www.blacksheepdeli.com.*

Fodor'sChoice
★
☾

Eric Carle Museum of Picture Book Art. If you have kids in tow—or if you just love children's books art—"The Carle" is a must-see. This light-filled museum celebrates and preserves not only the works of renowned children's book author Eric Carle (who penned *The Very Hungry Caterpillar*), but also Maurice Sendak, Lucy Cousins, Petra Mathers, Tomie DePaola, and Leo and Diane Dillon. Puppet shows, lectures, author events, and storytelling are part of the museum's ongoing calendar of events. Children are invited to create their own works of art in the museum's studio or read a few classics (or discover new authors) in the library. ⊠ *125 W. Bay Rd.* ☎ *413/658–1100* ⊕ *www.picturebookart. org* ☞ *$9* ☾ *Tues.–Fri. 10–4, Sat. 10–5, Sun. noon–5.*

★ **The Yiddish Book Center.** Founded in 1980 by Aaron Lansky, this non-profit organization has become a major force in the effort to preserve the Yiddish language and Jewish culture, by rescuing over one million Yiddish books that would otherwise have been lost. Built in 1997 on the campus of Hampshire College, the center is housed in a split-roof building that resembles a cluster of houses in a traditional Eastern European *shtetl*, or village. Inside, a contemporary space contains more than 100,000 books, a kosher dining room, and a visitor center with changing exhibits, as well as occasional lectures, films, concerts, and other performances. ⊠ *1021 West St. (Hwy. 116)* ☎ *413/256–4900* ⊕ *www. yiddishbookcenter.org* ☞ *Suggested Donation: $8* ☾ *Sun.–Fri. 10–4, Closed Sun. in winter.*

SHOPPING

Atkins Farms. An institution in the Pioneer Valley, the Atkins Farms are surrounded by apple orchards and gorgeous views of the Holyoke Ridge. Children's events happen throughout the year. Inside, you'll find a bakery and deli; the market sells produce, baked goods, and specialty foods. ⊠ *1150 West St. (Hwy. 116)* ☎ *413/253–9528* ⊕ *www. atkinsfarms.com.*

NIGHTLIFE AND THE ARTS

Amherst Brewing Company. Head to "the ABC" for its lounge, game room, and a vast selection of beers brewed on the premises. ⊠ *10 University Dr.* ☎ *413/253–4400* ⊕ *www.amherstbrewing.com.*

The Harp. This is a small but cozy Irish tavern with live music on Thursday afternoon and Friday night. ⊠ *163 Sunderland Rd.* ☎ *413/548–6900* ⊕ *www.theharp.net.*

WHERE TO EAT AND STAY

For expanded hotel reviews, visit Fodors.com.

$ BARBECUE ★ 🍴 **Bub's Bar-B-Q.** This rib joint, open for more than three decades, is one of the best in the state. Maybe it's the tangy, homemade sauce; maybe it's the sides, like wilted collard greens, orange-glazed sweet potatoes, black-eyed corn, and spicy ranch beans; likely, it's the heaping platters of fall-off-the-bone ribs and pulled pork. There's plenty of outdoor seating when the weather cooperates. [$] *Average main: $13* ✉ *676 Amherst Rd. (Hwy. 116), north of Amherst town line, Sunderland* ☎ *413/548–9630* 🌐 *www.bubsbbq.com* 🕒 *Closed Mon. No lunch Tues.–Fri.*

$$ AMERICAN Fodor's Choice ★ 🍴 **Judie's.** Since 1977, academic types have crowded around small tables on the glassed-in porch, ordering traditional dishes like grilled chicken topped with lobster ravioli, steak and potatoes, seafood gumbo, and probably the best bowl of French onion soup the town has to offer. Your best bet? Try the more creative popover specials in flavors like gumbo and shrimp scampi. The atmosphere is hip and artsy; a painting covers each tabletop. [$] *Average main: $15* ✉ *51 N. Pleasant St.* ☎ *413/253–3491* 🌐 *www.judiesrestaurant.com* ✍ *Reservations not accepted.*

$ B&B/INN 🏨 **Allen House Inn and Amherst Inn.** A rare find, these late-19th-century inns a block apart from each other have been gloriously restored in accordance with the aesthetics of the Victorian era. **Pros:** lots of charm and elegance; great linens; free parking. **Cons:** rooms chock-full of ornate furnishings may be a bit much for some; tiny baths. [$] *Rooms from: $125* ✉ *599 Main St. and 257 Main St.* ☎ *413/253–5000* 🌐 *www.allenhouse.com* 🛏 *14 rooms* 🍽 *Breakfast.*

DEERFIELD

10 miles northwest of Amherst.

In Deerfield, a horse pulling a carriage clip-clops past perfectly maintained 18th-century homes, neighbors tip their hats to strangers, kids play ball in fields by the river, and the bell of the impossibly beautiful brick church peals from a white steeple. This is the perfect New England village, though not without a past darkened by tragedy. Its original Native American inhabitants, the Pocumtucks, were all but wiped out by deadly epidemics and a war with the Mohawks. English pioneers eagerly settled into this frontier outpost in the 1660s and 1670s, but two bloody massacres at the hands of the Native Americans and the French caused the village to be abandoned until 1707, when construction began on the buildings that remain today.

GETTING HERE AND AROUND

While you can take the train to Springfield, the most direct public transportation to Deerfield is a Peter Pan bus. If you're driving, take Route 10 from the south or Route 2 from the west. Aside from walking around Historic Deerfield, however, you won't get far without a car.

EXPLORING

Fodor's Choice ★ **Historic Deerfield.** Although it has a turbulent past, this village now basks in a genteel aura. With 52 buildings on 93 acres, Historic Deerfield provides a vivid glimpse into 18th- and 19th-century America. Along the tree-lined main street are 13 museum houses, built between 1720 and

Historic Deerfield is one of many places in the region to experience America's past through living history.

1850; two are open to the public on self-guided tours, and the remainder can be seen by guided tours that begin on the hour. At the **Wells-Thorn House,** various rooms depict life as it changed from 1725 to 1850. The adjacent **Frary House** has arts and crafts from the 1900s on display; the attached Barnard Tavern was the main meeting place for Deerfield's villagers. Also of note is the **Hinsdale and Anna Williams House,** the stately home for an affluent early New England couple. There's a visitors center at Hall Tavern at 80 Old Main Street. Plan at least one full day at Historic Deerfield. ☎ *413/775–7214* ⊕ *www.historic-deerfield. org* ✉ *$12* ⊙ *Apr.–Dec., daily 9:30–4:30 (except Thanksgiving and Christmas); Jan.–Mar., Flynt Center weekends 9:30–4:30, house museums open by appointment only.*

Flynt Center of Early New England Life. This traditional museum contains two galleries of silver and pewter as well as needlework, textiles, and clothing dating back to the 1600s. The lobby cases house rotating exhibitions. ✉ *37-D Old Main St.* ⊙ *Weekends 9:30–4:30.*

QUICK BITES
Richardson's Candy Kitchen. A short drive from Historic Deerfield, Richardson's Candy Kitchen makes and sells luscious cream-filled chocolates, truffles, and other handmade chocolates and confections. ✉ *500 Greenfield Rd.* ☎ *413/772–0443* ⊕ *www.richardsonscandy.com.*

Fodor'sChoice
★
☺
Magic Wings Butterfly Conservatory & Gardens. This lush place has a glass conservatory filled with more than 4,000 fluttering butterflies, as well as an extensive three-season outdoor garden filled with plants that attract local species. Observe the butterfly nursery, where newborns first take flight. An extensive garden shop sells butterfly-friendly plants; there are also

Sunday-afternoon children's programs and events, a snack bar, and gift shop. ✉ *281 Greenfield Rd., South Deerfield* ☎ *413/665–2805* 🌐 *www.magicwings.net* 🎟 *$12* 🕓 *Daily 9–5 (to 6 Memorial Day–Labor Day).*

WHERE TO EAT AND STAY

For expanded hotel reviews, visit Fodors.com.

$$$ AMERICAN Fodor's Choice ★ 🍴 **Chandler's.** On the grounds of Yankee Candle Village, devoted to candle making and selling, is one of the area's best restaurants. Though it's quite large, the restaurant retains a very intimate feel aided by candlelit dining every night, and the staff could not be more attentive. Start out with a pan-seared crab cake with fennel, basil, and lemon juice or a selection of local cheeses, then enjoy entrées like grilled salmon with artichoke risotto and duck breast in a blood orange demi-glace. Even though this is fine dining, Chandler's also has an excellent kids' menu. [$] *Average main: $27* ✉ *25 Deerfield Rd., South Deerfield* ☎ *413/665–1277* 🌐 *chandlers.yankeecandle.com* 🕓 *No dinner Mon. and Tues.*

$ B&B/INN 🏨 **Sunnyside Farm Bed & Breakfast.** Homey atmosphere, reasonable prices, and a quiet, out-of-the-way location make this countryside B&B a favorite with older couples and outdoor lovers; maple antiques and family heirlooms decorate the circa-1800 Victorian farmhouse's country-style rooms, all of which are hung with fine-art reproductions and have views across the strawberry fields. **Pros:** quiet and serene; wallet-pleasing prices. **Cons:** you're miles from anywhere; shared bathrooms. [$] *Rooms from: $100* ✉ *21 River Rd., Whately* ☎ *413/665–3113* 🛏 *5 rooms without bath* 💳 *No credit cards* 🍽 *Breakfast.*

SHELBURNE FALLS

18 miles northwest of Deerfield.

A tour of New England's fall foliage wouldn't be complete without a trek across the famed Mohawk Trail, a 63-mile section of Highway 2 that runs past picturesque Shelburne Falls. The community, separated from neighboring Buckland by the Deerfield River, is filled with little art galleries and surrounded by orchards, farm stands, and sugar houses.

GETTING HERE AND AROUND

Shelburne Falls lies on Route 2, otherwise known as the Mohawk Trail. Useful not only for driving through town, but heading off to the Berkshires as well.

EXPLORING

★ **Bridge of Flowers.** From April to October, an arched, 400-foot trolley bridge is transformed into this promenade bursting with color. ✉ *Water St.* ☎ *413/625–2544* 🌐 *bridgeofflowersmass.org.*

SPORTS AND THE OUTDOORS

RAFTING **Zoar Outdoor.** White-water rafting, canoeing, and kayaking in the Class II–III rapids of the Deerfield River is a popular summer activity. From April to October, Zoar Outdoor conducts (child-friendly) daylong rafting trips along 10 miles of challenging rapids, as well as floats along gentler sections of the river. Zip line tours are also offered, consisting of 11 zip lines and 2 suspended bridges. ✉ *7 Main St., off Hwy. 2, Charlemont* ☎ *800/532–7483* 🌐 *www.zoaroutdoor.com.*

Connecticut

WORD OF MOUTH

"New Haven's pizza is justifiably famous, with Frank Pepe's, Sally's, and Modern Apizza all top-notch examples of the type. . . . Louis' Lunch claims to have invented the hamburger, and it's an eccentrically fun place to try once (they . . . use toast instead of rolls, and serve potato salad instead of fries)."

—bachslunch

WELCOME TO CONNECTICUT

TOP REASONS TO GO

★ **Country Driving:** Follow the rolling, twisting roads of Litchfield County, such as U.S. 7, U.S. 44, and Route 63, through the charmed villages of Kent, Salisbury, and Litchfield.

★ **Maritime History:** The village of Mystic is packed with interesting nautical attractions related to Connecticut's rich seafaring history.

★ **Urban Exploring:** Anchored by Yale University, downtown New Haven now (finally) buzzes with hip restaurants, smart boutiques, and acclaimed theaters.

★ **Literary Giants:** In the same historic Hartford neighborhood, you can explore the homes— and legacies—of Mark Twain and Harriett Beecher Stowe.

★ **Antique Hunting:** You'll find numerous fine shops, galleries, and auction houses specializing in antiques all over the state. Two standout towns: Woodbury and Putnam.

1 Southwestern Connecticut. Enjoy a mix of moneyed bedroom communities and small, dynamic cities, with miles of gorgeous Long Island Sound shoreline. Shop Greenwich Avenue's boutiques, catch a show at the Westport Playhouse, and end with a nightcap in Norwalk's lively SoNo neighborhood.

2 Hartford and the Connecticut River Valley. Get your arts-and-culture fix in Hartford with a visit to the historic Old State House, the Connecticut Science Center, or the Wadsworth Atheneum. Drive south through the Connecticut River Valley for a scenic, small-town New England experience.

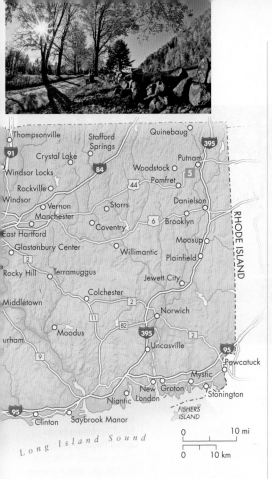

Thompsonville
Stafford Springs
Quinebaug
91
Crystal Lake
84
Putnam
395
Windsor Locks
Woodstock
5
44
Pomfret
Rockville
Windsor
Vernon
Storrs
Danielson
Manchester
6
Brooklyn
Coventry
East Hartford
Moosup
Glastonbury Center
Willimantic
Plainfield
Rocky Hill
Terramuggus
Jewett City
Colchester
2
Middletown
11
Norwich
82
Durham
Moodus
395
2
9
Uncasville
95
Pawcatuck
Mystic
New Groton
London
Stonington
Niantic
FISHERS ISLAND
95
Clinton
Saybrook Manor

Long Island Sound

RHODE ISLAND

0   10 mi

0   10 km

GETTING ORIENTED

Connecticut's coastline runs east–west, from the towns of Stonington and Mystic at the Rhode Island border, down to Greenwich in the southwest corner of the state. Head north from the Greenwich vicinity to the hills of Litchfield County in the northwest, bordered by New York and Massachusetts. In the center of the state, you'll find the capital, Hartford: travel south from here to tour the small towns of the Connecticut River Valley. Northeast of Hartford is the less-traveled Quiet Corner, whose rural towns abut Massachusetts and Rhode Island.

5

3 The Litchfield Hills. Litchfield County's pastoral countryside is the perfect setting for an autumn weekend: nestle into a romantic country inn, leaf peep around Lake Waramaug, and hunt for undiscovered treasures in the antiques shops of Woodbury.

4 New Haven to Mystic. Wander through Yale's campus or visit the dinosaurs at the Peabody Museum of Natural History before dining at a chic New Haven eatery.

Head east along the coastline for unspoiled seaside towns or roll the dice and head inland to the casinos at Foxwoods or Mohegan Sun.

5 The Quiet Corner. The scenic drive along Route 169 through Brooklyn toward Woodstock affords glimpses of authentic Colonial homes, rolling hills, and bucolic views. Try the local wines at Sharpe Hill Vineyard in Pomfret and or go antiquing in downtown Putnam.

CONNECTICUT FALL FOLIAGE DRIVE

Hidden in the heart of Litchfield County is the crossroads village of New Preston, perched above a 40-foot waterfall on the Aspetuck River. Just north of here you'll find Lake Waramaug, nestled in the rolling foothills and Mt. Tom, both ablaze with rich color every fall.

Start in New Milford and stroll along historic Main Street. Here you'll find New England's longest green and many shops, galleries, and restaurants within a short walk. Hop in the car and drive south on Main Street, then turn left to head north on wooded Route 202. About 4 miles north of the town green is the **Silo at Hunt Hill Farm Trust.** The former property of the late Skitch Henderson, onetime music director of NBC and the New York Pops, consists of a gallery, cooking school, and gift store housed in the buildings of two farms dating to the 1700s. Continue north on Route 202 to the junction of Route 45 and follow signs for Lake Waramaug.

—Bethany Cassin Beckerlegge

BEST TIME TO GO

Peak foliage in Connecticut occurs between October 9 and November 9, according to the state's Department of Environmental Protection (☎ 800/282–6863 ⊕ www. ct.gov/dep). In season, their website includes daily updates on leaf color. Hope for a wet spring, warmer fall days, and cool nights (but not freezing) for the most dramatic color display.

Route 45 will bring you through the tiny village center of New Preston; stop here for a bit of shopping at **Dawn Hill Antiques.** Take 45 north and follow signs for Lake Waramaug. The 8-mile drive around the lake is stunning in autumn with the fiery foliage of the red maples, rusty brown oaks, and yellow birches reflected in the water. The beach area of **Lake Waramaug State Park** (about halfway around the lake) is a great place for a picnic, or perhaps even a quick dip on a warm fall day. **Hopkins Vineyard** is open daily for wine tasting; head to their Hayloft Wine Bar to enjoy a glass of wine and the spectacular lake views.

After completing a loop of Lake Waramaug, head back to Route 202 North toward Litchfield. Another excellent leaf-peeping locale is **Mt. Tom State Park,** about 3 miles or so from the junction of Routes 45 and 202. Here you can hike the mile-long trail to the summit and climb to the top of a stone tower that provides 360-degree views of the countryside's colors—the vibrant magenta-reds of the sugar maples are always among the most dazzling. After your hike, continue north on Route 202, ending your journey in the quintessential New England town of Litchfield. Peruse the shops and galleries in the town center and end the day with a dinner at the chic **West Street Grill.**

It's only about 30 miles from New Milford to the center of Litchfield, but with stops at the Silo at Hunt Hill, Lake Waramaug, and Mt. Tom you could easily spend half the day enjoying the scenery.

NEED A BREAK?

Dawn Hill Antiques. Dawn Hill Antiques is filled with antiques that the owners have discovered on their regular trips to Sweden. ⊠ *11 Main St., New Preston* ☎ *860/868-0066* ⊕ *www.dawnhillantiques. com.*

Hopkins Vineyard. This vineyard offers wine tastings and produces more than 13 varieties of wine, from sparkling to dessert. A wine bar in the hayloft serves a fine cheese-and-pâté board and has views of the lake. ⊠ *25 Hopkins Rd., off N. Shore Rd., New Preston* ☎ *860/868-7954* ⊕ *www.hopkinsvineyard. com* ⊟ *$6.50 for a tasting, $10 for a tour* ⊙ *Hours vary.*

5

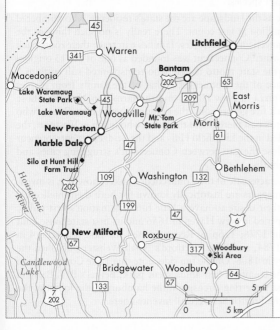

Updated by Bethany Cassin Beckerlegge

You can travel from just about any point in Connecticut to any other in less than two hours, yet the land you traverse— fewer than 60 miles top to bottom and 100 miles across—is as varied as a drive across the country.

Connecticut's 253 miles of shoreline blows salty sea air over such beach communities as Old Lyme and Stonington. Patchwork hills and peaked mountains fill the state's northwestern corner, and once-upon-a-time mill towns line rivers such as the Housatonic. Connecticut has seemingly endless farmland in the northeast, where cows might outnumber people, as well as chic New York City bedroom communities such as Greenwich and New Canaan, where boutique shopping bags seem to be the dominant species.

Just as diverse as the landscape are the state's residents, who numbered close to 3.5 million at last count. There really is no such thing as the definitive Connecticut Yankee. Yes, families can trace their roots back to the 1600s, when Connecticut was founded as one of the 13 original colonies, but the state motto is "He who transplanted still sustains." And so the face of the Nutmegger is that of the family from Naples now making pizza in New Haven and the farmer in Norfolk whose land dates back five generations, the grandmother in New Britain who makes the state's best pierogi and the ladies who lunch in Westport, the celebrity nestled in the Litchfield Hills and the Bridgeport entrepreneur working to close the gap between Connecticut's struggling cities and its affluent suburbs.

A unifying characteristic of the Connecticut Yankee, however, is inventiveness. Nutmeggers are historically known for both their intellectual abilities and their desire to have a little fun. The nation's first public library was opened in New Haven in 1656 and its first statehouse built in Hartford in 1776; Tapping Reeve opened the first law school in Litchfield in 1784; and West Hartford's Noah Webster published the first dictionary in 1806. On the fun side, note that Lake Compounce in Bristol was the country's first amusement park; Bethel's P. T. Barnum staged the first three-ring circus; and the hamburger, the lollipop, the Frisbee, and the Erector Set were all invented here.

Not surprisingly, Nutmeggers have a healthy respect for their history. For decades, Mystic Seaport, which traces the state's rich maritime past, has been the premier tourist attraction. Today, however, Foxwoods Casino near Ledyard, run by the Mashantucket Pequots, is the world's largest casino, drawing more than 40,000 visitors per day. Thanks in large part to these lures, not to mention rich cultural attractions, cutting-edge restaurants, shopping outlets, first-rate lodgings, and abundant natural beauty (including 92 state parks and 30 state forests), tourism is one of the state's leading industries. Exploring Connecticut reveals a small state that's big in its appeal.

PLANNING

WHEN TO GO

Connecticut is lovely year-round, but fall and spring are particularly appealing times to visit. A fall drive along the state's back roads or the Merritt Parkway (a National Scenic Byway) is a memorable experience. Leaves of yellow, orange, and red color the fall landscape, but the state blooms in springtime, too—town greens are painted with daffodils and tulips, and blooming trees punctuate the rich green countryside. Summer, of course, is prime time for most attractions; travelers have the most options then but also plenty of company, especially along the shore.

PLANNING YOUR TIME

The Nutmeg State is a confluence of different worlds, where farm country meets country homes, and fans of the New York Yankees meet Down-Easter Yankees. To get the best sense of this variety, start in the scenic Litchfield Hills, where you can see historic town greens and trendy cafés. If you have a bit more time, head south to the wealthy southwestern corner of the state and then over to New Haven, with its cultural pleasures. If you have five days or a week, take in the capital city of Hartford and the surrounding towns of the Connecticut River Valley and head down to the southeastern shoreline.

GETTING HERE AND AROUND

AIR TRAVEL

People visiting Connecticut from afar can fly into New York City, Boston, or Providence or smaller airports in or near Hartford and New Haven.

Bradley International Airport. North of Hartford, this airport is served by most major airlines and has direct flights from most major cities. ⊠ *11 Schoephoester Rd., Windsor Locks* ☎ *860/292–2000* ⊕ *www. bradleyairport.com.*

Tweed New Haven Airport. There are several flights per day on US Airways to Philadelphia from this regional airport. ⊠ *155 Burr St., New Haven* ☎ *203/466–8888* ⊕ *www.flytweed.com.*

CAR TRAVEL

The interstates are the quickest routes between many points in Connecticut, but they can be busy and ugly. From New York City head north on Interstate 95, which hugs the Connecticut shoreline into Rhode Island, or, to reach the Litchfield Hills and Hartford, head north on

Interstate 684, then east on Interstate 84. From central New England, go south on Interstate 91, which bisects Interstate 84 in Hartford and Interstate 95 in New Haven. From Boston take Interstate 95 south through Providence or take the Massachusetts Turnpike west to Interstate 84. Interstate 395 runs north–south from southeastern Connecticut to Massachusetts.

Often faster because of less traffic, the historic Merritt Parkway (Route 15) winds between Greenwich and Middletown; U.S. 7 and Route 8, extending between Interstate 95 and the Litchfield Hills; Route 9, which heads south from Hartford through the Connecticut River Valley to Old Saybrook; and scenic Route 169, which meanders through the Quiet Corner.

TRAIN TRAVEL

Amtrak. Amtrak runs from New York to Boston, stopping in Stamford, Bridgeport, and New Haven before heading north through Hartford and several other towns or east to Old Saybrook and Mystic. ☎ 800/872–7245 ⊕ www.amtrak.com.

Metro-North Railroad. Metro-North Railroad trains from New York stop locally between Greenwich and New Haven, and a few head inland to New Canaan, Danbury, and Waterbury. ☎ 877/690–5114 ⊕ www. mta.info.

RESTAURANTS

Call it the fennel factor or the arugula influx: southern New England has witnessed a gastronomic revolution. Preparation and ingredients reflect the culinary trends of nearby Manhattan and Boston; indeed, the quality and diversity of Connecticut restaurants now rival those of such sophisticated metropolitan areas. Although traditional favorites remain—such as New England clam chowder, buttery lobster rolls, Yankee pot roast, and fish-and-chips—Grand Marnier is now favored on ice cream over hot fudge sauce; sliced duck is wrapped in phyllo and served with a ginger-plum sauce (the orange glaze decidedly absent); and everything from lavender to fresh figs is used to season and complement dishes. Dining is increasingly international: you'll find Indian, Vietnamese, Thai, Malaysian, South American, and Japanese restaurants—even Spanish tapas bars—in cities and suburbs. Designer martinis are quite the rage, brewpubs have popped up around the state, and even caviar is making a comeback. The one drawback of this turn toward sophistication is that finding a dinner entrée for less than $10 is difficult. *Prices in the reviews are the average cost of a main course at dinner or, if dinner is not served, at lunch.*

HOTELS

Connecticut has plenty of business-oriented chain hotels and low-budget motels, along with many of the more unusual and atmospheric inns, resorts, bed-and-breakfasts, and country hotels that are typical of New England. You'll pay dearly for rooms in summer on the coast and in autumn in the hills, where thousands of visitors peek at the changing foliage. Rates are lowest in winter, but so are the temperatures, making spring the best time for bargain seekers to visit. *Prices in the reviews are the lowest cost of a standard double room in high season.*

VISITOR INFORMATION

Connecticut Commission on Culture & Tourism ✉ *1 Constitution Plaza, 2nd Fl., Hartford* ☎ *860/256–2800, 888/288–4748* ⊕ *www.ctvisit.com.*

SOUTHWESTERN CONNECTICUT

Southwestern Connecticut is a rich swirl of old New England and new New York. This region consistently reports the highest cost of living and most expensive homes of any area in the country. Its bedroom towns are home primarily to white-collar executives; some still make the hour-plus dash to and from New York, but many drive to Stamford, which is reputed to have more corporate headquarters per square mile than any other U.S. city.

Venture away from the wealthy communities, and you'll discover cities struggling in different stages of urban renewal: Stamford, Norwalk, Bridgeport, and Danbury. These four have some of the region's best cultural and shopping opportunities, but the economic disparity between Connecticut's troubled cities and its upscale towns is perhaps most visible in Fairfield County.

ESSENTIALS

Visitor Information Coastal Fairfield County Convention and Visitors Bureau *203/767–8273* ⊕ *www.coastalctinc.com.*

GREENWICH

28 miles northeast of New York City, 64 miles southwest of Hartford.

You'll have no trouble believing that Greenwich is one of the wealthiest towns in the United States when you drive along U.S. 1 (called Route 1 by the locals, as well as West Putnam Avenue, East Putnam Avenue, and the Post Road). The streets here are lined with ritzy car dealers, posh boutiques, oh-so-chic restaurants, and well-heeled, well-to-do residents. Though real estate prices have come down, the median home price in Greenwich still hovers around $1.1 million. So bring your platinum card.

GETTING HERE AND AROUND

If you are traveling north from New York City, Greenwich will be the first town in Connecticut once you cross the state border. It's easily accessible from I–95 or the Merritt Parkway if you are coming by car, and is also serviced by Metro-North commuter trains.

EXPLORING

Audubon Greenwich. Established in 1942 as the National Audubon Society's first nature-education facility, this center in northern Greenwich is the best location in the area for bird-watching. During the Fall Hawk Watch Festival you can see over 16 species of hawks, eagles, and vultures migrate over the site. Other annual events are the Spring into Audubon Festival and the summer and Christmas bird counts. The center is filled with "real-life" interactive exhibits, galleries, and classrooms, a wildlife observation room, and an observation deck that offers sweeping views of wildlife activity. Outside, the sanctuary includes protected wildlife habitats and 7 miles of hiking trails on 285 acres of woodland, wetland, and meadow. ✉ *613 Riversville Rd.* ☎ *203/869–5272* 🌐 *greenwich.audubon.org/* 🎟 *$3* 🕒 *Daily 9–5.*

★ **Bruce Museum of Arts and Science.** In 1908, the owner of this then-private home (built in 1853), wealthy textile merchant Robert Moffat Bruce, bequeathed it to the town of Greenwich with the stipulation that it be used "as a natural history, historical, and art museum." Today this diversity remains reflected in the museum's collection of some 15,000 objects in fine and decorative arts, natural history, and anthropology—including paintings by Childe Hassam, sculptures by Auguste Rodin, and stained glass by Dale Chihuly—from which the museum selects items for changing exhibitions. Permanently on display is the spectacular mineral collection. Kids enjoy the touchable meteorite and glow-in-the-dark minerals, as well as the fossilized dinosaur tracks. ✉ *1 Museum Dr., off I–95 (Exit 3)* ☎ *203/869–0376* 🌐 *www.brucemuseum.org* 🎟 *$7, free Tues.* 🕒 *Tues.–Sat. 10–5, Sun. 1–5.*

WHERE TO EAT AND STAY

For expanded hotel reviews, visit Fodors.com.

$$$$ FRENCH Fodor's Choice ★ 🍴 **Jean-Louis.** Chef Jean-Louis Gerin specializes in what he calls "la nouvelle classique" French cuisine, a style based on stocks and reductions—and his own dedication to excellence. A five-course degustation menu explores the day's special offerings, which might include sea salt–encrusted foie gras with aged sherry vinegar and a duck *à l'orange* reduction or a seared ostrich fillet with buttery mashed potatoes. Heady roses, signature fine china, custom glassware, and touches of lace create a romantic, sophisticated atmosphere. [$] *Average main: $45* ✉ *61 Lewis St.* ☎ *203/622–8450* 🌐 *www.restaurantjeanlouis.com* 🕒 *Closed Sun. No lunch Sat.*

$$ ASIAN FUSION 🍴 **Tengda Asian Bistro.** This hopping Asian-fusion hot spot offers consistently good Japanese cuisine with European accents. In a turn-of-the-20th-century house, the dining room has a rustic yet industrial feel, with exposed brick cozying up next to sculpted steel. Tuck into the crispy firecracker shrimp, sample the spicy mango chicken, or dive into a fresh lobster tempura roll while sipping an exotic cocktail from the diverse drink list. [$] *Average main: $16* ✉ *21 Field Point Rd.* ☎ *203/625–5338* 🌐 *asianbistrogroup.com.*

$$$$ HOTEL 🏨 **Delamar Greenwich Harbor Hotel.** This three-story luxury hotel, just blocks from downtown Greenwich, resembles a villa on the Italian Riviera. **Pros:** waterfront location; posh spa; easy walk to downtown restaurants and shopping. **Cons:** super-pricey. [$] *Rooms from: $309* ✉ *500 Steamboat Rd.* ☎ *203/661–9800, 866/335–2627* 🌐 *www.thedelamar.com* 🛏 *74 rooms, 8 suites* 🍽 *No meals.*

STAMFORD

6 miles northeast of Greenwich, 38 miles southwest of New Haven.

Office buildings, chain hotels, and major department stores dominate the face of Stamford. Quality restaurants, nightclubs, and shops line Atlantic and lower Summer streets, however, and have given the city some much-needed leisure time attractions.

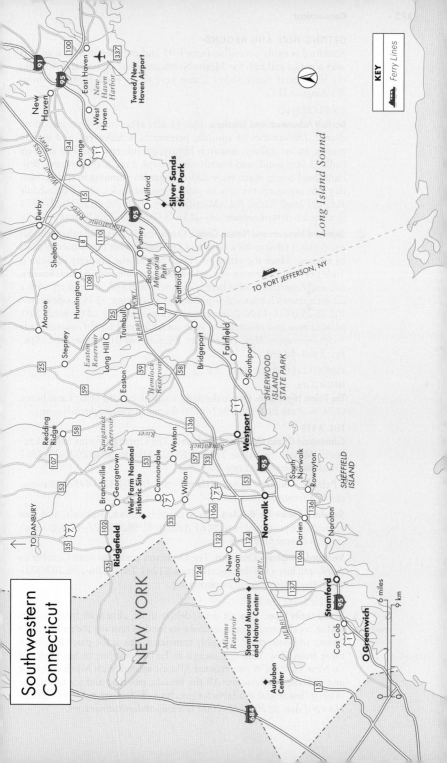

Southwestern Connecticut

NEW YORK

TO DANBURY

Long Island Sound

KEY

⛴ Ferry Lines

91

95

100

337

East Haven

New Haven Harbor

Tweed/New Haven Airport

New Haven

West Haven

34

Orange

11

Wilbur Cross Pkwy.

Housatonic River

Derby

5

Shelton

8

110

95

Milford

Putney

◆ Silver Sands State Park

108

Huntington

Monroe

Easton Reservoir

25

Trumbull

Long Hill

Stepney

MERRITT PKWY.

25

59

Easton

59

Hemlock Reservoir

Boothe Memorial Park

Stratford

8

Fairfield

Southport

Bridgeport

58

136

SHERWOOD ISLAND STATE PARK

TO PORT JEFFERSON, NY ⛴

Redding Ridge

58

Saugatuck Reservoir

Saugatuck River

107

Branchville

Georgetown

53

53

Cannondale

Weston

57

33

136

Westport

11

95

Weir Farm National Historic Site ◆

7

Wilton

7

53

53

South Norwalk

Rowayton

SHEFFIELD ISLAND

35

102

Ridgefield

35

7

33

106

123

124

Norwalk

136

Darien

Noroton

106

New Canaan

124

PKWY.

137

Stamford

95

15

Miamus Reservoir

Stamford Museum and Nature Center ◆

MERRITT

Cos Cob

Greenwich

Audubon Center ◆

15

684

0 miles 6

0 km 9

GETTING HERE AND AROUND

Stamford is easily accessible from I–95 and the Merritt Parkway. It is also a major rail hub for Metro-North commuter trains and Amtrak; the high-speed Acela makes a stop here on its route from Boston to Washington D.C.

EXPLORING

Bartlett Arboretum and Gardens. This 91-acre arboretum is home to more than 2,000 varieties of annuals, perennials, wildflowers, and woody plants, an art gallery, research library, greenhouse, marked ecology trails, 2-acre pond, and boardwalk through a red maple swamp. Brilliant, bold colors make the wildflower garden stunning in spring. Sunday afternoons are the time to visit for guided walks. ⊠ *151 Brookdale Rd., off High Ridge Rd. (Merritt Pkwy., Exit 35)* ☎ *203/322–6971* ⊕ *www.bartlettarboretum.org* ⊠ *$6* ⊙ *Grounds daily 9–dusk.*

Stamford Museum and Nature Center. Oxen, sheep, pigs, and other animals roam this 118-acre New England farmstead with many nature trails to explore. Once the estate of Henri Bendel, the property includes a Tudor-revival stone mansion, which houses exhibits on natural history, art, and Americana. Also here is a planetarium and observatory with a 22-inch research telescope—perfect for stargazing. ⊠ *39 Scofieldtown Rd.* ☎ *203/322–1646* ⊕ *www.stamfordmuseum.org* ⊠ *Grounds $10, planetarium and observatory each an additional $3* ⊙ *Grounds daily 9–5; observatory May–Labor Day, Fri. 8:30 pm–10:30 pm; Sept.–Apr., Fri. 8 pm–10 pm.*

NIGHTLIFE AND THE ARTS

NIGHTLIFE

The Palms Night Club. Dance the night away here to the latest Latin beats. ⊠ *78 W. Park Pl.* ☎ *203/961–9770* ⊕ *www.palmsnightclub.com.*

THE ARTS

Connecticut Grand Opera and Orchestra. The Opera performs from October to May at the Palace Theater. ⊠ *307 Atlantic St.* ☎ *203/327–2867* ⊕ *www.ctgrandopera.org.*

Palace Theatre ⊠ *61 Atlantic St.* ☎ *203/325–4466* ⊕ *www.stamfordcenterforthearts.org.*

Stamford Center for the Arts. Plays, comedy shows, musicals, and film festivals are presented here. ⊠ *61 Atlantic St.* ☎ *203/325–4466* ⊕ *www.stamfordcenterforthearts.org.*

Stamford Symphony Orchestra. The Orchestra performs from October to April, and has a family concert series. ⊠ *263 Tresser Blvd.* ☎ *203/325–1407* ⊕ *www.stamfordsymphony.org.*

WHERE TO EAT

$ ✕ **City Limits Diner.** This art deco, deluxe diner, alive with bright colors
AMERICAN and shiny chrome, likes to describe its food as running the gamut from "haute to homespun." Roughly translated, this is the place for everything from New York egg creams to French martinis to hot pastrami on New York rye to pan-roasted Atlantic salmon with Israeli couscous and shiitake mushrooms. All the breads, pastries, and ice cream are made in-house and available for purchase. $ *Average main: $15* ⊠ *135 Harvard Ave.* ☎ *203/348–7000* ⊕ *www.citylimitsdiner.com.*

NORWALK

14 miles northeast of Stamford, 47 miles northeast of New York City.

In the 19th century, Norwalk became a major New England port and also manufactured pottery, clocks, watches, shingle nails, and paper. It later fell into neglect, in which it remained for much of the 20th century. In the early 1990s, however, Norwalk's coastal business district was the focus of major redevelopment, which has turned it into a hot spot for trendy shopping, culture, and dining, much of it along the main drag, Washington Street. The stretch is known as SoNo (South Norwalk), and in the evening it is the place to be seen if you're young, single, and living it up in Fairfield County.

YANKEE DOODLE DANDY

Norwalk is the home of Yankee Doodle Dandies: in 1756, Colonel Thomas Fitch threw together a motley crew of Norwalk soldiers and led them off to fight at Ft. Crailo, near Albany, New York. Supposedly, Norwalk's women gathered feathers for the men to wear as plumes in their caps to give them some appearance of military decorum. Upon the arrival of these foppish warriors, one of the British officers sarcastically dubbed them "macaronis"—slang for dandies. The name caught on, and so did the song.

GETTING HERE AND AROUND

If you are traveling by car, Norwalk is most easily reached by I–95 and the Merritt Parkway. Metro-North commuter trains also stop here. Exit at the South Norwalk stop to put yourself within walking distance of SoNo shops, restaurants, and bars.

EXPLORING

★ ☮ **Maritime Aquarium at Norwalk.** This 5-acre waterfront center, the cornerstone of the SoNo district, explores the marine life and maritime culture of Long Island Sound. The aquarium's more than 20 habitats include some 1,000 creatures indigenous to the sound. You can see toothy bluefish and sand tiger sharks in the 110,000-gallon Open Ocean Tank, dozens of jellyfish performing their ghostly ballet in "Jellyfish Encounter," stately loggerhead sea turtles, winsome river otters, and happy harbor seals. The center also operates an Environmental Education Center and marine-mammal cruises aboard the *Oceanic* and has a towering IMAX theater. ⊠ *10 N. Water St.* ☎ *203/852–0700* ⊕ *www.maritimeaquarium. org* ☞ *Aquarium $12.95, IMAX theater $9, combined $19.45* ☉ *Labor Day–June, daily 10–5; July–Labor Day, daily 10–6.*

Sheffield Island & Lighthouse. The 3-acre park here is a prime spot for a picnic. The 1868 lighthouse has four levels, 10 rooms to explore, and is adjacent to the Stewart B. McKinney U.S. Fish and Wildlife Refuge. Clambakes are held Thursday evenings from June through September. ⊠ *Ferry service from Hope Dock, at corner of Washington and North Water Sts.* ☎ *203/838–9444 ferry and lighthouse* ⊕ *www.seaport.org* ☞ *Round-trip ferry service and lighthouse tour $22* ☉ *Ferry Memorial Day through Labor Day, weekdays at 11 and 3, weekends at 11, 2, and 3:30.*

Norwalk's Maritime Aquarium is a great way to get eye-to-eye with animals endemic to Long Island Sound, like loggerhead turtles.

WHERE TO EAT AND STAY

For expanded hotel reviews, visit Fodors.com.

$$$ MODERN AMERICAN 🍴 **Match.** In the heart of SoNo, Match cooks up fresh local ingredients to create inventive New American dishes. High ceilings, exposed brick, and industrial fixtures provide a sleek, urban look. Indulge in one of the signature wood-fired pizzas straight out of the oven, or savor the handmade herbed-ricotta ravioli in a tomato and olive oil ragu. Complete your meal with a melt-in-your-mouth hot chocolate soufflé topped with raspberries and vanilla gelato. [$] *Average main: $28* ✉ *98 Washington St.* ☎ *203/852–1088* 🌐 *www.matchsono.com* ⏲ *No lunch.*

$$ B&B/INN 🏨 **Silvermine Tavern Bed & Breakfast.** The simple rooms at this venerable, late-18th-century inn on a quiet road near the New Canaan and Wilton border are furnished with hooked rugs, canopy beds, and antiques—vintage New England. **Pros:** nice alternative to the area's many chain hotels; reasonable rates; tranquil setting. **Cons:** rooms lack phones and TVs; old-fashioned vibe isn't everybody's cup of tea; it's a drive to South Norwalk's shopping and dining. [$] *Rooms from: $125* ✉ *194 Perry Ave.* ☎ *203/847–4558* 🌐 *www.silverminetavern.com* 🛏 *10 rooms, 1 suite* 🍽 *Breakfast.*

RIDGEFIELD

11 miles north of New Canaan, 43 miles west of New Haven.

In Ridgefield you'll find a rustic Connecticut atmosphere within an hour of Manhattan. The inviting town center is a largely residential sweep of lawns and majestic homes, with a feel more reminiscent of the peaceful Litchfield Hills, even though the town is in the northern reaches of Fairfield County.

GETTING HERE AND AROUND

From I–95 or the Merritt Parkway, head north on Route 7 to Route 33 to reach Ridgefield or take Metro-North to the Branchville station.

EXPLORING

★ **Aldrich Contemporary Art Museum.** Cutting-edge art is not exactly what you'd expect to find in a stately 18th-century Main Street structure that was once a general store, Ridgefield's first post office, a private home, and, for 35 years, a church. Nicknamed "Old Hundred," this historic building now houses the Aldrich's administrative offices since the 2004 completion of the new museum building. The 25,000 square foot space puts its own twist on traditional New England architecture with an abstract design recognized by the American Institute of Architects. The white clapboard and granite structure houses 12 galleries, a screening room, a sound gallery, a 22-foot-high project space for large installations, a 100-seat performance space, and an education center. Outside is a 2-acre sculpture garden. ⊠ *258 Main St.* ☎ *203/438–4519* ⊕ *www.aldrichart.org* 🖾 *$7, free Tues.* ⊗ *Tues.–Sun. noon–5.*

WHERE TO EAT AND STAY

For expanded hotel reviews, visit Fodors.com.

$$ ✕ **Luc's Cafe and Restaurant.** A cozy bistro set inside a stone building with
FRENCH low ceilings, closely spaced tables, and a handy location in Ridgefield's quaint downtown, Luc's charms patrons with carefully prepared food and low-key, friendly service. You can opt for a simple salade niçoise or *croque monsieur* (hot ham-and-cheese) sandwich or enjoy a classic steak au poivre with a velvety Roquefort sauce and crispy *frites*. There's an extensive wine list, plus a range of aperitifs and single-malt whiskies. Enjoy live jazz on some evenings. $ *Average main: $19* ⊠ *3 Big Shop Lane* ☎ *203/894–8522* ⊕ *www.lucscafe.com* ⊗ *Closed Sun.*

$$ 🏨 **Stonehenge Inn.** The manicured lawns and bright white-clapboard
B&B/INN buildings of Stonehenge are visible just off U.S. 7. **Pros:** neatly kept grounds; polished service; terrific restaurant. **Cons:** not within walking distance of downtown Ridgefield. $ *Rooms from: $150* ⊠ *35 Stonehenge Rd., off U.S. 7* ☎ *203/438–6511* ⊕ *www.stonehengeinn-ct.com* 🛏 *12 rooms, 4 suites* ⦿| *Breakfast.*

WESTPORT

15 miles southeast of Ridgefield, 47 miles northeast of New York City.

Westport, an artists' community since the turn of the 20th century, continues to attract creative types. Despite commuters and corporations, the town remains more artsy and cultured than its neighbors: if the rest of Fairfield County is stylistically five years behind Manhattan, Westport lags by just five months.

GETTING HERE AND AROUND

You can reach Westport by car via I–95 (Exit 17 will put you closest to the center of town and main shopping areas) or the Merritt Parkway. Metro-North also has two stops here, Westport (closer to town) and Greens Farms (farther east).

THE ARTS

The Levitt Pavilion for the Performing Arts. Enjoy an excellent series of mostly free summer concerts here that range from jazz to classical, folk rock to blues. ✉ *40 Jesup Rd.* ☎ *203/221–2153* 🌐 *www.levittpavilion.com.*

Westport Country Playhouse. Long associated with benefactors Joanne Woodward and the late Paul Newman, the venerable and intimate Westport Country Playhouse presents high-quality plays throughout the year. ✉ *25 Powers Ct.* ☎ *203/227–4177* 🌐 *www.westportplayhouse.org.*

WHERE TO EAT

$$ AMERICAN Fodor's Choice ★

🍴 **Dressing Room.** Opened by the late Paul Newman and renowned cookbook author Michel Nischan in 2006, this pretheater favorite, beside the Westport Playhouse, celebrates regional American, farm-to-table cuisine. Many ingredients on the menu are sourced locally; others come from prominent ranches and farms around the country. Highlights include the baby back ribs, served with an apple-cabbage slaw, and seasonal items like the Connecticut lobster succotash with fresh corn, zucchini, and roasted peppers. A huge fieldstone fireplace warms the rustic-chic dining room, with its sturdy ceiling beams and barn-board walls. [$] *Average main: $20* ✉ *27 Powers Ct.* ☎ *203/226–1114* 🌐 *www.dressingroomhomegrown.com* ⏲ *Closed Mon. No lunch Tues.*

HARTFORD AND THE CONNECTICUT RIVER VALLEY

Westward expansion in the New World began along the meandering Connecticut River. Dutch explorer Adrian Block first explored the area in 1614, and in 1633 a trading post was set up in what is now Hartford. Within five years, throngs of restive Massachusetts Bay colonists had settled in this fertile valley. What followed were more than three centuries of shipbuilding, shad hauling, and river trading with ports as far away as the West Indies and the Mediterranean.

Less touristy than the coast and northwest hills, the Connecticut River Valley is a swath of small villages and uncrowded state parks punctuated by a few small cities and a large one: the capital city of Hartford. South of Hartford, with the exception of industrial Middletown, genuinely quaint hamlets vie for attention with antiques shops, scenic drives, and romantic French restaurants and country inns.

ESSENTIALS

Visitor Information Connecticut's Heritage River Valley–Central Regional Tourism District ✉ *1 Constitution Plaza, 2nd fl., Hartford* ☎ *860/787–9640* 🌐 *www.visitctriver.com.*

Connecticut
River Valley

ESSEX

29 miles east of New Haven.

Essex, consistently named one of the best small towns in the United States, looks much as it did in the mid-19th century, at the height of its shipbuilding prosperity. So important to the young country was Essex's boat manufacturing that the British burned more than 40 ships here during the War of 1812. Gone are the days of steady trade with the West Indies, when the aroma of imported rum, molasses, and spices hung in the air. Whitewashed houses—many the former roosts of sea captains—line Main Street, which has shops that sell clothing, antiques, paintings and prints, and sweets.

GETTING HERE AND AROUND

The best way to reach Essex is by car; take I–95 to Route 9 north.

EXPLORING

★ **Connecticut River Museum.** In an 1878 steamboat warehouse at the foot of Main Street, this museum tells the story of the Connecticut River through paintings, maritime artifacts, interactive displays, and ship models. The riverfront museum even has a full-size working reproduction of the world's first submarine, the *American Turtle*; the original was built by David Bushnell in 1775 as a "secret weapon" to win the Revolutionary War. ✉ *At dock, 67 Main St.* ☎ *860/767–8269* 🌐 *www.ctrivermuseum.org* 🎫 *$8* 🕒 *Tues.–Sun. 10–5.*

SCENIC TRIP

Essex Steam Train and Riverboat. This ride offers some of the best views of the Connecticut River Valley from the vantage point of a restored train (1920s coaches pulled by a vintage steam locomotive) and an old-fashioned Mississippi-style riverboat. The train, traveling along the Connecticut River through the lower valley, makes a 12-mile round-trip from Essex Station to Deep River Station; from there, if you wish to continue, you board the riverboat for a ride to East Haddam (the open promenade deck on the third level has the best views). Special trains, including a dinner train and a wine train, as well as a Santa Special and hugely popular visits by Thomas the Tank Engine, occur periodically. ✉ ***Valley Railroad Company, 1 Railroad Ave. (Rte. 9), Exit 3*** ☎ ***860/767-0103*** 🌐 ***www.essexsteamtrain.com*** 🎫 ***Train fare $17, train-boat fare $26*** 🕒 ***May–Dec.; call for schedule.***

WHERE TO EAT

$$$ FRENCH Fodor's Choice ★

🍴 **Brasserie Pip.** Within the Copper Beech Inn is this hip and relaxed brasserie, which serves superbly authentic fare, and has outdoor seating in warm weather on a porch overlooking the inn's extensive gardens. You could make a night of the cheese and charcuterie plates, plus a selection of fresh oysters on the half shell. Or opt for more substantial fare, like the ricotta gnocchi with spring vegetables or classic steak frites. Pip's cocktail bar makes its own flavored vodkas—such as blood-orange-and-coriander—to prepare memorable martinis. [$] *Average main: $26* ✉ *46 Main St., Ivoryton, 4 miles west of Essex* ☎ *860/767–0330* 🌐 *copperbeechinn.com* 🕒 *Closed Mon. No lunch.*

Ride through the Connecticut River Valley on a vintage Essex Steam Train.

EAST HADDAM

7 miles north of Chester, 28 miles southeast of Hartford.

Fishing, shipping, and musket making were the chief enterprises at East Haddam, the only town in the state that occupies both banks of the Connecticut River. This lovely community retains much of its old-fashioned charm, most of it centered around its historic downtown.

GETTING HERE AND AROUND

The best way to reach East Haddam is by car. From I-95, take Route 9 north to Route 82 east to Route 154 north.

EXPLORING

★ **Gillette Castle State Park.** The outrageous 24-room oak-and-fieldstone hilltop castle, modeled after medieval castles of the Rhineland and built between 1914 and 1919 by the eccentric actor and dramatist William Gillette, is the park's main attraction. You can tour the castle and hike on trails near the remains of the 3-mile private railroad that chugged about the property until the owner's death in 1937. Gillette, who was born in Hartford, wrote two famous plays about the Civil War and was beloved for his play *Sherlock Holmes* (in which he performed the title role). In his will, he demanded that the castle not fall into the hands of "some blithering saphead who has no conception of where he is or with what surrounded." ⊠ *67 River Rd., off Rte. 82* ☎ *860/526-2336* ⊕ *www.friendsofgillettecastle.org* 🎫 *Park free, castle $6* ⊗ *Park daily 8-sunset; castle Memorial Day-Columbus Day, daily 10-4:30.*

★ **Goodspeed Opera House.** This magnificent 1876 Victorian-gingerbread "wedding cake" theater on the Connecticut River—so called for all its turrets, mansard roof, and grand filigree—is widely recognized for its role in the preservation and development of American musical theater. More than 16 Goodspeed productions have gone on to Broadway, including *Annie*. Performances take place from April to early December. ✉ *6 Main St. (Rte. 82)* ☎ *860/873–8668* ⊕ *goodspeed.org/* 🎟 *Tour $5* 🕙 *Tours June–Oct; call for times.*

MIDDLETOWN

15 miles northwest of East Haddam, 24 miles northeast of New Haven.

With its Connecticut River setting, easy access to major highways, and historic architecture, Middletown is a popular destination for recreational boaters and tourists alike. The town's High Street is an architecturally eclectic thoroughfare. Charles Dickens once called it "the loveliest Main Street in America" (Middletown's actual Main Street runs parallel to it a few blocks east).

GETTING HERE AND AROUND
Middletown is best reached by car. From Hartford, follow I–91 south to Route 9 south. From the coast, take I–95 to Route 9 north.

EXPLORING
Wesleyan University. Founded in 1831 and one of the oldest Methodist institutions of higher education in the United States, Wesleyan University has roughly 2,700 undergrads, 600 graduate students, and a vibrant science-and-arts scene, which gives Middletown a contemporary college-town feel. On campus, note the massive, fluted Corinthian columns of the Greek-Revival Russell House (circa 1828) at the corner of Washington Street, across from the pink Mediterranean-style Davison Art Center, built 15 years later; farther on are gingerbreads, towering brownstones, Tudors, and Queen Annes. A few hundred yards up on Church Street, which intersects High Street, is the Olin Library. The 1928 structure was designed by Henry Bacon, the architect of the Lincoln Memorial. The school bookstore is at 45 Broad St. ✉ *High St., 45 Wyllys Ave.* ☎ *860/685–2000* ⊕ *www.wesleyan.edu.*

OFF THE BEATEN PATH

Lyman Orchards. Looking for a quintessential New England outing? These orchards just south of Middletown are not to be missed. Get lost in the sunflower maze and then pick your own fruits and vegetables—berries, peaches, pears, apples, and even pumpkins from June to October. ✉ *Rtes. 147 and 157, Middlefield* ☎ *860/349–1793* ⊕ *www.lymanorchards.com* 🕙 *Nov.–Aug., daily 9–6; Sept. and Oct., daily 9–7.*

SPORTS AND THE OUTDOORS
Dinosaur State Park. See some 500 tracks left by the dinosaurs that once roamed the area around this park north of Middletown. The tracks are preserved under a giant geodesic dome. You can even make plaster casts of tracks on a special area of the property; call ahead to learn what materials you need to bring. ✉ *400 West St., Rocky Hill, east of I–91 Exit 23* ☎ *860/529–8423* ⊕ *www.dinosaurstatepark.org* 🎟 *$6* 🕙 *Exhibits Tues.–Sun. 9–4:30, trails daily 9–4:30.*

CLOSE UP

Connecticut's Historic Gardens

Eight extraordinary Connecticut gardens form Connecticut's Historic Gardens, a "trail" of natural beauties across the state.

Harriet Beecher Stowe Center. A high-Victorian texture garden, a wild-flower meadow, Connecticut's largest magnolia tree, an antique rose garden, a 100-year-old pink dogwood, and a blue cottage garden are the highlights of the grounds at the Harriet Beecher Stowe Center. ⊠ *77 Forest St., Hartford* ☎ *860/522–9258* ⊕ *www.harrietbeecherstowecenter.org* ⊒ *$9.*

Griswold Museum in Old Lyme

Butler-McCook House & Garden. Landscape architect Jacob Weidenmann created a Victorian garden oasis amid downtown city life here. ⊠ *396 Main St., Hartford* ☎ *860/522–1806* ⊕ *www.ctlandmarks.org.*

Hill-Stead Museum. The centerpiece of the Hill-Stead Museum is a circa-1920 sunken garden by Beatrix Farrand enclosed in a yew hedge and surrounded by a wall of rough stone; at the center of the octagonal design is a summerhouse with 36 flower beds and brick walkways radiating outward. ⊠ *35 Mountain Rd., Farmington* ☎ *860/677–4787* ⊕ *www.hillstead.org* ⊒ *$12.*

Promisek Beatrix Farrand Garden. Farrand also designed the garden at Promisek Beatrix Farrand Garden, which overflows with beds of annuals and perennials such as hollyhocks, peonies, and always-dashing delphiniums. ⊠ *694 Skyline Ridge Rd., Bridgewater* ☎ *860/350–8226* ⊕ *www.promisek.org.*

Glebe House Museum. Legendary British garden writer and designer Gertrude Jekyll designed only three gardens in the United States, and the one at the Glebe House Museum is the only one still in existence. The garden is a classic example of Jekyll's ideas of color harmonies and plant combinations; a hedge of mixed shrubs encloses a mix of perennials. ⊠ *49 Hollow Rd., Woodbury* ☎ *203/263–2855* ⊕ *www.theglebehouse.org* ⊒ *$5.*

The Bellamy-Ferriday House & Garden. An apple orchard and a circa-1915 formal parterre garden that blossoms with peonies, historic roses, and lilacs are the highlights of this garden. ⊠ *9 Main St. N, Bethlehem* ☎ *203/266–7596* ⊕ *www.ci.bethlehem.ct.us* ⊒ *$7.*

Roseland Cottage. At Roseland Cottage, the boxwood parterre garden includes 21 flower beds surrounded by boxwood hedge. ⊠ *556 Rte. 169, Woodstock* ☎ *860/928–4074* ⊕ *www.historicnewengland.org* ⊒ *$8.*

Florence Griswold Museum. The gardens at the historic Florence Griswold Museum, once the home of a prominent Old Lyme family and then a haven for artists, have been restored to their 1910 appearance and feature hollyhocks and black-eyed Susans. ⊠ *96 Lyme St., Old Lyme* ☎ *860/434–5542* ⊕ *www.flogris.org* ⊒ *$9.*

5

SHOPPING

Wesleyan Potters. Jewelry, clothing, baskets, pottery, weavings, and more are available here. The nonprofit guild also runs classes and workshops. Don't miss the Annual Exhibit & Sale from the day after Thanksgiving to mid-December, when the best of the juried art and crafts are on sale. ✉ *350 S. Main St.* ☎ *860/347–5925* 🌐 *www.wesleyanpotters.com.*

NIGHTLIFE AND THE ARTS

THE ARTS

★ **Wesleyan University Center for the Arts.** See modern dance or a provocative new play, hear top playwrights and actors discuss their craft, and take in an art exhibit or concert here. ✉ *283 Washington Terr.* ☎ *860/685–3355 box office* 🌐 *www.wesleyan.edu/cfa.*

NIGHTLIFE

Eli Cannon's. At last count, Eli Cannon's had more than 30 beers on draft and an extensive bottled selection. ✉ *695 Main St.* ☎ *860/347–3547* 🌐 *www.elicannons.com.*

WHERE TO EAT

$ AMERICAN ★ 🍴 **O'Rourke's Diner.** A devastating fire closed this beloved steel, glass, and brick diner in 2007, but the owners—partly through donations from the community—have rebuilt it better than ever. It's been featured on Food Network's *Diners, Drive-Ins and Dives,* and it's the place to go for top-notch diner fare, including creative specialties like the omelet stuffed with roasted portobello mushrooms, Brie, and asparagus. The steamed cheeseburgers are another favorite. Arrive early: lines are often out the door and the diner closes at 3 pm. [$] *Average main: $13* ✉ *728 Main St.* ☎ *860/346–6101* 🌐 *www.orourkesmiddletown.com* ⏲ *No dinner.*

WETHERSFIELD

7 miles northeast of New Britain, 32 miles northeast of New Haven.

Wethersfield, a vast Hartford suburb, dates from 1634 and has the state's largest—and, some say, most picturesque—historic district, with more than 100 pre-1849 buildings. Old Wethersfield has the oldest firehouse in the state, the oldest historic district in the state, and the oldest continuously operating seed company. Today, this "old" community has new parks and new shops, but history is still its main draw.

GETTING HERE AND AROUND

Wethersfield is only a few miles south of Hartford, and most easily reached by car. From there, take I–91 south to Route 3 south.

EXPLORING

Comstock Ferre & Co. Original tin signs still adorn the inviting post-and-beam buildings of the Comstock Ferre & Co., the country's oldest continuously operating seed company, founded in 1820. The company sells more than 800 varieties of seeds and more than 2,000 varieties of perennials, as well as special seed collections so that you can create your own magical moonlight, Italian herb, or shade garden. ✉ *263 Main St.* ☎ *860/571–6590* 🌐 *www.comstockferre.com* ⏲ *Sun.–Fri. 10–4.*

Webb-Deane-Stevens Museum. For a true sample of Wethersfield's historic past, stop by the Joseph Webb House, the Silas Deane House, and the

Isaac Stevens House, next door to each other along Main Street and all built in the mid- to late 1700s. These well-preserved examples of Georgian architecture reflect their owners' lifestyles as, respectively, a merchant, a diplomat, and a tradesman. The Webb House, a registered National Historic Landmark, was the site of the strategy conference between George Washington and the French general Jean-Baptiste Rochambeau that led to the British defeat at Yorktown. ✉ *211 Main St., off I–91, Exit 26* ☎ *860/529–0612* ⊕ *www.webb-deane-stevens. org* ✉ *$10* ◷ *May–Oct., Mon. and Wed.–Sat. 10–4, Sun. 1–4; Apr. and Nov., Sat. 10–4, Sun. 1–4; other times by appointment.*

★ **New Britain Museum of American Art.** An important stop for art lovers in a small industrial city 8 miles west of Wethersfield, this museum more than doubled its exhibit space with the opening of a new building in 2006. The 100-year-old museum's collection of more than 10,000 works from 1740 to the present had seriously outgrown the turn-of-the-20th-century house that held it. Among the treasures are paintings by artists of the Hudson River and Ash Can schools; by John Singer Sargent, Winslow Homer, Georgia O'Keeffe, and others on up through op-art works and sculpture by Isamu Noguchi. Deserving of special note is the selection of impressionist artists, including Mary Cassatt, William Merritt Chase, Childe Hassam, and John Henry Twachtman, as well as Thomas Hart Benton's five-panel mural *The Arts of Life in America.* The museum also has a café, a large shop, and a library of art books. ✉ *56 Lexington St., New Britain* ☎ *860/229–0257* ⊕ *www.nbmaa.org* ✉ *$10, free Sat. 10-noon* ◷ *Tues., Wed., and Fri. 11–5; Thurs. 11–8; Sat. 10–5; Sun. noon–5.*

HARTFORD

4 miles north of Wethersfield, 45 miles northwest of New London, 81 miles northeast of Stamford.

Midway between New York City and Boston, Hartford is Connecticut's capital city. Founded in 1635 on the banks of the Connecticut River, Hartford was at various times home to authors Mark Twain and Harriet Beecher Stowe, inventors Samuel and Elizabeth Colt, landscape architect Frederick Law Olmsted, and Ella Grasso, the first woman to be elected a state governor. Today, Hartford, where America's insurance industry was born in the early 19th century, is poised for change, with a new convention center and science museum, Connecticut Science Center. The city is a destination on the verge of discovery.

GETTING HERE AND AROUND

Hartford is centrally located in the middle of the state. Two main highways meet here; I–91 runs north–south from Western Massachusetts straight through Hartford and on to the Connecticut coastline. I–84 runs generally east to west from Union at the northeast border with Massachusetts to near Danbury at the border of New York. Amtrak also has service to Hartford on its Northeast Regional line. Bradley International Airport in Windsor Locks, 15 minutes north of Hartford, offers flights to more than 30 destinations in the United States, Canada, and the Caribbean.

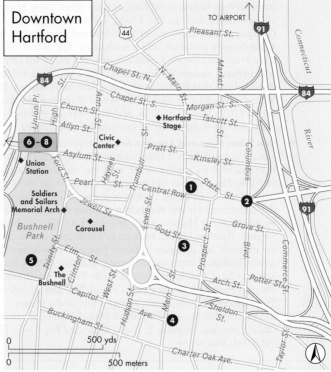

EXPLORING

TOP ATTRACTIONS

★ **Children's Museum.** A life-size walk-through replica of a 60-foot sperm
whale greets patrons at this museum, formerly known as the Science
Center of Connecticut. In West Hartford, 5 miles west of downtown,
the museum has a wildlife sanctuary and real-life images "beamed"
in from NASA, plus an exhibit on rocks and fossils that will make a
geologist out of your little one. ✉ *950 Trout Brook Dr., West Hartford*
☎ *860/231–2824* ⊕ *www.thechildrensmuseumct.org* 🎫 *Museum and
one planetarium show $11* ☉ *Tues.–Sat. 9–4, Sun. 11–4.*

Fodor's Choice **Connecticut Science Center.** Scientists of all ages will delight in Hartford's
★ science center. The strikingly modern building, designed by world-
renowned architect César Pelli, houses 40,000 square feet of exhibit
space under a wavelike roofline that appears to float over the structure.
Dive into a black hole and examine the moon's craters in the Space
Exploration exhibit, race mini-sailboats and magnetic trains at Forces in
Motion, and discover your hidden athletic talents in the Sports Lab. Kid
Space is perfect for the 3- to 6-year-old crowd, with a water play area,
"I Spy" adventure activities, and magnetic ball wall. Complete your
visit by taking in a movie in the 3-D digital theater. The café empha-
sizes locally sourced cuisine. ✉ *250 Columbus Blvd.* ☎ *860/724–3623*
⊕ *www.ctsciencecenter.org* 🎫 *$17* ☉ *Tues.–Sun. 10–5.*

★ **Harriet Beecher Stowe Center.** Stowe (1811–96) spent her final years at this 1871 Victorian Gothic cottage, on the Connecticut Freedom Trail. The center was built around the cottage, created as a tribute to the author of the antislavery novel *Uncle Tom's Cabin.* Stowe's personal writing table and effects are inside the home. ✉ *77 Forest St.* ☎ *860/522–9258* ⊕ *www.harrietbeecherstowecenter.org* 🎟 *$9* ⊙ *Year-round Wed.–Fri. 9:30–4:30, Sat. 9:30–5:30, Sun. noon–4:30; June–Oct. additionally open Tues. 9:30–4:30.*

Fodor'sChoice **The Mark Twain House & Museum.** Built in 1874, this building was the
★ home of Samuel Langhorne Clemens, better known as Mark Twain, until 1891. While he and his family lived in this 19-room Victorian mansion, Twain published seven major novels, including *Tom Sawyer, Huckleberry Finn,* and *The Prince and the Pauper.* The home is one of only two Louis Comfort Tiffany–designed domestic interiors open to the public. A contemporary museum on the grounds presents an up-close look at the author and shows an outstanding Ken Burns documentary on his life. ✉ *351 Farmington Ave., at Woodland St.* ☎ *860/247–0998* ⊕ *www.marktwainhouse.org* 🎟 *$16* ⊙ *Apr.–Dec., Mon.–Sat. 9:30–5:30, Sun. noon–5:30; Jan.–Mar., Mon. and Wed.– Sat. 9:30–5:30, Sun. noon–5:30.*

Fodor'sChoice **Wadsworth Atheneum Museum of Art.** With more than 50,000 artworks
★ and artifacts spanning 5,000 years, this is the nation's oldest public art museum. The first American museum to acquire works by Salvador Dalí and the Italian artist Caravaggio, it also houses 7,000 items documenting African-American history and culture in partnership with the Amistad Foundation. Particularly impressive are the museum's baroque, impressionist, and Hudson River school collections. ✉ *600 Main St.* ☎ *860/278–2670* ⊕ *www.wadsworthatheneum.org* 🎟 *$10* ⊙ *Wed.–Fri. 11–5 (1st Thurs. of most months until 8), weekends 10–5.*

WORTH NOTING

Butler-McCook Homestead. Built in 1782, this home housed four generations of Butlers and McCooks until it became a museum in 1971. Inside is Hartford's oldest intact collection of art and antiques, including furnishings, family possessions, and Victorian-era toys that show the evolution of American tastes over nearly 200 years. The beautifully restored Victorian garden was originally designed by Jacob Weidenmann. ✉ *396 Main St.* ☎ *860/522–1806, 860/247–8996 Education dept.* ⊕ *www. ctlandmarks.org* 🎟 *$7* ⊙ *Apr., Oct–Dec., Sat.–Sun. 11–4; May–Sept. Thurs.–Sun. 11–4.*

QUICK
BITES
Mozzicato–De Pasquale's Bakery, Pastry Shop & Caffé. Located in Hartford's Little Italy neighborhood along Franklin Avenue, this shop serves delectable Italian pastries in the bakery and espresso, cappuccino, and gelato in the café. ✉ *329 Franklin Ave.* ☎ *860/296–0426* ⊕ *www. mozzicatobakery.com.*

Old State House. This Federal-style house with an elaborate cupola and roof balustrade was designed in the early 1700s by Charles Bulfinch, architect of the U.S. Capitol. It served as Connecticut's state capitol until a new building opened in 1879, then became Hartford's city hall until 1915. In the 1820 Senate Chamber, where everyone from Abraham Lincoln to George Bush has spoken, you can view a portrait of George Washington by Gilbert Stuart, and in the Courtroom you can find out about the trial of the *Amistad* Africans in the very place where it was first held. In summer, enjoy concerts and a farmers' market; don't forget to stop by the Museum of Natural and Other Curiosities. ⊠ *800 Main St.* ☎ *860/522–6766* ⊕ *www.ctosh.org* ⌑ *$6* ☉ *Sept.–June weekdays 10–5; July and Aug., Tues.–Sat. 10–5.*

State Capitol. The gold-leaf dome of the State Capitol rises above Bushnell Park. Built in 1878, the building houses the state's executive offices and legislative chamber as well as historical memorabilia. On a tour, you can walk through the Hall of Flags, see a statue of Connecticut state hero Nathan Hale, and observe the proceedings of the General Assembly, when in session, from the public galleries. ⊠ *210 Capitol Ave.* ☎ *860/240–0222* ⊕ *www.cga.ct.gov/capitoltours* ⌑ *Free* ☉ *Building weekdays 9–3. Tours given hourly, Sept.–June, weekdays 9:15–1:15; July and Aug., weekdays 9:15–2:15.*

OFF THE BEATEN PATH

Noah Webster House & West Hartford Historical Society. This 18th-century farmhouse is the birthplace of the famed author (1758–1843) of the *American Dictionary*. Inside is Webster memorabilia and period furnishings; outside there is a garden planted with herbs, vegetables, and flowers that would have been available to the Websters when they lived here. ⊠ *227 S. Main St., West Hartford* ☎ *860/521–5362* ⊕ *www.noahwebsterhouse.org* ⌑ *$7* ☉ *Thurs.–Mon. 1–4.*

SPORTS AND THE OUTDOORS

Bushnell Park. Fanning out from the State Capitol building, this city park, created in 1850, was the first public space in the country with natural landscaping. The original designer, a Swiss-born landscape architect and botanist named Jacob Weidenmann, planted 157 varieties of trees and shrubs to create an urban arboretum. Added later were the Soldiers and Sailors Memorial Arch, dedicated to Civil War soldiers; the Corning Fountain; the Bushnell Park Carousel (open May through September), intricately hand-carved in 1914 by the Artistic Carousel Company of Brooklyn, New York; the Pumphouse Gallery; and a performance venue. An oasis of green, the park has a pond and about 750 trees, including four state-champion trees. ⊠ *Asylum and Trinity Sts.* ☎ *860/232–6710* ⊕ *www.bushnellpark.org.*

NIGHTLIFE AND THE ARTS

NIGHTLIFE

Black-Eyed Sally's. For barbecue and blues head to Black-Eyed Sally's. ⊠ *350 Asylum St.* ☎ *860/278–7427* ⊕ *www.blackeyedsallys.com.*

THE ARTS **Bushnell.** The Bushnell hosts the Hartford Symphony Orchestra and tours of major musicals. ⊠ *166 Capitol Ave.* ☎ *860/987–6000, 888/824–2874* ⊕ *www.bushnell.org.*

Hartford Symphony Orchestra. The second-largest orchestra in New England, the Hartford Symphony Orchestra plays classical, chamber, and popular music. ⊠ *99 Pratt St., Suite 500* ☎ *860/244–2999* ⊕ *www.hartfordsymphony.org*

Hartford Conservatory. The conservatory presents musical theater, concerts, and dance performances, with an emphasis on traditional works. ✉ *61 Woodland St.* ☎ *860/246–2588* 🌐 *www.hartfordconservatory.org.*

Hartford Stage Company. The Tony Award–winning Hartford Stage Company puts on classic and new plays from around the world. ✉ *50 Church St.* ☎ *860/527–5151* 🌐 *www.hartfordstage.org.*

Real Art Ways. Modern and experimental musical compositions are presented here in addition to avant-garde and foreign films. ✉ *56 Arbor St.* ☎ *860/232–1006* 🌐 *www.realartways.org.*

TheatreWorks. This is the Hartford equivalent of off-Broadway, where experimental new dramas are presented. ✉ *233 Pearl St.* ☎ *860/527–7838* 🌐 *www.theaterworkshartford.org.*

TAKE A TOUR

Connecticut Freedom Trail. More than 50 historic sights associated with the state's African American heritage can be found on the trail. ✉ *One Constitution Plaza* ☎ *860/256–2800* 🌐 *www.ctfreedomtrail.ct.gov.*

Connecticut Art Trail. This self-guided tour takes you through 14 museums and sites important to the 19th-century American impressionist movement. 🌐 *www.arttrail.org.*

Connecticut Wine Trail. The wine trail travels among 24 member vineyards. ☎ *860/677–5467* 🌐 *www.ctwine.com.*

5

WHERE TO EAT

$$ PIZZA ★ 🍴 **First and Last Tavern.** What looks to be a simple neighborhood joint south of downtown is actually one of the state's most hallowed pizza parlors, serving superb thin-crust pies (locals love the puttanesca) since 1936. The old-fashioned wooden bar in one room is jammed most evenings with suburbia-bound daily-grinders. The main dining room, which is just as noisy, has a brick outer wall covered with celebrity photos. This is the original, but other branches have opened around the state. [$] *Average main: $18* ✉ *939 Maple Ave.* ☎ *860/956–6000* 🌐 *www.firstandlasttavern.com* ✍ *Reservations not accepted.*

$$$$ AMERICAN Fodor's Choice ★ 🍴 **Max Downtown.** With its contemporary design, extensive array of martinis and wines, and sophisticated cuisine, Max Downtown is a favorite with the city's well-heeled and a popular after-work spot. Creative entrées include sesame crusted ahi tuna with yuzu soy sauce, sourdough-crusted New Bedford cod with lobster-potato gnocchi, and a wide range of perfectly prepared steaks with toppings like foie-gras butter and cognac-peppercorn cream. Desserts, such as the chocolate-chip ice cream cake or malted milk ball crème brûlée, are not to be missed. This restaurant is part of a small empire of excellent Hartford-area restaurants that includes Max's Oyster in West Hartford, Max a Mia in Avon, and several others. [$] *Average main: $33* ✉ *185 Asylum St.* ☎ *860/522–2530* 🌐 *www.maxrestaurantgroup.com/downtown* ✍ *Reservations essential* ⌚ *No lunch weekends.*

$$$ ITALIAN 🍴 **Peppercorn's Grill.** This mainstay of Hartford's restaurant scene presents contemporary Italian cuisine in both a lively (colorful murals) and formal (white linens) setting. Enjoy house-made potato gnocchi, ravioli,

Connecticut's Victorian Gothic state capitol rises from Hartford's Bushnell Park.

and top-quality steaks, but save room for the warm chocolate bread pudding and the Valrhona chocolate cake. $ *Average main: $30* ✉ *357 Main St.* ☎ *860/547–1714* ⊕ *www.peppercornsgrill.com* ☉ *Closed Sun. No lunch Sat.*

WHERE TO STAY

For expanded hotel reviews, visit Fodors.com.

$$$ 🏨 **Hartford Marriott Downtown.** This upscale hotel is connected to the
HOTEL   Connecticut Convention Center and conveniently located within walking distance of the Connecticut Science Center, the Wadsworth Atheneum, the Old State House, and other attractions. **Pros:** close to major attractions; in the heart of downtown. **Cons:** convenient location comes at a price. $ *Rooms from: $179* ✉ *200 Columbus Blvd.* ☎ *860/249–8000, 866/373–9806* ⊕ *www.marriott.com* ⮑ *401 rooms, 8 suites* ⦿| *No meals.*

$$$ 🏨 **Residence Inn Hartford-Downtown.** Part of the rehabilitation project
HOTEL   at the historic Richardson building, the all-suites Residence Inn is convenient to Pratt Street, Hartford Stage, and the Old State House. **Pros:** spacious rooms; great value; right in middle of downtown. **Cons:** right in the middle of downtown; cookie-cutter furnishings. $ *Rooms from: $199* ✉ *942 Main St.* ☎ *860/524–5550, 800/960–5045* ⊕ *www. marriott.com* ⮑ *120 suites* ⦿| *Breakfast.*

FARMINGTON

5 miles southwest of West Hartford.

Farmington, incorporated in 1645, is a classic river town with lovely estates, a perfectly preserved main street, and the prestigious Miss Porter's School, the late Jacqueline Kennedy Onassis's alma mater. This bucolic and affluent suburb of Hartford oozes historical charm. Antiques shops are near the intersection of Routes 4 and 10, along with some excellent house museums.

GETTING HERE AND AROUND

Farmington is most easily reached by car. From Hartford, take I–84 west to Route 4 west.

EXPLORING

★ **Hill-Stead Museum.** Converted from a private home into a museum by its talented owner, Theodate Pope, a turn-of-the-20th-century architect, the house has a superb collection of French impressionist art displayed in situ, including Claude Monet's *Haystacks* and Edouard Manet's *Guitar Player* hanging in the drawing room. Poetry readings by nationally known writers take place in the elaborate Beatrix Farrand–designed sunken garden every other week in summer. ✉ *35 Mountain Rd.* ☎ *860/677–4787* 🌐 *www.hillstead.org* 🎟 *$12* 🕒 *Tues.–Sun. 10–4.*

5

WHERE TO EAT AND STAY

For expanded hotel reviews, visit Fodors.com.

$$$ AMERICAN 🍴 **Apricots Restaurant and Pub.** This white Colonial with windows overlooking gardens and the Farmington River is a long-term staple of Hartford area dining. American classics such as scrumptious oven-roasted Maine crab cakes and sautéed Atlantic salmon with fava bean and sweet corn succotash are presented in a formal dining room; less-expensive fare is served in the downstairs pub. [$] *Average main: $27* ✉ *1593 Farmington Ave.* ☎ *860/673–5405* 🌐 *www.apricotsrestaurant.com.*

$$ HOTEL 🏨 **Avon Old Farms Hotel.** A country hotel at the base of Avon Mountain, this 20-acre compound of Colonial-style buildings with manicured grounds is midway between Farmington and Simsbury. **Pros:** attractive pool area; central location; well-kept rooms. **Cons:** rooms need a little upgrading. [$] *Rooms from: $129* ✉ *279 Avon Mountain Rd., Avon* ☎ *860/677–1651* 🌐 *www.avonoldfarmshotel.com* 🛏 *160 rooms* 🍽 *Breakfast.*

THE LITCHFIELD HILLS

★ Here in the foothills of the Berkshires is some of the most spectacular and unspoiled scenery in Connecticut. Two highways, Interstate 84 and Route 8, form the southern and eastern boundaries of the region. New York, to the west, and Massachusetts, to the north, complete the rectangle. Grand old inns are plentiful, as are sophisticated eateries. Rolling farmlands abut thick forests, and trails—including a section of the Appalachian Trail—traverse the state parks and forests. Two rivers, the Housatonic and the Farmington, attract anglers and canoeing enthusiasts, and the state's three largest natural lakes, Waramaug,

Bantam, and Twin, are here. Sweeping town greens and stately homes anchor Litchfield and New Milford. Kent, New Preston, and Woodbury draw avid antiquers, and Washington and Norfolk provide a glimpse into New England village life as it might have existed two centuries ago.

ESSENTIALS

Visitor Information **Litchfield Hills–Northwest Connecticut Convention and Visitors Bureau** *860/567-4506* ⊕ *www.northwestct.com.*

NEW MILFORD

28 miles west of Waterbury, 46 miles northeast of Greenwich.

If you're approaching the Litchfield Hills from the south, New Milford is a practical starting point to begin a visit. It was also a starting point for a young cobbler named Roger Sherman, who, in 1743, opened his shop at the corner of Main and Church streets. A Declaration of Independence signatory, Sherman also helped draft the Articles of Confederation and the Constitution. You'll find old shops, galleries, and eateries all within a short stroll of New Milford green.

GETTING HERE AND AROUND

New Milford is best visited by car. From Danbury and points south, take Route 7 to Route 202 to reach the town.

EXPLORING

Silo at Hunt Hill Farm Trust. The former property of the late Skitch Henderson, onetime music director of NBC and the New York Pops, consists of several attractions in the old buildings of two farms dating back to the 1700s. Inside a barn is the Silo Store, packed with objets de cookery, crafts, and assorted goodies and sauces; the Silo gallery presents art shows and literary readings; and the Silo cooking school draws culinary superstars to teach cooking classes between March and December. The Skitch Henderson Living Museum focuses on Henderson's collections of musical memorabilia, including rare recordings and scores, as well as other items as diverse as the Steinway he used at NBC and an antique marble soda fountain. ✉ *44 Upland Rd., 4 miles north of the New Milford town green on U.S. 202* ☎ *860/355-0300* ⊕ *www.thesilo.com* 🔅 *Donation suggested* ⊗ *Wed.–Sat. 10–5, Sun. noon–5.*

WHERE TO EAT AND STAY

For expanded hotel reviews, visit Fodors.com.

$$$

AMERICAN

✕ **Adrienne.** Set in an 18th-century farmhouse with terraced gardens, Adrienne serves New American cuisine from a seasonal menu. You may be lucky enough to encounter Maine lobster cakes on a roasted corn sauce, or grilled American lamb chops with mashed blue Peruvian potatoes and French green beans. Sunday brunch (think eggs Florentine, seafood crepes, and vegetable scampi) on the outdoor terrace is also popular and there is live jazz on the first Sunday of every month. $ *Average main: $25* ✉ *218 Kent Rd.* ☎ *860/354-6001* ⊕ *www. adriennerestaurant.com* ⊗ *Closed Mon. No dinner Sun.*

$$

B&B/INN

▢ **The Homestead Inn.** High on a hill overlooking New Milford's town green, this building was built in 1853 and opened as an inn in 1928. **Pros:** reasonably priced; close to shops and restaurants. **Cons:** on a busy

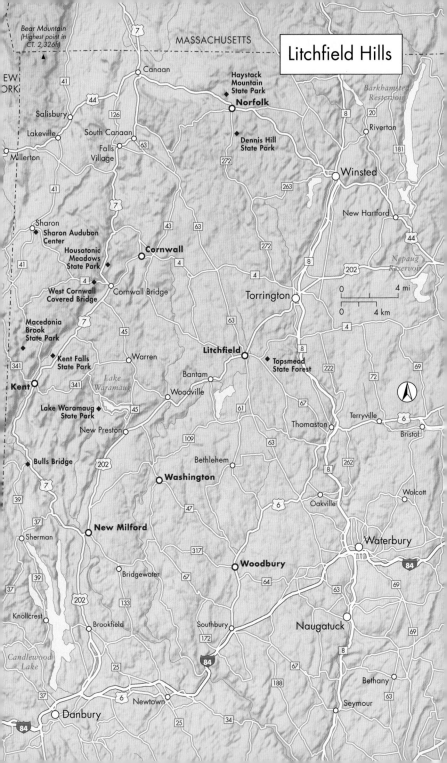

street. $ *Rooms from: $145* ⊠ *5 Elm St.* ☎ *860/354–4080* ⊕ *www. homesteadct.com* ⊃ *14 rooms, 1 suite* ⊚ *Breakfast.*

KENT

12 miles northwest of New Preston.

Kent has the area's greatest concentration of art galleries, some nationally renowned. Home to a prep school of the same name, Kent once held many ironworks. The Schaghticoke Indian Reservation is also here. During the Revolutionary War, 100 Schaghticokes helped defend the Colonies by transmitting messages of army intelligence from the Litchfield Hills to Long Island Sound along the hilltops by way of shouts and drumbeats.

GETTING HERE AND AROUND

To reach Kent by car, travel north on Route 7 from New Milford.

EXPLORING

Sloane-Stanley Museum. Hardware-store buffs and vintage-tool aficionados will feel right at home at this museum. Artist and author Eric Sloane (1905–85) was fascinated by Early American woodworking tools, and his collection showcases examples of American craftsmanship from the 17th to the 19th centuries. The museum contains a re-creation of Sloane's last studio and also encompasses the ruins of a 19th-century iron furnace. Sloane's books and prints, which celebrate vanishing aspects of Americana such as barns and covered bridges, are on sale here. ⊠ *31 Kent-Cornwall Rd. (U.S. 7)* ☎ *860/927–3849* ⊕ *www.ct.gov* ⊠ *$8* ⊙ *Late May–late Oct., Wed.–Sun. 10–4.*

SPORTS AND THE OUTDOORS

Appalachian Trail. The Appalachian Trail's longest river walk, off Route 341, is the almost-8-mile hike from Kent to Cornwall Bridge along the Housatonic River.

Macedonia Brook State Park. The early-season trout fishing is superb at 2,300-acre Macedonia Brook State Park, where you can also hike and cross-country ski. ⊠ *159 Macedonia Brook Rd., off Rte. 341* ☎ *860/927–3238* ⊕ *www.ct.gov.*

SHOPPING

Belgique. You'll find sublime handmade chocolates, plus gelato and sorbet and—perfect on a winter day—pure and decadently rich Belgian hot chocolate here. ⊠ *1 Bridge St.* ☎ *860/927–3681* ⊕ *www.belgiqueonline. com.*

Pauline's Place. This store specializes in Victorian, Georgian, art deco, Edwardian, and contemporary jewelry. ⊠ *79 N. Main St.* ☎ *860/927– 4475* ⊕ *www.paulinesplacejewelry.com.*

EN ROUTE

Kent Falls State Park. Heading north from Kent toward Cornwall, you'll pass the entrance to 295-acre Kent Falls State Park, where you can hike a short way to one of the most impressive waterfalls in the state and picnic in the green meadows at the base of the falls. ⊠ *U.S. 7* ☎ *860/927–3238.*

CORNWALL

12 miles northeast of Kent.

Connecticut's Cornwalls can get confusing. There's Cornwall, Cornwall Bridge, West Cornwall, Cornwall Hollow, East Cornwall, and North Cornwall. This quiet corner of the Litchfield Hills is known for its fantastic vistas of woods and mountains and its covered bridge, which spans the Housatonic.

GETTING HERE AND AROUND
Head north on Route 7 to reach Cornwall from Kent.

EXPLORING
West Cornwall Bridge. A romantic reminder of the past, the wooden, barn-red, one-lane bridge, not to be confused with the town of Cornwall Bridge (which was named for an earlier covered bridge that stood originally on that site), is several miles up U.S. 7 on Route 128 in West Cornwall. The bridge was built in 1841 and incorporates strut techniques that were copied by bridge builders around the country. ⊕ *www. coveredbridgesite.com.*

SPORTS AND THE OUTDOORS
Housatonic Meadows State Park. The park is marked by its tall pine trees near the Housatonic River and has terrific riverside campsites. Fly-fishers consider this 2-mile stretch of the river among the best places in New England to test their skills against trout and bass. ⊠ *U.S. 7, Cornwall Bridge* ☎ *860/672–6772 seasonal camping info* ⊕ *www.ct.gov.*

☼ **Sharon Audubon Center.** With 11 miles of hiking trails, this 1,147-acre property—a mixture of forests, meadows, wetlands, ponds, and streams—provides myriad hiking opportunities. It's also home to Princess, an American crow, who shares the visitor center with small hawks, an owl, and other animals in a live-animal display. Also here is a natural-history museum and children's adventure center. An aviary houses a bald eagle, a red-tailed hawk, and two turkey vultures. ⊠ *325 Cornwall Bridge Rd., Sharon* ☎ *860/364–0520* ⊕ *www.sharon. audubon.org* ⊉ *$3* ☉ *Tues.–Sat. 9–5, Sun. 1–5, trails daily dawn–dusk.*

CANOEING AND KAYAKING
Clarke Outdoors. This outfitter rents canoes, kayaks, and rafts and operates 10-mile trips from Falls Village to Housatonic Meadows State Park. ⊠ *163 Route 7(1 mile south of the covered bridge), West Cornwall* ☎ *860/672–6365* ⊕ *www.clarkeoutdoors.com.*

FISHING
Housatonic Anglers. Take a half- or full-day tour, evening outing, or fly-fishing lesson here and fish for trout and bass on the Housatonic and its tributaries. ⊠ *26 Bolton Hill Rd.* ☎ *860/672–4457* ⊕ *www. housatonicanglers.com.*

Housatonic River Outfitters. This outfitter operates a full-service fly shop; leads guided trips of the region; runs classes in fly-fishing, fly-tying, and casting; and stocks a good selection of vintage and antique gear. ⊠ *24 Kent Rd., Cornwall Bridge* ☎ *860/672–1010* ⊕ *www.dryflies.com.*

Be patient on back roads: Many covered bridges, like this one in West Cornwall, are one-lane only.

WHERE TO STAY
For expanded hotel reviews, visit Fodors.com.

$$$
B&B/INN

Cornwall Inn. This 19th-century inn on scenic U.S. 7 combines country charm with contemporary elegance; eight rooms in the adjacent "lodge" are slightly more private and rustic in tone and have white cedar-post beds. **Pros:** tranquil setting; lovely grounds; welcoming toward kids and pets. **Cons:** a bit far from neighboring towns. $ *Rooms from: $199* ✉ *270 Kent Rd. South(U.S. 7)* ☎ *860/672–6884, 800/786–6884* ⊕ *www.cornwallinn.com* ⤢ *12 rooms, 1 suite* ⧉ *Breakfast.*

NORFOLK

14 miles east of Salisbury, 59 miles north of New Haven.

Norfolk, thanks to its severe climate and terrain, is one of the best-preserved villages in the Northeast. Notable industrialists have been summering here for two centuries, and many enormous homesteads still exist. The striking town green, at the junction of Route 272 and U.S. 44, has a fountain designed by Augustus Saint-Gaudens and executed by Stanford White at its southern corner. It stands as a memorial to Joseph Battell, who turned Norfolk into a major trading center.

GETTING HERE AND AROUND
To reach Norfolk by car from points north or south, use Route 272.

SPORTS AND THE OUTDOORS
Dennis Hill State Park. Dr. Frederick Shepard Dennis, former owner of the 240 acres now making up the park, lavishly entertained guests, among them President William Howard Taft and several Connecticut

governors, in the stone pavilion at the summit of the estate. From its 1,627-foot height, you can see Haystack Mountain, New Hampshire, and, on a clear day, New Haven harbor, all the way across the state. Picnic on the park's grounds or hike one of its many trails. ✉ *Rte. 272* ☎ *860/482–1817* 🌐 *www.ct.gov* 🎟 *Free* 🕒 *Daily 8 am–dusk.*

Haystack Mountain State Park. One of the most spectacular views in the state can be seen from this park via its challenging trail to the top or a road halfway up. ✉ *Rte. 272* ☎ *860/482–1817.*

SHOPPING

Norfolk Artisans Guild. The shop carries works by more than 60 local artisans—from hand-painted pillows to handcrafted baskets. ✉ *10 Station Pl.* ☎ *860/542–5055* 🕒 *Mon.–Sun. 10–5.*

THE ARTS

★ **Norfolk Chamber Music Festival.** The Norfolk Chamber Music Festival, at the Music Shed on the 70-acre Ellen Battell Stoeckel Estate at the northwest corner of the Norfolk green, presents world-renowned artists and ensembles on Friday and Saturday summer evenings. Students from the Yale School of Music perform on Thursday evening and Saturday morning. Early arrivals can stroll or picnic on the 70-acre grounds or visit the art gallery. ☎ *860/542–3000 June–Aug., 203/432–1966 Sept.–May* 🌐 *www.yale.edu/norfolk.*

WHERE TO STAY

For expanded hotel reviews, visit Fodors.com.

$$$ B&B/INN Fodor's Choice ★ 🏨 **Manor House Inn.** Among this 1898 Bavarian Tudor's remarkable appointments are its bibelots, mirrors, carpets, antique beds, and prints—not to mention the 20 stained-glass windows designed by Louis Comfort Tiffany. **Pros:** sumptuous decor; lavish breakfasts; secluded and peaceful setting. **Cons:** no phone or TV in the rooms (and cell phone reception is iffy in these parts); no Internet offered. [$] *Rooms from: $215* ✉ *69 Maple Ave.* ☎ *860/542–5690, 866/542–5690* 🌐 *www.manorhouse-norfolk.com* 🛏 *8 rooms, 1 suite* 🍴 *Breakfast.*

LITCHFIELD

19 miles southwest of Riverton, 34 miles west of Hartford.

Everything in Litchfield, the wealthiest and most noteworthy town in the Litchfield Hills, seems to exist on a larger scale than in neighboring burgs, especially the impressive Litchfield Green and the white Colonial and Greek-Revival homes that line the broad elm-shaded streets. Harriet Beecher Stowe, author of *Uncle Tom's Cabin,* and her brother, abolitionist preacher Henry Ward Beecher, were born and raised in Litchfield, and many famous Americans earned their law degrees at the Litchfield Law School. Today, lovely but exceptionally expensive boutiques and hot restaurants line the downtown.

GETTING HERE AND AROUND

To reach Litchfield by car from points north or south, take Route 8 to Route 118 west.

EXPLORING

Litchfield History Museum. Furniture, clothing, household objects, and paintings provide glimpses into the evolution of this small New England town from its earliest days to the present, and seven well-organized galleries highlight family life and work during the 50 years after the American Revolution. The extensive reference library has information about the town's historic buildings, including the Sheldon Tavern (where George Washington slept on several occasions) and the Litchfield Female Academy, where in the late 1700s Sarah Pierce taught girls not just sewing and deportment but mathematics and history. ⊠ *7 South St., at Rtes. 63 and 118* ☎ *860/567–4501* ⊕ *www.litchfieldhistoricalsociety. org* 🖼 *$5 (includes Tapping Reeve House and Litchfield Law School)* ☉ *Mid-Apr.–late Nov., Tues.–Sat. 11–5, Sun. 1–5.*

★ **Tapping Reeve House and Litchfield Law School.** In 1773, Judge Tapping Reeve enrolled his first student, Aaron Burr, in what became the first law school in the country. (Before Judge Reeve, students studied the law as apprentices, not in formal classes.) This school is dedicated to Reeve's achievement and to the notable students who passed through its halls: Oliver Wolcott Jr., John C. Calhoun, Horace Mann, three U.S. Supreme Court justices, and 15 governors, not to mention senators, congressmen, and ambassadors. This museum is one of the state's most worthy attractions, with multimedia exhibits, an excellent introductory film, and restored facilities. ⊠ *82 South St.* ☎ *860/567–4501* ⊕ *www.litchfieldhistoricalsociety.org* 🖼 *$5 (includes Litchfield History Museum)* ☉ *Mid-Apr.–late Nov., Tues.–Sat. 11–5, Sun. 1–5.*

SPORTS AND THE OUTDOORS

Fodor's Choice ★ **The White Memorial Conservation Center.** At the heart of the White Memorial Foundation, this 4,000-acre nature preserve houses top-notch natural-history exhibits and a gift shop. The foundation, one of the state's prime birding areas, contains some 30 bird-watching platforms; two self-guided nature trails; several boardwalks; campgrounds; boating facilities; fishing areas; and 35 miles of hiking, cross-country skiing, and horseback-riding trails. ⊠ *Off U.S. 202 (2 miles west of village green), 80 Whitehall Rd.* ☎ *860/567–0857* ⊕ *www.whitememorialcc. org* 🖼 *Conservation center $6, grounds free* ☉ *Conservation center Mon.–Sat. 9–5, Sun. noon–5; grounds daily dawn to dusk.*

HORSEBACK RIDING **Lee's Riding Stable.** This stable conducts trail and pony rides. ⊠ *57 E. Litchfield Rd.* ☎ *860/567–0785* ⊕ *www.windfieldmorganfarm.com/ lees.html.*

SHOPPING

Jeffrey Tillou Antiques. This antiques store specializes in 18th- and 19th-century American furniture and paintings. ⊠ *39 West St.* ☎ *860/567– 9693* ⊕ *www.tillouantiques.com.*

WHERE TO EAT AND STAY

For expanded hotel reviews, visit Fodors.com.

$$ AMERICAN ✕ **The Village Restaurant.** Beloved by visitors and locals alike, this storefront eatery in a redbrick town house serves tasty, unfussy food—inexpensive pub grub in one room, updated contemporary American cuisine in the other. Whether you order a burger or herb-crusted pork

Explore White Memorial Conservation Center on the boardwalks, nature trails, and bird-watching platforms.

chops, you're bound to be pleased. [$] *Average main: $22* ✉ *25 West St.* ☎ *860/567–8307* 🌐 *www.village-litchfield.com.*

$$$ AMERICAN ★ 🍴 **West Street Grill.** This sophisticated dining room on the town green is *the* place to see and be seen, both for patrons and for the state's up-and-coming chefs, many of whom got their start here. Imaginative grilled fish, steak, poultry, and lamb dishes are served with fresh vegetables and pasta or risotto. The ice cream and sorbets, made by the restaurant, are worth every calorie. [$] *Average main: $30* ✉ *43 West St.* ☎ *860/567–3885* 🌐 *www.weststreetgrill.net.*

$$$$ B&B/INN 🏨 **The Litchfield Inn.** This reproduction Colonial-style inn's guest rooms underwent a complete renovation in 2012. **Pros:** well-kept property; updated rooms; efficient staff; good location for exploring entire region. **Cons:** on busy road; not within walking distance of downtown shopping and dining. [$] *Rooms from: $300* ✉ *432 Bantam Rd. (Rte. 202)* ☎ *860/567–4503* 🌐 *www.litchfieldinnct.com* 🛏 *32 rooms.*

$$$$ RESORT ALL-INCLUSIVE Fodor's Choice ★ 🏨 **Winvian.** This ultra-posh, 113-acre hideaway adjacent to the grounds of the White Memorial Foundation consists of 19 of the most imaginatively themed and luxuriously outfitted cottages you'll ever lay eyes on. **Pros:** whimsical and super-plush accommodations; outstanding cuisine; stunning setting. **Cons:** super-pricey. [$] *Rooms from: $650* ✉ *155 Alain White Rd., Morris* ☎ *860/567–9600* 🌐 *www.winvian.com* 🛏 *19 cottages, 1 suite* 🍽 *Multiple meal plans.*

WASHINGTON

11 miles west of Bethlehem.

The beautiful buildings of The Gunnery prep school mingle with stately Colonials and churches in Washington, one of the best-preserved Colonial towns in Connecticut. The Mayflower Inn, south of The Gunnery on Route 47, attracts an exclusive clientele. Washington, which was settled in 1734, in 1779 became the first town in the United States to be named for the first president.

GETTING HERE AND AROUND

Washington is best visited by car. Route 47 runs through town, connecting it with New Preston to the north and Woodbury to the south.

EXPLORING

The Institute for American Indian Studies. The exhibits in this small but excellent and thoughtfully arranged collection detail the history and continuing presence of more than 10,000 years of Native American life in New England. Highlights include nature trails, a simulated archaeological site, and an authentically constructed Algonquian Village with wigwams, a longhouse, a rock shelter, and more. The Collections and Research Center has a research library, a large exhibit hall, and a gift shop that presents the work of some of the country's best Native American artists. The institute is at the end of a forested residential road (just follow the signs from Route 199 South). ✉ *38 Curtis Rd., off Rte. 199* ☎ *860/868–0518* 🌐 *www.iaismuseum.org* 🎟 *$5* 🕒 *Mon.–Sat. 10–5, Sun. noon–5.*

WHERE TO EAT AND STAY

For expanded hotel reviews, visit Fodors.com.

$$$$ AMERICAN ★ 🍴 **Mayflower Inn.** In the refined and romantic restaurant of the chic Mayflower Inn & Spa, gaze out from the dining room's large windows—or from your seat on the terrace in warm weather—toward the formal English gardens while enjoying deftly prepared regional American cuisine. The menu changes seasonally but might list Block Island swordfish with rosemary, white-bean stew, and tangerine-glazed pancetta or Kobe-beef carpaccio with Parmesan aioli. After dinner, stop by the paneled library for a glass of cognac. [$] *Average main: $37* ✉ *118 Woodbury Rd. (Rte. 47)* ☎ *860/868–9466* 🌐 *www.mayflowerinn.com.*

$$$$ RESORT Fodor's Choice ★ 🏨 **Mayflower Inn & Spa.** Though the most-expensive suites at this inn cost upwards of $1000 a night, the Mayflower is often booked months in advance. **Pros:** idyllic and perfected landscaped grounds; solicitous but relaxed service; outstanding spa. **Cons:** some rooms starting to show a little age; very pricey. [$] *Rooms from: $800* ✉ *118 Woodbury Rd. (Rte. 47)* ☎ *860/868–9466* 🌐 *www.mayflowerinn.com* 🛏 *19 rooms, 11 suites* 🍽 *No meals.*

WOODBURY

10 miles southeast of Washington.

More antiques shops may be in the quickly growing town of Woodbury than in all the towns in the rest of the Litchfield Hills combined. Five

Continued on page 306

ANTIQUES AND CRAFTS SHOPPING
SOMETHING OLD, SOMETHING NEW

By Christina Valhouli

Forget the mall. In New England, shoppers can pick up serious antiques or quirky bric-a-brac in old mills and converted barns. Or hit funky galleries or annual craft fairs to meet artisans and buy one-of-a-kind products. Your souvenirs will be as memorable as the shopping experience.

Alongside New England's wealth of early American history is some of the best antique and craft shopping in the country—and often in beautiful settings perfect for browsing. You can explore galleries in converted farmhouses, craft shops clustered around the village green, or a picturesque Main Street (Woodstock, Vermont, or Camden, Maine, are good bets). Drive through historic coastal towns, like Essex, Massachusetts, where finds such as sun-bleached, centuries-old wooden tables or antique compasses evoke the area's maritime heritage. Picture-perfect towns like Blue Hill, Maine, and Chester, Connecticut, are home to plenty of contemporary artists' galleries and cooperatives, like the Connecticut River Artisans, which showcases handmade quilts, jewelry, and ceramics; or try your luck at the Frog Hollow Craft Center in Burlington, Vermont.

Top Left, Hand-blown glass. Top right, Brimfield Antique Show. Bottom, antique pocket watch.

GREAT FINDS: CRAFTS

When most people think of a typical New England look, the austere lines of a Shaker table or the colorful patterns in a quilt come to mind. Artisans here still make crafts the old-fashioned way, but a new generation of glassblowers, potters, and weavers is creating products that will appeal to modernistas.

QUILTS. Today's quilters continue to produce traditional quilts, but there are plenty of contemporary styles available. Instead of star patterns, go for bold stripes or blocky squares made from funky fabrics. Buy one for your bed or to hang; baby quilts start around $100.

SHAKER-STYLE FURNITURE. The Shakers believed that form must follow function, and a typical Shaker design is clean, straight-lined, and devoid of decoration. Carpenters still make Shaker-inspired furniture, including ladderback chairs, tables, and bookcases. Chairs start around $300.

FELT. Humble felt is simply unspun wool that has been rolled and beaten into a solid form, but it's one of the most versatile (and eco-friendly) products around. Contemporary artists fashion felt into handbags, rugs, and even lightweight sculptures. Handbags start at $60.

CERAMICS. Visit a pottery studio or an art gallery and choose from ceramic plates and mugs or sturdier stoneware products that can survive the dishwasher. Small ceramic pieces start at $25.

WOOD-TURNED BOWLS. Hand- or wood-turned bowls are individually shaped on a lathe from solid blocks of wood. Each piece has a unique size, shape, grain pattern, and color. Look for rare spalted wood bowls—highly valued for their patterns and rich contrasts. Bowls are around $40 and up.

BLOWN GLASS. It's worth a trip to a glass-blowing studio just to see the artisans blow a gob of molten glass into a beautiful object. Best bets include colorful vases, bowls, and sculptures; handblown glass is typically $100 to $500.

GREAT FINDS: ANTIQUES

Antiques can run the gamut from auction-worthy pieces to decorative trinkets and vintage items from the '40s, '50s and '60s. Antique trends come and go, but popular New England buys include "smalls" like old prints and glass bottles. Don't be put off if you don't know a lot about antiques—however, do keep in mind that a true antique must be at least 100 years old.

KITCHEN TOOLS. Although you won't be tempted to cook with an old iron cauldron, items like engraved stove plates, mortar and pestles, and spoon racks look great on display for about $40–$180.

■TIP→

Start a collection easily with two or more of the same item (salt and pepper shakers) or style (speckled graniteware).

JEWELRY. Cuff links, earrings, and brooches make great gifts and will take up little room in your luggage. Antique jewelry runs the gamut from fun beaded necklaces to delicate Art Deco pieces. Prices start at $20.

MAPS. Frame an old nautical chart or map of a town you vacationed in for a stylish memento. Reproductions are easier on the wallet but still look good. Prices start at $40 for prints and run up to the thousands for antiques.

PENS. Hardly anyone writes letters anymore, which makes collecting old pens even more special. Parker pens from the 1970s are airplane inspired, while antique fountain pens are sheathed in beautiful wood or mother of pearl (and a joy to use). Prices are $100 up to thousands.

AMERICANA. This can be anything from painted signs to photographs of historic villages or kitschy porcelain figurines that evoke what it means to be American. Items inspired by the Stars and Stripes make colorful decorative accents for a country home feel. Postcards and other small items start at $5.

MIRRORS. If your taste runs toward the ornate, browse for 19th-century Federal and Queen Anne–style gilt mirrors. For something smaller and more understated, try a concave or vintage sunburst mirror. Prices range from $200–$2,000.

TOP SHOPPING ROUTES & SIGHTS

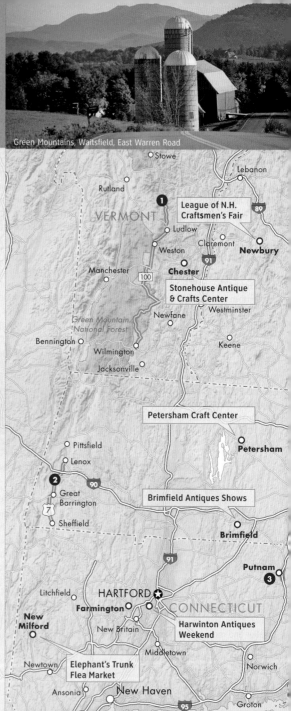

Green Mountains, Waitsfield, East Warren Road

One of the most effective and fun ways to shop is to hop in the car and drive through sleepy, scenic towns. On several key shopping routes in New England, stretches of road are absolutely packed with shops. Charles Street in Boston and downtown Providence and Portland are ideal, compact urban shopping areas for walking. If you do have wheels, try these routes.

1 Route 100. One of the most picturesque drives in the Green Mountain State, this winding road goes from Wilmington north all the way up to Stowe. You'll pass craft studios, general stores like the Vermont Country Store in Weston, and plenty of red barns and covered bridges.

2 Route 7, Berkshire County. Practically the entire route is chock-a-block with antiques stores. The Berkshire County Antiques Dealers Association (⊕ www.berkshireantiquesandart.com) publishes a handy guide to the various shops. Key Western Massachusetts shopping towns include Great Barrington, Sheffield, and Lenox.

3 Main Street, Putnam. Most of the town has a stuck-in-time quality, so it's a great place to spend the day the northeastern part of the state. The majority of antique stores are clustered around Main Street and its offshoots. Start your hunt at the massive Antiques Marketplace.

Map Labels

1 League of N.H. Craftsmen's Fair

Stonehouse Antique & Crafts Center

Petersham Craft Center

Brimfield Antiques Shows

Harwinton Antiques Weekend

Elephant's Trunk Flea Market

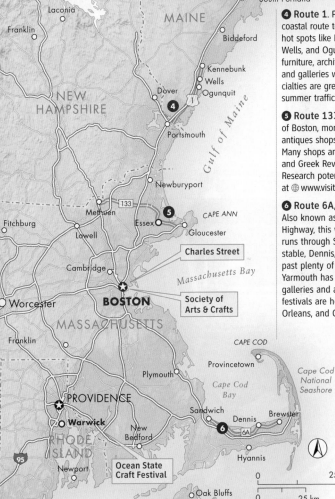

ANTIQUES

Antique Shop, Snefield, Berkshires   White Elephant Shop, Essex

4 Route 1. Pick up this Maine coastal route to hit shopping hot spots like Kennebunk, Wells, and Ogunquit. Colonial furniture, architectural antiques, and galleries with quirky specialties are great breaks from summer traffic.

5 Route 133, Essex. North of Boston, more than 30 antiques shops line this road. Many shops are in old Colonial and Greek Revival buildings. Research potential shops online at ⊕ www.visitessexma.com).

6 Route 6A, Cape Cod. Also known as the Old King's Highway, this winding route runs through Sandwich, Barnstable, Dennis, and Brewster past plenty of antiques shops. Yarmouth has several art galleries and annual crafts festivals are held in Falmouth, Orleans, and Chatham.

DID YOU KNOW?

Antiques can be more than just decoration: clocks can be fixed to tell time, dressers are great for storage, and old-fashioned oil lamps can illuminate today's homes, too.

WHERE TO GET THE GOODS

Depending on your budget, there are plenty of places to shop. Take your pick from artisan studios, art galleries, auction houses, and multi-dealer antique centers. Some antiques shops are one step above flea markets, so prices can vary widely. Antiques shows and craft fairs also offer excellent one-stop shopping opportunities.

TOP ANTIQUES SHOWS

⭐ **Brimfield Antique and Collectible Shows**, Brimfield, Massachusetts. May, July and September (⊕ *www.brimfieldshow.com*).

Elephant's Trunk Country Flea Market, New Milford, Connecticut. Most Sundays except in December and March (⊕ *www.etflea.com*).

Harwinton Antiques Weekend, Connecticut. June and September (⊕ *www.farmingtonantiques weekend.com*).

Maine Antiques Festival, Union, Maine. August (⊕ *www.maineantique fest.com*).

Top, Ceramics sold along Route 100, Vermont.

Right, antique rocking horse.

TOP CRAFT FAIRS AND CENTERS

Center for Maine Crafts West Gardiner, Maine (⊕ *mainecrafts.org*).

⭐ **League of New Hampshire Craftsmen's Fair**, Newbury, New Hampshire. August (⊕ *www.nhcrafts.org*).

Ocean State Artisans Holiday Craft Festival, Warwick, Rhode Island. November (⊕ *www.oceanstateartisans.com*).

Petersham Craft Center, Petersham, Massachusetts (⊕ *www.petershamcraftcenter.org*).

Society of Arts and Crafts, Boston, Massachusetts (⊕ *www.societyofcrafts.org*).

Stonehouse Antique and Crafts Center, Chester, Vermont (☎ 802/875–4477).

5

IN FOCUS ANTIQUES AND CRAFTS SHOPPING

SHOPPING KNOW-HOW

Many shops are often closed on Sundays and Mondays. Call ahead to confirm. Before you whip out the credit card (or a wad of cash), there are a few other things to remember.

■ Unless you're an expert, it can be difficult to tell if an item is a reproduction or a genuine antique. Buy a price guide or a reference book like Miller's *Antiques & Collectibles* or *Kovel's* to have an idea of a fair value.

■ To ensure you are buying from a legitimate source, make sure the dealer belongs to a professional organization.

■ Think carefully about shipping costs for bulky items. It's also a good idea to carry with you some key measurements from your house.

■ If you find a piece that you love, check it carefully for any flaws. Point out any dings or scratches and use it as a bargaining chip when negotiating a price.

■ Always remember the golden rule: Buy what you love at a price you can afford.

magnificent churches and the Greek-Revival King Solomon's Temple, formerly a Masonic lodge, line U.S. 6; they represent some of the best-preserved examples of Colonial religious architecture in New England.

GETTING HERE AND AROUND

To reach Woodbury by car from Washington, take Route 47 south to Route 6.

EXPLORING

Glebe House Museum and The Gertrude Jekyll Garden. This property consists of the large, antiques-filled, gambrel-roof Colonial in which Dr. Samuel Seabury was elected the first Episcopal bishop in the United States, in 1783, and its historic garden. The latter was designed in the 1920s by renowned British horticulturist Gertrude Jekyll. Though small, it is a classic, old-fashioned English-style garden and the only one of the three gardens Jekyll designed in the United States still in existence. ✉ *149 Hollow Rd.* ☎ *203/263–2855* 🌐 *www.theglebehouse.org* 🎫 *$5* 🕒 *May–Oct., Wed.–Sun. 1–4; Nov., weekends 1–4.*

SHOPPING

Country Loft Antiques. This antiques shop specializes in 18th- and 19th-century country French antiques. ✉ *557 Main St. S* ☎ *203/266–4500* 🌐 *www.countryloftantiques.com.*

David Dunton. This store offers pieces from respected dealer of formal American Federal–style furniture David Dunton. ✉ *Rte. 132 off Rte. 47, 35 Weekeepeemee Rd.* ☎ *203/263–5355* 🌐 *www.daviddunton.com.*

Mill House Antiques. The Mill House carries formal and country English and French furniture and has the state's largest collection of Welsh dressers. ✉ *1068 Main St. N* ☎ *203/263–3446* 🌐 *www.millhouseantiques-ct.com.*

Monique Shay Antiques & Designs. The six barns that make up Monique Shay's are lined with French Canadian country antiques. ✉ *920 Main St. S* ☎ *203/263–3186* 🌐 *www.moniqueshay.com.*

WHERE TO EAT AND STAY

For expanded hotel reviews, visit Fodors.com.

$$$ AMERICAN Fodor's Choice ★ 🍴 **Good News Café.** Carole Peck is a well-known name throughout New England, and since this café opened in 1992, foodies have been flocking to Woodbury to sample her superb cuisine. The emphasis is on healthy, innovative, and surprisingly well-priced fare: wok-seared Gulf shrimp with new potatoes, grilled green beans, and a garlic aioli or Cuban-style black-bean cassoulet with duck confit, pork, chorizo, and wild boar are good choices. In the simpler room next to the bar, you can order from a less expensive café menu. [$] *Average main: $27* ✉ *694 Main St. S* ☎ *203/266–4663* 🌐 *www.good-news-cafe.com* 🕒 *Closed Tues.*

$$$ B&B/INN ★ 🏨 **Cornucopia at Oldfield.** A Federal Colonial house in northern Southbury, a short drive from Woodbury antiques shops and restaurants, Cornucopia has a bounty of pleasing comforts: from high-quality antiques and soft Kingdown-brand bedding to floral gardens and a pool surrounded by a private hedge. **Pros:** fine antiques; beautifully kept grounds; modern in-room amenities. **Cons:** on somewhat busy road. [$] *Rooms from: $175* ✉ *782 N. Main St., Southbury* ☎ *203/267–6772* 🌐 *www.cornucopiabnb.com* 🛏 *3 rooms, 2 suites* 🍽 *Breakfast.*

NEW HAVEN TO MYSTIC

As you drive northeast along Interstate 95, culturally rich New Haven is the final urban obstacle between southwestern Connecticut's over-developed coast and southeastern Connecticut's quieter shoreline. The remainder of the jagged coast, which stretches to the Rhode Island, consists of small coastal villages, quiet hamlets, and relatively undisturbed beaches. The only interruptions along this seashore are the industry and piers of New London and Groton. Mystic, Stonington, Old Saybrook, Clinton, and Guilford are havens for fans of antiques and boutiques. North of Groton, near the town of Ledyard, the Mashantucket Pequot Reservation owns and operates Foxwoods Casino and the Mashantucket Pequot Museum & Research Center. The Mohegan Indians run the Mohegan Sun casino in Uncasville. These two properties have added noteworthy hotels and marquee restaurants in recent years.

NEW HAVEN

9 miles east of Milford, 46 miles northeast of Greenwich.

New Haven's history goes back to the 17th century, when its squares, including a lovely central green for the public, were laid out. The city is home to Yale University. The historic district surrounding Yale and the distinctive shops, prestigious museums, and highly respected theaters downtown are a major draw—New Haven has developed an acclaimed restaurant scene in recent years.

GETTING HERE AND AROUND

New Haven is accessible by car from both I–95 and the Rt. 15. Amtrak's Northeast Regional and high-speed Acela trains also stop here, and New Haven is the end of the line for Metro-North commuter trains from New York City. Shore Line East train service connect New Haven and New London.

ESSENTIALS

Visitor Information Greater New Haven Convention and Visitors Bureau ✉ *127 Washington Ave., 4th Fl. West, North Haven* ☎ *203/777–8550, 800/332–7829* ⊕ *www.newhavencvb.org.*

TOP ATTRACTIONS

Fodor's Choice ★ **Yale Center for British Art.** With the largest collection of British art outside Britain, the center surveys the development of English art, life, and thought from the Elizabethan period to the present. The skylighted galleries of architect Louis I. Kahn's final work (completed after his death) contain works by John Constable, William Hogarth, Thomas Gainsborough, Joshua Reynolds, and J. M. W. Turner, to name but a few. You'll also find rare books and paintings documenting English history. ✉ *1080 Chapel St.* ☎ *203/432–2800* ⊕ *britishart.yale.edu* 🎫 *Free* ⊙ *Tues.–Sat. 10–5, Sun. noon–5.*

★ **Yale University.** New Haven as a manufacturing center dates from the 19th century, but the city owes its fame to merchant Elihu Yale. In 1718 Yale's contributions enabled the Collegiate School, founded in 1701 at Saybrook, to settle in New Haven, where it changed its name

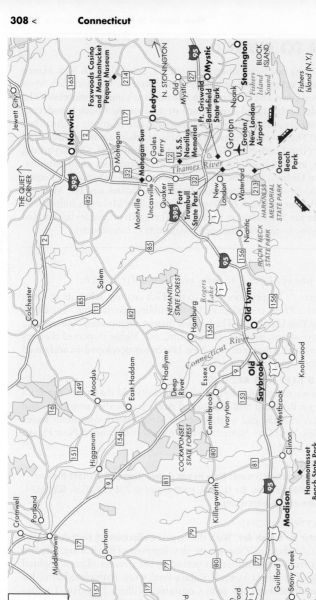

New Haven to Mystic

KEY

⛴ Ferry Lines

Jewett City

165

THE QUIET CORNER

Norwich

2

395

82

Foxwoods Casino and Mashantucket Pequot Museum

214

117

Ledyard

N. STONINGTON

27

Old Mystic

Mystic

Stonington

Noank

BLOCK ISLAND

Fishers Island Sound

Fishers Island (N.Y.)

Mohegan

Mohegan Sun

Gales Ferry

12

U.S.S. Nautilus Memorial

Ft. Griswold Battlefield State Park

Groton

Groton/ New London Airport

32

Thames River

New London

New London Airport

2

Montville

Uncasville

Quaker Hill

Fort Trumbull State Park

32

Waterford

213

Ocean Beach Park

HARKNESS MEMORIAL STATE PARK

Plum Island (N.Y.)

85

1

Niantic

95

156

Salem

11

82

NEHANTIC STATE FOREST

Rogers Lake

ROCKY NECK STATE PARK

Colchester

85

Hamburg

156

1

Old Lyme

156

Orient Point

Connecticut River

Long Island Sound

149

East Haddam

Hadlyme

Deep River

Essex

9

Old Saybrook

1

Knollwood

Moodus

16

151

Higganum

154

COCKAPONSET STATE FOREST

Centerbrook

Ivoryton

153

80

Westbrook

Cromwell

Portland

9

81

Clinton

81

Madison

Long Island (N.Y.)

Middletown

17

Durham

79

Killingworth

Hammonasset Beach State Park

95

1

157

77

80

1

11

77

Thimble Islands

10 miles

15 km

Wallingford

5

68

15

North Haven

17

Northford

Lake Gaillard

North Branford

Guilford

Stony Creek

Branford

1

New Haven
see detail
map

East Haven

Milford

Tweed/New Haven Airport

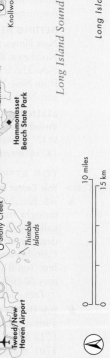

CLOSE UP

Connecticut Lobster Rolls

Behold the lobster roll. Sweet, succulent, and sinfully rich, it's the ultimate buttery icon of a Connecticut summer. Other New England states may prefer to chill out with lobster rolls created from a cool mix of lobster meat, mayonnaise, and chopped celery, but Nutmeggers like their one-of-a-kind rolls served hot, hot, hot.

The traditional Connecticut lobster roll, said to have been invented in the early 1930s at Perry's, a now-defunct seafood shack on the Boston Post Road in Milford, consists of nothing more than plump chunks of hot lobster meat and melted butter served on a butter-toasted roll. In other words: heaven on a bun. From seafood shanties along the shore to more gourmet getaways farther inland, Connecticut is fairly swimming with eateries that offer these revered rolls. Three favorites:

Abbott's Lobster in the Rough. A lobster roll at Abbott's Lobster in the

Rough is best enjoyed seated at a picnic table at the edge of Noank Harbor watching the boats bob by. ⊠ *117 Pearl St., Noank* ☎ *860/536–7719* ⊕ *www.abbotts-lobster.com* ⊗ *Closed mid-Oct.–May.*

Lenny and Joe's Fish Tale. At Lenny and Joe's Fish Tale, kids of all ages love to eat their lobster rolls or fried seafood outdoors by a hand-carved Dentzel carousel with flying horses (and a whale, frog, lion, seal, and more), which the restaurant runs from early May through early October. ⊠ *1301 Boston Post Rd., Madison* ☎ *203/245–7289* ⊕ *www.ljfishtale. com.*

Marnick's. You can take your lobster roll to go for a picnic on a small beach on the Long Island Sound, or enjoy a leisurely after-dinner stroll along the sea wall here. ⊠ *10 Washington Pkwy., Stratford* ☎ *203/377–6288* ⊕ *www.marnicks.com.*

5

to Yale University. This is one of the nation's great universities, and its campus holds some handsome neo-Gothic buildings and noteworthy museums. The university's guides conduct one-hour walking tours that include Connecticut Hall in the Old Campus, which has had a number of illustrious past residents. ⊠ *Yale Visitor Center, 149 Elm St.* ☎ *203/432–2302* ⊕ *www.yale.edu/visitor* 🎟 *Free* ⊗ *Tours weekdays at 10:30 and 2, weekends at 1:30* ☞ *Tours start from 149 Elm St. on north side of New Haven Green.*

WORTH NOTING

Beinecke Rare Book and Manuscript Library. The collections here include a Gutenberg Bible, illuminated manuscripts, and original Audubon bird prints, but the building is almost as much of an attraction—the walls are made of marble cut so thin that the light shines through, making the interior a breathtaking sight on sunny days. ⊠ *121 Wall St.* ☎ *203/432–2977* ⊕ *www.library.yale.edu/beinecke* 🎟 *Free* ⊗ *Mon.–Thurs. 9–7, Fri. 9–5, Sat. noon–5.*

New Haven Green. Bordered on the west side by the Yale campus, the green is a fine example of early urban planning. As early as 1638, village elders set aside the 16-acre plot as a town common. Three

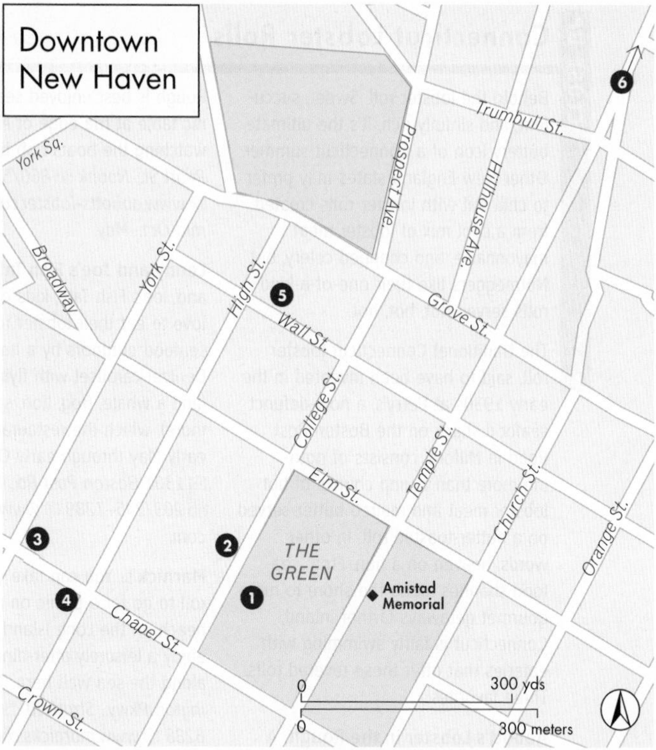

early-19th-century churches—the Gothic-style **Trinity Episcopal Church,** the Georgian-style **Center Congregational Church,** and the predominantly Federal-style **United Church**—contribute to its present appeal. ✉ *Between Church and College Sts.*

Peabody Museum of Natural History. Opened in 1876, the Peabody, with more than 11 million specimens, is one of the largest natural history museums in the nation. In addition to exhibits on Andean, Mesoamerican, and Pacific cultures, the venerable museum has an excellent collection of birds, including a stuffed dodo and passenger pigeon. The main attractions for children and amateur paleontologists alike are some of the world's earliest reconstructions of dinosaur skeletons. ✉ *170 Whitney Ave.* ☎ *203/432–5050* 🌐 *www.peabody.yale.edu* *$9* ⏲ *Mon.–Sat. 10–5, Sun. noon–5.*

Yale University Art Gallery. Since its founding in 1832, this art gallery has amassed more than 200,000 works from around the world, dating from ancient Egypt to the present day. Highlights include works by Vincent van Gogh, Edouard Manet, Claude Monet, Pablo Picasso, Winslow Homer, and Thomas Eakins, as well as Etruscan and Greek vases, Chinese ceramics and bronzes, early Italian paintings, and a collection of American decorative arts that is considered one of the world's finest. The gallery's landmark main building is also of note. Opened in 1953, it was

Louis I. Kahn's first major commission and the first modernist building on the neo-Gothic Yale campus. Over the years, its extensive open spaces were subdivided into galleries, classrooms, and offices, but a major renovation, completed in 2006, restored it to Kahn's original conception. ⊠ *1111 Chapel St.* ☎ *203/432–0600* ⊕ *www.yale.edu/ artgallery* ⊡ *Free* ☾ *Sept.–June, Tues., Wed., Fri., and Sat. 10–5, Thurs. 10–8, Sun. 1–6; July and Aug., Tues.–Sat. 10–5, Sun. 1–6.*

NIGHTLIFE AND THE ARTS
NIGHTLIFE
Anna Liffey's. This is one of the city's liveliest Irish pubs. ⊠ *17 Whitney Ave.* ☎ *203/773–1776* ⊕ *www. annaliffeys.com.*

> **DID YOU KNOW?**
>
> Yale University—including both undergraduate and graduate schools—has matriculated five U.S. presidents (William Howard Taft, Gerald Ford, Bill Clinton, and both George Bushes). Other standouts have included commentator William F. Buckley, writers James Fenimore Cooper and Tom Wolfe, artist Mark Rothko, composer Cole Porter, cartoonist Garry Trudeau, lexicographer Noah Webster, architect Eero Saarinen, and actors Jodie Foster, Edward Norton, Meryl Streep, Sam Waterston, and Sigourney Weaver.

BAR. This spot is a cross between a nightclub, a brick-oven pizzeria, and a brewpub. ⊠ *254 Crown St.* ☎ *203/495–1111* ⊕ *www.barnightclub. com.*

Toad's Place of New Haven. Alternative and traditional rock bands play at Toad's Place. ⊠ *300 York St.* ☎ *203/624–8623* ⊕ *www.toadsplace.com.*

THE ARTS **Long Wharf Theatre.** The well-regarded Long Wharf Theatre presents works by contemporary writers and revivals of neglected classics. ⊠ *222 Sargent Dr.* ☎ *203/787–4282* ⊕ *www.longwharf.org.*

New Haven Symphony Orchestra. The New Haven Symphony Orchestra plays at Yale University's Woolsey Hall. ☎ *203/865–0831* ⊕ *www. newhavensymphony.org.*

Woolsey Hall. Built in 1901 to commemorate Yale's bicentennial, Woolsey Hall hosts performances by the New Haven Symphony Orchestra, the Philharmonia Orchestra of Yale, and recitals on the Newberry Memorial Organ. ⊠ *500 College St., at Grove St.*

Shubert Performing Arts Center. Broadway musicals and dramas plus dance and classical-music performances are held here. ⊠ *247 College St.* ☎ *203/624–1825* ⊕ *www.shubert.com.*

Yale Repertory Theatre. The theater premieres new plays and mounts fresh interpretations of the classics. ⊠ *1120 Chapel St.* ☎ *203/432–1234* ⊕ *www.yale.edu/yalerep.*

Yale School of Music. Most events in the impressive roster of performances by the Yale School of Music take place in Sprague Hall. ⊠ *98 Wall St.* ☎ *203/432–4158* ⊕ *www.yale.edu/music.*

Sprague Memorial Hall. Many Yale School of Music performances are held here in the Morse Recital Hall. ⊠ *470 College St., at Wall St.*

SHOPPING

Atticus Bookstore & Café. This independent bookseller in the heart of Yale University offers a full café menu you can enjoy while devouring the latest bestseller. ✉ *1082 Chapel St.* ☎ *203/776–4040* ⊕ *atticusbookstorecafe.com.*

Chapel Street. This street, near the town green, has a pleasing assortment of shops and eateries. ✉ *Chapel St., btwn. Park and Church St.*

WHERE TO EAT

$$
WINE BAR
✕ **Barcelona.** There's no need to take a transatlantic flight for authentic Spanish cuisine when you can feast on tapas right here in New Haven. Barcelona has locations throughout Connecticut, and this outpost delivers in both dining and decor (think a 200-bottle wine cellar, open kitchen, and massive wall-sized mural of a Spanish bullfighter). There are entrées on the menu, but the tapas are a better bet: the chorizo with sweet and sour figs offers an intensely rich bite; the organic greens with goat cheese croquettes is a nice balance of tastes and textures; and the *gambas al ajillo* (sautéed shrimp with garlic, sherry, and *guindilla* peppers) is full of flavor. $ *Average main: $22* ✉ *155 Temple St., in the Omni New Haven Hotel, Downtown* ☎ *203/848–3000* ⊕ *www.barcelonawinebar.com* ⌂ *Reservations essential* ☾ *No lunch.*

$$$
MALAYSIAN
✕ **Bentara.** With so many wonderful Asian restaurants in New Haven, it's hard to single out one stellar selection, but Bentara has plenty going for it—a cuisine (Malaysian) somewhat uncommon in America, a charismatic and talented chef with a penchant for innovative preparations, and a charmed setting inside a vintage redbrick building on an up-and-coming downtown street. Apart from traditional noodle stir-fries and soups, watch for such tempting dishes as grilled salmon with a coconut-turmeric-lime sauce. $ *Average main: $25* ✉ *76 Orange St.* ☎ *203/562–2511* ⊕ *www.bentara.com.*

$$
AMERICAN
✕ **Caseus Fromagerie Bistro.** The aroma of high-quality aged cheese will hit you as you walk into this two-level bistro and fromagerie. On the bottom floor you can buy cheeses to-go, in addition to other goodies like artisanal chocolates, jams, and olive oils. Visit the upstairs bistro to linger over a meal centered on the key ingredient. The decadent mac and cheese is made in three different varieties (chevre, raclette, and comte), the grilled cheese is said to be made with the bistro's "best melting cheeses," and the onion soup gratin is topped with no fewer than six varieties. All the ingredients are all natural and organic, and dishes that do not include cheese, like the half chicken roasted with fresh thyme butter or the heirloom tomato and seared day-boat scallops, are equally delightful. $ *Average main: $20* ✉ *93 Whitney Ave., New Haven* ☎ *203/624–3373* ⊕ *www.caseusnewhaven.com* ☾ *Closed Sun.*

$$$
AMERICAN
✕ **Heirloom.** Heirloom isn't your typical hotel restaurant. In half of the lobby of The Study hotel, this contemporary American eatery has casually refined decor and a chalkboard menu. Dine during the day if you want to enjoy the sunlight pouring in through the floor-to-ceiling windows. Menu highlights include perfectly cooked Atlantic salmon with oyster mushrooms, cippolini onions, and sorrel sauce and the crowd-pleasing lobster fried rice with sweet egg and vegetable stir-fry. The bar is great for a pre- or post-dinner cocktail. $ *Average main: $25* ✉ *1157*

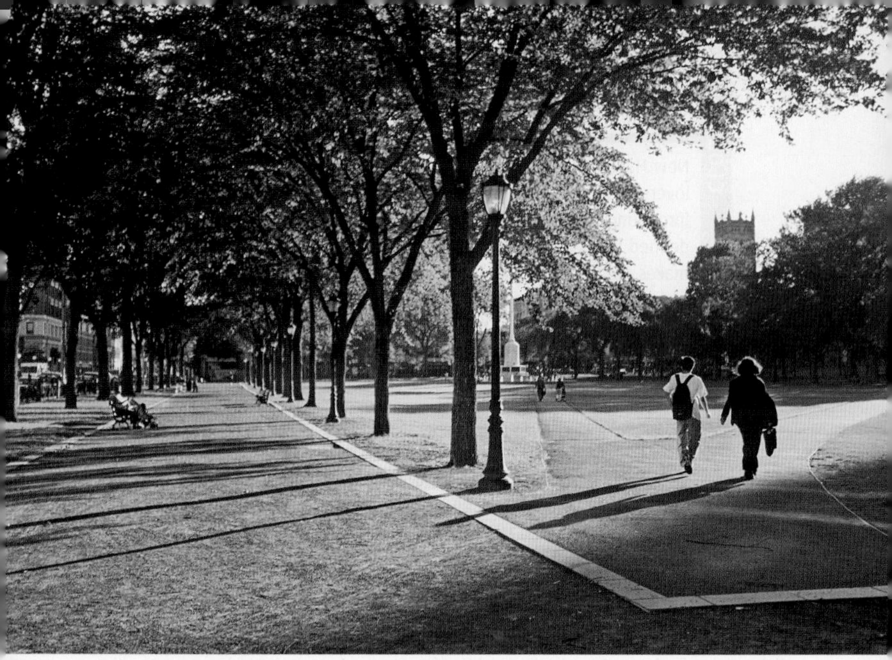

Yale's leafy campus is home to many Neo-Gothic buildings.

Chapel St., at The Study at Yale, Downtown ☎ *203/503–3900* 🌐 *www.studyhotels.com.*

$$$$ SPANISH Fodor's Choice ★ 🍴 **Ibiza.** Owner Ignacio Blanco and chef Luis Bollo are *the* names in Spanish cuisine in the state. Tall ceilings, multipaned windows, exposed brick, and vibrant murals create a backdrop for such extraordinary dishes as Catalan noodle paella with codfish, salmon, shrimp, bay scallops, and cockles, and ravioli stuffed with braised oxtail and wild mushrooms, with sweet potato purée and scallion vinaigrette. A tasting menu is available Monday–Saturday. [$] *Average main: $32* ✉ *39 High St.* ☎ *203/865–1933* 🌐 *www.ibizanewhaven.com* 🕒 *Closed Sun. No lunch Fri.–Wed.*

$ AMERICAN 🍴 **Louis' Lunch.** This all-American luncheonette on the National Register of Historic Places claims to be the birthplace of the American hamburger. Its first-rate burgers are cooked in an old-fashioned, upright broiler and served with either a slice of tomato or cheese on two slices of toast. As most customers who come from far and wide for these tasty morsels agree, it doesn't get much better than that. Louis' is open until 2 am Thursday–Saturday and is cash only. [$] *Average main: $10* ✉ *263 Crown St., Downtown* ☎ *203/562–5507* 🌐 *www.louislunch.com* 💳 *No credit cards* 🕒 *Closed Sun. and Mon. No dinner Tues. and Wed.*

$$ PIZZA ★ 🍴 **Pepe's Pizzeria.** Does this place serve the best pizza in the world, as so many reviewers claim? If it doesn't, it comes close. Pizza is the only thing prepared here—try the justifiably famous white-clam pie (it's especially good with bacon on top). Expect to wait an hour or more for a table—or, on weekend evenings, come after 10. [$] *Average main: $16* ✉ *157 Wooster St., Downtown* ☎ *203/865–5762* 🌐 *www.pepespizzeria.com* ✍ *Reservations not accepted* 💳 *No credit cards.*

CLOSE UP

New Haven Pizza 101

New Haven has been on pizza-lovers' radar for decades. The apizza (pronounced "ah-beetz" by locals) is defined by its thin, chewy crust, which makes for a unique—and, some would argue, superior—pizza experience. From white clam pies to mashed potato–topped concoctions, here are our picks for the area's best pizzas.

Frank Pepe's bacon spinach pie.

FRANK PEPE PIZZERIA NAPOLETANA

This is where it all began: in 1925 Frank Pepe opened this eponymous pizza place (✉ 157 Wooster St. ☎ 203/865–5762 ⊕ www.pepespizzeria.com) and created what would become the iconic New Haven–style pizza. Eager customers line up for hours to get a taste of the famous thin-crust pies, in particular, Frank Pepe's pièce de résistance—the white clam pizza. This masterful creation consists of olive oil, garlic, oregano, grated Parmesan cheese, and little-neck clams atop a thin crust.

SALLY'S APIZZA

Just two blocks from Frank Pepe's on Wooster Street (considered to be New Haven's Little Italy) is Sally's Apizza (✉ 237 Wooster Street ☎ 203/624–5271 ⊕ www.sallysapizza.com), a rival of Frank Pepe's since 1938, when Salvatore Consiglio, Pepe's nephew, decided to break away from his relatives and open his own pizzeria. The result of this family feud is two competing pizzerias and a divided city: those who believe Frank Pepe's serves the best pizza and those who are devoted to Sally's. If you want to judge for yourself, head to Frank Pepe's first; Sally's doesn't open until 5 (and is closed Monday).

MODERN APIZZA

It's not what Modern Apizza (✉ 874 State St. ☎ 203/776–5306 ⊕ www.modernapizza.com) has that sets it apart from the rest, but rather what it doesn't have: toppings. The pizzeria's signature "plain" pie is a thin crust with a layer of tomato sauce and just a sprinkling of Parmesan cheese. If you want mootz (mozzarella in New Haven–speak), then you have to ask for it. But why mess with a classic? Modern Apizza has been serving its signature pies since 1934, and business is still booming.

BAR

It doesn't surprise us that BAR (✉ 254 Crown St. ☎ 203/495–8924 ⊕ www.barnightclub.com), a nightclub-cum-microbrewery, is in a college town and that its signature pie just happens to be bacon-and-mashed-potato-topped pizza—a college student's comfort-food dream. BAR is a relative newcomer (it opened in 1991), but it's giving the old-timers a run for their money. If you want to taste what this place does best, push aside any creeping thoughts of carbs and calories, and go for the masterpiece, a slightly charred, crispy-crusted pizza, topped with a thin layer of creamy mashed potatoes and bits of bacon.

—Carolyn Galgano

$ **Sugar Bakery and Sweet Shop.** Winning Food Network's *Cupcake Wars*
BAKERY put this little East Haven bakery on the map. Stop in to try one of the
25 different types of cupcakes rotated daily. With flavors like cannoli,
cookie dough, and the Elvis (banana cupcake with peanut-butter-and-
jelly-butter cream frosting) you're bound to find a cupcake or five to
fuel your perfect sugar high. $ *Average main: $10* ⊠ *422 Main St., East
Haven* ☎ *203/469–0851* ⊕ *www.thesugarbakery.com.*

WHERE TO STAY
For expanded hotel reviews, visit Fodors.com.

$$$ **Omni Hotels & Resorts.** This comfortable hotel is near the heart of
HOTEL New Haven and outfitted with all the modern amenities. **Pros:** upscale
furnishings; nice gym and spa; walking distance from many shops and
restaurants. **Cons:** somewhat steep rates; in busy part of downtown.
$ *Rooms from: $200* ⊠ *155 Temple St.* ☎ *203/772–6664* ⊕ *www.
omnihotels.com* ↪ *299 rooms, 7 suites* ⦿ *No meals.*

$$$ **The Study at Yale.** Overlooking the sea of brick buildings that make up
HOTEL Yale University, this boutique hotel is designed to fit in with its erudite
surroundings. **Pros:** destination restaurant; attentive staff. **Cons:** small
gym; only one computer in the lobby. $ *Rooms from: $219* ⊠ *1157
Chapel Street, New Haven* ☎ *203/503–3900* ⊕ *www.studyhotels.com*
↪ *117 rooms, 7 suites* ⦿ *No meals.*

MADISON

5 miles east of Guilford, 62 miles northeast of Greenwich.

Coastal Madison has an understated charm. Ice cream parlors, antiques
stores, and quirky gift boutiques prosper along U.S. 1, the town's main
street. Stately Colonial homes line the town green, site of many a summer antiques fair and arts-and-crafts festival. The Madison shoreline,
particularly the white stretch of sand known as Hammonasset Beach
and its parallel boardwalk, draws visitors year-round.

GETTING HERE AND AROUND
Madison is accessible by car and train. Drive north on I–95 from New
Haven, or take the Shore Line East train to the Madison stop.

SPORTS AND THE OUTDOORS
★ **Hammonasset Beach State Park.** Hammonasset Beach State Park, the
largest of the state's shoreline sanctuaries, has 2 miles of white-sand
beaches, a top-notch nature center, excellent birding, and a hugely popular campground with about 550 sites. ⊠ *I–95, Exit 62, 1288 Boston
Post Rd.* ☎ *203/245–2785 park, 203/245–1817 campground* 🖾 *Park
$13–$22 mid-Apr.–mid-Oct., free off-season* ☉ *Park daily 8 am–dusk.*

WHERE TO STAY
For expanded hotel reviews, visit Fodors.com.

$$ **The Inn at Lafayette.** Skylights, painted murals, and handcrafted wood-
B&B/INN work are among the design accents at this hostelry in a converted 1830s
church. **Pros:** steps from shopping and restaurants; excellent restau-
rant. **Cons:** busy street. $ *Rooms from: $160* ⊠ *725 Boston Post Rd.*
☎ *203/245–7773, 866/623–7498* ⊕ *www.innatlafayette.com* ↪ *5
rooms* ⦿ *Breakfast.*

OLD SAYBROOK

9 miles east of Madison, 29 miles east of New Haven.

Old Saybrook, once a lively shipbuilding and fishing town, bustles with summer vacationers and antiques shoppers. Its downtown is an especially pleasing place for a window-shopping stroll. At the end of the afternoon, stop at the old-fashioned soda fountain, where you can share a sundae with your sweetie.

GETTING HERE AND AROUND

Drive north on I–95 to Route 154 to reach Old Saybrook. The town is also serviced by Amtrak's Northeast Regional trains, and the Shore Line East commuter trains.

SHOPPING

Beautiful Impressions. In this historic former general store and pharmacy, you'll find rubber stamps and inks along with ice-cream sodas for sale. ✉ *30 Westbrook Pl., Westbrook* ☎ *860/399–8855* 🌐 *www.beautiful-impressions.com.*

North Cove Outfitters. This is Connecticut's version of L.L. Bean. ✉ *75 Main St.* ☎ *866/437–6707* 🌐 *www.northcove.com.*

Saybrook Country Barn. You'll find everything you need to outfit a home in country style, from tiger-maple dining-room tables to hand-painted pottery. ✉ *2 Main St.* ☎ *860/388–0891* 🌐 *www.saybrookcountrybarn.com.*

WHERE TO EAT AND STAY

For expanded hotel reviews, visit Fodors.com.

$$$ FRENCH ★ 🍴 **Café Routier.** Grilled trout with lyonnaise potatoes and a whole-grain mustard sauce, fried oysters with a chipotle rémoulade, and a duck-and-wild-mushroom ragout are among the favorites at this bistro, which specializes in regional favorites and seasonal dishes. [$] *Average main: $26* ✉ *1353 Boston Post Rd., 5 miles west of Old Saybrook, Westbrook* ☎ *860/399–8700* 🌐 *www.caferoutier.com* ⏲ *No lunch.*

$$$$ HOTEL ★ 🏨 **Saybrook Point Inn & Spa.** Rooms at the cushy Saybrook are furnished mainly in 18th-century style, with reproductions of British furniture and impressionist art—many have fireplaces. **Pros:** swanky rooms; top-notch service; superb restaurant. **Cons:** pricey; you'll need a car to get to downtown shops and dining. [$] *Rooms from: $279* ✉ *2 Bridge St.* ☎ *860/395–2000, 800/243–0212* 🌐 *www.saybrook.com* 🛏 *82 rooms, some condos also available* 🍽 *No meals.*

OLD LYME

4 miles east of Old Saybrook, 40 miles south of Hartford.

Old Lyme, on the other side of the Connecticut River from Old Saybrook, is renowned among art lovers for its past as the home of the Lyme Art Colony, the most famous gathering of impressionist painters in the United States. Artists continue to be attracted to the area for its lovely countryside and shoreline. The town also has handsome old houses, many built for sea captains.

GETTING HERE AND AROUND

Old Lyme is best reached by car. Drive north on I–95 from Old Saybrook.

EXPLORING

Fodor's Choice ★ **Florence Griswold Museum.** Central to Old Lyme's artistic reputation is this grand late-Georgian-style mansion owned by Miss Florence Griswold that served as a boardinghouse for members of the Lyme Art Colony in the first decades of the 20th century. When artists such as Willard Metcalf, Clark Voorhees, Childe Hassam, and Henry Ward Ranger flocked to the area to paint its varied landscape, Miss Florence offered housing as well as artistic encouragement. The house was turned into a museum in 1947 and underwent a major restoration completed in 2006 to restore it to its 1910 appearance, when the colony was in full flower (clues to the house's layout and decor in that era were gleaned from members' paintings). The museum's 10,000-square-foot Krieble Gallery, on the riverfront, hosts changing exhibitions of American art. ✉ *96 Lyme St.* ☎ *860/434–5542* 🌐 *www.florencegriswoldmuseum.org* 🎟 *$9* 🕒 *Tues.–Sat. 10–5, Sun. 1–5.*

WHERE TO STAY

For expanded hotel reviews, visit Fodors.com.

$$$$ B&B/INN Fodor's Choice ★ 🏨 **Bee and Thistle Inn and Spa.** Behind a weathered stone wall in the Old Lyme historic district is a three-story 1756 Colonial house with 5½ acres of broad lawns, formal gardens, and herbaceous borders. **Pros:** a short walk from Griswold Museum; lovely old home; fantastic restaurant. **Cons:** can hear noise from I–95; historic rooms don't have many modern amenities. [$] *Rooms from: $242* ✉ *100 Lyme St.* ☎ *860/434–1667, 800/622–4946* 🌐 *www.beeandthistleinn.com* 🛏 *11 rooms* 🍴 *Breakfast.*

NORWICH

15 miles north of New London, 37 miles southeast of Hartford.

Outstanding Georgian and Victorian structures surround the triangular town green in Norwich, and more can be found downtown by the Thames River. The former mill town is hard at work at restoration and rehabilitation efforts. So eye-catching are these brightly colored structures that the Paint Quality Institute has designated the town one of the "Prettiest Painted Places in New England."

GETTING HERE AND AROUND

To reach Norwich from the coast by car, take I–95 to I–395 north to Route 82 east.

EXPLORING

Slater Memorial Museum & Converse Art Gallery. The Slater Memorial Museum & Converse Art Gallery, on the grounds of the Norwich Free Academy, houses one of the country's largest collections of Greek, Roman, and Renaissance plaster casts of some of the world's greatest sculptures, including the Winged Victory, Venus de Milo, and Michelangelo's *Pietà*. The Converse Art Gallery, adjacent to the museum, hosts six to eight shows a year, many of which focus on Connecticut artists and craftsmen as well as student work. ✉ *108 Crescent St.* ☎ *860/887–2506* 🌐 *www.norwichfreeacademy.com* 🎟 *$3* 🕒 *Tues.–Fri. 9–4, weekends 1–4.*

WHERE TO STAY

For expanded hotel reviews, visit Fodors.com.

$$$$ B&B/INN 🏨 **Spa at Norwich Inn.** This Georgian-style inn is on 42 rolling acres right by the Thames River. **Pros:** one of the best spas in the state; beautiful grounds. **Cons:** oriented toward spa guests; tired room decor in need of an upgrade. [$] *Rooms from: $339* ✉ *607 W. Thames St. (Rte. 32)* ☎ *860/425–3500, 800/275–4772* 🌐 *www.thespaatnorwichinn.com* 🛏 *49 rooms, 54 villas* 🍴 *No meals.*

LEDYARD

10 miles south of Norwich, 37 miles southeast of Hartford.

Ledyard, in the woods of southeastern Connecticut between Norwich and the coastline, is known first and foremost for the vast Mashantucket Pequot Tribal Nation's Foxwoods Resort Casino. With the opening of the excellent Mashantucket Pequot Museum & Research Center, however, the tribe has moved beyond gaming to educating the public about its history, as well as that of other Northeast Woodland tribes.

GETTING HERE AND AROUND

Driving is probably the best way to get to Ledyard; take I–95 to Route 2 west. If you are only planning to visit Foxwoods, there are many coach bus companies that run charter trips directly there. See 🌐 *www.foxwoods.com/bybus.aspx* for more information.

EXPLORING

Fodor's Choice ★ 👶 **Mashantucket Pequot Museum & Research Center.** A large complex a mile from the Foxwoods Resort Casino, this museum brings the history and culture of Northeastern Woodland tribes in general and the Pequots in particular to life in exquisite detail. Some highlights include re-creations of an 18,000-year-old glacial crevasse that you can travel into, a caribou hunt from 11,000 years ago, and a 17th-century fort. Perhaps most remarkable is a sprawling "immersion environment"—a 16th-century village with more than 50 life-size figures and real smells and sounds. Audio devices provide detailed information about the sights. The research center, open to scholars and schoolchildren free, holds some 150,000 volumes. Also on-site is a full-service restaurant that serves both Native and traditional American cuisine. ✉ *110 Pequot Tr., Mashantucket* ☎ *800/411–9671* 🌐 *www.pequotmuseum.org* 🎟 *$15* 🕒 *Wed.–Sat. 10–4.*

TOP EXPERIENCE: CASINOS

Foxwoods Resort Casino. On the Mashantucket Pequot Indian Reservation near Ledyard, Foxwoods is the world's largest resort casino. The skylighted compound draws 40,000-plus visitors daily to its more than 6,200 slot machines, 380 gaming tables, 3,200-seat high-stakes bingo parlor, poker rooms, Keno station, theater, and Race Book room. This 4.7-million-square-foot complex includes the Grand Pequot Tower, the Great Cedar Hotel, and the Two Trees Inn, which have more than 1,400 rooms combined, as well as a full-service spa, retail concourse, food court, and numerous restaurants. In spring 2008 Foxwood unveiled the MGM Grand at Foxwoods, an ultraluxury branch of the Las Vegas gaming resort that added another 825 posh rooms and suites, plus several notable restaurants. ✉ *350 Trolley Line Blvd., Mashantucket* ☎ *800/369–9663* 🌐 *www.foxwoods.com* 🕒 *Daily 24 hrs.*

Mohegan Sun. The Mohegan Indians, known as the Wolf People, operate this casino west of Ledyard and just south of Norwich, which has more than 300,000 square feet of gaming space, including 6,000 slot machines and more than 250 gaming tables. Also part of the complex: the Kids Quest family entertainment center, a 130,000-square-foot shopping mall, more than 30 restaurants and food-and-beverage suppliers, and a 34-story, 1,200-room luxury hotel with a full-service spa. Free entertainment is presented nightly in the Wolf Den; a 10,000-seat arena hosts major national acts and is home to the WNBA's Connecticut Sun; and a swanky 300-seat cabaret hosts intimate shows and comedy acts. Mohegan After Dark is a 22,000-square-foot complex with three nightclubs. ✉ *1 Mohegan Sun Blvd., off I–395, Uncasville* ☎ *888/226–7711* 🌐 *www.mohegansun.com* 🕒 *Daily 24 hrs.*

5

WHERE TO EAT

$$ AMERICAN ★ 🍴 **Trade Winds at Stonecroft.** The sunny dining room at this peaceful, elegant 1807 inn serves creative country fare at resonable prices. Favorites from the seasonally changing menu have included curried sweet-corn-and-lump-crab bisque and seared double-thick pork chops with Granny Smith apple and raisin chutney. [$] *Average main: $19* ✉ *515 Pumpkin Hill Rd.* ☎ *860/572–0771, 800/772–0774* 🌐 *www.stonecroft.com* 🕒 *Closed Mon. and Tues. No lunch.*

WHERE TO STAY

For expanded hotel reviews, visit Fodors.com.

$$$ HOTEL 🏨 **Grand Pequot Tower.** Mere steps from the gaming floors, this expansive 17-story showpiece contains deluxe rooms and suites in pleasantly neutral tones. **Pros:** elegant rooms; easy access to the casino; nice views from upper floors. **Cons:** not much to entice if you're not gambling. [$] *Rooms from: $199* ✉ *350 Trolley Line Blvd., at Foxwoods Resort Casino, Mashantucket* ☎ *860/312–5044, 800/369–9663* 🌐 *www.foxwoods.com* 🛏 *824 rooms* 🍽 *No meals.*

$$$ HOTEL 🏨 **MGM Grand at Foxwoods.** This lavishly appointed hotel, which opened in 2008, offers stylish accommodations just seconds away from the casino's action. **Pros:** elegant rooms; easy access to the casino; nice views from upper floors. **Cons:** if you're not a gambler, this might not be your scene. [$] *Rooms from: $199* ✉ *350 Trolley Line Blvd., at Foxwoods Resort Casino, Mashantucket* ☎ *800/369–9663* 🌐 *www.foxwoods.com* 🛏 *825 rooms* 🍽 *No meals.*

$$$ HOTEL ★ 🏨 **Mohegan Sun.** The emphasis of this 34-story hotel is on luxury. **Pros:** numerous fine restaurants are steps from lobby; incredible views from upper floors; excellent spa and fitness center. **Cons:** better like casinos. [$] *Rooms from: $199* ✉ *1 Mohegan Sun Blvd., Uncasville* ☎ *888/777–7922* 🌐 *www.mohegansun.com* 🛏 *1,020 rooms, 180 suites* 🍽 *No meals.*

$$$
B&B/INN
★

Stonecroft. A sunny 1807 Georgian Colonial on 6½ acres of green meadows, woodlands, and rambling stone walls is the center of Stonecroft. **Pros:** scenic and verdant grounds; cheerful service. **Cons:** secluded location requires a car to get around. $ *Rooms from: $179* ⊠ *515 Pumpkin Hill Rd.* ☎ *860/572–0771, 800/772–0774* ⊕ *www.stonecroft. com* 🖙 *10 rooms* ⏏ *Breakfast.*

MYSTIC

8 miles east of Groton.

Mystic has devoted itself to recapturing the seafaring spirit of the 18th and 19th centuries. Some of the nation's fastest clipper ships were built here in the mid-19th century; today's Mystic Seaport is the state's most popular museum. Downtown Mystic has an interesting collection of boutiques and galleries.

GETTING HERE AND AROUND

By car, take I–95 to Route 27 south to reach Mystic. Amtrak's Northeast Regional train service also stops here.

ESSENTIALS

Visitor Information Mystic Country–Eastern Regional Tourism District ⊠ *27 Coogan Blvd., Bldg. 3A* ☎ *860/536–8822* ⊕ *mysticcountry.com.*

EXPLORING

Fodor'sChoice
★
☾

Mystic Aquarium. The animals here go through 1,000 pounds of herring, capelin, and squid each day. Juno, a male beluga whale, is responsible for consuming 85 pounds of that himself. He calls the aquarium's Arctic Coast exhibit home. This exhibit—which holds 800,000 gallons of water, measures 165 feet at its longest point by 85 feet at its widest point, and ranges from just inches to 16½ feet deep—is just a small part of this revered establishment. ■ TIP→ **For an unforgettable up-close-and-personal experience with a beluga whale, take part in the Train-A-Whale or Beluga Encounter program ($145). Both allow you to touch and interact with these magnificent animals and learn more about how trainers teach the whales.** You can also check out world-renowned ocean explorer Dr. Robert Ballard's Institute for Exploration and its new Nautilus Live Theater which brings live video from the *E/V Nautilus* ship and and two-way communications as it explores wrecks. The new Titanic–12,450 Feet Below exhibition captures the excitement of finding the *Titanic* and its history. You can also see African penguins, harbor seals, graceful sea horses, Pacific octopuses, and sand tiger sharks. ■ TIP→ **Try not to miss feeding time at the Ray Touch Pool, where rays suction sand eels right out of your hand.** ⊠ *55 Coogan Blvd.* ☎ *860/572–5955* ⊕ *www. mysticaquarium.org* 🎟 *$29* ⊗ *Mar., Nov. daily 9–4; Apr.–Oct., daily 9–5, Dec.–Feb., daily 10–4.*

Fodor'sChoice
★
☾

Mystic Seaport. The world's largest maritime museum, Mystic Seaport encompasses 37 acres of indoor and outdoor exhibits with more than 1 million artifacts that provide a fascinating look at the area's rich shipbuilding and seafaring heritage. In the narrow streets and historic homes and buildings (some moved here from other sites), craftspeople give demonstrations of open-hearth cooking, weaving, and other skills

Mystic Seaport includes a number of vessels you can tour, including the *Charles W. Morgan*.

of yesteryear. The museum's more than 500 vessels include the *Charles W. Morgan*, the last remaining wooden whaling ship afloat, and the 1882 training ship *Joseph Conrad*. You can climb aboard for a look or for sail-setting demonstrations and reenactments of whale hunts. Special events are held throughout the year. Children younger than five are admitted free. ⊠ *75 Greenmanville Ave., 1 miles south of I–95, Exit 90* ☎ *860/572–0711* ⊕ *www.mysticseaport.org* ⊠ *$24* ⊙ *Apr.–Oct., daily 9–5; Nov., daily 10–4, Dec.–Mar., Thurs.–Sun. 10–4.*

SHOPPING

Finer Line Gallery. This gallery exhibits nautical and other prints, including some local scenes. ⊠ *48 W. Main St.* ☎ *860/536–8339* ⊕ *www.finerlinegallery.com.*

Olde Mistick Village. A re-creation of an early 1700s American village, Olde Mistick Village has more than 50 shops that sell everything from crafts and clothing to souvenirs and munchies. ⊠ *Coogan Blvd., off I–95, Exit 90* ☎ *860/536–4941* ⊕ *www.oldemistickvillage.com.*

Whyevernot. This is a colorful spot for clothing, jewelry, pottery, linens, handmade papers, and much more. ⊠ *17 W. Main St.* ☎ *860/536–6209* ⊕ *www.whyevernot.com.*

WHERE TO EAT

$$
SEAFOOD
Fodor's Choice
★

✕ **Abbott's Lobster in the Rough.** If you want some of the state's best lobsters, mussels, crabs, or clams on the half shell, head down to this unassuming seaside lobster shack in sleepy Noank, a few miles southwest of Mystic. Most seating is outdoors or on the dock, where the views of Noank Harbor are magnificent. $ *Average main: $18* ⊠ *117 Pearl St., Noank* ☎ *860/536–7719* ⊕ *www.abbotts-lobster.com* ⊙ *Closed*

Columbus Day–1st Fri. in May and weekdays Labor Day–Columbus Day ☞ *BYOB.*

$$$ SEAFOOD ★ 🍴 **Go Fish.** In this town by the sea, one hungers for seafood, and this sophisticated restaurant captures all the tastes—and colors—of the ocean. There's a raw bar, wine bar, coffee bar, and a black granite sushi bar, which, with its myriad tiny, briny morsels, is worth the trip in itself. The glossy blue tables in the two large dining rooms perfectly complement the signature saffron-scented shellfish bouillabaisse. The menu lists options for vegetarians and carnivores as well, but the lobster ravioli in a light cream sauce is a must-try. [$] *Average main: $25* ✉ *Olde Mistick Village, Coogan Blvd., off I–95, Exit 90* ☎ *860/536–2662* 🌐 *www.gofishct.com.*

SETTING SAIL AT MYSTIC SEAPORT

Kids can learn the ropes—literally—of what it takes to be a sailor during Mystic Seaport's many sailing classes and camps. Younger children and those who wish to stay on shore can sign up for courses on building boats (including how to varnish them), blacksmithing, carving, and roping (from knotting to splicing). The Seaport's planetarium also offers instruction on navigating a ship by the stars. Prices for classes vary. Call Mystic Seaport (☎ *860/572–5322*) or see its website (🌐 *www.mysticseaport.org*) for details.

WHERE TO STAY

For expanded hotel reviews, visit Fodors.com.

$$$ B&B/INN 🏨 **Old Mystic Inn.** This cozy inn, built in 1784, was once a bookshop specializing in antique books and maps. **Pros:** beautifully kept historic house; quiet neighborhood; friendly host. **Cons:** need a car to get into downtown. [$] *Rooms from: $205* ✉ *52 Main St.* ☎ *860/572–9422* 🌐 *www.oldmysticinn.com* 🛏 *8 rooms* 🍴 *Breakfast.*

$$$ HOTEL 🏨 **Whaler's Inn.** A perfect compromise between a chain motel and a country inn, this complex with public rooms furnished with lovely antiques is one block from the Mystic River and downtown. **Pros:** within walking distance of downtown shopping; excellent restaurant. **Cons:** rooms in motel-style building have less character; on a busy street. [$] *Rooms from: $190* ✉ *20 E. Main St.* ☎ *860/536–1506, 800/243–2588* 🌐 *www.whalersinnmystic.com* 🛏 *49 rooms* 🍴 *Breakfast.*

STONINGTON

7 miles southeast of Mystic, 57 miles east of New Haven.

The pretty village of Stonington pokes into Fishers Island Sound. A quiet fishing community clustered around white-spired churches, Stonington is far less commercial than Mystic. In the 19th century, though, it was a bustling whaling, sealing, and transportation center. Historic buildings line the town green and border both sides of Water Street up to the imposing Old Lighthouse Museum.

GETTING HERE AND AROUND

From Mystic by car, take Route 1 north (you'll actually be heading due east so don't be concerned) to Route 1A.

EXPLORING

Old Lighthouse Museum. This museum occupies a lighthouse that was built in 1823 and moved to higher ground 17 years later. Climb to the top of the tower for a spectacular view of Long Island Sound and three states. Six rooms of exhibits depict the varied history of the small coastal town. ✉ *7 Water St.* 📞 *860/535–1440* ⊕ *www.stoningtonhistory.org/light.htm* 💲 *$9* 🕙 *May–Oct., daily 10–6; Nov. and Apr., weekends 10–4.*

Stonington Vineyards. At this small coastal winery, you can browse through the works of local artists in the gallery or enjoy a picnic lunch on the grounds. The vineyard's Seaport White, a Vidal-Chardonnay blend, is a nice accompaniment. ✉ *523 Taugwonk Rd.* 📞 *860/535–1222, 800/421–9463* ⊕ *www.stoningtonvineyards.com* 💲 *$12 tasting, free tour* 🕙 *May–Nov., daily 11–5, tours at 2; Jan.–Apr. weekdays 12–4, weekends 11–5.*

WHERE TO STAY

For expanded hotel reviews, visit Fodors.com.

$$$
B&B/INN
Fodor's Choice
★

Inn at Stonington. The views of Stonington Harbor and Fishers Island Sound are spectacular from this waterfront inn in the heart of Stonington Village. **Pros:** smartly furnished rooms; walking distance from village shops and dining; great water views. **Cons:** no restaurant on-site. 💲 *Rooms from: $220* ✉ *60 Water St.* 📞 *860/535–2000* ⊕ *www.innatstonington.com* 🛏 *18 rooms* 🍽 *Breakfast.*

THE QUIET CORNER

Few visitors to Connecticut experience the old-fashioned ways of the state's "Quiet Corner," a vast patch of sparsely populated towns that seem a world away from the rest of the state. The Quiet Corner has a reclusive allure: people used to leave New York City for the Litchfield Hills; now many leave for northeastern Connecticut, where the stretch of Route 169 from Brooklyn past Woodstock has been named a National Scenic Byway.

The cultural capital of the Quiet Corner is Putnam, a small mill city on the Quinebaug River whose formerly industrial town center has been transformed into a year-round antiques mart. Smaller jewels are Pomfret and Woodstock—two towns where authentic Colonial homesteads still seem to outnumber the contemporary, charmless clones that are springing up all too rapidly across the state.

POMFRET

51 miles north of Stonington; 6 miles north of Brooklyn.

Pomfret, one of the grandest towns in the region, was once known as the inland Newport because it attracted the wealthy, who summered here in large "cottages." Today it is a quiet stopping-off point along Route 169, designated one of the most scenic byways in the country by the National Scenic Byway Program.

GETTING HERE AND AROUND

Pomfret is best visited by car; Route 169 runs right through the center of town. From I–395, take Route 44 west to Route 169 south.

EXPLORING

Sharpe Hill Vineyard. Centered on an 18th-century-style barn in the hills of Pomfret, this vineyard gives tastings and serves lunch and dinner in a European-style wine garden and its restaurant, Fireside Tavern, Friday through Sunday, depending on the season (advance reservations are essential). Its Ballet of Angels, a heavenly semidry white, just may be New England's top-selling wine. ⊠ *108 Wade Rd.* ☎ *860/974–3549* ⊕ *www.sharpehill.com* 🖾 *Tastings $7-$12* ☉ *Fri.–Sun. 11–5.*

SPORTS AND THE OUTDOORS

Connecticut Audubon Society. Adjacent to the Connecticut Audubon Bafflin Sanctuary's more than 700 acres of rolling meadows, grassland habitats, forests, and streams, this nature center presents environmental-education programs for all ages, seasonal lectures and workshops, and natural-history exhibits. Miles of trails provide excellent birding. ⊠ *218 Day Rd.* ☎ *860/928–4948* ⊕ *www.ctaudubon.org* 🖾 *Free* ☉ *Sanctuary daily dawn–dusk; center weekdays 9–4, weekends, noon–4.*

WHERE TO EAT

$$$$
EUROPEAN
Fodor's Choice
★

✕ **Golden Lamb Buttery.** Connecticut's most unusual dining experience has achieved almost legendary status. Eating here, in a converted barn on a 1,000-acre farm, is far more than a chance to enjoy good Continental food: it's a social and gastronomical event. There is one seating each for lunch and dinner; choose from one of four entrées, which might include roast duck or chateaubriand. The dinner prix fixe is $75, but lunch has an a la carte menu. Owners Bob and Virginia "Jimmie" Booth have a hay wagon that you can ride before dinner (a musician accompanies you). $ *Average main: $75* ⊠ *499 Wolf Den Rd., off Rte. 169, Brooklyn* ☎ *860/774–4423* ⊕ *www.thegoldenlamb.com* ⌁ *Reservations essential* 🏛 *Jacket and tie* ☉ *Closed Sun. and Mon. No dinner Tues.–Thurs.*

$$$
AMERICAN

✕ **The Harvest.** This romantic country restaurant is alive with fresh flowers, glimmering candles, antiques, and touches of chintz. The menu focuses heavily on steaks with a wide range of cuts and sauces, as well as such contemporary American fare like sesame-seared yellowfin tuna and lobster and lump crab strudel. There's an excellent Sunday brunch. $ *Average main: $25* ⊠ *37 Putnam Rd.* ☎ *860/928–0008* ⊕ *www.harvestrestaurant.com* ☉ *Closed Mon. No lunch Sat.*

$$
AMERICAN
★

✕ **Vanilla Bean Café.** Homemade soups, sandwiches, and baked goods have long been a tradition at this café inside a restored 19th-century barn. Dinner specials might include herb-crusted sea bass with sweet corn and heirloom tomatoes or shepherd's pie made with lamb. Belgian waffles and blueberry pancakes are breakfast highlights. There are also an art gallery and folk entertainment. $ *Average main: $16* ⊠ *450 Deerfield Rd.(off U.S. 44, Rte. 97, and Rte. 169)* ☎ *860/928–1562* ⊕ *www. thevanillabeancafe.com* ☉ *No dinner Mon. and Tues.*

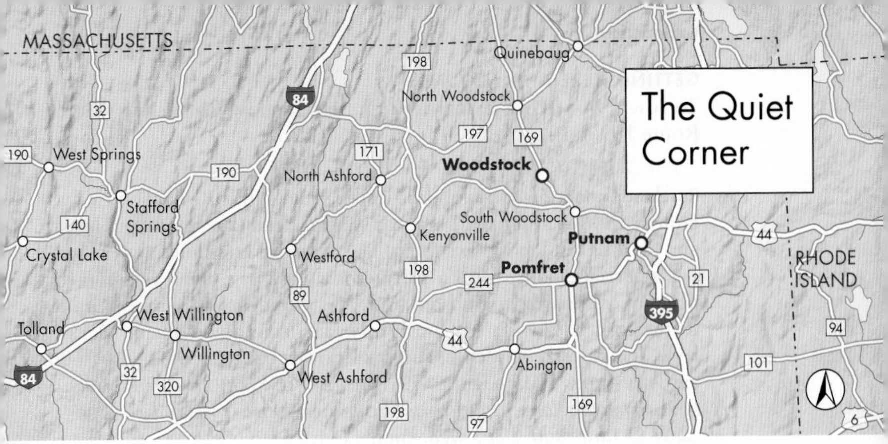

PUTNAM

5 miles northeast of Pomfret.

Ambitious antiques dealers have reinvented Putnam, a mill town 30 miles west of Providence, Rhode Island, that was neglected after the Depression. Putnam's downtown, with more than 400 antiques dealers, is the heart of the Quiet Corner's antiques trade.

GETTING HERE AND AROUND

By car, take Route 44 east from Pomfret to reach Putnam.

SHOPPING

Antiques Marketplace. The four-level Antiques Marketplace houses the wares of nearly 300 dealers, from fine furniture to tchotchkes. ✉ *109 Main St.* ☎ *860/928–0442* 🌐 *www.antiquesmarketplace.com.*

Arts & Framing. Head here for antique art and art restoration and framing services. ✉ *112 Main St.* ☎ *860/963–0105* 🌐 *www.artsandframingputnam.com.*

WHERE TO EAT

$$$ AMERICAN 🍴 **85 Main.** This stylish trattoria/bistro is *the* place to go for a break from antiquing. Typical lunchtime offerings include roasted corn and clam chowder, pesto chicken salad, and a burger and fries; dinner could be maple-glazed pan-seared sea scallops or veal bolognese. There is also a raw bar and a full sushi bar. [$] *Average main: $27* ✉ *85 Main St.* ☎ *860/928–1660* 🌐 *www.85main.com.*

WOODSTOCK

5 miles northwest of Putnam.

The landscape of this enchanting town is splendid in every season—the rolling hills seem to stretch for miles. Scenic roads lead past antiques shops, a country inn in the grand tradition, orchards, grassy fields and grazing livestock, and the fairgrounds of one of the state's oldest agricultural fairs, held each Labor Day weekend.

GETTING HERE AND AROUND

To reach Woodstock by car from Putnam, follow Route 171 west to Route 169 north.

EXPLORING

★ **Roseland Cottage.** This pink board-and-batten Gothic Revival house was built in 1846 as a summer home for New York silk merchant, publisher, and abolitionist Henry C. Bowen. The house and outbuildings (including a carriage house with a private bowling alley) hold a prominent place in history, having hosted four U.S. presidents (Ulysses S. Grant, Rutherford B. Hayes, William Henry Harrison, and William McKinley). The parterre garden includes 21 flower beds surrounded by 600 yards of boxwood hedge. ✉ *556 Rte. 169* ☎ *860/928–4074* 🌐 *www.historicnewengland.org/historic-properties/homes/roseland-cottage* 🎟 *$8* 🕒 *June–mid-Oct., Wed.–Sun. 11–4.*

SHOPPING

Christmas Barn. Christmas Barn has 12 rooms of country and Christmas goods. ✉ *835 Rte. 169* ☎ *860/928–7652* 🌐 *www.thechristmasbarnonline.com.*

Scranton's Shops. This store sells the wares of 60 regional artisans. ✉ *300 Rte. 169* ☎ *860/928–3738* 🌐 *www.scrantonsshops.com.*

Whispering Hill Farm. Supplies for rug hooking and braiding, quilting, and needlework, plus an assortment of antiques are all on sale here. ✉ *18 Castle Rock Rd. (Route 169)* ☎ *860/928–0162* 🌐 *whisperinghill.com.*

WHERE TO STAY

For expanded hotel reviews, visit Fodors.com.

$$$ B&B/INN 🏨 **The Inn at Woodstock Hill.** This inn overlooking the countryside has rooms with antiques, four-poster beds, fireplaces, pitched ceilings, and timber beams. **Pros:** beautiful grounds; many rooms have fireplaces; very good restaurant. **Cons:** traditional decor is very old-fashioned; somewhat remote. [$] *Rooms from: $175* ✉ *94 Plaine Hill Rd., South Woodstock* ☎ *860/928–0528* 🌐 *www.woodstockhill.com* 🛏 *21 rooms* 🍴 *Breakfast.*

Rhode Island

WORD OF MOUTH

"I would suggest an afternoon stroll around the Italian Federal Hill area [in Providence]. Shop for some yummy things, have a great lunch, sit and people-watch. . . ."

—dfrostnh

"Cliff Walk and Beavertail are two of my summer/fall favorites."

—janie

WELCOME TO RHODE ISLAND

TOP REASONS TO GO

★ **Mansions:** See how the one-percenters lived during Newport's Gilded Age with a tour of Cornelius Vanderbilt's opulent 70-room "summer cottage" known as The Breakers.

★ **Historic Street:** Follow along Benefit Street on Providence's East Side for a mile of history and see ornate homes built by leading Colonial merchants.

★ **Nature:** Block Island is one of the most serene spots on the Eastern Seaboard, especially at Rodman's Hollow, a glacial outwash basin, where winding paths lead to the sea.

★ **Sand:** Take your pick from South County's numerous sugary-white beaches, including Scarborough State Beach in Narragansett.

★ **Food Enclave:** From food trucks to upscale dining, Providence has an exciting culinary scene fueled in large part by young Johnson & Wales University–trained chefs.

1 Providence. Visit Rhode Island's capital city on an empty stomach so you can fill up on its exciting culinary scene, anchored by one of New England's most treasured Little Italy neighborhoods, Federal Hill. Prestigious colleges give Providence intellectual and cultural vitality while restored Colonial houses on the East Side preserve its history.

2 The Blackstone Valley. The Blackstone River powered the factories that led America's industrial revolution in the 19th century. Now it's the focal point of renewed interest in northern Rhode Island as a destination where several fascinating museums document the rise of industry over the past 200 years.

3 South County. Visit some of southern New England's most accessible and scenic stretches of beach and you'll be happy to discover the ocean warm and welcoming in the summer. Explore nature preserves or take a fishing charter trip out of Galilee, Snug Harbor, or Jerusalem. Get off the beaten path on Route 1A and stop in antiques shops and galleries along the way.

4 Newport County and East Bay. No socks required in this longtime yachting enclave where boat crews unwind after a day on the water with a dark and stormy. Take in the beaches, Colonial architecture, professional tennis, and the dramatic views of the Newport Pell Bridge. Go fly a kite in Brenton Point State Park.

5 Block Island. This laid-back island with 17 miles of beaches—including Crescent Beach, one of New England's best beaches—offers an idyllic seaside escape in summer. Best of all, it's less crowded than Martha's Vineyard and Nantucket. Relax at one of its rambling Victorian inns and B&Bs (most lacking in-room TVs and phones) and take in busy shops and restaurants.

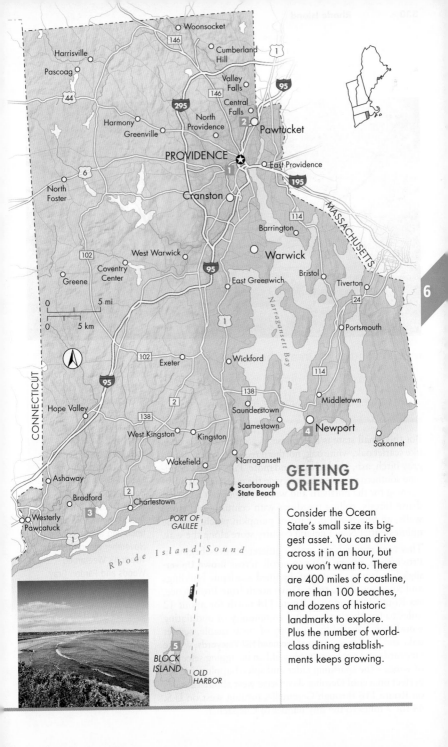

Woonsocket

146

Cumberland
Hill

1

Harrisville

95

Pascoag

Valley
Falls

146

Central
Falls

44

295

2

Pawtucket

North
Providence

Harmony

Greenville

PROVIDENCE

East Providence

6

195

North
Foster

Cranston

MASSACHUSETTS

114

Barrington

West Warwick

102

95

Warwick

Coventry
Center

Bristol

Greene

East Greenwich

Tiverton

Narragansett Bay

24

0   5 mi

Portsmouth

0   5 km

102

Exeter

Wickford

138

Middletown

Hope Valley

95

114

CONNECTICUT

2

Saunderstown

138

West Kingston

Jamestown

Newport

4

Kingston

Ashaway

Wakefield

Narragansett

Sakonnet

Bradford

2

1

GETTING
ORIENTED

3

Charlestown

Westerly
Pawcatuck

Scarborough
State Beach

PORT OF
GALILEE

1

Rhode Island Sound

Consider the Ocean
State's small size its biggest asset. You can drive
across it in an hour, but
you won't want to. There
are 400 miles of coastline,
more than 100 beaches,
and dozens of historic
landmarks to explore.
Plus the number of world-
class dining establish-
ments keeps growing.

5

BLOCK
ISLAND

OLD
HARBOR

RHODE ISLAND FALL FOLIAGE DRIVE

Rhode Island's state tree is the red maple, which turns shades of gold, purple, and scarlet in fall and is common across the state.

BEST TIME TO GO

Foliage peaks in most of Rhode Island in the second week of October, especially in the state's northwest corner where the elevation is highest. Color can last a good two weeks in a year with no big storms and lots of cool, crisp fall nights. Autumn splendor can continue into the beginning of November along the coast. Tiverton's Weetamoo Woods and Pardon Gray Preserve and Little Compton's Wilbour Woods have great walking trails.

But this small state is also home to a diversity of species like scarlet oak, white oak, northern red oak, yellow birch, gray birch, ash, black cherry and more. Pine forests dominate southern woodlands, reserving the most dramatic leaf peeping for the northern and western regions. You'll find dense forests, rolling meadows with centuries-old stone walls, an occasional orchard or pumpkin patch, and the quintessential New England country store along the way.

This tour through the state's quieter corners begins in Providence, where you can stroll across **Brown University's** handsome campus of dignified academic buildings and towering shade trees. Drive north from Providence, via Route 112 and then Route 114 north for about 12 miles to Cumberland, a rural community of undulating woodland crowned by a canopy of sugar maple, scarlet oak, and birch trees. Stop at **Diamond Hill Vineyards**, whose vineyards and apple orchards yield an intriguing selection of wines—the sparkling cider and spiced-apple wine are perfect on a cool October day. Drive west about 12 miles on Route 116 through Greenville, turning west on U.S. 44 for 7 miles to the tiny hamlet of Chepachet.

The rest of the tour meanders through some of Rhode Island's most pastoral countryside. In quaint Chepachet, Colonial and Victorian buildings contain antiques shops and quirky stores. Don't miss **Brown & Hopkins**, one of the country's oldest continuously operating general stores (including an old-fashioned candy counter), or the **Tavern on Main**, a rambling 18th-century restaurant that's perfect for a lunch stop.

Follow U.S. 44 west 5 miles through the burst of changing leaves in **Pulaski Memorial State Forest**. Turn left onto Route 94 and follow this for about 13 miles to Route 102, and then continue southeast another 20 miles to Exeter. The most undeveloped route from Chepachet to Exeter is lined with pristine hardwood forests, with an abundance of red maple, white oak, beech, elm, and poplar trees.

From Route 102, detour south in Exeter 1½ miles down Route 2 to **Schartner Farm** for a corn maze or hayride and cider and pumpkin pie. Backtrack to Route 102 and continue east 4 miles to the Colonial seaport of Wickford, whose pretty harbor opens to Narragansett Bay. The town's oak- and beech-shaded lanes are perfect for a late-afternoon stroll among the gift shops, galleries, and boutiques.

The drive is a total of about 80 miles and takes from four to eight hours, depending on stops.

NEED A BREAK?

Brown & Hopkins Country Store. Opened in 1809, this store carries candles, reproduction antiques, penny candy, and handmade soaps. ⊠ *1179 Putnam Pike, Chepachet* ☏ *401/568–4830* ⊕ *www.brownandhopkins.com* ⊙ *Mon.–Sat. 10–5, Sun. 11–5.*

Diamond Hill Vineyards. This winery produces wine from Pinot Noir grapes as well as peaches and apples grown here or locally. ⊠ *3145 Diamond Hill Rd., Cumberland* ☏ *401/333–2751* ⊕ *www.favorlabel.com* ⊙ *Thurs.–Sat. noon–5, Sun. 11–3.*

Schartner Farm. This farm store is popular during the fall for cider, pumpkin pie, and hayrides. ⊠ *1 Arnold Pl., Exeter* ☏ *401/294–2044* ⊕ *www.schartnerfarms.com* ⊙ *Daily 8–sunset; hayrides and corn maze weekends, 11–4:30.*

Tavern on Main. For lunch, try the tavern burger topped with bourbon sauce or the lobster roll. ⊠ *1157 Putnam Pike, Chepachet* ☏ *401/710–9788* ⊕ *www.tavernonmainri.com* ⊙ *Closed Mon.–Tues.*

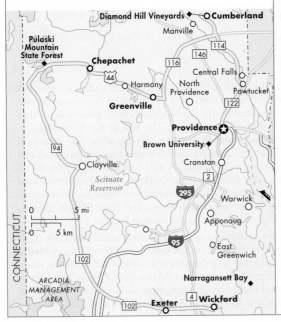

Updated
by Janine
Weisman

"Rhode Island: 3% Bigger at Low Tide," reads a bestselling T-shirt by designer Hilary Treadwell. It's a bit of an exaggeration: the state geologist actually calculates .5%. But the smallest state's size is a big source of pride given all there is to do and see within its 1,500 square miles (one third of those are water). The visitor may find it hard to choose from so many experiences: historic tours, fine dining, and Water-Fire in Providence; apple picking and canal boat rides in the Blackstone Valley; fishing trips and hitting the beach in South County or Block Island; pedaling along Bristol's bike path; and taking sunset sails and touring Gilded Age mansions in Newport.

Rhode Island and Providence Plantations, the state's official name, has a long history of forward thinking and a spirit of determination and innovation symbolized by the 11-foot-tall bronze Independent Man atop its marble domed State House. The first of the 13 colonies to declare independence from Britain can also claim the first successful textile mill in Pawtucket, America's oldest synagogue in Newport, and the first lunch wagon in Providence. A state founded on the principle of religious liberty drew Baptists, Jews, Quakers, and others throughout the 17th and 18th centuries, then flourished with factories, silver foundries and jewelry companies that drew workers from French Canada, Italy, Ireland, England, Portugal, and Eastern Europe.

The state's leaders keep working to make Rhode Island a dynamic place to live and work in and to visit for the 21st century. They moved a highway to carry on the revitalization of Downtown Providence, made infrastructure improvements at Fort Adams State Park in Newport to host international yacht-racing events, extended commuter rail service linking Providence to T. F. Green Airport and Wickford, and planned bike-path expansions in South County and Blackstone Valley. Rhode Island's 39 cities and towns—none more than 50 miles apart—offer natural attractions, inspired culinary artistry, and many opportunities to relax and take in its scenic vistas.

PLANNER

WHEN TO GO

Summer, with its renowned arts and music festivals and gorgeous beach days, is a great time to visit Rhode Island. But visitors will find fun and exciting things to do here all year-round. The shoulder seasons of April–May and September–October offer pleasant weather and more affordable accommodations. Late fall, winter and early spring have their own charms such as popular restaurant weeks in Providence, Newport, and Narragansett when restaurants join together to promote special three-course prix-fixe menus.

Newport has the Newport Jazz and Newport Folk festivals in late July and early August as well as the Newport Music Festival for classical music fans in July. Take the ferry to Block Island for a fun day trip or relaxing overnight stay and experience its low-key, less crowded beaches.

Late October is a good time to catch fall foliage in the Blackstone Valley, around the University of Rhode Island or in picturesque Tiverton and Little Compton. The return of students to the several colleges of Providence gives the capital city energy and a youthful vibe.

PLANNING YOUR TIME

By car it's an hour or less from any one place in Rhode Island to another. Though the distances are short, the state is densely populated, so allow extra time for traffic congestion.

Most of the sights in Providence can be seen in one day. The Blackstone Valley can also occupy a day (potentially as an afternoon side trip from Providence). Newport, though not even 12 square miles, offers enough to see in two days. The same can be said for South County, with its superb beaches. With a week, you can visit all four regions of the state as well as Block Island.

GETTING HERE AND AROUND

AIR TRAVEL

Rhode Island's main airport is T. F. Green in Warwick, which is served by most domestic air carriers. Boston's Logan Airport is only an hour away. The major car-rental agencies have branches at both airports.

Air Contacts T. F. Green Airport ✉ *U.S. 1 (Exit 13 off I–95), 2000 Post Rd., Warwick* ☎ *401/691–2471, 888/268–7222* ⊕ *www.pvdairport.com.*

CAR TRAVEL

New England's main interstate, Route 95, cuts diagonally through Rhode Island, spanning 43 miles from the Connecticut border to the Massachusetts line.

Interstate 195 southeast from Providence leads to New Bedford, Massachusetts, and Cape Cod. Route 146 northwest from Providence leads to Worcester, Massachusetts, and Interstate 90, passing through the Blackstone Valley. U.S. 1 follows much of the Rhode Island coast east from Connecticut before turning north to Providence. Route 138 heads east from Route 1 to Jamestown, Newport, and Portsmouth, in easternmost Rhode Island. Route 114 leads south from East Providence down through the East Bay community of Bristol and then to Newport.

Once you're here, a car is your best way to get around the state, although it's quite practical to explore Providence and Newport on foot and using public transportation. Parking is easy to find outside of cities, though challenging and sometimes expensive in Downtown Providence and Newport.

RESTAURANTS

Rhode Island's restaurant scene has flourished over the past decade, fueled by the creative passion of award-winning chefs, many in their 20s and early 30s, who have elevated fine dining to an art form. Abundant fresh seafood also makes for outstanding fish-and-chips, clam chowder, and stuffed quahogs (the hard clam that is the official state shell), which are all best enjoyed at one of the state's many clam shacks. Then there is regional fare such as the thin corn pancake cooked on a griddle known as the johnnycake, as well as coffee milk, Del's frozen lemonade, and Gray's Ice Cream. Authentic Italian restaurants can be found in Providence's Federal Hill neighborhood. *Prices in the reviews are the average cost of a main course at dinner or, if dinner is not served, at lunch.*

HOTELS

The major chain hotels are represented in Rhode Island, but the state's many smaller B&Bs and other inns provide a more intimate experience. Rates are very seasonal; in Newport, for example, winter rates are often half those of summer. Many inns in coastal towns are closed in winter. *Prices in the reviews are the lowest cost of a standard double room in high season.*

VISITOR INFORMATION

Rhode Island Department of Economic Development, Tourism Division
☎ 800/556–2484 ⊕ *www.visitrhodeisland.com.*

PROVIDENCE

Big-city sophistication with small-city charm, Providence has the best of both worlds. The capital city's thriving arts community, prestigious academic institutions, Brown University and the Rhode Island School of Design (RISD), renowned restaurant scene and revitalized Downtown make it an exciting place to be. And Providence's convenient location, close to Boston without being too close, warrants a stop on any New England tour.

The city underwent a renaissance in the 1990s when the two rivers that merge to form the Providence River were uncovered and moved to create Waterplace Park, now the setting for the popular summer evening series of bonfires on the river known as WaterFire. The relocation of I–195 has again changed the city's landscape, leading to the impressive new Providence River Bridge, reconnecting Downtown and the Jewelry District, and allowing improvements to India Point Park.

GETTING ORIENTED

The narrow Providence River cuts through the city's Downtown from north to south. West of the river lies the compact business district. A largely Italian neighborhood, Federal Hill, pushes west from here along Atwells Avenue. On the north side of Downtown is the white-marble State House. South Main and Benefit streets run parallel to the river, on the East Side. College Hill constitutes the western half of the East Side. At the top of College Hill, Thayer Street runs north to south. Don't confuse the city of East Providence with Providence's East Side.

GETTING HERE AND AROUND

AIR TRAVEL T. F. Green Airport, 10 miles south of Providence, has scheduled daily flights by most major airlines, including Air Canada, Cape Air, Delta, Jet Blue, Southwest, United, and US Airways. By cab, the ride from T. F. Green Airport to Downtown Providence takes about 15 minutes and costs about $28 to $32. The Airport Taxi & Limousine Service shuttle, running from the airport to Downtown hotels, Rhode Island School of Design, and Brown University, costs $11 per person each way.

BUS TRAVEL At Kennedy Plaza in Downtown Providence, you can board the local Rhode Island Public Transit Authority (RIPTA) buses or trolleys. The Route 92 trolley links Federal Hill to the East Side and the Route 6 trolley links Downtown to the Roger Williams Park & Zoo. RIPTA fares are $2 per ride; an all-day pass is $6. Exact-cash fare is needed when boarding buses or change is distributed back in a fare card. RIPTA buses also service T. F. Green Airport; Route 14 links the airport to Kennedy Plaza.

TRAIN TRAVEL When traveling between New York City and Boston, Amtrak makes stops at Westerly, Kingston, and Providence. The Massachusetts Bay Transportation Authority (MBTA) commuter rail service connects Boston and Providence to T. F. Green Airport and Wickford Junction during weekday morning and evening rush hours for a little more than half the cost of an Amtrak ride. MBTA provides weekday service year-round with runs scheduled from early morning to noon and late afternoon to approximately 10:15 pm. The fare from the airport to Providence is $2.25 per person or $8.25 between T. F. Green and Boston's South Station.

PARKING Overnight parking is not allowed on Providence streets, though the city was in the process of implementing a parking permit program for residents at this writing. During the day it can be difficult to find curbside parking, especially Downtown and on Federal and College hills. A large parking garage exists at Providence Place mall.

TOURS **Providence Preservation Society.** The Providence Preservation Society publishes five booklets describing self-guided walking tours of the city available for $3 each at its headquarters. The tours include Benefit Street, the city's waterfront, downtown, the Elmwood section, and the Armory District. ⊠ *21 Meeting St.* ☏ *401/831–7440* ⊕ *www.ppsri.org* ⊙ *Headquarters open Mon.–Fri. 9–5.*

ESSENTIALS

Transportation Contacts Airport Taxi & Limousine Service ☎ 401/737–2868 ⊕ www.airporttaxiri.com. **Amtrak** ☎ 800/872-7245 ⊕ www.amtrak.com. **Massachusetts Bay Transportation Authority** (*MBTA*). ☎ 617/722-3200, 617/222-3538 ⊕ www.mbta.com. **Rhode Island Public Transit Authority** (*RIPTA*). ✉ *Kennedy Plaza Passenger Terminal, 1 Kennedy Plaza, Downtown* ☎ 401/781-9400 ⊕ www.ripta.com.

Visitor Information Providence Warwick Convention & Visitors Bureau ✉ *144 Westminster St.* ☎ 401/456–0200, 800/233-1636 ⊕ www.goprovidence.com.

DOWNTOWN

TOP ATTRACTIONS

★ **Federal Hill.** You're as likely to hear Italian as English in this neighborhood. The stripe down Atwells Avenue is painted in red, white, and green, and a huge *pignoli* (pine nut), an Italian symbol of abundance and quality, hangs on an arch soaring over the street. Grocers sell pastas, pastries, and usually hard-to-find Italian groceries. During the Federal Hill Stroll (usually held in early June) festival goers enjoy music and sample signature cuisine at numerous eateries within a ¾-mile stretch of Atwells Avenue. ✉ *379 Atwells Ave., Federal Hill* ⊕ *www.federalhillprov.com.*

★ **First Baptist Church in America.** This historic house of worship was built in 1775 for a congregation established in 1638 by Roger Williams and his fellow Puritan dissenters. One of the finest examples of Georgian architecture in Colonia America, the church was built to seat 1,200 people and to this day is used for Brown University's baccalaureate ceremony. The 185-foot steeple was put up in 3½ days. The auditorium's large crystal chandelier from Ireland was installed in 1792. Self-guided tour booklets are available in multiple languages. ✉ *75 N. Main St., Downtown* ☎ *401/454-3418* ⊕ *www.fbcia.org* 🎫 *$2 includes self-guided tour booklet* ⊙ *Mon.–Fri. 10–noon and 1–3. Guided tours Memorial Day through Labor Day. Closed Sat.*

OFF THE
BEATEN
PATH

Roger Williams Park and Zoo. Plan a full day to take in this regal 435-acre Victorian park where you can picnic, feed the ducks in the lakes, rent a swan paddleboat, or ride a Victorian-style carousel. The 40-acre **zoo**—one of the nation's oldest—has African elephants, Masai giraffes, zebras, red pandas, snow leopards, moon bears, gibbons, giant ant eaters, river otters, and more in naturalistic settings. The **Museum of Natural History** has a collection of more than 250,000 specimens, including preserved animals, plants, rocks, fossils, and ethnographic objects. The **Cormack Planetarium** has a 2 pm show on weekends year-round and daily in the summer months. The **Botanical Center** has two greenhouses and 12,000 square feet of indoor gardens. ✉ *1000 Elmwood Ave., South Providence* ✛ *From downtown, take Route 95 South to Exit 17 (Elmwood Avenue); the park is the first left turn* ☎ *401/785-9450 museum, botanical center, 401/785-3510 zoo* ⊕ *www.rogerwilliamsparkzoo. org and providenceri.gov/museum* 🎫 *zoo: $14.95; planetarium and museum $3; museum only: $2; botanical center $3* ⊙ *Zoo: daily 9–4;*

Providence

0 — 500 yards
0 — 500 meters

Doyle Ave.

Camp St.

Hope St.

Olney St.

146

95

1

Douglas Ave.

Orms St.

44

Smith St.

Jewett St.

Smith St.

44

Olney St.

Barnes St.

Lloyd Ave.

Arlington Ave.

1

2

N. Main St.

Pratt St.

Lloyd Ave.

Prospect St.

Brown St.

Thayer St.

Hope St.

EAST SIDE

TO WAYLAND SQUARE

Canal St.

Meeting St.

Promenade St.

95

6

3

Steeple St.

Angell St.

15

4

Waterman St.

Brook St.

Cooke St.

Ives St.

Gano St.

Memorial Blvd.

5

College St.

6 **7**

George St.

Exchange Terr.

8

Benevolent St.

Benevolent St.

Kennedy Plaza

9

Charles Field St.

Washington St.

S. Main St.

10

Power St.

1

Arcade

Williams St.

FEDERAL HILL

Dorrance St.

Benefit St.

Hope St.

Atwells Ave.

14

Fountain St.

Westminster St.

Pine St.

Friendship St.

S. Water St.

Providence

Arnold St.

Transit St.

Broadway

Green St.

Empire St.

6

Sheldon St.

Wickenden St.

Washington St.

11

India Point Park

River

India St.

95

Pine St.

Friendship St.

Hospital St.

Davol Square

12

Point St.

Iway Bridge

India St.

Broad St.

Lockwood St.

Crary St.

95

S. Water St.

195

Providence Harbor

1

Alberts Ave.

TO ROGER WILLIAMS PARK AND ZOO

13

In the last 20 years, the Providence riverfront has been beautified, highlighting the river that divides the city.

museum: daily 10–5; botanical center: Tues.–Sun. 11–4 ⊘ Botanical Center closed Mon.

WORTH NOTING

Providence Children's Museum. At Rhode Island's only hands-on children's museum, kids ages 1–11 and their families play and learn in vibrant interactive environments including Water Ways, a playscape of pumps and fountains; Coming to Rhode Island, a time-traveling adventure through state history; and Littlewoods, with a cave and a climbing tree for toddlers. You can also investigate the awesome power of air, explore a two-story-high climbing maze, and enjoy a picnic in the Children's Garden. ⊠ *100 South St., Downtown* ☎ *401/273–5437* ⊕ *www.childrenmuseum.org* 🖃 *$8.50* ⊘ *Sept.–Mar., Tues.–Sun. 9–6; Apr.–Labor Day., daily 9–6.*

Rhode Island State House. Designed by the noted firm of McKim, Mead & White and built between 1895 and 1904, Rhode Island's capitol is the fourth-largest self-supporting marble dome in the world. The gilded Independent Man statue that tops the dome was struck by lightning 27 times before lightning rods were installed in 1975. The State Library on the north side of the second floor has the military accoutrements of Nathaniel Greene, Washington's

---

TASTE OF ITALY TOUR

Savoring Federal Hill. For an insider's tour of Providence's own "Little Italy," sign up for a Cindy Salvato's three-hour walking and tasting tour ($50) that takes you into a half dozen of Federal Hill's long standing establishments (including a bakery, an Italian specialty store, and wine shop). ☎ *401/934–2149* ⊕ *savoringrhodeisland.com.*

Roger Williams

It was an unthinkable idea: a complete separation of church and state. Break the tie between church and state and where would the government get its authority? The answer threatened the Puritan way of life. And that's why in the winter of 1636 the Massachusetts Bay Colony banished a certain preacher with radical opinions named Roger Williams. He fled south into the wilderness with the goal of establishing a new colony of religious tolerance and arranged to buy land from the Narragansett Sachems Cononicus and Miantonomo at the confluence of the Woonasquatucket and Moshassuck rivers. Word spread that this new settlement Williams named Providence was a place where civil power rested in the hands of the people. Those persecuted for their beliefs flocked to Providence, which grew into a prosperous Colonial shipping port. What started out as a radical experiment became the basis of American democracy.

second-in-command during the Revolutionary War, plus the state flag on board Apollo 11's first lunar landing mission in 1969 and moon rocks collected at the time. In the State Room is a full-length portrait of George Washington by Rhode Islander Gilbert Stuart. A steel vault in front of the Senate Chamber holds the original 1663 parchment charter granted by King Charles II to the colony of Rhode Island "to hold for a lively experiment," i.e., a civil state observing religious freedom. Fifty-minute-long guided tours are offered weekday mornings. ⊠ *82 Smith St., Downtown* ☎ *401/222–3983* ⊕ *www.sos.ri.gov/publicinfo/tours* ⊗ *Weekdays 8:30–4:30; tours weekdays 9, 10, and 11.*

Roger Williams National Memorial. This 4½-acre park dedicated to Rhode Island's founder has a symbolic well to mark the site of the spring around which Roger Williams built Providence's original settlement in 1636. Several picnic tables are here along with demonstration gardens showing how Native Americans grew corn, beans, and squash and English colonists grew herbs. A visitor's center has exhibits and a five-minute film about the park's namesake and his firm belief in religious liberty. The park has 20 free parking spaces, though a two-hour limit is strictly enforced. ⊠ *282 N. Main St., Downtown* ☎ *401/521–7266* ⊕ *www.nps.gov/rowi* 🎟 *Free* ⊗ *Memorial Day–Columbus Day, daily 9–5; mid-Oct.–May daily 9–4:30.*

Waterplace Park and Riverwalk. Romantic Venetian-style footbridges, cobblestone walkways, and an amphitheater encircling a tidal pond set the tone at this 4-acre tract. The Riverwalk passes the junction of three rivers—the Woonasquatucket, Providence, and Moshassuck—a nexus of the shipping trade during the city's early years that by the mid-20th century had been covered over with highways and parking lots. An urban-renewal project uncovered the buried rivers, rerouted them, and surrounded them with amenities for pedestrians rather than cars to create Waterplace Park, now a gathering place for free concerts in the summer. It's also the site of the popular **WaterFire**, a multimedia installation featuring music and nearly 100 burning braziers that rise from the water and are tended from boats; the dusk-to-midnight WaterFire show happens approximately 16 times a year and attracts nearly 1 million visitors annually. Four times a season, a popular open-air ballroom night has 3,000+ people dancing under the stars on the streets of Providence. ⊠ *At Memorial Blvd., Steeple St., and Exchange St., Downtown* ☎ *401/273–1155* ⊕ *www.waterfire.org.*

OFF THE BEATEN PATH

Culinary Arts Museum. This offbeat, fascinating museum on the Harborside campus of Johnson & Wales University celebrates the joy of cooking and eating throughout human history. See exhibits of vintage menus, an authentic 1920s diner, ancient Chinese culinary vessels, displays of mayonnaise makers, marshmallow beaters, other kitchen gadgets, and more. Check out the original letters by assorted past United States presidents to friends and food providers who supplied gourmet gifts on various occasions. ⊠ *315 Harborside Blvd., South Providence* ☎ *401/598–2805* ⊕ *www.culinary.org* 🎟 *$7* ⊘ *Tues.–Sun. 10–5* ⊘ *Closed Mon.*

EAST SIDE

TOP ATTRACTIONS

Fodor's Choice
★

Benefit Street. The centerpiece of any visit to Providence is this "mile of history" where the city's wealthiest families lived in the 18th and early 19th centuries. Benefit Street is home to the one of the highest concentrations of Colonial architecture and passes through the campuses of Brown University and the Rhode Island School of Design.

Providence Preservation Society. The Providence Preservation Society distributes maps and pamphlets with self-guided tours. ⊠ *21 Meeting St., at Benefit St., East Side* ☎ *401/831–7440* ⊕ *www.ppsri.org*

Rhode Island Historical Society. The Rhode Island Historical Society conducts summer (mid-June–mid-Oct.) walks on Benefit Street. The 90-minute tours cost $12 per person and depart from the John Brown House Museum Tuesday–Saturday at 11 am. ⊠ *52 Power St.* ☎ *401/273–7507* ⊕ *www.rihs.org* 🎟 *$12* ⊠ *Benefit St.*

Brown University. Founded in 1764, this Ivy League institution is the nation's seventh-oldest college and has more than 40 academic departments, The Graduate School, Warren Alpert Medical School, and School of Engineering. A stroll through the College Hill campus encounters Gothic and Beaux-Arts structures as well as the imposing Prospect Street gates, which open twice a year—in fall to welcome the students and spring to bid them farewell. Free one-hour university tours conducted by current undergraduate students depart from the Stephen Robert '62 Campus Center on the Main Green. Public events include student-produced outdoor Shakeseare performances and a summer outdoor movie series hosted by the Granoff Center for the Creative Arts. The Haffenreffer Museum of Anthropology on the ground floor of Manning Hall has exhibits showcasing artifacts from around the world. The David Winton Bell Gallery in the List Art Center hosts several major art exhibitions a year. ⊠ *Stephen Robert '62 Campus Center, 75 Waterman St., East Side* ☎ *401/863–2378 tour schedule* ⊕ *www.brown.edu.*

The Independent Man atop Rhode Island's marble domed capitol building symbolizes the smallest state's spirit of free thinking.

EN ROUTE **Thayer Street.** Bustling Thayer Street bears a proud old New England name and is very much a part of life at Brown University. You'll find restaurants from Greek to Korean, fashion boutiques, shops selling vintage clothing and funky gifts, and the Avon Cinema in the blocks between Waterman and Bowen streets. ⊠ *Thayer St., between Waterman and Bowen Sts., East Side.*

★ **John Brown House Museum.** Rhode Island's most famous 18th-century home was the stately residence of John Brown, a wealthy businessman and privateer, slave trader, politician, and China Trade merchant. Built in 1786–88, John Brown's stately, three-story brownstone-trimmed, brick mansion was designed by his brother Joseph Brown, who also designed the First Baptist Meeting House. The house is a perfect example of late-Georgian-early-Federal design and made quite the impression on John Quincy Adams, who called it "the most magnificent and elegant private mansion that I have ever seen on this continent." An ardent patriot, John Brown was a famous participant in the burning of the British customs ship *Gaspee* in 1772. ⊠ *52 Power St., East Side* ☎ *401/273–7507* ⊕ *www.rihs.org* ⊡ *$8* ☉ *Tours Apr.–Nov., Tues.–Fri. 1:30 and 3, Sat. 10:30, noon, 1:30, and 3; Dec.–Mar., Fri and Sat. 10:30, noon, 1:30, and 3* ☉ *Closed Sun. and Mon.*

Fodor's Choice
★
☺ **Museum of Art, Rhode Island School of Design.** The largest wooden Buddha outside of Japan and an ancient Egyptian mummy reside at this superb museum in a multilevel complex with entrances on both Benefit and North Main streets. Its permanent collection of more than 86,000 works of art spans from ancient Egypt, Greece, and Rome and all periods from Asia, Europe, and the Americas, up to the latest in contemporary art.

The collection covers painting, sculpture, prints, drawings, textiles and fashion, furniture, and more. Artists represented include major figures like Cézanne, Chanel, Copley, Degas, Hirst, Homer, LeWitt, Matisse, Manet, Picasso, Rothko, Sargent, Turner, Twombly, van Gogh, and Warhol. The museum has a vibrant exhibition schedule and hosts lectures, concerts, and films. Admission includes the adjoining **Pendleton House,** a replica of an early-19th-century Providence house.

The Rhode Island School of Design (RISD) museum houses more than 86,000 objects—ranging from ancient art to work by contemporary artists from across the globe. Highlights include impressionist paintings, 20th-century design, Gorham silver, Newport furniture, an ancient Egyptian (332–30 BCE) mummy, and a 12th-century Buddha—the largest historic Japanese wooden sculpture in the United States. Artists represented include major figures in the history of visual art and culture, including Cézanne, Chanel, Copley, Degas, Hirst, Homer, LeWitt, Matisse, Manet, Picasso, Rothko, Sargent, Turner, Twombly, van Gogh, and Warhol—to name a few. The museum presents special exhibitions throughout the year, along with public programs and events for all ages, inspiring lifelong relationships with art and design. ⊠ *224 Benefit St., East Side* ☎ *401/454–6500* ⊕ *www.risdmuseum.org* ⊠ *$10; pay what you wish Sun. 10–1; free last Sat. of the month* ☉ *Open Tues.–Sun. 10–5, Thurs. 10–9* ☉ *Closed Mon.*

★ **Providence Athenaeum.** Philadelphia architect William Strickland designed this Greek Revival building that opened in 1838, absorbing the collections of two disbanded libraries: Providence Library Company and an earlier Athenaeum library. Here Edgar Allan Poe courted poet Sarah Helen Whitman and signed a periodical in the collection containing a piece he published anonymously. An 1870s Manet print that illustrated Poe's "The Raven" hangs in the rare-book room, which also contains two medieval illuminated manuscripts. Raven signs are posted at eight points of interest on a self-guided library tour. Among them is a special cabinet modeled after an Egyptian temple to house the library's multi-volume imperial edition of *Description de l'Egypte* (1809-1822), commissioned by Napoleon. ■ TIP→ The library has Wi-Fi. ⊠ *251 Benefit St., East Side* ☎ *401/421–6970* ⊕ *www.providenceathenaeum.org* ⊠ *Free* ☉ *Labor Day–Memorial Day, Mon.–Thurs. 9–7, Fri. and Sat., 9–5, Sun. 1–3; Memorial Day-Labor Day, Mon.–Thurs. 9–7, Fri. and Sat. 9–1* ☉ *Closed first 2 wks in Aug. and Sun. Memorial Day–Labor Day.*

WORTH NOTING

First Unitarian Church of Providence. This Romanesque house of worship made of Rhode Island granite was built in 1816. Its steeple houses a 2,500-pound bell, the largest ever cast in Paul Revere's foundry. ⊠ *1 Benevolent St., at Benefit St., East Side* ☎ *401/421–7970* ⊕ *www.firstunitarianprov.org* ⊠ *Free* ☉ *Open Mon.–Fri., 9–4; closed last two weeks of July.*

John Hay Library. Built in 1910 and named for Abraham Lincoln's secretary, the "Hay" houses Brown University Library's collections of rare books and manuscripts, the University Archives, and special collections. Notable areas of strength include American literature and popular culture, political, military, and diplomatic history, the history of science, magic, book arts, and graphics. World-class collections of Lincoln-related items, H. P. Lovecraft letters, and toy soldiers are of particular interest. The library is open to the public but you need to present a photo ID to enter. ⊠ *20 Prospect St., East Side* ☎ *401/863– 2146* ⊕ *library.brown.edu/about/hay* ⊡ *Free* ☉ *Sept.–mid-Dec. and Feb.–May, Mon.–Thurs., 10–6, Fri. 10–5; mid-Dec.–Jan., Mon.–Fri., 10–5; Memorial Day–Labor Day, Mon.–Fri., 10–5.*

QUICK BITES

Seven Stars Bakery. For first-rate coffee and espresso drinks with artful foam, venture up Hope Street to the bustling Seven Stars Bakery, located in a converted garage. You'll also find pecan sticky buns, brownies, cookies, and sandwiches on fresh baguettes. But you won't find Internet access here. ⊠ *820 Hope St., East Side* ☎ *401/521–2200* ⊕ *www.sevenstarsbakery. com* ☉ *Mon.–Fri., 6 am–6:30 pm; Sat. and Sun. 7–6.*

Wickenden Street. Named for a Baptist minister who was one of Providence's first settlers, this main artery in the Fox Point district is home to antiques stores, galleries, and trendy cafés. Formerly a working-class Portuguese neighborhood, Wickenden Street has seen steady gentrification with artists, professors, and other new residents. But Our Lady of the Rosary Church on Traverse Street still conducts two Sunday morning Masses in Portuguese and publishes its church bulletin in both Portuguese and English. ⊠ *Wickenden St.*

SPORTS AND THE OUTDOORS

BIKING

East Bay Bicycle Path. The 14½-mile East Bay Bicycle Path connects Providence's India Point Park to Independence Park in Bristol. Along the way, you pass neighborhoods, schools, business districts, a total of eight parks, and deck bridges with views of coves and saltwater marshes. ☎ *401/253–7482* ⊕ *www.dot.ri.gov/bikeri/east_bay_bike_path.asp.*

BOATING

Prime boating areas include the Providence River, the Seekonk River, and Narragansett Bay.

SHOPPING

Providence has a handful of small but engaging shopping areas. In Fox Point, Wickenden Street contains many antiques stores and several art galleries. Near Brown University, Thayer Street has a number of boutiques though there has been an influx of chain stores. Downtown's Westminster Street has morphed into a strip of independently owned fashion boutiques, galleries, and design stores.

DOWNTOWN

ANTIQUES AND HOME FURNISHINGS

Craftland. Etsy fans will rejoice in the array of arts and crafts to be found at Craftland. Jewelry, note cards, prints, silk-screened T-shirts, fashion accessories, bags, and other sparkly handmade objects by local artists are for sale at this colorful shop and gallery. ⊠ *235 Westminster St., Downtown, Providence* ☎ *401/272–4285* ⊕ *www.craftlandshop.com* ⊗ *Mon.–Sat., 10–6; Sun. 11–6.*

HomeStyle. Along increasingly gentrified Westminster Street, drop by HomeStyle for eye-catching objets d'art, stylish housewares, and other decorative items. ⊠ *229 Westminster St., Downtown* ☎ *401/277–1159* ⊕ *www.homestyleri.com.*

Tilden-Thurber Gallery. At the corner of Mathewson and Westminster streets, this gallery carries high-end Colonial- and Federal-era furniture and antiques. ⊠ *292 Westminster St., Downtown* ☎ *401/272–3200* ⊕ *www.tildenthurber.com* ⊗ *Sat. 11–5 and by appointment.*

ART GALLERIES

risd|works. risdlworks has a selection of quirky kitchen gadgets, diverse jewelry, handblown art glass, and fine art prints by Rhode Island School of Design faculty and alumni, including *Family Guy* creator Seth Mac-Farlane's custom RISD T-shirt. ⊠ *20 North Main St., Downtown* ☎ *401/277–4949* ⊕ *www.risdworks.com* ⊗ *Tues.–Sun. 10–5, Thurs. 10–9* ⊗ *Closed Mon.*

FOOD

Tony's Colonial Food store. This superb Italian grocery and deli stocks freshly prepared foods. ⊠ *311 Atwells Ave., Downtown* ☎ *401/621–8675* ⊕ *www.tonyscolonial.com* ⊗ *Mon.–Thurs. 8:30–6, Fri. 8–6:30, Sat. 8–6, Sun. 8–5.*

Venda Ravioli. Venda Ravioli carries an amazing selection of imported and homemade Italian foods. ⊠ *275 Atwells Ave., Downtown* ☎ *401/ 421–9105* ⊕ *www.vendaravioli.com.*

MALLS

Arcade. The Arcade, built in 1828, is America's oldest shopping mall. At this writing renovations to the Greek Revival building were creating about a dozen shops and restaurants on the first floor and micro-lofts on the second and third floors. A National Historic Landmark, the building has entrances on Westminster and Weybosset streets. ⊠ *65 Weybosset St., Downtown* ☎ *401/454–4568* ⊕ *www.arcadeprovidence.com.*

Copacetic Rudely Elegant Jewelry. Expect the unusual at this shop, which sells handmade jewelry, gadgets and clocks created by more than 100 artists. ⊠ *17 Peck St., Downtown* ☎ *401/273–0470* ⊕ *www. copaceticjewelry.com* ⊗ *Mon –Fri. 10–6, Sat. 10–4* ⊗ *Closed Sun.*

EAST SIDE

ANTIQUES AND HOME FURNISHINGS

Butterfield. Owner Mindy Matouk has an eye for edgy but elegant home decor like cowhide rugs, contemporary crystal chandeliers, and all kinds of artsy pillows. ⊠ *187 Wayland Ave., East Side, Providence* ☎ *401/273–3331.*

Frog + Toad. Browse the eclectic selection of home decor, jewelry, and fashion from local designers at this small Hope Street curiosity shop and gift boutique. ⊠ *795 Hope St., East Side, Providence* ☎ *401/831–3434* ⊕ *hopestreetprov.com/frog-toad* ⊗ *Mon.–Sat. 10–6, Sun. noon–6.*

ART GALLERIES

Bert Gallery. The Bert Gallery displays late-19th- and early-20th-century paintings by regional artists. ⊠ *540 S. Water St., East Side* ☎ *401/751–2628* ⊕ *www.bertgallery.com.*

The Peaceable Kingdom. This gallery stocks folk art from around the world, including tribal weavings and rugs, international clothing and jewelry, masks, musical instruments, and paintings. ⊠ *116 Ives St., East Side* ☎ *401/351–3472* ⊕ *www.pkgifts.com.*

FEDERAL HILL
FOOD

Scialo Bros. Bakery. Get your cannoli fix at this family-owned and -operated bakery that has been around since 1916. ⊠ *257 Atwells Ave., Federal Hill, Providence* ☎ *401/421–0986, 877/421–0986* ⊕ *www. scialobakery.com.*

NIGHTLIFE AND THE ARTS

For events listings, consult the daily *Providence Journal* or the website ⊕ *golocalprov.com.* The weekly *Providence Phoenix* or *Providence Monthly* are both free in restaurants and shops.

NIGHTLIFE
DOWNTOWN

BARS   **Mirabar.** Long-running Mirabar is one of the most popular gay bars in Providence. It has a mezzanine overlooking the first-story dance floor and a third-floor mahogany and marble bar area. ⊠ *35 Richmond St., Downtown* ☎ *401/331–6761* ⊕ *www.mirabar.com.*

MUSIC CLUBS   **AS220.** Hear uncensored, unjuried, original music from techno-pop and
★   hip-hop to folk and jazz at this gallery and performance space. Spoken word and poetry slams, comedy nights, and open mikes are also scheduled. The bar always has a dozen rotating beers on tap. ⊠ *115 Empire St., Downtown* ☎ *401/861–9190* ⊕ *www.as220.org.*

Lupo's Heartbreak Hotel. Housed in a historic, five-story theater, this music venue hosts national alternative, rock, blues, and punk bands. ⊠ *79 Washington St., Downtown* ☎ *401/331–5876* ⊕ *www.lupos.com.*

Rí Rá Irish Pub. Corned beef and cabbage is on the menu year-round at Rí Rá Irish Pub. Pop and rock cover bands play Thursday through Sunday nights here while a traditional Irish session also takes place on Sundays from 6–9 pm. The pub is inside the vintage Union Station building Downtown, and the interior was shipped here, piece by piece, from an 1880s pub in County Mayo, Ireland. ⊠ *50 Exchange Terr., Downtown* ☎ *401/272–1953* ⊕ *www.rira.com.*

EAST SIDE

BARS   **Hot Club.** Hot Club is fashionable with young professionals, university professors, politicians, and others. Summer nights find a crowd on the outdoor deck overlooking the Providence River and Fox Point Hurricane Barrier. A limited menu features $5 burgers cooked on a charcoal grill. Sundays have live music. ⊠ *575 S. Water St., East Side* ☎ *401/861–9007.*

FEDERAL HILL

BARS **Lili Marlene's.** An easygoing bar and with cozy booths, Lili Marlene's cultivates a loyal following among in-the-know locals who like martinis and beer, good burgers, and free pool. ⊠ *422 Atwells Ave., Federal Hill* ☎ *401/751–4996.*

THE ARTS

FILM

Cable Car Cinema & Cafe. This espresso-café-cum-movie-theater showcases a fine slate of foreign and independent flicks; seating is on couches and old-school movie chairs. They also offer beer and wine concessions. ⊠ *204 S. Main St., Downtown* ☎ *401/272–3970* ⊕ *www. cablecarcinema.com.*

GALLERY TOURS

Gallery Night Providence. During Gallery Night, held the third Thursday evening of every month March through November, some 25 participating art galleries and museums hold open houses and mount special exhibitions. ■ TIP→ Park free at One Regency Plaza and take a free guided two-hour art bus tour organized by themes. ☎ *401/490–2042* ⊕ *www. gallerynight.info.*

MUSIC

Providence Performing Arts Center. Narrowly escaping demolition in the 1970s, the 3,200-seat Providence Performing Arts Center, is listed on the National Register of Historic Places. Major renovations in the 1990s restored the stage, lobby, and arcade to their original splendor when it opened in 1928 as a Loew's Movie Palace. The theater and concert hall hosts touring Broadway shows, concerts, and other large-scale events. Its five-manual mighty Wurlitzer pipe organ is a source of pride and joy. ⊠ *220 Weybosset St., Downtown* ☎ *401/421–2787* ⊕ *www.ppacri.org.*

Rhode Island Philharmonic. The Rhode Island Philharmonic Orchestra presents a series of classical, "rush hour," pops, and education concerts at The Vets from September to May and Summer Pops concerts throughout the state, including the annual 4th of July Concert at India Point Park in Providence. ⊠ *667 Waterman Ave., East Providence* ☎ *401/248–7000* ⊕ *www.ri-philharmonic.org.*

Veterans Memorial Auditorium. Located next door to the Renaissance Providence Hotel, the 1,900-seat Veterans Memorial Auditorium has a proscenium stage and exquisite interior and hosts concerts, opera, and dance performances. ⊠ *1 Ave. of the Arts, Downtown* ☎ *401/272–4862* ⊕ *www.vmari.com.*

THEATER

Brown University Theater. Brown University mounts productions of contemporary works as well as classics. Every winter, its renowned graduate playwriting program presents a Writing is Live Festival of new plays. A lively summer theater program through the university's partnership with Trinity Rep offers professional productions for the cost of a movie ticket. Dance concerts take place in the Ashamu Dance studio and in the Stuart Theatre. ⊠ *Catherine Bryan Dill Center for the Performing Arts, 77 Waterman St., East Side* ☎ *401/863–2838* ⊕ *www.brown.edu/tickets.*

★ **Trinity Repertory Company.** The Trinity Repertory Company and the professional resident actors and participants from Brown University's MFA theater program present classics, foreign plays, intimate musicals, new works by young playwrights, and an annual version of *A Christmas Carol.* ✉ *201 Washington St., Downtown* ☎ *401/351–4242* 🌐 *www.trinityrep.com* 🕒 *Box office: Tues.–Sun., noon–8.*

WHERE TO EAT

The hard part is deciding which one of Providence's many superb dining spots to visit. If you're in the mood for Italian, you'll enjoy a stroll through Federal Hill on Atwells Avenue. Downtown is home to excellent fine-dining establishments while the East Side has great neighborhood and upscale casual restaurants as well as an assortment of those with hip ambience and international cuisine.

DOWNTOWN

$$$ ITALIAN Fodor's Choice ★ 🍴 **Bacaro.** The two floors at this lively Italian restaurant founded by Chef Brian Kingsford and partner Jennifer Matta, both formerly of Al Forno, offer a unique dining experience. The informal first floor and bar has a deli case stocked with cured salami, cheeses, olives, and traditional Italian-style tapas. Upstairs is a more traditional dining room with impressive views of the Providence River. Every table receives a separate *salumeria cicchetteria* menu checklist and selections come on a beautifully presented board. Rely on the very knowledgeable servers to guide you around the frequently changing menu, which emphasizes seasonal, local ingredients. The pan-seared duck breast with creamy red wine risotto inspires as much awe as the high ceilings and exposed wood beams overhead. The hard part is saving room for dessert—the pear and walnut crisp tart for two can actually feed four. [$] *Average main: $27* ✉ *262 S. Water St., Downtown* ☎ *401/751–3700* 🌐 *www.bacarorestaurant.net* 🕒 *Closed Sun. and Mon. No lunch.*

$$ MODERN AMERICAN 🍴 **The Dorrance.** The opulent first floor of what was once the Union Trust Building is home to Providence's newest purveyor of farm-to-table food. Siena marble, ornate plaster detailing, and stained glass lends a Newport mansion vibe, but the long bar is populated by young professionals in jeans enjoying handcrafted creative cocktails. A one-page menu of small and large plates offers creative dishes from local, fresh ingredients. For example, the Maine Jonah Crab is served simply yet elegantly with shaved vegetables, grilled leeks, and aioli. Also try the roasted dry-aged duck. The Up N' Cumber cocktail with cucumber vodka, St-Germain, lime juice, and ginger beer is divine. [$] *Average main: $20* ✉ *60 Dorrance St., Downtown* ☎ *401/521–6000* 🌐 *www.thedorrance.com* 🕒 *Closed Sun. and Mon. No lunch Sat.–Mon.*

$$$ MODERN AMERICAN ★ 🍴 **Gracie's.** The best table in Providence for a romantic dinner for two is table 21 in a cozy, private alcove at Ellen Gracyalny's stellar Downtown restaurant. Located across the street from Trinity Rep, Gracie's mixes sophistication with whimsy in the main dining room with star-themed decor. Young Executive Chef Matthew Varga is known for wowing guests with pleasant little surprises. The amazing triple-cooked potato medallion accompanying mouthwatering Chatham cod loin might

make you reevaluate your low-carb diet. The service here is excellent. A three-course prix-fixe menu for $35 is available nightly, but for true excitement, opt for Varga's five- or seven-course tasting and see what delights come your way. [$] *Average main: $29* ✉ *194 Washington St., Downtown* ☎ *401/272–7811* 🌐 *www.graciesprov.com* 🕒 *Closed Sun. and Mon. No lunch.*

$$$ SEAFOOD ★ 🍴 **Hemenway's Seafood Grill & Oyster Bar.** Before "Providence" and "renaissance" were used in the same sentence, Hemenway's had already established itself as a great fine-dining seafood destination. That's still the case even as newer restaurants garner more excitement and attention. The menu includes New England staples like a perfectly cracked baked stuffed lobster with lump crab and scallop stuffing, fried whole-belly clams, and baked, fried, or grilled George's Bank sea scallops. Inspired chef's specialties include a prosciutto-wrapped rainbow trout and a Portuguese-style grilled littleneck clam appetizer with *chourico* (spicy Portugese sausage), savory broth, and grilled bread. The wine list is extensive and martini lovers will have a hard time making a decision here. High ceilings and huge windows grace the dining room, which looks out on the city's World War II Memorial. In warm weather, dine outside on the front patio. [$] *Average main: $29* ✉ *121 South Main St., Downtown* ☎ *401/351–8570* 🌐 *www.hemenwaysrestaurant.com.*

$$ AMERICAN 🍴 **Local 121.** In what was the lobby of the former Dreyfus Hotel is now an elegant restaurant where the focus is on locally raised foods from area farms, fishermen, and food artisans. Local 121's posh dining room has a dark brown-and-white color scheme, stylish light fixtures, and comfortable round booths, while the casual Tap Room has a long wood bar and stained-glass windows. The varied menu changes seasonally and features a fresh pasta and local catch of the day. The grilled hanger steak comes with a divine house-made steak sauce. Close to Trinity Rep, Local 121 has a three-course $30 pre-theater dinner menu Sunday through Friday before 6 pm. [$] *Average main: $22* ✉ *121 Washington St., Downtown* ☎ *401/274–2121* 🌐 *www.local121.com* 🕒 *No lunch Mon.*

$$$ MODERN AMERICAN ★ 🍴 **Mill's Tavern.** The lasagna-inspired Cobb salad served as a square of perfectly chopped egg, vegetables, and bacon on a bed of Bibb lettuce is just one of many examples of culinary artistry you'll find here. This upscale tavern has redbrick walls and vaulted casement ceilings. The menu, which includes a raw bar and selections from the wood-burning oven and rotisserie, consists of contemporary American, French-influenced fare that changes quarterly to emphasize local and seasonal ingredients. If you decide not to go for the Angus all-natural rib eye with house-made steak sauce, the pan-roasted Scottish salmon over French lentils with citrus tomato jam is noteworthy. Take advantage of the $29 three-course fixed price menu on weeknights. [$] *Average main: $30* ✉ *101 N. Main St., Downtown* ☎ *401/272–3331* 🌐 *www.millstavernrestaurant.com* 🕒 *No lunch.*

$ AMERICAN 🍴 **The ROI.** Executive Chef Paul Shire's meatloaf masterpiece made with Jack Daniels gravy and rolled quick oats instead of breadcrumbs, made famous at DownCity, is now available at this Jewelry District upstart. Located in the former Century Lounge, The ROI menu aims to please with polenta fries, grilled pizza, and half-pound burgers made with antibiotic-free beef. Live music plays on the sizable stage on weekends. Specialty cocktails include Point Street Punch made with vodka-infused pineapple slices. [S] *Average main: $13* ⊠ *150 Chestnut St., Downtown* ☎ *401/272–2161* ⊕ *theroiprov.com* ☾ *Closed Mon.*

$ **✕ Tazza.** Skip the bland buffet at your hotel and head to this great, light-filled "caffe" where the real coffee drinkers congregate. They come for CAFÉ
★ Tazza's robust coffee brewed mad-scientist style with siphon pots that boil water heated by halogen lamps. The result is a cup of joe without bitterness or acidity. You can also opt to get your brew hand-poured over coffee grounds directly into your cup for the freshest possible coffee experience. The unique brunch menu combines lunch fare, like grilled pizza and a trio of Black Angus bacon burgers, with a variety of sweet and savory breakfast options, like beignets and shrimp and cheddar grits. Plan to return for weeknight raw-bar specials, great cocktails, and the adventurous dinner menu ($$$) featuring fricassee of rabbit and caramelized pineapple–wrapped salmon. ■ TIP➜ Tazza **sponsors free outdoor movie nights in the lot next door on Thursdays June through October.** [S] *Average main: $9* ⊠ *250 Westminster St., Downtown* ☎ *401/421–3300* ⊕ *www.tazzacaffe.com.*

EAST SIDE

$$$ **✕ Chez Pascal.** You know this French bistro will be welcoming and BISTRO unpretentious from its logo, a trio of pigs in striped shirts and berets. ★ Located in a peaceful residential neighborhood, Chez Pascal seats 80, yet a dividing wall makes it feel intimate and romantic. The menu always offers escargot baked in butter, garlic, and parsley and a house butchered pork of the day, but also reflects locally available seasonal produce. There is a three-course $35 tasting menu Tuesday through Thursday. ■ TIP➜ **There is a takeout window serving house-made sausages and sandwiches during the day.** [S] *Average main: $26* ⊠ *960 Hope St., East Side* ☎ *401/421–4422* ⊕ *www.chez-pascal.com* ☾ *Closed Sun.*

$$ **✕ Red Stripe.** A giant fork hangs on the outside of this lively neighbor-FRENCH hood brasserie on Wayland Square. They do things big here, from the popular 10-ounce Angus burger to the everything-but-the-kitchen-sink chopped salad. The *moules* (Prince Edward Island mussels) come with a choice of savory broth and hand-cut *frites* and are uncovered table-side with a flourish, releasing aromatic steam. Menu highlights include lavender-scented brick chicken and cider beer–brined pork tenderloin. [S] *Average main: $16* ⊠ *465 Angell St., East Side* ☎ *401/437–6950* ⊕ *redstriperestaurants.com.*

FEDERAL HILL

$ **✕ Angelo's Civita Farnese.** Since 1924, boisterous Angelo's has been serv-ITALIAN ing up reliably good home-style red-sauce fare with old-world charm. The third-generation, family-owned restaurant in the heart of Federal Hill has a little bar and affordable prices. Locals come for the chicken Parmesan, veal and peppers, and broiled or fried hand-cut pork chops. [S] *Average main: $12* ⊠ *141 Atwells Ave., Federal Hill* ☎ *401/621–8171* ⊕ *www.angelosonthehill.com.*

Finish off a meal at Mill's Tavern with their signature Portuguese bread pudding.

$$$ MODERN AMERICAN Fodor's Choice ★ 🍴 **Nick's on Broadway.** What might pass for a no-frills luncheonette from the street is actually a trendy neighborhood restaurant with some of the best breakfast food in Rhode Island, plus extraordinary lunches and dinners. Young chef Derek Wagner delights morning patrons with vanilla-battered French toast with warm fruit compote; later in the day, he prepares a knockout pulled-pork sandwich with cheddar and caramelized onion. Foodies will appreciate Wagner's passionate embrace of the farm-to-table movement, not to mention his attention to detail—his outstanding homemade mustard may occupy a small place on the charcuterie plate but it speaks volumes. Ask for a seat at the polished wood counter for a front-row view of the well-choreographed show in the open kitchen, and try the chocolate-bacon bread pudding for dessert. [$] *Average main: $24* ✉ *500 Broadway, Federal Hill* ☎ *401/421–0286* 🌐 *www.nicksonbroadway.com* 🕒 *Closed Mon. and Tues. No dinner Sun.*

$$$ ITALIAN 🍴 **Pane e Vino.** This popular Federal Hill spot, whose name means "bread and wine" in Italian, offers fresh ingredients presented in a straightforward way. Portions are big: appetizers like the braised escarole, house-made sausage, and cannellini beans over grilled artisan bread are more like a lunch portion. Share a starch course if you dare but keep in mind the veal chop may rival the one that tipped over Fred Flintstone's car. The dining-room staff provides excellent service, and tables in front near the window are especially suited for a romantic dinner. **TIP→ A gluten-free menu is also available.** [$] *Average main: $25* ✉ *365 Atwells Ave., Federal Hill* ☎ *401/223–2230* 🌐 *www.panevino.net* 🕒 *No lunch.*

$$ ITALIAN ★ 🍴 **Siena.** Among Federal Hill's 30 or so restaurants, Siena generates the most buzz and for good reason: the *branzino* (Chilean sea bass) with scallops in a creamy scallion sauce and the *bolognese* are legendary. It's

best to split an appetizer as portions here are huge, though you might want to keep the delicious *involtini di melanzane*, eggplant rolled with prosciutto and ricotta and baked in tangy marinara sauce, all to yourself. The silky white *pasta e fagioli* under the menu's antipasti section is a meal in itself. The excellent wine list is usually augmented by special additions available by bottle or glass, and the well-trained waitstaff offers guidance to help you make the perfect pairing. ■ TIP→ When reserving a table, try for one up front by the large windows as the stylish back dining room can get noisy. $ *Average main: $21* ⊠ *238 Atwells Ave., Federal Hill* ☎ *401/521–3311* ⊕ *www.sienari.com* ☉ *No lunch*.

WHERE TO STAY

For expanded hotel reviews, visit Fodors.com.

DOWNTOWN

$$
B&B/INN
★

Christopher Dodge House. Rooms on the east side of this three-story 1858 Italianate brick town house have direct views of the State House, though Route 95 lies between the two. **Pros:** huge windows in rooms; guests receive free passes to health club one block away. **Cons:** Route 95 may be too close for comfort for some. $ *Rooms from: $149* ⊠ *11 W. Park St., Downtown* ☎ *401/351–6111* ⊕ *www.providence-hotel. com* ⇘ *14 rooms* ◎| *Breakfast*.

$$
HOTEL
★

Hotel Providence. In the heart of the city's Arts and Entertainment District, this intimate boutique hotel sets a new standard for elegant decor and attentive service. **Pros:** attentive staff; central location; plush rooms; a lobby "doggie lounge" has treats for pets. **Cons:** late risers may not appreciate the 8 am pealing of Grace Church's 16 bells right next door. $ *Rooms from: $159* ⊠ *139 Mathewson St., Downtown* ☎ *401/861–8000, 800/861–8990* ⊕ *www.hotelprovidence.com* ⇘ *64 rooms, 16 suites*.

$$
HOTEL
★

Providence Biltmore. The city's grand dame and beloved landmark with its skyscraping neon sign has endured hurricanes and economic upheaval that saw it pushed into state receivership in 2011. **Pros:** spacious suites; great location. **Cons:** the new owner has no immediate plans to repair the external glass elevator which has been out of service for several years. $ *Rooms from: $164* ⊠ *Kennedy Plaza, 11 Dorrance St., Downtown* ☎ *401/421–0700, 800/294–7709* ⊕ *www. providencebiltmore.com* ⇘ *292 rooms, 185 suites* ◎| *No meals*.

$$$
HOTEL
Fodor's Choice
★

Renaissance Providence Downtown Hotel. This luxury hotel adjoining Veterans Memorial Auditorium opened in 2007 inside one of Providence's most mysterious buildings, a stately nine-story neoclassical building constructed as a Masonic temple but never occupied. **Pros:** terrific location next door to Providence Place Mall and State House lawn; super-comfortable linens and bedding. **Cons:** some rooms have small windows. $ *Rooms from: $209* ⊠ *5 Ave. of the Arts, Downtown* ☎ *401/919–5000, 800/468–3571* ⊕ *www.renaissanceprovidence.com* ⇘ *272 rooms, 7 suites*.

6

EAST SIDE

$$ 🔅 **The Old Court Bed & Breakfast.** Parents of Brown and RISD students
B&B/INN book their stays in this three-story Italianate inn on historic Benefit Street a few years before graduation. **Pros:** on a regal residential street; elegant furnishings; friendly service. **Cons:** small bathrooms; closets sized for 19th-century wardrobes. $ *Rooms from: $145* ⊠ *144 Benefit St., East Side* ☎ *401/751–2002* ⊕ *www.oldcourt.com* ⇗ *10 rooms* ❡❍❡ *Breakfast.*

FEDERAL HILL

$ 🔅 **Hotel Dolce Villa.** This small, well-managed inn is the only accom-
HOTEL modation actually in Federal Hill—it overlooks DePasquale Square and its vibrant cafés, gelato stands, and gourmet markets. **Pros:** great value; fun location with sister restaurant Caffe Dolce Vita next door; huge suites. **Cons:** modern white decor and carpets starting to show wear; no gym. $ *Rooms from: $159* ⊠ *63 DePasquale Sq., Federal Hill* ☎ *401/383–7031* ⊕ *www.dolcevillari.com* ⇗ *14 suites* ❡❍❡ *No meals.*

THE BLACKSTONE VALLEY

In 1790, young British engineer Samuel Slater arrived in Providence with the knowledge he gained from apprenticing in English cotton mills. It was a crime to export machinery designs for cotton-cloth making, but Slater had memorized much of what he saw. He found backers and partners and three years later, a mill opened at Pawtucket Falls in the Blackstone River. Eventually hundreds of mills were operating up and down the river from Worcester to Providence, transforming a young nation's agriculture-dominated economy and launching an industrial revolution. The Blackstone Valley helped make America the world's industrial powerhouse for a century and a half, luring immigrants to the region to work in its factories to make textiles as well as barbed wire, space suits, and even Mr. Potato Head. Much of that industry is now gone and many old mills have been renovated and converted to condominiums, offices, and gallery space. But the scenic river, the focus of ongoing environmental remediation efforts, remains a main attraction to the region, which includes the Rhode Island communities of Woonsocket, Pawtucket, Central Falls, Cumberland, Lincoln, North Smithfield, Smithfield, Glocester, and Burrillville. The Blackstone River Valley National Heritage Corridor designation aims to preserve and interpret the area's landscape and history.

GETTING HERE AND AROUND

TOURS **Blackstone Valley Explorer.** Running from Central Falls (June through mid-August) and Woonsocket (late August through late October), the 40-passenger riverboat Blackstone Valley Explorer offers tours on Sunday afternoons on the Blackstone River. The 45-minute narrated tour describes the area's ecology and industrial history. ⊠ *Central Falls Landing, 45 Madeira Ave., Central Falls* ☎ *800/454–2882, 401/724–2200* ⊕ *www.rivertourblackstone.com* ⊴ *$10.*

ESSENTIALS

Visitor Information Blackstone Valley Visitor Center ⊠ *175 Main St., Pawtucket* ☎ *401/724–2200, 800/454–2882* ⊕ *www.tourblackstone.com.*

PAWTUCKET

5 miles north of Providence.

Northeast of Providence, Pawtucket is Rhode Island's fourth-largest city with a population of more than 71,000 living in its 8.7 square miles. In Algonquian, "petuket" means "at the falls in the river." In 1671, ironworker Joseph Jenks built a forge and gristmill on the west bank of the Seekonk River at the falls where the Blackstone River reaches sea level, establishing a village that would grow on both sides of the fast-running river. The city shaped the Industrial Revolution, reaching its manufacturing peak in the late 19th century. Many industries moved south or died out in the 20th century, leaving numerous vacant mills for which city officials continue to pursue adaptive reuse projects. Pawtucket is still home to the headquarters of toy manufacturer Hasbro. Its thriving arts and cultural scene includes the Sandra Feinstein-Gamm Theatre, originally founded in Providence and now occupying the annex of the historic Pawtucket Armory, and the Hope Artiste Village, a mix of art studios, lofts, retail shops, light industrial workshops and the Met music venue.

ESSENTIALS

Visitor Information The Blackstone Valley Visitor Center. The Blackstone Valley Visitor Center, across the street from Slater Mill, has staffed information kiosks, maps, a gift shop, and the Pawtucket Arts Collaborative gallery. ⊠ *175 Main St.* ☎ *401/724–2200, 800/454–2882* ⊕ *www.tourblackstone.com* ⊠ *Free* ⊙ *Mon.–Sat. 10–5, Sun. 1–5.*

EXPLORING

Fodor'sChoice ★ ☺ **Slater Mill Museum.** Concord and Lexington may lay legitimate claim to what Ralph Waldo Emerson called "the shot heard round the world" in 1776, but Pawtucket's Slater Mill would provide the necessary economic shot in the arm through its own industrial revolution and secure America's sovereign independence in the decades that followed. Built in 1793, this National Historic Landmark was the first successful water-powered spinning mill in America and spawned the textile manufacturing industry. The museum complex explores America's second revolution, with expert interpretive guides dressed in period clothing who demonstrate the fiber-to-yarn and the yarn-to-fabric processes, and discuss how industrialization forever changed this nation. On-site are collections of hand-operated and powered machinery, a 120-seat theater, two gift shops, a gallery, and a recreational park. ⊠ *67 Roosevelt Ave.* ☎ *401/725–8638* ⊕ *www.slatermill.org* ⊠ *$12* ⊙ *Mar. and Apr., weekends 11–3; May–Oct., Tues.–Sun. 10–4, Nov. weekends 10–4, Dec.–Feb. tours by appointment.*

☺ **Slater Memorial Park.** Within the stately grounds of this park along Ten Mile River are picnic tables, tennis courts, a playground, and a river walk. The park's **Looff Carousel,** built by Charles I. D. Looff in 1894, has 39 horses, three dogs, a lion, a camel, a giraffe, and two chariots that are the earliest examples of the Danish immigrant's work. The carousel animals don't go up and down, but they move fast. Rides are only 25¢. The Pawtucket chapter of the Daughters of the American Revolution gives tours by appointment of the park's **Daggett House**, which dates to 1685. ✉ *825 Armistice Blvd.* ☎ *401/728–0500 park information* 🎟 *Free* 🕓 *Park: daily dawn–dusk. Carousel: July and August, daily 11–5; May and June, Sept. and Oct. weekends 11–5.*

SPORTS AND THE OUTDOORS

Pawtucket Red Sox. From April through early September, the Pawtucket Red Sox, the Triple-A international league affiliate of the Boston Red Sox, play approximately 70 home games at the 10,000-seat **McCoy Stadium.** ✉ *1 Ben Mondor Way* ☎ *401/724–7300* 🌐 *www.pawsox.com* 🎟 *Tickets $7–$11.*

NIGHTLIFE AND THE ARTS

Sandra Feinstein–Gamm Theatre. Known for its Shakespearean performances, the theatre also produces edgy productions of classic and contemporary works in an intimate 137-seat setting. Its season runs from fall through spring. ✉ *172 Exchange St.* ☎ *401/723–4266* 🌐 *www.gammtheatre.org.*

WHERE TO EAT

$ DINER ★ 🍴 **Modern Diner.** The line is often out the door on weekends for a seat in this 1941 Sterling Streamliner eatery. Breakfast—try the hash Benedict, lobster cheese grits, or cranberry pecan pancakes—is served all day, meaning until this family-run diner closes at 2. The burgundy and tan railway car simulation was the first diner to be listed on the National Register of Historic Places. It's attached to a modern addition with retro counter seating. [$] *Average main: $8* ✉ *364 East Ave.* ☎ *401/726–8390* 💳 *No credit cards* 🕓 *No dinner.*

$ INDIAN ★ 🍴 **Rasoi.** Taking its name from the Hindi word for kitchen, Rasoi has an affordable menu featuring cuisine from 27 regions of India. Just over the Providence line into Pawtucket, young professionals flock here for the grilled lamb barra kebab, Bengali seafood stew, chicken tikka labadar, and numerous vegetarian options. The menu indicates spicy, gluten-free, and vegan selections. The stylish dining room has a rectangular bar and warm orange walls, gold-specked blue floors, and red decorative panels. ■ **TIP➔ Check the website for the schedule of monthly cooking classes.** [$] *Average main: $15* ✉ *727 East Ave.* ☎ *401/728–5500* 🌐 *www.rasoi-restaurant.com.*

WOONSOCKET

10 miles north of Pawtucket, 15 miles north of Providence.

A city with a population of 41,000 encompassing 7.7 square miles, Woonsocket borders Massachusetts. Two theories exist regarding the origin and meaning of the city's name, both attributed to the language of the Native Americans who lived here before white settlers. One definition joins "woone" meaning thunder and "socket" meaning mist, given the city's location at the largest falls of the Blackstone River. Historians also suggest the name refers to the Woonsocket Hill in present

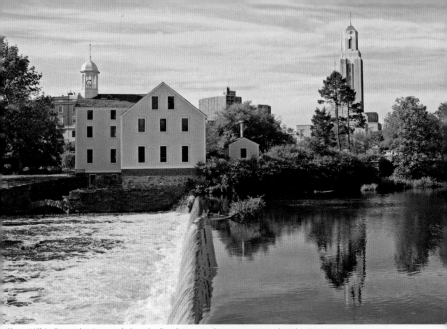

Slater Mill in Pawtucket is regarded as the first factory in the country; it produced cotton using waterpower.

day North Smithfield, some 3 miles southwest of the city, which was mentioned by Roger Williams in a 1660 letter. Woonsocket is home to one of the best museums about immigrant factory life and textile milling in the country. It is also home to the headquarters of Fortune 500 company CVS Corporation.

EXPLORING

Fodor's Choice ★ ☾ **Museum of Work and Culture.** Set up in a former textile mill, this interactive museum examines the lives of American factory workers and owners during the Industrial Revolution. Focusing on French Canadian immigrants to Woonsocket's mills, the museum's cleverly laid-out walk-through exhibits begin with a 19th-century Québécois farmhouse, then continue with displays of life in a 20th-century tenement, Catholic school, church, and on the shop floor. The genesis of the textile workers' union is described, as are the events that led to the National Textile Strike of 1934. There is also an engaging presentation about child labor. ⊠ *42 S. Main St.* ☎ *401/769-9675* ⊕ *www.rihs.org* ✉ *$8* ☾ *Tues.–Fri., 9:30–4, Sat. 10–4, Sun. 1–4. Closed Mon.*

NIGHTLIFE AND THE ARTS

Chan's. Hear renowned blues and jazz performers along with folk, cabaret, and comedy acts, and enjoy fine Chinese cuisine at Chan's. Reservations are advisable; tickets generally run about $10 to $25. ⊠ *267 Main St.* ☎ *401/765-1900* ⊕ *www.chanseggrollsandjazz.com.*

WHERE TO EAT AND STAY

For expanded hotel reviews, visit Fodors.com.

$ B&B/INN **The Pillsbury House Bed & Breakfast.** Tucked away on historic Prospect Street, a half mile from the Blackstone River, is this lovely 1875 Victorian. **Pros:** stunning architecture; great rates. **Cons:** old-fashioned decor isn't for everyone. [$] *Rooms from: $95* ✉ *341 Prospect St.* ☎ *401/766–7983, 800/205–4112* 🌐 *www.pillsburyhouse.com* 🛏 *3 rooms, 1 suite* 🍴 *Breakfast.*

SOUTH COUNTY

Although officially called Washington County, the southwestern region of Rhode Island is home to beautiful seaside villages, unspoiled beaches, and parks and management areas that offer great hiking, kayaking, and running opportunities. More laid-back than Newport and Providence, the area has always been a summertime destination, but South County's 11 towns have grown into a region of year-round residents. With a student body of more than 13,000 undergraduate and 3,000 graduate students, the University of Rhode Island occupies a 1,200-acre campus in Kingston as well as a 153-acre waterfront campus in Narragansett where its Graduate School of Oceanography is located.

ESSENTIALS

Visitor Information South County Tourism Council ✉ *4808 Tower Hill Rd., Suite 101, Wakefield* ☎ *401/789–4422, 800/548–4662* 🌐 *www.southcountyri.com.*

WESTERLY

50 miles southwest of Providence, 100 miles southwest of Boston, 140 miles northeast of New York City.

The picturesque downtown business district in this town of 18,000 people bordering Pawcatuck, Connecticut, has more than 55 structures on the National Register of Historic Places, galleries and artist studios and a 14.5-acre Victorian strolling park. Once a busy little railroad town in the late 19th century, Westerly is now a stop on the New York–Boston Amtrak corridor. The town was once known for its red granite used in monuments around the country. It has since sprawled out along U.S. 1 and grown to include seven villages—Westerly itself, or downtown Westerly, Watch Hill, Dunn's Corners, Misquamicut, Bradford, Shelter Harbor, and Weekapaug—encompassing a 33-square-mile area.

GETTING HERE AND AROUND

When traveling between New York City and Boston, Amtrak makes stops at Westerly, Kingston, and Providence.

ESSENTIALS

Transportation Information Amtrak ☎ *800/872–7245* 🌐 *www.amtrak.com.*

SPORTS AND THE OUTDOORS

Westerly Public Library and Wilcox Park. Designed and created in 1898 by Warren Manning (an associate of Frederick Law Olmsted), this 14.5-acre Victorian strolling park in the heart of downtown Westerly boasts a pond, meadow, arboretum, perennial garden, sculptures, fountains, and monuments. Every June there is a Summer Pops concert featuring the Chorus of Westerly and Boston Pops with fireworks. A garden market, arts festivals, and Shakespeare-in-the-park productions are held periodically. ⊠ *44 Broad St.* ☎ *401/596–2877* ⊕ *www.westerlylibrary.org.*

NIGHTLIFE

Knickerbocker Cafe. The band Roomful of Blues was born at "The Knick" and still gigs at this music club near the Westerly train station. The venue hosts roots, R&B, jazz, blues, and alt-country touring acts and dance parties. ⊠ *35 Railroad Ave.* ☎ *401/315–5070* ⊕ *www.theknickerbockercafe.com.*

WHERE TO EAT AND STAY

For expanded hotel reviews, visit Fodors.com.

$$
AMERICAN
✕ **Bridge.** On the site of the former upscale Up River Cafe is a more casual restaurant that opened three months after the devastating flood in March 2010. Named for the bridge spanning the Pawcatuck River that runs beside it, the restaurant offers affordable American regional cuisine with an emphasis on local seafood and comfort food. The menu includes a flavorful meat loaf, lobster mac 'n' cheese, and chicken potpie along with popular grilled fish tacos. The riverside bar and outdoor patio is great for taking in summer concerts in the park right across the narrow river in Connecticut or watching the annual Westerly-Pawcatuck Duck Race, when 20,000 rubber duckies are cast into the river to raise money for local schools and nonprofits. $ *Average main: $18* ⊠ *37 Main St.* ☎ *401/348–9700.*

$$$
B&B/INN
⌂ **Shelter Harbor.** Set back off Route 1, this early 19th-century farmhouse inn and restaurant in the village of Shelter Harbor is a quiet retreat 5 miles from downtown Westerly. **Pros:** quiet location; beautiful grounds; great water views; men's and women's locker rooms with showers, towels, and soaps near hot tub. **Cons:** bathrooms could use updating. $ *Rooms from: $192* ⊠ *10 Wagner Rd., off U.S. 1, Shelter Harbor* ☎ *401/322–8883, 800/468–8883* ⊕ *www.shelterharborinn.com* ↵ *24 rooms* ¶⊙¶ *Breakfast.*

WATCH HILL

6 miles south of downtown Westerly.

★ The quintessential New England seaside village has quite the inventory of well-kept summerhouses owned by wealthy families for generations. Parking can be difficult on Bay Street, the tiny business district with boutiques, cafés, and the historic carousel. Watch Hill has almost 2 miles of gorgeous beaches including Napatree Point Conservation Area, a great spot to see shorebirds and raptors and take in the sunset.

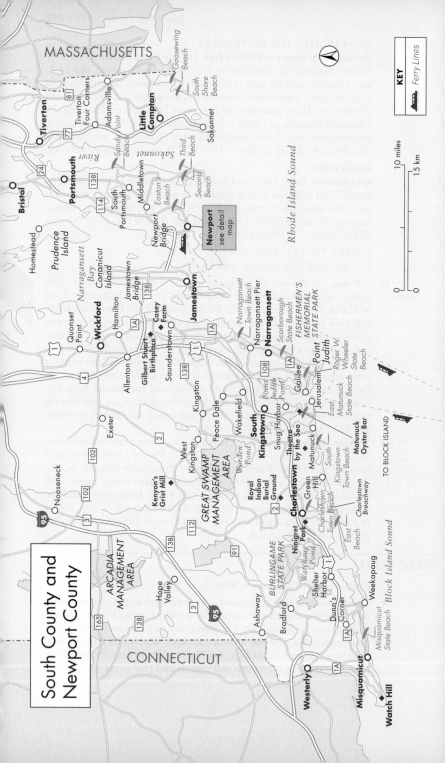

EXPLORING

Flying Horse Carousel. At the beach end of Bay Street is one of the oldest carousels in America, built by the Charles W. F. Dare Company of New York City and part of a traveling carnival that came to Watch Hill before 1883. The carved wooden horses with real horsehair manes and leather saddles are suspended from chains attached to the ceiling, creating the impression the horses are flying. Riders must be between ages two and 12. ⊠ *151 Bay St.* ☎ *401/348–6007* 💲 *$1.50 outside horses; $1 inside* ☻ *Mid-June–Labor Day, weekdays 10–9, weekends and holidays 9–9; Memorial Day–mid-June and Labor Day–Columbus Day, weekends 9–9.*

Watch Hill Lighthouse. A tiny museum on the site of this 1808 lighthouse contains the original Fresnal light, a binnacle, mariner sea chests, photographs of the hurricane of 1938, and shots of 19th- and early-20th-century sailing vessels off Watch Hill. Parking is for the handicapped and senior citizens only; everyone else must walk along a private road off Larkin Road. ⊠ *14 Lighthouse Rd.* ☎ *401/596–7761* ⊕ *www. watchhilllighthousekeepers.org* 💲 *Free* ☻ *Grounds daily 8–8. Museum July–Labor Day, Tues. and Thurs. 1–3.*

WHERE TO STAY

For expanded hotel reviews, visit Fodors.com.

$$$$
RESORT
Fodor's Choice
★
⊞ Ocean House. High on bluffs overlooking Block Island Sound is this extraordinary replica of the Victorian grand hotel of the same name built on the same spot in 1868. **Pros:** exceptional service; private sand beach with cabanas; full-size championship croquet lawn; spa with 25-meter lap pool; complimentary cooking classes led by a resident "food forager." **Cons:** rooms start at $715 a night during high season; two-night minimum on weekends; traditionalists may dislike no-gratuity policy resulting from $32-per-night resort fee. 💲 *Rooms from: $715* ⊠ *1 Bluff Ave., Watch Hill* ☎ *401/315-0579* ⊕ *www.oceanhouseri.com* ⌂ *49 rooms, 23 residences, 10 signature suites* ¶○¶ *Multiple meal plans.*

$$$$
RENTAL
⊞ Watch Hill Inn Residences. Comprising an 1845 Victorian-style inn and a modern 2007 addition, this upscale condominium complex has sunny one- and two-bedroom condos and apartments rented nightly, weekly, or monthly. **Pros:** steps from beaches and shops; many units have private decks; amenities include beach towels, in-room coffeemaker, treadmills, and Wi-Fi. **Cons:** two-night minimum stay required. 💲 *Rooms from: $350* ⊠ *38–44 Bay St.* ☎ *401/348–6300* ⊕ *www.watchhillinn. com* ⌂ *24 apartments* ¶○¶ *No meals.*

MISQUAMICUT

2½ miles northeast of Watch Hill.

The Native American name for this 7-mile-long strip of sandy beachfront stretching from Watch Hill to Weekapaug means "Red Fish," referencing Atlantic salmon, common to the Pawcatuck River and also the original name for the entire Westerly area settled in 1661. Today it's a family-oriented summer vacation destination with amusement parks featuring a carousel, minigolf, go-carts, batting cages, waterslides, and kiddie rides. Hop on a Jet Ski, paddle a kayak, or find a spot for sunbathing. Evenings bring concerts and movies on the beach.

EXPLORING

Atlantic Beach Park. The largest and most popular of the several kid-oriented amusements along Misquamicut Beach, this festive facility has lots to keep families busy, including a carousel, bumper cars, a mini golf course, waterslides, batting cages, and a large arcade with more than 75 video and other games. ✉ *323 Atlantic Ave.* ☎ *401/322–0504* 🌐 *www.atlanticbeachpark.com* 🎟 *Free general admission; $2 per ride excluding water park* 🕒 *Mid-June–Labor Day, daily; weekends only mid-May–mid-June and Labor Day–mid-Oct.; hours vary depending on the ride or game.*

SPORTS AND THE OUTDOORS

Misquamicut State Beach. Half-mile-long Misquamicut State Beach is the state's longest beach, part of the several-mile-long stretch that makes up Misquamicut. Expect the 2,100-space parking lot to fill up on sunny summer holiday weekends. Facilities include showers, changing rooms, first-aid, concessions, and restrooms. ✉ *Atlantic Ave., 257 Atlantic Ave., Westerly* ☎ *401/596–9097* 🌐 *www.riparks.com/misquamicut.htm* 🕒 *May–Memorial Day, weekends 9–6; Memorial Day–Labor Day, daily 9–6.*

WHERE TO EAT AND STAY

For expanded hotel reviews, visit Fodors.com.

$$ MEDITERRANEAN 🍴 **Maria's Seaside Cafe.** This family-owned lunch and dinner spot across the street from the beach is a standout on a strip of ice cream stands, take-out shacks, and motels that have seen better days. Maria's Mediterranean menu has such refined choices as pan-seared Stonington scallops over Italian couscous with lobster meat and black-truffle essence. The ahi tuna sashimi appetizer with avocado, tomatoes, and crispy tortilla strips is also notable. There is a great wine list and raw bar selections. Outdoor seating is cleverly divided into a section with quiet tables for two on one side and larger tables to accommodate families on the other. [$] *Average main: $21* ✉ *132 Atlantic Ave.* ☎ *401/596–6886* 🌐 *www.mariasseasidecafe.com* 🕒 *Closed early-Oct.–May.*

$$$ HOTEL ★ 🏨 **Breezeway Resort.** This well-maintained boutique motel with cheery rooms owned by the Bellone family since 1970 is only two-tenths of a mile away from the ocean. **Pros:** spotless rooms; nice range of room configurations; comfortable mattresses; beach towels provided; washer/dryer on-site; 10% discount at nearby Maria's Seaside Cafe, also owned by the Bellones. **Cons:** a bit noisy with so many kids; most rooms don't have Wi-Fi. [$] *Rooms from: $189* ✉ *70 Winnapaug Rd.* ☎ *401/348–8953, 800/462–8872* 🌐 *www.breezewayresort.com* 🛏 *30 rooms, 25 suites* 🕒 *Closed late Oct. through early May* 🍽 *Breakfast.*

CHARLESTOWN

12 miles northeast of Misquamicut.

Named after King Charles II, Charlestown had previously been a part of Westerly until it was incorporated in 1738. The 37-square-mile town of about 7,800 people is centrally located between New London, Connecticut, and Providence, both a 40-minute drive. Approximately 20% of Charlestown is conservation and recreation land, including Burlingame State Park, Ninigret Wildlife Refuge, Ninigret Park, and East Beach. Its secluded coastline makes the town a great spot for swimming, sailing, surfing, beachcombing, and boating. Charlestown is also home to the Narragansett Indian Tribe Reservation, which holds the oldest recorded annual powwow in North America every August.

SPORTS AND THE OUTDOORS

PARKS

Burlingame State Park. This 2,100-acre park has nature trails, picnic and swimming areas, and campgrounds, as well as boating and fishing on crystal clear Watchaug Pond. Parking at the picnic area is free but there is a $2 rental fee for a table. ⊠ *1 Burlingame Rd.* ☎ *401/322–8910.*

★ **Ninigret National Wildlife Refuge.** Spring brings great opportunities to view the male American woodcock's mating ritual at this 400-acre sanctuary. But bird-watchers flock here year-round to commune with nature among 9 miles of trails and diverse upland and wetland habitats, including grasslands, shrublands, wooded swamps, and freshwater ponds. There are two stretches of beach lands and marshes, plus the abandoned naval air station on Ninigret Pond, the state's largest coastal salt pond and a great place to watch the sunset. Explore an impressive collection of wildlife and natural history displays at the Kettle Pond Visitor Center on the other side of Route 1. ⊠ *50 Bend Rd., off Rte. 1* ☎ *401/364–9124* ⊕ *www.fws.gov/ninigret/complex* ☜ *Free* ☉ *Daily dawn–dusk, visitor center daily 10–4.*

Ninigret Park. This 227-acre park off Old Post Road on the site of a World War II–era naval air training base features picnic grounds, ball fields, a playground, a bike path, tennis and basketball courts, nature trails, a disc golf course, and a 3-acre spring-fed swimming pond. Ninigret Park is also the site for summer music festivals and the Charlestown Seafood Festival every August. ⊠ *On Rte. 1A just off Rte. 1, 5 Park Lane* ☎ *401/364–1222* ☉ *Daily 8–sunset.*

Frosty Drew Nature Center & Observatory. This nature center, located within Ninigret Park, has a Meade 16-inch telescope and presents free nature and Friday night astronomy programs. The observatory also opens for viewing special astronomical events like meteor showers, lunar eclipses, and comets. ⊠ *4870 Old Post Rd.* ☎ *401/364–9508* ⊕ *www.frostydrew.org*

BEACHES

Charlestown Town Beach. The Town of Charlestown owns 450 feet of oceanfront and has concessions and new bathroom facilities with outdoor rinsing stations. Lifeguards are on duty weather permitting 9–5 weekdays and 8–5 weekends and holidays. The town also owns Blue Shutters Beach at the end of East Road, which also has a new pavilion where you can see Block Island and Long Island from the shaded deck. ⊠ *557 Charlestown Beach Rd.* ☎ *401/364–1208* ☜ *Parking $20 weekends and holidays; $15 weekdays.*

★ **East Beach.** This unspoiled narrow barrier beach and campground accessible from Route 1 is the place for tranquillity. Spanning 3 miles of shoreline that fronts and separates Ninigret Pond from the ocean, it's quite a contrast to Narragansett's bustling Scarborough beach. A small portion of the beach is staffed with lifeguards on a seasonal basis. Facilities include composting toilets and changing rooms. ⊠ *Ninigret Conservation Area, E. Beach Rd.* ☎ *401/322–0450* ⌖ *Parking on weekends: $28 nonresidents, $14 residents; weekdays $20 nonresidents, $10 residents.*

BOATING

Ocean House Marina. This full-service marina has fuel, fishing supplies, and boat rentals. ⊠ *60 Town Dock Rd., at Cross Mills exit off U.S. 1* ☎ *401/364–6040* ⊕ *www.oceanhousemarina.com.*

SHOPPING

★ **Fantastic Umbrella Factory.** The hippy dippy, kid-friendly Fantastic
☾ Umbrella Factory has four rustic shops built around a wild garden. For sale are hardy perennials and unusual daylilies, jewelry, vintage eyewear, pottery, blown glass, penny candy, greeting cards, crafts, and incense. There is also the BYOB Small Axe Cafe serving organic foods. For 50¢ you can scoop a cone full of seeds to feed the fenced-in emus, guinea hens, and ducks. ⊠ *4820 Old Post Rd., off U.S. 1* ☎ *401/364–1060* ⊕ *www.fantasticumbrellafactory.com* ☺ *Memorial Day–Labor Day, daily 10–6; rest of the year, daily 10–5.*

RHODE ISLAND TREATS

Coffee Milk. The official state drink, coffee milk is like chocolate milk but made instead with coffee-flavored syrup; the preferred coffee syrup is Autocrat Coffee Syrup.

Del's Frozen Lemonade. A finalist for official state drink, you can get one of these refreshingly cold drinks from one of many Del's trucks making the rounds in the summer or a Del's storefront.

NY System Wieners. Try a hot dog "done all the way"—topped with meat sauce, mustard, onions, and celery salt; they are said to be a great hangover cure.

SOUTH KINGSTOWN

10 miles northeast of Charlestown.

Originally incorporated in 1674 as Kings Town, this rural community was the site of the Great Swamp Fight in 1675, the battle in which Colonial soldiers gave King Philip his greatest defeat. Almost a third of South Kingstown's 57 square miles is protected open space. There are two beaches, three rivers, and several salt ponds, making it a great place for fishing and boating. The town of about 30,000 people claims a total of 14 distinct villages, including Wakefield, Snug Harbor, Matunuck, and Kingston, home of the University of Rhode Island.

SPORTS AND THE OUTDOORS
BEACHES

East Matunuck State Beach. East Matunuck State Beach is popular with the college crowd and older beachgoers for its heavier surf and white sand, picnic areas, and new green-energy pavilion with showers and concessions. ⚠ **The open water is not suitable for small children.** ⊠ *950 Succotash Rd.* ☎ *401/789–8585* ⊕ *www.riparks.com/eastmatunuck. htm* 🚗 *Parking nonresidents: $28 weekends, $20 weekdays; residents: $14 weekends, $10 weekdays.*

South Kingstown Town Beach. The 1/3-mile long South Kingstown Town Beach, with a playground, picnic tables, grills, and showers, cannot be seen from the road and doesn't fill as quickly as the nearby state beaches. The beach has moderate surf. ⊠ *719 Matunuck Beach Rd.* ☎ *401/789–9301* 🚗 *Parking $20 nonresidents, $10 residents.*

BOATING AND FISHING

Snug Harbor Marina. On the docks at Snug Harbor, an annual shark tournament the weekend after July 4th means you'll see mako, blue, and the occasional tiger shark being weighed in. The harbor is also a fine spot for kayaking. Snug Harbor Marina sells bait, arranges fishing charters, and rents sea kayaks. ⊠ *410 Gooseberry Rd., Wakefield* ☎ *401/783–7766* ⊕ *www.snugharbormarina.com.*

NIGHTLIFE AND THE ARTS

Ocean Mist. Ocean Mist has an outside deck right on the beach where you can watch the surfers on the point and catch some rays. Live bands, including rock and reggae acts, perform nightly in summer and on weekends off-season. ⊠ *895 Matunuck Beach Rd., Matunuck* ☎ *401/782–3740* ⊕ *www.oceanmist.net* ☉ *Mon.–Fri. 11:30 am–1 am, weekends 9 am–1 am.*

Fodor's Choice ★ **Theatre by the Sea.** Enjoy summer stock as it was meant to be performed at this old 500-seat barn-theater a quarter mile from the ocean. Broadway musicals get the royal treatment here with directors, choreographers, and many actors and singers coming from New York City. The season extends from late May through early September. On the National Register of Historic Places, a summer theater has been on the site since 1933, although hurricanes, World War II, and economic hardships kept some summers dark. The nonprofit Ocean State Theater Company now produces classics and newer musicals, as well as a play each year; tickets run $35–$54. The Bistro by the Sea restaurant features casual contemporary cuisine. ⊠ *364 Cards Pond Rd., Matunuck* ☎ *401/782–8587* ⊕ *www.theatrebythesea.com.*

WHERE TO EAT

$$ SEAFOOD Fodor's Choice ★ ✕ **Matunuck Oyster Bar.** Shuckers are hard at work at the raw bar in this awesome, waterside restaurant Perry Raso opened in 2009 as an offshoot of his Matunuck Oyster Farm, located just 200 yards away in Potter Pond. This year-round business committed to mixing fresh local produce with farm-raised and wild-caught seafood draws a crowd. Thankfully a valet ensures you're able to park your vehicle. Sunset is the best time to visit and take in the view with a glass of wine while enjoying Point Judith calamari with cherry peppers and arugula, whole-belly

Point Judith Lighthouse is just one of 21 such beacons in the Ocean State.

fried clams and different varieties of crisp, briny Rhode Island oysters, cherrystones, and littleneck clams. ■ **TIP→ Be prepared to wait, and snag a table outside if you can.** [$] *Average main: $20* ✉ *629 Succotash Road, East Matunuck* ☎ *401/783–4202* 🌐 *www.rhodyoysters.com* ✍ *Reservations not accepted.*

NARRAGANSETT

5 miles east of Wakefield.

A popular summer resort destination during the Victorian era, Narragansett still has as its main landmark, The Towers, the last remaining section of the famous 1886 Narragansett Pier Casino designed by McKim, Mead, and White. The town is home to a large commercial fishing fleet and four beaches. Take a scenic drive down Route 1A to see the ocean and grand old shingle-style homes. You'll eventually wind up at Point Judith Lighthouse, which has been in operation since the 19th century.

EXPLORING

👶 **Port of Galilee.** This little corner of Narragansett is a working fishing village where you can watch fishermen unload their catch, eat at a fish shack, or go for a swim at two state beaches: Captain Roger Wheeler State Beach or Salty Brine State Beach. The port is the major hub for year-round ferry service to Block Island. ✉ *301 Great Island Rd., Galilee* ☎ *401/783–5551* 🌐 *www.dem.ri.gov/programs/bnatres/coastal/index.htm.*

Block Island Ferry. Interstate Navigation Company, Inc. operates the Block Island Ferry from Point Judith with high-speed ferry service available Memorial Day through Columbus Day and traditional service offered year-round. The high-speed ferry, which takes 30 minutes, is for passengers and bicycles only. If you're bringing a car, you must take the one-hour trip on the traditional ferry. ⊠ *Galilee State Pier, 304 Great Island Rd.* ☎ *401/783–7996, 866/783–7996* ⊕ *www. blockislandferry.com*

Point Judith Lighthouse. From the port of Galilee it's a short drive to this 1857 lighthouse with a beautiful ocean view. The lighthouse is on an active Coast Guard Station; the public may access the grounds. ⊠ *1470 Ocean Rd.* ☎ *401/789–0444* ☒ *Free* ☉ *Daily dawn–dusk.*

☺ **South County Museum.** Set on part of early-19th-century Rhode Island governor William Sprague's former estate (now a town park), the museum founded in 1933 holds 25,000 artifacts dating from pre-European settlement to mid-20th century. The campus consists of six exhibit buildings, including a print shop, blacksmith and carpentry shops, and textile arts center. A living history farm has Romney sheep, Nubian goats, Narragansett turkeys, and a flock of Rhode Island Red Heritage chickens, the state bird. ⊠ *115 Strathmore St., off Rte 1A* ☎ *401/783–5400* ⊕ *www.southcountymuseum.org* ☒ *$6* ☉ *May, June and Sept., Fri. and Sat. 10–4; July and Aug., Wed.-Sat. 10–4.*

SPORTS AND THE OUTDOORS

BEACHES

Narragansett Town Beach. Covering approximately 19 acres, Narragansett Town Beach offers four large parking areas along with food, restrooms, first-aid, a popular surfing area, and a beautiful sandy beachfront. ⊠ *39 Boston Neck Rd.* ☎ *401/783–6430* ⊕ *www.narragansettri.gov* ☒ *$6 per person; parking $10 weekdays, $15 weekends.*

Roger W. Wheeler State Beach. Roger W. Wheeler State Beach has fine white sand, calm water, and a slight drop-off. There is a playground area, picnic tables, a bathhouse, and parking. ⊠ *100 Sand Hill Cove Rd., Galilee* ☎ *401/789–3563.*

Fodor's Choice ★ **Scarborough State Beach.** The 42-acre Scarborough State Beach has stunning views of where Narragansett Bay empties into the ocean and generally moderate surf. Two pavilions have hot and cold showers and concessions. There is also a concrete boardwalk with gazebos and an observation tower. ⊠ *870 Ocean Rd.* ☎ *401/789–2324* ☒ *Parking nonresidents: $28 weekends, $20 weekdays; residents: $14 weekends, $10 weekdays.*

FISHING

The Frances Fleet. The Frances Fleet, with four vessels, operates day and overnight fishing trips as well as whale-watching cruises. ⊠ *33 State St., Point Judith* ☎ *401/783–4988, 800/662–2824* ⊕ *www.francesfleet.com.*

Prowler. International Game Fish Association's Fishing Hall of Famer Captain Al Anderson—credited with tagging more fish for science than anyone worldwide—can take you fishing for tuna, bluefish, and striped bass on the 42-foot *Prowler.* ⊠ *State Charter Boat Dock, State St.* ☎ *401/783–8487* ⊕ *www.prowlercharters ri.com.*

6

Seven B's V. The Seven B's V is an 80-foot open party and fishing boat that holds up to 120 passengers. ✉ *Port of Galilee, Dock RR, 30 State St.* ☎ *401/789–9250* 🌐 *www.sevenbs.com.*

WHALE-WATCHING

Lady Frances. During July and August, whale-watching excursions aboard *Lady Frances* depart at 1 pm and return at 5:30. ✉ *33 State St., Point Judith* ☎ *401/783–4988* 🌐 *www.francesfleet.com* 🎫 *$45* 🕒 *July–Aug., Tues., Thurs.–Sat.*

SURFING

Narragansett Surf & Skate Shop. Narragansett Surf and Skate rents surfboards, body boards, and wetsuits, and offers surf and stand-up paddle lessons for individuals and groups. ✉ *74 Narragansett Ave.* ☎ *401/789–7890, 401/789–1954 surf report* 🌐 *narragansettsurfandskate.com.*

WHERE TO EAT

$$ SEAFOOD Fodor's Choice ★ 👶

🍴 **Aunt Carrie's.** The perfectly textured clam cakes are the size of baseballs at this authentic Point Judith seafood dinner hall where you can choose to eat in the 125-seat dining hall or order at the takeout window and use the picnic tables across the street. You won't find a better lobster roll anywhere else: mounds of fresh lobster meat with lettuce and just enough mayo are pressed between two hulking grilled slices of freshly baked bread. There's even a lobster BLT. The clam chowder comes three ways: red, white, and clear. Family-owned for four generations, the recipes for several varieties of namesake Carrie Cooper's pies are still in use. The lines can get pretty long in the thick of summer, but the wait is worth it. The waitstaff is friendly and attentive and the restaurant is BYOB. [$] *Average main: $19* ✉ *1240 Ocean Rd., Point Judith* ☎ *401/783–7930* 🌐 *www.auntcarriesri.com* ✍ *Reservations not accepted* 🕒 *Closed Oct.–Mar.*

$$ SEAFOOD ★

🍴 **Coast Guard House.** A plaque on the dining room wall commemorates how this Ocean Road landmark can't be any closer to the sea: the dining room was underwater when Hurricane Bob hit in August 1991. While the two open decks draw a crowd in nice weather, enjoy a table by the huge bank of windows inside when the sea is stormy. Originally built in 1888 as a U.S. Life Saving Service Station, many of the property's architectural details have been preserved and historic photos line the walls in the spacious and sleek bar area. The lightly fried calamari with a citrus vinaigrette and sushi-grade ahi tuna are especially pleasing. Seafood often comes from the nearby Port of Galilee. [$] *Average main: $21* ✉ *40 Ocean Rd.* ☎ *401/789–0700* 🌐 *www.thecoastguardhouse.com* 🕒 *Closed Jan.*

$ ECLECTIC

🍴 **Crazy Burger Cafe & Juice Bar.** Vegetarians, vegans, and omnivores flock to this funky BYOB café not far from Narragansett Town Beach for smoothies, creative juice blends like pear-ginger-apple, eclectic burgers, and sweet-potato fries. Breakfast, served until 4 pm every day, features popular Mexican-style eggs and spinach crepes. White Christmas lights and colorful cloth napkins are part of the decor as is a red phone booth behind the counter housing condiments (Crazy Burger makes its own ketchup). The waitstaff is friendly but usually very busy. Expect a bit of a wait until you can settle into a comfy booth and contemplate the extensive menu. $ *Average main: $10* ✉ *144 Boon St.* ☎ *401/783–1810* ⊕ *www.crazyburger.com* ⌕ *Reservations not accepted.*

$$
SEAFOOD

✕**George's of Galilee.** Owned by the same family since 1948, this local landmark right by Salty Brine State Beach serves arguably the best "stuffies" (baked stuffed quahogs) and clam cakes in the state. Get your fried and broiled seafood here at reasonable prices; George's buys fish directly from the boats in Galilee. The real draw is the large outside second-floor bar where you can enjoy a fruity rum punch in a fish bowl you can take home as a souvenir. A major renovation over the winter of 2011–2012 gutted and redesigned the first floor and stairway and added a sleek black granite bar, mahogany trim, a new outdoor patio, and fire pit. $ *Average main: $17* ✉ *250 Sand Hill Cove Rd.* ☎ *401/783–2306* ⊕ *www.georgesofgalilee.com* ⌕ *Reservations not accepted* ☉ *Closed Jan.–mid-Feb.; no dinner Feb. and March, Mon.–Thurs.*

WHERE TO STAY

For expanded hotel reviews, visit Fodors.com.

$$
B&B/INN

🏨**Blueberry Cove Inn.** This warmly furnished, historic inn is set along an attractive tree-lined residential street. **Pros:** four-tenths of a mile from Narragansett Town Beach; beach towels and chairs available; close to restaurants; outstanding breakfasts. **Cons:** two-night stay required July, August, and most weekends May–November; three-night stays required for summer holidays. $ *Rooms from: $150* ✉ *75 Kingstown Rd.* ☎ *401/792–9865, 800/478–1426* ⊕ *www.blueberrycoveinn.com* ⇆ *7 rooms, 2 suites* ⍟ *Breakfast.*

$$
B&B/INN
★

🏨**The Richards Bed & Breakfast.** The white rope hammock behind this secluded 8,500-square-foot circa-1884 English-style stone mansion is where you want to be. **Pros:** lots of quiet; remarkable architecture; great breakfast; reasonable rates. **Cons:** a bit of a walk from the beach; no TV in rooms. $ *Rooms from: $160* ✉ *144 Gibson Ave.* ☎ *401/789–7746* ⊕ *www.therichardsbnb.com* ⇆ *3 rooms, 1 suite* ▭ *No credit cards* ⍟ *Breakfast.*

WICKFORD

12 miles north of Narragansett Pier, 15 miles south of Providence.

★ A quaint village on a small harbor, Wickford has dozens of 18th- and 19th-century homes, historical churches, antiques shops, and boutiques selling jewelry, home accents and gifts, and clothing. Wickford hosts Daffodil Days in the spring, an annual arts festival in July and the Festival of Lights in December.

EXPLORING

Casey Farm. This 1751 farmstead overlooks Narragansett Bay off Route 1A south of Wickford. In the 19th century, this was the summer residence of the Casey family, who leased the land to tenant farmers. Today this community-supported farm is operated by resident managers who raise organically grown vegetables. Nearly 30 miles of stone walls surround the 300-acre farmstead. ■**TIP→ A weekly farmers' market takes place Saturdays from May to October.** ✉ *2325 Boston Neck Rd.,*

Saunderstown ☎ *401/295–1030* ⊕ *www.historicnewengland.org* ✉ *$4* ⊙ *June–mid-Oct., Tues.–Thurs., 1–5, Sat. 9–2.*

★ **Smith's Castle.** Built in 1678 by Richard Smith Jr., this beautifully preserved saltbox plantation house replaced an earlier fortified house built by Smith's father. The former house had been burned during hostilities in King Philip's War. Originally the site of a trading post established by Roger Williams, it also includes a marked mass grave where 40 colonists killed in the Great Swamp battle of 1676 are buried. The land was part of a great plantation during the 18th century, spanning more than 3,000 acres worked by slaves and indentured laborers, and was later a large dairy farm. Saved from the wrecking ball by preservationists in 1949, the castle today appears much like it was in 1740. Smith's Castle hosts an annual Strawberry Festival each June and other special events. ✉ *55 Richard Smith Dr., 1 mile north of Wickford* ☎ *401/294–3521* ⊕ *www.smithscastle.org* ✉ *$6* ⊙ *May and Sept.–mid-Oct., noon–4; Fri.–Sun., noon–4; June–Aug. Thurs.–Sun., noon–4; tours given on the hour, last tour at 3.*

SPORTS AND THE OUTDOORS

BOATING

Kayak Centre. In Wickford Harbor, the Kayak Centre sells and rents kayaks and stand-up paddleboards and provides lessons. ✉ *9 Phillips St.* ☎ *401/295–4400* ⊕ *www.kayakcentre.com* ⊙ *Mon.–Wed., and Fri., 10–6; Thurs., 10–7; Sat., 10–5; Sun., noon–5.*

SHOPPING

Wickford Art Association. The Wickford Art Association operates a gallery that hosts juried arts shows and puts on the annual Wickford Art Festival every July. ✉ *36 Beach St.* ☎ *401/294–6840* ⊕ *www.wickfordart. org* ⊙ *Sun. noon–3, Mon. noon–4, Tues.–Sat., 11–3.*

Five Main. The small fine-art gallery Five Main represents local and nationally known artists, photographers, and jewelry designers. You'll find inspired landscapes and seascapes as well as a collection of vintage pottery. ✉ *5 Main St.* ☎ *401/294–6280* ⊕ *www.fivemain.com.*

The Mermaid's Purl. This welcoming yarn shop has a great selection of organic cotton, bamboo, alpaca, merino wool, and cashmere yarns, felting supplies, beads, buttons, books, patterns, knitting and crochet needles, and accessories. Classes are held at least three nights a week. Wednesday morning and evening "knit-ins" invite you to bring in a work in progress and get help if needed. ✉ *1 West St.* ☎ *401/268–3899* ⊕ *www.themermaidspurl.com* ⊙ *Mon.–Sat., 10–5, Sun., noon–5.*

NEWPORT COUNTY AND EAST BAY

Newport is one of the great sailing cities of the world and the host to world-class jazz, blues, folk, classical music, and film festivals. Colonial houses and Gilded Age mansions grace the city. Besides Newport itself, Newport County also encompasses the two other communities of Aquidneck Island—Middletown and Portsmouth—plus Conanicut Island, also known as Jamestown, to the west, and Tiverton and Little Compton, abutting Massachusetts to the east. Little Compton is a remote, idyllic town that presents a strong contrast to Newport's quick pace. Narrow and scenic Mount Hope Bridge carries traffic north from Aquidneck Island to Bristol, the most charming of the three towns that make up the East Bay region, which is encompassed entirely within Bristol County, one of the nation's smallest geographically.

GETTING HERE AND AROUND

You'll need to cross at least one of four major bridges to reach Newport County. The largest is the Newport Pell Bridge, spanning Narragansett Bay's East Passage via Route 138 and linking the island community of Jamestown and Newport. Motorists without a Rhode Island-issued EZ-Pass transponder have to pay $5 to cross it. Newport anchors Aquidneck Island, also home to the towns of Middletown and Portsmouth. From the north end of Portsmouth, Route 24 takes you across the Sakonnet River Bridge to Tiverton. Follow Route 77 south through Tiverton to reach quiet Little Compton. From the northwest end of Portsmouth, you cross the Mount Hope Bridge to reach the charming town of Bristol in Bristol County, home to the oldest continuous 4th of July parade in the country. The Jamestown-Verrazano Bridge connects Jamestown to North Kingstown over Narragansett Bay's West Passage.

CAB TRAVEL Cozy Cab runs a daily shuttle service ($25 each way) between T. F. Green Airport (in Warwick) and the Newport Visitors' Information Center, as well as major hotels.

FERRY TRAVEL Visitors headed to Newport from the west can save themselves the hassle of parking in Newport and the Newport Pell Bridge toll by parking their cars for free in Jamestown and boarding the Jamestown Newport Ferry. Conanicut Marine operates the 40-foot passenger ferry from One East Ferry Wharf in Jamestown and offers free van shuttle service to a large parking area at nearby Taylor Point. The ferry runs daily mid-June through Labor Day and on weekends Memorial Day weekend through mid-June and late September through Columbus Day. The ferry links the village of Jamestown to Rose Island, Fort Adams State Park, Perrotti Park, Bowen's Wharf, and Waites Wharf. An $18 round-trip rate is good for all day but one-way passage rates and bicycle rates are available. Ferry service starts at 9:15 am in Jamestown, and the last run leaves Newport around 7:20 (or around 11 pm on weekends.)

Oldport Marine Services operates a harbor shuttle service Monday through Thursday from noon to 6 pm and Friday, Saturday, and Sunday from 11 am to 7 pm ($10 all day, $6 round-trip, $3 one-way). The shuttle lands at Perrotti Park, Bowen's Wharf, Ann Street Pier, International Yacht Restoration School, the Sail Newport dock, Fort Adams, and Goat Island.

PARKING In Newport, a number of lots around town offer pay parking (the largest and most economical is the garage behind the Newport Visitors' Information Center); street parking can be difficult to find in summer.

ESSENTIALS

Transportation Contacts Cozy Cab ✉ *129 Connell Hwy., Newport* ☎ *401/846–2500, 800/846–1502* ⊕ *www.cozytrans.com.* **Jamestown Newport Ferry** ☎ *401/423–9900* ⊕ *www.jamestownnewportferry.com* 🎫 *$18*

roundtrip, $10 one-way, bicycles $3 each way. **Oldport Marine Services**
☎ 401/847–9109 ⊕ www.oldportmarine.com.

Visitor Information Discover Newport ⊠ *The Newport Visitors Center,
23 America's Cup Ave., Newport* ☎ *401/845–9130, 800/976–5122* ⊕ *www.
gonewport.com* ⊙ *Daily 9–5; summer daily 9–6.*

JAMESTOWN

25 miles south of Providence, 3 miles west of Newport.

Surrounded by Narragansett Bay's East and West passages, Conanicut
Island comprises the town of Jamestown. About 9 miles long and 1
mile-wide, the island is home to beautiful state parks, historic Beavertail Lighthouse, farmland, and a downtown village with a quaint mix
of shops and restaurants.

EXPLORING

Jamestown Windmill. Once common in Rhode Island, the English-
designed windmill built in 1787 ground corn for more than 100 years—
and it still works. You can enter the three-story, octagonal structure
and see how the 18th-century technology worked. ⊠ *378 North Main
Rd.* ☎ *401/423–0784* ⊕ *www.jamestownhistoricalsociety.org* 🎟 *Free*
⊙ *Mid-June–Columbus Day, weekends 1–4.*

Watson Farm. In 1789, Job Watson purchased this piece of rich farmland
on Conanicut Island, and five generations of his family cultivated the
land for the next two centuries. Thomas Carr Watson bequeathed the
265 acres to the Society for the Preservation of New England Antiquities, now called Historic New England, when he died in 1979. Still a
working farm using sustainable practices, the farm produces grass-fed
beef and lamb as well as wool blankets for local markets. The annual
Sheep Shearing Day takes place on the second Saturday in May when
you can visit the baby lambs, see the flock being shorn by local shearers
and watch spinning and weaving demonstrations. Visitors can explore
the farm fields with grazing livestock, stroll 2 miles of trails, and view
seasonal farm activities. ⊠ *455 North Rd.* ☎ *401/423–0005* ⊕ *www.
spnea.org/visit/homes/watson.htm* 🎟 *$4* ⊙ *June–mid-Oct., Tues.,
Thurs., and Sun. 1–5.*

SPORTS AND THE OUTDOORS

PARKS

Beavertail State Park. Water conditions range from tranquil to harrowing
at this park straddling the southern tip of Conanicut Island. However,
on a clear, calm day, the park's craggy shoreline seems intended for
sunning, hiking, and climbing. Grilling is not allowed. There are restrooms with composting toilets open daily year-round. On several dates
between May and October, the Beavertail Lighthouse Museum Association opens the historic **Beavertail Lighthouse** tower to allow visitors to
climb 49 steps to enjoy the magnificent panorama from the observation deck. The present granite lighthouse was constructed in 1856 but
the first tower was built in 1749. A museum is in what was the lighthouse keeper's quarters, and the old steam engine room has a saltwater
aquarium with local species. ⊠ *800 Beavertail Rd.* ☎ *401/423–3270*

⊕ *www.beavertaillight.org* 🔗 *Free* ☉ *Park daily dawn–dusk; museum mid-June–Labor Day, daily 10–4; Memorial Day–mid-June and Labor Day–Columbus Day, weekends 10–3.*

Fort Wetherill State Park. An outcropping of stone cliffs at the tip of the southeastern peninsula, this green space has 26 picnic tables and walking paths with scenic overlooks. There's also a boat ramp. The park is a favorite of scuba divers. Public restrooms are open daily from April through October. ⊠ *3 Fort Wetherill Rd.* 🕿 *401/423–1771* 🔗 *Free* ☉ *Daily dawn–dusk.*

BEACHES

ⓒ **Mackerel Cove Beach.** Sandy Mackerel Cove Beach is sheltered from the currents of Narragansett Bay, making it a great spot for families. ⊠ *Beavertail Rd.*

GOLF

Jamestown Golf Course. Jamestown Golf Course has a crisp 9-hole course for $18 weekdays and $19 on weekends. At the 5th hole you can see both the Jamestown and Newport bridges and Mt. Hope Bridge. A limited pro shop and full bar and grill are on-site. ⊠ *245 Conanicus Ave.* 🕿 *401/423–9930* ⊕ *www.jamestowngolf.com.*

WHERE TO EAT AND STAY

For expanded hotel reviews, visit Fodors.com.

$$$
SEAFOOD
★
✕ **Jamestown FiSH.** This upscale Jamestown newcomer showcases the ocean's underappreciated species like sable, char, and cuttlefish. The adventurous menu changes often to reflect available fresh seafood and produce. Try the spicy fish tomato bisque that's a refreshing alternative to New England clam chowder, though you can get that here, too. The downstairs has a cool blue dining room with white table linens, Italian blue water glasses, and a gas fireplace. The upstairs bar area has a patio offering great views of Newport Bridge lit up at night. Patio seating is first-come, first-served, though you can make reservations for the indoor dining room. $ *Average main: $28* ⊠ *14 Narragansett Ave.* 🕿 *401/423–3474* ⊕ *www.jamestownfishri.com.*

$$$
ITALIAN
✕ **Trattoria Simpatico.** A jazz trio plays Monday through Thursday evenings and Sunday afternoons while patrons dine alfresco under a copper beech tree at this popular spot. An herb garden, fieldstone walls, and white linen complete the picture of this casual, yet fine-dining restaurant. Seating is also in the tented garden or formal dining rooms. The menu features splendid salads, Northern Italian pasta dishes, meats and seafood prepared with a Continental flair, and a handful of Asian-fusion dishes. The food is so good it's hard to choose just one or two memorable entrées, but the maple-soy glazed tuna pad thai and chocolate "sushi" for dessert are noteworthy. Reservations are essential on summer weekends. $ *Average main: $25* ⊠ *13 Narragansett Ave.* 🕿 *401/423–3731* ⊕ *www.trattoriasimpatico.com* ☉ *No lunch Mon.–Fri.*

$$
B&B/INN
🛏 **East Bay B&B.** This 1893 Victorian is peaceful day and night, even though it's only a block from Jamestown's two main streets and wharf. **Pros:** great value compared to Newport accommodations; large rooms; close to restaurants; fireplace in common area. **Cons:** small showers;

only three parking spaces and on-street parking can be tough in summer; no kids under 12. [$] *Rooms from: $149* ✉ *14 Union St.* ☎ *401/423-0330, 800/243-1107* 🌐 *www.eastbaybnb.com* 🛏 *4 rooms* 🍴 *Breakfast.*

NEWPORT

30 miles south of Providence, 80 miles south of Boston.

Established in 1639 by a small band of religious dissenters led by William Coddington and Nicholas Easton, the city by the sea became a haven for those who believed in religious freedom. Newport's deep-water harbor at the mouth of Narragansett Bay ensured its success as a leading Colonial port, and a building boom produced hundreds of houses and many landmarks that still survive today. These include the Wanton-Lyman-Hazard House and the White Horse Tavern, both built during the 17th century, plus Trinity Church, Touro Synagogue, the Colony House, and the Redwood Library, all built in the 18th century.

British troops occupied Newport from 1776–1779, causing half the city's population to flee and ending a golden age of prosperity. The economic downturn that followed may not have been so great for its citizens but it certainly was for preserving Newport's architectural heritage as few had the capital to raze buildings and replace them with bigger and better ones. By the mid-19th century, the city had gained a reputation as the summer playground for the very wealthy who built enormous mansions overlooking the Atlantic. These so-called "summer cottages," occupied for only six to eight weeks a year by the Vanderbilts, Berwinds, Astors, and Belmonts, helped establish the best young American architects. The presence of these wealthy families also brought the New York Yacht Club, which made Newport the venue for the America's Cup races beginning in 1930 until the 1983 loss to the Australians.

The Gilded Age mansions of Bellevue Avenue are what many people associate most with Newport. These late-19th-century homes are almost obscenely grand, laden with ornate rococo detail and designed with a determined one-upmanship (⇨ *Mansions of Newport*).

Pedestrian-friendly Newport has so much else to offer in a relatively small geographical area— beaches, seafood restaurants, galleries, shopping, and cultural life. The city boasts more than 2,300 rooms in hotels, motels, inns, B&Bs, and time-shares. Summer can be crowded but fall and spring are increasingly popular times of the year to visit.

EXPLORING

DOWNTOWN NEWPORT

More than 200 pre-Revolutionary buildings (mostly private residences) remain in Newport. But you'll also find other noteworthy landmarks such as St. Mary's Church at the corner of Spring Street and Memorial Boulevard West where John Fitzgerald Kennedy and Jacqueline Bouvier were married on September 12, 1953. In summer, traffic is thick, and the narrow one-way streets can be frustrating. Consider parking in a pay lot and leaving your car behind to walk the downtown area. The Ocean Drive and Bellevue Avenue are nice to see from a bicycle.

Colony House. Completed in 1741, this National Historic Landmark on Washington Square was the center of political activity in Colonial Newport. The Declaration of Independence was read from its steps on July 20, 1776, and later British troops used this structure as a barracks during their occupation of Newport. In 1781, George Washington met here with French commander Count Rochambeau, cementing the alliance that led to the American victory at Yorktown. The Newport Historical Society manages the Colony House and offers guided tours. ⊠ *Washington Sq.* 🖀 *401/841–8770* ⊕ *www.newporthistory.org* 🖀 *Tour $12.*

Common Burial Ground. Among those buried in this graveyard, which dates back to the 17th century, are several governors, a Declaration of Independence signer, famous lighthouse keeper Ida Lewis, and Desire Tripp, whose unusual February 1786 gravestone commemorates the amputation of her arm. Many tombstones were made in the stone carving shop of John Stevens, which opened in 1705 and is still in operation. ⊠ *Farewell St.* 🖀 *401/841–8770* ⊕ *www.newporthistory.org* 🖀 *Free; Newport Historical Society walking tour $12.*

Great Friends Meeting House. The oldest house of worship in Rhode Island reflects the quiet reserve and steadfast faith of Colonial Quakers, who gathered here to discuss theology, peaceful alternatives to war, and the abolition of slavery. Built in 1699, the two-story shingle structure has wide-plank floors, simple benches, balcony, and beam ceiling. ⊠ *29 Farewell St.* 🖀 *401/841–8770* ⊕ *www.newporthistory.org.*

Newport Art Museum. Celebrating its centennial in 2012, the Newport Art Museum and Art Association has three buildings: the 1864 Griswold House designed by Richard Morris Hunt (a National Historic Landmark), the Cushing Gallery and its art school, the Coleman Center for Creative Studies. The galleries exhibit works from the museum's impressive holdings and the local and regional contemporary art scene. In the museum's permanent collection are works by Fitz Henry Lane, George Inness, William Trost Richards, John La Farge, Nancy Elizabeth Prophet, Gilbert Stuart, and Helena Sturtevant as well as contemporary artists like Dale Chihuly, Howard Ben Tre, and Joseph Norman. The museum offers concerts, live theater, art and book talks, family programming, and special events throughout the year. ⊠ *76 Bellevue Ave.* 🖀 *401/848–8200* ⊕ *www.newportartmuseum.org* 🖀 *$10, $8 seniors, $6 students and military, free children 5 and under* ☉ *Nov.–April, Tues.–Sat. 10–4, Sun. noon–4; May–Oct., Tues.–Sat. 10–5, Sun. noon–5* ☉ *Mon.*

Newport Historical Society Museum & Shop at Brick Market. The Newport Historical Society's guided walking and site tours depart from this information center and museum in the 1762 Brick Market on Washington Square. Designed by Peter Harrison, the building houses a gift shop and a Newport history exhibit. ⊠ *127 Thames St.* 🖀 *401/841–8770* ⊕ *www.newporthistory.org* 🖀 *Suggested donation $4* ☉ *Daily 10–5.*

★ **Redwood Library & Athenaeum.** In 1747, Abraham Redwood gave 500 pounds sterling to purchase a library of arts and sciences; three years later, this Georgian-Palladian style building opened with 751 titles. More than half the original collection vanished during the British

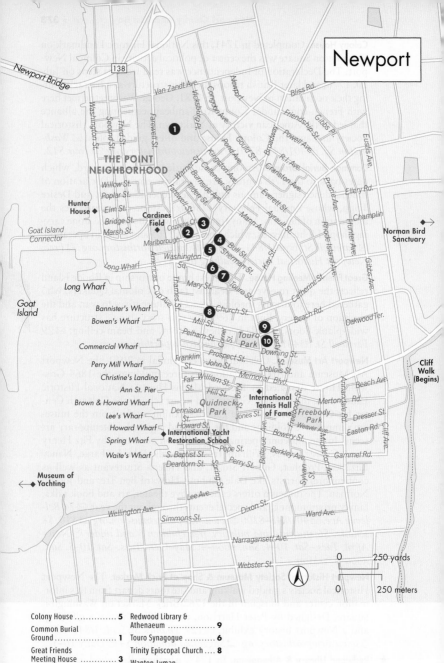

Newport

138

Newport Bridge

Van Zandt Ave.

THE POINT NEIGHBORHOOD

Willow St.
Poplar St.
Elm St.
Bridge St.
Marsh St.

Hunter House ◆

Cardines Field

Goat Island Connector

Long Wharf

Goat Island

Bannister's Wharf
Bowen's Wharf

Commercial Wharf

Perry Mill Wharf

Christine's Landing
Ann St. Pier

Brown & Howard Wharf
Lee's Wharf
Howard Wharf
Spring Wharf
Waite's Wharf

Museum of Yachting ◆

Washington St.
Second St.
Third St.
Farewell St.

Marlborough

Washington Sq.

Thames St.

America's Cup Ave.

Mill St.
Pelham St.
Franklin St.
Fair St.
William St.
Hill St.
Dennison St.
Howard St.
Pope St.
S. Baptist St.
Dearborn St.

Quidneck Park

International Yacht Restoration School ◆

Lee Ave.
Wellington Ave.
Simmons St.

Norman Bird Sanctuary →

Bliss Rd.
Friendship St.
Gibbs St.
Eustis Ave.

Broadway
Powell Ave.
R.I. Ave.
Cranston Ave.
Everett St.
Avrault St.
Ellery Rd.
Champlin
Rhode Island Ave.
Hunter Ave.
Gibbs Ave.

Hicksburg Pl.
Congdon Ave.
Gould St.
Pond Ave.
Kingston Ave.
Callender Ave.
Tilden Ave.
Burnside Ave.
Warner St.
Cozzens Ct.

Mann Ave.
Bull St.
Sherman St.
Kay St.

Touro St.
Mary St.
Church St.
Catherine St.
Beach Rd.
Oakwood Ter.

Touro Park

Liberty St.
Downing St.
Prospect St.
John St.
Memorial Blvd.
Deblois St.
Freebody Park
Annandale Rd.
Beach Ave.
Mertondale Rd.
Dresser St.
Easton Rd.
Cliff Ave.

Cliff Walk (Begins) →

International Tennis Hall of Fame ◆

Jones St.
Bowery St.
Weaver Ave.
Bellevue Ave.
Berkley Ave.
Perry St.
Spring St.
Gammel Rd.
Sylvan St.
Middleton Ave.

Dixon St.
Ward Ave.
Narragansett Ave.
Webster St.

0 ——— 250 yards
0 ——— 250 meters

occupation of Newport, but 90% has been recovered or replaced. The country's oldest surviving lending library is open to the public but supported by members who pay an annual fee. (Qualified scholars and researchers can use the collection for free.) Paintings on display include five portraits by Gilbert Stuart. Look for the portrait of the Colonial governor's wife whose low neckline later led to the commissioning of Stuart's daughter Jane to paint a bouquet over her cleavage. A guided 35-minute tour is offered daily at 2 pm. ⊠ *50 Bellevue Ave.* ☎ *401/847–0292* ⊕ *www.redwoodlibrary.org* ☑ *Free, tour $5* ☉ *Mon.–Wed., Fri., and Sat. 9:30–5:30, Thurs. 9:30–8, Sun. 1–5.*

Fodor'sChoice
★
Touro Synagogue. In 1658, more than a dozen Jewish families whose ancestors had fled Spain and Portugal during the Inquisition founded a congregation in Newport. A century later, Peter Harrison designed a two-story Palladian house of worship for the congregation. George Washington wrote a famous letter to the congregation in which he pledged the new American nation "would give to bigotry no sanction, to persecution no assistance." Now the oldest surviving synagogue in the United States, it was dedicated in 1763, and its simple exterior and elegant interior remain virtually unchanged. A small trapdoor in the platform upon which the Torah is read symbolizes the days of persecution when Jews were forced to worship in secret. The John L. Loeb Visitors Center opened in 2009 with two floors of state-of-the-art exhibits and multimedia presentations interpreting early American Jewish life and Newport's Colonial history. ■ TIP➔ The last synagogue tour is generally one hour before the visitor center closes. ⊠ *85 Touro St.* ☎ *401/847–4794* ⊕ *www.tourosynagogue.org* ☑ *$12* ☉ *Jan.–Apr. and Nov.–Mar., Sun. only 11:30–2:30; May–June, Sun.–Fri. 11:30–2:30; July–Aug., Sun.–Fri. 9:30–4:30; Sept.–Oct., Sun–Fri. 10–2:30.*

QUICK BITES

la maison de COCO. Enjoy your tea-infused *chocolat chaud* in a bowl at this little French café across from the Hotel Viking. Owner and pastry chef Michele De Luca-Verley makes truffles daily with fresh cream from a Tiverton dairy farm. ⊠ *28 Bellevue Ave.* ☎ *401/845–2626* ⊕ *www. lamaisondecoco.com.*

Rosemary & Thyme. The Brie, pear, and prosciutto sandwich on a grilled baguette (known affectionately as the "BPP" to locals) has a cult following at this little Spring Street boulangerie and café. But you may have a hard time deciding between several outstanding European street food–inspired sandwiches. ⊠ *382 Spring St.* ☎ *401/619–3338.*

Trinity Episcopal Church. George Washington once sat in the distinguished visitor pew close to the distinctive three-tier wineglass pulpit. Completed in 1726, the church is similar to Boston's Old North Church, both inspired by the designs of Sir Christopher Wren. Trinity's 1733 London-made organ is believed to be the first big pipe organ in the 13 colonies. Among those buried in the churchyard's historic cemetery is French Admiral D'Arsac de Ternay, commander of the allied French Navy in Newport who was buried with special permission in 1780 as there were then no Roman Catholic cemeteries in New England. ⊠ *Queen Anne*

Sq., 145 Spring St. ☎ *401/846–0660* ⊕ *www.trinitynewport.org* ✉ *Suggested donation* ⊙ *May–mid-June, weekdays 10–12:30; mid-June–early July, weekdays 10–3; early July–Aug., Mon.–Sat. 10–3; Sept.–mid-Oct., weekdays 10–3; mid-Oct.–late Oct., weekdays 10–12:30. Sun. services at 8 and 10. Wed. Holy Eucharist noon.*

Wanton-Lyman-Hazard House. As Newport's oldest house museum, this late-17th-century residence presents a window on the city's Colonial and Revolutionary history. The dark-red building was the site of the city's Stamp Act riot of 1765. After the British Parliament levied a tax on most printed material, the Sons of Liberty stormed the house, which was occupied by a prominent Loyalist. ⊠ *17 Broadway* ☎ *401/846–0813* ⊕ *www.newporthistory.org.*

White Horse Tavern. America's oldest tavern was originally built in 1652 as a two-room, two-story residence but was converted to a tavern in 1673 by William Mayes Sr., father of a notorious pirate. It served as a meeting place of the Colony's General Assembly, Criminal Court, and City Council. Now a fine-dining restaurant, the White Horse's gambrel roof, low dark-beam ceilings, cavernous fireplace, and uneven plank floors convey Newport's Colonial charm. ⊠ *26 Marlborough St.* ☎ *401/849–3600* ⊕ *whitehorsetavern.us.*

GREATER NEWPORT

Just outside of downtown you can begin discovering elaborate, stunning mansions. Along the waterfront, these "summer cottages" were built by wealthy families in the late 1800s and early 1900s as seasonal residences. ⇨ *See Mansions of Newport.*

★ **International Tennis Hall of Fame & Museum.** Tennis fans and lovers of history, art, and architecture will enjoy visiting the birthplace of American tournament tennis and its museum containing clothing worn by the sport's biggest stars, video highlights of great matches, and the 1874 patent from Queen Victoria for the game of lawn tennis among other memorabilia. The 6-acre site is home to the shingle-style Newport Casino, which opened in 1880 and was designed by architects McKim, Mead, and White, a grandstand, and the recently restored Casino Theatre. The 13 grass tennis courts, one clay court, and an indoor tennis facility are open to the public for play. In early July, the Hall of Fame hosts the prestigious Campbell's Hall of Fame Tennis Championships, the only men's pro tournament in the nation held on grass courts, and the induction ceremony for its newest Hall of Famers. ⊠ *194 Bellevue Ave.* ☎ *401/849–3990* ⊕ *www.tennisfame.com* ✉ *$12, $15 with audio tour, $3 grounds pass only* ⊙ *Daily 9:30–5.*

International Yacht Restoration School. Visitors to IYRS can watch work being done on historically significant sailboats and powerboats from an elevated catwalk inside the 1903 Restoration Hall —a large brick building that was once an electric power plant. The 2½-acre campus on lower Thames Street is also home to the 1831 Aquidneck Mill which has on its top floor a maritime reference library with more than 4,000 nautical titles, including some 100 rare books, logbooks, yacht registers, and yacht club directories. Also see ongoing restoration of the 1885 racing schooner *Coronet.* ⊠ *449 Thames St.* ☎ *401/848–5777*

⊕ *www.iyrs.org* ⊙ *Mon.–Fri. 9–5; library Tues.–Thurs. noon–6 and Fri. and Sat. noon–5.*

★ **National Museum of American Illustration.** This museum exhibits original work by Norman Rockwell, J. C. Leyendecker, Maxfield Parrish, N. C. Wyeth, and many others spanning the "Golden Age of American Illustration" (1895–1945). All 323 printed *Saturday Evening Post* covers are on display. For all its treasured artwork, the museum has a surprisingly low profile at Vernon Court on Bellevue Avenue. The 1898 Beaux-Arts adaptation of an 18th-century French chateau was designed by the same architects responsible for the New York Public Library, the U.S. Senate and House office buildings, and other landmarks. Frederick Law Olmsted designed the adjacent grounds. ✉ *492 Bellevue Ave.* ☎ *401/851–8949* ⊕ *www.americanillustration.org* 🎟 *$18* ⊙ *Memorial Day–Labor Day, Fri., Sat., and Sun. 11–5, with a guided tour Friday at 3 or by advanced reservation. Open year-round by advance reservation.*

★ **Norman Bird Sanctuary.** Stroll through the woods or hike to the top of
☾ Hanging Rock for a spectacular view at this 325-acre sanctuary for more than 300 species of birds, plus deer, foxes, minks, turtles, and rabbits. The sanctuary has about 7 miles of trails, ranging from ¼ to 1¼ miles long. The visitor center in a 19th-century barn highlights Rhode Island's natural history with a variety of wildlife and ecosystem exhibits spanning from the time of Native Americans before white settlers arrived to the present. ✉ *583 Third Beach Rd., Middletown* ☎ *401/846–2577* ⊕ *www.normanbirdsanctuary.org* 🎟 *$6* ⊙ *Daily 9–5.*

SPORTS AND THE OUTDOORS

BASEBALL

☾ **Cardines Field.** One of America's oldest ballparks with a circa-1908 original backdrop is home to the Newport Gulls of the New England Collegiate Baseball League. Home games from June through early August draw a family-friendly crowd to watch some of tomorrow's major leaguers play ball. ✉ *20 America's Cup Ave., Downtown* ⊕ *www. newportgulls.com* 🎟 *$4.*

BEACHES

Easton's Beach. Easton's Beach, also known as First Beach, is a ¾-mile-long surf beach with a boardwalk, 1950s carousel, aquarium, and playground. Public facilities include restrooms, indoor and outdoor showers, skate park, an elevator and beach wheelchairs for persons with disabilities. The snack bar's twin lobster rolls are very popular and a great deal. ✉ *175 Memorial Blvd.* ☎ *401/845–5810* ⊕ *www. cityofnewport.com/departments/enterprise-fund/beach/home.cfm* ⊙ *Memorial Day–Labor Day, daily 9–6.*

☾ **Fort Adams State Park.** The largest coastal fortification in the United States is at Fort Adams State Park, home to the Newport Folk and Jazz Festivals. From mid-May through Columbus Day, the nonprofit Fort Adams Trust offers guided and self-guided tours of the fort where soldiers lived from 1824 to 1950. The park has a small, protected beach on Newport Harbor with a picnic area, concession stand, and lifeguards in summer. A public boat ramp is by the beach. Public restrooms are open May 1–Oct. 31. ✉ *Harrison Ave., 90 Fort Adams Dr.* ☎ *401/841–0707*

Continued on page 388

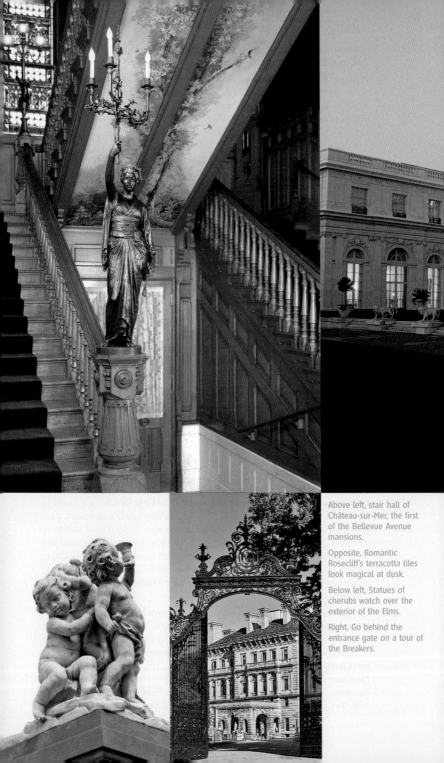

Above left, stair hall of
Château-sur-Mer, the first
of the Bellevue Avenue
mansions.

Opposite, Romantic
Rosecliff's terracotta tiles
look magical at dusk.

Below left, Statues of
cherubs watch over the
exterior of the Elms.

Right, Go behind the
entrance gate on a tour of
the Breakers.

The Mansions of Newport

GILDED AGE GEMS

By Andrew Collins, Debbie Harmsen, and Janine Weisman

Would you call a home with 70 rooms a cottage? If not, you're obviously not Cornelius Vanderbilt II. The Breakers, the "summer cottage" of the 19th-century multimillionaire, is one of a dozen mansions in Newport that are now by far the city's top attractions. Many of the homes are open to the public for tours, giving you a peek into the lives of the privileged.

THE SOCIAL SCENE

The Breakers dining room, just one of the opulent mansion's 70 rooms.

To truly appreciate a visit to Newport's mansions, you need to understand the times and the players—those who built these opulent homes and summered here for six weeks a year.

Newport at the turn of the 20th century was where the socialites of Boston, New York, and Philadelphia came for the summer. They were among the richest people in America at the time—from railroad tycoons and coal barons to plantation owners.

The era during which they lived here, the late 1800s up through the 1920s, is often referred to as the Gilded Age, a term coined by Mark Twain and co-author Charles Dudley Warner in a book by the same name. It was a time when who you knew was everything. Caroline Schermerhorn Astor was the queen of New York and Newport society; her list of the "Four Hundred" was the first social register. Three übersocialites were Alva Vanderbilt Belmont, Mary Ann (Mamie) Fish, and Tessie Oelrichs. These ladies who seriously lunched threw most of *the* parties in Newport.

While the women gossiped, planned soirees, and dressed and redressed thoughout the summer days, the men were usually off yachting.

In terms of the deepest pockets, the two heavyweight families during Newport's Gilded Age were the Vanderbilts and the Astors.

Madeleine Force was only 19 when she married John Jacob Astor IV at the Beechwood mansion in 1911; he was 47.

LEADING FAMILIES

Alva Vanderbilt Belmont

Beechwood will soon be reinvented as an art museum.

Cornelius Vanderbilt

THE VANDERBILTS Cornelius Vanderbilt I, called Commodore Cornelius Vanderbilt, built his empire on steamships and railroads. Cornelius had amassed almost $100 million before he died in 1877. He gave most of it to his son William Henry, who, also shrewd in the railroading business, nearly doubled the family fortune over the next decade. William Henry Vanderbilt willed $70 million to his son Cornelius Vanderbilt II, who became the chairman and president of New York Central Railroad; and $55 million to son William K. Vanderbilt, who also managed railroads for a while and saw his yacht, *The Defender*, win the America's Cup in 1895. One of Cornelius Vanderbilt II's sons, Alfred Gwynne Vanderbilt, died on the *Lusitania*, which sank three years after the *Titanic*. **Visit:** The Breakers, Marble House.

John Jacob Astor IV

THE ASTORS Meanwhile, in the Astor camp, John Jacob Astor IV, who perished on the *Titanic*, had the riches his great-granddad had made in the fur trade as well as his own millions earned from successful real estate ventures, including New York City hotels such as the St. Regis and the Astoria (later the Waldorf–Astoria). His mother was Caroline Astor. Her mansion, Beechwood, is now owned by Oracle CEO Larry Ellison.

John Jacob Astor

6

IN FOCUS: THE MANSIONS OF NEWPORT

WHICH MANSION SHOULD I VISIT?

Even though the 11 Newport "summer cottages" were inhabited for only six weeks each year, it would take you almost that long to explore all the grand rooms and manicured grounds. Each mansion has its own style and unique features. Here are the characteristics of each to help you choose those you'd like to visit:

Beechwood: The home of Social Register founder Caroline Astor is now owned by Larry Ellison and not open to the public; he plans to restore it to house 18th and 19th century art.

Belcourt Castle: An incredible (and quirky) collection of furnishings and art; based on French 18th-century hunting lodge; ghost tours.

⭐ **The Breakers:** The most opulent; enormous Italian Renaissance mansion built by Cornelius Vanderbilt II; tours are often big and very crowded; open most of the year.

Château-sur-Mer: The prettiest gardens and grounds; High Victorian–style mansion built in 1852; enlarged and modified in 1870s by Richard Morris Hunt.

Portrait of Mrs. Cornelius Vanderbilt II circa 1880, The Breakers.

Chepstow: Italianate villa with a fine collection of art; a bit less wow factor; summer hours only.

⭐ **The Elms:** A French chatea-style home with 10 acres of stunningly restored grounds; new guided servant quarters tour takes you into a hidden dormitory, roof, and basement; open most of the year.

Hunter House: Fantastic collection of Colonial furniture; downtown location, not on Bellevue Avenue; pricey admission; summer hours only.

Isaac Bell House: Currently undergoing restoration; less dramatic shingled Victorian displays an unusual mix of influences; less visited; summer hours only.

Kingscote: Gothic Revival–style home includes early Tiffany glass; one of the first summer cottages built in 1841; summer hours only.

⭐ **Marble House:** Outrageously opulent and sometimes crowded; former Vanderbilt home modeled on Petit Trianon in Versailles; tour at your own pace with

MANSION TOURS

Preservation Society of Newport County. The Preservation Society maintains 11 historic properties and the Newport Mansions Store on Bannister's Wharf. Both guided tours and audio tours are available; you can purchase a combination ticket to see multiple properties for a substantial discount. The hours and days the houses are open in fall and winter vary. ☎ 401/847–1000 ⊕ www.newportmansions. org. 🎧 The Newport Mansions Experience (admission to any 5 properties excluding Hunter House) $31.50.

digital audio tour; open most of the year.

Rosecliff: Romantic 1902 mansion; modeled after Grand Trianon in Versailles; somewhat crowded tours.

Rough Point: More contemporary perspective in 20th-century furniture; 1889 English manor–style home; tours are expensive and have limited availability.

Consider viewing mansions from the Cliff Walk for a different perspective.

Marble House at night.

TOP EXPERIENCE

★ **Cliff Walk.** See the backyards of Newport's famous oceanfront Gilded Age mansions while strolling along this 3½-mile public access walkway. The designated National Recreation Trail stretches from Memorial Boulevard at the west end of Easton's Beach (also called First Beach) southerly to the east end of Bailey's Beach. Along the way you'll pass the Breakers, Rosecliff, and Marble House and its Chinese Tea House. The north half of the walk is paved but the trail turns to large flat boulders south of Ruggles Avenue. Be prepared for increasingly rough terrain not suitable for small children, strollers, or people with mobility problems. Park on either Memorial Boulevard or Narragansett Avenue.

Belcourt Castle

Chateau-sur-Mer

Belcourt Castle

The Breakers great hall

BELCOURT CASTLE. Richard Morris Hunt based his design for this 60-room mansion, built in 1894 for wealthy bachelor Oliver H.P. Belmont, on the hunting lodge of Louis XIII. The home, privately owned by the Tinney family since 1956, has been up for sale since 2009, when it was listed for $7.2 million. Harle Tinney, the sole surviving member of the family, continues to operate the mansion in the meantime. It is filled with treasures from more than 30 countries. Admire the stained glass and carved wood throughout. Don't miss the Golden Coronation Coach and inquire about the haunted chair and suit of armor. The mansion's 5 pm Thursday and Saturday ghost tours are great fun. ⊠ *657 Bellevue Ave.* ☎ *401/846–0669* ⊕ *www.belcourtcastle.com* ⊠ *$25* ⊙ *Tour days and times vary.*

Fodor'sChoice★ **THE BREAKERS.** The 70-room summer estate of Cornelius Vanderbilt II, president of the New York Central Railroad, was built in 1895. Architect Richard Morris Hunt modeled the four-story residence after the 16th-century Italian Renaissance palaces. This mansion is not only big but also grand—be sure to look for the sculpted figures tucked above the pillars. The interior includes rare marble, alabaster, and gilded rooms, with open-air terraces revealing magnificent ocean views. Noteworthy are a blue marble fireplace, rose alabaster pillars in the dining room, and a porch with a mosaic ceiling that took Italian artisans six months, lying on their backs, to install. ⊠ *44 Ochre Point Ave.* ☎ *401/847–1000* ⊕ *www.newportmansions.org* ⊠ *$19.50* ⊙ *Jan.–Mar., daily 10–4; mid-Mar.–June, daily 9–6; Jul.–Labor Day, 9–7; Sept.–mid-Nov. 9–6; mid-Nov.–Jan. 1, 9–5.*

CHATEAU-SUR-MER. Built in 1852 as an Italianate-style villa for China trade merchant William Shepard Wetmore, Chateau-sur-Mer was Newport's first grand residence until the construction of the Vanderbilt houses 40 years later. In 1857 Wetmore threw an extravagant, unprecedented gala for 2,500 people, ushering in the Gilded Age in Newport. The house is a treasure trove

of Victorian architecture, furniture, wallpapers, ceramics, and stenciling. See hand-carved Italian woodwork, Chinese porcelains, and Japanese and Egyptian Revival stenciled wallpapers. The grounds have some rare trees from Mongolia. ⊠ *474 Bellevue Ave.* ☎ *401/847–1000* ⊕ *www.newportmansions.org* 🖃 *$14.50* 🕙 *Mid-Mar.–mid-Nov., daily 10–6.*

CHEPSTOW. Though not as grand as other Newport mansions, this Italianate-style villa with a mansard roof houses a remarkable collection of art and furniture gathered by the Morris family of New York City. Its collection of important 19th-century American paintings includes Hudson River landscapes. Built in 1861, the home was designed by Newport architect George Champlin Mason. ⊠ *120 Narragansett Ave.* ☎ *401/847–1000* ⊕ *www.newportmansions.org* 🖃 *$14.50* 🕙 *Late May–June and Labor Day–Columbus Day, open weekends and holidays 10–6; late June–Labor Day, daily 10–6.*

Chateau-sur-Mer

Fodor'sChoice★ **THE ELMS.** Architect Horace Trumbauer modeled this graceful 48-room French neoclassical mansion and its grounds after the Château d'Asnières near Paris. The Elms was built for Edward Julius Berwind, a bituminous-coal baron, in 1901 and was one of the first in Newport to be fully electrified. At the foot of the 10-acre estate is a spectacular sunken garden. The Behind the Scenes tours, which offer a glimpse into the life of staff and the operations (such as the boiler room and kitchen) of the mansion, is one of the best of any of these mansion tours. ⊠ *367 Bellevue Ave.* ☎ *401/847–1000* ⊕ *www.newportmansions.org* 🖃 *$14.50* 🕙 *Mid-Apr.–Dec., daily 10–5; Jan.–Mar., weekends 10–4.*

Chepstow

The Elms sunken garden

The Elms

Hunter House

Kingscote

Hunter House

HUNTER HOUSE. The oldest house owned and maintained by the Preservation Society of Newport, the 1748 Hunter House served as the Revolutionary War headquarters of French admiral Charles Louis d'Arsac de Ternay after its Loyalist owner fled the city. Characterized by a balustraded gambrel roof and heavy stud construction, it is an excellent example of an early Georgian frame residence. A collection of Colonial furniture includes pieces crafted by Newport's famed 18th-century Townsend-Goddard family of cabinetmakers and paintings by Cosmo Alexander, Gilbert Stuart, and Samuel King. The house is named after ambassador William Hunter. ⊠ *54 Washington St.* ☎ *401/847–1000* ⊕ *www.newportmansions. org* 🎫 *$28* ☽ *Memorial Day–Labor Day, daily 10–6, last tour at 5.*

Isaac Bell House

ISAAC BELL HOUSE. Revolutionary in its design when it was completed in 1883, the shingle-style Isaac Bell House combines Old English and European architecture with Colonial American and exotic details, such as a sweeping open floor plan and bamboo-style porch columns. It was designed by McKim, Mead, and White for wealthy cotton broker Isaac Bell. ⊠ *70 Perry St., at Bellevue Ave.* ☎ *401/847–1000* ⊕ *www. newportmansions.org* 🎫 *$14.50* ☽ *Late May–early Sept., daily 10–6; Sept.–early Oct., Sat. and Sun. 10–6.*

KINGSCOTE. This Gothic Revival mansion completed in 1841 for Georgia plantation owner Geoge Noble Jones was one of Newport's first summer cottages. Richard Upjohn designed Kingscote which was rebuilt in 1881 for the King family. The dining room contains one of the first installations of Tiffany glass windows and a cork ceiling. Furnishings reflect the King family's involvement in the China trade. ⊠ *253 Bellevue Ave.* ☎ *401/847–1000* ⊕ *www.newportmansions.org* 🎫 *$14.50* ☽ *July–early Oct., daily 10–5.*

★ **MARBLE HOUSE.** One of the most opulent of the Newport mansions, Marble House contains 500,000 cubic feet of marble. The house was built from 1888 to 1892

Kingscote-ivory silk dinner gown circa 1901

by William Vanderbilt, who gave it as a gift to his wife Alva for her 39th birthday. The house was designed by the architect Richard Morris Hunt, who took inspiration from the Petit Trianon at Versailles. The Vanderbilts divorced in 1895, and Alva married Oliver H.P. Belmont, moving down the street to Belcourt Castle. After his death, she reopened Marble House and had the Chinese Tea House built on the back lawn where she hosted "Votes for Women" rallies. ⊠ *596 Bellevue Ave.* ☎ *401/847–1000* ⊕ *www.newportmansions.org* ⊡ *$14.50* ⊙ *Mid-Mar.–mid-Nov., daily 10–6; Nov.-Jan. 1, daily 10–4.*

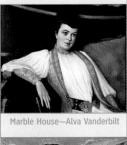

ROSECLIFF. Built in 1902, Newport's most romantic mansion was commissioned by Tessie Hermann Oelrichs, who inherited a Nevada silver fortune from her father. Stanford White modeled the palace after the Grand Trianon at Versailles. Rosecliff has a heart-shaped staircase and Newport's largest private ballroom. Rosecliff stayed in the Oelrichs family until 1941, went through several ownership changes, and then was purchased by Mr. and Mrs. J. Edgar Monroe of New Orleans in 1947. Some scenes from *The Great Gatsby* and *True Lies* were filmed here. ⊠ *548 Bellevue Ave.* ☎ *401/847–1000* ⊕ *www.newportmansions.org* ⊡ *$14.50* ⊙ *Mid-Mar.–mid-Nov., daily 10–5.*

Fodor'sChoice ★ ROUGH POINT. Tobacco heiress and preservationist Doris Duke furnished her 39,000-square-foot English manorial-style house at the southern end of Bellevue Avenue with family treasures and fine art and antiques she purchased on her world travels. Highlights include paintings by Renoir, van Dyck, and Gainsborough, numerous Chinese porcelains, Turkish carpets, and Belgian tapestries, and a suite of Louis XVI chairs. Duke bequeathed the oceanfront house with all its contents to the Newport Restoration Foundation to operate as a museum after her death. ⊠ *680 Bellevue Ave.* ☎ *401/847–8344* ⊕ *www.newportrestoration.org* ⊡ *$25* ⊙ *Mid-Apr.–mid-May, Thurs.–Sat. 10–2; mid-May–early Nov., Tues.–Sat. 9:45–3:45.*

NEWPORT TOURS

BOAT TOURS

More than a dozen yacht companies operate tours of Newport Harbor and Narragansett Bay. Outings usually run two hours and cost about $25 to $35 per person.

Madeleine. Madeleine, a 72-foot schooner, departs from Bannister's Wharf for 90-minute harbor and sunset sailing cruises. ⊠ *24 Bannister's Wharf* ☎ *401/847–0298* ⊕ *www. cruisenewport.com* 🖃 *$37 sunset cruise, $28 daytime cruise.*

Newport Majestic Cruises. The 92-foot double-decker luxury yacht *Majestic* takes passengers out on Narragansett Bay to see lighthouses, the Newport Pell Bridge, and other landmarks. Brunch, lunch, and sunset dinner cruises cost $45-$70 per person. Seal-watching tours are offered during the winter. ⊠ *2 Bowen's Ferry Landing, Newport* ☎ *401/849–3575* ⊕ *www.newportmajestic.com.*

RumRunner II. RumRunner II, a 1929 motor yacht built for two New Jersey mobsters to carry "hooch,"

leaves from Bannister's Wharf. ⊠ *24 Bannister's Wharf* ☎ *401/847–0298* ⊕ *www.cruisenewport.com* 🖃 *$26 Smuggler's Cocktail Cruise, $20 East Passage narrated tour.*

Sightsailing of Newport. The 80-foot schooner *Aquidneck* and two sailboats depart from Bowen's Wharf for up to two-hour tours of Newport Harbor and Narragansett Bay. ☎ *401/849–3333, 401/849–3333* ⊕ *www.sightsailing.com* 🖃 *$28.50-$37.*

TROLLEY TOURS

Viking Tours of Newport. Take a trolley tour of Newport daily from mid-April through October and on Saturdays November through early April. ☎ *401/847–6921* ⊕ *www.vikingtoursnewport.com* 🖃 *$25-$52.*

WALKING TOURS

Newport Historical Society. Various walking tours are available from April through December. ☎ *401/841-8770* ⊕ *www.newporthistorytours.org* 🖃 *$12.*

⊕ *www.fortadams.org* 🖃 *Park free; fort guided tours $12; self-guided tours $6* ☉ *Daily 7:30–dusk.*

Sachuest Beach. Sachuest Beach, or Second Beach, in Middletown, is a beautiful, 1¼-mile-long, sandy beach with a popular surfing spot on its west end. A pavilion has a concession stand, restrooms, and outdoor showers. Surfboard and stand-up paddleboard rentals are available. A 45-site RV campground across the street usually can take short-term reservations. Parking fees are $10 on weekdays and $20 on weekends and holidays. ■TIP→ The town stops charging for parking after 4 pm. ⊠ *Sachuest Point Rd., 305 Sachuest Point Rd., Middletown* ☎ *401/849–2822* ⊕ *www.middletownri.com/government/6/43/sachuest-beaches-campground* ☉ *Memorial Day–Labor Day, daily 8–6.*

Third Beach. Third Beach on the Sakonnet River is more peaceful than the nearby ocean beaches and is a great spot for families. It has a boat ramp and is a favorite of windsurfers. You'll find a mobile concession stand on weekends. ⊠ *Third Beach Road, Middletown* ☎ *401/849–2822* ⊕ *www.middletownri.com/government/6/43/sachuest-beaches-campground.*

BIKING

The 12-mile swing down Bellevue Avenue to Ocean Drive and back, offers amazing coastal views.

Ten Speed Spokes. Ten Speed Spokes rents hybrid bikes for $35 for a day and $15 for each additional day. Road bikes are $45 per day. ⊠ *18 Elm St.* ☎ *401/847–5609* ⊕ *www. tenspeedspokes.com.*

BOATING AND DIVING

Sail Newport. Take a private two-hour sailing lesson or rent 19- or 22-foot sailboats or kayaks at Sail Newport, New England's largest public sailing center. ⊠ *60 Ft. Adams Dr., Ft. Adams State Park* ☎ *401/846–1983* ⊕ *www.*

SCENIC DRIVE

Ocean Drive. There really isn't a street called Ocean Drive, but the name has come to indicate the roughly 10-mile scenic route from Bellevue Avenue at the intersection of Memorial Boulevard, heading south to Ocean Avenue and out to Castle Hill Avenue, Ridge Road, and Harrison Avenue. About halfway, you'll come to the 89-acre Brenton Point State Park, a premiere destination for kite enthusiasts and picnickers with free parking.

sailnewport.org ⊘ *Memorial Day–Labor Day, daily 8:30–8:30; Labor Day–Columbus Day 9–5.*

The Dive Shop. The Dive Shop rents, sells, and services dive equipment, refills Nitrox and air tanks, offers PADI instruction and certification and conducts group "fun dives" close to shore. ⊠ *550 Thames St.* ☎ *401/847–9293* ⊕ *theridiveshop.com.*

FISHING

Fishin' Off. This outfitter runs charter fishing trips in Narragansett Bay and coastal Rhode Island waters on a 36-foot Trojan cabin cruiser. ⊠ *88 McIntosh Dr., Portsmouth* ☎ *401/683–8080* ⊕ *www.fishinoff.com.*

The Saltwater Edge. The Saltwater Edge conducts guided trips, gives lessons, and sells tackle for both fly-fishing and surf-casting. ⊠ *47 Valley Rd., Middletown* ☎ *401/842–0062* ⊕ *www.saltwateredge.com.*

POLO

Newport International Polo Series. Teams from around the U.S. and the world compete in Saturday evening matches. Spectators are invited to stomp divets at the half and then mingle with players and pet the horses after the match. Arrive early with a picnic for a choice tailgating spot. Concession stand has a bar and grilled fare. ☎ *401/846–0200* ⊕ *www.nptpolo.com* ▱ *$15 box sets; $10 lawn and bleachers* ⊘ *June–Sept.*

SHOPPING

Many of Newport's shops and art and crafts galleries are on Thames Street, Spring Street, and at Bowen's and Bannister's wharves. The Brick Market area—between Thames Street and America's Cup Avenue—has more than 40 shops. Bellevue Avenue just south of Memorial Boulevard (near the International Tennis Hall of Fame) contains a strip of high-end fashion and home decor boutiques and gift shops.

Newport's naturally well-protected harbor has made the city a sailing capital.

ANTIQUES

★ **Aardvark Antiques.** Aardvark Antiques specializes in distinctive architectural salvage such as wrought ironwork, mantels, doors, stained glass, fountains, and garden statuary and rents unusual pieces to movie sets and photo shoots. ⊠ *9 Connell Hwy.* ☎ *401/849–7233* ⊕ *www. aardvarkantiques.com.*

ART AND CRAFTS GALLERIES

Arnold Art. Arnold Art exhibits original paintings and prints of landscapes and seascapes by Rhode Island artists. ⊠ *210 Thames St.* ☎ *401/847–2273* ⊕ *www.arnoldart.com.*

Harbor Fine Art. Harbor Fine Art has oil paintings by several notable artists around the region who specialize in landscapes and seascapes in oil. Also on display are handmade stained glass and jewelry by local artists. ⊠ *134 Spring St.* ☎ *401/848–9711* ⊕ *www.harborfineart.com* ⊗ *Daily 10-6.*

Thames Glass. Watch Matthew Buechner and his team of glassblowers at work making blown-glass gifts through a window in the gallery at Thames Glass. Sign up for a lesson ($30–$145) to make an ornament, paperweight, or vase out of hot, molten glass. Your creation will take two days to cool but can be shipped to you if you're leaving town sooner. ⊠ *688 Thames St.* ☎ *401/846–0576* ⊕ *www.thamesglass.com* ⊗ *Jan.–June: Mon.–Sat. 10–5, Sun. noon–5; July-Dec.: Mon.–Sat. 10–6, Sun. noon–5.*

BEACH GEAR

Water Brothers. This is the place to go for surf supplies, including bathing suits, wet suits, sunscreen, sunglasses, surfboards, and all styles of skateboards. Owner Sid Abruzzi records a new surf report daily to keep surfers apprised of local waves. ✉ *23 Memorial Blvd.* ☎ *401/846–7873, 401/848–9283 surf report, 401/849–9283 surf report* ⊕ *originalwaterbrothers.com.*

CLOTHING

Angela Moore. Look to Angela Moore for stylish, mod resort threads and signature hand-painted beaded jewelry. ✉ *190 Bellevue Ave.* ☎ *401/619–1900* ⊕ *www.angelamoore.com.*

FOOD

Newport Spice Company. There are at least five kinds of paprika, plus a variety of blends for exotic dishes, salts, peppers and teas, spice grinders, and other gift ideas at this specialty shop. At the urging of Tallulah on Thames Chef Jake Rojas, the shop now blends its own version of the popular meat rub Ras el Hanout. ✉ *24 Franklin St.* ☎ *401/846–8400* ⊕ *www.newportspice.com* ☽ *10–6 daily, May–Dec.; 10–5 Wed.–Mon., Jan.–Apr.* ☽ *Closed Tues., Jan.–Apr.*

Newport Wine Cellar. This specialty wine and craft beer merchant offers lively Wednesday night wine classes next door at its sister gourmet foods and artisan cheese shop, le petit gourmet. ✉ *24 Bellevue Ave.* ☎ *401/619–3966* ⊕ *www.newportwinecellar.com.*

JEWELRY

Alloy. RISD MFA grad Tamar Kern displays her signature stackable cone rings plus unique designs by two-dozen other leading contemporary artists here. ✉ *125 Bellevue Ave.* ☎ *401/619–2265* ⊕ *www.alloygallery.com.*

NIGHTLIFE AND THE ARTS

To sample Newport's lively nightlife, you need only stroll down Thames Street or the southern end of Broadway after dark. Pick up the free *Newport Mercury* or *Newport This Week* or visit ⊕ *www.newportri.com* for entertainment listings and news on featured events.

BARS

Candy Store. The Candy Store in the Clarke Cooke House is the best place to sip a dark and stormy and rub elbows with yacht crews. The walls are covered with photos from the halcyon days of Newport's America's Cup supremacy. If you're up for dancing, head downstairs to the Boom Boom Room. ✉ *Bannister's Wharf* ☎ *401/849–2900* ⊕ *www.clarkecooke.com.*

The Fifth Element. This chic Broadway lounge offers specialty martinis and gourmet pizza. Live bands like the popular Honky Tonk Knights draw a hip crowd. It's also a good Sunday brunch spot. ✉ *111 Broadway* ☎ *401/619–2552* ⊕ *www.thefifthri.com.*

FESTIVALS

★ **Newport Folk Festival.** Bob Dylan made his premiere national performance at the 1963 Newport Folk Festival. Two years later, some fans booed when he went electric, marking a shift in his own musical trajectory and the start of a larger cultural shift from folk to rock. Held over the last weekend in July at Fort Adams State Park, the folk fest continues stretching boundaries and keeping things fresh with multiple stages and acts spanning folk, blues, country, bluegrass, folk rock, alt-country, indie folk, and folk punk. In 2005, The Pixies pulled a reverse Dylan and played acoustic. Lineups mix veteran performers like Jackson Browne, Patty Griffin, and Arlo Guthrie with younger stars like Conor Oberst, Brandi Carlile, and Deer Tick. The festival is held rain or shine, and seating is general admission on a large uncovered lawn. ✉ *Fort Adams State Park, Harrison Ave.* ☎ *401/848–5055* 🌐 *www.newportfolkfest.net* 🎫 *$84 per day, $74 advance.*

Newport Jazz Festival. The grandfather of all jazz festivals, founded by George Wein in 1954, takes place the first weekend in August at Fort Adams State Park and features both jazz veterans and up-and-coming artists. Newport Jazz Festival performers in recent years have included Esperanza Spalding, Wynton Marsalis, Dianne Reeves, the Bad Plus with Bill Frisell, Dr. John, and Maria Schneider Orchestra. The festival is held rain or shine with open-air lawn seating. ✉ *Fort Adams State Park, Harrison Ave.* ☎ *401/848–5055, 800/745–3000* 🌐 *newportjazzfest.net* 🎫 *$84 per day, $74 advance.*

Fodor's Choice ★ **Newport Music Festival.** A great way to experience a Newport mansion is to take in one of the 60 or so classical music concerts presented every July during the Newport Music Festival. Morning, afternoon, evening, and even midnight performances by world-class artists are scheduled at The Elms, The Breakers, and other venues. Selected works are chosen from 19th-century chamber music, vocal repertoire, and Romantic-era piano literature. Every year features at least one American debut and a tribute to a composer. (The 2013 season will pay tribute to the bicentenary of Wagner and Verdi.) ✉ *Box Office, 850 Aquidneck Ave., Middletown* ☎ *401/849–0700, 401/846–1133* 🌐 *www.newportmusic.org* 🎫 *Tickets $20-$75.*

FILM

👶 **newportFILM.** Enjoy sneak peeks of films before they open elsewhere thanks to this nonprofit group that hosts outdoor screenings and mini-festivals with programming for adults and kids throughout the year. ✉ *174 Bellevue Ave., Suite 314* ☎ *401/649–2784* 🌐 *www.newportfilm.com.*

WHERE TO EAT

$$$$ STEAKHOUSE Fodor's Choice ★ 🍴 **22 Bowen's Wine Bar & Grille.** Excellent service, world-class steaks, and an extensive, award-winning wine list make dinner here a memorable experience. The USDA Prime Beef and Premium Hereford center-cut filets are handpicked and aged a minimum of 14 and 21 days, respectively, for premium flavor and texture. It's pricey but comparable to what you'd expect at a big-city steak house. Sushi-grade tuna, Rhode Island-style calamari (with hot peppers), and Maine lobster are on the menu, too. Floor-to-ceiling windows allow you to watch the world go by on the wharf outside. It's a great choice for a special-occasion dinner. [$] *Average main: $36* ✉ *22 Bowen's Wharf* ☎ *401/841–8884* 🌐 *www.22bowens.com.*

$$$$ AMERICAN Fodor's Choice ★ 🍴 **Castle Hill Inn.** No other place can compete with the spectacular water views from the Sunset Room, one of four dining rooms inside the historic main inn. A perfect spot for a romantic dinner, it's also fitting that Castle Hill has a great value two-course lunch menu that allows for watching clouds and fishing boats pass by while savoring ethereal cuisine. The three-course prix-fixe menu displays a passion for simple New England food done well, recreating a clambake with littlenecks and a plump Georges Bank scallop in smoked seaweed-infused Vinho Verde broth. Produce comes from local growers listed right on the menu. The popular Sunday brunch offers lobster hash and house-made German charcuterie. [$] *Average main: $75* ✉ *590 Ocean Dr.* ☎ *888/466–1355, 401/849–3800* 🌐 *www.castlehillinn.com* ✍ *Reservations essential.*

$$$ WINE BAR ★ 🍴 **Fluke Wine, Bar & Kitchen.** Cocktails made with fresh-pressed juices are the stars at this modern hot spot. But the menu also has a well-conceived mix of snacks, cheeses, and charcuterie plus rotating small and large plate offerings. Seafood options like pan-seared scallops are compelling choices for freshness and imaginative side pairings like celery root, unsmoked Italian bacon, and pumpkin seed pesto. Try the grilled maple mustard–glazed pork belly. Finish off with goat cheesecake with candied kumquats. [$] *Average main: $28* ✉ *41 Bowen's Wharf* ☎ *401/849–7778* 🌐 *www.flukewinebar.com* ⏲ *No lunch. Closed Jan.*

6

$ DINER 🍴 **Franklin Spa.** A local landmark where the line can be out the door on summer weekend mornings, the satisfying breakfast served here by a friendly staff is worth the wait. The Portuguese Sailor (grilled *chourico* and egg with melted cheese on Portuguese sweet bread) is a house specialty. Healthy options include egg-white omelets, fresh-squeezed orange juice, and fruit smoothies made with fat-free yogurt. Owner and avid fisherman Rocky Botelho is at the grill most days. [$] *Average main: $7* ✉ *229 Spring St.* ☎ *401/847–3540* ✍ *Reservations not accepted* 💳 *No credit cards.*

$$$ FRENCH 🍴 **Restaurant Bouchard.** Regional takes on French cuisine fill the menu at this upscale yet homey establishment inside a stately gambrel-roof 1785 Colonial on Thames Street. Nightly specials are based on the fresh catch from Rhode Island waters, which might include scallops, swordfish, and clams, as well as classics like sautéed duck breast with a ground-coffee crust, finished with a brandy balsamic sauce. The wine list offers a nice range of New- and Old-World varietals. [$] *Average main: $29* ✉ *505 Thames St.* ☎ *401/846–0123* 🌐 *www.restaurantbouchard.com* ⏲ *No lunch.*

$$$$ MODERN AMERICAN Fodor's Choice ★ 🍴 **Spiced Pear.** For atmosphere, service, and exceptional food, the Spiced Pear at the Chanler at Cliff Walk is the ultimate fine-dining triple threat. Overlooking Easton's Beach and the north end of the Cliff Walk, this refined open-kitchen restaurant has attentive tuxedoed waiters, an extensive wine list, and a creative New England dinner menu. Selections include a substantial organic beet salad as well as butter-poached Maine lobster and a flavorful Rohan duck. Lunchtime has the absurdly delicious Kobe beef GQ burger ($26). The Bar, which has lighter fare and a signature martini, hosts a popular Friday night jazz series. [$] *Average main: $38* ✉ *117 Memorial Blvd.* ☎ *401/847–2244* 🌐 *www.thechanler.com/dining.*

$$$$ MODERN AMERICAN ★ 🍴 **Tallulah on Thames.** The menu here changes a few times a week in order to use the freshest, locally sourced seafood and produce available. But you can always count on an imaginative take on traditional New England fare and artful presentation. Deconstructed chowder and other soups are poured right at your table. Wednesdays from November through April draw a cult following for Blackbird Farms' grass-fed beef burgers and fries. An attentive and knowledgable staff offers expertise on wine selections from boutique vineyards and prix-fixe selections. Artisan chocolates make an exquisite end to every meal. [$] *Average main: $34* ✉ *464 Thames St.* ☎ *401/849–2433* 🌐 *tallulahonthames.com* 🕒 *Closed Jan. and Tues. No lunch.*

WHERE TO STAY

For expanded hotel reviews, visit Fodors.com.

$$ B&B/INN 🏨 **Architect's Inn.** Built in 1873 by noted Newport architect George Champlin Mason (Chepstow, Fort Adams Commandant House), this distinctive Swiss chalet–inspired house just off Bellevue Avenue has five good-sized rooms in classic Victorian style but with modern comforts like TVs, DVD players, individual climate control, and luxury bedding. **Pros:** friendly hosts cater to any and all dietary restrictions, including separate kosher kitchen; central but quiet location; fireplace in every room. **Cons:** guests are politely asked to leave their shoes at the door to protect wood floors; some may find the decor too knickknacky. [$] *Rooms from: $150* ✉ *2 Sunnyside Pl.* ☎ *401/845–2547, 877/466–2547* 🌐 *www.architectsinn.com* 🛏 *5 suites* 🍴 *Breakfast.*

$$$$ HOTEL Fodor's Choice ★ 🏨 **Castle Hill Inn and Resort.** Built as a summerhouse in 1874 for scientist and explorer Alexander Agassiz, this luxurious and romantic Ocean Drive getaway on a 40-acre peninsula is 3 miles from downtown Newport with its own private beach and trails to the Castle Hill Lighthouse. **Pros:** stunning views; superb restaurant; variety of rooms. **Cons:** you need a car to get into town; expensive. [$] *Rooms from: $682* ✉ *590 Ocean Dr.* ☎ *401/849–3800, 888/466–1355* 🌐 *www.castlehillinn.com* 🛏 *35 rooms, 3 suites* 🍴 *Breakfast.*

$$$$ HOTEL Fodor's Choice ★ 🏨 **The Chanler at Cliff Walk.** The custom-designed rooms at this landmark boutique hotel on the Cliff Walk represent the most unique and luxurious accommodations in Newport. **Pros:** panoramic water views from many rooms; two or three flat-screen TVs per room; great on-site restaurant. **Cons:** no elevator (one room is handicapped accessible); some rooms have steps to access bathroom; Memorial Blvd. traffic can be noisy. [$] *Rooms from: $599* ✉ *117 Memorial Blvd.* ☎ *401/847–1300, 401/847–1300* 🌐 *www.thechanler.com* 🛏 *7 rooms, 13 suites* 🍴 *Breakfast.*

$$$$ B&B/INN ★ 🏨 **Francis Malbone House.** The design of this stately painted-brick house is attributed to Peter Harrison, the same architect behind Touro Synagogue and the Redwood Library. **Pros:** steps from many restaurants and shops; highly professional service; working fireplaces in each room. **Cons:** Thames Street abounds with tourists in summer. [$] *Rooms from: $275* ✉ *392 Thames St.* ☎ *401/846–0392, 800/846–0392* 🌐 *www.malbone.com* 🛏 *17 rooms, 3 suites* 🍴 *Breakfast.*

$$$$ HOTEL ★ 🏨 **Hydrangea House Inn.** Rosie the house bichon frisé keeps watch at this mid-19th-century inn across the street from the Hotel Viking with decadent suites and rooms that exude romance. **Pros:** central location; huge rooms; highly personal service. **Cons:** slightly over-the-top decor. [$] *Rooms from: $295* ✉ *16 Bellevue Ave.* ☎ *401/846–4435, 800/945–4667* 🌐 *www.hydrangeahouse.com* 🛏 *3 rooms, 7 suites* 🍴 *Breakfast.*

$$ B&B/INN 🏨 **Spring Street Inn.** Centrally located accommodations in downtown Newport for under $200 a night sounds too good to be true. **Pros:** on a quiet but centrally located street; breakfast is terrific and afternoon snacks are included. **Cons:** small showers. [$] *Rooms from: $159* ✉ *353 Spring St.* ☎ *401/847–4767* 🌐 *www.springstreetinn.com* 🛏 *6 rooms, 1 suite* 🍴 *Breakfast.*

$$$$ HOTEL Fodor's Choice ★ 🏨 **Vanderbilt Grace.** Built in 1909 by Alfred Gwynne Vanderbilt for his mistress Agnes O'Brien Ruiz, this Grace Hotel property aims to impress and does. **Pros:** highly personalized service; full-service spa and indoor and outdoor pools; stylish snooker room. **Cons:** on a narrow street that's busy in summer; municipal parking lot next door. [$] *Rooms from: $495* ✉ *41 Mary St.* ☎ *401/846–6200* 🌐 *www.vanderbiltgrace.com* 🛏 *33 rooms, 29 suites.*

6

PORTSMOUTH

11 miles north of Newport.

Founded by religious dissident Anne Hutchinson, who led a group of settlers to the area in 1638 after being banished from the Massachusetts Bay Colony, Portsmouth is Rhode Island's second-oldest community. The town was the site of the Battle of Rhode Island on August 29, 1778, when American troops, who included a locally recruited African American regiment, withdrew to Bristol and Tiverton leaving Aquidneck Island under British control. Covering a 23.3-mile area, Portsmouth has a population of more than 17,000. The town is also home to many yacht builders and boat dealers.

EXPLORING

👶 **Green Animals Topiary Garden.** Fanciful animals, a sailing ship, and geometric shapes populate this large topiary garden on a Victorian estate that served as a Fall River, Massachusetts, textile mill owner's summer residence. Also here are flower gardens, winding pathways, a variety of trees, and the 1872 white clapboard house, which displays original family furnishings and an antique toy collection. A self-guided tour of the house is included with admission. ✉ *380 Cory's La., off Rte. 114* ☎ *401/683–1267* 🌐 *www.newportmansions.org* 🎫 *$14.50* 🕒 *Mid-May–Oct., daily 10–6.*

SPORTS AND THE OUTDOORS

BEACHES

Sandy Point Beach. Sandy Point Beach is a choice spot for families and beginning windsurfers because of the calm surf along the Sakonnet River. Lifeguards are on duty Memorial Day through Labor Day. ✉ *Sandy Point Ave.* 🎫 *$7 weekdays, $12 weekends.*

A horse, an elephant, and a bunny are just some of the creatures at Green Animals Topiary Garden in Portsmouth.

BRISTOL

5 miles north of Portsmouth, 20 miles southeast of Providence.

Midway between Newport and Providence—each a 30-minute drive—patriotic Bristol sits on a 10-square-mile peninsula between Narragansett Bay on its west and Mount Hope Bay on its east. The main thoroughfare through the town's charming business district, Hope Street, is painted with a red-white-and-blue center stripe in honor of the town's annual 4th of July Celebration dating back to 1785, making it the oldest continuous celebration of its kind in the United States. Bristol was once a boatbuilding center; the Herreshoff Manufacturing Company built five consecutive America's Cup Defenders between 1893 and 1920. Roger Williams University's 143-acre campus is located here. The southern end of the East Bay Bike Path lies at Independence Park. The bike path crosses the access road for Colt State Park, a great spot for picnics and kite flying.

EXPLORING

Blithewold Mansion, Garden & Arboretum. Starting with a sea of daffodils in April, the grounds of this 33-acre estate and historic public garden situated on Bristol Harbor bloom with color all the way until fall. Highlights include fruity, fragant pink chestnut roses and one of the largest giant sequoia trees on the East Coast. The 45-room English-style manor house is filled with original antiques and artwork. ⊠ *101 Ferry Rd.* ☎ *401/253–2707* ⊕ *www.blithewold.org* ✉ *$11* ⊙ *Grounds daily 10–5, mansion Apr.–mid-Oct., Tues.–Sat. 10–4, Sun. and most Mon. holidays 10–3.*

★ **Herreshoff Marine Museum/America's Cup Hall Of Fame.** This maritime museum on the site of the former Herreshoff Manufacturing Company (1878-1946) honors the maker of yachts for eight consecutive America's Cup defenses as well as the sport of yachting. Its collection includes more than 60 boats, ranging from the 8½-foot dinghy *Nathanael* to 75-foot successful America's Cup defender *Defiant*. The **Hall of Fame** was founded in 1992 as an arm of the museum by Halsey Herreshoff, a four-time America's Cup defender and grandson of yacht designer Nathanael Herreshoff. The museum hosts classic yacht regattas, sponsors symposia on classic yacht design and restoration, and operates a sailing school for kids and adults. ⊠ *1 Burnside St.* ☎ *401/253–5000* ⊕ *www.herreshoff.org* ☞ *$10* ☉ *Late Apr.–early Nov., daily 10–5.*

OFF THE
BEATEN
PATH

Warren. The town of Warren, located north of Bristol, has the distinction of being the smallest town in the smallest county in the smallest state in the United States. Home to a thriving arts scene, the town is one of nine "Tax-Free Arts Districts" in Rhode Island allowing sales tax–free purchases at its galleries. The East Bay Bike Path travels through its commercial district allowing for easy stops to get a Del's frozen lemonade or other treat. Warren also claims the stellar **2nd Story Theatre** (⊕ *www.2ndstorytheatre.com*) which stages cutting-edge comedies and dramas during its regular season and summer months. ⊠ *Warren* ⊕ *discoverwarren.com.*

WHERE TO EAT AND STAY

For expanded hotel reviews, visit Fodors.com.

$ ✕ **Beehive Cafe.** This aptly named busy two-story café is a favorite spot for local college students and foodies who appreciate fresh-baked bread and the famous Butternut Sandwich ($9), made with roasted butternut squash, tangy-sweet pesto and tomato with baby spinach, and carmelized onions and Vermont cheddar. The breakfast menu served every day until 3:30 includes gingerbread pancakes, sweet potato biscuits, and homemade granola. Dinner is served Thursday, Friday, and Saturday nights. $ *Average main: $9* ⊠ *10 Franklin St.* ☎ *401/396–9994* ⊕ *www. thebeehivecafe.com* ☉ *Sun.–Wed. 7–4, Thurs.–Sat. 7–9.*

$$$ ✕ **DeWolf Tavern.** A notorious 1818 rum distillery is now one of the
ECLECTIC state's most distinctive restaurants with its timber ceilings, African gran-
Fodor's Choice ite from slave-ship ballasts in the walls, and framed sections of early-
★ 19th-century-graffiti-covered plaster. Chef Sai Viswanath reinvents traditional New England fare with lobster roasted in a 900-degree tandoor oven, seared local sea scallops with chestnut spaetzle and a thymegaram masala sauce, and seafood stew simmered in coconut, coriander, star anise, and mustard-seed broth. Save room for the homemade cardamom or sour cream ice cream. Alfresco dining on the second-story back deck at sunset is one of summer's greatest pleasures. Planning a romantic night out for two during colder months? Ask to reserve table 36 with the waterview window near the fireplace in the upstairs dining room. $ *Average main: $28* ⊠ *259 Thames St.* ☎ *401/254–2005* ⊕ *www.dewolftavern.com* ☞ *Reservations essential.*

$$$
MODERN
AMERICAN
★
✕**Persimmon.** This intimate neighborhood bistro just off Bristol's main street only has seating for 38 patrons so reservations are essential on summer weekends. Neutral walls, white table linens, and simple but elegant china focus your attention on the artfully composed dishes of Chef Champe Speidel, who owns the restaurant with his wife Lisa. The kitchen staff even uses tweezers to arrange the petite greens on each plate. The meats, bacon, and sausage on the seasonal menu come from the owner's new Barrington butcher shop Persimmon Provisions. Appetizers include an excellent pan-seared foie gras. $ *Average main: $27* ✉ *31 State St.* ☎ *401/254–7474* ⊕ *www.persimmonbristol.com* ☾ *Closed Mon. Closed Sun. Jan.–April; no lunch.*

$$
ITALIAN
★
✕**Roberto's.** The East Bay's best Italian restaurant can compete with any establishment on Federal Hill with its delicious braciole, 10 different classic veal and chicken preparations, and owner Robert Vanderhoof's thoughtful wine list covering Italy, France, Australia, and California. After 11 years occupying part of a historic house on Bristol's parade route, Roberto's moved two blocks north in the spring of 2012 to new digs with a third-larger seating capacity and expanded bar area. The extra space means walk-ins may have better luck getting a table, though reservations are essential on busy summer weekends. Be prepared to wait; this place is bustling every night of the week. One wall of the new elegant dining room has a lovely mural of Tuscany painted by renowned local artist Kendra Ferreira, the mother of Roberto's Johnson & Wales University–trained chef Christian Ferreira. $ *Average main: $22* ✉ *450 Hope St.* ☎ *401/254–9732* ⊕ *www.robertosofbristol.com* ☾ *No lunch.*

$$
HOTEL
▦ **Bristol Harbor Inn.** Part of Thames Street Landing in the Bristol waterfront, this 40-room hotel was constructed with timber and architectural detailing from an 1818 rum distillery and warehouse once on the site. **Pros:** reasonably priced for a waterfront hotel; stellar restaurant; Pilates studio on-site; convenient location near retail shop and bars. **Cons:** other than shops and marina, there are no exterior grounds. $ *Rooms from: $135* ✉ *259 Thames St.* ☎ *401/254–1444, 866/254–1444* ⊕ *www.bristolharborinn.com* ⇆ *40 rooms, 8 suites* ▯⊙▯ *Breakfast.*

SPORTS AND THE OUTDOORS

BIKING

East Bay Bike Path. Flat and affording majestic views of Narragansett Bay, the 14½-mile East Bay Bike Path connects Providence to Bristol's charming downtown. ✉ *Colt State Park, Hope St./Rte. 114* ☎ *401/253–7482* ⊕ *www.riparks.com/eastbay.htm.*

TIVERTON/LITTLE COMPTON

10 miles south of Bristol to Tiverton Four Corners.

The southeastern corner of Rhode Island was originally inhabited by the Sakonnet tribe, led by Awashonks, a cousin of Metacomet (known as King Philip). The name means "the black goose comes." Tiverton and Little Compton were part of Massachusetts until 1747.

From Route 24 at the Sakonnet River Bridge, take Rte. 77 (Main Road) south for about 5¾ miles to reach historic Tiverton Four Corners, where you'll find Gray's Ice Cream, art galleries, an artisanal cheese

Rhode Island isn't just about regattas; working boats are common on the water, too.

shop, an arts center, and the 1730 Chase-Cory House. Continuing south to Little Compton you'll pass rolling estates, lovely homes, farmlands, woods, and a gentle western shoreline. The distance from Tiverton Four Corners to Sakonnet Point is 9 miles. Consider a hike in Tiverton's Weetamoo Woods or Little Compton's Wilbur Woods. Options for dining and accommodations are rather limited in the area, though you will find it a pleasant afternoon drive from Newport or Bristol. Open from mid-May through mid-November is the Stone House at Sakonnet Point, an intimate 13-room hotel with a restaurant, The Tap Room, serving New England comfort food.

EXPLORING

Tiverton Four Corners. From Route 24, head south on Main Road (Route 77) to historic Tiverton Four Corners, the intersection of Main Road with East and Neck roads. Located here are the Four Corners Arts Center in the Soule-Seabury House, built circa 1800, which hosts an annual antiques show, art festivals, exhibits, concerts, outdoor dance, sculpture, theater, and other special events. There's also Gray's Ice Cream, the 1730 Chase-Cory House, an artisanal cheese shop, art galleries, shops, and boutiques. ⊠ *Tiverton* ⊕ *www.tivertonfourcorners.com.*

Little Compton Commons. This quintessential rural New England town square is actually more of a long triangle anchored by the Georgian-style United Congregational Church and a Colonial cemetery. Among the headstones you'll find one for Elizabeth Padobie, said to be the first white girl born in New England. Surrounding the green are a rock wall and all the elements of a small community: town hall, community center, police station, school, library, general store, and restaurant. ✉ *40 Commons* ⊕ *www.little-compton.com.*

Sakonnet Point. A scenic drive down Route 77 ends at this quiet, southeastern corner of Rhode Island and an Army Corp of Engineers breakwater people like to fish off or walk along to view the harbor. The 1884 Sakonnet Lighthouse on Little Cormorant Rock is not open to the public. Much of the land is privately owned, and parking is limited in the area. ✉ *Sakonnet Point, 19 Bluff Head Ave.*

★ **Sakonnet Vineyard.** The plantable 50 acres at this vineyard produce about 20,000 cases a year, including an award-winning crisp, tarty peach-lemon-flavored Vidal Blanc and a dark fruity blend of Cabernet Franc and Chancellor named Rhode Island Red. For $10, you can enjoy a tasting of six different wines and keep the glass. Free tours are daily at noon and 3 pm. The Coop Cafe serving lighter fare is open Friday through Sunday Memorial Day through Columbus Day. ✉ *162 W. Main Rd.* ☎ *401/635–8486, 800/919–4637* ⊕ *www.sakonnetwine.com* 🏷 *Free* ⊙ *Memorial Day–Columbus Day, daily 10–6; Nov.–Memorial Day, daily 11–5.*

SPORTS AND THE OUTDOORS
HIKING

★ **Weetamoo Woods.** Combined with Pardon Gray Preserve there are more than than 10 miles of walking trails in this 850-acre nature preserve that's home to a coastal oak-holly forest, Atlantic white cedar swamp, two grassland meadows, early American cellar holes, and the remains of a mid-19th-century village sawmill. The main entrance to Weetamoo Woods is on East Road (Rte. 179), a quarter-mile east of Tiverton Four Corners, and has a parking area and kiosk with maps. An entrance to Pardon Gray Preserve is off Main Road (Rte. 77). Weetamoo Woods takes its name from the last sachem of the Pocasset Tribe of Wampanoag Indians. She supported Metacom (King Philip) in the King Philip's War and died in that conflict. ✉ *Tiverton* ☎ *401/625–1300* ⊕ *www. tivertonlandtrust.org.*

Wilbur Woods. Wilbur Woods, a 30-acre hollow with picnic tables and a waterfall, is a good place for a casual hike along a 1-mile marked loop that winds along and over Dundery Brook. ✉ *111 Swamp Road.*

BLOCK ISLAND

Block Island, 12 miles off Rhode Island's southern coast, is the smallest state's answer to nearby bigger and ritzier Martha's Vineyard and Nantucket. Only 10 square miles but boasting 17 miles of beaches that unlike many on its Massachusetts sister islands are open to everyone, it has been a vacation destination since the 19th century. Despite the number of summer visitors and thanks to the efforts of local conservationists, the island's beauty remains intact (more than 43% of the land is preserved); its 365 freshwater ponds support thousands of species of birds that migrate seasonally along the Atlantic Flyway.

The original inhabitants of the island were Native Americans who called it Manisses, or "isle of the little god." Following a 1614 visit by Dutch

Block Island

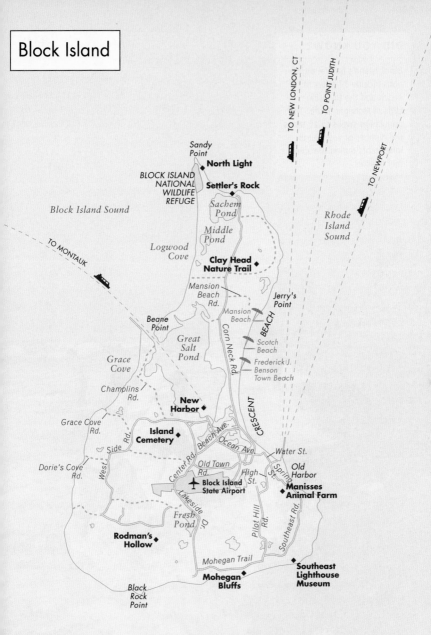

Block Island Sound

BLOCK ISLAND NATIONAL WILDLIFE REFUGE

Sandy Point

North Light

Settler's Rock

Sachem Pond

Middle Pond

Logwood Cove

Clay Head Nature Trail

Mansion Beach Rd.

Jerry's Point

Mansion Beach

BEACH

Scotch Beach

Corn Neck Rd.

Frederick J. Benson Town Beach

Beane Point

Great Salt Pond

Grace Cove

Champlins Rd.

New Harbor

Grace Cove Rd.

CRESCENT

Side Rd.

West Rd.

Dorie's Cove Rd.

Island Cemetery

Beach Ave.

Ocean Ave.

Water St.

Center Rd.

Old Town Rd.

High St.

Spring St.

Old Harbor

Lakeside Dr.

Block Island State Airport

Manisses Animal Farm

Fresh Pond

Pilot Hill Rd.

Southeast Rd.

Rodman's Hollow

Mohegan Trail

Mohegan Bluffs

Southeast Lighthouse Museum

Black Rock Point

TO MONTAUK

TO NEW LONDON, CT

TO POINT JUDITH

TO NEWPORT

Rhode Island Sound

ATLANTIC OCEAN

0 — 1/2 mile

0 — 1 km

explorer Adrian Block, the island was given the name Adrian's Eyelant, and later Block Island. In 1661 it was settled by farmers and fishermen from Massachusetts Bay Colony, who gave it what remains its second official name, the Town of New Shoreham, when it became part of Rhode Island in 1672.

Block Island, with 950 year-round residents, is a laid-back community. You can dine at any of the island's establishments in shorts and a T-shirt. The busiest season, when the population explodes to about 15,000, is between May and Columbus Day—at other times, most restaurants, inns, stores, and visitor services close down. If you plan to stay overnight in summer, make reservations well in advance; for weekends in July and August, March is not too early.

GETTING HERE AND AROUND

AIR TRAVEL   You can reach Block Island either by air or ferry. New England Airlines operates scheduled flights from Westerly to Block Island Airport.

FERRY TRAVEL   There's year-round car-and-passenger ferry service to Block Island from the Port of Galilee, in the town of Narragansett in South County. Seasonal passenger-only ferry service is available from Newport; New London, Connecticut; and Montauk, New York. All of the ferry companies permit bicycles, with the fares for these ranging from $3 to $10 each way.

The most heavily trafficked route is Block Island Ferry's traditional car-passenger service and high-speed passenger service between Block Island's Old Harbor and Galilee. By conventional ferry, the one-hour trip is about $14 one-way for passengers (rates fluctuate with oil prices) and $50 for automobiles, and runs from one or two times a day in winter to 10 times a day in peak season. Make auto reservations well ahead by telephone. Foot passengers may make reservations online; with or without a reservation, arrive 45 minutes ahead in high season to allow time to find parking in the pay lots that surround the docks ($10 to $15 a day). From early June to mid-October the high-speed service makes four to six daily 30-minute trips ($19 one-way) along the same route. There is no auto service on the high-speed; passenger reservations are recommended.

Block Island Ferry also operates a seasonal service from Newport's Fort Adams State Park to Old Harbor. The passengers-only ferry leaves Newport for Block Island once a day from July through Labor Day at 9:15 am and leaves Block Island at 4:45 pm. One-way rates are about $11 (no reservations or credit cards are accepted in Newport). Approximate sailing time is two hours.

From late May to mid-October, a high-speed passenger-only ferry operated by Block Island Express runs between New London, Connecticut, and Old Harbor. The ferry departs New London every three hours, three or four times a day, and takes a little more than an hour. Tickets are $25 one-way. Reservations are recommended.

Viking Fleet runs high-speed passenger service from Montauk, Long Island, to Block Island from late May to mid-October. The boat departs Montauk at 10 am and leaves Block Island at 5 pm, plus an additional trip on Sundays in July and August that departs Block Island at 11:30

6

am and Montauk at 3:30 pm. Fare is $50 one-way. Travel time is one hour; the ferry docks at New Harbor.

GETTING
AROUND
Block Island has two harbors, Old Harbor and New Harbor. Approaching the island by sea from New London, Newport, or Point Judith, you'll see Old Harbor, the island's only village, and its group of Victorian hotels, the largest left intact on the New England coast. Most of the smaller inns, shops, and restaurants are also here, and it's a short walk from the ferry landing to most of the interesting sights as well as many accommodations.

A car isn't necessary but can be helpful if you're staying far from Old Harbor or visiting for long. You can rent one at Block Island Car Rental.

ESSENTIALS

Transportation Contacts Block Island Bike and Car Rental ⊠ *Ocean Ave.* ☎ *401/466–2297.* **Block Island Express** ⊠ *2 Ferry St., New London* ☎ *401/466–2212, 860/444–4624* ⊕ *www.goblockisland.com.* **Block Island Ferry** ⊠ *Galilee State Pier, Narragansett* ☎ *866/783–7996* ⊕ *www.blockislandferry.com.* **New England Airlines** ⊠ *Westerly State Airport, 56 Airport Rd., Westerly* ☎ *800/243–2460* ⊕ *www.block-island.com/nea.* **Viking Fleet** ⊠ *Viking Dock, 462 Westlake Dr., Montauk, New York* ☎ *631/668–5700* ⊕ *www.vikingfleet.com.*

Visitor Information Block Island Chamber of Commerce ⊠ *Drawer D, 1 Water St.* ☎ *401/466–2982, 800/383–2474* ⊕ *www.blockislandchamber.com.*

EXPLORING

TOP ATTRACTIONS

★ **Mohegan Bluffs.** The 200-foot cliffs along Mohegan Trail, the island's southernmost road, are named for an Indian battle in which the local Manisses defeated an attacking band of Mohegans. From Payne Overlook, west of the Southeast Lighthouse, you can see to Montauk Point, New York, and beyond. An intimidating set of stairs leads down almost to the bottom; erosion means there's then a short but treacherous rocky scramble before you reach the beach. It is pebbly at the base of the stairs but sandy in the cove to the west, with lively surf that attracts surfers. ■ TIP→ Wear walking shoes and don't attempt the descent unless you're in reasonably good shape. ⊠ *Mohegan Trail.*

★ **North Light.** This 1867 granite lighthouse on the northernmost tip of the Block Island National Wildlife Refuge serves as a maritime museum. The refuge is home to American oystercatchers, piping plovers, and other rare migrating birds. From a parking lot at the end of Corn Neck Road, it's a ¾-mile hike over sand to the lighthouse. The building's tower was rebuilt in 2009, and a small wind turbine powers the museum. Seals sun themselves on nearby Sandy Point during winter months; during the summer, charter fishing boats work the riptide to the north, where two ocean currents converge over a shallow shoal. ⚠ Not safe for swimming. ⊠ *Corn Neck Rd., Block Island National Wildlife Refuge* ☎ *401/466–3213* 💲 *Donation suggested* ☼ *July 5–Labor Day, daily 10–4.*

Rodman's Hollow boasts cliffside trails that may be enjoyed on foot or horseback.

Rodman's Hollow. This easy-to-find nature preserve off Cooneymus Road is many visitors' first point of contact with the island's Greenway Trail system and an enduring testament to the island's conservation ethic. The main trail runs south about 1 mile to clay bluffs with great ocean views, from which a winding path descends to the rocky beach below. Side trails cross the 50-acre hollow, offering longer hikes and the allure of getting mildly lost. The striking, if muted, natural beauty makes it easy to understand why, 40 years ago, this was the property that first awoke the local land conservation movement, now close to achieving its goal of preserving half the island. Geology buffs will delight in this fine example of a glacial outwash basin; nature lovers may enjoy looking for the Block Island meadow vole, the state-threatened northern harrier, and federally endangered American burying beetle. A small parking lot sits just south of Cooneymus Road near a stone marker. ⊠ *Cooneymus Rd.*

Southeast Lighthouse Museum. The small repository is inside a "rescued" 1873 redbrick beacon with gingerbread detail that was moved back 360 feet from the eroded clay cliffs. The lighthouse is a National Historic Landmark; tours are offered during the summer. ⊠ *Mohegan Trail* ☎ *401/466–5009* ⊠ *$5* ☉ *Memorial Day–Labor Day, daily 10–4.*

West Side. To explore the island's lovely West Side, head west from New Harbor on West Side Road; after the Island Cemetery, you'll pass the converted West Side Baptist Church and a horse farm. To reach the tranquil west shore, turn right on Grace's Cove Road, Dorie's Cove Road, or Cooneymus Beach Road, dirt roads that dead-end in small coves with sunset ocean views. The road jogs left and turns into Cooneymus

Road, which overlooks Rodman's Hollow; ¼ mile further, it intersects with Lakeside Drive. Turn right to encounter Painted Rock, a knee-high boulder that islanders paint with messages that memorialize birthdays, weddings, and other life-changing events. ⊠ *West Side Rd.*

WORTH NOTING

☺ **Manisses Animal Farm.** When the kids have had enough of the beach, they'll be wowed by this hobby farm, run by the owners of the Hotel Manisses in meadows behind the gracious Victorian hotel. Camels, llamas, emus, fainting goats (goats whose legs stiffen when excited causing them to fall over), black swans, kangaroos, and a zedonk (cross between a zebra and a donkey) roam outside and will take handouts of the pellets provided; lemurs leap around their own enclosure. A herd of gentle alpacas helps provide fibers for the adjacent North Light Fibers textile mill, while a little closer to the road, herb and vegetable gardens provide ingredients for the Manisses' fine-dining restaurant. ⊠ *Off Spring St.* 🕾 *401/466–2421* 🖃 *Free* ☺ *Daily dawn–dusk.*

★ **New Harbor.** The Great Salt Pond has a culture all its own, centered on the three marinas, two hotels, and five restaurants clustered along its southern shore that make up this commercial area about a 20-minute walk from Old Harbor. Up to 2,000 boats create a forest of masts on summer weekends, drawn by sail races and fishing tournaments, while on the quiet north and east shores, clammers and windsurfers claim the tidal flats. Two landmark buildings preserved in the island's historic red-and-white idiom overlook the waters: the decommissioned Coast Guard Building at the cut where oceangoing boats enter and leave and the Narragansett Inn, the only Victorian hotel still run by the family that built it. The hotel is a lovely spot for sunset cocktails or dining. The Montauk Ferry docks at Champlin's, the largest of the marinas. ⊠ *Great Salt Pond.*

SPORTS AND THE OUTDOORS

BEACHES

The east side of the island has a number of beaches, which, like the rest of Rhode Island's coastline, offer temperate, warm waters that are ideal for swimming from June through around September.

Fodor'sChoice **Crescent Beach.** This 3-mile beach runs north from Old Harbor, and its
★ white sands become wider and crowds thinner the further away from town you go. It is divided into three smaller beaches, each with its own access point from Corn Neck Road. Furthest north is Mansion Beach. Look for the Mansion Beach Road sign, then follow the dirt road to the right to park in the two-level ruins of the old Searles Ball Mansion. It's a short hike to reach what is easily one of New England's most beautiful beaches; in the morning, you may spot deer on the dunes, while surfers dot Jerry's Point to the north. Closer to Old Harbor, Scotch Beach, with its small parking lot directly off Corn Neck Road, is a mecca for young adults who party, play volleyball, skimboard, and surf cast for striped bass. ⊠ *Corn Neck Rd.*

Digging for clams is a fun pastime on Block Island's beaches.

Frederick J. Benson Town Beach. This busy, family-oriented beach less than 1 mile from Old Harbor, has parking lots and plenty of space to lock up bicycles. There's a beach pavilion with a snack bar, showers, and chair and umbrella rentals. Surf here tends to be calmer, making it ideal for kids, and there are lifeguards. ⊠ *Corn Neck Rd.*

BIKING

The best way to explore Block Island is by bicycle (about $20 to $30 a day to rent) or moped (about $45 for an hour; $85 to $115 for the day). Most rental places are open spring through fall and have child seats for bikes, and all rent bicycles in a variety of styles and sizes, including mountain bikes, hybrids, tandems, and children's bikes.

Island Moped and Bike Rentals. Behind the Harborside Inn on Water Street, Island Moped and Bike Rentals has bikes of all kinds for daily and weekly rentals, and mopeds for hourly to half-day rentals (mopeds may not be driven after dusk). ⊠ *Weldon's Way, Chapel St.* ☎ *401/741–2329* ⊕ *www.bimopeds.com.*

Old Harbor Bike Shop. Descend from the Block Island Ferry and get right on a bike at Old Harbor Bike Shop, which also has a location at the Boat Basin marina in New Harbor that's convenient for boaters and travelers from Montauk. Bicyles, mopeds, Jeeps and, if you book early, convertibles are available. ⊠ *South of ferry dock* ☎ *401/466–2029* ⊕ *www.blockislandtransportation.com/about.htm.*

BOATING

Aldo's Boat Rentals. Just off the Champlin's Marina docks, Aldo's Boat Rentals offers all sorts of fun on the quiet waters of the Great Salt Pond, from leisurely, no-skill-required pontoon boats to small, zippy Hobe

Cat sailboats. Bumper boats and paddleboats are fun for kids, or fish for fluke from center-console powerboats. ⊠ *Champlin's Marina, West Side Rd., New Harbor* ☎ 401/466–2700.

Block Island Boat Basin. The boat basin has a small grocery store with marina supplies for boaters. ⊠ *West Side Rd., New Harbor* ☎ 401/ 466–2631.

Pond & Beyond. Pond & Beyond offers guided, wildlife-oriented kayak trips around the Great Salt Pond from its location behind Smuggler's Cove Restaurant. Children 12 and older can take custom tours designed to their skill level, while younger kids will be happy to hang out at the sea life touch tanks run nearby by the Block Island Maritime Institute. ⊠ *Ocean Ave., New Harbor* ☎ 401/578–2773 ⊕ *www.blockisland.com/ kayakbi.*

FISHING

Most of Rhode Island's record fish have been caught on Block Island. In fact, it's held the striped bass record (currently a 77.4-pound whopper caught in 2011) since 1984. From almost any beach, skilled anglers can land tautog and bass. The New Harbor channel is a good spot to hook bonito and fluke. Shellfishing licenses ($20 a week) may be obtained at the harbormaster's building at the Boat Basin in New Harbor.

Block Island Fishworks. The tiny Block Island Fishworks in New Harbor sells a wide range of tackle including hand-tied fly-fishing leaders, and offers charter fishing trips—inshore for bass and blues, offshore for tuna and shark—guide services, and spearfishing lessons. ⊠ *Ocean Ave.* ☎ 401/742–3992 ⊕ *www.bifishworks.com.*

Twin Maples. Twin Maples Tackle Shop has been selling bait and hand-made lures, sophisticated fishing tackle, and coveted "Eat Fish" T-shirts from its rustic salt-pond setting for more than 60 years. ⊠ *Beach Ave.* ☎ 401/466–5547 ⊕ *www.twinmaplesblockisland.com.*

HIKING

★ **Clay Head Nature Trail.** The outstanding Clay Head Nature Trail meanders past Clay Head Swamp and along 150-foot clay bluffs. Songbirds chirp and flowers bloom along the paths; stick close to the ocean for a stunning hike that ends at Sachem Pond, or venture into the interior's intertwining paths for hours of wandering and blackberrying in an area called the Maze. The trailhead is recognizable by a simple white post marker that lies on the east side of Corn Neck Road about 2 miles north of Old Harbor. Stop at the Nature Conservancy on High Street for trail maps. ⊠ *Corn Neck Rd., Clay Head Trail Rd.*

Greenway. The Greenway, a well-maintained trail system, meanders for more than 25 miles across the island, crossing stone walls and allowing access to parts of the island you can't reach any other way. The beaches that ring the island also offer great hikes, from sandy strolls to cliffside bouldering. Trail maps for the Greenway are available at the Chamber of Commerce on Water Street (*800/383–2474, www. blockislandchamber.com*).

Nature Conservancy. The Nature Conservancy distributes maps of the Greenway and trail maps of Clay Head Nature Trail. They also conduct nature walks; call for times or check the *Block Island Times*. ⊠ *352 High St.* ☎ *401/466–2129.*

WATER SPORTS

Diamondblue Surf Shop. There is a full range of surfing gear, as well as kiteboarding lessons and stand-up paddleboard rentals here. ⊠ *Bridgegate Square, Intersection of Dodge St. and Corn Neck Rd.* ☎ *401/466–3145* ⊕ *www.diamondbluebi.com.*

Island Outfitters. This shop sells wet suits, spearguns, and scuba gear, as well as beach gear and bathing suits. ⊠ *227 Weldon's Way* ☎ *401/466–5502.*

Block Island Parasail & Watersports. Block Island Parasail & Watersports will take you parasailing and also rents five-person jet boats and 10-person banana boats. ⊠ *Old Harbor Basin, Water St.* ☎ *401/864–2474* ⊕ *www.blockislandparasail.com.*

SHOPPING

Golddiggers. This jewelry story carries handmade pendants, rings, and bracelets with maritime and Block Island–themed designs. ⊠ *90 Chapel St.* ☎ *401/466–2611* ⊕ *www.blockislandgolddiggers.com.*

Island Bound Bookstore. Island Bound Bookstore has a good selection of fiction and nonfiction titles, including excellent histories of the island, as well as art supplies and crafts for kids. ⊠ *New Post Office Bldg.* ☎ *401/466–8878* ⊕ *www.islandboundbookstore.com.*

Jessie Edwards Studios. This gallery showcases photographs, sculptures, and paintings, often with nautical themes. Owner Jessie Edwards does home portraits by commission, and operates the island's only framing shop. ⊠ *New Post Office Bldg., 2nd Floor* ☎ *401/466–5314* ⊕ *www.jessieedwardsgallery.com.*

Lazy Fish. The eclectic collection of home accessories found here is curated by a careful eye; the owner is also an interior designer who blends old with new to colorful but harmonious effect. ⊠ *235 Dodge St.* ☎ *401/466–2990.*

North Light Fibers. North Light Fibers opened in a barn near Manisses Animal Farm in 2010 and uses the fleeces from its alpacas, llamas, yaks, and sheep to make beautiful yarns, knitwear, blankets, and craft kits. ⊠ *Manisses Animal Farm, Spring St.* ☎ *401/466–2050* ⊕ *www.northlightfibers.com.*

NIGHTLIFE

Nightlife, at least in season, is one of Block Island's highlights, and you have approximately two-dozen places to grab a drink. Check the *Block Island Times* for band listings.

Atlantic Inn. Of the island's many gracious Victorian hotel porches, the Atlantic Inn's is still the best one to begin your summer evening. Locals and visitors alike gather on the hilltop porch and sloping lawn below, clustering in Adirondack chairs to enjoy inventive cocktails, an award-winning wine list, well-prepared tapas, and an unparalleled view of Old

Harbor and Block Island Sound in the setting sun. Croquet mallets are available at the front desk. ✉ *359 High St.* ☎ *401/466–5883* 🌐 *www.atlanticinn.com.*

Captain Nick's Rock N' Roll Bar. Captain Nick's Rock N' Roll Bar sets itself apart from the other bars that surround nightlife epicenter Bridgegate Square by hosting June's Block Island Music Festival, a free roundup of to-be-discovered bands from around the country. Later in the summer it becomes a fortress of summertime fun, with bars on two floors, live music inside and out, and a suntanned crowd to ogle. Quieter Piano Bar evenings are hosted by its owner, a gifted pianist and singer, on Tuesday and Wednesday evenings; Fat Head Sushi, available Thursday to Sunday evenings, is the best light dinner deal in town. ✉ *34 Ocean Ave.* ☎ *401/466–5670* 🌐 *www.captainnicks.com.*

Mahogany Shoals. Mahogany Shoals is still, principally, a tiny shack built over the water at Payne's Dock where Irish Sea chanteys are the evening entertainment of choice. It has expanded, gracefully, with an outdoor bar, plenty of seating, and an upper-level deck, but remains the best place on the island to get a quiet evening drink, peer at people's yachts, and catch a breeze on even the hottest of nights. ✉ *Payne's Dock, 133 Ocean Ave.*

WHERE TO EAT

$$$ MODERN AMERICAN Fodor's Choice ★

🍴 **The 1661 Inn and Hotel Manisses.** The chef at the island's premier restaurant for American cuisine uses herbs and vegetables from the hotel's garden and locally caught seafood to prepare superb dishes such as lobster johnnycakes with sweet corn salsa and fennel pollen butter or grilled swordfish with lobster mashed potatoes and a lemon beurre blanc. Fans of red meat appreciate the tandoori beef tenderloin skewers with chickpea salad, grilled naan, and raita, or the kalbi braised short ribs with house-made kimchi, garlicky spinach, and sushi rice. A wide selection of small plates make this a place to splurge without breaking the bank, and the garden seating around a fountain is tranquil. [$] *Average main: $26* ✉ *1 Spring St.* ☎ *401/466–2421* 🌐 *www.blockislandresorts.com* 🕒 *Closed Nov.–Apr.*

$$ AMERICAN ★

🍴 **The Beachead.** The food—especially the Rhode Island clam chowder—is consistently great, the price is right, and you won't feel like a tourist at this locals' favorite. Catch ocean breezes on the patio, or in stormy weather, sit at the bar and watch breakers roll in 30 feet away. The menu and service are unpretentious; you can stop in for a grilled tuna or chicken sandwich at lunch, or try more ambitious fare, such as Portuguese mussels linguica or steak au poivre, at dinner. The kitchen brings its talent for reliability and quality to Payne's Dock, where it runs the Burger Bar at lunch and dinner during boating season. [$] *Average main: $18* ✉ *585 Corn Neck Rd.* ☎ *401/466–2249* 🌐 *thebeachead.com* ✍ *Reservations not accepted* 🕒 *Closed Dec.–April.*

$$$ AMERICAN ★

🍴 **Eli's.** This intimate bistro is the source of some of Block Island's most creative cuisine. An appetizer of tuna poke, wakame salad, sriracha aioli, and homemade wonton chips is too popular not to be a menu constant, but other seasonal dishes might include spring lamb osso bucco with ceci beans and a citrus-herb gremolata, or seared red snapper with baby bok choy and grilled Chinese-style pork belly. The pastry chef enjoys local fame for her bread pudding. Wait times can be long and the tiny bar, a favorite of locals, is prime real estate. $ *Average main: $25* ⊠ *456 Chapel St.* ☎ *401/466–5230* ⊕ *www.elisblockisland. com* ⚑ *Reservations not accepted* ⊘ *Closed Nov.–March. No lunch.*

$$$
SEAFOOD

✕ **Finn's.** A Block Island institution, Finn's serves fresh, reliable fried and broiled seafood and a wonderful smoked bluefish pâté. The island's best bet for simple steamed lobster, this is also the spot for an unfussy lunch such as the Workman's Special—a burger, coleslaw, and fries. Eat inside or out on the deck, or get food to go from the takeout window and raw bar. Finn's Fish Market is in the same building and its lobster tanks and ice tables are the best source for local seafood to cook at home or over a beach fire. $ *Average main: $26* ⊠ *Ferry Landing, 212 Water St.* ☎ *401/466–2473* ⊕ *finnsseafood.com* ⚑ *Reservations not accepted* ⊘ *Closed mid-Oct.–May.*

$
VEGETARIAN

✕ **Froozies.** What began as a smoothie bar on the back porch of the National Hotel has evolved into a standout sandwich joint, with hearty but healthy options, a varied vegetarian menu, and good people-watching. Active types stop by at 7:30 am for a black bean and avocado breakfast burrito and fair-trade coffee. Night owls roll in late-morning for hangover-cure smoothies and the Grilled Pondsider, one of the best takes on a grilled cheese ever invented with pesto, mozzarella, sun-dried tomatoes, sunflower seeds, and spinach. $ *Average main: $8* ⊠ *26 Dodge St.* ☎ *401/466–2230* ⊕ *www.frooziesblockisland.com* ⚑ *Reservations not accepted* ⊘ *Closed Oct.–May.*

WHERE TO STAY

It's advisable to book lodgings well in advance, especially for weekends in July and August, when many hotels ask for a two-night minimum; the Chamber of Commerce runs a room reservation service that's handy for last-minute trips. Many visitors rent homes for stays of a week or more.

For expanded hotel reviews, visit Fodors.com.

Ballard Hall Real Estate. This reliable agent has hundreds of vacation rental homes, from tiny budget cottages to swank beachside mansions. ⊠ *Bridegate Square, 1 Ocean Ave.* ☎ *401/466–8883* ⊕ *www. blockislandproperty.com.*

Block Island Reservations. Block Island Reservations books rooms for a number of hotels, inns and B&Bs, as well as some vacation home and apartment rentals, both nightly and weekly. ⊠ *Harborside Inn, 213 Water St.* ☎ *800/825–6254* ⊕ *www.blockislandreservations.com.*

$$$
HOTEL
★

🏨 **The Atlantic Inn.** Perched on a hill of floral gardens and undulating lawns, away from the hubbub of the Old Harbor area, this long, white, classic 1879 Victorian resort has big windows, high ceilings, a sweeping staircase, and lovely views. **Pros:** spectacular hilltop location; beautiful veranda for whiling away the afternoon; grand decor. **Cons:** no TVs or high-speed Internet in rooms. $ *Rooms from: $200* ⊠ *359 High St. 401/466–5883, 800/224–7422* ⊕ *www.atlanticinn.com* ⇱ *20 rooms, 1 suite* ⊘ *Closed late Oct.–mid-Apr.* ⦿*❘ Breakfast.*

$$ B&B/INN **Blue Dory Inn.** This Old Harbor district inn, with a main building and three small shingle-and-clapboard outbuildings, has been a guesthouse since its construction in 1898. **Pros:** great in-town location; relatively affordable. **Cons:** some units are small. [$] *Rooms from: $165* ✉ *61 Dodge St. 401/466–5891, 800/992–7290* 🌐 *www.blockislandinns.com* *11 rooms, 4 cottages, 3 suites* 🍴 *Breakfast.*

$$$$ B&B/INN Fodor's Choice ★ **Payne's Harbor View Inn.** This 2002 inn, designed to blend with the island's historic architecture, occupies a breezy hillside overlooking the Great Salt Pond and just minutes from Crescent Beach. **Pros:** relatively inexpensive for luxurious feel; kayak rentals; Wi-Fi and TVs. **Cons:** bar does not serve hard alcohol. [$] *Rooms from: $235* ✉ *Ocean Ave. and Beach Ave.* ☎ *401/466–5758* *10 rooms* 🍴 *Breakfast.*

$$$$ B&B/INN **The Rose Farm Inn.** With simple accommodations in a late-19th-century, pale blue, restored farmhouse and more luxurious units across a country lane inside a Colonial-style 1990s structure, this property set on a 20-acre pastoral farmstead offers two distinct styles. **Pros:** Captain Rose rooms have whirlpool tubs; bike-rental shop next door; quiet setting yet easy walk to Old Town. **Cons:** bathrooms in Farm House a bit rustic; few in-room amenities. [$] *Rooms from: $234* ✉ *Off High Street, Roslyn Rd.* ☎ *401/466–2034* 🌐 *www.rosefarminn.com* *19 rooms, 17 with bath* ⏲ *Closed mid-Oct.–early May* 🍴 *Breakfast.*

Vermont

WORD OF MOUTH

"We headed up to Burlington where we had a wonderful dim sum lunch at A Single Pebble, explored the Church Street Marketplace and the magnificent waterfront. We loved the feel of Burlington and the presence of the water and the mountains."

—jubilada

WELCOME TO VERMONT

TOP REASONS TO GO

★ **Small-town charm:** Vermont rolls out a seemingly never-ending supply of tiny, charming towns made of steeples, general stores, village squares, red barns, and B&Bs.

★ **Ski resorts:** The East's best skiing takes place in uncrowded, modern facilities, with great views and lots and lots of fresh snow.

★ **Fall foliage:** Perhaps the most vivid colors in North America wave from the trees in September and October, when the whole state is ablaze.

★ **Gorgeous landscapes:** This sparsely populated, heavily forested state is an ideal place to find peace and quiet amid the mountains, valleys, and lakes.

★ **Tasty and healthy eats:** The state's rich soil and focus on local farming and ingredients yields great cheeses, dairies, orchards, vineyards, local food resources, and restaurants.

1 Southern Vermont. Most people's introduction to the state is southern Vermont, accessible by car from New York and Boston. Like elsewhere across the state, you'll find unspoiled towns, romantic B&Bs, rural farms, and pristine forests. There are two notable exceptions: sophisticated little Manchester has upscale shopping, and independent Brattleboro is a hippie outpost and environmentally conscious town.

2 Central Vermont. Similar to southern Vermont in character and geography, central Vermont's star is Stowe, the quintessential ski town east of the Mississippi. Warren, Waitsfield, and Middlebury are among its charming small towns.

3 Northern Vermont. The northernmost part of the state is a place of contrasts. Burlington, with dramatic views of Lake Champlain and the Adirondacks, is the state's most populous city at around 60,000 residents; it's an environmentally sensitive, laid-back college town with a sophisticated local food scene. To the east, the landscape becomes desolate, with natural beauty and almost no significant population, making the Northeast Kingdom a refuge for nature lovers and aficionados of wide-open northern beauty.

GETTING ORIENTED

Vermont can be divided into three regions. The southern part of the state, flanked by Bennington on the west and Brattleboro on the east, played an important role in Vermont's Revolutionary War–era drive to independence (yes, there was once a Republic of Vermont) and its eventual statehood. The central part is characterized by rugged mountains and the gently rolling dairy lands near Lake Champlain. Northern Vermont is home to the state's capital, Montpelier, and its largest city, Burlington, as well as its most rural area, the Northeast Kingdom. The Green Mountains run from north to south up the center of the state; this central spinal corridor is unpopulated, protected national forest.

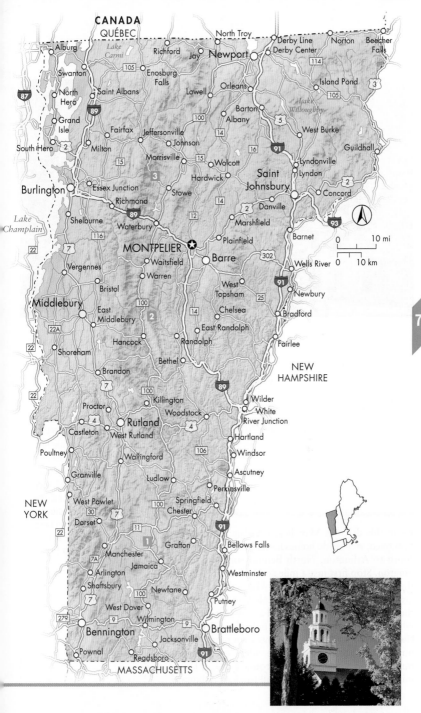

CANADA
QUÉBEC

Lake Carmi

Alburg
Swanton
North Troy
Richford
Jay
Newport
Derby Line
Derby Center
Norton
Beecher Falls
105
Enosburg Falls
Orleans
Island Pond
114
North Hero
Saint Albans
Lowell
3
105
87
Grand Isle
Fairfax
Jeffersonville
Albany
Barton
Lake Willoughby
West Burke
Guildhall
South Hero
Milton
Johnson
100
14
16
91
Lyndonville
89
Morrisville
15
Wolcott
5
Lyndon
2
Burlington
Essex Junction
3
Hardwick
Saint Johnsbury
Concord
Stowe
2
Danville
Richmond
14
Marshfield
Barnet
89
Shelburne
Waterbury
12
Plainfield
93
116
MONTPELIER
Waitsfield
Barre
302
Wells River
7
22
Vergennes
Warren
West Topsham
91
Newbury
Bristol
100
25
Middlebury
East Middlebury
14
Chelsea
Bradford
22A
2
East Randolph
Fairlee
22
Hancock
Randolph
Shoreham
Bethel
NEW HAMPSHIRE
7
Brandon
89
100
Killington
Wilder
22
Proctor
Woodstock
White River Junction
4
Rutland
West Rutland
4
Hartland
Castleton
106
Windsor
Poultney
Wallingford
Ascutney
Granville
Ludlow
Perkinsville
NEW YORK
West Pawlet
30
Springfield
Chester
22
Dorset
100
91
11
1
Grafton
Bellows Falls
7A
Manchester
Jamaica
Arlington
Westminster
Shaftsbury
100
Newfane
7
West Dover
Putney
279
9
Wilmington
9
Brattleboro
Bennington
Jacksonville
91
Pownal
Readsboro
MASSACHUSETTS

0   10 mi
0   10 km

7

VERMONT FALL FOLIAGE DRIVE

Eighty percent of Vermont is forested, and since cities are few and far between, the interior of Vermont is a rural playground for leaf peepers and widely considered to have the most intense range of foliage colors anywhere on the continent. The few distractions from the dark reds and yellow, oranges and russets—the tiny towns and hamlets—are as pristine as nature itself.

Begin this drive in Manchester Village, along the old-fashioned, well-to-do homes lining Main Street, and drive south to Arlington, North Bennington, and Old Bennington. Stop first just a mile south along 7A at **Hildene**, the Lincoln family home. The 412 acres of explorable grounds here are ablaze with color, and the views over the Battenkill Valley are as good as any you can find anywhere. Continue south another mile along 7A to **Equinox Nursery**, where you can pick your own pumpkin from a huge patch, try delicious apple cider and cider doughnuts, and take in the stunning countryside. A few more miles south along 7A is the small town of Arlington.

BEST TIME TO GO

Late September and early October are the times to go, with the southern area peaking about a week later than the north. Remember to book hotels in advance. The state has a Fall Foliage Hotline and an online interactive map (☎ 800/VERMONT ⊕ www.foliage-vermont.com). The drive from Manchester to Bennington outlined here is just 30 minutes, but a relaxed day is best to take in all the sights.

From 7A in Arlington, you can take two adventurous and stunning detours. One is pure foliage: follow 313 west a few miles to the New York state border for more beautiful views. Or head east a mile to East Arlington where delightful shops await you, including **Grist Mill Antiques**, which is set right above a wonderfully cascading brook. (You can continue even farther east from this spot to Kelly Stand Road leading into the Green Mountains; this is a little-known route that can't be beat.) Back on 7A South in Arlington, stop at the **Cheese House**, the delightfully cheesy roadside attraction.

Farther south into Shaftsbury is **Clear Brook Farm**, a brilliant place for cider and fresh produce and pumpkins. Robert Frost spent much of his life in South Shaftsbury, and you can learn about his life at his former home, the **Stone House.** From South Shaftsbury take Route 67 through North Bennington and continue on to Route 67A in Old Bennington. Go up the 306-foot-high **Bennington Battle Monument** to survey the seasonal views across four states. Back down from the clouds, walk a few serene blocks to the cemetery of the **Old First Church**, where Robert Frost is buried, and contemplate his autumnal poem, "Nothing Gold Can Stay."

NEED A BREAK?

Equinox Valley Nursery. This nursery carries fresh produce, seasonal snacks, and is full of family-friendly fall activities— a corn maze, pumpkin golf (mini golf played with small pumpkins and croquet mallets), hay rides, and pumpkin carving. ⊠ *1158 Main St.(7A), Manchester* ☎ *802/362-2610* ⊕ *www. equinoxvalleynursery.com* ⊠ *Free* ⏲ *Apr.–Dec., Mon.– Sat. 8:30–5, Sun. 9–4.* **Clear Brook Farm.** Set on more than 20 acres, Clear Brook Farm sells their own organic produce, in addition to baked goods and other seasonal treats. ⊠ *47 Hidden Valley Rd., Manchester* ☎ *802/442-4273* ⊕ *www. clearbrookfarm.com* ⏲ *May–Aug., daily 9–6; Sept.–Oct., daily 10–6.* **The Cheese House.** Get your Vermont cheddar fix at the Cheese House, which also sells maple syrup and other local products and gifts. ⊠ *5187 Vermont Rte. 7A, Arlington* ☎ *802/375-9033* ⊕ *www. thevermontcheesehouse. com* ⊠ *Free* ⏲ *Wed.–Mon. 10–5. Closed Tues.*

7

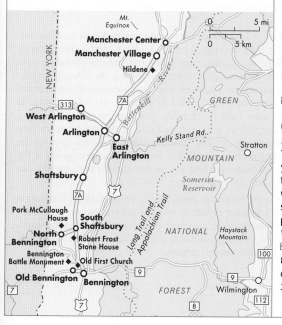

Updated by
Eliot Sloan

Vermont is an entire state of hidden treasures and unspoiled scenery. Wander anywhere in the state—80% is forest—and you'll travel a pristine countryside dotted with farms and framed by mountains. Tiny towns with church steeples, village greens, and clapboard Colonial-era houses are perfect for exploring.

Sprawl has no place here. Highways are devoid of billboards by law, and on some roads cows still stop traffic twice a day en route to and from the pasture. In spring, sap boils in sugarhouses, some built generations ago, and up the road a chef trained at the New England Culinary Institute in Montpelier might use the resulting maple syrup to glaze a pork tenderloin.

It's the landscape, for the most part, that attracts people to Vermont. The rolling hills belie the rugged terrain underneath the green canopy of forest growth. In summer, clear lakes and streams provide ample opportunities for swimming, boating, and fishing; the hills attract hikers and mountain bikers. The more than 14,000 miles of roads, many of them only intermittently traveled by cars, are great for biking. In fall, the leaves have their last hurrah, painting the mountainsides a stunning show of yellow, gold, red, and orange. Vermont has the best ski resorts in the eastern United States, centered along the spine of the Green Mountains north to south. The traditional heart of skiing is the town of Stowe. Almost anywhere you go, any time of year, it will make you smile and reach for your camera.

Vermont may seem locked in time, but technological sophistication appears where you least expect it: wireless Internet access in a 19th-century farmhouse-turned-inn and cell phone coverage from the state's highest peaks. Like an old farmhouse under renovation, Vermont's historic exterior is still the main attraction.

PLANNING

WHEN TO GO

In summer, the state is lush and green, although in winter, the hills and towns are blanketed with snow and skiers travel from around the East Coast to challenge Vermont's peaks. Fall is one of the most amazing times to come. If you have never seen a kaleidoscope of autumn colors, a trip to Vermont is worth braving the slow-moving traffic and paying the extra money for fall lodging. The only time things really slow down is during "mud" season—otherwise known as late spring. Even innkeepers have told guests to come another time. Activities in the Champlain Islands come essentially to a halt in the winter, except for ice fishing and snowmobiling. Two of the state's biggest attractions, Shelburne Farms and the Shelburne Museum, are closed mid-October through April. Otherwise, though everything looks completely different depending on the season, Vermont is open all year.

PLANNING YOUR TIME

There are many ways to take advantage of Vermont's beauty: skiing or hiking its mountains, biking or driving its back roads, fishing or sailing its waters, shopping for local products, visiting its museums and sights, or simply finding the perfect inn and never leaving the front porch.

Distances are relatively short, yet the mountains and many back roads will slow a traveler's pace. You can see a representative north–south section of Vermont in a few days; if you have up to a week, you can hit the highlights. Note that many inns have two-night-minimum stays on weekends and holidays.

GETTING HERE AND AROUND

AIR TRAVEL

Continental, Delta, JetBlue, United, Porter Airlines, and US Airways fly into Burlington International Airport. Rutland State Airport has daily service to and from Boston on Cape Air.

BOAT TRAVEL

Lake Champlain Ferries. This company operates three ferry crossing routes between the lake's Vermont and New York shores: Grand Isle–Plattsburgh, NY; Burlington–Port Kent, NY; and Charlotte–Essex, NY. ☎ 802/864–9804 ⊕ www.ferries.com.

CAR TRAVEL

Vermont is divided by a mountainous north–south middle, with a main highway on either side: scenic Route 7 on the western side and Interstate 91 (which begins in New Haven and runs through Hartford, central Massachusetts, and along the Connecticut River in Vermont to the Canadian border) on the east. Interstate 89 runs from New Hampshire across central Vermont from White River Junction to Burlington and up to the Canadian border. For current road conditions, call ☎ 800/429–7623.

TRAIN TRAVEL

Amtrak. Amtrak has daytime service linking Washington, D.C., with Brattleboro, Bellows Falls, White River Junction, Montpelier, Waterbury, Essex Junction, and St. Albans via its Vermonter line. Amtrak's

Ethan Allen Express connects New York City with Fair Haven and Rutland. ☎ *800/872–7245* ⊕ *www.amtrak.com.*

RESTAURANTS

Everything that makes Vermont good and wholesome is distilled in its eateries, making the regional cuisine much more defined than neighboring states. With an almost political intensity, farmers and chefs have banded together to insist on utilizing Vermont's wonderful bounty. Especially in summer, the produce and meats are impeccable. Many of the state's restaurants belong to the Vermont Fresh Network (⊕ *www. vermontfresh.net*), a partnership that encourages chefs to create menus from local produce.

Great chefs are coming to Vermont for the quality of life, and the New England Culinary Institute is a recruiting ground for new talent. Seasonal menus use local fresh herbs and vegetables along with native game. Look for imaginative approaches to native New England foods such as maple syrup (Vermont is the largest U.S. producer), dairy products (especially cheese), native fruits and berries, "new Vermont" products such as salsa and salad dressings, and venison, quail, pheasant, and other game.

Your chances of finding a table for dinner vary with the season: lengthy waits are common at peak times (a reservation is always advisable); the slow months are April and November. Some of the best dining is at country inns. *Prices in the reviews are the average cost of a main course at dinner or, if dinner is not served, at lunch.*

HOTELS

Vermont's only large chain hotels are in Burlington and Rutland. Elsewhere it's just quaint inns, bed-and-breakfasts, and small motels. The many lovely and sometimes quite luxurious inns and B&Bs provide what many people consider the quintessential Vermont lodging experience. Most areas have traditional base ski condos; at these you sacrifice charm for ski-and-stay deals and proximity to the lifts. Rates are highest during foliage season, from late September to mid-October, and lowest in late spring and November, although many properties close during these times. Winter is high season at Vermont's ski resorts. *Prices in the reviews are the lowest cost of a standard double room in high season.*

VISITOR INFORMATION

Vermont Department of Tourism and Marketing ⊠ *6 Baldwin St., Drawer 33, Montpelier* ☎ *802/828–3237, 800/837–6668* ⊕ *www.vermontvacation.com.*

Foliage and Snow Hot Line. This useful hotline has tips on peak foliage viewing locations and times, up-to-date snow conditions, and events in Vermont. ☎ *802/828–3239.*

SOUTHERN VERMONT

Cross into the Green Mountain State from Massachusetts on Interstate 91, and you might feel as if you've entered a new country. There isn't a town in sight. What you see are forested hills punctuated by rolling pastures. When you reach Brattleboro, no fast-food joints or strip malls

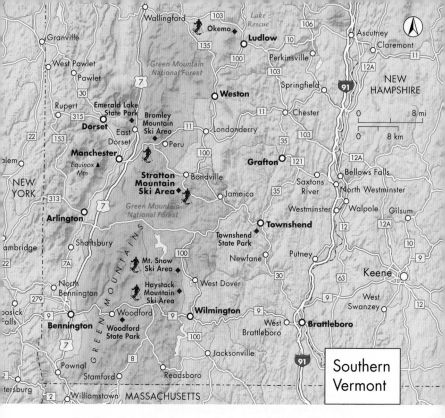

line the exits to signal your arrival at southeastern Vermont's gateway city. En route to downtown, you pass by Victorian-era homes on tree-lined streets. From Brattleboro, you can cross over the spine of the Green Mountains toward Bennington and Manchester.

The state's southwest corner is the southern terminus of the Green Mountain National Forest, dotted with lakes, threaded with trails and old forest roads, and home to four big ski resorts: Bromley, Stratton, Mount Snow, and Haystack Mountain.

⇨ *The towns are listed in counterclockwise order in this section, beginning in the east in Brattleboro, then traveling west along Route 9 toward Bennington, then north to Manchester and Weston and south along scenic Routes 100 and 30 back to Townshend and Newfane.*

BRATTLEBORO

60 miles south of White River Junction.

Brattleboro has drawn political activists and earnest counter-culturists since the 1960s. Today, the arty town of 12,000 is still politically and culturally active, making it Vermont's most offbeat outside of Burlington.

OUTDOOR ACTIVITIES

Biking: Vermont, especially the often-deserted roads of the Northeast Kingdom, is great bicycle-touring country. Many companies lead weekend tours and weeklong trips throughout the state. If you'd like to go it on your own, most chambers of commerce have brochures highlighting good cycling routes in their area.

Canoeing and Kayaking: Getting on Vermont's many rivers and lakes is a great way to experience nature. Outfitters can be found almost anywhere there's water.

Fishing: Central Vermont is the heart of the state's warm-water lake and pond fishing area. Lake Champlain, stocked annually with salmon and lake trout, has become the state's ice-fishing capital.

Hiking: Vermont is an ideal state for hiking—80% of the state is forest, and trails are everywhere. The Appalachian Trail runs the length of the state. In fact, it was the first portion of the trail to be completed, and in Vermont it is called the Long Trail. Many bookstores in the state have numerous volumes dedicated to local hiking.

Skiing: The Green Mountains run through the middle of Vermont like a bumpy spine, visible from almost every point in the state; generous accumulations of snow make them an ideal site for skiing. Route 100 is also known as Skier's Highway, passing by 13 of the state's ski areas.

GETTING HERE AND AROUND

Brattleboro is near the intersection of Route 9, the principal east–west highway also known as the Molly Stark Trail, and Interstate 91. For downtown, use Exit 2 from Interstate 91.

ESSENTIALS

Visitor Information Brattleboro Area Chamber of Commerce ⊠ *180 Main St.* ☎ *802/254–4565, 877/254–4565* ⊕ *www.brattleborochamber.org.*

EXPLORING

Brattleboro Museum and Art Center. Downtown is the hub of Brattleboro's art scene, with this museum in historic Union Station at the forefront. It presents changing exhibits created by locally, nationally, and internationally renowned artists. ⊠ *10 Vernon St.* ☎ *802/257–0124* ⊕ *www.brattleboromuseum.org* 🎟 *$6, free 1st Fri. each month 5–8:30* ⊗ *Thurs.–Mon. 11–5, 1st Fri. each month 11–8:30.*

OFF THE BEATEN PATH

Putney. Nine miles upriver, this small town, with a population of just over 2,000, is the country cousin of bustling Brattleboro and is a haven for writers, artists, and craftspeople. There are dozens of pottery studios to visit and a few orchards. In 2009, a fire burned down the world-class general store that had served as the heart of the community, but there is talk of rebuilding. ⊠ *Putney.*

The Green Mountain Spinnery. Watch wool being spun into yarn at the Green Mountain Spinnery. The factory shop, which is open daily all year, sells yarn, knitting accessories, and patterns. Tours are conducted at 1:30 on the first and third Tuesday of the month. ⊠ *7 Brickyard Lane,* *off I–91, Exit 4, Putney* ☎ *802/387–4528, 800/321–9665* ⊕ *www. spinnery.com*

Harlow's Sugar House. Two miles north of Putney, Harlow's Sugar House has a working cider mill and sugarhouse, as well as seasonal apple and berry picking. The family has been sugaring on this farm since 1927. You can buy cider, maple syrup, and other items in the gift shop. ⊠ *563 Bellows Falls Rd., Putney* ☎ *802/387–5852* ⊕ *www. vermontsugar.com*

SPORTS AND THE OUTDOORS
BIKING
Brattleboro Bicycle Shop. This shop rents and repairs hybrid bikes. ⊠ *165 Main St.* ☎ *802/254–8644* ⊕ *www.bratbike.com.*

CANOEING
Vermont Canoe Touring Center. Canoes and kayaks are available for rent here. ⊠ *451 Putney Rd.* ☎ *802/257–5008.*

SHOPPING
ART
Gallery in the Woods. This store sells art, jewelry, and glassware from around the world. ⊠ *145 Main St.* ☎ *802/257–4777* ⊕ *www. galleryinthewoods.com.*

Through the Music. To get a sense of the vibrant works being produced by young local artists, head to the back of the **Turn it Up** record shop to find Through the Music, an otherwise easy-to-miss gallery. The excellent contemporary art spans genres from painting to pottery. ⊠ *2 Elliot St.* ☎ *802/779–3188* ⊕ *www.throughthemusic.com.*

Vermont Artisan Designs. Ceramics, glass, wood, clothing, jewelry, and furniture from more than 300 artists are on display here. ⊠ *106 Main St.* ☎ *802/257–7044* ⊕ *www.vtartisans.com.*

BOOKS
★ **Brattleboro Books.** With more than 75,000 used books this is a great spot to browse. It's also a good source for local goings-on. ⊠ *36 Elliot St.* ☎ *802/257–7777* ⊕ *brattleborobooks.com* ⊘ *Mon–Sat. 10–6, Sun. 11–5.*

NIGHTLIFE AND THE ARTS
ARTS
Brattleboro has an evening gallery walk on the first Friday of each month from 5:30 to 8:30.

Latchis Theater. This throwback art deco movie theater complete with velvet curtains shows four films at a time and hosts art exhibits when movies aren't playing. ⊠ *50 Main St.* ☎ *802/254–6300* ⊕ *www.latchis.com.*

NIGHTLIFE
Metropolis Wine Bar & Cocktail Lounge. This popular new cocktail lounge serves up signature infused cocktails, tapas, wine, local beer, and live music in a hip, festive atmosphere. ⊠ *55 Elliot St., Brattleboro* ☎ *802/490–2255* ⊕ *www.metropoliswinebar.com.*

NEED A BREAK?

Mocha Joe's Roasting Co. The gathering spot in town for coffee and conversation is Mocha Joe's Roasting Co., which takes great care in sourcing beans from places like Kenya, Ethiopia, and Guatemala. This is ground zero for Brattleboro's contemporary bohemian spirit. ✉ *82 Main St., Corner of Main and Elliot Sts.* ☎ *802/257–5637* 🌐 *www.mochajoes.com.*

BILLBOARDS AND VERMONT

Did you know that there are no billboards in Vermont? The state banned them in 1967 (similar laws exist in Maine, Alaska, and Hawaii), and the last one came down in 1975, so when you look out your window, you see trees and other scenic sights, not advertisements. (It may make playing the Alphabet Game with your child a bit difficult.)

WHERE TO EAT

$ AMERICAN 🍴 **Brattleboro Food Co-op.** Soon to be further upgraded, this is one of the best foodie stops in the state to stock up on Vermont's finest artisanal products. Its charms include different grades of self-serve maple syrup and reusable containers to store your bounty. Pick up a premade sandwich or order a plate of curry chicken at the deli counter, then eat it in this busy market's small sitting area. Natural and organic is the focus, with everything from tofu sandwiches to beef *satay* (skewered grilled meat). The delicatessen is connected to a natural-foods market and serves breakfast. [$] *Average main: $6* ✉ *2 Main St.* ☎ *802/257–0236* 🌐 *www.brattleborofoodcoop.com.*

$ ITALIAN 🍴 **Fireworks.** Stop by this trendy, airy, and colorful trattoria-style restaurant for flatbread pizzas, pastas, and salads any night of the week. In nice weather, check out their back patio. Try the daily specials and well-mixed cocktails. [$] *Average main: $14* ✉ *69-73 Main St., Brattleboro* ☎ *802/254-2073* 🌐 *fireworksrestaurant.net* 🕒 *7 days.*

$$$ STEAKHOUSE ★ 🍴 **Peter Havens.** In a town better known for tofu than toniness, this chic little bistro knows just what to do with a filet mignon: serve it with Roquefort walnut butter. One room is painted a warm red, another in sage; both are punctuated by copies of Fernando Botero paintings, creating a look that is one of the most sophisticated in the state. Try the house-cured gravlax made with lemon vodka or the fresh seasonal seafood, which even includes a spring fling with soft-shell crabs. The wine list is superb. [$] *Average main: $30* ✉ *32 Elliot St.* ☎ *802/257–3333* 🌐 *www.peterhavens.com* 🕒 *Closed Sun., Mon., Tues. No lunch.*

$$$$ AMERICAN Fodor's Choice ★ 🍴 **T.J. Buckley's.** It's easy to miss this tiny restaurant, but it's worth seeking out as one of the most romantic little eateries in Vermont. Open the doors to the sleek black 1920s diner and enter what amounts to a very intimate theater, with a mere 18 seats for the show. The stage is an open kitchen, the flames a few feet away, and working under the whisper of vocal jazz and candlelight is the star of the show: Michael Fuller, the dashing owner and sole chef, who has been at the helm for 25 years. The contemporary menu is conveyed verbally each day and is based on locally available ingredients. It's dinner theater for culinary fans, a romantic triumph. [$] *Average main: $35* ✉ *132 Elliot St.* ☎ *802/257–4922* 🌐 *www.tjbuckleys.com* ✍ *Reservations essential* 🕒 *Closed Mon. and Tues. No lunch.*

$ SOUTHERN 🍴 **Top of the Hill Grill.** Hickory-smoked ribs, beef brisket, apple-smoked turkey, and pulled pork are a few of the favorites at this seasonal barbecue outside town. Larger parties can opt for "family-style" dinners;

The rolling green hills of Putney are home to many organic farm operations.

homemade pecan pie is the dessert of choice. The best seats are outdoors at picnic tables overlooking the West River. $ *Average main: $15* ✉ *632 Putney Rd.* ☎ *802/258–9178* ⊕ *www.topofthehillgrill.com* ▭ *No credit cards* ☺ *Closed Nov.–mid-Apr.*

$
CAFÉ
✕ **The Works.** Right in the center of town, this spot is filled with natural light and people on laptops sitting at long wooden tables or enjoying coffee and a book in one of their comfy armchairs. Try their fresh fruit smoothies, veggie panini, wraps, and salads. This is a perfect breakfast or lunch stop or just a place to catch up on email. $ *Average main: $6* ✉ *118 Main St., Brattleboro* ☎ *802/579–1851.*

WHERE TO STAY
For expanded hotel reviews, visit Fodors.com.

$$$
B&B/INN
⌂ **Forty Putney Road.** Engaging hosts Tim and Amy Brady run this French-style manse and have restored some of its more interesting original features (like nickel-plated bathroom fixtures) and added new ones (like flat-screen TVs). **Pros:** caring hosts; clean, remodeled rooms. **Cons:** short walk into town; rates vary and spike during busy periods. $ *Rooms from: $200* ✉ *192 Putney Rd.* ☎ *802/254–6268, 800/941–2413* ⊕ *www.fortyputneyroad.com* ☞ *5 rooms, 1 suite* ⍾ *Breakfast.*

$$
B&B/INN
Fodor's Choice
★
⌂ **Hickory Ridge House.** If you're looking for a relaxing country get-away, this 1808 Federal-style mansion, a former sheep farm set on a wide meadow, is a sure bet. **Pros:** peaceful, scenic property; terrific house; great breakfast; quintessential B&B experience. **Cons:** not walking distance from town. $ *Rooms from: $165* ✉ *53 Hickory Ridge Rd., Putney11 miles north of Brattleboro* ☎ *802/387–5709, 800/380–9218* ⊕ *www.hickoryridgehouse.com* ☞ *6 rooms, 1 cottage* ⍾ *Breakfast.*

$ HOTEL **Latchis Hotel.** To stay in the heart of town at a low rate, you can do no better than the Latchis. **Pros:** heart-of-town location; good value. **Cons:** clean but dull furnishings; less personality than area B&Bs. [$] *Rooms from: $95* ✉ *50 Main St.* ☎ *802/254-6300, 800/798-6301* 🌐 *www.latchis.com* 🛏 *30 rooms, 3 suites* 🍴 *Breakfast.*

WILMINGTON

18 miles west of Brattleboro.

The village of Wilmington, with its classic Main Street lined with 18th- and 19th-century buildings, anchors the Mount Snow Valley. Most of the valley's lodging and dining establishments, however, line Route 100, which travels 5 miles north to West Dover and Mount Snow, where skiers flock on winter weekends. The area abounds with cultural activity year-round, from concerts to art exhibits.

GETTING HERE AND AROUND

Wilmington is at the junction of Routes 9 and 100. West Dover and Mount Snow are a few miles to the north along Route 100.

ESSENTIALS

Visitor Information Mount Snow Valley Chamber of Commerce ✉ *21 W. Main St.* ☎ *802/464-8092, 877/887-6884* 🌐 *www.visitvermont.com.*

EXPLORING

★ 👶 **Adams Farm.** At this working farm you can collect fresh eggs from the chicken coop, feed a rabbit, milk a goat, ride a tractor or a pony, and jump in the hay—plus run through the corn maze in summer and take sleigh rides in winter. The indoor livestock barn is open Wednesday through Sunday, November to mid-June; an outdoor version is open daily the rest of the year. The farm store sells more than 200 handmade quilts and sweaters. ✉ *15 Higley Hill Rd., 3 miles north of Wilmington, off Rte. 100* ☎ *802/464-3762* 🌐 *www.adamsfamilyfarm.com* 🎟 *$6.96–$14.95* 🕒 *Wed.–Sun. 10–5.*

👶 **Southern Vermont Natural History Museum.** This museum, 5 miles east of Wilmington on Route 9, houses one of New England's largest collections of mounted birds, including three extinct birds and a complete collection of mammals native to the Northeast. The museum also has live hawk and owl exhibits. ✉ *7599 Rte. 9* ☎ *802/464-0048* 🌐 *www.vermontmuseum.org* 🎟 *$5* 🕒 *June–late Oct., daily 10–5; late Oct.–May, most weekends 10–4, call ahead.*

SPORTS AND THE OUTDOORS

BOATING

Green Mountain Flagship Company. Canoes, kayaks, and sailboats are available for rent from May to late October on Lake Whitingham. ✉ *389 Rte. 9, 2 miles west of Wilmington* ☎ *802/464-2975.*

SKI AREA

Mount Snow. The closest major ski area to all of the Northeast's big cities, Mount Snow, is also one of the state's premier family resorts and has a full roster of year-round activities. The almost 800-acre facility encompasses a hotel, 10 condo developments, an 18-hole golf course, a health

CLOSE UP

Vermont Maple Syrup

Vermont is one of the country's smallest states, but it's the largest producer of maple syrup. A visit to a maple farm is a great way to learn all about sugaring, the process of taking maple tree sap and making syrup. Sap is stored in a sugar maple tree's roots in the winter, and in the spring when conditions are just right, the sap runs up and is capable of being tapped. Tapping season takes place in March and April, which is when all maple in the state is produced.

Maple sap is collected in buckets.

One of the best parts of visiting a maple farm is getting to taste the four grades of syrup. As the sugaring season goes on and days get warmer, the sap becomes progressively darker and stronger flavored. Color, clarity, and flavor define the four grades of syrup. Is one grade better than another? Nope. It's just a question of taste. Sap drawn early in the season produces the lightest color, and has the most delicate flavor: this is called Vermont Fancy. Vermont Grade A Medium Amber has a mellow flavor. Vermont Grade A Dark Amber is much more robust, and Vermont Grade B is the most flavorful, making it often the favorite of first-time tasters.

Is one syrup better than another? Can you actually tell the difference? You'd need an exceptionally nuanced palate to discern between one Vermont syrup and another, but aesthetics can alter taste, and authenticity counts. So when visiting a maple farm, make sure that this is a place that actually makes its own syrup, as opposed to just bottling or selling someone else's.

Vermont Maple Syrup. There are approximately 50 maple farms that are free and open all year to the public. The official industry website for Vermont Maple Syrup is a great resource that has a map of maple farms that host tours, a directory of producers open year-round, and a list of places you can order maple by mail. In addition, you can learn about the Annual Maple Open House weekend, which is when sugarhouses throughout the state open their doors to the public. ⊕ www.vermontmaple.org.

Morse Farm Maple Sugarworks. Sugarhouses are located throughout the state, but there's no better introduction to Vermont mapling than a visit to Morse Farm Maple Sugarworks in Montpelier, Vermont. Burr Morse's family has been mapling for more than 200 years, longer than anyone else in the state. Attractions here include a free tour of a sugarhouse, tastings, and an outdoor museum and woodshed theater. ⊠ 1168 County Rd., Montpelier ☎ 800/242–2740 ⊕ www.morsefarm.com.

Jed's Maple Products. If you're traveling with children, Jed's Maple Products, far in the Northeast Kingdom, is a good option as owners Steve and Amy Wheeler take kids into the woods to show how to tap trees. Always call ahead if you're planning a visit. ⊠ 475 Carter Rd., Westfield ☎ 802/744–2095, 866/478–7388 ⊕ www.jedsmaple.com.

—Michael de Zayas

During the spring sugaring season, water is boiled off the maple sap to concentrate the syrup's flavor.

club and spa, 45 miles of mountain-biking trails, and an extensive network of hiking trails.

Mount Snow prides itself on its 250 snowmaking fan guns, which let it open earlier than any ski area in the state. More than half of the 80 trails down its 1,700-foot vertical summit are intermediate, wide, and sunny. There are four major downhill areas. The main mountain is mostly beginners' slopes, especially toward the bottom, while the north face includes the majority of the expert terrain. Corinthia used to be a separate ski mountain, but is now connected with a mix of trail levels. The south face, Sunbrook, has wide, sunny trails. The trails are served by 20 lifts, including three high-speed quads. Snowmaking covers 85% of the terrain. There are 98 acres of glades. The ski school's instruction program is designed to help skiers of all ages and abilities. Mount Snow also has eight terrain parks of different skill levels and a 400-foot half-pipe with 18-foot walls. Skiing programs start with the Cub Camp, designed for kids age three. Snow Camp teaches kids four to six, and Mountain Camp and Mountain Riders are for kids seven to 14; there's also a well-organized child-care center. ⊠ *39 Mount Snow Rd., West Dover* ☎ *802/464–3333, 802/464–2151 snow conditions, 800/245–7669 lodging* ⊕ *www.mountsnow.com.*

Two cross-country ski centers near Mount Snow provide more than 68 miles of varied terrain.

Timber Creek. This appealingly small cross-country ski and snow shoe center has 9 miles of groomed loops, equipment rentals, and ski lessons. ⊠ *R1 Tomber Creek Rd., at Rte. 100, north of Mount Snow, West Dover* ☎ *802/464–0999* ⊕ *www.timbercreekxc.com.*

SNOWMOBILE TOURS

High Country. This outfitter runs one-hour, two-hour, and half-day snowmobile tours from the base of Mount Snow. ✉ *Mount Snow base lodge, Rte. 100, West Dover* ☎ *802/464–2108* 🌐 *www.high-country-tours.com.*

SHOPPING

Downtown Wilmington is lined with unique shops and galleries.

Quaigh Design Centre. This store sells great pottery and artwork from Britain and New England—including works by Vermont woodcut artists Sabra Field and Mary Azarian—and Scottish woolens. ✉ *11 W. Main St.(Rte. 9)* ☎ *802/464–2780.*

WHO WAS MOLLY STARK?

In the heart of Wilmington, to the side of Crafts Inn (built by Stanford White in 1902) is a sculpture in honor of Molly Stark, the wife of Revolutionary War general John Stark. The general was said to have roused his troops in the Battle of Bennington, vowing victory over the British: "They are ours, or this night Molly Stark sleeps a widow!" He lived, and the victory path across Vermont, now Route 9, is called the Molly Stark Trail.

WHERE TO STAY

For expanded hotel reviews, visit Fodors.com.

$$$ B&B/INN 🏨 **Deerhill Inn.** The picture of a quintessential New England inn, this is a truly charming spot. **Pros:** great restaurant; nicely renovated rooms. **Cons:** must drive to town and resort. [$] *Rooms from: $225* ✉ *14 Valley View Rd., West Dover* ☎ *802/464–3100, 800/993–3379* 🌐 *www.deerhill.com* 🛏 *12 rooms, 2 suites* 🍴 *Multiple meal plans.*

$$$ RESORT 👶 🏨 **Grand Summit Hotel.** The 200-room base lodge at Mount Snow is an easy choice for skiers who don't care about anything but getting on the slopes as quickly as possible. **Pros:** easy ski access; modern property. **Cons:** somewhat bland decor in rooms; not a historic option. [$] *Rooms from: $200* ✉ *39 Mount Snow Rd., West Dover* ☎ *800/451–4211* 🌐 *www.mountsnow.com* 🛏 *104 rooms, 96 suites* 🍴 *No meals.*

$$ B&B/INN 🏨 **The Inn at Sawmill Farm.** Full of character and charm, this inn in a converted barn has common rooms elegantly accented with English chintzes, antiques, and Oriental rugs. **Pros:** spacious grounds; attentive service. **Cons:** overload of floral prints in some rooms; room size varies. [$] *Rooms from: $175* ✉ *7 Crosstown Rd., at Rte 100, West Dover 802/464–8131, 800/493–1133* 🌐 *www.theinnatsawmillfarm.com* 🛏 *21 rooms* ⏲ *Closed early-Apr.–late May* 🍴 *Multiple meal plans.*

$$$ B&B/INN 🏨 **White House of Wilmington.** It's hard to miss this 1915 Federal-style mansion standing imposingly atop a high hill off Route 9 east of Wilmington. **Pros:** intriguing, big, old-fashioned property; intimate dining. **Cons:** not in town, so you have to drive to everything; no children under eight. [$] *Rooms from: $235* ✉ *178 Rte. 9* ☎ *802/464–2135, 800/541–2135* 🌐 *www.whitehouseinn.com* 🛏 *24 rooms, 1 cottage* 🍴 *Breakfast.*

OUTDOOR OUTFITTERS AND INFORMATION

BIKING

P.O.M.G. Bike Tours of Vermont. This outfitter, whose name stands for peace of mind guaranteed, leads weekend and five-day bike tours. ☎ 802/434-2270, 888/635-2453 ⊕ www.pomgbike.com.

Vermont Bicycle Touring (VBT). This guide company leads bike tours in the state. ✉ 614 Monkton Rd., Bristol ☎ 802/453-4811, 800/245-3868 ⊕ www.vbt.com.

CANOEING AND KAYAKING

BattenKill Canoe. This outfitter organizes canoe tours (some are inn-to-inn) and fishing trips. ✉ 6328 Historic Rte. 7A, Sunderland ☎ 802/362-2800, 800/421-5268 ⊕ www.battenkill.com.

True North Kayak Tours. This tour company operates a guided kayak tour of Lake Champlain and a natural-history tour; they also customize lessons, single-day and multiday trips and coordinate special trips for kids. ✉ 25 Nash Pl., Burlington ☎ 802/238-7695 ⊕ www.vermontkayak.com.

Umiak Outdoor Outfitters. A full-service outfitter, Umiak has canoe and kayak excursions as well as rentals. ✉ 849 S. Main St., Stowe ☎ 802/253-2317 ⊕ www.umiak.com.

FISHING

Vermont Fish and Wildlife Department. For information about fishing, including licenses, call the Vermont Fish and Wildlife Department. ✉ 103 South Main St. ☎ 802/241-3700 ⊕ www.vtfishandwildlife.com.

HIKING

Green Mountain Club. The Green Mountain Club publishes hiking maps and guides. The club also manages the Long Trail. ✉ 4711 Waterbury-Stowe Rd. (Rte. 100), Waterbury Center ☎ 802/244-7037 ⊕ www.greenmountainclub.org.

SKIING

Ski Vermont/Vermont Ski Areas Association. For skiing information, contact Ski Vermont/Vermont Ski Areas Association. ✉ 26 State St. Montpelier ☎ 802/223-2439 ⊕ www.skivermont.com.

SPORT TOURS

Country Inns Along the Trail. This company arranges self-guided hiking, skiing, and biking trips from inn to inn in Vermont. 802/247-3300, 800/838-3301 ⊕ www.inntoinn.com.

BENNINGTON

21 miles west of Wilmington.

Bennington is the commercial focus of Vermont's southwest corner and home to the renowned Bennington College. It's really three towns in one: Downtown Bennington, Old Bennington, and North Bennington. Downtown Bennington has retained much of the industrial character it developed in the 19th century, when paper mills, gristmills, and potteries formed the city's economic base. The outskirts of town are commercial and not worth a stop, so make your way right into Downtown and Old Bennington to appreciate the true charm of the area.

The poet Robert Frost is buried in Bennington at the Old First Church, "Vermont's Colonial Shrine."

GETTING HERE AND AROUND

The heart of modern Bennington is at the intersection of U.S. 7 and Route 9. Old Bennington is a couple of miles west on Route 9, at Monument Avenue. North Bennington is a few miles north on Route 67A.

ESSENTIALS

Visitor Information Bennington Area Chamber of Commerce ⌧ *100 Veterans Memorial Dr. (U.S. 7)* ☎ *802/447–3311, 800/229–0252* ⊕ *www.bennington. com.*

EXPLORING

TOP ATTRACTIONS

Bennington Battle Monument. This 306-foot stone obelisk—with an elevator to the top—commemorates General John Stark's victory over the British, who attempted to capture Bennington's stockpile of supplies. Inside the monument you can learn all about the battle, which took place near Walloomsac Heights in New York State on August 16, 1777, and helped bring about the surrender of the British commander "Gentleman Johnny" Burgoyne two months later. The summit provides commanding views of the Massachusetts Berkshires, the New York Adirondacks, and the Vermont Green Mountains. ⌧ *15 Monument Circle, Old Bennington* ☎ *802/447–0550* ⊕ *www.bennington.com/ chamber/walking/monumentdescription.html* ⌨ *$2* ☯ *Mid-Apr.–Oct., daily 9–5.*

Bennington Museum. The rich collections at this museum include military artifacts, early tools, dolls, toys, and the Bennington Flag, one of the oldest of the Stars and Stripes in existence. One room is devoted to early Bennington pottery, and two rooms cover the history of American glass (fine Tiffany specimens are on display). The museum displays the largest public collection of the work of Grandma Moses (1860–1961), the popular self-taught artist who lived and painted in the area. ⌧ *75 Main St. (Rte. 9), Old Bennington* ☎ *802/447–1571* ⊕ *www.benningtonmuseum.com* ⌧ *$10* ⊘ *July–Oct. daily 10–5; Nov.–Dec. and Feb.–June, Thurs.–Tues. 10–5, closed Wed. and Jan.*

North Bennington. North of Old Bennington is this village, home to Bennington College, lovely mansions, Lake Paran, three covered bridges, and a wonderful old train depot. ⌧ *North Bennington.*

   Bennington College. Contemporary stone sculpture and white-frame neo-Colonial dorms surrounded by acres of cornfields punctuate the green meadows of the placid campus of Bennington College. ⌧ *Rte. 67A off U.S. 7, look for stone entrance gate, One College Dr., North Bennington* ☎ *802/442–5401* ⊕ *www.bennington.edu.*

   Park-McCullough House. The architecturally significant Park-McCullough House is a 35-room classic French Empire–style mansion, built in 1865 and furnished with period pieces. Several restored flower gardens grace the landscaped grounds, and a stable houses a collection of antique carriages. Call for details on the summer concert series. ⌧ *1 Park St., at West St., North Bennington* ☎ *802/442–5441* ⊕ *www.parkmccullough.org* ⌧ *$10* ⊘ *Mid-May–mid-Oct., daily 10–4; last tour at 3.*

Robert Frost Stone House Museum. A few miles north along Route 7A is the town of Shaftsbury. It was here that Frost came in 1920 "to plant a new Garden of Eden with a thousand apple trees of some unforbidden variety." The museum tells the story of the nine years (1920–29) Frost spent living in the house with his wife and four children. (He passed the 1930s in a house up the road in Shaftsbury, now owned by a Hollywood movie producer.) It was here that he penned "Stopping by Woods on a Snowy Evening" and published two books of poems. Seven of the Frost family's original 80 acres can be wandered. Among the apple boughs you just might find inspiration of your own. ⌧ *75 Main St. (Rte. 9), Shaftsbury* ☎ *802/447–6200* ⊕ *www.frostfriends.org* ⌧ *$5* ⊘ *May–Nov.; Tues.–Sun. 10–5.*

WORTH NOTING

Old Bennington. West of Downtown, Old Bennington is a National Register Historic District centered along the axis of Monument Avenue and well endowed with stately Colonial and Victorian mansions. Here, at the Catamount Tavern (now a private home north of Church Street), Ethan Allen organized the Green Mountain Boys, who helped capture Fort Ticonderoga in 1775. ⌧ *Old Bennington.*

The Old First Church. In the graveyard of this church, the tombstone of the poet Robert Frost proclaims, "I had a lover's quarrel with the world." ⌧ *1 Church La., at Monument Ave., Old Bennington* ☎ *802/447–1223* ⊕ *www.oldfirstchurchbenn.org* ⌧ *Free.*

SPORTS AND THE OUTDOORS

Lake Shaftsbury State Park. There is a swimming beach, nature trails, boat and canoe rentals, and a snack bar here. ⊠ *Rte. 7A, 10½ miles north of Bennington, 262 Shaftsbury State Park Rd.* ☎ *802/375–9978* ⊕ *www. vtstateparks.com/htm/shaftsbury.htm.*

Woodford State Park. This park has an activities center on Adams Reservoir, a playground, boat and canoe rentals, and nature trails. ⊠ *Rte. 9, 10 miles east of Bennington, 142 State Park Rd.* ☎ *802/447–7169* ⊕ *www.vtstateparks.com/htm/woodford.htm.*

SHOPPING

The Apple Barn & Country Bake Shop. This shop sells home-baked goodies, fresh cider, Vermont cheeses, maple syrup, and apples! Thirty varieties are grown in its orchards. You can pick berries here, too, making it a fun family stop. You can watch them making cider donuts at the bakery and café on weekends most of the year. ⊠ *604 Rte. 7S., 1½ miles south of Downtown Bennington* ☎ *888/827–7537* ⊕ *theapplebarn.com.*

Bennington Potters Yard. The showroom at the Bennington Potters Yard stocks first-quality pottery and seconds from the famed Bennington Potters. Take a free tour on weekdays from 10 to 3 when the potters are working, or follow a self-guided tour around the yard. ⊠ *324 County St.* ☎ *802/447–7531, 800/205–8033* ⊕ *www.benningtonpotters.com.*

BOOKS

Now & Then Books. This great used bookstore, located in an upstairs shop, has nearly 50,000 volumes in stock. ⊠ *439 Main St.* ☎ *802/442–5566* ⊕ *www.nowandthenbooksvt.com.*

The Bennington Bookshop. This bookstore sells new books and gifts and has free Wi-Fi. ⊠ *467 Main St.* ☎ *802/442–5059.*

THE ARTS

Bennington Center for the Arts. Cultural events, including exhibitions by local and national artists, take place here. ⊠ *44 Gypsy La.* ☎ *802/442–7158* ⊕ *www.thebennington.org.*

Oldcastle Theatre Co. The on-site Oldcastle Theatre Co. hosts fine regional theater from May through October. ⊠ *44 Gypsy La., at Vermont Rte. 9 West* ☎ *802/447–0564* ⊕ *oldcastletheatre.org.*

Basement Music Series. This series, run by the nonprofit Vermont Arts Exchange, is a funky basement cabaret venue in an old factory building. Purchase tickets in advance for the best contemporary music performances in town. ⊠ *29 Sage St., North Bennington* ☎ *802/442–5549* ⊕ *www.vtartxchange.org/bms.php.*

WHERE TO EAT

$ ✕ **Blue Benn Diner.** Breakfast is served all day in this authentic diner,
DINER where the eats include turkey hash and breakfast burritos with scrambled eggs, sausage, and chilis, plus pancakes of all imaginable varieties. The menu lists many vegetarian selections. Lines may be long, especially on weekends: locals and tourists alike can't stay away. $ *Average main: $10* ⊠ *314 North St.* ☎ *802/442–5140* ⚓ *Reservations not accepted* ⊟ *No credit cards.*

$$$
EUROPEAN

✗ **Four Chimneys Inn.** It's a treat just to walk up the long path to this classic Old Bennington mansion, the most refined setting around. The dining room is a discreet, quiet room lit by candles and a gas fireplace. Chef Pete Jaenecke creates a sophisticated seasonal menu. If you're lucky, it might include handcrafted *agnolotti* (ravioli) pasta filled with Angus beef, braised in port with a shallot confit and cherry ragout and topped with a local blue cheese, or maybe the poached salmon in a lemon-dill beurre blanc sauce. The restaurant is open seasonally for dinner, but all year for private events. $ *Average main: $29* ⊠ *21 West Rd. (Rte. 9), Old Bennington* ☎ *802/447–3500* ⊕ *www.fourchimneys. com* ⚄ *Reservations essential* ⊘ *No lunch.*

$$
ECLECTIC
★

✗ **Pangaea Lounge.** Don't let the dusty old storefront and scuffed-up floor fool you. Bennington's in-the-know crowd comes here before anywhere else for affordable comfort food and an excellent bar. Directly next door is Pangaea, the restaurant's fancier twin, which is somewhat overpriced and not as intimate. The eclectic pub fare includes such dishes as pot roast chimichangas, Cobb salad with Danish blue cheese, salmon burgers, and seared pork loin with a potato croquette. On weekends in warmer months, follow the crowd out back to the deck. $ *Average main: $17* ⊠ *3 Prospect St., 3 miles north of Bennington, North Bennington* ☎ *802/442–4466* ⊕ *www.vermontfinedining.com* ⊘ *No lunch.*

WHERE TO STAY

For expanded hotel reviews, visit Fodors.com.

$
B&B/INN
★

🏠 **The Eddington House Inn.** You can thank Patti Eddington for maintaining this three-bedroom house, the best value in all of Vermont. **Pros:** budget prices for great B&B; privacy and gentle service. **Cons:** slightly off usual tourist track; only three rooms so it fills up fast. $ *Rooms from: $139* ⊠ *21 Main St., North Bennington* ☎ *802/442–1511* ⊕ *www. eddingtonhouseinn.com* ↪ *3 rooms* ⫴⦾⫴ *Breakfast.*

$$
B&B/INN
Fodor's Choice
★

🏠 **Four Chimneys Inn.** This is the quintessential Old Bennington mansion and one of the best inns in Vermont. **Pros:** stately mansion that's extremely well kept; formal dining; very clean, spacious, renovated rooms. **Cons:** common room/bar closes early. $ *Rooms from: $150* ⊠ *21 West Rd. (Rte. 9), Old Bennington* ☎ *802/447–3500* ⊕ *www. fourchimneys.com* ↪ *9 rooms, 2 suites* ⫴⦾⫴ *Breakfast.*

ARLINGTON

15 miles north of Bennington.

Smaller than Bennington and more down to earth than upper-crust Manchester to the north, Arlington exudes a certain Rockwellian folksiness, and it should. Illustrator Norman Rockwell lived here from 1939 to 1953, and many of his neighbors served as models for his portraits of small-town life.

GETTING HERE AND AROUND

Arlington is at the intersection of Routes 313 and 7A. Take 313 West to reach West Arlington.

EXPLORING

West Arlington. A covered bridge leads to the quaint town green of West Arlington, where Norman Rockwell once lived. River Road runs along the south side of the Battenkill River, a scenic drive. If you continue west along Route 313, you'll come to the Wayside General Store, a real charmer, where you can pick up sandwiches and chat with locals. The store is frequently mentioned (anonymously) in the Vermont columns written by Christopher Kimball, editor of *Cooks Illustrated.* ✉ *West of Arlington on Rte. 313 W.*

SPORTS AND THE OUTDOORS

★ **BattenKill Canoe.** This outfitter rents canoes for trips along the Battenkill River, which runs directly behind the shop. If you're hooked, they also run bigger white-water trips as well as inn-to-inn tours. ✉ *6328 Historic Rte. 7A, Sunderland* ☎ *802/362–2800, 800/421–5268* 🌐 *www.battenkill.com.*

SHOPPING

ANTIQUES

East Arlington Antiques Center. More than 70 dealers display their wares at East Arlington Antiques Center, which is in a converted 1930s movie theater. Among the finds is one of the country's best stoneware collections. Manager Jon Maynard is a charmer. ✉ *1152 East Arlington Rd., East Arlington* ☎ *802/375–6144* 🕒 *Daily 10–5.*

Fodor's Choice ★ **Gristmill Antiques.** This beautiful two-floor antiques shop in a historic mill looks out over Roaring Brook. ✉ *316 Old Mill Rd., East Arlington* ☎ *802/375–2500.*

GIFTS

👶 **The Village Peddler.** The Village Peddler has a "chocolatorium" chocolate museum where you can learn all about chocolate. It sells fudge and other candies and has a large collection of teddy bears for sale. ✉ *261 Old Mill Rd., East Arlington* ☎ *802/375–6037* 🌐 *www.villagepeddlervt.com.*

NIGHTLIFE AND THE ARTS

Friday Night Fireside Music Series. Held in the cozy tavern at the West Mountain Inn, this music series features great live music acts every other Friday evening from November through May for a $10 cover. ✉ *144 West Mountain Inn Rd., at River Rd. and Rte. 313, West Arlington* ☎ *802/375–6516* 🌐 *www.westmountaininn.com.*

WHERE TO STAY

For expanded hotel reviews, visit Fodors.com.

$$$ B&B/INN 🏨 **The Arlington Inn.** Greek Revival columns at this 1848 home lend it an imposing presence in the middle of town, but the atmosphere is friendly and old-fashioned. **Pros:** heart-of-town location; friendly atmosphere. **Cons:** rooms are dated; expensive dining. [$] *Rooms from: $209* ✉ *3904 VT Rte. 7A* ☎ *802/375–6532, 800/443–9442* 🌐 *www.arlingtoninn.com* 🛏 *13 rooms, 5 suites* 🍴 *Multiple meal plans.*

$$ B&B/INN 👶 🏨 **Hill Farm Inn.** Simple cottages and the best views in the Manchester area make this former dairy farm a winner. **Pros:** lovely open meadow setting; farm animals on-site; cabins offer privacy and fun. **Cons:** rooms are quite simple, not luxurious. [$] *Rooms from: $155* ✉ *458 Hill Farm*

7

Rd., off Rte. 7A, Sunderland ☎ *802/375–2269, 800/882–2545* 🌐 *www.hillfarminn.com* 🛏 *6 rooms, 5 suites, 4 cabins* 🍴 *Breakfast.*

$$ B&B/INN **West Mountain Inn.** This 1810 farmhouse sits on 150 acres on the side of a mountain, offering hiking trails and easy access to the Battenkill River, where you can canoe or go tubing. **Pros:** mountainside location; great for families; outdoor activities. **Cons:** outdated bathrooms and carpets; unimpressive food; not luxurious. [$] *Rooms from: $195* ✉ *144 West Mountain Inn Rd., at River Rd. and Route 313* ☎ *802/375–6516* 🌐 *www.westmountaininn.com* 🛏 *16 rooms, 6 suites* 🍴 *Multiple meal plans.*

MANCHESTER

9 miles northeast of Arlington.

★ Well-to-do Manchester has been a popular summer retreat since the mid-19th century, when city dwellers traveled north to take in the cool clean air at the foot of 3,816-foot Mt. Equinox. Manchester Village's tree-shaded marble sidewalks and stately old homes—Main Street here could hardly be more picture perfect—reflect the luxurious resort lifestyle of more than a century ago. A mile north on 7A, Manchester Center is the commercial twin to Colonial Manchester Village, as well as where you'll find the town's famed upscale factory outlets doing business in attractive faux-Colonial shops.

Manchester Village also houses the world headquarters of Orvis, the outdoor goods brand that began here in the 19th century and has greatly influenced the town ever since. Its complex includes a fly-fishing school with lessons in its casting ponds and the Battenkill River.

GETTING HERE AND AROUND

Manchester is the main town for the ski resorts of Stratton and Bromley and is roughly 15 minutes from either on Routes 11 and 30. It's 15 minutes north of Arlington, 30 minutes north of Bennington and south of Rutland on Routes 7 and 7A. Take 7A for a more scenic drive.

ESSENTIALS

Visitor Information Chamber of Commerce, Manchester and the Mountains ✉ *5046 Main St.* ☎ *802/362–2100, 800/362–4144* 🌐 *www.manchestervermont.net.* **Green Mountain National Forest Visitor Center** ✉ *2538 Rte. 30* ☎ *802/362–2307* 🌐 *www.fs.fed.us/r9/gmfl* 🕓 *Weekdays 8–4:30.*

EXPLORING

American Museum of Fly Fishing. This museum houses the world's largest collection of angling art and angling-related objects. Rotating exhibitions draw from a permanent collection of more than 1,500 rods, 800 reels, 30,000 flies, and the tackle of notables like Winslow Homer, Bing Crosby, and Jimmy Carter. Every August the museum organizes a fly-fishing festival with kids' activities and vendors selling antique equipment. ✉ *4104 Main St.* ☎ *802/362–3300* 🌐 *www.amff.com* 🎟 *$5* 🕓 *Tues.–Sat 10–4.*

Fodor's Choice ★ **Hildene.** The Lincoln Family Home is a twofold treat, providing historical insight into the life of the Lincolns while escorting you through the lavish Manchester life of the 1900s. Abraham had only one son who survived to adulthood, Robert Todd Lincoln, who served as secretary

The formal gardens and mansion at Robert Todd Lincoln's Hildene are a far cry from his father's log cabin.

of war and head of the Pullman Company. Robert bought the beautifully preserved 412-acre estate and built a 24-room mansion where he and his descendants lived from 1905–75. The entire grounds are open for exploration—you can hike, picnic, and ski; see the astronomical observatory; loll in beautiful gardens; and walk through the sturdy Georgian Revival house, which holds the family's original furniture, books, and possessions. One of three surviving stovepipe hats owned by Abraham, a Lincoln Bible, a gorgeously restored Pullman car, and Robert's Harvard University yearbook are among the treasures you'll find. When the 1,000-pipe aeolian organ is played, the music reverberates as though from the mansion's very bones.

Rising from a 10-acre meadow, the new Hildene Farm, which opened in 2010, is magnificent. The agriculture center is built in a traditional style—post-and-beam construction of timber felled and milled on the estate—and as an exemplar of renewable energy, from the closed-loop cordwood heating system to the solar panels covering the roof. A herd of goats and informative farming displays recall the Lincolns' use of this land. Best of all, you can watch goat cheese being made and take some home.

The highlight, though, may be the elaborate formal gardens: in June a thousand peonies bloom. When snow conditions permit, you can cross-country ski and snowshoe on the property. Robert's carriage house now houses the gorgeous museum store and visitor center—the nicest of its kind in the state—that showcases, among other things, a live bee exhibit and Mary Todd Lincoln's 1928 vintage Franklin car. Allow half a day for exploring Hildene. ⊠ *940 Hildene Rd., at Rte. 7A* ☎ *802/362–1788* ⊕ *www.hildene.org* 🖅 *Tour $16, grounds pass $5* ☉ *Daily 9:30–4:30.*

Southern Vermont Arts Center. Rotating exhibits and a permanent collection of more than 700 pieces of 19th- and 20th-century American art are showcased at this 12,500-square-foot museum. The original building, a graceful Georgian mansion set on 407 acres, is the frequent site of concerts, performances, and film screenings. In summer and fall, a pleasant restaurant with magnificent views serves lunch. ⊠ *930 SVAC Dr., West Rd.* ☎ *802/362–1405* ⊕ *www.svac.org* 🖅 *$8* ☉ *Tues.–Sat. 10–5, Sun. noon–5.*

SPORTS AND THE OUTDOORS

BIKING

Battenkill Sports Bicycle Shop. This shop rents, sells, and repairs bikes and provides maps and route suggestions. ⊠ *1240 Depot St.(U.S. 7, Exit 4)* ☎ *802/362–2734, 800/340–2734* ⊕ *www.battenkillsports.com.*

FISHING

Battenkill Anglers. Teaching the art and science of fly-fishing, Battenkill Anglers offers both private and group lessons. ⊠ *6204 Main St.* ☎ *802/379–1444* ⊕ *www.battenkillangler.com.*

Orvis Fly-Fishing School. This nationally renowned school offers courses mid-April to mid-October, ranging from two-hour pond trips with casting lessons and fishing with private instructors to three-day advanced classes on the Battenkill. The company opened a new building just for the fly school across the street from its flagship store in 2009. ⊠ *6204 Rte. 7A, Manchester Center* ☎ *802/362–4604, 802/362–3184* ⊕ *www. orvis.com/schools.*

HIKING

There are bountiful hiking trails in the Green Mountain National Forest. Shorter hikes begin at the Equinox Resort, which owns about 1,000 acres of forest and has a great trail system open to the public.

Long Trail. One of the most popular segments of Vermont's Long Trail starts from a parking lot on Route 11/30 five minutes out of town and goes to the top of Bromley Mountain. The strenuous 6-mile round-trip takes about four hours. ⊠ *Route 11/30* ⊕ *www.greenmountainclub.org.*

Lye Brook Falls. A moderate four-hour hike starts off Manchester East Road and ends at Vermont's most impressive cataract, Lye Brook Falls. ⊠ *Manchester East Rd.*

Mountain Goat. Stop here for hiking and backpacking equipment as well as snowshoe, cross-country, and Telemark ski rentals. ⊠ *4886 Main St.* ☎ *802/362–5159* ⊕ *mountaingoat.com.*

ICE-SKATING

Riley Rink at Hunter Park. The Olympic-size indoor Riley Rink at Hunter Park has ice-skating rentals and a concession stand. ⊠ *410 Hunter Park Rd.* ☎ *802/362–0150* ⊕ *www.rileyrink.com.*

SHOPPING
ART AND ANTIQUES
Long Ago & Far Away. This store specializes in fine indigenous artwork, including Inuit stone sculpture. ⊠ *Green Mountain Village Shops, 4963 Main St.* ☎ *802/362–3435* ⊕ *www.longagoandfaraway.com.*

Tilting at Windmills Gallery. The large Tilting at Windmills Gallery displays and sells the paintings and sculpture of nationally known artists. ⊠ *24 Highland Ave.* ☎ *802/362–3022* ⊕ *www.tilting.com.*

BOOKS
Fodor's Choice ★ ☾ **Northshire Bookstore.** The heart of Manchester Center, this bookstore is adored by visitors and residents for its ambience, selection, and service. Up the central black iron staircase is a second floor dedicated to children's books, toys, and clothes. Connected to the bookstore is the Spiral Press Café, where you can sit for a grilled pesto-chicken sandwich or a latte and scone. ■TIP→ Adding to the gravitational draw: the entire town has a Wi-Fi connection. ⊠ *4869 Main St.* ☎ *802/362–2200, 800/437–3700* ⊕ *www.northshire.com.*

CLOTHING
Manchester Designer Outlets. Spread out across Manchester Center, Manchester Designer Outlets is the most upscale collection of stores in northern New England—and every store is a discount outlet! Adding to the allure, town ordinances decree the look of the shops be in tune with the surrounding historic homes, making these the most attractive and decidedly Colonial-looking outlets you'll ever see. The long list of upscale clothiers who call Manchester home include Kate Spade, Kenneth Cole, Michael Kors, Betsey Johnson, Ann Taylor, Tumi, BCBG, Armani, Coach, Polo Ralph Lauren, Brooks Brothers, and Theory. There are also less expensive brand outlets like Pacsun, Gap, and Banana Republic. ⊠ *97 Depot St.* ☎ *802/362–3736, 800/955–7467* ⊕ *www.manchesterdesigneroutlets.com.*

★ **Orvis Flagship Store.** The two-story, lodgelike Orvis Flagship Store has a trout pond as well as the company's latest clothing and accessories. It's a required shopping destination for many visitors—the Orvis name is pure Manchester. ⊠ *4200 Rte. 7A* ☎ *802/362–3750* ⊕ *www.orvis.com.*

NIGHTLIFE AND THE ARTS
Falcon Bar. This bar at the Equinox Resort has a sophisticated setting with music on weekends, or you can take in the wonderful outdoor deck. In winter the place to be is under the heating lamps surrounding the giant Vermont slate fire pit. ⊠ *3567 Main St.(Rte. 7A)* ☎ *800/362–4747* ⊕ *www.equinoxresort.com.*

Perfect Wife. This is a local hang out, with music three to four nights a week. ⊠ *2594 Depot St.(Rte. 11/30)* ☎ *802/362–2817* ⊕ *www.perfectwife.com* ☉ *Tues.–Sat. 4–close. Closed Sun.–Mon.*

WHERE TO EAT
$$$ FRENCH ✕**Bistro Henry.** The active presence of chef-owner Henry Bronson accounts for the continual popularity of this friendly place that's about $5 per dish cheaper than the other good restaurants in town. The menu works off a bistro foundation, with a peppery steak au poivre and a

Manchester Designer Outlets' Colonial-style architecture helps blend upscale discount shopping with the surrounding town.

medium rare duck breast served with a crispy leg, and mixes things up with eclectic dishes like seared tuna with wasabi and soy; crab cakes in a Cajun rémoulade; and a delicious scallop dish with Thai coconut curry and purple sticky rice. The wine list is extensive, and Dina Bronson's desserts are memorable—indulge in the "gooey chocolate cake," a great molten treat paired with a homemade malt ice cream. $ *Average main: $29* ✉ *1942 Depot St., 3 miles east of Manchester Center* ☎ *802/362–4982* ⊕ *www.bistrohenry.com* ☉ *Closed Mon. No lunch.*

$$$$ ✕ **Chantecleer.** There is something wonderful about eating by candlelight
EUROPEAN in an old barn. Chantecleer's dining rooms (in winter ask to sit by the great fieldstone fireplace) are wonderfully romantic, even with a collection of roosters atop the wooden beams. The menu leans toward the Continental with starters like a fine escargot glazed with Pernod in a hazelnut-and-parsley butter. Crowd pleasers include Colorado rack of lamb and whole Dover sole filleted tableside. A recipe from the chef's Swiss hometown makes a winning winter dessert: Basel Rathaus Torte, a delicious hazelnut layer cake. $ *Average main: $38* ✉ *8 Reed Farm La., off Rte. 7A, 3½ miles north of Manchester, East Dorset* ☎ *802/362–1616* ⊕ *www.chantecleerrestaurant.com* ⌂ *Reservations essential* ☉ *Closed Nov. and April. Closed Mon. and Tues. No lunch.*

$$$$ ✕ **Chop House.** Walk to the very back room of the Equinox Resort's
STEAKHOUSE Marsh Tavern, past a velvet curtain, and you'll have entered a different eatery—a wonderful, very expensive steakhouse called the Chop House. The dining room has a bit of history—the marble above the fireplace is chiseled L. L. ORVIS 1832 (and way before he claimed the spot the Green Mountain Boys gathered here to plan their resistance). Today, you'll yield to USDA Prime aged corn- or grass-fed beef broiled

at 1,700 degrees and finished with herb butter. The New York strip, 32-ounce rib eye, 16-ounce milk-fed veal chops, filet mignon, lamb, and seafood are delicious, a must for deep-pocketed lovers of steaks and seafood. $ *Average main: $44* ⊠ *3567 Main St.* ☎ *802/362–4700* ⊕ *www.equinoxresort.com.*

$$ **✕ Depot 62 Bistro.** The best pizzas in town are topped with terrific fresh
PIZZA ingredients and served in the middle of a high-end antiques showroom, making this Turkish-Mediterranean restaurant a local secret worth knowing about. The wood-fired oven yields masterful results—like the arugula pizza, a beehive of fresh greens atop a thin-crust base. This a great place for lunch or an inexpensive but satisfying dinner. Sit on your own or at the long communal table. $ *Average main: $18* ⊠ *515 Depot St.* ☎ *802/366–8181* ⊕ *www.depot62cafe.com.*

$$$ **✕ Mistral's.** This classic French restaurant is tucked in a grotto off Route
FRENCH 11/30 on the climb to Bromley Mountain. The two dining rooms are perched over the Bromley Brook, and at night lights magically illuminate a small waterfall. Ask for a window table. Specialties include Chateaubriand béarnaise and rack of lamb with rosemary for two. Chef Dana Markey's crispy sweetbreads with porcini mushrooms are a favorite. $ *Average main: $25* ⊠ *10 Toll Gate Rd.* ☎ *802/362–1779* ☾ *Closed Wed. No lunch.*

$$$ **✕ Perfect Wife.** Owner-chef Amy Chamberlain, the self-proclaimed aspir-
ECLECTIC ing flawless spouse, creates freestyle cuisine like turkey schnitzel and grilled venison with a caramelized shallot and dried cranberry demiglace. There are two entrances to the restaurant, and we recommend the hilltop tavern, which looks over the more formal dining room below. The tavern is one of the livelier local spots in town, with live music on weekends and a pub menu with burgers, potpies in winter, and Vermont microbrews on tap. $ *Average main: $27* ⊠ *2594 Depot St.(Rte. 11/30), 2½ miles east of Manchester Center* ☎ *802/362–2817* ⊕ *www.perfectwife.com* ☾ *Closed Sun. No lunch.*

$$$$ **✕ The Reluctant Panther Inn & Restaurant.** The dining room at this luxurious
AMERICAN inn is a large, modern space, where dark wood and high ceilings meld into a kind of Nouveau Vermont aesthetic. The food is indulgent and rich as well as very expensive, making this a special-occasion kind of place. The dinner menu includes maple-rubbed Vermont lamb, scallops, and a duet of Long Island duck breast and confit of leg cannelloni. In the warmer months, sit outside on the lovely landscaped patio. $ *Average main: $37* ⊠ *39 West Rd.* ☎ *800/822–2331* ⊕ *www.reluctantpanther.com* ☾ *No lunch Jan.–Apr. closed weekdays.*

$$$ **✕ The Silver Fork.** This popular, intimate bistro with Caribbean flair
ECLECTIC is owned by husband-and-wife team Mark and Melody French. The
Fodor's Choice owners spent years living in Puerto Rico and the flavors of the island
★ are reflected in their menu. Start with savory olive tapenade and warm rosemary flatbread, then try the salmon seared on mango with greens, or dig into crispy crab cakes. There are also more Continental offerings on the sophisticated international menu like veal ragu and warm apple cinnamon beignets. Be sure to reserve one of the six tables ahead of time, or sit at the wine bar for a casual and romantic dinner with a bottle from the impressive wine list or a maple martini. $ *Average*

main: $26 ✉ *4201 Main St., across from huge Orvis fly-fishing store* ☎ *802/768–8444* ✍ *Reservations essential* ⏲ *Closed Sun. No lunch Sun.–Mon.*

$$ AMERICAN 🍴 **Ye Olde Tavern.** This 200-year-old Colonial inn serves up Yankee favorites like pot roast and cheddar and ale onion soup along with plenty of local New England charm. A favorite of regulars and visitors alike, the Tavern offers excellent food in a casual, colorful setting with a fireplace. Their cozy tap room is also a nice spot to stop for a drink and a taste of Vermont. [$] *Average main: $19* ✉ *5183 Main St.* ☎ *802/362–0611* 🌐 *www.yeoldetavern.net.*

WHERE TO STAY

For expanded hotel reviews, visit Fodors.com.

$$$$ RESORT Fodor's Choice ★ 🏨 **The Equinox Resort.** The Equinox defines the geographic center and historic heart of Manchester Village and has been *the* fancy hotel in town—and in the state—since the 18th century. **Pros:** heart-of-town location; full-service hotel; great golf and spa. **Cons:** big-hotel feeling; overrun by New Yorkers on weekends. [$] *Rooms from: $294* ✉ *3567 Main St. (Rte. 7A)* ☎ *802/362–4700, 888/367–7625* 🌐 *www.equinoxresort.com* 🛏 *164 rooms, 29 suites* 🍽 *No meals.*

$$ B&B/INN 🏨 **Wilburton Inn.** A few miles south of Manchester and overlooking the Battenkill Valley from a hilltop all its own, this turn-of-the-century complex is centered on a Tudor mansion with 11 bedrooms and suites and richly paneled common rooms containing part of the owners' vast art collection. **Pros:** beautiful setting with easy access to Manchester; fine dining. **Cons:** rooms in main inn, especially, need updating; limited indoor facilities; popular wedding site. [$] *Rooms from: $190* ✉ *257 River Rd.* ☎ *802/362–2500, 800/648–4944* 🌐 *www.wilburton.com* 🛏 *30 rooms, 4 suites* 🍽 *Breakfast.*

DORSET

7 miles north of Manchester.

★ Lying at the foot of many mountains and with a village green surrounded by white clapboard homes and inns, Dorset has a solid claim to the title of Vermont's most picture-perfect town. The town has just 2,000 residents but two of the state's best and oldest general stores.

The country's first commercial marble quarry was opened here in 1785. Dozens followed suit, providing the marble for the main research branch of the New York City Public Library and many Fifth Avenue mansions, among other notable landmarks, as well as the sidewalks here and in Manchester. A remarkable private home made entirely of marble can be seen on Dorset West Road, a beautiful residential road west of the town green. The marble Dorset Church on the green features two Tiffany stained-glass windows.

EXPLORING

Fodor's Choice ★ **Dorset Quarry.** On hot summer days the sight of dozens of families jumping, swimming, and basking in the sun around this massive swimming hole makes it one of the most wholesome and picturesque recreational spots in the United States. First mined in 1785, this is the oldest marble quarry in the United States. The popular area visible from Route 30 is actually just the lower quarry, and footpaths lead to the quiet upper quarry. ✉ *Rte. 30, 1 mile south of Dorset Green* 🎟 *Free.*

★ 🐤 **Merck Forest & Farmland Center.** This 3,100-acre farm and forest is a nonprofit educational center with 30 miles of nature trails for hiking, cross-country skiing, snowshoeing, and horseback riding. You can visit the farm, which grows organic fruits and vegetables (and purchase them at the farm stand), and check out the pasture-raised horses, cows, sheep, pigs, and chickens. There are also remote cabins and tent sites for rental. ✉ *3270 Rte. 315, Rupert* ☎ *802/394–7836* 🌐 *www.merckforest.org* 🎟 *Free* 🕒 *Daily, dawn–dusk.*

SPORTS AND THE OUTDOORS

Emerald Lake State Park. This park has a small beach, a marked nature trail, an on-site naturalist, boat rentals, and a snack bar. ✉ *U.S. 7, 65 Emerald Lake La., East Dorset* ☎ *802/362–1655* 🌐 *www.vtstateparks.com/htm/emerald.htm* 🎟 *$3.*

SHOPPING

Dorset Union Store. The Dorset Union Store first opened in 1816 as a village co-op. Today this privately owned general store makes good prepared dinners, has a big wine selection, rents DVDs, and sells food and gifts. ✉ *Dorset Green* ☎ *802/867–4400* 🌐 *www.dorsetunionstore.com* 🕒 *Mon–Sat 7–7, Sun. 8–6.*

H. N. Williams General Store. The H. N. Williams General Store is the most authentic and comprehensive general store in the state. It was started in 1840 by William Williams and has been run by the same family for six generations. This is one of those unique places where you can buy both maple syrup and ammo and catch up on posted town announcements. A farmers' market (🌐 *www.dorsetfarmersmarket.com*) is held outside on Sundays in summer. ✉ *2732 VT Rte. 30* ☎ *802/867–5353* 🌐 *www.hnwilliams.com.*

THE ARTS

Dorset Playhouse. Dorset is home to a prestigious summer theater troupe that presents the annual Dorset Theater Festival. Plays are held in a wonderful converted pre-Revolutionary barn, the Dorset Playhouse, in which the playhouse also hosts a community group in winter. ✉ *104 Cheney Rd., off town green* ☎ *802/867–2223, 802/867–5777* 🌐 *www.dorsetplayers.org.*

WHERE TO EAT

$$ AMERICAN 🍴 **The Dorset Inn.** Since 1796, the inn that houses this restaurant has been continuously operating, and even today you can count on three meals a day, every day of the year. The comfortable tavern, which serves the same menu as the more formal dining room, is popular with locals, and Patrick, the amiable veteran bartender, will make you feel at home. The menu highlights ingredients from local farms. Popular choices include yam fritters served in maple syrup and a lightly breaded chicken breast saltimbocca, stuffed with prosciutto and mozzarella. [$] *Average main: $22* ✉ *8 Church St., Dorset Green at Rte. 30* ☎ *802/867–5500* 🌐 *www.dorsetinn.com.*

$$$ ECLECTIC ★ 🍴 **Inn at West View Farm.** Chef-owner Raymond Chen was the lead line cook at New York City's Mercer Kitchen under Jean-Georges Vongerichten before opening this local ingredient–friendly restaurant. You'll find traditional floral wallpaper and soft classical music, but that's where the similarities to Dorset's other eateries end. Chen's dishes are skillful and practiced, starting with an *amuse-bouche* such as *brandade* (salt cod) over pesto. French influences are evident in the sautéed mushrooms and mascarpone ravioli in white truffle oil. Asian notes are evident, too, as in the lemongrass ginger soup with shiitake mushrooms that's ladled over grilled shrimp. A tavern serves enticing, inexpensive small dishes. [$] *Average main: $30* ✉ *2928 Rte. 30* ☎ *802/867–5715, 800/769–4903* 🌐 *www.westviewfarm.com* 🕑 *Closed Tues. and Wed.*

WHERE TO STAY

For expanded hotel reviews, visit Fodors.com.

$$ B&B/INN 🏨 **Inn at West View Farm.** Although these rooms could use a little attention, they offer an inexpensive way to stay in an old farmhouse with comfortable common rooms—along with easy access to an amazing dining room. **Pros:** great restaurant; good value. **Cons:** rooms aren't perfectly maintained. [$] *Rooms from: $150* ✉ *2928 Rte. 30* ☎ *802/867–5715* 🌐 *www.innatwestviewfarm.com* 🛏 *9 rooms, 1 suite* 🍽 *Breakfast.*

$$$ B&B/INN 🏨 **Squire House Bed & Breakfast.** There are three rooms in this big house that combines modern comforts and antique fixtures on a wonderfully quiet road. **Pros:** big estate feels like your own; well-maintained. **Cons:** bathrooms less exciting than rooms; no credit cards. [$] *Rooms from: $210* ✉ *3395 Dorset West Rd.* ☎ *802/867–0281* 🌐 *www.squirehouse.com* 🛏 *2 rooms, 1 suite* 💳 *No credit cards* 🍽 *Breakfast.*

STRATTON

26 miles southeast of Dorset.

Stratton is really Stratton Mountain Resort—a mountaintop ski resort with a self-contained "town center" of shops, restaurants, and lodgings clustered at the base of the slopes. When the snow melts, golf, tennis, and a host of other summer activities are big attractions, but the ski village remains quiet. For those arriving from the north along Route 30, Bondville is the town at the base of the mountain. At the junction of Routes 30 and 100 is the tiny Vermont village of Jamaica, with its own cluster of inns and restaurants on the east side of the mountain.

GETTING HERE AND AROUND

From Manchester or Route 7, follow Route 11/30 east until they split. Route 11 continues past Bromley ski mountain while Route 30 turns south 10 minutes toward Bondville, the town closest to Stratton Mountain.

SPORTS AND THE OUTDOORS

SKI AREAS

Bromley. About 20 minutes from Stratton, Bromley is a favorite with families. The 46 trails are evenly divided between beginner, intermediate, and expert. The resort runs a child-care center for kids ages six weeks to four years and hosts children's programs for ages 3–12. An added bonus: the trails face south, making for glorious spring skiing and warm winter days. ✉ *3984 Vermont Rte. 11, Peru* ☎ *802/824–5522, 800/865–4786* ⊕ *www.bromley.com.*

★ **Stratton Mountain.** About 30 minutes from Manchester, sophisticated, exclusive Stratton Mountain draws affluent families and young professionals from the New York–southern Connecticut corridor. An entire village, with a covered parking structure for 700 cars, is at the base of the mountain. Activities are afoot year-round. Stratton has 15 outdoor tennis courts, 27 holes of golf, hiking accessed by a gondola to the summit, and instructional programs in tennis and golf. The sports center, open year-round, has two indoor tennis courts, three racquetball courts, a 25-meter indoor saltwater swimming pool, a hot tub, a steam room, and a fitness facility with yoga and cycling studios, cardio center, and weight room. Accommodations include hotels, condominiums with underground parking, and spacious mountain homes. Adjacent to the base lodge are a condo-hotel, restaurants, and shops lining a pedestrian mall.

In terms of downhill skiing, Stratton prides itself on its immaculate grooming, making it excellent for cruising. The lower part of the mountain is beginner to low-intermediate, served by several chairlifts, including one high-speed six-passenger. The upper mountain is served by several chairlifts, including a six-passenger and a 12-passenger gondola. Down the face are the expert trails, and on either side are intermediate cruising runs with a smattering of wide beginner slopes. The third sector, the Sun Bowl, is off to one side with two high-speed, six-passenger lifts and two expert trails, a full base lodge, and plenty of intermediate terrain, plus three terrain parks and a half-pipe. Snowmaking covers 95% of the slopes. Every March, Stratton hosts the U.S. Open Snowboarding Championships. A Learning Park provides its own Park Packages for novice skiers and snowboarders. In all, Stratton has 13 lifts that service 94 trails and 100+ acres of glades. There is a ski and snowboard school for children ages 4–12. The resort also has more than 11 miles (18 km) of cross-country skiing and the Sun Bowl Nordic Center. An on-site day-care center takes children from six weeks to five years old for indoor activities and outdoor excursions. ✉ *5 Village Rd., Bondville. Turn off Rte. 30 and go 4 miles up access road* ☎ *800/787–2886, 802/297–4211 snow conditions, 800/787–2886 lodging* ⊕ *www.stratton.com.*

NIGHTLIFE AND THE ARTS

Fodor's Choice
★
Johnny Seesaw's. Near Bromley Mountain, Johnny Seesaw's is a classic rustic ski lodge with two huge fireplaces and a relaxed attitude. There's live music on weekends and an excellent comfort food menu. It's closed April through Memorial Day. ✉ *3574 VT Rte. 11, Peru* ☎ *802/824–5533* ⊕ *www.jseesaw.com.*

Mulligan's. Popular Mulligan's hosts bands or DJs in the late afternoon and on weekends in winter. ✉ *Stratton Village Sq. 11B, Mountain Rd., Bondville* ☎ *802/297–9293* ⊕ *www.mulligans.ie.*

Red Fox Inn. Year-round, the Red Fox Inn is the best après-ski nightlife spot in southern Vermont. It hosts Irish music Wednesday night; an open mike Thursday night; and rock and roll at other times. ✉ *103 Winhall Hollow Rd., Bondville* ☎ *802/297–2488* 🌐 *www.redfoxinn.com.*

WHERE TO EAT

$$$ AMERICAN ★ 🍴 **The Red Fox Inn.** This two-level converted barn has the best nightlife in southern Vermont and a fun dining room to boot. The restaurant has been here since 1979, but you'd believe since 1900. The upper level is the dining room—the big A-frame has wagon wheels and a carriage suspended from the ceiling. Settle in near the huge fireplace for rack of lamb, free-range chicken, or penne à la vodka. Downstairs is the tavern where there's Irish music, half-price Guinness, and fish-and-chips on Wednesday. Other nights there might be live music, karaoke, or video bowling. The bar operates daily year-round. [$] *Average main: $29* ✉ *103 Winhall Hollow Rd., Bondville* ☎ *802/297–2488* 🌐 *www.redfoxinn.com* ⏲ *No lunch. Closed Mon.–Wed. June–Oct.*

$$$ CONTEMPORARY Fodor's Choice ★ 🍴 **Three Mountain Inn.** If you're in the Stratton area and can splurge on an expensive meal, don't miss dinner at this charming inn. The prix-fixe meal includes *amuse-bouche*, starter, salad, entrée, and dessert for $55, plus the best restaurant bread in Vermont, a homemade herb focaccia. A starter might be baked Malpeque oysters with a chorizo and fennel jam; entrées include grilled swordfish with toasted couscous and a mint cucumber sauce. Each dining room has a fireplace, and common areas have terrific original wall and ceiling beams, making the restaurant a romantic winner. [$] *Average main: $35* ✉ *3732 Rte. 30/100, Jamaica* ☎ *802/874–4140* 🌐 *www.threemountaininn.com* ⏲ *No dinner Mon. and Tues. No lunch.*

WHERE TO STAY

For expanded hotel reviews, visit Fodors.com.

$$ RENTAL 🏨 **Long Trail House.** Directly across the street from Stratton's ski village, this fairly new condo complex is one of the best choices close to the slopes. **Pros:** across from skiing; good rates available; outdoor heated pool. **Cons:** room decor varies; two-night stay required on weekends. [$] *Rooms from: $150* ✉ *1 Stratton Mtn. Rd., Bondville* ☎ *802/297–2200, 800/787–2886* 🌐 *www.stratton.com* 🛏 *100 units.*

$ B&B/INN 🏨 **Red Fox Inn.** Stay here for great mid-week rates (50% off Sunday through Thursday) and relaxed, no-frills accommodations off the noisy mountain. **Pros:** great nightlife and food next door; real local hosts; secluded. **Cons:** a 10-15 minute drive to ski areas; weekends overpriced. [$] *Rooms from: $125* ✉ *103 Winhall Hollow Rd., Bondville* ☎ *802/297–2488* 🌐 *www.redfoxinn.com* 🛏 *8 rooms, 1 suite* 🍽 *No meals.*

$$$ B&B/INN Fodor's Choice ★ 🏨 **Three Mountain Inn.** A 1780s tavern, this romantic inn in downtown Jamaica (10 miles northeast of Stratton) feels authentically Colonial, from the wide paneling to the low ceilings. **Pros:** charming, authentic, romantic, small-town B&B; well-kept rooms; great dinners. **Cons:** can be expensive. [$] *Rooms from: $234* ✉ *3732 Rte. 30/100, Jamaica* ☎ *802/874–4140* 🌐 *www.threemountaininn.com* 🛏 *14 rooms, 1 suite* 🍽 *Breakfast.*

WESTON

17 miles north of Stratton.

Best known for the Vermont Country Store, Weston was one of the first Vermont towns to discover its own intrinsic loveliness—and marketability. With its summer theater, classic town green with a Victorian bandstand, and an assortment of shops, the little village really lives up to its vaunted image.

SHOPPING

★ **The Vermont Country Store.** The Vermont Country Store is an old-fashioned emporium selling all manner of items. The store was first opened in 1946 and is still run by the Orton family, though it has become something of an empire, with a large catalog and online business. One room is set aside for Vermont Common Crackers and bins of fudge and other candy. In others you'll find nearly forgotten items such as Lilac Vegetol aftershave and horehound drops, as well as practical items such as sturdy outdoor clothing and even typewriters. Nostalgia-evoking implements dangle from the store's walls and rafters. (There's a second location on Route 103 in Rockingham.) ⊠ *657 Main St.(Rte. 100)* ☎ *802/824–3184* ⊕ *www.vermontcountrystore.com.*

THE ARTS

Kinhaven Music School. In July and August, the Kinhaven Music School stages free student classical music concerts on Friday at 4 and Sunday at 2:30. Faculty concerts are Saturday at 8 pm. ⊠ *354 Lawrence Hill Rd.* ☎ *802/824–4332* ⊕ *www.kinhaven.org.*

Weston Playhouse. The members of the Weston Playhouse, the oldest professional theater in Vermont, produce Broadway plays, musicals, and other works. Their season runs from late June to early September. ⊠ *703 Main St., Village Green, off Rte. 100* ☎ *802/824–5288* ⊕ *www. westonplayhouse.org.*

WHERE TO STAY

For expanded hotel reviews, visit Fodors.com.

$$$
B&B/INN **Inn at Weston.** Highlighting the country elegance of this 1848 inn, a short walk from the town green, is innkeeper Bob Aldrich's collection of 500 orchid species—rare and beautiful specimens surround the dining table in the gazebo, and others enrich the indoors. **Pros:** great rooms; terrific town location. **Cons:** top-end rooms are expensive. $ *Rooms from: $200* ⊠ *630 Main St.(Rte 100)* ☎ *802/824–6789* ⊕ *www.innweston.com* 🛏 *13 rooms* ⏹ *Breakfast.*

LUDLOW

9 miles northeast of Weston.

Ludlow is a largely nondescript industrial town whose major draw is Okemo, one of Vermont's largest and most popular ski resorts.

You never know what you'll find at a rambling general store like Weston's Vermont Country Store.

SPORTS AND THE OUTDOORS

SKI AREAS **Okemo Mountain Resort.** Family-owned since 1982 and still run by Tim and Diane Mueller, Okemo Mountain Resort has evolved into a major year-round resort, now with two base areas. Known for its wide, well-groomed trails, it's a favorite among intermediates.

At 2,200 feet, Okemo has the highest vertical drop of any resort in southern Vermont. The beginner trails extend above both base areas, with more challenging terrain higher on the mountains. Intermediate trails are the theme here, but experts will find steep trails and glades at Jackson Gore and on the south face. Of the 113 trails, 36% have an intermediate rating, 32% are rated novice, and 32% are rated for experts. They are served by an efficient system of 24 lifts, including nine quads, three triple chairlifts, and six surface lifts; 95% of the trails are covered by snowmaking. Okemo has four terrain parks for skiers and snowboarders, including one for beginners; two 400-foot-long super-pipes, and a mini half-pipe. For cross-country skiing, the Okemo Valley Nordic Center has 14 miles of groomed cross-country trails and 8 miles of dedicated snowshoe trails and rents equipment.

If you're looking for non-snow-related activities, you can play basketball and tennis at the Ice House next to Jackson Gore Inn or perfect your swing at the 18-hole, par-70, 6,400-yard, heathlands-style course at the Okemo Valley Golf Club. Seven target greens, four outdoor putting greens, a golf academy, an indoor putting green, swing stations, and a simulator provide plenty of ways to improve your game year-round.

Jackson Gore, a second base village north of Ludlow off Route 103, has an inn, restaurants, a child-care center, and shops. The resort offers numerous ski and snowboarding packages. There's also ice-skating at the Ice House, a covered, open-air rink open 10–9 daily in the winter. The Spring House, next to the entrance of Jackson Gore Inn, has a great kids' pool with slides, a racquetball court, fitness center, and sauna. The yoga and Pilates studio has classes a few times a week. A day pass is $14. ✉ *77 Okemo Ridge Rd.* ☎ *802/228–4041, 802/228–5222 snow conditions, 800/786–5366 lodging* 🌐 *www.okemo.com.*

Tater Hill Golf Course. The newer of Okemo's two golf courses, the off-site 18-hole Tater Hill Golf Course has a pro shop, putting green, and a driving range. The course is located in Windham, 22 miles south of Ludlow. ✉ *6802 Popple Dungeon Rd., Windham* ☎ *802/875–2517*

WHERE TO EAT

$$ AMERICAN 🍴 **Coleman Brook Tavern.** Slope-side at the Jackson Gore Inn, Coleman Brook is the fanciest and most expensive of Okemo's 19 places to eat, but it's not formal—you'll find ski-boot-wearing diners crowding the tables at lunch. Big wing chairs and large banquettes line window bays. Ask to sit in the Wine Room, a separate section where tables are surrounded by the noteworthy collection of wines. Start with a pound of clams steamed in butter, garlic, white wine, and fresh herbs. Then move on to the sesame seed–crusted ahi tuna served over green-tea soba noodles in a ginger-miso broth. The s'mores dessert is cooked with a tabletop "campfire." [$] *Average main: $20* ✉ *111 Jackson Gore Rd., Okemo* ☎ *802/228–1435.*

$ PIZZA 👶 🍴 **Goodman's American Pie.** This pizzeria has the best wood-fired oven pizza in town. It also has character to spare—sit in chairs from old ski lifts and order from a counter that was once a purple VW bus. Though it's on Main Street, it's set back and kind of hidden—you may consider it your Ludlow secret. Locals and Okemo regulars already in the know stop by to design their own pizza from 25 ingredients; there is also a section of six specials. The Rip Curl has mozzarella, Asiago, ricotta, chicken, fresh garlic, and fresh tomatoes. Slices are available. Arcade games are in the back. [$] *Average main: $8* ✉ *106 Main St.* ☎ *802/228–4271* 💳 *No credit cards* 🕒 *Closed Wed.*

$$ ECLECTIC 🍴 **Harry's.** The local favorite when you want to eat a little out of town, this casual roadside restaurant 5 miles northwest of Ludlow has a number of international influences. Traditional contemporary entrées such as pork tenderloin are at one end of the menu and Mexican dishes at the other. The large and tasty burrito, made with fresh cilantro and black beans, is one of the best bargains around. Chef-owner Trip Pearce also owns the equally popular Little Harry's in Rutland. [$] *Average main: $19* ✉ *3621 Rte. 103, Mount Holly* ☎ *802/259–2996* 🌐 *www.harryscafe.com* 🕒 *Closed Mon. and Tues. No lunch.*

$$ ECLECTIC Fodor's Choice ★ 🍴 **The Inn at Weathersfield.** One of Vermont's best restaurants, hidden 15 miles east of Ludlow, this is a culinary gem inside an 18th-century countryside inn. A chalkboard in the foyer lists the area farms that grow the food you'll eat here on any given night, and it's no gimmick: chef Jason Tostrup (a former sous chef at Thomas Keller's Bouchon in Napa Valley, and a veteran of New York's Vong, Daniel, and Jean Georges) is passionate about local ingredients. Its farm-to-table cuisine is created with a sophistication that many less principled restaurants

lack. A daily five-course "Verterra" prix-fixe menu ($57) might feature stuffed local quail in a cider-soy glaze or local "humanely raised" veal served two ways. Service is excellent, and the wine list is large and reasonably priced. If it's summer, enjoy your meal on the patio. $ *Average main: $21* ⌧ *1342 Rte. 106, Perkinsville* ☎ *802/263–9217* ⊕ *www. innatweathersfield.com* ⊘ *No lunch. Closed Mon. and Tues. and Apr. and beginning of Nov.*

WHERE TO STAY

For expanded hotel reviews, visit Fodors.com.

$$
B&B/INN

Inn at Water's Edge. Former Long Islanders Bruce and Tina Verdrager converted their old ski house and barns into this comfortably refined haven, perfect for those who want to ski but don't want to stay in town. **Pros:** bucolic setting on a lakefront; interesting, big house. **Cons:** ordinary B&B rooms; 5 miles north of town. $ *Rooms from: $175* ⌧ *45 Kingdom Rd.* ☎ *802/228–8143, 888/706–9736* ⊕ *www. innatwatersedge.com* ⤴ *9 rooms, 2 suites* ⏏ *Multiple meal plans.*

$$
B&B/INN
★

Inn at Weathersfield. Once you discover the food and charming rooms at Weathersfield, you won't want to go home. **Pros:** dynamite restaurant and tavern; comfy, relaxed inn; quiet. **Cons:** 15-mile drive from the Okemo slopes. $ *Rooms from: $179* ⌧ *1342 Rte. 106, Perkinsville* ☎ *802/263–9217* ⊕ *www.innatweathersfield.com* ⤴ *12 rooms* ⊘ *Closed first two weeks in Nov.* ⏏ *Breakfast.*

$$$
HOTEL
☼

Jackson Gore Inn. This slope-side base lodge is the place to stay if your aim is convenience to Okemo's slopes. **Pros:** ski-in, ski-out at base of mountain; good for families. **Cons:** chaotic and noisy on weekends; expensive. $ *Rooms from: $162* ⌧ *77 Okemo Ridge Rd., off Rte. 103* ☎ *802/228–1400, 800/786–5366* ⊕ *www.okemo.com* ⤴ *263 rooms* ⏏ *Breakfast.*

GRAFTON

★

8 miles south of Chester.

Out-of-the-way Grafton is as much a historical museum as a town. During its heyday, citizens grazed some 10,000 sheep and spun their wool into sturdy yarn for locally woven fabric. When the market for wool declined, so did Grafton. Then in 1963, the Windham Foundation—Vermont's second-largest private foundation—commenced the town's rehabilitation. Not only was the Old Tavern preserved (now called The Grafton Inn), but so were many other commercial and residential structures in the village center.

EXPLORING

Historical Society Museum. The Historical Society Museum documents the town's history with exhibits that change yearly. ⌧ *10 Main St. (Rte. 121)* ☎ *802/843–2584* ⊕ *www.graftonhistory.info* 🎟 *$3* ⊘ *Memorial Day–Columbus Day, Thurs.–Mon. 10–4. Closed Tues. and Wed.*

SHOPPING

Gallery North Star. Oils, watercolors, lithographs, and sculptures of Vermont-based artists are on display here. ⌧ *151 Townshend Rd.* ☎ *802/843–2465* ⊕ *www.gnsgrafton.com* ⊘ *Daily 10–5.*

Vermont Artisanal Cheese

Vermont is the artisanal cheese capital of the country, with more than 40 creameries (and growing fast) that are open to the public—carefully churning out hundreds of different cheeses. Many creameries are "farmstead" operations, meaning that the animals that provide the milk are on-site where their milk is made into cheese. If you eat enough cheese during your time in the state, you may be able to differentiate between the many types of milk (cow, goat, sheep, or even water buffalo), as well as make associations between the geography and climate of where you are and the taste of the cheese you eat.

This is one of the reasons why taking a walk around a dairy is a great idea: you can see the process in action, from grazing to aging to eating. Almost all dairies welcome visitors, though it's universally recommended that you call ahead to plan your visit.

Shelburne Farms. At Shelburne Farms, a chalkboard stands in the cheese-making facility and notes which part of the complex cheese-making process visitors can witness at various times throughout the day. ⊠ *1611 Harbor Rd., Shelburne* ☎ *802/985–8686* ⊕ *www.shelburnefarms.org* ⟶ *$8.*

Vermont Butter & Cheese Creamery. One of the leaders of the artisanal cheese movement, Vermont Butter & Cheese invites curious cheese aficionados to visit their 4,000-square-foot creamery where gemlike goat cheeses such as Bonne Bouche—a perfectly balanced, cloudlike cheese—are made Monday through Friday. ⊠ *40 Pitman Rd, Websterville* ☎ *800/884–6287* ⊕ *www.vermontcreamery.com.*

Consider Bardwell Farm. This farm in West Pawlet was the first cheese

Vermont sheep's milk cheese.

cooperative in the state, founded in 1864, and today, a new generation of cheese makers make nine goat and cow milk cheeses on-site, including the bright, nutty, and exceptionally delicious Pawlet. Visit their website for information regarding cheese-making workshops and classes offered at the farm. ⊠ *1333 Rte. 153, West Pawlet* ☎ *802/645–9928* ⊕ *www.considerbardwellfarm.com.*

Cabot Visitors Center. For a taste of the classic Vermont cheddar, head to Cabot Creamery to take a tour of the factory and see how the many varieties of cheddars are made. ⊠ *2878 Main St., Cabot* ☎ *800/837–4261* ⊕ *www.cabotcheese.coop.*

The Vermont Cheese Council. The Cheese Council has developed the Vermont Cheese Trail, a map of 38 creameries with contact information for each. ☎ *866/261–8595* ⊕ *www.vtcheese.com.*

Vermont Cheesemakers Festival. If you're a real cheese lover, definitely plan your trip to Vermont around the state's world-class food event, the annual Vermont Cheesemakers Festival at Shelburne Farms. Each July more than 40 cheese makers gather to sell and sample their various cheeses. ⊕ *www.vtcheesefest.com.*

—Michael de Zayas

7

Grafton Village Cheese Company. Sample the best of Vermont cheddar at the Grafton Village Cheese Company. ✉ *533 Townshend Rd.* ☎ *800/472–3866* 🌐 *www.graftonvillagecheese.com.*

WHERE TO STAY

For expanded hotel reviews, visit Fodors.com.

$$$ B&B/INN ★ 🏨 **The Grafton Inn.** This 1801 classic (formerly The Old Tavern at Grafton) is one of the oldest operating inns in the country and still one of Vermont's greatest lodging assets. **Pros:** classic Vermont inn and tavern; professionally run; appealing common areas. **Cons:** rooms are attractive but not stellar. [$] *Rooms from: $225* ✉ *92 Main St. (Rte. 121)* ☎ *802/843–2231, 800/843–1801* 🌐 *www.graftoninnvermont.com* 🛏 *39 rooms, 7 suites* 🍴 *Breakfast.*

TOWNSHEND

9 miles south of Grafton.

One of a string of attractive villages along the banks of the West River, Townshend embodies the Vermont ideal of a lovely town green presided over by a gracefully proportioned church spire. The spire belongs to the 1790 Congregational Meeting House, one of the state's oldest houses of worship. North on Route 30 is the Scott Bridge, the state's longest single-span covered bridge. It makes for a pretty photo although it is closed to foot and vehicle traffic.

OFF THE BEATEN PATH

Newfane. With a village green surrounded by pristine white buildings, Newfane, 6 miles southeast of Townshend, is sometimes described as the quintessential New England small town. The 1839 First Congregational Church and the Windham County Court House, with 17 green-shuttered windows and a rounded cupola, are often open. The building with the four-pointed spire is Union Hall, built in 1832. ✉ *Newfane.*

SPORTS AND THE OUTDOORS

Townshend State Park. At Townshend State Park you'll find a sandy beach on the West River and a trail that parallels the river for 2½ miles, topping out on Bald Mountain Dam. Up the dam, the trail follows switchbacks literally carved into the stone apron. ✉ *Rte. 30 N, 2755 State Forest Rd.* ☎ *802/365–7500* 🌐 *www.vtstateparks.com/htm/townshend.htm.*

SHOPPING

🧸 **Big Black Bear Shop.** The Big Black Bear Shop at Mary Meyer Stuffed Toys Factory, the state's oldest stuffed toy company, offers discounts of up to 70% on stuffed animals of all sizes. ✉ *Rte. 30, 3/4¾ miles north of town, Newfane* ☎ *802/365–4160, 888/758–2327* 🌐 *www.bigblackbear.com.*

Newfane Country Store. You'll find homemade fudge and other Vermont foods, gifts, crafts, and many quilts—which can also be custom ordered—here. ✉ *598 Rte. 30, Newfane* ☎ *802/365–7916* 🌐 *www.newfanecountrystore.com.*

WHERE TO EAT

$ DINER — 🍴 **Townshend Dam Diner.** Folks come from miles around to enjoy traditional fare such as Mom's meat loaf, chili, and roast beef croquettes, as well as Townshend-raised bison burgers and creative daily specials. Breakfast, served all day every day, includes such tasty treats as raspberry chocolate-chip walnut pancakes and homemade French toast. You can sit at any of the collection of 1930s enamel-top tables or in the big swivel chairs at the U-shaped counter. The diner is a few miles northwest of the village on Route 30. [$] *Average main: $8* ✉ *5929 Rte. 30, West Townshend* ☎ *802/874–4107* 💳 *No credit cards* 🕒 *Closed Tues.*

$$$$ EUROPEAN — 🍴 **Windham Hill Inn.** This remote inn is a fine choice for a romantic, four-course prix fixe dinner ($68). Chef Graham Gill heads up the Frog Pond dining room (don't worry; there are no frogs' legs on the menu). Start with a spiced Vermont quail, served with hand-rolled pappardelle and a wild mushroom ragout. Entrées include a fig-and-balsamic-glazed seared duck breast served with roasted pear and garden Swiss chard and a *cipollini* onion and fingerling potato sauté. There's a remarkably large wine list. [$] *Average main: $68* ✉ *311 Lawrence Dr., West Townshend* ☎ *802/874–4080* 🌐 *www.windhamhill.com* ✍ *Reservations essential.*

WHERE TO STAY

For expanded hotel reviews, visit Fodors.com.

$ B&B/INN — 🏨 **Boardman House.** This handsome Greek Revival home on the town green combines modern comfort with the relaxed charm of a 19th-century farmhouse. **Pros:** inexpensive; perfect village green location. **Cons:** no phone and cell-phone reception is bad. [$] *Rooms from: $85* ✉ *Townshend Green* ☎ *802/365–4086* 🛏 *4 rooms, 1 suite* 💳 *No credit cards* 🍽 *Breakfast.*

$$$ B&B/INN ★ — 🏨 **Four Columns Inn.** Rooms and suites in this white-columned, 1834 Greek Revival mansion were designed for luxurious romantic getaways. **Pros:** great rooms; center of town location. **Cons:** little area entertainment in town. [$] *Rooms from: $220* ✉ *Newfane Green, 6 miles southeast of Townshend, 21 West St., Newfane* ☎ *802/365–7713, 800/787–6633* 🌐 *www.fourcolumnsinn.com* 🛏 *6 rooms, 9 suites* 🍽 *Breakfast.*

$$$ B&B/INN ★ — 🏨 **Windham Hill Inn.** As there's not too much to do nearby, you might find yourself sitting by a fire or swimming in the outdoor pool at this calm, quiet retreat, and that's a good thing. **Pros:** quiet getaway; good food; lovely setting. **Cons:** rural location makes entertainment not an option; spotty cell service; expensive dinners. [$] *Rooms from: $250* ✉ *311 Lawrence Dr., West Townshend* ☎ *802/874–4080, 800/944–4080* 🌐 *www.windhamhill.com* 🛏 *21 rooms* 🍽 *Breakfast.*

CENTRAL VERMONT

Central Vermont's economy once centered on marble quarrying and mills. But today, as in much of the rest of the state, tourism drives the economic engine. The center of the dynamo is Killington, the East's largest downhill resort, but central Vermont has more to discover than high-speed chairlifts and slope-side condos. The old mills of Quechee and

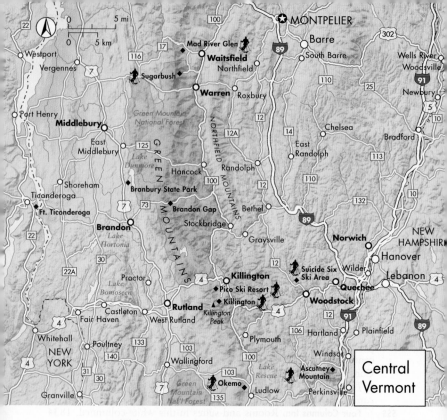

Middlebury are now home to restaurants and shops, giving wonderful views of the waterfalls that once powered the mill turbines. Woodstock has upscale shops and a national historic park. Away from these settlements, the protected (except for occasional logging) lands of the Green Mountain National Forest are laced with hiking trails.

Our coverage of towns begins with Norwich, on U.S. 5 near Interstate 91 at the state's eastern edge, winds west toward U.S. 7, then continues north to Middlebury before heading over the spine of the Green Mountains to Waitsfield.

NORWICH

6 miles north of White River Junction.

On the shores of the Connecticut River, Norwich boasts beautifully maintained 18th- and 19th-century homes set about a handsome green. Norwich is the Vermont sister to sophisticated Hanover, New Hampshire (home of Dartmouth College), over the river.

GETTING HERE AND AROUND

Most attractions are off Interstate 91; the town sits a mile to the west.

EXPLORING

★ **Montshire Museum of Science.** Numerous hands-on exhibits here explore
☾ nature and technology. Kids can make giant bubbles, watch fish and
turtles swim in enormous aquariums, explore wind, and wander a maze
of outdoor trails by the river. An ideal destination for a rainy day,
this is one of the finest museums in New England. ⊠ *1 Montshire Rd.*
☎ *802/649–2200* ⊕ *www.montshire.org* 🎟 *$12* ☾ *Daily 10–5.*

SHOPPING

★ **King Arthur Flour Baker's Store.** Are you a baker? King Arthur Flour Baker's Store is a must-see for those who love bread. The shelves are stocked
with all the ingredients and tools in the company's *Baker's Catalogue,*
including flours, mixes, and local jams and syrups. The bakery has a
viewing area where you can watch products being made, and you can
buy baked goods or sandwiches. A separate education center has evening and weekend classes and weeklong baking packages. ⊠ *135 U.S.*
Rte. 5 South ☎ *802/649–3881, 800/827–6836* ⊕ *www.bakerscatalogue.*
com ☾ *Mon.–Fri. 7:30–6, Sat. 8:30–6.*

QUECHEE

11 miles southwest of Norwich, 6 miles west of White River Junction.

A historic mill town, Quechee sits just upriver from its namesake gorge,
an impressive 165-foot-deep canyon cut by the Ottauquechee River.
Most people view the gorge from U.S. 4. To escape the crowds, hike
along the gorge or scramble down one of several trails to the river.

EXPLORING

Fodor's Choice **Simon Pearce.** The main attraction in the village is this glassblowing fac-
★ tory, store, and restaurant, which an Irish glassmaker by the same name
☾ set up in 1981 in a restored woolen mill by a waterfall. Waterpower still
drives the factory's furnace. Visitors may take a free self-guided tour
of the freshly updated downstairs factory floor and see the amazing
glassblowers at work (great for kids, too!). A perfect place for unique
gifts and souvenirs, the store in the mill sells beautifully crafted contemporary glass and ceramic tableware and stunning home furnishings,
such as glass lamps, vases, and wooden bowls. Seconds and discon-
tinued items are reduced 25%. An excellent, sophisticated restaurant
with outstanding views of the falls uses the Simon Pearce glassware
and is justly popular. ■TIP→ Make an afternoon of it: watch the glassblowers, check out the shop, have lunch, and be sure not to miss the small
but elegant art gallery across the street, which showcases local artists in
a tasteful, serene setting. ⊠ *The Mill, 1760 Main St.* ☎ *802/295–2711*
⊕ *www.simonpearce.com* ☾ *Store daily 9–9; glassblowing Tues.–Sat.*
9–9, Sun. and Mon. 9–5.

☾ **Vermont Institute of Natural Science (VINS) Nature Center.** Next to Quechee
Gorge, this science center has 17 raptor exhibits, including bald eagles,
peregrine falcons, and owls. All the caged birds have been found injured
and are unable to survive in the wild. Predators of the Sky, a 30-minute
live bird program, starts daily at 11, 1, and 3:30. ⊠ *6565 Woodstock*

Rd. (Rte. 4) ☎ *802/359–5000* 🌐 *www.vinsweb.org* 🎟 *$12* 🕐 *May–Oct., daily 10–5; Nov.–Apr., daily 10–4.*

SPORTS AND THE OUTDOORS

Wilderness Trails & the Vermont Fly Fishing School. This school leads workshops, rents fishing gear and mountain bikes, and arranges canoe and kayak trips. In winter, the company conducts cross-country and snowshoe treks. ✉ *1119 Main St.* ☎ *802/295–7620* 🌐 *www.scenesofvermont.com/wildernesstrails.*

SHOPPING

ANTIQUES AND CRAFTS

Quechee Gorge Village. More than 350 dealers sell their wares at the Quechee Gorge Village, an antiques and crafts mall in an immense reconstructed barn that also houses a country store and a classic diner. A merry-go-round and a small-scale working railroad operate when weather permits. ✉ *573 Woodstock Rd., off U.S. 4* ☎ *802/295–1550, 802/295–1550* 🌐 *www.quecheegorge.com.*

CLOTHING AND MORE

Scotland by the Yard. This store sells all things Scottish, from kilts to Harris tweed jackets and tartan ties. ✉ *8828 Woodstock Rd. (U.S. 4)* ☎ *802/295–5351, 800/295–5351* 🌐 *www.scotlandbytheyard.com.*

WHERE TO EAT AND STAY

For expanded hotel reviews, visit Fodors.com.

$$ AMERICAN Fodor's Choice ★ 🍴 **Simon Pearce.** Candlelight, sparkling glassware from the studio downstairs, exposed brick, and large windows overlooking the falls of the roaring Ottauquechee River create an ideal setting for contemporary American cuisine. The food is widely considered to be worthy of a pilgrimage. Horseradish-crusted blue cod with crispy leeks, herb mashed potatoes, and balsamic shallot reduction as well as roast duck with mango chutney sauce are house specialties; the wine cellar holds several hundred vintages. The lunch menu might include a roasted duck quesadilla or Mediterranean lamb burger. [$] *Average main: $21* ✉ *The Mill, 1760 Main St.* ☎ *802/295–2711* 🌐 *www.simonpearce.com.*

$$$ B&B/INN 🏨 **The Parker House Inn.** This beautiful 1857 house on the National Historic Register was once home to the mill owner who ran the textile mill next door (which is now Simon Pearce). **Pros:** in-town; riverfront location; spacious, cute rooms. **Cons:** no yard. [$] *Rooms from: $245* ✉ *1792 Main St.* ☎ *802/295–6077* 🌐 *www.theparkerhouseinn.com* 🛏 *7 rooms, 1 suite* 🍽 *Breakfast.*

$$$ B&B/INN 🏨 **Quechee Inn at Marshland Farm.** Each room in this handsomely restored 1793 country home has Queen Anne–style furnishings and period antiques. **Pros:** historic; spacious property. **Cons:** bathrooms are dated. [$] *Rooms from: $200* ✉ *1119 Main St.* ☎ *802/295–3133, 800/235–3133* 🌐 *www.quecheeinn.com* 🛏 *22 rooms, 3 suites* 🍽 *Breakfast.*

WOODSTOCK

4 miles west of Quechee.

★ Woodstock is a Currier & Ives print come to life. Well-maintained Federal-style houses surround the tree-lined village green, which is not

Simon Pearce is a glassblowing factory, store, and restaurant; the factory's furnace is still powered by hydroelectricity from Quechee Falls.

far from a covered bridge. The town owes much of its pristine appearance to the Rockefeller family's interest in historic preservation and land conservation and to native George Perkins Marsh, a congressman, diplomat, and conservationist who wrote the pioneering book *Man and Nature* (1864) about humanity's use and abuse of the land. Only busy U.S. 4 detracts from the town's quaintness.

ESSENTIALS

Visitor Information Woodstock Vermont Area Chamber of Commerce ⊠ *18 Central St.* ☎ *802/457–3555, 888/496–6378* ⊕ *www.woodstockvt.com.*

EXPLORING

Billings Farm and Museum. Founded by Frederick Billings in 1871 as a model dairy farm, this is one of the oldest dairy farms in the country and sits on the property that was the childhood home of George Perkins Marsh. Concerned about the loss of New England's forests to overgrazing, Billings planted thousands of trees and put into practice Marsh's conservationist farming ideas. Exhibits in the reconstructed Queen Anne farmhouse, school, general store, workshop, and former Marsh homestead demonstrate the lives and skills of early Vermont settlers. ⊠ *5302 River Rd. (Rte. 12), ½ mile north of Woodstock* ☎ *802/457–2355* ⊕ *www.billingsfarm.org* ⊠ *$12* ⊙ *May–late Oct., daily 10–5; call for winter holiday and weekend schedules.*

Marsh-Billings-Rockefeller National Historical Park. This 555-acre park is Vermont's only national park and the nation's first to focus on natural resource conservation and stewardship. The pristine and stunning park encompasses the forestland planned by Frederick Billings according to Marsh's principles, as well as Frederick Billings's mansion, gardens,

The upscale Woodstock area is known as Vermont's horse country.

and carriage roads. The entire property was the gift of Laurance S. Rockefeller, who lived here with his late wife, Mary, Billings's granddaughter. You can learn more at the visitor center, tour the residential complex with a guide every hour on the hour, and explore the 20 miles of trails and old carriage roads that climb Mt. Tom. ⊠ *54 Elm St.* ☎ *802/457–3368* ⊕ *www.nps.gov/mabi* ✉ *Tour $8* ☉ *May–Oct., mansion and garden tours 10–5; grounds daily dawn–dusk.*

SPORTS AND THE OUTDOORS

BIKING

The Start House. The Start House rents, sells, and services bikes and skis and distributes a free touring map for biking. ⊠ *28 Central St.* ☎ *802/457–3377* ⊕ *www.starthouseskiandbike.com.*

GOLF

Woodstock Inn & Resort Golf Club. Robert Trent Jones Sr. designed the 18-hole, 6,000-yard, par-70 course at the Woodstock Inn & Resort Golf Club. Greens fees are $70 weekdays, $95 weekends. ⊠ *14 The Green* ☎ *802/457–1100* ⊕ *www.woodstockinn.com.*

HORSEBACK RIDING

Kedron Valley Stables. Kedron Valley Stables conducts one-hour guided trail rides and horse-drawn sleigh and wagon rides. ⊠ *Rte. 106 S, 4342 South Rd., South Woodstock* ☎ *802/457–1480, 800/225–6301* ⊕ *www. kedron.com.*

SHOPPING

Collective. This funky and attractive shop sells local artwork and crafts, including jewelry, glass, pottery, clothing, and home decor. ✉ *47 Central St., Woodstock* ☎ *802/457–1298* 🌐 *www.collective-theartofcraft.com* 🕑 *Mon.–Sat.10–5, Sun. 11–4.*

FOOD

Sugarbush Farm. Take the Taftsville covered bridge off Route 4 east of town to Sugarbush Farm, where you'll learn how maple sugar is made and get to taste as much syrup as you'd like. The farm also makes excellent cheeses and is open 10 to 5 year-round. ✉ *591 Sugarbush Farm Rd.* ☎ *802/457–1757, 800/281–1757* 🌐 *www.sugarbushfarm.com.*

Taftsville Country Store. East of town, the Taftsville Country Store sells a wide selection of Vermont cheeses, moderately priced wines, and Vermont specialty foods. ✉ *404 Woodstock Rd. (U.S. 4), Taftsville* ☎ *802/457–1135, 800/854–0013* 🌐 *www.taftsville.com.*

Village Butcher. This emporium of Vermont edibles has great sandwiches, cheeses, local beers, and delicious baked goods—perfect for a picnic or lunch-on-the-go. ✉ *18 Elm St.* ☎ *802/457–2756.*

Woodstock Farmers' Market. The Woodstock Farmers' Market is a year-round buffet of local produce, fresh fish, and excellent sandwiches and pastries. The maple-walnut scones go fast so get there early. The market is closed on Monday. ✉ *468 Woodstock Rd. (U.S. 4)* ☎ *802/457–3658* 🌐 *www.woodstockfarmersmarket.com* 🕑 *Tues.–Sat. 7:30–7, Sun. 9–6; closed Mon.*

WHERE TO EAT

$$$$ AMERICAN ★ 🍴 **The Barnard Inn Restaurant & Max's Tavern.** The dining room in this 1796 brick farmhouse breathes 18th century, but the food is decidedly 21st century. Former San Francisco restaurant chef-owners Will Dodson and Ruth Schimmelpfennig create inventive three-and four-course prix-fixe menus ($65–$75) with delicacies such as venison carpaccio and chili and sesame-encrusted ahi tuna. In the back is a local favorite, Max's Tavern, which serves upscale pub fare such as beef with Gorgonzola mashed potatoes and panfried trout with almond *beurre noisette* (browned butter). [$] *Average main: $65* ✉ *5518 Rte. 12, 8 miles north of Woodstock, Barnard* ☎ *802/234–9961* 🌐 *barnardinn.com* ✍ *Reservations essential* 🕑 *Closed Sun.–Tues. No lunch.*

$$$ AMERICAN ★ 🍴 **Cloudland Farm.** Representative of the wildly popular local food scene in Vermont, Cloudland Farm offers twice-weekly prix-fixe dinners—Thursday and Saturday—with all local and seasonal ingredients fresh from their farm. Meals feature the farm's own pork and beef in entrees such as maple-glazed ham roast with apple and onion compote or beef shank osso buco with sautéed kale and beef bacon. Desserts, such as homemade carrot cake with red wine caramel and carrot jam, are delicious. With the table literally on the farm, this is a unique farm-to-table experience and worth the short drive from Woodstock. [$] *Average main: $30* ✉ *1101 Cloudland Rd., North Pomfret* ☎ *802/457–2599* 🌐 *www.cloudlandfarm.com* ✍ *Reservations essential* 🕑 *No lunch; closed March and Fri., Sun.–Wed.*

$$ 🍴 **Keeper's Café.** Creative, moderately priced fare draws customers from all over the region to this café. Chef Eli Morse's menus include such light dishes as pancetta salad and fresh corn soup and such elaborate entrées as herb garlic roast chicken with a sherry caper sauce. Blackboard specials change daily. Housed inside a former general store, the small dining room feels relaxed, with locals table-hopping to chat with friends. [$] *Average main: $21* ✉ *Rt. 106 and Bailey's Mills Rd., 12 miles south of Woodstock, Reading* ☎ *802/484–9090* 🌐 *www.keeperscafe.com* 🕓 *Closed Sun. and Mon. No lunch.*
CAFÉ

$$ 🍴 **Pane e Saluto.** Don't let the size fool you—meals at this little upstairs restaurant are exciting and memorable, thanks to young couple Deirdre Heekin and Caleb Barker. Reserve well in advance as the small space fills up fast. Hip contemporary decor, an intimately small space, and Heekin's discreetly passionate front-of-house direction all come together to complement the Barker's slow-food-inspired passion for flavorful, local and farm-raised dishes. Try *ragu d'agnello e maiale* (spaghetti with an *abruzzese* ragu from roasted pork and lamb) followed by *cotechino e lenticche* (a garlic sausage with lentils). You might expect such an *osteria* in Berkeley or Brooklyn, but this tiny spot pumps life into the blood of old Woodstock. Ask about the culinary tours the team leads each year in Italy. [$] *Average main: $21* ✉ *61 Central St.* ☎ *802/457–4882* 🌐 *www.osteriapaneesalute.com* ✍ *Reservations essential* 🕓 *Closed Mon, Tues., and Wed. and Apr. and Nov. No lunch.*
ITALIAN
Fodor's Choice ★

$$ 🍴 **The Prince & The Pauper.** Modern French and American fare with a Vermont accent is the focus of this candlelit Colonial restaurant off the Woodstock Green. The grilled duck breast might have an Asian five-spice sauce, and lamb and pork sausage in puff pastry comes with a honey-mustard sauce. A three-course prix-fixe menu is available for $49; a less-expensive bistro menu can be ordered from in the lounge. [$] *Average main: $21* ✉ *24 Elm St.* ☎ *802/457–1818* 🌐 *www.princeandpauper.com* 🕓 *No lunch.*
FRENCH ★

WHERE TO STAY

For expanded hotel reviews, visit Fodors.com.

$$$ 🏨 **The Fan House.** If you are searching for an authentic home in the heart of a very small, quaint Vermont town, take the one-minute walk from the perfect general store in Barnard to this 1840 white Colonial. **Pros:** center of old town; homey comforts; good library. **Cons:** upstairs rooms can be cool in winter. [$] *Rooms from: $200* ✉ *6296 Rte. 12 N 802/234–6704* 🌐 *www.thefanhouse.com* 🛏 *3 rooms* 💳 *No credit cards* 🕓 *Closed Apr.* 🍽 *Breakfast.*
B&B/INN

$$$$ 🏨 **Kedron Valley Inn.** You're likely to fall in love at the first sight of this 1828 three-story brick building that forms the centerpiece of this quiet, elegant retreat. **Pros:** good food; quiet setting. **Cons:** 5 miles south of Woodstock. [$] *Rooms from: $259* ✉ *10671 South Rd. (Rte. 106), South Woodstock* ☎ *802/457–1473, 800/836–1193* 🌐 *www.kedronvalleyinn.com* 🛏 *21 rooms, 6 suites* 🕓 *Closed Apr.* 🍽 *Breakfast.*
B&B/INN

$$ 🏨 **The Shire Riverview Motel.** Some rooms in this immaculate motel have decks—and almost all have views—overlooking the Ottauquechee River. **Pros:** inexpensive access to the heart of Woodstock; views. **Cons:** dull rooms; unexciting exterior. [$] *Rooms from: $158* ✉ *46*
HOTEL

Pleasant St. ☎ *802/457–2211* ⊕ *www.shiremotel.com* ⇔ *42 rooms, 1 suite* ◯ *No meals.*

$$$$
RESORT
ALL-INCLUSIVE
Fodor's Choice
★

🏠 **Twin Farms.** Let's just get it out: Twin Farms is the best lodging choice in Vermont. **Pros:** impeccable service; stunning rooms; sensational meals. **Cons:** astronomical prices; must drive to town/Woodstock. $ *Rooms from: $1600* ✉ *1 Stage Rd., Barnard* ☎ *802/234–9999* ⊕ *www. twinfarms.com* ⇔ *3 rooms, 10 cottages* ⊙ *Closed Apr.* ◯ *All-inclusive.*

$$$$
RESORT
Fodor's Choice
★

🏠 **The Woodstock Inn & Resort.** If this is your first time in Woodstock and you want to feel that you're in the middle of it all, stay here. **Pros:** attractive and historic property; excellent food; brand-new spa; contemporary furnishings; professionally run. **Cons:** can lack intimacy. $ *Rooms from: $300* ✉ *Fourteen the Green* ☎ *802/457–1100, 800/448–7900* ⊕ *www.woodstockinn.com* ⇔ *135 rooms, 7 suites* ◯ *No meals.*

KILLINGTON

15 miles east of Rutland.

With only a gas station, post office, motel, and a few shops at the intersection of Routes 4 and 100, it's difficult to tell that the East's largest ski resort is nearby. The village of Killington is characterized by unfortunate strip development along the access road to the ski resort. But the 360-degree views atop Killington Peak, accessible by the resort's gondola, make it worth the drive.

SPORTS AND THE OUTDOORS

BIKING

True Wheels Bike Shop. This bike shop sells and rents bicycles and has information on local routes. ✉ *2886 Killington Rd.* ☎ *802/422–3234* ⊕ *www.truewheels.com.*

FISHING

Gifford Woods State Park. Kent Pond in Gifford Woods State Park is a terrific fishing spot. ✉ *Rte. 100, ½ mile north of U.S. 4, 34 Gifford Woods Rd.* ☎ *802/775–5354* ⊕ *www.vtstateparks.com/htm/gifford.cfm.*

GOLF

Killington Golf Course. At its namesake resort, Killington Golf Course has a challenging 18-hole, par-72 course. Greens fees are $50 midweek and $60 weekends inclusive of carts. Twilight rates are slightly less. ✉ *4763 Killington Rd.* ☎ *802/422–6200* ⊕ *www.killington.com/ summer/golf_course.*

SKI AREAS

★ **Killington.** "Megamountain," "The Beast of the East," and plain "huge" are apt descriptions of Killington. Powder Corp. operates Killington and its neighbor, **Pico**, and over the past several years has improved lifts and snowmaking capabilities. Thanks to its extensive snowmaking system, the resort typically opens in early November, and the lifts often run into late April or early May. Après-ski activities are plentiful and have been rated the best in the East by national ski magazines. With a single call to Killington's hotline or a visit to its website, skiers can plan an entire vacation: choose accommodations, book air or railroad transportation, and arrange for rental equipment and ski or snowboard lessons. Killington ticket holders can also ski at Pico Mountain: a shuttle connects the two areas.

The Killington–Pico complex has a host of activities, including a lift-served tubing park, snowcat-drawn sleigh rides, world-class on-snow events and festivals, mountain biking, hiking, golf course and an 18-hole disc golf course. The resort rents mountain bikes and advises hikers. The K-1 Express Gondola takes you up the mountain to Vermont's second-highest summit.

In terms of downhill skiing, it would probably take several weeks to test all 192 trails on the seven mountains of the Killington complex, even though all except Pico interconnect. About 80% of the 1,017 acres of skiing terrain can be covered with machine-made snow. Transporting skiers to the peaks of this complex are 29 lifts, including 2 gondolas, 11 quads (including 7 high-speed express quads), 5 triples, and a Magic Carpet. The K-1 Express Gondola goes to the area's highest elevation, 4,241-foot Killington Peak. The Skyeship Gondola starts on U.S. 4, far below Killington's main base lodge. ■TIP➜ Savvy skiers park at the base of the Skyeship Gondola to avoid the more crowded access road. After picking up more passengers at a midstation, the Skyeship tops out on Skye Peak. Although Killington has a vertical drop of 3,050 feet, only gentle trails—Juggernaut and Great Eastern—go from top to bottom. The skiing includes everything from Outer Limits, the East's steepest and longest mogul trail, to 6½-mile Great Eastern. In the glades, underbrush and low branches have been cleared to provide tree skiing. Killington's 22-foot superpipe is one of the best rated in the East. Instruction programs are available for youngsters ages 3–8; those 6–12 can join an all-day program. ⊠ *4763 Killington Rd.* ☎ *802/422–6200, 802/422–6200 snow conditions, 800/621–6867 lodging* ⊕ *www.killington.com.*

Pico. When weekend hordes hit Killington, the locals head to Pico. One of Killington's "seven peaks," Pico is physically separated from its parent resort. The 52 trails range from elevator-shaft steep to challenging intermediate trails near the summit, with easier terrain near the bottom of the mountain's 2,000-foot vertical. The learning slope is separated from the upper mountain, so hotshots won't bomb through it. The lower express quad can get crowded, but the upper one rarely has a line. ⊠ *4763 Killington Rd.* ☎ *802/422–6200, 866/667–7426* ⊕ *www.picomountain.com.*

CROSS-COUNTRY SKIING

The Mountain Top Inn & Resort. This resort has 40 miles of hilly trails groomed for Nordic skiing, 37 miles of which can be used for skate skiing. You can also enjoy snowshoeing, dogsledding, ice-skating, and snowmobile and sleigh rides. In the summer there's horseback riding, fishing, hiking, biking, and water sports. The Inn is also a lovely place to stay (➩ *see separate listing*) or to have a meal after skiing. ⊠ *195 Mountaintop Rd., Chittenden* ☎ *802/483–6089, 802/483–2311* ⊕ *www.mountaintopinn.com.*

NIGHTLIFE AND THE ARTS

Inn at Long Trail. On weekends, listen to live music and sip draft Guinness at the Inn at Long Trail. ✉ *U.S. 4, 709 Rte. 4, Sherburne Pass* ☎ *800/325–2540* 🌐 *www.innatlongtrail.com.*

Pickle Barrel Night Club. During ski season, the Pickle Barrel Night Club has a band every happy hour on Friday and Saturday. After 8, the crowd moves downstairs for dancing, sometimes to big-name bands. ✉ *1741 Killington Rd.* ☎ *802/422–3035* 🌐 *www.picklebarrelnightclub.com.*

Taboo. Taboo serves all-you-can-eat pizza on Monday nights in winter, and $3 Long Trail pints on Sunday. It's open year-round. ✉ *2841 Killington Rd.* ☎ *802/422–9885.*

Wobbly Barn. Twentysomethings prefer to dance at the Wobbly Barn, open only during ski season. ✉ *2229 Killington Rd.* ☎ *802/422–6171* 🌐 *www.wobblybarn.com.*

WHERE TO STAY

For expanded hotel reviews, visit Fodors.com.

$$$ B&B/INN 🏨 **Birch Ridge Inn.** A slate-covered carriageway about a mile from Killington base stations leads to one of the area's most popular off-mountain stays, a former executive retreat in two renovated A-frames. **Pros:** quirky; well maintained. **Cons:** oddly furnished; outdated, older building style. [$] *Rooms from: $200* ✉ *37 Butler Rd.* ☎ *802/422–4293, 800/435–8566* 🌐 *www.birchridge.com* 🔑 *10 rooms* 🕓 *Closed May* 🍴 *Multiple meal plans.*

$$$ RESORT 👶 🏨 **The Mountain Top Inn & Resort.** This Nordic skiers' and horseback riders' haven has stunning views and laid-back luxury accommodations. **Pros:** family friendly, and a great spot for outdoor activities and events. **Cons:** expensive for what it is. [$] *Rooms from: $245* ✉ *195 Mountain Top Rd., Chittenden* ☎ *802/483–2311* 🌐 *www.mountaintopinn.com* 🔑 *30 rooms, 5 cabins* 🍴 *Breakfast.*

$$$$ RESORT 🏨 **The Woods Resort & Spa.** These clustered upscale two- and three-bedroom town houses stand in wooded lots along a winding road leading to the spa. **Pros:** contemporary facility; clean, spacious rooms; lots of room choices. **Cons:** lacks traditional Vermont feel. [$] *Rooms from: $250* ✉ *53 Woods La.* ☎ *802/422–3139, 800/642–1147* 🌐 *www.woodsresortandspa.com* 🔑 *107 units* 🍴 *No meals.*

RUTLAND

15 miles southwest of Killington, 32 miles south of Middlebury.

On and around U.S. 7 in Rutland are strips of shopping centers and a seemingly endless row of traffic lights—very un-Vermont. Two blocks west, however, stand the mansions of the marble magnates. The county farmers' market is held in Depot Park Saturdays 9–2. Note: While Rutland is a good central base to grab a bite and see some interesting marble, it's not a place to spend too much time sightseeing.

ESSENTIALS

Visitor Information **Rutland Region Chamber of Commerce** ✉ *50 Merchants Row* ☎ *802/773–2747, 800/756–8880* 🌐 *www.rutlandvermont.com.*

EXPLORING

Chaffee Art Center. The beautiful former mansion of the local Paramount Theatre's founder, this arts center exhibits the work of more than 200 Vermont artists. ⊠ *16 S. Main St.* ☎ *802/775–0356* ⊕ *www. chaffeeartcenter.org* ✉ *Free* ⊙ *Tues.–Sat. 10–5, Sun. noon–4.*

New England Maple Museum and Gift Shop. Maple syrup is Vermont's signature product, and this museum north of Rutland explains the history and process of turning maple sap into syrup with murals, diorama exhibits, and a slide show. If you don't get a chance to visit a sugarhouse, this is a fine place to sample the four different grades and pick up some souvenirs. ⊠ *4578 U.S. 7, 9 miles south of Brandon, Pittsford* ☎ *802/483–9414* ⊕ *www.maplemuseum.com* ✉ *Museum $2.50* ⊙ *Late May–Oct., daily 8:30–5:30; Nov., Dec., and mid-Mar.–late May, daily 10–4.*

Paramount Theatre. The highlight of downtown is this 700-seat, turn-of-the-20th-century gilded playhouse, designed in the spirit of a Victorian opera house. The gorgeous, fully renovated theater holds over a thousand people and is home to music, theater and a film series highlighting its past as a 1930s motion picture theater. ⊠ *30 Center St.* ☎ *802/775–0570* ⊕ *www.paramountvt.org* ✉ *Event ticket prices vary.*

Vermont Marble Museum. North of Rutland, this monument to marble highlights one of the main industries in this region and illustrates marble's many industrial and artistic applications. The hall of presidents has a carved bust of each U.S. president, and in the marble chapel is a replica of Leonardo da Vinci's *Last Supper.* Elsewhere you can watch a sculptor-in-residence shape the stone into finished works of art, compare marbles from around the world, and check out the Vermont Marble Company's original "stone library." Factory seconds and foreign and domestic marble items are for sale. A short walk away is the original marble quarry in Proctor. Marble from here became part of the U.S. Supreme Court building and the New York Public Library. ⊠ *52 Main St., 4 miles north of Rutland, off Rte. 3, Proctor* ☎ *802/459–2300, 800/427–1396* ⊕ *www.vermont-marble.com* ✉ *$7* ⊙ *Mid-May–Oct., daily 9–5:30.*

Wilson Castle. As you drive a long country road just outside Rutland, the opulent vision of this 32-room mansion will surprise you. Completed in 1867, it was built over the course of eight years by a Vermonter who married a British aristocrat. The current owner, Blossom Wilson Davine Ladabouche, still makes her summer home in the old servants' quarters. Within the mansion are 84 stained-glass windows (one inset with 32 Australian opals), hand-painted Italian frescoes, and 13 fireplaces. It's magnificently furnished with European and Asian objets d'art. ⊠ *W. Proctor Rd., Proctor* ☎ *802/773–3284* ⊕ *www.wilsoncastle.com* ✉ *$10* ⊙ *Late May–mid-Oct., daily 9–6, last tour at 5.*

SPORTS AND THE OUTDOORS

BOATING

Lake Bomoseen Marina. Rent pontoon boats, speedboats, waterskiing boats, Wave Runners, and water toys at Lake Bomoseen Marina. ⊠ *145 Creek Rd., off Rte. 4A, 1½ miles west of Castleton* ☎ *802/265–4611.*

HIKING

Deer's Leap. Deer's Leap is a 3-mile round-trip hike to a great view overlooking Sherburne Gap and Pico Peak. ✉ *Starts at the Inn at Long Trail on Rte. 4 west of Rutland.*

Mountain Travelers. Mountain Travelers sells hiking maps and guidebooks, gives advice on local hikes, rents kayaks, and sells sporting equipment. ✉ *147 Rte. 4 E* ☎ *802/775–0814.*

WHERE TO EAT

$$ ECLECTIC ✕ **Little Harry's.** Locals have packed this restaurant ever since chef-owners Trip (Harry) Pearce and Jack Mangan brought Vermont cheddar ravioli and lamb lo mein to downtown Rutland in 1997. (It's the "little" to the bigger Harry's near Ludlow.) The 17 tabletops are adorned with laminated photos of the regulars. For big appetites on small budgets, the pad thai and veggie thai red curry are huge meals for under $8. [$] *Average main: $18* ✉ *121 West St.* ☎ *802/747–4848* 🌐 *littleharrys.com* ⏲ *No lunch.*

BRANDON

15 miles northwest of Rutland.

Thanks to an active artists' guild, tiny Brandon is making a name for itself. In 2003 the Brandon Artists Guild, led by American folk artist Warren Kimble, auctioned 40 life-size fiberglass pigs painted by local artists. The "Really Really Pig Show" raised money for the guild and has brought small-town fame ever since to this community through its yearly shows. Brandon is also home to the Basin Bluegrass Festival, held in July.

ESSENTIALS

Visitor Information Brandon Visitor Center ✉ *4 Grove St. (Rte. 7 at 73 W)* ☎ *802/247–6401* 🌐 *brandon.org.*

EXPLORING

Stephen A. Douglas Museum. The famous early American statesman was born in Brandon in this house in 1813. He left 20 years later to establish himself as a lawyer, becoming a three-time U.S. senator and arguing more cases before the U.S. Supreme Court than anyone else. This museum, which opened in 2009, recounts the early Douglas years, early Brandon history, and the anti-slavery movement in Vermont—the first state to abolish it. ✉ *4 Grove St., at U.S. 7* ☎ *802/247–6401* 🌐 *www.brandon.org* 🎟 *Free* ⏲ *Daily 9–5.*

SPORTS AND THE OUTDOORS

Moosalamoo Association. The Moosalamoo Association manages, protects, and provides stewardship for more than 20,000 acres of the Green Mountain National Forest, northeast of Brandon. More than 60 miles of trails take hikers, mountain bikers, and cross-country skiers through some of Vermont's most gorgeous mountain terrain. Attractions include Branbury State Park, on the shores of Lake Dunmore; secluded Silver Lake; and sections of both the Long Trail and Catamount Trail (the latter is a Massachusetts-to-Québec ski trail). The Blueberry Hill Inn has direct public access to trails. ☎ *800/448–0707.*

GOLF

Neshobe Golf Club. This golf course has 18 holes of par-72 golf on a bent-grass course totaling nearly 6,500 yards. The greens fee is $28–$49 and the Green Mountain views are terrific. Several local inns offer golf packages. ⊠ *224 Town Farm Rd., Rte. 73 east of Brandon* ☎ *802/247–3611* ⊕ *www.neshobe.com.*

HIKING

Mt. Horrid. For great views from a vertigo-inducing cliff, hike up the Long Trail to Mt. Horrid. The steep, hour-long hike starts at the top of Brandon Gap (about 8 miles east of Brandon on Route 73). ⊠ *Rte. 73.*

Falls of Lana. A large turnout on Route 53 marks a moderate trail to the Falls of Lana. ⊠ *Rte. 53.*

Mt. Independence. West of Brandon, four trails—two short ones of less than 1 mile each and two longer ones—lead to the abandoned Revolutionary War fortifications at Mt. Independence. To reach them, take the first left turn off Route 73 west of Orwell and go right at the fork. The road will turn to gravel and fork again; take a sharp left-hand turn toward a small marina. The parking lot is on the left at the top of the hill.

SHOPPING

★ **The Inside Scoop and Antiques by the Falls.** A husband-and-wife team runs these two separate and equally fun-loving businesses under one roof: a colorful ice cream stand and penny candy store and an antiques store filled floor to ceiling with Americana. ⊠ *22 Park St., East Brandon* ☎ *802/247–6600.*

WHERE TO EAT AND STAY

For expanded hotel reviews, visit Fodors.com.

$$ CAFÉ × **Café Provence.** Robert Barral, a former Chicago Four Seasons chef and 16-year director of the New England Culinary Institute, graces Brandon with this delicious informal eatery named after his birthplace. One story above the main street, the café with hints of Provence—flowered seat cushions and dried-flower window valences—specializes in eclectic farm-fresh dishes. Goat-cheese cake with mesclun greens, braised veal cheeks and caramelized endive, and a portobello pizza from the restaurant's hearth oven are just a few of the choices. Breakfast offerings include buttery pastries, eggs Benedict, and breakfast pizza, and outdoor seating can be had under large umbrellas. $ *Average main: $20* ⊠ *11 Center St.* ☎ *802/247–9997* ⊕ *www.cafeprovencevt.com.*

$$$$ B&B/INN Fodor's Choice ★ **Blueberry Hill Inn.** In the Green Mountain National Forest, 5½ miles off a mountain pass on a dirt road, you'll find this secluded inn with its lush gardens and a pond with a wood-fired sauna on its bank. **Pros:** peaceful setting within the national forest; terrific property with lots to do; great food. **Cons:** forest setting not for those who want to be near town. $ *Rooms from: $322* ⊠ *1307 Goshen–Ripton Rd., Goshen* ☎ *802/247–6735, 800/448–0707* ⊕ *www.blueberryhillinn.com* ⇄ *12 rooms* ◎ *Some meals.*

MIDDLEBURY

17 miles north of Brandon, 34 miles south of Burlington.

★ In the late 1800s Middlebury was the largest Vermont community west of the Green Mountains, an industrial center of river-powered wool and grain mills. This is Robert Frost country: Vermont's late poet laureate spent 23 summers at a farm east of Middlebury. Still a cultural and economic hub amid the Champlain Valley's serene pastoral patchwork and the home of topnotch Middlebury College, the picturesque town and rolling countryside invite a day of exploration.

EXPLORING

Middlebury College. Founded in 1800, Middlebury College was conceived as a more godly alternative to the worldly University of Vermont but has no religious affiliation today. In the middle of town, the early-19th-century stone buildings contrast provocatively with the postmodern architecture of the Center for the Arts and the sports center. Music, theater, and dance performances take place throughout the year at the **Wright Memorial Theatre** and **Center for the Arts.** ⊠ *38 College St.* ☎ *802/443–5000* ⊕ *www.middlebury.edu.*

Robert Frost Interpretive Trail. About 10 miles east of town on Route 125 (1 mile west of Middlebury College's Bread Loaf campus), this easy ¾-mile trail winds through quiet woodland. Plaques along the way bear quotations from Frost's poems. A picnic area is across the road from the trailhead. ⊠ *Rte. 125.*

☺ **UVM Morgan Horse Farm.** The Morgan horse—Vermont's official state animal—has an even temper, stamina, and slightly truncated legs in proportion to its body. The University of Vermont's Morgan Horse Farm, about 2½ miles west of Middlebury, is a breeding and training center where in summer you can tour the stables and paddocks. ⊠ *74 Battell Dr., off Morgan Horse Farm Rd. (follow signs off Rte. 23), Weybridge* ☎ *802/388–2011* ⊕ *www.uvm.edu/morgan* ⊠ *$4* ⊙ *May–Oct., daily 9–4.*

Vermont Folklife Center. In the Masonic Hall, exhibits include photography, antiques, folk paintings, manuscripts, and other artifacts and contemporary works that examine facets of Vermont life. ⊠ *88 Main St.* ☎ *802/388–4964* ⊕ *www.vermontfolklifecenter.org* ⊠ *Donations accepted* ⊙ *Gallery May–Dec., Tues.–Sat. 11–4.*

Vermont State Craft Center/Frog Hollow. More than a crafts store, this arts center mounts changing exhibitions and displays exquisite works in wood, glass, metal, clay, and fiber by more than 250 Vermont artisans. The center, which overlooks Otter Creek, sponsors classes taught by some of those artists. Burlington and Manchester also have centers. ⊠ *1 Mill St.* ☎ *802/863–6458* ⊕ *www.froghollow.org* ⊙ *Call for hrs.*

OFF THE BEATEN PATH

Fort Ticonderoga Ferry. Established in 1759, the Fort Ti cable ferry crosses Lake Champlain between Shoreham and Fort Ticonderoga, New York, at one of the oldest ferry crossings in North America. The trip takes seven minutes. ⊠ *3143 Richville Rd., Shoreham* ☎ *802/897–7999* ⊕ *www.forttiferry.com* ⊠ *Cars, pickups, and vans with driver and*

7

passenger $8; bicycles $2; pedestrians $1 ⊙ *May–last Sun. of Oct., daily 8–5:45.*

SHOPPING

Historic Marble Works. This renovated marble manufacturing facility has a collection of unique shops set amid quarrying equipment and factory buildings. ⊠ *2 Maple St.* ☎ *802/388–3701.*

Danforth Pewter. This store sells lovely handcrafted pewter vases, lamps, jewelry, and tableware. ⊠ *52 Seymour St.* ☎ *800/222–3142* ⊕ *www.danforthpewter.com*

WHERE TO EAT

$ ✕ **American Flatbread at the Marble Works.** On weekends this is the most
PIZZA happening spot in town, and no wonder: the pizza is extraordinary, and
★ the attitude is pure Vermont. Wood-fired clay domes create masterful thin crusts from organically grown wheat. Besides the innovative, delicious pizzas, try an organic mesclun salad tossed in the house raspberry-ginger vinaigrette. If you love pizza and haven't been here, you're in for a treat. There are also locations in Waitsfield and Burlington. $ *Average main: $12* ⊠ *137 Maple St., at the Marble Works* ☎ *802/388–3300* ⊕ *www.americanflatbread.com* ⌂ *Reservations not accepted* ⊙ *Closed Sun. and Mon. No lunch.*

$$ ✕ **The Bobcat Cafe & Brewery.** Worth the drive from Middlebury to the
AMERICAN small, quaint town of Bristol, The Bobcat is the place to be in the area.
★ Fun, funky, and hip, this charming eatery is nice enough for a date but casual enough for the whole family. Choose from a wide range of great offerings from burgers to seared scallops and wash it down with excellent house-brewed beer. For something special, try the Caribbean jerk pork loin and coconut flan for dessert. $ *Average main: $18* ⊠ *5 Main St., Bristol* ☎ *802/453–3311* ⊕ *www.bobcatcafe.com* ⊙ *No lunch.*

$$$ ✕ **Mary's at Baldwin Creek.** People drive from the far reaches of Vermont
AMERICAN to eat at this restaurant just beyond the charming, little-known town
Fodor'sChoice of Bristol, 13 miles northeast of Middlebury. Plan time to visit the
★ huge vegetable gardens that surround this beautiful property. A slow approach to locally grown foods finds life here with hearty fare like summer lasagna, a prime showcase for the flavors of the veggies grown 50 feet from your table, and the near-legendary garlic soup, a creamy year-round staple that seems genetically engineered to please. Desserts are hit or miss. $ *Average main: $25* ⊠ *1868 North Rte. 116, Bristol* ☎ *802/453–2432* ⊕ *www.innatbaldwincreek.com* ⊙ *Closed Mon. and Tues. No lunch.*

$$ ✕ **The Storm Cafe.** There is no setting in town quite like the deck over-
MODERN looking the Otter Creek Falls at one end of the long footbridge over
AMERICAN the creek. Even if you're not here in summer, the eclectic ever-changing menu at this small restaurant in the old Frog Hollow Mill makes it worth a visit any time of year. "Stormy" Jamaican jerk–seasoned pork tenderloin and melt-in-your-mouth desserts like an apricot soufflé are favorites, as are their large salads. $ *Average main: $20* ⊠ *3 Mill St.* ☎ *802/388–1063* ⊕ *www.thestormcafe.com* ⊙ *No dinner Mon.*

WHERE TO STAY

For expanded hotel reviews, visit Fodors.com.

$$ B&B/INN **Inn on the Green.** The 1803 National Historic Register inn and separate carriage house is situated right in the center of bucolic Middlebury and near the stunning Middlebury College campus. **Pros:** ideal location; great breakfast. **Cons:** rooms can be small and close together. *[$] Rooms from: $179 ✉ 71 S. Pleasant St. ☎ 802/388–7512 🌐 www.innonthegreen.com 🛏 9 rooms, 2 suites 🍴 Breakfast.*

$$ B&B/INN **Swift House Inn.** The 1824 Georgian home of a 19th-century governor showcases white-panel wainscoting, mahogany furnishings, and marble fireplaces. **Pros:** attractive, spacious, well-kept rooms; professionally run. **Cons:** near to but not quite in the heart of town. *[$] Rooms from: $169 ✉ 25 Stewart La. ☎ 866/388–9925 🌐 www.swifthouseinn.com 🛏 20 rooms 🍴 Breakfast.*

WAITSFIELD AND WARREN

32 miles northeast (Waitsfield) and 25 miles east (Warren) of Middlebury.

Skiers discovered the high peaks overlooking the pastoral Mad River Valley in the 1940s. Now the valley and its two towns, Waitsfield and Warren, attract the hip, the adventurous, and the low-key. Warren is tiny and adorable, with a general store that attracts tour buses. The gently carved ridges cradling the valley and the swell of pastures and fields lining the river seem to keep notions of ski-resort sprawl at bay. With a map from the Sugarbush Chamber of Commerce you can investigate back roads off Route 100 that have exhilarating valley views.

ESSENTIALS

Visitor Information Sugarbush Chamber of Commerce ✉ *Rte. 100* ☎ *802/496–3409, 800/828–4748* 🌐 *www.madrivervalley.com.*

SPORTS AND THE OUTDOORS

GOLF

Sugarbush Resort. Great views and challenging play are the trademarks of the Robert Trent Jones–designed 18-hole mountain course at Sugarbush Resort. The greens fee runs from $50 to $100. ✉ *1840 Sugarbush Access Rd., Warren* ☎ *802/583–6725* 🌐 *www.sugarbush.com.*

MULTI-SPORT OUTFITTER

Clearwater Sports. This outfitter rents canoes, kayaks, tubing, and camping equipment and leads guided river trips and white-water instruction in the warm months. In winter, the store leads snowshoe and backcountry ski tours and rents Telemark equipment, snowshoes, and one-person Mad River Rocket sleds. ✉ *4147 Main St. (Rte. 100), Waitsfield* ☎ *802/496–2708* 🌐 *clearwatersports.com.*

SLEIGH RIDES

Mountain Valley Farm. This farm offers horse-drawn carriage and sleigh rides with reservations. ✉ *1719 Common Rd., Waitsfield* ☎ *802/496–9255* 🌐 *mountainvalleyfarm.com.*

Sheep's cheese is just one of the many food products that contribute to great fresh local meals in Vermont.

SKI AREAS

Blueberry Lake Cross-Country Ski Area. This ski area has 18 miles of trails through thickly wooded glades. ✉ *424 Plunkton Rd., East Warren* ☎ *802/496–6687* ⊕ *www.blueberrylakeskivt.com.*

Mad River Glen. The hundreds of shareholders who own Mad River Glen are dedicated, knowledgeable skiers devoted to keeping skiing what it used to be—a pristine alpine experience. Mad River's unkempt aura attracts rugged individualists looking for less-polished terrain: the area was developed in the late 1940s and has changed relatively little since then. It remains one of only three resorts in the country that ban snowboarding.

Mad River is steep, with natural slopes that follow the mountain's fall lines. The terrain changes constantly on the 45 interconnected trails, of which 33% are beginner, 27% are intermediate, and 41% are expert. Intermediate and novice terrain is regularly groomed. Five lifts—including the world's last surviving single chairlift—service the mountain's 2,037-foot vertical drop. Most of Mad River's trails are covered only by natural snow. The kids' ski school runs classes for little ones ages 4 to 12. The nursery is for infants to 6-year-olds; reservations are recommended.

Known as the capital of free-heel skiing, Mad River Glen sponsors Telemark programs throughout the season. Every March, the North America Telemark Organization (NATO) Festival attracts up to 1,400 visitors. Snowshoeing is also an option. There is a $5 fee to use the snowshoe trails, and rentals are available. ✉ *Rte. 17, Fayston*

☎ *802/496–3551, 802/496–2001 snow conditions, 800/850–6742 cooperative office* ⊕ *www.madriverglen.com.*

Sugarbush. Sugarbush has remade itself as a true skier's mountain, with steep, natural snow glades and fall-line drops. Not as rough around the edges as Mad River Glen, Sugarbush also has well-groomed intermediate and beginner terrain. A computer-controlled system for snowmaking has increased coverage to 70%. At the base of the mountain are condominiums, restaurants, shops, bars, and a sports center.

Sugarbush is two distinct, connected mountain complexes connected by the Slide Brook Express quad. Lincoln Peak, with a vertical of 2,400 feet, is known for formidable steeps, especially on Castlerock. Mount Ellen has more beginner runs near the bottom, with steep fall-line pitches on the upper half of the 2,650 vertical feet. There are 111 trails in all: 22% beginner, 46% intermediate, 32% expert. The resort has 18 lifts: seven quads (including four high-speed versions), three triples, four doubles, and four surface lifts. There's half- and full-day instruction available for children ages 4–12, ski/day care for 3-year-olds, and supervised ski and ride programs for teens. Sugarbear Forest, a terrain garden, has fun bumps and jumps. The Sugarbush Day School accepts children ages 6 weeks to 6 years. ⊠ *1840 Sugarbush Access Rd., accessible from Rte. 100 or 17, Warren 802/583–6300, 802/583–7669 snow conditions, 800/537–8427 lodging* ⊕ *www.sugarbush.com.*

SHOPPING

All Things Bright and Beautiful. This eccentric 12-room Victorian house is jammed to the rafters with stuffed animals of all shapes, sizes, and colors as well as folk art, prints, and collectibles. One of the rooms is a coffee and ice cream shop. ⊠ *27 Bridge St., Waitsfield* ☎ *802/496–3997* ⊕ *www.allthingsbright.com.*

The Warren Store. This general store has everything you'd hope to find in a tiny but sophisticated Vermont: local beer and a nice wine selection, cheese, a bakery, strong coffee, delicious sandwiches and prepared foods, cards, and clothing. ■TIP→ You can snag a copy of the New York Times if you need a news or crossword fix. In summer, grab a quick lunch on their small deck by the water; in winter, by their cozy woodstove. Stop in after a day of skiing or hiking for a tasting in their wine shop and take in the lively local scene. ⊠ *284 Main St., Warren* ☎ *802/496–3864* ⊕ *www.warrenstore.com* ⊙ *Daily 8–7.*

NIGHTLIFE AND THE ARTS

NIGHTLIFE

Purple Moon Pub. Live bands play most weekends at Purple Moon Pub. ⊠ *6163 Main St. (Rte. 100), Waitsfield* ☎ *802/496–3422* ⊕ *www. purplemoonpub.com.*

★ **Tracks.** Downstairs in the Pitcher Inn, Tracks is a tavern and bar run by the Relais & Châteaux property. Housed in a comfortable but tasteful lodge-style setting with a fireplace and a giant moose head, Tracks has a terrific full tavern menu—try the grilled local steak with aioli and fries or the smoked pulled pork sandwich. There is also an excellent wine selection, billiards, darts, and a fun shuffleboard game played on a long table with sawdust. ⊠ *275 Main St, Warren* ☏ *802/493–6350* ⊕ *www.pitcherinn.com.*

ARTS

Green Mountain Cultural Center. The Green Mountain Cultural Center hosts concerts, art exhibits, and educational workshops. ⊠ *Inn at the Round Barn Farm, 1661 E. Warren Rd., Waitsfield* ☏ *802/496–7722* ⊕ *www.theroundbarn.com.*

Valley Players. The Valley Players present musicals, dramas, follies, and more. ⊠ *4254 Main St., Waitsfield(Rte. 100)* ☏ *802/583–1674* ⊕ *www. valleyplayers.com.*

WHERE TO EAT

$ · PIZZA · Fodor'sChoice ★ **✕ American Flatbread–Waitsfield.** Is this the best pizza experience in the world? It just may be. In summer, dining takes place outside around fire pits in the beautiful valley, a setting and meal not to be forgotten. The secret is in the love, but some clues to the magic are in the organically grown flour and vegetables and the wood-fired clay ovens. The "new Vermont sausage" pizza is Waitsfield pork in a maple-fennel sausage baked with sundried tomatoes, caramelized onions, cheese, and herbs; it's a dream, as are the more traditional pizzas. As a restaurant, it's open evenings Thursday through Sunday, but the retail bakery is open Monday–Thursday 7:30 am–8 pm; if you're here during that time anything in the oven is yours for $10. This is the original American Flatbread location—plan your trip around it. $ *Average main: $15* ⊠ *46 Lareau Rd., off Rte. 100, Waitsfield* ☏ *802/496–8856* ⊕ *www. americanflatbread.com* ⌂ *Reservations not accepted* ⊗ *Restaurant closed Mon.–Wed. No lunch.*

$$$ · MODERN AMERICAN **✕ Common Man.** A local institution (but recently under new ownership), this restaurant is in a big 1800s barn with hand-hewn rafters and crystal chandeliers hanging from the beams. That's the Common Man for you: fancy and après-ski all at once. Bottles of Moët & Chandon signed by the customers who ordered them sit atop the beams. The eclectic, sophisticated New American cuisine highlights locally grown produce and meats. The menu might include a roasted beet salad with goat cheese and fennel in an orange vinaigrette, duck breast with butternut squash purée, or seared black bass with sticky rice and bok choy. Dinner is served by candlelight. Couples sit by the big fireplace. $ *Average main: $25* ⊠ *3209 German Flats Rd., Warren* ☏ *802/583–2800* ⊕ *www. commonmanrestaurant.com* ⊗ *Closed Sun. and Mon. No lunch.*

WHERE TO STAY

For expanded hotel reviews, visit Fodors.com.

$$$ · B&B/INN ★ **The Inn at Round Barn Farm.** A Shaker-style round barn (one of only five in Vermont) is the physical hallmark of this B&B, but what you'll remember when you leave is how comfortable a stay here is. **Pros:** great trails, gardens, and rooms; nice breakfast; unique architecture. **Cons:** no restaurant. $ *Rooms from: $205* ⊠ *1661 E. Warren Rd., Waitsfield* ☏ *802/496–2276* ⊕ *www.theroundbarn.com* ⇢ *11 rooms, 1 suite* ⦿ *Breakfast.*

$$$$ B&B/INN Fodor's Choice ★ [🏨] **The Pitcher Inn.** *Sublime* is a word that comes to mind when thinking about a night at the elegant Pitcher Inn, one of three of Vermont's Relais & Châteaux properties. **Pros:** exceptional service; fabulous restaurant; great bathrooms; fun pub; beautiful location. **Cons:** at some point, you have to go home. [$] *Rooms from: $425* ✉ *275 Main St., Warren* ☎ *802/496–6350, 888/867–4824* 🌐 *www.pitcherinn.com* 🛏 *9 rooms, 2 suites* 🍴 *Breakfast.*

NORTHERN VERMONT

Vermont's northernmost region reveals the state's greatest contrasts. To the west, Burlington and its suburbs have grown so rapidly that rural wags now say that Burlington's greatest advantage is that it's "close to Vermont." The north country also harbors Vermont's tiny but charming capital, Montpelier, and its highest mountain, Mt. Mansfield, site of the famous Stowe ski resort. To the northeast of Montpelier is a sparsely populated and heavily wooded territory that former Senator George Aiken dubbed the "Northeast Kingdom." It's the domain of loggers, farmers, and avid outdoors enthusiasts.

Our coverage of towns begins in the state capital, Montpelier, moves west toward Stowe and Burlington, then goes north through the Lake Champlain Islands, east along the boundary with Canada toward Jay Peak, and south into the heart of the Northeast Kingdom.

MONTPELIER

38 miles southeast of Burlington, 115 miles north of Brattleboro.

With only about 8,000 residents, little Montpelier is the country's smallest capital city. But it has a youthful energy—and certainly an independent spirit—that makes it seem almost as large as Burlington. The well-preserved downtown bustles with state and city workers walking to meetings and restaurants, or students heading to one of the funky coffee shops.

EXPLORING

★ **Morse Farm Maple Sugarworks.** With eight generations of sugaring, the Morses are the oldest maple family in existence, so you're sure to find an authentic maple farm experience here. Burr Morse heads up the operation now, along with his son Tom. You can see an earlier generation, Burr's father, Harry Morse, hamming it up in a hilarious video playing at the theater. More than 3,000 trees produce the syrup (sample all the grades), candy, cream, and sugar that are sold in their gift shop. ✉ *1168 County Rd.* ☎ *800/242–2740* 🌐 *www.morsefarm.com* 🎟 *Free.*

Vermont Museum. The Vermont Historical Society runs this engaging museum recounting more than 150 years of state history. The collection here was begun in 1838 and features all things Vermont, from a catamount (the now extinct Vermont cougar) to Ethan Allen's shoe buckles. The museum store has a great collection of books, prints, and gifts. ✉ *109 State St.* ☎ *802/479–8500* 🌐 *www.vermonthistory.org* 🎟 *$5* 🕒 *May–Oct., Tues.–Sat. 10–4.*

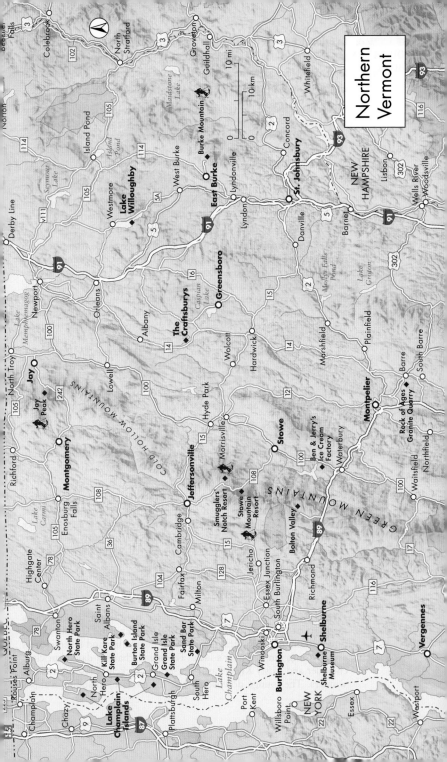

Northern Vermont

QUICK BITES

La Brioche Bakery. This is a great downtown stop for breakfast and lunch. New England Culinary Institute students are up at 4 am preparing breads for thankful locals. There's a nice selection of soups, salads, and sandwiches. ✉ *89 Main St.* ☎ *802/229–0443* 🌐 *www.neci.edu/labrioche.*

★ **Vermont State House.** The regal, gold-domed capitol surrounded by forest is emblematic of this proud rural state. With the gleaming dome and columns of Barre granite 6 feet in diameter, the statehouse is home to the oldest legislative chambers in their original condition in the United States. Half-hour tours take you through the governor's office and the house and senate chambers. The goddess of agriculture tops the gilded dome. Interior paintings and exhibits make much of Vermont's sterling Civil War record. ✉ *115 State St.* ☎ *802/828–2228* 🎟 *Donations accepted* 🕓 *Weekdays 8–4; tours July–mid-Oct., weekdays every ½ hr 10–3:30 (last tour at 3:30), Sat. 11–3 (last tour at 2:30).*

OFF THE BEATEN PATH

Rock of Ages Granite Quarry. The attractions here range from the awe-inspiring (the quarry resembles the Grand Canyon in miniature) to the mildly ghoulish (you can consult a directory of tombstone dealers throughout the country) to the whimsical (an outdoor granite bowling alley). You might recognize the sheer walls of the quarry from *Batman and Robin,* the film starring George Clooney and Arnold Schwarzenegger. At the crafts center, skilled artisans sculpt monuments; at the quarries themselves, 25-ton blocks of stone are cut from sheer 475-foot walls by workers who clearly earn their pay. ✉ *560 Graniteville Rd., Exit 6 off I–89, follow Rte. 63, 7 miles southeast of Montpelier, Graniteville* ☎ *802/476–3119* 🌐 *www.rockofages.com* 🎟 *Tour of active quarry $5, craftsman center and self-guided tour free* 🕓 *Visitor center May–Oct., Mon.–Sat. 8:30–5, Sun. 10–5; narrated tour on Sat. (call for times).*

SHOPPING

Unique shops attract locals and tourists alike to Montpelier.

Zutano. For hip children's clothing made in Vermont, head to Zutano. ✉ *79 Main St.* ☎ *802/223–2229* 🌐 *www.zutano.com.*

WHERE TO EAT

$$$ ECLECTIC

🍴 **Ariel's.** Well off the beaten path, this small restaurant overlooking a lake is worth the drive down a dirt road. The chef prepares eclectic treats such as scallop, lobster, and shrimp ravioli in a ginger shiitake broth. The wine selection is excellent. The full menu is offered Friday and Saturday; a pub menu ($–$$) is served Wednesday, Thursday, and Sunday. [$] *Average main: $26* ✉ *29 Stone Hill Rd., 8 miles south of Montpelier, Brookfield* ☎ *802/276–3939* 🌐 *www.arielsrestaurant.com* 🕓 *Closed Nov. and Apr.; Mon. and Tues. May–Oct.; Mon.–Thurs. Dec.–Mar.*

$$ AMERICAN

🍴 **NECI on Main.** Nearly everyone working here (formerly known as the Main Street Grill) is a student at the New England Culinary Institute. Although this is a training ground, the quality and inventiveness are anything but beginner's luck. The menu changes daily, but clam chowder and Misty Knoll Farm free-range chicken breast are reliable winners. The lounge downstairs has lighter fare, including a tapas menu. Sunday brunch is popular. [$] *Average main: $20* ✉ *118 Main St.* ☎ *802/223–3188* 🌐 *www.neci.edu* 🕒 *Closed Mon. No dinner Sun.*

$$ ITALIAN 🍴 **Sarducci's.** Legislative lunches have been a lot more leisurely since Sarducci's came along to fill the trattoria void in Vermont's capital. These bright, cheerful rooms alongside the Winooski River are a local favorite for pizza fresh from wood-fired ovens, wonderfully textured homemade Italian breads, and imaginative pasta dishes such as pasta *pugliese,* which marries penne with basil, black olives, roasted eggplant, portobello mushrooms, and sun-dried tomatoes. [$] *Average main: $17* ✉ *3 Main St.* ☎ *802/223–0229* 🌐 *www.sarduccis.com* 🕒 *No lunch Sun.*

$ CAFÉ 👶 🍴 **The Skinny Pancake.** This healthy, fun, dine-in creperie, with locations in Montpelier and Burlington, makes a great stop for breakfast, lunch, or an easy dinner. The Breakfast Monster, made with eggs and local Cabot cheddar, is a winner. For lunch, try the spinach and feta crepes, the Veggie Monster, or the Lamb Fetatastic, made with local lamb sausage, baby spinach, Vermont feta, and kalamata olives. If you're in the mood for dessert, sample the Nutella crepe or the Pooh Bear served with warm local honey and cinnamon. [$] *Average main: $8* ✉ *89 Main St.* ☎ *802/262–2253* 🌐 *www.skinnypancake.com.*

$ ECLECTIC ★ 🍴 **Three Penny Taproom.** The new kid on the block in downtown Montpelier, this lively, hip taproom is getting rave reviews. The Three Penny serves a wide array of craft beer and imaginative artisanal small plates—try the maple roasted pork belly sandwich with grain mustard raclette or the cheese plate with Bayley Hazen blue and figs—in a fun, European pub atmosphere that feels straight out of an artsy neighborhood in Brussels but is all Vermont. [$] *Average main: $15* ✉ *108 Main St* ☎ *802/223–8277* 🌐 *www.threepennytaproom.com.*

WHERE TO STAY

For expanded hotel reviews, visit Fodors.com.

$$ B&B/INN 🏨 **Inn at Montpelier.** There are just a few places to stay around town and this is the most charming option. **Pros:** beautiful home; relaxed central setting; amazing porch. **Cons:** some rooms are small. [$] *Rooms from: $180* ✉ *147 Main St.* ☎ *802/223–2727* 🌐 *www.innatmontpelier.com* 🛏 *19 rooms* 🍴 *Breakfast.*

EN ROUTE

Ben & Jerry's Ice Cream Factory. On your way to Stowe from Interstate 89, be sure to stop at Ben & Jerry's Ice Cream Factory, a must for ice cream lovers. Ben Cohen and Jerry Greenfield began selling ice cream from a renovated gas station in Burlington in the 1970s. The tour only skims the surface of the behind-the-scenes goings-on at the plant—a flaw forgiven when the free samples are dished out. ✉ *1281 Waterbury-Stowe Rd. (Rte. 100), 1 mile north of I–89, Waterbury* ☎ *802/846–1500* 🌐 *www.benjerry.com* 🎟 *Tour $4* 🕒 *Late Oct.–June, daily 10–6; July–mid-Aug., daily 9–9; mid-Aug.–late Oct., daily 9–7. Tours run every half hour.*

Cabot Creamery. The major cheese producer in the state, midway between Barre and St. Johnsbury, has a visitor center with an audio-visual presentation about the dairy and cheese industry. You can taste samples, purchase cheese and other Vermont products, and tour the plant. ✉ *2878 Main St., 3 miles north of U.S. 2, Cabot* ☎ *800/837–4261*

⊕ *www.cabotcheese.coop* ⌧*$2* ⊗ *June–Oct., daily 9–5; Nov., Dec., and Feb.–May, Mon.–Sat. 9–4; Jan., Mon.–Sat. 10–4; call ahead to check cheese-making days.*

STOWE

22 miles northwest of Montpelier, 36 miles east of Burlington.

Fodor's Choice
★
Long before skiing came to Stowe in the 1930s, the rolling hills and valleys beneath Vermont's highest peak, 4,395-foot Mt. Mansfield, attracted summer tourists looking for a reprieve from city heat. Most stayed at one of two inns in the village of Stowe. When skiing made the town a winter destination, the arriving skiers outnumbered the hotel beds, so locals took them in. This spirit of hospitality continues, and many of these homes are now lovely country inns. The village itself is tiny, just a few blocks of shops and restaurants clustered around a picture-perfect white church with a lofty steeple, but it serves as the anchor for Mountain Road, which leads north past restaurants, lodges, and shops on its way to Stowe's fabled slopes.

ESSENTIALS
Visitor Information Stowe Area Association ☎ *802/253-7321, 877/467-8693* ⊕ *www.gostowe.com.*

EXPLORING
Gondola. Mt. Mansfield's "Chin" area is accessible by the eight-seat gondola. ⊠ *1 Mountain Rd., 8 miles off Rte. 100* ☎ *802/253-3000* ⊕ *www.stowe.com* ⌧ *Gondola $14* ⊗ *Mid-June–mid-Oct., daily 10–5; early Dec.–late Apr., daily 8–4; closed in Nov. and May.*

Cliff House Restaurant. At the gondola's summit station is the Cliff House Restaurant, where lunch is served daily 11–3. ☎ *802/253-3558* ⊕ *www.stowe.com.*

Mt. Mansfield. With its elongated summit ridge resembling the profile of a recumbent man's face, Mt. Mansfield has long attracted the adventurous. The mountain is ribboned with hiking and ski trails.

Trapp Family Lodge. Built by the von Trapp family, of *Sound of Music* fame, this Tyrolean lodge and its surrounding pastureland are the site of a popular outdoor music series in summer and an extensive cross-country ski-trail network in winter. Its bakery/café overlooking a breathtaking mountain vista serves food and local beers; a ski-accessible-only cabin offers homemade soups, sandwiches, and hot chocolate; the resort also has a fine dining restaurant and a more casual bar. ⊠ *700 Trapp Hill Rd.* ☎ *802/253-8511, 800/826-7000* ⊕ *www.trappfamily.com.*

Vermont Ski Museum. The state's skiing history is documented here with myriad exhibits. ⊠ *1 Main St.* ☎ *802/253-9911* ⊕ *www. vermontskimuseum.org.*

SPORTS AND THE OUTDOORS
CANOEING AND KAYAKING
Umiak Outdoor Outfitters. This full-service outfitter rents canoes and kayaks for day trips and leads overnight excursions. The store also operates a rental outpost at Lake Elmore State Park in Elmore, on the Winooski

Continued on page 491

LET IT SNOW
WINTER ACTIVITIES IN VERMONT

by Elise Coroneos

SKIING AND SNOWBOARDING IN VERMONT

Less than 5 mi from the Canadian border, Jay Peak is Vermont's northernmost ski resort.

Ever since America's first ski tow opened in a farmer's pasture near Woodstock in January 1934, skiers have headed en masse to Vermont in winter. Today, 18 alpine and 30 nordic ski areas range in size and are spread across the state, from Mount Snow in the south to Jay Peak near the Canadian border. The snowmaking equipment has also become more comprehensive over the years, with more than 70% of the trails in the state using man-made snow. Here are some of the best ski areas by various categories:

GREAT FOR KIDS **Smugglers' Notch, Okemo,** and **Bromley Mountain** all offer terrific kids' programs, with classes organized by age categories and by skill level. Kids as young as 3 (4 at some ski areas) can start learning. Child care, with activities like stories, singing, and arts and crafts, are available for those too young to ski; some ski areas, like Smuggler's Notch, offer babysitting with no minimum age daytime and evening.

BEST FOR BEGINNERS Beginner terrain makes up nearly half of the mountain at **Stratton,** where options include private and group lessons for first-timers. Also good are small but family-friendly **Bolton Valley** and **Bromley Mountains,** which both designate a third of their slopes for beginners.

EXPERT TERRAIN The slopes at **Jay Peak** and massive **Killington** are most notable for their steepness and pockets of glades. About 40% of the runs at these two resorts are advanced or expert. Due to its far north location, Jay Peak tends to get the most snow, making it ideal for those skilled in plowing through fresh powder. Another favorite with advanced skiers is Central Vermont's **Mad River Glen,** where many slopes are ungroomed (natural) and the motto is "Ski it if you can." In addition, **Sugarbush, Stowe,** and **Smugglers' Notch** are all revered for their challenging untamed side country.

Mount Mansfield is better known as Stowe.   Stratton Mountain clocktower

7

IN FOCUS LET IT SNOW

NIGHT SKIING Come late afternoon, **Bolton Valley** is hopping. That's because it's the only location in Vermont for night skiing. Ski and ride under the lights from 4 until 8 Wednesday through Saturday, followed by a later après-ski scene.

APRÈS-SKI The social scenes at **Killington, Sugarbush,** and **Stowe** are the most noteworthy (and crowded). Warm up after a day in the snow in Killington with all-you-can-eat pizza on Monday nights and daily happy hour specials at the Outback, or stop by the always popular Wobbly Barn. For live music, try Castlerock Pub in Sugarbush or the Matterhorn Bar in Stowe.

SNOWBOARDING Boarders (and some skiers) will love the latest features for freestyle tricks in Vermont. Home to the Burton US Open, **Stratton** has a half pipe, rail garden, and four other parks. **Mount Snow's** Carinthia Peak is an all-terrain park–dedicated mountain, the only of its kind in the state. Head to **Killington** for Burton Stash, another beautiful all-natural features terrain park. **Okemo** has a superpipe and five terrain parks, including a new gladed park with all-natural features. Note that snowboarding is not allowed at skiing cooperative **Mad River Glen.**

CROSS-COUNTRY To experience the best of cross-country skiing in the state, simply follow the Catamount Trail, a 300-mile nordic route from southern Vermont to Canada. **The Trapp Family Lodge** in Stowe has 40 miles of groomed cross-country trails and 60 miles of back-country trails. Another top option is **The Mountain Top Inn & Resort,** just outside of Killington. Its Nordic Ski and Snowshoe Center provides instruction for newcomers, along with hot drinks and lunches when it is time to take a break and warm up.

TELEMARK Ungroomed snow and tree skiing are a natural fit with free-heel skiing at **Mad River Glen.** Jay Peak also has telemark rentals and instruction.

MOUNTAIN-RESORT TRIP PLANNER

TIMING

■ **Snow Season.** Winter sports time is typically from Thanksgiving through April, weather permitting. Holidays are the most crowded.

■ **March Madness.** Most of the season's snow tends to come in March, so that's the time to go if you want to ski on fresh, nature-made powder. To increase your odds, choose a ski area in the northern part of the state.

■ **Summer Scene.** During summertime, many ski resorts reinvent themselves as prime destinations for golfers, zipline and canopy tours, mountain bikers, and weddings. Other summer visitors come to the mountains to enjoy hiking trails, climbing walls, aquatic centers, chairlift and horseback rides, or a variety of festivals.

■ **Avoid Long Lift Lines.** Try to hit the slopes early—many lifts start at 8 or 9 AM, with ticket windows opening a half-hour earlier. Then take a mid-morning break as lines start to get longer and head out again when others come in for lunch.

SAVINGS TIPS

■ **Choose a Condo.** Especially if you're planning to stay for a week, save money on food by opting for a condominum unit with a kitchen. You can shop at the supermarket and cook breakfast and dinner.

■ **Rent Smart.** Consider ski rental options in the villages rather than those at the mountain. Renting right at the ski area may be more convenient, but it may also cost more.

■ **Discount Lift Tickets.** Online tickets are often the least expensive; multi-day discounts and and ski-and-stay packages will also lower your costs. Good for those who can plan ahead, early-bird tickets often go on sale before the ski season even starts.

■ **Hit the Peaks Off-peak.** In order to secure the best deals at the most competitive rates, avoid booking during school holidays. President's Week in February is the busiest, because that's when Northeastern schools have their spring break.

Top left, Killington's six mountains make up the largest ski area in Vermont. Top right, Stratton has a Snowboard-cross course.

THINK WARM THOUGHTS

It can get cold on the slopes, so be prepared. Consider proper face warmth and smart layering, plus ski-specific socks, or purchase a pair each of inexpensive hand and feet warmers that fit easily in your gloves and boots. Helmets, which can also be rented, provide not only added safety but warmth.

VERMONT SKI AREAS BY THE NUMBERS

Okemo's wide slopes attract snowbirds to Ludlow in Central Vermont.

Numbers are a helpful way to compare mountains, but remember that each resort has a distinct personality. This list is composed of ski areas in Vermont with at least 100 skiable acres. For more information, see individual resort listings.

SKI AREA	Vertical Drop	Skiable Acres	# of Trails & Lifts	Terrain Type ●	■	◆/◆◆	Snowboarding Options
Bolton Valley	1,704	165	70/6	34%	36%	30%	Terrain park
Bromley	1,334	177	46/9	28%	37%	35%	Terrain park
Burke Mountain	2,011	250	50/8	14%	42%	44%	Terrain park
Jay Peak	2,153	385	76/8	20%	39%	41%	Terrain park
Killington	3,050	752	140/22	34%	30%	36%	Terrain park, Half-pipe
Mad River Glen	2,037	120	49/5	33%	27%	41%	Snowboarding not allowed
Mount Snow	1,700	590	80/23	15%	68%	18%	Terrain park, Half-pipe
Okemo	2,200	632	119/24	32%	36%	32%	Terrain park, Superpipe, RossCross terrain cross park
Pico Mountain	1,967	252	52/9	17%	46%	37%	Triple Slope
Smugglers' Notch	2,610	310	78/8	17%	51%	32%	Terrain park
Stowe	2,360	485	116/16	16%	59%	25%	Terrain park, Half-pipe
Stratton	2,003	600+	96/13	41%	32%	27%	Terrain park, Half-pipe, Snowboardcross course
Sugarbush	2,600	508	111/16	22%	46%	32%	Terrain park, Half-pipe

CONTACT THE EXPERTS

Ski Vermont (☎ 802/223-2439 ⊕ www.skivermont.com), a non-profit association in Montpelier, Vermont, and **Vermont Department of Tourism** (⊕ www.vermontvacation.com) are great resources for travelers planning a wintertime trip to Vermont.

KNOW YOUR SIGNS

On trail maps and the mountains, trails are rated and marked:

● Beginner   ◆ Advanced

■ Intermediate   ◆◆ Expert

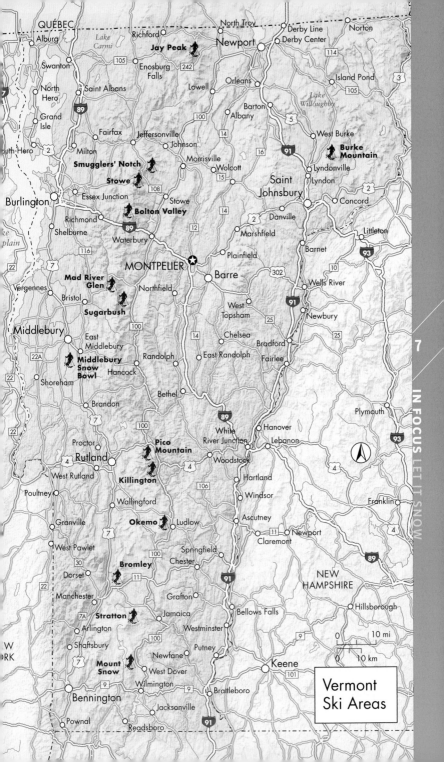

MORE WINTER FUN

A horse and sleigh ride in South Woodstock

DOG SLEDDING

Being pulled through the woods by a team of of up to eight adult Siberian Huskies, you might feel like you are a pioneer taking on the elements—or like you're in Alaska's Iditarod.

Pros: unique experience; kids love it.
Cons: dogs can be stubborn; pricey.

■ **Peacepups Dog Sledding** (☏ 802/888-7733 ⊕ www.peacepupsdogsledding.com) at Lake Elmore, 15 miles from Stowe, offers two-hour day tours using a team of eight dogs. Choose between sitting back and riding inside a padded toboggan while your driver (and the dogs) do the work, or join in the driving using a two-person tandem sled. Either cost $120 per adult ($60 for kids under 12). Tours head out every Wednesday, Friday, Saturday, and Sunday at 10 AM, noon, and 2 PM from mid-December to the end of March, weather permitting.

■ Twilight dog sledding tours leave the **Stowe Mountain Resort** (☏ 802/253-3656 ⊕ www.stowe.com) for one hour every Tuesday and Thursday. The cost is $150 for guests of the resort or $160 for nonguests. This is a sit-down ride inside a padded toboggan.

■ For a taste of how the professionals do it, head to Burke Mountain during **Vermont's Annual Dog Sled Dash** (⊕ www.sleddogdash.com). Usually held in February, the event is the largest of its kind in New England, with more than 100 teams entering for part of the $10,000 purse. Vacationers come to witness the event—put on some snowshoes and trek in to find the best vantage points. If you fancy your own dog-sledding skills, you can register online.

ICE SKATING

If you want outdoor activity but want to stay in one spot and not be outside for a long time—or not even outside at all, but just feel like you are—ice skating might be just your thing. In Vermont you can skate surrounded by the nearby snowcapped mountains or in the comfort of an indoor professional facility.

Pros: excellent activity for groups; easy access (venues are often close to your lodging); inexpensive.
Cons: can be crowded.

■ **The Ice Station at Okemo** (☏ 802/228-1406 ⊕ www.okemo.com), near the Jackson Gore base, is a roof-covered natural ice rink with a warming area for those with comfort in mind. Open mid-December through April from 2 to 9 PM on weekdays and 10 AM to 9 PM on weekends. The cost is $4 for rink access plus $4 to rent skates.

■ Check out **Jay Peak's** (☏ 802/988-2611 ⊕ www.jaypeakresort.com) new, $7 million NHL-sized rink, which opened in 2010 and seats 400 spectators. It costs $6.

■ For the ultimate outdoor skating experience, head to **Lake Morey** in Fairlee, home to America's longest natural ice skating trail. From December to April, the lake freezes over and is groomed for ice skating, providing a magical 4-mi stretch of ice amid forested hillsides. It is maintained by the **Upper Valley Trails Alliance** (☏ 802/649-9075 ⊕ www.uvtrails.org). Bring your own skates or find rentals at the nearby **Nordic Skater** (☏ 866/244-2570 ⊕ www.nordicskater.com), which also runs outdoor skating workshops for $30.

Snowmobiling

Snowshoeing at Trapp Family Lodge

SLEDDING AND TUBING

Want down-the-mountain action but prefer not to ski or board? Tubing is offered at many Vermont ski areas with lifts to tow riders back up, or you can just ask the locals for the best sledding hills. Either way it is especially popular with kids: get ready to hear the question "Can we do it again?" multiple times.

Pros: fun for families and groups; cheaper than skiing.

Cons: rides can be bumpy; not for very young (and short) kids.

■ A standout is Stratton's **Coca Cola Tubing Park** (☎ 800/787–2886 ⊕ www.stratton. com). Careen down any one of four lanes that stretch up to 750 feet long. Kids must be 5 years or older to ride. Open 4 to 8 PM Friday, noon to 8 PM Saturday, and noon to 4 PM Sunday. Tickets are $20 for one hour and $22 for two hours.

■ **Okemo** (☎ 866/706–5366 ⊕ www. okemo.com) offers a tubing facility at its Jackson Gore base area as an après-ski activity from 3 to 6 PM on Friday and Saturday (hours may vary). Take a conveyor-style lift to the top of the hill and then ride down one of four groomed lanes. Tubes rent for $10 an hour. Kids must be at least 42 inches tall to ride.

■ For extra adventure, visitors at **Smugglers' Notch** (☎ 800/419–4615 ⊕ www. smuggs.com) can try airboarding, which uses an inflated sled. First-timers must enroll in an two-hour clinic ($25), after which they can rent and ride for $20 (plus a valid lift ticket) from 2 to 4 PM. Riders must be at least 10 years old and 48 inches tall.

SLEIGH RIDES

Riding a sleigh in Vermont is not quite dashing through the snow on a one-horse open sleigh—the speed is gentle enough that you can sip hot cocoa on the ride, and the sleigh is big, so it usually takes two horses. But you will see Christmas-card-like settings as the sleigh takes you down trails lined with fir trees. Many farms and some resorts offer sleigh rides from December through April, weather permitting. When there is no snow on the ground, horse-drawn carriage rides may be available. The Woodstock area is known as Vermont's horse country, and many local stables have different types of riding options year-round.

Pros: great way to see scenery; fun group activity.

Cons: slow speed; not comfortable if it's windy or snowing hard.

■ The **Mountain Top Inn & Resort** (☎ 802/483–2311 ⊕ www.mountaintopinn.com) just 11 mi from Killington, offers a Sleigh and Dinner Package for $150 for two adults (includes tax and gratuity). The sleigh ride through the resort's wooded trails followed by a three-course dinner is the perfect nightcap. Call for the regularly scheduled 30 minute rides starting at $25 per person, with discounts for children. Private rides are also available.

■ The **Kedron Valley Stables** (☎ 802/457–1480 ⊕ www.kedron.com), in South Woodstock, runs hour-long sleigh rides for up to two people for $125, or for three to seven people for $150. For groups of ten or more, there's an extra charge of $20 per each additional person.

Okemo Resort

Tubing down Magic Mountain.

SNOWMOBILING

Travel a snow-covered highway through densely forested valleys, past snow-capped mountains, and into friendly villages—all without exerting your own energy. Thanks to the extensive trails administered through the state's VAST (Vermont Association of Snow Travelers) system, it's possible to see extensive back country normally beyond the realm of visitors. Snowmobiles usually hold two riders.

Pros: you can cover a lot of ground.
Cons: can be noisy; expensive; controversial because of environmental impact.

■ Snowmobile rentals are available at several ski areas, including **Killington** (☎ 802/422-2121 ⊕ www.killingtonsnowmobiletours.com) and **Okemo** (☎ 800/328-8725 ⊕ www.killingtonsnowmobiletours.com/okemo). Both have one-hour guided tours across groomed ski trails ($94 for one person, $119 for two). If you are feeling more adventurous, take the two-hour backcountry tour through 25 mi of the Calvin Coolidge State Forest ($149 for one person, $195 for two). Helmets and boots are included.

■ For an after-hours perspective, try night snowmobiling at **Smugglers' Notch Resort** (☎ 802/644-8851 ⊕ www.smuggs.com) and **Stratton** (☎ 802/824-5399 ⊕ www.stratton.com). Smugglers' evening tours depart daily on the hour from 5–8 PM from around mid-December to early April, weather permitting. Stratton night tours are available on Saturday nights and holiday nights at from 5–8:30 PM, with additional nights available upon request. The cost is $90 per snowmobile per hour.

SNOWSHOEING

Hikers wanting to explore nature in the winter can do so in depth thanks to snowshoes, which easily attach to your boots. Showshoeing allows you to get up close and personal with the surrounding wilderness. Tranquil trails are easy to find in the Green Mountain State; just avoid those shared with snowmobiles. Some alpine resorts now have networks of snowshoeing trails. Many places that rent cross-country ski gear, like the Trapp Family Lodge, also rent snowshoes. Poles help snowshoers stabilize, especially on uneven and steep terrain.

Pros: inexpensive; great exercise; easy to do (no lesson required).
Cons: small children might get worn out quickly; can be a lot of work; colder than cross-country skiing because you're not moving fast.

■ **Mount Olga Trail** (⊕ www.trails.com) is the most popular snowshoeing destination in Vermont. Located in Wilmington's Molly Stark State Park, the trail is 2.3 mi long. The hike is relatively easy, climaxing with a 360-degree view of southern Vermont and northern Massachusetts.

■ Northeast Vermont's **Kingdom Trails** (☎ 802/626-6005 ⊕ www.kingdomtrails.org) is a network of more than 100 mi of trails used for snowshoeing (hiking and mountain biking in summer). A day pass is $10 for adults, $5 for kids ages 8–15, and free for kids 7 and under. Guests at East Burke's **Inn at Mountain View Farm** (☎ 800/572-4509, ⊕ www.innmtnview.com), the closest inn to the beginning of the trails, receive free access.

River off Route 2 in Waterbury, at North Beach in Burlington, and on the Lamoille River in Jeffersonville. ✉ *849 S. Main St. (Rte. 100), south of Stowe Village* ☎ *802/253–2317* ⊕ *www.umiak.com.*

FISHING

The Fly Rod Shop. This shop provides a guiding service; gives fly-tying, casting, and rod-building classes in winter; rents fly tackle; and sells equipment, including classic and collectible firearms. ✉ *2703 Waterbury Rd. (Rte. 100), 1½ miles south of Stowe* ☎ *802/253–7346, 800/535–9763* ⊕ *www.flyrodshop.com.*

GOLF

Stowe Country Club. Stowe Country Club has a scenic 18-hole, par-72 course; a driving range; and a putting green. Greens fees are $65-$105; cart rental is $18. ✉ *1 Mountain Rd.* ☎ *802/253–4893.*

HIKING

Mt. Mansfield. Ascending Mt. Mansfield makes for a scenic and challenging day hike. Trails lead from Route 108 (Mountain Road) to the summit ridge, where they meet the north-to-south Long Trail. Views from the summit take in New Hampshire's White Mountains, New York's Adirondacks across Lake Champlain, and southern Québec. The Green Mountain Club publishes a trail guide.

ICE-SKATING

Jackson Arena. This is a public ice-skating rink, with skate rentals available. ✉ *1 Park St.* ☎ *802/253–6148.*

SKI AREA

★ **Stowe Mountain Resort.** To be precise, the name of the village is Stowe and the name of the mountain is Mt. Mansfield, but to generations of skiers, the area, the complex, and the region are just plain Stowe. Stowe Mountain Resort is a classic that dates from the 1930s. Even today, the area's mystique attracts as many serious skiers as social ones. Improved snowmaking, new lifts, and free shuttle buses that gather skiers from lodges, inns, and motels along Mountain Road have added convenience to the Stowe experience. Yet the traditions remain: the Winter Carnival in January, the Sugar Slalom in April, ski weeks all winter. Three base lodges provide the essentials, including two on-mountain restaurants.

The resort provides hiking, in-line skating, an alpine slide, gondola rides, and an 18-hole golf course. It also has 27 miles of groomed cross-country trails and 18 miles of backcountry trails. Four interconnecting cross-country ski areas have more than 90 miles of groomed trails within the town of Stowe.

Mt. Mansfield, with an elevation of 4,395 feet and a vertical drop of 2,360 feet, is one of the giants among eastern ski mountains. The mountain's symmetrical shape allows skiers of all abilities long, satisfying runs from the summit. The famous Front Four (National, Liftline, Starr, and Goat) are the intimidating centerpieces for tough, expert runs, yet there is plenty of mellow intermediate skiing, with 59% of the runs rated at that level and 116 trails total. One long beginner trail, the Toll Road Trail, is 3½ miles. Mansfield's satellite sector is a network of intermediate trails and one expert trail off a basin served by a gondola. Spruce Peak, separate from the main mountain, is a teaching hill and offers a pleasant experience for intermediates and beginners. In addition to the high-speed, eight-passenger gondola, Stowe has 16 lifts, including two quads, two triples, and five double chairlifts, plus one handle tow, to service its 116 trails. Night-skiing trails are accessed by the gondola. The resort has 80% snowmaking coverage. Snowboard facilities include a half-pipe and two terrain parks—one for beginners, at Spruce Peak, and one for experts, on the Mt. Mansfield side. Children's programs are headquartered at Spruce Peak, with ski-school programs for ages 4 to 12. ⊠ *5781 Mountain Rd.* ☎ *802/253–3000, 802/253–3600 snow conditions, 800/253–4754 lodging* ⊕ *www.stowe.com.*

SHOPPING

In Stowe, Mountain Road is lined with shops from town up toward the ski area. North of Stowe, shops line Route 100 from Interstate 89.

Cabot Cheese Annex Store. On Route 100 south toward Waterbury, between the cider mill and Ben & Jerry's, you can visit the Cabot Cheese Annex Store. ⊠ *2657 Waterbury-Stowe Rd.(Rte. 100), 2½ miles north of I–89* ☎ *802/244–6334* ⊕ *www.cabotcheese.coop.*

★ **Cold Hollow Cider Mill.** Watch apples pressed into cider at the Cold Hollow Cider Mill. The on-site store sells cider, fabulous cider doughnuts and baked goods, Vermont produce, and specialty foods. Sample all the cold cider you like; kids get free cider popsicles. ⊠ *Rte. 100, 3 miles north of I–89, 3600 Waterbury-Stowe Rd., Waterbury Center* ☎ *800/327–7537, 800/327–7537* ⊕ *www.coldhollow.com.*

NIGHTLIFE AND THE ARTS

THE ARTS

Spruce Peak Performing Arts Center. The Spruce Peak Performing Arts Center sponsors a wide variety of visual and performing arts in the Stowe area, including theater, music, and dance. ⊠ *122 Hourglass Dr.* ☎ *802/760–4634* ⊕ *www.sprucepeakarts.com.*

Stowe Theater Guild. This theater guild performs musicals in summer and plays in September. ⊠ *67 Main St.* ☎ *802/253–3961 summer only* ⊕ *www.stowetheatre.com.*

NIGHTLIFE

Matterhorn Night Club. This nightclub hosts live music and dancing Thursday–Saturday nights and has a separate martini bar. ⊠ *4969 Mountain Rd.* ☎ *802/253–8198* ⊕ *www.matterhornbar.com.*

Rusty Nail. This bar rocks to live music on weekends. ⊠ *1190 Mountain Rd.* ☎ *802/253–6245* ⊕ *rustynailbar.com.*

WHERE TO EAT

$$
AMERICAN

✕ **Harrison's Restaurant.** For an excellent dinner at a warm and unpretentious American bistro, go no farther than Harrison's in downtown Stowe. A lively local scene, cozy booth seating by the fireplace, and a creative menu paired with a variety of fine wines and local beers make this a perfect spot for couples and families alike. Stop in for braised short ribs in blackberry chipotle barbecue sauce, fresh local salads, a sirloin bistro steak, or lobster mac 'n' cheese made with Cabot cheddar. The bar is also inviting—it's a nice place to dine alone or chat over a drink with a local. $ *Average main: $20* ⊠ *25 Main Street, behind*

TD Bank ☎ *802/253–7773* ⊕ *www.harrisonsstowe.com* ⌂ *Reservations essential.*

$$$ ╳ **Hen of the Wood.** Ask any great chef in Vermont where they go to find
ECLECTIC a tremendous meal and Hen of the Wood will inevitably be at the top
★ of their list. The setting is riveting: a converted 1835 gristmill beside
a waterfall. Inside the underground level of the mill a sunken pit for-
merly housing the grindstone is now filled with tables, and uneven stone
walls are dotted floor to ceiling with tiny candles—decidedly romantic.
Sophisticated dishes showcase the abundance of local produce, meat,
cheese, and more. A typical plate on the daily changing menu may fea-
ture sheep milk's gnocchi, a local farm pork loin, short ribs, grassfed rib
eye, and a wild Alaskan halibut. This is a very-near-to-perfect Vermont
dining experience. In the warmer months, beg for a coveted patio table
overlooking a dramatic series of falls. $ *Average main: $25* ✉ *92 Stowe
St., Waterbury* ☎ *802/244–7300* ⊕ *www.henofthewood.com* ⌂ *Reser-
vations essential* ☉ *Closed Sun. and Mon. No lunch.*

$$$ ╳ **Michael's on the Hill.** Swiss-born chef Michael Kloeti trained in Europe
EUROPEAN and New York before opening this dining establishment in a 19th-
century farmhouse outside Stowe. In addition to à la carte options,
Michael's four-course prix-fixe menus ($60) highlight European cuisine
such as roasted rabbit with mirepoix or ravioli with braised autumn
vegetables. There's live piano music weekends. $ *Average main: $32*
✉ *4182 Stowe-Waterbury Rd. (Rte. 100), 6 miles south of Stowe,
Waterbury Center* ☎ *802/244–7476* ⊕ *www.michaelsonthehill.com*
☉ *Closed Tues. No lunch.*

$$ ╳ **Norma's.** With lovely floor-to-ceiling windows in a tasteful, bistrolike
AMERICAN setting overlooking breathtaking Mt. Mansfield, Norma's at Topnotch
Resort and Spa has become much more than a resort restaurant: its
popularity also attracts locals and traveling foodies. After a spa service,
stop by for a plentiful salad made with local organic greens and just-
gathered mushrooms served with a plate of Vermont cheeses or seared
salmon. Drive up for dinner at sunset on the outdoor, torch-lit patio and
sip a lavender blueberry martini or a chili lime margarita. After a day
on the slopes, bring the whole family to enjoy hearty portions from a
creative seasonal menu—crispy duck breast, seared scallops and roasted
fennel, rib eye steak with Bayley Hazen blue cheese and asparagus, and
house-baked desserts. An extensive wine list, friendly atmosphere, and
excellent service make this a top choice. $ *Average main: $24* ✉ *4000
Mountain Rd., Stowe* ☎ *802/451–8686* ⊕ *www.topnotchresort.com*
⌂ *Reservations essential* ☉ *Closed Mon. and Tues.*

$ ╳ **Red Hen Baking Co.** If you're a devotee of artisanal bakeries, it'd be
CAFÉ a mistake not to trek the 15 miles away from Stowe to have lunch,
pick up fresh-baked bread, or try a sweet treat here. Try the ham-and-
cheese croissants, sticky buns, homemade soups, and sandwiches. Red
Hen supplies bread to some of the state's best restaurants, including
Hen of the Wood, and is open 7 am to 6 pm daily. $ *Average main: $8*
✉ *961 Rte. 2, Middlesex* ☎ *802/223–5200* ⊕ *www.redhenbaking.com*
⌂ *Reservations not accepted* ☉ *No dinner.*

WHERE TO STAY

For expanded hotel reviews, visit Fodors.com.

$$ B&B/INN 👶 🏨 **Green Mountain Inn.** Welcoming guests since 1833, this classic redbrick inn is across from the landmark Community Church and gives you access to the buzz of downtown. **Pros:** fun location; lively tavern. **Cons:** farther from skiing than other area hotels. [$] *Rooms from: $169* ✉ *18 Main St.* ☎ *802/253–7301, 800/253–7302* 🌐 *www.greenmountaininn.com* 🛏 *105 rooms* 🍴 *No meals.*

$$$$ B&B/INN 🏨 **Stone Hill Inn.** A contemporary B&B where classical music plays in the halls, each soundproof guest room has a king-size bed. **Pros:** clean and new; very comfortable. **Cons:** expensive; a bit stiff. [$] *Rooms from: $299* ✉ *89 Houston Farm Rd.* ☎ *802/253–6282* 🌐 *www.stonehillinn.com* 🛏 *9 rooms* 🍴 *Breakfast.*

$ HOTEL 👶 🏨 **Stowe Motel & Snowdrift.** This family-owned motel sits on 16 acres across the river from the Stowe recreation path. **Pros:** cheap; complimentary bikes and games. **Cons:** basic, motel-style accommodations. [$] *Rooms from: $125* ✉ *2043 Mountain Rd. (Rte. 108)* ☎ *802/253–7629, 800/829–7629* 🌐 *www.stowemotel.com* 🛏 *52 rooms, 4 suites, 4 houses* 🍴 *Breakfast.*

$$$ RESORT Fodor's Choice ★ 🏨 **Stowe Mountain Lodge.** At the base of Stowe's skiing mountain, this 2008 addition to the Stowe lodging scene would be king of the hill for location alone, but a luxury stay here also includes many ski lodge perks. **Pros:** ski valet and perfect setting; great concierge; activities galore. **Cons:** somewhat sterile in feel; no separate kids' pool. [$] *Rooms from: $250* ✉ *7412 Mountain Rd.* ☎ *802/253–3560* 🌐 *www.stowemountainlodge.com* 🛏 *139 rooms* 🍴 *No meals.*

$$$$ RESORT 🏨 **Stoweflake Mountain Resort and Spa.** Stoweflake has one of the largest spas in the area (along with Topnotch and Stowe Mountain Lodge) and accommodations that range from standard hotel rooms to luxurious suites with fireplaces, refrigerators, double sinks, and whirlpool tubs. **Pros:** nice spa. **Cons:** urban-style resort feels slightly outdated; average food and service. [$] *Rooms from: $279* ✉ *1746 Mountain Rd* ☎ *802/253–7355* 🌐 *www.stoweflake.com* 🛏 *94 rooms, 30 town houses* 🍴 *No meals.*

$$$ RESORT Fodor's Choice ★ 🏨 **Topnotch Resort and Spa.** On 120 acres overlooking Mt. Mansfield, this posh property has a contemporary look and outstanding spa.**Pros:** near the mountain; impressive tennis center and hiking trails; family-friendly; outdoor heated pool and hot tub facing the mountains; beautiful natural setting; good dining; top spa. **Cons:** the big city-style look and feel may not be for everyone. [$] *Rooms from: $250* ✉ *4000 Mountain Rd.* ☎ *802/253–8585, 800/451–8686* 🌐 *www.topnotchresort.com* 🛏 *71 rooms, 9 suites, 14 town houses* 🍴 *Multiple meal plans.*

$$$$ HOTEL 👶 🏨 **Trapp Family Lodge.** Located a few miles up above the town of Stowe, the resort (built by the von Trapp family of *Sound of Music* fame) caters to families and events, offering lodge rooms, villas, and large guesthouses. **Pros:** amazing cross-country ski trails and gorgeous views. **Cons:** caters to families, events, and large tourist groups; can be crowded and lacks an intimate feel. [$] *Rooms from: $270* ✉ *700 Trapp Hill Rd.* ☎ *802/253–8511* 🌐 *www.trappfamilylodge.com* 🛏 *96 rooms* 🍴 *No meals.*

CLOSE UP

Spa Vacations

Vermont's destination spas have come a long way since its *au naturel* mineral springs attracted affluent 19th-century city dwellers looking to escape the heat, but the principle remains the same: a natural place to restore mind and body. There are three big spas in Stowe one in Manchester, and one in Woodstock.

Equinox Resort's Avanyu Spa. The Equinox Resort's Avanyu Spa, with mahogany doors and beadboard wainscoting, feels like a country estate. At one end is an NCAA-length indoor pool and outdoor hot tub; at the other end are the treatment rooms. The signature 80-minute Spirit of Vermont combines Reiki, reflexology, and massage. In the co-ed relaxation room, spa goers can nestle into overstuffed chairs next to a two-sided fireplace made of Vermont gneiss. ⊠ *3567 Rte. 7A, Manchester* ☏ *802/362–4700* ⊕ *www.equinoxresort.com/.*

Spa at Stoweflake. One of the largest spas in New England, Spa at Stoweflake features a massaging hydrotherapeutic waterfall, a Hungarian mineral pool, 30 treatment rooms, a hair and nail salon, and 120 services, such as the Bingham Falls Renewal, named after a local waterfall. This treatment begins with a seasonal body scrub, rinsed off in a Vichy shower, followed by an aromatherapy oil massage. ⊠ *1746 Mountain Rd. (Rte. 108)* ☏ *802/760–1083, 800/253–2232* ⊕ *www.stoweflake.com.*

Spa at Topnotch. The Spa at Topnotch provides an aura of calm, with its birch wood doors and accents, natural light, and cool colors. Signature services include a Vermont wildflower or woodspice treatment, which includes a warm herb wrap, exfoliation, and massage. The spa also has a full-service salon and shop, and classes in tai chi, yoga, and Pilates are offered in the nearby fitness center. ⊠ *4000 Mountain Rd. (Rte. 108)* ☏ *802/253–8585* ⊕ *www.topnotchresort.com.*

The Spa and Wellness Center at Stowe Mountain Lodge. This is a state-of-the-art facility with 19 treatment rooms. Besides the expected array of facials, scrubs, and massages, the spa offers contemporary services like body composition analysis. ⊠ *7412 Mountain Rd. (Rte. 108)* ☏ *802/253–3560* ⊕ *www.stowemountainlodge.com.*

The Spa at the Woodstock Inn and Resort. The newest spa in the state, the Spa at the Woodstock Inn and Resort features a stunning 10,000-square-foot nature-inspired facility with ten treatment rooms, a full-service salon, and sophisticated shop. The spa's elegant, minimalist design accentuates its beautiful setting: natural light pours into the sparkling dressing rooms and the comfortable firelit Great Room, and an outdoor meditation courtyard with a hot soaking pool and Scandinavian-style sauna faces open sky. ⊠ *14 The Green, Woodstock* ☏ *802/457–1100* ⊕ *www.woodstockinn.com/Activities/Spa.*

The Woods Resort and Spa. At Killington, the Woods Resort and Spa is a European spa within an upscale condo complex. At the resort's clubhouse, the spa has a 75-foot indoor pool, sauna, steam room, and weight room. Spa services include massages, hot-stone therapies, facials, salt scrubs, maple-sugar polishes, and mud treatments. ⊠ *53 Woods La., Killington* ☏ *802/422–3139* ⊕ *www.woodsresortandspa.com.*

7

THE CRAFTSBURYS

27 miles northeast of Stowe.

The three small villages of the Craftsburys—Craftsbury Common, Craftsbury, and East Craftsbury—are among Vermont's finest and oldest towns. Handsome white houses and barns, the requisite common, and terrific views make them well worth the drive. Craftsbury General Store in Craftsbury Village is a great place to stock up on picnic supplies and local information. The rolling farmland hints at the way Vermont used to be: the area's sheer distance from civilization and its rugged weather have kept most of the state's development farther south.

WHERE TO STAY

For expanded hotel reviews, visit Fodors.com.

$$ HOTEL **Craftsbury Outdoor Center.** If you think simplicity is bliss and love the outdoors, give this place a try. **Pros:** outdoor focus; activities galore. **Cons:** many rooms have a shared bath; many are sparely furnished. [$] *Rooms from: $199* ✉ *535 Lost Nation Rd., Craftsbury Common* ☎ *802/586–7767, 802/586–7767* 🌐 *www.craftsbury.com* 🛏 *49 rooms, 10 with bath; 4 cabins; 2 suites* 🍴 *Some meals.*

JEFFERSONVILLE

36 miles west of Greensboro, 18 miles north of Stowe.

Jeffersonville is just over Smugglers' Notch from Stowe but miles away in feel and attitude. In summer, you can drive over the notch road as it curves precipitously around boulders that have fallen from the cliffs above, then pass open meadows and old farmhouses and sugar shacks on the way down to town. Below the notch, Smugglers' Notch Ski Resort is the hub of activity year-round. Downtown Jeffersonville, once home to an artists' colony, is quiet but has excellent dining and nice art galleries.

EXPLORING

Boyden Valley Winery. West of Jeffersonville in Cambridge, this winery conducts tours and tastings and showcases an excellent selection of Vermont specialty products and local handicrafts, including fine furniture. Its Big Barn Red is satisfyingly full-bodied, and it makes a brilliant line of ice wines. ✉ *Junction of Rtes. 15 and 104, Cambridge* ☎ *802/644–8151* 🌐 *www.boydenvalley.com* 🕓 *Daily May–Dec. 10–5, Jan.–Apr., Fri.–Sun. 10–5; tours at 11:30 and 1.*

SPORTS AND THE OUTDOORS

KAYAKING

Green River Canoe & Kayak. At the junction of Routes 15 and 108 behind The Family Table Restaurant, this outfitter rents canoes and kayaks on the Lamoille River and leads guided canoe trips to Boyden Valley Winery. ✉ *4807 Rte. 15* ☎ *802/644–8336.*

LLAMA RIDES

Applecheek Farm. Applecheek Farm runs daytime and evening (by lantern) hay and sleigh rides, llama treks, and farm tours. ✉ *567 McFarlane Rd., Hyde Park* ☎ *802/888–4482* 🌐 *www.applecheekfarm.com.*

Northern Vermont Llama Co. The llamas carry everything, including snacks and lunches on half- and full-day treks from May through October along the cross-country ski trails of Smugglers' Notch. Advance reservations are essential. ✉ *766 Lapland Rd., Waterville* ☎ *802/644–2257* ⊕ *www.northernvermontllamaco.com.*

SKI AREA

★ **Smugglers' Notch.** "The granddaddy of all family resorts," Smugglers'
Notch consistently wins accolades for its family programs. Its children's ski school is one of the best in the country—possibly *the* best—but skiers of all levels come here. Smugglers' was the first ski area in the East to designate a triple-black-diamond run—the Black Hole. All the essentials are available in the village at the base of the Morse Mountain lifts, including lodgings, restaurants, and several shops. Smugglers' has a full roster of summertime programs, including pools, complete with waterfalls and waterslides; the Giant Rapid River Ride (the longest water ride in the state); lawn games; mountain biking and hiking programs; and craft workshops for adults. The Treasures Child Care Center accepts children 6 weeks and older.

The self-contained village has outdoor ice-skating and sleigh rides. The numerous snowshoeing programs include family walks and backcountry trips. SmuggsCentral has an indoor pool, hot tub, Funzone playground with slides and miniature golf, and a teen center, open from 5 pm until midnight. In terms of Nordic skiing, the area has 18 miles of groomed and tracked trails and 12 miles of snowshoe trails.

For downhill skiing, Smugglers' has three mountains. The highest, Madonna, with a vertical drop of 2,610 feet, is in the center and connects with a trail network to Sterling (1,500 feet vertical). The third mountain, Morse (1,150 feet vertical), is adjacent to Smugglers' "village" of shops, restaurants, and condos; it's connected to the other peaks by trails and a shuttle bus. The wild, craggy landscape lends a pristine wilderness feel to the skiing experience on the two higher mountains. The tops of each of the mountains have expert terrain—a couple of double-black diamonds (and the only triple-black-diamond trail in the East) make Madonna memorable. Intermediate trails fill the lower sections. Morse has many beginner and advanced beginner trails. Smugglers' 70 trails are served by eight lifts, including six chairs and two surface lifts. Top-to-bottom snowmaking on all three mountains allows for 62% coverage. There are four progression terrain parks, including one for early beginners. Night skiing and snowboarding classes are given at the new Learning and Fun Park.

Ski camps for kids ages 3–17 provide excellent instruction, plus movies, games, and other activities. Wednesday, Thursday, and Saturday are kids' nights at Treasures, with dinner and supervised activities for children ages 3–11. ✉ *4323 VT Rte. 108 South* ☎ *802/644–8851, 800/419–4615* ⊕ *www.smuggs.com.*

SHOPPING
ANTIQUES
Route 15 between Jeffersonville and Johnson is dubbed the "antiques highway."

Green Apple Antique Center. This antiques store has a large collection of pottery, tools, furniture, and more. There's also a good bakery in the back of the store. ✉ *60 Main St.* ☎ *802/644–2989* 🌐 *www.tggweb.com/posies/.*

Smugglers' Notch Antique Center. This shop sells antiques and collectibles from 60 dealers in a rambling barn. ✉ *906 Rte. 108 South* ☎ *802/644–2100* 🌐 *smugglersnotchantiques.com.*

CLOTHING

Fodor's Choice ★ **Johnson Woolen Mills.** This authentic factory store has deals on woolen blankets, yard goods, and the famous Johnson outerwear. ✉ *51 Lower Main St. E, 9 miles east of Jeffersonville, Johnson* ☎ *802/635–2271* 🌐 *www.johnsonwoolenmills.com.*

WHERE TO EAT AND STAY

For expanded hotel reviews, visit Fodors.com.

$ AMERICAN 🍴 **158 Main Restaurant & Bakery.** It's worth the short drive from Smugglers' Notch to try the best and most popular restaurant in neighboring Jeffersonville. Menu selections range from sesame-seared yellowfin tuna with jasmine rice and wasabi to the locals' favorite breakfast, the "Two Eggs Basic," which comes with two eggs any style, homemade toast, and home fries for $3.18. Portions are big; prices are not. Sunday brunch is served 8 am–2 pm. [$] *Average main: $15* ✉ *158 Main St.* ☎ *802/644–8100* 🌐 *www.158Main.com* ✍ *Reservations not accepted* ⏲ *Closed Mon. No dinner Sun.*

$$$$ RESORT Fodor's Choice ★ 🖐 🏨 **Smugglers' Notch Resort.** From watercolor workshops to giant water parks to weeklong camps for kids, this family resort has a plethora of activities. **Pros:** great place for families and to learn to ski. **Cons:** not a romantic getaway for couples. [$] *Rooms from: $388* ✉ *4323 Rte. 108 South* ☎ *802/644–8851, 800/419–4615* 🌐 *www.smuggs.com* 🛏 *550 condominiums* 🍽 *No meals.*

BURLINGTON

31 miles southwest of Jeffersonville, 76 miles south of Montreal, 349 miles north of New York City, 223 miles northwest of Boston.

Fodor's Choice ★ As you drive along Main Street toward downtown Burlington, it's easy to see why this five-college city is so often called one of the most livable small cities in the United States. Downtown is filled with hip restaurants and bars, art galleries, and the Church Street Marketplace—a bustling pedestrian mall with trendy shops, craft vendors, street performers, and sidewalk cafés. Just beyond, Lake Champlain shimmers beneath the towering Adirondacks on the New York shore. On the shores of the lake, Burlington's revitalized waterfront teems with outdoors enthusiasts who bike or stroll along its recreation path, picnic on the grass, and ply the waters in sailboats and motor craft in summer.

EXPLORING

★ 🖐 **ECHO Lake Aquarium and Science Center/Leahy Center for Lake Champlain.** Part of the waterfront's revitalization, this aquarium and science center gives kids a chance to check out 100 hands-on, interactive wind and

BURLINGTON'S LOCAL FOOD MOVEMENT

Burlington is exploding on the national food scene as one of the hubs of the local food movement. Known for its excellent soil and abundance of local organic farms—as is showcased in its huge weekly farmers' market (Saturdays, May through October) and popular outdoor summertime farm suppers—this health-conscious and liberal city is home to restaurants and markets with a foodie's focus on fresh, high-quality ingredients rivaling those of a much larger city. Burlington residents heading home from work are likely to be seen biking to pick up their weekly CSA-share at the Intervale (the city's huge web of community gardens), doing some weeding in their own urban garden plots, or stopping by one of the farms to pick berries or flowers on their way to a dinner party.

water exhibits and a sunken shipwreck. ⊠ *1 College St.* ☎ *802/864– 1848* ⊕ *www.echovermont.org* ⊠ *$12.50* ⊙ *Daily 10–5, Thurs. until 8.*

The Ethan Allen Homestead Museum. One of the earliest residents of the Intervale area was Ethan Allen, Vermont's Revolutionary-era guerrilla fighter, who remains a captivating figure. Exhibits at the on-site visitor center answer questions about his flamboyant life. The house holds such frontier hallmarks as rough saw-cut boards and an open hearth for cooking. A re-created Colonial kitchen garden resembles the one the Allens would have had. After the tour and multimedia presentation, you can stretch your legs on scenic trails along the Winooski River. ⊠ *1 Ethan Allen Homestead, off Rte. 127, north of Burlington* ☎ *802/865–4556* ⊕ *www.ethanallenhomestead.org* ⊠ *$5* ⊙ *May–Oct., Mon.–Sat. 10–4, Sun. 1–4.*

University of Vermont. Crowning the hilltop above Burlington is the campus of the University of Vermont, known simply as UVM for the abbreviation of its Latin name, Universitas Viridis Montis—the University of the Green Mountains. With more than 10,000 students, UVM is the state's principal institution of higher learning. The most architecturally interesting buildings have gorgeous lake views and face the green, which has a statue of UVM founder Ira Allen, Ethan's brother. ⊠ *85 South Prospect St.* ☎ *802/656–3131* ⊕ *www.uvm.edu.*

Magic Hat Brewing Company. You can tour the Magic Hat brewery—a leader in Vermont's microbrewery revolution—which puts out 400 bottles a minute. The tour includes free beer samples and their Growler Bar has 48 beers on tap. ⊠ *5 Bartlett Bay Rd., South Burlington* ☎ *802/658– 2739* ⊕ *magichat.net* ⊠ *Free* ⊙ *Open Mon.–Sat. 10–6, Sun. noon–5. Tours Thurs. and Fri. 3, 4, and 5; Sat. 1, 2, 3, 4, and 5; Sun. 1:30.*

SPORTS AND THE OUTDOORS

BEACHES

North Beaches. The North Beaches are on the northern edge of Burlington. Leddy Beach (on Leddy Park Road off North Avenue) is a good spot for sailboarding, and the smaller beaches a bit further north for kiteboarding. ⊠ *North Beach Park off North Ave., 52 Institute Rd.* ☎ *802/864–0123* ⊕ *www.enjoyburlington.com/northbeach.cfm.*

BIKING

Burlington's 10-mile Cycle the City loop runs along the waterfront, connecting several city parks and beaches. It also passes the Community Boathouse and runs within several blocks of downtown restaurants and shops.

North Star Sports. North Star Sports rents bicycles and provides maps of bicycle routes. ⊠ *100 Main St.* ☎ *802/863–3832* ⊕ *northstarsportsvt.com.*

Ski Rack. Ski Rack rents and services bikes and skis, sells a wide array of sports clothing and equipment, and provides maps. ⊠ *85 Main St.* ☎ *802/658–3313, 800/882–4530* ⊕ *www.skirack.com.*

BOATING

Burlington Community Boathouse. Burlington Community Boathouse rents 19-foot sailboats and also houses the city's marina and summertime waterfront watering hole, Splash, which is the best place to have a drink and watch the sunset over the lake. ⊠ *Foot of College St., Burlington Harbor* ☎ *802/865–3377.*

Shoreline Cruises. Shoreline Cruise's *Spirit of Ethan Allen III,* a 500-passenger, three-level cruise vessel, has narrated cruises and dinner and sunset sailings with awesome views of the Adirondacks and Green Mountains. ⊠ *Burlington Boat House, 348 Flynn Ave.* ☎ *802/862–8300* ⊕ *www.soea.com* ☎ *$12* ⊗ *Cruises late May–mid-Oct., daily 10–9.*

Waterfront Boat Rentals. Waterfront Boat Rentals rents kayaks, canoes, rowboats, skiffs, and Boston Whalers. Affordable sailing lessons are available. ⊠ *Foot of Maple St. on Perkins Pier, Burlington Harbor* ☎ *802/864–4858* ⊕ *www.waterfrontboatrentals.com.*

SKI AREA

Bolton Valley Resort. About 25 miles from Burlington, Bolton Valley Resort is a family favorite. In addition to 61 downhill ski trails (more than half rated for intermediates), Bolton has night skiing Wednesday–Saturday, 62 miles of cross-country and snowshoe trails, and a sports center. ⊠ *4302 Bolton Valley Access Rd., Bolton* ☎ *802/434–3444, 877/926–5866* ⊕ *www.boltonvalley.com.*

OFF THE BEATEN PATH

Green Mountain Audubon Nature Center. This is a wonderful place to discover Vermont's outdoor wonders. The center's 300 acres of diverse habitats are a sanctuary for all things wild, and the 5 miles of trails provide an opportunity to explore the workings of differing natural communities. Events include dusk walks, wildflower and birding rambles, nature workshops, and educational activities for children and adults. The center is 18 miles southeast of Burlington. ⊠ *255 Sherman Hollow Rd., Huntington* ☎ *802/434–3068* ☎ *Donations accepted* ⊗ *Grounds daily dawn–dusk, center Mon.–Sat. 8–4.*

Vermont by Bike

CLOSE UP

Road biking in the Green Mountains.

Vermont has more than 14,000 miles of roads, and almost 80% of them are town roads that see little high-speed traffic, making them ideal for scenic bike rides. The state is also threaded with thousands of miles of dirt roads suitable for mountain biking. Although mountain-bike trails and old farm and logging roads wind through the Green Mountain State, most are on private property and are, therefore, not mapped. Several mountain-biking centers around the state have extensive trail networks (and maps) that will keep avid fat-tire fans happy for a few hours or a few days. To road bike in Vermont, you'll want a map and preferably a bicycle with at least 10 gears. The only roads that prohibit cycling are the four-lane highways and Routes 7 and 4 in Rutland.

TOP ROAD BIKING ROUTES:
To make a relatively easy 16-mile loop, begin at the blinker on U.S. 7 in **Shelburne** and follow Mt. Philo Road south to Hinesburg Road, then west

to Charlotte. Lake Road, Orchard Road, and Mouth of River Road go past orchards and berry fields. Bostwick Road returns to U.S. 7.

In the heart of the central Green Mountains is a moderate 18-mile loop on Routes 4, 100, and 100A that passes Calvin Coolidge's home in **Plymouth Notch.**

West of **Rutland** is a beautiful 27-mile ride on Routes 140, 30, and 133 that passes swimming holes, then hugs the shore of Lake St. Catherine. Start in Middletown Springs.

A scenic 43-mile ride in the **Northeast Kingdom** passes through pleasant Peacham and the birches and maples of Groton State Forest. Start in Danville and follow Peacham Road, then Routes 302 and 232 and U.S. 2.

For a real test, try the 48-mile ride over **Middlebury and Brandon Gaps** on Routes 125 and 73, which connect via Routes 153 and 100.

7

SHOPPING

CRAFTS

Bennington Potters North. In addition to its popular pottery, Bennington Potters North stocks interesting gifts, glassware, furniture, and other housewares. ⊠ *127 College St.* ☎ *802/863–2221, 800/205–8033* ⊕ *www.benningtonpotters.com.*

Vermont State Craft Center/Frog Hollow. Vermont State Craft Center/Frog Hollow is a nonprofit collective that sells contemporary and traditional crafts by more than 200 Vermont artisans. ⊠ *85 Church St.* ☎ *802/863–6458* ⊕ *www.froghollow.org.*

FOOD

★ **Lake Champlain Chocolates.** This chocolatier makes sensational truffles, caramels, hot chocolate, candies, and wonderful gift baskets. The chocolates are all-natural, made in Vermont, and make a great edible souvenir. ■TIP→ The factory store is on Pine Street, but they also have a smaller store in town (on Church Street). ⊠ *750 Pine St., Burlington* ☎ *800/465–5909* ⊕ *www.lakechamplainchocolates.com.*

MARKETS

Fodor's Choice ★ **Burlington Farmers' Market.** Burlington's lively farmers' market is an absolute must-see when visiting in summer or fall. Located in the center of town, the market is jam-packed with local farmers selling their colorful array of organic produce, flowers, baked goods, maple syrup, meats, cheeses, prepared foods, and crafts. There's live music on the green, fresh cider and doughnuts in the fall, and the best people-watching in the state. ■TIP→ Bring your own bag; you'll need it! ⊠ *City Hall Park, corner of College St. and St. Paul St.* ☎ *802/310–5172* ⊕ *www.burlingtonfarmersmarket.org* ⊘ *Late May–Oct., Sat. 8:30–2, Nov.–Apr. every other Sat.10–2 indoors at Memorial Auditorium.*

Church Street Marketplace. This pedestrian thoroughfare is lined with boutiques, cafés, restaurants, and street vendors. Check out some of the local handcrafted favorites, including Champlain Chocolates and Danforth Pewter. ⊠ *2 Church St., Suite 2A* ☎ *802/863–1648* ⊕ *www.churchstmarketplace.com.*

NIGHTLIFE AND THE ARTS

THE ARTS

Fire House Art Gallery. The Fire House Art Gallery exhibits works by local artists. ⊠ *135 Church St.* ☎ *802/865–7165* ⊕ *www.burlingtoncityarts.com.*

★ **Flynn Theatre for the Performing Arts.** A grandiose old structure, the Flynn Theatre is the cultural heart of Burlington. It schedules the Vermont Symphony Orchestra, theater, dance (Alvin Ailey company comes each year), big-name musicians like Feist, Lucinda Williams, and the like, and lectures, recently from writer David Sedaris. ⊠ *153 Main St.* ☎ *802/652–4500 information, 802/863–5966 tickets* ⊕ *www.flynncenter.org.*

Saint Michael's Playhouse. Saint Michael's Playhouse stages performances in the McCarthy Arts Center, about a 10-minute drive out of Burlington. ⊠ *1 Winooski Park, St., Michael's College, Rte. 15, Colchester* ☎ *802/654–2281 box office, 802/654–2281 administrative office* ⊕ *www.saintmichaelsplayhouse.org.*

Vermont Symphony Orchestra. The Vermont Symphony Orchestra performs throughout the state year-round and at the Flynn from October through May. ✉ *2 Church St.* ☎ *802/864–5741* 🌐 *www.vso.org.*

NIGHTLIFE

★ **The Farmhouse Tap & Grill.** The Tap Room, downstairs from the hugely popular Farmhouse Tap & Grill, serves a wide range of local artisan beers, wines, and small plates in a cozy and buzzing fireside setting reminsicent of a Colorado lodge tavern. Featuring local foods—try the great cheese plates—and a seasonal outdoor beer garden in summertime, this is the place to see and be seen in downtown Burlington. ✉ *160 Bank St.* ☎ *802/859–0888* 🌐 *www.farmhousetg.com.*

Higher Ground. National and local musicians come to Higher Ground, a local music venue about 10 minutes out of town. ✉ *1214 Williston Rd., South Burlington* ☎ *802/652–0777* 🌐 *www.highergroundmusic.com.*

Leunig's Bistro & Cafe. Right in the center of town, Leunig's has a Parisian bistro feel and is a great place to go for a glass of wine or a cocktail. ✉ *115 Church St.* ☎ *802/863–3759* 🌐 *www.leunigsbistro.com.*

Nectar's. The band Phish got its start at Nectar's, which is always jumping to the sounds of local bands and never charges a cover. ✉ *188 Main St.* ☎ *802/658–4771* 🌐 *www.liveatnectars.com.*

The Vermont Pub & Brewery. The Vermont Pub & Brewery makes its own beer and is one of the most popular casual spots in town. Folk musicians play here regularly. ✉ *144 College St.* ☎ *802/865–0500* 🌐 *www.vermontbrewery.com.*

7

WHERE TO EAT

$$ PIZZA Fodor's Choice ★ 🍴 **American Flatbread–Burlington Hearth.** It might be worth going to college in Burlington just to be able to gather with friends at this wildly popular, charming, and delicious organic pizza place. Seating is first-come, first-served and the scene is bustling with locals and visitors sipping on house-made brews. The wood-fired clay-dome oven plus all-organic ingredients creates masterful results like the Punctuated Equilibrium, which has kalamata olives, roasted red peppers, local goat cheese, fresh rosemary, red onions, mozzarella, and garlic, or the "new Vermont sausage," topped with local nitrate-free maple-fennel sausage. Fresh salads topped with local goat or blue cheese are also a popular favorite. Here's to the college life! There are also locations in Middlebury and Waitsfield. [$] *Average main: $17* ✉ *115 St. Paul St.* ☎ *802/861–2999* 🌐 *americanflatbread.com* ✍ *Reservations not accepted.*

$ AMERICAN ★ 🍴 **Farmhouse Tap & Grill.** Farmhouse is one of the two most popular restaurants in town (the other being American Flatbread), but don't be put off by the line on a typical weekend night—it's worth it! Known for their all-local beef, cheese, and produce, this farm-to-table experience is laid-back in style but one of the finest meals in the area. Specialities include excellent burgers, chicken and biscuits, wonderful local cheese and charcuterie plates, and a great wine and craft beer selection. ■ TIP→ **Put your name on the list and have a drink at their cozy downstairs Tap Room or outdoor beer garden while you wait.** Or, if the wait feels too long, try El Cortijo, their small Mexican taqueria just down the street, for a locally raised beef or chicken taco and a terrific margarita.

$ *Average main: $15* ⊠ *160 Bank St., Burlington* ☎ *802/859–0888* ⊕ *www.farmhousetg.com.*

$$$ ✕ **Leunig's Bistro & Cafe.** Church Street's popular café delivers alfresco bis-
CAFÉ tro cuisine, a friendly European-style bar, and live jazz Tuesday–Thurs-
day evenings in warm weather. Favorite entrées include salade nicoise,
soupe au pistou, and lavender-and-peppercorn-crusted tuna; if you're
a fan of crème brûlée, theirs is the best in town. An expanded upstairs
lounge offers cocktails, a nice wine selection, and lighter fare, such as a
local cheese plate. A prix-fixe dinner for two for $30, served daily 5–6,
is one of the city's best bargains. ■TIP→ This is a great spot for week-
end brunch. $ *Average main: $25* ⊠ *115 Church St.* ☎ *802/863–3759*
⊕ *www.leunigsbistro.com.*

$ ✕ **Penny Cluse Cafe.** This popular breakfast and brunch spot is often busy
AMERICAN and buzzing with activity. Weekend lines can be long, but locals think
♻ it's worth the wait for their famous gingerbread blueberry pancakes,
warm buscuits with herb gravy, huevos rancheros, and homemade
banana bread. $ *Average main: $10* ⊠ *169 Cherry St.* ☎ *802/651–8834*
⊕ *www.pennycluse.com* ⊗ *No dinner.*

$$$ ✕ **Trattoria Delia.** Didn't manage to rent that villa in Umbria this year?
ITALIAN The next best thing is this charming Italian country eatery around the
corner from City Hall Park. Game and fresh produce are the stars; try
the wild boar braised in red wine, tomatoes, rosemary, and sage served
on soft polenta. Wood-grilled items are also a specialty. ■TIP→ In winter, try to reserve a table near the fire. $ *Average main: $25* ⊠ *152 St.*
Paul St. ☎ *802/864–5253* ⊕ *www.trattoriadelia.com* ☖ *Reservations*
essential ⊗ *No lunch.*

$$ ✕ **A Single Pebble Restaurant.** The creative, authentic Chinese selections
CHINESE served on the first floor of this charming residential row house include
traditional clay-pot dishes as well as wok specialties, such as beef pre-
pared with fresh baby bok choy and kung pao chicken. The dry-fried
green beans (sautéed with flecks of pork, black beans, preserved veg-
etables, and garlic) are a house specialty, as is "mock eel," braised
shiitake mushrooms served in a crispy ginger sauce. All dishes can be
made without meat. ■TIP→ Try their dim sum on Sundays from 11:30–
1:45. $ *Average main: $21* ⊠ *133 Bank St.* ☎ *802/865–5200* ⊕ *www.*
asinglepebble.com ☖ *Reservations essential.*

AMERICAN ✕ **Stone Soup.** A perfect place to stop for a delicious and healthful lunch
or early dinner, Stone Soup offers all-local produce and organic ingre-
dients showcased in their fresh salads, wonderful soups, homemade
breads, and wide array of baked goods. There are many veggie and
vegan options here. $ *Average main: $12* ⊠ *211 College St.* ☎ *802/862–*
7616 ⊕ *www.stonesoupvt.com* ▭ *No credit cards* ⊗ *Closed Sun.*

WHERE TO STAY

For expanded hotel reviews, visit Fodors.com.

$$$ ⛉ **Courtyard Burlington Harbor.** A relatively new property a block from the
HOTEL lake and a five-minute walk into town, this clean, attractive hotel has
♻ a pretty bar and lobby area with a fireplace and couches, cookies upon
arrival, and excellent beds. **Pros:** right in town; clean and convenient
to everything. **Cons:** lacks local charm; a bit sterile in feel. $ *Rooms*

Burlington's pedestrian-only Church Street Marketplace and the nearby shores of Lake Champlain are great for exploring.

from: $229 ✉ *25 Cherry St.* ☎ *802/864–4700* ⊕ *www.marriott.com* 🛏 *150 rooms* ⏍ *No meals.*

$$$$
HOTEL

🏨 **The Essex.** "Vermont's Culinary Resort" is a hotel and conference center about 10 miles from downtown Burlington, with two restaurants run by the New England Culinary Institute. **Pros:** daily cooking classes; free airport shuttle. **Cons:** odd location in suburb of Burlington; sterile feel; no local scene. ⑂ *Rooms from: $350* ✉ *70 Essex Way, off Rte. 289, Essex Junction* ☎ *802/878–1100, 800/727–4295* ⊕ *www.vtculinaryresort.com* 🛏 *60 rooms, 60 suites* ⏍ *No meals.*

$$
B&B/INN
★

🏨 **The Lang House on Main Street.** Within walking distance of downtown but in the historic hill section of town, this grand 1881 Victorian home is full of fine woodwork, plaster detailing, and stained-glass windows. **Pros:** family-friendly; interesting location; well-run. **Cons:** street can be busy. ⑂ *Rooms from: $185* ✉ *360 Main St.* ☎ *802/652–2500, 877/919–9799* ⊕ *www.langhouse.com* 🛏 *11 rooms* ⏍ *Breakfast.*

$$
B&B/INN
★

🏨 **Willard Street Inn.** High in the historic hill section of Burlington, this ivy-covered grand house with an exterior marble staircase and English gardens incorporates elements of Queen Anne and Colonial/Georgian Revival styles. **Pros:** lovely old mansion loaded with character; friendly attention. **Cons:** long walk to downtown; feels a bit "stuffy." ⑂ *Rooms from: $180* ✉ *349 S. Willard St.* ☎ *802/651–8710, 800/577–8712* ⊕ *www.willardstreetinn.com* 🛏 *14 rooms* ⏍ *Breakfast.*

SHELBURNE

5 miles south of Burlington.

A few miles south of Burlington, the Champlain Valley gives way to fertile farmland, affording stunning views of the rugged Adirondacks across the lake. In the middle of this farmland is the village of Shelburne (and just farther south, beautiful and more rural Charlotte), chartered in the mid-18th century and partly a bedroom community for Burlington. Stunning Shelburne Farms is worth at least a few hours of exploring, as are Shelburne Orchards in fall when you can pick your own apples and drink fresh cider while admiring breathtaking views of the lake and mountains beyond.

GETTING HERE AND AROUND

Shelburne is south of Burlington after the town of South Burlington, notable for its very un-Vermont traffic and commercial and fast food–franchised stretch of U.S. 7. It's easy to confuse Shelburne Farms—2 miles west of town on the lake, with Shelburne Museum, which is just south of town directly on Route 7, but you'll want to make time for both.

EXPLORING

Fodor's Choice
★
🧒
Shelburne Farms. Founded in the 1880s as a private estate for two very rich New Yorkers, this 1,400-acre farm is much more than an exquisite landscape: it's an educational and cultural resource center with, among other things, a working dairy farm, a Children's Farmyard (with hands-on workshops throughout the day), daily viewings of various stages of the farm's famous cheese being made, and a bakery whose aroma of fresh bread and pastries is an olfactory treat. It's a brilliant place for parents to expose their kids to the dignity of farm work and the joys of compassionate animal husbandry—indeed, children and adults alike will get a kick out of hunting for eggs in the oversize coop and milking a cow. Frederick Law Olmsted, co-creator of New York's Central Park, designed the magnificent grounds overlooking Lake Champlain. If you fall in love with the scenery, arrange a romantic dinner at the lakefront mansion or spend the night. ⊠ *West of U.S. 7, 1611 Harbor Rd.* ☎ *802/985–8498* ⊕ *www.shelburnefarms.org* 🔁 *$8* ⊙ *Visitor center and shop daily 10–5; tours mid-May–mid-Oct. (last tour at 3:30); walking trails daily 10–4, weather permitting.*

Fodor's Choice
★
Shelburne Museum. You can trace much of New England's history simply by wandering through the 45 acres and 37 buildings of this museum. The outstanding 80,000-object collection of Americana consists of 18th- and 19th-century period homes and furniture, fine and folk art, farm tools, more than 200 carriages and sleighs, John James Audubon prints, an old-fashioned jail, and even a private railroad car from the days of steam. The museum also has an assortment of duck decoys, an old stone cottage, a display of early toys, and the *Ticonderoga*, a side-wheel steamship, grounded amid lawn and trees. ⊠ *5555 Shelburne Rd. (U.S. 7)* ☎ *802/985–3346* ⊕ *www.shelburnemuseum.org* 🔁 *$20* ⊙ *May–Oct., daily 10–5.*

Shelburne Vineyard. South of Shelburn Museum on Route 7 you'll see rows of organically grown vines. Visit the attractive tasting room and learn how wine is made. ✉ *6308 Shelburne Rd. (Rte. 7)* ☎ *802/985–8222* 🌐 *www.shelburnevineyard.com* 🎟 *$5.*

Vermont Teddy Bear Company. On the 25-minute tour of this fun-filled factory you'll hear more puns than you ever thought possible and learn how a few homemade bears, sold from a cart on Church Street, have turned into a multimillion-dollar business. A children's play tent is set up outdoors in summer, and you can wander the beautiful 57-acre property. ✉ *6655 Shelburne Rd.* ☎ *802/985–3001* 🌐 *www.vermontteddybear.com* 🎟 *Tour $2* ⏲ *Tours Mon.–Sat. 9:30–5, Sun. 10:30–4; store daily 9–6.*

WORD OF MOUTH

"Shelburne Farms is very very cool.... [The] view from the back lawn over Lake Champlain that's like being in Italy looking out at Lake Como.... Swimming in the lake. Lots and lots of bike trails. The Farm Barn like a castle in Normandy with cows kids can milk, and roosters strutting around and sheep looking sheepish.... We played billiards and sat on Adirondack chairs looking at the lake for a long time. We had afternoon tea at 3:30 and dinner at 8:30. It was wonderful."

—santamonica

SHOPPING

The Shelburne Country Store. When you enter the The Shelburne Country Store, you'll step back in time. Walk past the potbellied stove and take in the aroma emanating from the fudge neatly piled behind huge antique glass cases. The store specializes in candles, weather vanes, glassware, and local foods. ✉ *29 Falls Rd., Village Green off U.S. 7* ☎ *800/660–3657* 🌐 *www.shelburnecountrystore.com/.*

WHERE TO EAT

$$ ECLECTIC 🍴 **The Bearded Frog.** This is the top restaurant in the Shelburne area, perfect for a casual dinner in its cozy bar or for a more upscale ambience in the attractive, sophisticated dining room. In the bar, try the soups, quiche, burgers, and terrific cocktails. The somewhat more formal dining room serves fresh local salads topped with local blue cheese, seared scallops, excellent grilled fish, steaks, and decadent desserts. [$] *Average main: $20* ✉ *5247 Shelburne Rd.* ☎ *802/985–9877* 🌐 *www.thebeardedfrog.com* ⏲ *No lunch.*

$$$ AMERICAN Fodor's Choice ★ 🍴 **The Dining Room at the Inn at Shelburne Farms.** Dinner here will make you dream of F. Scott Fitzgerald. Piano music wafts from the library, and you can carry a drink through the rooms of this 1880s mansion, gazing across a long lawn and formal gardens on the shore of dark Lake Champlain—you'll swear Jay Gatsby is about to come down the stairs. Count on just-grown ingredients that come from the market gardens as well as flavorful locally grown venison, beef, pork, and chicken. On weekends a spectacular spread of produce is set up next to a cocktail bar with fresh specialties. The dining room overlooks the lake shore, and Sunday brunch (not served in May) is the area's best. Breakfast is served

Shelburne Museum's many attractions include the Ticonderoga steamship and other pieces from New England's past.

as well. $ *Average main: $27* ✉ *1611 Harbor Rd.* ☎ *802/985–8498* ⊕ *www.shelburnefarms.org* ⊙ *Closed mid-May–mid-Oct.*

WHERE TO STAY

For expanded hotel reviews, visit Fodors.com.

$$$
B&B/INN
Fodor'sChoice
★

The Inn at Shelburne Farms. It's hard not to feel a little bit like an aristocrat at this exquisite turn-of-the-20th-century Tudor-style inn, one of the most memorable properties in the country. **Pros:** stately lakefront setting in a fantastic historic mansion; great service; wonderful value; great restaurant. **Cons:** some may miss not having a TV in the room; closed in winter; must book far in advance. $ *Rooms from: $225* ✉ *1611 Harbor Rd.* ☎ *802/985–8498* ⊕ *www.shelburnefarms. org* ⇗ *24 rooms, 17 with bath; 2 cottages* ⊙ *Closed mid-Oct.–mid-May* ⦿ *No meals.*

VERGENNES

12 miles south of Shelburne.

Vermont's oldest city, founded in 1788, is also the third oldest in New England. The downtown area is a compact district of restored Victorian homes and public buildings with a few good eateries sprinkled throughout. Main Street slopes down to Otter Creek Falls, where cannonballs were made during the War of 1812. The statue of Thomas MacDonough on the green immortalizes the victor of the Battle of Plattsburgh in 1814.

ESSENTIALS

Visitor Information Addison County Chamber of Commerce ✉ *93 Court St., Middlebury* ☎ *802/388–7951, 800/733–8376* 🌐 *www.addisoncounty.com.*

OFF THE BEATEN PATH

Lake Champlain Maritime Museum. This museum documents centuries of activity on the historically significant lake. Climb aboard a replica of Benedict Arnold's Revolutionary War gunboat moored in the lake, learn about shipwrecks, and watch craftsmen work at traditional boatbuilding and blacksmithing. Among the exhibits are a nautical archaeology center, a conservation laboratory, and a restaurant. ✉ *Basin Harbor Rd., 7 miles west of Vergennes, 4472 Basin Harbor Rd., Basin Harbor* ☎ *802/475–2022* 🌐 *www.lcmm.org* 🎟 *$10* 🕒 *May–mid-Oct., daily 10–5.*

SHOPPING

Dakin Farm. Cob-smoked ham, aged cheddar cheese, maple syrup made on-site, and other specialty foods can be found here. You can also visit the ham smokehouse and watch the waxing and sealing of the cheeses. ✉ *5797 Rte. 7, 5 miles north of Vergennes* ☎ *800/993–2546* 🌐 *www.dakinfarm.com.*

WHERE TO EAT AND STAY

For expanded hotel reviews, visit Fodors.com.

$$ ECLECTIC

🍴 **Starry Night Café.** This chic restaurant is one of the hottest spots around, and it's increased in size to meet growing demand. Appetizers include house specials such as honey-chili-glazed shrimp and gazpacho. Among the French-meets-Asian entrées are lobster-stuffed sole, pan-seared scallops, and grilled New York steak. [$] *Average main: $24* ✉ *5371 Rte. 7, 5 miles north of Vergennes, Ferrisburg* ☎ *802/877–6316* 🌐 *www.starrynightcafe.com* ✍ *Reservations essential* 🕒 *Closed Mon. and Tues. No lunch.*

$$$$ RESORT Fodor's Choice ★ 👶

🏨 **Basin Harbor Club.** On 700 acres overlooking Lake Champlain, this ultimate family resort provides luxurious accommodations and a full roster of amenities, including an 18-hole golf course, boating (with a 40-foot tour boat), a 3,200-foot grass airstrip, and daylong children's programs. **Pros:** gorgeous lakeside property; activities galore. **Cons:** open only half the year; pricey. [$] *Rooms from: $370* ✉ *4800 Basin Harbor Rd.* ☎ *802/475–2311, 800/622–4000* 🌐 *www.basinharbor.com* 🛏 *36 rooms, 2 suites in 3 guesthouses, 77 cottages* 🕒 *Closed mid-Oct.–mid-May* 🍽 *Breakfast.*

LAKE CHAMPLAIN ISLANDS

43 miles north of Vergennes, 20 miles northwest of Shelburne, 15 miles northwest of Burlington.

Lake Champlain, which stretches more than 100 miles south from the Canadian border, forms the northern part of the boundary between New York and Vermont. Within it is an elongated archipelago composed of several islands—Isle La Motte, North Hero, Grand Isle, South Hero—and the Alburg Peninsula. With a temperate climate, the islands hold several apple orchards and are a center of water recreation in summer and ice fishing in winter. A scenic drive through the islands on U.S.

2 begins at Interstate 89 and travels north to Alburg Center; Route 78 takes you back to the mainland.

ESSENTIALS

Visitor Information Lake Champlain Regional Chamber of Commerce ⊠ *60 Main St., Suite 100, Burlington* ☎ *802/863–3489, 877/686–5253* ⊕ *www. vermont.org.* **Lake Champlain Islands Chamber of Commerce** ⊠ *3501 US Rte. 2, Suite 100, North Hero* ☎ *802/372–8400, 800/262–5226* ⊕ *www. champlainislands.com.*

EXPLORING

Herrmann's Royal Lipizzan Stallions. These beautiful stallions, cousins of the noble white horses bred in Austria since the 16th century, perform intricate dressage maneuvers for delighted spectators for a brief period each summer on North Hero. These acrobatic horses are descendants of animals rescued from the turmoil of World War II by General George Patton and members of the Herrmann family. ⊠ *U.S. 2, North Hero* ☎ *802/372–5683* ☞ *Barn visits free between performances, shows $17* ☉ *Early July–late Aug., Thurs. and Fri. at 6 pm, weekends at 2:30 pm.*

Snow Farm Vineyard and Winery. Vermont's first vineyard and grape winery was started here in 1996; today it specializes in nontraditional botanical hybrid grapes to withstand the local climate. Take a self-guided tour, sip some samples in the tasting room, and picnic and listen to music at the free concerts on the lawn Thursday evenings mid-June through Labor Day. ⊠ *190 W. Shore Rd., South Hero* ☎ *802/372–9463* ⊕ *www.snowfarm.com* ☞ *Free* ☉ *May–Dec., daily 10–5; tours May–Oct. at 11 and 2.*

St. Anne's Shrine. This spot marks the site where French soldiers and Jesuits put ashore in 1665 and built a fort, creating Vermont's first European settlement. The state's first Roman Catholic Mass was celebrated here on July 26, 1666. ⊠ *92 St. Anne's Rd., Isle La Motte* ☎ *802/928–3362* ⊕ *www.saintannesshrine.org* ☞ *Free* ☉ *Mid-May–mid-Oct., daily 9–4.*

SPORTS AND THE OUTDOORS

Apple Island Resort. Apple Island Resort rents sailboats, rowboats, canoes, kayaks, and motorboats. ⊠ *71 US Rte. 2, South Hero* ☎ *802/372–3800* ⊕ *appleislandresort.com.*

Hero's Welcome. Hero's Welcome rents bikes, canoes, kayaks, and paddleboats. ⊠ *3537 U.S. 2, North Hero* ☎ *802/372–4161, 800/372–4376* ⊕ *heroswelcome.com.*

Missisquoi National Wildlife Refuge. On the mainland east of the Alburg Peninsula, Missisquoi National Wildlife Refuge consists of 6,642 acres of federally protected wetlands, meadows, and woods. It's a beautiful area for bird-watching, canoeing, or walking nature trails. ⊠ *29 Tabor Rd., 36 miles north of Burlington, Swanton* ☎ *802/868–4781* ⊕ *missisquoi.fws.gov.*

Sand Bar State Park. Sand Bar State Park has one of Vermont's best swimming beaches, a snack bar, changing room, and boat rental concession. ⊠ *1215 U.S. 2, South Hero* ☎ *802/893–2825* ⊕ *www.vtstateparks.com/ htm/sandbar.htm* ☞ *$3.50* ☉ *Mid-May–early-Sept., daily dawn–dusk.*

WHERE TO STAY

For expanded hotel reviews, visit Fodors.com.

$$$ B&B/INN **North Hero House Inn and Restaurant.** This inn has four buildings right on Lake Champlain, including the 1891 Colonial Revival main house with nine guest rooms, the restaurant, a pub room, library, and sitting room. **Pros:** relaxed vacation complex; superb lakefront setting. **Cons:** open just May to November. [$] *Rooms from: $225* ✉ *U.S. 2, 3643 US Rural Rte. 2, North Hero* ☎ *802/372–4732, 888/525–3644* 🌐 *www.northherohouse.com* 🛏 *26 rooms* 🕘 *Closed Dec.–Apr.* 🍴 *Breakfast.*

$ HOTEL **Ruthcliffe Lodge & Restaurant.** Good food and splendid scenery make this off-the-beaten-path motel directly on Lake Champlain a great value. **Pros:** inexpensive; serene setting; laid-back. **Cons:** rooms simple, not luxurious. [$] *Rooms from: $149* ✉ *1002 Quarry Rd., Isle La Motte* ☎ *802/928–3200* 🌐 *www.ruthcliffe.com* 🛏 *7 rooms* 🕘 *Closed Columbus Day–mid-May* 🍴 *Breakfast.*

MONTGOMERY/JAY

32 miles east of St. Albans, 51 miles northeast of Burlington.

Montgomery is a small village near the Canadian border and Jay Peak ski resort. Amid the surrounding countryside are seven covered bridges.

OFF THE BEATEN PATH

Lake Memphremagog. Vermont's second-largest lake, Lake Memphremagog extends from Newport 33 miles north into Canada. Prouty Beach in Newport has camping facilities, tennis courts, and paddleboat and canoe rentals. ✉ *386 Prouty Beach Rd., Newport* ☎ *802/334–7951 Prouty Beach.*

East Side Restaurant. Watch the sun set from the deck of the East Side Restaurant, which serves excellent burgers and prime rib. ✉ *47 Landing St., Newport* ☎ *802/334–2340* 🌐 *www.eastsiderestaurant.net*

SPORTS AND THE OUTDOORS

SKI AREA

Hazen's Notch Cross Country Ski Center and B&B. Delightfully remote at any time of the year, this center has 40 miles of marked and groomed trails and rents equipment and snowshoes. ✉ *4850 Rte. 58* ☎ *802/326–4799.*

★ **Jay Peak.** Sticking up out of the flat farmland, Jay Peak averages 355 inches of snow a year—more than any other Vermont ski area. Its proximity to Québec attracts Montréalers and discourages Eastern Seaboarders; hence, the prices are moderate and the lift lines shorter than at other resorts. The area is renowned for its glade skiing and powder.

Off-season, Jay Peak runs tram rides to the summit from mid-June through Labor Day and mid-September through Columbus Day ($10). The child-care center for youngsters ages 2–7 is open from 9 am to 9 pm. If you're staying at Hotel Jay and Jay Peak Condominiums, you receive this nursery care free, as well as evening care and supervised dining at the hotel. Infant care is available on a fee basis with advanced reservations. In the winter, snowshoes can be rented, and guided walks are led by a naturalist. Telemark rentals and instruction are available.

Jay Peak has two interconnected mountains for downhill skiing, the highest reaching nearly 4,000 feet with a vertical drop of 2,153 feet.

DID YOU KNOW?

Long and skinny Lake Champlain is sometimes called the sixth Great Lake. Several small and scenic islands, like Grand Isle, are popular seasonal getaways in warm weather.

The smaller mountain has straight-fall-line, expert terrain that eases midmountain into an intermediate pitch. The main peak is served by Vermont's only tramway and transports skiers to meandering but challenging intermediate trails. Beginners should stick near the bottom on trails off the Metro lift. Weekdays at 9:30 am and 1:30 pm, mountain ambassadors conduct a free tour. The area's 76 trails, including 21 glades and two chutes, are served by eight lifts, including the tram and the longest detachable quad in the East. The area also has two quads, a triple, and a double chairlift; one T-bar; and a moving carpet. Jay has 80% snowmaking coverage. The area also has four terrain parks, each rated for different abilities, and a brand new state-of-the art ice arena for hockey and figure skating. There are ski-school programs for children ages 3–18. ⊠ *830 Jay Peak Rd., Jay* ☎ *802/988–2611, 800/451–4449 outside VT* ⊕ *www.jaypeakresort.com.*

WHERE TO STAY

For expanded hotel reviews, visit Fodors.com.

$$$$ ⊞ **Hotel Jay & Jay Peak Condominiums.** Centrally located in the ski resort's
HOTEL base area, the hotel and its simply furnished rooms are a favorite for
🕭 families. **Pros:** great for skiers and summer mountain adventurers.
Cons: not an intimate, traditional Vermont stay. $ *Rooms from: $250*
⊠ *4850 Rte. 242* ☎ *802/988–2611, 800/451–4449 outside VT* ⊕ *www.jaypeakresort.com* 🛏 *48 rooms, 94 condominiums* ⦿ *Some meals.*

$ ⊞ **Inn on Trout River.** Guest rooms at this 100-year-old riverside inn
B&B/INN sport a country-cottage style, and all have down quilts and flannel sheets in winter. **Pros:** traditional B&B. **Cons:** rooms heavy on the florals. $ *Rooms from: $57* ⊠ *241 S. Main St., Montgomery Center* ☎ *802/326–4391, 800/338–7049* ⊕ *www.troutinn.com* 🛏 *9 rooms, 1 suite* ⦿ *Multiple meal plans.*

EN **Northeast Kingdom.** Routes 14, 5, 58, and 100 make a scenic drive
ROUTE around the Northeast Kingdom, named for the remoteness and stalwart independence that have helped preserve its rural nature. You can extend the loop and head east on Route 105 to the city of Newport on Lake Memphremagog. Some of the most unspoiled areas in all Vermont are on the drive south from Newport on either U.S. 5 or Interstate 91 (the latter is faster, but the former is prettier). ■ TIP→ **As "The Kingdom" is remote and there are not many great places to stay, consider instead renting a cabin or house on VRBO or HomeAway; there are many great options in this area.**

LAKE WILLOUGHBY

30 miles southeast of Montgomery (summer route; 50 miles by winter route), 28 miles north of St. Johnsbury.

Lake Willoughby. The cliffs of Mt. Pisgah and Mt. Hor drop to the edge of Lake Willoughby on opposite shores, giving this beautiful, deep, glacially carved lake a striking resemblance to a Norwegian fjord. The trails to the top of Mt. Pisgah reward hikers with glorious views. ⊠ *Westmore.*

EXPLORING

★ 👶 **Bread and Puppet Museum.** This ramshackle barn houses a surrealistic collection of props used by the world-renowned Bread and Puppet Theater. The troupe has been performing social and political commentary with the towering (they're supported by people on stilts), eerily expressive puppets for about 30 years and performs at the museum every Sunday June–August at 3. ✉ *753 Heights Rd. (Rte. 122), 1 mile east of Rte. 16, Glover* ☎ *802/525–3031* 🌐 *www.breadandpuppet.org* 🎟 *Donations accepted* ⏲ *June–Oct., daily 10–6.*

EAST BURKE

17 miles south of Lake Willoughby.

Once a sleepy village, East Burke is now the Northeast Kingdom's outdoor-activity hub. The Kingdom Trails attract thousands of mountain bikers in summer and fall. In winter, many trails are groomed for cross-country skiing.

ESSENTIALS

Visitor Information Kingdom Trails Association *802/626–0737* 🌐 *www.kingdomtrails.org.*

SPORTS AND THE OUTDOORS

Contact the Kingdom Trails Association for details and maps.

East Burke Sports. East Burke Sports rents mountain bikes, kayaks, and skis, and provides guides for cycling, hiking, paddling, skiing, and snowshoeing. ✉ *439 Rte. 114* ☎ *802/626–3215* 🌐 *www.eastburkesports.com.*

The Village Sport Shop. The Village Sport Shop rents bikes, canoes, kayaks, paddleboats, rollerblades, skis, and snowshoes. ✉ *511 Broad St., Lyndonville* ☎ *802/626–8448* 🌐 *www.villagesportshop.com.*

Burke Mountain. About an hour's drive from Montpelier is Burke Mountain. Racers stick to the Training Slope, served by its own poma lift. The other 44 trails and glades are a quiet playground. ✉ *1 Mountain Rd.* ☎ *802/626–3322* 🌐 *www.skiburke.com.*

WHERE TO EAT AND STAY

For expanded hotel reviews, visit Fodors.com.

$ AMERICAN 🍴 **River Garden Café.** You can eat lunch, dinner, or brunch outdoors on the enclosed porch, on the patio amid perennial gardens, or inside this bright and cheerful café. The excellent fare includes lamb tenderloin, warm artichoke dip, bruschetta, pastas, and fresh fish, and the popular salad dressing is bottled for sale. [$] *Average main: $12* ✉ *427 Rte. 114* ☎ *802/626–3514* 🌐 *www.rivergardencafe.com* ⏲ *Closed Mon. and Tues. Nov.–Apr.*

$$$ RESORT 👶 🏨 **The Wildflower Inn.** The hilltop views are breathtaking at this rambling, family-oriented complex of old farm buildings on 570 acres. **Pros:** mega kid-friendly nature resort; best of the Northeast Kingdom's expansiveness; relaxed. **Cons:** most rooms are simply furnished. [$] *Rooms from: $200* ✉ *2059 Darling Hill Rd., 5 miles west of East Burke, Lyn-*

Catch a show and some social commentary at the Bread and Puppet Theater in summer, or visit the museum year-round.

donville ☎ *802/626–8310, 800/627–8310* ⊕ *www.wildflowerinn.com* 🛏 *10 rooms, 13 suites, 1 cottage* ⊗ *Closed Apr. and Nov.* ⏀ *Breakfast.*

ST. JOHNSBURY

16 miles south of East Burke, 39 miles northeast of Montpelier.

St. Johnsbury, the southern gateway to the Northeast Kingdom, was chartered in 1786. But its identity was established after 1830, when Thaddeus Fairbanks invented the platform scale, a device that revolutionized weighing methods. The Fairbanks family's philanthropic efforts gave the city a strong cultural and architectural imprint. Today St. J, as the locals call it, is the friendly, adventure-sports-happy hub of the Northeast Kingdom.

EXPLORING

★ **Dog Mountain.** Artist Stephen Huneck was famous for his colorful folk
☺ art sculptures and paintings of dogs. Much more than an art gallery–gift shop, this deeply moving place is complete with a chapel where animal lovers can reflect on their deceased and living pets. Above all, this is a place to bring your dog: there is a swimming pond, an agility course, and hiking trails. ⊠ *143 Parks Rd., off Spaulding Rd.* ☎ *800/449–2580* ⊕ *www.dogmt.com* 🎫 *Free* ⊗ *Daily 10–5.*

Fodor's Choice **Fairbanks Museum and Planetarium.** This odd and deeply thrilling little
★ museum displays the eccentric collection of Franklin Fairbanks, who
☺ surely had one of the most inquisitive minds in American history. He built this magnificent barrel-vaulted two-level gallery in 1889 just to house the specimens of plants, animals, mounted birds, mammals,

reptiles, plants, and collections of folk art and dolls—and a seemingly unending variety of beautifully mounted curios—he had picked up around the world. The museum showcases over 175,000 items, but it's surprisingly easy to feast your eyes on everything here without getting a museum headache. There's also a popular 45-seat planetarium, the state's only public planetarium; as well the Eye on the Sky Weather Gallery, home to live NPR weather broadcasts. ✉ *1302 Main St.* ☎ *802/748–2372* 🌐 *www.fairbanksmuseum.org* 🎫 *Museum $8; planetarium $5* 🕒 *May–mid-Oct., Mon.–Sat. 9–5, Sun. 1–5; mid-Oct.–Apr., Tues.–Sat. 9–5, Sun. 1–5. Planetarium shows July and Aug., daily at 11 and 1:30; Sept.–June, weekends at 1:30.*

Fodor's Choice ★ **St. Johnsbury Athenaeum.** With its dark, rich paneling, polished Victorian woodwork, and ornate circular staircases, this building is both the town library (one of the nicest you're likely to ever come across) and one of the oldest art galleries in the country, housing more than 100 original works mainly of the Hudson River school. Albert Bierstadt's enormous (15 feet by 10 feet) *Domes of Yosemite* dominates the beautiful painting gallery. ✉ *1171 Main St.* ☎ *802/748–8291* 🌐 *www.stjathenaeum.org* 🎫 *Free* 🕒 *Mon. and Wed. 10–8; Tues., Thurs., and Fri. 10–5:30; Sat. 9:30–4.*

OFF THE BEATEN PATH

Peacham. Tiny Peacham, 10 miles southwest of St. Johnsbury, is on almost every tour group's list of must-sees. With views extending to the White Mountains of New Hampshire and a white-steeple church, Peacham is perhaps the most photographed town in New England. The movie adaptation of *Ethan Frome*, starring Liam Neeson, was filmed here. Next door, the **Peacham Corner Guild** sells local handcrafts. ✉ *Peacham* 🌐 *www.peacham.net.*

Peacham Store. One of the town's gathering spots, the Peacham Store, sells specialty soups and stews. ✉ *641 Bayley-Hazen Rd., Peacham* ☎ *802/592–3310*

WHERE TO STAY

For expanded hotel reviews, visit Fodors.com.

$$$ B&B/INN ★ 🏨 **Rabbit Hill Inn.** Few inns in New England have the word-of-mouth buzz that Rabbit Hill seems to earn from satisfied guests. **Pros:** attractive, spacious rooms; romantic; lovely grounds; good food. **Cons:** might be too quiet a setting for some. [$] *Rooms from: $210* ✉ *Rte. 18, 11 miles south of St. Johnsbury, 48 Lower Waterford Rd., Lower Waterford* ☎ *802/748–5168, 802/748–5168* 🌐 *www.rabbithillinn.com* 🛏 *19 rooms* 🕒 *Closed 1st 3 wks in Apr., 1st 2 wks in Nov.* 🍴 *Multiple meal plans.*

New Hampshire

WORD OF MOUTH

"In New Hampshire, Jackson is a picture-perfect mountain village. You might also want to check out the quiet and scenic agricultural towns along the Connecticut River. Hanover, NH, is the ultimate New England Ivy League town with good dining, a nice museum, and the beautiful Dartmouth campus."

—zootsi

WELCOME TO NEW HAMPSHIRE

TOP REASONS TO GO

★ **The White Mountains:** Great for hiking and skiing, these rugged, dramatic peaks and notches are unforgettable.

★ **Lake Winnipesaukee:** Water parks, arcades, boat cruises, and classic summer camps make for a family fun summer.

★ **Fall Foliage:** Head to the Kancamagus Highway in the fall for one of America's best drives or seek out a lesser-known route that's just as stunning.

★ **Portsmouth:** Less than an hour from Boston, this great American city has coastline allure, colorful Colonial architecture, and the right amount of energy.

★ **Pristine Towns:** Jaffrey Center, Walpole, Tamworth, Center Sandwich, and Jackson are among the most charming tiny villages in New England.

1 The Seacoast. You can find historical sites, hopping bars, beaches, whale-watching, and deep-sea fishing all packed in along New Hampshire's 18 miles of coastline. Hampton Beach is the center of summertime activities, while Portsmouth is a hub of nightlife, dining, and Colonial history.

2 Lakes Region. Throughout central New Hampshire are lakes and more lakes. The largest, Lake Winnipesaukee, has 240 miles of coastline and attracts all sorts of water sports enthusiasts, but there are many more secluded and quiet lakes with enchanting bed-and-breakfasts where relaxation is the main activity.

3 The White Mountains. Skiing, snowshoeing, and snowboarding in the winter; hiking, biking, and riding scenic railways in the summer—the Whites, as locals call their mountains, have plenty of natural wonders within a stone's throw from the roads, but other spots call for lung-busting hikes. Mount Washington, the tallest mountain in the Northeast, can be conquered by trail, train, or car.

4 Dartmouth-Lake Sunapee. Quiet villages can be found throughout the region. Many of them are barely removed from Colonial times, but some thrive as centers of arts and education and are filled with quaint shops. Hanover, the home of 240-year-old Dartmouth College, retains that true New England college town feel, with ivy-draped buildings and cobblestone walkways. Lake Sunapee is a wonderful place to swim, fish, or enjoy a cruise.

5 The Monadnocks and Merrimack Valley. The southwest region of the Granite State exemplifies both the vanguards of new technology economic activity—the cities of Manchester and Nashua—and the values of old New England in the hills surrounding Mt. Monadnock. High-tech firms have set up shop in old brick factory buildings while small towns still celebrate tradition and history.

GETTING ORIENTED

Although New Hampshire has three interstates running through it (I–95, I–93, and I–89), most of its regions are accessible only on smaller roads. From Boston or Portland, Maine, I–95 provides the best access to Portsmouth and the beaches along the coast, though many people like to drive along Route 1A, which parallels the coast. North of Portsmouth, Route 16 leads to the White Mountains, whose precipitous peaks seem to rise out of nowhere, and the lakes region, home to Lake Winnipesaukee. From there, I–93 cuts north toward Franconia and Littleton and south into Concord, Manchester, and Nashua. State roads east and north of I–93 lead to Dixville Notch, which casts the first vote in presidential elections, and the Connecticut Lakes. Following the Connecticut River takes you to Hanover, home of Dartmouth College, Claremont, Charleston, Walpole, and Keene. From Concord, travelers head west to reach the Monadnock Region.

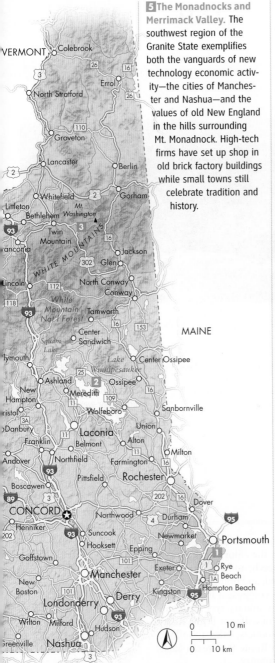

NEW HAMPSHIRE FALL FOLIAGE DRIVE

With its quaint villages graced with green commons, white town halls, and covered bridges, southwestern New Hampshire is dominated by the imposing rocky summit of Mt. Monadnock and brilliant colors in fall. Kancamagus Highway is another classic foliage route, but for more solitude and less traffic, try this more accessible route that peaks a few weeks later than the state's far north.

BEST TIME TO GO

Early October is best time to view foliage in southern New Hampshire, but the time can vary by up to four weeks. Call or check online for daily leaf changes (☎ 800/258–3608 ⊕ www.visitnh.gov).

PLANNING YOUR TIME

Expect to travel about 55 miles. The journey can take up to a full day if you stop to explore along the way.

The Granite State is the second most forested state in the nation; by Columbus Day, the colors of the leaves of its maple, birch, elm, oak, beech, and ash trees range from green to gold, purple to red, and orange to auburn. Routes 12, 101, 202, and 124 compose a loop around Mt. Monadnock, named for its solitary type of mountain. Start in Keene with a cup of coffee at Prime Roast; for New Hampshire–made products, take a walk on Main Street or detour west on Route 9 to reach **Stonewall Farm** for something more country.

From Keene, travel east on Route 101 through Dublin and over Pack Monadnock, a 2,290-foot peak (not to be confused with the 3,165-foot Grand, or Mt. Monadnock). In quaint **Peterborough**, browse the local stores, whose attitude and selection matches the state's independent spirit.

Then turn south on Route 202, stopping at **Colls Farmstand** for some seasonal treats before reaching Jaffrey Village. Just west on 124, in historic Jaffrey Center, be sure to visit the **Meeting House Cemetery** on the common where author Willa Cather is buried. A side trip, 4 miles south on 202, leads to the majestic **Cathedral of the Pines** in Rindge, one of the best places in the region for foliage viewing because the evergreens offset the brilliant shades of red.

Heading west on 124, you can take Dublin Road to the main entrance of **Monadnock State Park** or continue along to the Old Toll Road parking area for one of the most popular routes up the mountain, the **Halfway House Trail**. All of the hiking trails have great views, including the area's many lakes. Continuing on 124 you come to Fitzwilliam and Route 12; turn north back to Keene.

NEED A BREAK?

Stonewall Farm. Stonewall Farm is a nonprofit working farm that teaches visitors about the importance of agriculture. There's an active schedule of special events that feature maple sugaring, farm animals, and other farm activities such as horse-drawn hayrides and a pumpkin patch. ✉ *242 Chesterfield Rd., Keene* ☎ *603/357-7278* ⊕ *www.stonewallfarm.org* ⊙ *Grounds dusk–dawn. Learning center and gift shop weekdays 8:30–4:30. Farm stand daily 9–4:30.*

Colls Farmstand. Colls Farmstand carries maple syrup, jams, and other New Hampshire–made products, as well as fruit, vegetables, and an on-site deli for fresh meats and sandwiches. ✉ *16 Colls Farm Rd., Jaffrey* ☎ *603/532-7540* ⊕ *www. collsfarmllc.com* ⊙ *Mon.–Sat. 9–6, Sun. 9–5.*

8

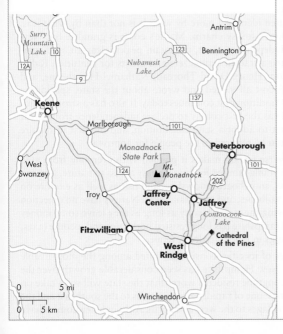

Surry Mountain Lake 10
12A
9
Keene
Antrim
123
Bennington
Nubanusit Lake
137
Marlborough 101
Monadnock State Park
Peterborough
101
West Swanzey
124
Mt. Monadnock
202
Troy
Jaffrey Center
Jaffrey
Contoocook Lake
Fitzwilliam
Cathedral of the Pines
West Rindge
0   5 mi
0   5 km
Winchendon

Updated by Laura V. Scheel

New Hampshire residents have often been called cantankerous, but beneath that crusty exterior is often hospitality and friendliness. The state's motto was coined by New Hampshire native General John Stark, who led the Colonial Army in its hard-fought battle of Bennington, Vermont, in 1777. "Live free or die; death is not the worst of evils," he said, in a letter written 20 years after the battle. The residents of the Granite State have taken "Live Free or Die" to heart, defining themselves by that principle for more than 200 years.

The state is often identified more by what it is not than by what it is. It lacks Vermont's folksy charm. Maine's coast is grander. But New Hampshire's independent spirit, mountain peaks, clear air, and sparkling lakes have attracted trailblazers and artists for centuries. Ralph Waldo Emerson, Henry David Thoreau, Nathaniel Hawthorne, and Louisa May Alcott all visited and wrote about the state, sparking a strong literary tradition that continues today. It also has a strong political history: it was the first colony to declare independence from Great Britain, the first to adopt a state constitution, and the first to require that constitution be referred to the people for approval.

The state's diverse terrain makes it popular with everyone from avid adventurers to young families looking for easy access to nature. You can hike, climb, ski, snowboard, snowshoe, and fish as well as explore on snowmobiles, sailboats, and mountain bikes. Natives have no objection to others enjoying the state's beauty as long as they leave some money behind. New Hampshire has long resisted both sales and income taxes, so tourism brings in much-needed revenue.

With a number of its cities consistently rated among the most livable in the nation, New Hampshire has seen considerable growth over the past decade. Longtime residents worry that the state will soon take on two personalities: one of rapidly growing cities to the southeast and the other of quiet villages to the west and north. Although newcomers have brought change, the independent nature of the people and the state's natural beauty remain constant.

PLANNING

WHEN TO GO

Summer and fall are the best times to visit most of New Hampshire. Winter is a great time to travel to the White Mountains, but most other tourist sites in the state, including the Portsmouth museums and many attractions in the Lakes Region, are closed due to snow and cold weather. In summer, people flock to beaches, mountain trails, and lake boat ramps. In the cities, festivals showcase music, theater, and crafts. Fall brings leaf peepers, especially to the White Mountains and along the Kancamagus Highway (Route 112). Skiers and snowboarders take to the slopes in winter, when Christmas lights and carnivals brighten the long, dark nights. Spring's unpredictable weather—along with April's mud and late May's black flies—tends to deter visitors. Still, the season has its joys, not the least of which is the appearance of the state flower, the purple lilac, from mid-May to early June as well as colorful rhododendrons.

PLANNING YOUR TIME

Some people come to New Hampshire to hike or ski the mountains, fish and sail the lakes, or cycle along the back roads. Others prefer to drive through scenic towns, visiting museums and shops. Although New Hampshire is a small state, roads curve around lakes and mountains, making distances longer than they appear. You can get a taste of the coast, lake, and mountain areas in three to five days; eight days gives you time to make a more complete loop.

GETTING HERE AND AROUND

AIR TRAVEL

Manchester Boston Regional Airport is the state's largest and has non-stop service to more than 20 cities. Boston's Logan Airport is within one to three hours of most places in New Hampshire as is Bradley International in Hartford, Connecticut.

CAR TRAVEL

New Hampshire is an easy drive north from Boston and serves as a good base for exploring northern New England. Many destinations are near major highways, so getting around by car is a great way to travel. Interstate 93 stretches from Boston to Littleton and on into neighboring Vermont. Interstate 89 will get you from Concord to Hanover and eventually to Burlington, Vermont. To the east, Interstate 95, which is a toll road, passes through southern New Hampshire's coastal area on its way from Massachusetts to Maine. Throughout the state are quiet backcountry lanes and winding roads that might take a little longer but can make for some of the best parts of the journey.

Speed limits on interstate and limited-access highways are usually 65 mph, except in heavily settled areas, where 55 mph is the norm. On state and U.S. routes, speed limits vary considerably. On any given stretch, the limit may be anywhere from 25 mph to 55 mph, so watch the signs carefully. Right turns on red lights are permitted unless otherwise indicated.

TRAIN TRAVEL

Amtrak. Amtrak runs its Downeaster service from Boston to Portland, Maine, with stops in Exeter, Durham, and Dover. ☎ 800/872–7245 ⊕ www.amtrak.com.

RESTAURANTS

New Hampshire prides itself on seafood—not just lobster but also salmon pie, steamed mussels, fried clams, and seared tuna. Across the state you'll find country taverns with upscale Continental and American menus, many of them embracing regional ingredients. Alongside a growing number of contemporary eateries are such state traditions as greasy-spoon diners, pizzerias, and pubs that serve hearty comfort fare. Reservations are almost never required, and dress is casual in nearly every eatery. *Prices in the reviews are the average cost of a main course at dinner or, if dinner is not served, at lunch.*

HOTELS

In the mid-19th century, wealthy Bostonians retreated to imposing New Hampshire country homes in summer months. Grand hotels were built across the state, especially in the White Mountains, when the area competed with Saratoga Springs, Newport, and Bar Harbor to draw the nation's elite vacationers. Today a handful of these hotel-resorts survive, with their large cooking staffs and tradition of top-notch service. Many of the vacation houses have been converted into inns and B&Bs. The smallest have only a couple of rooms and are typically done in period style. The largest contain 30 or more rooms and suites and have in-room fireplaces and even hot tubs. You'll also find a great many well-kept, often family-owned motor lodges—particularly in the White Mountains and Lakes regions. In the ski areas expect the usual ski condos and lodges. In the Merrimack River valley, as well as along major highways, chain hotels and motels prevail. There are numerous campgrounds across the state, which accommodate RVs as well. The White Mountains provide an excellent base for camping and hiking.

Country Inns in the White Mountains handles reservations for a wide variety of B&Bs and inns throughout the region. For long-term rentals try Preferred Vacation Rental, Inc. and Strictly Rentals, Inc. *Prices in the reviews are the lowest cost of a standard double room in high season.*

THE SEACOAST

New Hampshire's 18-mile stretch of coastline packs in a wealth of scenery and diversions. The honky-tonk of Hampton Beach gets plenty of attention, good and bad, but first-timers are often surprised by the significant chunk of shoreline that remains pristine—especially through the town of Rye. This section begins in the regional hub, Portsmouth, cuts down the coast to the beaches, branches inland to the prep-school town of Exeter, and runs back up north through Dover, Durham (home of the University of New Hampshire), and Rochester. From here it's a short drive to the Lakes Region.

OUTDOOR ACTIVITIES

Hitting the trails by boot and ski, fishing, kayaking and canoeing, biking, or just plain old walking will undoubtedly be a part of your visit.

Biking: Many ski resorts in the White Mountains offer mountain biking opportunities, providing chairlift rides to the top and trails for all skill levels at the bottom. Some of the state's best road biking is along the Kancamagus Highway and around Lake Sunapee.

Hiking: For the more adventurous, hiking the trails in the White Mountains or along the Appalachian Trail, also known as the Long Trail, is their reason for visiting. For those more interested in less arduous treks, there are plenty of day hikes in the White Mountain National Forest and state parks such as Pisgah, the state's largest, in Cheshire County, the Crawford Notch and Franconia Notch state parks in the Whites, and Mt. Monadnock.

Skiing: Ski areas abound in New Hampshire—try Mt. Sunapee, Waterville Valley, Loon Mountain, or Canon Mountain. For cross-country skiing, nothing beats Gunstock Mountain Resort, with 32 miles of trails, also open for snowshoeing. Or visit Franconia Village, which has 37 miles of cross-country trails.

ESSENTIALS
Visitor Information Seacoast New Hampshire & South Coast Maine
☎ *603/427–2020* ⊕ *www.seacoastnh.com.*

PORTSMOUTH

8

47 miles southeast of Concord; 50 miles southwest of Portland, Maine; 56 miles north of Boston.

★ Settled in 1623 as Strawbery Banke, Portsmouth became a prosperous port before the Revolutionary War, and, like similarly wealthy Newport, Rhode Island, it harbored many Tory sympathizers throughout the campaign. Filled with grand residential architecture spanning the 18th through early 20th centuries, this city of 23,000 has many house museums, including the collection of 40-plus buildings that make up the Strawbery Banke Museum. With hip eateries, quirky shops, swank cocktail bars, respected theaters, and jumping live-music venues, this sheltered harbor city is a hot destination. Downtown, especially around elegant Market Square, buzzes with conviviality.

GETTING HERE AND AROUND
Interstate 95 and Route 1 run through Portsmouth. From the west take Route 101 and from the north take Route 16. Amtrak runs through Durham, which is a short drive to the coast. Once in Portsmouth, you can walk about the downtown, though you'll want a car for further attractions. COAST Trolley's downtown loop hits most of the city's historical sights during the summer.

ESSENTIALS
Bus and Trolley COAST Bus ☎ *603/743–5777* ⊕ *www.coastbus.org.*

New Hampshire Coast

Taxi Anchor Taxi ☎ *603/436–1888.* Portsmouth Taxi ☎ *603/431–6811.*

Visitor Information Greater Portsmouth Chamber of Commerce ✉ *Box 239, 500 Market St.* ☎ *603/610–5510* ⊕ *www.portsmouthchamber.org.*

EXPLORING

TOP ATTRACTIONS

Albacore Park. The USS *Albacore,* built here in 1953, is docked at this museum/visitor center in Albacore Park. You can board the proto-type submarine, which was a floating laboratory designed to test an innovative hull design, dive brakes, and sonar systems for the Navy. The nearby Memorial Garden and its reflecting pool are dedicated to those who have lost their lives in submarine service. ✉ *600 Market St.* ☎ *603/436–3680* ⊕ *www.ussalbacore.org* 🖳 *$5* ⊙ *Daily 9:30–5 Memorial Day–Columbus Day; Thurs.–Mon. Columbus Day–Memorial Day. Call ahead for short winter closure.*

John Paul Jones House. The yellow, hip-roof home was a boardinghouse when the Revolutionary War hero lived here while supervising ship-building for the Continental Navy. The 1758 structure displays furni-ture, costumes, glass, guns, portraits, and documents from the late 18th century. The collection specializes in textiles, particularly some extraor-dinary embroidery samplers from the early 19th century. ✉ *43 Middle*

SIGHTSEEING TRAILS AND TROLLEYS

TRAILS

Discover Portsmouth Center.
This is the place to find out about daily art events, history tours, walking trails, and other local happenings. Sign up for a guided walking, kayak, and even a two-wheeled Segway tour here; you can also get maps and plenty of information about embarking on the Portsmouth Harbour Trail, a route which passes more than 70 points of scenic and historical significance. ⊠ *Corner of Islington and Middle Sts.* ☎ *603/436–8433* ⊕ *www. portsmouthhistory.org.*

Portsmouth Black Heritage Trail.
Important sites of African American history are along the self-guided walk on the Portsmouth Black Heritage Trail. Included are the **New Hampshire Gazette Printing Office**, where skilled slave Primus Fowle operated the paper's printing press for some 50 years beginning in 1756, and the city's 1866 **Election Hall**, outside of which the city's black citizens held annual celebrations of the Emancipation Proclamation. Guided tours can be arranged by phone. ⊠ *Downtown, starting at Prescott Park wharf, 143 Pleasant St.* ☎ *603/380–1231* ⊕ *www.pbhtrail. org* ⊠ *Donations welcome.*

TROLLEYS

Downtown Loop Coast Trolley.
Portsmouth is also served by the Downtown Loop Coast Trolley, which makes numerous stops at popular downtown attractions, public parking areas, and the waterfront. This service operates from late June to late August, from 10:30 to 5:30 p.m. ⊠ *Departs from Market Sq. every half hour, 42 Sumner Dr., Dover* ☎ *603/743–5777* ⊕ *www.coastbus. org/routes/downtownloop.html* ⊠ *50¢.*

St. ☎ *603/436–8420* ⊕ *www.portsmouthhistory.org* ⊠ *$6* ⊙ *May–Oct., daily 11–5.*

Redhook Ale Brewery. Tours here end with a beer tasting, but if you don't have time for the tour, stop in the Cataqua Public House to sample the fresh ales and have a bite to eat (open daily for lunch and dinner). The building is visible from the Spaulding Turnpike. ⊠ *Pease International Tradeport, 1 Redhook Way* ☎ *603/430–8600* ⊕ *www.redhook.com* ⊠ *$1* ⊙ *Check website for hours and tour info.*

★ **Strawbery Banke Museum.** The first English settlers named the area around today's Portsmouth for the wild strawberries along the shores of the Piscataqua River. The name survives in this 10-acre neighborhood, continuously occupied for more than 300 years and now doing duty as an outdoor history museum, one of the largest in New England. The compound has 46 buildings dating from 1695 to 1820—some restored and furnished to a particular period, some used for exhibits, and some viewed from the outside only—as well as period gardens. Half the interior of the Drisco House, built in 1795, depicts its use as a dry-goods store in Colonial times, whereas the living room and kitchen are decorated as they were in the 1950s, showing how buildings were adapted over time. The Shapiro House has been restored to reflect the life of the Russian Jewish immigrant family who lived in the home in the early 1900s. Perhaps the most opulent house, done in decadent Victorian style, is the 1860 Goodwin Mansion, former home of Governor Ichabod Goodwin. ⊠ *14 Hancock St.* ☎ *603/433–1100* ⊕ *www.strawberybanke.org* 🎟 *$15* ⊗ *May 1–Oct. 31, daily 10–5; special December tours.*

WORTH NOTING

Moffatt-Ladd House and Garden. The period interior of this 1763 home tells the story of Portsmouth's merchant class through portraits, letters, and furnishings. The Colonial Revival garden includes a horse chestnut tree planted by General William Whipple when he returned home after signing the Declaration of Independence in 1776. ⊠ *154 Market St.* ☎ *603/436–8221* ⊕ *www.moffattladd.org* 🎟 *Garden and house tour $6, garden only $2* ⊗ *Early June–mid-Oct., Mon.–Sat. 11–5, Sun. 1–5.*

QUICK BITES

Annabelle's Natural Ice Cream. Drop by Annabelle's Natural Ice Cream for a dish of New Hampshire pure maple walnut or rich vanilla ice cream made with golden egg yolks. ⊠ *49 Ceres St.* ☎ *603/436–3400* ⊕ *www.annabellesicecream.com.*

Breaking New Grounds. Breaking New Grounds is a big hangout in town and serves coffee, pastries, and gelato. ⊠ *14 Market Sq.* ☎ *603/436–9555.*

Wentworth-Coolidge Mansion Historic Site. A National Historic Landmark now part of Little Harbor State Park, this home site was originally the residence of Benning Wentworth, New Hampshire's first royal governor (1753–70). Notable among its period furnishings is the carved pine mantelpiece in the council chamber. Wentworth's imported lilac trees bloom each May. The visitor center stages lectures and exhibits and contains a gallery with changing exhibits. ⊠ *375 Little Harbor Rd., near South Street Cemetery* ☎ *603/436–6607* ⊕ *www.nhstateparks.org* ⊗ *late June–early Sept., Wed.–Sun. 10–4; late May–late June and early Sept.–mid Oct., weekends 10–4.*

OFF THE BEATEN PATH

New Castle. Though it consists of a single square mile of land, the small island of New Castle, 3 miles southeast from downtown via Route 1B, was once known as Great Island. The narrow roads and coastal lanes are lined with pre-Revolutionary houses, making for a beautiful drive or stroll. **Wentworth-by-the-Sea** (☎ *603/422–7322* ⊕ *www.wentworth.com*), the last of the state's great seaside resorts, towers over the southern end of New Castle on Route 1B. It was the site of the signing of the Russo-Japanese Treaty in 1905, when Russian and Japanese delegates stayed at the resort and signed an agreement ending the Russo-Japanese War that would win President Theodore Roosevelt a Nobel Peace Prize. The property was vacant for 20 years before it reopened as a luxury resort in 2003.

Ft. Constitution Historic Site. Also on New Castle, Ft. Constitution Historic Site was built in 1631 and then rebuilt in 1666 as Ft. William and Mary, a British stronghold overlooking Portsmouth Harbor. The fort earned its fame in 1774, when patriots raided it in one of Revolutionary America's first overtly defiant acts against King George III. The rebels later used the captured munitions against the British at the Battle

Strawbery Banke Museum includes period gardens and 46 historic buildings.

of Bunker Hill. Panels explain its history. Park at the dock and walk into the Coast Guard installation to the fort. ⊠ *Wentworth St. off Rte. 1B, at the Coast Guard Station* ☎ *603/436–1552* ⊕ *www.nhstateparks.org* ☞ *Free* ☾ *Parking lot 8:30–dusk in summer, park itself is always open*

OFF THE BEATEN PATH

Isles of Shoals. Many of these nine small, rocky islands (eight at high tide) retain the earthy names—Hog and Smuttynose to cite but two—given them by transient 17th-century fishermen. A history of piracy, murder, and ghosts surrounds the archipelago, long populated by an independent lot who, according to one writer, hadn't the sense to winter on the mainland. Not all the islands lie within the state's borders: after an ownership dispute, five went to Maine and four to New Hampshire.

Celia Thaxter, a native islander, romanticized these islands with her poetry in *Among the Isles of Shoals* (1873) and celebrated her garden in *An Island Garden* (1894; now reissued with the original color illustrations by Childe Hassam). In the late 19th century, **Appledore Island** became an offshore retreat for Thaxter's coterie of writers, musicians, and artists. The island is now used by the Marine Laboratory of Cornell University. **Star Island** contains a nondenominational conference center and is open for guided tours. ⊠ *315 Market St.* ☎ *800/441–4620* ⊕ *www.islesofshoals.com.*

SPORTS AND THE OUTDOORS

PARKS

Great Bay Estuarine Research Reserve. Just inland from Portsmouth is one of southeastern New Hampshire's most precious assets. Amid its 4,471 acres of tidal waters, mudflats, and about 48 miles of inland shoreline,

A boat tour of Portsmouth Harbor is popular in warm weather, and a great introduction to the city's maritime heritage.

you can spot blue herons, ospreys, and snowy egrets, particularly during spring and fall migrations. Winter eagles also live here.

Great Bay National Estuarine Research Reserve. The best public access is via the Great Bay National Estuarine Research Reserve. The facility has year-round interpretive programs, indoor and outdoor exhibits, a library and bookshop, and a 1,700-foot boardwalk as well as other trails through mudflats and upland forest. ⊠ *89 Depot Rd., off Rte. 33, Greenland* ☎ *603/778–0015* ⊕ *www.greatbay.org* ☉ *Visitor center open May–Sept., Wed.–Sun. 10–4; Oct., weekends 10–4; grounds open dawn to dusk year-round.*

Prescott Park. Picnicking is popular at this waterfront park. A large formal garden with fountains is perfect for whiling away an afternoon. The park contains Point of Graves, Portsmouth's oldest burial ground, and two 17th-century warehouses. ⊠ *Between Strawbery Banke Museum and the Piscataqua River* ☎ *603/436–2848* ⊕ *www.prescottpark.org.*

Prescott Park Arts Festival. Prescott Park is home to the seasonal Prescott Park Arts Festival, a summer-long packed schedule that kicks off with the Chowder Festival in early June and includes a multitude of concerts, outdoor movies, musical theater, and food festivals. All events are free; bring your beach blanket and chairs to find space on the grass. ☎ *603/436–2848* ⊕ *www.prescottpark.org*

Urban Forestry Center. This 180-acre park has gardens and marked trails appropriate for short hikes. ⊠ *45 Elwyn Rd.* ☎ *603/431–6774* ⊕ *www. nhdfl.org.*

Water Country. New Hampshire's largest water park has a river tube ride, large wave pool, white-water rapids, and 12 waterslides. ✉ *2300 Lafayette Rd.* ☎ *603/427–1111* ⊕ *www.watercountry.com* 💲 *$38* ⊙ *Mid-June–Labor Day, hours vary.*

BOAT TOURS

Isles of Shoals Steamship Company. The Isles of Shoals Steamship Company runs a three-hour Isles of Shoals, lighthouses, and Portsmouth Harbor cruise out of Portsmouth aboard the *Thomas Laighton,* a replica of a Victorian steamship, from April through December (twice daily in summer). Lunch and light snacks are available on board, or you can bring your own. There are also fall foliage cruises, narrated sunset cruises visiting five local lighthouses, and special holiday cruises. ✉ *Barker Wharf, 315 Market St.* ☎ *603/431–5500, 800/441–4620* ⊕ *www.islesofshoals.com.*

Portsmouth Harbor Cruises. From May to October, Portsmouth Harbor Cruises operates tours of Portsmouth Harbor, foliage trips on the Cocheco River, and sunset cruises aboard the MV *Heritage.* ✉ *64 Ceres St.* ☎ *603/436–8084, 800/776–0915* ⊕ *www.portsmouthharbor.com.*

Portsmouth Kayak Adventures. Explore the waters, sites, and sea life of the Piscataqua River Basin and the New Hampshire coastline on a guided kayak tour with Portsmouth Kayak Adventures. Beginners are welcome (instruction is included). Tours are run daily from June through mid-October, at 10 and 2. Sunset tour times vary. ✉ *185 Wentworth Rd.* ☎ *603/559–1000* ⊕ *www.portsmouthkayak.com.*

SHOPPING

Market Square, in the center of town, has gift and clothing boutiques, book and card shops, and exquisite crafts stores.

Byrne & Carlson. Byrne & Carlson produces handmade chocolates in the European tradition. ✉ *121 State St.* ☎ *888/559–9778* ⊕ *www.byrneandcarlson.com.*

Nahcotta. Nahcotta is a wonderful contemporary art gallery and has a well-chosen selection of contemporary housewares, artist-crafted jewelry, and glassware. ✉ *110 Congress St.* ☎ *603/433–1705* ⊕ *www.nahcotta.com.*

N.W. Barrett Gallery. N.W. Barrett Gallery specializes in leather, jewelry, pottery, and other arts and crafts. It also sells furniture, including affordable steam-bent oak pieces and one-of-a-kind lamps and rocking chairs. ✉ *53 Market St.* ☎ *603/431–4262* ⊕ *www.nwbarrett.com.*

NIGHTLIFE AND THE ARTS

THE ARTS

Seven galleries participate in the Art 'Round Town Reception, a gallery walk that takes place the first Friday of each month. Check out ⊕ *www.artroundtown.org* for more information.

Kennedy Gallery. The Kennedy Gallery is one of the galleries that participates in the Art 'Round Town Reception, a gallery walk that takes place the first Friday of each month. ✉ *41 Market St.* ☎ *603/436–7007* ⊕ *www.kennedygalleryandframing.com.*

Music Hall. Beloved for its acoustics, the 1878 Music Hall brings the best touring events to the seacoast—from classical and pop concerts to dance and theater. The hall also hosts art-house film series. ⊠ *28 Chestnut St.* ☏ *603/436–2400, 603/436–9900 film line* ⊕ *www.themusichall.org.*

Players' Ring. Throughout the year, the Players' Ring stages more than 15 original and well-known plays and performances by local theater groups. ⊠ *105 Marcy St.* ☏ *603/436–8123* ⊕ *www.playersring.org.*

Prescott Park Arts Festival. This outdoor festival presents theater, dance, and musical events from June through August. ⊠ *105 Marcy St.* ☏ *603/436–2848* ⊕ *www.prescottpark.org.*

Three Graces Gallery. The gallery showcases an unusual mix of paintings, sculpture, jewelry and other art; watch for monthly changing exhibitions. ⊠ *105 Market St.* ☏ *603/436–1988* ⊕ *www.threegracesgallery.com.*

NIGHTLIFE

BARS **The Library Restaurant.** If vodka is your thing, you'll do no better than the book-lined English oak bar in The Library Restaurant, which has more than 120 brands of vodka and 96 kinds of martinis. ⊠ *401 State St.* ☏ *603/431–5202* ⊕ *www.libraryrestaurant.com.*

Two Ceres Street. Try one of the original martinis such as the Lumberjack, with Maker's Mark and maple syrup, or the Hot and Dirty, with Grey Goose vodka, pepperoncini, and olive juice. ⊠ *2 Ceres St.* ☏ *603/433–2373* ⊕ *www.twoceresstreet.com.*

MUSIC **Portsmouth Gas Light Co.** This brick-oven pizzeria and restaurant hosts local rock bands in its lounge, courtyard, and slick upstairs space. ⊠ *64 Market St.* ☏ *603/430–9122* ⊕ *www.portsmouthgaslight.com.*

The Press Room. People come from Boston and Portland just to hang out at the Press Room, which showcases folk, jazz, blues, and bluegrass performers nightly. ⊠ *77 Daniel St.* ☏ *603/431–5186* ⊕ *www. pressroomnh.com.*

The Red Door Lounge. Discover the local music scene at The Red Door Lounge, which has a bar, a live music series, and DJs nightly. Indie music fans shouldn't miss Monday nights at 8 for the acclaimed live acts as part of the Hush Hush Sweet Harlot Music Series. ⊠ *107 State St.* ☏ *603/373–6827* ⊕ *www.reddoorportsmouth.com.*

WHERE TO EAT

$$ ✕**Blue Mermaid Island Grill.** This is a fun, colorful place for great fish,
ECLECTIC sandwiches, and quesadillas, as well as house-cut yucca chips. Specialties include plantain-encrusted cod topped with grilled mango vinaigrette and served with grilled banana–sweet potato hash, a chipotle-and-honey-marinated sirloin, and braised short ribs with an island rub. In summer you can eat on a deck that overlooks the adorable Colonial homes of the Hill neighborhood. Live music includes soul, bluegrass, rock, and even yodeling Wednesday through Saturday. $ *Average main:* $20 ⊠ *409 The Hill* ☏ *603/427–2583* ⊕ *www.bluemermaid.com.*

$ ✕**Friendly Toast.** The biggest and best breakfast in town (as well as lunch
AMERICAN and dinner) is served at this funky, wildly colorful diner-style restaurant
★ loaded with bric-a-brac. Almond Joy cakes (buttermilk pancakes, choc-
☾ olate chips, coconut, and almonds), raspberry and orange French toast,

and hefty omelets are favorites. Also enjoy the homemade breads and muffins. A late-night crowd gathers after the bars close; Friendly Toast is open 24 hours on weekends. $ *Average main: $12* ⊠ *113 Congress St.* ☎ *603/430–2154* ⊕ *www.thefriendlytoast.net.*

$$ ✕ **Jumpin' Jay's Fish Cafe.** A wildly popular downtown spot, this offbeat,
SEAFOOD dim-lighted eatery has a changing menu of fresh seafood from local fishermen and exotic locales such as New Zealand and Ecuador. Try the steamed Prince Edward Island mussels with a spicy ginger and saffron sauce, a Portuguese fisherman's stew, or the haddock piccata (served in a sauce of lemon, white wine, and capers). Singles like to gather at the central bar for dinner and furtive glances. $ *Average main: $23* ⊠ *150 Congress St.* ☎ *603/766–3474* ⊕ *www.jumpinjays.com.*

$$$$ ✕ **Library Restaurant.** This former luxury hotel has been made over into
STEAKHOUSE a country library–themed restaurant. The 12-foot hand-painted dining
★ room ceiling was constructed by the Pullman Car Woodworkers in 1889. Hand-carved Spanish mahogany paneling covers the walls, and the marble bar top used to be the check-in desk. Although the kitchen churns out light dishes such as crab cakes and barbecue shrimp, the mainstays are thick-cut steaks and chops. The crushed-peppercorn–encrusted steak is meat heaven. The English-style pub serves nearly 100 martinis made from vodkas such as Fris, Mezzaluna, Boomsma, and Thor's Hammer. Sunday brunch is also available. $ *Average main: $40* ⊠ *401 State St.* ☎ *603/431–5202* ⊕ *www.libraryrestaurant.com.*

$ ✕ **Poco's Bow Street Cantina.** The boisterous downstairs bar and spacious
LATIN AMERICAN outside deck are a local hangout, but the upstairs dining room turns out
★ exceptional Southwestern and Pan-Latin cuisine. Snapper tacos, fried calamari, and lobster quesadilla are among the better choices. Most tables have great views of the Piscataqua River. $ *Average main: $12* ⊠ *37 Bow St.* ☎ *603/431–5967* ⊕ *www.pocosbowstreetcantina.com.*

WHERE TO STAY
For expanded hotel reviews, visit Fodors.com.

$$$ ⌨ **The Governor's House.** Among Portsmouth's inns and small hotels,
B&B/INN the Governor stands apart. **Pros:** great rooms and home; free bicycle
Fodor'sChoice rental; great location. **Cons:** 15-minute bike ride to the beach. $ *Rooms*
★ *from: $239* ⊠ *32 Miller Ave.* ☎ *603/427–5140, 866/427–5140* ⊕ *www. governors-house.com* ⋑ *5 rooms* ⦿⦾ *Breakfast.*

$$ ⌨ **Martin Hill Inn.** You may fall in love with this adorable yellow 1815
B&B/INN house surrounded by gardens once you see it from the street. **Pros:** very clean; real antiques, excellent resources for local attractions. **Cons:** not in historic district; early breakfast. $ *Rooms from: $185* ⊠ *404 Islington St.* ☎ *603/436–2287* ⊕ *www.martinhillinn.com* ⋑ *4 rooms, 3 suites* ⦿⦾ *Breakfast.*

$$$$ ⌨ **Wentworth by the Sea.** What's not to love about this white colossus
RESORT overlooking the sea on New Castle Island. **Pros:** great spa and res-
Fodor'sChoice taurants; sense of history; oceanfront perch. **Cons:** not in downtown
★ Portsmouth. $ *Rooms from: $349* ⊠ *588 Wentworth Rd., New Castle* ☎ *603/422–7322, 866/240–6313* ⊕ *www.wentworth.com* ⋑ *127 rooms, 34 suites.*

Four of the nine rocky Isles of Shoals belong to New Hampshire, the other five belong to Maine.

RYE

8 miles south of Portsmouth.

On Route 1A as it winds south through Rye you'll pass a group of late-19th- and early-20th-century mansions known as **Millionaires' Row.** Because of the way the road curves, the drive south along this route is breathtaking. In 1623 the first Europeans established a settlement at Odiorne Point in what is now the largely undeveloped and picturesque town of Rye, making it the birthplace of New Hampshire. Today the area's main draws are a lovely state park, oceanfront beaches, and the views from Route 1A. Strict town laws have prohibited commercial development in Rye, creating a dramatic contrast with its frenetic neighbor Hampton Beach.

SPORTS AND THE OUTDOORS

PARKS

★ **Odiorne Point State Park.** This site encompasses more than 330 acres
☪ of protected land, on the site where David Thompson established the first permanent European settlement in what is now New Hampshire. Several nature trails with interpretive panels describe the park's military history, and you can enjoy vistas of the nearby Isles of Shoals. The rocky shore's tidal pools shelter crabs, periwinkles, and sea anemones. Throughout the year, the **Seacoast Science Center** conducts guided walks and interpretive programs and has exhibits on the area's natural history. Displays trace the social history of Odiorne Point back to the Ice Age, and the tidal-pool touch tank and 1,000-gallon Gulf of Maine deepwater aquarium are popular with kids. Day camp is

offered for grades K–8 throughout summer and during school vacations. Popular music concerts are held Thursday evenings in summer. ✉ *570 Ocean Blvd.(Rte. 1A), north of Wallis Sands, Rye Harbor State Beach* ☎ *603/436–8043 science center, 603/436–1552 park* 🌐 *www.seacoastsciencecenter.org* 🎟 *$5 science center, $4 park* 🕓 *Science center Apr.–Oct., daily 10–5; Nov.–Mar., Mon.–Sat. 10–5; park daily 8–dusk.*

👶 **Rye Airfield.** If you've got active kids with you, consider spending the day at this extreme-sports park with an indoor in-line skate, scooter, and skateboard arena and two BMX tracks. ✉ *U.S. 1, 170 Lafayette Rd.* ☎ *603/964–2800* 🌐 *www.ryeairfield.com.*

BEACHES

Jenness State Beach. Good for swimming and sunning, Jenness State Beach is a favorite with locals. The facilities include a bathhouse, lifeguards, and metered parking. ✉ *Route 1A* ☎ *603/436–1552* 🌐 *www.nhstateparks.org* 🎟 *$5.*

Wallis Sands State Beach. Wallis Sands State Beach is a swimmers' beach with bright white sands, picnic area, a bathhouse, a store, and plenty of parking. ✉ *Route 1A* ☎ *603/436–9404* 🌐 *www.nhstateparks.org* 🎟 *$15 per car.*

FISHING AND WHALE WATCHING

Atlantic Fleet. For a full- or half-day deep-sea angling charter, try Atlantic Fleet (whale-watching trips are also scheduled). ✉ *1870 Ocean Blvd., Harbor* ☎ *603/964–5220, 800/942–5364* 🌐 *www.atlanticwhalewatch.com.*

Granite State Whale Watch, Inc. Granite State Whale Watch, Inc. conducts naturalist-led whale-watching tours aboard the 150-passenger MV *Granite State* out of Rye Harbor State Marina from May to early October and narrated Isles of Shoals and fireworks cruises weekly in July and August. ✉ *Rye Harbor State Marina, 1860 Ocean Blvd. (Rte. 1A)* ☎ *603/964–5545, 800/964–5545* 🌐 *www.granitestatewhalewatch.com* 🎟 *$36.*

WHERE TO EAT

$$$ AMERICAN ★ 🍴 **The Carriage House.** Walk across scenic Ocean Boulevard from Jenness Beach to this elegant cottage eatery that serves innovative dishes with a Continental flair. Standouts include crab cakes served with a spicy jalapeño sauce, penne *alla vodka* teeming with fresh seafood, creative Madras curries, and steak au poivre. Upstairs is a rough-hewn-wood–paneled tavern serving lighter fare. Savor a hot fudge–ice cream croissant for dessert. [$] *Average main: $25* ✉ *2263 Ocean Blvd.* ☎ *603/964–8251* 🌐 *www.carriagehouserye.com* 🕓 *No lunch.*

HAMPTON BEACH

8 miles south of Rye.

👶 Hampton Beach, from Route 27 to where Route 1A crosses the causeway, is an authentic seaside amusement center—the domain of fried-dough stands, loud music, arcade games, palm readers, parasailing, and bronzed bodies. An estimated 150,000 people visit the town and its free public beach on the 4th of July, and it draws plenty of people until late

8

September, when things close up. The 3-mile boardwalk, where kids play games and see how saltwater taffy is made, looks like a leftover from the 1940s; in fact, the whole community remains remarkably free of modern franchises. Free outdoor concerts are held on many a summer evening, and once a week there's a fireworks display. Each August, locals hold a children's festival, and they celebrate the end of the season with a huge seafood feast on the weekend after Labor Day.

GETTING HERE AND AROUND
Interstate 95 is the fastest way to get to Hampton, but the town is best seen by driving on Route 1A, which follows the coast and offers access to a number of beaches. Route 1 is the quickest way to get around, but be prepared for strip malls and stoplights.

ESSENTIALS
Visitor Information Hampton Area Chamber of Commerce ⊠ *1 Lafayette Rd.* ☎ *603/926–8718* ⊕ *www.hamptonchamber.com.*

SPORTS AND THE OUTDOORS
BEACHES
Hampton Beach State Park. Hampton Beach State Park, at the mouth of the Hampton River, is a long stretch of sand on the southwestern edge of town. The park has just had a major overhaul: you'll find a brand new visitor center, multiple picnic areas, a store (seasonal), and several bathhouses. ⊠ *Rte. 1A* ☎ *603/926–3784* ⊕ *www.nhstateparks.org* ⊠ *$15 per car May–Oct., free Nov.–Apr.*

FISHING AND WHALE-WATCHING
Several companies conduct whale-watching excursions as well as half-day, full-day, and nighttime cruises. Most leave from the Hampton State Pier on Route 1A.

Al Gauron Deep Sea Fishing. This company maintains a fleet of three boats for whale-watching cruises and fishing charters. ⊠ *State Pier* ☎ *603/926–2469* ⊕ *www.algauron.com.*

Eastman's Docks. Eastman's Docks offers whale-watching and fishing cruises, with evening and morning charters. ⊠ *River St., Seabrook* ☎ *603/474–3461* ⊕ *www.eastmansdocks.com.*

Smith & Gilmore. Enjoy half- or full-day deep-sea fishing expeditions with Smith & Gilmore. ⊠ *State Pier* ☎ *603/926–3503, 877/272–4005* ⊕ *www.smithandgilmore.com.*

NIGHTLIFE
Hampton Beach Casino Ballroom. Despite its name, the Hampton Beach Casino Ballroom isn't a gambling establishment but a late-19th-century, 2,000-seat performance venue that has hosted everyone from Janis Joplin to Jerry Seinfeld, George Carlin, and B.B. King. Performances are scheduled weekly from April through October. ⊠ *169 Ocean Blvd.* ☎ *603/929–4100* ⊕ *www.casinoballroom.com.*

WHERE TO EAT AND STAY
For expanded hotel reviews, visit Fodors.com.

$$$
AMERICAN
✕ **Ron's Landing.** Amid the motels lining Ocean Boulevard is this casually elegant restaurant. Try the sesame-seared ahi tuna with a pineapple,

orange, and cucumber salsa for a starter. Good seafood entrées include the oven-roasted salmon with a hoisin glaze, a Frangelico cream sauce, slivered almonds, and sliced apple and the baked haddock stuffed with scallops and lobster and served with lemon-dill butter. From many tables you can enjoy a sweeping Atlantic view. Brunch is served Sundays, October to May. $ *Average main: $28* ⌧ *379 Ocean Blvd.* ☎ *603/929–2122* ⊕ *www.ronslanding.com* ⊙ *Closed Mon. No lunch.*

$$$$ ⊡ **Ashworth by the Sea.** You'll be surprised how contemporary this
HOTEL center-of-the-action, across-from-the-beach hotel is, even though it's been around for a century. **Pros:** center-of-town location and across from beach; open all year. **Cons:** breakfast not included; very busy. $ *Rooms from: $349* ⌧ *295 Ocean Blvd.* ☎ *603/926–6762, 800/345–6736* ⊕ *www.ashworthhotel.com* ⇥ *105 rooms.*

EN ROUTE **Applecrest Farm Orchards.** At the 400-acre Applecrest Farm Orchards, you can pick your own apples and berries or buy fresh fruit pies and cookies, homemade ice cream, and many other tasty treats. Fall brings cider pressing, hayrides, pumpkins, and music on weekends. In winter a cross-country ski trail traverses the orchard. Author John Irving worked here as a teenager, his experiences inspiring the book *The Cider House Rules.* ⌧ *133 Rte. 88, Hampton Falls* ☎ *603/926–3721* ⊕ *www. applecrest.com* ⊙ *May–Dec., daily 8–6.*

EXETER

9 miles northwest of Hampton, 52 miles north of Boston, 47 miles southeast of Concord.

★ In the center of Exeter, contemporary shops mix well with the esteemed Phillips Exeter Academy, which opened in 1783. During the Revolutionary War, Exeter was the state capital, and it was here amid intense patriotic fervor that the first state constitution and the first Declaration of Independence from Great Britain were put to paper. These days Exeter shares more in appearance and personality with Boston's blue-blooded satellite communities than the rest of New Hampshire—indeed, plenty of locals commute to Beantown. A handful of cheerful cafés and coffeehouses are clustered in the center of town.

GETTING HERE AND AROUND

Amtrak's Downeaster service stops here between Boston and Portland, Maine. On the road, it's 9 miles northwest of Hampton on Route 111. Route 101 is also a good way to get to Exeter from the east or west. The town itself is easy to walk around.

ESSENTIALS

Visitor Information Exeter Area Chamber of Commerce ⌧ *24 Front St., #101* ☎ *603/772–2411* ⊕ *www.exeterarea.org.*

EXPLORING

American Independence Museum. Adjacent to Phillips Exeter Academy in the Ladd-Gilman House, this museum celebrates the birth of the nation. The story unfolds during the course of a guided tour focusing on the Gilman family, who lived in the house during the Revolutionary era. See drafts of the U.S. Constitution and the first Purple Heart as well as letters and documents written by George Washington and the household furnishings of John Taylor Gilman, one of New Hampshire's early governors. In July the museum hosts the American Independence Festival. ✉ *1 Governor's Lane* ☎ *603/772–2622* 🌐 *www.independencemuseum.org* 🎟 *$6* 🕑 *Mid-May–Oct., Wed.–Sat. 10–4 (last tour at 3).*

Phillips Exeter Academy. Above all else, the town is energized by the faculty and 1,000 high school students of the Phillips Exeter Academy. The grounds of the academy's 129 buildings, open to the public, resemble an elite Ivy League university campus. The Louis Kahn–designed library contains the largest secondary-school book collection in the world. ✉ *20 Main St.* ☎ *603/772–4311* 🌐 *www.exeter.edu.*

Rockingham Recreation Trail. The New Hampshire Division of Parks and Recreation maintains the Rockingham Recreation Trail, which wends 25 miles from Newfields, just north of Exeter, to Manchester and is open to hikers, bikers, equestrians, snowmobilers, and cross-country skiers.

SHOPPING

Exeter Fine Crafts. Prestigious Exeter Fine Crafts shows an impressive selection of juried pottery, paintings, jewelry, textiles, glassware, and other fine creations by some of northern New England's top artists. ✉ *61 Water St.* ☎ *603/778–8282* 🌐 *www.exeterfinecrafts.com.*

A Picture's Worth a Thousand Words. A Picture's Worth a Thousand Words stocks antique and contemporary prints, old maps, town histories, and rare books. ✉ *65 Water St.* ☎ *603/778–1991* 🌐 *www.apwatw.com.*

Travel and Nature. Find a wide selection of outdoor sporting goods items, clothing, and travel books, including guides to New Hampshire hiking spots and other specialized titles. ✉ *45 Water St.* ☎ *603/772–5573.*

Water Street Books. Water Street Books carries new fiction and nonfiction with an emphasis on New Hampshire authors. ✉ *125 Water St.* ☎ *603/778–9731* 🌐 *www.waterstreetbooks.com.*

WHERE TO EAT

$ AMERICAN Fodor's Choice ★

🍴 **Loaf and Ladle.** There are three components to this extraordinary place: quality, price, and location. The name refers to homemade bread—more than 30 kinds—and soup—more than 100 varieties are offered on a rotating basis. A bowl of soup, which is a full meal, is $6.25, and it's hard to spend more than that here. Choose a chunk of Anadama bread, made with cornmeal and molasses, to go with your soup, and take your meal to one of the two decks that hover over the Exeter River. It's simple and homey. [$] *Average main: $6* ✉ *9 Water St.* ☎ *603/778–8955* ✍ *Reservations not accepted.*

$$ AMERICAN

🍴 **The Tavern At River's Edge.** A convivial downtown gathering spot on the Exeter River, this downstairs tavern pulls in parents of prep-school kids, University of New Hampshire (UNH) students, and suburban yuppies. It may be informal, but the kitchen turns out surprisingly sophisticated chow. Start with sautéed ragout of portobello and shiitake mushrooms, sun-dried tomatoes, roasted shallots, garlic, and Asiago cheese. Move on to a lobster risotto with wild mushrooms and asparagus. In the bar, lighter fare is served daily 3–10. [$] *Average main: $22* ✉ *163 Water St.* ☎ *603/772–7393* 🌐 *www.tavernatriversedge.com* 🕑 *No lunch.*

WHERE TO STAY

For expanded hotel reviews, visit Fodors.com.

$$ B&B/INN ★ **The Exeter Inn.** This elegant brick Georgian-style inn on the Phillips Exeter Academy campus has been the choice of visiting parents since it opened in the 1930s. **Pros:** contemporary, well-designed, clean rooms; near Academy. **Cons:** not close to town shops; you may not want to be on a prep-school campus. [$] *Rooms from: $189* ✉ *90 Front St.* ☎ *603/772–5901, 800/782–8444* 🌐 *www.theexeterinn.com* 🛏 *41 rooms, 5 suites.*

$$$ B&B/INN ★ **Inn by the Bandstand.** If you're visiting someone at the academy and want to stay in a B&B, we recommend this place in the heart of town. **Pros:** perfect location in town; richly furnished rooms. **Cons:** early breakfast. [$] *Rooms from: $229* ✉ *Six Front St.* ☎ *603/772–6352, 877/239–3837* 🌐 *www.innbythebandstand.com* 🛏 *7 rooms, 2 suites* 🍴 *Breakfast.*

DURHAM

12 miles north of Exeter, 11 miles northwest of Portsmouth.

Settled in 1635 and the home of General John Sullivan, a Revolutionary War hero and three-time New Hampshire governor, Durham was where Sullivan and his band of rebel patriots stored the gunpowder they captured from Ft. William and Mary in New Castle. Easy access to Great Bay via the Oyster River made Durham a maritime hub in the 19th century. Among the lures today are the water, farms that welcome visitors, and the University of New Hampshire (UNH), which occupies much of the town's center.

GETTING HERE AND AROUND

By car, Durham can be reached on Route 108 from the north or south and Route 4 from Portsmouth from the east or Concord from the west. The Downeaster Amtrak train stops here between Boston and Portland, Maine. A good place to begin your exploration of Durham is at the art galleries on the campus of the University of New Hampshire.

ESSENTIALS

Visitor Information **University of New Hampshire** ☎ *603/862–1234* 🌐 *www.unh.edu.*

EXPLORING

Museum of Art. This UNH gallery occasionally exhibits items from a permanent collection of about 1,100 pieces but generally uses its space to host traveling exhibits. Noted items in the collection include 19th-century Japanese woodblock prints and American landscape paintings. ✉ *Paul Creative Arts Center, 30 College Rd.* ☎ *603/862–3712* 🌐 *www.unh.edu/moa* 🎟 *Free* ⏲ *Sept.–May, Mon.–Wed. 10–4, Thurs. 10–8, weekends 1–5. Closed Fri.*

8

SPORTS AND THE OUTDOORS

Wagon Hill Farm. You can hike several trails or picnic at 130-acre Wagon Hill Farm, overlooking the Oyster River. The old farm wagon on the top of a hill is one of the most photographed sights in New England. Park next to the farmhouse and follow walking trails to the wagon and through the woods to the picnic area by the water. Sledding and cross-country skiing are winter activities. ✉ *U.S. 4 across from Emery Farm.*

SHOPPING

Emery Farm. In the same family for 11 generations, Emery Farm sells fruits and vegetables in summer (including pick-your-own raspberries, strawberries, and blueberries), pumpkins in fall, and Christmas trees in December. The farm shop carries breads, pies, and local crafts. Children can pet the resident goats and sheep and attend the storytelling events that are often held on Tuesday mornings in July and August. ✉ *135 Piscataqua Rd. (Rte. 4)* ☎ *603/742–8495* 🌐 *www.emeryfarm.com* 🕒 *May–Dec., daily 9–6.*

NIGHTLIFE AND THE ARTS

THE ARTS

Celebrity Series. At UNH, the Celebrity Series brings music, theater, and dance to several venues. ☎ *603/862–2290* 🌐 *www.unh.edu/celebrity.*

UNH Department of Theater and Dance. A variety of shows are produced by the UNH Department of Theater and Dance. ✉ *Paul Creative Arts Center, 30 Academic Way* ☎ *603/862–2919* 🌐 *www.unh.edu/theatre-dance.*

Whittemore Center Arena. UNH's Whittemore Center Arena hosts everything from Boston Pops concerts to home shows, plus college sports. ✉ *128 Main St.* ☎ *603/862–4000* 🌐 *www.whittcenter.com.*

NIGHTLIFE

Stone Church. Students and local yupsters head to the Stone Church —in an authentic 1835 former Methodist church—to listen to live rock, jazz, blues, and folk. The restaurant on the premises serves dinner Wednesday through Sunday; local craft beers are a specialty. ✉ *5 Granite St., Newmarket* ☎ *603/659–7700* 🌐 *www.stonechurchrocks.com.*

WHERE TO EAT AND STAY

For expanded hotel reviews, visit Fodors.com.

$$$ AMERICAN ★ 🍴 **ffrost Sawyer Tavern.** That's not a typo, but an attempt to duplicate a quirk in obsolete spelling (the way capital letters used to be designated) of an old resident of this hilltop house. The eccentric stone basement tavern has its original beams, from which hang collections of mugs, hats, and—no way around it—bedpans. There's a terrific old bar. Choose from fine fare like pan-seared sea scallops or pecan-battered fried chicken breast; standards include burgers, pizza, and fish-and-chips. [$] *Average main: $25* ✉ *17 Newmarket Rd.* ☎ *603/868–7800* 🌐 *www.threechimneysinn.com.*

$$ B&B/INN 🏨 **Three Chimneys Inn.** This stately yellow structure has graced a hill overlooking the Oyster River since 1649. **Pros:** intimate inn experience; afternoon social hour. **Cons:** have to walk or drive into town. [$] *Rooms from: $169* ✉ *17 Newmarket Rd.* ☎ *603/868–7800, 888/399–9777* 🌐 *www.threechimneysinn.com* 🛏 *23 rooms* 🍽 *Breakfast.*

CLOSE UP

New Hampshire Farmers' Markets

Winter squash is in season in New Hampshire from September to October.

Bedford Farmers' Market. Just outside Manchester, the Bedford Farmers' Market has a particularly rich mix of local growers and food purveyors, selling seasonal jams, pasture-raised lamb and chicken, homemade treats for dogs and cats, goats' milk soaps and balms, and even New Hampshire wines from Jewell Towne Vineyard. There's usually live music and activities for children at hand. ✉ *Benedictine Park, Wallace Rd., Bedford* ⊕ *bedfordfarmersmarket.org* ⊗ *June–Oct., Tues. 3–6 pm.*

Exit 20 Farmers' Market at Tanger Outlets. At the Exit 20 Farmers' Market at Tanger Outlets you'll find folk art and country crafts in addition to food. ✉ *I–93, Exit 20, Tanger Outlet shops, Tilton* ⊕ *www.tangeroutlet.com* ⊗ *June–Sept., Wed. 3–6 pm.*

Lebanon Farmers' Market. Lebanon Farmers' Market draws more than 50 vendors from throughout the northern Connecticut River Valley. ✉ *Colburn Park, 51 North Park St.,* *Lebanon* ☎ *603/448–5121* ⊕ *www.lebanonfarmersmarket.org* ⊗ *Late May–late Sept., Thurs. 4–7 pm.*

Portsmouth Farmers' Market. One of the best and longest-running farmers' markets in New Hampshire is the Portsmouth Farmers' Market, which features live music and regional treats, such as maple syrup and artisanal cheeses, in addition to bountiful produce. ✉ *1 Junkins Ave., Portsmouth* ⊗ *May–early Nov., Sat. 8 am–1 pm.*

Me & Ollie's. Don't miss the award-winning breads of the much-beloved bakery Me & Ollie's at the Portsmouth Farmers' Market. ☎ *603/436–7777* ⊕ *www.meandollies.com.*

Seacoast Growers Association. The Portsmouth Farmers' market is part of the Seacoast Growers Association, which also has weekly markets in Dover, Durham, Exeter, Hampton, and Kingston. ⊕ *www.seacoastgrowers.org.*

—Andrew Collins

8

LAKES REGION

Lake Winnipesaukee, a Native American name for "smile of the great spirit," is the largest of the dozens of lakes scattered across the eastern half of central New Hampshire. With about 240 miles of shoreline of inlets and coves, it's the largest in the state. Some claim Winnipesaukee has an island for each day of the year—the total, though impressive, falls short: 274.

In contrast to Winnipesaukee, which bustles all summer long, is the more secluded Squam Lake. Its tranquillity is no doubt what attracted the producers of *On Golden Pond*; several scenes of the Academy Award–winning film were shot here. Nearby Lake Wentworth is named for the state's first royal governor, who, in building his country manor here, established North America's first summer resort.

Well-preserved Colonial and 19th-century villages are among the region's many landmarks, and you'll find hiking trails, good antiques shops, and myriad water-oriented activities. This section begins at Wolfeboro and more or less circles Lake Winnipesaukee clockwise, with several side trips.

ESSENTIALS

Visitor Information Lakes Region Association ☎ *603/286–8008, 800/605–2537* ⊕ *www.lakesregion.org.*

WOLFEBORO

40 miles northeast of Concord, 49 miles northwest of Portsmouth.

Quietly upscale and decidedly preppy Wolfeboro has been a resort since Royal Governor John Wentworth built his summer home on the shores of the lake in 1768. The town bills itself as the oldest summer resort in the country, and its center, bursting with tony boutiques, fringes Lake Winnipesaukee and sees about a tenfold population increase each summer. In 2007 French president Nicolas Sarkozy summered here. Mitt Romney is another summer resident. The century-old, white clapboard buildings of the Brewster Academy prep school bracket the town's southern end. Wolfeboro marches to a steady, relaxed beat, comfortable for all ages.

GETTING HERE AND AROUND

Enter on the west side of Lake Winnipesaukee on Route 28. Be prepared for lots of traffic in the summertime.

ESSENTIALS

Visitor Information Wolfeboro Area Chamber of Commerce ⊠ *32 Central Ave.* ☎ *603/569–2200* ⊕ *www.wolfeborochamber.com.*

EXPLORING

New Hampshire Boat Museum. Two miles northeast of downtown, this museum celebrates the Lakes Region's boating legacy with displays of vintage Chris-Crafts, Jersey Speed Skiffs, three-point hydroplanes, and other fine watercraft, along with model boats, antique engines, racing photography and trophies, and old-timey signs from marinas. You can

With 240 miles of shoreline, Lake Winnipesaukee is so much more than just the town of Wolfeboro.

also take a ride in a reproduction triple-cockpit HackerCraft on the lake. ⊠ *399 Center St.* ☎ *603/569–4554* ⊕ *www.nhbm.org* ✉ *$7* ⊗ *Memorial Day–Columbus Day, Mon.–Sat. 10–4; Sun. noon–4.*

Wright Museum. Uniforms, vehicles, and other artifacts at this museum illustrate the contributions of those on the home front to the U.S. World War II effort. ⊠ *77 Center St.* ☎ *603/569–1212* ⊕ *www.wrightmuseum.org* ✉ *$8* ⊗ *May–Oct., Mon.–Sat. 10–4; Sun. noon–4; Feb.–Apr., Sun. noon–4.*

QUICK BITES

Lydia's Cafe. Brewster Academy students and summer folk converge upon groovy little Lydia's Cafe for espresso, sandwiches, homemade soups, bagels, and desserts. ⊠ **33 N. Main St.** ☎ **603/569–3991** ⊕ **www.lydiascafewolfeboro.com.**

Kelly's Yum Yum Shop. Picking up pastries, cookies, freshly baked breads, and other sweets in the Kelly's Yum Yum Shop has been a tradition since 1948—the butter-crunch cookies are highly addictive. ⊠ **16 N. Main St.** ☎ **603/569–1919** ⊕ **www.yumyumshop.net** ⊗ **Closed Jan–Apr.**

SPORTS AND THE OUTDOORS
BEACH
Wentworth State Beach. Wentworth State Beach has good swimming, fishing, picnicking areas, ball fields, and a bathhouse on the shores of Wentworth Lake. ⊠ *Rte. 109* ☎ *603/569–3699* ⊕ *www.nhstateparks.org* ✉ *$4.*

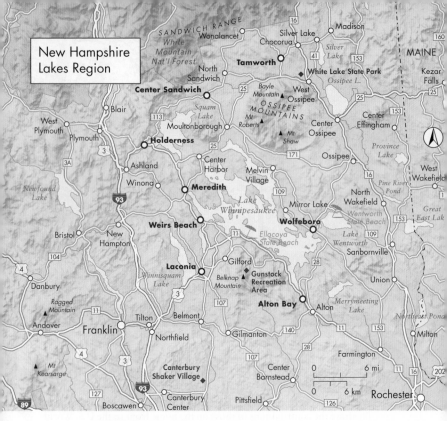

New Hampshire Lakes Region

HIKING

Abenaki Tower. A short (¼-mile) hike to the 100-foot post-and-beam Abenaki Tower, followed by a more rigorous climb to the top, rewards you with a view of Lake Winnipesaukee and the Ossipee mountain range. The trailhead is on Route 109 in Tuftonboro.

WATER SPORTS

Scuba divers can explore *The Lady*, the 125-foot-long cruise ship that sank in 30 feet of water off Glendale in 1895.

Dive Winnipesaukee Corp. Dive Winnipesaukee Corp runs charters out to wrecks and offers rentals, repairs, scuba sales, boat rentals, and lessons in waterskiing. ⊠ *4 N. Main St.* ☎ *603/569–8080* ⊕ *www.divewinnipesaukee.com.*

SHOPPING

The Country Bookseller. You'll find an excellent regional-history section and plenty of children's titles at the Country Bookseller, Wolfeboro's fine general-interest bookstore. ⊠ *23A N. Main St.* ☎ *603/569–6030* ⊕ *www.thecountrybookseller.com.*

Hampshire Pewter. The artisans at Hampshire Pewter use 16th-century techniques to make pewter tableware and accessories. Come to shop or take a free tour Memorial Day through Columbus Day, weekdays

OUTDOOR OUTFITTERS AND RESOURCES

BIKING

Bike New England. This is an excellent Web resource for maps, tours, and routes for cyclists all over New England. ✉ *Wolfeboro* 🌐 *www.bikenewengland.com.*

Bike the Whites. Bike the Whites organizes custom bike tours in New Hampshire and Vermont. ☎ *800/421–1785* 🌐 *www.bikethewhites.com.*

HIKING

U.S. Forest Service. ☎ *603/536–6100* 🌐 *www.fs.fed.us/r9/forests/white_mountain.*

Appalachian Mountain Club. ☎ *800/372–1758* 🌐 *amc-nh.org/index.php.*

New England Hiking Holidays. ☎ *603/356–9696, 800/869–0949* 🌐 *www.nehikingholidays.com.*

New Hampshire State Parks. ✉ *172 Pembroke Rd., Concord* ☎ *603/271–3556* 🌐 *www.nhstateparks.org.*

SKIING

Ski New Hampshire. ☎ *603/745–9396, 800/887–5464* 🌐 *www.skinh.com.*

at 10, 11, 1, 2, and 3. ✉ *43 Mill St.* ☎ *603/569–4944, 800/639–7704* 🌐 *www.hampshirepewter.com.*

Made on Earth. Here you can find new-age gifts, clothing, books, and crafts. ✉ *33 Main St.* ☎ *603/569–9100* 🌐 *www.madeonearthwolfeboro.com.*

WHERE TO EAT

$$ ASIAN 🍴 **East of Suez.** In a countrified lodge on the south side of town, this friendly restaurant serves creative Pan-Asian cuisine, with an emphasis on Philippine fare, such as *lumpia* (pork-and-shrimp spring rolls with a sweet-and-sour fruit sauce) and *pancit canton* (panfried egg noodles with sautéed shrimp and pork and Asian vegetables with a sweet oyster sauce). You can also sample Thai red curries, Japanese tempura, and Korean-style flank steak. [$] *Average main: $19* ✉ *775 S. Main St.* ☎ *603/569–1648* 🌐 *www.eastofsuez.com* 🕒 *Closed Oct.–mid-May.*

WHERE TO STAY

For expanded hotel reviews, visit Fodors.com.

$$ B&B/INN ★ 🏨 **Topsides B & B.** At this stylish retreat, refined rooms convey the allure of a particular region, from coastal France to Martha's Vineyard to British fox-hunting country. **Pros:** great location; clean, simple rooms. **Cons:** some rooms are upstairs. [$] *Rooms from: $195* ✉ *209 S. Main St.* ☎ *603/569–3834* 🌐 *www.topsidesbb.com* 🛏 *5 rooms* 🍽 *Breakfast.*

$$$$ B&B/INN ★ 🏨 **The Wolfeboro Inn.** This 1812 inn has a commanding lakefront location and is a perennial favorite for those visiting Lake Winnipesaukee. **Pros:** lakefront setting; interesting pub. **Cons:** availability sometimes limited due to weddings and corporate groups. [$] *Rooms from: $269* ✉ *90 N. Main St.* ☎ *603/569–3016, 800/451–2389* 🌐 *www.wolfeboroinn.com* 🛏 *41 rooms, 3 suites* 🍽 *Breakfast.*

8

ALTON BAY

10 miles southwest of Wolfeboro.

Lake Winnipesaukee's southern shore is alive with visitors from the moment the first flower blooms until the last maple sheds its leaves. Two mountain ridges hold 7 miles of the lake in Alton Bay, which is the name of both the inlet and the town at its tip. Cruise boats dock here, and small planes land year-round on the water and the ice. There's a dance pavilion, along with miniature golf, a public beach, and a Victorian-style bandstand.

EXPLORING

Mt. Major. Mt. Major, 5 miles north of Alton Bay on Route 11, has a 2.5-mile trail up a series of challenging cliffs. At the top is a four-sided stone shelter built in 1925, but the reward is the spectacular view of Lake Winnipesaukee.

WHERE TO EAT

$$$$ AMERICAN ★ 🍴 **The Crystal Quail.** This four-table BYOB restaurant with seating for 12, inside an 18th-century farmhouse, is worth the drive for the sumptuous meals prepared by longtime proprietors Harold and Cynthia Huckaby, who use free-range meats and mostly organic produce and herbs in their cooking. The prix-fixe menu changes daily but might include saffron-garlic soup, a house pâté, mushroom and herb quail, or goose confit with apples and onions. No credit cards are accepted. [$] *Average main: $70* ✉ *202 Pitman Rd., 12 miles south of Alton Bay, Center Barnstead* ☎ *603/269–4151* 🌐 *www.crystalquail.com* ✍ *Reservations essential* 💳 *No credit cards* 🕒 *Closed Mon. and Tues. No lunch* ☞ *BYOB.*

WEIRS BEACH

17 miles northwest of Alton Bay.

👶 Weirs Beach is Lake Winnipesaukee's center for arcade activity. Anyone who loves souvenir shops, fireworks, waterslides, and hordes of children will feel right at home. Cruise boats also depart from here.

GETTING HERE AND AROUND

Weirs Beach is just north of Laconia and south of Meredith on Route 3.

EXPLORING

👶 **Funspot.** The mother ship of Lake Winnipesaukee's several family-oriented amusement parks, Funspot claims to be the largest arcade in the world, but it's much more than just a video-game room. Indeed, you can work your way through a miniature golf course, a driving range, an indoor golf simulator, 20 lanes of bowling, cash bingo, and more than 500 video games. Some outdoor attractions are closed in winter months. ✉ *Rte. 3, 579 Endicott St. N* ☎ *603/366–4377* 🌐 *www.funspotnh.com* 🕒 *Mid-June–Labor Day, daily 9 am–11 pm; Labor Day–mid-June, Sun.–Thurs. 10–10, Fri. and Sat. 10 am–11 pm.*

Fodor's Choice ★ 👶 **MS Mount Washington.** This 230-foot boat makes 2½-hour scenic cruises of Lake Winnipesaukee from Weirs Beach from mid-May to late October, with stops in Wolfeboro, Alton Bay, Center Harbor, and Meredith (you can board at any of these). Evening cruises include live music and a buffet dinner and have nightly music themes, so check ahead to make sure it's music you like. The same company operates the MV *Sophie C.* ($24), which has been the area's floating post office for more than a century. The boat departs from Weirs Beach with mail and passengers and lets you see areas of the lake not accessible by larger ships. Additionally, you can ride the MV *Doris E.* ($16–24) on one- and two-hour scenic cruises of Meredith Bay and the lake islands throughout summer. ☎ 603/366–5531, 888/843–6686 ⊕ *www.cruisenh.com* ☒ *$27* ☉ *Day cruises, departures daily every few hours mid-June–late Oct. Special cruises, departure times vary.*

★ **Winnipesaukee Railroad.** The period cars of this railroad carry you along the lakeshore on one- or two-hour rides; boarding is at Weirs Beach or Meredith. Special trips that include dinner are also available, as are foliage trains in fall and special Santa trains in December. ☒ *U.S. 3* ☎ *603/279–5253, 603/745–2135 (Lincoln location)* ⊕ *www.hoborr. com* ☒ *$15* ☉ *July–mid-Sept., daily; Memorial Day–late June and mid-Sept.–mid-Oct., weekends only. Call for hours.*

SPORTS AND THE OUTDOORS

BEACH AND BOATING

Ellacoya State Beach & RV Park. The beach and park cover 600 feet along the southwestern shore of Lake Winnipesaukee. ☒ *Rte. 11, Gilford* ☎ *603/293–7821* ⊕ *www.nhstateparks.org* ☒ *$4* ☉ *Mid-May–Labor Day.*

Thurston's Marina. The marina rents watercraft such as pontoon boats and powerboats. ☒ *18 Endicott St. N* ☎ *603/366–4811* ⊕ *www. thurstonsmarina.com.*

GOLF

Pheasant Ridge. One of the several courses run by Play Golf New England, this one has an 18-hole layout with great mountain views. Greens fees range from $20 to $45. ☒ *140 Country Club Rd., Gilford* ☎ *603/524–7808* ⊕ *www.playgolfne.com.*

SKI AREAS

Gunstock Mountain Resort. High above Lake Winnipesaukee, this all-purpose recreation area, originally a WPA project, dates from 1937. In recent years, it has invested $10 million to increase snowmaking, options for beginning skiers, and amenities such as private ski lessons and slope-side dining. Thrill Hill, a snow-tubing park, has four runs, a lift service, and a 12-acre terrain park with jumps, rails, and tabletops for snowboarders looking for a challenge, and a racing program. The ski area has 51 trails, 21 open for night skiing, and 32 miles of cross-country and snowshoeing trails available. In summer enjoy the swimming pool, playground, hiking trails, mountain-bike rentals and trails, a skateboarding and blading park, guided horseback rides, pedal boats, and a campground. ☒ *719 Cherry Valley Rd., Gilford* ☎ *603/293–4341, 800/486–7862* ⊕ *www.gunstock.com.*

SHOPPING

Pepi Herrmann Crystal. Take a tour and watch artists at work crafting the hand-cut crystal chandeliers and stemware sold here. Closed Monday. ☒ *3 Waterford Pl.* ☎ *603/528–1020* ⊕ *www.handcut.com.*

8

What's your vessel of choice for exploring New Hampshire's Lakes Region: kayak, canoe, powerboat, or sailboat?

NIGHTLIFE AND THE ARTS

New Hampshire Music Festival. The New Hampshire Music Festival presents award-winning orchestras on Thursdays, Fridays, and alternate Saturdays, from early July to mid-August; concerts occur at the Festival House on Symphony Lane in Center Harbor or at the Silver Cultural Arts Center on Main Street in Plymouth. ⊠ *52 Symphony La.* ☎ *603/279–3300* ⊕ *www.nhmf.org.*

LACONIA

4 miles west of Gilford, 27 miles north of Concord.

The arrival in Laconia—then called Meredith Bridge—of the railroad in 1848 turned the once-sleepy hamlet into the Lakes Region's chief manufacturing hub. It acts today as the area's supply depot, a perfect role given its accessibility to both Winnisquam and Winnipesaukee lakes as well as Interstate 93. It also draws bikers from around the world for Laconia Motorcycle Week in June.

GETTING HERE AND AROUND

The best way to Laconia is on Route 3 or Route 11. Scenic rides from the south include Route 106 and Route 107.

EXPLORING

Belknap Mill. The oldest unaltered, brick-built textile mill in the United States (1823), Belknap Mill contains a knitting museum devoted to the textile industry and a year-round cultural center that sponsors concerts, workshops, exhibits, and a lecture series. ⊠ *Mill Plaza, 25 Beacon St. E* ☎ *603/524–8813* ⊕ *www.belknapmill.org* ⏲ *Free* ☉ *Weekdays 9–5.*

OFF THE BEATEN PATH

Canterbury Shaker Village. Shaker furniture and inventions are well regarded, and this National Historic Landmark helps illuminate the world of the people who created them. Established as a religious community in 1792, the village flourished in the 1800s and practiced equality of the sexes and races, common ownership, celibacy, and pacifism. The last member of the community passed away in 1992. Shakers invented such household items as the clothespin and the flat broom and were known for the simplicity and integrity of their designs. Engaging 90-minute tours pass through some of the 694-acre property's more than 25 restored buildings, many of them still with original Shaker furnishings, and crafts demonstrations take place daily. The Shaker Table restaurant ($$–$$$$) serves lunch daily and candlelight dinners Thursday–Sunday (reservations essential); the food blends contemporary and traditional Shaker recipes to delicious effect. A large shop sells fine Shaker reproductions. ✉ *288 Shaker Rd., 15 miles south of Laconia via Rte. 106, Canterbury* ☎ *603/783–9511, 866/783–9511* 🌐 *www.shakers.org* 🎟 *$17 for a 2-day pass* 🕒 *Mid-May–Oct., daily 10–5.*

SPORTS AND THE OUTDOORS

Bartlett Beach. Bartlett Beach on Lake Winnisquam has a playground and picnic area and no fee. ✉ *Winnisquam Ave.*

Opechee Park. On Lake Opechee, Opechee Park has dressing rooms, a baseball field, tennis courts, and picnic areas. ✉ *N. Main St.*

SHOPPING

Tanger Outlets. The more than 50 stores at the Tanger Outlets include Brooks Brothers, Eddie Bauer, Coach, and Mikasa. ✉ *120 Laconia Rd., I–93 Exit 20, Tilton* ☎ *603/286–7880* 🌐 *www.tangeroutlet.com.*

WHERE TO STAY

For expanded hotel reviews, visit Fodors.com.

$$ B&B/INN 🏨 **The Lake House at Ferry Point.** Four miles southwest of Laconia, this home across the street from Lake Winnisquam is a quiet retreat with easy access to a dock, and a small beach. **Pros:** affordable, lovely setting. **Cons:** best for relaxed do-it-yourselfers. [$] *Rooms from: $185* ✉ *100 Lower Bay Rd., Sanbornton* ☎ *603/524–0087* 🌐 *www.lakehouseatferrypoint.com* 🛏 *9 rooms, 1 suite* 🍴 *Breakfast.*

MEREDITH

11 miles north of Laconia.

Meredith is a favored spot for water-sports enthusiasts and anglers. Lodgers will love the luxurious beds at the Inns at Mill Falls, which are next to an old factory filled with gift and clothing shops. For a true taste of Meredith, take a walk down Main Street, just one block from busy Route 3, which is dotted with intimate coffee shops, salons and barber shops, family restaurants, redbrick buildings, antiques stores, and a gun shop. You can pick up area information at a kiosk across from the town docks. One caveat: on busy weekends, getting into town from the west can mean sitting in traffic for 30 minutes or more.

ESSENTIALS

Visitor Information Meredith Area Chamber of Commerce ☎ *877/279-6121* ⊕ *www.meredithareachamber.com.*

SPORTS AND THE OUTDOORS

BOATING

Meredith is near the quaint village of Center Harbor, another boating hub that's in the middle of three bays at the northern end of Lake Winnipesaukee.

Meredith Marina. Rent powerboats and jet-skis at Meredith Marina. ⊠ *2 Bayshore Dr.* ☎ *603/279-7921* ⊕ *www.meredithmarina.com.*

Wild Meadow Canoes & Kayaks. Wild Meadow Canoes & Kayaks has canoes and kayaks for rent. ⊠ *6 Whittier Way, in Center Harbor* ☎ *603/253-7536, 800/427-7536* ⊕ *www.wildmeadowcanoes.com.*

HIKING

Red Hill. Red Hill, a hiking trail on Bean Road off Route 25, northeast of Center Harbor and about 7 miles northeast of Meredith, really does turn red in autumn. The reward at the end of the route is a view of Squam Lake and the mountains.

SHOPPING

The Annalee Outlet. The Annalee Outlet sells, at a discount, the seasonal decorations and dolls of the Annalee company, famous for its felt dolls that Annalee Davis Thorndike began making here in 1933. ⊠ *Olde Province Commons, 71 U.S. 104* ☎ *800/433-6557* ⊕ *www.annalee. com* ⊙ *Daily 10-6.*

The Inns & Spa at Mill Falls. The Inns & Spa at Mill Falls, part of the Inns at Mill Falls, contain shops with clothing, gifts, and books set around the old factory waterfall that runs through it. ⊠ *312 Daniel Webster Hwy.* ☎ *800/622-6455* ⊕ *www.millfalls.com.*

Keepsake Quilting. Keepsake Quilting, reputedly America's largest quilt shop, contains 5,000 bolts of fabric, hundreds of quilting books, and countless supplies, as well as handmade quilts. ⊠ *Senters Market, 12 Main St., Rte. 25B, Center Harbor, 5 miles northeast of Meredith* ☎ *603/253-4026, 800/525-8086* ⊕ *www.keepsakequilting.com.*

★ **League of NH Craftsmen.** The League of NH Craftsmen sells works by over 200 area artisans; demonstrations are scheduled regularly. It's next to the Inn at Church Landing. ⊠ *279 U.S. 3* ☎ *603/279-7920* ⊕ *www. nhcrafts.org/meredith/.*

Old Print Barn. The Old Print Barn carries rare prints—Currier & Ives, antique botanicals, and more—from around the world. ⊠ *343 Winona Rd., New Hampton* ☎ *603/279-6479* ⊕ *www.theoldprintbarn.com.*

THE ARTS

Interlakes Summer Theatre. Broadway musicals are presented at the Interlakes Summer Theatre during its 10-week season of summer stock. ⊠ *One Laker Lane, Interlakes Auditorium, Rte. 25* ☎ *888/245-6374* ⊕ *www.interlakestheatre.com.*

View simple yet functional furniture, architecture, and crafts at Canterbury Shaker Village.

WHERE TO EAT AND STAY

For expanded hotel reviews, visit Fodors.com.

$$ AMERICAN 🍴 **Lakehouse Grille.** With perhaps the best lake views of any restaurant in the region, this restaurant might be forgiven for ambitious dishes that fall short of being really good. Come here to be near the lake, especially in the convivial bar area, and you'll leave quite happy. The setting is an upscale lodge and is one of the Common Man restaurants. The best dishes are old reliables like steak, ribs, and pizza. Breakfast is served daily. [$] *Average main: $21* ✉ *Church Landing, 281 Daniel Webster Hwy.(Route 3), Ashland* ☎ *603/279–5221* 🌐 *www.thecman.com.*

$$ AMERICAN 🍴 **Mame's.** This 1820s tavern, once the home of the village doctor, now contains a warren of dining rooms with exposed-brick walls, wooden beams, and wide-plank floors. Expect a wide variety of beef, seafood, and chicken plates, but don't be afraid to order the "Luncheon Nightmare," pumpernickel-rye bread topped with turkey, ham, broccoli, and bacon and baked in a cheese sauce. You can also find vegetarian dishes, burgers, sandwiches, and wonderful soups and salads on the menu. Save room for the bread pudding with apples and rum sauce. A cozy tavern upstairs features pub food. [$] *Average main: $23* ✉ *8 Plymouth St.* ☎ *603/279–4631* 🌐 *www.mamesrestaurant.com.*

$$$$ B&B/INN Fodor's Choice ★ 🏨 **Inns and Spa at Mill Falls.** There are four separate hotels here: two newer properties are on the shore of Lake Winnipesaukee, one is connected to a 19th-century mill (now a lively shopping area) and its roaring falls, and the last has views overlooking the lake. **Pros:** many lodging choices and prices; lakefront rooms; fun environment. **Cons:** expensive; two buildings are not on lakefront. [$] *Rooms from: $329* ✉ *312 Daniel*

Webster Hwy.(Rte 3), at Rte. 25 ☎ 603/279–7006, 800/622–6455 🌐 www.millfalls.com 🛏 154 rooms, 15 suites 🍴 Breakfast.

HOLDERNESS

8 miles southeast of Plymouth; 8 miles northwest of Meredith.

Routes 25B and 25 lead to the prim small town of Holderness, between Squam and Little Squam lakes. *On Golden Pond,* starring Katharine Hepburn and Henry Fonda, was filmed on Squam, whose quiet beauty attracts nature lovers.

EXPLORING

Fodor's Choice ★ **Squam Lakes Natural Science Center.** Trails on this 200-acre property include a ¾-mile path that passes black bears, bobcats, otters, mountain lions, and other native wildlife in trailside enclosures. The "Up Close to Animals" series in July and August allows visitors to see a species at an educational presentation in an amphitheater. Children's activities include learning about bugs, watercolor painting of plants and animals, and wilderness survival skills. The boat ride is the best way to tour the lake: naturalists explain its science and describe the animals that make their home here, including fascinating stuff about the loon. ✉ *Rte. 113, 23 Science Center Rd.* ☎ *603/968–7194* 🌐 *www.nhnature.org* 🎟 *$15* 🕒 *May–Oct., daily 9:30–4:30 (last entry at 3:30).*

WHERE TO EAT

$$$$ AMERICAN 🍴 **Manor on Golden Pond Restaurant.** Leaded glass panes and wood paneling set the decidedly romantic tone at this wonderful inn's dining rooms on a hill overlooking Squam Lake. The main dining room is in the manor's original billiard room and features woodwork from 1902. Two other dining rooms have very separate looks: one features white linen, fresh flowers, and candlelight; the other is in the style of a Parisian bistro. The menu changes weekly but might include lobster risotto, filet mignon, quail, or monkfish. Breakfast is also served. A fabulous seven-course tasting menu is $80. [$] *Average main: $35* ✉ *31 Manor Dr., on the corner of Rte. 3 and Shepard Dr.* ☎ *603/968–3348* 🌐 *www.manorongoldenpond.com* ✍ *Reservations essential.*

$$ AMERICAN 🍴 **Walter's Basin.** A former bowling alley in the heart of Holderness makes an unlikely but charming setting for meals overlooking Little Squam Lake—local boaters dock right beneath the dining room. Among the specialties on this seafood-intensive menu are crostini with panfried rainbow trout. Burgers and sandwiches are served in the adjoining tavern. [$] *Average main: $22* ✉ *859 U.S. Rte. 3* ☎ *603/968–4412* 🌐 *www.waltersbasin.com* 🕒 *Call for winter schedule.*

WHERE TO STAY

For expanded hotel reviews, visit Fodors.com.

$$$ B&B/INN 🏨 **Glynn House.** Pam, Ingrid, and Glenn Heidenreich operate this upscale 1890s Queen Anne–style Victorian with a turret and wraparound porch and, next door, a handsome 1920s carriage house. **Pros:** luxurious; well run; social atmosphere. **Cons:** not much to do in town. [$] *Rooms from: $209* ✉ *59 Highland St., Ashland* ☎ *603/968–3775, 866/686–4362* 🌐 *www.glynnhouse.com* 🛏 *5 rooms, 8 suites* 🍴 *Breakfast.*

$$ B&B/INN **Inn on Golden Pond.** Sweet-as-pie Bill and Bonnie Webb run this comfortable and informal B&B at a slight walk from the lake, to which they provide hiking trail maps. **Pros:** friendly innkeepers; very clean rooms and common spaces. **Cons:** 5-minute walk to access lake; not luxurious. [$] *Rooms from: $185* ✉ *1080 U.S. Rte. 3* ☎ *603/968–7269* 🌐 *www.innongoldenpond.com* 🛏 *6 rooms, 2 suites* 🍴 *Breakfast.*

$$$$ B&B/INN Fodor's Choice ★ **The Manor on Golden Pond.** A name like that is a lot to live up to. **Pros:** wood fireplaces; comfy sitting rooms; great food; welcoming hosts. **Cons:** expensive. [$] *Rooms from: $285* ✉ *U.S. 3 and Shepard Hill Rd.* ☎ *603/968–3348, 800/545–2141* 🌐 *www.manorongoldenpond.com* 🛏 *21 rooms, 2 suites, 1 cottage.*

$$ B&B/INN **Squam Lake Inn.** Graceful, simple Victorian furnishings fill the nine stylish rooms and suites at this peaceful farmhouse inn just a short stroll from Squam Lake. **Pros:** quiet setting; comfortable beds; big breakfasts. **Cons:** short walk to lake. [$] *Rooms from: $185* ✉ *Rte. 3 and Shepard Hill Rd.* ☎ *603/968–4417, 800/839–6205* 🌐 *www.squamlakeinn.com* 🛏 *9 rooms* ⏲ *Closed Dec.–Mar.* 🍴 *Breakfast.*

CENTER SANDWICH

12 miles northeast of Holderness on Route 103.

★ With Squam Lake to the west and the Sandwich Mountains to the north, Center Sandwich claims one of the prettiest settings of any Lakes Region community. So appealing are the town and its views that John Greenleaf Whittier used the Bearcamp River as the inspiration for his poem "Sunset on the Bearcamp." The town attracts artisans—crafts shops abound among its clutch of charming 18th- and 19th-century buildings.

ESSENTIALS

Visitor Information Squam Lakes Area Chamber of Commerce ☎ *603/968–4494* 🌐 *www.visitsquam.com.* **Sandwich HIstorical Society** ☎ *603/284–6269* 🌐 *www.sandwichhistorical.org.*

EXPLORING

Castle in the Clouds. This wonderful mountaintop estate was built in 1913–14 without nails. The elaborate mansion has 16 rooms, eight bathrooms, and doors made of lead. Owner Thomas Gustave Plant spent $7 million, the bulk of his fortune, on this project and died penniless in 1941. A tour includes the mansion and the Castle Springs spring-water facility on this 5,200-acre property overlooking Lake Winnipesaukee; there are also hiking and pony and horseback rides. ✉ *Rte. 171, 455 Old Mountain Rd., Rte. 171, Moultonborough* ☎ *603/476–5900* 🌐 *www.castleintheclouds.org* 🎟 *$16* ⏲ *Mid-May–early June weekends only; early June–late Oct., daily 10–4:30.*

Historical Society Museum. This museum traces Center Sandwich's history through the faces of its inhabitants. Works by mid-19th-century portraitist and town son Albert Gallatin Hoit hang alongside a local photographer's exhibit portraying the town's mothers and daughters. The museum houses a replica country store, local furniture, and other items. ✉ *4 Maple St.* ☎ *603/284–6269* 🌐 *www.sandwichhistorical.org* 🎟 *$3* 🕒 *Late June–early Oct., Tues.–Sat. 10–4.*

Loon Center. The Loon Center and **Frederick and Paula Anna Markus Wildlife Sanctuary** is the headquarters of the Loon Preservation Committee, an Audubon Society project. The loon, recognizable for its eerie calls and striking black-and-white coloring, resides on many New Hampshire lakes but is threatened by boat traffic, poor water quality, and habitat loss. Two trails wind through the 200-acre property; vantage points on the Loon Nest Trail overlook the spot resident loons sometimes occupy in late spring and summer. ✉ *183 Lee's Mills Rd.* ☎ *603/476–5666* 🌐 *www.loon.org* 🎟 *Free* 🕒 *Columbus Day–Dec, Mon.–Sat. 9–5; Jan.–Apr., Thurs–Sat. 9–5; May–June, Mon.–Sat. 9–5; July–Columbus Day, daily 9–5.*

SHOPPING

Old Country Store and Museum. The store has been selling maple products, cheeses aged on-site, penny candy, and other items since 1781. Much of the equipment still used in the store is antique, and the museum (free) displays old farming and forging tools. ✉ *1011 Whittier Hwy., Moultonborough* ☎ *603/476–5750* 🌐 *www.nhcountrystore.com/.*

WHERE TO EAT

$$ AMERICAN 🍴 **Corner House Inn.** This restaurant, in a converted barn adorned with local arts and crafts, serves classic American fare. Salads with local greens are a house specialty, but also try the chef's lobster-and-mushroom bisque or the shellfish sauté. Lunch and Sunday brunch are served, and on Thursday evenings there's storytelling (October–May) with dinner. [$] *Average main: $18* ✉ *22 Main St.* ☎ *603/284–6219* 🌐 *www.cornerhouseinn.com* 🕒 *No lunch mid-June–mid-Oct.*

$$$ AMERICAN 🍴 **The Woodshed.** Farm implements and antiques hang on the walls of this enchanting 1860 barn. The fare is mostly traditional New England—prime rib, rack of lamb, marinated chicken—but with some surprises, such as Cajun-blackened pork tenderloin. Either way, the exceptionally fresh ingredients are sure to please. [$] *Average main: $26* ✉ *128 Lee Rd., Moultonborough* ☎ *603/476–2311* 🌐 *www.thewoodshedrestaurant.com* 🕒 *Closed Mon. No lunch.*

TAMWORTH

13 miles east of Center Sandwich, 20 miles southwest of North Conway.

President Grover Cleveland summered in what remains a village of almost unreal quaintness—it's equally photogenic in verdant summer, during the fall foliage season, or under a blanket of winter snow. Cleveland's son, Francis, returned and founded the acclaimed Barnstormers Theatre in 1931, one of America's first summer theaters and one that continues to this day. Tamworth has a clutch of villages within its borders. At one of them—Chocorua—the view through the birches of Chocorua Lake has been so often photographed that you may experience déjà vu. Rising above the lake is Mount Chocorua (3,490 feet), which has many good hiking trails.

GETTING HERE AND AROUND

The five villages of Tamworth boast six churches, which are worth a half-day's casual drive to admire their white clabbered elegance. Downtown Tamworth is tiny and can be strolled in a few minutes, but you might linger in the hope to meet one of the town's many resident poets and artists.

EXPLORING

Remick Country Doctor Museum and Farm. For 99 years (1894–1993) Dr. Edwin Crafts Remick and his father provided medical services to the Tamworth area and operated a family farm. After the younger Remick died, these two houses were turned into the Remick Country Doctor Museum and Farm. The exhibits focus on the life of a country doctor and on the activities of the still-working farm. You can tour the farm daily, and each season features a special activity such as maple syrup making or building without nails. The second floor of the house has been kept as it was when Remick passed away; it's a great way to see the life of a true Tamworth townsman. ⊠ *58 Cleveland Hill Rd.* ☎ *603/323–7591, 800/686–6117* ⊕ *www.remickmuseum.org* ⊠ *$3* ☉ *Labor Day–mid-June, weekdays 10–4; mid-June–Labor Day., Mon.–Fri. 10–4, Sat. 10–3.*

SPORTS AND THE OUTDOORS

White Lake State Park & Campground. The 72-acre stand of native pitch pine here is a National Natural Landmark. The park has hiking trails, a sandy beach, trout fishing, canoe rentals, two camping areas, a picnic area, and swimming. ⊠ *1632 White Mountain Hwy.* ☎ *603/323–7350* ⊕ *www.nhstateparks.org* ⊠ *$4* ☉ *Late May–mid-June, weekends dawn–dusk; mid-June–early Sept., daily dawn–dusk.*

SHOPPING

Chocorua Dam Ice Cream & Gift Shop. The many rooms with themes—Christmas, bridal, and children's among them—at the Chocorua Dam Ice Cream & Gift Shop contain handcrafted items. Don't forget to try the ice cream, coffee, or tea and scones. ⊠ *Rte. 16, Chocorua* ☎ *603/323–8745* ☉ *Closed Oct.–mid-May.*

THE ARTS

Arts Council of Tamworth. The Arts Council of Tamworth produces concerts—soloists, string quartets, revues, children's programs—from September through June and an arts show in late July. ⊠ *77 Main St.* ☎ *603/323–8104* ⊕ *www.artstamworth.org/.*

Barnstormers Theatre. Barnstormers Theatre puts on eight dramatic and comedic theater productions during July and August; you'll likely find community events and concerts the rest of the year. ⊠ *104 Main St.* ☎ *603/323–8500* ⊕ *www.barnstormerstheatre.org/.*

WHERE TO EAT AND STAY

For expanded hotel reviews, visit Fodors.com.

$ ╳ **Jake's Seafood and Grill.** Oars and nautical trappings adorn the wood-
SEAFOOD paneled walls at this stop between West and Center Ossipee, about 8 miles southeast of Tamworth. The kitchen serves some of eastern New Hampshire's freshest and tastiest seafood, notably lobster pie, fried

8

clams, and seafood casserole; other choices include steak, ribs, and chicken dishes. [$] *Average main: $15* ✉ *2055 Rte. 16, West Ossipee* ☎ *603/539–2805* 🌐 *www.jakesseafoodco.com* 🕓 *Closed April.*

$ SOUTHERN ★ 🍴 **Yankee Smokehouse.** Need a rib fix? This down-home barbecue joint's logo depicting a happy pig foreshadows the gleeful enthusiasm with which patrons dive into the hefty sandwiches of sliced pork and smoked chicken and immense platters of baby back ribs and smoked sliced beef. Ample sides of slaw, beans, fries, and garlic toast complement the hearty fare. Even Southerners have been known to come away impressed. [$] *Average main: $14* ✉ *Rtes. 16 and 25, about 5 miles southeast of Tamworth* ☎ *603/539–7427* 🌐 *www.yankeesmokehouse.com.*

$$ B&B/INN ★ 🏨 **Lazy Dog Inn.** If you travel with your dog, you've just found your new favorite B&B. **Pros:** mega dog-friendly; super clean. **Cons:** some rooms share bath; some people don't like dogs. [$] *Rooms from: $160* ✉ *201 Rte. 16, Chocorua* ☎ *603/323–8350, 888/323–8350* 🌐 *www.lazydoginn.com* 🛏 *7 rooms, 4 with bath* 🍽 *Breakfast.*

THE WHITE MOUNTAINS

Sailors approaching East Coast harbors frequently mistake the pale peaks of the White Mountains—the highest range in the northeastern United States—for clouds. It was 1642 when explorer Darby Field could no longer contain his curiosity about one mountain in particular. He set off from his Exeter homestead and became the first European to climb what would later be called Mt. Washington. The 6,288-foot peak must have presented Field with formidable obstacles—its summit claims the highest wind velocity in the world ever recorded (231 mph in 1934) and can see snow every month of the year.

Today an auto road and a cog railway lead to the top of Mt. Washington, and people come by the tens of thousands to hike and climb, photograph the vistas, and ski. The peak is part of the Presidential Range, whose peaks are named after early presidents, and part of the White Mountain National Forest, which has roughly 770,000 acres that extend from northern New Hampshire into southwestern Maine. Among the forest's scenic notches (deep mountain passes) are Pinkham, Kinsman, Franconia, and Crawford. From the notches lead trailheads for short hikes and multiday adventures, which are also excellent spots for photographing the majestic White Mountains

⇨ *This section of the guide begins in Waterville Valley, off Interstate 93, and continues to North Woodstock. It then follows portions of the White Mountains Trail, a 100-mile loop designated as a National Scenic and Cultural Byway.*

ESSENTIALS

Visitor Information White Mountains Visitors Bureau ✉ *Exit 32 off Rte. I–93, North Woodstock* ☎ *800/346–3687* 🌐 *www.visitwhitemountains.com.* **White Mountain National Forest** ☎ *603/536–6100* 🌐 *www.fs.fed.us/r9/forests/white_mountain.*

WATERVILLE VALLEY

60 miles north of Concord.

The first visitors began arriving in Waterville Valley in 1835. A 10-mile cul-de-sac follows the Mad River and is surrounded by mountains. The valley was first a summer resort and then more of a ski area. Although it's now a year-round getaway, it still has a small-town charm. There are inns, condos, restaurants, shops, conference facilities, a grocery store, and a post office.

GETTING HERE AND AROUND

Depot Camp is a great starting point for hiking, snowshoeing, and cross-country skiing. In town, the Schuss bus has regular stops at the shops in Village Square, the lodges and condos, the Waterville Valley Conference Center, and the ski area. There's enough to do in this small village to keep outdoor enthusiasts busy for several days.

SPORTS AND THE OUTDOORS

White Mountain Athletic Club. The White Mountain Athletic Club has tennis, racquetball, and squash as well as a 25-meter indoor pool, a jogging track, exercise equipment, whirlpools, saunas, steam rooms, and a games room. The club is free to guests of many area lodgings. ⊠ *Rte. 49* ☎ *603/236–8303* ⊕ *www.wmacwv.com.*

Waterville Valley Resort. Former U.S. ski-team star Tom Corcoran designed this family-oriented resort. The lodgings and various amenities are about 1 mile from the slopes, but a shuttle renders a car unnecessary. This ski area has hosted more World Cup races than any other in the East, so most advanced skiers will be challenged. Most of the 52 trails are intermediate: straight down the fall line, wide, and agreeably long. A 7-acre tree-skiing area adds variety. One hundred percent snowmaking coverage ensures good skiing even when nature doesn't cooperate. The Waterville Valley cross-country network, with the ski center in the town square, has over 70 km of trails, about two thirds of which are groomed; the rest are backcountry. ⊠ *1 Ski Area Rd.* ☎ *603/236–8311, 800/468–2553 snow conditions, 800/468–2553 lodging* ⊕ *www.waterville.com.*

WHERE TO STAY

For expanded hotel reviews, visit Fodors.com.

$$$
HOTEL
Black Bear Lodge. This family-friendly property has one-bedroom suites that sleep up to six and have full kitchens. **Pros:** affordable. **Cons:** basic in its decor and services. $ *Rooms from: $205* ⊠ *3 Village Rd.* ☎ *603/236–4501, 800/349–2327* ⊕ *www.blackbearlodgenh.com* ⇌ *107 suites.*

$$
HOTEL
Golden Eagle Lodge. Waterville's premier condominium property—with its steep roof punctuated by dozens of gabled dormers—recalls the grand hotels of an earlier era. **Pros:** most reliable accommodation in town. **Cons:** somewhat bland architecture and decor. $ *Rooms from: $179* ⊠ *28 Packard's Rd.* ☎ *888/703–2453* ⊕ *www.goldeneaglelodge. com* ⇌ *139 condominiums.*

$ HOTEL **Snowy Owl Inn & Resort.** You're treated to afternoon wine and cheese in the atrium lobby, which has a three-story fieldstone fireplace and prints and watercolors of snowy owls. **Pros:** affordable. **Cons:** bland. [$] *Rooms from: $149* ✉ *41 Village Rd.* ☎ *603/236–8383, 800/766–9969* 🌐 *www.snowyowlinn.com* *85 rooms* 🍴 *Breakfast.*

LINCOLN/NORTH WOODSTOCK

64 miles north of Concord.

These neighboring towns at the southwestern end of the White Mountains National Forest and one end of the Kancamagus Highway (Route 112) are a lively resort area, especially for Bostonian families who can make an easy day trip straight up Interstate 93 to Exit 32. Festivals, such as the New Hampshire Scottish Highland Games in mid-September, keep Lincoln swarming with people year-round. The town itself is not much of an attraction. Tiny North Woodstock maintains more of a village feel.

GETTING HERE AND AROUND

Lincoln and North Woodstock are places to spend a day shopping in their quaint shops, which are within easy walking distance of each other. It's a pleasant 1-mile stroll between the two towns. On Route 112, which connects the two villages, there is a state visitor center.

ESSENTIALS

Visitor Information Lincoln–Woodstock Chamber of Commerce ☎ *603/745–6621* 🌐 *www.lincolnwoodstock.com.*

EXPLORING

Clark's Trading Post. This old-time amusement park is a kids' favorite and chock full of hokum. It consists of a bear show, circus performers, half-hour train rides over a 1904 covered bridge, a museum of Americana inside an 1880s firehouse, a restored gas station filled with antique cars, and a replica of the Old Man of the Mountain that you can climb on. Tour guides tell tall tales and vendors sell popcorn, ice cream, pizza, and snacks. There's also a mammoth gift shop and a penny-candy store. ✉ *U.S. 3, off I–93 (Exit 33), 110 Daniel Webster Hwy., North Lincoln* ☎ *603/745–8913* 🌐 *www.clarkstradingpost.com* *$19* *Memorial Day–Columbus Day, daily 9–5 (until 9 pm Sat. July 5–Aug. 16).*

FUN TOUR

Hobo Railroad. A ride on the Hobo Railroad yields scenic views of the Pemigewasset River and the White Mountain National Forest. The narrated excursions take 80 minutes. ✉ ***Kancamagus Hwy. (Rte. 112), 64 Railroad St.*** ☎ ***603/745–2135*** 🌐 ***www.hoborr.com*** ***$15*** ***Late June–early Sept., daily; May–late June and early Sept.–Oct., weekends; call for schedule.***

SPORTS AND THE OUTDOORS

Loon Mountain. Wide, straight, and consistent intermediate trails prevail at Loon, a modern resort on the western edge of the Kancamagus Highway (Route 112) and the Pemigewasset River. Beginner trails and slopes are set apart. The most advanced among the 61 runs are grouped on the North Peak section, with 2,100 feet of vertical skiing, farther

The White Mountains

Detail Map (inset)

Highlands
Gorham
2
16
Mt. Madison △
Mt. Jefferson △   △ Mt. Adams
Mt. Clay △   Mt. Washington
                    Auto Road
Cog Railway •   Mt. Washington
Observatory •   State Park
Fabyan   ▲ Mount
                  Washington   Pinkham
                                Notch
Crawford
Notch
16
Crawford Notch
State Park
302
WHITE MOUNTAINS
Glen •   Story
                Land
Bartlett
Echo Lake State Park •
0   4mi
0   4 km
North Conway

Main Map

CANADA
QUÉBEC
257
3
First
Connecticut
Lake
Pittsburg
Aziscohos
Lake
Lake
Francis
Beecher Falls
Wilsons Mills
16
3
Colebrook
Dixville Notch
102   MAINE
Dixville Notch
State Park
26
Errol
26
105
North Stratford
16   Upton
114   Umbagog
                    Lake
5   0   8mi
Lake   0   8 km
Willoughby
Maidstone
Lake
VERMONT   110
West Burke   Groveton   West
                            Milan   Milan
Lyndonville   Guildhall   16
Lyndon
                 Lancaster
5   Berlin
2   Jefferson
Concord   See Detail Above
91   Gorham   Gilead
anville   2
Saint   Whitefield   113
Johnsbury
                            Mount
                            Adams ▲
Barnet   Littleton   Twin   Mt.
                             Mountain Washington
91   Franconia Bethlehem Fabyan   Pinkham Notch
                                       Bretton Wildcat
                            3   Woods
                 Franconia   North
302   Notch State Park   Chatham
Lisbon   White
2   Mountain 302   Black
Wells River   Cannon   National   Mountain
Woodsville   Mt.   Forest   Jackson   Story Land
112   Attitash Glen
5   WHITE MOUNTAINS Ski Area Echo Lake
                 93   State Park
Newbury   Lincoln/North Loon   Kancamagus   N. Conway
10   Woodstock   Mountain Hwy.   Bartlett
91   49   Bear   Cranmore Fryeburg
25   118   Lincoln   Notch Rd. Moutain
Bradford   112
TO   Waterville Mount   16   153
HANOVER   Waterville Valley   Chocurua   TO   Conway
         118   Valley   TO   SNOWVILLE,
         TO   CONCORD ↓   EAST MADISON ↓ Conway
         CONCORD ↓   Lake

from the main mountain. Snowboarders have a half-pipe and their own park; an alpine garden with bumps and jumps provides thrills for skiers. In the base lodge and around the mountain are the usual food-service and lounge facilities. Day and night lift-served snow tubing is on the lower slopes; there's also a winter zipline. The touring center at Loon Mountain has 20 km of cross-country trails, and there's ice-skating on an outdoor rink. ⊠ *Kancamagus Hwy. (Rte. 112), 60 Loon Mountain Rd.* ☎ *603/745–8111, 603/745–8100 snow conditions, 800/229–5666 lodging* ⊕ *www.loonmtn.com.*

Lost River Gorge in Kinsman Notch. At Lost River Gorge in Kinsman Notch parents can enjoy the looks of wonder on their children's faces as they negotiate a wilderness of wooden boardwalks and stairs that snake up and down a granite gorge carved by the waters of the Lost River. Kids can also wiggle through a series of caves such as the Lemon Squeezer and pan for gems and fossils. A cafeteria, gift shop, and garden round out the amenities. ⊠ *Kancamagus Hwy. (Rte. 112), 6 miles west of North Woodstock* ☎ *603/745–8720, 800/346–3687* ⊕ *www.findlostriver.com* ☞ *$17 adults, $13 children* ☉ *Check website for hours.*

Pemi Valley Moose Tours. Eager to see a mighty moose? Embark on a moose-watching bus tour into the northernmost White Mountains with Pemi Valley Moose Tours. The nearly three-hour trips depart in the early evening for the best wildlife sighting opportunities. ⊠ *36 Main St., off I–93 (Exit 32)* ☎ *603/745–2744* ⊕ *www.moosetoursnh.com.*

Whale's Tale Waterpark. At Whale's Tale Waterpark you can float on an inner tube along a gentle river, careen down one of five water-slides, take a trip in a multipassenger tube, or bodysurf in the large wave pool. Whale Harbor and Orca Park Play Island contain water activities for small children and toddlers. ⊠ *U.S. 3, off I–93 (Exit 33), 481 Daniel Webster Hwy., North Lincoln* ☎ *603/745–8810* ⊕ *www. whalestalewaterpark.net* ☞ *$34* ☉ *Mid-June–Labor Day, daily 10–6.*

NIGHTLIFE

Black Diamond Lounge. Skiers head to the Black Diamond Lounge in the Mountain Club at the Loon Mountain resort. ⊠ *60 Loon Mountain Rd.* ☎ *603/745–2244* ⊕ *www.mtnclub.com.*

North Country Center for the Arts. Theater for children and adults and art exhibitions run from July through October at the North Country Center for the Arts. ⊠ *Papermill Theatre, 25 Mountain Brook Cir.* ☎ *603/745–6032, 603/745–2141 box office* ⊕ *www.papermilltheatre.org.*

Thunderbird Lounge. The draws at the Thunderbird Lounge are regularly scheduled entertainment year-round and a large dance floor. ⊠ *Indian Head Resort, 664 U.S. 3, North Lincoln* ☎ *603/745–8000.*

WHERE TO EAT AND STAY
For expanded hotel reviews, visit Fodors.com.

$$
AMERICAN

✕ **Woodstock Inn, Station & Brewery.** If you like eateries loaded with character, don't miss these two restaurants inside the former Lincoln Railroad Station of the late 1800s. More formal is the Clement Room Grille, serving seafood, local meat, and wild game; down the hall is a great brewery and pub that serves 13 handcrafted brews and is decorated

Continued on page 572

A WALK IN THE WOODS

Hiking the Appalachian Trail

By Melissa Kim

Tucked inside the nation's most densely populated corridor, a simple footpath in the wilderness stretches more than 2,100 miles, from Georgia to Maine. The Appalachian Trail passes through some of New England's most spectacular regions, and daytrippers can experience the area's beauty on a multitude of accessible, rewarding hikes.

Running along the spine of the Appalachian Mountains, the trail was fully blazed in 1937 and designed to connect anyone and everyone with nature. Within a day's drive of two-thirds of the U.S. population, it draws an estimated four million people every year. Through-hikers complete the whole trail in one daunting six-month season, but all ages and abilities can find renewal and perspective here in just a few hours. One-third of the AT passes through New England, and it's safe to say that the farther north you go, the harder the trail gets. New Hampshire and Maine challenge experienced hikers with windy, cold, and isolated peaks.

Top, hiking in New Hampshire's White Mountains. Above, autumn view of Profile Lake, Pemigewasset, NH.

ON THE TRAIL

New England's prime hiking season is in late summer and early fall, when the blaze of foliage viewed from a high peak is unparalleled. Popular trails see high crowds; if you seek solitude, try hiking at sunrise, a peaceful time that's good for wildlife viewing. You'll have to curb your enthusiasm in spring and early summer to avoid mud season in late April and black flies in May and June.

With the right gear, attitude, and preparation, winter can also offer fine opportunities for hiking, snowshoeing, and cross-country skiing.

FOLLOW THE TRAIL

Most hiking trails are marked with blazes, blocks of colored paint on a tree or rock. The AT, and only the AT, is marked by vertical, rectangular 2- by 6-inch white blazes. Two blazes mark route changes; turn in the direction of the top blaze. At higher elevations, you might also see cairns, small piles of rocks carefully placed by trail rangers to show the way when a blaze might be obscured by snow or fog.

Scenic U.S. 302—and the AT—pass through Crawford Notch, a spectacular valley in New Hampshire's White Mountains.

Hikers gather outside Lakes of the Clouds Hut, near the peak of Mount Washington.

TRIP TIPS

WHAT TO WEAR: For clothes, layer with a breathable fabric like polypropylene, starting with a shirt, a fleece, and a wind- or water-resistant shell. Bring gloves, a hat, and a change of socks.

WHAT TO BRING: Carry plenty of water and lightweight high-energy food. Don't forget sunscreen and insect repellent. Bring a map and compass. Just in case: a basic first-aid kit, a flashlight or headlamp, whistle, multi-tool, and matches.

PLAN AHEAD: In your car, leave a change of clothing, especially dry socks and shoes, as well as extra water and food.

PLAY IT SAFE: Tell someone your hiking plan and take a hiking partner. Carry a rescue card with emergency contact information and allergy details.

BE PREPARED: Plan your route and check the weather forecast in advance.

REMEMBER YOUR BEGINNINGS: Look back at the trail especially at the trailhead and at tricky junctions. If you've got a digital camera, photograph trail maps posted at the trailhead or natural landmarks to help you find your way.

WHERE TO STAY

Day hikers looking to extend the adventure can also make the experience as hard or as soft as they choose. Through-hikers combine camping with overnight stays in primitive shelters, mountain huts, comfortable lodges, and resorts just off the trail.

Rustic cabins and lean-tos provide basic shelter in Maine's Baxter State Park. In Maine and New Hampshire, the Appalachian Mountain Club runs four-season lodges as well as a network of mountain huts for backcountry hikers. A hiker code of camaraderie and conviviality prevails in these huts. Experience a night and you might just find yourself dreaming of a through-hike.

FOR MORE INFORMATION

Appalachian Trail Conservancy
(🌐 www.appalachiantrail.org)

Appalachian National Scenic Trail
(🌐 www.nps.gov/appa)

Appalachian Mountain Club
(🌐 www.outdoors.org)

ANIMALS ALONG THE TRAIL

❶ Black bear

Black bears are the most common—and smallest—bear in North America. Clever and adaptable, these adroit mammals will eat whatever they can (though they are primarily vegetarian, favoring berries, grasses, roots, blossoms, and nuts). Not naturally aggressive, black bears usually make themselves scarce when they hear hikers. The largest New England populations are in New Hampshire and Maine.

❷ Moose

Spotting a moose in the wild is unforgettable: their massive size and serene gaze are truly humbling. Treasure the moment, then slowly back away. At more than six feet tall, weighing 750 to 1,000 pounds, a moose is not to be trifled with, particularly during rutting and calving seasons (fall and spring, respectively). Dusk and dawn are the best times to spot the iconic animal; you're most likely to see one in Maine, especially in and around ponds.

⚠ Black flies

Especially fierce in May and June, these pesky flies can upset the tranquility of a hike in the woods as they swarm your face and bite your neck. To ward them off, cover any exposed skin and wear light colors. You'll get some relief on a mountain peak; cold weather and high winds also keep them at bay.

❸ Bald eagles

Countless bird species can be seen and heard along the AT, but what could be more exciting than to catch a glimpse of our national bird as it bounces back from near extinction? Now it's not uncommon to see the majestic bald eagle with its tremendous wing span, white head feathers, and curved yellow beak. The white head and tail distinguish the bald from the golden eagle, a bit less rare but just as thrilling to see. Most of New England's bald eagles are in Maine, but they are now present—albeit in small numbers—in all six states.

WILDFLOWERS ALONG THE TRAIL

❹ Mountain laurel

The clusters of pink and white blooms of the mountain laurel look like bursts of fireworks. Up close, each one has the delicate detail of a lady's parasol. Blooms vary in color, from pure white to darker pink, and have different amounts of red markings. Connecticut's state flower, mountain laurel flourishes in rocky woods, blooming in May and June. Look for the shrub in southern New England; it's rare along the Appalachian trail in Vermont and Maine.

❺ Mountain avens

A member of the rose family, these showy yellow flowers abound in New Hampshire's White Mountains. You can't miss the large buttercup-like blooms on long green stems when they are in bloom from June through August. So common here, yet extremely rare: the only other place in the whole world where you can find mountain avens is on an island off the coast of Nova Scotia.

❻ Painted trillium

You might smell a trillium before you see it; these flowers have an unpleasant odor that may attract the flies that pollinate it. To identify this impressive flower, look for sets of three: three large pointed blue-green leaves, three sepals (small leaves beneath the petals), and three white petals with a brilliant magenta center. It can take four or five years for a trillium to produce one flower, which blooms in May and June in wet woodlands.

❼ Pink lady slippers

These delicate orchids can grow from 6 to 15 inches high and favor specific wet wooded areas in dappled sunlight. The slender stalk rises from a pair of green leaves, then bends a graceful neck to suspend the paper-thin pale pink closed flower. The slow-growing plant needs help from fungus and bees to survive and can live to be 20 years old. New Hampshire's state wildflower, the pink lady slipper blooms in June throughout New England.

8

IN FOCUS A WALK IN THE WOODS

● = Somewhat Common ● = Rare

CHOOSE YOUR DAY HIKE

MAINE

GULF HAGAS, Greenville

Difficult, 8-plus mi round-trip, 6–7 hours

This National Natural Landmark in the North Maine Woods is a spectacular sight for the adventurous day hiker. It involves a long drive on logging roads east from Greenville *(see Inland Maine section)* to a remote spot and a slippery, sometimes treacherous 8-mile hike around the rim of what's been dubbed Maine's Grand Canyon. Swimming in one of the sparkling pools under a 30-foot-high waterfall and admiring the views of cliffs, cascades, gorges, and chasms in this slate canyon, otherwise unthinkable in New England, will take your breath away.

TABLE ROCK, Bethel

Medium, 2.4 mi round-trip, 2 hours

Maine's Mahoosuc Range is thought to be one of the most difficult stretches of the entire AT, but north of Bethel at Grafton Notch State Park, day hikes range from easy walks in to cascading waterfalls to strenuous climbs up Old Speck's craggy peak. The Table Rock trail offers interesting sights—great views of the notch from the immense slab of granite that gives this trail its name, as well as one of the state's largest system of slab caves—narrow with tall openings unlike underground caves.

NEW HAMPSHIRE

ZEALAND TRAIL, Berlin

Easy, 5.6 mi round-trip, 3.5–4 hours

New Hampshire's Presidential range gets so much attention and traffic that sometimes the equally spectacular Pemigewasset Wilderness, just to its west, gets overlooked. Follow State Route 302 to the trailhead on Zealand Rd. near Bretton Woods. For an easy day hike to one of the Appalachian Mountain Club's excellent overnight huts, take the mostly flat Zealand Trail over bridges and past a beaver swamp to Zealand Pond. The last tenth of a mile is a steep ascent to the mountain retreat, where you might spot an AT through-hiker taking a well-deserved rest. (Most north-bound through-hikers reach this section around July or August.) In winter, you can get here by a lovely cross-country ski trip.

TRAIL NAMES

For through-hikers, doing the AT can be a life-altering experience. One of trail's most respected traditions is the taking of an alter ego: a trail name. Lightning Bolt: fast hiker. Pine Knot: tough as one. Bluebearee: because a bear got all her food on her very first night on the trail.

VERMONT

HARMON HILL, Bennington

Medium to difficult, 3.6 mi round-trip, 3–4 hours

This rugged hike in the Green Mountains goes south along the AT where it coincides with the Long Trail, Vermont's century-old "footpath in the wilderness." From the trailhead on Route 9 just east of Bennington, the first half mile or so is strenuous, with some rock and log staircases and hairpins. The payback is the sweeping view from the top; you'll see Mount Anthony, Bennington and its iconic war monument, and the rolling green hills of the Taconics to the west.

STRATTON MOUNTAIN, Stratton

Difficult, 6.6 mi round-trip, 5–6 hours

A steep and steady climb from the trailhead on Kelly Stand Rd. (between West Wardsboro and Arlington) up the 3,936-foot-high Stratton Mountain follows the AT and Long Trail through mixed forests. It's said that this peak is where Benton MacKaye conceived of the idea for the Appalachian Trail in 1921. An observation tower at the summit gives you a great 360-degree view of the Green Mountains. From July to October, you can park at Stratton resort and ride the gondola up (or down) and follow the .75-mi Fire Tower Trail to the southern true peak.

MASSACHUSETTS

MOUNT GREYLOCK, North Adams

Easy to difficult, 2 mi round-trip, less than 1 hour

There are many ways to experience Massachusetts's highest peak. From North Adams, follow Route 2 to the Notch Rd. trailheads. For a warm-up, try the Rounds Rock trail (Easy, 0.7 mi) for some spectacular views. Or drive up the 8-mi-long summit road and hike down the Robinson's Point trail (Difficult, 0.8 mi) for the best view of the Hopper, a glacial cirque that's home to an old-growth red spruce forest. At the summit, the impressive **Bascom Lodge**, built in the 1930s by the Civilian Conservation Corps, provides delicious meals and overnight stays (⊕ www.bascomlodge.net).

CONNECTICUT

LION'S HEAD, Salisbury

Medium, 4.6 mi round-trip, 3.5–4 hours

The AT's 52 miles in Connecticut take hikers up some modest mountains, including Lion's Head in Salisbury. From the trailhead on State Route 41, follow the white blazes of the AT for two easy miles, then take the blue-blazed Lion's Head Trail for a short, steep push over open ledges to the 1,738-foot summit with its commanding views of pastoral southern New England. Try this in summer when the mountain laurels—Connecticut's state flower—are in bloom.

EXPERIENCE MOUNT WASHINGTON

Looking at Mt. Washington from Mt. Bond in the Pemigewasset Wilderness Area, New Hampshire.

Mount Washington is the Northeast's peak of superlatives: worst weather in the world, highest spot in the northeast, windiest place on Earth. It snows in the summer, there are avalanches in winter, and it's foggy 60 percent of the time. Strong 35-mile-per-hour winds are the average, and extreme winds of 100 miles per hour with higher gusts blow year-round. Here, you can literally get blown away.

Explorers, scientists, artists, and botanists have been coming to the mountain for hundreds of years, drawn by its unique geologic features, unusual plants, and exceptional climate.

WHY SO WINDY? The 6,288-foot-high treeless peak is the highest point for miles around, so nothing dampens the force of the wind. Also, the sharp vertical rise causes wind to accelerate. Dramatic changes in air pressure also cause strong, high winds. Add to that the fact that three major storm tracks converge here, and you've got a mountain that has claimed more than 135 lives in the past 150 years.

GOING UP THE MOUNTAIN

An ascent up Mount Washington is for experienced hikers who are prepared for severe, unpredictable weather. Even in summer, cold, wet, foggy, windy conditions prevail. The most popular route to the top is on the eastern face up the Tuckerman Ravine Trail. But countless trails offer plenty of moderate day hikes, like the Alpine Garden Trail, as an alternative to a summit attempt. Start at the Pinkham Notch Visitor Center on Route 16 to review your options.

BACKPACKING ON THE MOUNTAIN

Lakes of the Clouds Hut perches 5,050 feet up the southern shoulder, providing bunkrooms and meals in summer; reservations are required. On the eastern face, the **Hermit Lake Shelter Area** has shelters and tent platforms; to camp here you'll need a first-come, first-served permit from the Visitors Center. Both are operated by the **AMC** (☎ 603/466-2727; ⊕ www.outdoors.org).

In the summer, the **Auto Road** (☎ 603/466-3988 ⊕ www.mountwashington autoroad.com) and the **Cog Railway** (☎ 800/922-8825 ⊕ www.thecog.com) present alternate ways up the mountain; both give you a real sense of the mountain's grandeur. In winter, a **Snow-Coach** (☎ 603/466-2333 ⊕ www.greatglentrails.com) hauls visitors 4.5 miles up the Auto Road with an option to cross-country ski, telemark, or snowshoe back down.

with old maps and memorabilia. You come here as much to mix with locals and enjoy the vibe as to eat. The menu is standard pub fare: pizza, burgers, steaks, quesadillas, wings, chicken, and seafood. $ *Average main: $24 ⊠ Exit 32, off I–93, 135 Main St., North Woodstock* 🕾 *603/745–3951* ⊕ *www.woodstockinnbrewery.com.*

$$
RESORT
☺

▨ **Indian Head Resort.** This is the place for families on a budget. **Pros:** best place for kids at a great price. **Cons:** crowded and sometimes hard to get a reservation. $ *Rooms from: $179 ⊠ 664 U.S. Route 3, 5 miles north of North Woodstock, North Lincoln* 🕾 *603/745–8000, 800/343–8000* ⊕ *www.indianheadresort.com* ⬎ *98 rooms, 40 cottages.*

$$$
RESORT

▨ **Mountain Club on Loon.** If you want a ski-in, ski-out stay on Loon Mountain, this is your best and only option. **Pros:** easy skiing access; clean, basic rooms; close to national forest. **Cons:** very busy place in winter. $ *Rooms from: $225 ⊠ 90 Loon Mountain, Kancamagus Hwy. (Rte. 112)* 🕾 *603/745–2244, 800/229–7829* ⊕ *www.mtnclub. com* ⬎ *117 rooms, 117 suites.*

FRANCONIA

16 miles northwest of Lincoln/North Woodstock on I–93.

Travelers have long passed through the White Mountains via Franconia Notch, and in the late 18th century a town evolved just to the north. It and the region's jagged rock formations and heavy coat of evergreens have stirred the imaginations of Washington Irving, Henry Wadsworth Longfellow, and Nathaniel Hawthorne, who penned a short story about the craggy cliff known as the Old Man of the Mountain. There is almost no town proper to speak of here, just a handful of stores, touched though it is by Interstate 93 (the Franconia Notch Parkway).

Four miles west of Franconia, Sugar Hill is a town of about 500 people. It's famous for its spectacular sunsets and views of the Franconia Mountains, best seen from Sunset Hill, where a row of grand hotels and mansions once stood.

GETTING HERE AND AROUND

Franconia is a small town with not much to offer tourists, but it is an access point for many ski areas and the villages of Sugar Hill, Easton, Bethlehem, Bretton Woods, Littleton, Lincoln, and North Woodstock, towns replete with white church steeples, general stores, country inns, and picturesque farms.

ESSENTIALS

Visitor Information Franconia Notch Chamber of Commerce. 🕾 *603/823–5661* ⊕ *www.franconianotch.org.*

EXPLORING

Flume Gorge. This 800-foot-long chasm has narrow walls that cause an eerie echo from the gorge's running water. A wooden boardwalk and a series of stairways wind their way to the top of the falls that thunder down the gorge, followed by a 1-mile hike back to the visitor center. There's a gift shop, café, and dog walk on-site. ⊠ *Franconia Notch Pkwy., Exit 34A* 🕾 *603/745–8391* ⊕ *www.nhstateparks.org* ▱ *$14* *adults, $11 children, or a combined Cannon Mtn. Tram ride and Flume entrance for $26 adults, $20 children* ⊙ *Early May–late Oct., daily 9–5.*

Frost Place. Robert Frost's year-round home from 1915 to 1920 and his summer home for 19 years, this is where the poet soaked up the New England life. This place is imbued with the spirit of his work, down to the rusted mailbox in front that's painted "R. Frost" in simple lettering. Two rooms host occasional readings and contain memorabilia and signed editions of his books. Out back, you can follow short trails marked with lines from his poetry. A visit here will slow you down and remind you of the intense beauty of the surrounding countryside. Poetry readings are scheduled during many evenings in summer. ⊠ *158 Ridge Rd.* ☎ *603/823–5510* ⊕ *www.frostplace.org* ✉ *$5* ⊙ *Open Memorial Day–mid-October.*

Old Man of the Mountain. This naturally formed profile in the rock high above Franconia Notch, a famous New Hampshire geological site, crumbled unexpectedly on May 3, 2003, from the strains of natural erosion. The iconic image had defined New Hampshire, and the Old Man's "death" stunned and saddened residents. You can still stop at the posted turnouts from Interstate 93 north- or southbound. In Franconia Notch State Park on the northbound side of the highway there is a pull-off; on the southbound side take Exit 34B and follow the signs. Another option is to go along the shore of Profile Lake for the best views of the mountain face. There's a small, free Old Man of the Mountain Museum administered by Franconia Notch State Park at the southbound viewing area (by the Cannon Mountain Tram parking area) open daily 9–5.

SPORTS AND THE OUTDOORS
SKI AREAS

Cannon Mountain. The staff at this state-run facility in Franconia Notch State Park is attentive to skier services, family programs, snowmaking, and grooming. One of the nation's first ski areas, Cannon has 55 trails that present challenges rarely found in New Hampshire—for instance, the narrow, steep pitches off the peak of a 2,146-foot vertical rise. There are also two glade-skiing trails—Turnpike and Banshee—and a tubing park with lift service. Thirty-seven miles of cross-country trails are available to Nordic skiers. In summer, for $14 round-trip, the Cannon Mountain Aerial Tramway can transport you up 2,022 feet. It's an eight-minute ride to the top, where marked trails lead to an observation platform. The tram runs daily from mid-May through late October. ⊠ *9 Franconia Notch State Park* ☎ *603/823–8800* ⊕ *www.cannonmt.com.*

Franconia Village Cross-Country Ski Center. The cross-country ski center at the Franconia Inn has over 65 km of groomed and backcountry trails. One popular route leads to Bridal Veil Falls, a great spot for a picnic lunch. You can also enjoy horse-drawn sleigh rides and ice-skating on a lighted rink. ⊠ *1172 Easton Rd.* ☎ *603/823–5542, 800/473–5299* ⊕ *www.franconiainn.com/cross_country_ski_center.php.*

WHERE TO EAT AND STAY

For expanded hotel reviews, visit Fodors.com.

$ AMERICAN ★ 🍴 **Polly's Pancake Parlor.** In the Dexter family for three generations, Polly's has been serving up pancakes, waffles, and French toast since the 1930s. Since then, smoked bacon and ham, sandwiches on homemade bread, desserts such as raspberry pie, delicious baked beans, and even gluten-free items have been added to the menu. Much of the food is made from grains ground on-site. Home mixes and maple syrup, cream, and sugar are for sale year-round. The restaurant closes for the cold season. [$] *Average main: $8* ✉ *672 Rte. 117* ☎ *603/823–5575* 🌐 *www.pollyspancakeparlor.com* 🕒 *Open daily 7–2, mid-May–mid-Oct; from mid-Mar–mid May, weekends only. No dinner.*

$$$$ AMERICAN 🍴 **Sugar Hill Inn.** This 1789 farmhouse is the fine-dining option in the area. Chef Val Fortin serves American fare such as peppercorn-crusted sirloin steak with grilled mushrooms and truffle oil and free-range duck breast with wild mushrooms, prosciutto, and chili-glazed scallops; the homemade desserts are always delicious. A four-course prix-fixe meal is $60. [$] *Average main: $60* ✉ *116 NH Rte. 117* ☎ *603/823–5621* 🌐 *www.sugarhillinn.com* ✍ *Reservations essential* 🕒 *Closed Tues. and Wed. No lunch.*

$$ RESORT 🏨 **Franconia Inn.** At this 120-acre family-friendly resort, you can play tennis on four clay courts, swim in the outdoor heated pool or hot tub, mountain bike, and hike. **Pros:** good for kids; amazing views; outdoor heated pool. **Cons:** may be too remote for some. [$] *Rooms from: $169* ✉ *1300 Easton Rd.* ☎ *603/823–5542, 800/473–5299* 🌐 *www.franconiainn.com* 🛏 *34 rooms, 3 suites, 2 2-bedroom cottages* 🕒 *Restaurant closed Apr.–mid-May.*

$$$ B&B/INN ★ 🏨 **Sugar Hill Inn.** The nicest place in Franconia for a romantic retreat is the Sugar Hill Inn. **Pros:** romantic, classic B&B; fine dinners. **Cons:** expensive. [$] *Rooms from: $210* ✉ *116 NH Rte. 117, Sugar Hill* ☎ *603/823–5621, 800/548–4748* 🌐 *www.sugarhillinn.com* 🛏 *10 rooms, 4 suites* 🍽 *Multiple meal plans.*

LITTLETON

7 miles north of Franconia and 86 miles north of Concord, on I–93.

One of northern New Hampshire's largest towns (this isn't saying much, mind you) is on a granite shelf along the Ammonoosuc River, whose swift current and drop of 235 feet enabled the community to flourish as a mill center in its early days. Later, the railroad came through, and Littleton grew into the region's commerce hub. In the minds of many, it's more a place to stock up on supplies than a bona fide destination, but few communities have worked harder at revitalization. Today, intriguing shops and eateries line the adorable Main Street, with its tidy 19th- and early-20th-century buildings that suggest a set in a Jimmy Stewart movie.

EXPLORING

Littleton Grist Mill. Stop by this restored 1798 mill just off Main Street on the Ammonoosuc River. It contains a small shop selling stone-ground flour products and a museum downstairs showcasing the original mill equipment. ⊠ *18 Mill St.* ☎ *603/259–3205* ⊕ *littletongristmillonline. com/* ⊙ *July–Dec., daily 10–5; Apr.–June, Tues.–Sat. 10–4.*

OFF THE
BEATEN
PATH

Whitefield. Like Dixville Notch and Bretton Woods, Whitefield, 11 miles northeast of Littleton, became a prominent summer resort in the late 19th century, when wealthy industrialists flocked to the small village in a rolling valley between two precipitous promontories to golf, ski, play polo, and hobnob with each other. The sprawling, yellow clapboard Mountain View Grand Hotel, which was established in 1865 and had grown to grand hotel status by the early 20th century, only to succumb to changing tourist habits and close by the 1980s, has been fully refurbished and is now open again as one of New England's grandest resort hotels. It's worth driving through the courtly Colonial center of town—Whitefield was settled in the early 1800s—and up Route 116 just beyond to see this magnificent structure atop a bluff overlooking the Presidentials.

Bethlehem. In the days before antihistamines, hay-fever sufferers came by the trainload to this enchanting village, 5 miles southeast of Littleton, whose crisp air has a blissfully low pollen count. Today this hamlet is notable for its distinctive arts and crafts, Victorian and Colonial homes, art deco movie theater, and shops and eateries on its main street.

Lancaster. About 8 miles north of Whitefield via U.S. 3, the affable seat of Coos County sits at the confluence of the Connecticut and Israel rivers, surrounded by low serrated peaks. Before becoming prosperous through commerce, Lancaster was an agricultural stronghold; at one time the only acceptable currency here was the bushel of wheat. It's still an intimate mountain town. Like Littleton, it has restored much of its main street, which now has a dapper mix of Victorian homes, funky artisan and antiques shops, and prim churches and civic buildings.

SPORTS AND THE OUTDOORS

The Society for the Protection of New Hampshire Forests owns two properties open to visitors in Bethlehem, 5 miles southeast of Littleton.

Bretzfelder Park. Bretzfelder Park, a 77-acre nature and wildlife park, has a picnic shelter, hiking, and cross-country ski trails. ⊠ *Prospect St., Bethlehem* ☎ *603/444–6228.*

Rocks Christmas Tree Farm. The Rocks Christmas Tree Farm is a working Christmas-tree farm (select your own) with walking trails, historic buildings, and educational programs. ⊠ *4 Christmas Lane, Bethlehem* ☎ *603/444–6228.*

SHOPPING

Main Street and Union Street are filled with great little shops.

Potato Barn Antiques Center. You'll find several dealers under one roof at Potato Barn Antiques Center—specialties include vintage farm tools, clothing, and costume jewelry. ⊠ *960 Lancaster Rd., 6 miles north of Lancaster, Northumberland* ☎ *603/636–2611* ⊕ *www. potatobarnantiques.com.*

Village Book Store. There is good selection of both nonfiction and fiction titles at the Village Book Store. ⊠ *81 Main St.* ☎ *603/444–5263* ⊕ *www. booksmusictoys.com.*

8

Bretton Woods is a year-round destination, and especially popular with families.

QUICK BITES

Miller's Cafe & Bakery. Beside the Littleton Grist Mill, Miller's Cafe & Bakery serves coffees, microbrews and wines, baked goods, sandwiches, and salads. ✉ *16 Mill St.* ☎ *603/444–2146* 🌐 *www.millerscafeandbakery.com* 🕓 *Closed Sun. and Mon. Oct.–May.*

WHERE TO EAT AND STAY

For expanded hotel reviews, visit Fodors.com.

$$ AMERICAN ★ 🍴 **Tim-bir Alley.** This is a rare find in New Hampshire: an independent restaurant in a contemporary setting that's been around a long time (since 1983) and yet still takes its food seriously. If you're in town, don't miss it. Tim Carr's menu changes weekly and uses regional American ingredients in creative ways. Main dishes might include an eggplant pâté with feta cheese, red pepper, and a tomato-herb marmalade or a basil-and-olive-oil-flavored salmon with a spinach-Brie-pecan pesto. Save room for such desserts as white chocolate–coconut cheesecake. [$] *Average main: $23* ✉ *7 Main St.* ☎ *603/444–6142* 💳 *No credit cards* 🕓 *Closed Jan.–Apr. Closed Mon. and Tues. No lunch.*

$ B&B/INN Fodor's Choice ★ 🏨 **Thayers Inn.** This stately 1843 Greek Revival hotel is the essence of Littleton. **Pros:** one of the best values in New England. **Cons:** Continental breakfast only. [$] *Rooms from: $129* ✉ *111 Main St.* ☎ *603/444–6469, 800/634–8179* 🌐 *www.thayersinn.com* 🛏 *27 rooms, 13 suites* 🍽 *Breakfast.*

BRETTON WOODS

14 miles southeast of Bethlehem; 28 miles northeast of Lincoln/ Woodstock.

In the early 1900s private railcars brought the elite from New York and Philadelphia to the Mount Washington Hotel, the jewel of the White Mountains. A visit to the hotel, which was the site of the 1944 United Nations conference that created the International Monetary Fund and the International Bank for Reconstruction and Development (and the birth of many conspiracy theories), is not to be missed. The area is also known for its cog railway and Bretton Woods ski resort.

GETTING HERE AND AROUND

Bretton Woods is in the heart of the White Mountains on Route 302. A free shuttle helps get you around the various facilities at the resort. Helpful advice on how to enjoy your stay can be found at the concierge and activities desk in the main lobby of the Mount Washington Hotel.

EXPLORING

Fodor's Choice
★
☼
Mount Washington Cog Railway. In 1858 Sylvester Marsh petitioned the state legislature for permission to build a steam railway up Mt. Washington. A politico retorted that he'd have better luck building a railroad to the moon. But 11 years later, the Mount Washington Cog Railway chugged its way up to the summit along a 3-mile track on the west side of the mountain, and today it's one of the state's most beloved attractions—a thrill in either direction. The train runs from May until early December, with varying departure times. A full trip ($62) is three hours including one hour at the summit. ⊠ *U.S. 302, 6 miles northeast of Bretton Woods* ☎ *603/278–5404, 800/922–8825* ⊕ *www.thecog. com* ⊠ *$62.*

SPORTS AND THE OUTDOORS

SKI AREA

Fodor's Choice
★
☼
Bretton Woods. Skiing with your family New Hampshire's largest ski area is one of the best family ski resorts in the country. It's also probably the best place in New England to learn to ski. (If it's your first time, get started at the free area serviced by a rope tow.) The views of Mt. Washington alone are worth the visit to Bretton Woods; the scenery is especially beautiful from the **Top of Quad restaurant,** which is open during ski season.

Trails appeal mostly to novice and intermediate skiers, including two magic carpet lifts for beginners. There are some steeper pitches near the top of the 1,500-foot vertical and glade skiing to occupy the experts in the family, as well as night skiing and snowboarding on weekends and holidays. Snowboarders enjoy the four terrain parks, including the all-natural Wild West Park and a half-pipe. A cross-country ski center has 62 miles of groomed and double-track trails, some of them lift-serviced. The Nordic Ski Center near the hotel offers access to 55 miles of cross-country trails and doubles as the golf clubhouse in summer.

Options for kids are plentiful. The Hobbit Ski and Snowboard School for ages 4–12 has full- and half-day instruction. Hobbit Ski and Snow-play program, for ages 3–5, is an introduction to skiing and fun on

8

the snow. The ski area also offers an adaptive program for children and adults with disabilities. There are also organized activities in the nursery. The complimentary Kinderwoods Winter Playground has a sled carousel, igloos, and a zip line. Parents can buy an interchangeable family ticket that allows parents to take turns skiing while the other watches the kids—both passes come for the price of one.

A new addition is the year-round Canopy Tour, which has 10 zip lines, two sky bridges, and three rappel stations. Small groups, guided by experienced climbers and ski patrollers, leave every half hour. The tour, at $110, is one of the longest in the United States and is an exhilarating introduction to flora and fauna of the White Mountains and the history of the area. Kids are welcome but must weigh more than 70 lbs. ✉ *U.S. 302* ☎ *603/278–3320, 603/278–1000 weather conditions, 800/232–2972 information, 800/258–0330 lodging* 🌐 *www.brettonwoods.com.*

WHERE TO EAT

$$$ AMERICAN 🍴 **The Bretton Arms Dining Room.** You're likely to have the best meal in the area at this intimate setting. Though the same executive chef oversees the Mount Washington Hotel dining room, the latter is immense, and the Bretton Arms is cozier. Three small, interconnected rooms are separated by fireplaces. The menu is seasonal and might include Maine lobster tossed with fresh pasta and free-range Long Island duck breast; it also features locally sourced food. [$] *Average main: $26* ✉ *U.S. 302* ☎ *603/278–1000* 🌐 *www.mtwashingtonresort.com* ⏲ *No lunch.*

$$$$ AMERICAN ★ 🍴 **The Dining Room.** You'd be hard-pressed to find a larger or grander dining room in New Hampshire (only the Balsams can compare). The Mount Washington Hotel's enormous octagonal dining room, built in 1902, is adorned with Currier & Ives reproductions, Tiffany glass, chandeliers up the wazoo, massive windows that open to the Presidential Range, and a nightly musical trio. This may be the only restaurant in the state that requires a jacket (except in winter); if you forgot yours, they have about 30 you can borrow. Try seasonal dishes such as seared haddock and shrimp fricassee, lemon lobster ravioli with shrimp and scallops, or roast pork with onions and mushrooms. The Dining Room offers a "Gold Sash Dinner" at a chef's table with a customized menu and wine pairings. [$] *Average main: $36* ✉ *In Mount Washington Hotel, U.S. 302* ☎ *603/278–1000* 🌐 *www.mtwashingtonresort.com* ✍ *Reservations essential* 👔 *Jacket required.*

$$ AMERICAN 🍴 **Fabyan's Station.** In 1890, 60 tourist trains a day passed through this station, now a casual restaurant. If you're looking for an easygoing meal, Fabyan's cooks up delicious clam chowder in a bread bowl and a 16-ounce T-bone grilled to perfection. Half the restaurant is a tavern with a long bar, and the other half serves sandwiches, fish, and steaks. There's a kids' menu, too, and a model train circles the dining room. [$] *Average main: $17* ✉ *Rte. 302, 1 mile north of Bretton Woods ski area* ☎ *603/278–2222* ✍ *Reservations not accepted.*

The views of Mt. Washington and the Presidential range from the porch of Mt. Washington Resort can't be beat.

WHERE TO STAY

For expanded hotel reviews, visit Fodors.com.

$
HOTEL
★

🏨 **The Lodge.** A stay at this inexpensive roadside motel run by Bretton Woods gives you free access to all of the resort facilities at Mount Washington Hotel, including the pools, gym, and arcade, which makes it a great deal. **Pros:** cheap; free access to Mount Washington amenities; free ski shuttle. **Cons:** across street from resort amenities; Continental breakfast only. 💲*Rooms from: $139* ✉ *U.S. 302* ☎ *603/278–1000, 800/680–6600* ⊕ *www.mtwashington.com* 🛏 *50 rooms* ⦿*Breakfast.*

$$
RESORT
Fodor's Choice
★
☾

🏨 **Mount Washington Resort.** The two most memorable sights in the White Mountains would have to be Mount Washington and the Mount Washington Hotel. **Pros:** beautiful resort; loads of activities; free shuttle to skiing and activities. **Cons:** kids love to run around the hotel; Internet access expensive. 💲*Rooms from: $199* ✉ *U.S. 302* ☎ *603/278–1000* ⊕ *brettonwoods.com* 🛏 *177 rooms, 23 suites* ⦿*Multiple meal plans.*

$$$$
B&B/INN
Fodor's Choice
★

🏨 **The Notchland Inn.** Built in 1862 by Sam Bemis, America's grandfather of landscape photography, the house conveys mountain charm on a scale unmatched in New England. **Pros:** middle-of-the-forest setting; marvelous house and common rooms; original fireplaces; good dinner. **Cons:** at 15 miles from the Bretton Woods ski area, will be too isolated for some; rooms could be better equipped (better bedding, for example). 💲*Rooms from: $265* ✉ *2 Morey Rd., Harts Location* ☎ *603/374–6131* ⊕ *www.notchland.com* 🛏 *8 rooms, 5 suites, 2 cottages* ⦿*Breakfast.*

EN
ROUTE

Crawford Notch State Park. Scenic U.S. 302 winds through the steep, wooded mountains on either side of spectacular Crawford Notch, southeast of Bretton Woods, and passes through Crawford Notch State

8

Park, where you can picnic and take a short hike to Arethusa Falls or the Silver and Flume cascades. The park has a number of roadside photo opportunities. The visitor center has a gift shop and a cafeteria; there's also a **campground**. ✉ *2059 U.S. Rte. 302, Harts Location* ☎ *603/374–2272, 603/374–2272 campground* 🌐 *www.nhstateparks.org* 🎟 *$4.*

BARTLETT

18 miles southeast of Bretton Woods.

With Bear Mountain to its south, Mt. Parker to its north, Mt. Cardigan to its west, and the Saco River to its east, Bartlett, incorporated in 1790, has an unforgettable setting. Lovely Bear Notch Road (closed in winter) has the only midpoint access to the Kancamagus Highway (Route 112). There isn't much town here (dining options are in Glen). It's best known for the Attitash Ski Resort, within walking distance.

SPORTS AND THE OUTDOORS

SKI AREA

Attitash Ski Resort. Attitash, with a vertical drop of 1,760 feet, and Attitash Bear Peak, with a 1,450-foot vertical, have massive snowmaking operations and full-service base lodges. The bulk of the skiing and boarding is geared to intermediates and experts, with some steep pitches and glades. At 500 feet, the Ground Zero half-pipe is New England's longest. The Attitash Adventure Center has a rental shop, lessons desk, and children's programs. Attitash also has summer activities such as an alpine slide, guided horseback rides, and a scenic sky ride. ✉ *U.S. 302* ☎ *800/223–7669* 🌐 *www.attitash.com.*

WHERE TO EAT

$$ SOUTHWESTERN 🍴 **Margarita Grill.** Après-ski and hiking types congregate here in the dining room in cold weather and on the covered patio when it's warm for homemade salsas, wood-fired steaks, ribs, burgers, and a smattering of Tex-Mex and Southwestern specialties. Unwind with a margarita at the bar after a day on the mountains. [$] *Average main: $17* ✉ *78 U.S. 302, Glen* ☎ *603/383–6556* 🌐 *www.margaritagrillnh.com* 🕒 *No lunch weekdays.*

$$ AMERICAN 🍴 **Red Parka Steakhouse & Pub.** This downtown Glen pub has been an institution for nearly 40 years. A family-dining–oriented menu features an all-you-can-eat salad bar, baked stuffed shrimp, scallops, and hand-cut steaks. The barbecue sauce is made on-site, and beer is served in Mason jars. Plan to spend some time reading the dozens and dozens of license plates that adorn the walls of the downstairs pub. [$] *Average main: $18* ✉ *3 Station St., Glen* ☎ *603/383–4344* 🌐 *www.redparkapub.com* ✍ *Reservations not accepted* 🕒 *No lunch; pub opens at 3.*

WHERE TO STAY

For expanded hotel reviews, visit Fodors.com.

$$ HOTEL 🏨 **Attitash Mountain Village Resort.** Across the street from the entrance to Attitash, you can't see this cluster of units from the road because they're in the pine trees (there are also a few slopeside condos), but they're there, along with hiking trails, a playground, a clay tennis court, two heated pools, an arcade, and a free stocked fishing pond. **Pros:** simple,

no-frills family place; playground. **Cons:** a bit rundown. [$] *Rooms from: $159* ✉ *784 U.S. 302* ☎ *603/374–6501, 800/862–1600* 🌐 *www.mtwashingtonvalleyaccommodations.com* 🛏 *350 units.*

$ HOTEL 🏨 **Attitash Grand Summit Hotel & Conference Center.** This ski hotel is the choice for those who want ski-in, ski-out convenience. **Pros:** ski-in, ski-out; nice pool and hot tubs; cheaper with ski package; full breakfast included. **Cons:** generally bland accommodations. [$] *Rooms from: $129* ✉ *U.S. 302* ☎ *603/374–1900, 800/223–7669* 🌐 *www.attitash.com* 🛏 *143 rooms.*

JACKSON

5 miles north of Glen.

★ Just off Route 16 via a red covered bridge, Jackson has retained its storybook New England character. Art and antiques shopping, tennis, golf, fishing, and hiking to waterfalls are among the draws. When the snow falls, Jackson becomes the state's cross-country skiing capital. Four downhill ski areas are nearby. Hotels and B&Bs offer a ski shuttle. Visit Jackson Falls for a wonderful photo opportunity.

ESSENTIALS

Visitor Information **Jackson Area Chamber of Commerce** ☎ *603/383–9356* 🌐 *www.jacksonnh.com.*

EXPLORING

👶 **Story Land.** That cluster of fluorescent buildings along Route 16 is a theme park with life-size storybook and nursery-rhyme characters. The 21 rides and five shows include a flume ride, Victorian-theme river-raft ride, farm tractor–inspired kiddie ride, pumpkin coach, variety show, and swan boats. ✉ *850 Rte. 16, Glen* ☎ *603/383–4186* 🌐 *www.storylandnh.com* 🎟 *$29* 🕒 *Memorial Day–early Oct. Check website for dates and hours.*

SPORTS AND THE OUTDOORS

Black Mountain. Friendly, informal Black Mountain has a warming southern exposure. The Family Passport allows two adults and two juniors to ski at discounted rates. Midweek rates ($35) are usually the lowest in Mt. Washington Valley. The 40 trails and glades on the 1,100-foot mountain are evenly divided among beginner, intermediate, and expert. There's a nursery for kids six months and up. Enjoy guided horseback riding in the summer. ✉ *373 Black Mountain Rd.* ☎ *603/383–4490, 800/475–4669 snow conditions* 🌐 *www.blackmt.com.*

★ **Jackson Ski Touring Foundation.** One of the nation's top four cross-country skiing areas, Jackson Ski Touring Foundation has 97 miles of trails. Many of the trails are groomed for regular cross-country and skate skiing. You can arrange lessons and rentals at the lodge, in the center of Jackson Village. ✉ *153 Main St.* ☎ *603/383–9355* 🌐 *www.jacksonxc.org.*

Nestlenook Estate and Resort. Nestlenook Estate and Resort maintains an outdoor ice-skating rink with rentals, music, and a bonfire. Snowshoeing and sleigh rides are other winter options; in summer you can fly-fish

8

or ride in a horse-drawn carriage. ✉ *Dinsmore Rd.* ☎ *603/383–7101* 🌐 *www.nestlenookfarm.com.*

WHERE TO EAT

$ AMERICAN 🍴 **Red Fox Bar & Grille.** Some say this big family restaurant overlooking the Wentworth Golf Club gets its name from a wily fox with a penchant for stealing golf balls off the fairway. The wide-ranging menu has barbecued ribs and wood-fired pizzas as well as more refined dishes such as seared sea scallops with Grand Marnier sauce. The Sunday breakfast buffet is very popular. [$] *Average main: $16* ✉ *49 Rte. 16* ☎ *603/383–4949* 🌐 *www.redfoxpub.com* ⏲ *Lunch on Tues and Wed., summer only.*

$$$ AMERICAN ★ 🍴 **Thompson House Eatery.** One of the most innovative restaurants in generally staid northern New Hampshire, this eatery inside a rambling red farmhouse serves comfort food such as a wonderful meat loaf made with local beef, salads with in-season greens, maple scallops sautéed with a cream sauce, and a chocolate espresso pudding that will make your eyes roll with delight. [$] *Average main: $28* ✉ *193 Main St.* ☎ *603/383–9341* 🌐 *www.thompsonhouseatery.com* ⏲ *Closed Apr.–mid-May.*

$$$ AMERICAN Fodor's Choice ★ 🍴 **Thorn Hill.** This famous inn serves up one of New England's most memorable meals. In warm months dine on the romantic porch, which overlooks the Presidential mountain range. The wine list is the state's most lauded, with 1,900 labels. The curated and changing "Top 50" list of reasonably priced bottles is a sure guide. You'll find subtle and flavorful dishes such as a New York strip with chanterelle mushrooms and bordelaise sauce and salmon grilled with Mediterranean spices and served with hummus and cucumber *raita* (Indian yogurt sauce). The menu changes regularly. [$] *Average main: $26* ✉ *42 Thorn Hill Rd.* ☎ *603/383–4242, 800/289–8990* 🌐 *www.innatthornhill.com* ✍ *Reservations essential* ⏲ *No lunch.*

WHERE TO STAY

For expanded hotel reviews, visit Fodors.com.

$$ B&B/INN 🏨 **Christmas Farm Inn and Spa.** Despite its wintery name, this 1778 inn is an all-season retreat. **Pros:** kids welcome; nice indoor and outdoor pools, very close to Black Mt. Ski area. **Cons:** can be very busy with kids [$] *Rooms from: $189* ✉ *3 Blitzen Way, Rte. 16B* ☎ *603/383–4313, 800/443–5837* 🌐 *www.christmasfarminn.com* 🛏 *18 rooms, 16 suites, 7 cottages* 🍽 *Breakfast.*

$$ B&B/INN Fodor's Choice ★ 🏨 **Inn at Jackson.** This B&B is impeccably maintained, charmingly furnished, and bright. **Pros:** super-clean rooms; great value; peaceful setting. **Cons:** third-floor rooms lack fireplaces. [$] *Rooms from: $189* ✉ *Corner of Main St. and Thorn Hill Rd.* ☎ *603/383–4321, 800/289–8600* 🌐 *www.innatjackson.com* 🛏 *14 rooms* 🍽 *Breakfast.*

$$$$ B&B/INN Fodor's Choice ★ 🏨 **The Inn at Thorn Hill & Spa.** This house, modeled after the 1891 Stanford White Victorian that burned down a decade ago, offers spacious rooms with a relaxed elegance. **Pros:** great meals and service; romantic setting. **Cons:** Wi-Fi works on main floor only; not in-room. [$] *Rooms from: $340* ✉ *42 Thorn Hill Rd.* ☎ *800/289–8990, 800/289–8990* 🌐 *www.innatthornhill.com* 🛏 *15 rooms, 7 suites, 3 cottages* 🍽 *Some meals.*

MT. WASHINGTON

20 miles northwest of Jackson.

★ **Mt. Washington.** Mt. Washington is the highest peak (6,288 feet) in the northeastern United States and the site of a weather station that recorded the world's highest winds, 231 mph, in 1934. You can drive to the top, which climbs 4,600 feet in 7.5 miles, in the summer. A number of trailheads circle the mountain and the other peaks in the Presidential Range, but all of them are strenuous and for the hearty. For the best information on trails in the Presidents, visit the website. The Mt. Washington Cog Railway, which operates in the summer only, climbs 3,500 feet in 3 miles, at grades averaging 25%. *(⇨ Bretton Woods for information on the Mt. Washington Cog Railway.)* ⊕ *www.mountwashington.org.*

ESSENTIALS

Visitor Information Mount Washington Observatory ☎ *603/356–2137* ⊕ *www.mountwashington.org.* **White Mountain National Forest** ✉ *71 White Mountain Dr., Clampton* ☎ *603/536–6100* ⊕ *www.fs.fed.us/r9/forests/ white_mountain.*

EXPLORING

Great Glen Trails SnowCoach. In winter, when the road is closed to private vehicles, you can opt to reach the top of Mt. Washington via a guided tour in one of the four-wheel-drive vehicles that leave from Great Glen Trails Outdoor Center, just south of Gorham, on a first-come, first-served basis. Great Glen's nine-passenger vans are refitted with snowmobile-like treads and can travel to just above the tree line. You have the option of cross-country skiing or snowshoeing down. ✉ *Rte. 16, Pinkham Notch* ☎ *603/466–2333* ⊕ *www.greatglentrails.com/winter/ outdoor-center/snowcoach/* 🎟 *$45 (includes all-day trail pass)* ☾ *Dec.– Mar., snow necessary, most days, beginning at 8:30.*

Mt. Washington Auto Road. Opened in 1861, this route begins at the Glen House, a gift shop and rest stop 15 miles north of Glen on Route 16, and winds its way up the east side of the mountain, ending at the top, a 7.5-mile and approximately half-hour drive later. At the summit is the Sherman Adams Summit Building, built in 1979 and containing a visitor center and a museum focusing on the mountain's geology and extreme weather conditions; you can stand in the glassed-in viewing area to hear the wind roar. The Mt. Washington Observatory is at the building's western end. Rules limit what cars may use the road. For instance, cars with automatic transmission must be able to shift down into first gear. A guided bus tour is available or you can reach the top along several rough hiking trails; those who hoof it can make the return trip via shuttle, tickets for which are sold at the Stage Office, at the summit at the end of the cog railway trestle. Remember that the temperature atop Mt. Washington will be much colder than down below—the average year-round is below freezing, and the average wind velocity is 35 mph. ✉ *Rte. 16, Pinkham Notch* ☎ *603/466–3988* ⊕ *www.mountwashingtonautoroad. com* 🎟 *Car and driver $25, each additional adult passenger $8* ☾ *Check the website for hours of operation; closed late Oct.–early May.*

Reward your vehicle for tackling the auto road with the obligatory bumper sticker: "This Car Climbed Mt. Washington."

SPORTS AND THE OUTDOORS

Appalachian Mountain Club Pinkham Notch Visitor Center. The Appalachian Mountain Club Pinkham Notch Visitor Center has lectures, workshops, slide shows, and outdoor skills instruction year-round. Accommodations include the adjacent Joe Dodge Lodge, the Highland Center at Crawford Notch with 100-plus beds and a 16-bed bunkhouse next to it, and the club's eight high-mountain huts spaced one day's hike from each other in the White Mountain National Forest portion of the Appalachian Trail. The huts provide meals and dorm-style lodging from June to late September or early October; the rest of the year they are self-service. ⊠ *Rte. 16, Gorham* ☎ *603/466–2721, 603/466–2727 reservations* ⊕ *www.outdoors.org.*

Great Glen Trails Outdoor Center. Amenities at this fabulous lodge at the base of Mt. Washington include a huge ski-gear and sports shop, food court, climbing wall, observation deck, and fieldstone fireplace. In winter it's renowned for its dramatic 24-mile cross-country trail system. Some trails have snowmaking, and there's access to more than 1,100 acres of backcountry. It's even possible to ski or snowshoe the lower half of the Mt. Washington Auto Road. Trees shelter most of the trails, so Mt. Washington's infamous weather isn't such a concern. In summer it's the base from which hikers, mountain bikers, and trail runners can explore Mt. Washington. The center also has programs in canoeing, kayaking, and fly-fishing. ⊠ *Rte. 16* ☎ *603/466–2333* ⊕ *www.greatglentrails.com.*

Pinkham Notch. Although not a town per se, scenic Pinkham Notch covers Mt. Washington's eastern side and has several ravines, including

Tuckerman Ravine, famous for spring skiing. The Appalachian Mountain Club maintains a large visitor center here on Route 16 that provides information to hikers and travelers and has guided hikes, outdoor skills workshops, a cafeteria, lodging, regional topography displays, and an outdoors shop. ☎ 603/466–2721 ⊕ *www.outdoors.org.*

Wildcat Mountain. Glade skiers favor Wildcat, with 28 acres of official tree skiing. The 47 runs include some stunning double-black-diamond trails. Skiers who can hold a wedge should check out the 2½-mile-long Polecat. Experts can zip down the Lynx. Views of Mt. Washington and Tuckerman Ravine are superb. The trails are classic New England—narrow and winding. Wildcat's expert runs deserve their designations and then some. Intermediates have mid-mountain to base trails, and beginners will find gentle terrain and a broad teaching slope. Snowboarders have several terrain parks and the run of the mountain. In summer you can go to the top on the four-passenger gondola ($15), ride a zip line, and hike the many well-kept trails. ⊠ *Rte. 16, Jackson* ☎ *603/466–3326, 888/754–9453 snow conditions, 800/255–6439 lodging* ⊕ *www.skiwildcat.com.*

DIXVILLE NOTCH

63 miles north of Mt. Washington, 66 miles northeast of Littleton, 149 miles north of Concord.

Just 12 miles from the Canadian border, this tiny community is known for two things: the Balsams, one of New Hampshire's oldest and most celebrated resorts, and the fact that Dixville Notch and another New Hampshire community, Hart's Location, are the first election districts in the nation to vote in presidential general elections. When the 30 or so Dixville Notch voters file into the little Balsams meeting room on the eve of Election Day and cast their ballots at the stroke of midnight, they invariably make national news.

TOURS

Northern Forest Moose Tours. One of the favorite pastimes in this area is spotting moose, those large, ungainly, yet elusive members of the deer family. Although you may catch sight of one or more yourself, Northern Forest Moose Tours conducts bus tours of the region that have a 97% success rate for spotting moose. ☎ 603/466–3103, 877/986–6673 ☞ *$25* ⊙ *May–Oct. Bus leaves at 6:30 pm.*

OFF THE BEATEN PATH

Pittsburg. Well north of the White Mountains, in the Great North Woods, Pittsburg contains the four Connecticut Lakes and the springs that form the Connecticut River. The state's northern tip—a chunk of about 250 square miles—lies within the town's borders, the result of a dispute between the United States and Canada that began in 1832 and was resolved in 1842, when the international boundary was fixed. Remote though it is, this frontier town teems with hunters, boaters, fishermen, hikers, and photographers from early summer through winter. Especially in the colder months, moose sightings are common. The town has more than a dozen lodges and several informal eateries. It's about a 90-minute drive from Littleton and 40 minutes from Dixville Notch; add another 30 minutes to reach Fourth Connecticut Lake, nearly at the Canadian border. On your way, you pass the village of Stewartson, exactly midway between the Equator and the North Pole.

SPORTS AND THE OUTDOORS

Dixville Notch State Park. Dixville Notch State Park, in the northernmost notch of the White Mountains, has picnic areas, a waterfall, two mountain brooks, and hiking trails. ✉ *Rte. 26* ☎ *603/538–6707* ⊕ *www. nhstateparks.org.*

WHERE TO EAT AND STAY

For expanded hotel reviews, visit Fodors.com.

$
FRENCH
Fodor's Choice
★

✕ **Le Rendez Vous.** You might not expect to find an authentic French bakery and pastry shop in the small workaday village of Colebrook, 10 miles west of Dixville Notch, but Le Rendez Vous serves fabulous tarts and treats—the owners came here directly from Paris. Drop in to this quaint café—furnished with several tables and armchairs— for coffee, hand-dipped Belgian chocolates, croissants, a tremendous variety of fresh-baked breads, and all sorts of gourmet foods, from dried fruits and nuts to lentils, olive oils, and balsamic vinegar. $ *Average main: $5* ✉ *121 Main St., Colebrook* ☎ *603/237–5150* ⊕ *www. lerendezvousbakerynh.com/.*

$$
RESORT

🛏 **The Glen.** Each of this resort's seven cabins sits alone in the forest with private views of the First Connecticut Lake and cedar siding with decks that have Adirondack chairs to enjoy the bucolic view. **Pros:** rustic; remote setting; charming lodge. **Cons:** remote; not luxurious. $ *Rooms from: $150* ✉ *118 Glen Rd., 1 mile off U.S. 3, Pittsburg* ☎ *603/538–6500, 800/445–4536* ⊕ *www.theglennh.com* ⇄ *6 rooms, 9 cabins* ▭ *No credit cards* ⊗ *Closed mid-Oct.–mid-May* ⦿ *All meals.*

NORTH CONWAY

76 miles south of Dixville Notch; 7 miles south of Glen; 41 miles east of Lincoln/North Woodstock.

Before the arrival of the outlet stores, the town drew visitors for its inspiring scenery, ski resorts, and access to White Mountain National Forest. Today, however, the feeling of natural splendor is gone. Shopping is the big sport, and businesses line Route 16 for several miles. You'll get a close look at them because traffic slows to a crawl here. You can take scenic West Side Road from Conway to Intervale to circumvent the traffic and take in splendid views.

GETTING HERE AND AROUND

On Route 16/302 avoid the stores on the south side of town by parking near the fire station on Main Street and spend half a day visiting the unique shops and restaurants in this part of town. Taxis can get you around between Conway, North Conway, and Jackson.

ESSENTIALS

Taxi Taxi Village Taxi ☎ *603/356–3602.*

Visitor Information North Country Chamber of Commerce ☎ *603/237– 8939, 800/698–8939* ⊕ *www.northcountrychamber.org.*

EXPLORING

Ⓒ **Conway Scenic Railroad.** The Conway Scenic Railroad operates trips aboard vintage trains from historic North Conway Station. The Notch Train, through Crawford Notch to Crawford Depot (a 5-hour round-trip) or Fabyan Station (5½ hours), offers wonderful scenic views from the domed observation coach. The Valley Train provides views of Mt. Washington countryside on a 55-minute round trip to Conway or a 1¾-hour trip to Bartlett—lunch and dinner are served on some departures. The 1874 station displays lanterns, old tickets and timetables, and other railroad artifacts. Reserve your spot early during foliage season for the dining excursions. ✉ *38 Norcross Cir.* ☎ *603/356–5251, 800/232–5251* ⊕ *www.conwayscenic.com* 🖃 *$15–$75* ⊙ *Mid-Apr.– mid Dec; call for times.*

Ⓒ **Hartmann Model Railroad Museum.** This building houses about 2,000 engines, more than 5,000 cars and coaches, and 14 operating layouts (from G to Z scales) in addition to a café, a crafts store, a hobby shop, and an outdoor miniature train that you can sit on and ride. ✉ *15 Town Hall Rd. at Rte. 16 (U.S. 302), Intervale* ☎ *603/356–9922* ⊕ *www. hartmannrr.com* 🖃 *$6* ⊙ *Open daily 10–5 in July and Aug. Closed Tues. June, Sept., and Oct. Closed Mar.–mid-May.*

Weather Discovery Center. The hands-on exhibits at this meteorological educational facility demonstrate how weather is monitored and how it affects us. The center is a collaboration between the National Oceanic and Atmospheric Administration Forecast Systems lab and the Mt. Washington Observatory at the summit of Mt. Washington. ✉ *2779 Main St.* ☎ *603/356–2137* ⊕ *www.mountwashington.org* ⊙ *Daily 10–5.*

SPORTS AND THE OUTDOORS

Echo Lake State Park. You needn't be a rock climber to catch views from the 700-foot White Horse and Cathedral ledges. From the top you'll see the entire valley, including Echo Lake, which offers fishing and swimming and on quiet days an excellent opportunity to shout for echoes. ✉ *Off U.S 302* ☎ *603/271–3556* ⊕ *www.nhstateparks.org* 🖃 *$4.*

CANOEING AND KAYAKING

Outdoors Saco Bound. River outfitter Outdoors Saco Bound rents canoes, kayaks, and tubes (with transportation) for gentle floats down the Saco River. ✉ *2561 E. Main St., Rte. 302, Conway Center* ☎ *603/447–2177* ⊕ *www.sacobound.com.*

FISHING

North Country Angler. As one of the best tackle shops in the state, North Country Angler offers guided fly-fishing trips throughout the region as well as casting clinics. ✉ *2888 White Mountain Hwy.* ☎ *603/356–6000* ⊕ *www.northcountryangler.com.*

SKI AREAS

Cranmore Mountain Adventure Park. This downhill ski area has been a favorite of families since it began operating in 1938. Five glades have opened more skiable terrain. The 50 trails are well laid out and fun to ski. Most runs are naturally formed intermediates that weave in and out of glades. Beginners have several slopes and routes from the summit;

Sit back and enjoy the view on the Conway Scenic Railroad.

experts must be content with a few short, steep pitches. In addition to the trails, there's snow tubing, a mountain coaster, and snowboarders have a terrain park and a half-pipe. Night skiing is offered Thursday–Saturday and holidays. ✉ *1 Skimobile Rd.* ☎ *603/356–5543, 603/356–5544 snow conditions, 800/786–6754 lodging* ⊕ *www.cranmore.com.*

King Pine Ski Area at Purity Spring Resort. Some 9 miles south of Conway, this family-run ski area has been going strong since the late 19th century. Some ski-and-stay packages include free skiing for midweek resort guests. King Pine's 16 gentle trails are ideal for beginner and intermediate skiers; experts won't be challenged except for a brief pitch on the Pitch Pine trail. There's tubing on weekend afternoons and night skiing and tubing on Friday and Saturday evenings, plus 9 miles of cross-country skiing. Indoors, you can enjoy a pool and fitness complex and go ice-skating. In summer the resort is a destination for waterskiing, kayaking, loon watching, tennis, hiking, and other activities. ✉ *1251 Eaton Rd., Route 153, East Madison* ☎ *603/367–8896, 800/373–3754* ⊕ *www.kingpine.com.*

Mt. Washington Valley Ski Touring and Snowshoe Foundation. Forty miles of groomed cross-country trails weave through North Conway and the countryside along the Mt. Washington Valley Ski Touring and Snowshoe Foundation. Equipment rentals are available. ✉ *279 Rte. 16, U.S. 302, Intervale* ☎ *603/356–9920* ⊕ *www.mwvskitouring.org.*

SHOPPING

ANTIQUES

Richard Plusch Antiques. Richard Plusch Antiques deals in period furniture and accessories, including glass, sterling silver, Oriental porcelains, rugs, and paintings. ✉ *2584 White Mountain Hwy.* ☎ *603/356–3333.*

CLOTHING

More than 150 factory outlets—including L. L. Bean, Timberland, Pfaltzgraff, Lenox, Polo, Nike, Anne Klein, and Woolrich—line Route 16.

Joe Jones' Sun & Ski Sports–North Conway. A top pick for skiwear is Joe Jones' Sun & Ski Sports–North Conway. ✉ *2709 White Mountain Hwy.* ☎ *603/356–9411* 🌐 *www.joejonessports.com.*

CRAFTS

Handcrafters Barn. Handcrafters Barn stocks the work of 150 area artists and artisans. ✉ *2473 White Mountain Hwy.* ☎ *603/356–8996* 🌐 *www.handcraftersbarn.com.*

League of New Hampshire Craftsmen. This store carries the creations of the state's best artisans. ✉ *2526 Main St.* ☎ *603/356–2441* 🌐 *www.nhcrafts.org.*

Zeb's General Store. This old-fashioned country store sells food items, crafts, and other products made in New England. ✉ *2675 Main St.* ☎ *603/356–9294, 800/676–9294* 🌐 *www.zebs.com.*

WHERE TO EAT

$$ AMERICAN 🍴 **Delaney's Hole in the Wall.** This casual sports tavern displays its memorabilia such as autographed baseballs and an early photo of skiing at Tuckerman Ravine. Entrées range from fajitas to mussels and scallops sautéed with spiced sausage and Louisiana seasonings. Live music is featured on Wednesday nights. [$] *Average main: $18* ✉ *2966 White Mountain Hwy. (Rte. 16), ¼ mile north of North Conway Village* ☎ *603/356–7776* 🌐 *www.delaneys.com.*

$ AMERICAN 🍴 **Muddy Moose Restaurant & Pub.** This family restaurant buzzes with the noise of children. Its mac and cheese, blueberry-glazed ribs, burgers, and salads will satisfy kids and parents alike. A unique side dish of carrots with a hint of maple syrup is a pleasant surprise. The Muddy Moose Pie, made of ice cream, fudge, and crumbled Oreos, can feed a family of four. [$] *Average main: $16* ✉ *2344 White Mountain Hwy.* ☎ *603/356–7696* 🌐 *www.muddymoose.com* ✍ *Reservations not accepted.*

WHERE TO STAY

For expanded hotel reviews, visit Fodors.com.

$$ B&B/INN 🏨 **The Buttonwood Inn.** A tranquil 6-acre oasis in this busy resort area, the Buttonwood is on Mt. Surprise, 2 miles northeast of North Conway Village. **Pros:** good bedding and amenities; tranquil; clean. **Cons:** unexciting for those not wanting a remote getaway. [$] *Rooms from: $159* ✉ *64 Mt. Surprise Rd.* ☎ *603/356–2625, 800/258–2625* 🌐 *www.buttonwoodinn.com* 🛏 *10 rooms, 1 suite* 🍽 *Breakfast.*

$$ B&B/INN 🏨 **Darby Field Inn.** After a day in the White Mountains, warm up by the fieldstone fireplace in the living room. **Pros:** clean; romantic; remote. **Cons:** better for couples than families. [$] *Rooms from: $170*

8

New Hampshire's Diners

CLOSE UP

Friendly Toast. In the historic coastal city of Portsmouth, the Friendly Toast might be the most vaunted breakfast spot in the state. Creative fare like Almond Joy pancakes (with coconut, chocolate chips, and almonds) and the "Flying Fish scramble" (eggs with smoked salmon, fresh dill, and cheddar) keep hungry bellies coming back again and again. ⊠ *113 Congress St., Portsmouth* ☎ *603/430–2154* ⊕ *www.thefriendlytoast.net.*

Lou's Restaurant. Dartmouth students and professors hobnob over stellar breakfast victuals at Lou's Restaurant, a cheap-and-cheerful storefront diner that serves up prodigious portions of corned-beef hash and eggs Benedict, as well as artfully decorated cupcakes and house-made donuts. Just beware of the long lines on weekend mornings. ⊠ *30 S. Main St., Hanover* ☎ *603/643–3321* ⊕ *www.lousrestaurant.net.*

Red Arrow Diner. Once named one of the country's "top 10 diners" by *USA Today*, the bustling Red Arrow Diner is open 24/7 and caters to politicos, students, artists, and regular Janes and Joes in the heart of the Granite State's largest city. The 1922 diner's daily "Blue Plate Specials" are served on actual blue plates, and you'll find such regular items as kielbasa and beans and house-brewed Arrow root beer and cream soda. ⊠ *61 Lowell St., Manchester* ☎ *603/626–1118* ⊕ *www.redarrowdiner.com* ⊠ *63 Union Sq., Milford* ☎ *603/249–9222* ⊕ *www.redarrowdiner.com.*

Sunny Day Diner. Up in the skiing and hiking haven of Lincoln, outdoorsy souls fuel up on hearty fare like banana-bread French toast

Red Arrow Diner in Manchester.

and cherry pie à la mode at the cozy Sunny Day Diner, a handsomely restored building from the late 1950s. ⊠ *U.S. 3, just off I–93, Exit 33, Lincoln* ☎ *603/745–4833.*

Tilt'n Diner. Travelers to the state's Lakes Region have long been familiar with the flashy pink exterior and neon signage of the Tilt'n Diner, a convivial 1950s-style restaurant that's known for its baked shepherd's pie and Southern breakfast—sausage gravy, biscuits, and baked beans with two eggs—served all day. On sunny days, dine at one of the picnic tables. ⊠ *61 Laconia Rd., Tilton* ☎ *603/286–2204* ⊕ *www.thecman.com.*

—Andrew Collins
Red Arrow Diner in Manchester

✉ *185 Chase Hill, Albany* ☎ *603/447–2181, 800/426–4147* 🌐 *www.darbyfield.com* 🛏 *13 rooms* 🕒 *Closed Apr.* 🍴 *Breakfast.*

$$ RESORT 🏨 **White Mountain Hotel and Resort.** West of the traffic of North Conway, the scenery becomes splendid and rooms in this hotel at the base of Whitehorse Ledge have mountain views. **Pros:** scenic setting that's close to shopping; lots of activities. **Cons:** two-night-minimum summer weekends. [$] *Rooms from: $189* ✉ *2560 West Side Rd.* ☎ *800/533–6301* 🌐 *www.whitemountainhotel.com* 🛏 *69 rooms, 11 suites* 🍴 *Multiple meal plans.*

EN ROUTE A great place to settle in to the White Mountains, take in one of the greatest panoramas of the mountains, and get visitor info is at the **Intervale Scenic Vista.** The stop, off Route 16 a few miles north of North Conway, is run by the DOT, has a helpful volunteer staff, features a wonderful large topographical map, and has terrific bathrooms.

KANCAMAGUS HIGHWAY

36 miles between Conway and Lincoln/North Woodstock.

★ **The Kancamagus Highway.** Interstate 93 is the fastest way to the White Mountains, but it's hardly the most appealing. The section of Route 112 known as the Kancamagus Highway passes through some of the state's most unspoiled mountain scenery—it was one of the first roads in the nation to be designated a National Scenic Byway. The Kanc, as it's called by locals, is punctuated by overlooks and picnic areas, erupts into fiery color each fall, when photo-snapping drivers really slow things down. A number of campgrounds are off the highway. In bad weather, check with the White Mountains Visitors Bureau for road conditions. 🌐 *www.kancamagushighway.com.*

SPORTS AND THE OUTDOORS

Lincoln Woods Trail. A couple of short hiking trails off the Kancamagus Highway (Route 112) yield great rewards with relatively little effort. The Lincoln Woods Trail starts from the large parking lot of the Lincoln Woods Visitor Center, 4 miles east of Lincoln. Here you can purchase the recreation pass ($5 per vehicle, good for seven consecutive days) needed to park in any of the White Mountain National Forest lots or overlooks; stopping briefly to take photos or to use the restrooms at the visitor center is permitted without a pass. The trail crosses a suspension bridge over the Pemigewasset River and follows an old railroad bed for 3 miles along the river. 🌐 *www.fs.usda.gov/whitemountain.*

Sabbaday Falls. The parking and picnic area for Sabbaday Falls, about 15 miles west of Conway, is the trailhead for an easy ½-mile route to a multilevel cascade that plunges through two potholes and a flume. Swimming is not allowed here; only viewing. ✉ *Off Kancamagus Highway.*

8

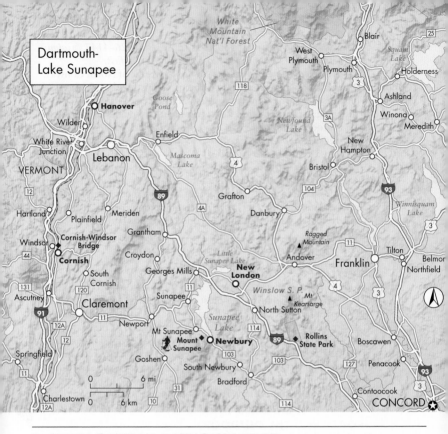

DARTMOUTH–LAKE SUNAPEE

In the west-central part of the state, the towns around prestigious Dartmouth College and rippling Lake Sunapee vary from sleepy, old-fashioned outposts that haven't changed much in decades to bustling, sophisticated towns rife with cafés, art galleries, and boutiques. Among the latter, Hanover and New London are the area's main hubs, both of them increasingly popular as vacation destinations and with telecommuters seeking a quieter, more economical home base. Although distinct from the Lakes Region, greater Lake Sunapee looks like a miniature Lake Winnipesaukee, albeit with far less commercial development. For a great drive, follow the Lake Sunapee Scenic and Cultural Byway, which runs for about 25 miles from Georges Mills (a bit northwest of New London) down into Warner, tracing much of the Lake Sunapee shoreline. When you've tired of climbing and swimming and visiting the past, look for small studios of area artists. This part of the state, along with the even quieter Monadnock area to the south, has long been an informal artists' colony where people come to write, paint, and weave in solitude.

ESSENTIALS

Visitor Information Lake Sunapee Region Chamber of Commerce
☎ *603/526–6575, 877/526–6575* ⊕ *www.sunapeevacations.com.*

NEW LONDON

16 miles northwest of Warner, 25 miles west of Tilton.

New London, the home of Colby-Sawyer College (1837), is a good base for exploring the Lake Sunapee region. A campus of stately Colonial-style buildings fronts the vibrant commercial district, where you'll find several cafés and boutiques.

GETTING HERE AND AROUND

From the south take Exit 11 on Interstate 93 to Crockett Corner and then north on Route 114. From the north take Exit 12 and travel south on Route 114. Mount Sunapee Ski Area offers a ski shuttle to and from many of the area hotels and B&Bs.

OFF THE BEATEN PATH

Mt. Kearsarge Indian Museum, Education and Cultural Center. Take a tour of this complex, which holds an extensive collection of Native American artistry, including moose-hair embroidery, quilt work, and basketry. Signs on the Medicine Woods trail identify plants and explain how they are used as foods, medicines, and dyes. Tours leave on the hour. The museum is about 15 miles southeast of New London. ⊠ *Kearsarge Mountain Rd., Warner* ☎ *603/456–2600* ⊕ *www.indianmuseum.org* ⊡ *$8.50* ☺ *May–Oct., Mon.–Sat. 10–5, Sun. noon–5; Nov., Sat. 10–5, Sun. noon–5.*

SPORTS AND THE OUTDOORS

Rollins State Park. A 3½-mile scenic auto road at Rollins State Park snakes up the southern slope of Mt. Kearsarge, where you can hike a ½-mile trail to the summit. The road often closes in winter due to hazardous conditions. ⊠ *Off Rte. 103, Main St., Warner* ☎ *603/456–3808* ⊕ *www.nhstateparks.org* ⊡ *$4.*

SHOPPING

Artisan's. Artisan's carries jewelry, glass, and other local handicrafts. ⊠ *Corner of Main and Pleasant Sts.* ☎ *603/526–4227* ⊕ *www.artisansnewlondon.com.*

THE ARTS

New London Barn Playhouse. Broadway-style and children's plays are presented here every summer in New Hampshire's oldest continuously operating theater. ⊠ *84 Main St.* ☎ *603/526–6710* ⊕ *www.nlbarn.org.*

WHERE TO EAT AND STAY

For expanded hotel reviews, visit Fodors.com.

$ ✕ **Ellie's Cafe & Deli.** From its eggs Benedict to its oven-baked breakfast
CAFÉ chimichanga to its pancakes with candied walnuts and crème brulée
Fodor'sChoice French toast, the food at Ellie's is made for comfort and to fill you up.
★ You can also linger over a cup of hot coffee in the rustic atmosphere of wood floors and exposed posts and beams. Lunch includes flatbread sandwiches or a veggie "tower," a baguette stuffed with portobello mushrooms, red onion, cucumber, and roasted red peppers. $ *Average*

8

main: $9 ✉ *207 Main St.* ☎ *603/526–2488* 🌐 *www.elliescafeanddeli.com.*

$$ AMERICAN 🍴 **Flying Goose Brew Pub & Grille.** With 12 handcrafted beers and additional seasonal varieties made with hops grown on-site, this inviting restaurant and pub is a hit with beer connoisseurs. Standouts include a meatloaf made with locally raised beefalo, paper-thin onion rings, fresh-cut steaks, and turkey pot pie. The menu changes twice a year, in the summer and fall. Thursday evenings have live music. [$] *Average main: $18* ✉ *40 Andover Rd., at the intersection of Rtes. 11 and 114* ☎ *603/526–6899* 🌐 *www.flyinggoose.com.*

$$ B&B/INN 🏨 **Follansbee Inn.** Built in 1840, this quintessential country inn on the shore of Kezar Lake is the kind of place that almost automatically turns strangers into friends. **Pros:** relaxed lakefront setting; clean rooms. **Cons:** bar serves only wine and beer. [$] *Rooms from: $159* ✉ *Rte. 114, 2 Keyser St., North Sutton* ☎ *603/927–4221, 800/626–4221* 🌐 *www.follansbeeinn.com* 🛏 *17 rooms* 🍽 *Breakfast.*

$$ B&B/INN ★ 🏨 **The Inn at Pleasant Lake.** This 1790s inn lies across Pleasant Lake from majestic Mt. Kearsarge.**Pros:** lakefront with a small beach; boating. **Cons:** away from town activities. [$] *Rooms from: $165* ✉ *853 Pleasant St.* ☎ *603/526–6271, 800/626–4907* 🌐 *www.innatpleasantlake.com* 🛏 *10 rooms* 🍽 *Breakfast.*

EN ROUTE **Sunapee Harbor.** About midway between New London and Newbury on the west side of the lake, Sunapee Harbor is an old-fashioned, all-American summer resort community that feels like a miniature version of Wolfeboro, with a large marina, a handful of restaurants and shops on the water, a tidy village green with a gazebo, and a small museum in a Victorian stable run by the historical society. A plaque outside Wild Goose Country Store details some of Lake Sunapee's attributes—that it's one of the highest lakes in New Hampshire, at 1,091 feet above sea level, and one of the least polluted. An interpretive path runs along a short span of the Sugar River, the only outflow from Lake Sunapee, which winds for 18 miles to the Connecticut River. ✉ *17 Garnet St.* 🌐 *www.sunapeevacations.com.*

NEWBURY

8 miles southwest of New London.

Newbury is on the edge of Mt. Sunapee State Park. The mountain, which rises to an elevation of nearly 3,000 feet, and the sparkling lake are the region's outdoor recreation centers. The popular League of New Hampshire Craftsmen's Fair, the nation's oldest crafts fair, is held at the base of Mt. Sunapee each August.

GETTING HERE AND AROUND

From New London, take 114 West to 103A South, which follows the eastern coast of Lake Sunapee to Newbury.

EXPLORING

The Fells Historic Estate & Gardens. John M. Hay, who served as private secretary to Abraham Lincoln and secretary of state for Presidents William McKinley and Theodore Roosevelt, built the Fells on Lake Sunapee as a summer home in 1890. House tours offer a glimpse of early-20th-century life on a New Hampshire estate. The grounds include a 100-foot-long perennial garden and a rock garden with a brook flowing through it. Miles of hiking trails can also be accessed from the estate. The building houses art and history exhibits and hosts educational programs for children all year. The estate is sometimes rented for weddings and other events. ⊠ *456 Rte. 103A* ☎ *603/763–4789* ⊕ *www.thefells.org* ⊐ *$10* ⊘ *Late June – Labor Day, daily 10–4; late May – late June and Labor Day–Columbus Day, weekends 10–4; grounds open all year dawn–dusk.*

SPORTS AND THE OUTDOORS

BEACHES AND FISHING

Mt. Sunapee State Park Beach. Sunapee State Beach has picnic areas, a beach, and a bathhouse. You can rent canoes, too. ⊠ *Rte. 103* ☎ *603/763–5561* ⊕ *www.nhstateparks.org* ⊐ *$4* ⊘ *Daily dawn–dusk.*

Lake Sunapee. Lake Sunapee has brook and lake trout, salmon, smallmouth bass, and pickerel. Note that anglers over the age of 16 need a state fishing license, available at most local tackle or sporting goods shops.

BOAT TOURS

Lake Sunapee Cruises. Narrated cruises aboard the Lake Sunapee Cruises provide a closer look at Lake Sunapee's history and mountain scenery and run from late May through mid-October, daily in summer and on weekends in spring and fall; the cost is $19. ⊠ *81 Main St., Sunapee Harbor* ☎ *603/938–6465* ⊕ *www.sunapeecruises.com.*

MV Kearsarge. Dinner cruises are held on the MV *Kearsarge* and leave from the dock at Sunapee Harbor, June through mid-October, Tuesday–Sunday evenings; the cost is $36 and includes a buffet dinner. ☎ *603/938–6465* ⊕ *www.mvkearsarge.com.*

SKI AREA

Mount Sunapee. Although the resort is state-owned, it's managed by Vermont's Okemo Mountain Resort (in Ludlow). The agreement has allowed the influx of capital necessary for operating extensive lifts, snowmaking (97% coverage), and trail grooming. This mountain is 1,510 vertical feet and has 65 trails, mostly intermediate. Experts can take to a dozen slopes, including three nice double black diamonds. Boarders have a 420-foot-long half-pipe and a terrain park with music. In summer, the Sunapee Express Quad zooms you to the summit, there's a zip-line canopy tour, and several other warm season activities. From here, it's just under a mile hike to Lake Solitude. Mountain bikers can use the lift to many trails, and an in-line skate park has beginner and advanced sections (plus equipment rentals). ⊠ *1398 Rte. 103* ☎ *603/763–3500, 603/763–4020 snow conditions, 877/687–8627 lodging* ⊕ *www.mtsunapee.com.*

SHOPPING

Outspokin' Bicycle and Sport. Overlooking Lake Sunapee's southern tip, Outspokin' Bicycle and Sport has a tremendous selection of biking, hiking, skateboarding, waterskiing, skiing, and snowboarding clothing and equipment. ⊠ *4 Old Route 3, Sunapee Harbor* ☎ *603/763–9500* ⊕ *www.outspokin.com.*

Wild Goose Country Store. Right on the harbor in Sunapee village, on the marina, Wild Goose Country Store carries quirky gifts, teddy bears, penny candy, pottery, and other engaging odds and ends. ✉ *77 Main St., Sunapee* ☎ *603/763–5516.*

WHERE TO EAT

$ AMERICAN 🍴 **Anchorage at Sunapee Harbor.** Fans of this long gray restaurant with a sprawling deck overlooking Sunapee Harbor's marina come as much for the great views as for the dependable—and occasionally creative—American chow. It's as likely a place for a burger or fried seafood platter as for homemade lobster spring rolls. There's also live entertainment some nights—in fact, this is where the founders of the rock band Aerosmith first met back in the early 1970s. [$] *Average main: $15* ✉ *71 Main St., Sunapee Harbor* ☎ *603/763–3334* 🌐 *www.theanchorageatsunapeeharbor.com* 🕒 *Closed mid-Oct.–mid-May. and Mon.*

WHERE TO STAY

For expanded hotel reviews, visit Fodors.com.

$$$ RENTAL ★ 🏨 **Sunapee Harbor Cottages.** This charming collection of six private cottages is within a stone's throw of Sunapee Harbor. **Pros:** attractive, spacious units, no minimum stays. **Cons:** main house blocks view of the harbor. [$] *Rooms from: $200* ✉ *4 Lake Ave., Sunapee Harbor* ☎ *603/763–5052, 866/763–5052* 🌐 *www.sunapeeharborcottages.com* 🛏 *6 cottages.*

HANOVER

12 miles northwest of Enfield; 62 miles northwest of Concord.

Eleazer Wheelock founded Hanover's Dartmouth College in 1769 to educate the Abenaki "and other youth." When he arrived, the town consisted of about 20 families. The college and the town grew symbiotically, with Dartmouth becoming the northernmost Ivy League school. Hanover is still synonymous with Dartmouth, but it's also a respected medical and cultural center for the upper Connecticut River Valley.

GETTING HERE AND AROUND

Lebanon Municipal Airport, near Dartmouth College, is served by US Airways Express from New York. By car, Interstate 91 North or Interstate 89 are the best ways to get to Lebanon, Hanover, and the surrounding area. Plan on spending a day visiting Hanover and to see all the sights on the Dartmouth campus.

Shops, mostly of the independent variety but with a few upscale chains sprinkled in, line Hanover's main street. The commercial district blends almost imperceptibly with the Dartmouth campus. West Lebanon, south of Hanover on the Vermont border, has many more shops.

ESSENTIALS

Airport Lebanon Municipal Airport ✉ *5 Airport Rd., West Lebanon* ☎ *603/298–8878* 🌐 *www.flyleb.com.*

Taxi Big Yellow Taxi ☎ *603/643–8294* 🌐 *www.bigyellowtaxis.com.*

19 28

Visitor Information Hanover Area Chamber of Commerce ⊠ *Nugget Arcade Bldg., 53 S. Main St., Suite 216* ☎ *603/643–3115* ⊕ *www.hanoverchamber.org.*

EXPLORING

★ **Dartmouth College.** Robert Frost spent part of a brooding freshman semester at this Ivy League school before giving up college altogether. The buildings that cluster around the green include the **Baker Memorial Library**, which houses such literary treasures as 17th-century editions of William Shakespeare's works. The library is also well known for Mexican artist José Clemente Orozco's 3,000-square-foot murals that depict the story of civilization in the Americas. ⊠ *N. Main and Wentworth Sts.* ☎ *603/646–1110* ⊕ *www.dartmouth.edu.*

Hopkins Center for the Arts. If the towering arcade at the entrance to the Hopkins Center for the Arts appears familiar, it's probably because it resembles the project that architect Wallace K. Harrison completed just after designing it: New York City's Metropolitan Opera House at Lincoln Center. The complex includes a 900-seat theater for film showings and concerts, a 400-seat theater for plays, and a black-box theater for new plays. The Dartmouth Symphony Orchestra performs here, as does the Big Apple Circus. ⊠ *2 East Wheelock St.* ☎ *603/646–2422* ⊕ *hop.dartmouth.edu.*

Hood Museum of Art. In addition to African, Peruvian, Oceanic, Asian, European, and American art, the Hood Museum of Art owns the Pablo Picasso painting *Guitar on a Table*, silver by Paul Revere, and a set of Assyrian reliefs from the 9th century BC. The range of contemporary works, including pieces by John Sloan, William Glackens, Mark Rothko, Fernand Léger, and Joan Miró, is particularly notable. Rivaling the collection is the museum's architecture: a series of austere, copper-roofed, redbrick buildings arranged around a courtyard. Free campus tours are available on request. ⊠ *Wheelock St.* ☎ *603/646–2808* ⊕ *www.hoodmuseum.dartmouth.edu* ⊠ *Free* ☉ *Tues. and Thurs.–Sat. 10–5, Wed. 10–9, Sun. noon–5.*

QUICK BITES

Dirt Cowboy. Take a respite from museum hopping with a cup of espresso, a ham-and-cheese scone, or a freshly baked brownie at the Dirt Cowboy, a café across from the green and beside a used-book store. ⊠ *7 S. Main St.* ☎ *603/643–1323* ⊕ *www.dirtcowboycafe.com.*

Boloco. A local branch of a Boston chain, Boloco, occupies a slick basement space with comfy sofas and has a small patio to the side. Drop by for an ample selection of burritos (or bowls, if you wish to forgo the wrap), salads, and smoothies. ⊠ *35 S. Main St.* ☎ *603/643–0202* ⊕ *boloco.com.*

★ **Enfield Shaker Museum.** In 1782, two Shaker brothers from Mount Lebanon, New York, arrived on Lake Mascoma's northeastern side, about 12 miles southeast of Hanover. Eventually, they formed Enfield, the ninth of 18 Shaker communities in the United States, and moved it to the lake's southern shore, where they erected more than 200 buildings. The Enfield Shaker Museum preserves the legacy of the Shakers, who numbered 330 members at the village's peak. By 1923, interest in the society had dwindled, and the last 10 members joined the Canterbury community, south of Laconia. A self-guided walking tour takes you through 13 of the remaining buildings, among them the Great Stone Dwelling (overnight stays are available May–October; $135) and an 1849 stone mill. Demonstrations of Shaker crafts techniques and numerous special events take place year-round. ✉ *447 NH Rte. 4A, Enfield* ☎ *603/632–4346* 🌐 *www.shakermuseum.org* 🎟 *$8.50* 🕐 *May–Oct. Mon.–Sat. 10–5, Sun. noon–5; Nov.–Apr. Mon.–Sat. 10–4, Sun. noon–4.*

OFF THE BEATEN PATH

Upper Valley. From Hanover, you can make a 60-mile drive up Route 10 all the way to Littleton for a highly scenic tour of the upper Connecticut River Valley. You'll have views of the river and Vermont's Green Mountains from many points. The road passes through groves of evergreens, over leafy ridges, and through delightful hamlets. Grab gourmet picnic provisions at the general store on Lyme's village common—probably the most pristine of any in the state—and stop at the bluff-top village green in historical Haverhill (28 miles north of Hanover) for a picnic amid the panorama of classic Georgian- and Federal-style mansions and faraway farmsteads. You can follow this scenic route all the way to the White Mountains region or loop back south from Haverhill—along Route 25 to Route 118 to U.S. 4 west—to Enfield, a drive of about 45 miles (75 minutes).

Ledyard Canoe Club of Dartmouth. Ledyard Canoe Club of Dartmouth provides canoe and kayak rentals on the swift-flowing Connecticut River, which isn't suitable for beginners and is safest after mid-June. ☎ *603/643–6709.*

WHERE TO EAT

$$ AMERICAN

🍴 **Canoe Club.** Bedecked with canoes, paddles, and classic Dartmouth paraphernalia, this festive spot presents live jazz and folk music most nights. The mood may be casual, but the kitchen presents rather imaginative food, including a memorable starter of a roasted beet medley with spiced chocolate sauce and orange glaze. Among the main courses, the seafood cioppino, with shrimp, scallops, onion, and sweet pepper, is a favorite. There's also a lighter, late-night menu. [$] *Average main: $19* ✉ *27 S. Main St.* ☎ *603/643–9660* 🌐 *www.canoeclub.us.*

$ AMERICAN ★

🍴 **Lou's.** This is one of two places in town where students and locals really mix. After all, it's hard to resist. A Hanover tradition since 1948, this diner-cum-café-cum-bakery serves possibly the best breakfast in the valley—a plate of *migas* (eggs, cheddar, salsa, and guacamole mixed with tortilla chips) can fill you up for the better part of the day; blueberry-cranberry buttermilk pancakes also satisfy. Or grab a seat at the old-fashioned soda fountain and order an ice-cream sundae. [$] *Average main: $8* ✉ *30 S. Main St.* ☎ *603/643–3321* 🌐 *lousrestaurant.net* 🕐 *No dinner.*

$$ ITALIAN

🍴 **Lui Lui.** The creatively topped thin-crust pizzas and huge pasta portions are only part of the draw at this chatter-filled eatery; the other is its dramatic setting inside a former power station on the Mascoma River. Pizza picks include the Tuscan (mozzarella topped with tomato and roasted garlic) and the grilled chicken with barbecue sauce. Pasta fans should dive into a bowl of linguine with homemade clam sauce.

The Cornish–Windsor Bridge is the second-longest covered bridge in the United States, at 460 feet.

$ *Average main: $17* ⊠ *8 Glen Rd., West Lebanon* ☎ *603/298–7070* ⊕ *www.luilui.com.*

$$
ECLECTIC
✕ **Murphy's On the Green.** Students, visiting alums, and locals regularly descend upon this wildly popular pub, which has walls lined with shelves of old books. The varied menu features burgers and salads as well as meat loaf, crusted lamb sirloin, and eggplant filled with tofu. Check out the extensive beer list. $ *Average main: $19* ⊠ *11 S. Main St.* ☎ *603/643–4075* ⊕ *www.murphysonthegreen.com.*

WHERE TO STAY

For expanded hotel reviews, visit Fodors.com.

$$$$
HOTEL
★
🏨 **The Hanover Inn.** If you're in town for a Dartmouth event, you'll want to stay on the town's—and the college's—main square. **Pros:** center of campus and town; well managed. **Cons:** breakfast not included; over-priced. $ *Rooms from: $349* ⊠ *The Green, 2 S. Main St.* ☎ *603/643–4300, 800/443–7024* ⊕ *www.hanoverinn.com* ⌂ *108 rooms, 15 suites.*

$$
B&B/INN
🏨 **Trumbull House.** The sunny guest rooms of this white Colonial-style house—on 16 acres on Hanover's outskirts—have king- or queen-size beds, writing desks, feather pillows, and other comfortable touches, as well as Wi-Fi. **Pros:** quiet setting; lovely home; big breakfast. **Cons:** 3 miles east of town. $ *Rooms from: $169* ⊠ *40 Etna Rd.* ☎ *603/643–2370, 800/651–5141* ⊕ *www.trumbullhouse.com* ⌂ *4 rooms, 1 suite, 1 cottage* ⦿ *Breakfast.*

CORNISH

22 miles south of Hanover.

Today Cornish is best known for its four covered bridges and for being the home of reclusive late author J. D. Salinger, but at the turn of the 20th century the village was known primarily as the home of the country's then most popular novelist, Winston Churchill (no relation to the British prime minister). His novel *Richard Carvell* sold more than a million copies. Churchill was such a celebrity that he hosted Teddy Roosevelt during the president's 1902 visit. At that time Cornish was an enclave of artistic talent. Painter Maxfield Parrish lived and worked here, and sculptor Augustus Saint-Gaudens set up his studio and created the heroic bronzes for which he is known.

GETTING HERE AND AROUND

About 5 miles west of town on Route 44, the Cornish-Windsor Bridge crosses the Connecticut River between New Hampshire and Vermont. The Blacksmith Shop covered bridge is 2 miles east of Route 12A on Town House Road, and the Dingleton Hill covered bridge is 1 mile east of Route 12A on Root Hill Road. Cornish itself is small enough to see in one morning.

EXPLORING

Cornish-Windsor Bridge. This 460-foot bridge, 1½ miles south of the Saint-Gaudens National Historic Site, connects New Hampshire to Vermont across the Connecticut River. It dates from 1866 and is the longest covered wooden bridge in the United States. The notice on the bridge reads: "Walk your horses or pay two dollar fine."

Fodor'sChoice **Saint-Gaudens National Historic Site.** Just south of Plainfield, where River
★ Road rejoins Route 12A, a small lane leads to this historic site, where you can tour sculptor Augustus Saint-Gaudens' house, studio, gallery, and 150 acres of grounds and gardens. Scattered throughout are full-size casts of his works. The property has two hiking trails, the longer of which is the Blow-Me-Down Trail. Concerts are held every Sunday afternoon in July and August. The museum is about 1½ miles north of the Cornish-Windsor Bridge on Route 12A. ⊠ *Off Rte. 12A, 139 Saint-Gaudens Rd.* ☎ *603/675–2175* ⊕ *www.nps.gov/saga* ✉ *$5, good for 7-day reentry* ☉ *Buildings Memorial Day–Oct., daily 9–4:30; grounds daily dawn–dusk.*

SPORTS AND THE OUTDOORS

North Star Canoe Rentals. North Star Canoe Rentals rents canoes and kayaks for half- or full-day trips on the Connecticut River. It makes for a lazy and relaxing paddle down the river, with stops for swimming and sunbathing at your leisure. ⊠ *Rte. 12A, Balloch's Crossing* ☎ *603/542–6929* ⊕ *www.kayak-canoe.com.*

8

THE MONADNOCKS AND MERRIMACK VALLEY

Southwestern and south-central New Hampshire mix village charm with city hustle and bustle across two distinct regions. The Merrimack River Valley has the state's largest and fastest-growing cities: Nashua, Manchester, and Concord. To the west, in the state's sleepy southwestern corner, is the Monadnock region, one of New Hampshire's least developed and most naturally stunning parts. Here you'll find plenty of hiking trails as well as peaceful hilltop hamlets that appear barely changed in the past two centuries. Mt. Monadnock, southern New Hampshire's largest peak, stands guard over the Monadnock region, which has more than 200 lakes and ponds. Rainbow trout, smallmouth and largemouth bass, and some northern pike swim in Chesterfield's Spofford Lake. Goose Pond, just north of Keene, holds smallmouth bass and white perch.

⇨ *The towns are listed in counterclockwise order, beginning with Nashua and heading north to Manchester and Concord; then west to Charleston; south to Walpole; southwest to Keene and Jaffrey; and finally northeast to Peterborough.*

NASHUA

98 miles south of Lincoln/North Woodstock; 48 miles northwest of Boston; 36 miles south of Concord; 50 miles southeast of Keene.

Once a prosperous manufacturing town that drew thousands of immigrant workers in the late 1800s and early 1900s, Nashua declined following World War II, as many factories shut down or moved to where labor was cheaper. Since the 1970s, however, the metro area has jumped in population, developing into a charming, old-fashioned community. Its low-key downtown has classic redbrick buildings along the Nashua River, a tributary of the Merrimack River. Though not visited by tourists as much as other communities in the region, Nashua (population 90,000) has some good restaurants and an engaging museum.

GETTING HERE AND AROUND

A good place to start exploring Nashua is at Main and High streets, where a number of fine restaurants and shops are located. Downtown Nashua has free Wi-Fi.

ESSENTIALS

Taxi SK Taxi ☎ *603/882–5155.* **D & E Taxi** ☎ *603/889–3999.*

WHERE TO EAT

$$ BISTRO Fodor's Choice ★

🍴 **MT's Local Kitchen and Wine Bar.** Part hip bistro, part jazzy wine bar MT's is so popular that even foodies from Massachusetts drive here. The regularly changing menu highlights local products and might include pork scallopini with a cognac soaked raisin pan sauce or wood-grilled Vermont chicken with marinated mushrooms. Wood-fired pizzas are also a specialty—try the one topped with sopressata, stewed dates, caramelized onions, ricotta, and pecans. [$] *Average main: $24* ✉ *212 Main St.* ☎ *603/595–9334* 🌐 *www.mtslocal.com/.*

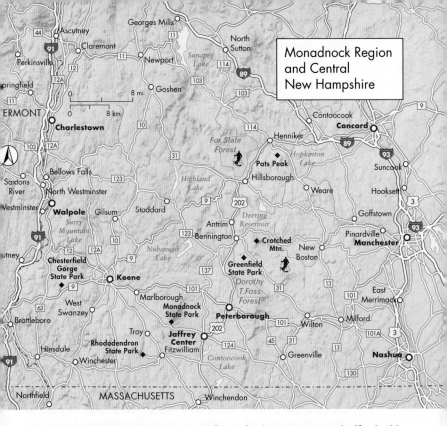

Monadnock Region and Central New Hampshire

$$\text{\$\$} \quad \times \textbf{Villa Banca.} \text{ On the ground floor of a dramatic, turreted office build-}$$

ITALIAN ing, this spot with high ceilings and tall windows specializes in traditional and contemporary Italian cooking. Start with Gorgonzola artichokes and move on to pasta Alfredo. The butternut squash ravioli is a sweet delight, and the macadamia nut–encrusted tilapia will satisfy the fish lover at your table. Note the exotic-martini menu, a big draw at happy hour. $ *Average main: $21* ⊠ *194 Main St.* ☎ *603/598–0500* ⊕ *www.villabanca.com* ☉ *No lunch on weekends.*

MANCHESTER

18 miles north of Nashua, 53 miles north of Boston.

Manchester, with 108,000-plus residents, is New Hampshire's largest city. The town grew up around the Amoskeag Falls on the Merrimack River, which fueled small textile mills through the 1700s. By 1828, Boston investors had bought the rights to the Merrimack's water power and built the Amoskeag Mills, which became a testament to New England's manufacturing capabilities. In 1906 the mills employed 17,000 people and weekly churned out more than 4 million yards of cloth. This vast enterprise served as Manchester's entire economic base; when it closed in 1936, the town was devastated.

Today Manchester is mainly a banking and business center. The old mill buildings have been converted into warehouses, classrooms, restaurants, museums, and office space. The city has the state's major airport, as well as the Verizon Wireless Arena, which hosts minor-league hockey matches, concerts, and conventions.

GETTING HERE AND AROUND

Manchester Airport, the state's largest airport, has rapidly become a cost-effective, hassle-free alternative to Boston's Logan Airport, with nonstop service to more than 20 cities. Manchester can be hard to get around, but it offers a number of taxi services.

ESSENTIALS

Airport Manchester-Boston Regional Airport ⊠ *1 Airport Rd.* ☎ *603/624–6556* ⊕ *www.flymanchester.com.*

Taxi Evergreen Limousine ☎ *603/624–0801* ⊕ *evergreenmata.com.* **Manchester Taxi** ☎ *603/623–2222.*

Visitor Information Greater Manchester Chamber of Commerce ⊠ *54 Hanover St.* ☎ *603/666–6600* ⊕ *www.manchester-chamber.org/.*

EXPLORING

Amoskeag Fishways. From May to mid-June, salmon, shad, and river herring "climb" the fish ladder at this spot near the Amoskeag Dam. The visitor center has an underwater viewing window, year-round interactive exhibits and programs about the Merrimack River, and a hydroelectric-station viewing area. ⊠ *6 Fletcher St.* ☎ *603/626–3474* ⊕ *www.amoskeagfishways.org* ☉ *Mon.–Sat. 9–5.*

Fodor's Choice
★
☉
Amoskeag Mills. There are miles of hallways in the brick buildings that comprise this former textile mill. To get a sense of what they are and what they meant to Manchester, visit the two key museums housed here: the SEE Science Center and the Millyard Museum. ⊠ *Mill No. 3, 200 Bedford St.(entrance at 255 Commercial St.).*

SEE Science Center. The SEE Science Center is a hands-on science lab and children's museum with more than 70 exhibits. If you're in Manchester, child or adult, don't miss it. The world's largest permanent LEGO installation of regular-sized LEGOs is here, depicting the city's Amoskeag Millyard and the city of Manchester as it was in 1915. This mind-blowing exhibit is made up of 3 million LEGOs across 2,000 square feet. More important, the exhibit also conveys the massive size and importance of the mills, which ran a mile on each side of the Merrimack. ⊠ *200 Bedford St.* ☎ *603/669–0400* ⊕ *www.see-sciencecenter.org* ☎ *$8* ☉ *Weekdays 10–4, weekends 10–5.*

Millyard Museum. Upstairs in theAmoskeag Mills building, state-of-the-art exhibits depict the region's history from when Native Americans lived alongside and fished the Merrimack River to the heyday of Amoskeag Mills. The interactive Discovery Gallery is geared toward kids; there's also a lecture/concert hall and a large museum shop. ⊠ *200 Bedford St.* ☎ *603/622–7531* ⊕ *www.manchesterhistoric.org* ☎ *$8* ☉ *Tues.–Sat. 10–4.*

At the Currier Museum of Art, you can enjoy European and American classics, or visit a nearby Frank Lloyd Wright house.

Fodor's Choice
★

Currier Museum of Art. A modern Sol LeWitt mural faces the original 1929 Italianate entrance to a permanent collection of European and American paintings, sculpture, and decorative arts from the 13th to the 20th century, including works by Edouard Monet, Picasso, Edward Hopper, Andrew Wyeth, and Georgia O'Keeffe. Also run by the Currier (tours depart from the museum) is the nearby Frank Lloyd Wright–designed Zimmerman House, built in 1950. Wright called this sparse, utterly functional living space "Usonian," an invented term used to describe 50 such middle-income homes he built with his vision of distinctly American architecture. It's New England's only Frank Lloyd Wright–designed residence open to the public. ⊠ *150 Ash St.* ☎ *603/669–6144, 603/626–4158 Zimmerman House tours* ⊕ *www.currier.org* ✉ *$10, free Sat. 10–noon; $20 combo with Zimmerman House (reservations essential)* ⊙ *Sun., Mon., Wed., and Fri. 11–5; first Thurs. of every month 11–8; Sat. 10–5; call for Zimmerman House tour hrs.*

NIGHTLIFE AND THE ARTS

THE ARTS

The Palace Theatre. Musicals and plays are presented throughout the year at the Palace Theatre. It also hosts musical and comedy acts, the state's philharmonic and symphony orchestras and the Opera League of New Hampshire. ⊠ *80 Hanover St.* ☎ *603/668–5588 box office* ⊕ *www. palacetheatre.org.*

NIGHTLIFE

Club 313. New Hampshire's most popular disco for gays and lesbians also has karaoke and drag shows. It's open Tuesday–Sunday. ⊠ *93 S. Maple St.* ☎ *603/628–6813* ⊕ *club313nh.com.*

The Yard. Revelers come from all over to drink at the Yard, which is also a steak and seafood restaurant. Saturday nights are for country line dancing with live music and dj tunes. ✉ *1211 S. Mammoth Rd.* ☎ *603/623–3545* 🌐 *www.theyardrestaurant.com.*

WHERE TO EAT

$$ AMERICAN ★ 🍴 **Cotton.** Inside one of the old Amoskeag Mills buildings mod lighting and furnishings and a patio set in an arbor give this restaurant a swanky atmosphere. A blunt neon sign that reads FOOD belies its sophisticated menu. The kitchen specializes in putting a new spin on comfort food. Start with pan-seared crab cakes or the lemongrass chicken salad. The menu changes four times a year but might include 16-ounce all-natural Delmonico steak or wood-grilled scallops as well as superb sweet-potato hash. For the past eight years Cotton's has been voted best martinis in New Hampshire by *New Hampshire Magazine.* [$] *Average main: $19* ✉ *75 Arms St.* ☎ *603/622–5488* 🌐 *www.cottonfood.com* ⏲ *No lunch weekends.*

$ AMERICAN Fodor's Choice ★ 🍴 **Red Arrow Diner.** This tiny diner is ground zero for presidential hopefuls in New Hampshire come primary season. The rest of the time, a mix of hipsters and oldsters, including comedian and Manchester native Adam Sandler, favor this neon-streaked, 24-hour greasy spoon, which has been going strong since 1922. Filling fare—platters of kielbasa, French toast, liver and onions, chicken Parmesan with spaghetti, and the diner's famous panfries—keeps patrons happy. Homemade sodas and éclairs round out the menu. [$] *Average main: $10* ✉ *61 Lowell St.* ☎ *603/626–1118* 🌐 *redarrowdiner.com.*

WHERE TO STAY

For expanded hotel reviews, visit Fodors.com.

$$ B&B/INN 🏨 **Ash Street Inn.** Because it's in an attractive residential neighborhood of striking Victorian homes, staying in this five-room B&B will give you the best face of Manchester. **Pros:** spotless newly decorated rooms; within walking distance of the Currier Museum. **Cons:** not a full-service hotel. [$] *Rooms from: $159* ✉ *118 Ash St.* ☎ *603/668–9908* 🌐 *www.ashstreetinn.com* 🛏 *5 rooms* 🍽 *Breakfast.*

$$$ B&B/INN ★ 🏨 **Bedford Village Inn.** If you trade direct downtown access for a lovely manor outside of town, you'll be rewarded by the comforts of this beautiful and well-run property. **Pros:** relaxing property just outside Manchester; exceptional grounds; great restaurant. **Cons:** outside of town. [$] *Rooms from: $208* ✉ *2 Olde Bedford Way, Bedford* ☎ *603/472–2001, 800/852–1166* 🌐 *www.bedfordvillageinn.com* 🛏 *12 suites, 2 apartments, 1 cottage.*

$$ HOTEL 🏨 **Radisson Hotel Manchester Downtown.** Of Manchester's many chain properties, the 12-story Radisson has the most central location—a short walk from Amoskeag Mills and great dining along Elm Street. **Pros:** central downtown location. **Cons:** fee for parking; unexciting chain hotel. [$] *Rooms from: $159* ✉ *700 Elm St.* ☎ *603/625–1000, 800/967–9033* 🌐 *www.radisson.com/manchester-hotel-nh-03101/nhmanch* 🛏 *244 rooms, 6 suites.*

CONCORD

20 miles northwest of Manchester, 67 miles northwest of Boston, 46 miles northwest of Portsmouth.

New Hampshire's capital (population 42,000) is a quiet town that tends to the state's business but little else—the sidewalks roll up promptly at 6. Stop in town to get a glimpse of New Hampshire's State House, which is crowned by a gleaming gold, eagle-topped dome.

GETTING HERE AND AROUND

Taxis can help get you around town, though Main Street is easy to walk about. Event information can be found at ⊕ *www.ci.concord.nh.us.*

ESSENTIALS

Taxi Concord Cab ☎ *603/225–4222.*

Visitor Information Concord Chamber of Commerce ✉ *49 S. Main St.* ☎ *603/224–2508* ⊕ *www.concordnhchamber.com.*

EXPLORING

Concord on Foot. The **Concord on Foot** walking trail winds through the historic district.

The Greater Concord Chamber of Commerce. Maps for the walk can be picked up at the Greater Concord Chamber of Commerce or stores along the trail. ✉ *49 S. Main St.* ☎ *603/224–2508* ⊕ *www. concordnhchamber.com*

⟳ **McAuliffe-Shepard Discovery Center.** In a 40-foot dome theater, shows on the solar system, constellations, and space exploration abound. The planetarium was named for the Concord teacher who was killed in the Space Shuttle *Challenger* explosion in 1986. Children love seeing the tornado tubes, magnetic marbles, and other hands-on exhibits. Outside, explore the scale-model planet walk and the human sundial. ✉ *New Hampshire Technical Institute campus, 2 Institute Dr.* ☎ *603/271–7827* ⊕ *www.starhop.com* 🖃 *$9; $4 planetarium shows* ⊗ *Daily in summer and school vacation weeks; Thurs.–Sun. 10–5, Fri. 6:30–9; call for show times and reservations.*

New Hampshire Historical Society. Steps from the state capitol, the society's museum is a great place to learn about the Concord coach, the stagecoach that was a popular mode of transportation before railroads. Rotating exhibitions may include New Hampshire quilts and their stories and historical protraits of residents. ✉ *6 Eagle Sq.* ☎ *603/228-6688* ⊕ *www.nhhistory.org* 🖃 *$5.50* ⊗ *Tue.–Sat. 9:30–5, Sun. noon–5; Mon. 9:30–5 July–mid. Oct. & Dec.*

Pierce Manse. Franklin Pierce lived in this Greek Revival home before he moved to Washington to become the 14th U.S. president. He's buried nearby. ✉ *14 Horseshoe Pond La.* ☎ *603/225–4555* ⊕ *www. piercemanse.org* 🖃 *$7* ⊗ *Mid-June–early Sept. Tues.–Sat., 11–3; mid-Sept.–mid-Oct., Fri. and Sat, 12–3; otherwise by appt.*

Fodor's Choice ★ **State House.** A self-guided tour of the neoclassical, gilt-domed statehouse, built in 1819, is a real treat. You get total access to the House and Senate galleries. This is the oldest capitol building in the nation in which the legislature uses its original chambers. In January through June

8

you can watch the assemblies in action once a week: the 24 senators of the New Hampshire Senate (the fourth-smallest American lawmaking body) meet once a week. In a wild inversion, the state's representatives number 400—one representative per 3,000 residents, a ratio that is a world record. At the visitor center you'll see paraphernalia from decades of presidential primaries. ✉ *41 Green St.* ☎ *603/271–2154* 🌐 *www.ci.concord.nh.us/tourdest/statehs/* 🎟 *Free* 🕘 *Weekdays 8–4:30.*

NIGHTLIFE AND THE ARTS

Capitol Center for the Arts. The Center has been restored to reflect its Roaring Twenties' origins. It hosts touring Broadway shows, dance companies, and musical acts. ✉ *44 S. Main St.* ☎ *603/225–1111* 🌐 *www.ccanh.com.*

Hermanos Cocina Mexicana. The lounge at Hermanos Cocina Mexicana stages live jazz Sunday through Thursday nights. ✉ *11 Hills Ave.* ☎ *603/224–5669* 🌐 *www.hermanosmexican.com.*

SHOPPING

Capitol Craftsman Jewelers. Fine jewelry and handicrafts are sold at Capitol Craftsman Jewelers. ✉ *16 N. Main St.* ☎ *603/224–6166* 🌐 *www.capitolcraftsman.com.*

League of New Hampshire Craftsmen. Shop for crafts in many media at the League of New Hampshire Craftsmen. ✉ *36 N. Main St.* ☎ *603/228–8171* 🌐 *www.nhcrafts.org.*

Mark Knipe Goldsmiths. Antique stones are set in rings, earrings, and pendants here; pieces by other designers are also on hand. ✉ *2 Capitol Plaza, Main St.* ☎ *603/224–2920* 🌐 *www.knipegold.com.*

WHERE TO EAT AND STAY

For expanded hotel reviews, visit Fodors.com.

$ AMERICAN ★ 🍴 **Arnie's Place.** If you need a reason to make the 1½-mile detour from Interstate 93, then more than 50 kinds of homemade ice cream should do the trick. Try the toasted-coconut, raspberry, or vanilla flavors. The chocolate shakes are a real treat for chocoholics. The lemon freeze will give you an ice cream headache in no time, but it's worth it. A small dining room is available for dishes such as a barbecue platter (smoked on the premises), hamburgers, and hot dogs, but the five walk-up windows and picnic benches are the way to go. [$] *Average main: $12* ✉ *164 Loudon Rd., Concord Heights* ☎ *603/228–3225* 🌐 *www.arniesplace.com* 🕘 *Closed mid-Oct.–late Feb.*

$ ECLECTIC 🍴 **Barley House.** A lively, old-fashioned tavern practically across from the capitol building and usually buzzing with a mix of politicos, business folks, and tourists, the Barley House serves dependable chow: chorizo-sausage pizzas, burgers smothered with peppercorn-whiskey sauce and blue cheese, chicken potpies, Cuban sandwiches, beer-braised bratwurst, and Mediterranean chicken salad—it's an impressive melting pot of a menu. The bar turns out dozens of interesting beers, on tap and by the bottle, and there's also a decent wine list. It's open until 1 am. [$] *Average main: $14* ✉ *132 N. Main St.* ☎ *603/228–6363* 🌐 *www.thebarleyhouse.com* ✍ *Reservations not accepted* 🕘 *Closed Sun.*

$ THAI 🍴 **Siam Orchid.** This dark, attractive Thai restaurant with a colorful rickshaw gracing its dining room serves spicy and reasonably authentic Thai food. It draws a crowd from the capitol each day for lunch. Try the fiery broiled swordfish with shrimp curry sauce or the pine-nut chicken in an aromatic ginger sauce. There's a second location in Manchester. [$] *Average main: $15* ✉ *158 N. Main St.* ☎ *603/228–3633* 🌐 *www.siamorchid.net* 🕓 *No lunch weekends.*

$$ HOTEL 🏨 **The Centennial.** This is the most modern hotel in New Hampshire, and it's home to Granite, the state's most contemporary restaurant ($$) and bar, making it a draw for the state's politicians and those doing business here. **Pros:** super sleek hotel; very comfortable and clean rooms; great bar and restaurant. **Cons:** busy. [$] *Rooms from: $189* ✉ *96 Pleasant St.* ☎ *603/227–9000, 800/360–4839* 🌐 *www.thecentennialhotel.com* 🛏 *27 rooms, 5 suites.*

CHARLESTOWN

Charlestown has the state's largest historic district. About 60 homes, handsome examples of Federal, Greek Revival, and Gothic Revival architecture, are clustered about the town center; 10 of them were built before 1800. Several merchants on the main street distribute brochures that describe an interesting walking tour of the district.

GETTING HERE AND AROUND

You can reach Charlestown from Interstate 91, but it's best to follow Route 12 North from Keene for a gorgeous scenic route. Walking about downtown Charlestown should take only 15 minutes of your day, but it's worth admiring the buildings in the town center. The Fort at No. 4 is less than 2 miles from downtown, north on Route 11.

EXPLORING

👶 **Fort at No. 4.** In 1747, this fort was an outpost on the periphery of Colonial civilization. That year fewer than 50 militiamen at the fort withstood an attack by 400 French soldiers, ensuring that northern New England remained under British rule. Today, costumed interpreters at this living-history museum cook dinner over an open hearth and demonstrate weaving, gardening, and candle making. Each year the museum holds reenactments of militia musters and battles of the French and Indian War. ✉ *267 Springfield Rd., ½ mile north of Charlestown* ☎ *603/826–5700, 603/826–5700* 🌐 *www.fortat4.com* 🎟 *$10* 🕓 *May–Oct., Mon.–Sat. 10–4:30, Sun. 10–4; extended hours in July & Aug.*

SPORTS AND THE OUTDOORS

Morningside Flight Park. On a bright, breezy day you might want to detour to the Morningside Flight Park, considered to be among the best flying areas in the country. Watch the bright colors of gliders as they take off from the 450-foot peak, or take hang-gliding lessons yourself. ✉ *357 Morningside Lane, off Rte. 12/11, 5 miles north of Charlestown* ☎ *603/542–4416* 🌐 *flymorningside.kittyhawk.com.*

8

WALPOLE

13 miles south of Charlestown.

Walpole possesses one of the state's most perfect town greens. Bordered by Elm and Washington streets, it's surrounded by homes built about 1790, when the townsfolk constructed a canal around the Great Falls of the Connecticut River and brought commerce and wealth to the area. The town now has 3,200 inhabitants, more than a dozen of whom are millionaires. Walpole is home to Florentine Films, Ken Burns's production company.

GETTING HERE AND AROUND

It's a short jaunt off Route 12, north of Keene. The small downtown is especially photogenic.

OFF THE BEATEN PATH

Sugarhouses. Maple-sugar season occurs about the first week in March when days become warmer but nights are still frigid. A drive along maple-lined back roads reveals thousands of taps and buckets catching the labored flow of unrefined sap. Plumes of smoke rise from nearby sugarhouses, where "sugaring off," the process of boiling down this precious liquid, takes place. Many sugarhouses are open to the public; after a tour and demonstration, you can sample the syrup. ⊕ *www. nhmapleproducers.com.*

Bascom Maple Farm. Bascom Maple Farm has been family-run since 1853 and produces more maple syrup than anyone in New England. Visit the 2,200-acre farm and get maple products from candy to syrup. ⊠ *56 Sugarhouse Rd., Alstead* ☎ *603/835–6361* ⊕ *www. bascommaple.com.*

Stuart & John's Sugar House & Pancake Restaurant. Stuart & John's Sugar House & Pancake Restaurant conducts a tour and sells syrup and maple gifts in a roadside barn. It also serves breakfast, lunch, and ice cream weekends mid-February–April and mid-September–November. ⊠ *Junction Routes 12 and 63, Westmoreland* ☎ *603/399–4486* ⊕ *www. stuartandjohnssugarhouse.com.*

SHOPPING

★ **Boggy Meadow Farm.** At Boggy Meadow Farm you can watch the cheese process unfold, from the 200 cows being milked to the finer process of cheese making. The farmstead's raw-milk cheeses can be sampled and purchased in the store. It's worth a trip just to see the beautiful 400-acre farm. ⊠ *13 Boggy Meadow Lane* ☎ *603/756–3300, 877/541–3953* ⊕ *www.boggymeadowfarm.com.*

WHERE TO EAT

$$
FRENCH
Fodor's Choice
★

✕ **The Restaurant at L. A. Burdick Chocolate.** Famous candy maker Larry Burdick, who sells his artful hand-filled and hand-cut chocolates to top restaurants around the Northeast, is a Walpole resident. This restaurant has the easygoing sophistication of a Parisian café and may tempt you to linger over an incredibly rich hot chocolate. The Mediterranean-inspired menu utilizes fresh, often local ingredients and changes daily. Of course, dessert is a big treat here, featuring Burdick's tempting chocolates and pastries. For dinner, you might start with a selection of artisanal cheeses or reduction trio of pâtés, followed by a house beef stew or homemade sausages. $ *Average main: $17* ⊠ *47 Main St.* ☎ *603/756–2882* ⊕ *www.burdickchocolate.com* ☉ *No dinner Sun. and Mon.*

KEENE

17 miles southeast of Walpole; 20 miles northeast of Brattleboro, Vermont; 56 miles southwest of Manchester.

Keene is the largest city in the state's southwest corner. Its rapidly gentrifying main street, with several engaging boutiques and cafés, is America's widest (132 feet). Each year, on the Saturday before Halloween, locals use the street to hold a Pumpkin Festival, where the small town competes with big cities such as Boston for the most jack-o'-lanterns in one place at one time.

ESSENTIALS

Visitor Information Greater Keene Chamber of Commerce ⊠ *48 Central Sq.* ☎ *603/352–1303* ⊕ *www.keenechamber.com.* **Monadnock Travel Council** *800/432–7864* ⊕ *www.monadnocktravel.com.*

EXPLORING

Keene State College. This hub of the local arts community is on the tree-lined main street and has a worthwhile art gallery and an art-house movie theater. ⊠ *229 Main St.* ☎ *603/358–2263* ⊕ *www.keene.edu.*

Thorne-Sagendorph Art Gallery. The gallery contains a permanent collection including works by George Rickey, Robert Mapplethorpe, and Vargian Bogosian and presents traveling exhibits. ⊠ *229 Main St.* ☎ *603/358–2720* ⊕ *www.keene.edu/tsag.*

Putnam Theater. Foreign and art films are shown here September through May. ⊠ *229 Main St.* ☎ *603/358–2160* ⊕ *www.keene.edu/ Putnam.*

OFF THE BEATEN PATH

Chesterfield's Route 63. If you're in the mood for a country drive or bike ride, head west from Keene along Route 9 to Route 63 (about 11 miles) and turn left toward the hilltop town of Chesterfield. This is an especially rewarding journey at sunset, as from many points along the road you can see west out over the Connecticut River Valley and into Vermont. The village center consists of little more than a handful of dignified granite buildings and a small general store. You can loop back to Keene via Route 119 east in Hinsdale and then Route 10 north—the entire journey is about 40 miles.

NIGHTLIFE AND THE ARTS

Colonial Theatre. Opened in 1924 as a vaudeville stage, the Colonial Theatre now hosts comedy performers, music concerts and ballet and has the town's largest movie screen. ⊠ *95 Main St.* ☎ *603/357–1233* ⊕ *www.thecolonial.org.*

Elm City Restaurant & Brewery. Located at the Colony Mill, the brewery serves light food and draws a mix of college students and young professionals. ⊠ *222 West St.* ☎ *603/355–3335* ⊕ *www.elmcitybrewing.com.*

Redfern Art Center on Brickyard Pond. At Keene State College, the Redfern Art Center on Brickyard Pond has year-round music, theater, and

8

dance performances in two theaters and a recital hall. ⊠ *229 Main St.* ☎ *603/358–2168* ⊕ *www.keene.edu/racbp.*

SHOPPING

★ **Colony Mill Marketplace.** This old mill building holds 20-plus stores and boutiques such as the Toadstool Bookshop, which carries many children's and regional travel and history books, and Antiques at Colony Mill, which sells the wares of more than 120 dealers and has a food court. ⊠ *222 West St.* ☎ *781/273–5555* ⊕ *www.colonymill.com.*

Hannah Grimes Marketplace. Shop here for mostly New Hampshire–made pottery, toys, kitchenware, soaps, greeting cards, and specialty foods. ⊠ *42 Main St.* ☎ *603/352–6862* ⊕ *hannahgrimesmarketplace.com.*

WHERE TO EAT AND STAY

For expanded hotel reviews, visit Fodors.com.

$$
MEDITERRANEAN
Fodor's Choice
★

✕ **Luca's.** A deceptively simple storefront bistro overlooking Keene's graceful town square, Luca's dazzles with epicurean creations influenced by Italy, France, Greece, Spain, and North Africa. Enjoy sautéed shrimp with cilantro pesto and plum tomatoes, three-cheese ravioli with artichoke hearts, or grilled salmon marinated in cumin and coriander. For a real treat, ask Luca to surprise you with a sampler of items from his extensive menu, and don't forget to ask for the locally made gelato or sorbet for dessert. $ *Average main: $20* ⊠ *10 Central Sq.* ☎ *603/358–3335* ⊕ *www.lucascafe.com.*

$$
B&B/INN
★

🏨 **Chesterfield Inn.** Surrounded by gardens, the Chesterfield Inn sits above Route 9, the main road between Keene and Brattleboro, Vermont. **Pros:** attractive gardens; close to the Connecticut River. **Cons:** breakfast ends early. $ *Rooms from: $174* ⊠ *20 Cross Rd., West Chesterfield* ☎ *603/256–3211, 800/365–5515* ⊕ *www.chesterfieldinn.com* 📞 *13 rooms, 2 suites* ☽ *Closed Christmas; no dinner on Sun.* 🍴 *Breakfast.*

$
RESORT
☾

🏨 **The Inn at East Hill Farm.** If you have kids, and they like animals, meet bliss: a family resort with daylong kids' programs on a 160-acre 1830 farm overlooking Mt. Monadnock. **Pros:** rare agritourism and family resort; activities galore; beautiful setting. **Cons:** remote location; noisy mess-hall dining. $ *Rooms from: $119* ⊠ *460 Monadnock St., Troy* ☎ *603/242–6495, 800/242–6495* ⊕ *www.east-hill-farm.com* 📞 *65 rooms* 🍴 *All meals.*

$
HOTEL

🏨 **The Lane Hotel.** You can get a rare touch of urbanity in the sleepy Monadnocks in this upscale redbrick boutique hotel in the middle of Main Street. **Pros:** spacious and comfortable rooms; center of town. **Cons:** no gym. $ *Rooms from: $130* ⊠ *30 Main St.* ☎ *603/357–7070, 888/300–5056* ⊕ *www.thelanehotel.com* 📞 *33 rooms, 7 suites.*

JAFFREY CENTER

16 miles southeast of Keene.

Novelist Willa Cather came to Jaffrey Center in 1919 and stayed in the Shattuck Inn, which now stands empty on Old Meeting House Road. Not far from here, she pitched the tent in which she wrote several chapters of *My Ántonia*. She returned nearly every summer thereafter until her death and was buried in the Old Burying Ground, which also

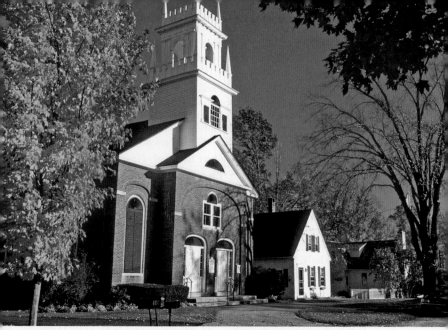
Jaffrey Center is known for its historic buildings and its proximity to Mount Monadnock.

contains the remains of Amos Fortune, a former slave who bought his freedom in 1863 and moved to town when he was 71. Fortune, who was a tanner, also bought the freedom of his two wives. He died at the age of 91.

GETTING HERE AND AROUND

Jaffrey Center's historic district is on Route 124 and is home to a number of brick buildings. It should take less than an hour to view it in its entirety. Two miles east of town on Route 124 can be found the Old Burying Ground, which is behind the Meeting House.

ESSENTIALS

Visitor Information Jaffrey Chamber of Commerce ☎ *603/532–4549* ⊕ *www.jaffreychamber.com.*

EXPLORING

Cathedral of the Pines. This outdoor memorial pays tribute to Americans who have sacrificed their lives in service to their country. There's an inspiring view of Mt. Monadnock and Mt. Kearsarge from the Altar of the Nation, which is composed of rock from every U.S. state and territory. All faiths are welcome to hold services here; organ music for meditation is played at midday from Tuesday through Thursday in July and August. The Memorial Bell Tower, with a carillon of bells from around the world, is built of native stone. Norman Rockwell designed the bronze tablets over the four arches. Flower gardens, an indoor chapel, and a museum of military memorabilia share the hilltop. It's 8 miles southeast of Jaffrey Center. ⊠ *10 Hale Hill Rd., off Rte. 119, Rindge* ☎ *603/899–3300, 866/229–4520* ⊕ *www.cathedralofthepines. org* ⬚ *Free* ☉ *May–Oct., daily 9–5.*

SPORTS AND THE OUTDOORS

★ **Monadnock State Park.** The oft-quoted statistic about Mt. Monadnock is that it's America's most-climbed mountain—second in the world to Japan's Mt. Fuji. Whether this is true or not, locals agree that it's never lonely at the top. Some days, especially during foliage season, more than 400 people crowd its bald peak. Monadnock rises to 3,165 feet, and on a clear day the hazy Boston skyline is visible from its summit. The park maintains picnic grounds and a small campground (RVs welcome, but no hookups) with 28 sites. Five trailheads branch into more than two-dozen trails of varying difficulty that wend their way to the top. Allow between three and four hours for any round-trip hike. A visitor center has free trail maps as well as exhibits documenting the mountain's history. In winter, you can cross-country ski along roughly 12 miles of groomed trails on the lower elevations of the mountain. ✉ *Off Rte. 124, 2½ miles north of Jaffrey Center* ☎ *603/532–8862* 🌐 *www.nhstateparks.org* 🎟 *$4* 🕒 *Daily dawn–dusk* ☞ *No pets.*

Rhododendron State Park. More than 16 acres of wild rhododendrons bloom in mid-July at this park, which has the largest concentration of *Rhododendron maximum* north of the Allegheny Mountains. Bring a picnic lunch and sit in a nearby pine grove or follow the marked footpaths through the flowers. On your way here, be sure to pass through Fitzwilliam's well-preserved historic district of Colonial and Federal-style houses, which have appeared on thousands of postcards. ✉ *Rte. 119 W, off Rte. 12, 10 miles southwest of Jaffrey Center, Fitzwilliam* ☎ *603/532–8862* 🌐 *www.nhstateparks.org* 🎟 *$4* 🕒 *May–Nov., daily 8–sunset.*

SHOPPING

Bloomin' Antiques. You'll find about 35 dealers at Bloomin' Antiques. ✉ *3 Templeton Turnpike, Fitzwilliam Center* ☎ *603/585–6688.*

WHERE TO EAT AND STAY

For expanded hotel reviews, visit Fodors.com.

$ AMERICAN 🍴 **J.P. Stephens Restaurant and Tavern.** An appealing choice either for lunch or dinner, this rustic-timbered dining room overlooks a small mill pond in Rindge, about 8 miles south of Jaffrey Center. The 1790 building used to house a sawmill, a gristmill, a forge, and a blacksmith. The sole meunière is delicate and flavorful and the apple brandy and walnut chicken is sweet and brazen. There's live music and karaoke most nights in the tavern. [$] *Average main: $16* ✉ *377 U.S. 202, Rindge* ☎ *603/899–3322* 🌐 *www.jpstephensrestaurant.com* 🕒 *Closed Mon.*

$ B&B/INN 🏨 **Benjamin Prescott Inn.** Thanks to the dairy farm surrounding this 1853 Colonial house—with its stenciling and wide pine floors—you feel as though you're miles out in the country rather than just minutes from Jaffrey Center. **Pros:** inexpensive; homey and comfortable. **Cons:** 2 miles east of town. [$] *Rooms from: $110* ✉ *433 Turnpike Rd. (Rte. 124 E)* ☎ *603/532–6637* 🌐 *www.benjaminprescottinn.com* 🛏 *7 rooms, 3 suites* 🍽 *Breakfast.*

$ B&B/INN 🏨 **The Monadnock Inn.** Rooms in this 1830s home are painted in lively lavenders, yellows, or peaches, a cheery presence in the heart of pristine Jaffrey Center, and a perfect place to get away from it all. **Pros:**

well-lit rooms with lacy curtains; feels like grandma's house. **Cons:** limited amenities. [$] *Rooms from: $110* ✉ *379 Main St.* ☎ *603/532–7800, 877/510–7019* 🌐 *www.monadnockinn.com* 🛏 *9 rooms, 2 suites* 🍴 *Breakfast.*

$$ B&B/INN 🏨 **Woodbound Inn.** A favorite with families and outdoors enthusiasts, this 1819 farmhouse became an inn in 1892. **Pros:** relaxed, lakefront resort; new focus on food. **Cons:** older; simple furnishings, no WiFi or cell phone service in cabins. [$] *Rooms from: $178* ✉ *247 Woodbound Rd., Rindge* ☎ *603/532–8341, 800/688–7770* 🌐 *www.woodboundinn.com* 🛏 *44 rooms; 11 cabins* 🍴 *Breakfast.*

PETERBOROUGH

9 miles northeast of Jaffrey Center, 30 miles northwest of Nashua, on Route 101.

Thornton Wilder's play *Our Town* was based on Peterborough. The nation's first free public library opened here in 1833. The town, which was the first in the region to be incorporated (1760), is still a commercial and cultural hub.

GETTING HERE AND AROUND

Parking is just off Main Street, with shopping, coffee, and food all close by. Stand on the bridge and watch the roiling waters of the Nubanusit River on the north end of Main Street.

ESSENTIALS

Visitor Information **Greater Peterborough Chamber of Commerce** ☎ *603/924–7234* 🌐 *www.greater-peterborough-chamber.com.*

EXPLORING

MacDowell Colony. Composer Edward MacDowell and his wife, Marian, founded this place in 1907 as an artists' retreat at their farm. Willa Cather wrote part of *Death Comes for the Archbishop* here. Wilder was in residence when he wrote *Our Town* (Peterborough's resemblance to the play's Grover's Corners is no coincidence). Today, MacDowell is the country's most famous artists' colony, functioning year-round. Top emerging and established artists of all genres are awarded fellowships during which they're given a private cottage in the woods in which to work, typically for about five weeks. Group dinners each evening are designed to spark new ideas. Only a small portion of the colony is open to visitors. ✉ *100 High St.* ☎ *603/924–3886* 🌐 *www.macdowellcolony.org.*

👶 **Mariposa Museum.** You can play instruments or try on costumes from around the world and indulge your cultural curiosity at this nonprofit museum dedicated to hands-on exploration of international folklore and folk art. The three-floor museum is inside a historic redbrick Baptist church, across from the Universalist church in the heart of town. The museum hosts a number of workshops and presentations on dance and arts and crafts. There's also a children's reading nook and a library. ✉ *26 Main St.* ☎ *603/924–4555* 🌐 *www.mariposamuseum.org* 🎟 *$5* 🕒 *July and Aug., daily 11–5; Sept.–June, Wed.–Sun. 11–5.*

SPORTS AND THE OUTDOORS

PARK

Miller State Park. About 3 miles east of town, an auto road takes you almost 2,300 feet up Pack Monadnock Mountain. The road is closed mid-November through mid-April. ⊠ *Rte. 101* ☎ *603/924–3672* ⊕ *www.nhstateparks.org* ☐ *$4.*

SKI AREA

Crotched Mountain. New Hampshire's southernmost skiing and snowboarding facility has 17 trails, half of them intermediate, and the rest divided pretty evenly between beginner and expert. There's an 875-foot vertical drop. The slopes have ample snowmaking capacity, ensuring good skiing all winter long. Crotched is famous for its night skiing and a Midnight Madness lift ticket (5 pm–3 am). Other facilities include a 40,000-square-foot lodge with a couple of restaurants, a ski school, and a snow camp for youngsters. ⊠ *615 Francestown Rd. (Rte. 47), Bennington* ☎ *603/588–3668* ⊕ *www.crotchedmountain.com.*

GOLF

Crotched Mountain Golf Club. At the Donald Ross–designed Crotched Mountain Golf Club, you'll find a hilly, rolling 18-hole layout with a nice view of the Monadnocks. Greens fees are $60 (weekends). ⊠ *740 Francestown Rd., Francestown* ☎ *603/588–2923* ⊕ *www. crotchedmountaingolfclub.com.*

SHOPPING

Eastern Mountain Sports. The corporate headquarters and retail outlet of Eastern Mountain Sports sells everything from tents to skis to hiking boots, offers hiking and camping classes, equipment rentals, and conducts kayaking and canoeing demonstrations. ⊠ *1 Vose Farm Rd., off Rte. 124* ☎ *603/924–7231* ⊕ *www.ems.com.*

Harrisville Designs. Hand-spun and hand-dyed yarn as well as looms are sold at Harrisville Designs. The shop also conducts classes in knitting and weaving. ⊠ *43 Main St., Harrisville* ☎ *603/827–3996* ⊕ *www. harrisville.com.*

Sharon Arts Center. Locally made pottery and fabric are exhibited here, as well as woodwork and other crafts. ⊠ *20-40 Depot St.* ☎ *603/924– 2787* ⊕ *www.sharonarts.org.*

THE ARTS

Monadnock Music. From early July to late August Monadnock Music produces a series of solo recitals, chamber music concerts, and orchestra and opera performances by renowned musicians. Events take place throughout the area on Wednesday through Saturday evenings at 8 and on Sunday at 4; many are free. ⊠ *2A Concord St.* ☎ *603/924–7610, 800/868–9613* ⊕ *www.monadnockmusic.org.*

Peterborough Folk Music Society. The society presents folk music concerts by artists such as John Gorka, Greg Brown, and Cheryl Wheeler; concerts are held monthly October through April in a fantastic old barn. ⊠ *Hadley Rd.* ☎ *603/827–2905* ⊕ *pfmsconcerts.org.*

8

Peterborough Players. The Players have performed since 1933 and productions are staged in a converted barn from late June through mid-September. ✉ *55 Hadley Rd.* ☎ *603/924–7585* 🌐 *www.peterboroughplayers.org.*

WHERE TO STAY

For expanded hotel reviews, visit Fodors.com.

$ B&B/INN 🏠 **Birchwood Inn.** Henry David Thoreau slept here, probably on his way to climb Monadnock or to visit Jaffrey or Peterborough. **Pros:** nice tavern. **Cons:** remote small town great for some, not for others. [$] *Rooms from: $99* ✉ *340 Rte. 45, Temple* ☎ *603/878–3285* 🌐 *www.thebirchwoodinn.com* 🛏 *2 rooms, 3 suites* 🍴 *Breakfast.*

$ B&B/INN ★ 🏠 **The Hancock Inn.** This Federal-style 1789 inn is the real Colonial deal—the oldest in the state and the pride of this idyllic town 8 miles north of Peterborough. **Pros:** quintessential Colonial inn in a perfect New England town; cozy rooms. **Cons:** remote location. [$] *Rooms from: $115* ✉ *33 Main St., Hancock* ☎ *603/525–3318, 800/525–1789* 🌐 *www.hancockinn.com* 🛏 *13 rooms* 🕒 *Closed first two weeks of Nov. and Mar.* 🍴 *Breakfast.*

$ B&B/INN 🏠 **The Inn at Crotched Mountain.** Three of the nine fireplaces in this 1822 inn are in Colonial-style guest rooms. **Pros:** spectacular country setting. **Cons:** too remote for some. [$] *Rooms from: $130* ✉ *534 Mountain Rd., 12 miles northeast of Peterborough, Francestown* ☎ *603/588–6840* 🌐 *www.innatcrotchedmt.com* 🛏 *13 rooms, 8 with private baths* 💳 *No credit cards* 🕒 *Closed Apr. and Nov.* 🍴 *Breakfast.*

$ HOTEL ★ 🏠 **Jack Daniels Motor Inn.** With so many dowdy motels in southwestern New Hampshire, it's a pleasure to find one as bright and clean as the Jack Daniels, just ½ mile north of downtown Peterborough. **Pros:** affordable rooms; low-key atmosphere. **Cons:** basic motel-style rooms; have to drive or walk into town. [$] *Rooms from: $139* ✉ *80 Concord St. (U.S. 202)* ☎ *603/924–7548* 🌐 *www.jackdanielsmotorinn.com* 🛏 *17 rooms.*

Inland Maine

WORD OF MOUTH

"My travel through the North Woods was done in different segments. . . . Hundreds of small lakes, ponds, and rivers dotted the
landscape, and the entire scene was pastoral and relaxing. . . .
[Baxter State Park] is truly the forest primeval, and I could spend
a lot of time there."

—dwooddon

WELCOME TO INLAND MAINE

TOP REASONS TO GO

★ **Baxter State Park:** Mt. Katahdin, the state's highest peak stands as a sentry over Baxter's forestland in its "natural wild state."

★ **Moosehead Lake:** Surrounded by mountains, Maine's largest lake—dotted with islands and chiseled with inlets and coves—retains the rugged beauty that so captivated author Henry David Thoreau in the mid-1800s.

★ **Water sports:** It's easy to get out on the water with scheduled cruises on large inland lakes; marinas and outfitters renting boats, canoes, and kayaks throughout the region; and white-water-rafting trips on several rivers.

★ **Winter pastimes:** Downhill skiing, snowmobiling, snowshoeing, cross-country skiing, and dogsledding are all popular winter sports.

★ **Foliage drives:** Maine's best fall foliage is inland, where hardwoods outnumber spruce, fir, and pine trees in many areas.

1 Western Lakes and Mountains. Lakes both quiet and busy, classic New England villages, and ski resorts fit perfectly in the forested landscape. In winter, this is ski country; snowmobiling and snowshoeing are also popular. In summer, the woods and water draw vacationers for a cool escape. In fall, foliage drives invite exploration of the region's national forest and state parks. In spring, there are no crowds, but fishermen, white-water rafters, and canoeists make their way here.

2 The North Woods. Much of the North Woods' private forestland is open for public recreation and best experienced by paddling a canoe or raft, hiking, snowshoeing, snowmobiling, or fishing. Some great destinations are mostly undeveloped: Moosehead Lake, Baxter State Park, and Allagash Wilderness Waterway. Greenville, a laidback and woodsy resort town, is a good base for day trips—take a drive (go slow!) down a "moose alley."

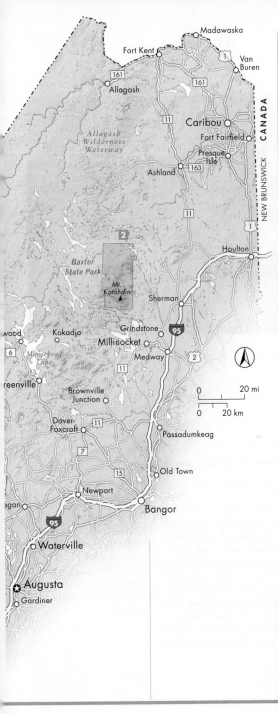

GETTING ORIENTED

Though Maine is well known for its miles of craggy coastline, the inland part of the state is surprisingly vast and much less populated. Less than an hour's drive from the bays and ocean, huge swaths of forestland are dotted with lakes (sometimes called "ponds" despite their size). Summer camps, ski areas, and small villages populate the western part of the state, which stretches north along the New Hampshire border to Québec. Quiet waters are easy to find in the more remote inland areas, but busier Sebago Lake is just north of coastal Portland, Maine's largest city. The northwest area is more rugged and remote while in the north-central part of the state, wilderness areas beckon outdoor lovers to the North Woods, which extend north and west to Canada.

9

INLAND MAINE FALL FOLIAGE DRIVE

Pine, spruce, and fir trees offset the red, orange, and yellow of maples and birches in the fall. This route follows Western Maine's mountains, passing by or near stunning overlooks, waterfalls, hiking trails, and a lakeside state park.

From Mexico, Route 17 heads north from U.S. 2, passing old homesteads and fields along the Swift River Valley before making the winding, mountainous ascent to **Height of Land**, the drive's literal pinnacle. This must-stop overlook, overhauled in 2011, has off-road parking, interpretive panels, stone seating, and a path to the nearby **Appalachian Trail**. Mountain vistas are reflected in the many (and often connected) lakes, ponds, rivers, and streams. On a clear day you can see west to New Hampshire and Canada. **Mooselookmeguntic Lake** and **Upper Richardson Lake** seem to float in the sea of forestland below. A few miles north of here at the Rangeley overlook observe how the east end of town forms a small isthmus between Rangeley Lake and Haley Pond.

BEST TIME TO GO

Fall color usually peaks in the Rangeley area in the first or second week of October. Get fall foliage updates at ⊕ *www.mainefoliage.com.*

PLANNING YOUR TIME

The Rangeley Lakes National Scenic Byway (⊕ *www.byways.org*) makes up much of this 59-mile drive (1½ hours without stops), but plan for a relaxed full day of exploring.

In tiny, welcoming Oquossoc, where Routes 17 and 4 meet, **The Farmer's Daughter** welcomes passersby with displays of pumpkins and mums during autumn. You can pick up apple cider and picnic items at this specialty foods store. Or stop for the **Gingerbread House Restaurant** for a meal, or just ice cream or baked goods. After a snack break, cross the street to the **Rangeley Outdoor Sporting Heritage Museum** (⇨ Rangely), where you can learn why visitors have come here to fish, hunt, and enjoy the outdoors since the mid-1800s.

Rangeley, 7 miles along Route 4, has restaurants, inns, waterfront parks, and outdoorsy shops. The countryside sweeps into view along public hiking trails at both **Saddleback Maine** ski resort and the 175-acre **Wilhelm Reich Museum**.

The road to **Rangeley Lake State Park** is accessible from both Routes 4 and 17, as is the **Appalachian Trail**. Overhanging foliage frames waterfalls at the scenic rest areas at or near each end of the drive that are perfect for picnics: Smalls Falls on Route 4, the byway's eastern terminus, and Coos Canyon on Route 17. Both of these popular spots have several falls, swimming holes, and paths with views of the drops. Coos Canyon is part of the Swift River, a destination for recreational gold panning. You can rent or buy panning equipment and get a demonstration at **Coos Canyon Rock and Gift**, right across Route 17 from its namesake. It also sells sandwiches and snacks.

NEED A BREAK?

The Farmer's Daughter. At The Farmer's Daughter specialty foods store, produce comes from the family farm. At the bakery counter, you can buy a cup of coffee, or apple cider in season. ⊠ 13 Rumford Rd. (Rte. 17), Oquossoc ☎ 207/864–2492.

Wilhelm Reich Museum. This museum showcases the life and work of controversial physician-scientist Wilhelm Reich (1897–1957). There are magnificent views from the observatory and the many trails on the 175-acre grounds. ⊠ 19 Orgonon Circle, Rangeley ☎ 207/864–3443 ⊕ www.wilhelmreichtrust.org 🏛 Museum $6, grounds free ⊙ Museum July and Aug., Wed.–Sun. 1–5; Sept., Sat. 1–5. Grounds daily 9–5.

Rangeley Lakes Heritage Trust. This trust protects 13,000 acres of area land. Contact them for trail maps and information about outdoor recreation in the area. ⊠ 52 Carry Rd. (Rte. 4), Oquossoc ☎ 207/864–7311 ⊕ www.rlht.org.

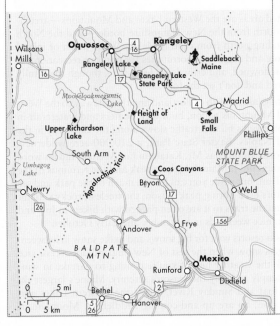

9

By Mary Ruoff   Unlike Maine's more famous, more populated, and more visited coast, inland Maine is a four-season destination. With strings of lakes and rivers framed by mountainous terrain, hilly pastoral stretches, classic New England villages with restaurants and shops that entice but don't overwhelm, and the region's most extensive wilderness areas, Maine's interior lures visitors in summer, fall, winter, and spring (yes, the slow season, but canoeists, fishermen, and white-water rafters venture inland).

The most visited areas are the Western Lakes and Mountains—stretching west and north from the New Hampshire border—and the North Woods—extending north from central Maine. While much of inland Maine is remote and rugged, opportunities for outdoor recreation are plentiful and renowned, and crowds do form here, though thankfully they're scattered and don't set the tone.

Sebago and Long lakes, north of Portland and the gateway to the Western Lakes and Mountains region, hum with boaters and watercraft in the summer. Sidewalks fill and traffic slows along the causeway in the tourist hub of Naples. Baxter State Park, a 210,000-acre wilderness park in the North Woods has Mt. Katahdin (an Abenaki Indian word for "Great Mountain"), Maine's highest peak and the terminus of the Appalachian Trail. But while you can hike in much of the park and see few other visitors even during peak season, the treeless, rocky summit of Katahdin and the trails to it are often packed with hikers in July and August and on nice weekends in September and early October.

Come winter, ski resorts wait for big snows and make snow in between. Maine often gets snow when the rest of New England doesn't, or vice versa, so track the weather here if you're coming to partake in winter sports or simply to enjoy the season's serenity. Maine's largest ski resorts, Sugarloaf and Sunday River, are in the Western Lakes and Mountains region. So are up-and-coming Saddleback Mountain in

Rangeley and Shawnee Peak in Bridgton, both family-friendly resorts. But not to worry, the lift lines don't get too long. Though they didn't come in the winter, "rusticators" began flocking to Maine to vacation in the mid-1800s, arriving at inland destinations by train or steamship, just as they did on Maine's coast. Escaping the summer heat and city pollution, these wealthy urbanites headed to the mountains to hike, swim, canoe, fish, hunt, and relax, staying at rustic sporting camps or at the grand hotels that cropped up in some of the most scenic spots. Moosehead Lake's Mt. Kineo—a walled outcropping north of Greenville where Indian tribes from throughout the Northeast came for flint—gave rise to one of the nation's largest and fanciest hotels in the late 1800s. Rangeley was discovered for its sport fishing in the mid-1800s and is still a haven for anglers, who come to fish for "world-class" brook trout and land-locked salmon. Modern streamer fly-fishing was born in the Rangeley region, and many of the local waters are restricted to fly-fishing.

The legacy of the rusticators and the locals who catered to them lives on at the sporting camps still found on inland Maine's remote lakes and rivers, albeit in fewer numbers. It also survives through Maine's unique system of licensed outdoor guides, known as Registered Maine Guides. These days they may lead kayak trips, hiking expeditions, white-water rafting excursions, and moose safaris as well as fishing, hunting, and canoe trips. Guides are happy to show you their license—it's the law that they have one, and some also opt to wear a badge.

PLANNING

WHEN TO GO

Inland's Maine's most popular hiking trails and beaches may get busy in warm weather, but if splendid isolation is what you crave, you can easily find it. In summer, traffic picks up but rarely creates jams, except in a few spots. Peak lodging rates apply, but moderate weather makes this a great time to visit. Inland Maine gets hotter than the coast, though less so along lakes and at higher elevations. July and August are warmest; September is less busy.

Western Maine is the state's premier destination for leaf peepers—hardwoods are more abundant here than on the coast. Late September through mid-October is peak foliage season.

Maine's largest ski areas can make their own snow; they usually open in mid-November and often operate into April. Inland Maine typically has snow cover by Christmas, so cross-country skiing, snowshoeing, and snowmobiling are in full swing by the end of the year. In ski towns, many lodgings charge peak rates in the winter.

Snowmelt ushers in mud season in early spring. Mid-May to mid-June is black fly season; they're especially pesky in the woods but less bothersome in town. Spring is a prime time for canoeing and fishing.

PLANNING YOUR TIME

Inland Maine locales are often destinations where visitors stay their entire trip. That's certainly true of those who come to ski at a resort, fish at a remote sporting camp, or just relax at a lakeside cabin. After a day hike on a mountain trail reached by driving gravel logging roads, visitors are unlikely to hurry on to another town. Vacation rental homes and cottages often require a week's stay, as do lakeside cottage resorts. Generally speaking, the farther inland you go, the farther it is between destinations.

GETTING HERE AND AROUND

AIR TRAVEL

Two primary airports serve Maine: Portland International (PWM ⊕ *www.portlandjetport.org*) and Bangor International (BGR ⊕ *www.flybangor.com*). Portland is closer to the Western Lakes and Mountains area; Bangor is more convenient to the North Woods. Regional flying services, operating from regional and municipal airports, provide access to remote lakes and wilderness areas and offer scenic flights.

CAR TRAVEL

Because Maine is large and rural, a car is essential. U.S. 2 is the major east–west thoroughfare in Western Maine, winding from Bangor to New Hampshire. Interstate 95 is a departure point for many visitors to inland Maine, especially the North Woods. The highway heads inland at Brunswick and is a toll road, the Maine Turnpike, from the New Hampshire border to Augusta. Because of the hilly terrain and abundant lakes and rivers, inland Maine roads are often curvy. Traffic rarely gets heavy, though highways often pass right through instead of around the larger towns, which can slow your trip a bit.

There are few public roads in Maine's North Woods, though private logging roads there are often open to the public (sometimes by permit and fee). When driving these roads, always give lumber-company trucks the right of way; loggers must drive in the middle of the road and often can't move over or slow down for cars. Be sure to have a full tank of gas before heading onto the many private roads in the region.

RESTAURANTS

Fear not, lobster lovers: this succulent, emblematic Maine food is on the menu at many inland restaurants, from fancier establishments to roadside places. Lobster dishes are more common than boiled lobster dinners, but look for daily specials. Shrimp, scallops, and other seafood are also menu mainstays, and you may find surprises like bison burgers or steaks from a nearby farm. Organic growers and natural foods producers are planted throughout the state and often sell their food to finer restaurants nearby. Seasonal foods like pumpkins, blackberries, and strawberries make their way into homemade desserts, as do Maine's famed blueberries. Many lakeside resorts and sporting camps have a reputation for good food; some of the latter will cook the fish you catch. *Prices in the reviews are the average cost of a main course at dinner or, if dinner is not served, at lunch.*

HOTELS

Although there is a higher concentration of upscale inns on the coast than inland, Bethel, Bridgton, the Kingfield area, and Rangeley have sophisticated hotels and inns. At lodgings near ski resorts, peak-season rates may apply in winter and summer. Both Sebago and Kezar lakes have full-service cottage resorts (usually a week's stay is required). The two largest ski resorts, Sunday River and Sugarloaf, offer a choice of hotels and condos. Greenville has the largest selection of lodgings in the North Woods region, with a nice mix of fine and homey inns. Lakeside sporting camps, from the primitive to the upscale, are popular around Rangeley and the North Woods. Many have cozy cabins heated with woodstoves and serve three hearty meals a day. In Maine's mountains, as on its coast, many small inns and B&Bs don't have air-conditioning. *Prices in the reviews are the lowest cost of a standard double room in high season.*

Maine State Parks Campsite Reservations Program. For information on Maine's 12 state park campgrounds, contact the Maine State Parks Campsite Reservations Program. Note: It does not serve Baxter State Park, which is not part of the Bureau of Parks and Lands. ⊠ *22 SHS, 18 Elkins Lane, East Side Campus, Augusta* ☎ *207/624–9950, 800/332–1501 in Maine* ⊕ *www.campwithme.com.*

VISITOR INFORMATION
Maine Tourism Association ⊠ *327 Water St., Hallowell* ☎ *207/623–0363, 800/767–8709* ⊕ *www.mainetourism.com.*

WESTERN LAKES AND MOUNTAINS

From Sebago Lake, less than 20 miles northwest of Portland, the sparsely populated Western Lakes and Mountains stretch north along the New Hampshire border to Québec. Each season offers different outdoor highlights: you can choose from snow sports, hiking, mountain biking, leaf peeping, fishing, and paddling. The Sebago Lake area bustles with activity in summer. Harrison and the Waterfords are quieter, Center Lovell is a dreamy escape, and Bridgton is a classic New England town. So is Bethel, in the valley of the Androscoggin River; Sunday River, one of Maine's two major ski resorts, is nearby. The more rural Rangeley Lake area brings long stretches of pine, beech, spruce, and sky and more classic inns. Carrabassett Valley, just north of Kingfield, is home to Sugarloaf, a major ski resort with a challenging golf course.

SEBAGO LAKE AREA

20 miles northwest of Portland.

GETTING HERE AND AROUND
Sebago Lake, gateway to Maine's Western Lakes and Mountains, is about 20 miles from Portland on U.S. 302.

ESSENTIALS
Vacation Rentals Krainin Real Estate ⊠ *1539 Roosevelt Tr.(Rte. 302), Raymond* ☎ *207/655–3811* ⊕ *www.krainin.com.*

Visitor Information Sebago Lakes Region Chamber of Commerce ⊠ *747 Roosevelt Tr. (U.S. 302), Windham* ☎ *207/892–8265* ⊕ *www. sebagolakeschamber.com.*

CLOSE UP

Outdoor Activities

People visit inland Maine year-round for hiking, biking (mountain biking is big at ski resorts off-season), camping, fishing, boating, canoeing, kayaking, white-water rafting, downhill and cross-country skiing, snowshoeing, and snowmobiling.

BICYCLING

Bicycle Coalition of Maine. For information on bicycling in Maine, contact the Bicycle Coalition of Maine. ☎ 207/623–4511 ⊕ www.bikemaine. org.

FISHING

Maine Department of Inland Fisheries and Wildlife. For information about fishing licenses, contact the Maine Department of Inland Fisheries and Wildlife. ☎ 207/287–8000 ⊕ www.mefishwildlife.com.

Maine Professional Guides Association. For assistance in finding a fishing guide, contact the Maine Professional Guides Association, which represents Registered Maine Guides. These guides are also available through most wilderness camps, sporting goods stores, and outfitters. ⊕ www.maineguides.org.

HIKING

Maine Trail Finder. Visitors can find Maine trails to hike, mountain bike, snowshoe, and ski on this website, which includes trail descriptions, photos, user comments, directions, links to maps, weather conditions, and more. If trails aren't listed for a particular area, it doesn't mean there aren't any: the nonprofit site, launched in 2010, is gradually adding listings statewide. ☎ 207/778–0900 ⊕ www. mainetrailfinder.com.

RAFTING

The Kennebec and Dead rivers, which converge at The Forks in Western Maine, and the West Branch of the Penobscot River, near Millinocket in the North Woods, provide thrilling white-water rafting. These rivers are dam-controlled, so day and multi-day guided trips run rain or shine daily from spring (mid-April on the Kennebec, May on the Dead and the Penobscot) to mid-October. Many rafting outfitters operate resort facilities in their base towns.

SKIING

Ski Maine. For alpine and cross-country skiing information, contact Ski Maine. ☎ 207/773–7669 ⊕ www. skimaine.com.

SNOWMOBILING

Maine Snowmobile Association. The Maine Snowmobile Association distributes an excellent statewide trail map of about 3,500 miles of trails. ☎ 207/622–6983 ⊕ www.mesnow. com.

EXPLORING

Sebago Lake. Sebago Lake is Maine's second largest lake after Moosehead and provides all the drinking water for Greater Portland. Many wilderness camps and year-round homes surround Sebago, which is popular with water-sports enthusiasts. Naples occupies an enviable location between Long and Sebago lakes. The town swells with seasonal residents and visitors in summer and, though winter is the slow season, things heat up in the first half of February with a winter carnival

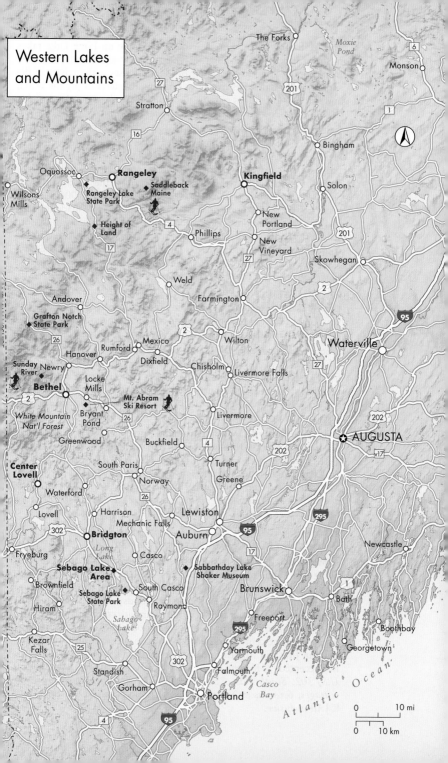

Western Lakes and Mountains

The Forks

Moxie Pond

Monson

6

Stratton

27

201

16

Bingham

Oquossoc

Rangeley

Rangeley Lake State Park

Saddleback Maine

Kingfield

Solon

1

Wilsons Mills

Height of Land

New Portland

New Vineyard

17

Phillips

4

27

Skowhegan

201

Weld

Farmington

2

Waterville

Andover

Grafton Notch State Park

26

Hanover

Rumford

Mexico

Dixfield

Chisholm

Wilton

95

Sunday River

Newry

Locke Mills

Mt. Abram Ski Resort

Livermore Falls

27

Bethel

2

White Mountain Nat'l Forest

Bryant Pond

26

Livermore

202

Greenwood

Buckfield

4

Turner

AUGUSTA

17

Center Lovell

South Paris

Norway

Greene

Waterford

26

Lovell

Harrison

Mechanic Falls

Lewiston

302

Bridgton

Long Lake

Auburn

95

295

Newcastle

Fryeburg

Casco

17

Sabbathday Lake Shaker Museum

Sebago Lake Area

Brownfield

South Casco

Sebago Lake State Park

Raymond

Brunswick

1

Bath

Hiram

Sabago Lake

Boothbay

Kezar Falls

25

Freeport

295

Georgetown

Standish

302

Yarmouth

Gorham

Falmouth

Casco Bay

95

4

Portland

Atlantic Ocean

0   10 mi

0   10 km

and ice-fishing derby. On clear days, the view up Long Lake takes in snowcapped Mt. Washington. The causeway separating Long Lake from Brandy Pond in the center of Naples pulses with activity in the summer. Open-air cafés overflow, boats and watercraft ply the water, and throngs of families parade along the sidewalk edging Long Lake. ☎ *207/892–8265* 🌐 *www.sebagolakeschamber.com.*

OFF THE BEATEN PATH

Sabbathday Lake Shaker Village. Established in the late 18th century, this is the last active Shaker community in the United States, with fewer than 10 members. Open for guided tours are four buildings with rooms of Shaker furniture, folk art, tools, farm implements, and crafts from the 18th to the early 20th century: the 1794 Meetinghouse; the 1839 Ministry's Shop, where the elders and eldresses lived until the early 1900s; the 1821 Sister's Shop, where household goods and candies were made for sale; and the 1816 Spinhouse, where changing exhibits are housed. A store sells herbs and goods handcrafted by the Shakers. Visitors can tour the community's herb garden on Tuesday and Thursday afternoons. ✉ *707 Shaker Rd.(turn off Rte. 26), New Gloucester* ☎ *207/926–4597* 🌐 *www.shaker.lib.me.us* 🎟 *Tour $7* ⏲ *Late May–early Oct., Mon.–Sat. 10–4:30.*

SPORTS AND THE OUTDOORS

U.S. 302 cuts through Naples, and in the center at the Naples causeway you'll find rental craft for fishing or cruising. Sebago and Long lakes are popular areas for sailing, fishing, and motorboating.

Sebago Lake State Park. This 1,400-acre park on the north shore of the lake provides swimming, picnicking, camping (250 sites), boating, and fishing (salmon and togue). Come winter, the 6 miles of hiking trails are groomed for cross-country skiing. ✉ *11 Park Access Rd., Casco* ☎ *207/693–6231, 207/693–6613 May–Oct. 15 only; camping information* 🌐 *www.parksandlands.com* 🎟 *$4.50* ⏲ *9–sunset.*

🖐 **Songo River Queen II.** Departing from the Naples causeway, *Songo River Queen II*, a 93-foot stern-wheeler, takes passengers on hour, hour-and-a-half, and two-hour cruises on Long Lake. ✉ *841 Roosevelt Tr. (U.S. 302)* ☎ *207/693–6861* 🌐 *www.songoriverqueen.net* 🎟 *$12 (one-hour), $16 (one-and-a-half-hour) and $20 (two-hour)* ⏲ *Early May–mid-June and early Sept.–mid-Oct., 1 cruise daily on weekends; mid-June–Labor Day, 5 cruises daily.*

WHERE TO STAY

For expanded hotel reviews, visit Fodors.com.

$$$$ RESORT ALL-INCLUSIVE ★ 🖐

🏨 **Migis Lodge.** The pine-paneled cottages scattered under canopied pines along the ½ mile of shorefront at this 125-acre resort have fieldstone fireplaces and porches and are handsomely furnished with colorful rugs and handmade quilts. **Pros:** exclusive woodsy resort with access to private island; daily outdoor cocktail hour with complimentary drinks on Monday and Friday; open-air gym, wood-fired sauna, and, in quiet locale, massage center and outdoor exercise classes. **Cons:** week minimum in July and August (unless shorter openings occur); credit cards not accepted. [$] *Rooms from: $325* ✉ *30 Migis Lodge Rd., turn off U.S. 302, South Casco* ☎ *207/647–3472* 🌐 *www.migis.com* 🛏 *35 cottages, 6 rooms* 💳 *No credit cards* ⏲ *Closed mid-Oct.–early June* 🍴 *All-inclusive.*

BRIDGTON

8 miles north of Naples, 30 miles south of Bethel.

Bridgton's winding Main Street (U.S. 302) reveals picturesque New England townscapes at every curve. On steamy summer days, kids dive off the dock at the town beach tucked at the end of Highland Lake, just past storefronts with restaurants, galleries, and shops. Just steps from downtown a covered pedestrian bridge leads to 66-acre Pondicherry Park, a nature preserve with wooded trails and two streams. The town has 10 lakes that are popular for boating and fishing. Come winter, people arrive to ski at Shawnee Peak.

The combination of woods, lakes, views, and several public reserves where they can be enjoyed, makes the surrounding countryside a good choice for leaf peepers and outdoor lovers. A few miles north, Harrison anchors the northern end of Long Lake. Tiny Waterford is a National Historic District. Come fall, Fryeburg, on the New Hampshire border, is home to the famed Fryeburg Fair (⊕ *www.fryeburgfair.com*), New England's largest agricultural fair.

GETTING HERE AND AROUND

U.S. 302 runs from Portland, along the east side of Sebago Lake to Naples, then up the west side of Long Lake to Bridgton.

ESSENTIALS

Vacation Rentals Maine Lakeside Getaways ⊠ *12 Hawk Ridge Rd., Harrison* ☎ *207/647–4000, 866/647–8557* ⊕ *www.mainelakesidegetaways.com.*

Visitor Information Greater Bridgton Lakes Region Chamber of Commerce ⊠ *101 Portland Rd. (U.S. 302)* ☎ *207/647–3472* ⊕ *www.mainelakeschamber.com.*

EXPLORING

Rufus Porter Museum and Cultural Heritage Center. Local youth Rufus Porter became a leading folk artist, painting landscape and harbor murals on the walls of New England homes in the early 1800s, including those in the museum's red Cape Cod–style house. Also an inventor, Porter founded *Scientific American* magazine. Early issues are showcased, as are some of his inventions and miniature portraits. Changing exhibits feature 19th-century folk and decorative arts. By summer 2013, the museum plans to relocate to 121 Main Street, occupying an 1840s house and moving the Cape home to the grounds. ⊠ *67 N. High St.* ☎ *207/647–2828* ⊕ *www.rufusportermuseum.org* ⌖ *$8* ⊙ *Mid-June–mid-Oct., Wed.–Sat. noon–4.*

SPORTS AND THE OUTDOORS

Shawnee Peak. Just an hour's drive from Portland and a few miles from Bridgton's downtown, Shawnee Peak appeals to families and those who enjoy nighttime skiing—beginner, intermediate, and expert trails are lit most evenings. Five lifts serve 40 trails, four glades, and two terrain parks. There are slope-side condominiums and two base lodges with cafeterias. The main lodge also has a deck-fronted restaurant, babysitting, ski school and rentals, and a ski shop. ⊠ *119 Mountain Rd., turn off U.S. 302* ☎ *207/647–8444* ⊕ *www.shawneepeak.com.*

WHERE TO STAY

For expanded hotel reviews, visit Fodors.com.

$ **Bear Mountain Inn.** On 25 acres above lake-size Bear Pond, this 1825
B&B/INN homestead is meticulously decorated with country furnishings and
★ bear decor. **Pros:** sweeping lawn has 80-foot lake-view deck with fireplace; private beach has boat and swimming docks, canoes, and kayaks; benches and hammocks along riverside trail; great courtesy snack
choices. **Cons:** one suite is considerably smaller; two rooms share a hall
bath, one has a private hall bath. *$ Rooms from: $120 ⊠ 364 Waterford Rd., Waterford ☎ 207/583–4404 ⊕ www.bearmtninn.com ⇨ 8
rooms, 6 with bath; 2 suites, 1 cabin ⎮◎⎮ Breakfast.*

$$ **Noble House Inn.** In town but on a quiet road, this 1903 estate above
B&B/INN Highland Lake beach offers convenience and quietude. **Pros:** bottom-
less cookie jar; ski packages; two plush suites have sitting rooms with
TV and DVD; family suite has bunk beds. **Cons:** near lake with beach
but not great lake views *$ Rooms from: $165 ⊠ 81 Highland Rd.
☎ 207/647–3733, 888/237–4880 ⊕ www.noblehousebb.com ⇨ 5
rooms, 4 suites ⎮◎⎮ Breakfast.*

CENTER LOVELL

17 miles northwest of Harrison, 23 miles south of Bethel.

At Center Lovell you can glimpse secluded Kezar Lake to the west, the
retreat of wealthy and very private people. Only town residents and
property owners can use the town beaches, but there is a public boat
launch. Sabattus Mountain, which rises behind Center Lovell, has a
public hiking trail.

WHERE TO EAT AND STAY

For expanded hotel reviews, visit Fodors.com.

$$$ ✕ **Center Lovell Inn Restaurant.** The eclectic furnishings in this eye-catching
CONTEMPORARY cupola-topped property from 1805 blend the mid-19th and mid-20th
centuries in a pleasing, homey style. In summer the best tables for dining are on the wraparound porch, which has sunset views of the White
Mountains. Inside, one dining room has mountain views and the other
an original iron fireplace. Entrées may include pan-seared Muscovy
duck, fillet of bison, or fresh swordfish. Breakfast is by reservation
only (no lunch). Nine lodging rooms (some shared baths; some rooms
can be combined as suites) are upstairs and in the adjacent Harmon
House. *$ Average main: $27 ⊠ 1107 Main St. (Rte. 5) ☎ 207/925–
1575, 800/777–2698 ⊕ www.centerlovellinn.com ☾ Closed Nov.–late
Dec. and Apr.–mid-May.*

$$$ **Quisisana.** This delightful summer-only cottage resort on Kezar
RESORT Lake makes music a focus. **Pros:** unique musical theme; plethora of
ALL-INCLUSIVE watersports; regular activities like Tuesday cocktail party and dinner-
hour children's program. **Cons:** one-week minimum in peak season
(unless shorter openings occur); no Wi-Fi in cottages; cash or check
only. *$ Rooms from: $215 ⊠ 42 Quisisana Dr., off Pleasant Point
Rd. ☎ 207/925–3500 ⊕ www.quisisanaresort.com ⇨ 11 rooms in 2
lodges, 46 cottage units ⊟ No credit cards ☾ Closed Sept.–mid-June
⎮◎⎮ All-inclusive.*

BETHEL

28 miles north of Lovell; 65 miles north of Portland.

Bethel is pure New England, a town with white clapboard houses, white-steeple churches, and a mountain vista at the end of every street. In winter, this is ski country: Sunday River ski area in Newry is only a few miles north. Bethel WinterFest is usually held in February. On the third weekend in July, Mollyockett Days, which includes a parade, fireworks, and frog-jumping contest, honors a Pequawket Indian renowned for her medicinal cures in the early days of white settlement.

GETTING HERE AND AROUND

From the south, Route 35 winds along the east side of Long Lake to Harrison, through the Waterfords, and on to Bethel. Route 5 leads to Bethel from Center Lovell. The two roads overlap en route to Bethel, then split off from each other several miles south of town. Either road will get you there, but Route 5 is a little shorter and especially pretty come fall, with lots of overhanging trees. From the west, U.S. 2 passes through the White Mountain National Forest as it enters Maine from New Hampshire and continues to Bethel and nearby Newry, home of Sunday River ski resort.

ESSENTIALS

Vacation Rentals Four Seasons Realty & Rentals ✉ *32 Parkway Plaza, Suite 1* ☎ *207/824–3776* ⊕ *fourseasonsrealtymaine.com.*

Visitor Information Bethel Area Chamber of Commerce ✉ *8 Station Pl.* ☎ *207/824–2282, 800/442–5826* ⊕ *www.bethelmaine.com.*

EXPLORING

Bethel Historical Society Regional History Center. Start your stroll in Bethel here, across from the Village Common. The center's campus comprises two buildings: the 1821 O'Neil Robinson House and the 1813 Dr. Moses Mason House, both of which are listed on the National Register of Historic Places. The Robinson House has changing exhibits pertaining to the region's history; the Moses Mason House has nine period rooms and a front hall and stairway wall decorated with Rufus Porter School folk art murals. Pick up a self-guided walking tour of Bethel Hill Village, or print it from the museum's website. ✉ *10–14 Broad St.* ☎ *207/824–2908, 800/824–2910* ⊕ *www.bethelhistorical.org* ☞ *$3 Mason House; O'Neil Robinson House free* ☉ *O'Neil Robinson House Jan.–April Tues.–Thurs. 10–4; May–Dec. Tues.–Fri.10–4; July and Aug. also Sat. 1–4. Dr. Moses Mason House July and Aug. Tues.–Sat. 1–4 and by appointment year-round.*

SPORTS AND THE OUTDOORS

CANOEING AND KAYAKING

Bethel Outdoor Adventure and Campground. This outfitter rents canoes, kayaks, and bikes and guides fishing, kayak, and canoe trips. It also operates a hostel and riverside campground. Maine Mineralogy Expeditions is based here, offering mineral mine tours and an open-air facility where you can sluice for gems and minerals to keep. ✉ *121 Mayville Rd. (U.S. 2)* ☎ *207/824–4224, 800/533–3607* ⊕ *www.betheloutdooradventure.com.*

9

DOGSLEDDING

Mahoosuc Guide Service. This guide company leads day and multiday dogsledding expeditions on the Maine–New Hampshire border, as well as canoeing trips. ⊠ *1513 Bear River Rd. (Rte. 26), Newry* ☎ *207/824–2073* ⊕ *www.mahoosuc.com.*

Mahoosuc Mountain Lodge. Mahoosuc Mountain Lodge has two dorms and a farmhouse with guest rooms. ⊠ *1513 Bear River Rd. (Rte. 26), Newry* ⊕ *www.mahoosucmountainlodge.com.*

MULTI-SPORT OUTFITTERS

Northwoods Outfitters. Northwoods Outfitters outfits for moose-watching, biking, skiing, snowmobiling, snowboarding, canoeing, kayaking, camping, and fishing. They lead trips for many of these activities as well as rent canoes, kayaks, bikes, snowmobiles, snowshoes, ATVs, and more. Shop, get trail advice, and kick back in the Internet café at its downtown outfitters store. They also run an inn and lake rentals as well as shuttle service. ⊠ *5 Lilly Bay Rd.* ☎ *207/695–3288, 866/223–1380* ⊕ *www.maineoutfitter.com.*

Sun Valley Sports. Sun Valley Sports guides snowmobile and ATV trips (rental included). It also operates fly-fishing trips, moose and wildlife safaris, and rents canoes and kayaks. ⊠ *129 Sunday River Rd.* ☎ *207/824–7533, 877/851–7533* ⊕ *www.sunvalleysports.com.*

PARKS

Grafton Notch State Park. Route 26 runs through this park, which stretches along the Bear River Valley 14 miles north of Bethel and is a favorite foliage drive. It's an easy walk from the roadside parking areas to Mother Walker Falls, Moose Cave, and the spectacular Screw Auger Falls. You can also hike to the summit of Old Speck Mountain, the state's third-highest peak. If you have the stamina, the equipment, and several days, you can pick up the Appalachian Trail here, hike over Saddleback Mountain, and continue on to Mt. Katahdin. The Appalachian Trailhead parking lot is cleared in the winter for snowshoers and cross-country skiers who use the snowmobile trail along Route 26 through the park (no staff in winter). ⊠ *Rte. 26, Newry* ☎ *207/824–2912 mid-May–mid-Oct., 207/624–6080* ⊕ *www.parksandlands.com* ⊙ *Daily, 9–sunset (no staff mid-Oct.–mid-May).*

Maine Appalachian Trail Club. The Maine Appalachian Trail Club publishes seven Appalachian Trail maps and a Maine trail guide. ⊕ *www.matc.org.*

White Mountain National Forest. This forest straddles New Hampshire and Maine, with the highest peaks on the New Hampshire side. The Maine section, though smaller, has magnificent rugged terrain, camping and picnic areas, and hiking, from hour-long nature loops to a day hike up Speckled Mountain. The mountain is part of the 11,000-acre Caribou-Speckled Mountain Wilderness Area, one of several in the forest, but the only one entirely within Maine. The most popular Maine access to the forest is Route 113 from its intersection with U.S. 2 in Gilead, 10 miles from downtown Bethel. Most of the highway is the Maine Pequawket Trail Scenic Byway, and the section through the forest is spectacular come fall. This forest road is closed in winter but is used by snowmobilers and cross-country skiers. The first few miles of Route 113 from U.S. 2 are plowed (park along road or in parking area). ☒ *Route 113, turn off U.S. 2, Gilead* ☏ *603/466–2713* ⊕ *www.fs.fed.us/r9/white* 🎫 *Day pass $3 per car, week pass $5 per car.*

New Hampshire Visitor Center. The New Hampshire Visitor Center, within the White Mountain National Forest, has interactive exhibits for kids and displays on the forest's history and natural setting. ☒ *Androscoggin Ranger Station Visitor Center, 300 Glen Rd.(Rte. 16), Gorham* ☉ *Late May–mid-Oct., daily 8–4:30; late Oct.–mid-May, weekdays 8–4:30.*

SKI AREAS

Carter's Cross-Country Ski Center. This cross-country ski center offers about 30 miles of trails for all levels of skiers, lessons, and rentals—snowshoes, skis, and sleds to pull children are available. It also rents lodge rooms and ski-in cabins (trail passes included). ☒ *786 Intervale Rd.* ☏ *207/824–3880, 207/539–4848* ⊕ *www.cartersxcski.com.*

Sunday River. What was once a sleepy ski area with minimal facilities has evolved into a sprawling resort that attracts skiers from as far away as Europe. Spread throughout the valley at Sunday River are three base areas, two condominium hotels, a less costly lodge-style inn, trailside condominiums, town houses, and a ski dorm. Sunday River is home to the Maine Handicapped Skiing program, which provides lessons and services for skiers with disabilities. Rentals, lessons, children's programs, day care, and slope-side dining are all here, too; 16 lifts service 132 trails, five terrain parks, and a superpipe. There's plenty else to do, including cross-country skiing, ice-skating, tubing, and, come summer and fall, hiking, mountain biking, and scenic lift rides. ☒ *15 S. Ridge Rd., turn on Sunday River Rd. from U.S. 2, Newry* ☏ *207/824–3000 main number, 207/824–3000 snow conditions, 800/543–2754 reservations* ⊕ *www.sundayriver.com.*

Mt. Abram. Family-friendly Mt. Abram, south of Bethel, has 44 trails and glade areas, five lifts, two base lodges, day care, and ski lessons. It's open Thursday through Sunday during the ski season. ☒ *308 Howe Hill Rd., turn off Route 26, Greenwood* ☏ *207/875–5000* ⊕ *www.skimtabram.com.*

EN ROUTE
Artist's Bridge. The routes north from Bethel to the Rangeley district are all scenic, particularly in autumn when the maples are aflame with color. In the town of Newry, make a short detour to the Artist's Bridge (turn off Route 26 onto Sunday River Road and drive about 4 miles), the most painted and photographed of Maine's eight covered bridges. ☒ *Sunday River Rd., Newry.*

Grafton Notch State Park. From Newry, Route 26 continues north from U.S. 2 to the gorges and waterfalls of Grafton Notch State Park and on to Upton. This 21-mile stretch is the state's Grafton Notch Scenic Byway. Drive carefully and keep a lookout: this is one of Maine's moose alleys. At Errol, New Hampshire, Route 16 will return you east around the north shore of Mooselookmeguntic Lake, through Oquossoc, and into Rangeley. ☒ *1941 Bear River Rd. (Rte. 26), Newry.*

One of the Rangeley Lakes, Mooselookmeguntic is said to mean "portage to the moose feeding place" in the Abenaki language.

Height of Land. A direct but still stunningly scenic route from Bethel to Rangeley is U.S. 2 east to the twin towns of Rumford and Mexico, where Route 17 heads north to Oquossoc, about an hour's drive. The high point of this route, part of the Rangeley Lakes National Scenic Byway, is Height of Land, with its unforgettable views of mountains and the island-studded blue mass of Mooselookmeguntic Lake. In Oquossoc, turn right on Route 4 towards Rangeley. ⊠ *Rte. 17 overlook, Rangeley.*

RANGELEY

66 miles north of Bethel.

Rangeley, on the north side of Rangeley Lake on Route 4/16, has long lured anglers and winter-sports enthusiasts to its more than 40 lakes and ponds and 450 square miles of woodlands. A few blocks from Main Street, Lakeside Park ("Town Park" to locals) has a large swimming area and boat launch. Equally popular in summer or winter, Rangeley has a rough, wilderness feel to it.

GETTING HERE AND AROUND

To reach Rangeley on a scenic drive, take Route 17 north from U.S. 2 to Route 4 in Oquossoc, then head east. Route 16 soon joins the highway and from Rangeley continues east to Kingfield and Sugarloaf ski resort.

ESSENTIALS

Vacation Rentals Morton and Furbish Rental Agency ⊠ *2478 Main St.* ☎ *207/864–9065, 888/218–4882* ⊕ *www.rangeleyrentals.com.*

CLOSE UP

Whoopie Pies

When a bill aiming to make the whoopie pie Maine's official dessert was debated in the state legislature in early 2011, some lawmakers countered that blueberry pie (made with Maine wild blueberries, of course) should have the honor. In the end it did, but what could have been a civil war ended civilly, with whoopie pies designated the "official state treat." Spend a few days anywhere in Maine and you'll notice just how popular the treat is.

The name is misleading: it's a pie only in the sense of a having a filling between two "crusts"—namely, a thick layer of sugary frosting sandwiched between two saucers of rich cake, usually chocolate. It's said to have Pennsylvania Dutch roots and may have acquired its distinctive moniker from the jubilant yelp farmers emitted after discovering it in their lunchboxes. Many Mainers dispute this, claiming the whoopie pie originated here. Typically, the filling is made with butter or shortening; some recipes add Marshmallow Fluff. Many bakers have indulged the temptation to experiment with flavors and ingredients, particularly in the filling but also in the cake, yielding pumpkin, raspberry, oatmeal cream, red velvet, peanut butter, and more.

Try some of these:

Labadies Bakery. Labadies Bakery in Lewiston boasts 87 years of baking whoopie pies (which, over time, have grown from whoopie to whopping: they top out at 16 inches in diameter!). Though most of its business is wholesale, it has a storefront bakery. ⊠ *161 Lincoln St., Lewiston* ☎ *207/784–7042* ⊕ *www. labadiesbakery.com.*

Wicked Whoopies. Made by Isamax Snacks in Gardiner, these whoopie pies are stocked in supermarkets and convenience stores throughout Maine and sold at the company's coffee shops in Freeport and Farmingdale. ⊠ *621 Maine Ave., Farmingdale* ☎ *207/622–8860* ⊕ *www. wickedwhoopies.com* ⊠ *32 Main St., Freeport* ☎ *207/865–3100.*

Cranberry Island Kitchen. Cranberry Island Kitchen supplies Williams-Sonoma and ships nationwide, but about half of its "gourmet" whoopie pies (free-range eggs, Maine-made butter) are sold at its store near Portland's Old Port, where the offerings include seashell-shaped whoopie pies and filling flavors like espresso chocolate chip and Chambord. ⊠ *52 Danforth St., Portland* ☎ *207/829–5200* ⊕ *www.cranberryislandkitchen.com.*

Friars' Bakehouse. Friars' Bakehouse was voted to have the best whoopie pies in the Bangor area by respondents to a *Bangor Daily News* poll. The bakery and restaurant is run by two Franciscan friars, one of whom spent time in highly regarded culinary programs. ⊠ *21 Central St., Bangor* ☎ *207/947–3770.*

Moody's Diner. This diner makes pies of considerable size, prized for their filling above all. ⊠ *1885 Atlantic Hwy, Waldoboro* ☎ *207/832–7785* ⊕ *www. moodysdiner.com.*

Two Fat Cats Bakery. This bakery's whoopie pies are delicately proportioned, with a smooth and light marshmallow cream filling, and conservative with flavors—no peanut-butter-mint-chocolate-chip pies to be found here. ⊠ *47 India St., Portland* ☎ *207/347–5144* ⊕ *www. twofatcatsbakery.com.*

9

Visitor Information Rangeley Lakes Maine Chamber of Commerce ⊠ *6 Park Dr.* ☎ *207/864–5364, 800/685–2537* ⊕ *www.rangeleymaine.com.*

EXPLORING

Rangeley Outdoor Sporting Heritage Museum. Spruce railings and siding on the Rangeley Outdoor Sporting Heritage Museum's facade replicate a local taxidermy shop from about 1900. Inside, the welcome center is a reassembled log sporting camp cabin from the same period, when grand hotels and full-service sporting camps drew well-to-do rusticators on long stays. Visitors like to linger here before viewing displays on the Rangeley area's rich history as a fishing, hunting, and outdoor mecca, from the Native Americana period through the rusticator era to today. One of the big lures is the exhibit on local fly-tier Carrie Stevens, whose famed streamer flies (the world's largest collection is here) increased the region's fly-fishing fame in the 1920s. ⊠ *8 Rumford Rd.(Rte. 17), Oquossoc* ☎ *207/864–3091* ⊕ *www.rangeleyoutdoormuseum.org* 🎫 *$5* ☉ *Memorial Day–June and Labor Day–Columbus Day, Fri. and Sat. 10–2; July and Aug., Wed–Sun. 10–2.*

SPORTS AND THE OUTDOORS

BOATING AND FISHING

Rangeley and Mooselookmeguntic lakes are good for canoeing, sailing, fishing, and motorboating. Several outfits rent equipment and provide guide service if needed. Lake fishing for brook trout and landlocked salmon is at its best in May, June, and September. The Rangeley area's rivers and streams are especially popular with fly-fishers, who enjoy the sport from May through October.

GOLF

Mingo Springs Golf Course. Mingo Springs Golf Course is known for its mountain and water views as well as challenging play on its 18-hole course. Greens fees start at $32 for 9 holes and $42 for 18 holes. You can also take in the views and spot wildlife on the Mingo Springs Trail & Bird Walk, an easy 3-mile loop trail through woods along the course. ⊠ *43 Country Club Rd.* ☎ *207/864–5021* ⊕ *www.mingosprings.com.*

PARKS

Rangeley Lake State Park. On the south shore of Rangeley Lake, this 869-acre park has superb lakeside scenery, swimming, picnic tables, a boat ramp, and 50 campsites. ⊠ *S. Shore Dr., turn off Rte. 17 or Rte. 4* ☎ *207/864–3858 May 15–Oct. 1 only, 207/624–6080* ⊕ *www. parksandlands.com* 🎫 *$4.50* ☉ *Daily 9–sunset (Oct.–mid-May no staff, roads not open or plowed).*

SKI AREAS

Rangeley Lakes Trails Center. Rangeley Lakes Trails Center rents cross-country skis and snowshoes and has about 25 miles of groomed trails surrounding Saddleback Mountain. The snack bar is open in the winter, and you can hike, mountain bike, and run on the trails in warmer weather. ⊠ *524 Saddleback Mountain Rd., Dallas* ☎ *207/864–4309* ⊕ *www.xcskirangeley.com.*

Saddleback Maine. A family atmosphere prevails at Saddleback Maine, where the quiet, lack of crowds, and spectacularly wide valley views draw return visitors. The 66 trails and glades, accessed by five lifts, are divided among 33% novice, 30% intermediate, and 37% advanced. A fieldstone fireplace anchors the post-and-beam base lodge. You can also find a day-care center, ski school, rental and retail shop, and trailside condominium lodging on-site. Hiking (the Appalachian Trail crosses Saddleback's summit ridge), mountain biking, canoeing, kayaking, fly-fishing, moose tours, and birding are big draws in warm weather, as are music concerts, which continue in winter. On the second weekend in August, the annual Saddleback Mountain Bluegrass Festival draws thousands. ✉ *976 Saddleback Mountain Rd., follow signs from Rte. 4, Dallas* ☎ *207/864–5671, 866/918–2225, 207/864–5441, 207/864–5671 reservations* ⊕ *www.saddlebackmaine.com.*

WHERE TO EAT AND STAY

For expanded hotel reviews, visit Fodors.com.

$$$
AMERICAN
✕ **Gingerbread House Restaurant.** A big fieldstone fireplace, well-spaced tables, wrap-around deck, and antique marble soda fountain, all with views of the woods beyond, make for comfortable surroundings inside what really looks like a giant gingerbread house. Breakfast, lunch, and dinner are served; folks also stop in for baked goods or ice cream. Soups, salads, and sandwiches at lunch give way to entrées such as lobster macaroni and cheese and barbecued ribs with blueberry chipotle sauce and maple syrup. At lunch and dinner, many order the popular Maine crab cakes appetizer as a main course and you can sit at outdoor tables in the summer. $ *Average main: $23* ✉ *55 Carry Rd. (Rte. 4), Oquossoc* ☎ *207/864–3602* ⊕ *gingerbreadhouserestaurant.net* ⊗ *Closed Nov. and Apr.; and Mon.–Wed., Dec.–Mar. No lunch or dinner Sun., mid-Sept.–mid-June (except on holiday weeks and weekends).*

$
B&B/INN
⟳
▦ **Country Club Inn.** Built in 1920 as the country club for the adjacent Mingo Springs Golf Course, this secluded hilltop retreat has sweeping lake and mountain views. **Pros:** loads of lawn and board games; lots of photos of Rangeley's long-gone resorts; regular, B&B, and Modified American Plan rates. **Cons:** smallish rooms in main building. $ *Rooms from: $119* ✉ *56 Country Club Rd.* ☎ *207/864–3831* ⊕ *www.countryclubinnrangeley.com* ⇱ *19 rooms* ⊗ *Closed Nov. and Apr.* ⧀ *Multiple meal plans.*

$
HOTEL
▦ **The Rangeley Inn.** From Main Street you see only the large three-story blue inn, built in 1907 for wealthy urbanites on vacation. **Pros:** this historic hotel is the last of its kind in the region; canoes for Haley Pond; some marble baths and whirlpool tubs; motel rooms have refrigerators and microwaves. **Cons:** no Rangeley Lake views; restaurants are dinner-only. $ *Rooms from: $84* ✉ *2443 Main St.* ☎ *207/864–3341, 800/666–3687* ⊕ *www.rangeleyinn.com* ⇱ *35 inn rooms, 13 motel rooms (including 1 suite)* ⊗ *Hotel and restaurants (not motel) closed Apr., May, Nov., and Dec.; dinning room restaurant also closed Jan.–March and June* ⧀ *No meals.*

9

KINGFIELD

38 miles east of Rangeley

In the shadows of Mt. Abram and Sugarloaf Mountain, home to its namesake ski resort, Kingfield has everything a "real" New England town should have: a general store, historic inns, and white clapboard churches. Sugarloaf has golf and tennis in summer.

ESSENTIALS

Visitor Information Franklin County Chamber of Commerce ⊠ *248 Wilton Rd., Farmington* ☎ *207/778–4215* ⊕ *www.franklincountymaine.org.*

SPORTS AND THE OUTDOORS

SKI AREAS

★ **Sugarloaf Mountain Resort.** Abundant natural snow, a huge mountain, and the only above-tree-line lift-service skiing in the East have made Sugarloaf Mountain Resort one of Maine's best-known ski areas with 14 lifts, 153 trails and glades, ski school, and rentals. Two slope-side hotels and hundreds of slope-side condominiums provide ski-in, ski-out access, and the base village has restaurants and shops. The Outdoor Center has more than 60 miles of cross-country ski trails as well as snowshoeing, snow tubing, and ice-skating. There's also plenty for the kids, from day care to special events. Once you are here, a car is unnecessary—a shuttle connects all mountain operations. Summer is much quieter than winter, but you can mountain bike, fish, hike, ride a chairlift, and zip line, plus golf at the superb 18-hole, Robert Trent Jones Jr.–designed golf course ($59–$89 with cart, cost varies by season). ⊠ *5092 Access Rd., Carrabassett Valley* ☎ *207/237–2000, 207/237–6808 snow conditions, 800/843–5623 reservations* ⊕ *www.sugarloaf.com/index.html.*

THE NORTH WOODS

Moosehead Lake, the four-season resort town of Greenville, Baxter State Park, and the Allagash Wilderness Waterway are dispersed within Maine's remote North Woods. This vast area in the north-central section of the state is best experienced by canoe or raft; via hiking, snowshoe, or snowmobile; or on a fishing trip. Maine's largest lake, Moosehead supplies more in the way of rustic camps, guides, and outfitters than any other northern locale. Its 400-plus miles of shorefront, three-quarters of which is owned by lumber companies or the state, is virtually uninhabited.

GREENVILLE

155 miles northeast of Portland; 70 miles northwest of Bangor.

Greenville, tucked at the southern end of island-dotted, mostly forest-lined Moosehead Lake, is an outdoors-lover's paradise. Boating, fishing, and hiking are popular in summer, while snowmobiling, skiing, and ice fishing reign in winter. The town also has the greatest selection of shops, restaurants, and inns in the North Woods region. Restaurants and lodgings are also clustered 20 miles north in Rockwood, where the

CLOSE UP

North Woods Outfitters

BOATING

Allagash Canoe Trips. This tour operator provides guided canoe trips on the Allagash Waterway, plus the Moose, Penobscot, and St. John rivers. It also guides white-water rafting trips on the Kennebec and Dead rivers. ⊠ *8 Bigelow, Carrabassett Valley* ☎ *207/237-3077* ⊕ *www.allagashcanoetrips.com.*

Beaver Cove Marina. At this marina, you can rent power and pontoon boats, sailboats, fishing skiffs, and canoes and kayaks. ⊠ *16 Coveside Rd., Beaver Cove* ☎ *207/695-3526* ⊕ *www.beavercovemarina.com.*

Katahdin Outfitters. Katahdin Outfitters outfits canoe and kayak expeditions on the St. John River, the West Branch of the Penobscot River, and the Allagash Wilderness Waterway. ⊠ *Baxter State Park Road, 1/8 mile from Millinocket town line, Millinocket* ☎ *207/723-5700* ⊕ *www.katahdinoutfitters.com.*

If requested, most canoe-rental operations will also arrange transportation, help plan your route, and provide a guide. Transportation to wilderness lakes can be handled through various regional flying services.

MULTI-SPORT

North Woods Ways. Run by two Registered Maine Guides who've authored books on outdoor adventure skills, North Woods Ways offers wilderness workshops that attract visitors from as far away as Japan and Scandinavia. On day and overnight trips, you can learn canoe and backcountry travel and camping skills (winter and summer). Paddle-making workshops are also offered. ⊠ *2293 Elliottsville Rd., Willimantic* ☎ *207/997-3723* ⊕ *www.northwoodsways.com.*

RAFTING

North Country Rivers. From spring through fall, North Country Rivers runs white-water rafting trips on the Dead and Kennebec rivers in The Forks in Western Maine, and on the West Branch of Penobscot River outside Millinocket in the North Woods. North Country's 55-acre resort south of The Forks in Bingham has cabin and cottage rentals, tent and RV campgrounds, and a lodge with a restaurant, pub, and store. Its Millinocket base is at Big Moose Inn, Cabins & Campground. The outfitter also offers moose and wildlife safaris; rents ATVs, snowmobiles, bikes, and kayaks; and guides trips for many outdoor activities. ⊠ *Gadabout Gaddis Airport, 36 Main St., Bingham* ☎ *207/672-4814, 800/348-8871* ⊕ *www.northcountryrivers.com.*

9

Moose River flows through the village and—across from Mt. Kineo's majestic cliffs—into the lake.

GETTING HERE AND AROUND

To reach Greenville from Interstate 95, get off at Exit 157 in Newport and head north, successively, on Routes 7, 23, and 15.

ESSENTIALS

Vacation Rentals Northwoods Camp Rentals ⊠ *14 Lakeview St.* ☎ *800/251-8042* ⊕ *mooseheadrentals.com.*

DID YOU KNOW?

Mt. Katahdin's summit—Baxter Peak, the northern terminus of the Appalachian Trail—can be reached by several routes, including the white-blazed Hunt Trail (officially part of the AT), the rocky Cathedral Trail, or the less strenuous Saddle Trail. The precarious Knife Edge links Baxter and Pamola peaks.

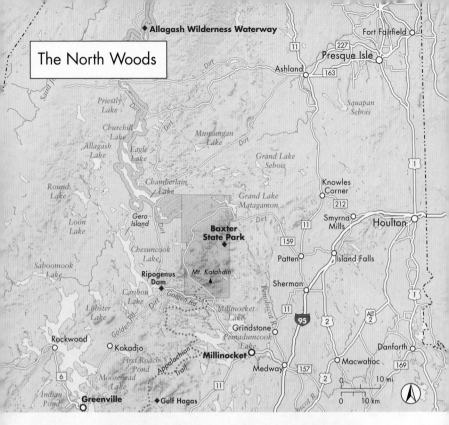

The North Woods

Moosehead Historical Society & Museums. At its main property, the historical society leads guided tours of the Eveleth-Crafts-Sheridan House, a late-19th-century Victorian mansion filled with period antiques, most original to the home. Special exhibits and displays change annually. The Lumberman's Museum, about the region's logging history, is in the carriage house. Several blocks away the former Universalist Church in downtown Greenville is home to the society's Center for Moosehead History and Moosehead Lake Aviation Museum. The former has a fine exhibit of Native American artifacts from the Moosehead Lake region, dating from 9,000 BC to the 1700s, as well as changing exhibits. The latter highlights the impact of aviation on the area, from the early bush pilots to Greenville's annual International Seaplane Fly-in. ✉ *444 Pritham Ave. (Rte. 15)* ☎ *207/695–2909* ⊕ *www.mooseheadhistory.org* 🖾 *Eveleth-Crafts-Sheridan House $5, other museums free* 🕐 *Eveleth-Crafts-Sheridan House mid-June–mid-Oct., Wed.–Fri. 1–4; Lumberman's Museum Tues.–Fri. 9–4; Center for Moosehead History and Moosehead Lake Aviation Museum mid-June–mid-Oct., Thurs.–Sat. 10–4; museums also open by appointment.*

Mt. Kineo. Once a thriving summer resort for the wealthy, the Mt. Kineo House was accessed primarily by steamship. The resort—home to one of the nation's busiest hotels in the late 1800s and set below its namesake cliffs—was torn down around 1940. But Kineo, where for centuries Native Americans from throughout the Northeast came for flint, remains a pleasant day trip. An islandlike peninsula, it's only easy access is by boat. You can take the Kineo Shuttle, which departs from the State Dock in Rockwood, or rent a motorboat in Rockwood and make the journey across the lake in about 15 minutes. It's an easy hike on the Bridal Trail to Kineo's summit for awesome views down the lake. A map is available at the Moosehead Lake Region Chamber of Commerce. ✉ *Village Road, turn off of Rte. 15, Rockwood* ✚ *To depart from State Dock in Rockwood, from Greenville go 20 miles north on Rte. 15, turn right on Village Rd., go about ¼ mile to dock.*

SPORTS AND THE OUTDOORS

FISHING

Togue (lake trout), landlocked salmon, smallmouth bass, and brook trout lure thousands of anglers to the region from ice-out in mid-May until September; the hardiest return in winter to ice fish.

BIKING

Mountain biking is popular in the Greenville area, but bikes are not allowed on some logging roads. Expect to pay about $25 per day to rent a bicycle. Northwoods Outfitters (⇨ *see North Woods Outfitters*) rents mountain bikes, kids' bikes, and more.

MULTI-SPORT OUTFITTER

Moose Country Safaris & Eco Tours. In the Greenville area, Moose Country Safaris & Eco Tours leads moose, bird-watching, and loon safaris. They also have Jeep, snowshoe, hiking, canoe, waterfall, and come late summer, meteor-shower tours. ✉ *191 North Dexter Rd., Sangerville* ☎ *207/876–4907* ⊕ *www.moosecountrysafaris.com.*

PARKS

Lily Bay State Park. Nine miles northeast of Greenville on Moosehead Lake, this park has good lakefront swimming, a 2-mile walking trail with water views, two boat-launching ramps, a playground, and two campgrounds with a total of 90 sites. In winter, the entrance road is plowed to access the groomed cross-country ski trails and the lake for ice fishing and snowmobiling. ✉ *State Park Rd., turn off Lily Bay Rd., Beaver Cove* ☎ *207/695–2700 mid-May–mid-Oct. only, 207/941–4014* ⊕ *www.parksandlands. com* 🖼 *$4.50* ☉ *Daily 9–sunset (mid-Oct.–mid-May no staff, roads not open except on a limited basis during snow season).*

TOURS

★ **Katahdin Cruises.** The Moosehead Marine Museum runs three- and four-and-a-half-hour afternoon trips on Moosehead Lake aboard the *Katahdin,* a 115-foot 1914 steamship converted to diesel. There are also a number of special cruises, including themed evening cruises, a July 4th fireworks trip, and, on the last Saturday in September, the annual eight-hour "Head of the Lake Cruise." Also called *The Kate,* the ship carried passengers to Mt. Kineo until 1938 and then was used in the logging industry until 1975. The boat and the free shoreside museum have displays about the steamships that transported people and cargo on the lake more than 100 years ago. ✉ *12 Lily Bay Rd.* ☎ *207/695–2716* 🌐 *www.katahdincruises.com* 🎟 *3-hr trips $33, 4½-hr trips $38* 🕐 *Late June–Columbus Day, 3-hr cruises Tues.–Sat. 12:30, except on select Wednesdays, when trips are 4½ hrs; also special cruises* ☞ *Board on shoreline by museum.*

OFF THE BEATEN PATH

Gulf Hagas. In a very remote area east of Greenville accessed by gravel roads, hiking trails lead from Katahdin Iron Works Road to Gulf Hagas, a National Natural Landmark with chasms, cliffs, six large waterfalls, pools, exotic flora, and rock formations. Slippery rocks make for difficult hiking along the gorge rim. Hiking from either of the two parking areas to the gorge and around a loop that includes the rim trail is an 8-mile, all-day affair. Or you can hike to the first waterfall en route and then back to the parking lot. It's about 3 miles round-trip from both the Upper Gulf Parking Area to Stairs Falls on the gorge's west end and from the Gulf Hagas Parking Area to Screw Auger Falls—the gulf's most spectacular drop—on its east end. You must ford the Pleasant River near the outset of this trail. This is easily done in summer when the water (about 150 feet wide) is knee-deep, but use extra caution in spring or after heavy rains, when the river is swifter and deeper. The Hermitage, a rare patch of old-growth pine, rises beyond the waterway. From Greenville, take Pleasant Street east (road becomes gravel) 11 miles to the Hedgehog checkpoint, follow signs to the Upper Gulf Parking Area (2½ miles) or the Gulf Hagas Parking Area (about 6½ miles). From Millinocket, take Route 11 south about 32 miles to the Katahdin Iron Works Road sign, continue 7 miles on a dirt road to the Katahdin Iron Works checkpoint, follow signs to the Gulf Hagas Parking Area (about 7 miles) or the Upper Gulf Parking Area (about 12 miles). From mid-May to mid-October, fees are charged at checkpoints (closed in April, late October, and November, but roads are still accessible), where you can buy trail maps and get hiking and parking information. ✉ *15 miles east of Greenville, access is by logging roads.*

North Maine Woods. North Maine Woods manages the private gravel roads to this very isolated area—yield to logging trucks. ✉ *92 Main St., Ashland* ☎ *207/435–6213* 🌐 *www.northmainewoods.org*

WHERE TO STAY

For expanded hotel reviews, visit Fodors.com.

$$$$ B&B/INN Fodor's Choice ★

🏨 **Blair Hill Inn.** Beautiful gardens and a hilltop location with marvelous views over the lake distinguish this 1891 estate, as do the mansion's fine antiques, plush bedding, and elegant baths, most with oversize tubs (one is an original claw-foot). **Pros:** bar open (5 to 9 pm) for guests-only when restaurant is closed; music series in July and August; 15 acres with stone paths, wooded picnic area, and trout pond; veranda, third-floor deck run the length of the inn. **Cons:** no direct lake access. [$] *Rooms from: $350* ✉ *351 Lily Bay Rd.* ☎ *207/695–0224* 🌐 *www.blairhill.com* 🛏 *7 rooms, 1 suite* 🕐 *Closed Apr. and Nov.* 🍴 *Breakfast.*

$$ RESORT ★

🏨 **Little Lyford Lodge and Cabins.** When you want to get away from everything, head to this rustic wilderness retreat on 66,500 acres of conservation land, part of the Appalachian Mountain Club's lodging network.

Pros: woodsy getaway; cedar sauna in winter; loaner snowshoes. **Cons:** winter access is by cross-country ski, snowshoe, or snowmobile transport (for a fee); few indoor amenities. [$] *Rooms from: $125* ✉ *About 16 miles east of Greenville, access via logging roads* ☎ *603/466–2727* 🌐 *www.outdoors.org/mainelodges* 🛏 *9 cabins, 12-bed bunkhouse* ⏲ *Closed Apr.–mid-May and Oct.–late Dec.* 🍴 *All meals.*

MILLINOCKET

67 miles north of Bangor, 88 miles northwest of Greenville via Routes 6 and 11.

Millinocket, a paper-mill town with a population of about 4,000, is a gateway to Baxter State Park and Maine's North Woods. Although it has a smattering of motels and restaurants, Millinocket is the place to stock up on supplies, fill your gas tank, or grab a hot meal or shower before heading into the wilderness. Numerous rafting and canoeing outfitters and guides are based here.

GETTING HERE AND AROUND

From Interstate 95, take Route 157 (Exit 244) west to Millinocket. From here take Millinocket Lake Road (becomes Baxter Park Road) to Baxter State Park, Togue Pond Gate (southern entrance, 18 miles from Millinocket).

ESSENTIALS

Visitor Information **Katahdin Area Chamber of Commerce** ✉ *1029 Central St.* ☎ *207/723–4443* 🌐 *www.katahdinmaine.com.*

SPORTS AND THE OUTDOORS

MULTI-SPORT OUTFITTERS

New England Outdoor Center. New England Outdoor Center, with two locations en route to Baxter State Park, offers a host of guided trips, some of which take place within the park. Snowmobile, fishing, canoe, hiking, and moose-watching trips are based out of the center's Twin Pine Camps on Millinocket Lake, 9 miles from Baxter's southern gate. You can also rent a canoe, kayak, or snowmobile, or sign up for canoe instruction. Twin Pine is also home to 17 lakeside rental cabins (including upscale "green" units) and the popular River Driver's Restaurant. Just 4 miles from the park, the center's Penobscot Outdoor Center is the base for white-water rafting trips. This locale has a seasonal open-air pub and a campground with tent sites, canvas tents (cots, solar or gas lights), and simple wood-frame cabins (bunk beds and cots, solar lights). ✉ *30 Twin Pines Rd.* ✥ *From Millinocket, take Millinocket Lake Rd. about 8 miles to Black Cat Rd., turn right; go 1 mile to Twin Pines Rd., turn left* ☎ *207/723–5438, 800/766–7238* 🌐 *www.neoc.com.*

PARKS

★ **Allagash Wilderness Waterway.** A spectacular 92-mile corridor of lakes and rivers, the waterway cuts through northern Maine's vast commercial forests, beginning at the northwest corner of Baxter State Park and running north to the town of Allagash, 10 miles from the Canadian border. From May to mid-October, this is prime canoeing and camping country, but trips should not be undertaken lightly. The complete

9

92-mile course requires 7 to 10 days. The best bet for a novice is to go with a guide; a good outfitter will help plan your route and provide your craft and transportation. ✉ *Maine Bureau of Parks and Lands, 106 Hogan Rd., Bangor* ☎ *207/941–4014* ⊕ *www.parksandlands.com.*

Northern Forest Canoe Trail. The Alagash Wilderness Waterway is part of the 740-mile Northern Forest Canoe Trail, which runs from New York to Maine. ☎ *802/496–2285* ⊕ *www.northernforestcanoetrail.org.*

Fodor's Choice **Baxter State Park.** A gift from Governor Percival Baxter, this is the jewel
★ in the crown of northern Maine, a 210,000-acre wilderness area that surrounds **Mt. Katahdin,** Maine's highest mountain (5,267 feet at Baxter Peak) and the terminus of the Appalachian Trail. Katahdin draws thousands of hikers every year for the daylong climb to the summit and the stunning views of woods, mountains, and lakes. Three parking lot trailheads lead to its peak; some routes include the hair-raising Knife Edge Ridge. The crowds climbing Katahdin can be formidable on clear summer days, so if you crave solitude, tackle one of the 45 other mountains in the park, 17 of which exceed an elevation of 3,000 feet and all of which are accessible from an extensive network of trails. South Turner can be climbed in a morning (if you're fit), and its summit has a great view of Katahdin across the valley. On the way you'll pass Sandy Stream Pond, where moose are often seen at dusk. The Owl, the Brothers, and Doubletop Mountain are good day hikes. ■ TIP→ Reserve a day-use parking space at the Katahdin trailheads if you plan to hike the mountain between May 15 and October 15. Check the park website for information; without a reservation you may have to hike elsewhere in the park. No pets, domestic animals, oversize vehicles, radios, all-terrain vehicles, motorboats, or motorcycles are allowed in the park; roads are unpaved, narrow, and winding, and there are no pay phones, gas stations, stores, running water, or electricity. The camping is primitive at the park's 10 campgrounds, which must be reserved online within four months of your trip. There are also cabins at Daicey Pond and Kidney Pond campgrounds. The visitor center is at the southern entrance outside Millinocket. You can also get information about Baxter in town at park headquarters. ✉ *Headquarters: 64 Balsam Dr.* ✛ *Togue Pond Gate (southern entrance): 18 miles northwest of Millinocket via Rte. 157 and Millinocket Lake Road (becomes Baxter Park Road); Matagamon Gate (northern entrance): Grand Lake Rd., 26 miles northwest of Patten via Rte. 159 and Grand Lake Rd.* ☎ *207/723–5140, 207/723–4636 hiking hotline* ⊕ *www.baxterstateparkauthority.com* 🎫 *$14 per vehicle (free to Maine residents).*

Maine Coast

WORD OF MOUTH

"Riding to the top of Cadillac Mountain [in Acadia National Park] on our motorcycles was something I will never regret and will always cherish. The loop drive through the park was amazing."

—annikany

WELCOME TO MAINE COAST

TOP REASONS TO GO

★ **Perfection on a Bun:** It's not a Maine vacation without sampling the "lobster roll," lobster with a touch of mayo nestled in a buttery grilled New England–style hot-dog bun (opens on top).

★ **Boating:** The coastline of Maine was made for boaters. Whether it's your own boat, a friend's, or a charter, make sure you get out on the water.

★ **Wild Maine Blueberries:** They may be tiny, but the wild blueberries pack a flavorful punch in season (late July to early September).

★ **Cadillac Mountain:** Drive the winding 3½-mile road to the 1,530-foot summit in Acadia National Park for the sunrise.

★ **Perfect Souvenir:** Buy a watercolor, hand-painted pottery, or handcrafted jewelry—artists and craftspeople abound.

★ **Ice Cream:** Summer in Maine means ice cream. Stop at one of the many stands selling Maine-made Gifford's, or savor homemade at a storefront ice cream parlor: you can't go wrong.

1 **The Southern Coast.** Stretching north from Kittery to just outside Portland, this is Maine's most-visited region. The towns along the shore and miles of sandy expanses cater to summer visitors. Old Orchard Beach features Coney Island–like amusements, while Kittery, the Yorks, Wells, and the Kennebunks are more low-key getaways.

2 **Portland.** Maine's largest and most cosmopolitan city, Portland balances its historic role as a working harbor with its newer identity as a center of sophisticated arts and shopping, and innovative restaurants.

3 **The Mid-Coast Region.** North of Portland, from Brunswick to Monhegan Island, the craggy coastline winds its way around pastoral peninsulas. Its villages boast maritime museums, antiques shops, and beautiful architecture.

Watervil

☆ Augusta

Lewiston

Auburn

Waldobor

Newcastle

Damariscot

Brunswick

Freeport

Bath

Phippsburg

Boothba

Yarmouth

Georgetown

Falmouth

Portland

Casco Bay

Saco

Old Orchard Beach

Sanford

Biddeford

0   20 mi

Kennebunk

0   20 km

Kennebunkport

Wells

Ogunquit

York

Kittery

Portsmouth

NEW HAMPSHIRE

4 Penobscot Bay. This region combines lively coastal towns with dramatic natural scenery. Camden is one of Maine's most picture-perfect towns, with its pointed church steeples, antique homes, cozy harbor, and historic windjammer fleet.

5 Blue Hill Peninsula. Art galleries are plentiful here, and the entire region is ideal for biking, hiking, kayaking, and boating. For many, the peninsula defines the silent beauty of the Maine Coast.

6 Acadia National Park and Mount Desert Island. Millions come to enjoy Acadia National Park's stunning peaks and vistas of the island's mountains. Bar Harbor is more of a visitor's haven, while Southwest Harbor and Bass Harbor offer quieter retreats.

7 Way Down East. This is the "real" Maine, some say, and it unfurls in thousands of acres of wild blueberry barrens, congestion-free coastlines, and a tangible sense of rugged endurance.

GETTING ORIENTED

10

Much of the appeal of the Maine Coast lies in its geographical contrasts, from its long stretches of swimming and walking beaches in the south to the cliff-edged, rugged rocky coasts in the north. And not unlike the physical differences of the coast, each town along the way reveals a slightly different character.

Updated by
Mary Ruoff

As you drive across the border into Maine, a sign announces: "The way life should be." Romantics luxuriate in the feeling of a down comforter on a yellow-pine bed or in the sensation of the wind and salt spray on their faces while cruising in a historic windjammer. Families love the unspoiled beaches and safe inlets dotting the shoreline. Hikers are revived while roaming the trails of Acadia National Park, and adventure seekers kayak along the coast.

The Maine Coast is several places in one. Portland may be Maine's largest metropolitan area, but its attitude is decidedly more big town than small city. South of Portland, Ogunquit, Kennebunkport, Old Orchard Beach, and other resort towns predominate along a reasonably smooth shoreline. North of Portland and Casco Bay, secondary roads turn south off U.S. 1 onto so many oddly chiseled peninsulas that it's possible to drive for days without retracing your route. Slow down to explore the museums, galleries, and shops in the larger towns and the antiques and curio shops and harborside lobster shacks in the smaller fishing villages. Freeport is an entity unto itself, a place where numerous name-brand outlets and specialty stores have sprung up around the retail outpost of famous outfitter L. L. Bean. And no description of the coast would be complete without mention of popular Acadia National Park, with its majestic mountains that are often shrouded in mist.

If you come to Maine seeking an untouched fishing village with locals gathered around a potbellied stove in the general store, you'll likely come away disappointed; that innocent age has passed in all but the most remote spots like Way Down East. Tourism has supplanted fishing, logging, and potato farming as Maine's number-one industry, and most areas are well equipped to receive the annual onslaught of visitors. But whether you are stepping outside a cabin for a walk in the woods or watching a boat rock at its anchor, you can sense the wilderness nearby, even on the edges of the most urbanized spots.

PLANNING

WHEN TO GO

Maine's dramatic coastline and pure natural beauty welcome visitors year-round, but note that many smaller museums and attractions are open only for high season—from Memorial Day to mid-October—as are many of the waterside attractions and eateries.

Summer begins in earnest on July 4th, and many smaller inns, B&Bs, and hotels from Kittery on up to the Bar Harbor region are booked a month or two ahead on weekends through August. That's also the case come fall, when the fiery foliage draws leaf peepers. After Halloween, hotel rates drop significantly until ski season begins around Thanksgiving. Along the coast, bed-and-breakfasts that remain open will often rent rooms at far lower prices than in summer.

In spring, the fourth Sunday in March is designated as Maine Maple Sunday, and farms throughout the state open their doors to visitors not only to watch sap turn into golden syrup but to sample the sweet results.

PLANNING YOUR TIME

You could easily spend a lifetime's worth of vacations along the Maine Coast and never truly see it all. But if you are determined to travel the coast from end to end, allot at least two weeks to travel comfortably.

Driving in Coastal Maine		
	Miles	Time
Boston–Portland	112	2 hours
Kittery–Portland	50	50 minutes
Portland–Freeport	18	20 minutes
Portland–Camden	80	2 hours
Portland–Bar Harbor	175	3 hours, 20 minutes

GETTING HERE AND AROUND

AIR TRAVEL

Maine has two major international airports, Portland International Jetport and Bangor International Airport, to get you to or close to your coastal destination. Manchester-Boston Regional Airport in New Hampshire is about 45 minutes away from the southern end of the Maine coastline. Boston's Logan Airport is the only truly international airport in the region; it's about 90 minutes south of the Maine border.

CAR TRAVEL

Once you are here the best way to experience the winding back roads of the craggy Maine Coast is in a car. There are miles and miles of roads far from the larger towns that have no bus services, and you won't want to miss discovering your own favorite ocean vista while on a scenic drive.

TRAIN TRAVEL

Amtrak offers regional service from Boston to Portland via its Downeaster line that originates at Boston's North Station and makes four stops in Maine: Wells, Saco, Old Orchard Beach (seasonal), and finally Portland.

Starting in fall 2012, service will be expanded to Freeport and Brunswick. Greyhound and Concord Coach Lines also offer bus service from Boston to many towns along the Maine Coast. Concord has express service between Portland and Boston's Logan Airport and South Station. Both Concord and Amtrak operate out of the Portland Transportation Center at ⊠ *100 Thompson's Pt. Road.*

RESTAURANTS

Many breakfast spots along the coast open as early as 6 am to serve the going-to-work crowd (in fishing areas as early as 4 am). Lunch generally runs 11–2:30; dinner is usually served 5–9. Only in the larger cities will you find full dinners being offered much later than 9, although in larger towns you can usually find a bar or bistro serving a limited menu late into the evening.

Many restaurants in Maine are closed Monday, though this isn't true in resort areas in high season. However, resort-town eateries often shut down completely in the off-season. *Unless otherwise noted in reviews, restaurants are open daily for lunch and dinner.*

Credit cards are accepted for meals throughout Maine, even in some of the most modest establishments.

The one signature dinner on the Maine Coast is, of course, the lobster dinner. It generally includes boiled lobster, a clam or seafood chowder, corn on the cob, and coleslaw or perhaps a salad. Lobster prices vary from day to day, but generally a full lobster dinner should cost around $25; without all the add-ons, about $18. *Prices in the reviews are the average cost of a main course at dinner or, if dinner is not served, at lunch.*

HOTELS

Beachfront and roadside motels and historic-home B&Bs and inns make up the majority of accommodation options along the Maine Coast. There are a few large luxury resorts, such as the Samoset Resort in Rockport or the Bar Harbor Inn in Bar Harbor, but most accommodations are simple and relatively inexpensive. You will find hotel chains in larger cities and towns, including major tourist destinations like Freeport and Bar Harbor. Many properties close during the off-season—mid-October until mid-May; some that stay open drop their rates dramatically. There is a 7% state hospitality tax on all room rates. *Prices in the reviews are the lowest cost of a standard double room in high season.*

THE SOUTHERN COAST

Maine's southernmost coastal towns—Kittery, the Yorks, Ogunquit, the Kennebunks, and the Old Orchard Beach area—reveal a few of the stunning faces of the state's coast, from the miles and miles of inviting sandy beaches to the beautifully kept historic towns and carnival-like attractions. There is something for every taste, whether you seek solitude in a kayak or prefer being caught up in the infectious spirit of fellow vacationers.

CLOSE UP

Outdoor Activities

No visit to the Maine Coast is complete without some outdoor activity—be it generated by two wheels, two feet, two paddles, or pulling a bag full of clubs.

Bicycling: The Bicycle Coalition of Main and Explore Maine by Bike are excellent sources for trail maps and other riding information. The Bicycle Coalition's website includes where to rent bikes.

Bicycle Coalition of Maine
☎ 207/623–4511 ⊕ www.bikemaine.org.

Explore Maine by Bike ⊕ www.exploremaine.org/bike.

Hiking: Exploring the Maine Coast on foot is a quick way to acclimate to the relaxed pace of life here.

Healthy Maine Walks. Healthy Maine Walks has comprehensive listings for walks that can be done in an hour or less, from park paths to routes that follow roads and streets. ⊕ www.healthymainewalks.com.

Kayaking: Nothing gets you literally off the beaten path like plying the salt waters in a graceful sea kayak.

Maine Association of Sea Kayaking Guides and Instructors. Maine Association of Sea Kayaking Guides and Instructors are state-licensed and offer instructional classes and guided tours, plan trips, and rent equipment. ⊕ www.maskgi.org.

Maine Island Trail Association. More seasoned paddlers can join the Maine Island Trail Association ($45, $65 for a family) for a map of and full access to Maine's famous sea trail: 200 islands and mainland sites; most private but open to members, on a 375-mile path from the southernmost coast to the Canadian Maritimes. Member benefits also include discounts at outfitters and retailers, including L.L. Bean. Join online or at businesses like kayak outfitters. The website also lists a handful of free public kayaking sites. ☎ 207/761–8225 ⊕ www.mita.org.

North of Kittery, long stretches of hard-packed white-sand beach are closely crowded by nearly unbroken ranks of beach cottages, motels, and oceanfront restaurants. The summer colonies of York Beach and Wells brim with family crowds, T-shirt and gift shops, and shorefront development; nearby wildlife refuges and land reserves promise an easy quiet escape. York Village evokes yesteryear sentiment with its acclaimed historic district, while upscale Ogunquit tantalizes visitors with its array of shops and a cliff-side walk.

More than any other region south of Portland, the Kennebunks—and especially Kennebunkport—provide the complete Maine Coast experience: classic townscapes where white-clapboard houses rise from manicured lawns and gardens; rocky shorelines punctuated by sandy beaches; quaint downtown districts packed with gift shops, ice cream stands, and visitors; harbors with lobster boats bobbing alongside yachts; rustic, picnic-tabled restaurants serving lobster and fried seafood; and well-appointed dining rooms. As you continue north, the scents of friend dough and cotton candy mean you've arrived at Maine's version of Coney Island, Old Orchard Beach.

10

KITTERY

65 miles north of Boston; 3 miles north of Portsmouth, New Hampshire.

One of the earliest settlements in the state of Maine, Kittery suffered its share of British, French, and Native American attacks throughout the 17th and 18th centuries, yet rose to prominence as a vital shipbuilding center. The tradition continues; despite its New Hampshire name, the Portsmouth Naval Shipyard is part of Maine and has been building U.S. submarines since World War I and was founded in 1800 and built its first warship in 1815. It's not open to the public, but those on boats can pass by and get a glimpse.

Known as the "Gateway to Maine," Kittery has come to more recent light as a major shopping destination thanks to its complex of factory outlets. Flanked on either side of U.S. 1 are more than 120 stores, which attract hordes of shoppers year-round. For something a little less commercial, head east on Route 103 to the hidden Kittery most people miss: the lands around **Kittery Point.** Here you can find hiking and biking trails and great views of the water. With Portsmouth, New Hampshire, across the water, Whaleback Ledge Lighthouse, and the nearby Isles of Shoals, Kittery is a picturesque place to pass some time. The isles and the light, as well as two others, can be seen from two forts along or near this winding stretch of Route 103: Ft. McClary State Historic Site and Ft. Foster, a town park (both closed to vehicles off-season).

GETTING HERE AND AROUND

Three bridges—on U.S. 1 (closed until July 2013 as a new span is constructed), U.S. 1 Bypass, and Interstate 95—cross the Piscataqua River from Portsmouth, New Hampshire to Kittery. Interstate 95 has three Kittery exits. Route 103 is a scenic coastal drive through Kittery Point to York.

ESSENTIALS

Visitor Information Greater York Region Chamber of Commerce ✉ *1 Stonewall Lane, off U.S. 1, York* ☎ *207/363–4422* 🌐 *www.gatewaytomaine.org.*

WHERE TO EAT

$$ SEAFOOD ★ 🍴 **Chauncey Creek Lobster Pound.** From the road you can barely see the red roof hovering below the trees, but chances are you can see the cars parked at this popular outdoor restaurant along the high banks of the tidal river, beside a working pier. Brightly colored picnic tables fill the deck and an enclosed eating area. The menu has lots of fresh lobster choices and a raw bar with offerings like clams and oysters. Bring your own beer or wine if you desire alcohol. You can also bring sides and desserts that aren't on the menu. [$] *Average main: $22* ✉ *16 Chauncey Creek Rd., Kittery Point* ☎ *207/439–1030* 🌐 *www.chaunceycreek.com* 🕒 *Closed after Columbus Day–Fri. before Mother's Day and Mon. between Labor Day and Columbus Day.*

DID YOU KNOW?

Maine may not have many sandy beaches or warm water, but the rocky shoreline, powerful ocean, and contrasting evergreens have inspired photographers and artists for years.

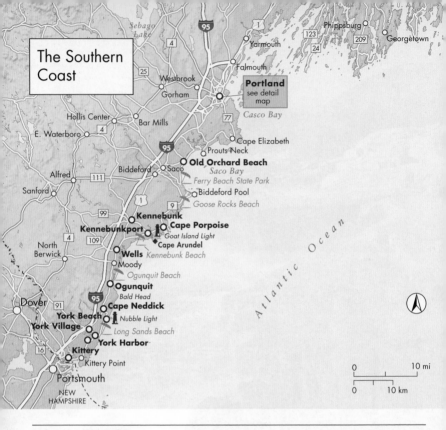

YORK VILLAGE

8 miles north of Kittery via Interstate 95, U.S. 1, and U.S. 1A.

The actual village of York is quite small, housing the town's basic components of post office, town hall, several shops and galleries, and a stretch of antique homes. As subdued as the town may feel today, the history of York Village reveals a far different character. One of the first permanently settled areas in the state of Maine, it was once witness to great destruction and fierce fighting during the French, Indian, and British wars; towns and fortunes were sacked, yet the potential for prosperity encouraged the area's citizens continually to rebuild and start anew. Colonial York citizens enjoyed great wealth and success from fishing and lumber as well as a penchant for politics. Angered by the British-imposed taxes, York held its own little-known tea party in 1775 in protest.

GETTING HERE AND AROUND

York is Exit 7 on Interstate 95; follow signs to U.S. 1, the modern commercial strip. From here U.S. 1A winds to the village center and on to York Harbor and York Beach before looping back up to U.S. 1 in Cape Neddick.

ESSENTIALS

Greater York Region Chamber of Commerce ✉ *1 Stonewall Lane, off U.S. 1, York* ☎ *207/363-4422* ⊕ *www.gatewaytomaine.org.* **York Trolley Co.** York Trolley Company ☎ *207/363-9600* ⊕ *www.yorktrolley.com.*

EXPLORING

Museums of Old York. Nine historic 18th- and 19th-century buildings, clustered on York Street and along Lindsay Road and the York River, highlight York's rich history starting in early Colonial times. The Old York Gaol (1719) was once the King's Prison for the Province of Maine; inside are dungeons, cells, and the jailer's quarters. The many period rooms in the Emerson-Wilcox House—the main part was built in 1742—display items from daily life here in centuries past, including furniture from as early as the 1600s and an impressive ceramic dishware collection. The 1731 Elizabeth Perkins House reflects the Victorian style of its last occupants, the prominent Perkins family. You can buy tickets at the Parsons Education Center, which has changing exhibits, or at the Gaol. A ticket for all the buildings (many are self-guided) is good for the season. ✉ *Parsons Education Center, 6 Lindsay Rd.* ☎ *207/363-4974* ⊕ *www.oldyork.org* 🎫 *All buildings $12 (valid for the season); $6 for one building* ⊙ *Early June–Sat. before Columbus Day, most buildings Mon.–Sat. 9:30–4.*

George Marshall Store Gallery. Storefront windows and bead board trim at the George Marshall Store Gallery, built in 1867, pay homage to its past as a general store, but the focus here is on the present. Changing exhibits of works by prominent and up-and-coming regional artists change every five weeks from April through December. ✉ *140 Lindsay Road* ☎ *207/351-1083* ⊕ *www.georgemarshallstoregallery. com* ⊙ *Early June–Columbus Day weekend, Tues.–Sat. 10–5, Sun. 1–5; mid-Oct.–early June, Wed.–Sun. but hours vary.*

Stonewall Kitchen. You've probably seen the kitchen's smartly labeled jars of gourmet chutneys, jams, jellies, salsas, and sauces in specialty stores back home. York is the headquarters and processing center for them. The Stonewall complex houses the expansive flagship company store, which carries kitchenware and home decor items, too. There's also a bustling café and take-out restaurant, a viewing area of the bottling process, and stunning gardens. Sample all the mustards, salsas, and dressings you can stand, or have lunch at the café. Takeout is available during store hours. Breakfast (until 11) and lunch (11–3) are served daily; dine garden-side in season. The campus also houses a cooking school where participants can join in evening or daytime courses. Reservations are required; most classes cost $45–$80 and are shorter than two hours. ✉ *2 Stonewall La., just off U.S. 1, next to York area information center* ☎ *207/351-2712 store, 877/899-8363 cooking school* ⊕ *www.stonewallkitchen.com* ⊙ *Sun. 9–6.; Mon.–Sat. 8–8 late May–early Sept., 8–6 early Sept.–late Nov. and late Dec.–late May, 8–7 late Nov.–late Dec.*

10

SHOPPING

Gateway Farmers' Market. Bring a basket for morning shopping at the Gateway Farmers' Market, held in the back lot at the Greater York Region Chamber of Commerce visitors center from 9–1 on Saturday, June until Columbus Day weekend, and also on Thursday in July and August. You'll find fresh local produce as well as flowers, lots of baked goods and artisan breads, specialty foods, local seafood and meat, and handcrafted items like soaps and candles. It's a good place to gather the makings for a beach picnic. ⊠ *1 Stonewall Lane, just off U.S. 1* ⊕ *www. gatewayfarmersmarket.com.*

Bradley's Custom Framing & Gallery. Watercolors, oils, pastels, and pottery are among the artworks that can be had at Bradley's Custom Framing & Gallery, where many local artists are represented, including the photographer-owner. ⊠ *244 York St.(U.S. 1A)* ☎ *207/351–3110* ⊕ *www.bradley-s-custom-framing-and-gallery.com.*

YORK HARBOR

1 mile below York Village via U.S. 1A.

Just a few miles from the village proper, York Harbor opens up to the water and offers many places to linger and explore. The harbor is busy with boats of all kinds, while the harbor beach is a good stretch of sand for swimming. Much more formal than the northward York Beach and much quieter, the area retains a somewhat more exclusive air. Perched along the cliffs on the north side of the harbor are huge "cottages" built by wealthy summer residents in the late 1800s, when the area became a premier seaside resort destination with several grand hotels.

GETTING HERE AND AROUND

After passing through York Village to York Harbor, originally called Lower Town, U.S. 1A winds around and heads north to York Beach's village center, a four-mile trip.

ESSENTIALS

Greater York Region Chamber of Commerce. ⊠ *1 Stonewall Lane, off U.S. 1, York* ☎ *207/363–4422* ⊕ *www.gatewaytomaine.org.*

EXPLORING

Sayward-Wheeler House. Built in 1718, the waterfront home was remodeled in the 1760s by Jonathan Sayward, a local merchant who had prospered in the West Indies trade. By 1860 his descendants had opened the house to the public to share the story of their Colonial ancestors. The house, accessible only by guided tour, reveals the decor of a prosperous New England family at the outset of the Revolutionary War. The parlor—considered one of the country's "best preserved Colonial interiors," with a tall clock and mahogany Chippendale-style chairs—looks pretty much as it did when Sayward lived here. ⊠ *9 Barrell Lane Extension* ☎ *207/384–2454* ⊕ *www.historicnewengland.org* ⊡ *$5* ☾ *June– mid-Oct., 2nd and 4th Sat. of month 11–5; last tour at 4.*

SPORTS AND THE OUTDOORS

BIKING

Berger's Bike Shop. Berger's Bike Shop rents all manner of bikes for local excursions. ✉ *241 York St.(U.S. 1A), No. 1, York Village* ☎ *207/363–4070* ⊕ *www.bergersbikeshop.com.*

FISHING

Fish Tale Charters. Fish Tale Charters takes anglers on fly-fishing or light tackle charters in search of stripers or juvenile bluefin tuna; trips depart from Town Dock No. 2 in York Harbor. ✉ *York* ☎ *207/363–3874* ⊕ *www.maineflyfishing.net.*

Rip Tide Charters. Rip Tide Charters goes where the fish are—departure points vary, from Ogunquit to York and Portsmouth, New Hampshire. They specialize in fly-fishing and light tackle for stripers, mackerel, and bluefish. ✉ *York* ☎ *207/337–3608* ⊕ *www.mainestriperfishing.com.*

Shearwater Charters. Shearwater Charters offers light tackle and fly-fishing charters in the York River and along the shoreline from Kittery to Ogunquit. Bait-fishing trips are also available. Departures are from Town Dock No. 2 in York Harbor. *207/363–5324* ⊕ *www.mainestripers.net.*

HIKING AND WALKING

Cliff Walk/Fisherman's Walk. Two walking trails traverse the shore from near Harbor Beach. Just beside it in a small park, the Cliff Walk ascends its granite namesake, running past the summer "cottage" mansions at the harbor entrance. There are some steps, but as signs caution, tread carefully because of erosion. Fisherman's Walk, on the other hand, is an easy stroll. Starting across Stage Neck Road from the beach, it passes waterfront businesses, historic homes, and rocky harbor beaches on the way to York's beloved Wiggly Bridge. This pedestrian suspension bridge alongside Route 103 (there is minimal parking here) leads to Steedman Woods, a public preserve with a shaded loop trail along the York River estuary's ambling waters. You can also enter the preserve near the George Marshall Store in York Village ✉ *Stage Neck Road, turn off U.S. 1.*

Cutts Island Trail. For a peek into the Rachel Carson National Wildlife Refuge, take this approximately 2-mile trail, part of the refuge's 800-acre Brave Boat Harbor Division. It's one of only a handful of trails in its 11 divisions. It's a prime bird-watching area. There's a kiosk at the trailhead. ✉ *Seapoint Road, Kittery* ⊹ *From Rte. 103 turn on Cutts Island Lane, continue on Seapoint Road, watch for sign* ⊕ *www.fws.gov/northeast/rachelcarson.*

WHERE TO EAT

$$$

SEAFOOD

★

✕ **Dockside Restaurant.** On an island-like peninsula overlooking York Harbor, this restaurant has plenty of seafood on the menu, including popular dishes like haddock stuffed with Maine shrimp and "drunken" lobster—sautéed lobster, scallops, shallots, and herbs in an Irish whiskey cream. There's also treats like beef tenderloin and slow-roasted duckling. Start with seafood chowder or cakes of native crab and wild mushroom. Floor-to-ceiling windows in the stair-stepped modern dinning space transport diners to the water beyond; every seat has a water

10

view. Lighter fare is served in the cozy mahogany bar. Dockside is part of a 7-acre property with lodging rooms and suites in several buildings, from a grand 1895 summer home to condo-style quarters. [$] *Average main: $25* ✉ *22 Harris Island Rd., just off Rte. 103, York* ☎ *207/363–2722* 🌐 *www.docksidegq.com* 🕑 *Closed late Oct.–mid-June and Tues. in June, Sept., and Oct. (sometimes no lunch on weekends because of weddings).*

$$$ SEAFOOD 🍴 **Foster's Downeast Clambake.** Save your appetite for this one. Specializing in the traditional Maine clambake—a feast consisting of rich clam chowder, a pile of mussels and steamers, Maine lobster, corn on the cob, roasted potatoes and onions, bread, butter, and Maine blueberry crumb cake (phew!)—this massive complex provides musical entertainment as well as belly-busting meals. There are also several barbeque offerings. For pickup orders there's a 10-meal minimum and for deliveries a 20-meal minimum. [$] *Average main: $23* ✉ *5 Axholme Rd., at U.S. 1A, York* ☎ *207/363–3255, 800/552–0242* 🌐 *www.fostersclambake.com* 🕑 *Early Sept.–late May. Weekends only late May–mid-June.*

WHERE TO STAY

For expanded hotel reviews, visit Fodors.com.

$$$ B&B/INN ★ 🏨 **Inn at Tanglewood Hall.** The inn's artfully painted floors, lush wallpapers, and meticulous attention to detail are the fruits of a former designation as a designers' showcase home. **Pros:** elegant, authentic historic lodging; serene setting amid gardens, grand trees; short walk to beaches, nature trails. **Cons:** no water views. [$] *Rooms from: $185* ✉ *611 York St.* ☎ *207/351–1075* 🌐 *www.tanglewoodhall.com* 🛏 *4 rooms, 2 suites* 🍽 *Breakfast.*

$$$$ ★ 🏨 **Stage Neck Inn.** Since the 1870s successive hotels have perched on this tiny rock-clad peninsula beside York Harbor's entrance. **Pros:** elaborate full-breakfast buffet with scrumptious baked goods and artfully arrayed fruits; poolside service and snack bar in season; rooms have balconies or deck areas. **Cons:** no suites. [$] *Rooms from: $312* ✉ *8 Stage Neck Rd., turn off U.S. 1A, York* ☎ *207/363–3850* 🌐 *www.stageneck.com* 🕑 *Closed for 2 wks after Jan. 1.*

$$$ B&B/INN ★ 🏨 **York Harbor Inn.** A rebuilt mid-17th-century fishing cabin with dark timbers and a fieldstone fireplace form the heart of the historic main inn, while several wings and neighboring buildings have been added over the years. **Pros:** many rooms have harbor views; close to beaches, scenic walking trails. **Cons:** rooms vary greatly in style, size, and appeal. [$] *Rooms from: $199* ✉ *480 York St. (U.S. 1A), York* ☎ *207/363–5119* 🌐 *www.yorkharborinn.com* 🛏 *54 rooms, 2 suites* 🍽 *Breakfast.*

YORK BEACH

6 miles north of York Harbor via U.S. 1A.

Like many shorefront towns in Maine, York Beach has a long history of entertaining summer visitors. Take away today's bikinis and iPods and it's easy to imagine squealing tourists adorned in the full-length bathing garb of the late 19th century. Just as they did back then, visitors today come here to eat ice cream, enjoy carnival-like novelties, and indulge in the sun and sea air.

York Beach is a real family destination, devoid of all things staid and stuffy—children are meant to be seen and heard here. Just beyond the sands of Short Sand Beach are a host of amusements, from bowling to indoor mini golf and the Fun-O-Rama arcade. Nubble Light is the tip of the separating Long Sands and Short Sands beaches. The latter is mostly lined with unpretentious seasonal homes, though motels and restaurants are mixed in.

GETTING HERE AND AROUND

It's a scenic six miles to York Beach via the loop road U.S. 1A from its southern intersection with U.S. 1, next the York exit from Interstate 95. But though two miles longer, it's generally faster to continue north on U.S. 1A to Cape Neddick and take U.S 1A south to the village center, home to Short Sands Beach. It's just a mile. Here, U.S. 1A is known as Ocean Avenue as it heads north from York Harbor along Long Sands Beach en route to York Beach village and Short Sands Beach. A trolley along U.S. 1 links the beaches in summer. You can also get from beach to beach on a series of residential streets that wind around Nubble Point between these beaches.

York Trolley Co. From late June through Labor Day, York Trolley Co.'s bright red trolleys link Short Sands Beach in York Beach village and nearby Long Sands Beach, running along U.S. 1A with a number of stops. Route maps can be picked up throughout York and at the local chamber; fares are $1.50 one-way and $3 for the round-trip. You can also connect with a shuttle service to Ogunquit. The trolley is part of the Shoreline Explorer network (☎ *207/324–5762 Ext. 2932* ⊕ *www. shorelineexplorer.com*), which links seasonal trolleys in southern Maine beach towns from the Yorks to the Kennebunks, allowing visitors to travel between towns without their cars. ☎ *207/363–9600* ⊕ *www. yorktrolley.com.*

ESSENTIALS

Visitor Information Greater York Region Chamber of Commerce. ✉ *1 Stonewall Lane, off U.S. 1, York* ☎ *207/363–4422* ⊕ *www.gatewaytomaine.org.*

EXPLORING

10

Nubble Light. On a small island just off the tip of the cape jutting dramatically into the Atlantic Ocean between Long Sands Beach and Short Sands Beach is one of the most photographed lighthouses on the globe. Direct access is prohibited, but the small Sohier Park right across from the light has parking, historical placards, benches, and an information center, open in peak season, that shares the 1879 light's history. The light is at the tip of the geographical Cape Neddick, and that is the light's official name, but it's mostly known as Nubble Light or the Nub. ■ TIP→ Cape Neddick is also the name of the community at the north end of York, on the opposite side of York Beach from the light. Ask a local where Cape Neddick is and they will likely send you there. ✉ *End of Nubble Road, turn off U.S. 1A, York* ☎ *207/363–3569 Memorial Day weekend–Labor Day* ⊕ *www.nubblelight.org* ☉ *Park, daily; information center, Memorial Day weekend–Labor Day.*

☺ **York's Wild Kingdom.** Between the zoo and the carnival rides, it's sometimes hard to distinguish the wild animals from the kids here. The zoo, ringed by woods, has an impressive variety of exotic animals and is home to the state's only white Bengal tiger. The amusement park has a nostalgic charm. Combination tickets can be purchased to visit the zoo and ride the amusements, and discounts are available for kids under 13—the target market, since there are no large thrill rides. Nor is there a charge to enter the amusement park, which also sells ride tokens. Many York Beach visitors come just to enjoy the ocean views from the Ferris wheel and share (hopefully!) the "seaboard's largest fried dough." ⊠ *23 Railroad Ave., parking entrance on U.S. 1* ✢ *Parking entrance is on U.S. 1 about 2½ miles from Interstate 95 Exit 7 (look for the 40-foot sign); Railroad Avenue entrance is walk-in* ☎ *207/363–4911, 800/456–4911* ⊕ *www.yorkzoo.com* ⊠ *$14.75 zoo only; $21.25 zoo and rides (adults)* ☉ *Late May–late Sept. Zoo-only weekdays from late May–mid-June and after Labor Day, and on last weekend of the season.*

NIGHTLIFE

Inn on the Blues. Inn on the Blues is a hopping music club that attracts national bands. Entertainment here includes funk, jazz, and reggae as well as blues. It's open April through December and weekends only in the shoulder seasons. ⊠ *7 Ocean Ave.(U.S. 1A), York* ☎ *207/351–3221* ⊕ *www.innontheblues.com.*

WHERE TO EAT AND STAY

For expanded hotel reviews, visit Fodors.com.

$

AMERICAN

✕ **The Goldenrod.** If you wanted to—and you are on vacation—you could eat nothing but the famous taffy here, made just about the same way today as it was back in 1896. The famous Goldenrod Kisses, some 50 tons of which are made per year, are a great attraction, and people line the windows to watch the taffy being made. Aside from the famous candy (there's penny candy, too), this eating place is family oriented, very reasonably priced, and a great place to get ice cream from the old-fashioned soda fountain. Breakfast is served all day, while the simple lunch menu of sandwiches and burgers doubles as dinner, along with a handful of entrées like baked haddock and meatloaf. $ *Average main: $10* ⊠ *2 Railroad Ave.* ☎ *207/363–2621* ⊕ *www.thegoldenrod.com* ☉ *Closed mid-Oct.–mid-May.*

$$$

HOTEL

▥ **Union Bluff Hotel.** Although this hotel had to be rebuilt after a devastating fire, the face of the massive, turreted structure remains very similar to its mid-19th-century beginnings. **Pros:** many spectacular, uninterrupted ocean views; right in the midst of the York Beach action. **Cons:** rooms lack any charm or character befitting of inn's origins; not for those looking for a quiet getaway. $ *Rooms from: $179* ⊠ *8 Beach St.* ☎ *207/363–1333, 800/833–0721* ⊕ *www.unionbluff.com* ⤸ *36 rooms, 6 suites in main inn, 21 rooms in adjacent motel, 8 rooms in Meeting House.*

CAPE NEDDICK

1 mile north of York Beach via U.S. 1A.

Cape Neddick is one of the less developed of York's areas, running up from the water just after York Beach and stretching toward Ogunquit on the town's north side, but there's not much public access to the water. It has many modest residential homes, with a sprinkling of businesses catering to locals and visitors. There are a few restaurants and inns but no distinct village hub. Cape Neddick Harbor is at its southern end, beyond York Beach village.

GETTING HERE AND AROUND

U.S. 1A returns to U.S. 1 in Cape Neddick after its 7-mile loop down to the coast starting in southern York near Exit 7 of Interstate 95. U.S. 1 continues north to Ogunquit.

EXPLORING

Mount Agamenticus Park. A park sits atop this humble summit of 692 feet, one of the highest points along the Atlantic seaboard. That may not seem like much, but if you choose to hike to the top, you will be rewarded with incredible views all the way to the White Mountains in New Hampshire. If you don't want to hoof it (though it's not very steep), there is parking at the top. The park is part of the Mount Agamenticus Conservation Region, which has more than 10,000 acres and attracts hikers, equestrians, ATV riders, and mountain bikers (you can use a road bike on the paved summit road). ✉ *Mountain Road, turn off U.S. 1, follow signs* ☎ *207/361–1102* 🌐 *www.agamenticus.org* 🕒 *Daily dawn–dusk.*

WHERE TO EAT

$ AMERICAN ★ 🍴 **Flo's Steamed Hot Dogs.** Yes, it seems crazy to highlight a hot-dog stand, but this is no ordinary place. Who would guess that a hot dog could make it into *Saveur* and *Gourmet* magazines? There is something grand about this shabby, red-shingle shack that has been dealing dogs since 1959. The line is out the door most days, but this place is so efficient that the wait isn't long. Flo has passed on, but her son and daughter-in-law keep the business going, selling countless thousands of hot dogs each year. The classic here has mayo and the special sauce—consisting of, among other things, onions and molasses (you can buy a bottle to take home, and you'll want to). [$] *Average main: $3* ✉ *1359 U.S. 1* 🌐 *www.floshotdogs.com* 💳 *No credit cards* 🕒 *Closed Wed.*

$$$ ECLECTIC ★ 🍴 **Frankie & Johnny's Restaurant.** If you've had about all the fried seafood you can stand, try this hip spot that focuses on creative cuisine served with flair. The chef and his co-owner wife have developed a strong following since opening in 1992. There are lots of seafood, poultry, and meat options, homemade pasta choices, and always a few vegetarian dishes (special requests like gluten-free are happily accommodated). The toasted peppercorn-seared sushi-grade tuna, served with coconut risotto on gingered vegetables, is excellent. Pork served with a sweet pear cream sauce is also a signature dish. Even the breads and most desserts are made by the chef. Entrées include really large dinner salads with fruit and nuts as well as veggies atop the greens. You're welcome to bring your own libations; only cash and checks are accepted. [$] *Average main: $28* ✉ *1594 U.S. 1* ☎ *207/363–1909* 🌐 *www.frankie-johnnys.com* 💳 *No credit cards* 🕒 *Closed mid-Dec.–early Feb. Closed Mon. and Tues. July and Aug., also Wed. mid-Feb.–June and Sept.–early Dec. No lunch.*

Ogunquit's Perkins Cove is a pleasant place to admire the boats—and wonder at the origin of their names.

SHOPPING

Jeremiah Campbell & Co. Reproductions of 18th- and 19th-century home furnishings are the specialty of Jeremiah Campbell & Co. Everything here is handcrafted, from rugs, decoys, furniture, and lighting to glassware. The shop is closed Wednesday. ✉ *1537 U.S. 1* ☎ *207/363–8499* ⊕ *www.jeremiahcampbell.com.*

SPORTS AND THE OUTDOORS

FISHING

Eldredge Bros. Fly Shop. Offering various guided fishing trips, private casting lessons, and, come June, striper and trout "schools" (fly-tying and rod-building seminars are offered off-season) is Eldredge Bros. Fly Shop. Kayak rentals and rod-and-reel rentals are also available. ✉ *1480 U.S. 1* ☎ *207/363–9269, 877/427–9345* ⊕ *www.eldredgeflyshop.com.*

KAYAKING

Excursions Coastal Maine Outfitting Co. Hop on one of the regularly scheduled guided kayak trips with Excursions Coastal Maine Outfitting Co. You can cruise along the shoreline or sign up for an overnight paddle. Reservations are recommended; trips start at $60. Kayak classes are also offered. ✉ *1740 U.S. 1* ☎ *207/363–0181* ⊕ *www.excursionsinmaine.com.*

OGUNQUIT

8 miles north of the Yorks via U.S. 1.

A resort village since the late 19th century, stylish Ogunquit gained fame as an artists' colony. Today it has become a mini Provincetown, with a gay population that swells in summer. Many inns and small clubs cater to a primarily gay and lesbian clientele. The nightlife in Ogunquit revolves around the precincts of Ogunquit Square and Perkins Cove, where people stroll, often enjoying an after-dinner ice-cream cone or espresso. For a scenic drive, take Shore Road from downtown to the 175-foot Bald Head Cliff; you'll be treated to views up and down the coast. On a stormy day the surf can be quite wild here.

GETTING HERE AND AROUND

Ogunquit Trolley. Parking in the village and the beach is costly and limited, so leave your car at the hotel, and hop the trolley. It costs $1.50 a trip and runs Memorial Day weekend until Columbus Day, with weekend-only service for the first few weeks. From Perkins Cove the trolley runs through town along Shore Road and then down to Ogunquit Beach; it also stops along U.S. 1. The trolley is part of the Shoreline Explorer network (☎ 207/324–5762 Ext. 2932 ⊕ www.shorelineexplorer.com), which links seasonal trolleys in southern Maine beach towns from the Yorks to the Kennebunks. You can connect with a Shoreline shuttle to York, or take the Shoreline Trolley to Wells and, if you want, continue on to the Kennebunks by shuttle. ☎ 207/646–1411 ⊕ www. ogunquittrolley.com.

ESSENTIALS

Transportation Information Ogunquit Trolley ☎ 207/646–1411 ⊕ www. ogunquittrolley.com 🖾 $1.50.

Visitor Information Ogunquit Chamber of Commerce ✉ 36 Main St.(U.S. 1) ☎ 207/646–2939 ⊕ www.ogunquit.org.

EXPLORING

★ **Perkins Cove.** This neck of land off Shore Road in the lower part of Oqunquit village has a jumble of sea-beaten fish houses and buildings that were part of an art school. These have largely been transformed by the tide of tourism into shops and restaurants. ■ TIP→ This touristy spot is known as Perkins Cove, but technically speaking, the thin strip of land divides Perkins and Oarweed coves. When you've had your fill of browsing, stroll out along **Marginal Way,** a mile-long footpath that hugs the shore of a rocky promontory known as Israel's Head. Benches allow you to appreciate the open sea vistas, flowering bushes, and million-dollar homes. ✉ Perkins Cove Rd., off Shore Rd.

WHERE TO EAT AND STAY

For expanded hotel reviews, visit Fodors.com.

$ ✕ **Amore Breakfast.** One could hardly find a more-satisfying, full-bodied

AMERICAN breakfast than at this smart and busy joint just shy of the entrance to

★ Perkins Cove. A lighthearted mix of retro advertising signs adorns the walls of this bright, open, and very bustling dining room. You won't find tired standards here—the only pancakes are German potato. The Oscar Madison omelet combines crabmeat with asparagus and Swiss, topped with a béarnaise sauce. For a real decadent start, opt for the Banana Foster: pecan-coated, cream cheese–stuffed French toast with a side of sautéed bananas in rum syrup. Next door at the Cafe Amore, which is open until 8 pm in July and August, you can pick up sandwiches, baked goods, and gift items. [$] *Average main: $10* ✉ *309 Shore Rd.* ☎ *207/646–6661* 🌐 *www.amorebreakfast.com* ⏲ *Closed mid-Dec.–Fri. before Apr. 1, and Wed. and Thurs. in spring and fall. No dinner except in café (light fare) in July and Aug.*

$$$$ ECLECTIC Fodor's Choice ★ 🍴 **Arrows.** Elegant simplicity is the hallmark of this renowned restaurant in an 18th-century farmhouse 2 miles up a back road. You'll find delicacies such as lamb loin with huckleberry gastrique, and a serving of oysters cooked three ways—in green goddess sauce, poached in cream with spinach and shallots, and chilled with green garlic and chives—on the regularly changing menu. Much of what appears depends on what is ready for harvest in the restaurant's abundant garden. The full-course "Chef's Collection" is $95, the 10-course "Indulgence Menu" is prepared "at the whim of the chef" for $135, and the Friday night bistro menu is $39.95. Guests are encouraged to dress up (jackets, men!); no shorts, but jeans are OK. [$] *Average main: $40* ✉ *41 Berwick Rd.* ☎ *207/361–1100* 🌐 *www.markandclarkrestaurants.com* ✍ *Reservations essential* ⏲ *Closed Mon. and Jan.–March. No lunch.*

$$$ HOTEL 🏨 **Ogunquit Resort Motel.** Right along U.S. 1 just a mile north of Ogunquit village, this is a great choice for families and affordable for the area. **Pros:** large room for the Continental breakfast; good-size rooms; fitness center. **Cons:** close to highway; no lawns or grounds. [$] *Rooms from: $199* ✉ *719 Main St. (U.S. 1)* ☎ *877/646–8336* 🌐 *www.ogunquitresort.com* 🛏 *77 rooms, 10 suites* 🍽 *Breakfast.*

WELLS

5 miles north of Ogunquit via U.S. 1.

Lacking any kind of noticeable village center, Wells could be easily overlooked as nothing more than a commercial stretch on U.S. 1 between Ogunquit and the Kennebunks. But look more closely—this is a place where people come to enjoy some of the best beaches on the coast. The town included Ogunquit until 1980. Today this family-oriented beach community has 7 miles of densely populated shoreline, along with nature preserves where you can explore salt marshes and tidal pools.

GETTING HERE AND AROUND

Shoreline Trolley. Just $1 per trip, this seasonal trolley serves Wells Beach and Crescent Beach and has many stops along U.S. 1 at motels, campgrounds, restaurants, and so on. You can also catch it at the Wells Transportation Center when the Downeaster (the Amtrak train from Boston to Maine) pulls in. The trolley is part of the Shoreline Explorer network, which links seasonal trolleys in southern Maine beach towns from York to the Kennebunks, allowing visitors to travel between them without their cars. Besides serving the Wells area, it runs north to downtown Kennebunk and the town's Lower Village, where a shuttle connects with the trolley serving the Kennebunks, and south to Ogunquit, where you can connect with the local trolley or take a shuttle on to York Beach. ☎ *207/324–5762* 🌐 *www.shorelineexplorer.com.*

ESSENTIALS

Transportation Information Shoreline Trolley ☎ *207/324–5762* 🌐 *www.shorelineexplorer.com* 🎟 *$1.*

Visitor Information Wells Chamber of Commerce ✉ *136 Post Rd. (U.S. 1)*
☎ *207/646–2451* ⊕ *www.wellschamber.org.*

QUICK
BITES

Congdon's Doughnuts. How would you like a really superior doughnut that the same family has been making since 1945, originally in Kennebunk? Congdon's Doughnuts makes about 40 different varieties, though the plain one really gives you an idea of just how good these doughnuts are. Plain, honey-dipped, and black raspberry jelly are the biggest sellers. There are drive-through and takeout windows, or you can sit inside and have breakfast or lunch. Waits can be long for breakfast in summer. ✉ *1090 Post Rd. (U.S. 1)* ☎ *207/646–4219* ⊕ *www.congdons.com* ☉ *Mon.–Wed. Nov.–mid-April, Mon. and Tues. late April–mid-June, Wed. mid-Sept.–Oct.*

SPORTS AND THE OUTDOORS
BEACHES
With its thousands of acres of marsh and preserved land, Wells is a great place to spend a lot of time outdoors. Nearly 7 miles of sand stretch along the boundaries of Wells, making beach-going a prime occupation. Tidal pools sheltered by rocks are filled with all manner of creatures awaiting discovery. During the summer season, a pay-and-display metered (no quarters, receipt goes on dashboard) parking system is in place at the public beaches, but the summer trolley serves **Crescent Beach**, along Webhannet Drive, and **Wells Beach** at the end of Mile Road off U.S. 1. There is another metered lot but no trolley stop at the north end of Atlantic Avenue, which runs north along the shore from the end of Mile Road. Stretching north from the jetty at Wells Harbor is **Drakes Island Beach** (end of Drakes Island Road off U.S. 1). Lifeguards are on hand at all the beaches, and all have public restrooms.

Wheels and Waves. Rent bikes, surfboards, wet suits, Boogie boards, kayaks, and all sorts of outdoor gear at Wheels and Waves. ✉ *365 Post Rd.(U.S. 1)* ☎ *207/646–5774* ⊕ *www.wheelsnwaves.com.*

STATE PARKS AND REFUGES
Rachel Carson National Wildlife Refuge. At the headquarters of the Rachel Carson National Wildlife Refuge, which has 11 divisions from Kittery to Cape Elizabeth, is the Carson Trail, a one-mile loop. The trail traverses a salt marsh and a white-pine forest where migrating birds and waterfowl of many varieties are regularly spotted, and it borders Branch Brook and the Merriland River. ✉ *321 Port Rd.(Rte. 9)* ☎ *207/646–9226* ⊕ *www.fws.gov/northeast/rachelcarson* ☉ *Daily, sunrise to sunset.*

WHERE TO EAT AND STAY
For expanded hotel reviews, visit Fodors.com.

$$
\text{SEAFOOD}
$$

\$\$
SEAFOOD ✕ **Billy's Chowder House.** Locals and families and couples on vacation all head to this classic roadside seafood restaurant in the midst of a salt marsh en route to Wells Beach. They come for the generous lobster rolls, haddock sandwiches, seafood entrées, and chowders, but there are plenty of non-seafood choices, too. Big windows in the bright dining rooms overlook the marsh, part of the Rachel Carson National

10

WALKING TOURS IN THE KENNEBUNKS

To take a little walking tour of Kennebunk's most notable structures, begin from the Federal-style Brick Store Museum ⊠ *117 Main Street*. Head south on Main Street (turn left out of the museum) to see several extraordinary 18th- and early 19th-century homes, including the **Lexington Elms** at 99 Main St. (1799), the **Horace Porter House** at ⊠ *92 Main St.* (1848), and the **Benjamin Brown House** at ⊠ *85 Main St.* (1788).

When you've had your fill of historic homes, head back up toward the museum, pass the 1773 **First Parish Unitarian Church** (its Asher Benjamin–style steeple contains an original Paul Revere bell), and turn right onto **Summer Street**. This street is an architectural showcase, revealing an array of styles from Colonial to Federal. Walking past these grand

beauties will give you a real sense of the economic prowess and glamour of the long-gone shipbuilding industry.

For a guided 90-minute architectural walking tour of Summer Street, contact the museum at ☎ *207/985–4802*. You can also purchase a $4.95 map that marks historic buildings or a $15.95 guidebook, *Windows on the Past*.

For a dramatic walk along Kennebunkport's rocky coastline and beneath the views of Ocean Avenue's grand mansions, head out on the **Parson's Way Shore Walk**, a paved 4.8-mile round-trip. Begin at Dock Square and follow Ocean Avenue along the river, passing the Colony Hotel and St. Ann's Church, all the way to Walker's Point. Simply turn back from here.

Wildlife Refuge. $ *Average main: $15* ⊠ *216 Mile Rd.* ☎ *207/646–7558* ⊕ *www.billyschowderhouse.com* ⊘ *Closed mid-Dec.–mid-Jan.*

$
DINER
✕ **Maine Diner.** One look at the 1953 exterior and you start craving good diner food. You'll get a little more than you're expecting; how many greasy spoons make an award-winning lobster pie? That's the house favorite, as well as a heavenly seafood chowder. There's plenty of fried seafood in addition to the usual diner fare, and breakfast is served all day. Check out the adjacent gift shop, Remember the Maine. $ *Average main: $10* ⊠ *2265 Post Rd.(U.S.1)* ☎ *207/646–4441* ⊕ *www.mainediner.com* ⊘ *Closed at least 1 wk in Jan.*

$$$$
B&B/INN
Fodor'sChoice
★
🛏 **Haven by the Sea.** Once the summer mission of St. Martha's Church in Kennebunkport, this exquisite inn has retained many of the original details from its former life as a seaside church. **Pros:** unusual structure with elegant appointments; tucked away message room. **Cons:** not an in-town location. $ *Rooms from: $239* ⊠ *59 Church St.* ☎ *207/646–4194* ⊕ *www.havenbythesea.com* 🛏 *7 rooms, 2 suites, 1 apartment (weekly rental)* ❍⏐ *Breakfast.*

KENNEBUNK

5 miles north of Wells via U.S. 1.

Sometimes bypassed on the way to its sister town of Kennebunkport, Kennebunk has its own appeal. In the 19th century the town was a major shipbuilding center; docks lined the river with hundreds of workers busily crafting the vessels that would bring immense fortune to some of the area's residents. Although the trade is long gone, the evidence that remains of this great wealth exists in Kennebunk's mansions. Kennebunk is a classic small New England town, with an inviting shopping district, steepled churches, and fine examples of 18th- and 19th-century brick and clapboard homes. There are also plenty of natural spaces for walking, swimming, birding, and biking—the Kennebunks' major beaches are here. Kennebunk's main village—downtown means here–is along U.S. 1, mostly extending west from the Mousam River. The Lower Village is along Routes 9 and 35, three miles down Route 35 from the main village. Route 9 runs right across the Kennebunk River to Kennebunkport's touristy downtown, forming one commercial area with restaurants, shops, boat cruises, and galleries. The drive down Route 35 keeps visitors agog with the splendor of the area's mansions, spread out on both sides of the road. To get to the grand and gentle beaches of Kennebunk, continue straight (road becomes Beach Avenue) at the intersection with Route 9.

GETTING HERE AND AROUND

Intown Trolley. Narrated 45-minute jaunts run daily from Memorial Day weekend through Columbus Day. The $16 fare is valid for the day, so you can hop on and off—or start your journey—at any of the stops. The route includes Kennebunk's beaches and Lower Village as well as neighboring Kennebunkport's scenery and sights. The main stop is at 21 Ocean Ave. in Kennebunkport, around the corner from Dock Square. The trolley is part of the Shoreline Explorer (☎ 207/324–5762 Ext. 2932 ⊕ www.shorelineexplorer.com) network, which links seasonal trolleys in southern Maine beach towns from the Yorks to the Kennebunks. So, you can make connections to continue by shuttle or trolley to beach towns south of here. ☎ 207/967–3686 ⊕ www.intowntrolley.com.

ESSENTIALS

Visitor Information Intown Trolley ☎ 207/967–3686 ⊕ www.intowntrolley. com ☒ $16 all-day fare ☉ Memorial Day weekend–Columbus Day, daily 10–3 in spring and fall, until 4 in summer. **Kennebunk-Kennebunkport Chamber of Commerce** ☎ 207/967–0857 ⊕ www.visitthekennebunks.com.

EXPLORING

Brick Store Museum. The cornerstone of this block-long preservation of early-19th-century commercial and residential buildings is **William Lord's Brick Store.** Built as a dry-goods store in 1825 in the Federal style, the building has an openwork balustrade across the roofline, granite lintels over the windows, and paired chimneys. Exhibits chronicle the Kennebunk area's history and Early American decorative and fine arts. The museum leads architectural walking tours of Kennebunk's National Historic District by appointment from late May through September. You can also purchase a $4.95 map that marks historic buildings or a $15.95 guidebook, *Windows on the Past.* ☒ 117 Main St. ☎ 207/985–4802 ⊕ www.brickstoremuseum.org ☒ $5 donation suggested ☉ Tues.–Fri. 10–4:30, Sat. 10–1.

10

First Parish of Kennebunk Unitarian Universalist Church. Built in 1773, just before the American Revolution, this stunning church is a marvel. The 1804 Asher Benjamin–style steeple stands proudly atop the village, and the sounds of the original Paul Revere bell can be heard for miles. The church holds Sunday services at 10:30 am, and all are welcome. ⊠ *114 Main St.* ☎ *207/985–3700* ⊕ *www.uukennebunk.org.*

SHOPPING

Maine Art Shows. Selling works by artists from Maine and New England, Maine Art Shows has two galleries in Kennebunk's Lower Village. The main two-story gallery is at the corner of Western Avenue and Chill Hill Road and has a sculpture garden. A few doors down, a modern window-filled gallery has art shows in the summer. ⊠ *10 Chase Hill Rd.* ☎ *207/967–0049* ⊕ *www.maine-art.com.*

SPORTS AND THE OUTDOORS

Kennebunk Beaches. Kennebunk has three beaches, each following the other along Beach Avenue, which is lined with cottages and old Victorians. The mostly northerly, and closest to downtown Kennebunkport, is Gooch's Beach, the main swimming beach. Next is stony Kennebunk Beach, followed by Mother's Beach, which is popular with families. There's a small playground and tidal puddles for splashing, and rock outcroppings lessen the waves. A permit is needed to park here from June 15 to Sept. 15; the cost is $15 daily, $50 weekly, and $100 for the season. ■TIP→ You can buy one at town hall on Route 35 (1 Summer St. 207/985–2102) or at the chamber. ⊠ *Beach Avenue.*

Kennebunk Plains. For an unusual exploring treat, visit the Kennebunk Plains, a 135-acre protected grasslands habitat that is home to several rare and endangered species of vegetation and wildlife. Locally known as the blueberry plains, a good portion of the area is abloom with the hues of ripening wild blueberries in late July; after August 1 visitors are welcome to pick and eat all the berries they can find. The roads take you through vast grasslands and scrub-oak woods and by ponds. The area is maintained by the Nature Conservancy and is open daily from sunrise to sunset. ⊠ *Route 99* ✛ *From U.S. 1 take Route 9A west, turn right on Route 99, watch for sign* ☎ *207/729–5181 Nature Conservancy in Maine office* ⊕ *www.nature.org.*

Kennebunkport Town Hall. You can pick up a parking permit ($15 a day, $50 a week) at the Kennebunkport Town Hall or at the police department on Route 9 on the way to the beach. ⊠ *6 Elm St., Kennebunkport* ☎ *207/967–4243* ⊙ *Weekdays 8–4:30.*

Cast-Away Fishing Charters. Find and catch fish with Cast-Away Fishing Charters. The captain also offers a lobstering trip that's fun for families with kids–they can help haul the traps. ⊠ *Departs from Performance Marine, 4-A Western Ave., Kennebunkport 04046* ☎ *207/284–1740* ⊕ *www.castawayfishingcharters.com.*

First Chance. First Chance leads whale-watching cruises on 85-foot *Nick's Chance.* You get a ticket–no expiration–for another trip if whales aren't sighted. Scenic lobster cruises are also offered aboard 65-foot *Kylie's Chance.* Trips run daily in summer and on weekends in the shoulder seasons. ✉ *Performance Marine, 4-A Western Ave.* ☎ *207/967–5507, 800/767–2628* 🌐 *www.firstchancewhalewatch.com.*

WHERE TO EAT

$$ AMERICAN 🍴 **Duffy's Tavern & Grill.** Every small town needs its own lively and friendly tavern, and this bustling spot is Kennebunk's favorite, housed in a former shoe factory with exposed brick, soaring ceilings, and hardwood floors. Right outside are the tumbling waters of the Mousam River as it flows from the dam. There's a large bar with overhead televisions and plenty of seating in the main room, plus a less-captivating back section. You'll find lots of comfortable standards, like burgers, pizza, and the popular fish-and-chips. Onion rings are hand-dipped. [$] *Average main: $16* ✉ *4 Main St.* ☎ *207/985–0050* 🌐 *www.duffyskennebunk.com.*

$$ AMERICAN 🍴 **Federal Jack's.** Run by the Kennebunkport Brewing Co., this two-story complex is directly on the water before the bridge from Lower Village into Kennebunkport. All beers are handcrafted on-site, including Blue Fin Stout and Goat Island Light—try the sampler if you can't decide. Upstairs in the restaurant the food is American pub style, with plenty of seafood elements; the clam chowder is rich and satisfying. There's also a Sunday brunch buffet. The restaurant has two dining rooms and a huge deck that packs in the crowds in the summer. There's a poolroom and live entertainment Thursday through Saturday (Sunday in summer). Brew tours are available. [$] *Average main: $14* ✉ *8 Western Ave.* ☎ *207/967–4322* 🌐 *www.federaljacks.com.*

WHERE TO STAY

For expanded hotel reviews, visit Fodors.com.

$$$ B&B/INN 🏨 **Bufflehead Cove Inn.** On the Kennebunk River at the end of a winding dirt road, this gray-shingle B&B sits amid fields and apple trees. **Pros:** beautiful and peaceful pastoral setting; ideal riverfront location; perfect for a serene getaway. **Cons:** two-night minimum stay on weekends. [$] *Rooms from: $185* ✉ *18 Bufflehead Cove Rd.* ☎ *207/967–3879* 🌐 *www.buffleheadcove.com* 🛏 *4 rooms, 1 suite, 1 cottage* ⏲ *Closed Dec.–Apr.* 🍽 *Breakfast.*

$$$$ HOTEL 👶 🏨 **The Seaside.** This handsome seaside property has been in the hands of the Severance family since 1667. **Pros:** great ocean views from upper-floor rooms; Continental breakfast; rates drop more than 50 percent in winter (except during Christmas Prelude). **Cons:** rooms are motel standard and a little outdated; not an in-town location. [$] *Rooms from: $249* ✉ *80 Beach Ave.* ☎ *207/967–4461, 800/967–4461* 🌐 *www.kennebunkbeachmaine.com* 🛏 *22 rooms* 🍽 *Breakfast.*

$$$$ B&B/INN ★ 🏨 **White Barn Inn.** For a romantic overnight stay, you need look no further than the exclusive White Barn Inn, known for its attentive, pampering service. **Pros:** about 10 minutes walk to both Dock Square and the beach; elegant spa offers it all; concierge. **Cons:** prices are steep. [$] *Rooms from: $499* ✉ *37 Beach Ave.* ☎ *207/967–2321* 🌐 *www.whitebarninn.com* 🛏 *13 rooms, 9 suites, 5 cottages* 🍽 *Breakfast.*

Kennebunk is a classic New England town, while Kennebunkport (pictured) has more upscale inns and shopping.

KENNEBUNKPORT

Approximately 6 miles north of Wells via U.S. 1 and Route 9.

Kennebunkport has been a resort area since the 19th century, but its most famous residents have made it even more popular—the presidential Bush family is often in residence in their immense home, which sits dramatically out on Walker's Point on Cape Arundel. The amount of wealth here is as tangible as the sharp sea breezes and the sounds of seagulls overhead. Newer mansions have sprung up alongside the old; a great way to see them is to take a slow drive out along the cape on Ocean Avenue. The area focused around the water and Dock Square in downtown Kennebunkport is where you can find the most activity (and crowds) in the Kennebunks. Winding alleys disclose shops and restaurants geared to the tourist trade, right in the midst of a hardworking harbor. Often called the "the Port," downtown's commercial activity continues right across the harbor bridge to Kennebunk's Lower Village. It's all seamless to visitors; many don't realize they have crossed into another town.

GETTING HERE AND AROUND

Intown Trolley. Narrated 45-minute jaunts run daily from Memorial Day weekend through Columbus Day, leaving every hour starting at 10 am at the main stop at 21 Ocean Ave., around the corner from downtown's Dock Square. The route includes sites and scenery in Kennebunkport as well as neighboring Kennebunk's beaches and Lower Village. The $16 fare is valid for the day, so you can hop on and off—or start your journey—at any of the stops. You can also connect with a shuttle to the Shoreline Trolley, which runs from Kennebunk to Ogunquit. Both trolleys and the shuttle are part of the Shoreline Explorer network (☎ 207/324–5762 *Ext. 2932* ⊕ *www.shorelineexplorer.com*), which links seasonal trolleys in southern Maine beach towns from the Yorks to the Kennebunks, allowing visitors to travel between towns without their cars. ☎ 207/967–3686 ⊕ *www.intowntrolley.com.*

ESSENTIALS

Visitor Information Kennebunk-Kennebunkport Chamber of Commerce. ☎ *207/967–0857* ⊕ *www.visitthekennebunks.com.*

Transportation Information Intown Trolley ☎ *207/967–3686* ⊕ *www. intowntrolley.com* ▧ *$16 all-day fare* ☉ *Memorial Day weekend–Labor Day, daily 10–3 in spring and fall, until 4 in summer.*

EXPLORING

Dock Square. The heart and pulse of busy little Kennebunkport is this town center. Boutiques, T-shirt shops, art galleries, gift stores, and restaurants line the square and spread out alongside streets and alleys. Walk onto the drawbridge to admire the tidal Kennebunk River. Cross to the other side and you are in the Lower Village of neighboring Kennebunk.

Goose Rocks. Three-mile-long Goose Rocks, about a 10-minute drive north of town off Route 9, has plenty of shallow pools for exploring and a good long stretch of smooth sand. It's a favorite of families with small children. You will need to pick up a parking permit during the summer season. You can get a $15 daily permit at Goose Rocks Beach General Store (⊠ *3 Dyke Road* ☎ *207/967–2289*), just before the beach on the left. Daily, weekly ($50), and seasonal ($100) passes are available at Kennebunkport Town Hall (⊠ *6 Elm St.* ☎ *207/967–4243*) or the town police department just off Route 9 (⊠ *101 Main St.* ☎ *207/967–2454*). ⊠ *Dyke Road, turn off Rte. 9.*

Nott House. Also known as White Columns, the imposing Greek Revival mansion with Doric columns is furnished with the belongings of four generations of the Perkins-Nott family. In July and August, the 1853 house is open for guided tours and also serves as a gathering place for village walking tours. It is owned by the Kennebunkport Historical Society, located about a mile away at 125–135 North Street, where it has five other historical buildings, including an old jail and schoolhouse, and a modern structure where changing exhibits are shown. The society is open Tuesday–Friday 10–4 year-round. ⊠ *8 Maine St.* ☎ *207/967–2751* ⊕ *www.kporthistory.org* ▧ *$10 for house tour; $10 for walking tour; $15 for house and walking tour* ☉ *House: July and Aug., Thur.–Sat. 11–3, 45-minute tours starting at quarter past the hour (last tour at 2:15). Walking tours: July and Aug., Thurs.–Sat. at 11.*

★ **Seashore Trolley Museum.** Here streetcars built from 1872 to 1972, includ-
☾ ing trolleys from major metropolitan areas and world capitals (Boston to Budapest, New York to Nagasaki, San Francisco to Sydney), are all beautifully restored and displayed. Best of all, you can take a trolley ride for nearly 4 miles on the tracks of the former Atlantic Shoreline trolley line, with a stop along the way at the museum restoration

10

shop, where trolleys are transformed from junk into gems. The outdoor museum is self-guided. ✉ *195 Log Cabin Rd.* ☎ *207/967–2712* 🌐 *www.trolleymuseum.org* 🎫 *$10* 🕒 *Memorial Day–Columbus Day, daily 10–5; weekends only earlier in May and and through end of October.*

SHOPPING

Abacus. Abacus sells eclectic crafts, jewelry, and furniture. ✉ *2 Ocean Ave., Dock Sq.* ☎ *207/967–0111* 🌐 *www.abacusgallery.com.*

Mast Cove Galleries. Since 1979, Mast Cove Galleries has been selling paintings and sculpture by artists from New England and beyond. It occupies the barn and first floor of the owner's 1851 village home, which has a sculpture garden. The gallery is open March through December but hosts indoor jazz and blues concerts year-round. ✉ *2 Mast Cove Ln.* ☎ *207/967–3453* 🌐 *www.mastcove.com.*

SPORTS AND THE OUTDOORS

👶 ***Rugosa.*** Lobster-trap hauling trips in the scenic waters off the Kennebunks run daily aboard the *Rugosa* from Memorial Day weekend through early October. ✉ *Depart from Nonantum Resort, 95 Ocean Ave.* ☎ *207/468–4095* 🌐 *www.rugosacharters.com.*

WHERE TO EAT

$$ SEAFOOD 🍴 **Mabel's Lobster Claw.** Since the 1950s Mabel's has been serving lobsters, homemade pies, and lots of seafood for lunch and dinner in this tiny dwelling out on Ocean Avenue. Decor includes paneled walls, wooden booths, autographed photos of various TV stars (plus members of the Bush family). There's outside seating, too, and paper place mats that illustrate how to eat a Maine lobster. The house favorite is the Lobster Savannah—split and filled with scallops, shrimp, and mushrooms and baked in a Newburg sauce. Save room for the peanut butter ice cream pie. There's also a takeout window where you can order ice cream and food. [$] *Average main: $20* ✉ *124 Ocean Ave.* ☎ *207/967–2562* 🌐 *www.mabelslobster.com* 🕒 *Closed Nov.–early Apr.*

$$$ MODERN AMERICAN 🍴 **Pier 77 Restaurant & the Ramp Bar & Grille.** The view takes center stage at this dual establishment. On the ground level, Pier 77 is the fine-dining portion with large windows overlooking the harbor. Every seat has a nice view at the restaurant, which serves up sophisticated fare, focusing on meats and seafood. The place is vibrant with live music in summer and a great place for cocktails on the water. Tucked down below, the tiny, tiny but oh-so-funky-and-fun Ramp pays homage to a really good burger, fried seafood, and other pub-style choices. [$] *Average main: $25* ✉ *77 Pier Rd., Cape Porpoise* ☎ *207/967–8500* 🌐 *www.pier77restaurant.com* 🕒 *Jan.–mid-March, Pier closed, Ramp closed Mon. and Tues.; mid-March–April and Nov. and Dec., both closed Tues.*

WHERE TO STAY

For expanded hotel reviews, visit Fodors.com.

$$$$ B&B/INN 🏨 **Cape Arundel Inn.** This shingle-style 19th-century inn, originally a summer "cottage" like the mansions nearby, commands a magnificent ocean view that takes in the Bush estate at Walker's Point. **Pros:** extraordinary views from most rooms; across the road from rockbound coast. **Cons:** not for the budget-minded. [$] *Rooms from: $335* ✉ *208 Ocean*

Ave. ☎ *207/967–2125* 🌐 *www.capearundelinn.com* 🛏 *14 rooms, 1 suite* 🕒 *Closed late Dec.–early Feb.* 🍴 *Breakfast.*

$$$$ B&B/INN Fodor's Choice ★ 🏨 **The Captain Lord Mansion.** Of all the mansions in Kennebunkport's historic district that have been converted to inns, the 1814 Captain Lord Mansion is the stateliest and most sumptuously appointed. **Pros:** beautiful landscaped grounds; bikes for guests; putting green. **Cons:** not a beachfront location. [$] *Rooms from: $329* ✉ *6 Pleasant St.* ☎ *207/967–3141, 800/522–3141* 🌐 *www.captainlord.com* 🛏 *18 rooms, 2 suites* 🍴 *Breakfast.*

$$$ RESORT Fodor's Choice ★ 👶 🏨 **The Colony Hotel.** You can't miss this place—it's grand, white, and incredibly large, set majestically atop a rise overlooking the ocean. **Pros:** private beach; heated saltwater swimming pool; activities and entertainment for all ages. **Cons:** not intimate. [$] *Rooms from: $179* ✉ *140 Ocean Ave.* ☎ *207/967–3331, 800/552–2363* 🌐 *www.thecolonyhotel.com/maine* 🛏 *112 rooms, 11 suites, 2 cottages* 🕒 *Closed Nov.–mid-May* 🍴 *Breakfast.*

EN ROUTE

For a rewarding drive that goes into the reaches of the coastline on the way to Old Orchard Beach, head out of Kennebunkport on Route 9. You'll soon come to the fishing village of Cape Porpoise. Don't drive through without heading down Point Road to the pier, where there are wondrous views, lobster boats in the harbor, and a place to take it all in whatever the mood: Pier 77 Restaurant has an upstairs dining room and a funky pub tucked below. Continuing on Route 9, plan to do some beach walking at Goose Rocks Beach or Fortunes Rocks Beach, both ideal for stretching your legs or just looking for shells or critters in the tide pools. Just don't venture here in peak season without a parking permit. You can pick up one for Goose Rocks at the Kennebunkport police station en route; Fortunes Rock Beach is in neighboring Biddeford and also requires a permit. Route 9 winds through wooded areas, then heads through this slightly weary-looking old mill town. You can't miss the humongous old brick mill by the falls on the Saco River, now apartments and the anchor for a revitalization project. Across the river is Saco, a busy town where commerce and its accompanying traffic continues. Once you get past here, Route 9 returns to its peaceful curves and gentle scenery, leaving crowded civilization behind and winding through the charming resort villages of Camp Ellis and Ocean Park. You could pack a picnic and spend some time at Ferry Beach State Park (look for the entrance just off Route 9 on Bayview Road, beyond Camp Ellis). The varied landscapes in here include forested sections, swamp, beach, a rare stand of tupelo (black gum) trees, and lots of dunes. There are a few miles of marked trails to hike.

OLD ORCHARD BEACH AREA

15 miles north of Kennebunkport; 18 miles south of Portland.

Back in the late 19th century, Old Orchard Beach was a classic, upscale, place-to-be-seen resort area. The railroad brought wealthy families looking for entertainment and the benefits of the fresh sea air. Although a good bit of this aristocratic hue has dulled in more recent times—admittedly, the place is more than a little pleasantly tacky these days—Old Orchard Beach remains a good place for those looking for entertainment by the sea. Many visitors are French Canadian.

The center of the action is a 7-mile strip of sand beach and its accompanying amusement park. Despite the summertime crowds and fried-food odors, the atmosphere can be captivating. During the 1940s and '50s, the pier had a dance hall where stars of the time performed. Fire claimed the end of the pier—at one time it jutted out nearly 1,800 feet into the sea—but booths with games and candy concessions still line both sides. In summer the town sponsors fireworks (on Thursday night). Places to stay run the gamut from cheap motels to cottage colonies to full-service seasonal hotels. You won't find free parking in town, but there are ample lots. Amtrak has a seasonal stop here.

GETTING HERE AND AROUND

From Interstate 95 get off at Exit 32 and follow signs. Traveling from the south on U.S. 1, Route 5 heads into town. To continue north on U.S. 1, return on Route 98.

ESSENTIALS

Visitor Information Old Orchard Beach Chamber of Commerce ⊠ *11 First St.* ☎ *207/934–2500, 800/365–9386* ⊕ *www.oldorchardbeachmaine.com.*

EXPLORING

Ocean Park. A world away from the beach scene lies Ocean Park, on the southwestern edge of town. Locals and visitors like to keep the separation distinct, touting their area as a more peaceful and wholesome family-style village (to that end, there are no alcohol or tobacco sales in this little haven). This vacation community was founded in 1881 by Free Will Baptist leaders as a summer assembly with both religious and educational purposes, following the example of Chautauqua, New York. Today the community hosts an impressive variety of cultural happenings, including movies, concerts, sand sculpture contest, and workshops. Interdenominational religious services featuring guest preachers are held in the 1881 octagonal Temple, which is on the National Register of Historic Places. Although the religious nature of the place is apparent in its worship schedule and some of its cultural offerings, most of its programs and activities are secular; all are welcome. There's even a public shuffleboard area for vacationers not interested in the neon carnival attractions about a mile up the road. Get an old-fashioned raspberry lime rickey at the Ocean Park Soda Fountain (near the library, at Furber Park); it's also a good place for breakfast or a light lunch. ⊠ *14 Temple Ave., Ocean Park* ☎ *207/934–9068 Ocean Park Association* ⊕ *www.oceanpark.org.*

SPORTS AND THE OUTDOORS

Scarborough Marsh Audubon Center. Not far from Old Orchard Beach is this Maine Audubon Society–run nature center. You can explore this natural haven by foot or canoe on your own, or by signing up for a guided walk or paddle. The salt marsh is Maine's largest and is an excellent place for bird-watching and peaceful paddling along its winding ways. The center has a discovery room for kids, programs for all ages ranging from basket making to astronomy, and a good gift shop. Tours include birding walks. ⊠ *Pine Point Rd.(Rte. 9), Scarborough*

☎ 207/883–5100 🌐 *www.maineaudubon.org* 🎫 *Free; guided tours begin at $5* ⏲ *Daily, 9:30–5:30 mid-June–Labor Day; weekends only Memorial Day weekend–mid-June and through Sept. after Labor Day.*

WHERE TO EAT

$$ ECLECTIC ★ 🍴 **The Landmark.** This restaurant in a 1910 Victorian home almost feels as if it doesn't belong here. Tables are set either on the glassed-in porch or within high, tin-ceiling rooms. Candles and a collection of giant fringed art nouveau lamps provide a gentle light. The menu has a good selection of seafood and meats, many treated with flavors from various parts of the globe. It's the kind of menu that encourages you to try new things, and you definitely won't be disappointed. From July through Labor Day you can eat outside on the stone patio, sheltered by umbrellas, and order from an "in the rough" dinner menu, with everything cooked on the adjacent grill. Choose from clambake-style meals, charbroiled and marinated skewers, and BBQ ribs. [$] *Average main: $19* ✉ *28 E. Grand Ave.* ☎ *207/934–0156* 🌐 *www.landmarkfinedining.com* ⏲ *Closed late Nov.–Mar, Mon.–Thurs. mid-April to mid-May, Mon. mid-May–mid-June and in Oct. after Columbus Day. No lunch.*

$$$ SEAFOOD 🍴 **Yellowfin's Restaurant.** Inside this diminutive restaurant housed in an impeccably kept yellow Victorian, it is fresh, bright, and appropriately beachy. A giant tank bubbles quietly in the background while its resident colorful fish in the tank survey the landscape of white linen–covered tables adorned with sand and shell centerpieces. White cloth panels draped along the ceiling add an enveloping sense of comfort to the lively space. Not surprisingly, the house specialty is ahi yellowfin tuna, pan-seared and treated with a wasabi ginger sauce; other choices include seared scallops, lamb, and a savory seafood *fra diavolo* (spicy tomato sauce). Brunch is offered Sunday year-round. In Ocean Park it's BYOB—you'll have to stock up in nearby Old Orchard Beach. [$] *Average main: $23* ✉ *5 Temple Ave.* ☎ *207/934–1100* 🌐 *yellowfinsrestaurantme.com* ⏲ *No lunch mid-June–early Sept. or Sun. Sept.–mid June (Sunday brunch year-round).*

PORTLAND

28 miles from Kennebunk via Interstates 95 and 295.

Maine's largest city is considered small by national standards—its population is just 64,000—but its character, spirit, and appeal make it feel much larger. In fact, it is a cultural and economic center for a metropolitan area of 230,000 residents—almost one-quarter of Maine's entire population. Over the past several years it's landed on a number of lists of the best places to live in and travel to. Portland and its environs are well worth at least a day or two of exploration.

A city of many names throughout its history, including Casco and Falmouth, Portland has survived many dramatic transformations. Sheltered by the nearby Casco Bay Islands and blessed with a deep port, Portland was a significant settlement right from its start in the early 17th century. Settlers thrived on fishing and lumbering, repeatedly building up the area while the British, French, and Native Americans continually

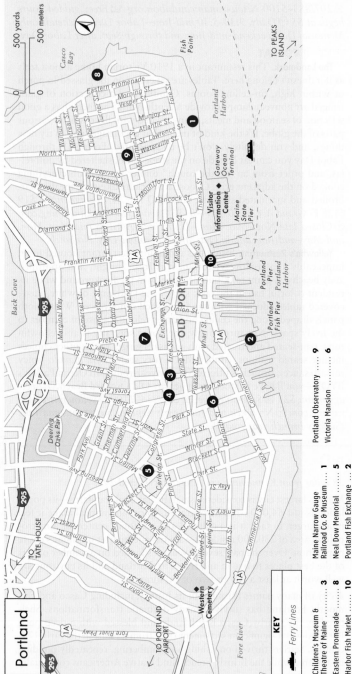

Portland

500 yards
500 meters

Casco Bay

Fish Point

TO PEAKS ISLAND

Eastern Promenade

Morning St.
Vesper St.
Munjoy St.
Atlantic St.
St. Lawrence St.
Waterville St.

Walnut St.
Montreal St.
Melbourne St.
Quebec St.
North St.

Portland Harbor

Fore St.
Monument St.

Hammond St.
Anderson St.
Cove St.

Sheridan Ave.
Washington Ave.
Tomaso Ln.

Mountfort St.
Hancock St.

Diamond St.

Anderson St.
E. Oxford St.
India St.

Back Cove

Franklin Arterial

Congress St.
Federal St.
Newbury St.
Middle St.

Thames St.

Gateway Ocean Terminal

♦ Visitor Information Center

Maine State Pier

Pearl St.
Marginal Way
Somerset St.
Lancaster St.
Oxford St.
Cumberland Ave.
Market St.
Fore St.
Milk St.

Portland Pier

OLD PORT
Union St.

Portland Fish Pier

Portland Harbor

Preble St.
Elm St.
Chapel St.
Alder St.
Parris St.
Forest Ave.
High St.

Exchange St.
Free St.
Spring St.
Pearl St.
Pleasant St.
Union St.
Wharf St.
Commercial St.

Deering Oaks Park

State St.
Grant St.
Sherman St.
Cumberland Ave.
Deering St.
Mellen St.
Park Ave.
Carleton St.
Pine St.

Congress St.
Park St.
State St.
High St.
Winter St.
Brackett St.
Clark St.
Danforth St.
York St.

Bramhall St.
Brackett St.
Neal St.
Vaughan St.
Chadwick St.
Carroll St.
Gilman St.
Bowdoin St.

May St.
Emery St.
Thomas St.
Spring St.
Danforth St.

Commercial St.

Western Cemetery

St. John St.
Valley St.

Fore River

TO TATE HOUSE

TO PORTLAND AIRPORT

Fore River Pkwy

KEY

⚓ Ferry Lines

Children's Museum &
Theatre of Maine **3**
Eastern Promenade **8**
Harbor Fish Market **10**
Longfellow House **7**

Maine Narrow Gauge
Railroad Co. & Museum ... **1**
Neal Dow Memorial **5**
Portland Fish Exchange ... **2**
Portland Museum of Art ... **4**

Portland Observatory **9**
Victoria Mansion **6**

PORTLAND TOURS

AUTO TOURS
Portland Discovery Land & Sea Tours. The informative trolley tours of Portland Discovery Land & Sea Tours detail Portland's historical and architectural highlights from Memorial Day through October. Options include combining a city tour with a bay or lighthouse cruise; the latter goes by four lights. Trolley tours and cruises, which are on an 80-passenger boat, are each $21. ⊠ *Long Wharf, 170 Commercial St.* ☎ *207/774–0808* ⊕ *www.portlanddiscovery.com.*

WALKING TOURS
Maine Foodie Tours. Learn about Portland's culinary history and sample local delights like lobster hors d'oeuvres, organic cheese, and the famous Maine whoopie pie with

Maine Foodie Tours. The culinary foot tours include stops at fishmongers, bakeries, and cheese shops that provide product to Portland's famed restaurants. Most purveyors extend a discount on a purchase. From summer into early fall, you can also take a chocolate tour, a bike-and-brewery tour, or a trolley tour with a stop (one of seven) at a microbrewery. Tours begin at various locales in the Old Port; prices start at $33. ☎ *207/233–7485* ⊕ *www.mainefoodietours.com.*

Portland Freedom Trail. Portland Freedom Trail provides a self-guided tour, available for free download online, of sites associated with the Underground Railroad and the antislavery movement. ☎ *207/591–9980* ⊕ *www.portlandfreedomtrail.org.*

sacked it. Many considered the region a somewhat dangerous frontier, but its potential for prosperity was so apparent that settlers came anyway to tap its rich natural resources.

In 1632, Portland's first home was built on the Portland Peninsula in the area now known as Munjoy Hill. The British burned the city in 1775, when residents refused to surrender arms, but it was rebuilt and became a major trading center. Much of Portland was destroyed again in the Great Fire on July 4, 1866, when a flicked ash or perhaps a celebratory firecracker started a fire in a boatyard that grew into conflagration; 1,500 buildings burned to the ground.

Today, there are excellent microbrew and restaurant scenes—many visitors come here just for the food—and a great art museum. The waterfront is a lively place to walk around well into the evening.

GETTING HERE AND AROUND
From Interstate 95, take Interstate 295 to get downtown and onto the Portland Peninsula. Commercial Street runs along the harbor, Fore Street is in one block up in heart of the Old Port, and the Arts District stretches along diagonal Congress Street. Munjoy Hill is on the eastern end of the peninsula and the West End on the opposite side.

ESSENTIALS
Contacts Greater Portland Convention and Visitors Bureau ⊠ *Visitor Information Center, 14 Ocean Gateway Pier* ☎ *207/772–5800* ⊕ *www.visitportland.com.* **Downtown Portland** ⊠ *549 Congress St.* ☎ *207/772–6828* ⊕ *www.portlandmaine.com.*

THE OLD PORT

Fodor's Choice
★

A major international port and a working harbor since the early 17th century, the Old Port bridges the gap between the city's historical commercial activities and those of today. It is home to fishing boats docked alongside whale-watching charters, luxury yachts, cruise ships, and oil tankers from around the globe. Commercial Street parallels the water and is lined with brick buildings and warehouses that were built following the Great Fire of 1866. In the 19th century candle makers and sail stitchers plied their trades here; today specialty shops, art galleries, and restaurants have taken up residence.

As with much of the city, it's best to park your car and explore the Old Port on foot. You can park at the city garage on Fore Street (between Exchange and Union streets) or opposite the U.S. Custom House at the corner of Fore and Pearl streets. A helpful hint: look for the "Park & Shop" sign on garages and parking lots and get one hour of free parking for each stamp collected at participating shops. Allow a couple of hours to wander at leisure on Market, Exchange, Middle, and Fore streets. The city is very pedestrian-friendly. Maine state law requires vehicles to stop for walkers in crosswalks.

Harbor Fish Market. A Portland favorite since 1968, this freshest-of-the-fresh seafood market ships lobsters and other Maine delectables almost anywhere in the country. A bright-red facade on a working wharf opens into a bustling space with bubbling lobster pens and fish, clams, and other shellfish on ice; employees are as skilled with a fillet knife as sushi chefs. There is also a retail store. ⊠ *9 Custom House Wharf* ☎ *207/775–0251, 800/370–1790* ⊕ *www.harborfish.com* ✉ *Free.*

⟲ **Maine Narrow Gauge Railroad Museum.** Whether you're crazy about old trains or just want to see the sights from a different perspective, the railroad museum has an extensive collection of locomotives and rail coaches and offers scenic tours on narrow-gauge railcars. The 3-mile jaunts run on the hour and take you along Casco Bay, at the foot of the Eastern Promenade. The operating season caps off with a Halloween ride (wear your costumes). During the Christmas season the trains run (museum is closed) for Polar Express rides, based on the popular children's book. ⊠ *58 Fore St.* ☎ *207/828–0814* ⊕ *www. mainenarrowgauge.org* ✉ *Train $10 (includes admission), museum $3* ⊙ *May–Oct., daily 10–4 (last ride at 3); April, weekends 10–4 (also open daily Maine school break week).*

Portland Fish Exchange. You may want to hold your nose for this glimpse into the Old Port's active fish business when you drop by the 20,000-square-foot Portland Fish Exchange. Peek inside coolers teeming with cod, flounder, and monkfish and watch fishermen repairing nets outside. Auctions take place Sunday through Thursday at 11 am, and while these days most buyers bid online, you can follow the action on a computer screen in the lobby. The exchange opens at 7 and closes up around 3 or 4. ⊠ *6 Portland Fish Pier* ☎ *207/773–0017* ⊕ *www. pfex.org* ✉ *Free.*

Portland's busy harbor is full of working boats, pleasure craft, and ferries headed to the Casco Bay Islands.

THE ARTS DISTRICT

This district starts at the top of Exchange Street, near the upper end of the Old Port, and extends west past the Portland Museum of Art. Congress Street is the district's central artery. Art galleries, specialty stores, and a score of restaurants line Congress Street. Parking is tricky; two-hour meters dot the sidewalks, but there are several nearby parking garages.

TOP ATTRACTIONS

Children's Museum & Theatre of Maine. Touching is okay at Portland's small but fun Children's Museum, where kids can pretend they are lobstermen, veterinarians, shopkeepers, or actors in a play. Most exhibits, many of which have a Maine theme, are best for children 10 and younger. An outside pirate ship play area is a great play to have a picnic lunch, and don't miss the life-size inflatable humpback whale rising to the ceiling at the whale exhibit. Have a Ball! teaches about the science of motion, letting kids build ramps that make balls speed up, slow down and leap across tracks. Camera Obscura, an exhibit about optics, provides fascinating panoramic views of the city. It's aimed at adults and older children, so you can purchase a separate admission. ⊠ *142 Free St.* ☎ *207/828–1234* ⊕ *www.kitetails.org* ✉ *Museum $9; Camera Obscura only, $4* ⊘ *Memorial Day–Labor Day, Mon.–Sat. 10–5, Sun. noon–5; day after Labor Day–day before Memorial Day, Tues.–Sat. 10–5, Sun. noon–5.*

Longfellow House. The boyhood home of the famous American poet is the first brick house in Portland and the oldest building on the peninsula.

It's particularly interesting because most of the furnishings, including the young Longfellow's writing desk, are original. Wallpaper, window coverings, and a vibrant painted carpet are period reproductions. Built in 1785, the large dwelling (a third floor was added in 1815) sits back from the street and has a small portico over its entrance and four chimneys surmounting the roof. It's part of the Maine Historical Society, which includes an adjacent museum with exhibits about Maine life and a research library. After your guided tour, stay for a picnic in the Longfellow Garden; it's open to the public during museum hours. ⊠ *489 Congress St.* ☎ *207/774–1822* ⊕ *www.mainehistory.org* 🖅 *House and Maine Historical Society Museum $8; museum only, $5; garden, free* ☉ *House and museum, May–Oct., Mon.–Sat. 10–5, Sun. noon–5 (last house tour at 4); check for weekend and holiday hours in Nov. and Dec. Museum only: Nov.–April, Mon.–Sat. 10–5.*

★ **Portland Museum of Art.** Maine's largest public art institution's collection includes fine seascapes and landscapes by Winslow Homer, John Marin, Andrew Wyeth, Edward Hopper, Marsden Hartley, and other American painters. Homer's *Weatherbeaten,* a quintessential Maine Coast image, is here, and the museum owns and displays, on a rotating basis, 16 more of his paintings, plus more than 400 of his illustrations. In 2006, it bought the artist's mansard-roofed seaside studio on Prouts Neck in Scarborough; reservation-only 2½-hour tours depart from the museum in spring and fall. The museum has works by Monet and Picasso, as well as the Joan Whitney Payson Collection of impressionist and postimpressionist art, which includes works by Degas, Renoir, and Chagall. I. M. Pei designed the strikingly modern Charles Shipman Payson building, which fittingly displays modern art. The nearby L. D. M. Sweat Galleries showcase the collection of 19th-century American art. Special events are held in the gorgeous Federal-style 1801 McLellan House. ⊠ *7 Congress Sq.* ☎ *207/775–6148* ⊕ *www.portlandmuseum.org* 🖅 *$12, free Fri. 5–9* ☉ *Late May–mid-Oct., Mon.–Thurs. and weekends 10–5, Fri. 10–9. Closed Mon. late-Oct.–mid-May.*

★ **Victoria Mansion.** Built between 1858 and 1860, this Italianate mansion is widely regarded as the most sumptuously ornamented dwelling of its period remaining in the country. Architect Henry Austin designed the house for hotelier Ruggles Morse and his wife, Olive. The interior design—everything from the plasterwork to the furniture (much of it original)—is the only surviving commission of New York designer Gustave Herter. Behind the elegant brownstone exterior of this National Historic Landmark are colorful frescoed walls and ceilings, ornate marble mantelpieces, gilded gas chandeliers, a magnificent 6-foot-by-25-foot stained-glass ceiling window, and a freestanding mahogany staircase. Guided tours run about 45 minutes and cover all the architectural highlights. Victorian era–themed gifts and art are sold in the museum shop. ⊠ *109 Danforth St.* ☎ *207/772–4841* ⊕ *www. victoriamansion.org* 🖅 *$15* ☉ *May–Oct., Mon.–Sat. 10–4, Sun. 1–5; Christmas tours day after Thanksgiving–Jan. 3, daily 11–5.*

WHAT'S ON TAP: MICROBREWERIES

One of the nation's microbrew hotbeds, Maine is home to more than 30 breweries, and several of the larger ones—Allagash, Geary's, and Shipyard—are in and around Portland. These breweries are open for tours and tastings, but beer lovers may prefer the smaller brewpubs that make their own beer and serve it fresh from their own taps in neighborhood taverns. In the Old Port you'll find Gritty McDuff's and Sebago Brewing Company. In South Portland there's Sea Dog Brewing Company. If you're in town in November, check out the Maine Brewer's Festival (⊕ *www.mainebrew. com*). Pick up the Maine Beer Trail, a guide to Maine's breweries, at a local brew pub, or download it at the Maine Brewers' Guild website (⊕ *www.mainebrewersguild.org*).

WORTH NOTING

Eastern Promenade. Of the two promenades, this one, often overlooked by tourists, has by far the best view. Gracious Victorian homes, many now converted to condos and apartments, border one side of the street. On the other is 68 acres of hillside parkland that includes Ft. Allen Park and, at the base of the hill, the Eastern Prom Trail and tiny East End Beach and Boat Launch. On a sunny day the Eastern Prom is a lovely spot for picnicking and people-watching. ⊠ *From Washington St. south to end of Fore St. (becomes Eastern Promenade).*

Neal Dow Memorial. Now the headquarters of the Maine Women's Christian Temperance Union as well as a museum, this majestic 1829 Federal-style home is open for guided tours that start on the hour. The mansion, once a stop on the Underground Railroad, was the home of Civil War Gen. Neal Dow, who became known as the "Father of Prohibition." He was responsible for Maine's adoption of the antialcohol bill in 1851, which spurred a national movement. ⊠ *714 Congress St.* ☎ *207/773–7773* ⊕ *www.mewctu.org* ✉ *Free ($3 donation suggested)* ⊗ *Weekdays 11–4 or by appointment.*

Portland Observatory. This octagonal observatory on Munjoy Hill was built in 1807 by Captain Lemuel Moody, a retired sea captain, as a maritime signal tower. Moody used a telescope to identify incoming ships and flags to signal to merchants where to unload their cargo. Held in place by 122 tons of ballast, it's the last remaining historic maritime signal station in the country. The guided tour leads all the way to the dome, where you can step out on the deck and take in views of Portland, the islands, and inland towards the White Mountains. ⊠ *138 Congress St.* ☎ *207/774–5561* ⊕ *www.portlandlandmarks.org* ✉ *$8* ⊗ *Memorial Day weekend–Columbus Day, daily 10–5; Thurs. evening sunset tours mid-July–early Sept.*

10

OFF THE
BEATEN
PATH

Tate House Museum. Built astride rose granite steps and a period herb garden overlooking the Stroudwater River on the outskirts of Portland, this magnificent 1755 house was built by Captain George Tate. Tate had been commissioned by the English Crown to organize "the King's Broad Arrow"—the marking and cutting down of gigantic forest trees, which were shipped to England to be fashioned as masts for the British Royal Navy. The house has several period rooms, including a sitting room with some fine English Restoration chairs. With its clapboard still gloriously unpainted, its impressive Palladian doorway, dogleg stairway, unusual clerestory, and gambrel roof, this house will delight all lovers of Early American decorative arts. There are special holiday programs during December. The gift shop is open with limited hours off-season. ✉ *1267 Westbrook St.* 📞 *207/774–6177* ⊕ *www.tatehouse. org* 💲 *$8* ⊘ *Early June–early Oct., 9–4 Wed.–Sat. (last tour at 3), by appt. off-season.*

THE WEST END

A leisurely walk through Portland's West End, beginning at the top of the Arts District, offers a real treat to historic architecture buffs. The neighborhood, on the National Register of Historic Places, reveals an extraordinary display of architectural splendor, from High Victorian Gothic to lush Italianate, Queen Anne, and Colonial Revival.

A good place to start is at the head of the Western Promenade, which has benches and a nice view. From the Old Port, take Danforth Street all the way up to Vaughn Street; take a right on Vaughn and then an immediate left onto Western Promenade. Pass by the Western Cemetery, Portland's second official burial ground, laid out in 1829 (inside is the ancestral plot of famous poet Henry Wadsworth Longfellow), and look for street parking.

Greater Portland Landmarks. You could easily spend an hour or two wandering the backstreets of the West End; longer if you bring a picnic to enjoy in the grassy park alongside the Western Promenade. If you're interested in particular buildings, download or pick up a self-guided walking tour from Greater Portland Landmarks. The cost is $2, or $6 for all four of its Portland tours. ✉ *93 High St.* 📞 *207/774–5561* ⊕ *www.portlandlandmarks.org* ⊘ *Weekdays 9–5.*

WHERE TO EAT

Portland is blessed with exceptional restaurants rivaling those of a far larger city: in 2009 *Bon Appétit* declared it America's "Foodiest Small Town." Fresh seafood, including the famous Maine lobster, is still popular and prevalent, but there are plenty more cuisines to be enjoyed. More and more restaurants are using local meats, seafood, and organic and local produce as much as possible; changing menus reflect what is available in the region at the moment. As sophisticated as many of these establishments have become, the atmosphere is generally casual; with a few exceptions, you can leave your jacket and tie at home.

Smoking is banned in all restaurants, taverns, and bars in Maine. As always, reservations are recommended and allowed unless we state otherwise.

$$ ✕ **Becky's Diner.** You won't find a more local or unfussy place—or one
DINER that is more abuzz with conversation at 4 am—than this waterfront institution, way down on the end of Commercial Street. Sitting next to

Exchange Street, in the Old Port, is a popular place to explore for restaurants, shopping, and summer treats.

you at the counter or in a neighboring booth could be rubber-booted fishermen back from sea, college students soothing a hangover, or suited business folks with Blackberries. From the upstairs deck you can watch the working waterfront in action. The food is cheap, generous in proportion, and has that satisfying, old-time diner quality. Breakfast and lunch are served all day; dinner is available from 4 pm until closing. Nightly specials add to the large menu of fried seafood platters, salads, and sandwiches. Get a pie, cake, or pudding to go. $ *Average main: $14* ✉ *390 Commercial St.* ☎ *207/773–7070* ⊕ *www.beckysdiner.com.*

$ ✕ **Duckfat.** Even in midafternoon in March this small, hip sandwich shop in the Old Port's east end is packed. The folks who started well-known Hugo's restaurant down the street sold it to concentrate on serving everyday farm-to-table fare here. The signature Belgian fries are made with Maine potatoes cooked, yes, in duck fat, and served in paper cones. Sandwiches are made with panini bread; choices like tuna melt with Thai chili mayo change seasonally, but the meatloaf and BGT (bacon, tomato, goat cheese) are standards. There's also charcuterie. Drink choices include gelato milk shakes, French press coffee, lime-mint fountain sodas, beer, and wine. $ *Average main: $10* ✉ *43 Middle St.* ☎ *207/774–8080* ⊕ *www.duckfat.com* ⊘ *Reservations not accepted.*

MODERN
AMERICAN

$$$$ ✕ **Five Fifty-Five.** Classic dishes are cleverly updated at this classy Congress Street spot. The menu changes seasonally to reflect ingredients available from local waters, organic farms, and food purveyors, but seared local diver scallops, served in a buttery carrot-vanilla emulsion, are an exquisite mainstay. So is the mac and cheese, which boasts artisanal cheeses and shaved black truffle. You may also find dishes such as milk-braised rabbit with Himalayan red rice and lemon-dressed local

MODERN
AMERICAN
Fodor'sChoice
★

greens. You can try the $60 tasting menu, or come for Sunday brunch. The space, with exposed brick and copper accents, is a former 19th-century firehouse. A new sister restaurant, Petite Jacqueline bistro in Longfellow Square, has also earned accolades and fans. [$] *Average main: $29* ✉ *555 Congress St.* ☎ *207/761–0555* 🌐 *www.fivefifty-five.com* 🕒 *No lunch (Sunday brunch).*

$ PIZZA ★ 👶 🍴 **Flatbread.** Families, students, and bohemian types gather at this popular pizza place, known locally as Flatbread's. Two giant wood-fire ovens, where the pies are cooked, are the heart of the soaring, warehouselike space; in summer you can escape the heat by dining on the deck overlooking the harbor. The simple menu has eight signature pizzas plus weekly veggie and meat specials; everything is homemade, organic, and nitrate-free. Be sure to order the delicious house salad with toasted sesame seeds, seaweed, blue or goat cheese, and ginger-tamarind vinaigrette. Waits can be long on weekends and in summer, and there are no reservations for parties of less than 10, but you can call a half hour ahead to get on the waiting list. [$] *Average main: $10* ✉ *72 Commercial St.* ☎ *207/772–8777* 🌐 *www.flatbreadcompany.com.*

$$$$ MODERN AMERICAN ★ 🍴 **Fore Street.** One of Maine's best chefs, Sam Hayward, opened this restaurant in a renovated warehouse on the edge of the Old Port in 1996. The menu changes daily to reflect the freshest ingredients from Maine's farms and waters. Every copper-top table in the main dining room has a view of the enormous brick oven and soapstone hearth that anchor the open kitchen, where sous-chefs seem to dance as they create such dishes as turnspit-roasted dry-rubbed pork loin, wood-grilled Maine island land chop with sun-root purée, and Maine mussels oven-roasted in garlic and almond butter. Desserts include artisanal cheeses. In July or August, try to book reservations two months in advance, and a week or more at other times. But last-minute planners take heart: each night a third of the tables are reserved for walk-in diners. [$] *Average main: $30* ✉ *288 Fore St.* ☎ *207/775–2717* 🌐 *www.forestreet.biz* 🕒 *No lunch.*

$$ SEAFOOD ★ 🍴 **Gilbert's Chowder House.** This is the real deal, as quintessential as Maine dining can be. Clam rakes and nautical charts hang from the walls of this unpretentious waterfront diner. The flavors are from the depths of the North Atlantic, prepared and presented simply: fish, clam, and seafood chowders (corn, too); fried shrimp; haddock; clam strips; and extraordinary clam cakes. A chalkboard of daily specials often features fish-and-chips and various entrée and chowder combinations. Don't miss out on the lobster roll—a toasted hot-dog bun bursting with claw and tail meat lightly dressed with mayo but otherwise unadulterated. It's classic Maine, fuss-free and presented on a paper plate. [$] *Average main: $17* ✉ *92 Commercial St.* ☎ *207/871–5636* 🌐 *www.gilbertschowderhouse.com.*

$$$$ ECLECTIC ★ 🍴 **Hugo's.** James Beard Award–winning chef-owner Rob Evans turned stylish Hugo's into one of the city's best restaurants and sold it in 2012 to former staff. If you're adventurous, the eight-course "blind-tasting" menu ($90 per person) is a lot of fun—if you don't mind not knowing what you're going to be served. You also can mix and match $10 to $20 items from the à la carte menu, such as crispy skin pork belly and crepe-wrapped arctic char. Portions are small, as they're meant to be part of

a four- to six-course meal. Serving the freshest local organic foods is a high priority here, so the menu changes almost every day. Next door is a sister business, Eventide Oyster Co.; the setting and fare here is more casual. $ *Average main: $18* ⊠ *88 Middle St.* ☎ *207/774–8538* ⊕ *www. hugos.net* �》 *Closed Sun. and Mon. No lunch.*

$$$

MEDITERRANEAN

Fodor'sChoice

★

✕ **Local 188.** There's an infectious vibe at this eclectic Arts District eatery, which is a foodie hot spot but also a favorite place for locals to eat or come for a drink. The 2,000-square-foot space has lofty tin ceilings and worn maple floors. Mismatched chandeliers dangle over the dining area, and a pair of antlers crowns the open kitchen. Regulars chat with servers about what just-caught seafood will decorate the paella and which fresh local, organic veggies are starring in the tortillas, one of several tapas choices. You'll find entrées like Casco Bay hake with herb salsa verde, poached purple potatoes, smoked aioli, and beets. Reservations aren't taken for the large bar side. Many of the 10 or so draft brews are Maine-crafted; there are some 150 mostly European wines. $ *Average main: $22* ⊠ *685 Congress St.* ☎ *207/761–7909* ⊕ *www.local188.com* ☛ *No lunch weekdays; brunch on weekends.*

$$$

ECLECTIC

✕ **Walter's.** A fixture in the Old Port since the late 1980s and at its second locale, this relaxed, busy place with a chic modern interior is popular with suits and tourists alike. The seasonally changing menu nicely balances local seafood and meats with Asian and other international flavors. You'll find appetizers like calamari dressed with lemon and cherry pepper aioli and entrées such as crispy duck breast served with spaetzle, baby bok choy, and plum sauce. An inviting bar has a lighter menu; try the mussels or the Greek lamb sliders. $ *Average main: $26* ⊠ *2 Portland Sq.* ☎ *207/871–9258* ⊕ *www.waltersportland.com* ☛ *Closed Sun. No lunch Sat.*

WHERE TO STAY

As Portland's popularity as a vacation destination has increased, so have its options for overnight visitors. Though several large hotels—geared toward high-tech, amenity-obsessed guests—have been built in the Old Port, they have in no way diminished the success of smaller, more intimate lodgings. Inns and B&Bs have taken up residence throughout the West End, often giving new life to the grand mansions of Portland's 19th-century wealthy businessmen. For the least expensive accommodations, investigate the chain hotels near the Interstate and the airport.

Expect to pay from about $150 a night for a pleasant room (often with complimentary breakfast) within walking distance of the Old Port during high season, and more than $400 for the most luxurious of suites. In the height of the summer season many places are booked; make reservations well in advance, and ask about off-season specials.

For expanded hotel reviews, visit Fodors.com.

10

$$$$

B&B/INN

★

⌂ **Danforth Inn.** A stunning showpiece, the stylish decor at this convenient inn a short walk from downtown befits what was one of Portland's grandest Federal-style dwellings when it was built in 1823. **Pros:** basement billiards room; city views from cupola. **Cons:** small windows in some third-floor rooms. $ *Rooms from: $275* ⊠ *163 Danforth St.*

CLOSE UP

The Eastern Prom Trail

To experience the city's busy shoreline and grand views of Casco Bay, walkers, runners, and cyclists head out on the 2.1-mile Eastern Prom Trail.

Beginning at the intersection of Commercial and India streets, this paved trail runs along the water at the bottom of the Eastern Promenade, following an old rail bed and running alongside the still-used railroad tracks of the Maine Narrow Gauge Railroad Co. & Museum. There are plenty of places with benches and tables for a picnic break along the way. From the trailhead, it's about 1 mile to the small East End Beach.

Continuing along the trail, you'll pass underneath busy Interstate 295, and emerge at the Back Cove Trail, a popular 3½-mile loop you can connect with for a long trek. To return to the Old Port, backtrack along the trail or head up the steep path to the top of the promenade. Here you can continue along the promenade sidewalk or take the trails through this 68-acre stretch of parkland to the lovely picnic area and playground.

Continuing along the sidewalk toward the Old Port, a gazebo and several old cannons to your left indicate you're at the small Fort Allen Park. Use one of the coin-operated viewing scopes to view Civil War–era Ft. Gorges, which never saw action.

Where the Eastern Prom becomes Fore Street, continue on for a few blocks to India Street and take a left, which will bring you back to where you started. Or, continue into the Old Port.

Plan at least an hour to walk the trail with brief stops, or two if you continue along the Back Cove Trail. But if can, make time for the Prom—it's truly an urban jewel.

☎ 207/879–8755, 800/991–6557 🌐 www.danforthmaine.com 🛏 8 rooms 🍴 Breakfast.

$$$ B&B/INN 🏨 **Inn on Carleton.** Though operating for years, this West End inn was completely redone after it was sold in 2010 to the attentive resident innkeeper. **Pros:** most rooms have electric fireplaces; English garden with fountain. **Cons:** not an easy walk to the Old Port. [$] *Rooms from: $185 ✉ 46 Carleton St. ☎ 207/775–1910, 800/639–1770 🛏 6 rooms.*

$$ B&B/INN 🏨 **Morrill Mansion.** Portland's newest B&B has tastefully appointed rooms with well-executed color schemes: blue is a favorite accent color here. **Pros:** close to Arts District; parlors on each floor for relaxing. **Cons:** in West End but not on a grand block. [$] *Rooms from: $149 ✉ 249 Vaughan St. ☎ 207/774–6900 🌐 www.morrillmansion.com 🛏 6 rooms, 2 suites 🍴 Breakfast.*

$$$ B&B/INN Fodor's Choice ★ 🏨 **Pomegranate Inn.** The classic facade of this handsome 1884 Italianate in the architecturally rich Western Promenade area gives no hint of the surprises within. **Pros:** many rooms have gas fireplaces; close to Western Promenade. **Cons:** not an easy walk from Old Port. [$] *Rooms from: $189 ✉ 49 Neal St. ☎ 207/772–1006, 800/356–0408 🌐 www.pomegranateinn.com 🛏 7 rooms, 1 suite 🍴 Breakfast.*

$$$$ HOTEL ★ [icon] **Portland Harbor Hotel.** Making luxury its primary focus, the Harbor Hotel has become a favorite with business travelers seeking meetings on a more intimate scale and vacationing guests who want high-quality service and amenities, like the free shuttle service to local restaurants and sites. **Pros:** luxurious extras; amid the action of the Old Port and waterfront. **Cons:** lobby charms with fireplace but is on the small side. [$] *Rooms from: $229* ✉ *468 Fore St.* ☎ *207/775–9090, 888/798–9090* 🌐 *www.portlandharborhotel.com* 🛏 *87 rooms, 14 suites.*

$$$$ HOTEL [icon] **The Portland Regency Hotel & Spa.** Not part of a chain despite the "Regency" name, this brick building in the center of the Old Port was Portland's armory in the late 19th century. **Pros:** easy walk to sites; lots of room variety for a hotel. **Cons:** lower-than-standard ceilings in most rooms. [$] *Rooms from: $289* ✉ *20 Milk St.* ☎ *207/774–4200, 800/727–3436* 🌐 *www.theregency.com* 🛏 *85 rooms, 10 suites.*

NIGHTLIFE

Portland's nightlife scene is largely centered around the bustling Old Port and a few smaller, artsy spots on Congress Street. There's a great emphasis on local, live music and pubs serving award-winning local microbrews. Several hip wine bars have cropped up, serving appetizers along with a full array of specialty wines and whimsical cocktails. It's a fairly youthful scene in Portland, in some spots even rowdy and rough-around-the-edges, but there are plenty of places where you don't have to shout over the din to be heard.

The Big Easy. To see live local and national acts any night of the week, try the Big Easy. Everything from blues, jazz, and soul to Grateful Dead covers are played here. Occasionally closed on Sundays. ✉ *55 Market St.* ☎ *207/775–2266* 🌐 *www.bigeasyportland.com.*

Bull Feeney's. For nightly themed brew specials, plenty of Guinness, and live entertainment, head to Bull Feeney's, a lively two-story Irish pub and restaurant. ✉ *375 Fore St.* ☎ *207/773–7210.*

Gritty McDuff's Portland Brew Pub. Maine's original brewpub serves fine ales, British pub fare and seafood dishes. There's between six and eight ales on tap, and there's always a seasonal offering. Come on Tuesday and Saturday nights for live music. ✉ *396 Fore St.* ☎ *207/772–2739* 🌐 *www.grittys.com.*

Novare Res Bier Café. At tucked-away Novare Res Bier Café, choose from 33 rotating drafts and more than 300 bottled brews, relax on an expansive deck, and munch on antipasti or a meat and cheese plate. The Maine tap tower features eight of the state's microbrews; others are on the main tower along with beers from around the world. ✉ *4 Canal Plaza, off Exchange St. between Middle St. and Fore St.* ☎ *207/761–2437* 🌐 *www.novareresbiercafe.com.*

Rí Rá. Happening Irish pub and restaurant Rí Rá has live music Thursday through Saturday nights; for a mellower experience, settle into a couch at the upstairs bar. ✉ *72 Commercial St.* ☎ *207/761–4446* 🌐 *www.rira.com.*

Sonny's. In a landmark Victorian-era former bank with arched windows overlooking an Old Port square, this stylish bar and lounge packs in the late-night crowd. It has quite a list of cocktails, many using house-infused liquors—try the chili tequila. A funk-influenced band plays on Thursday; there's a DJ on Saturday. The Latin American cuisine is a winner, too. At night you can order lighter fare like a poblano cheeseburger with yam fries as well as entrées such as hangar steak and the braised-brisket enchilada. Food is served until 10:30 on weekends. ✉ *83 Exchange St.* ☎ *207/772–7774* ⊕ *www.sonnysportland.com.*

THE ARTS

Art galleries and studios have spread throughout the city, infusing with new life many abandoned yet beautiful old buildings and shops. Many are concentrated along the Congress Street downtown corridor; others are hidden amid the boutiques and restaurants of the Old Port and the East End. A great way to get acquainted with the city's artists is to participate in the First Friday Art Walk, a self-guided, free tour of galleries, museums, and alternative art venues that happens—you guessed it—on the first Friday of each month. Brochures and maps are available on the organization's website: ⊕ *www.firstfridayartwalk.com.*

Merrill Auditorium. Merrill Auditorium has numerous theatrical and musical events, including performances by the Portland Symphony Orchestra, Portland Ovations (performing arts), and Portland Opera Repertory Theatre. Every other Tuesday from mid-June to the end of August, organ recitals (suggested $15 donation) are given on the auditorium's huge 1912 Kotzschmar Memorial Organ. ✉ *20 Myrtle St.* ☎ *207/842–0800* ⊕ *www.porttix.com.*

Portland Stage. Portland Stage mounts theatrical productions from September to May on its two stages. ✉ *25-A Forest Ave.* ☎ *207/774–0465* ⊕ *http://www.portlandstage.com.*

Space Gallery. Space Gallery sparkles as a contemporary art gallery and alternative arts venue, opening its doors to everything from poetry readings to live music and play and documentary film showings. The gallery is open daily Wednesday through Saturday (unless shows are changing). Performances are typically in the evenings. ✉ *538 Congress St.* ☎ *207/828–5600* ⊕ *www.space538.org.*

SHOPPING

Exchange Street is great for arts and crafts and boutique browsing, while Commercial Street caters to the souvenir hound—gift shops are packed with nautical items, and lobster and moose emblems are emblazoned on everything from T-shirts to shot glasses.

ART AND ANTIQUES

Abacus. Abacus, an appealing crafts gallery, has gift items in glass, wood, and textiles, eclectic furniture, plus fine modern jewelry. ✉ *44 Exchange St.* ☎ *207/772–4880* ⊕ *www.abacusgallery.com.*

Gleason Fine Art. Gleason Fine Art exhibits sculpture and paintings by Maine and New England artists from the 19th to 21st centuries. Shows change monthly from May through October; the gallery is open by chance or appointment off-season. ⊠ *545 Congress St.* ☎ *207/699– 5599* ⊕ *www.gleasonfineart.com.*

Greenhut Galleries. Greenhut Galleries shows contemporary art by seasonal and year-round artists from Maine. Artists represented include David Driskell, an artist and leading African American art scholar. ⊠ *146 Middle St.* ☎ *207/772–2693, 888/772–2693* ⊕ *www. greenhutgalleries.com.*

Portland Architectural Salvage. A fixer-upper's dream, Portland Architectural Salvage has four floors of unusual reclaimed finds from old buildings, including fixtures, hardware, and stained-glass windows, and also assorted antiques. ⊠ *131 Preble St.* ☎ *207/780–0634* ⊕ *www. portlandsalvage.com.*

BOOKS
Longfellow Books. Longfellow Books is known for its good service and thoughtful literary collection. Both new and used books are sold. There's a little of everything here (you can order ebooks, too). Author readings are scheduled regularly. ⊠ *1 Monument Way* ☎ *207/772–4045* ⊕ *www.longfellowbooks.com.*

CLOTHING
Bliss. Hip boutique Bliss stocks T-shirts, dresses, jewelry, and accessories by cutting-edge designers, plus jeans by big names like J Brand and Mother. There's also a great selection of Frye boots. ⊠ *58 Exchange St.* ☎ *207/879–7125* ⊕ *www.blissboutiques.com.*

Hélène M. Photos of style icon Audrey Hepburn grace the walls of Hélène M., where you'll find classic, fashionable pieces by designers like Tory Burch, Diane von Furstenberg, and Rebecca Taylor. ⊠ *425 Fore St.* ☎ *207/772–2564* ⊕ *www.helenem.com.*

Material Objects. With an eclectic combination of good-quality consignment and new jewelry and clothing for both men and women, Material Objects makes for an affordable and unusual shopping spree. ⊠ *500 Congress St.* ☎ *207/774–1241.*

Sea Bags. At Sea Bags, totes made from recycled sailcloth and decorated with bright, graphic patterns are sewn right in the store. ⊠ *25 Custom House Wharf* ☎ *888/210–4244* ⊕ *www.seabags.com.*

HOUSEHOLD ITEMS/FURNITURE
Angela Adams. Maine islander Angela Adams specializes in simple but bold geometric motifs parlayed into dramatic rugs (custom, too), canvas totes, bedding, and other home accessories. The shop also carries sleek wood furniture from her husband's woodshop. ⊠ *273 Congress St.* ☎ *800/255–9454, 800/255–9454* ⊕ *www.angelaadams.com.*

10

SPORTS AND THE OUTDOORS

When the weather's good, everyone in Portland heads outside. There are also many green spaces nearby Portland, including Fort Williams Park, home to Portland Head Light; Crescent Beach State Park; and Two Lights State Park. All are on the coast south of the city in suburban Cape

CLOSE UP

Lobster Shacks

If it's your first time to the Maine Coast, it won't be long before you stumble upon the famous and quint-essential seaside eatery, the lobster shack. Also known as a lobster "pound," especially in other parts of New England, this humble establish-ment serves only two kinds of fresh seafood—lobster and clams. Lobster shacks are essentially wooden huts with picnic tables set around the waterfront. The menu is simplicity itself: steamed lobster or clams by the pound, or a lobster roll. Sides may include potato chips, coleslaw, or corn on the cob. Some pounds are even BYOB—no, not bring your own bib; those are usually provided—but bring your own beer or refreshments.

A lobster roll: perfection on a bun.

most important of all, a beautiful unob-structed view of working lobster boats in a scenic Maine harbor.

A few of our favorites sit on side-by-side piers right on Moscungus Bay: **Round Pond Fisherman's Coop.** ⊠ *25 Town Landing Rd., Round Pond* ☎ *207/529-5725.*

Moscungus Bay Lobster Co. ⊠ *28 Town Landing Rd., Round Pond* ☎ *207/529-5528* ⊕ *www. mainefreshlobster.com.*

Waterman's Beach Lobster. Waterman's Beach Lobster in South Thomaston is authentic, inexpensive, and scenic, overlooking islands in the Atlantic. You can eat lunch or dinner under the pavilions right next to the beach and pier, or get ever closer to the water at picnic tables. It's BYOB, and in addition to the seafood favorites, Waterman's also sells freshly baked pies and locally made ice cream. ⊠ *343 Waterman's Beach Rd., Thomaston* ☎ *207/596-7819, 207/594-7518* ⊕ *www. watermansbeachlobster.com.*

Maine Lobster Council. You can find out more about Maine lobster from the Maine Lobster Council. ⊠ *2 Union St., Suite 204, Portland* ☎ *207/541-9310* ⊕ *www.lobsterfrommaine.com.*

—Michael de Zayas

A signature item at a lobster shack is the lobster dinner. Although this can vary from pound to pound, it generally means the works: a whole steamed lobster, steamed clams, corn on the cob, and potato chips. If the lobster dinner sounds like a bit much, then go for the classic lobster roll, a buttered New England–style hot dog roll filled with chunks of lobster meat and a bit of mayo. Some pounds will serve it with lemon, some will serve it with butter, and some with even a touch of lettuce or herbs. Purists will serve no toppings at all (and why bother when the unadulterated taste of fresh, sweet lobster meat can't be beat). Most shacks will even have a tank with live lobsters; few will let you pick your own.

We can say this much: the best place to get a lobster dinner or lobster roll is at a shack, and the only authentic ones are right next to the water. There's a general sense that the "purest" pounds are the ones that are the simplest: a wooden shack, right on the water with wooden picnic tables, and perhaps

A traditional clambake may also include lobsters and corn. It's best enjoyed outside—just add drawn butter.

Elizabeth and offer walking trails, picnic facilities, and water access. Bradbury Mountain State Park, in Pownal, has incredible vistas from its easily climbed peak. In Freeport is Wolfe's Neck Woods State Park, where you can take a guided nature walk and see nesting ospreys. Both are north of Portland. ⇨ *Side Trips from Portland for more on these.*

BICYCLING

Bicycle Coalition of Maine. For state bike trail maps, club and tour listings, or hints on safety, contact the Bicycle Coalition of Maine. ⊠ *341 Water St., 10, Augusta* ☎ *207/623–4511* ⊕ *www.bikemaine.org.*

Cycle Mania. Rent bikes downtown at Cycle Mania. The rental rate is only $25 and includes a helmet and lock. ⊠ *59 Federal St.* ☎ *207/774–2933* ⊕ *www.cyclemania1.com.*

Gorham Bike and Ski. You can rent several types of bikes, including hybrid, tandem, and comfort bikes, starting at $25 per day. ⊠ *693 Congress St.* ☎ *207/773–1700* ⊕ *www.gorhambike.com.*

Portland Trails. For local biking information, contact Portland Trails. They can tell you about designated paved routes that wind along the water, through parks, and beyond. For a map, call or get one online. ⊠ *305 Commercial St.* ☎ *207/775–2411* ⊕ *www.trails.org.*

BOATING

Various Portland-based skippers offer whale-, dolphin-, and seal-watching cruises; excursions to lighthouses and islands; and fishing and lobstering trips. Board the ferry to see the nearby islands. Self-navigators can rent kayaks or canoes.

Casco Bay Lines. Casco Bay Lines operates the ferry service to the six bay islands with year-round populations. Summer offerings include music cruises, tours past lighthouses, and a trip to Bailey Island with a stop-over for lunch. ⊠ *Maine State Pier, 56 Commercial St.* ☎ *207/774–7871* ⊕ *www.cascobaylines.com.*

Lucky Catch Cruises. Lucky Catch Cruises sets out to sea in a real lobster boat so passengers can get the genuine experience, which includes haul-ing traps and the chance to purchase the catch. ⊠ *Long Wharf, 170 Commercial St.* ☎ *207/761–0941* ⊕ *www.luckycatch.com* ☉ *Memorial Day weekend–late Oct.*

Odyssey Whale Watch. Odyssey Whale Watch leads whale-watching and deep-sea–fishing trips, which run from mid-May to mid-October. Whale-watching trips are $48, 2.5-hour mackeral fishing trips $35, and six-hour cod fishing trips $69. ⊠ *Long Wharf, 170 Commercial St.* ☎ *207/775–0727* ⊕ *www.odysseywhalewatch.com.*

Portland Discovery Land & Sea Tours. For tours of the harbor and Casco Bay, including a trip to Eagle Island and an up-close look at several light-houses, try Portland Discovery Land & Sea Tours. ⊠ *Long Wharf, 170 Commercial St.* ☎ *207/774–0808* ⊕ *http://www.portlanddiscovery.com.*

Portland Schooner Co. Portland Schooner Co. offers daily windjammer cruises aboard the vintage schooners Bagheera and Wendameen. There are two-hour sails and also, on the Wendameen, overnight bed and breakfast trips. ⊠ *Maine State Pier, 56 Commercial St.* ☎ *207/766–2500* ⊕ *www.portlandschooner.com.*

HOT-AIR BALLOON RIDES

Hot Fun First Class Balloon Flights. Hot Fun First Class Balloon Flights flies mainly sunrise trips and can accommodate up to three people. The price of $300 per person includes a post-flight champagne toast, snacks, and shuttle to the lift-off site. ☎ *207/799–0193* ⊕ *www.hotfunballoons.com.*

SIDE TRIPS FROM PORTLAND

CASCO BAY ISLANDS

The islands of Casco Bay are also known as the Calendar Islands because an early explorer mistakenly thought there was one for each day of the year (in reality there are only some 140) These islands range from ledges visible only at low tide to populous Peaks Island, a suburb of Portland. Some are uninhabited; others support year-round com-munities as well as stores and restaurants. Fort Gorges commands Hog Island Ledge, and Eagle Island is the site of Arctic explorer Admiral Robert Peary's home. The brightly painted ferries of Casco Bay Lines are the islands' lifeline. There is frequent service to the most populated ones, including Peaks, Long, Little Diamond, and Great Diamond.

There is little in the way of overnight lodging on the islands; the popula-tion swells during the warmer months due to summer residents. There are few restaurants or organized attractions other than the natural beauty of the islands themselves. Meandering about by bike or on foot is a good way to explore on a day trip.

GETTING HERE AND AROUND

Casco Bay Lines provides ferry service from Portland to the islands of Casco Bay. The CAT, a stunning, modern high-speed ferry, travels between Portland and Yarmouth, Nova Scotia.

ESSENTIALS

Transportation Information Casco Bay Lines ☎ *207/774–7871* 🌐 *www.cascobaylines.com.*

CAPE ELIZABETH TO PROUTS NECK

EXPLORING

Fodor's Choice ★ **Portland Head Light.** Familiar to many from photographs and Edward Hopper's painting *Portland Head Light* (1927), this lighthouse was commissioned by George Washington in 1790. The towering white stone structure stands over the keeper's quarters, a white home with a blazing red roof, now the Museum at Portland Head Light. The lighthouse is in 90-acre Fort Williams Park, a sprawling green space with walking paths, picnic facilities, a beach and—you guessed it—a cool old fort. ✉ *Museum, 1000 Shore Rd., Cape Elizabeth* ☎ *207/799–2661* 🌐 *www.portlandheadlight.com* 🎟 *$2* 🕒 *Memorial Day–mid-Oct., daily 10–4; Apr., May, Nov., and Dec., weekends 10–4.*

WHERE TO EAT AND STAY

For expanded hotel reviews, visit Fodors.com.

$$$ SEAFOOD 🍴 **Joe's Boathouse.** The two simple dining rooms of this dockside establishment are finished in blues, with large windows looking out to a marina and Ft. Gorges. Favorites here include lobster fettuccine and seafood jambalaya; for lunch try the grilled-crab and avocado club or Asian-inspired crispy salmon salad. In summer, eat out on the patio. An in-between menu is served between 3 and 5—don't worry, you can always order steamed lobster. [$] *Average main: $24* ✉ *1 Spring Point Dr., South Portland* ☎ *207/741–2780* 🌐 *www.joesboathouse.com.*

$$ SEAFOOD 🍴 **The Lobster Shack at Two Lights.** You can't beat the location—right on the water, below the lighthouse pair that gives Two Lights State Park its name—and the food's not bad either. Enjoy fresh lobster whole or piled into a hot-dog bun with a dollop of mayo. Other menu must-haves include chowder, fried clams, and fish-and-chips. It's been a classic spot since the 1920s. Eat inside or out. [$] *Average main: $18* ✉ *225 Two Lights Rd., Cape Elizabeth* ☎ *207/799–1677* 🌐 *www.lobstershacktwolights.com* 🕒 *Closed late Oct.–late Mar.*

$$$$ RESORT 🏨 **Black Point Inn.** Toward the tip of the peninsula that juts into the ocean at Prouts Neck stands this stylish, tastefully updated 1878 resort inn with spectacular views up and down the coast. **Pros:** sleek geothermally heated pool; discounts near 25% in shoulder seasons. **Cons:** 18% "guest service charge" is tacked on to room rate. [$] *Rooms from: $480* ✉ *510 Black Point Rd., Scarborough* ☎ *207/883–2500* 🌐 *www.blackpointinn.com* 🛏 *20 rooms, 5 suites* 🕒 *Closed late Oct.–early May* 🍽 *Some meals.*

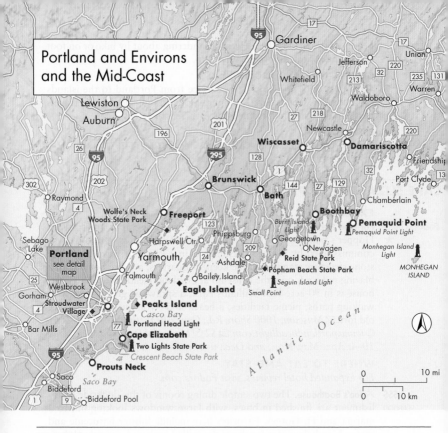

Portland and Environs
and the Mid-Coast

FREEPORT

17 miles north of Portland via Interstate 295.

Those who flock straight to L.L. Bean and see nothing else of Freeport are missing out. The city's charming backstreets are lined with historic buildings and old clapboard houses, and there's a pretty little harbor on the south side of the Harraseeket River. It's true, many who come to the area do so simply to shop—L.L. Bean is the store that put Freeport on the map, and plenty of outlets and some specialty stores have settled here. Still, if you choose, you can stay a while and experience more than fabulous bargains; beyond the shops are bucolic nature preserves with miles of walking trails and plenty of places for leisurely ambling that don't require the overuse of your credit cards.

GETTING HERE AND AROUND

Interstate 295 has three Freeport exits and passes by on the edge of the downtown area. U.S. 1 is Main Street here.

Freeport Historical Society. Pick up a village walking map and check out the historical exhibits at the Freeport Historical Society, located in Harrington House, a hybrid Federal- and Greek Revival-style home built in the 1830s. ⊠ *45 Main St.(U.S. 1)* ☎ *207/865–3170* ⊕ *www. freeporthistoricalsociety.org* ⊘ *Mon.–Fri. 10–5, Sat. 10–2.*

Pettengill Farm. The grounds of the Freeport Historical Society's salt-water Pettengill Farm—140 acres along Harraseeket River estuary, with trails, fields, orchards, and gardens—are open to the public. It's about a 15-minute walk from the parking area down a farm road to the circa 1800 saltbox farmhouse, which is open by appointment. Little changed since it was built, it has rare etchings (sgraffitti) of ships and sea monsters on three bedroom walls. There are no period displays. ⊠ *Pettengill Road* ✛ *From U.S. 1 in downtown Freeport, take Bow Street east 1½ miles, turn right on Pettengill Road, watch for sign* ⊕ *www.freeporthistoricalsociety.org* ☉ *Daily, dawn to dusk.*

SPORTS AND THE OUTDOORS

CLASSES **L.L. Bean Outdoor Discovery Schools.** It shouldn't come as a surprise that one of the world's largest outdoor outfitters also provides its customers with instructional adventures to go with its products. L.L. Bean's year-round Outdoor Discovery Schools offer courses in canoeing, shooting, biking, kayaking, fly-fishing, snowshoeing, cross-country skiing, and other outdoor sports. Depending on the activity, the flagship Freeport store offers $20 2.5-hour classes as well as half-, full-, and multi-day courses. ☎ *888/552–3261* ⊕ *www.llbean.com/ods.*

SHOPPING

Edgecomb Potters. Nationally known Edgecomb Potters produces vibrantly colored, hand-thrown porcelain tableware finished with an unusual crystalline glaze. It also sells jewelry, glassware, glass sculptures, and gifts for the home, almost all made by American artisans. ⊠ *8 School St.* ☎ *207/865–1705* ⊕ *www.edgecombpotters.com.*

Freeport Visitors Guide. *Freeport Visitors Guide* lists the more than 200 stores on Main Street, Bow Street, and elsewhere, including Coach, Brooks Brothers, Banana Republic, J. Crew, and Cole Haan. You can pick it up around town or at FreeportUSA, the local merchants association. ⊠ *23 Depot St.* ☎ *207/865–1212, 800/865–1994* ⊕ *www.freeportusa.com.*

Fodor's Choice **L.L. Bean.** Founded in 1912 as a mail-order merchandiser after its name-★ sake invented a hunting boot, L.L. Bean's giant flagship store attracts more than 3 million shoppers annually and is open 365 days a year in the heart of Freeport's outlet shopping district. You can still find the original hunting boots, along with cotton and wool sweaters; outerwear of all kinds; casual clothing, boots, and shoes for men, women, and kids; and camping equipment. Nearby are the company's home furnishings store, bike, boat, and ski store, and outlet. ⊠ *95 Main St. (U.S. 1)* ☎ *877/755–2326* ⊕ *www.llbean.com.*

R. D. Allen Freeport Jewelers. R. D. Allen Freeport Jewelers specializes in brightly colored tourmaline and other gemstones mined in Maine. Most of the pieces are the work of Maine artisans. Watermelon tourmaline is a specialty. ⊠ *13 Middle St.* ☎ *207/865–1818, 877/837–3835* ⊕ *www.rdallen.com.*

Thos. Moser Cabinetmakers. Famed local furniture company Thos. Moser Cabinetmakers sells artful, handmade wood pieces with clean, classic lines. The store has information on tours at the workshop half an hour away in Auburn. They are scheduled in the summer and by

10

appointment the rest of the year. ✉ *149 Main St.* ☎ *207/865–4519* 🌐 *www.thosmoser.com.*

NIGHTLIFE AND THE ARTS

L.L. Bean Summer Concert Series. Throughout the summer, L.L.Bean hosts free activities, including concerts, at L.L. Bean Discovery Park. It's set back from Main Street, along a side street that runs between the company's flagship and home furnishings stores. ✉ *95 Main St.* ☎ *877/755–2326* 🌐 *http://www.llbean.com/events.*

WHERE TO EAT AND STAY

For expanded hotel reviews, visit Fodors.com.

$$ SEAFOOD 🍴 **Harraseeket Lunch & Lobster Co.** Harraseeket Lunch & Lobster Co. Seafood baskets and lobster dinners are the focus at this popular, bare-bones place beside the town landing in South Freeport. Order at the counter, find a seat inside or out, and expect long lines in summer. [$] *Average main: $18* ✉ *On pier, 36 S. Main St., South Freeport* ☎ *207/865–4888* 🌐 *www.harraseeketlunchandlobster.com* ✍ *Reservations not accepted* 💳 *No credit cards* 🕒 *Closed mid-Oct.–Apr.*

$$$$ HOTEL Fodor's Choice ★ 🏨 **Harraseeket Inn.** Despite some modern appointments, including elevators, this large hotel has a country-inn ambience throughout. **Pros:** full breakfast and afternoon tea; outdoor fire pit; walk to shopping district. **Cons:** additions have diminished some authenticity. [$] *Rooms from: $235* ✉ *162 Main St.* ☎ *207/865–9377, 800/342–6423* 🌐 *www.harraseeketinn.com* 🛏 *82 rooms, 2 suites, 9 town houses* 🍽 *Breakfast.*

THE MID-COAST REGION

Lighthouses dot the headlands of Maine's Mid-Coast region, where thousands of miles of coastline wait to be explored. Defined by chiseled peninsulas stretching south from U.S. 1, this area has everything from the sandy beaches and sandbars of Popham Beach to the jutting cliffs of Monhegan Island. If you are intent on hooking a trophy-size fish or catching a glimpse of a whale, there are plenty of cruises available. If you want to explore deserted beaches and secluded coves, kayaks are your best bet. Put in at the Harpswells, or on the Cushing and Saint George peninsulas, or simply paddle among the lobster boats and other vessels that ply the waters here.

Tall ships often visit Maine, sometimes sailing up the Kennebec River for a stopover at Bath's Maine Maritime Museum, on the site of the old Percy & Small Shipyard. Next door to the museum, the Bath Iron Works still builds the U.S. Navy's Aegis-class destroyers.

Along U.S. 1, charming towns, each unique, have an array of attractions. Brunswick, while a bigger, commercial city, has rows of historic brick and clapboard homes and is home to Bowdoin College. Bath is known for its maritime heritage. Wiscasset has arguably the best antiques shopping in the state. On its waterfront you can choose from a variety of seafood shacks competing for the best lobster rolls. Damariscotta, too, is worth a stop for its lively main street and good seafood restaurants.

South along the peninsulas the scenery opens to glorious vistas of working lobster harbors and marinas. It's here you find the authentic lobster pounds where you can watch your catch come in off the traps. Boothbay Harbor is the quaintest town in the Mid-Coast and a busy tourist destination come summer, with lots of little stores that are perfect for window-shopping. It's one of three towns where you can take a ferry to Monhegan Island, which seems to be inhabited exclusively by painters at their easels, depicting the cliffs and weathered homes with colorful gardens.

ESSENTIALS

Visitor Information Southern Midcoast Maine Chamber ⊠ *Border Trust Business Center, 2 Main St., Topsham* ☎ *877/725–8797* ⊕ *www.midcoastmaine.com.* **State of Maine Visitor Information Center** ⊠ *1100 U.S. 1, take I–95, Exit 17, follow signs, Yarmouth* ☎ *207/846–0833, 888/624–6345* ⊕ *www.mainetourism.com.*

BRUNSWICK

10 miles north of Freeport via U.S. 1.

Lovely brick and clapboard buildings are the highlight of Brunswick's Federal Street Historic District, which includes Federal Street and Park Row and the stately campus of Bowdoin College. From the intersection of Pleasant and Maine streets, in the center of town, you can walk in any direction and discover an impressive array of restaurants. Seafood? German cuisine? A Chinese buffet that beats out all the competition? It's all here. So are bookstores, gift shops, boutiques, and jewelers.

Below Brunswick are Harpswell Neck and the more than 40 islands that make up the town of Harpswell, known collectively as the Harpswells. Route 123 runs down Harpswell Neck, where small coves shelter lobster boats, and summer cottages are tucked away among birch and spruce trees. On your way down from Cook's Corner to Land's End at the end of Route 24, you cross Sebascodegan Island. Heading east here leads to East Harpswell and Cundy's Harbor. Continuing straight south down 24 leads to Orr's Island. Stop at Mackerel Cove to see a real fishing harbor; there are a few parking spaces where you can stop to picnic and look for beach glass or put in your kayaks. Inhale the salt breeze as you cross the world's only cribstone bridge (designed so that water flows freely through gaps between the granite blocks) on your way to Bailey Island, home to a lobster pound made famous thanks in part to a Visa commercial.

10

GETTING HERE AND AROUND

From Interstate 295 take the Coastal Connector to U.S. 1 in Brunswick. From here Route 24 runs to Bailey Island and Route 123 down Harpswell Neck.

SPORTS AND THE OUTDOORS

★ **H2Outfitters.** The coast near Brunswick is full of hidden nooks and crannies waiting to be explored by kayak. H2Outfitters, at the southern end of Orr's Island just before the Cribstone Bridge, is the place in Harpswell to get on the water. It provides top-notch kayaking instruction and also offers half-day, full-day, bed-and-breakfast, and camping trips in

Low tide is the perfect time to explore tidal flats, tide pools, or fish from the shore at Popham Beach State Park.

the waters off its home base and elsewhere in Maine. ✉ *1894 Harpswell Island Road(Rte. 24), Orr's Island* ☎ *207/833–5257, 800/205–2925* 🌐 *www.h2outfitters.com.*

WHERE TO EAT

$$$ SEAFOOD Fodor's Choice ★ 🐤 🍴 **Cook's Lobster House.** What began as a lobster shack on Bailey's Island in 1955 has grown into a huge, internationally famous family-style restaurant with a small gift shop. The restaurant still catches its own fish and seafood, so you can count on the lobster casserole and the haddock sandwich to be delectable. Along with fame come prices; the shore dinners are $40-plus, and the most expensive include a 1¼-pound baked stuffed lobster with a choice of steamed mussels or clams or fried shrimp or clams, a choice of sides, and a bowl of fish chowder or lobster stew. But there's lots of less pricey fare, and a basic 1-pound lobster dinner is $20. Whether you choose inside or deck seating, you can watch the activity on the water as men check lobster pots and kayakers fan across the bay. [$] *Average main: $24* ✉ *68 Garrison Cove Rd., Bailey Island* ☎ *207/833–2818* 🌐 *www.cookslobster.com* ✍ *Reservations not accepted* ⏲ *Closed early Jan.–mid-Feb.*

BATH

11 miles north of Brunswick via U.S. 1.

Bath has been a shipbuilding center since 1607. The result of its prosperity can be seen in its handsome mix of Federal, Greek Revival, and Italianate homes along Front, Centre, and Washington streets. In the heart of Bath's historic district are some charming 19th-century homes, including the 1820 Federal-style home at 360 Front St., the 1810 Greek Revival–style mansion at 969 Washington St., covered with gleaming white clapboards, and the Victorian gem at 1009 Washington St., painted a distinctive shade of raspberry. All three operate as inns. An easily overlooked site is the town's City Hall. The bell in its tower was cast by Paul Revere in 1805.

The venerable Bath Iron Works completed its first passenger ship in 1890. During World War II, BIW—as it's locally known—launched a new ship every 17 days. It is still building today, turning out destroyers for the U.S. Navy. BIW is one of the state's largest employers, with about 5,600 workers. It's a good idea to avoid U.S. 1 on weekdays from 3:15 pm to 4:30 pm, when a major shift change takes place. You can tour BIW through the Maine Maritime Museum.

GETTING HERE AND AROUND

U.S. 1 passes through downtown and across the Kennebec River at Bath. Downtown is on the north side of the highway along the river.

EXPLORING

Fodor's Choice ★ **Maine Maritime Museum.** No trip to Bath is complete without a visit to this cluster of buildings that once made up the historic Percy & Small Shipyard. Plan on at least half a day—tickets are good for two days during any seven-day period because there's so much to see at this museum, which examines the world of shipbuilding and is the only way to tour Bath Iron Works (May to mid-October). From mid-June through Columbus Day, five nature and lighthouse boat tours cruise the scenic Kennebec River—one takes in 10 lights. The 142-foot Grand Banks fishing schooner *Sherman Zwicker* docks here during the same period and is included in the admission; others ships come for a time. Inside the main museum building, exhibits use ship models, paintings, photographs, and historical artifacts to tell the maritime history of the region. Also during the peak season, hour-long tours of the shipyard show how these massive wooden ships were built. In the boat shop, you can watch boatbuilders wield their tools. A separate historic building houses a fascinating lobstering exhibit. It's worth coming here just to watch the 18-minute video on lobstering written and narrated by E. B. White. Changing exhibits cover everything from fishing to maritime art to war. A gift shop and bookstore are on the premises, and you can grab a bite to eat in the café or bring a picnic to eat on the grounds. Kids ages five and younger get in free. ⊠ *243 Washington St.* ☎ *207/443–1316* ⊕ *www.mainemaritimemuseum.org* 🖃 *$15 (good for 2 days within 7-day period)* ☉ *Daily 9:30–5.*

10

OFF THE BEATEN PATH

Popham Beach State Park. Popham Beach State Park has bathhouses and picnic tables. At low tide you can walk several miles of tidal flats and also out to a nearby island, where you can explore tide pools or fish off the ledges. The park is on a peninsula facing the open Atlantic, between the mouths of the Kennebec and Morse rivers. ⊠ *10 Perkins Farm Lane, turn off Rte. 209, Phippsburg* ☎ *207/389–1335* ⊕ *www.parksandlands. com* 🖃 *$6* ☉ *Daily, 9 to sunset.*

Percy's Store. About a mile from Popham Beach State Park, the road ends at the Civil War–era Fort Popham State Historic Site, an unfinished semicircular granite fort on the sea. Just before the fort you can dine in and enjoy the beach views at Spinney's Restaurant, or grab a quick bite next door at Percy's Store, which has picnic tables and a path to the beach. It's a beautiful, secluded end-of-the-road locale. ✉ *6 Sea St.* ☎ *207/389–2010* 🌐 *www.percysstore.com*

WHERE TO EAT AND STAY

For expanded hotel reviews, visit Fodors.com.

$$ BARBECUE 🍴 **Beale Street Barbecue.** Ribs are the thing at Maine's oldest barbecue joint, opened in 1996. Hearty eaters should ask for one of the platters piled high with pulled pork, pulled chicken, or shredded beef. Fried calamari with habanero mayo and chili served with corn bread are popular appetizers. Enjoy a Maine microbrew at the bar while waiting for your table. [$] *Average main: $13* ✉ *215 Water St.* ☎ *207/442–9514* 🌐 *www.mainebbq.com.*

$$$$ RESORT Fodor's Choice ★ 🏨 **Sebasco Harbor Resort.** A destination family resort spread across 575 acres on the water near the foot of the Phippsburg Peninsula, the resort has a wide range of accommodations and a host of amenities. **Pros:** golf course; cottages good for families; kids' activities. **Cons:** no sand beach. [$] *Rooms from: $229* ✉ *29 Kenyon Rd., off Rte. 217, Phippsburg* ☎ *207/389–1161, 877/389–1161* 🌐 *www.sebasco.com* 🛏 *107 rooms, 8 suites, 23 cottages* ⏲ *Closed late Oct.–mid-May* 🍽 *Some meals.*

WISCASSET

10 miles north of Bath via U.S. 1.

Settled in 1663, Wiscasset sits on the banks of the Sheepscot River. It bills itself "Maine's Prettiest Village," and it's easy to see why: it has graceful churches, old cemeteries, and elegant sea captains' homes (many converted into antiques shops or galleries), and a good wine and specialty foods shop called Treats (stock up here if you're heading north).

Pack a picnic and take it down to the dock on Water Street, where you can watch the fishing boats or grab a lobster roll from Red's Eats or the lobster shack nearby. Wiscasset has expanded its wharf, and this is a great place to catch a breeze on a hot day. U.S. 1 becomes Main Street, and traffic often slows to a crawl come summer. You can walk to all galleries, shops, restaurants, and other attractions. ■ **TIP→ You'll likely have success if you try to park on Water Street rather than Main.**

SHOPPING

Edgecomb Potters. Not to be missed is Edgecomb Potters, which makes vibrantly colored, exquisitely glazed porcelain that is nationally known. Its store also carries jewelry, glassware, glass sculptures, and gifts for the home, almost all made by American artisans. ✉ *727 Boothbay Rd., Edgecomb* ☎ *207/882–9493* 🌐 *www.edgecombpotters.com.*

Sheepscot River Pottery. Sheepscot River Pottery boasts beautifully glazed kitchen tiles as well as kitchenware and home accessories, including sinks. Jewelry and other items by Maine artisans are also sold. ✉ *34 U.S. 1, Edgecomb* ☎ *207/882–9410* 🌐 *www.sheepscot.com.*

At the Maine Maritime Museum, a boatbuilder works on a yacht tender, used to ferry people to shore.

WHERE TO EAT

$

FAST FOOD

✕ **Red's Eats.** You've probably driven right past this little red shack on the Wiscasset side of the bridge if you've visited this area and seen the long line of hungry customers. Red's is a local landmark famous for its hamburgers, hot dogs, lobster and crab rolls, and crispy onion rings and clams fried in their own housemade batters. Maine-made Round Top ice cream is also sold (try blueberry or black raspberry). Enjoy views of the tidal Sheepscot River from picnic tables on the two-level deck or down on the grass by the water. $ *Average main: $12* ✉ *41 Water St.* ☎ *207/882–6128* ⌕ *Reservations not accepted* ▭ *No credit cards* ⊘ *Closed mid-Oct.–mid-Apr.*

10

OFF THE
BEATEN
PATH

The town of Boothbay includes the village center, Boothbay Harbor, as well as East Boothbay. The shoreline of the Boothbay Peninsula is a craggy stretch of inlets where pleasure craft anchor alongside trawlers and lobster boats. Boothbay Harbor is like a smaller version of Bar Harbor—touristy but friendly and fun—with pretty, winding streets and lots to explore. Commercial Street, Wharf Street, Townsend Avenue, and the By-Way are lined with shops and ice-cream parlors.

In season, boat trips to Monhegan Island leave from the piers off Commercial Street. Drive out to Ocean Point in East Boothbay for some incredible scenery. Boothbay is 13 miles south of Wiscasset via U.S. 1 and Route 27.

Coastal Maine Botanical Garden. You can browse for hours in the trinket shops, crafts galleries, clothing stores, and boutiques around the harbor or take a walk around the 248-acre Coastal Maine Botanical Garden

Continued on page 714

MAINE'S LIGHTHOUSES
GUARDIANS OF THE COAST   By John Blodgett

Perched high on rocky ledges, on the tips of wayward islands, and sometimes seemingly on the ocean itself are the more than five dozen lighthouses standing watch along Maine's craggy and ship-busting coastline.

Marshall Point Light

LIGHTING THE WAY: A BIT OF HISTORY

Portland Head Light

Most lighthouses were built in the first half of the 19th century to protect the vessels from running aground at night or when the shoreline was shrouded in fog. Along with the mournful siren of the foghorn and maritime lore, these practical structures have come to symbolize Maine throughout the world.

SHIPWRECKS AND SAFETY

These alluring sentinels of the eastern seaboard today have more form than function, but that certainly was not always the case. Safety was a strong motivating factor in the erection of the lighthouses. Commerce also played a critical role. For example, in 1791 Portland Head light was completed, partially as a response to local merchants' concerns about the rocky entrance to Portland Harbor and the varying depths of the shipping channel, but approval wasn't given until a terrible accident in 1787 in which a 90-ton sloop wrecked. In 1789, the federal government created the U.S. Lighthouse Establishment (later the U.S. Lighthouse Service) to manage them. In 1939 the U.S. Coast Guard took on the job.

Some lighthouses in Maine were built in a much-needed venue, but the points and islands upon which they sat were prone to storm damage. Along with poor construction, this meant that over the years many lighthouses had to be rebuilt or replaced.

LIGHTHOUSES TODAY

In modern times, many of the structures still serve a purpose. Technological advances, such as GPS and radar, are mainly used to navigate through the choppy waters, but a lighthouse or its foghorns are helpful secondary aids, and sometimes the only ones used by recreational boaters. The numerous channel-marking buoys still in existence also are testament to the old tried-and-true methods.

Of the 66 lighthouses along this far northeastern state, 52 are still working, alerting ships (and even small aircraft) of the shoreline's rocky edge. Government agencies, historic preservation organizations, and mostly private individuals own the decommissioned lights.

KEEPERS OF THE LIGHT

Some keepers also used bells and sirens, like this Fog Signal Station on Manana Island in 1898.

Pemaquid Point's fourth-order Fresnel lens

LIFE OF A LIGHTKEEPER

One thing that has changed with the modern era is the disappearance of the lighthouse keeper. In the early 20th century, lighthouses began the conversion from oil-based lighting to electricity. A few decades later, the U.S. Coast Guard switched to automation, phasing out the need for an on-site keeper.

While the keepers of tradition were no longer needed, the traditions of these stalwart, 24/7 employees live on through museum exhibits and retellings of Maine's maritime history, legends, and lore. The tales of a lighthouse keeper's life are the stuff romance novels are made of: adventure, rugged but lonely men, and a beautiful setting along an unpredictable coastline.

The lighthouse keepers of yesterday probably didn't see their own lives so romantically. Their daily narrative was one of hard work and, in some cases, exceptional solitude. A keeper's primary job was to ensure that the lamp was illuminated all day, every day. This meant that oil (whale or coal oil and later kerosene) had to be carried about and wicks trimmed on a regular basis. When fog shrouded the coast, they sounded the solemn horn to pierce through the damp darkness that hid their light. Their quarters were generally small and often attached to the light tower itself. The remote locations of the lights added to the isolation a keeper felt, especially before the advent of radio and telephone, let alone the Internet. Though some brought families with them, the keepers tended to be men who lived alone.

THE LIGHTS 101

Over the years, Fresnel (fray-NELL) lenses were developed in different shapes and sizes so that ship captains could distinguish one lighthouse from another. Invented by Frenchman Augustin Fresnel in the early 19th century, the lens design allows for a greater transmission of light perfectly suited for lighthouse use. Knowing which lighthouse they were near helped captains know which danger was present, such as a submerged ledge or shallow channel. Some lights, such as those at Seguin Island Light, are fixed and don't flash. Other lights are colored red.

DID YOU KNOW?

A lighthouse's personality shines through its flash pattern. For example, Bass Harbor Light (pictured) blinks red every four seconds. Some lights, such as Seguin Island Light, are fixed and don't flash.

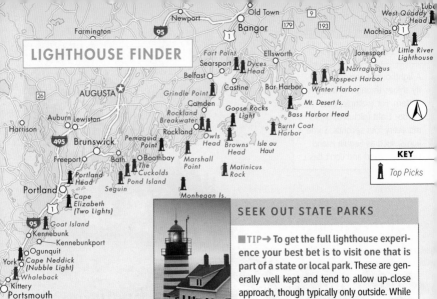

Lubec
West Quoddy Head
Old Town
Newport
Bangor
Farmington
Machias
95
179
9
193
1
Little River Lighthouse
Fort Point
Ellsworth
Jonesport
Searsport
Dyces Head
Belfast
Narraguagus
Prospect Harbor
AUGUSTA
Castine
Bar Harbor
Winter Harbor
26
Grindle Point
Mt. Desert Is.
Camden
Goose Rocks Light
Bass Harbor Head
Auburn Lewiston
Rockland Breakwater
Harrison
Rockland
Burnt Coat Harbor
495
Brunswick
Pemaquid Point
Owls Head
Browns Head
Isle au Haut
Freeport
Bath
Boothbay
Marshall Point
The Cuckolds
Matinicus Rock
Portland Head
Pond Island
Seguin
Portland
Monhegan Is.
Cape Elizabeth (Two Lights)
95
Goat Island
Kennebunk
Kennebunkport
Ogunquit
York
Cape Neddick (Nubble Light)
Whaleback
Kittery
Portsmouth

KEY

Top Picks

West Quoddy Head

SEEK OUT STATE PARKS

■ TIP➔ To get the full lighthouse experience your best bet is to visit one that is part of a state or local park. These are generally well kept and tend to allow up-close approach, though typically only outside. While you're at the parks you can picnic or stroll on the trails. Wildlife is often abundant in and near the water; you might spot sea birds and even whales in certain locations (try West Quoddy Head, Portland Head, or Two Lights).

VISITING MAINE'S LIGHTHOUSES

As you travel along the Maine Coast, you won't see lighthouses by watching your odometer—there were no rules about the spacing of lighthouses. The decision as to where to place a lighthouse was a balance between a region's geography and its commercial prosperity and maritime traffic.

Lighthouses dot the shore from as far south as York to the country's easternmost tip at Lubec. Accessibility varies according to location and other factors. A handful are so remote as to be outright impossible to reach (except perhaps by kayaking and rock climbing). Some don't allow visitors according to Coast Guard policies, though you can enjoy them through the zoom lens of a camera. Others you can walk right up to and, occasionally, even climb to the top. Lighthouse enthusiasts and preservation groups restore and maintain many of them. All told, approximately 30 lighthouses allow some sort of public access.

MUSEUMS, TOURS, AND MORE

Most keeper's quarters are closed to the public, but some of the homes have been converted to museums, full of intriguing exhibits on lighthouses, the famous Fresnel lenses used in them, and artifacts of Maine maritime life in general. Talk to the librarians at the **Maine Maritime Museum** in Bath (⊕ *www.mainemaritimemuseum.org*) or sign up for one of the museum's daily lighthouse cruises to pass by no fewer than ten on the Lighthouse Lovers Cruise. In Rockland, the **Maine Lighthouse Museum** (⊕ *www.mainelighthousemuseum.org*) has the country's largest display of Fresnel lenses. The museum also displays keepers' memorabilia, foghorns, brassware, and more. Maine Open Lighthouse Day is the third Saturday in September; you can tour and even climb lights usually closed to the public.

For more information, check out the lighthouse page at Maine's official tourism site: ⊕ *www.visitmaine.com/attractions/sightseeing_tours/lighthouse.*

SLEEPING LIGHT: STAYING OVERNIGHT

Goose Rocks, where you can play lighthouse keeper for a week.

Want to stay overnight in a lighthouse? There are several options to do so. ■ TIP → Book lighthouse lodgings as far in advance as possible, up to one year ahead.

Our top pick is **Pemaquid Point Light** (*Newcastle Square Vacation Rentals* ☎ *207/563–6500* ⊕ *www.mainecoast-cottages.com*) because it has one of the most dramatic settings on the Maine coast. Two miles south of **New Harbor**, the second floor of the lighthouse keeper's house is rented out on a weekly basis early May through mid-November to support upkeep of the grounds. When you aren't enjoying the interior, head outdoors: the covered front porch has a rocking-chair view of the ocean. The one-bedroom, one-bath rental sleeps up to a family of four.

Situated smack dab in the middle of a major maritime thoroughfare between two Penobscot Bay islands, **Goose Rocks Light** (☎ *207/867–4747* ⊕ *www.beacon-preservation.com*) offers lodging for the adventuresome—the 51-foot "spark plug" lighthouse is completely surrounded by water. Getting there requires a ferry ride from Rockland to nearby **North Haven**, a 5- to 10-minute ride by motorboat, and then a climb up an iron-rung ladder from the pitching boat—all based on high tide and winds, of course. There's room for up to eight people. It's a bit more cushy experience than it was for the original keepers: there's a flat-screen TV with DVD player and a selection of music and videos for entertainment. In addition, a hammock hangs on the small deck that encircles the operational light; it's a great place from which to watch the majestic windjammers and the fishing fleet pass by.

Little River Lighthouse (☎ *207/259–3833* ⊕ *www.littleriverlight.org*), along the far northeastern reaches of the coast in **Cutler**, has three rooms available for rent in July and August. You're responsible for food and beverages, linens, towels, and other personal items (don't forget the bug spray), but kitchen and other basics are provided. The lighthouse operators will provide a boat ride to the island upon which the lighthouse sits.

TOP LIGHTHOUSES TO VISIT

BASS HARBOR LIGHT

One Maine lighthouse familiar to many because it is the subject of countless photographs is Bass Harbor Light, at the southern end of **Mount Desert Island.** It is within Acadia National Park and 17 miles from the town of Bar Harbor. The station grounds are open year-round, but the former keeper's house is now a private home for a Coast Guard family. This lighthouse is so close to the water it seems as if a blustery wind could tip it over the rocks right into the North Atlantic. ■ TIP➜ To photograph Bass Harbor, get up close, or walk a short trail for a horizontal shot of the lighthouse and its outbuildings. Also use a tripod or stand firm in the salted wind.

Bass Harbor

CAPE ELIZABETH LIGHT

Two Lights State Park, is so-named because it's next to two lighthouses. Both of these **Cape Elizabeth** structures were built in 1828, the first twin lighthouses to be erected on the Maine coast. The western light was converted into a private residence in 1924; the eastern light, Cape Elizabeth Light, still projects its automated cylinder of light 17 mi out to sea, from a height of 129 feet, and is the subject of Edward Hopper's *Lighthouse at Two Lights* (1929). The grounds immediately surrounding the building and the lighthouse itself are closed to the public, but the structure is easily viewed and photographed from nearby at the end of Two Lights Road. Explore the tidal pools for the small snails known as periwinkles. ■ TIP➜ If it's foggy, don't stand too close to the foghorn, and in season (late March through late October) be sure to eat a lobster roll at the Lobster Shack Restaurant—but do not feed the seagulls; you will be publicly chastised on the restaurant's loudspeaker if you do.

Two Lights, Eastern Light

CAPE NEDDICK LIGHT

More commonly known as Nubble Light for the smallish offshore expanse of rock it rests upon, Cape Neddick Light sits a few hundred feet off a rock point in **York Beach.** With such a precarious location, its grounds are inaccessible to visitors, but close enough to be exceptionally photogenic, especially during the Christmas season when the Town of York hangs Christmas lights and wreaths from the lighthouse and its surrounding buildings (Santa Claus makes an appearance via lobster boat at the annual lighting celebration). It's right across and easily viewed from Sohier Park, which has a seasonal information center. Notice that it emits a red light.

Cape Neddick

MONHEGAN ISLAND LIGHT

Only the adventuresome and the artistic see this light, because **Monhegan Island**, known both for its fishing and artistic communities, is accessible by an approximately one-hour ferry ride. To reach the lighthouse, you have an additional half-mile walk uphill from the ferry dock. But it's well worth the effort, especially if you enjoy island life—it's nothing but the rugged North Atlantic out here. The light was automated back in 1959, and since the early 1960s the former keeper's quarters has been home to the Monhegan Museum, which has exhibits about the island more so than the lighthouse. The tower itself is closed to the public. ■TIP→ If you've made it this far, stay a quiet night at one of a handful of lodging options on the island, lulled to sleep by muffled waves and the distance from the mainland.

Monhegan Island

PORTLAND HEAD LIGHT

The subject of Edward Hopper's painting *Portland Head-Light* (1927) and one of Maine's most photographed lighthouses (and its oldest), the famous Portland Head Light was completed in January 1791. Its first keeper, Revolutionary War veteran Captain Joseph Greenleaf, was appointed by George Washington. At the edge of Fort Williams Park, in **Cape Elizabeth**, the towering white stone lighthouse stands 101 feet above the sea. The United States Coast Guard operates it and it is not open for tours (except on Maine Open Lighthouse Day in September). However the adjacent keeper's dwelling, built in 1891, is now a museum, where you can inspect various lenses used in lighthouses. Visitors can also explore the numerous trails within the park, as well as its grassy areas, popular for picnics, kite flying, and watching ships from around the globe enter Portland Harbor.

Portland Head

WEST QUODDY HEAD LIGHT

Originally built in 1808 by mandate of President Thomas Jefferson, West Quoddy Head Light sits in **Lubec** on the easternmost tip of land in the mainland United States—so far east that at certain times of the year it's the first object in the country to be touched by the rising sun's rays. The 49-foot-high lighthouse, now famously painted with distinctive red and white candy stripes, is part of 541-acre Quoddy Head State Park, which has some of the state's best wildlife watching, including humpback, minke, and finback whales. Learn more in the lightkeeper's house-turned-museum. You can't climb the 50 steps to the top of the tower, but the museum shows a video of the interior.

West Quoddy Head

✉ *132 Botanical Gardens Drive, from Rte. 27 turn on Barters Island Rd.* ☎ *207/633–4333* ⊕ *www.mainegardens.org* 🎫 *$12.*

DAMARISCOTTA

8 miles north of Wiscasset via U.S. 1.

The Damariscotta region comprises several communities along the rocky coast. The town itself sits on the water and is a lively place filled with attractive shops and restaurants.

A few minutes' walk across the bridge over the Damariscotta River is the town of Newcastle, between the Sheepscot and Damariscotta rivers. Newcastle was settled in the early 1600s. The earliest inhabitants planted apple trees, but the town later became an industrial center, home to several shipyards and a couple of mills. The oldest Catholic church in New England, St. Patrick's, is here, and it still rings its original Paul Revere bell.

Bremen, which encompasses more than a dozen islands and countless rocky outcrops, has many seasonal homes along the water, and the main industries in the small community are fishing and clamming. Nobleboro, a bit north of here on U.S. 1, was settled in the 1720s by Colonel David Dunbar, sent by the British to rebuild the fort at Pemaquid. Neighboring Waldoboro is situated on the Medomak River and was settled largely by Germans in the mid-1700s. You can still visit the old German Meeting House, built in 1772. The Pemaquid Peninsula stretches south from Damariscotta to include Bristol, South Bristol, Round Pond, New Harbor, and Pemaquid.

GETTING HERE AND AROUND

In Newcastle, U.S. 1B runs from U.S. 1 across the Damariscotta River to Damariscotta. From this road take Route 129 south to South Bristol and Route 130 south to Bristol and New Harbor. From here you can return to U.S. 1 heading north on Route 32 through Round Pond and Bremen. In Waldoboro, turn off U.S. 1 on Jefferson Street to see the historic village center.

ESSENTIALS

Visitor Information **Damariscotta Region Chamber of Commerce** ☎ *207/563–8340* ⊕ *www.damariscottaregion.com.*

WHERE TO EAT AND STAY

For expanded hotel reviews, visit Fodors.com.

$$

AMERICAN

★

✕ **King Eider's Pub & Restaurant.** The classic pub right downtown bills itself as having the finest crab cakes in New England. Start with fresh local oysters and move on to entrées like seafood potpie, barbecued salmon topped with tomato vinaigrette, or a hand-cut steak, which you may also find on the daily chalkboard specials. With exposed brick walls and low wooden beams, it's a cozy place to enjoy your favorite ale. There is also seating on the deck, where you can see the Damariscotta River in the distance. Stop by on Thursday nights for live music. $ *Average main: $17* ✉ *2 Elm St.* ☎ *207/563–6008* ⊕ *www.kingeiderspub.com* 🍴 *Reservations essential.*

Lobster trap buoys are popular decorations in Maine; the markings represent a particular lobsterman's claim.

$$$ B&B/INN **Newcastle Inn.** A riverside location, tasteful decor, and lots of common areas (inside and out) make this a relaxing country inn. **Pros:** guests can order beer or wine; one suite-like room and two suites with sitting areas. **Cons:** not an in-town location. *Rooms from: $190 ✉ 60 River Rd., Newcastle ☎ 207/563–5685 🌐 www.newcastleinn.com 12 rooms, 2 suites 🍴 Breakfast.*

PEMAQUID POINT

10 miles south of Damariscotta via U.S. 1, U.S. 1B, and Route 130.

Pemaquid Point is the tip of the Pemaquid Peninsula, bordered by Muscongus and Johns bays. It's home to the famous lighthouse of the same name and its attendant fog bell and tiny museum. Also at the bottom on the peninsula, along the Muscongus Bay is the Nature Conservancy's Rachel Carson Salt Pond Preserve.

GETTING HERE AND AROUND

From U.S. 1, take U.S. 1B into Damariscotta and head south on Route 130 to Pemaquid Pt.

EXPLORING

★ **Pemaquid Point Light.** At the end of Route 130, this lighthouse at the tip of the Pemaquid Peninsula looks as though it sprouted from the ragged, tilted chunk of granite that it commands. Most days in the summer you can climb the tower to the light. The former keeper's cottage is now the Fishermen's Museum, which displays historic photographs, scale models, and artifacts that explore commercial fishing in Maine. Also here are the original fog bell and bell house. Pemaquid Art Gallery, on-site, mounts exhibitions by area artists in the summer. The museum is included in the $2 fee to be on the lighthouse property, a Bristol town park, during business hours in-season. There are restrooms and picnic tables. ✉ *3115 Bristol Rd. (Rte. 130), Pemaquid* ☎ *207/677–2492* 🌐 *www.bristolparks.org* 🕒 *Park: Daily (no fee off-season and when museum is closed in-season). Museum: Early May–Oct. daily 9–5.*

SPORTS AND THE OUTDOORS

CRUISES **Hardy Boat Cruises.** You can take a cruise to Monhegan (May through October) with Hardy Boat Cruises. It also offers seal and puffin watching trips and lighthouse and fall coastal cruises. ✉ *Shaw's Wharf, 132 State Rte. 32, New Harbor* ☎ *207/677–2026, 800/278–3346* 🌐 *www.hardyboat.com.*

WHERE TO STAY

For expanded hotel reviews, visit Fodors.com.

$$ B&B/INN 🏨 **Christmas Cove Inn.** If you're traveling with a dog, you'll find few more accommodating spots in Maine than this out-of-the-way place on Rutherford Island. **Pros:** great if you're traveling with dogs; long views of Pemaquid on clear days from lookout. **Cons:** dogs on premises. [$] *Rooms from: $140* ✉ *53 Coveside Rd., South Bristol* ☎ *207/644–1502, 866/644–1502* 🌐 *www.christmascoveinn.com* 🛏 *6 rooms* 🍴 *Breakfast.*

THOMASTON

10 miles northeast of Waldoboro, 72 miles northeast of Portland.

Thomaston is a delightful town, full of beautiful sea captains' homes and dotted with antiques and specialty shops. A National Historic District encompasses parts of High, Main, and Knox streets. The town is the gateway to the two peninsulas; you will see water on both sides as you arrive.

GETTING HERE AND AROUND

U.S. 1 is Main Street through Thomaston. Route 131 runs down the St. George Peninsula from here and Route 97 leads down the Cushing Peninsula and to Friendship.

WHERE TO EAT

$ AMERICAN ★ ✕ **Thomaston Cafe.** Here is a must-stop on the long, slow drive up U.S. 1. Works by local artists adorn the walls of this small downtown café, which uses local ingredients as much as possible. They serve an excellent breakfast, including homemade corned beef hash. For lunch there are scrumptious haddock chowder and delicious sandwiches. Try the pan-fried haddock sandwich lightly breaded with panko breadcrumbs, or a salad and crab cakes (sold at breakfast, too). Sunday brunch is served, and dinner on Friday and Saturday. Entrées include lobster ravioli and filet mignon with béarnaise sauce. [$] *Average main: $9* ✉ *154 Main St. (U.S. 1)* ☎ *207/354–8589* 🌐 *www.thomastoncafe.com* 🕒 *No dinner Sun.–Thurs.*

TENANTS HARBOR

10 miles south of Thomaston.

Tenants Harbor is a quintessential coastal harbor—dominated by lobster boats, its shores are rocky and slippery, and its village streets are lined with clapboard houses, a church, and a general store. It's a favorite with artists, and galleries and studios welcome browsers.

GETTING HERE AND AROUND

From U.S. 1 in Thomaston, Rte. 131 heads down the St. George Peninsula to Tenant's Harbor and continues all the way to Port Clyde at the tip.

PORT CLYDE

5 miles south of Tenants Harbor via Rte. 131.

The fishing village of Port Clyde sits at the end of the St. George Peninsula. The road leading here meanders along the St. George River, passing meadows and farmhouses and winding away from the river to the east side of the peninsula, which faces the Atlantic Ocean. Shipbuilding and granite quarrying were big industries here in the 1800s. Later seafood canneries opened here; you can still buy Port Clyde sardines. Lobster fishing is an economic anchor today, and the quiet village is a haven for artists, with a number of galleries. Marshall Point Lighthouse, right in the harbor, has a small museum.

MONHEGAN ISLAND

East of Pemaquid Peninsula, 10 miles south of Port Clyde by boat.

Fodor's Choice ★ Simple and artful living is the order of the day on remote Monhegan Island. To get here you'll need to take a ferry. A tiny hamlet greets you at the harbor. There are no paved roads, and everywhere you look artists stand before their canvases, rendering the landscape of serene gardened cottages and rugged coast.

The island was known to Basque, Portuguese, and Breton fishermen well before Christopher Columbus discovered America. About a century ago, Monhegan was discovered again by some of the finest American painters, including Rockwell Kent, Robert Henri, A.J. Hammond, and Edward Hopper, who sailed out to paint its open meadows, savage cliffs, wild ocean views, and fishermen's shacks. Tourists followed, and now three excursion boats dock here for a few hours each day in the warm months when harbor shops and artist studios bustle with activity.

You can escape the crowds on the island's 17 miles of hiking trails, which lead to the lighthouse and to the cliffs, or spend a night and feel some of the privacy that the island can afford. Note that if you're the kind of traveler who likes lots of activities, skip Monhegan. A day trip is typified by a little shopping and a hike across the island to view the bluffs. If the weather's bad, there's little to do. But if you enjoy a good hike, nature, or the concept of an island that's home to just artists and fishermen, the silence and serenity of the high cliffs at White Head,

Black Head, and Burnt Head and the serendipitous pleasures that the island creates will be unforgettable.

PENOBSCOT BAY

Few could deny that Penobscot Bay is one of Maine's most dramatically beautiful regions. Its more than 1,000 miles of coastline is made up of rocky granite boulders, often undeveloped shores, a sprinkling of colorful towns, and views of the sea and islands that are a photographer's dream.

Penobscot Bay stretches 37 miles from Port Clyde in the south to Stonington, the little fishing village at the tip of Deer Isle, in the north. The bay begins where the Penobscot River, New England's second-largest river system, ends, near Stockton Springs, and terminates in the Gulf of Maine, where it is 47 miles wide. It covers an estimated 1,070 square miles and is home to more than 1,800 islands.

Initially, shipbuilding was the primary moneymaker here. In the 1800s, during the days of the great tall ships (or Down Easters, as they were often called), more wooden ships were built in Maine than any other state in the country, and many were constructed along Penobscot Bay. This golden age of billowing sails and wooden sailing ships came to an end with the development of the steam engine. By 1900, sailing ships were no longer a viable commercial venture in Maine. However, as you will see when traveling the coast, the tall ships have not entirely disappeared—some, albeit tiny in number compared to the 1800s heyday, have been revived as recreational boats known as windjammers. Today, once again, there are more tall ships along Penobscot Bay than anywhere else in the country.

ROCKLAND

3 miles north of Thomaston via U.S. 1.

The town is considered the gateway to Penobscot Bay and is the first stop on U.S. 1 offering a glimpse of the often sparkling and island-dotted blue bay. Though once merely a place to pass through on the way to tonier ports like Camden, Rockland now gets attention on its own, thanks to a trio of attractions: the renowned Farnsworth Museum, the increasingly popular summer Lobster Festival, and the lively North Atlantic Blues Festival. Specialty shops and galleries line the main street, and one of the restaurants, Primo (between Camden and the little village of Owls Head), has become nationally famous. The town is still a large fishing port and the commercial hub of this coastal area.

Rockland Harbor bests Camden by one as home to the largest fleet of Maine windjammers. The best place in Rockland to view these beautiful vessels as they sail in and out of the harbor is the mile-long granite breakwater, which bisects the outer portion of Rockland Harbor. To get there, from U.S. 1, head east on Waldo Avenue and then right on Samoset Road; follow this short road to its end.

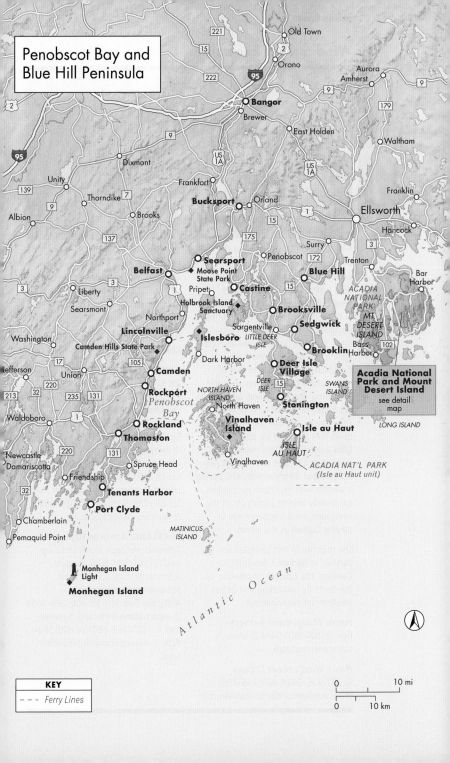

Penobscot Bay and Blue Hill Peninsula

Old Town
221
15
2
Orono
222
Brewer
Bangor
East Holden
Aurora
Amherst
9
179
Waltham
Dixmont
Frankfort
Orland
Bucksport
Ellsworth
Hancock
Franklin
Bar Harbor
Unity
139
Thorndike 7
Brooks
137
175
15
Surry
Penobscot
172
Trenton
ACADIA NATIONAL PARK
MT. DESERT ISLAND
Searsport
Moose Point State Park
Belfast
Pripet
Castine
Blue Hill
15
Holbrook Island Sanctuary
Brooksville
Sedgwick
Sargentville
Bass Harbor
102
Northport
LITTLE DEER ISLE
Brooklin
Lincolnville
Islesboro
Camden Hills State Park
Dark Harbor
Deer Isle Village
105
Camden
DEER ISLE
SWANS ISLAND

Acadia National Park and Mount Desert Island
see detail map

LONG ISLAND
Rockport
NORTH HAVEN ISLAND
Penobscot Bay
North Haven
Stonington
Rockland
Thomaston
Vinalhaven Island
ISLE AU HAUT
Spruce Head
Vinalhaven
ACADIA NAT'L PARK (Isle au Haut unit)
Friendship
Newcastle
Damariscotta
220
32
Tenants Harbor
Port Clyde
MATINICUS ISLAND
Chamberlain
Pemaquid Point
Atlantic Ocean
Monhegan Island Light
Monhegan Island

KEY
- - - Ferry Lines

0   10 mi
0   10 km

CLOSE UP

Windjammer Excursions

A windjammer cruise gives you a chance to admire Maine's dramatic coast from the water.

Nothing defines the Maine coastal experience more than a sailing trip on a windjammer. Windjammers were built all along the East Coast in the 19th and early 20th centuries. Designed primarily to carry cargo, these beauties (most are wood-hulled) have a rich past—the *Nathaniel Bowditch* served in World War II, while others plied the waters in the lumbering, granite, fishing, and oystering trades or served as pilot boats. They vary in size but can be as small as 46 feet and hold six passengers (plus a couple of crew members) or more than 130 feet and hold 40 passengers and 10 crew members. During a windjammer excursion passengers are usually able to participate in the navigation, be it hoisting a sail or playing captain at the wheel.

The majority of windjammers are berthed in Rockland, Rockport, or Camden. You can get information on the fleets by contacting one of two windjammer organizations:

Maine Windjammer Association ☎ 800/807-9463 ⊕ www. sailmainecoast.com.

Maine Windjammer Cruises ☎ 207/236-2938, 800/736-7981 ⊕ www.mainewindjammercruises.com.

Cruises can be anywhere from one to eight days. The price, ranging from $230 to $1,100, depending on length of trip, includes all meals. Trips leave from Camden, Rockland, and Rockport.

Here is a selection of some of the best windjammer cruises in the area.

CAMDEN–ROCKPORT: *Angelique* (☎ 207/785-6036 ⊕ www. sailangelique.com). *Appledore*, which can take you out for just a day sail (☎ 207/236-8353). *Mary Day*, Coastal Cruises (☎ 207/785-5670 ⊕ www.schoonermaryday.com). *Olad*, Downeast Windjammer Packet Co. (☎ 207/236-2323 ⊕ www. maineschooners.com); *Schooner Heron* (☎ 207/236-8605 or 800/599-8605 ⊕ www.woodenboatco.com).

ROCKLAND: *American Eagle* and *Schooner Heritage*, North End Shipyard (☎ 207/594-8007 ⊕ www. schoonerheritage.com or www. schooneramericaneagle.com). *Nathaniel Bowditch* (☎ 800/288-4098 ⊕ www.sailbowditch.com). *Summertime* (☎ 207/563-1605 or 800/562-8290 ⊕ www.schoonersummertime. com).

GETTING HERE AND AROUND

U.S. 1 runs along Main Street here, while U.S. 1A curves through the residential neighborhood west of the business district, offering a faster route if you are passing through.

Visitor Information Penobscot Bay Regional Chamber of Commerce ⊠ *Visitor Center, 1 Park Dr.* 🖀 *207/596–0376, 800/562–2529* ⊕ *www.therealmaine.com.*

EXPLORING

Fodor's Choice
★

Farnsworth Art Museum. One of the most important small museums in the country, much of its collection is devoted to Maine-related works of the famous Wyeth family: N. C. Wyeth, an accomplished illustrator whose works were featured in many turn-of-the-20th-century books; his late son Andrew, one of the country's best-known painters; and Andrew's son James, also an accomplished painter, who like his elders before him summers nearby. Galleries in the main building always display some of Andrew Wyeth's works, such as *The Patriot, Witchcraft,* and *Turkey Pond.* The **Wyeth Center,** a former church, shows art by his father and son. The museum's collection also includes works by Fitz Henry Lane, George Bellows, Frank W. Benson, Edward Hopper (as watercolors they may be "resting"), Louise Nevelson, and Fairfield Porter. Changing exhibits are shown in the **Jamien Morehouse Wing.** The **Farnsworth Homestead,** a handsome circa-1850 Greek Revival dwelling that is part of the museum, retains its original lavish Victorian furnishings (closed for maintenance, to reopen in 2013). ⊠ *16 Museum St.* 🖀 *207/596–6457* ⊕ *www.farnsworthmuseum.org* 🎟 *$12 for museum* ⊙ *Jan.–March, Wed.–Sun. 10–5; April, May, Nov., and Dec., Tues.–Sun. 10–5; June–Oct., Mon. and Tues. and Thurs.–Sun. 10–5, Wed. 10–8.*

Olson House. In Cushing, a tiny town about 10 miles south of Thomaston on the St. George River, the museum operates the Olson House, which is depicted in Andrew Wyeth's famous painting *Christina's World* as well as other works by the artist. The oldest part of the home was built in the late 1700s; guided tours only. ⊠ *384 Hawthorn Point Rd., Cushing* 🎟 *Museum and Olson house, $17; Olson house only, $10* ⊙ *Late May–June, Wed.–Sun. noon–5; July–early Oct., Tues.–Sun. 11–5 (last tour at 4).*

★
🐾

Maine Lighthouse Museum. The lighthouse museum has more than 25 Fresnel lighthouse lenses, as well as a collection of lighthouse artifacts and Coast Guard memorabilia. Permanent exhibits spotlight topics like lighthouse heroines—women who manned the lights when the keepers couldn't—and lightships. There are also changing exhibits. ⊠ *1 Park Dr.* 🖀 *207/594–3301* ⊕ *www.mainelighthousemuseum.org* 🎟 *$5* ⊙ *Late May–Oct., weekdays 9–5, weekends 10–4; Nov.–mid-May, 9–5 Thurs. and Fri. and 10–4 Sat.*

NIGHTLIFE AND THE ARTS

FESTIVALS
★
🐾

North Atlantic Blues Festival. About a dozen well-known artists gather for the North Atlantic Blues Festival, a two-day affair held the first full weekend after July 4th. The show officially takes place at the public landing on Rockland Harbor Park, but it also includes a Club Crawl Saturday night through downtown Rockland (for attendees of legal

10

THE PRETTIEST WALK IN THE WORLD

A few years ago *Yankee*, the quintessential magazine of New England, did a cover story on what it called "The Prettiest Walk in the World." The two-lane paved road, which winds up and down, with occasional views of the ocean and the village of Rockport, connects this town with Camden. To judge the merits of the journey of a few miles or so for yourself, you can travel on foot or by car. Begin at the intersection of U.S. 1 and Pascal Avenue. Take a right off U.S. 1 toward Rockport Harbor, then cross the bridge and go up the hill to Central Street. One block later, bear right on Russell Avenue, which becomes Chestnut Street at the Camden town line. Take this all the way to downtown Camden. Lining the way are some of the most beautiful homes in Maine, surrounded by an abundance of flora and fauna. Keep an eye out for Aldermere Farm and its Belted Galloway cows, as well as views of the sparkling ocean. For those who may not know, these rare cows get their name from the foot-wide white "belt" around their middles. The walk or drive is beautiful at any time of the year, but in fall it's breathtaking. Like the rest of New England, the coast of Maine gets a large number of fall-foliage "leaf peepers," and the reds and golds of the chestnut, birch, and elm trees along this winding route are especially beautiful.

age). Admission to the festival is $25 in advance, $35 at the gate. ☎ *207/596–6055* 🌐 *www.northatlanticbluesfestival.com.*

Maine Lobster Festival. Rockland's annual Maine Lobster Festival, in early August, started in 1947 and has become the biggest local event of the year. People come from all over the country to sample lobster in every possible form. During the few days of the festival about 10 tons of lobsters are steamed in a huge lobster cooker—you have to see it to believe it. The festival, held in Harbor Park, includes a parade, entertainment, craft and marine exhibits, food booths—and, of course, the crowning of the Maine Sea Goddess. ☎ *207/236–4404 Penobscot Bay Regional Chamber of Commerce* 🌐 *www.mainelobsterfestival.com.*

WHERE TO EAT

$$$$ MEDITERRANEAN Fodor's Choice ★ 🍴 **Primo.** Owner-chef Melissa Kelly and her world-class gourmet restaurant in a restored Victorian home have won many awards and been written up in *Gourmet, Bon Appétit,* and *O Magazine*. Upstairs the vibe is funky, downstairs is fancier. Wherever you eat it's farm-to-table here: Primo raises chickens and pigs, cures meats, produces eggs, and grows produce for its restaurant. Combining fresh Maine ingredients with Mediterranean influences, the daily-changing menu has dishes like kale salad with creamy garlic dressing, housemade pasta with local squid, and duck with sweet-and-sour rhubarb chutney. Pastry chef and co-owner Price Kushner creates delectable desserts like cannoli featuring crushed pistachios and amarena cherries. [$] *Average main: $35* ✉ *2 S. Main St.* ☎ *207/596–0770* 🌐 *www.primorestaurant.com* 🕒 *Open Wed.–Sun. No lunch. Closed mid-Jan.–mid-Apr.*

$$ DINER ★ 🍴 **Rockland Cafe.** It may not look like much from the outside, but Rockland Cafe is one of the most popular eating establishments in town. It's famous for the size of its breakfasts–get the fishcakes, also available for lunch and dinner, too. Breakfast is served until noon from May through October and until 4 from November through April. At dinner, the seafood combo of shrimp, scallops, clams, and haddock is excellent, or there's the classic liver and onions. [$] *Average main: $14* ✉ *441 Main St.* ☎ *207/596–7556* 🌐 *www.rocklandcafe.com.*

WHERE TO STAY

For expanded hotel reviews, visit Fodors.com.

$$$$ B&B/INN ★ 🏨 **Berry Manor Inn.** Originally the residence of Rockland merchant Charles H. Berry, this 1898 shingle-style B&B is in Rockland's National Historic District. **Pros:** in a nice, quiet neighborhood; within walking distance of downtown and the harbor; rooms have TVs and room-controlled air conditioners. **Cons:** not much of a view. [$] *Rooms from: $195* ✉ *81 Talbot Ave.* ☎ *207/596–7696, 800/774–5692* 🌐 *www.berrymanorinn.com* 🛏 *12 rooms* 🍴 *Breakfast.*

$$$ B&B/INN ★ 🏨 **LimeRock Inn.** In the center of town in Rockland's National Historic District, you can easily walk to the Farnsworth Museum or any of the other downtown attractions and restaurants from here. **Pros:** all rooms have TV/DVD and air conditioner; large in-town lot with gazebo. **Cons:** not on the water. [$] *Rooms from: $159* ✉ *96 Limerock St.* ☎ *207/594–2257, 800/546–3762* 🌐 *www.limerockinn.com* 🛏 *8 rooms* 🍴 *Breakfast.*

ROCKPORT

4 miles north of Rockland via U.S. 1.

Heading north on U.S. 1, you come to Rockport before you reach the tourist mecca of Camden. The most interesting part of Rockport—the harbor—is not right on U.S. 1. Originally called Goose River, the town was part of Camden until 1891. The cutting and burning of limestone was once a major industry in this area. The stone was cut in nearby quarries and then burned in hot kilns, and the resulting lime powder was used to create mortar. Some of the massive kilns are still here.

One of the most famous sights in Rockport is the **Rockport Arch**, which crosses Union Street at the town line and says "Camden" on the other side. It was constructed of wood and mortar in 1926, demolished in 1984, then rebuilt by popular demand in 1985. The arch has been displayed in a number of movies, including *Peyton Place* and *In the Bedroom.*

GETTING HERE AND AROUND

Rockport is off U.S. 1 between Rockland and Camden. Turn on Pascal Avenue to get to the village center.

ESSENTIALS

Visitor Information **Penobscot Bay Regional Chamber of Commerce**
✉ *Visitor Center, 2 Public Landing, Camden* ☎ *207/236–4404, 800/223–5459*
🌐 *www.mainedreamvacation.com.*

10

WHERE TO STAY

For expanded hotel reviews, visit Fodors.com.

$$$$ RESORT Fodor's Choice ★ **Samoset Resort.** Occupying 230 waterfront acres on the Rockland–Rockport town line, this all-encompassing resort offers luxurious rooms and suites, each with a private balcony or patio and most with ocean or garden views. **Pros:** full-service spa; children's activities in July and August; outdoor games galore, from basketball to croquet. **Cons:** no beach; can't walk to Rockland shops. [$] *Rooms from: $256* ✉ *220 Warrenton St.* ☎ *207/594–2511, 800/341–1650* 🌐 *www.samoset.com* 🛏 *160 rooms, 18 suites, 4 cottages, 72 time-share condominium rentals* 🍴 *Breakfast.*

CAMDEN

2 miles north of Rockport.

★ More than any other town along Penobscot Bay, Camden is the perfect picture-postcard of a Maine coastal village. It is one of the most popular destinations on the Maine Coast, so June through September the town is crowded with visitors, but don't let that scare you away; Camden is worth it. Just come prepared for busy traffic on the town's Main Street (U.S. 1) and make reservations for lodging and restaurants well in advance.

Camden is famous not only for its geography, but also for its large fleet of windjammers—relics and replicas from the age of sailing—with their romantic histories and great billowing sails. At just about any hour during the warm months you're likely to see at least one windjammer tied up in the harbor. The excursions, whether for an afternoon or a week, are best from June through September.

The town's compact size makes it perfect for exploring on foot: shops, restaurants, and galleries line Main Street, as well as side streets and alleys around the harbor. Especially worth inclusion on your walking tour is Camden's residential area. It is quite charming and filled with many fascinating old period houses from the time when Federal, Greek Revival, and Victorian architecture were the rage among the wealthy. Many of them are now B&Bs. The chamber of commerce, at the Public Landing, can provide you with a walking map. Humped on the north side of town are the Camden Hills. Drive or hike to the summit at Camden Hills State Park to enjoy mesmerizing views of the town, harbor, and island-dotted bay.

GETTING HERE AND AROUND

U.S. 1 runs right through Camden. Take Route 90 west from U.S. 1 and rejoin it in Warren to bypass Rockland—this is the quickest route south.

WHEN TO GO

FESTIVAL ★ 👶 **Windjammer Weekend.** One of the biggest and most colorful events of the year here is the Camden Windjammer Festival, which takes place on Labor Day weekend. The harbor is packed with historic vessels, and there are lots of good eats. Visitors can tour the ships. ☎ *207/236–4404 Penobscot Bay Regional Chamber, Camden office* 🌐 *www.camdenwindjammerfestival.com.*

The view from Camden Hills is a great way to see Penobscot Bay and the town of Camden.

SHOPPING

Camden's downtown area is a shopper's paradise with lots of interesting places to spend money. Most of the shops and galleries are along Camden's main drag. From the harbor, turn right on Bay View, and walk to Main/High Street. ■TIP→ U.S. 1 has lots of names as it runs through Maine. Three are within Camden's town limits—it starts as Elm Street, changes to Main Street, then becomes High Street.

Bayview Gallery. Bayview Gallery specializes in original art and prints with Maine themes. ⊠ *28 Bay View St.* ☏ *207/236–4534* ⊕ *www. bayviewgallery.com.*

Lily, Lupine & Fern. Lily, Lupine & Fern is a full-service florist and also offers a wonderful array of gourmet foods, chocolates, wines, imported beers, and cheeses. It stocks cigars, too. There's a small deck where you can enjoy harbor views and a cup of coffee. ⊠ *11 Main St.* ☏ *207/236– 9600* ⊕ *www.lilylupine.com.*

Planet. In this good-size storefront you'll find unique gifts and clothing, lots of books, and quality toys. Some of the gifts and toys are made in Maine. ⊠ *10 Main St. (U.S. 1)* ☏ *207/236–4410.*

WHERE TO EAT

$$$

SEAFOOD

✕ **Atlantica.** Right on the water's edge, the Atlantica is in a classic weathered, shingled building. Its lower deck is cantilevered over the water, offering a romantic setting with great views, and the interior decor is a mix of red walls and contemporary paintings. Fresh seafood with international accents is the specialty here. Favorites include pan-roasted split lobster tails with lemon butter, lobster stuffed with scallops, and pan-roasted king salmon. Everything is made right here from scratch,

10

including the tacos, breads, and desserts. There are small plates and lighter offerings like fish tacos. $ *Average main: $25* ⊠ *9 Bayview Landing* ☏ *207/236–6011, 888/507–8514* ⊕ *www.atlanticarestaurant. com* ⚑ *Reservations essential* ⊘ *Closed Nov.–April (but opens for special events and some holidays off-season) and Sun. and Mon. May–Oct. No lunch.*

$$
SEAFOOD
★

× **Cappy's Chowder House.** As you would expect from the name, Cappy's clam "chowdah" is the thing to order here—it's been written up in the *New York Times* and in *Bon Appétit* magazine—but there are plenty of other seafood specials at this restaurant. Don't be afraid to bring the kids—this place has many bargain meals, fun knicknacks about, and a "Crow's Nest" upper level. $ *Average main: $17* ⊠ *1 Main St.* ☏ *207/236–2254* ⊕ *www.cappyschowder.com* ⚑ *Reservations not accepted.*

$$$$
FRENCH
Fodor's Choice
★

× **Natalie's Restaurant.** What may be the most sought-after dining spot in Camden is the creation of Dutch owners Raymond Brunyanszki and Oscar Verest. Located in the Camden Harbour Inn, the restaurant is fine dining with a French flair. Order à la carte or from a variety of prix-fixe menus. "The Menu Saisonnier" is the chef's choice of the day; like all the offerings here it showcases fresh, seasonal ingredients. The "Homard Grand Cru" is a cascade of lobster dishes (they change seasonally but may include lobster gazpacho, lobster with squid ink, lobster with fiddleheads, lobster with beef cheek and foie-gras ravioli). In the lounge enjoy a predinner cocktail in front of the big fireplace. "Smart" casual attire is encouraged. $ *Average main: $42* ⊠ *83 Bay View St.* ☏ *207/236–7008* ⊕ *www.nataliesrestaurant.com* ⊘ *Closed Sun. June, Sept. and Oct. and also Mon. Nov.–May. No lunch.*

WHERE TO STAY

For expanded hotel reviews, visit Fodors.com.

$$$
B&B/INN
★

⬚ **Camden Hartstone Inn.** This downtown 1835 mansard-roofed Victorian home has been turned into a plush and sophisticated retreat and a fine culinary destination. **Pros:** extravagant breakfast may include lobster and asparagus quiche; some private entrances. **Cons:** not on water. $ *Rooms from: $194* ⊠ *41 Elm St. (U.S. 1)* ☏ *207/236–4259, 800/788–4823* ⊕ *www.hartstoneinn.com* ⇋ *12 rooms, 9 suites* ⊺⊙⊺ *Breakfast.*

$$$
HOTEL
★

⬚ **Lord Camden Inn.** If you want to be in the center of Camden and near the harbor, this is the place. **Pros:** large Continental breakfast; suite-like "premier" rooms have balconies and sitting areas. **Cons:** in the front rooms the U.S. 1 traffic may keep you awake. $ *Rooms from: $219* ⊠ *24 Main St. (U.S. 1)* ☏ *207/236–4325, 800/336–4325* ⊕ *www. lordcamdeninn.com* ⇋ *34 rooms, 2 suites* ⊺⊙⊺ *Breakfast.*

$$
B&B/INN
★

⬚ **Whitehall Inn.** The oldest part of the Whitehall is an 1834 white-clapboard sea captain's home, but much of this historic lodging was built in the early 1900s after an inn opened here. **Pros:** short walk to downtown and harbor; breakfast entrée choices. **Cons:** no good water views. $ *Rooms from: $169* ⊠ *52 High St. (U.S. 1)* ☏ *207/236–3391, 800/789–6565* ⊕ *www.whitehall-inn.com* ⇋ *37 rooms (2 share a bath), 4 suites* ⊘ *Closed mid-Oct.–mid-May* ⊺⊙⊺ *Breakfast.*

LINCOLNVILLE

6 miles north of Camden via U.S. 1.

Lincolnville's area of most interest—where there are a few restaurants, the ferry to Islesboro, and a swimming beach that attracts folks from neighboring Camden and Belfast—is Lincolnville Beach. The village is tiny; you could be through it in less than a minute. Still, it has a history going back to the Revolution, and you can see a small cannon on the beach here (never used) that was intended to repel the British in the War of 1812.

GETTING HERE AND AROUND

Lincolnville Beach is on U.S. 1 and the town of Lincolnville Center is inland on Route 173.

WHERE TO EAT

$$$ ✕ **Lobster Pound Restaurant.** If you're looking for an authentic place to
SEAFOOD have your Maine lobster dinner, this is it. This large restaurant has rustic
★ wooden picnic tables outside, an enclosed patio, and two dining rooms
☺ with a gift shop in between. Hundreds of live lobsters are in swimming tanks out back; just ask if you want to pick your own or let the kids take a look. There's a full bar; the wine list includes some local vintages. Right on U.S. 1 next to a small beach, the restaurant provides beautiful views from its indoor and outdoor seating. The classic "Shore Dinner Deluxe" consists of lobster stew or fish chowder, steamed clams or mussels, fried clams, 1½-pound lobster, potato or rice, salad, roll, and dessert. Because this is such a big place, you won't have to wait long even if it's busy . $ *Average main: $22* ⊠ *2521 Atlantic Hwy. (U.S. 1)* ☎ *207/789–5550* ⊕ *www.lobsterpoundmaine.com* ☂ *Closed Nov.–Apr.*

BELFAST

13 miles north of Lincolnville via U.S. 1.

A number of Maine coastal towns, such as Wiscasset and Damariscotta, like to think of themselves as the prettiest little town in Maine, but Belfast (originally to be named Londonderry) may be the true winner of this title. It has a full variety of charms: a beautiful waterfront; an old and interesting main street climbing up from the harbor; a delightful array of B&Bs, restaurants, and shops; and a friendly population. The downtown even has old-fashioned streetlamps, which set the streets aglow at night.

GETTING HERE AND AROUND

U.S. 1 runs through Belfast as it travels up the coast. From Interstate 95, take U.S. 3 in Augusta to get here. The highways join in Belfast heading north.

EXPLORING

In the mid-1800s Belfast was home to a number of wealthy business magnates, ship builders, ship captains, and so on. Their mansions still stand along High Street and in the residential area above it, offering excellent examples of Greek Revival and Federal architecture. In fact,

10

the town has one of the best showcases of Greek Revival homes in the state. Don't miss the "White House" where High and Church streets merge several blocks south of downtown.

Belfast Area Chamber of Commerce ⊠ *14 Main St.* ☎ *207/338–5900 information center, 207/338–3808* ⊕ *www.belfastmaine.org.*

NIGHTLIFE AND THE ARTS

★ **Rollie's Bar & Grill.** Rollie's Bar & Grill has been in business since 1972, and a bar operated here for years before that. The tavern is right downtown, up a bit from the harbor. The vintage bar is from an 1800s sailing ship. Rollie's is the most popular watering spot in town with the locals, and it just may serve the best hamburgers in the state. There are lots of booths and plenty of TVs for sports, and you'll see families here through the dinner hour. Then it's bar time until 1 am. Food is served until midnight on Friday and Saturday. ⊠ *37 Main St.* ☎ *207/338–4502* ⊕ *www.rollies.me.*

WHERE TO EAT

$$
AMERICAN
★
✕ **Darby's Restaurant and Pub.** Darby's, a charming old-fashioned restaurant and bar, is very popular with locals. The main part (it's expanded to three storefronts) has pressed-tin ceilings and has been a bar or a restaurant since it was built in the 1890s: the Brunswick bar is original. On the walls are works for sale by local artists and old murals of Belfast scenes. Pad thai and chicken chili with cashews are signature items; there's always several entrée specials. The menu also has hearty homemade soups and sandwiches, fish-and-chips, and dishes with an international flavor. Breakfast is served Friday through Sunday. $ *Average main: $18* ⊠ *155 High St.* ☎ *207/338–2339* ⊕ *www.darbysrestaurant.com* ☉ *Breakfast.*

$$$
SEAFOOD
★
✕ **Young's Lobster Pound.** The place looks more like a corrugated-steel fish cannery than a restaurant, but it is one of the best places to have an authentic Maine lobster dinner. Young's sits right on the edge of the water, across the harbor from downtown Belfast. When you first walk in, you'll see tanks and tanks of live lobsters of varying size. The traditional meal here is the Shore Dinner: fish or clam chowder or lobster stew; steamed clams or mussels; a 1½-pound boiled lobster; corn on the cob; and chips. Order your dinner at the counter, then find a table inside or on the deck. Surf-and-turf dinners and hot dogs are sold, too. It's BYOB. ■ TIP→ If you are enjoying your lobster at one of the outside tables, don't leave the table with no one to watch it. Seagulls are notorious thieves—and they LOVE lobster. $ *Average main: $25* ⊠ *2 Mitchell St., turn off U.S. 1* ☎ *207/338–1160* ☉ *Restaurant closed early Dec.–early April, boiled lobster sold to go year-round.*

SEARSPORT

6 miles north of Belfast via U.S. 1.

Searsport is well known as the antiques and flea-market capital of Maine and with good reason: the Antique Mall alone, on U.S. 1 just north of town, contains the offerings of 70 dealers, and flea markets during the visitor season line both sides of U.S. 1.

Learn about Maine's seafaring heritage at the Penobscot Marine Museum.

Searsport also has a rich history of shipbuilding and seafaring. In the early to mid-1800s there were 10 shipbuilding facilities in Searsport, and the population of the town was about 1,000 people more than it is today because of the ready availability of jobs. By the mid-1800s Searsport was home to more than 200 sailing-ship captains.

GETTING HERE AND AROUND

Downtown Searsport is right along U.S. 1, as is much of the town, which doesn't have lots of side streets. Just north of here in Stockton Springs U.S. 1A leads to Bangor.

ESSENTIALS

Visitor Information Belfast Chamber of Commerce Visitor Center. The information center has a large array of magazines, guidebooks, maps, and brochures that cover the entire Mid-Coast. It also can provide you with a free walking-tour brochure that describes the various historic homes and buildings, as well as the old business section in the harbor area. Ask the staff to tell you about the Museum in the Streets signage. ⊠ *14 Main St., a block from the harbor, Belfast* ☎ *207/338–5900* ⊕ *www.belfastmaine.org.*

EXPLORING

Fodor's Choice
★
☺
Penobscot Marine Museum. Along a street running up from Main Street in downtown Searsport, this museum explores the maritime culture of the Penobscot Bay region. Exhibits, artifacts, children's activities, and paintings are in six nearby buildings, most from the first half of the 19th century. The museum's other buildings include barns where small craft are displayed. One of the former sea captain's homes has period rooms. Outstanding marine art includes a notable collection of works by Thomas and James Buttersworth. There are photos of local

sea captains; an exhibit on fishing; a collection of China-trade merchandise; artifacts of life at sea; lots of scrimshaw; navigational instruments; tools from the area's history of logging, granite cutting, and ice cutting; treasures collected by seafarers from around the globe; models of famous ships; and changing exhibits. ⊠ *5 Church St.* ☎ *207/548–2529 administrative offices, 207/548–0334 store and admissions center; late May–late Oct. only* ⊕ *www.penobscotmarinemuseum.org* 💲 *$8* 🕙 *Late May–third weekend in Oct., Mon.–Sat. 10–5, Sun. noon–5.*

SHOPPING

ANTIQUES

Captain Tinkham's Emporium. In the very heart of town, Captain Tinkham's Emporium offers antiques, collectibles, vintage hand tools, jewelry, pottery, old books, magazines, records, paintings, and prints–a bit of everything. ⊠ *34 E. Main St.* ☎ *207/548–6465* ⊕ *www.jonesport-wood.com.*

Searsport Antique Mall. The biggest collection of antiques is in the Searsport Antique Mall, which has more than 70 dealers. ⊠ *149 E. Main St.(U.S. 1)* ☎ *207/548–2640* ⊕ *www.searsportantiquemall.com.*

BUCKSPORT

9 miles north of Searsport via U.S. 1.

The new Penobscot Narrows Bridge, spanning the Penobscot River, welcomes visitors to Bucksport, a town founded in 1763 by Jonathan Buck. Bucksport was the site of the second worst naval defeat in American history (the first was Pearl Harbor), in 1779, when a British Armada defeated the fledgling American Navy. It became known as "the disaster on the Penobscot." You can learn more about it at the museum in Bucksport or at the Penobscot Marine Museum in Searsport. Ft. Knox, Maine's largest historic fort, overlooks the town from across the river. There are magnificent views of the imposing granite structure from the pleasant riverfront walkway downtown.

GETTING HERE AND AROUND

U.S. 1 crosses a bridge into Bucksport; turn left for downtown and right to continue on the highway. Route 15 heads north to Bangor from here.

EXPLORING

Fodor'sChoice
★
☾

Penobscot Narrows Bridge & Observatory Tower/Fort Knox Historic Site. These neighboring attractions are owned by the state and managed together—observatory admission includes the fort. The 2,120-foot-long Penobscot Narrows Bridge, opened at the end of 2006 and replacing a 1931 span, has been declared an engineering marvel. It's certainly beautiful to drive over (no toll) or look at—from the surrounding countryside it pops up on the horizon like the towers of a fairy-tale castle. Spanning the Penobscot River across from Bucksport, the best part is the observation tower at the top of the western pylon, the first bridge observation tower in the country and, at 437 feet, the highest in the world. An elevator shoots you to the top. Don't miss it—the panoramic views, which take in the hilly countryside and the river as it widens into Penobscot Bay, are breathtaking.

Fort Knox is the largest historic fort in Maine and was built between 1844 and 1869, when despite a treaty with Britain settling boundary disputes, invasion was feared—the Brits controlled this region during the Revolutionary War and again during the War of 1812. The fort never saw any actual fighting, but it was used for troop training and as a garrison during the Civil War and the Spanish-American War. Visitors are welcome to explore the fort's passageways and many rooms. Guided tours are given daily during the summer and several days a week in the shoulder seasons. There are interpretive panels throughout the fort. ⊠ *711 Ft. Knox Rd., just after turning onto Rte. 174 from U.S. 1, Prospect* ☎ *207/469–6553* ⊕ *www.fortknox.maineguide.com* ⚊ *$7 observatory and fort, $4.50 fort only* ☉ *Observatory, Sept. and Oct. and Mary and June 9–5, July and Aug. 9–6. Park. Fort, May–Oct. 9–5; grounds daily 9–dusk.*

BANGOR

122 miles north of Portland via Interstate 95, 19 miles north of Bucksport via Rte. 15.

The second-largest metropolitan area in the state (Portland being the largest; Lewiston has a larger population for the city itself), Bangor is about 20 miles from the coast and is the unofficial capital of northern Maine. Back in the 19th century the "Queen City's" most important product and export was lumber from the state's vast North Woods. Now, because of its airport, Bangor has become a gateway to Mount Desert Island, Bar Harbor, and Acadia National Park. Along the revitalized waterfront, the American Folk Festival draws big crowds on the last weekend in August, and an outdoor stage attracts top bands and musicians throughout the summer.

GETTING HERE AND AROUND

Interstate 95 has five Bangor exits, 45 to 49. U.S. 1A loops up to Bangor from Stockton Springs and Ellsworth, near Bar Harbor, and connects with Interstate 395 on the western side of the Bangor area.

ESSENTIALS

Visitor Information Greater Bangor Convention & Visitors Bureau
☎ *207/947–5205, 800/916–6673* ⊕ *www.bangorcvb.org.*

EXPLORING

Maine Discovery Museum. The largest children's museum north of Boston, the Maine Discovery Museum has three floors with more than 60 interactive exhibits. Kids can explore Maine's ecosystem in Nature Trails, learn about other cultures in TradeWinds, step into classic children's books like *Charlotte's Web*—all written by Maine authors—in Booktown, and unearth true-to-size dinosaur "bones" in DINO Dig. There's also a drop-in art studio and daily programs on art and other topics. ■TIP→ Visitors to Acadia National Park often head here on a rainy day, and you can call ahead to sign kids up for one day of camp, space allowing. ⊠ *74 Main St.* ☎ *207/262–7200* ⊕ *www.mainediscoverymuseum.org* ⚊ *$7.50* ☉ *June–Sept., Mon.–Sat. 10–5, Sun. 12–5; Oct.–May, Tues.–Sat. 10–5, Sun. 12–5.*

10

For expanded hotel reviews, visit Fodors.com.

$ 🍽 **Lucerne Inn.** Nestled in the mountains, the Lucerne overlooks beauti-
HOTEL   ful Phillips Lake. **Pros:** golf course across the road. **Cons:** some dated
★   rooms. ⓢ *Rooms from: $119* ✉ *2517 Main Rd. (U.S. 1A), Dedham*
☎ *207/843–5123, 800/325–5123* ⊕ *www.lucerneinn.com* ⇖ *21 rooms,*
10 suites ⦿ *Breakfast.*

THE BLUE HILL PENINSULA

If you want to see unspoiled Down East Maine land- and seascapes, explore art galleries, savor exquisite meals, or simply enjoy life at an unhurried pace, you should be quite content on the Blue Hill Peninsula.

The large peninsula juts south into Penobscot Bay. Not far from the mainland are the islands of Little Deer Isle, Deer Isle, and, at the latter's tip, the picturesque fishing town of Stonington. A twisting labyrinth of roads winds through blueberry barrens and around picturesque coves, linking the towns of Blue Hill, Brooksville, Sedgwick, and Brooklin. Blue Hill and Castine are the area's primary business hubs. Painters, photographers, sculptors, and other artists are drawn to the area. You can find more than 20 galleries on Deer Isle and in Stonington and at least half as many on the mainland. With its small inns, charming B&Bs, and outstanding restaurants scattered across the area, the Blue Hill Peninsula may just persuade you to leave the rest of the coastline to the tourists.

VISITOR INFORMATION

Contacts Blue Hill Peninsula Chamber of Commerce ✉ *107 Main St., Blue Hill* ☎ *207/374–3242* ⊕ *www.bluehillpeninsula.org.* **Deer Isle–Stonington Chamber of Commerce** ☎ *207/348–6124* ⊕ *www.deerisle.com.*

CASTINE

18 miles north of Bucksport via U.S. 1 and Rtes. 175 and 166.

A summer destination for more than 100 years, Castine is a well-preserved seaside village rich in history. The French established a trading post here in 1613, naming the area Pentagoet. A year later Captain John Smith claimed the area for the British. The French regained control of the peninsula with the 1667 Breda Treaty, and Jean Vincent d'Abbadie de St. Castin obtained a land grant in the Pentagoet area, which would later bear his name. Castine's strategic position on Penobscot Bay and its importance as a trading post meant there were many battles for control until 1815. In the 19th century Castine was an important port for trading ships and fishing vessels. Larger ships, the Civil War, and the advent of train travel brought its prominence as a port to an end, but by the late 1800s some of the nation's wealthier citizens had discovered Castine as a pleasant summer retreat.

GETTING HERE AND AROUND

From U.S. 1 in Orland, near Bucksport, Route 175 heads south along the Penobscot River toward Castine. Continue on Route 166 at the crossroads of West Penobscot and after a bit you have the option of taking Route 166A into the village. The roads form a loop; the latter is especially scenic, passing expansive Wadsworth Cove at the mouth of the river as it enters its namesake bay.

EXPLORING

Federal- and Greek Revival–style architecture, rich history, and spectacular views of Penobscot Bay make Castine an ideal spot to spend a day or two. Explore its lively harbor front, two small museums (the Wilson Museum and the Castine Historical Society), and the ruins of a British fort. You can't miss the oversized historical signs throughout the village. An excellent self-guided walking tour is available at local businesses and the historical society. For a nice stroll, park your car at the landing and walk up Main Street toward the white Trinitarian Federated Church. Near hear turn right on Court Street and go one block to the town common. Among the white-clapboard buildings ringing this green space are the Ives House (once the summer home of poet Robert Lowell), the Adams School, the former Abbott School (home to the historical society), and the Unitarian Church, capped by a whimsical belfry. From lower Main Street, head out Perkins Street by foot, bike, or car. You'll pass summer "cottage" mansions and the Wilson Museum on the way to Dyces Head Lighthouse (private), where a path leads to cliffs (careful here) fronting Penobscot Bay, site of a major Revolutionary War battle. You can return on Battle Avenue to make a loop.

SPORTS AND THE OUTDOORS

Castine Kayak International Adventures. At Eaton's Wharf, Castine Kayak Adventures operates tours run by owner Karen Francoeur, a Registered Maine Guide. Sign up for a half-day of kayaking along the shore; a full day of kayaking by shipwrecks, reversing falls, and islands in Penobscot Bay; or nighttime bioluminescent trips—paddling stirs up a type of phytoplankton, causing them to light up like fireflies as they shoot through the water. The business also offers overnight kayak camping trips and instructional courses. It also rents mountain bikes and kayaks to experienced kayakers. ⊠ *17 Sea St.* ☎ *207/866–3506* ⊕ *www. castinekayak.com.*

WHERE TO EAT

$$ ✕ **Dennett's Wharf.** Originally built as a sail-rigging loft in the early
AMERICAN   1800s, this longtime favorite is a good place for oysters and fresh seafood of all kinds. The waterfront restaurant also serves burgers, sandwiches, and light fare. There are 23 microbrews on tap, including the tasty Dennett's Wharf Rat Ale. Eat in the dining room or outside on the deck–there are covered and open sections, another bar, and Adirondack chairs if you just stop by for a brew. $ *Average main: $16* ⊠ *15 Sea St.* ☎ *207/326–9045* ⊕ *www.dennettswharf.net* ◷ *Closed mid-Oct.–mid-April.*

10

BLUE HILL

20 miles east of Castine via Rtes. 166, 175, and 176.

Snuggled between 943-foot Blue Hill Mountain and Blue Hill Bay, the village of Blue Hill sits cozily beside its harbor. Originally known for its granite quarries, copper mines, and shipbuilding, today the town is known for its pottery and galleries, bookstores, antiques shops, and studios that line its streets. The Blue Hill Fair (⊕ *www.bluehillfair.com*), held Labor Day weekend, is a tradition in these parts, with agricultural exhibits, food, rides, and entertainment. A charming little park with a great playground is tucked away on the harbor downtown.

GETTING HERE AND AROUND

From U.S. 1 in Orland, Route 15 heads south to Blue Hill. To continue north on the highway, take Route 172 north to Ellsworth.

SHOPPING

ART GALLERIES

★ **Blue Hill Bay Gallery.** Blue Hill Bay Gallery sells oil and watercolor landscapes and seascapes of Maine and New England from the 19th through the 21st centuries. It also carries the owner's photography. ⊠ *11 Tenny Hill* ☎ *207/374–5773* ⊕ *www.bluehillbaygallery.com*.

POTTERY

North Country Textiles. Huge, old storefront windows fill this colorful corner store with light, adding to the delight of browsing the handcrafted rag rugs, ornate cotton jackets, felt puppets, many knitted items, and dyed artisan yarns. Almost everything sold at this shop in downtown's Levy Building is handcrafted in Maine. ⊠ *36 Main St.* ☎ *207/374–2715* ⊕ *www.northcountrytextiles.com*.

Rackliffe Pottery. In business since 1969, Rackliffe Pottery sells colorful pottery made with lead-free glazes. You can choose between water pitchers, dinnerware, serving platters, tea-and-coffee sets, and sets of canisters. ⊠ *126 Ellsworth Rd.* ☎ *207/374–2297* ⊕ *www. rackliffepottery.com*.

WINE

Blue Hill Wine Shop. Located in the restored barn at the rear of one of Blue Hill's earliest houses, the Blue Hill Wine Shop carries more than 1,200 carefully selected wines. Wine tastings are held the last Saturday of every month. Coffee, tea, cheeses, and prewrapped sandwiches are also available. ⊠ *123 Main St.* ☎ *207/374–2161* ⊕ *www. bluehillwineshop.com*.

WHERE TO EAT AND STAY

For expanded hotel reviews, visit Fodors.com.

$$$$
MODERN
AMERICAN
Fodor'sChoice
★

✕ **Arborvine.** Glowing gas fireplaces, period antiques, exposed beams, and hardwood floors covered with Oriental rugs adorn the four candlelit dining areas in this renovated Cape Cod–style house. Begin with a salad of mixed greens, sliced beets, and pears with blue cheese crumbled on top. For your entrée, choose from dishes such as crispy duck with rhubarb and lime glaze or roasted rack of lamb with a basil and pine nut crust; such preparations change seasonally. The fresh fish dishes are superb—try the crab cakes. Save room for desserts; ice cream (chocolate chili!) is homemade. Return when you're in a more casual mood: like the restaurant, the adjacent nautical-theme DeepWater Brew Pub serves dishes made with organic and local ingredients as much as possible—and of course its own beer. It's housed in an inviting space that opens to a lawn seating come summer. By summer 2013 the public should be able to watch the brewery in action in a restored 1780 barn. $ *Average main: $31* ⌧ *33 Tenney Hill* ☎ *207/374–2119* ⊕ *www.arborvine.com* ⊘ *Closed most of Nov. and March. Closed Mon.–Thurs. Dec.–Feb. and April–early May, Mon.–Wed. mid-May–mid-June, Mon. and Tues. late June–early July and mid-Sept.–Oct., Mon. July–early Sept. No lunch.*

$$$
B&B/INN
★
🛏 **Blue Hill Inn.** One side of this 1830 Federal-style inn was built as a home, but it soon became an inn, adding a wing with a matching facade in the 1850s. **Pros:** three first-floor rooms; modern suites with kitchens in separate building. **Cons:** some small rooms. $ *Rooms from: $185* ⌧ *40 Union St.* ☎ *207/374–2844, 800/826–7415* ⊕ *www.bluehillinn.com* ↪ *10 rooms, 3 suites* ⊘ *Closed Nov.–mid-May (2 suites in separate building open year-round)* 🍴 *Breakfast.*

SEDGWICK, BROOKLIN, AND BROOKSVILLE

Winding through the hills, the roads leading to the villages of Sedgwick, Brooklin, and Brooksville take you past rambling farmhouses, beautiful coves, and blueberry barrens studded with occasional masses of granite.

GETTING HERE AND AROUND
From Blue Hill, Route 175 runs along the bottom of the Blue Hill Peninsula, heading first to Brooklin, then through Sedgwick and Brooksville on its way to U.S. 1 in Orland. Route 176 traverses Sedgwick and Brooksville as it heads west from Blue Hill across the middle of the peninsula. Because this wide peninsula has lots of capes, points, and necks, take care when driving to make sure you're continuing on the right road and not unintentionally looping around. Use a map (don't rely on GPS)—there's a good one in the Blue Hill Peninsula Chamber of Commerce's visitors guide.

Sedgwick. Incorporated in 1789, Sedgwick runs along much of Eggemoggin Reach, the body of water separating the mainland from Deer Isle, Little Deer Isle, and Stonington.

Brooklin. The village of Brooklin, originally part of Sedgwick, established itself as an independent town in 1849. Today it's home to the world-famous Wooden Boat School, a 60-acre oceanfront campus offering courses in woodworking, boatbuilding, and seamanship, plus a few art classes on topics like painting seascapes. The public is welcome here. A small parklike area on the waterfront has a long pier and affords spectacular views of the area's chiseled coast. The gift store has some general-interest books with nautical tie-ins, plus T-shirts with Wooden Boat's cool ship's bow logo. The school is off the road to Naskeag Point, a sleepy, serenely beautiful spot at the end of the peninsula road with a small rock beach, teeny park, and a home peeking through the trees on the island across the harbor. As a stone marker notes, a Revolutionary War naval battle raged here.

10

Brooksville. The town of Brooksville, incorporated in 1817, is almost completely surrounded by water, with Eggemoggin Reach, Walker Pond, and the Bagaduce River marking its boundaries. Cape Rosier, remote and cove-lined even for this off-the-beaten-path peninsula, is home to Holbrook Island Sanctuary, a state park with hiking trails and a gravel beach.

WHERE TO EAT

$ × **Bagaduce Lunch.** Winner of a 2008 James Beard Award, this tidy fried-
SEAFOOD   fish specialist next to the reversing falls on the Bagaduce River, about
Fodor's Choice   10 miles west of Blue Hill, is the perfect place for an outdoor lunch (no
★   indoor seating). Picnic tables dot this nub of land with water on three
☼   sides, and there's a pier to tie up your kayak or boat, or to walk out
on to enjoy the lovely view. Clam, shrimp, haddock, or scallop baskets
come with onion rings or chips; there are also hot dogs, burgers, and
fried chicken fingers. Seals, bald eagles, and ospreys provide natural
entertainment in this rich tidal estuary. At low tide kids explore along
the shore. $ *Average main: $12* ⊠ *145 Franks Flat Rd. (Rte. 175),
Penobscot* ☎ *207/326–4197* ⊟ *No credit cards* ☼ *Closed mid-Sept.–late
April. No dinner Wed.*

$$$ × **Brooklin Inn.** At this small restaurant, in a 1920s bungalow-style build-
★   ing that was the dining room for a long-gone resort, the ambience is
pleasantly yesteryear. In summer, it expands to include seating in the
classic glass-enclosed wraparound porch. The changing menu embraces
traditional New England fare without clinging to the past, and all the
produce, meats, poultry, and fish are local and often organic. You'll find
dishes like crispy duckling with a rhubarb and lime glaze and French-
man Bay mussels in a Dijon herb cream reduction. Fare at the Irish
pub downstairs includes oysters, pizza, and sandwiches. The inn has
five homey guest rooms. $ *Average main: $25* ⊠ *22 Reach Road (Rte.
175), Brooklin* ☎ *207/359–2777* ⊕ *www.brooklininn.com* ☼ *Closed
Mon. and Tues. Nov.–April. No lunch.*

DEER ISLE VILLAGE

16 miles south of Blue Hill via Rtes. 176 and 15.

Around Deer Isle Village, thick woods give way to tidal coves. Stacks of
lobster traps populate the backyards of shingled houses, and dirt roads
lead to secluded summer cottages. This region is prized by artists, and
studios and galleries are plentiful.

GETTING HERE AND AROUND

From Sedgwick, Route 15 crosses a 1930s suspension bridge onto Little
Deer Isle and continues on to the larger Deer Isle.

EXPLORING

Haystack Mountain School of Crafts. Want to learn a new craft? This school
six miles from Deer Isle Village offers one- and two-week courses for
people of all skill levels in crafts such as blacksmithing, basketry, print-
making, and weaving. Artisans from around the world present free
evening lectures throughout summer. Tours of the facility are at 1 on
Wednesdays, June through about early September. ⊠ *89 Haystack*

School Dr., off Rte. 15 ☎ *207/348–2306* ⊕ *www.haystack-mtn.org* ✉ *$5 suggested donation* ⊙ *Daily, June–Sept.*

Edgar M. Tennis Preserve. Enjoy several miles of woodland and shore trails at the Edgar M. Tennis Preserve. Look for hawks, eagles, and ospreys and wander among old apple trees, fields of wildflowers, and ocean-polished rocks. ✉ *Tennis Rd., Deer Isle* ✛ *From Route 15 south, turn left onto Sunshine Rd., take it 2.5 miles to Tennis Rd., turn right and follow to preserve* ⊕ *www.islandheritagetrust.org* ✉ *Free* ⊙ *Daily dawn–dusk.*

SHOPPING

Nervous Nellie's Jams and Jellies. Nervous Nellie's Jams and Jellies sells jams and jellies made right on the property. There is a tearoom with homemade goodies and also a fanciful sculpture garden with everything from knights to witches to a lobster and a flamingo. They are the works of sculptor Peter Beerits, who operates Nervous Nellie's with his wife. ✉ *598 Sunshine Rd., turn off Rte. 15, Deer Isle* ☎ *207/348–6182, 800/777–6845* ⊕ *www.nervousnellies.com.*

STONINGTON

6 miles south of Deer Isle.

Stonington is at the southern end of Route 15, which has helped it retain its unspoiled small-town flavor. The boutiques and galleries lining Main Street cater mostly to out-of-towners, though the town remains a fishing and lobstering community at heart. The principal activity is at the waterfront, where boats arrive with the day's catch. The sloped island that rises to the south is Isle au Haut, which contains a remote section of Acadia National Park.

GETTING HERE AND AROUND

From Deer Isle village, Route 15 runs all the way to Stonington at the tip of the island. There is a ferry here to Isle au Haut.

EXPLORING

Deer Isle Granite Museum. This tiny museum documents Stonington's quarrying tradition. The museum's centerpiece is a working model of quarrying operations on Crotch Island and the town of Stonington at the turn of the last century. Granite was quarried here for Rockefeller Plaza in New York City and the John F. Kennedy Memorial in Arlington National Cemetery, among other well-known structures. ✉ *51 Main St.(Rte. 15)* ☎ *207/367–6331* ✉ *Free* ⊙ *July and Aug., Mon. and Tues. and Thurs.–Sun. 9–5.*

SPORTS AND THE OUTDOORS

★ **Old Quarry Ocean Adventures.** Old Quarry Ocean Adventures rents bikes, canoes, and kayaks and offers numerous boat trips and tours, starting at $37 per person. Departing from Webb Cove and passing Stonington Harbor en route to the outer islands, Captain Bill Baker's refurbished lobster boat takes visitors on puffin-watching, whale-watching, sunset, and lighthouse trips. There's also a three-hour Sightseeing and Natural History Eco-Cruise that goes by Crotch Island, which has one of the area's two active stone quarries, and stops at Green Island, where you

10

can take a dip in a water-filled quarry. You'll learn about the region's natural history and the history of Stonington and the local granite industry. There are all-day trips to bike or kayak on nearby islands, including Isle au Haut. ⊠ *130 Settlement Rd.* ☎ *207/367–8977* ⊕ *www. oldquarry.com.*

ISLE AU HAUT

6 miles south of Stonington via ferry.

Isle au Haut thrusts its steeply ridged back out of the sea south of Stonington. French explorer Samuel D. Champlain discovered Isle au Haut—or "High Island"—in 1604, but heaps of shells suggest that native populations lived on or visited the island prior to his arrival. The island is accessible only by mail boat, but the 45-minute journey is well worth the effort. A section of Acadia National Park is here, with miles of trails, and the boat will drop visitors off there in peak season. The island has some seasonal rentals but no inns. With only three stores, you wouldn't think folks would come here to shop. But some do, as the island is home to Black Dinah Chocolatiers (☎ *207/335–5010* ⊕ *www. blackdinahchocolatiers.com*), which makes artful high-end chocolates and has a small café (pastries, coffee, and of course chocolate).

GETTING HERE AND AROUND

Isle au Haut Boat Services (☎ *207/367–5193* ⊕ *www.isleauhaut.com*) operates daily ferry service between Stonington and Isle au Haut. During the summer season, trips increases from two to five Monday through Saturday and one to two on Sunday. From mid-June until late September, the boat also stops at Duck Harbor, in the island section of Acadia National Park (it will not unload bicycles, kayaks, or canoes). Ferry service is scaled back in the fall, then returns to the regular or "winter" schedule.

QUICK
BITES

Maine Lobster Lady. Come summer, this former island innkeeper sells yummy quick-eats, much of it made with fish from the local waters and her own organic garden produce. Her "food truck" (actually a tow trailer) is parked near the ranger's station at the Acadia National Park section on Isle au Haut. There are lobster rolls of course, or try a shrimp salad sandwich with paprika dill mayo on a homemade roll, or shrimp puffs served in a paper cone. Island scenes on the truck are graphics of works by an artist from across the water in Deer Isle. ⊠ *Isle au Haut* ☎ *207/335–5141* ⊕ *www.mainelobsterlady.com.*

ACADIA NATIONAL PARK AND MOUNT DESERT ISLAND

With some of the most dramatic and varied scenery on the Maine Coast and home to Maine's only national park, Mount Desert Island (pronounced "Mount Dessert" by locals) is Maine's most popular tourist destination, attracting 2 million visitors a year. Much of the

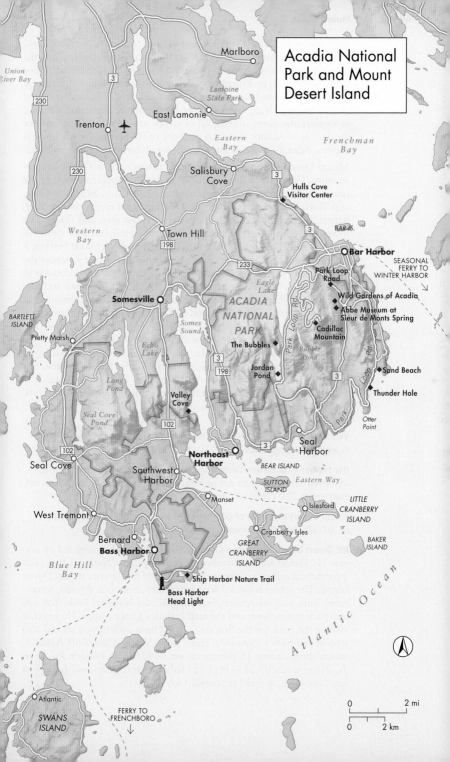

Acadia National Park and Mount Desert Island

Union River Bay

230

Marlboro

3

Lamoine State Park

East Lamoine

Trenton

230

Eastern Bay

Frenchman Bay

Salisbury Cove

3

Hulls Cove Visitor Center

Town Hill

198

233

BAR IS.

Bar Harbor

SEASONAL FERRY TO WINTER HARBOR

Western Bay

Somesville

Eagle Lake

ACADIA NATIONAL PARK

Park Loop Road

Wild Gardens of Acadia

Abbe Museum at Sieur de Monts Spring

Cadillac Mountain

BARTLETT ISLAND

Pretty Marsh

Somes Sound

Echo Lake

The Bubbles

Bubble Pond

Park Loop Rd.

3

Sand Beach

Jordan Pond

Thunder Hole

Long Pond

198

3

Park Loop Rd.

Seal Cove Pond

Valley Cove

102

Otter Point

102

Seal Cove

Southwest Harbor

Northeast Harbor

3

Seal Harbor

West Tremont

Manset

BEAR ISLAND

SUTTON ISLAND

Eastern Way

Islesford

LITTLE CRANBERRY ISLAND

Bernard

Bass Harbor

Cranberry Isles

GREAT CRANBERRY ISLAND

BAKER ISLAND

Blue Hill Bay

Ship Harbor Nature Trail

Bass Harbor Head Light

Atlantic Ocean

Atlantic

SWANS ISLAND

FERRY TO FRENCHBORO

0   2 mi

0   2 km

approximately 12-by-15-mile island belongs to Acadia National Park. The rocky coastline rises starkly from the ocean, appreciable along the scenic drives. Trails for hikers of all skill levels lead to the rounded tops of the mountains, providing views of Frenchman and Blue Hill bays and beyond. Ponds and lakes beckon you to swim, fish, or boat. Ferries and charter boats provide a different perspective on the island and a chance to explore the outer islands, all of which are part of Maine but not necessarily of Mount Desert. A network of old carriage roads lets you explore Acadia's wooded interior, filled with birds and other wildlife.

Mount Desert Island has four different towns, each with its own personality. The town of Bar Harbor is on the northeastern corner of the island and includes the little villages of Hulls Cove, Salisbury Cove, and Town Hill. The park aside, Bar Harbor is the major tourist destination, with plenty of accommodations, restaurants, and shops. The town of Mount Desert, in the middle of the island, has four main villages: Somesville, Seal Harbor, Otter Creek, and Northeast Harbor, a summer haven for the very wealthy. Southwest Harbor is across the water from Northeast Harbor, on the south side of the entrance to Somes Sound, which cuts up the center of the island. The town includes the smaller village of Manset south of the village center. Tremont is at the southernmost tip of the island and stretches up the western shore. It includes the villages of Bass Harbor, Bernard, and Seal Cove. Yes, Mount Desert Island is a place with three personalities: the hustling, bustling tourist mecca of Bar Harbor; the "quiet side" on the western half; and the vast natural expanse that is Acadia National Park. But though less congested and smaller, Northeast Harbor and especially Southwest Harbor are also home to inns, campgrounds, restaurants, ferries, galleries, and small museums.

ESSENTIALS

Visitor Information Bar Harbor Chamber of Commerce ☎ *888/540–9990* ⊕ *www.barharborinfo.com.*

Bar Harbor Information Center. The Bar Harbor Chamber of Commerce operates this information center just up from the water at the corner of Cottage and Main streets. ⊠ *2 Cottage St., Bar Harbor* ⊘ *Open early May–late Oct.*

Mount Desert Chamber of Commerce ⊠ *18 Harbor Dr., Northeast Harbor* ☎ *207/276–5040* ⊕ *www.mountdesertchamber.org.*

Mt. Desert Island Information Center at Thompson Island. Sponsored by several Mt. Desert Island chambers as well as Acadia National Park, this information center is along Route 3 just before it crosses to Mt. Desert Island. The center is loaded with pamphlets about island tours, restaurants, inns, and attractions, including Acadia National Park. You can buy park passes here, and the staff includes a park ranger. However, if visiting the park for the first time, or it's been awhile, you should also stop at the park's expansive Hulls Cove Visitor Center off Route 3, which shows a free 15-minute movie. ⊠ *1319 Bar Harbor Rd. (Rte. 3), Trenton* ☎ *207/288–3411* ⊘ *Daily 8–5 mid-May–mid-June, 8–6 late June–Aug., 8–5:30 Sept.–mid-Oct.*

BAR HARBOR

34 miles from Blue Hill via Rte. 172 and U.S. 1.

A resort town since the 19th century, Bar Harbor is the artistic, culinary, and social center of Mount Desert Island. It also serves visitors to Acadia National Park with inns, motels, and restaurants. Around the turn of the last century the island was known as the summer haven of the very rich because of its cool breezes. The wealthy built lavish mansions throughout the island, many of which were destroyed in a huge fire that devastated the island in 1947, but many of those that survived have been converted into businesses. Shops are clustered along Main, Mount Desert, and Cottage streets. Take a stroll down West Street, a National Historic District, where you can see some fine old houses.

The island and the surrounding Gulf of Maine are home to a great variety of wildlife: whales, seals, eagles, falcons, ospreys, and puffins (though not right offshore here), and forest dwellers such as deer, foxes, coyotes, and beavers.

GETTING HERE AND AROUND

In Ellsworth, Route 3 leaves U.S. 1 and heads to Bar Harbor. In season, free Island Explorer buses (⊕ *www.exploreacadia.com* ☎ *207/667–5796*) take visitors to Acadia National Park and other island towns. There is also a passenger ferry to Winter Harbor across Frenchman Bay.

SPORTS AND THE OUTDOORS

AIR TOURS

★ **Acadia Air Tours.** Acadia Air Tours provides scenic tours and flights over Bar Harbor and Acadia National Park. Most tours run from 25 minutes to an hour and range from $230 to $450 for two people. The sunset tour is $50 extra. ⊠ *968 Bar Harbor Rd.(Rte. 3), Trenton* ☎ *207/667–7627* ⊕ *www.acadiaairtours.com.*

BICYCLING

Acadia Bike. Acadia Bike rents bikes that are good for negotiating the carriage roads in Acadia National Park: mountain bikes, hybrids, and comfort bikes. ⊠ *48 Cottage St.* ☎ *207/288–9605, 800/526–8615* ⊕ *www.acadiabike.com.*

Bar Harbor Bicycle Shop. The Bar Harbor Bicycle Shop rents bikes by the half or full day. ⊠ *141 Cottage St.* ☎ *207/288–3886, 800/824–2453* ⊕ *www.barharborbike.com.*

Coastal Kayaking Tours. Coastal Kayaking Tours has been leading trips in the scenic waters off Mt. Dessert Island since 1982. Rentals are provided through its sister business, Acadia Outfitters, on the same downtown street. Trips are limited to no more than 12 people. The season is May through October. ⊠ *48 Cottage St., Bar Harbor* ☎ *207/288–9605, 800/526–8615.*

★ **Margaret Todd.** The big 151-foot four-masted schooner Margaret Todd operates 1½- to 2-hour trips three times a day among the islands of Frenchman's Bay from mid-May to October. The sunset sail has live music, and the 2 pm trip is narrated by an Acadia National Park ranger. Trips are $37.50 and depart from the pier at the Bar Harbor

10

Long ramps on Maine's many docks make it easier to access boats at either high tide or low tide.

Inn. ⊠ *Bar Harbor Inn pier, Newport Drive* ☎ *207/288–4585* ⊕ *www.downeastwindjammer.com.*

WHALE-WATCHING

★ **Bar Harbor Whale Watch Co.** Bar Harbor Whale Watch Co. has four
☾ boats, one of them a 140-foot jet-propelled double-hulled catamaran with spacious decks. It's one of two large catamarans used for whale-watching trips, some of which go at sunset or include a side trip to see puffins. The company also offers lighthouse, nature, and lobstering and seal-watching cruises, and a trip to Acadia National Park's Baker Island. ⊠ *1 West St.* ☎ *207/288–2386, 800/942–5374* ⊕ *www.whalesrus.com.*

SHOPPING

ART

Alone Moose Fine Crafts. Alone Moose Fine Crafts is the oldest made-in-Maine gallery in Bar Harbor. It offers bronze wildlife sculpture, jewelry, pottery, and watercolors. ⊠ *78 West St.* ☎ *207/288–4229* ⊕ *www.finemainecrafts.com.*

Eclipse Gallery. The Eclipse Gallery carries handblown glass, ceramics, wood and metal furniture, and home decor items like mirrors and lamps. The gallery is open from mid-May through October. ⊠ *12 Mount Desert St.* ☎ *207/288–9088* ⊕ *www.eclipsegallery.us.*

Island Artisans. Island Artisans sells basketry, pottery, fiber work, and jewelry created by about 150 Maine artisans. ⊠ *99 Main St.* ☎ *207/288–4214* ⊕ *www.islandartisans.com.*

Native Arts Gallery. Native Arts Gallery sells Native American silver and gold jewelry as well as crafts. The gallery is open from May through early November. ✉ *99 Main St.* ☎ *207/288–4474* 🌐 *www.nativeartsgallery.com.*

SPORTING GOODS

Cadillac Mountain Sports. One of the best sporting-goods stores in the state, Cadillac Mountain Sports has developed a following of locals and visitors alike. You can find top-quality climbing, hiking, boating, paddling, and camping equipment. In winter you can rent cross-country skis, ice skates, and snowshoes. ✉ *26 Cottage St.* ☎ *207/288–4532* 🌐 *www.cadillacmountainsports.com.*

WHERE TO EAT AND STAY

For expanded hotel reviews, visit Fodors.com.

$$$ SEAFOOD Fodor's Choice ★

🍴 **Burning Tree.** One of the top restaurants in Maine, this easy-to-miss gem is on Route 3 between Bar Harbor and Otter Creek, in the same building with a festive interior where it opened in 1988. The menu has standards but also changes with the seasons. It emphasizes freshly caught seafood, and seven species of fish are offered virtually every day, all from the Gulf of Maine. There is always monkfish; you may find it pan-sautéed, glazed with sweet chili sauce, and served with Thai-flavored eggplant and coconut rice. Oven-poached cod and stuffed gray sole are signature dishes. There are always two or three vegetarian options and an emphasis on organic produce, much of it from the owners' garden. [$] *Average main: $26* ✉ *69 Otter Creek Dr.(Rte. 3), Otter Creek* ☎ *207/288–9331* 🕓 *Closed mid-Oct.–mid-June; closed Tues. in season and also Mon. after Labor Day. No lunch.*

$$$ HOTEL Fodor's Choice ★

🏨 **Bar Harbor Inn & Spa.** Originally established in the late 1800s as a men's social club, this waterfront inn has rooms spread out over three buildings on well-landscaped grounds. **Pros:** right in town at the harbor; some two-level suites. **Cons:** not right near Acadia National Park. [$] *Rooms from: $209* ✉ *1 Newport Dr.* ☎ *207/288–3351, 800/248–3351* 🌐 *www.barharborinn.com* 🛏 *138 rooms, 15 suites* 🕓 *Closed late Nov.–mid-March* 🍽 *Breakfast.*

ACADIA NATIONAL PARK

3 miles from Bar Harbor via U.S. 3.

Fodor's Choice ★

With about 49,000 acres of protected forests, beaches, mountains, and rocky coastline, Acadia National Park is the second-most-visited national park in America (the first is Great Smoky Mountains National Park). According to the National Park Service, 2 million people visit Acadia each year. The park holds some of the most spectacular scenery on the Eastern Seaboard: a rugged coastline of surf-pounded granite and an interior graced by sculpted mountains, quiet ponds, and lush deciduous forests. Cadillac Mountain (named after a Frenchman who explored here in the late 1600s and later founded Detroit) the highest point of land on the East Coast, dominates the park. Although it's rugged, the park also has graceful stone bridges, miles of carriage roads (popular with walkers, runners, and bikers as well as horse-drawn carriages), and the Jordan Pond House restaurant (famous for its popovers).

CLOSE UP

Acadia's Best Campgrounds

Acadia National Park's two main campgrounds, Seawall and Blackwoods, don't have water views, but the price is right and the ocean is just a 10-minute walk away from each locale.

Blackwoods Campground. One of only two campgrounds inside inland Acadia National Park, Blackwoods is open throughout the year. ⊠ *Rte. 3, 5 miles south of Bar Harbor, Otter Creek*

📞 *207/288–3274, 800/365–2267, 877/444–6777* ⊕ *www.nps.gov*

Seawall Campground. On the "quiet side" of the island, about half the space at this campground does not accept reservations but offers space on a first-come, first-served basis, starting at 8 am. ⊠ *Rte. 102A, 4 miles south of Southwest Harbor, Manset* 📞 *207/244–3600, 877/444–6777 reservations* ⊕ *www.nps.gov*

The 27-mile Park Loop Road provides an excellent introduction, but to truly appreciate the park you must get off the main road and experience it by walking, hiking, biking, sea kayaking, or taking a carriage ride. If you get off the beaten path, you can find places you'll have practically to yourself. Mount Desert Island was once a preserve of summer homes for the very rich (and still is for some) and, because of this, Acadia is the first national park in the United States that was largely created by donations of private land. There are two smaller parts of the park: on Isle au Haut, 15 miles away out in the ocean, and on the Schoodic Peninsula, on the mainland across Frenchman Bay from Mt. Desert.

PARK ESSENTIALS

ADMISSION FEE

A user fee is required if you are anywhere in the park from May through Columbus Day—unless arriving on the Island Explorer buses that serve the park and island villages from June 23 through Columbus Day. They are free to ride and also offer free admittance to the park. The per-vehicle fee is $20 for a seven-consecutive-day pass from late June to Columbus Day, $10 from May through June 22 and from the day after Columbus Day through October. You can walk or ride in (bike or motorcycle) on a $5 individual pass, also good for seven days straight. Bus users are being encouraged to donate this sum for their enjoyment of the park. Or, use your National Park America the Beautiful Pass, which allows entrance to any national park in the United States. Check ⊕ *www.nps.gov* for details.

ADMISSION HOURS

The park is open 24 hours a day, year-round, but roads are closed from December through April 14 except for the Ocean Drive section of Park Loop Road and a small part of the road that provides access to Jordan Pond. Visitor center hours are 8–4:30 April 15–June and October, 8–5 in September, and until 6 in July and August.

PARK CONTACT INFORMATION

Acadia National Park ☎ 207/288–3338 ⊕ www.nps.gov/acad.

GETTING HERE AND AROUND

Route 3 leads to the island and Bar Harbor from Ellsworth and circles the eastern part of the island. Route 102 is the major road on the west side. Free Island Explorer buses serve the main villages and the park from June 23 through Columbus Day. There are scheduled stops, they also pick up and drop off passengers anywhere along the park it is safe to stop.

> ## BOOK A CARRIAGE RIDE
>
> If you would like to take a horse-drawn carriage ride down one of these roads, you can do so from mid-June to mid-October by making a reservation with Wildwood Stables (☎ 207/276–3622). One of their carriages can accommodate two wheelchairs each.

EXPLORING

HISTORIC SITES AND MUSEUMS

★ **Bass Harbor Head Light.** Built in 1858, this lighthouse is one of the most photographed lights in Maine. Now automated, it marks the entrance to Blue Hill Bay. The grounds and residence are Coast Guard property, but two trails around the facility provide excellent views. It's within Acadia National Park, and there is parking. ■TIP→ The best place to take a picture of this small but beautiful lighthouse is from the rocks below—but watch your step; they can be slippery. ⊠ *Lighthouse Rd., turn off Rte. 102A, Bass Harbor* ☞ *Free* ☉ *Daily 9–sunset.*

SCENIC DRIVES AND STOPS

★ **Cadillac Mountain.** At 1,530 feet, this is one of the first places in the United States to see the sun's rays at break of day. It is the highest mountain on the Eastern Seaboard north of Brazil. Dozens of visitors make the trek to see the sunrise or, for those less inclined to get up so early, sunset. From the smooth summit you have an awesome 360-degree view of the jagged coastline that runs around the island. A small gift shop and some restrooms are the only structures at the top. The road up the mountain is closed from December through April 14.

10

★ **Park Loop Road.** This 27-mile road provides a perfect introduction to
Ⓒ the park. If driving, you can do it in an hour, but allow at least half a day for the drive so that you can explore the many sites along the way. They are also served by the free Island Explorer buses, which will also pick up and drop off anywhere along the route where it's safe to stop. Traveling south on Park Loop Road toward Sand Beach, you'll reach a small ticket booth, where, if you haven't already, you will need to pay the park entrance fee (not charged from November through April, or to bus riders). Traffic is one-way from the Route 233 entrance to the Stanley Brook Road entrance south of the Jordan Pond House. The section known as Ocean Drive is open year-round, as is a small section that provides access to Jordan Pond from Seal Harbor.

VISITOR CENTER

Hulls Cove Visitor Center. At the Hulls Cove entrance to Acadia National Park northwest of downtown Bar Harbor, the Hulls Cove Visitor Center, operated by the National Park Service, is a great spot to get your bearings. A large relief map of Mount Desert Island gives you the lay of the land, and you can watch a free 15-minute video about everything the park has to offer. Pick up guidebooks, maps of hiking trails and carriage roads, schedules for ranger-led tours, and recordings for drive-it-yourself tours. Don't forget the *Acadia Beaver Log*, the park's free newspaper detailing guided hikes and other ranger-led events. Junior-ranger programs for kids, nature hikes, photography walks, tide-pool explorations, and evening talks are all popular. The visitor center is just off Route 3.

> **CAUTION**
>
> Every few years someone falls off one of the park's trails or cliffs and are swept out to sea. There is a lot of loose, rocky gravel along the shoreline, and sea rocks can often be slippery—so watch your step. Don't bring a sudden end to your visit by trying to get that "impossible" photo op.

The Acadia National Park Headquarters is just off Route 233 in the park not far from the north end of Eagle Lake and serves as the park's visitor center during the off-season. ⊠ *Route 3, turn into park entrance, watch for signs, Hulls Cove* ☎ *207/288–3338* ⊕ *www.nps.gov/acad* ⊙ *July and Aug., daily 8–6; mid-Apr.–June and Oct., daily 8–4:30, Sept. daily 8–5.*

SPORTS AND THE OUTDOORS

The best way to see Acadia National Park is to get out of your vehicle and explore on foot or by bicycle or boat. There are more than 45 miles of carriage roads that are perfect for walking and biking in the warmer months and for cross-country skiing and snowshoeing in winter. There are 125 miles of trails for hiking, numerous ponds and lakes for canoeing or kayaking, two beaches for swimming, and steep cliffs for rock climbing.

HIKING

Acadia National Park maintains more than 125 miles of hiking trails, from easy strolls around lakes and ponds to rigorous treks with climbs up rock faces and scrambles along cliffs. Although most hiking trails are on the east side of the island, the west side also has some scenic trails. For those wishing for a long climb, try the trails leading up Cadillac Mountain or Dorr Mountain. Another option is to climb Parkman, Sargeant, and Penobscot mountains. Most hiking is done from mid-May to mid-November. Snow falls early in Maine, so from as early as late November to the end of March, cross-country skiing and snowshoeing replace hiking. Volunteers groom most of the carriage roads if there's been 4 inches of snow or more.

■ TIP→ You can park at one end of any trail and use the free shuttle bus to get back to your starting point.

Distances for trails are given for the round-trip hike.

EASY **Ocean Path Trail.** This easily acces-
★ sible 4.4-mile round-trip trail runs
parallel to the Ocean Drive section
of the Park Loop Road from Sand
Beach to Otter Point. It has some
of the best scenery in Maine: cliffs
and boulders of pink granite at the
ocean's edge, twisted branches of
dwarf jack pines, and ocean views
that stretch to the horizon. Be sure
to save time to stop at **Thunder
Hole,** named for the sound the
waves make as they thrash through
a narrow opening in the granite

> ## ACADIA LEAF PEEPING
>
> The fall foliage in Maine can
> be spectacular. Because of the
> moisture, it comes later along the
> coast, around the middle of Octo-
> ber, than it does in the interior of
> the state. The best way to catch
> the colors along the coast is travel
> on the Acadia National Park Loop
> Road. For up-to-date information,
> go to ⊕ *www.mainefoliage.com.*

cliffs, into a sea cave, and whoosh up and out. Steps lead down to the
water, where you can watch the wave action close up, but use caution
here (access may be limited due to storms), and if venturing onto the
outer cliffs along this walk. ⊠ *Ocean Drive section of Park Loop Road,
Sand Beach or Otter Point parking areas.*

DIFFICULT **Acadia Mountain Trail.** This is the king of the trails. The 2½-mile round-
★ trip climb up Acadia Mountain is steep and strenuous, but the payoff is
grand: views of Somes Sound. If you want a guided trip, look into the
ranger-led hikes for this trail. ⊠ *Rte. 102, parking area and trailhead*
☎ *207/288–3338* ⊕ *www.nps.gov/acadia.*

SWIMMING

The park has two swimming beaches, Sand Beach and Echo Lake Beach.
Sand Beach, along Park Loop Road, has changing rooms, restrooms,
and a lifeguard on duty from the first full week of June to Labor Day.
The water temperature here rarely reaches above 55°F. Echo Lake
Beach, on the western side of the island just north of Southwest Harbor, has much warmer water, as well as changing rooms, restrooms,
and a lifeguard on duty throughout summer.

NORTHEAST HARBOR

12 miles south of Bar Harbor via Rtes. 3 and 198.

The summer community for some of the nation's wealthiest families,
Northeast Harbor has one of the best harbors on the coast, which
fills with yachts and powerboats during peak season. Some summer
residents rebuilt here after Bar Harbor's Great Fire of 1947 destroyed
mansions there.

It's a great place to sign up for a cruise around Somes Sound or to the
Cranberry Isles. Other than that, this quiet village has a handful of
restaurants, inns, boutiques, and art galleries.

SOMESVILLE

7 miles north of Northeast Harbor via Rte. 198.

Most visitors pass through Somesville on their way to Southwest Harbor, but this well-preserved village, the oldest on the island, is more than

10

a stop along the way. Originally settled by Abraham Somes in 1761, this was once a bustling commercial center with shingle, lumber, and wool mills; a tannery; a varnish factory; and a dye shop. Today Route 102, which passes through the center of town, takes you past a row of white-clapboard houses with black shutters and well-manicured lawns.

BASS HARBOR

10 miles south of Somesville via Rtes. 102 and 102A.

Bass Harbor is a tiny lobstering village with a relaxed atmosphere and a few accommodations and restaurants. If you're looking to get away from the crowds, consider using this hardworking community as your base. Although Bass Harbor does not draw as many tourists as other villages, the Bass Harbor Head Light in Acadia National Park is one of the region's most popular attractions and is undoubtedly one of the most photographed lighthouses in Maine. From Bass Harbor you can hike on the Ship Harbor Nature Trail or take a ferry to Frenchboro or Swans Island.

GETTING HERE AND AROUND

Maine State Ferry Service. From Bass Harbor the Maine State Ferry Service operates a ferry, the Captain Henry Lee, carrying both passengers and vehicles to Swans Island (40 minutes, round-trip $17.50 per person and $49 per car with driver) and Frenchboro (50 minutes, round-trip $11.25 per person and $32.25 per car with driver). The Frenchboro ferry doesn't run daily; there's also a passenger-only trip on a smaller boat (same price) from April through November. Excursion round-trips (you don't get off the boat) are $10. ⊠ *45 Granville Rd.* ☎ *207/244– 3254* ⊕ *www.maine.gov/mdot/msfs/.*

ESSENTIALS

Transportation Information Maine State Ferry Service. ⊠ *114 Grandville Rd.* ☎ *207/244–3254* ⊕ *www.maine.gov/mdot/msfs/swansisland.htm.*

WHERE TO EAT

$$ ✕ **Thurston's Lobster Pound.** Right on Bass Harbor, looking across to the
SEAFOOD village, Thurston's is easy to spot because of its bright yellow awning. You can buy fresh lobsters to go or sit at covered outdoor tables. Order everything from a grilled-cheese sandwich, soup, or hamburger to a boiled lobster served with clams or mussels. $ *Average main: $18* ⊠ *1 Thurston Rd., at Steamboat Wharf, Bernard* ☎ *207/244–7600* ⊕ *www. thurstonslobster.com* ⊘ *Closed mid-Oct.–mid-May.*

WAY DOWN EAST

Slogans such as "The Real Maine" ring truer Way Down East. The raw, mostly undeveloped coast in this remote region is more accessible than it is farther south. Even in summer here you're likely to have rocky beaches and shady hiking trails to yourself. The slower pace is as calming as a sea breeze.

One innkeeper relates that visitors who plan to stay a few days often opt for a week after learning more about the region's offerings, which include historic sites; museums on local history, culture, and art; national wildlife refuges; state parks and preserves; and increasingly, conservancy-owned public land. Cutler's Bold Coast, with its dramatic granite headlands, is protected from development. Waters near Eastport have some of the world's highest tides. Lakes perfect for canoeing and kayaking are sprinkled inland, and rivers snake through marshland as they near the many bays. Boulders are strewn on blueberry barrens. Rare plants thrive in coastal bogs and heaths, and dark-purple and pink lupines line the roads in late June.

VISITOR INFORMATION

Many chambers of commerce in the region distribute free copies of the pamphlet "Maine's Washington County: Just Off the Beaten Path," which is several cuts above the usual tourist promotion booklet.

Contacts DownEast & Acadia Regional Tourism ⊠ *87 Milbridge Rd., Cherryfield* ☎ *207/546–3600, 888/665–3278* ⊕ *www.downeastacadia.com.*

SCHOODIC PENINSULA

25 miles east of Ellsworth via U.S. Rte. 1 and Rte. 186.

The landscape of Schoodic Peninsula's craggy coastline, towering evergreens, and views over Frenchman Bay are breathtaking year-round. A drive through the well-to-do summer community of Grindstone Neck shows what Bar Harbor might have been like before so many of its mansions were destroyed in the Great Fire of 1947. Artists and artisans have opened galleries in and around Winter Harbor. Anchored at the foot of the peninsula, Winter Harbor was once part of Gouldsboro, which wraps around it. The southern tip of the peninsula is home to the Schoodic section of Acadia National Park.

GETTING HERE AND AROUND

From U.S. 1, Route 186 loops around the peninsula. Route 195 runs from U.S. 1 to Prospect Harbor and on to its end in Corea.

ESSENTIALS

Visitor Information Schoodic Chamber of Commerce ⊕ *www.acadiaschoodic.org.*

EXPLORING

Coastal Villages. Within Gouldsboro on the Schoodic Peninsula are several small coastal villages. You drive through **Wonsqueak** and **Birch Harbor** after leaving the Schoodic section of Acadia National Park. Near Birch Harbor you can find **Prospect Harbor,** a small fishing village nearly untouched by tourism.

> ### THE EARLY BIRD GETS THE SUN
>
> During your visit to Mount Desert, pick a day when you are willing to get up very early, such as 4:30 or 5 am. Drive with a friend to the top of Cadillac Mountain in Acadia National Park. Stand on the highest rock you can find and wait for the sun to come up. When it does, have your friend take a photo of you looking at it and label the photo something like "The first person in the country to see the sun come up on June 1, 2010."

10

In **Corea,** there's little to do besides watch the fishermen at work, wander along stone beaches, or gaze out to sea. ⊠ *Gouldsboro.*

Fodor's Choice   **Acadia National Park.** The only section of Maine's national park that sits
★   on the mainland is at the southern end of the Schoodic Peninsula in
the town of Winter Harbor. The park has a scenic 6-mile one-way loop
that edges along the coast and yields views of Grindstone Neck, Winter Harbor, Winter Harbor Lighthouse, and, across the water, Cadillac Mountain. At the tip of the point, huge slabs of pink granite lie
jumbled along the shore, thrashed unmercifully by the crashing surf
(stay away from the water's edge), and jack pines cling to life amid the
rocks. Fraser Point, at the beginning of the loop, is an ideal place for a
picnic. Work off lunch with a hike up Schoodic Head for the panoramic
views up and down the coast. During the summer season you can take
a passenger ferry to Winter Harbor from Bar Harbor, then catch the
free Island Explorer bus, which stops throughout the park. Admission
fees are not charged when you're just visiting Schoodic. A visitor center
is expected to open in summer 2013 at the park's Schoodic Education
Research Center. *For more information ⇨ see Acadia National Park
and Mount Desert Island.* ⊠ *End of Moore Road, turn off Rte. 186*
☎ *207/288–3338* ⊕ *www.nps.gov/acad* ☉ *Year-round, 24/7.*

Schoodic Education and Research Center. At the campus of a former
naval radio communications station within the Schoodic section of Acadia National Park, the Schoodic Education and Research Center offers
public lectures, workshops, and events like Junior Ranger Day. The goal
is to educate the public about science, nature, and the research work of
a nonprofit institute that is based here and works in partnership with the
park service. It's worth a drive by just to see the Rockefeller Building,
a massive 1935 French Eclectic- and Renaissance-style structure with a
stone and half-timber facade that housed naval offices and housing. In
summer 2013, a park visitor center and the main office of the Schoodic
Education and Research Center Institute are to open here. ⊠ *From Park
Loop Road, turn on Acadia Drive, watch for signs* ☎ *207/288–1310*
⊕ *www.sercinstitute.org*

SPORTS AND THE OUTDOORS

KAYAKING   **SeaScape Kayaking.** Led by a Registered Maine Guide, SeaScape's morning and afternoon kayak tours include an island stop and a blueberry
snack. The company also rents canoes, kayaks, and bikes from its location in Birch Harbor. ⊠ *18 E. Schoodic Dr., Birch Harbor* ☎ *207/963–
5806, 207/479–9912* ⊕ *www.seascapekayaking.com.*

SHOPPING

ANTIQUES   **U.S. Bells.** Hand-cast bronze doorbells and wind-bells are among the
AND MORE   items sold at U.S. Bells. You can also buy finely crafted quilts, wood-
fired pottery, and wood and bronze outdoor furniture, all made by
family members of the foundry owner. Ask for a tour of the foundry.
Open by appointment during the winter. ⊠ *56 W. Bay Rd.(Rte. 186),
Prospect Harbor* ☎ *207/963–7184* ⊕ *www.usbells.com.*

ART GALLERIES   **Lee Fusion Art Glass.** Window glass is fused in a kiln at Lee Fusion
Art Glass to create unusual glass dishware. Colorful enamel accents
depict birds, lighthouses, flowers, and designs made from doilies. The

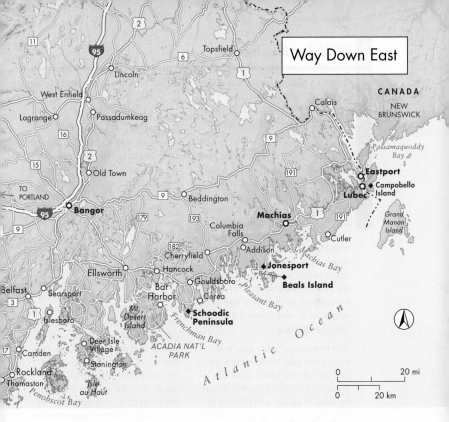

Way Down East

store is open Memorial Day weekend through Columbus Day. ✉ 679 S. Gouldsboro Rd. (Rt. 186), Gouldsboro ☎ 207/963–7280 🌐 www. leefusionartglass.com.

WHERE TO EAT AND STAY
For expanded hotel reviews, visit Fodors.com.

$ ✕ **Chase's Restaurant.** The orange booths may remind you of a fast-food joint, but this family restaurant has a reputation for serving good, basic
SEAFOOD fare. In this region that means a lot of fish. There are large and small fried seafood dinners and several more expensive seafood platters. Try the sweet-potato fries as a side. Lunch fare, sold all day, includes wraps and burgers. It's also open for breakfast. $ *Average main: $10* ✉ 193 *Main St. (Rte. 186)* ☎ 207/963–7171.

$ ✕ **J.M. Gerrish Restaurant.** Ice cream was sold here in the early 1900s,
CAFÉ and still is, and the name is the same, but ownership of this downtown fixture has changed over the years. Part of the old marble counter remains at what today is a café and bistro where folks bustle in for breakfast or lunch or linger over coffee inside and on the porch. The lunch menu has soups, salads, and sandwiches like chicken salad with grapes. Breads and baked goods are made in-house. Dinner is served Thursday through Saturday (it's open until 6 the rest of the week), offering traditional entrées like baked stuffed haddock and seafood

CLOSE UP

Wild for Blueberries

There's no need to inquire about the cheesecake topping if you dine out in August when the wild blueberry crop comes in. Anything but blueberries would be unthinkable.

Way Down East, wild blueberries have long been a favorite food and a key ingredient in cultural and economic life. Maine produces about a third of the commercial harvest, which totals about 70 million pounds annually, Canada supplying virtually all the rest. Washington County yields 65% of Maine's total crop, which is why the state's largest blueberry processors are here: Jasper Wyman & Son and the predecessor of what is now Cherryfield Foods were founded shortly after the Civil War.

Wild blueberries, which bear fruit every other year, thrive in the region's cold climate and sandy, acidic soil. Undulating blueberry barrens stretch for miles in Deblois and Cherryfield ("the Blueberry Capital of the World") and are scattered throughout Washington County. Look for tufts among low-lying plants along the roadways. In spring the fields shimmer as the small-leaf plants turn myriad shades of mauve, honey orange, and lemon yellow. White flowers appear in June. Fall transforms the barrens into a sea of red.

Amid Cherryfield's barrens, a plaque on a boulder lauds the late J. Burleigh Crane for helping advance an industry that's not as wild as it used to be. Honeybees have been brought in to supplement native pollinators, fields are irrigated, and barrens are burned and mowed to rid plants of disease and insects, reducing the need for pesticides. Most of the barrens in and around Cherryfield are owned by the large blueberry processors.

About 80% of Maine's crop is now harvested with machinery. That requires moving boulders, so the rest continues to be harvested by hand with blueberry rakes, which resemble large forks and pull the berries off their stems. Years ago, year-round residents did the work. Today migrant workers make up 90% of this seasonal labor force.

Blueberries get their dark color from anthocyanins, believed to provide antioxidants. Wild blueberries have more of these antiaging, anticancer compounds than their cultivated cousins. Smaller and more flavorful than cultivated blueberries, wild ones are mostly used in packaged foods. Less than 1% of the state's crop—about 500,000 pints—is consumed fresh, mostly in Maine. Look for fresh berries (sometimes starting in late July and lasting until early September) at roadside stands, farmers' markets, and supermarkets.

Wild Blueberry Land in Columbia Falls sells everything blueberry, from muffins and candy to socks and books. Find farm stores, stands, and markets statewide, many selling blueberries and blueberry jams and syrups, at ⊕ www.getrealmaine.com, a Maine Department of Agriculture site that promotes Maine foods.

—Mary Ruoff

fettuccine and good prices on wine by the bottle or glass. $ *Average main: $7* ⊠ *352 Main St.* ☎ *207/963–7320* ⊕ *www.jmgerrish.com* ⊘ *Closed mid-Oct.–mid-May.*

$ ⊡ **Bluff House Inn.** This homey lodge-style modern inn is on a secluded
B&B/INN   hillside with expansive views of Frenchman Bay. **Pros:** good value; larg-
ⓒ   est room has sitting area with pullout couch. **Cons:** only two rooms
have good water views; path to water a bit steep. $ *Rooms from: $85*
⊠ *57 Bluff House Rd., turn off Rte. 186, Gouldsboro* ☎ *207/963–7805*
⊕ *www.bluffinn.com* ↝ *8 rooms* ⦿ *Breakfast.*

$$ ⊡ **Oceanside Meadows Inn.** This place is a must for nature lovers. **Pros:**
B&B/INN   one of region's few sand beaches; staff share info about the area with
Fodor'sChoice   guests in parlor over tea. **Cons:** need to cross road to beach. $ *Rooms*
★   *from: $169* ⊠ *202 Corea Rd.(Rte. 195), Prospect Harbor* ☎ *207/963–*
ⓒ   *5557* ⊕ *www.oceaninn.com* ↝ *13 rooms, 2 suites* ⊘ *Closed mid-Oct.–*
mid-May ⦿ *Breakfast.*

JONESPORT AND BEALS ISLAND

48 miles northeast of Winter Harbor via Rte. 186, U.S. Rte. 1, and Rte. 187; 20 miles southwest of Machias.

The birding is superb around Jonesport and Beals Island, a pair of fishing communities joined by a bridge over Moosabec Reach. A handful of stately homes ring Jonesport's Sawyer Square, where Sawyer Memorial Congregational Church's exquisite stained-glass windows are illuminated at night. But the towns are less geared to travelers than those on the Schoodic Peninsula. Lobster traps are still piled in the yards, and lobster-boat races near Moosabec Reach are the highlight of the community's annual Independence Day celebration. Right next to Beals Island, Great Wass Island, connected to it by a bridge, is home to a namesake preserve with rugged trails to the coast.

GETTING HERE AND AROUND

In Columbia Falls Route 187, a loop road, heads down to Jonesport, where a bridge leads to Beals Island. Route 187 returns to U.S. 1 in Jonesboro.

MACHIAS

20 miles northeast of Jonesport.

The Machias area—Machiasport, East Machias, and Machias, the Washington County seat—lays claim to being the site of the first naval battle of the Revolutionary War, which took place in what is now Machiasport. Despite being outnumbered and out-armed, a small group of Machias men under the leadership of Jeremiah O'Brien captured the armed British schooner *Margaretta*. That battle, fought on June 12, 1775, is now known as the "Lexington of the Sea." The town's other claim to fame is wild blueberries. On the third weekend in August the annual Machias Wild Blueberry Festival is a community celebration complete with parade, crafts fair, concerts, and plenty of blueberry dishes.

ESSENTIALS

Visitor Information Machias Bay Area Chamber of Commerce ✉ *85 Main St., Suite 2* ☎ *207/255–4402* 🌐 *www.machiaschamber.org.*

> **LOOK UP!**
>
> With no large cities, Way Down East offers great stargazing. But if you want some new entertainment on a dark night, paddle a canoe on a lake and look down. Bioluminescent organisms in the water light up as you churn your paddle.

EXPLORING

★ **Burnham Tavern Museum.** It was in this gambrel-roofed tavern home that the men of Machias laid the plans that culminated in the capture of the *Margaretta* in 1775. After the Revolutionary War's first naval battle, wounded British sailors were brought here. Tour guides highlight exhibits and tell colorful stories of early settlers. Period furnishings and household items show what life was like in Colonial times. On the National Register of Historic Places, the dwelling is among the 21 in the country deemed most important to the Revolution. ✉ *14 Colonial Way (192)* ☎ *207/255–6930* 🌐 *www.burnhamtavern.com* 🎫 *$5* 🕒 *Mid-June–Sept., weekdays 9:30–4 (last tour at 3:30), or by appointment.*

WHERE TO EAT

$$$ MODERN AMERICAN ★ 🍴 **Riverside Inn & Restaurant.** A bright yellow exterior invites a stop at this delightful restaurant in a former sea captain's home perched on the bank of the Machias River, as are the restaurant's vegetable and herb gardens. Ask for a table in the intimate sunroom, which has water views and opens to the other dining room. You can enjoy a drink and snacks like fruit hummus and chips on the deck. The chef-owner brings a special flair to traditional dishes, such as pork served with a pistachio crust. His signature dish is salmon stuffed with crabmeat and shrimp. In summer months the menu includes dressed-up dinner salads—try pairing one with standout appetizers like hake cakes and red-tuna wontons. Also an inn (open daily except in early winter) with Victorian touches, Riverside has two guest rooms in the main house and two suites in the coach house. [$] *Average main: $28* ✉ *608 Main St., U.S. 1, East Machias* ☎ *207/255–4134, 888/255–4344* 🌐 *www.riversideinn-maine.com* 🕒 *Closed Jan.; Mon.–Wed. Feb.–May and Nov. and Dec.; Mon. June–Oct. No lunch.*

LUBEC

28 miles northeast of Machias via U.S. 1 and Rte. 189.

Lubec is one of the first places in the United States to see the sunrise. A popular destination for outdoor enthusiasts, it offers plenty of opportunities for hiking and biking, and the birding is renowned. It's a good base for day trips to New Brunswick's Campobello Island, reached by a bridge—the only one to the island—from downtown Lubec. The main attraction there, Roosevelt Campobello International Park, operates a visitor center that also provides information about the region generally on the U.S. side of the border. It's in Whiting at the corner of U.S. 1 and Route 189, the road to Lubec. The village is perched at the end of a narrow strip of land at the end of Route 189, so you often can

see water in three directions in this special off-the-beaten-path place.

GETTING HERE AND AROUND

In summer you can take a water taxi from here to Eastport— about a mile by boat but 40 miles by the circuitous northerly land route. From U.S. 1 in Whiting, Route 189 leads to Lubec; it's about 13 miles to the village.

WORD OF MOUTH

"Lubec is about as quaint and authentic as it gets. It is beautiful, has a beach and a dramatic, gorgeous trail next to [West] Quoddy Head Lighthouse, and also has some wonderful little restaurants. Eastport is great, too."

—dfrostnh

SPORTS AND THE OUTDOORS

★ **Quoddy Head State Park.** The easternmost point of land in the United States is marked by candy-striped West Quoddy Head Light. In 1806 President Thomas Jefferson signed an order authorizing construction of a lighthouse on this site. You can't climb the tower, but the former light keeper's house has a museum with a video showing the interior. The museum also has displays on Lubec's maritime past and the region's marine life. A gallery displays works by artists who live or summer in the area. A mystical 2-mile path along the cliffs here, one of five trails, yields magnificent views of Canada's cliff-clad Grand Manan Island. Whales can often be sighted offshore. The 540-acre park has a picnic area. ✉ *973 S. Lubec Rd., off Rte. 189* ☎ *207/733–0911* 🌐 *www.parksandlands.com* 🎟 *$3* 🕒 *Daily, 9–sunset.*

WHERE TO EAT AND STAY

For expanded hotel reviews, visit Fodors.com.

$$ SEAFOOD 🍴 **Uncle Kippy's.** There isn't much of a view from the picture windows, but locals don't mind—they come here for the satisfying seafood. The dining room is large and has a bar. Entrées include seafood dinners and combo platters and some chicken and meat dishes. There are burgers, too, and the fresh-dough pizza is popular. You can order from the lunch or dinner menu. A takeout window and ice cream bar are open May through September. [$] *Average main: $14* ✉ *170 Main St. (Rte. 189)* ☎ *207/733–2400* 🌐 *www.unclekippys.com* 🕒 *Closed Dec.–March and Mon. and Tues. April–June and Sept.–Nov.*

$ B&B/INN ★ 🏨 **Peacock House.** Five generations of the Peacock family lived in this white-clapboard house a few blocks up from downtown before it was converted into an inn. **Pros:** piano and fireplace in living room; lovely garden off deck; think-of-everything innkeepers direct guests to area's tucked-away spots. **Cons:** not on the water. [$] *Rooms from: $98* ✉ *27 Summer St.* ☎ *207/733–2403, 888/305–0036* 🌐 *www.peacockhouse.com* 🛏 *5 rooms, 2 suites* 🕒 *Closed Nov.–Apr.* 🍽 *Breakfast.*

CAMPOBELLO ISLAND, CANADA

28 miles east of Machias.

A popular excursion from Lubec, New Brunswick's Campobello Island has two fishing villages, Welshpool and Wilson's Beach. The only bridge is from Lubec, but in summer a car ferry shuttles passengers from

Campobello Island to Deer Island, where you can continue on to the Canadian mainland. (⇨ *See the Travel Smart section for information on passports or other documents U.S. citizens need when traveling between the United States and Canada.)*

GETTING HERE AND AROUND

After coming across the bridge from Lubec, Route 774 runs from one end of the island to the other, taking you through the two villages and to Roosevelt Campobello International Park.

EXPLORING

★ **Roosevelt Campobello International Park.** A joint project of the American and the Canadian governments, this park is crisscrossed with interesting hiking trails. Groomed dirt roads attract bikers. Eagle Hill Bog has a wooden walkway and signs identifying rare plants. Neatly manicured Campobello Island has always had a special appeal for the wealthy and famous. It was here that President Franklin Roosevelt and his family spent summers. You can take a self-guided tour of the 34-room Roosevelt Cottage that was presented to Eleanor and Franklin as a wedding gift. The wicker-filled structure looks essentially as it did when the family was in residence. A visitor center has displays about the Roosevelts and Canadian-American relations. Eleanor Roosevelt Teas are held at 11 and 3 daily in the neighboring Hubbard Cottage. ■ **TIP→ Note that the Islands are on Atlantic Time, which is an hour later than EST.** ✉ *459 Rte. 774, Welshpool, New Brunswick, Canada* ☎ *506/752–2922, 877/851–6663* 🌐 *www.fdr.net* 🎟 *Free.*

WHERE TO EAT

$$$ SEAFOOD ★ 👍 🍴 **Family Fisheries.** Seafood lovers know that fried fish doesn't have to be greasy. That's why people keep heading across the international bridge to eat at this family establishment in Wilson's Beach. The freshest seafood is delivered to the restaurant, where you can bring your own wine ($2 tipping fee). Order fried haddock, scallops, shrimp, or clams alone or as part of a platter. Eat in the large dining room or near the playground at picnic tables or in a screened room. Lobsters are cooked outside and also sold live or steamed to go. You can buy ice cream at the takeout window, and the restaurant serves breakfast in July and August. [$] *Average main: C$15* ✉ *1977 Rte. 774, Wilson's Beach, New Brunswick, Canada* ☎ *506/752–2470* ⏲ *Closed late Oct.–late Mar.*

EASTPORT

39 miles northeast of Lubec via Rte. 189, U.S. 1, and Rte. 190; 109 miles north of Ellsworth via U.S. 1 and Rte. 190.

Connected by a granite causeway to the mainland at Pleasant Point Reservation, Eastport has wonderful views of the nearby islands, and you can sometimes spot whales from the waterfront because the harbor is so deep. Known for its diverse architecture, the island city was one of the nation's busiest seaports in the early 1800s. In the late 19th century, 14 sardine canneries operated here. The industry's decline in the 20th century left the city economically depressed, but now the town has set its sights on shipping, salmon farming (though less so), tourism, and the arts—performing and visual arts are thriving here. On the weekend after Labor Day the Eastport Pirate Festival brings folks out in pirate attire for a ship race, parade, fireworks, cutlass "battles" by reenactors, and other events, including a children's breakfast and schooner ride with pirates.

Get downtown early to secure a viewing spot for Maine's largest July 4th parade. Canadian bagpipe bands make this an event not to be missed. The day culminates with fireworks over the bay. On the weekend of the second Sunday in August, locals celebrate Sipayik Indian Days at the Pleasant Point Reservation. This festival of Passamaquoddy culture includes canoe races, dancing, drumming, children's games, fireworks, and traditional dancing.

GETTING HERE AND AROUND

From U.S. 1 Route 190 leads to the Island City. Continue on Washington Street to the water. You can also take a water taxi from here to Lubec—1 mile or so by boat but about 40 by land—in the summer.

ESSENTIALS

Visitor Information Eastport Area Chamber of Commerce *207/853–4644* 🌐 *www.eastport.net.*

WHERE TO EAT

$$ SEAFOOD 👶 🍴 **Chowder House.** Just north of downtown Eastport, this expansive waterfront eatery sits on the pier next to where the ferry docks. Built atop an old cannery foundation, it has original details such as wood beams and a stone wall. Eat in the downstairs pub, upstairs in the dining room, or on the large deck. The house specialties include a smoked fish appetizer and seafood pasta in a wine-and-cheese sauce. Lunch, served until 4, includes fried seafood plates, burgers, wraps, and sandwiches. [$] *Average main: $17* ✉ *167 Water St.* ☎ *207/853–4700* 🌐 *www.eastportchowderhouse.net* 🕓 *Closed mid-Oct.–mid-May.*

$$$ MODERN AMERICAN Fodor's Choice ★ 🍴 **The Pickled Herring.** Linger near the open kitchen and you may hear diners pay homage to the chef at the wood-fire grill as he prepares dishes like duck with a maple-peppercorn glaze, linguini with Maine littleneck clams, and Maine-raised bone-in rib-eye steak. Thin wood-fired pizzettes with toppings like caramelized onions and lobster Alfredo is a lighter choice. Housed in a landmark downtown storefront with soaring windows and ceilings, this restaurant's wonderful food and atmosphere have made it a destination. Pictures of Eastport's former sardine plants hang on a brick wall, and gas-burning lanterns and streetlamp-like lights throw a soft glow. Urbanites will feel at home, but locals do, too. A fun bar area with low tables and banquettes hides behind an interior wall. Specialty cocktails like the Foghorn (Tanqueray, fresh-squeezed lime juice, and ginger ale) have a Down East twist, and 12 Maine microbrews and craft beers are on tap. [$] *Average main: $21* ✉ *32 Water St.* ☎ *207/853–2323* 🌐 *www.thepickledherring.com* 🕓 *Closed Jan.–April and Sun. and Mon. May–Dec. No lunch.*

Travel Smart
New England

GETTING HERE AND AROUND

New England's largest and most cosmopolitan city, Boston, is the region's major transportation and cultural center. Secondary hubs include Hartford, Connecticut, and Portland, Maine. Your best bet for exploring is to travel by car—flying within the region is expensive and driving distances between most attractions are short. Inside most cities, public transportation is a viable—and often preferable—means for getting around. Passenger ferry service is available to outlying islands (some vessels accommodate vehicles).

See the Getting Here and Around section at the beginning of each chapter for more transportation information.

▎AIR TRAVEL

Most travelers visiting New England head for a major gateway, such as Boston, Providence, Hartford/Springfield, Manchester, or even New York City or Albany, and then rent a car to explore the region. The New England states form a fairly compact region, with few important destinations more than six hours apart by car. It's costly and generally impractical to fly within New England, the exceptions being the island resort destinations of Martha's Vineyard and Nantucket in Massachusetts and Block Island in Rhode Island, which have regular service from Boston and a few other regional airports.

Boston's Logan Airport is one of the nation's most important domestic and international airports, with direct flights arriving from all over North America and internationally. New England's other major airports receive few international flights (mostly from Canada) but do offer a wide range of direct domestic flights to East Coast and Midwest destinations and, to a lesser extent, to the western United States. Some sample flying times to Boston are: from Chicago (2½ hours), London (6½ hours) and Los Angeles (6 hours).

Times from U.S. destinations are similar, if slightly shorter, to Albany and Hartford, assuming you can find direct flights.

AIRPORTS

The main gateway to New England is Boston's Logan International Airport (BOS). Bradley International Airport (BDL), in Windsor Locks, Connecticut, 12 miles north of Hartford, is convenient to Western Massachusetts and all of Connecticut. T. F. Green Airport (PVD), just outside Providence, Rhode Island, and Manchester Boston Regional Airport (MHT), in New Hampshire, are other major airports—and alternative gateways to Boston, which is a one-hour drive from each. Additional New England airports served by major carriers include Portland International Jetport (PWM) in Maine and Burlington International Airport (BTV) in Vermont. Other airports are in Albany, New York (ALB, near Western Massachusetts and Vermont); Westchester County, New York (HPN, near Southern Connecticut); Bangor, Maine (BGR); and Barnstable Municipal in Hyannis, Massachusetts (HYA). You can access Nantucket and Martha's Vineyard via ferries from Hyannis or fly directly to the islands' airports.

Airport Information Albany International Airport ☎ 518/242–2200 ⊕ www. albanyairport.com. **Bangor International Airport** ☎ 207/992–4600 ⊕ www.flybangor. com. **Barnstable Municipal Airport–Hyannis** ☎ 508/775–2020 ⊕ www.town.barnstable. ma.us/airport/. **Bradley International Airport–Hartford/Springfield** ☎ 860/292–2000 ⊕ www.bradleyairport.com. **Burlington International Airport** ☎ 802/863–1889 ⊕ www. burlingtonintlairport.com. **Logan International Airport–Boston** ☎ 800/235–6426 ⊕ www.massport.com. **Manchester Boston Regional Airport** ☎ 603/624–6539 ⊕ www. flymanchester.com. **Martha's Vineyard Airport** ☎ 508/693–7022 ⊕ www.mvyairport.com. **Nantucket Memorial Airport** ☎ 508/325–5300 ⊕ www.nantucketairport.com. **Portland**

International Jetport ☎ 207/874-8877 ⊕ www.portlandjetport.org. **T. F. Green Airport-Providence** ☎ 401/737-8222 ⊕ www.pvdairport.com. **Westchester County Airport-White Plains** ☎ 914/995-4850 ⊕ airport.westchestergov.com.

FLIGHTS

Numerous airlines fly to and from Boston; additionally, the discount carrier Southwest Airlines flies to Albany, Boston, Hartford/Springfield (Bradley International Airport), Providence, and Manchester, New Hampshire. Smaller or discount airlines serving Boston include AirTran, Cape Air, and JetBlue. Cape Air also provides service from Cape Cod and the islands to Providence and New Bedford. You can fly to Burlington from New York City on JetBlue, and you can fly to Boston from Atlantic City, Myrtle Beach, and Fort Lauderdale on Spirit Airlines. New England Airlines serves Block Island, with regularly scheduled flights from Westerly, Rhode Island.

Airline Contacts AirTran Airways ☎ 800/247-8726 ⊕ www.airtran.com. **American Airlines** ☎ 800/433-7300 ⊕ www.aa.com. **Cape Air** ☎ 800/352-0714 ⊕ www.capeair.com. **Delta Airlines** ☎ 800/221-1212 ⊕ www.delta.com. **JetBlue** ☎ 800/538-2583 ⊕ www.jetblue.com. **New England Airlines** ☎ 800/243-2460 ⊕ www.block-island.com/nea. **Southwest Airlines** ☎ 800/435-9792 ⊕ www.southwest.com. **Spirit Airlines** ☎ 800/772-7117 ⊕ www.spirit.com. **United Airlines** ☎ 800/864-8331 ⊕ www.united.com. **USAirways** ☎ 800/428-4322 ⊕ www.usairways.com.

▮ BOAT TRAVEL

Principal ferry routes in New England connect New Bedford on the mainland and Cape Cod with Martha's Vineyard and Nantucket, Boston with Provincetown, southern Rhode Island with Block Island, and Connecticut with New York's Long Island and Block Island. Other routes provide access to many islands off the Maine Coast. Ferries cross Lake Champlain between Vermont and upstate New York. International service between Portland, Yarmouth, and Bar Harbor, Maine, and Nova Scotia, is also available. With the exception of the Lake Champlain ferries—which are first-come, first-served—car reservations are advisable.

▮ BUS TRAVEL

Regional bus service is relatively plentiful throughout New England. It can be a handy and affordable means of getting around, as buses travel many routes that trains do not.

Concord Coach runs buses between Boston and Concord, New Hampshire, Portland, Maine, and Bangor, Maine. C&J sends Wi-Fi–equipped buses up the New Hampshire coast to Newburyport, Massachusetts, Dover, New Hampshire, Durham, New Hampshire, and Portsmouth, New Hampshire, and also provides service to New York City. Concord and C&J both leave from Boston's South Station (which is connected to the Amtrak station) and Logan Airport.

C&J ☎ 800/258-7111 ⊕ www.ridecj.com. **Concord Coach** ☎ 800/639-3317 ⊕ www.concordcoachlines.com.

BoltBus offers cheap fares in new Wi-Fi– and electrical outlet–equipped buses between Boston, New York, Philadelphia, and Washington, D.C., starting at just $1 if you reserve early enough. Megabus also offers low fares and its Wi-Fi–equipped buses serve New York City and many other points on the East Coast. BoltBus and Megabus use Boston's South Station. Major credit cards are accepted for all buses and for BoltBus you can only purchase tickets online.

Bus Information BoltBus ☎ 877/265-8287 ⊕ www.boltbus.com. **Megabus** ☎ 877/462-6342 ⊕ us.megabus.com.

▌CAR TRAVEL

New England is best explored by car. Areas in the interior are largely without heavy traffic and congestion. Coastal New England is more congested (especially getting to and from Cape Cod during the summer) and parking can be hard to find or expensive in Boston, Providence, and the many smaller resort towns along the coast. Still, a car is typically the best way to get around even on the coast (though you may want to park it at your hotel in Boston or on Cape Cod and use it as little as possible). In the interior, especially Western Massachusetts, Vermont, New Hampshire, and Maine, public transportation options are limited and a car is almost necessary. Note that Interstate 90 (the Massachusetts Turnpike) is a toll road throughout Massachusetts. If you rent a car at Logan International Airport, allow plenty of time to return it—as much as 60 minutes to be comfortable.

GASOLINE

Gas stations are easy to find along major highways and in most communities throughout the region. At this writing, the average price of a gallon of regular unleaded gas in New England is $3.89. However, prices vary from station to station within any city. The majority of stations are self-serve with pumps that accept credit cards, though you may find a holdout full-service station on occasion. Tipping is not expected at these.

PARKING

In Boston and other large cities, finding a spot on the street can be time- and quarter-consuming. Your best bet is to park in a garage, which can cost upward of $20 a day. In smaller cities, street parking is usually simpler, though parking garages are convenient and less expensive than their big-city counterparts. Pay attention to signs—some cities allow only residents to park on certain streets. In most small towns parking is not a problem, though some beach and lake parking areas are reserved for those with resident stickers.

ROAD CONDITIONS

Major state and U.S. routes are generally well maintained, with snowplows at the ready during the winter to salt and plow road surfaces soon after the flakes begin to fall. Traffic is heaviest around Boston, Hartford, and New Haven, especially during rush hour. Secondary state routes and rural roads can be a mixed bag; generally, Route 1 is well maintained, but with slower traffic that can get locally congested in even the smallest coastal towns.

Boston motorists are notorious for driving aggressively. Streets in the Boston area are confusing; a GPS unit can be very helpful.

ROADSIDE EMERGENCIES

Throughout New England, call 911 for any travel emergency, such as an accident or a serious health concern. For automotive breakdowns, 911 is not appropriate. Instead, find a local directory and dial a towing service. When out on the open highway, call the nonemergency central administration phone number of the State Police for assistance.

RULES OF THE ROAD

On city streets the speed limit is 30 mph unless otherwise posted; on rural roads, the speed limit ranges from 40 to 50 mph unless otherwise posted. Interstate speeds range from 50 to 65 mph, depending on how densely populated the area is. Throughout the region, you're permitted to make a right turn on red except where posted. Be alert for one-way streets in congested communities, such as Boston and Providence.

State law requires that drivers and all passengers wear seat belts at all times. Always strap children under age five or 40 pounds into approved child-safety seats.

You will encounter many traffic circles/rotaries if you drive in New England (especially in the Boston area). Remember that cars entering traffic circles must yield to cars that are already in the circle. Some rotaries have two lanes, which complicates things. If you're leaving the rotary at the next possible exit, enter from the right lane. If you're leaving the rotary at any exit after the first possible exit, enter from the left lane (which becomes the inner lane of the circle); you can also exit the circle directly from this lane—though check your right side so you don't side-swipe a driver who's incorrectly in the right lane.

CAR RENTAL

Because a car is the most practical way to get around New England, it's wise to rent one if you're not bringing your own. The major airports serving the region all have on-site car-rental agencies. If you're traveling to the area by bus or train, you might consider renting a car once you arrive. A few train or bus stations have one or two major car-rental agencies on-site.

Rates at the area's major airport, Boston's Logan Airport, begin at around $50 a day and $200 a week for an economy car with air-conditioning, automatic transmission, and unlimited mileage. The same car might go for around $70 a day and $300 a week at a smaller airport such as Portland International Jetport. These rates do not include state tax on car rentals, which varies depending on the airport but generally runs 12% to 15%. Generally, it costs less to rent a car outside of an airport, but factor into the value whether it is easy or difficult to get there with your luggage.

Most agencies won't rent to you if you're under the age of 21 and several major agencies will not rent to anyone under 25. When picking up a rental car, non-U.S. residents need a voucher for any prepaid reservation that was made in their home country, a passport, a driver's license, and a travel policy that covers each driver. Boston's Logan Airport is large, spread out, and usually congested, so if you will be returning a rental vehicle there, make sure to allow plenty of time to take care of it before heading for your flight.

Major Rental Agencies Alamo
☎ 877/222-9075 ⊕ www.alamo.com. **Avis**
☎ 800/331-1212 ⊕ www.avis.com. **Budget**
☎ 800/527-0700 ⊕ www.budget.com. **Hertz**

☎ 800/654-3131 ⊕ www.hertz.com. **National Car Rental** ☎ 877/222-9058 ⊕ www.nationalcar.com.

▌TRAIN TRAVEL

Amtrak offers frequent daily service along its Northeast Corridor route from Washington, D.C., Philadelphia, and New York to Boston. Amtrak's high-speed *Acela* trains link Boston and Washington, with stops at New York, Philadelphia, etc., along the way. The *Downeaster* connects Boston with Portland, Maine, with stops in coastal New Hampshire.

Other Amtrak services include the *Vermonter* between Washington, D.C., and St. Albans, Vermont, the *Ethan Allen Express* between New York and Rutland, Vermont, and the *Lake Shore Limited* between Boston and Chicago, with stops at Pittsfield, Springfield, Worcester, and Framingham, Massachusetts. These trains run on a daily basis. Allow 15 to 30 minutes to make train connections.

The Massachusetts Bay Transportation Authority (MBTA) connects Boston with outlying areas on the north and south shores of the state. Private rail lines have scenic train trips throughout New England, particularly during fall foliage season. Several use vintage steam equipment; the most notable is the Cog Railway to Mt. Washington in New Hampshire.

Metro-North Railroad's New Haven Line offers service from New York City along the Connecticut coast up to New Haven. The line also reaches as far north as Danbury and Waterbury.

Information Amtrak ☎ 800/872-7245
⊕ www.amtrak.com. **Mt. Washington Cog Railway** ☎ 603/278-5404, 800/922-8825
⊕ www.thecog.com. **Massachusetts Bay Transportation Authority** (*MBTA*).
☎ 617/222-3200, 800/392-6100 ⊕ www.mbta.com. **Metro-North Railroad** ☎ 212/532-4900, 877/690-5114 ⊕ www.mta.info/mnr.

ESSENTIALS

▮ ACCOMMODATIONS

In New England you can bed down in a chain hotel or a five-star palace, but unless you're staying in a city, this is really bed-and-breakfast land. Charming—and sometimes historic—inns, small hotels, and B&Bs dot the region and provide a glimpse of local life.

⇨ *Prices in the reviews are the lowest cost of a standard double room in high season.*

BED-AND-BREAKFASTS

Historic B&Bs and inns proliferate throughout New England. In many rural or less-touristy areas, B&Bs offer an affordable alternative to chain properties, but in tourism-dependent communities (i.e., most of the major towns in this region), expect to pay about the same or more for a historic inn as for a full-service hotel. Many of the state's finest restaurants are also in country inns. Although many B&Bs and smaller establishments continue to offer a low-key, homey experience, in recent years many such properties have begun offering amenities like Wi-Fi, whirlpool tubs, and TVs with DVD players. Quite a few inns and B&Bs serve substantial breakfasts.

Reservation Services Bed & Breakfast.com ☎ 512/322–2710, 800/462–2632 ⊕ www. bedandbreakfast.com. **Bed & Breakfast Inns Online** ☎ 800/215–7365 ⊕ www.bbonline. com. **BnB Finder.com** ☎ 888/469–6663 ⊕ www.bnbfinder.com.

HOUSE AND APARTMENT RENTALS

In New England, you are most likely to find a house, apartment, or condo rental in areas in which ownership of second homes is common, such as beach resorts and ski country. Home-exchange directories sometimes list rentals as well as exchanges. Another good bet is to contact real-estate agents in the area in which you are interested.

Contacts Forgetaway ⊕ www.forgetaway. com. **Home Away** ☎ 512/782–0805 ⊕ www. homeaway.com. **Interhome** ☎ 800/882–6864 ⊕ www.interhomeusa.com/. **Villas International** ☎ 415/499–9490, 800/221–2260 ⊕ www.villasintl.com.

HOTELS

Major hotel and motel chains are amply represented in New England. The region is also liberally supplied with small, independent motels, which run the gamut from the tired to the tidy. Don't overlook these mom-and-pop operations; they frequently offer cheerful, convenient accommodations at lower rates than the chains.

Reservations are always a good idea, particularly in summer and in winter resort areas, in college towns in September and at graduation time in spring; and at areas renowned for autumn foliage.

Most hotels and motels will hold your reservation until 6 pm; call ahead if you plan to arrive late. All will hold a late reservation for you if you guarantee your reservation with a credit-card number.

Note that in Massachusetts, by state law, all hotels are nonsmoking. All hotels listed have private baths unless otherwise noted.

▮ CHILDREN IN NEW ENGLAND

Throughout New England, you'll have no problem finding comparatively inexpensive child-friendly hotels and family-style restaurants—as well as some top children's museums, beaches, parks, planetariums, and lighthouses. Just keep in mind that a number of fine, antique-filled B&Bs and inns punctuate the landscape, and these places are not always suitable for kids—many flat-out refuse to accommodate children. Also, some of the more quiet and rural areas lack child-oriented attractions.

Favorite destinations for family vacations in New England include Boston, Cape Cod, the White Mountains, Mystic and southeastern Connecticut and coastal Maine, but in general, the entire region has plenty to offer families. Places that are especially appealing to children are indicated by a rubber-duckie icon (🦆) in the margin.

LODGING

Chain hotels and motels welcome children and New England has many family-oriented resorts with lively children's programs. You'll also find farms that accept guests and can be lots of fun for children. Rental houses and apartments abound, particularly around ski areas. In the off-season, these can be economical as well as comfortable touring bases. Some country inns, especially those with a quiet, romantic atmosphere and those furnished with antiques, are less enthusiastic about little ones. Many larger resorts and hotels will provide a babysitter at an additional cost. Others will provide a list of sitters in the area.

Most hotels in New England allow children under a certain age to stay in their parents' room at no extra charge, but others charge for them as extra adults; find out the cutoff age for children's discounts. Note that in Maine, by state law, hotels and inns (unless they have five or fewer rooms) cannot put age restrictions on children.

Most lodgings that welcome infants and small children will provide a crib or cot, but remember to give advance notice so that one will be available for you (and ask about any additional charges). Many family resorts make special accommodations for small children during meals.

TRANSPORTATION

Each New England state has specific requirements regarding age and weight requirements for children in car seats. If you're renting a car, ask about the state(s) you're planning to drive in. If you will need a car seat, make sure the agency you select provides them and reserve well in advance.

▮ COMMUNICATIONS

INTERNET

Most major chain hotels and many smaller motels throughout New England now offer Wi-Fi or other Internet access, both from individual rooms and in lobbies (which usually have a desktop computer available for guest use); ask about access fees when you book. Many coffee shops provide Wi-Fi (some for free), as do most libraries; the latter also provide computers with free Internet access. Cybercafes lists more than 4,000 Internet cafés worldwide.

Contacts Cybercafes ⊕ *www.cybercafes.com.*

▮ EATING OUT

Although certain ingredients and preparations are common to the region as a whole, New England's cuisine varies greatly from place to place. Especially in such urban areas as Boston, Providence, New Haven, and Portland and also in upscale resort areas such as Newport, Litchfield County, the Berkshires, Martha's Vineyard, Nantucket, and coastal Maine, you can expect to find stellar restaurants, many of them with culinary luminaries at the helm and a reputation for creative—and occasionally daring—menus.

Elsewhere, restaurant food tends more toward the simple, traditional, and conservative. Cities, collegiate communities, and other sophisticated New England areas also have a great variety of international restaurants, especially excellent Italian, French, Japanese, Indian, and Thai eateries. There are also quite a few diners, which typically present patrons with page after page of inexpensive, short-order cooking and often stay open until the wee hours.

The proximity to the ocean accounts for a number of restaurants, often tiny shacks, serving very fresh seafood, and the numerous boutique dairy, meat, and vegetable suppliers that have sprung up throughout New England account for other choice ingredients. In fact, menus in the more upscale and tourism-driven communities often note which Vermont dairy or Berkshires produce farm a particular goat cheese or heirloom tomato came from.

For information on food-related health issues, see Health below.

MEALS AND MEALTIMES

In general, the widest variety of mealtime options in New England is in larger cities and at resort areas, though you may be pleasantly surprised to hear about a creative café in a smaller town, especially along the Maine Coast.

For an early breakfast, pick places that cater to a working clientele. City, town, and roadside establishments specializing in breakfast for early workers often open their doors at 5 or 6 am. At country inns and B&Bs, breakfast is seldom served before 8 am; if you need to get an earlier start, ask ahead of time if your host or hostess can accommodate you. Lunch in New England generally runs from around 11 am to 2:30 pm; dinner is usually served from 6 to 9 pm (many restaurants have early-bird specials beginning at 5). Only in the larger cities will you find full dinners being offered much later than 9 pm. Many restaurants in New England are closed Monday and sometimes Sunday or Tuesday, although this is never true in resort areas in high season. However, resort-town eateries often shut down completely in the off-season.

Unless otherwise noted, the restaurants listed *in this guide* are open daily for lunch and dinner.

PAYING

For guidelines on tipping, see Tipping below.

Credit cards are accepted for meals throughout New England in all but the most modest establishments. ⇨ *Prices in the reviews are the average cost of a main*

course at dinner or, if dinner is not served, at lunch.

RESERVATIONS AND DRESS

It's a good idea to make a reservation if you can. We only mention them specifically when reservations are essential (there's no other way you'll ever get a table) or when they are not accepted. For popular restaurants, book as far ahead as you can (often 30 days) and reconfirm as soon as you arrive. (Large parties should always call ahead to check the reservations policy.) We mention dress only when men are required to wear a jacket or a jacket and tie.

WINE, BEER, AND SPIRITS

New England is no stranger to microbrews. The granddaddy of New England's independent beer makers is the Boston Beer Company (one of the largest American craft breweries and makers of Samuel Adams), producing brews available throughout the region since 1985. Following the Sam Adams lead in offering hearty English-style ales and special seasonal brews are breweries such as Vermont's Long Trail, Maine's Shipyard, and New Hampshire's Smuttynose Brewing Co. Green Mountain Cidery makes Woodchuck hard cider in Middlebury, Vermont.

New England is beginning to earn some respect as a wine-producing region. Varietals capable of withstanding the region's harsh winters have been the basis of promising enterprises such as Rhode Island's Sakonnet Vineyards, Chicama Vineyards on Martha's Vineyard, and Connecticut's Hopkins Vineyard (part of the Connecticut Wine Trail). Even Vermont is getting into the act with the Snow Farm Vineyard in the Lake Champlain Islands and Boyden Valley Winery in Cambridge.

Although a patchwork of state and local regulations affect the hours and locations of places that sell alcoholic beverages (for example, Connecticut prohibits the in-store sale of alcohol on Sundays and Massachusetts bans "happy hours"), New England licensing laws are fairly liberal. State-owned or -franchised stores sell hard liquor in New Hampshire, Maine, and Vermont; many travelers have found that New Hampshire offers the region's lowest prices. Look for state-run liquor "supermarkets" on interstate highways in the southern part of New Hampshire.

▐ HEALTH

Lyme disease, so named for its having been first reported in the town of Lyme, Connecticut, is a potentially debilitating disease carried by deer ticks, which thrive in dry, brush-covered areas, particularly on the coast. Always use insect repellent; the potential for outbreaks of Lyme disease make it imperative that you protect yourself from ticks from early spring through summer. To prevent bites, wear light-color clothing and tuck pant legs into socks. Look for black ticks about the size of a pinhead around hairlines and the warmest parts of the body. If you have been bitten, consult a physician, especially if you see the telltale bull's-eye bite pattern. Influenza-like symptoms often accompany a Lyme infection. Early treatment is imperative.

New England's two greatest insect pests are black flies and mosquitoes. The former are a phenomenon of late spring and early summer and are generally a problem only in the densely wooded areas of the far north. Mosquitoes, however, can be a nuisance just about everywhere in summer. The best protection against both pests is repellent containing DEET; if you're camping in the woods during black fly season, you'll also want to use fine mesh screening in eating and sleeping areas and even wear mesh headgear. A particular pest of coastal areas, especially salt marshes, is the greenhead fly. Their bite is nasty, they are hard to kill, and they are best repelled by a liberal application of Avon Skin So Soft or a similar product.

Coastal waters attract seafood lovers who enjoy harvesting their own clams, mussels, and even lobsters; permits are required and casual harvesting of lobsters is strictly forbidden. Amateur clammers should be aware that New England shellfish beds are periodically visited by red tides, during which microorganisms can render shellfish poisonous. To keep abreast of the situation, inquire when you apply for a license (usually at town halls or police stations) and pay attention to red tide postings as you travel.

▐ HOURS OF OPERATION

Hours in New England differ little from those in other parts of the United States. Within the region, shops and other businesses tend to keep slightly later hours in larger cities and along the coast, which is generally more populated than interior New England.

Most major museums and attractions are open daily or six days a week (with Monday being the most likely day of closing). Hours are often shorter on Saturday and especially Sunday, and some prominent museums stay open late one or two nights a week, usually Tuesday, Thursday, or Friday. New England also has quite a few smaller museums—historical societies, small art galleries, highly specialized collections—that open only a few days a week and sometimes only by appointment in winter or slow periods.

▌ MONEY

It costs a bit more to travel in most of New England than it does in the rest of the country, with the most costly areas being Boston and the coastal resort towns. There are also a fair number of somewhat posh inns and restaurants in the Berkshires, northwestern Connecticut, and parts of Vermont and New Hampshire. ATMs are plentiful and larger denomination bills (as well as credit cards) are readily accepted in tourist destinations during the high season.

Prices throughout this guide are given for adults. Substantially reduced fees are almost always available for children, students, and senior citizens.

CREDIT CARDS

Major credit cards are readily accepted throughout New England, though in rural areas you may encounter difficulties or the acceptance of only MasterCard or Visa (also note that if you'll be making an excursion into Canada, many outlets there accept Visa but not MasterCard).

Reporting Lost Cards American Express ☎ 800/528–4800 ⊕ www.americanexpress. com. **Diners Club** ☎ 800/234–6377 ⊕ www. dinersclub.com. **Discover** ☎ 800/347– 2683 ⊕ www.discover.com. **MasterCard** ☎ 800/627–8372 ⊕ www.mastercard.com. **Visa** ☎ 800/847–2911 ⊕ usa.visa.com.

▌ PACKING

The principal rule on weather in New England, is that there are no rules. A cold, foggy morning in spring can and often does become a bright, 60° afternoon. A summer breeze can suddenly turn chilly and rain often appears with little warning. Thus, the best advice on how to dress is to layer your clothing so that you can peel off or add garments as needed for comfort. Showers are frequent, so pack a raincoat and umbrella. Even in summer you should bring long pants, a sweater or two and a waterproof windbreaker, for evenings are often chilly and sea spray can make things cool.

Casual sportswear—walking shoes and jeans or khakis—will take you almost everywhere, but swimsuits and bare feet will not: shirts and shoes are required attire at even the most casual venues. Dress in restaurants is generally casual, except at some of the distinguished restaurants of Boston, Newport, and Maine Coast towns such as Kennebunkport, a few inns in the Berkshires, and in Litchfield and Fairfield counties in Connecticut. Upscale resorts, at the very least, will require men to wear collared shirts at dinner and jeans are often frowned upon.

In summer, bring a hat and sunscreen. Remember also to pack insect repellent; to prevent Lyme disease you'll need to guard against ticks from early spring through summer *(⇨ Health)*.

▌ SAFETY

Rural New England is one of the country's safest regions, so much so that residents often leave their doors unlocked. In the cities, particularly in Boston, observe the usual precautions. You should avoid out-of-the-way or poorly lighted areas at night; clutch handbags close to your body and don't let them out of your sight; and be on your guard in subways and buses, not only during the deserted wee hours but in crowded rush hours, when pickpockets are at work. Keep your valuables in hotel safes. Try to use ATMs in busy, well-lighted places such as bank lobbies.

If your vehicle breaks down in a rural area, pull as far off the road as possible, tie a handkerchief to your radio antenna (or use flares at night—check if your rental agency can provide them) and stay in your car with the doors locked until help arrives. Don't pick up hitchhikers. If you're planning to leave a car overnight to make use of off-road trails or camping facilities, make arrangements for a supervised parking area if at all possible. Cars left at trailhead parking lots are subject to theft and vandalism.

The universal telephone number for crime and other emergencies throughout New England is 911.

TIPPING GUIDELINES FOR NEW ENGLAND	
Bartender	$1 to $5 per round of drinks, depending on the number of drinks
Bellhop	$1 to $2 per bag, depending on the level of the hotel
Hotel Concierge	$5 or more, if he or she performs a service for you
Hotel Doorman	$1–$2 if he helps you get a cab
Hotel Maid	$1–$3 a day (either daily or at the end of your stay, in cash)
Hotel Room-Service Waiter	$1 to $2 per delivery, even if a service charge has been added
Porter at Airport or Train Station	$1 per bag
Skycap at Airport	$1 to $3 per bag checked
Taxi Driver	15%–20%, but round up the fare to the next dollar amount
Tour Guide	10% of the cost of the tour
Valet Parking Attendant	$1–$2, but only when you get your car
Waiter	15%–20%, with 20% being the norm at high-end restaurants; nothing additional if a service charge is added to the bill
Other Attendants	Restroom attendants in more expensive restaurants expect some small change or $1. Tip coat-check personnel at least $1–$2 per item checked unless there is a fee, then nothing.

TAXES

Sales taxes in New England are as follows: Connecticut 6.35%; Maine 5%; Massachusetts 6.25%; Rhode Island 7%; Vermont 6%. No sales tax is charged in New Hampshire. Some states and municipalities levy an additional tax (from 1% to 10%) on lodging or restaurant meals. Alcoholic beverages are sometimes taxed at a higher rate than that applied to meals.

TIME

New England operates on Eastern Standard Time and follows daylight saving time. When it is noon in Boston it is 9 am in Los Angeles, 11 am in Chicago, 5 pm in London, and 3 am the following day in Sydney. When taking a ferry to Nova Scotia, remember that the province operates on Atlantic Standard Time and, therefore, is an hour ahead.

TOURS

Insight Vacations offers a selection of fall foliage tours. Contiki Vacations, specialists in vacations for 18- to 35-year-olds, has a few tours available that pass through parts of New England as well as the rest of the Northeast.

Recommended Companies Contiki Vacations ☎ 866/266–8454 ⊕ contiki.com. **Insight Vacations** ☎ 888/680–1241 ⊕ www.insightvacations.com/us.

SPECIAL-INTEREST TOURS
BICYCLING AND HIKING
■TIP→ Most airlines accommodate bikes as luggage, provided they're dismantled and boxed.

Contacts Bike New England ☎ 978/979–6598 ⊕ www.bikenewengland.com. **TrekAmerica** ☎ 800/873–5872 ⊕ www.trekamerica.com. **Urban Adventours** ☎ 617/670–0637 ⊕ www.urbanadventours.com/.

CULINARY
Contacts Creative Culinary Tours ☎ 888/889–8681 ⊕ www.creativeculinarytours.com.

CULTURE
Contacts Northeast Unlimited Tours ☎ 800/759–6820 ⊕ www.newenglandtours.com. **New England**

Vacation Tours ☎ 800/742–7669 ⊕ www. newenglandvacationtours.com. **Wolfe Adventures & Tours** ☎ 888/449–6533 ⊕ www. wolfetours.com.

SKIING

Contacts New England Action Sports ☎ 800/477–7669 ⊕ www.skitrip.net. **New England Vacation Tours** ☎ 800/742–7669 ⊕ www.newenglandvacationtours.com.

▌ VISITOR INFORMATION

Each New England state provides a helpful free information kit, including a guidebook, map and listings of attractions and events. All include listings and advertisements for lodging and dining establishments. Each state also has an official website with material on sights and lodgings; most of these sites have a calendar of events and other special features.

Contacts Greater Boston Convention & Visitors Bureau ☎ 888/733–2678 ⊕ www. bostonusa.com. **Connecticut Commission on Culture and Tourism** ☎ 888/288–4748 ⊕ www.ctvisit.com. **Maine Office of Tourism** ☎ 888/624–6345 ⊕ www.visitmaine.com. **Massachusetts Office of Travel and Tourism** ☎ 800/227–6277, 617/973–8500 ⊕ www. massvacation.com. **New Hampshire Division**

of Travel and Tourism Development ☎ 800/386–4664, 603/271–2665 ⊕ www. visitnh.gov. **Rhode Island Tourism Division** ☎ 800/556–2484 ⊕ www.visitrhodeisland. com. **Vermont Department of Tourism and Marketing** ☎ 802/828–3237, 800/837–6668 brochures ⊕ www.vermontvacation.com.

ONLINE RESOURCES

Check out the official home page of each New England state for information on state government as well as links to state agencies with information on doing business, working, studying, living, and traveling in these areas. GORP is a terrific general resource for just about every kind of recreational activity. You can narrow your search using their "Park Finder" (found on the GORP homepage), where you'll have the option to choose from a myriad of topics, ranging from backpacking to sailing to nature viewing.

Yankee, New England's premier regional magazine, also publishes an informative travel website. Another great Web resource is Visit New England.

Online Info GORP ⊕ www.gorp.com. **Visit New England** ⊕ www.visitnewengland.com. **Yankee Magazine** ⊕ www.yankeemagazine. com/travel.

INDEX

A

Aardvark Antiques (shop), *390*
Abba ✕ , *188*
Abbott Hall, *134*
Abbott's Lobster in the Rough
✕ , *321–322*
Abenaki Tower, *546*
Acadia Air Tours, *741*
Acadia Mountain Trail, *749*
Acadia National Park, *16,
738–750, 752*
Acadia National Park Head-
quarters, *745*
Adams Farm, *426*
Adams National Historic Park,
144–145
Addison Choate Inn ☒ , *141*
African Meeting House, *208*
Air travel, *11, 764–765*
Connecticut, 267
Maine, 626, 653
*Massachusetts, 49, 157, 194,
199, 206, 219*
New Hampshire, 523, 596, 604
Rhode Island, 333, 335, 403
Vermont, 419
Alan Bilzerian (shop), *96*
Albacore Park, *527*
Alcott, Louisa May, *131*
Aldrich Contemporary Art
Museum, *275*
All Star Sandwich Bar ✕ , *115*
Allagash Wilderness Water-
way, *647–648*
Allen, Ethan, *499*
Alpamayo ✕ , *237–238*
Altar Rock, *212*
Alton Bay, NH, *548*
America's Cup hall of Fame,
397
American Flatbread at the
Marble Works ✕ , *470*
American Flatbread-Burlington
Hearth ✕ , *503*
American Flatbread-Waits-
field ✕ , *474*
American Independence
Museum, *537–538*
American Museum of Fly Fish-
ing, *436*
American Repertory Theater,
104
Amherst, MA, *256–258*
Amore Breakfast ✕ , *667–668*
Amoskeag Fishways, *604*
Amoskeag Mills, *604*

Anchor-In ☒ , *174*
Antique and crafts shopping
guide, *299–305*
Appalachian Trail, *16, 246,
292, 563*
Appalachian Trail Club
Pinkham Notch Visitor Cen-
ter, *584*
Applecrest Farm Orchards, *537*
Appledore Island, *529*
Aquinnah, MA, *205–206*
Aquinnah Cliffs, *205*
Aquinnah Lighthouse, *205–206*
Arborvine ✕ , *734–735*
Arlington, VT, *434–436*
Arnie's Place ✕ , *608*
Arrows ✕ , *668*
Artist's Bridge, *635*
Art's Dune Tours, *196*
Arts District (Portland, ME),
683–686
AS220 (music club), *345*
Astors' Beechwood (mansion),
382
Atlantic Beach Park, *360*
Atlantic Inn ☒ , *411*
Atlantic White Cedar Swamp,
190
Attitash Ski Area, *580*
Atwood House Museum, *185*
Audubon Greenwich, *269–270*
Aunt Carrie's ✕ , *366*

B

B & G Oysters, Ltd. ✕ , *105*
Bacaro ✕ , *347*
Baer's Den Bakery and Deli
✕ , *223*
Bagaduce Lunch ✕ , *736*
Bangor, ME, *731–732*
BAR ✕ , *314*
Bar Harbor, ME, *741–743*
Bar Harbor Inn & Spa ☒ , *743*
Bar Harbor Whale Watch Co.,
742
Barnard Inn Restaurant &
Max's Tavern ✕ , *459*
Barney's New York (depart-
ment store), *97*
Barnstable, MA, *175–176*
Bartholomew's Cobble (rock
garden), *246*
Bartlett, NH, *580–581*
Bartlett Arboretum and Gar-
dens, *272*
Bartlett Beach, *551*

Baseball, *46–47, 80–81, 354,
377*
Basin Harbor Club ☒ , *509*
Basketball, *93*
Bass Harbor, ME, *750*
Bass Harbor Head Light, *712,
745*
Bass Hole Boardwalk, *176*
Bath, ME, *702–704*
Battenkill Canoe, *435*
Battle Green (Lexington, MA),
126
Baxter State Park, *16–17, 648*
Bayside Resort ☒ , *178–179*
BeacHead ✕ , *410*
Beaches, *20, 26*
Connecticut, 315
*Maine, 62–663,669, 672, 703,
749*
*Massachusetts, 90–91, 139,
142, 154–155, 165, 173,
175, 179, 186, 187–188,
189, 192, 196, 201, 202, 209*
*New Hampshire, 535–536,
544, 549, 551, 595*
*Rhode Island, 360, 361, 362,
363, 365, 371, 377, 388,
395, 406–407*
Vermont, 499–500
Beals Island, ME, *756*
Bean & Cod (shop), *172*
Bear Mountain Inn ☒ , *632*
Beavertail Lighthouse Museum,
370
Beavertail State Park, *370–371*
Bed & breakfasts, *21, 768*
Bedford Village Inn ☒ , *606*
Bee & Thistle Inn and Spa ☒ ,
317
Beechwood Inn ☒ , *176*
Beinecke Rare Book and Manu-
script Library, *309*
Belcourt Castle, *382, 384*
Belfast, ME, *727–728*
Belfry Inn & Bistro ☒ , *162*
Belknap Mill, *550*
Bell in Hand Tavern, *99*
Bellamy-Ferriday House &
Garden, *281*
Ben & Jerry's Ice Cream Fac-
tory, *479*
Benefit Street (Providence RI),
340
Bennington, VT, *430–434*
Bennington Battle Monument,
431
Bennington College, *432*

PHOTO CREDITS

1, Kindra Clineff. 3, Kindra Clineff. 6-7, Kindra Clineff. 8, Natalia Bratslavsky/iStockphoto. 9 (left), Denis Jr. Tangney/iStockphoto. 9 (right), William Britten /iStockphoto. 13 (left), Michael Dwyer / Alamy. 13 (right), Rhona Wise/Icon Sports Media, Inc. 14, Chris Coe / age fotostock. 15, Jerry and Marcy Monkman/EcoPhotography.com/Aurora Photos. 16 (left), Ken Canning/iStockphoto. 16 (top right), Kindra Clineff. 16 (bottom right), iStockphoto. 17 (left), Chee-Onn Leong/Shutterstock. 17 (right), Kindra Clineff. 18 (left), drewthehobbit/Shutterstock. 18 (top center), Kindra Clineff. 18 (top right), T. Markley/Shutterstock. 18 (bottom right), Kindra Clineff. 19 (left), Kindra Clineff. 19 (top right), Natalia Bratslavsky/iStockphoto. 19 (bottom right), muffinman71xx/Flickr. 20, Dennis Curran/ Vermont Dept. of Tourism & Marketing. 21 (left), Rod Kaye/iStockphoto. 21 (right), Ken Canning/ Flickr. 22, Eric Foltz/iStockphoto. 23, Wikimedia Commons. 25, Michael Czosnek/iStockphoto. 26, Denis Jr. Tangney/iStockphoto. 27 (left) , Jeff Greenberg / age fotostock. 27 (right), Sheldon Kralstein/ iStockphoto. 28, Jason Ganser/iStockphoto. 29 (left), Hnin Khine/iStockphoto. 29 (right), kworth30/ wikipedia.org. 30, Denis Jr. Tangney/iStockphoto. 31, Kindra Clineff. 32, Kindra Clineff. 33, Jason Orender/iStockphoto. 36-37, Ken Canning/iStockphoto. 39 (top left), Micha≈Ç Krakowiak/iStock-photo. 39 (top center), Lisa Thornberg/iStockphoto. 39 (top right), Scott Cramer/iStockphoto. 39 (bottom left), Steffen Foerster Photography/Shutterstock. 39 (bottom center), iStockphoto. 39 (bottom right), Paul Aniszewski/Shutterstock. 40 (top), Denis Jr. Tangney/iStockphoto. 40 (bottom), Kevin Davidson/iStockphoto. 41, Kindra Clineff. 42, Kindra Clineff. Chapter 2: Boston: 43, Kindra Clineff. 44, Kindra Clineff. 45, ojbyrne/Flickr. 46, ChrisDag/Flickr. 47 (top), Kindra Clineff. 47 (bottom), Kin-dra Clineff. 48, David Eby/Shutterstock. 54-55, Kindra Clineff. 66, Kindra Clineff. 67 (top left), MCS@ flickr/Flickr. 67 (top center), A. H. C. / age fotostock. 67 (top right), cliff10666/Flickr. 67 (center left), Classic Vision / age fotostock. 67 (center right), Classic Vision / age fotostock. 67 (bottom), Kindra Clineff. 68, Kindra Clineff. 69 (top left), Kindra Clineff. 69 (top right), Freedom Trail Foundation. 69 (center left), Tony the Misfit/Flickr. 69 (center right), Kindra Clineff. 69 (bottom left), Tim Grafft/ MOTT . 69 (bottom center), Scott Orr/iStockphoto. 69 (bottom right), Kindra Clineff. 70 (top), Kindra Clineff. 70 (bottom), Jim Reynolds/Wikimedia Commons. 71 (top), revjim5000/Flickr. 71 (bottom), Kindra Clineff. 72, Kindra Clineff. 74, Kindra Clineff. 80, Kindra Clineff. 82, Allie_Caulfied/Flickr. 84, Isabella Stewart Gardner Museum, Boston. 88, Harvard Crimson. 93, Steve Dunwell / age fotostock. 100, Megapress / Alamy. 103, gkristo/Flickr. 110, Adam Gesuero. 112, StarChefs.com. 123 (top left), Charlesmark Hotel. 123 (top right), Fairmont Hotels & Resorts. 123 (center left), Boston Harbor Hotel. 123 (center right), Michael Weschler Photography. 123 (bottom left), The Charles Hotel. 123 (bottom right), Hotel Commonwealth. 130, Public Domain. 132, Kindra Clineff. 140, Kindra Clineff. 146, Kin-dra Clineff. Chapter 3: Cape Cod, Martha's Vineyard, and Nantucket: 149, Kindra Clineff. 151, Denis Jr. Tangney/iStockphoto. 152, Denis Jr. Tangney/iStockphoto. 153 (top), Kenneth Wiedemann/iStock-photo. 153 (bottom), Kindra Clineff. 154, (c) Mwaits I Dreamstime.com. 155 (top), (c) Jtunney I Dream-stime.com. 155 (bottom), (c) Ktphotog I Dreamstime.com. 156, Denis Jr. Tangney/iStockphoto. 163, Kindra Clineff. 166, Nantucket Historical Association. 167, Michael S. Nolan / age fotostock. 168, Kindra Clineff. 169 (top), Kindra Clineff. 169 (center), Penobscot Marine Museum. 169 (bottom left), Random House, Inc. 169 (bottom right), Kindra Clineff. 171, Jeff Greenberg / age fotostock. 177, Kin-dra Clineff. 182, Julie O'Neil/CCMNH. 191, Kindra Clineff. 193, Guido Caroti. 197, Kindra Clineff. 207, Denis Jr. Tangney/iStockphoto. 208, Kindra Clineff. 210, Kindra Clineff. Chapter 4: The Berk-shires and Western Massachusetts: 213, Kindra Clineff. 214, Denis Jr. Tangney/iStockphoto. 215 (top left), Allan Pospisil/iStockphoto. 215 (top right), Denis Jr. Tangney/iStockphoto. 215 (bottom), Denis Jr. Tangney/iStockphoto. 216, Denis Jr. Tangney/iStockphoto. 217, Denis Jr. Tangney/iStockphoto. 218, Kevin Kennefick. 225, Sterling and Francine Clark Art Institute, Williamstown, Massachusetts. 226-227, mkromer/Flickr. 232, Doug Baz. 233, Denis Jr. Tangney/iStockphoto. 237, Kindra Clineff. 241, wikipedia.org. 242, Denis Jr. Tangney/iStockphoto. 245, Kindra Clineff. 252, Kindra Clineff. 259, Kin-dra Clineff. Chapter 5: Connecticut: 261, Louis DiBacco /iStockphoto. 262, Rene, C Cartier/iStock-photo. 263 (top), Jaco le Roux/iStockphoto. 263 (bottom), Denis Jr. Tangney/iStockphoto. 264, Franz Marc Frei /age fotostock. 265, Calvin G. York /Hunt Hill Farm Trust. 266, Kindra Clineff. 274, Alex Nason. 279, Kindra Clineff. 281, Kindra Clineff. 288, Denis Jr. Tangney/iStockphoto. 294, Ken Wiede-mann/iStockphoto. 297, Kindra Clineff. 299 (left), Karen Gentry/Shutterstock. 299 (right), Jochen Tack / age fotostock . 299 (bottom), Marc Dietrich/Shutterstock. 300 (top left), Johann Helgason/Flickr. 300 (top right), Kindra Clineff. 300 (bottom left), robcocquyt/Shutterstock. 300 (center right), Cre8tive Images/Shutterstock. 300 (bottom right), Matthew Gough/Shutterstock. 301 (top left), Guitar75/Shut-terstock. 301 (top right), Artur Bogacki/Shutterstock. 301 (bottom left), Kindra Clineff. 301 (center right), libraryimages.net/Flickr. 301 (bottom right), iStockphoto. 302, Kindra Clineff. 303 (left), Kindra Clineff. 303 (right), Kindra Clineff. 304, Kindra Clineff. 305 (top), Kindra Clineff. 305 (bottom), Lise

Gagne/iStockphoto. 313, Kindra Clineff. 314, scaredy_kat/Flickr. 321, Kindra Clineff. Chapter 6: Rhode Island: 327, Kindra Clineff. 328 (top), Denis Jr. Tangney/iStockphoto. 328 (bottom), Steve Geer/ iStockphoto. 329, Steve Geer/iStockphoto. 330, Kindra Clineff. 331, Kindra Clineff. 332, Denis Jr. Tangney/iStockphoto. 338, Kenneth C. Zirkel/iStockphoto. 341, Denis Jr. Tangney/iStockphoto. 350, Michael Larson Photography. 355, iStockphoto. 364, Ken Wiedemann/iStockphoto. 378 (top left), The Preservation Society of Newport County. 378 (top right) & 379, The Preservation Society of Newport County. 378 (bottom left), Carolyn M Carpenter/Shutterstock. 378 (bottom right), The Preservation Society of Newport County. 380 (top), The Preservation Society of Newport County. 380 (bottom), Library of Congress Prints and Photographs Division. 381 (left), Kindra Clineff. 381 (top right), Library of Congress Prints and Photographs Division. 381 (right center top), wikipedia.org. 381 (right center bottom), Library of Congress Prints and Photographs Division. 381 (bottom right), Frymire Archive / Alamy. 382, The Preservation Society of Newport County. 383 (top left), Sergio Orsanigo. 383 (top right), The Preservation Society of Newport County. 383 (bottom), Travel Bug/Shutterstock. 384 (top left), The Preservation Society of Newport County. 384 (right), Michael Neelon / age fotostock. 384 (center left), Michael Neelon/ Alamy. 384 (bottom left), The Preservation Society of Newport County. 385 (top left), The Preservation Society of Newport County. 385 (top right), The Preservation Society of Newport County. 385 (center right top), exfordy/Flickr. 385 (center right), The Preservation Society of Newport County. 385 (center right bottom), The Preservation Society of Newport County. 385 (bottom right), dhan911/Flickr. 386 (top left), Nathan Benn / Alamy. 386 (top right), The Preservation Society of Newport County. 386 (left center top), The Preservation Society of Newport County. 386 (center left), Carolyn M Carpenter/Shutterstock. 386 (bottom left), The Preservation Society of Newport County. 387 (top left), The Preservation Society of Newport County. 387 (top right), Fraser Hall / age fotostock. 387 (center right top), The Preservation Society of Newport County. 387 (center right), The Preservation Society of Newport County. 387 (center right bottom), n ole/wikipedia.org. 387 (bottom right), Newport Restoration Foundation. 390, SuperStock/age fotostock. 396, Kindra Clineff. 399, Denis Jr. Tangney/iStockphoto. 402, Kindra Clineff. 405, Kindra Clineff. 407, Kindra Clineff. Chapter 7: Vermont: 413, Kindra Clineff. 414 (top), Marcio Silva/iStockphoto. 414 (bottom), Denis Jr. Tangney/ iStockphoto. 415, Denis Jr. Tangney/iStockphoto. 416, Heeb Christian / age fotostock. 417, Sarah Kennedy/iStockphoto. 418, S. Greg Panosian/iStockphoto. 425, Kindra Clineff. 427, Kindra Clineff. 428, Kindra Clineff. 431, Kindra Clineff. 437, Hildene. 440, Lee Krohn Photography, Manchester, Vermont. 448, Kindra Clineff. 451, Kindra Clineff. 457, Simon Pearce. 464–65, S. Greg Panosian/iStockphoto. 472, Kindra Clineff. 475, Fraser Hall / age fotostock. 481, Dennis Curran / age fotostock. 482, Skye Chalmers Photography, inc. 483 (left), Henryk T Kaiser / age fotostock. 483 (right), Hubert Schriebl. 484 (left), Marcio Silva/iStockphoto. 484 (right), Hubert Schriebl. 485, SMUGGLERS' NOTCH RESORT/Ski Vermont. 486, Okemo Mountain Resort. 488, Ellen Rooney / age fotostock. 489 (left), Barry Winiker / age fotostock. 489 (right), Don Landwehrle. 490 (left), OKEMO MOUNTAIN RESORT/Ski Vermont. 490 (right), Magic Mountain. 501, Kindra Clineff. 505, Skye Chalmers/State of Vermont. 508, Kindra Clineff. 512, Alan Copson / age fotostock. 515, Jack Sumberg. Chapter 8: New Hampshire: 517, Denis Jr. Tangney/iStockphoto. 518 (top), Denis Jr. Tangney/iStockphoto. 518 (bottom), Ken Canning/iStockphoto. 520, Mary Ann Alwan / Alamy. 521, iStockphoto. 522, Sebastien Cote/iStockphoto. 529, Kindra Clineff. 530, Kindra Clineff. 534, Denis Jr. Tangney/ iStockphoto. 540-541, cyanocorax/Flickr. 543, NHDTTD/Dave Martsolf. 545, DAVID NOBLE PHOTOGRAPHY / Alamy. 550, Kindra Clineff. 553, Roy Rainford / age fotostock. 563 (top), Jerry and Marcy Monkman/EcoPhotography.com / Alamy. 563 (bottom), Liz Van Steenburgh/Shutterstock. 564, Kindra Clineff. 565, Mike Kautz/AMC. 566 (left), nialat/Shutterstock. 566 (top right), RestonImages/ Shutterstock. 566 (bottom right), nialat/Shutterstock. 567 (top left), jadimages/Shutterstock. 567 (right), rebvt/Shutterstock. 567 (bottom left), Ansgar Walk/wikipedia.org. 567 (bottom center), J. Carmichael/wikipedia.org. 569, Matty Symons/Shutterstock. 570, Danita Delimont / Alamy. 571, Frank Siteman / age fotostock. 576, Kindra Clineff. 579, Kindra Clineff. 584, First Light / Alamy. 588, Kenneth C. Zirkel/iStockphoto. 590, gailf548/Flickr. 597, Kindra Clineff. 600, Jet Lowe/Wikimedia Commons. 605, Currier Museum of Art/Jose Martinez. 612, Franz Marc Frei / age fotostock. 614, Andre Jenny / Alamy. Chapter 9: Inland Maine: 619, Jeff Martone/Flickr. 620, Kenneth C. Zirkel/iStockphoto. 621, Stephen G Page/iStockphoto. 622, Denis Jr. Tangney/iStockphoto. 623, The Wilhelm Reich Infant Trust. 624, BrendanReals/Shutterstock. 636, D A Horchner / age fotostock. 642–643, Kazela/Shutterstock. Chapter 10: Maine Coast: 649, SuperStock/age fotostock. 650 (top), Denis Jr. Tangney/iStockphoto. 650 (bottom), Paul Tessier/iStockphoto. 651, Andrea Pelletier/iStockphoto. 652, Aimin Tang/ iStockphoto. 657, ARCO/L Weyers / age fotostock. 666, Perry B. Johnson / age fotostock. 674, Lucid Images / age fotostock. 683, SuperStock/age fotostock. 687, Jeff Greenberg / age fotostock. 694, Lee Coursey/Flickr. 695, Kindra Clineff. 702, Jim Kidd / Alamy. 705, Jeff Greenberg / Alamy. 706, Michael